LINCOLNOLOGY

THE LOCHLAINN SEABROOK COLLECTION

Everything You Were Taught About the Civil War is Wrong, Ask a Southerner!
Everything You Were Taught About American Slavery is Wrong, Ask a Southerner!
Everything You Were Taught About African-Americans and the Civil War is Wrong, Ask a Southerner!
Lincoln's War: The Real Cause, the Real Winner, the Real Loser
Abraham Lincoln Was a Liberal, Jefferson Davis Was a Conservative: The Missing Key to Understanding the American Civil War
Confederate Flag Facts: What Every American Should Know About Dixie's Southern Cross
Give This Book to a Yankee! A Southern Guide to the Civil War For Northerners
Women in Gray: A Tribute to the Ladies Who Supported the Southern Confederacy
The Unholy Crusade: Lincoln's Legacy of Destruction in the American South
Honest Jeff and Dishonest Abe: A Southern Children's Guide to the Civil War
Confederacy 101: Amazing Facts You Never Knew About America's Oldest Political Tradition
Slavery 101: Amazing Facts You Never Knew About America's "Peculiar Institution"
The Great Yankee Coverup: What the North Doesn't Want You to Know About Lincoln's War!
All We Ask Is To Be Let Alone: The Southern Secession Fact Book
Confederate Blood and Treasure: An Interview With Lochlainn Seabrook
The Ultimate Civil War Quiz Book: How Much Do You Really Know About America's Most Misunderstood Conflict?
A Rebel Born: A Defense of Nathan Bedford Forrest - Confederate General, American Legend (winner of the 2011 Jefferson Davis Historical Gold Medal)
A Rebel Born: The Screenplay
Nathan Bedford Forrest: Southern Hero, American Patriot - Honoring a Confederate Icon and the Old South
The Quotable Nathan Bedford Forrest: Selections From the Writings and Speeches of the Confederacy's Most Brilliant Cavalryman
Give 'Em Hell Boys! The Complete Military Correspondence of Nathan Bedford Forrest
Forrest! 99 Reasons to Love Nathan Bedford Forrest
Saddle, Sword, and Gun: A Biography of Nathan Bedford Forrest For Teens
Nathan Bedford Forrest and the Battle of Fort Pillow: Yankee Myth, Confederate Fact
Nathan Bedford Forrest and the Ku Klux Klan: Yankee Myth, Confederate Fact
Nathan Bedford Forrest and African-Americans: Yankee Myth, Confederate Fact
The Quotable Jefferson Davis: Selections From the Writings and Speeches of the Confederacy's First President
The Quotable Alexander H. Stephens: Selections From the Writings and Speeches of the Confederacy's First Vice President
The Alexander H. Stephens Reader: Excerpts From the Works of a Confederate Founding Father
The Quotable Robert E. Lee: Selections From the Writings and Speeches of the South's Most Beloved Civil War General
The Old Rebel: Robert E. Lee As He Was Seen By His Contemporaries
The Articles of Confederation Explained: A Clause-by-Clause Study of America's First Constitution
The Constitution of the Confederate States of America Explained: A Clause-by-Clause Study of the South's Magna Carta
The Quotable Stonewall Jackson: Selections From the Writings and Speeches of the South's Most Famous General
Abraham Lincoln: The Southern View - Demythologizing America's Sixteenth President
The Unquotable Abraham Lincoln: The President's Quotes They Don't Want You To Know!
Lincolnology: The Real Abraham Lincoln Revealed in His Own Words - A Study of Lincoln's Suppressed, Misinterpreted, and Forgotten Writings and Speeches
The Great Impersonator! 99 Reasons to Dislike Abraham Lincoln
Encyclopedia of the Battle of Franklin - A Comprehensive Guide to the Conflict that Changed the Civil War
Carnton Plantation Ghost Stories: True Tales of the Unexplained from Tennessee's Most Haunted Civil War House!
The McGavocks of Carnton Plantation: A Southern History - Celebrating One of Dixie's Most Noble Confederate Families and Their Tennessee Home
Jesus and the Law of Attraction: The Bible-Based Guide to Creating Perfect Health, Wealth, and Happiness Following Christ's Simple Formula
The Bible and the Law of Attraction: 99 Teachings of Jesus, the Apostles, and the Prophets
Christ Is All and In All: Rediscovering Your Divine Nature and the Kingdom Within
Jesus and the Gospel of Q: Christ's Pre-Christian Teachings As Recorded in the New Testament
Seabrook's Bible Dictionary of Traditional and Mystical Christian Doctrines
The Way of Holiness: The Story of Religion and Myth From the Cave Bear Cult to Christianity
Christmas Before Christianity: How the Birthday of the "Sun" Became the Birthday of the "Son"
Britannia Rules: Goddess-Worship in Ancient Anglo-Celtic Society - An Academic Look at the United Kingdom's Matricentric Spiritual Past
The Book of Kelle: An Introduction to Goddess-Worship and the Great Celtic Mother-Goddess Kelle, Original Blessed Lady of Ireland
The Goddess Dictionary of Words and Phrases: Introducing a New Core Vocabulary for the Women's Spirituality Movement
Aphrodite's Trade: The Hidden History of Prostitution Unveiled
UFOs and Aliens: The Complete Guidebook
The Caudills: An Etymological, Ethnological, and Genealogical Study - Exploring the Name and National Origins of a European-American Family
The Blakeneys: An Etymological, Ethnological, and Genealogical Study - Uncovering the Mysterious Origins of the Blakeney Family and Name
Princess Diana: Modern Day Moon-Goddess - A Psychoanalytical and Mythological Look at Diana Spencer's Life, Marriage, and Death (with Dr. Jane Goldberg)
Autobiography of a Non-Yogi: A Scientist's Journey From Hinduism to Christianity (with Dr. Amitava Dasgupta)

Five-Star Books & Gifts From the Heart of the American South

SeaRavenPress.com

LINCOLNOLOGY
THE REAL ABRAHAM LINCOLN

Revealed in His Own Words

A Study of Lincoln's Suppressed, Misinterpreted,
and Forgotten Writings and Speeches

ILLUSTRATED BY THE AUTHOR, "THE VOICE OF THE TRADITIONAL SOUTH," COLONEL

LOCHLAINN SEABROOK
JEFFERSON DAVIS HISTORICAL GOLD MEDAL WINNER

Diligently Researched for the Elucidation of the Reader

INTRODUCTION BY DR. J. MICHAEL HILL
FOREWORD BY MAYOR ROBERT LOVELL

2017
Sea Raven Press, Nashville, Tennessee, USA

LINCOLNOLOGY

Published by
Sea Raven Press, Cassidy Ravensdale, President
Southern Books, Real History!
PO Box 1484, Spring Hill, Tennessee 37174-1484 USA
SeaRavenPress.com • searavenpress@gmail.com

Copyright © 2011, 2017 Lochlainn Seabrook
in accordance with U.S. and international copyright laws and regulations, as stated and protected under the Berne Union for the Protection of Literary and Artistic Property (Berne Convention), and the Universal Copyright Convention (the UCC). All rights reserved under the Pan-American and International Copyright Conventions.

1st SRP paperback edition, 1st printing: May 2011, ISBN: 978-0-9827700-9-2
1st SRP paperback edition, 2nd printing: September 2017, ISBN: 978-0-9827700-9-2
1st SRP hardcover edition, 1st printing: September 2017, ISBN: 978-1-943737-56-7

ISBN: 978-0-9827700-9-2 (paperback)
Library of Congress Control Number: 2011921128

This work is the copyrighted intellectual property of Lochlainn Seabrook and has been registered with the Copyright Office at the Library of Congress in Washington, D.C., USA. No part of this work (including text, covers, drawings, photos, illustrations, maps, images, diagrams, etc.), in whole or in part, may be used, reproduced, stored in a retrieval system, or transmitted, in any form or by any means now known or hereafter invented, without written permission from the publisher. The sale, duplication, hire, lending, copying, digitalization, or reproduction of this material, in any manner or form whatsoever, is also prohibited, and is a violation of federal, civil, and digital copyright law, which provides severe civil and criminal penalties for any violations.

Lincolnology: The Real Abraham Lincoln Revealed In His Own Words—A Study of Lincoln's Suppressed, Misinterpreted, and Forgotten Writings and Speeches, by Lochlainn Seabrook. Introduction by Dr. J. Michael Hill. Foreword by Mayor Robert Lovell. Includes an index, notes, and bibliographical material.

Front and back cover design and art, book design, layout, and interior art by Lochlainn Seabrook
All images, graphic design, graphic art, and illustrations copyright © Lochlainn Seabrook
Cover photo: Abraham Lincoln, Library of Congress
Portions of this book have been adapted from the author's other works

The views on the American "Civil War" documented in this book are those of the publisher.

The paper used in this book is acid-free and lignin-free. It has been certified by the Sustainable Forestry Initiative and the Forest Stewardship Council and meets all ANSI standards for archival quality paper.

PRINTED & MANUFACTURED IN OCCUPIED TENNESSEE, FORMER CONFEDERATE STATES OF AMERICA

DEDICATION

To all the courageous and patriotic individuals, South and North, who challenged, resisted, and fought the Illinois Dictator between the years 1861 and 1865.

EPIGRAPH

My enemies pretend I am now carrying on this war for the sole purpose of abolition. So long as I am President, it shall be carried on for the sole purpose of restoring the Union.

A. Lincoln

AUGUST 15, 1864

CONTENTS

Books by Lochlainn Seabrook - 2
Foreword, by Mayor Robert Lovell - 8
Preface, by Lochlainn Seabrook - 11
Notes to the Reader - 15
Introduction, by Dr. J. Michael Hill - 19

1 LINCOLN AND THE PRESIDENCY - 23
2 LINCOLN AND SECESSION - 106
3 LINCOLN AND THE SO-CALLED "REBELLION" - 131
4 LINCOLN AND THE CONSTITUTION - 137
5 LINCOLN AND THE UNION - 178
6 LINCOLN AND THE CAUSE OF THE WAR - 189
7 LINCOLN AND THE START OF THE WAR - 216
8 LINCOLN AND ABOLITION - 273
9 LINCOLN AND SLAVERY, PART 1 - 306
10 LINCOLN AND SLAVERY, PART 2 - 416
11 LINCOLN, AFRICAN-AMERICANS, AND WHITE RACISM - 494
12 LINCOLN, BLACK COLONIZATION, AND WHITE SEPARATISM - 513
13 LINCOLN AND THE EMANCIPATION PROCLAMATION - 555
14 LINCOLN AND HIS WAR ON THE SOUTH - 610
15 LINCOLN AND HIS WAR ON THE NORTH - 628
16 LINCOLN AND HIS WAR CRIMES - 663
17 LINCOLN AND HIS PRESIDENTIAL ELECTIONS - 751
18 LINCOLN AND HIS BLACK SOLDIERS - 770
19 LINCOLN AND RELIGION - 799
20 LINCOLN AND RECONSTRUCTION - 817

Appendix A: Photos of Lincoln, His Vice Presidents, Cabinet, & Military Chiefs - 834
Appendix B: U.S. Presidents Who Influenced Lincoln & His Policies - 855
Appendix C: Chronology of the Lincoln-Douglas Debates - 856
Notes - 857
Bibliography - 926
Index - 985
Meet the Author - 1043
Meet the Introduction Writer - 1047
Meet the Foreword Writer - 1048

FOREWORD

BY MAYOR ROBERT LOVELL

One of the characters in my early life was my great, great Uncle Sydney Perry. Uncle Sydney was the last surviving son of a father who fought in the Mexican War and the War Between the States. His father was a local icon in a tiny Florida community which still bears his name to this very day. Needless to say, Uncle Sydney had many stories to tell about his father and especially concerning his two years as a Confederate infantryman in the Army of Northern Virginia. I loved to listen to his stories and to witness living history through a loved and revered ancestor. As a youngster, I of course, had only a cursive and superficial knowledge of American History. My information came from school text books, and teachers, mostly Northerners who had moved to Florida to take advantage of our wonderful climate, cheaper cost of living and lower taxes. At school, when the subject of Abraham Lincoln came up, we were always presented with a most positive and glowing image. However, at home and around my extended family, Lincoln was seen from an entirely different perspective!

I was especially enthralled by my great, great uncle's view of Abraham Lincoln. Uncle Sydney still viewed Lincoln as a contemporary political figure. Whenever the subject of Lincoln came up, it was if we were discussing a current president! Time had not dimmed his emotions on the subject! At the mention of Lincoln, Uncle Sydney's face would contort and his usual sweet and congenial countenance would harden. With his dark, piercing eyes narrowed, looking straight into my face, he would explode into a virulent diatribe. He would start by telling me in no uncertain terms that Abraham Lincoln was an evil man and no leader. He would cite his failure to avert the war and his murderous contempt for the people of the South that he had never even visited. He blamed Lincoln for the cruelty and arrogance of the invading Yankee army! Uncle Sydney said it was Lincoln who sent Sherman's army to loot, pillage, rob and burn the South!

He would emphasize that Abraham Lincoln was the one who didn't follow the Constitution. He would loudly point out that it was Lincoln who authorized his agents to arrest and execute folks without fair trial. Lincoln, he would say, was a dictator and a, "failure made into a saint by Yankee lies!"

Finally, Uncle Sydney would scoff at the notion that the war was over slavery. Uncle Sydney cited the fact that the Perry family was against slavery and had never supported it! He, of course said the war was over states rights and against Yankee tariffs and other economic sanctions. He would vigorously point to Yankee hypocrisy and arrogance over slavery.

Of course, his point of view was totally out of touch with what I was learning in school and what was portrayed in the movies and magazines. At the time, I felt Uncle Sydney was just an old timer, deluded and ignorant of the real facts and modern, erudite understanding of American history. He was more of an amusement to me and I certainly didn't take him seriously when it came to his analysis of the Lincoln era. I suppose I mostly looked on him as a curiosity or anachronism. In all other aspects of his life I considered him wise and understanding, but I was not willing to include his historical perspective. It would take a long time and many years of study before I began to appreciate his sagacity, experience and point of view.

Lincolnology is a book that discovers, identifies and documents the hidden man behind the Lincoln myth. The author has gone to great lengths to be accurate in his revelation of a historical figure that has not really stood the test of critical analysis. Lochlainn Seabrook takes you on a trip deep into undiscovered, hidden and I might say, forbidden territory. The elitist and politically correct pundits will not like this journey, nor will patriotic Americans feel comfortable along the way, but Americans need to "know the rest of the story." It is indeed painful to find that a revered marble statue is instead made of paper mache!

This work may contradict and offend our sensibilities because we are raised with the notion that Lincoln is beyond reproach and no one should or could question his motives or character! There is no room or tolerance in understanding the thinking of a Robert E. Lee, Jefferson Davis or for that matter, Uncle Sydney Perry. They had a very different grasp of this president than the myths and legends a politically correct America has created. In his book Seabrook attempts the un attemptable, to tell the truth, the whole truth and nothing but the truth!

But, one will ask, why is this message so important? Would the country not be better off if the issues were never raised? The answer is a resounding no! Ignorance is never a healthy idol to worship! This book is important for the souls of over three hundred thousand dead Confederate soldiers! It is important their memory not continue to be demeaned and denigrated by a society clueless of their sacrifice and suffering. To allow all semblance of honor, integrity and truth to be twisted by vitriolic resentment and hatred by the uncaring and ignorant is a crime against America. To allow this whitewash to obscure our past robs future generations of a genuine knowledge of their heritage and honor! It is therefore vitally important that the truth of the Southern cause be re-taught so that future generations might learn the meaning of duty, loyalty and sacrifice to the preservation of freedom and liberty!

In the final analysis, truth always wins out. It may be denied. It may be tried. It may be twisted and it may be changed. But, in the end it will prevail. In the words of James Russell Lowell, abolitionist, writer, poet, statesman, scholar and friend of the South: "Though the cause of evil prosper, yet the truth alone is strong! Though her portion be a scaffold and upon the throne be wrong! Yet, that scaffold sways the future and behind the dim unknown, standeth God within the shadows keeping watch over all his own."

Robert Lovell
Leesburg, Florida
April 2011

PREFACE

BY LOCHLAINN SEABROOK

Ever since the formation of the Southern Confederacy in 1861 it has been fashionable to use the term "anti-American" for conservative Southerners who are critical of Abraham Lincoln and his big spending, big government, Big Brother policies. Even more absurd, we are often dismissed as Lincolnphobic crusaders who want to "destroy the U.S." This is, of course, nothing more than anti-South propaganda and pro-North disinformation, spread by ill-informed often left-wing members of Lincoln's church.

As anyone who actually reads our works from cover to cover knows, the opposite is true. It is not his critics. It is Lincoln himself who was anti-American, which is why those of us who love the U.S. regularly take him to task. And, as I demonstrate repeatedly in this very book, it is Lincoln who hangs himself by his own petard. For as a liberal he plainly disliked, ignored, and even purposefully trampled over the Southern-inspired Constitution, a document whose principle author was one of the most conservative pro-American men who ever lived: Founding Father James Madison of Virginia.[1]

Not surprisingly, since the publication of my first book on Lincoln, *Abraham Lincoln: The Southern View*, some have accused me of "hating" our sixteenth president. What they do not seem to realize is that this is considered a compliment here in the traditional South, and I take it as such.

However, while I do not like Lincoln, I certainly do not hate him. Few could study Lincoln for as many years as I have and not come away with some kind of grudging respect, even sympathy, for our "Civil War president." For this was a man who suffered terribly due to the bloody, illegal, and pointless War he started, numerous family tragedies, and a host of personal demons. Lincoln himself said **"there are few things wholly evil or wholly good,"**[2] and I agree.

Despite my empathy in these areas, when it comes to his political life it is impossible to grant him any mercy. This is because he had numerous constructive choices before him concerning how to deal with the South, secession, and slavery. Yet, he always chose the most destructive path, always the one guaranteed to inflict the most suffering on Dixie.

For this reason alone it is justifiable to critique Lincoln; not personally (which I have no interest in), but politically. For it is as a traditional conservative Southerner that I take issue with him. And from this perspective there is much to take issue with!

In any analyzation of Lincoln the real question is always, what is genuine and what is fake?

The great problem with our sixteenth chief executive was his jaw-dropping duplicity and chameleon-like ability to be two people at once: the first, the "Great Emancipator," an anti-slavery proponent when in front of Northern audiences; the second, what I call the "Great Procrastinator," a slavery-tolerating proponent when in front of Southern audiences. This carefully crafted dual persona, which has been almost completely ignored by modern Lincoln scholars and educators, was much commented on by both his friends and his enemies.

This is only half of the difficulty, however. His devoted followers have taken great care to only allow the first Abraham Lincoln, the "Great Emancipator," to be revealed to the public, leading to a gross misrepresentation and a wholesale misunderstanding of who he really was. The result has been an appalling ignorance of the real Lincoln in the North and in the New South, and ongoing, often vicious, debates as to who he really was.

Since this, the *Northern* view of Lincoln—the only one known by the general public—has been studied, written, and discussed to death, I felt that a new appraisal of the man was called for, one that focuses on his other half, the part we in the traditional South call the "real Lincoln." Such an examination is particularly important in this, the sesquicentennial anniversary of Lincoln's War, for, as of the writing of this Preface on April 12, 2011, it has been exactly 150 years to the month that the unenlightened, the foolish, and the malicious have been hiding and dismissing the authentic Lincoln.

Thus it is that in *Lincolnology* we will be looking at the second Lincoln, the "Great Procrastinator," the side of himself that he usually only divulged to Southerners; the one his doting sycophants in the North and in the New South have deliberately from public view. This will be accomplished not by subjective opinion and *ad hominem* attacks. Rather, as my sub-subtitle suggests, my examination of the real Lincoln will come via the president himself; through a thorough study of his suppressed, misinterpreted, and forgotten writings and speeches.

In reading *Lincolnology* those not familiar with the real and complete Lincoln are sure to experience a range of emotions and reactions, from surprise and incredulity to outright shock and horror, leading many to wonder why he continues to be voted the number one "greatest American president" each year.

In fact, besides Lincoln's own guilefulness, prevarication, and obfuscation, the primary reason he is not hated today as much as Adolf Hitler and other dictators is because his more controversial and unsavory writings have been kept from public knowledge by his devotees. Is this anti-North hyperbole? Absolutely not. It is Lincoln's own words that damn him for all eternity. I am only the messenger.

Tragically for all of us, no matter what our political persuasion, a huge portion—perhaps even the vast majority—of Lincoln's original writings will never be known.

Many were *accidently* destroyed, such as when Lincoln's cousin, Elizabeth Todd Grimsley, for example, handed out some of his original papers as souvenirs; or when a family housemaid mistook some of his writings for garbage and tossed them into a fire.[3]

Lincoln himself contributed to the loss of many of his works. Before heading to Washington, D.C. in early 1861 to begin life in the White House, he threw out many of his own papers. Why? We will never know.

Far more sinister is the fact that an enormous quantity of Lincoln's documents were *intentionally* destroyed, not only by his followers, but by his work associates and family members. We know for a fact, based on countless sworn testimonies, that one of Lincoln's early employers, Samuel Hill, purposefully burned an atheistic book Lincoln wrote in the 1830s. According to its heretical author, the Bible is not the word of God, there is no such thing as a miracle, Jesus was a fraud,[4] and those who call themselves his followers (i.e., Christians) are **"ignoramuses."**[5] Hill's alleged purpose was to protect his young employee's future reputation[6]—and he succeeded. How different Lincoln would be viewed today had this important anti-Christian work not been lost.

The worst culprit from among the family category is unquestionably his son Robert Todd Lincoln, who was so concerned about his father's image that he would not even allow the president's official biographers, John G. Nicolay and John Hay, to include material he considered in any way injurious to his father's name in their ten-volume Lincoln biography.

After the deaths of Nicolay (in 1901) and Hay (in 1905), Robert took over ownership of his father's papers, carefully picking through them, discarding or burning anything that he deemed disparaging. It is safe to assume that untold thousands of President Lincoln's original writings went up the chimney at his sons hands, all in an effort to prevent them from getting out into the public forum.[7]

God only knows what incriminating speeches, scandalous letters, and sensational notes were incinerated, forever lost to the world.

We can be sure of one thing: if this material had not been destroyed, lost, or concealed, *and* it had become publicly known, there is no doubt that Lincoln would now be voted our "most detested president" rather than the idolized and apotheosized deity that he is today. In *Lincolnology* we will analyze what little remains of these surviving but buried writings.

I am a Christian. I have no interest in fomenting hatred toward our sixteenth president. However, I believe it is high time that the real Lincoln becomes known through an honest and objective examination of his own words. Hopefully someday his visage will be removed from our penny, five-dollar bill, and the Illinois license plate.

Even better, many of us would like to see his Pagan-styled memorial in Washington torn down to make way for a Christian-styled monument to a true Constitution-loving American patriot. I would suggest President Jefferson Davis.

Colonel Lochlainn Seabrook
Franklin, Tennessee, USA
April 12, 2011
150th Anniversary of Lincoln's War

NOTES TO THE READER

☛ To differentiate Lincoln's words from those of others in this book, I have **bolded** the president's. But please note that not all bolded words were created or written by Lincoln. In some cases he is merely quoting others in a particular letter or speech.

☛ In all cases I have retained the original spelling of early documents, speeches, and letters, including typographical errors. In the process I have done away with the arrogant [sic]. Quotes are thus exactly as originally written.

☛ American readers will understand my need to repeatedly give the first names of Northern and Southern individuals who are well-known here in the United States but who are far less familiar, if not completely unknown, to many foreigners.

☛ Any time we study the 19th Century it is important to bear in mind that Lincoln's party, the Republicans, and the opposing party, the Democrats, were the opposite of what they are today.[8] The Republicans of Lincoln's day (mainly Northerners) were big government liberals, while the Democrats (mainly Southerners) were small government conservatives. Thus while it is true that Lincoln was a Republican, he was nothing like the Republicans of the 21st Century.[9] He was what we would now call a liberal or a left-wing progressive, one who sought to enlarge the central government in power and scope while diminishing the powers and rights of the individual states. As Republican Lincoln said in his fiery Cooper Union Speech on February 27, 1860, to his opponents, the Democrats:

> **you say you are conservative—eminently conservative—while we are revolutionary, destructive, or something of the sort.**[10]

Lincoln disliked this view and fought against it,[11] but the Democrats were right: most liberals were, and are, Constitutional radicals who want to rewrite that document to suit their own political agendas. Lincoln himself made references to **"the political differences between Radicals and Conservatives,"** apparently placing himself somewhere in between.[12] He used the word "Radicals," of course, to mean abolitionists.

Today, however, true Conservatives certainly consider Lincoln himself a Radical. Not meaning an abolitionist (as in Lincoln's day),[13] but a liberal of the highest order, cut from the same progressive cloth as today's big government liberals, left-wingers like Hillary Clinton, Nancy Pelosi, Harry Reid, John Kerry, Barbara Boxer, Charles Rangel, Howard Dean, Dianne Feinstein, Maxine Waters, and Christopher Dodd, to name but a few. Had they lived in the mid 1800s all of these individuals would have belonged to the Republican party, just like their 19th-Century left-wing predecessor from Illinois.

During the presidential campaign of 1860, for example, traditional Southerners were publicly known as Democrats, or "conservatives," as they called themselves,[14] while Lincoln and most Northerners were publicly known as Republicans, or "liberals," as they referred to themselves.[15]

Lincoln, in his usual highly and antagonistic sectional manner, described the confusing situation in a letter written from Springfield, Illinois, on April 6, 1859:

> **Bearing in mind that about seventy years ago two great political parties were first formed in this country, that Thomas Jefferson was the head of one of them and Boston the headquarters of the other, it is both curious and interesting that those supposed to descend politically from the party opposed to Jefferson should now be celebrating his birthday in their own original seat of empire, while those claiming political descent from him have nearly ceased to breathe his name everywhere.**
>
> **Remembering, too, that the Jefferson party was formed upon its supposed superior devotion to the personal rights of men, holding the rights of property to be secondary only, and greatly inferior, and assuming that the so-called Democracy of to-day are the Jefferson, and their opponents the anti-Jefferson, party, it will be equally interesting to note how completely the**

two have changed hands as to the principle upon which they were originally supposed to be divided. The Democracy of to-day hold the liberty of one man to be absolutely nothing, when in conflict with another man's right of property; Republicans, on the contrary, are for both the man and the dollar, but in case of conflict the man before the dollar.[16]

Making the situation more complicated and confusing than it needs to be, however, the uninformed Lincoln sometimes incorrectly referred to the **"purpose"** of his liberal party as **"conservative,"** as he did September 16, 1859, in a speech at Columbus, Ohio:

The chief and real purpose of the Republican party is eminently conservative. It proposes nothing save and except to restore this government to its original tone in regard to this element of slavery, and there to maintain it, looking for no further change in reference to it than that which the original framers of the government themselves expected and looked forward to.[17]

While the first sentence of this paragraph is certainly true of today's Republican party, it was not true of them in 1859. In fact, Lincoln's statement here is a patent lie. His Republican party, the liberals of the day, wished to completely alter the Constitution in regard to the **"element of slavery"** in order to fit its own agenda. It was the Democrats, the conservatives of the day, who wanted to **"restore the government to its original tone."**

Simply stated, Lincoln was the 19th-Century's Franklin Delano Roosevelt, Barney Frank, or Barack Hussein Obama, while Jefferson Davis, the Confederacy's president, was the 19th-Century's Ronald Reagan, Ron Paul, or Sarah Palin. Without a basic understanding of these facts, the American "Civil War" will forever remain incomprehensible. For a full discussion of this topic see my book, *Abraham Lincoln Was a Liberal, Jefferson Davis Was a Conservative: The Missing Key to Understanding the*

American Civil War.

☞ To my foreign readers: the words "conservative" and "liberal" have different meanings around the world. In Canada, for example, they have the opposite meanings of those used here in the United States. Throughout this work I use the modern traditional American definitions:

> *Conservative*, a proponent of small government, powerful sovereign states, and self-reliant citizens.
> *Liberal*, a proponent of large government, weak subservient states, and government-dependent citizens.

☞ Gratitude to my wife Cassidy and my daughters Fiona and Dixie for their infinite patience. Special thanks to Dr. Hill and Mayor Lovell for their support and for their wonderful contributions to this book.

L.S.

INTRODUCTION

BY DR. J. MICHAEL HILL

No U.S. President is as controversial and divisive as Abraham Lincoln. On the one hand, he is praised as the greatest man to hold the office of President by establishment historians and other supporters of a consolidated American nation; on the other, he is reviled as a dictatorial tyrant by those who actually believe in the Founders' principles and have allowed the facts of their study of Lincoln to speak for themselves.

Lochlainn Seabrook falls into the latter category, and in his magisterial work, *Lincolnology: The Real Abraham Lincoln Revealed In His Own Words*, we have the sixteenth President laid bare according to his own testimony. What emerges is the picture of a man hardly recognizable as "Honest Abe" or the benign "Old Rail-splitter" of American folklore. Instead, we have a shady railroad lawyer beholden to the plutocratic interests of the northeast and a man who was clearly a sectional advocate in his checkered and mundane political career. Moreover, the Lincoln that is revealed in his own words is the champion of big, intrusive government, and in that sense he is an heir of the traditions of Alexander Hamilton and the Federalists.

It is understandable that the South, cleaving to the ideas of Patrick Henry and Thomas Jefferson and the States Rights principles found in the Articles of Confederation and the subsequent Bill of Rights (especially the 9th and 10th amendments), would oppose Lincoln—both then and now. Indeed, Lincoln's military subjugation of the Southern Confederacy in 1865 did not "save the Union," as mainstream establishment historians contend; rather, by invading the free and sovereign Southern States, preventing their legal secession, and forcing them back into what theretofore had been a voluntary union, actually destroyed the Founders' republic and the Constitution that was its fundamental law. What was born after Appomattox was an American Empire, and Abe Lincoln was its sire.

For those of us who have been fighting over the past two decades to return freedom and prosperity to the historic South, the myth of Lincoln as American Savior is as distasteful as it is untrue. It is, in fact, one of the major pillars on which the current regime (both Democrat and Republican) sits. For much too long, Southerners have been force-fed this myth, and many unfortunately have swallowed the lie. The regime understands how important Southern support (especially in the military) is for its ability to continue to rule. That is why the regime's supporters are quick to demonize anyone who challenges their sacred cows, of which the Lincoln Myth is one.

But truth eventually wins out. Thanks to the efforts of historians such as Lochlainn Seabrook, the Lincoln Myth is beginning to crumble. It is my sincere hope that this book ends up in the hands of every Southerner (and our righteous northern and western allies) and opens their eyes to the dangers of centralized tyranny, both in the 1860s and today.

Dr. J. Michael Hill
Killen, Alabama
April 2011

LINCOLNOLOGY
THE REAL ABRAHAM LINCOLN

Revealed in His Own Words

Lincoln & the Presidency

ACCORDING TO YANKEE MYTHOLOGY, LINCOLN was our greatest president. Indeed, he is annually voted the number one "most popular" and "best" president in American history by nescient citizens,[18] some even going so far as to call him "the greatest American in history."[19] His visage graces our penny and our five-dollar bill and, having been both immortalized and apotheosized, he is permanently ensconced in Washington, D.C. on his own Pagan-like throne in his own Pagan-like temple.

In the progressive, liberal, and socialist North, Lincoln has been likened to such beloved biblical figures as Melchizedek,[20] Abraham, Moses, and even "the Prince of Peace," Jesus of Nazareth. Lincoln's own mother, Nancy Hanks (a relative of actor Tom Hanks),[21] has even been compared to the Virgin Mary.[22] Some have actually referred to Lincoln as the "Redeemer President,"[23] a title traditional Southern Christians rightly consider both ridiculous and blasphemous.

While the North and the New South have been busy canonizing their favorite statesman, they have accused one of the Confederacy's greatest statesmen, our Jewish secretary of war and state, Judah P. Benjamin (proudly known here in Dixie as "the brains of the Confederacy"), of taking part in Lincoln's murder, portraying him as nothing less than a modern day "Judas Iscariot."[24]

One Lincoln cultist referred to his idol as the "one great man, and mystery and miracle of the nineteenth century." Another Northerner strained credulity when he referred to Lincoln as the "greatest, wisest and godliest man that has appeared on the earth since Christ."[25] Still another Yankee, Reverend Charles Francis Potter of New York, characterized the president as the "future social Christ" of America, and predicted the coming of an "American Church" and an "American Bible" in which the masses "will find in parallel columns the stories of Christ and of Lincoln."[26]

Despite the modern deification of our sixteenth president, during his two terms in office he was extremely disliked in both the North and the South.[27] Indeed, not only was Ulysses S. Grant far more popular,[28] in the 1860s a large percentage of the general public viewed Lincoln as the worst chief executive up to that time,[29] some even referring to him as "America's most hated president."[30]

According to his own words, there was certainly ample reason for concern.

Prior to his election to the Oval Office, Lincoln—a man who did not know precisely where he was born,[31] whose father and paternal ancestry are not known with certainty,[32] who had a psychic premonition that he would die if he became president,[33] and who was largely self-taught (with just one year of formal education)[34]—expressed little confidence in his ability to serve in the nation's highest office. On April 16, 1859, for example, here is what he said to an Illinois newspaper editor who suggested he make a run for the White House:

> . . . I must in candor say I do not think myself fit for the presidency. I certainly am flattered and gratified that some partial friends think of me in that connection; but I really think it best for our cause that no concerted effort, such as you suggest, should be made.[35]

A year earlier, in 1858, Lincoln met a German immigrant named Henry Villard waiting for a train. As it started to rain the pair ducked into an empty freight car for shelter. Villard recorded the incident in his *Memoirs*:

> He and I met accidentally, about nine o'clock on a hot, sultry evening, at a flag railroad station about twenty miles west of Springfield, on my return from a great meeting at Petersburg in Menard County. He had been driven to the station in a buggy and left there alone. I was already there. The train that we intended to take for Springfield was about due. After vainly waiting for half an hour for its arrival, a thunderstorm compelled us to take refuge in an empty freight-car standing on a side track, there being no

buildings of any sort at the station. We squatted down on the floor of the car and fell to talking on all sorts of subjects. It was then and there he told me that, when he was clerking in a country store, his highest political ambition was to be a member of the State Legislature. "Since then, of course," he said laughingly, "I have grown some, but my friends got me into this business [meaning the canvass]. I did not consider myself qualified for the United States Senate, and it took me a long time to persuade myself that I was. Now, to be sure," he continued, with another of his peculiar laughs, "I am convinced that I am good enough for it; but, in spite of it all, I am saying to myself every day: 'It is too big a thing for you; you will never get it.' Mary [Lincoln's wife] insists, however, that I am going to be Senator and President of the United States, too." These last words he followed with a roar of laughter, with his arms around his knees, and shaking all over with mirth at his wife's ambition. "Just think," he exclaimed, "of such a sucker as me as President!"[36]

Further evidence of his lack of political confidence comes from the seven Lincoln-Douglas Debates, which transpired between August 21, 1858, and October 15, 1858.[37] After losing that November to incumbent Stephen A. Douglas, Lincoln said:

> . . . I now sink out of view, and shall be forgotten.[38]

Years later, on June 9, 1864, Lincoln was apparently still of the same mind. It was on this date that he wrote his now famous "Reply to a Delegation from the National Union League" regarding his renomination for the 1864 election:

> Gentlemen: I can only say in response to the kind remarks of your chairman, as I suppose, that I am very grateful for the renewed confidence which has been accorded to me both by the convention and by the National League. I am not insensible at all to the personal compliment there is in this, and yet I do not allow myself to believe that any but a small portion of it is to be appropriated as a personal compliment. That really the convention and the Union League assembled with a higher view—that of taking care of the interests of the country for the present and the great future—and that the part I am entitled to appropriate as a compliment is

only that part which I may lay hold of as being the opinion of the convention and of the League, that I am not entirely unworthy to be intrusted with the place which I have occupied for the last three years. But I do not allow myself to suppose that either the convention or the League have concluded to decide that I am either the greatest or best man in America, but rather they have concluded that it is not best to swap horses while crossing the river, and have further concluded that I am not so poor a horse that they might not make a botch of it in trying to swap.[39]

Sincere humility is one thing. Self-negation, feigned or otherwise, is another.

In the winter of 1859 Jesse W. Fell asked Lincoln to write out a "sketch" of his life, a sort of 19th-Century biography that was to be used to educate the public about the Illinois politician. What follows is Lincoln's cover letter and self-written autobiography:

My dear Sir: Herewith is a little sketch, as you requested. There is not much of it, for the reason, I suppose, that there is not much of me. If anything be made out of it, I wish it to be modest, and not to go beyond the material. If it were thought necessary to incorporate anything from any of my speeches, I suppose there would be no objection. Of course it must not appear to have been written by myself. Yours very truly, A. Lincoln.

I was born February 12, 1809, in Hardin County, Kentucky. My parents were both born in Virginia, of undistinguished families—second families, perhaps I should say. My mother [Nancy], who died in my tenth year, was of a family of the name of Hanks, some of whom now reside in Adams, and others in Macon County, Illinois. My paternal grandfather, Abraham Lincoln, emigrated from Rockingham County, Virginia, to Kentucky about 1781 or 1782, where a year or two later he was killed by the Indians, not in battle, but by stealth, when he was laboring to open a farm in the forest. His ancestors, who were Quakers, went to Virginia from Berks County, Pennsylvania. An effort to identify them with the New England family of the same name ended in nothing more definite than a similarity of Christian names in both families, such as Enoch, Levi, Mordecai,

Solomon, Abraham, and the like.

My father [Thomas], at the death of his father, was but six years of age, and he grew up literally without education. He removed from Kentucky to what is now Spencer County, Indiana, in my eighth year. We reached our new home about the time the State came into the Union. It was a wild region, with many bears and other wild animals still in the woods. There I grew up. There were some schools, so called, but no qualification was ever required of a teacher beyond "readin', writin', and cipherin'" to the rule of three. If a straggler supposed to understand Latin happened to sojourn in the neighborhood, he was looked upon as a wizard. There was absolutely nothing to excite ambition for education. Of course, when I came of age I did not know much. Still, somehow, I could read, write, and cipher to the rule of three, but that was all. I have not been to school since. The little advance I now have upon this store of education, I have picked up from time to time under the pressure of necessity.

I was raised to farm work, which I continued till I was twenty-two. At twenty-one I came to Illinois, Macon County. Then I got to New Salem, at that time in Sangamon, now in Menard County, where I remained a year as a sort of clerk in a store. Then came the Black Hawk war; and I was elected a captain of volunteers, a success which gave me more pleasure than any I have had since. I went [on] the campaign, was elated, ran for the legislature the same year (1832), and was beaten—the only time I ever have been beaten by the people. The next and three succeeding biennial elections I was elected to the legislature. I was not a candidate afterward. During this legislative period I had studied law, and removed to Springfield to practise it. In 1846 I was once elected to the lower House of Congress. Was not a candidate for reelection. From 1849 to 1854, both inclusive, practised law more assiduously than ever before. Always a Whig [i.e., a liberal] in politics; and generally on the Whig electoral tickets, making active canvasses. I was losing interest in politics when the repeal of the Missouri compromise aroused me again. What I have done since then is pretty well known.

If any personal description of me is thought desirable, it may be said I am, in height, six feet four inches, nearly; lean in flesh, weighing on an average one hundred and eighty pounds; dark complexion, with coarse black hair and gray eyes. No other marks or brands recollected. Yours truly, A. Lincoln[40]

Compared to today's hyperbolic political bios, Lincoln's "sketch" of himself is the epitome of humility and self-negation.

Even upon hearing the news that he had been nominated for U.S. president in the spring of 1860, Lincoln displayed a reluctance that is almost shocking. In his reply to the Chicago Convention Committee, for example, he used the word **"painfully,"** noting that the nomination was

> a responsibility which I could almost wish had fallen upon some one of the far more eminent men and experienced statesmen whose distinguished names were before the convention . . .[41]

Even his election to president did nothing for his lack of self-love, as is evidenced in his February 18, 1861, address to the New York Legislature at Albany:

> It is true that . . . I hold myself, without mock modesty, the humblest of all individuals that have ever been elevated to the presidency . . .[42]

The next day, during his February 19 speech at Poughkeepsie, New York, Lincoln's poor self-image seems to have sunk even lower, even to the point where he states that the American public made a mistake in electing him:

> I do not say that in the recent election the people did the wisest thing that could have been done; indeed, I do not think they did; but I do say that in accepting the great trust committed to me, which I do with a determination to endeavor to prove worthy of it, I must rely upon you, upon the people of the whole country, for support . . .[43]

The next day, in a written reply to New York Mayor Fernando Wood, Lincoln said: **"I fear too great confidence may have been placed in me."**[44]

What was the source of this man's low self-esteem? We will never know for sure. The real question is this: would Americans today make a man president who said the following, as Lincoln did in a letter to Eliza Caldwell Browning (wife of Orville Hickman Browning) on April 1, 1838:

> I have now come to the conclusion never again to think of marrying, and for this reason—I can never be satisfied with any one who would be blockhead enough to have me.[45]

Right up to the end of his life it seems Lincoln was acutely aware that the occupation of U.S. president was one for which he was not qualified, one that he should not have pursued. On November 2, 1863, he wrote a letter to James H. Hackett that included the following:

> My note to you I certainly did not expect to see in print; yet I have not been much shocked by the newspaper comments upon it. Those comments constitute a fair specimen of what has occurred to me through life. I have endured a great deal of ridicule without much malice; and have received a great deal of kindness, not quite free from ridicule. I am used to it.[46]

These are unusual words for a sitting president two years into his first term, particularly because he must have known that even this small paragraph would be made public in the future. However, even this was far from being his most self-negating declaration.

In 1864, when he was asked what he thought of the anti-Lincoln Wade-Davis Bill, as well as a scathing speech given by his arch critic abolitionist Wendell Phillips, Lincoln replied:

> No, I have not seen them, nor do I care to see them. I have seen enough to satisfy me that I am a failure, not only in the opinion of the people in rebellion, but of many distinguished politicians of my own party.[47]

To this day most Southerners believe that Lincoln would have been better off had he followed the example of one of his generals, war criminal William Tecumseh Sherman (in Dixie still one of the most detested of all men). In 1884, when pressured to make a bid for the White house, Sherman wisely said: "I will not accept if nominated, and will not serve if elected."[48]

What may surprise modern readers even more than Lincoln's

admission that he was incapable of being president is that many of his own cabinet members, party members, military officers, and constituents agreed with him.

Yankee General Don Piatt, for instance, wrote the following about his leader, President Abraham Lincoln:

> The man who could open a Cabinet meeting called to discuss the Emancipation Proclamation by reading Artemus Ward,[49] who called for a comic song on the bloody battle-field,[50] was the same man who could guide with clear mind and iron hand the diplomacy that kept off the fatal interference of Europe, while conducting at home the most horrible of all civil wars that ever afflicted a people. He reached with ease the highest and the lowest level, and on the very field that he shamed with a ribald song he left a record of eloquence never reached by human lips before.[51]

In 1863, before the U.S. Congress, Yankee Senator Willard Saulsbury of Delaware stood up and, intimating that Lincoln was an "enemy of the country," declared the following:

> Thus has it been with Mr. Lincoln—a weak and imbecile man; the weakest man that I ever knew in a high place; for I have seen him and conversed with him, and I say here, in my place in the Senate of the United States, that I never did see or converse with so weak and imbecile a man as Abraham Lincoln, President of the United States. . . . if I wanted to paint a tyrant, if I wanted to paint a despot, a man perfectly regardless of every constitutional right of the people, who's sworn servant, not ruler, he is, I would paint the hideous form of Abraham Lincoln.[52]

Famed Yankee abolitionist William Lloyd Garrison said of Lincoln, he may be a giant in height, but he is a midget in intellect,[53] while one of Lincoln's officers, General George B. McClellan, felt that:

> The president is nothing more than a well meaning baboon. He is the original gorilla. What a specimen to be at the head of our affairs now![54]

Indiana Senator Albert Jeremiah Beveridge, also a lawyer and a historian, noted that early in Lincoln's political career—when he was a new and very active Congressman—scarcely anyone noticed him. Those few who did came away with a very "unfavorable impression."[55] George W.

Julian, Indiana Congressman under Lincoln, wrote of the U.S. leader:

> The President, his advisers, his commanding generals . . . whose shaping hands have had so much to do with the conduct of the war, must all of them be weighed in the balance by the people and the generations to come. "The great soul of the world is just," and sooner or later all disguises will be thrown off, and every historical character will stand forth as he is, in the light of his deeds and deserts. . . . Justice will be done; but that justice may brand as a crime the blunders proceeding from a feeble, timid, ambidextrous policy, resulting in great sacrifices of life and treasure, and periling the priceless interests at stake.[56]

On September 6, 1864, the New York *Daily Tribune* noted that Lincoln had been called the following names by his Northern political associates, many of them from his own party: "filthy story-teller," "despot," "big secessionist," "liar," "thief," "braggart," "buffoon," "usurper," "monster," "Ignoramus Abe," "old scoundrel," "perjurer," "robber," "swindler," "tyrant," "fiend," "butcher," and "land pirate."[57]

It is little wonder that Lincoln was so detested, even by many Northerners, at the time. For far from acting like a 19th-Century U.S. president, Lincoln's behavior was much more similar to an ancient Roman emperor, an imperial tyrant who viewed the American people as his docile and malleable subjects.

In order to achieve his true goal of installing big government in Washington and the northernization of the South, Lincoln did indeed quite consciously assume the role of a consolidating dictator, the head of Henry Clay's big government concept known as the "American System." This was, after all, part of the president's dream from the very beginning: just as liberals do today, Lincoln rejected both the natural rights principles of the Declaration of Independence and the idea of state sovereignty found in the U.S. Constitution. This after stating, on February 22, 1861, that

> **I have never had a feeling, politically, that did not spring from the sentiments embodied in the Declaration of Independence."**[58]

Eventually coming to believe instead in the supremacy of an all-powerful central government that lords over weak compliant states, as president he sought to totally control the economic and human resources of the American people, along with the nation's banking system and military establishment.[59] As Lincoln said in a November 20, 1863, letter to Edward Everett:

> The point made against the theory of the general government being only an agency, whose principles are the States, was new to me, and, as I think, is one of the best arguments for the national supremacy.[60]

This **"national supremacy"** was something Lincoln craved so obsessively that he was willing to use physical violence to attain it if necessary, as he intimated in June 26, 1857, speech at Springfield, Illinois:

> If it prove to be true, as is probable, that the people of Utah are in open rebellion to the United States . . . I say . . they ought to be somehow coerced to obedience . . .[61]

As president three years later, Lincoln put into practice what he had once only spoken of. For example, in the spring of 1861 he authorized a May 27 letter to Union General William Selby Harney of Missouri, that ended with the following statement:

> The authority of the United States is paramount, and whenever it is apparent that a movement, whether by color of State authority or not, is hostile, you will not hesitate to put it down.[62]

As we will see, such **"authority"** included suspending the writ of *habeas corpus* across the entire nation without just cause, illegally arresting, imprisoning, and torturing civilians, invading a foreign country without declaring war, instigating an illicit naval blockade, shutting down the legislatures of entire states, suppressing freedom of speech, confiscating and destroying private property, and the wholesale bombing of Southern towns and cities comprised solely of non-combatants.

Once, when confronted by the House of Representatives with a resolution to explain why he was arresting and imprisoning the police of Baltimore, Maryland, Lincoln gave this imperious reply:

> In answer to the resolution of the House of Representatives of the 24th instant asking the grounds, reason, and evidence upon which the police commissioners of Baltimore were arrested and are now

detained as prisoners at Fort McHenry, I have to state that it is judged to be incompatible with the public interest at this time to furnish the information called for by the resolution.[63]

Lincoln had no sympathy whatsoever for those Baltimore citizens he illegally arrested, illegally tried, and illegally imprisoned. One of these unfortunate souls was police officer John W. Davis, who refused to take Lincoln's equally illegal "Oath of Allegiance" to the U.S. government. Using the third person, here is how the tyrannical president (or one of his aids writing for him) replied to a protest against Davis' arrest on September 15, 1861:

> The President has read this letter, and he deeply commiserates the condition of any one so distressed as the writer seems to be. He does not know Mr. Davis—only knows him to be one of the arrested police commissioners of Baltimore because he says so in this letter. Assuming him to be one of those commissioners, the President understands Mr. Davis could at the time of his arrest, could at any time since, and can now, be released by taking a full oath of allegiance to the government of the United States, and that Mr. Davis has not been kept in ignorance of this condition of release. If Mr. Davis is still so hostile to the government, and so determined to aid its enemies in destroying it, he makes his own choice.[64]

Only an autocrat like Lincoln could possibly believe that a citizen who refuses to pledge an unlawful oath to an authoritarian government is an **"enemy"** seeking to **"destroy"** that government!

On February 19, 1862, big government Lincoln asked all Americans to celebrate the birthday of George Washington by reading his famous Farewell Address, issued on September 19, 1796. Said Lincoln:

> It is recommended to the people of the United States that they assemble in their customary places of meeting for public solemnities on the 22d day of February instant, and celebrate the anniversary of the birth of the Father of his Country, by causing to be read to them his immortal farewell address. A. Lincoln.[65]

Apparently Lincoln himself had never read it. For if he had he would have certainly noticed that the kind of authoritarian central government he so desperately desired was the exact type of government Washington warned Americans about in his address. Stating that he wished to leave office by offering several "all-important" sentiments, the "disinterested warnings of a parting friend," the nation's first president declared:

> The unity of government, which constitutes you one people, is also now dear to you. It is justly so; for it is a main pillar in the edifice of your real independence—the support of your tranquility at home, your peace abroad, of your safety, of your prosperity, of that very liberty which you so highly prize. But as it is easy to foresee that, from different causes and from different quarters, much pains will be taken, many artifices employed, to weaken in your minds the conviction of this truth; as this is the point in your political fortress against which the batteries of internal and external enemies will be most constantly and actively (though often covertly and insidiously) directed,—it is of infinite moment that you should properly estimate the immense value of your national union to your collective and individual happiness; that you should cherish a cordial, habitual, and immovable attachment to it; accustoming yourselves to think and speak of it as of the palladium of your political safety and prosperity; watching for its preservation with jealous anxiety; discountenancing whatever may suggest even a suspicion that it can, in any event, be abandoned; and indignantly frowning upon the first dawning of every attempt to alienate any portion of our country from the rest, or to enfeeble the sacred ties which now link together the various parts.[66]

Washington goes on to advise the citizens of the U.S. to avoid foreign alliances, becoming embroiled in wars, and

> over-grown military establishments, which, under any form of government, are inauspicious to liberty, and which are to be regarded as particularly hostile to republican liberty . . .[67]

Governmental change is allowed, even encouraged, Washington writes in his Farewell Address. But only by way of Constitutional amendments supported by the people. For changes brought about by force would surely lead to the destruction of self-government:

> . . . let there be no change by usurpation; for though this, in one instance, may be the instrument of good, it is the customary weapon by which free governments are destroyed.[68]

Sixty-five years later Lincoln would conveniently ignore all of these stern admonitions and destroy the free government that Southerner President Washington had helped to create.

Lincoln's vicious, monarchical, dictatorial impulses were certainly obvious to all Southerners. But they were obvious to many Northerners as well. At Alton, Illinois, on October 15, 1858, one of these, Stephen A. Douglas, made the following comments:

> Mr. Lincoln went on to tell you that he does not at all desire to interfere with slavery in the States where it exists, nor does his party. I expected him to say that down here. Let me ask him then how he expects to put slavery in the course of ultimate extinction everywhere, if he does not intend to interfere with it in the States where it exists? He says that he will prohibit it in all Territories, and the inference is, then, that unless they make free States out of them he will keep them out of the Union; for, mark you, he did not say whether or not he would vote to admit Kansas with slavery or not, as her people might apply (he forgot that, as usual); he did not say whether or not he was in favor of bringing the Territories now in existence into the Union on the principle of [Henry] Clay's compromise measures on the slavery question. I told you that he would not. His idea is that he will prohibit slavery in all the Territories, and thus force them all to become free States, surrounding the slave States with a cordon of free States and hemming them in, keeping the slaves confined to their present limits whilst they go on multiplying until the soil on which they live will no longer feed them, and he will thus be able to put slavery in a course of ultimate extinction by starvation. He will extinguish slavery in the Southern States as the French general extinguished the Algerines when he smoked them out. He is going to extinguish slavery by surrounding the slave States, hemming in the slaves, and starving them out of existence, as you smoke a fox out of his hole. He intends to do that in the name of humanity and Christianity, in order that we may get rid of the terrible crime and sin entailed upon our fathers of holding slaves. Mr. Lincoln makes out that line of policy, and appeals to the moral sense of justice and to the Christian feeling of the community to sustain him. He says that any man who holds to the contrary doctrine is in the position of the king who claimed to govern by divine right. Let us examine for a

moment and see what principle it was that overthrew the divine right of [King] George III to govern us. Did not these colonies rebel because the British parliament had no right to pass laws concerning our property and domestic and private institutions without our consent? We demanded that the British government should not pass such laws unless they gave us representation in the body passing them—and this the British government insisting on doing, we went to war, on the principle that the home government should not control and govern distant colonies without giving them a representation. Now Mr. Lincoln proposes to govern the Territories without giving them a representation, and calls on Congress to pass laws controlling their property and domestic concerns without their consent and against their will. Thus he asserts for his party the identical principle asserted by George III and the Tories of the Revolution.[69]

Douglas is right. In fact, it is this very attitude that has made despots, totalitarians, and dictators, whose chief aim is the total control of nations, come to idolize the socialist-styled President Lincoln.

One of these, arch socialist Adolf Hitler, head of the National Socialist German Workers Party (the Nazis), was fond of citing Lincoln as a shining example of how to destroy states' rights. In his book *Mein Kampf* ("My Struggle"), Hitler not only denies that the U.S.A. was originally a confederacy (it was actually called "the Confederacy" from 1781 to 1789[70] and was known by the nickname "the Confederate States of America" well into the 1800s)[71] he also repeats Lincoln's fantasy that a union always precedes (and thus creates) its states, and that therefore there is no such thing as state sovereignty.

In 1926 here is how the Führer presented Lincoln's theory: the question is, should Germany be turned into a Confederacy or a Union, and just what is a Confederacy? It is a voluntary union of free and independent states. By this definition, today there are no true confederacies anywhere in the world, Hitler asserted. The least like a confederacy is the United States of America, for her individual states do not have, could not have, and never had, any sovereignty. Why? Because, as he concluded, it was the Union that created the individual states, not vice versa.[72]

In short Hitler says that the idea of "sovereign states" has never existed in America, the same view that Lincoln held until the end of his life.

From this example alone there can be little question that Hitler used Lincoln's despotic, unhistorical, inaccurate, and self-serving ideas to justify demolishing states' rights as he rampaged his way across Europe.[73]

That Lincoln hated the idea of states' rights was clearly evident in a September 16, 1859, speech he gave at Columbus, Ohio. Here, after promoting his belief that blacks should not be made equal to whites, he makes numerous personal attacks on Douglas and the idea of "popular sovereignty" (states' rights), while promoting his notion that slavery should be limited to the South:

> . . . The giant [Douglas] himself has been here recently.[74] I have seen a brief report of his speech. If it were otherwise unpleasant to me to introduce the subject of the negro as a topic for discussion, I might be somewhat relieved by the fact that he dealt exclusively in that subject while he was here. I shall, therefore, without much hesitation or diffidence, enter upon this subject.
>
> The American people, on the first day of January, 1854, found the African slave-trade prohibited by a law of Congress. In a majority of the States of this Union, they found African slavery, or any other sort of slavery, prohibited by State constitutions. They also found a law existing, supposed to be valid, by which slavery was excluded from almost all the territory the United States then owned. This was the condition of the country, with reference to the institution of slavery, on the first of January, 1854. A few days after that, a bill was introduced into Congress, which ran through its regular course in the two branches of the national legislature, and finally passed into a law in the month of May, by which the act of Congress prohibiting slavery from going into the Territories of the United States was repealed. In connection with the law itself, and, in fact, in the terms of the law, the then existing prohibition was not only repealed, but there was a declaration of a purpose on the part of Congress never thereafter to exercise any power that they might have, real or supposed, to prohibit the extension or spread of slavery. This was a very great change: for the law thus repealed was of more than thirty years' standing. Following rapidly upon the heels of this action of Congress, a decision of the Supreme Court is made, by which it is declared that Congress, if it desires to prohibit the spread of slavery into the Territories, has no constitutional power to do so. Not only so, but that decision lays down principles, which, if pushed to their logical conclusion,—I say pushed to their logical conclusion,—would decide that the constitutions of free

States, forbidding slavery, are themselves unconstitutional. Mark me, I do not say the judges said this, and let no man say I affirm the judges used these words; but I only say it is my opinion that what they did say, if pressed to its logical conclusion, will inevitably result thus.

Looking at these things, the Republican party, as I understand its principles and policy, believes that there is great danger of the institution of slavery being spread out and extended, until it is ultimately made alike lawful in all the States of this Union; so believing, to prevent that incidental and ultimate consummation is the original and chief purpose of the Republican organization. I say "chief purpose" of the Republican organization; for it is certainly true that if the national house shall fall into the hands of the Republicans, they will have to attend to all the other matters of national house-keeping as well as this. The chief and real purpose of the Republican party is eminently conservative. It proposes nothing save and except to restore this government to its original tone in regard to this element of slavery, and there to maintain it, looking for no further change in reference to it than that which the original framers of the government themselves expected and looked forward to. [These last two sentences are false, and an intentional misrepresentation on Lincoln's part.]

The chief danger to this purpose of the Republican party is not just now the revival of the African slave-trade, or the passage of a congressional slave-code, or the declaring of a second Dred Scott decision, making slavery lawful in all the States. These are not pressing us just now. They are not quite ready yet. The authors of these measures know that we are too strong for them; but they will be upon us in due time, and we will be grappling with them hand to hand, if they are not now headed off. They are not now the chief danger to the purpose of the Republican organization; but the most imminent danger that now threatens that purpose is that insidious Douglas popular sovereignty. This is the miner and sapper. While it does not propose to revive the African slave-trade, nor to pass a slave-code, nor to make a second Dred Scott decision, it is preparing us for the onslaught and charge of these ultimate enemies when they shall be ready to come on, and the word of command for them to advance shall be given. I say this Douglas popular sovereignty—for there is a broad distinction, as I now understand it, between that article and a genuine popular sovereignty.

I believe there is a genuine popular sovereignty. I think a definition of genuine popular sovereignty, in the abstract, would be about this: That each man shall do precisely as he pleases with himself, and with all those things which exclusively concern him. Applied to government, this principle would be, that a general government shall do all those things which pertain to it, and all the local governments shall do precisely as they please in respect to those matters which exclusively concern them. I understand that this government of the United States, under which we live, is based upon this principle; and I am misunderstood if it is supposed that I have any war to make upon that principle.

Now, what is Judge Douglas's popular sovereignty? It is, as a principle, no other than that if one man chooses to make a slave of another man, neither that other man nor anybody else has a right to object. Applied in government, as he seeks to apply it, it is this: If, in a new Territory into which a few people are beginning to enter for the purpose of making their homes, they choose to either exclude slavery from their limits or to establish it there, however one or the other may affect the persons to be enslaved, or the infinitely greater number of persons who are afterward to inhabit that Territory, or the other members of the families of communities, of which they are but an incipient member, or the general head of the family of States as parent of all—however their action may affect one or the other of these, there is no power or right to interfere. That is Douglas's popular sovereignty applied.

He has a good deal of trouble with popular sovereignty. His explanations explanatory of explanations explained are interminable. The most lengthy and, as I suppose, the most maturely considered of his long series of explanations is his great essay in "Harper's Magazine." I will not attempt to enter on any very thorough investigation of his argument as there made and presented. I will nevertheless occupy a good portion of your time here in drawing your attention to certain points in it. Such of you as may have read this document will have perceived that the judge, early in the document, quotes from two persons as belonging to the Republican party, without naming them, but who can readily be recognized as being Governor [William H.] Seward, of New York, and myself. It is true that exactly fifteen months ago this day, I believe, I for the first time expressed a sentiment upon this subject, and in such a manner that it should get into print, that the public might see it beyond the circle of my hearers, and my expression of it at that time is the quotation that Judge Douglas makes. He has not made the quotation with accuracy, but justice to him requires me to say that it is sufficiently accurate not to change its sense.

The sense of that quotation condensed is this—that this slavery element is a durable element of discord among us, and that we shall probably not have perfect peace in this country with it until it either masters the free principle in our government, or is so far mastered by the free principle as for the public mind to rest in the belief that it is going to its end. This sentiment which I now express in this way was, at no great distance of time, perhaps in different language, and in connection with some collateral ideas, expressed by Governor Seward. Judge Douglas has been so much annoyed by the expression of that sentiment that he has constantly, I believe, in almost all his speeches since it was uttered, been referring to it, I find he alluded to it in his speech here, as well as in the copyright essay. I do not now enter upon this for the purpose of making an elaborate argument to show that we were right in the expression of that sentiment. I only ask your attention to this matter for the purpose of making one or two points upon it.

If you will read the copyright essay, you will discover that Judge Douglas himself says a controversy between the American colonies and the government of Great Britain began on the slavery question in 1699, and continued from that time until the Revolution; and, while he did not say so, we all know that it has continued with more or less violence ever since the Revolution.

Then we need not appeal to history, to the declaration of the framers of the government, but we know from Judge Douglas himself that slavery began to be an element of discord among the white people of this country as far back as 1699, or one hundred and sixty years ago, or five generations of men—counting thirty years to a generation. Now it would seem to me that it might have occurred to Judge Douglas, or to anybody who had turned his attention to these facts, that there was something in the nature of that thing, slavery, somewhat durable for mischief and discord.

There is another point I desire to make in regard to this matter before I leave it. From the adoption of the Constitution down to 1820 is the precise period of our history when we had comparative peace upon this question—the precise period of time when we came nearer to having peace about it than any other time of that entire one hundred and sixty years, in which he says it began, or of the eighty years of our own Constitution. Then it would be worth our while to stop and examine into the probable reason of our coming nearer to having peace then than at any other time. This was the precise period of time in which our fathers adopted, and during which they followed, a policy restricting the spread of slavery, and the whole Union was acquiescing in it. The whole country looked forward to the ultimate extinction of the institution. It was when a policy had been adopted and was prevailing, which led all just and right-minded men to suppose that slavery was gradually coming to an end, and that they might be quiet about it, watching it as it expired. I think Judge Douglas might have perceived that too, and, whether he did or not, it is worth the attention of fair-minded men, here and elsewhere, to consider whether that is not the truth of the case. If he had looked at these two facts, that this matter has been an element of discord for one hundred and sixty years among this people, and that the only comparative peace we have had about it was when that policy prevailed in this government, which he now wars upon, he might then, perhaps, have been brought to a more just appreciation of what I said fifteen months ago—that

> "a house divided against itself cannot stand. I believe this government cannot endure permanently half slave and half free. I do not expect the Union to be dissolved—I do not expect the house to fall; but I do expect it will cease to be divided. It will become all one thing or all the other. Either the opponents of slavery will arrest the further spread of it, and place it where the public mind will rest in the belief that it is in the course of ultimate

extinction, or its advocates will push it forward, until it shall become alike lawful in all the States, old as well as new, North as well as South."

That was my sentiment at that time. In connection with it I said:

"We are now far into the fifth year since a policy was initiated with the avowed object and confident promise of putting an end to slavery agitation. Under the operation of that policy, that agitation has not only not ceased, but has constantly augmented."

I now say to you here that we are advanced still farther into the sixth year since that policy of Judge Douglas—that popular sovereignty of his for quieting the slavery question—was made the national policy. Fifteen months more have been added since I uttered that sentiment, and I call upon you, and all other right-minded men, to say whether those fifteen months have belied or corroborated my words.

While I am here upon this subject, I cannot but express gratitude that the true view of this element of discord among us—as I believe it is—is attracting more and more attention. I do not believe that Governor Seward uttered that sentiment because I had done so before, but because he reflected upon this subject, and saw the truth of it. Nor do I believe, because Governor Seward or I uttered it, that Mr. [John] Hickman, of Pennsylvania, in different language, since that time, has declared his belief in the utter antagonism which exists between the principles of liberty and slavery. You see we are multiplying. Now, while I am speaking of Hickman, let me say, I know but little about him. I have never seen him, and know scarcely anything about the man; but I will say this much about him: Of all the anti-Lecompton Democracy that have been brought to my notice, he alone has the true, genuine ring of the metal. And now, without indorsing anything else he has said, I will ask this audience to give three cheers for Hickman. [The audience responded with three rousing cheers for Hickman.]

Another point in the copyright essay to which I

would ask your attention is rather a feature to be extracted from the whole thing, than from any express declaration of it at any point. It is a general feature of that document, and indeed, of all of Judge Douglas's discussions of this question, that the Territories of the United States and the States of this Union are exactly alike—that there is no difference between them at all—that the Constitution applies to the Territories precisely as it does to the States—and that the United States Government, under the Constitution may not do in a State what it may not do in a Territory, and what it must do in a State, it must do in a Territory. Gentlemen, is that a true view of the case? It is necessary for this squatter sovereignty; but is it true?

Let us consider. What does it depend upon? It depends altogether upon the proposition that the States must, without the interference of the General Government, do all those things that pertain exclusively to themselves—that are local in their nature, that have no connection with the General Government. After Judge Douglas has established this proposition, which nobody disputes or ever has disputed, he proceeds to assume, without proving it, that slavery is one of those little, unimportant, trivial matters, which are of just about as much consequence as the question would be to me whether my neighbor should raise horned cattle or plant tobacco; that there is no moral question about it, but that it is altogether a matter of dollars and cents; that when a new Territory is opened for settlement, the first man who goes into it may plant there a thing which, like the Canada thistle, or some other of those pests of the soil, cannot be dug out by the millions of men who will come thereafter; that it is one of those little things that is so trivial in its nature that it has no effect upon anybody save the few men who first plant upon the soil; that it is not a thing which in any way affects the family of communities composing these States, nor any way endangers the General Government. Judge Douglas ignores altogether the very well-known fact that we have never had a serious menace to our political existence, except it sprang from this thing, which he chooses to regard as only upon a par with onions and potatoes.

Turn it, and contemplate it in another view. He says that, according to his popular sovereignty, the General Government may give to the Territories governors, judges, marshals, secretaries, and all the other chief men to govern them, but they must not touch upon this other question. Why? The question of who shall be governor of a Territory for a year or two, and pass away, without his track being left upon the soil, or an act which he did for good or for evil being left behind, is a question of vast national magnitude. It is so much opposed in its nature to locality that the nation itself must decide it; while this other matter of planting slavery upon a soil—a thing which, once planted, cannot be eradicated by the succeeding millions who have as much right there as the first comers, or if eradicated, not without infinite difficulty and a long struggle—he considers the power to prohibit it as one of these little, local, trivial things that the nation ought not to say a word about; that it affects nobody save the few men who are there.

Take these two things and consider them together, present the question of planting a State with the institution of slavery by the side of a question of who shall be governor of Kansas for a year or two, and is there a man here—is there a man on earth—who would not say the governor question is the little one, and the slavery question is the great one? I ask any honest Democrat if the small, the local, and the trivial and temporary question is not, Who shall be governor?—while the durable, the important, and the mischievous one is, Shall this soil be planted with slavery?

This is an idea, I suppose, which has arisen in Judge Douglas's mind from his peculiar structure. I suppose the institution of slavery really looks small to him. He is so put up by nature that a lash upon his back would hurt him, but a lash upon anybody else's back does not hurt him. That is the build of the man, and consequently he looks upon the matter of slavery in this unimportant light.

Judge Douglas ought to remember, when he is endeavoring to force this policy upon the American people, that while he is put up in that way, a good many are not. He ought to remember that there was once in this country a man by the name of Thomas Jefferson, supposed to be a Democrat [i.e., at that time a conservative]—a man whose principles and policy are not very prevalent amongst Democrats to-day, it is true; but that man did not take exactly this view of the insignificance of the element of slavery which our friend

Judge Douglas does. In contemplation of this thing, we all know he [i.e., Jefferson] was led to exclaim, "I tremble for my country when I remember that God is just!" We know how he looked upon it when he thus expressed himself. There was danger to this country, danger of the avenging justice of God, in that little unimportant popular-sovereignty question of Judge Douglas. He supposed there was a question of God's eternal justice wrapped up in the enslaving of any race of men, or any man, and that those who did so braved the arm of Jehovah—that when a nation thus dared the Almighty, every friend of that nation had cause to dread his wrath. Choose ye between Jefferson and Douglas as to what is the true view of this element among us.

There is another little difficulty about this matter of treating the Territories and States alike in all things, to which I ask your attention, and I shall leave this branch of the case. If there is no difference between them, why not make the Territories States at once? What is the reason that Kansas was not fit to come into the Union when it was organized into a Territory, in Judge Douglas's view? Can any of you tell any reason why it should not have come into the Union at once? They are fit, as he thinks, to decide upon the slavery question—the largest and most important with which they could possibly deal; what could they do by coming into the Union that they are not fit to do, according to his view, by staying out of it? Oh, they are not fit to sit in Congress and decide upon the rates of postage, or questions of ad valorem or specific duties on foreign goods, or live-oak timber contracts; they are not fit to decide these vastly important matters, which are national in their import, but they are fit, "from the jump," to decide this little negro question. But, gentlemen, the case is too plain; I occupy too much time on this head, and I pass on.

Near the close of the copyright essay, the judge, I think, comes very near kicking his own fat into the fire. I did not think when I commenced these remarks that I would read from that article, but I now believe I will:

> [Lincoln quoting Douglas] "This exposition of the history of these measures shows conclusively that the authors of the compromise measures of 1850, and of the Kansas-Nebraska act of 1854, as well

> as the members of the Continental Congress in 1774, and the founders of our system of government subsequent to the Revolution regarded the people of the Territories and Colonies as political communities which were entitled to a free and exclusive power of legislation in their provincial legislatures, where their representation could alone be preserved, in all cases of taxation and internal polity."

When the judge saw that putting in the word "slavery" would contradict his own history, he put in what he knew would pass as synonymous with it—"internal polity." Whenever we find that in one of his speeches, the substitute is used in this manner; and I can tell you the reason. It would be too bald a contradiction to say slavery, but "internal polity" is a general phrase which would pass in some quarters, and which he hopes will pass with the reading community, for the same thing.

> [Lincoln continues quoting Douglas] "This right pertains to the people collectively, as a law-abiding and peaceful community, and not to the isolated individuals who may wander upon the public domain in violation of law. It can only be exercised where there are inhabitants sufficient to constitute a government, and capable of performing its various functions and duties, a fact to be ascertained and determined by—"

Who do you think? Judge Douglas says, "By Congress."

> "Whether the number shall be fixed at ten, fifteen, or twenty thousand inhabitants does not affect the principle."

Now I have only a few comments to make. Popular sovereignty, by his own words, does not pertain to the few persons who wander upon the public domain in violation of law. We have his words for that. When it does pertain to them is when they are sufficient to be formed into an organized political community, and he fixes the minimum for that at 10,000, and the maximum at 20,000. Now I would like to know what is to be done with the 9,000? Are they all to be treated, until they are large enough to be organized into a political community, as wanderers upon the public land in violation of law? And if so treated and driven out, at what point of time would there ever be ten thousand? If they were not driven out, but remained there as trespassers upon the public land in violation of the law, can they establish slavery there? No; the judge says popular sovereignty don't pertain to them then. Can they exclude it then? No; popular sovereignty don't pertain to them then. I would like to know, in the case covered by the essay, what condition the people of the Territory are in before they reach the number of ten thousand?

But the main point I wish to ask attention to is that the question as to when they shall have reached a sufficient number to be formed into a regular organized community is to be decided "by Congress." Judge Douglas says so. Well, gentlemen, that is about all we want. No; that is all the Southerners want. That is what all those who are for slavery want. They do not want Congress to prohibit slavery from coming into the new Territories, and they do not want popular sovereignty to hinder it; and as Congress is to say when they are ready to be organized, all that the South has to do is to get Congress to hold off. Let Congress hold off until they are ready to be admitted as a State, and the South has all it wants in taking slavery into and planting it in all the Territories that we now have, or hereafter may have. In a word, the whole thing, at a dash of the pen, is at last put in the power of Congress; for if they do not have this popular sovereignty until Congress organizes them, I ask if it at last does not come from Congress? If, at last, it amounts to anything at all, Congress gives it to them. I submit this rather for your reflection than for comment. After all that is said, at last, by a dash of the pen, everything that has gone before is undone, and he puts the whole question under the control of Congress. After fighting through more than three hours, if you will undertake to read it, he at last places the whole matter under the control of that power which he had been contending against, and arrives at a result directly contrary to what he had been laboring to do. He at last leaves the whole matter to the control of Congress.

There are two main objects, as I understand it, of this "Harper's Magazine" essay. One was to show, if possible, that the men of our Revolutionary times were in favor of his popular sovereignty; and the other was to show that the Dred Scott decision [i.e., that slaves are considered "property" under the Constitution] **had not entirely squelched out this popular sovereignty.** I do not propose, in regard to this argument drawn from the history of former times, to enter into a detailed examination of the historical statements he has made. I have the impression that they are inaccurate in a great many instances; sometimes in positive statement, but very much more inaccurate by the suppression of statements that really belong to the history. But I do not propose to affirm that this is so to any very great extent, or to enter into a very minute examination of his historical statements. I avoid doing so upon this principle—that if it were important for me to pass out of this lot in the least period of time possible, and I came to that fence and saw by a calculation of my own strength and agility that I could clear it at a bound, it would be folly for me to stop and consider whether I could or could not crawl through a crack. So I say of the whole history contained in his essay, where he endeavored to link the men of the Revolution to popular sovereignty. It only requires an effort to leap out of it—a single bound to be entirely successful. If you read it over you will find that he quotes here and there from documents of the Revolutionary times, tending to show that the people of the colonies were desirous of regulating their own concerns in their own way; that the British Government should not interfere; that at one time they struggled with the British Government to be permitted to exclude the African slave-trade; if not directly, to be permitted to exclude it indirectly by taxation sufficient to discourage and destroy it. From these and many things of this sort, Judge Douglas argues that they were in favor of the people of our own Territories excluding slavery if they wanted to, or planting it there if they wanted to, doing just as they pleased from the time they settled upon the Territory. Now, however his history may apply, and whatever of his argument there may be that is sound and accurate or unsound and inaccurate, if we can find out what these men did themselves do upon this very question of slavery in the Territories, does it not end the whole thing? If, after all this labor and effort to show that the men of the Revolution were in favor of his popular sovereignty and his mode of dealing with slavery in the Territories, we can show that these very men took hold of that subject, and dealt with it, we can see for ourselves how they dealt with it. It is not a matter of argument or inference, but we know what they thought about it.

It is precisely upon that part of the history of the country that one important omission is made by Judge Douglas. He selects parts of the history of the United States upon the subject of slavery, and treats it as the whole, omitting from his historical sketch the legislation of Congress in regard to the admission of Missouri, by which the Missouri Compromise was established, and slavery excluded from a country half as large as the present United States. All this is left out of his history, and in no wise alluded to by him, so far as I can remember, save once, when he makes a remark, that upon his principle the Supreme Court was authorized to pronounce a decision that the act called the Missouri Compromise was unconstitutional. All that history has been left out. But this part of the history of the country was not made by the men of the Revolution.

There was another part of our political history made by the very men who were the actors in the Revolution, which has taken the name of the ordinance of '87.[75] Let me bring that history to your attention. In 1784, I believe, this same Mr. [Thomas] Jefferson drew up an ordinance for the government of the country upon which we now stand; or rather a frame or draft of an ordinance for the government of this country, here in Ohio, our neighbors in Indiana, us who live in Illinois, and our neighbors in Wisconsin and Michigan. In that ordinance, drawn up not only for the government of that Territory, but for the Territories south of the Ohio River, Mr. Jefferson expressly provided for the prohibition of slavery. Judge Douglas says, and perhaps he is right, that that provision was lost from that ordinance. I believe that is true. When the vote was taken upon it, a majority of all present in the Congress of the Confederation [the

United States was originally known as "the Confederacy," particularly between 1781 and 1789, when our first Constitution was known as the "Articles of Confederation"][76] voted for it; but there were so many absentees that those voting for it did not make the clear majority necessary, and it was lost. But three years after that the Congress of the Confederation were together again, and they adopted a new ordinance for the government of this Northwest Territory, not contemplating territory south of the river, for the States owning that territory had hitherto refrained from giving it to the General Government; hence they made the ordinance to apply only to what the government owned. In that, the provision excluding slavery was inserted and passed unanimously, or at any rate it passed and became a part of the law of the land. Under that ordinance we live. First, here, in Ohio, you were a Territory, then an enabling act was passed, authorizing you to form a constitution and State government, provided it was Republican, and not in conflict with the ordinance of '87. When you framed your constitution and presented it for admission, I think you will find the legislation upon the subject will show that, "whereas you had formed a constitution that was Republican, and not in conflict with the ordinance of '87," therefore you were admitted upon equal footing with the original States. The same process in a few years was gone through with Indiana, and so with Illinois, and the same substantially with Michigan and Wisconsin.

Not only did that ordinance prevail, but it was constantly looked to whenever a step was taken by a new Territory to become a State. Congress always turned their attention to it, and in all their movements upon this subject they traced their course by that ordinance of '87. When they admitted new States they advertised them of this ordinance as a part of the legislation of the country. They did so because they had traced the ordinance of '87 throughout the history of this country. Begin with the men of the Revolution, and go down for sixty entire years, and until the last scrap of that Territory comes into the Union in the form of the State of Wisconsin, everything was made to conform to the ordinance of '87, excluding slavery from that vast extent of country.

I omitted to mention in the right place that the Constitution of the United States was in process of being framed when that ordinance was made by the Congress of the Confederation; and one of the first acts of Congress itself, under the new Constitution itself, was to give force to that ordinance by putting power to carry it out into the hands of new officers under the Constitution, in the place of the old ones, who had been legislated out of existence by the change in the government from the Confederation to the Constitution.[77] Not only so, but I believe Indiana once or twice, if not Ohio, petitioned the General Government for the privilege of suspending that provision and allowing them to have slaves. A report made by Mr. [Edmund Jennings] Randolph, of Virginia, himself a slaveholder, was directly against it, and the action was to refuse them the privilege of violating the ordinance of '87.

This period of history, which I have run over briefly, is, I presume, as familiar to most of this assembly as any other part of the history of our country. I suppose that few of my hearers are not as familiar with that part of history as I am, and I only mention it to recall your attention to it at this time. And hence I ask how extraordinary a thing it is that a man [i.e., Douglas] who has occupied a position upon the floor of the Senate of the United States, who is now in his third term, and who looks to see the government of this whole country fall into his own hands, pretending to give a truthful and accurate history of the slavery question in this country, should so entirely ignore the whole of that portion of our history—the most important of all. Is it not a most extraordinary spectacle, that a man should stand up and ask for any confidence in his statements, who sets out as he does with portions of history, calling upon the people to believe that it is a true and fair representation, when the leading part and controlling feature of the whole history is carefully suppressed?

But the mere leaving out is not the most remarkable feature of this most remarkable essay. His proposition is to establish that the leading men of the Revolution were for his great principle of non-intervention by the government in the question of slavery in the Territories; while history shows that they decided in the cases actually brought before them in exactly the contrary way, and he knows it. Not only did they so decide at that time, but they stuck to it during sixty years, through thick and thin, as long as there was one of the Revolutionary heroes upon the stage of political action. Through their whole course, from first to last, they clung to freedom. And now he asks the community to believe that the men of the Revolution were in favor of his great principle, when we have the naked history that they themselves dealt with this very subject matter of his principle, and utterly repudiated his principle, acting upon a precisely contrary ground. It is as impudent and absurd as if a prosecuting attorney should stand up before a jury, and ask them to convict A as the murderer of B, while B was walking alive before them.

I say again, if Judge Douglas asserts that the men of the Revolution acted upon principles by which, to be consistent with themselves, they ought to have adopted his popular sovereignty, then, upon a consideration of his own argument, he had a right to make you believe that they understood the principles of government, but misapplied them—that he has arisen to enlighten the world as to the just application of this principle. He has a right to try to persuade you that he understands their principles better than they did, and therefore he will apply them now, not as they did, but as they ought to have done. He has a right to go before the community, and try to convince them of this; but he has no right to attempt to impose upon any one the belief that these men themselves approved of his great principle. There are two ways of establishing a proposition. One is by trying to demonstrate it upon reason, and the other is, to show that great men in former times have thought so and so, and thus to pass it by the weight of pure authority. Now, if Judge Douglas will demonstrate somehow that this is popular sovereignty—the right of one man to make a slave of another, without any right in that other, or any one else, to object,—demonstrate it as Euclid demonstrated propositions,—there is no objection. But when he comes forward, seeking to carry a principle by bringing to it the authority of men who themselves utterly repudiate that principle, I ask that he shall not be permitted to do it.

I see, in the judge's speech here, a short sentence in these words: "Our fathers, when they formed this government under which we live, understood this question just as well and even better than we do now." That is true; I stick to that. I will stand by Judge Douglas in that to the bitter end. And now, Judge Douglas, come and stand by me, and truthfully show how they acted, understanding it better than we do. All I ask of you, Judge Douglas, is to stick to the proposition that the men of the Revolution understood this subject better than we do now, and with that better understanding they acted better than you are trying to act now.

I wish to say something now in regard to the Dred Scott decision, as dealt with by Judge Douglas. In that "memorable debate" between Judge Douglas and myself, last year, the judge thought fit to commence a process of catechizing me, and at Freeport I answered his questions, and propounded some to him. Among others propounded to him was one that I have here now. The substance, as I remember it, is: "Can the people of a United States Territory, under the Dred Scott decision, in any lawful way, against the wish of any citizen of the United States, exclude slavery from its limits, prior to the formation of a State constitution?" He answered that they could lawfully exclude slavery from the United States Territories, notwithstanding the Dred Scott decision. There was something about that answer that has probably been a trouble to the judge ever since.

The Dred Scott decision expressly gives every citizen of the United States a right to carry his slaves into the United States Territories. And now there was some inconsistency in saying that the decision was right, and saying, too, that the people of the Territory could lawfully drive slavery out again. When all the trash, the words, the collateral matter, was cleared away from it,—all the chaff was fanned out of it,—it was a bare absurdity: no less than that a thing may be lawfully driven away from where it has a lawful right to be. Clear it of all the verbiage, and that is the naked truth of his proposition—that a thing may be lawfully driven from the place where it has a lawful right to stay. Well, it was because the judge couldn't help seeing this that he has had so much trouble with it; and what I want to ask your especial attention to, just now, is to remind you, if you have not noticed the fact, that the judge does not any longer say that the people can exclude slavery. He does not say so in the copyright essay; he did not say so in the speech that he made here; and, so far as I know, since his reelection to the Senate, he has never said, as he did at Freeport, that the people of the Territories can exclude slavery. He desires that you, who wish the Territories to remain free, should believe that he stands by that position, but he does not say it himself. He escapes, to some extent, the absurd position I have stated by changing his language entirely. What he says now is something different in language, and we will consider whether it is not different in sense too. It is now that the Dred Scott decision, or rather the Constitution under that decision, does not carry slavery into the Territories beyond the power of the people of the Territories to control it as other property. He does not say the people can drive it out, but they can control it as other property. The language is different; we should consider whether the sense is different. Driving a horse out of this lot is too plain a proposition to be mistaken about; it is putting him on the other side of the fence. Or it might be a sort of exclusion of him from the lot if you were to kill him and let the worms devour him; but neither of these things is the same as "controlling him as other property." That would be to feed him, to pamper him, to ride him, to use and abuse him, to make the most money out of him, "as other property"; but, please you, what do the men who are in favor of slavery want more than this? What do they really want, other than that slavery, being in the Territories, shall be controlled as other property?

If they want anything else, I do not comprehend it. I ask your attention to this, first, for the purpose of pointing out the change of ground the judge has made; and, in the second place, the importance of the change—that that change is not such as to give you gentlemen who want his popular sovereignty the power to exclude the institution or drive it out at all. I know the judge sometimes squints at the argument that in controlling it as other property by unfriendly legislation they may control it to death, as you might in the case of a horse, perhaps, feed him so lightly and ride him so much that he would die. But when you come to legislative control, there is something more to be attended to. I have no doubt, myself, that if the Territories should undertake to control slave property as other property—that is, control it in such a way that it would be the most valuable as property, and make it bear its just proportion in the way of burdens as property,—really deal with it as property,—the Supreme Court of the United States will say, "God speed you, and amen." But I undertake to give the opinion, at least, that if the Territories attempt by any direct legislation to drive the man with his slave out of the Territory, or to decide that his slave is free because of his being taken in there, or to tax him to such an extent that he cannot keep him there, the Supreme Court will unhesitatingly decide all such legislation unconstitutional, as long as that Supreme Court is constructed as the Dred Scott Supreme Court is. The first two things they have already decided, except that there is a little quibble among lawyers between the words *dicta* and decision. They have already decided that a negro cannot be made free by territorial legislation.

What is that Dred Scott decision? Judge Douglas labors to show that it is one thing, while I think it is altogether different. It is a long opinion, but it is all embodied in this short statement: "The Constitution of the United States forbids Congress to deprive a man of his property without due process of law; the right of property in slaves is distinctly and expressly affirmed in that Constitution; therefore if Congress shall undertake to say that a man's slave is no longer his slave when he crosses a certain line into a Territory, that is depriving him of his property without due process of law, and is unconstitutional." There is the whole Dred Scott decision. They add that if Congress cannot do so itself, Congress cannot confer any power to do so, and hence any effort by the territorial legislature to do either of these things is absolutely decided against. It is a foregone conclusion by that court.

Now, as to this indirect mode by "unfriendly legislation," all lawyers here will readily understand that such a proposition cannot be tolerated for a moment, because a legislature cannot indirectly do that which it cannot accomplish directly. Then I say any legislation to control this property, as property, for its benefit as property, would be hailed by this Dred Scott Supreme Court, and fully sustained; but any legislation driving slave property out, or destroying it as property, directly or indirectly, will most assuredly by that court be held unconstitutional.

Judge Douglas says that if the Constitution carries slavery into the Territories, beyond the power of the people of the Territories to control it as other property, then it follows logically that every one who swears to support the Constitution of the United States must give that support to that property which it needs. And if the Constitution carries slavery into the Territories beyond the power of the people to control it as other property, then it also carries it into the States, because the Constitution is the supreme law of the land. Now, gentlemen, if it were not for my excessive modesty I would say that I told that very thing to Judge Douglas quite a year ago. This argument is here in print, and if it were not for my modesty, as I said, I might call your attention to it. If you read it, you will find that I not only made that argument, but made it better than he has made it since.

There is, however, this difference. I say now, and said then, there is no sort of question that the Supreme Court has decided that it is the right of the slaveholder to take his slave and hold him in the Territory; and, saying this, Judge Douglas himself admits the conclusion. He says if that is so, this consequence will follow; and because this consequence would follow, his argument is, the decision cannot therefore be that way— [Lincoln imitating Douglas] "that would spoil my popular sovereignty, and it cannot be possible that this great principle has been squelched out in this extraordinary way. It might be, if it were not for the extraordinary consequences of spoiling my humbug."

Another feature of the judge's argument about the Dred Scott case is an effort to show that that decision deals altogether in declarations of negatives; that the Constitution does not affirm anything as expounded by the Dred Scott decision, but it only declares a want of power, a total absence of power, in reference to the Territories. It seems to be his purpose to make the whole of that decision to result in a mere negative declaration of a want of power in Congress to do anything in relation to this matter in the Territories. I know the opinion of the judges states that there is a total absence of power; but that is, unfortunately, not all it states; for the judges add that the right of property in a slave is distinctly and expressly affirmed in the Constitution. It does not stop at saying that the right of property in a slave is recognized in the Constitution, is declared to exist somewhere in the Constitution, but says it is affirmed in the Constitution. Its language is equivalent to saying that it is embodied and so woven into that instrument that it cannot be detached without breaking the Constitution itself,—in a word, it is a part of the Constitution.

Douglas is singularly unfortunate in his effort to make out that decision to be altogether negative, when the express language at the vital part is that this is distinctly affirmed in the Constitution. I think myself, and I repeat it here, that this decision does not merely carry slavery into the Territories, but by its logical conclusion it carries it into the States in which we live. One provision of that Constitution is, that it shall be the supreme law of the land,—I do not quote the language,—any constitution or law of any State to the contrary notwithstanding. This Dred Scott decision says that the right of property in a slave is affirmed in that Constitution which is the supreme law of the land, any State constitution or law notwithstanding. Then I say that to destroy a thing which is distinctly affirmed and supported by the supreme law of the land, even by a State constitution or law, is a violation of that supreme law, and there is no escape from it. In my judgment there is no avoiding that result, save that the American people shall see that State constitutions are better construed than our Constitution is construed in that decision. They must take care that it is more faithfully and truly carried out than it is there expounded.

I must hasten to a conclusion. Near the beginning of my remarks I said that this insidious Douglas popular sovereignty is the measure that now threatens the purpose of the Republican party to prevent slavery from being nationalized in the United States. I propose to ask your attention for a little while to some propositions in affirmance of that statement. Take it just as it stands, and apply it as a principle; extend and apply that principle elsewhere, and consider where it will lead you. I now put this proposition, that Judge Douglas's popular sovereignty applied will reopen the African slave-trade; and I will demonstrate it by any variety of ways in which you can turn the subject or look at it.

The judge says that the people of the Territories have the right, by his principle, to have slaves if they want them. Then I say that the people in Georgia have the right to buy slaves in Africa if they want them, and I defy any man on earth to show any distinction between the two things—to show that the one is either more wicked or more unlawful: to show, on original principles, that one is better or worse than the other; or to show by the Constitution that one differs a whit from the other. He will tell me, doubtless, that there is no constitutional provision against people taking slaves into the new Territories, and I tell him that there is equally no constitutional provision against buying slaves in Africa. He will tell you that a people in the exercise of popular sovereignty ought to do as they please about that thing, and have slaves if they want them; and I tell you that the people of Georgia are as much entitled to popular sovereignty, and to buy slaves in Africa, if they want them, as the people of the Territory are to have slaves if they want them. I ask any man, dealing honestly with himself, to point out a distinction.

I have recently seen a letter of Judge Douglas's, in which, without stating that to be the object, he doubtless endeavors to make a distinction between the two. He says he is unalterably opposed to the repeal of the laws against the African slave-trade. And why? He then seeks to give a reason that would not apply to his popular sovereignty in the Territories. What is that reason? "The abolition of the African slave-trade is a compromise of the Constitution." I deny it. There is no truth in the proposition that the abolition of the African slave-trade is a compromise of the Constitution. No man can put his finger on anything in the Constitution, or on the line of history, which shows it. It is a mere barren assertion, made simply for the purpose of getting up a distinction between the revival of the African slave-trade and his "great principle."

At the time the Constitution of the United States was adopted it was expected that the slave-trade would be abolished. I should assert, and insist upon that, if Judge Douglas denied it. But I know that it was equally expected that slavery would be excluded from the Territories, and I can show by history that in regard to these two things public opinion was exactly alike, while in regard to positive action, there was more done in the ordinance of '87 to resist the spread of slavery than was ever done to abolish the foreign slave-trade. Lest I be misunderstood, I say again that at the time of the formation of the Constitution, public expectation was that the slave-trade would be abolished, but no more so than that the spread of slavery in the Territories should be restrained. They stand alike, except that in the ordinance of '87 there was a mark left by public opinion, showing that it was more committed against the spread of slavery in the Territories than against the foreign slave-trade.

Compromise! What word of compromise was there about it? Why, the public sense was then in favor of the abolition of the slave-trade; but there was at the time [in the North] a very great commercial interest involved in it, and extensive capital in that branch of trade. There were doubtless the incipient stages of improvement in the South in the way of farming, dependent on the slave-trade, and they made a proposition to Congress to abolish the trade after allowing it twenty years, a sufficient time for the capital and commerce engaged in it to be transferred to other channels. They made no provision that it should be abolished in twenty years; I do not doubt that they expected it would be; but they made no bargain about it. The public sentiment left no doubt in the minds of any that it would be done away. I repeat, there is nothing in the history of those times in favor of that matter being a compromise of the Constitution. It was the public expectation at the time, manifested in a thousand ways, that the spread of slavery should also be restricted.

Then I say if this principle is established, that there is no wrong in slavery, and whoever wants it has a right to have it; that it is a matter of dollars and cents; a sort of question as to how they shall deal with brutes; that between us and the negro here there is no sort of question, but that at the South the question is between the negro and the crocodile; that it is a mere matter of policy; that there is a perfect right, according to interest, to do just as you please—when this is done, where this doctrine prevails, the miners and sappers will have formed public opinion for the slave-trade. They will be ready for Jeff Davis and [Alexander Hamilton] Stephens, and other leaders of that company, to sound the bugle for the revival of the slave-trade, for the second Dred Scott decision, for the flood of slavery to be poured over the free States, while we shall be here tied down and helpless, and run over like sheep.

It is to be a part and parcel of this same idea to say to men who want to adhere to the Democratic party, who have always belonged to that party, and are only looking about for some excuse to stick to it, but nevertheless hate slavery, that Douglas's popular sovereignty is as good a way as any to oppose slavery. They allow themselves to be persuaded easily, in accordance with their previous dispositions, into this belief, that it is about as good a way of opposing slavery as any, and we can do that without straining our old party ties or breaking up old political associations. We can do so without being called negro-worshipers. We can do that without being subjected to the gibes and sneers that are so readily thrown out in place of argument where no argument can be found. So let us stick to this popular sovereignty—this insidious popular sovereignty. Now let me call your attention to one thing that has really happened, which shows this gradual and steady debauching of public opinion, this course of preparation for the revival of the slave-trade, for the territorial slave-code, and the new Dred Scott decision that is to carry slavery into the free States. Did you ever, five years ago, hear of anybody in the world saying that the negro had no share in the Declaration of National Independence; that it did not mean negroes at all, and when "all men" were spoken of negroes were not included?

I am satisfied that five years ago that proposition was not put upon paper by any living being anywhere. I have been unable at any time to find a man in an audience who would declare that be had ever known of anybody saying so five years ago. But last year there was not a "Douglas popular sovereignty" man in Illinois who did not say it. Is there one in Ohio but declares his firm belief that the Declaration of Independence did not mean negroes at all? I do not know how this is; I have not been here much; but I presume you are very much alike everywhere. Then I suppose that all now express the belief that the Declaration of Independence never did mean negroes. I call upon one of them to say that he said it five years ago.

If you think that now, and did not think it then, the next thing that strikes me is to remark that there has been a change wrought in you, and a very significant change it is, being no less than changing the negro, in your estimation, from the rank of a man to that of a brute. They are taking him down, and placing him, when spoken of, among reptiles and crocodiles, as Judge Douglas himself expresses it.

Is not this change wrought in your minds a very

important change? Public opinion in this country is everything. In a nation like ours this popular sovereignty and squatter sovereignty have already wrought a change in the public mind to the extent I have stated. There is no man in this crowd who can contradict it.

Now, if you are opposed to slavery honestly, as much as anybody, I ask you to note that fact, and the like of which is to follow, to be plastered on, layer after layer, until very soon you are prepared to deal with the negro everywhere as with the brute. If public sentiment has not been debauched already to this point, a new turn of the screw in that direction is all that is wanting; and this is constantly being done by the teachers of this insidious popular sovereignty. You need but one or two turns further until your minds, now ripening under these teachings, will be ready for all these things, and you will receive and support, or submit to, the slave-trade revived with all its horrors, a slave code enforced in our Territories, and a new Dred Scott decision to bring slavery up into the very heart of the free North. This, I must say, is but carrying out those words prophetically spoken by Mr. [Henry] Clay many, many years ago,—I believe more than thirty years,—when he told an audience that if they would repress all tendencies to liberty and ultimate emancipation, they must go back to the era of our independence and muzzle the cannon which thundered its annual joyous return on the Fourth of July; they must blow out the moral lights around us; they must penetrate the human soul, and eradicate the love of liberty; but until they did these things, and others eloquently enumerated by him, they could not repress all tendencies to ultimate emancipation.

I ask attention to the fact that in a preeminent degree these popular sovereigns are at this work: blowing out the moral lights around us; teaching that the negro is no longer a man, but a brute; that the Declaration has nothing to do with him; that he ranks with the crocodile and the reptile; that man, with body and soul, is a matter of dollars and cents. I suggest to this portion of the Ohio Republicans, or Democrats, if there be any present, the serious consideration of this fact, that there is now going on among you a steady process of debauching public opinion on this subject. With this, my friends, I bid you adieu.[78]

If anyone was **"debauching public opinion"** it was Lincoln!

He first misrepresents Douglas as a tyrant. But Douglas was a conservative who wanted freedom of choice. It was liberal Lincoln—the man who did not like to see blacks enslaved, but who had no problem enslaving whites under his autocratic government—who possessed dictatorial tendencies, and who wanted to impose his views indiscriminately across every state.

Lincoln here also totally misrepresents the idea of popular sovereignty, which he incorrectly defines as **"the right of one man to make a slave of another."** This definition would be laughable were it not for the fact that such words, coming as they did from the esteemed "Great Emancipator," have misled generations of Americans.

The fact is that big government, big spender Lincoln—the sectional Yankee politician whose main goal at this point seems to be have been trying to agitate war with the South—hated the very idea of states' rights so intensely that he could not even bring himself to discuss it openly and honestly. Nowhere is Lincoln's ignorance, or his guile, more evident than when he claims that the purpose behind popular sovereignty is to reopen the slave trade and nationalize slavery.

We should note here that it is probable that our sixteenth president did not even fully understand the distinction between state governments and the central government, as can be seen in the following November 29, 1862, letter to U.S. Attorney General Edward Bates:

> My dear Sir: Few things perplex me more than this question between [Missouri] **Governor** [Hamilton Rowan] **Gamble and the War Department**, as to whether the peculiar force organized by the former in Missouri are State troops or United States troops. Now, this is either an immaterial or a mischievous question. First, if no more is desired than to have it settled what name the force is to be called by, it is immaterial. Secondly, if it is desired for more than the fixing a name, it can only be to get a position from which to draw practical inferences; then it is mischievous. Instead of settling one dispute by deciding the question, I should merely furnish a nestful of eggs for hatching new disputes. I believe the force is not strictly either "State troops" or "United States troops." It is of mixed character. I therefore think it is safer, when a practical question arises, to decide that question directly, and not indirectly by deciding a

general abstraction supposed to include it, and also including a great deal more. Without dispute Governor Gamble appoints the officers of this force, and fills vacancies when they occur. The question now practically in dispute is: Can Governor Gamble make a vacancy by removing an officer or accepting a resignation? Now, while it is proper that this question shall be settled, I do not perceive why either Governor Gamble or the government here should care which way it is settled. I am perplexed with it only because there seems to be pertinacity about it. It seems to me that it might be either way without injury to the service; or that the offer of the Secretary of War to let Governor Gamble make vacancies, and he (the Secretary) to ratify the making of them, ought to be satisfactory. Yours truly, A. Lincoln.[79]

Lincoln certainly attached little or no importance to the matter of state versus federal governmental power; at least not in public.

In his September 16, 1859, speech Lincoln expresses his fear of the possibility of the **"nationalization of slavery"** by saying that he and the rest of the North would be **"tied down and helpless, and run over like sheep."** If he truly wanted to incorporate blacks into American society with full civil rights, why did he use this particular expression? The answer, as we will discover from his own words in Chapters 8, 11, and 12, is that he was not an abolitionist. He was a white supremacist, a white separatist, an advocate of American apartheid, and an emancipationist-colonizationist who wanted to restrict slavery then abolish it, for the sole purpose of then legally deporting all blacks out of the U.S.

Unlike bigoted liberal Lincoln, who wanted his tyrannical will, via the Federal government, forced upon the people, Douglas and the rest of the nation's conservatives followed the Constitution, specifically Amendments Nine and Ten, which tacitly promise states' rights, or "popular sovereignty," as it was called by some in 1859. According to this most sacred document, it was the individual states that were to decide on issues such as slavery, not the Federal government.

Lincoln's belief that states' rights would allow, and even promote, the nationalization of slavery is ludicrous, for while slavery was indeed more efficient, productive, and profitable than free labor in 1859, it was by then a thoroughly doomed institution.[80] For by the mid 1800s the reverberations of the Age of Enlightenment and the ever advancing technologies of the

Industrial Revolution, had made servitude more unappealing to Americans than ever before.

English philosopher John Locke, in particular, with his emphasis on natural law[81] (also known as natural rights),[82] had a profound impact on European-American, African-American, and Native-American slave owners, who began to reconsider the institution in light of his concepts. In his *The Second Treatise of Government* Locke wrote:

> Men being . . . all free, equal and independent, no one can be put out of this estate, and subjected to the political power of another, without his own consent.[83]

The concept of natural rights was adopted by the Founding Fathers. One of them was John Adams, America's second president. In 1765 Adams was speaking of the God-given freedoms of the people when he said:

> You have rights antecedent to all earthly governments; rights that cannot be repealed or restrained by human laws; rights derived from the Great Lawgiver of the Universe.[84]

Who could justify slavery after hearing such words? Many tried, but such words rang out like bells across the decades. They promised, however distant, complete emancipation and full civil rights. They would not go away, and Southerners in particular would not let them.

Black slaves themselves, having observed freedom all around them for several centuries, now longed for liberty more desperately than ever before.[85] The abolition train was in motion, and it could not be stopped.

By 1860, though it was still proving to be a very profitable institution (contrary to Yankee myth, from the 1840s onward, the American slave economy accelerated rapidly),[86] socially, politically, and culturally slavery was no longer acceptable to an American populace that had, by now, embraced the European Enlightenment. Criminalized by busybodies like Northerner William Lloyd Garrison,[87] slavery had become, in a word, obsolete, as nearly all Americans, both South and North, knew. By 1859, and certainly by mid-1863, white Southerners were well on their way to complete emancipation.[88] As even Lincoln noted in an October 16, 1854, speech:

> **How common is the remark now in the slave States, "If we were only clear of our slaves, how much better it**

would be for us."[89]

That sure knowledge that Southerners themselves would eventually and inevitably end slavery in their region, was due to a fact that you will not find in any Northern or New South history book: the American abolition movement got its start in the South, in Virginia to be exact,[90] with Southerners like George Washington, Thomas Jefferson, and George Mason pushing since the late 1700s to eradicate both the slave trade (buying and selling slaves) and slavery (owning slaves). Evidence of the Southern abolition movement is seen in the fact that in the early 1800s, four-fifths of the nation's abolition societies were located in the South, many with foundations dating back to the early 1700s.[91] It is not surprising then that most Southerners, 94 percent who did not own slaves, were anxious to rid the nation of the "peculiar institution."

Despite these bold facts, Lincoln believed that popular sovereignty (i.e., states' rights) would revitalize slavery and reopen the slave trade, both which he insinuates are centered in the South. These notions were nothing more than anti-South Yankee propaganda, for as is well-known here in the South, both the American slave trade and American slavery got their start in the North. While we are on this topic, let us examine these Northern-New South myths, so beloved by Lincoln, more closely, beginning with slavery.

It was not Mississippi, but Massachusetts that, in 1641, was the first state to legalize slavery,[92] and in 1700 the Bay State also became the first state to prohibit marriage between whites and blacks.[93]

Far earlier, in the 1620s, the state's first slaves were white, fellow colonists who were sold into slavery as punishment for committing crimes. By the 1630s Massachusetts Puritans were capturing, branding, and enslaving Native-Americans, which they either kept as personal servants or sold for profit to West Indian merchants.[94]

America imported her first African slaves in 1638 through Boston, Massachusetts, when Captain William Pierce brought New England's first shipload of Africans from the West Indies aboard the Salem vessel *Desire*.[95] By 1676 Boston slavers were routinely coming home with shiploads of human cargo from East Africa and Madagascar.[96] By the 1700s Massachusetts had 5,000 black slaves and 30,000 bondservants.[97]

By 1639 Connecticut had slaves, and by 1645 New Hampshire had them as well. The largest slave concentrations in New England were in Rockingham County, New Hampshire; Essex, Suffolk, Bristol, and

Plymouth Counties, Massachusetts; New London, Hartford, and Fairfield Counties, Connecticut; and Newport and Washington Counties, Rhode Island. There were so many slaves in Rhode Island's Narragansett region that they made up half the population.[98] At one time the state's slave traders owned and operated nearly 90 percent of America's slave trade.[99]

Lincoln seemed oblivious to all this, or at least he pretended to be. In his usual arrogant Yankee way here is what he said on March 6, 1860, at New Haven, Connecticut:

> **...here in Connecticut and at the North slavery does not exist, and we see it through no such medium. To us it appears natural to think that slaves are human beings; men, not property...**[100]

Would not Lincoln have been shocked to learn that while he was making this particular speech, there were still some 500,000[101] to 1 million slaves[102] working in the North, owned by 500,000 Northern white slave owners, 2.5 percent of the 20 million white Northerners in 1860?[103] Numbered among these were many famous Yanks, including Ulysses S. Grant,[104] as well as Winfield Scott, David G. Farragut, George H. Thomas, and the family of Lincoln's wife, Mary Todd.[105] The president himself once made reference to a slave-owning Yankee, the Honorable George Robertson, in a November 26, 1862, letter.[106]

Thus, Lincoln should not have been surprised to discover that at one time in the not too distant past, the slavers of Rhode Island and those of Massachusetts combined to make New England the leading slave-trading center in America and slavery "the hub of New England's economy." Two-thirds of Rhode Island's fleets and sailors alone were devoted to the trade. Even the states' governors participated in it, such as Jonathan Belcher (of Massachusetts) and Joseph Wanton (of Rhode Island). So integral was slavery to New England that without it she would have collapsed into financial ruin.[107]

Remnants of New England's "peculiar institution" are still obvious to this day, none more so than the pineapple. Though it is now seen as a "welcome" sign across the U.S., this is a corruption of its original meaning: when New England slave traders returned from their ocean expeditions to the tropics to pick up slaves, they would stick a pineapple on their fencepost to let everyone in town know that they were "welcome" to come in and shop for slave products, as well as for slaves themselves.[108]

Many notable New England families owe their present-day wealth and celebrity to the Northern slave trade.[109] Among them: the Cabots (ancestors of Massachusetts Senators Henry Cabot Lodge, Sr. and Jr.), the Belchers, the Waldos (ancestors of Ralph Waldo Emerson), the Faneuils (after whom Faneuil Hall is named), the Royalls, the Pepperells (after whom the town of Pepperell, Massachusetts, is named), the DeWolfs—the largest slave-trading family in Rhode Island, the Champlains (after whom Lake Champlain is named), the Ellerys, the Gardners (after whom Boston's Isabella Stewart Gardner Museum is named), the Malbones, the Robinsons, the Crowninshields (after whom Crowninshield Island, Massachusetts, is named), and the Browns (after whom Rhode Island's Brown University is named).[110]

The slave trading Royall family, who made millions from their slave plantations in Antigua, donated money and land to what would become the Harvard Law School. The educational center still uses a seal from the Royall family crest.[111] At least one half of the land in Brookline, Massachusetts, was once in the possession of slave owners, while in the town of Concord, Massachusetts, 50 percent of its government seats were occupied by slave owners. In this quaint New England borough, where slavery continued well into the 1830s (decades after the official "abolition" of slavery there), those blacks fortunate enough to be freed were then, unfortunately, exiled to the woods surrounding Walden Pond, where they struggled for survival in fetid squatter camps.[112]

It was also in Massachusetts that the now wholly disgraced and defunct field of "race science"—or "niggerology," as many Yankees referred to it—got its start, at Harvard University in Cambridge. It was this very pseudoscience, one which claimed that "blacks are inferior subhumans," that for hundreds of years allowed white Northerners to rationalize the exploitation of people of African descent.[113]

Little wonder that when William Lloyd Garrison went to Boston in 1830 to find support for the launch of his new antislavery newspaper, *The Liberator*, he was turned down by some of the city's most notable men, including William Ellery Channing, Daniel Webster, Jeremiah Evarts, and Jeremiah Mason. His plea was even rejected by Lyman Beecher, the town's most influential Christian leader and the father of abolitionist Harriet Beecher Stowe, the infamous author of the pro-North, anti-South fantasy *Uncle Tom's Cabin*. Garrison should not have been surprised: not only were many of Massachusetts' schools and churches segregated, nearly every one of Boston's clergymen was a member of the American Colonization Society, a Yankee-founded organization devoted to deporting all blacks out of the country.[114] (one of its future members would be the focus of this book, Abraham Lincoln).[115] Boston itself was once a major center of black colonization efforts.[116]

In 1788 the state of Massachusetts forbade the emigration of free blacks from outside its boundaries,[117] and well into the early 1800s restrictive Black Codes across New England prohibited African-Americans from voting, testifying in court, intermarrying with whites,[118] or gaining access to jobs, housing, and education. Banned from most restaurants and hotels, New England blacks were also subject to segregation on public transportation, and in theaters, churches, and hospitals.[119]

In the late 1830s the famous black civil rights leader Frederick Douglass, now a freedman, could not get a job as a caulker in New Bedford, Massachusetts, because of the color of his skin (white Yankee caulkers refused to work alongside him).[120] This type of Northern white racism worked to both justify and expedite Yankee slavery for centuries.

So great were the profits made by slave traders at Newport, Rhode Island,[121] that it has been said that the city was literally constructed over the graves of thousands of Africans.[122] By 1790, when Liverpool had become England's primary slave port, her only serious competition was from the Yankee slave ship owners of Bristol and Newport, Rhode Island.[123] Rhode Island's state flag still bears a ship's anchor, an apt reminder of her days as the nation's largest slave trader, one that imported 100,000 African slaves—20 percent of all those brought into the U.S.[124]

It was not just slave trading that Rhode Island was involved in. The state also possessed thousands of crop and cattle plantations which depended almost exclusively on slave labor.[125] In fact, due to the number of plantations that once dotted the Renaissance City, to this day the official name of the state of Rhode Island is "Rhode Island and Providence Plantations," a carryover from the 1600s when it was first named.[126]

Even after slavery was abolished in the North, both Rhode Island and Massachusetts continued to amass huge profits from the slave trade,[127] the same profits that would later help Lincoln fund his "Civil War" on the South.[128]

As for the capital of the American slave trade, it was not New Orleans, but New York City. In fact slavery would not begin in the South for another 100 years: in 1749, Georgia, the last of the thirteen original colonies, became the first Southern state to use slaves.[129] By 1756 New York state possessed some 13,000 adult black slaves, giving it the dubious distinction of having the largest slave force of any Northern colony at the time. That same year, slaves accounted for 25 percent of the population in Kings, Queens, Richmond, New York City, and Westchester, making this area the primary bastion of American slavery throughout the rest of the colonial period.[130]

Many of the most famous New York names—names such as the Lehman Brothers, John Jacob Astor, Junius and Pierpont Morgan, Charles Tiffany, Archibald Gracie, and many others—are only known today because of the tremendous riches they made from the town's "peculiar institution."[131] New York City, the center of America's cotton trade as early as 1815, was so deeply connected to the Yankee slave trade and to Southern slavery that it opposed all early attempts at abolition within its borders,[132] and, along with New Jersey, was the last Northern state to resist the passage of emancipation laws.[133]

Later, in December 1860, when the Southern states began seceding, New York City's mayor, Fernando Wood, advocated that the city secede as well, for its close relationship with King Cotton insured its economic stability.[134] When Lincoln's War finally erupted in April 1861, New York was one of the last states to recruit African-Americans: the state's governor, Horatio Seymour, refused to enlist them until he was forced to by the U.S. War Department.[135] This occurred on December 23, 1863, a year after the Emancipation Proclamation was issued and nearly three years after the War began.[136]

In fact, there is only one reason that New York City is today America's largest and wealthiest municipality: for centuries it served as the literal heart of North America's slaving industry.[137] As a result, according to the U.S. Census, to this day the Big Apple still possesses by far the largest population of blacks of any American city (twice as many as Chicago, the city in second place).[138] It was because of New York City's massive slaving business that it was also the center of many of America's earliest and most violent slave uprisings.[139]

Baltimore, Maryland, and Philadelphia, Pennsylvania, were also great slave ports.[140] Baltimore in particular was one of the nation's most important slave trade centers: her slave ships were said to be packed "like livestock" with black human cargo, with mortality rates reaching as high as 25 percent.[141] Another Maryland city, Annapolis, also became one of America's most prosperous towns due to its thriving slave trade. It was a Northern slave ship that brought Kunta Kinte, the lead character in Alex Haley's saga *Roots*, to Annapolis from West Africa in 1767.[142] The city still goes by the nickname the "sailing capital of the world."

In the 1860s, under Lincoln, Northern slavery continued unabated in America's Yankee capital city, Washington, D.C., until the middle of his administration. Up until that time, Lincoln turned down numerous opportunities to abolish the institution here.

The District—where blacks were once fined ($25), given twenty-five lashes (with a bull whip), jailed (for thirty days), then returned to slavery, just for receiving Garrison's abolitionist newspaper *The Liberator*;[143] where hospitals were strictly segregated so that blood plasma would not be used for both whites and blacks; and where even the White House press and photographers' pool was segregated (until the 1950s)[144]—had long been a major center for slave sales and boasted the nation's largest slave mart,[145] one located in full view of Northern members of Congress,[146] as Lincoln himself noted.[147] Numerous slave pens, located right across the street from the new Smithsonian building, overflowed with the human chattel of Yankee slave traders who lived and worked in the town. Northern politicians and statesmen alike passed by them on a daily basis without so much as a comment, criticism, or protest.[148]

It was these slaves, the *Northern* slaves from these *Northern* markets and pens, who built the White House, the U.S. Capitol, and numerous other Federal buildings in the city, along with many of her city streets.[149]

Apparently the sight of slave pens, slave jails, auction blocks, thousands of African slaves laboring throughout the city,[150] and Yankee slave boats plying up and down the Potomac River,[151] bothered neither Lincoln or the U.S. Congress, for the town's citizens were allowed to own and trade in slaves right up through the first year of the "Civil War."

Whites who lived in the capital were greatly interested in keeping down the number of blacks in their city, which, in 1850, stood at 26 percent of the total population. In contrast, blacks in slave-owning St. Louis, Missouri, represented only 5.4 percent. Cincinnati, Ohio, was only 2.8 percent black. To maintain, or even decrease, the local black populace, Washington whites widely approved of the new Fugitive Slave Act. Why? Under it, runaway slaves had to be returned to their owners. Those who escaped, however, would blend back into the city's free black population, thereby swelling African-American numbers.[152]

To counter this trend, numerous anti-black laws were revisited in order to make them more stringent. New amendments required black emigrants to Washington, D.C. to "apply for residence" within five days of their arrival, or face a fine, a sentence in the workhouse, and banishment from town. "Secret meetings" by blacks were prohibited and anyone of African descent had to obtain the permission of the mayor to gather in public.[153]

In a city where already severe Black Codes were rigidly enforced and where blacks merely suspected of petty crimes were often savagely beaten by Washington's police force, even law-abiding, hard-working blacks lived in constant fear, mainly of white gangs.[154] Without a "certificate of freedom," no free black in the city was safe from harassment and arrest by the police, who devoted the majority of their time to tracking down and capturing African-Americans. The "Negro business" was so profitable in the District that slave catchers were attracted to the town from far and wide.[155]

Throughout the 1850s white Washingtonians continued to reinforce slavery by endorsing the kidnaping of free blacks (to be sold into slavery) and engaging in the slave trade, even though it had been outlawed in 1850. And while blacks were three times as likely to be arrested as whites, black testimonies in court were regarded as both invalid and illegal, and overly harsh sentences were routinely handed out to black criminals.[156] Sometimes they were punished not so much for major crimes as for minor offenses, such as lighting off firecrackers, flying a kite in the wrong area, or swimming in the canal. The punishment? A "good whipping."[157]

It was not just the 1,800 black slaves in the District that caused Northern whites so much distress. It was also the 9,000 free blacks who lived and worked in the city, all of whom were habitually treated with "fear and hatred." The depth of this loathing can be seen in the name of an area of the Third Ward, known by Northern whites as "Nigger Hill."[158]

It was into the white racist world of Washington, D.C., that white racist Lincoln walked in the spring of 1861. If he was truly the "Great Emancipator," as Northern myth asserts, one would think that the first item on his agenda as president would have been to abolish slavery in the capital city. Instead, he stalled and deferred month after month, until over a year passed. As he himself had said just a few months prior to his inauguration:

> **I have no thought of recommending the abolition of slavery in the District of Columbia, nor the slave-trade among the slave States.**[159]

Lincoln's delay tactics in ridding Washington of slavery earned him yet another one of his many nicknames: "America's biggest slave owner." As an angry Charles Sumner put it:

> Do you know who, at this moment, is the largest slaveholder in this country? It is Abraham Lincoln; for he holds all of the three thousand slaves of the District, which is more than any other person in the country holds.[160]

On April 14, 1862, while Lincoln was still refusing to free Washington's slaves, noted black bishop, Daniel A. Payne, head of the African Methodist Episcopal Church, decided to pay him a visit. "Do you intend to sign a bill of emancipation or not?" he asked the president impatiently. Lincoln obfuscated, told stories and jokes. Forty-five minutes later, he still had not answered Payne's question, and the frustrated clergyman politely got up and left.[161]

Political expediency and constant pressure over the past year, including his meeting with Bishop Payne, finally forced Lincoln's hand, and two days later, on April 16, 1862, the country witnessed the passage of the District of Columbia Emancipation Act. Because of the president, it had not come easily.[162] In fact, the entire process, from bondage to emancipation, had taken hundreds of years! But finally, to the great relief of the North's handful of vociferous abolitionists, slavery had at last been banned in Washington, D.C.[163]

This "humanitarian" act was tainted, however, by several things. One was the fact that Lincoln's emancipation proclamation in Washington, D.C. turned out to be for the benefit of colonizationists like himself, not for the benefit of the slaves. For he had included a clause in the bill calling for their immediate deportation upon liberation.[164] The day the bill was signed into law, April 16, 1862, the president even wrote a letter to the House and Senate applauding them for recognizing his call for the deportation of the city's newly freed blacks and for setting aside funds for their colonization.[165]

There was also the anger of the city's whites, most who had no taste for abolition to begin with.[166] At the same time, antislavery advocates fumed over Lincoln's concomitant demand of Congress that it appropriate funding to deport, to Liberia and Haiti, the very blacks he had just freed (though the crafty president finally liberated the city's slaves, cleverly he had never promised that he would not attempt to colonize them outside the U.S.).[167]

Lincoln's half-hearted attempt at ending slavery in the nation's capital, of course, had little effect on the endemic Yankee trade there. In 1864, some two years after the District of Columbia Emancipation Act had been issued, former Northern slave Sojourner Truth discovered, to her horror, that whites near Washington, D.C. were kidnaping the black children of freed Southern servants and forcing them back into Northern slavery. The small community the freed blacks lived in, ironically called "Freedman's Village," had been set up by the U.S. army to help newly emancipated African-Americans adjust to living in free white society. Truth used the court system to have the children released and returned to their parents; but not before her own life was threatened by the violent and unrepentant Yankee slavers.

Lincoln, whose offices were not far away, must have been aware of these crimes, yet he did nothing. It was Lincoln's overt complicity in the institution of slavery that often prompted Truth to refer to the U.S. flag, not as the "Stars and Stripes," but as the "Scars and Stripes."[168]

America's capital city was so central to slavery that she probably would have become the nation's slave trading capital instead of New York City. The only reason Washington, D.C. did not was due to geography: at the time she was only a mere sixty-eight square miles, with no room to expand.[169] Nonetheless, a vestige of Washington's original function as a leading slave market is its black population, which peaked at 71 percent in 1970, one of the highest of any city in the U.S.[170]

As the founder of both the American slave trade and American slavery, and with her long history of deep economic ties to the slave industry, it should come as no surprise to learn that the top five American cities with the largest black populations today are all in the North and West (by rank they are New York City, New York; Chicago, Illinois; Detroit, Michigan; Philadelphia, Pennsylvania; and Los Angeles, California). Even the city with the highest percentage of blacks is in the North: Detroit.[171]

Now let us examine Lincoln's second piece of anti-South propaganda as inferred in his September 16, 1859, Columbus, Ohio, address; namely, that the South was the center of the American slave trade.

America's African slaves arrived here, not aboard Southern ships, but aboard Northern ones. For the only slave ships to ever sail from the U.S. left from Northern ports, and all were commanded by Northern captains and funded by Northern businessmen, and all operated under the auspices of the U.S. flag,[172] the Stars and Stripes,[173] as even foreigners like the British understood.[174]

The South, on the other hand, did not own slave ships, was not involved in the industry, and had no interest in it; thus no Africans were ever removed from their native land under the Confederate flag, the Stars and Bars.[175] This is why, when the Southern states formed the Confederacy,

February 4-9, 1861,[176] one of the first clauses they put into their Constitution was a prohibition against foreign slave trading.[177] Here, from the C.S. Constitution, Article 1, Section 9, Clause 1, is the exact wording:

> The importation of negroes of the African race, from any foreign country, other than the slaveholding States or Territories of the United States of America, is hereby forbidden; and Congress is required to pass such laws as shall effectually prevent the same.[178]

This was five years before the U.S. banned the foreign slave trade. Indeed the original U.S. Constitution, also Article 1, Section 9, Clause 1, allowed the

> . . . importation of such Persons as any of the States now existing shall think proper to admit . . .[179]

Those referred to here as "such Persons" were, of course, slaves.

If slavery was maintained in, fueled by, and run from the North, where then did the South get her "slaves"? Every one of the South's 3.5 million black servants was purchased, either directly or indirectly, from a Northern slave trader or Northern slave company. Thus, as pro-South historian Frank Lawrence Owsley writes, those truly responsible for Southern slavery are those who forced it on the South to begin with.[180]

As proof that those who forced slavery on the South were Yankees, consider the following. First, the only person ever tried, convicted, and executed for slaving was a Northerner: Captain Nathaniel Gordon, of New York, was put to death on February 21, 1862, by Lincoln's personal order.[181] Second, the last American slave ship to be captured by the U.S. government was a Northern one: the *Nightingale*, also from New York, confiscated on April 21, 1861. At the time of its seizure, this vessel, from the so-called "abolitionist North," had nearly 1,000 manacled Africans on board.[182] It was doing "business as usual" up until the first few weeks of Lincoln's War.[183]

In fact, it was the North's heavy dependence on the Yankee slave trade and on selling slaves to the South, that helped precipitate the War: when the Confederacy banned all slave trading with foreign nations, which included the U.S., the North panicked, deciding it was better to beat the South into submission than allow her to cut off one of the Yankees' primary streams of wealth.[184]

How can these things be true if they are not in our history books?

Let us examine the facts.

Though Southerner George Mason tried, unsuccessfully, to prohibit the U.S. slave trade as early as 1787[185] (he referred to it as a "wicked, cruel, and unnatural trade"),[186] and though Southern President Thomas Jefferson finally permanently banned it in 1808,[187] the law (as even Lincoln observed)[188] was routinely ignored by Northerners, who vigorously continued to illegally traffic in human chattel,[189] even through and after Lincoln's War.[190] Not a single slaving captain or trader was punished by the U.S. until Gordon in 1862,[191] and for good reason: the federal government was completely controlled by slave interests.[192] Indeed, this is how Lincoln funded his war: chiefly with the profits from Northern slavery and the Yankee slave trade, bought and paid for by Lincoln's "Wall Street Boys"; that is, the Northern business establishment, made up of Yankee robber barons, financiers, merchants, and industrialists.[193]

Yankee abolitionist, individualist, and natural rights advocate, Lysander Spooner, saw right through Lincoln's duplicitous treachery, correctly referring to the president's Wall Street Boys as the "lenders of blood money." Wrote Spooner:

> . . . these lenders of blood money had, for a long series of years previous to the war, been the willing accomplices of the slave-holders in perverting the government from the purposes of liberty and justice, to the greatest of crimes. They had been such accomplices *for a purely pecuniary consideration*, to wit, a control of the markets in the South; in other words, the privilege of holding the slave-holders themselves in industrial and commercial subjection to the manufacturers and merchants of the North (who afterwards furnished the money for the [Civil] war). And these Northern merchants and manufacturers, these lenders of blood money, were willing to continue to be the accomplices of the slaveholders in the future, for the same pecuniary considerations. But the slaveholders, either doubting the fidelity of their Northern allies, or feeling themselves strong enough to keep their slaves in subjection without Northern assistance, would no longer pay the price these Northern men demanded. And it was to enforce this price in the future—that is, to monopolize the Southern markets, to maintain their industrial and commercial control over the South—that these Northern manufacturers and merchants lent some of the profits of their former monopolies for the [Civil] war, in order to secure themselves the same, or greater, monopolies in the future. These—and not any love of liberty or justice—were the motives on which the money for the [Civil] war was lent by the

North.[194]

Having now exposed the lies in Lincoln's September 16th speech, let us examine one he made the next day, on September 17, 1859. Here, Lincoln continues to blast the idea of states' rights ("popular sovereignty") in a speech at Cincinnati, Ohio:

> My Fellow-citizens of the State of Ohio: This is the first time in my life that I have appeared before an audience in so great a city as this. I therefore—though I am no longer a young man—make this appearance under some degree of embarrassment. But I have found that when one is embarrassed, usually the shortest way to get through with it is to quit talking or thinking about it, and go at something else.
>
> I understand that you have had recently with you my very distinguished friend, Judge Douglas, of Illinois, and I understand, without having had an opportunity (not greatly sought, to be sure) of seeing a report of the speech that he made here, that he did me the honor to mention my humble name. I suppose that he did so for the purpose of making some objection to some sentiment at some time expressed by me. I should expect, it is true, that Judge Douglas had reminded you, or informed you, if you had never before heard it, that I had once in my life declared it as my opinion that this government cannot "endure permanently half slave and half free; that a house divided against itself cannot stand," and, as I had expressed it, I did not expect the house to fall; that I did not expect the Union to be dissolved, but that I did expect it would cease to be divided; that it would become all one thing or all the other; that either the opposition of slavery will arrest the further spread of it, and place it where the public mind would rest in the belief that it was in the course of ultimate extinction, or the friends of slavery will push it forward until it becomes alike lawful in all the States, old or new, free as well as slave. I did, fifteen months ago, express that opinion, and upon many occasions Judge Douglas has denounced it, and has greatly, intentionally or unintentionally, misrepresented my purpose in the expression of that opinion.
>
> I presume, without having seen a report of his speech, that he did so here. I presume that he alluded

also to that opinion in different language, having been expressed at a subsequent time by Governor [William H.] Seward, of New York, and that he took the two in a lump and denounced them; that he tried to point out that there was something couched in this opinion which led to the making of an entire uniformity of the local institutions of the various States of the Union, in utter disregard of the different States, which in their nature would seem to require a variety of institutions, and a variety of laws conforming to the differences in the nature of the different States.

Not only so: I presume he insisted that this was a declaration of war between the free and slave States—that it was the sounding to the onset of continual war between the different States, the slave and free States.

This charge, in this form, was made by Judge Douglas on, I believe; the 9th of July, 1858, in Chicago, in my hearing. On the next evening, I made some reply to it. I informed him that many of the inferences he drew from that expression of mine were altogether foreign to any purpose entertained by me, and in so far as he should ascribe these inferences to me, as my purpose, he was entirely mistaken; and in so far as he might argue that whatever might be my purpose, actions, conforming to my views, would lead to these results, he might argue and establish if he could; but, so far as purposes were concerned, he was totally mistaken as to me.

When I made that reply to him, I told him, on the question of declaring war between the different States of the Union, that I had not said I did not expect any peace upon this question until slavery was exterminated; that I had only said I expected peace when that institution was put where the public mind should rest in the belief that it was in course of ultimate extinction; that I believed, from the organization of our government until a very recent period of time, the institution had been placed and continued upon such a basis; that we had had comparative peace upon that question through a portion of that period of time, only because the public mind rested in that belief in regard to it, and that when we returned to that position in relation to that matter, I supposed we should again have peace as we previously had. I assured him, as I now assure you, that I neither then had, nor have, nor ever had, any purpose in any way of interfering with the institution of slavery where it exists. I believe we have no power, under the Constitution of the United States, or rather under the form of government under which we live, to interfere with the institution of slavery, or any other of the institutions of our sister States, be they free or slave States. I declared then, and I now re-declare, that I have as little inclination to interfere with the institution of slavery where it now exists, through the instrumentality of the General Government, or any other instrumentality, as I believe we have no power to do so. I accidentally used this expression: I had no purpose of entering into the slave States to disturb the institution of slavery. So, upon the first occasion that Judge Douglas got an opportunity to reply to me, he passed by the whole body of what I had said upon that subject, and seized upon the particular expression of mine, that I had no purpose of entering into the slave States to disturb the institution of slavery. "Oh, no," said he; "he [i.e., Lincoln] won't enter into the slave States to disturb the institution of slavery; he is too prudent a man to do such a thing as that; he only means that he will go on to the line between the free and slave States, and shoot over at them. This is all he means to do. He means to do them all the harm he can, to disturb them all he can, in such a way as to keep his own hide in perfect safety."

Well, now, I did not think, at that time, that that was either a very dignified or very logical argument; but so it was, and I had to get along with it as well as I could.

It has occurred to me here to-night that if I ever do shoot over the line at the people on the other side of the line, into a slave State, and propose to do so keeping my skin safe, that I have now about the best chance I shall ever have. I should not wonder if there are some Kentuckians about this audience; we are close to Kentucky; and whether that be so or not, we are on elevated ground, and by speaking distinctly I should not wonder if some of the Kentuckians would hear me on the other side of the river. For that reason I propose to address a portion of what I have to say to the Kentuckians.

I say, then, in the first place, to the Kentuckians, that I am what they call, as I understand it; a "Black Republican." I think slavery is wrong, morally and politically. I desire that it should be no further spread in these United States, and I should not object if it should gradually terminate in the whole Union. While I say this for myself, I say to you Kentuckians that I understand you differ radically with me upon this proposition; that you believe slavery is a good thing; that slavery is right; that it ought to be extended and perpetuated in this Union. Now, there being this broad difference between us, I do not pretend, in addressing myself to you Kentuckians, to attempt proselyting you; that would be a vain effort. I do not enter upon it. I only propose to try to show you that you ought to nominate for the next presidency, at Charleston, my distinguished friend, Judge Douglas. In all that there is no real difference between you and him; I understand he is as sincerely for you, and more wisely for you, than you are for yourselves. I will try to demonstrate that proposition. Understand now, I say that I believe he is as sincerely for you, and more wisely for you, than you are for yourselves.

What do you want more than anything else to make successful your views of slavery—to advance the outspread of it, and to secure and perpetuate the nationality of it? What do you want more than anything else? What is needed absolutely? What is indispensable to you? Why, if I may be allowed to answer the question, it is to retain a hold upon the North—it is to retain support and strength from the free States. If you can get this support and strength from the free States, you can succeed. If you do not get this support and this strength from the free States, you are in the minority, and you are beaten at once.

If that proposition be admitted,—and it is undeniable,—then the next thing I say to you is, that Douglas of all the men in this nation is the only man that affords you any hold upon the free States; that no other man can give you any strength in the free States. This being so, if you doubt the other branch of the proposition, whether he is for you,—whether he is really for you, as I have expressed it,—I propose asking your attention for a while to a few facts.

The issue between you and me, understand, is that I think slavery is wrong, and ought not to be outspread, and you think it is right, and ought to be extended and perpetuated. I now proceed to try to show to you that Douglas is as sincerely for you, and more wisely for you, than you are for yourselves.

In the first place, we know that in a government like this, a government of the people, where the voice of all the men of the country, substantially, enters into the administration of the government, what lies at the bottom of all of it is public opinion. I lay down the proposition that Judge Douglas is not only the man that promises you in advance a hold upon the North, and support in the North, but that he constantly molds public opinion to your ends; that in every possible way he can, he molds the public opinion of the North to your ends; and if there are a few things in which he seems to be against you,—a few things which he says that appear to be against you, and a few that he forbears to say which you would like to have him say,—you ought to remember that the saying of the one, or the forbearing to say the other, would lose his hold upon the North, and, by consequence, would lose his capacity to serve you.

Upon this subject of molding public opinion, I call your attention to the fact—for a well-established fact it is—that the judge never says your institution of slavery is wrong: he never says it is right, to be sure, but he never says it is wrong. There is not a public man in the United States, I believe, with the exception of Senator Douglas, who has not, at some time in his life, declared his opinion whether the thing is right or wrong; but Senator Douglas never declares it is wrong. He leaves himself at perfect liberty to do all in your favor which he would be hindered from doing if he were to declare the thing to be wrong. On the contrary, he takes all the chances that he has for inveigling the sentiment of the North, opposed to slavery, into your support, by never saying it is right. This you ought to set down to his credit. You ought to give him full credit for this much, little though it be in comparison to the whole which he does for you.

Some other things I will ask your attention to. He said upon the floor of the United States Senate, and he has repeated it, as I understand, a great many times, that he does not care whether slavery is "voted up or voted down." This again shows you, or ought to show you, if you would reason upon it, that he does not believe it to be wrong; for a man may say, when he sees nothing wrong in a thing, that he does not care whether it be voted up or voted down; but no man can logically say that he cares not whether a thing goes up or goes down which appears to him to be wrong. You therefore have a demonstration in this, that to Judge Douglas's mind your favorite institution, which you desire to have spread out and made perpetual, is no wrong.

Another thing he tells you, in a speech made at Memphis, in Tennessee, shortly after the canvass in Illinois, last year. He there distinctly told the people that there was a "line drawn by the Almighty across this continent, on the one side of which the soil must always be cultivated by slaves"; that he did not pretend to know exactly where that line was, but that there was such a line. I want to ask your attention to that proposition again—that there is one portion of this continent where the Almighty has designed the soil shall always be cultivated by slaves; that its being cultivated by slaves at that place is right; that it has the direct sympathy and authority of the Almighty. Whenever you can get these Northern audiences to adopt the opinion that slavery is right on the other side of the Ohio; whenever you can get them, in pursuance of Douglas's views, to adopt that sentiment, they will very readily make the other argument, which is perfectly logical, that that which is right on that side of the Ohio cannot be wrong on this, and that if you have that property on that side of the Ohio, under the seal and stamp of the Almighty, when by any means it escapes over here, it is wrong to have constitutions and laws "to devil" you about it. So Douglas is molding the public opinion of the North, first to say that the thing is right in your State over the Ohio River, and hence to say that that which is right there is not wrong here, and that all laws and constitutions here, recognizing it as being wrong, are themselves wrong, and ought to be repealed and abrogated. He will tell you, men of Ohio, that if you choose here to have laws against slavery, it is in conformity to the idea that your climate is not suited to it; that your climate is not suited to slave labor, and therefore you have constitutions and laws against it.

Let us attend to that argument for a little while, and see if it be sound. You do not raise sugar-cane (except the new-fashioned sugarcane, and you won't raise that long), but they do raise it in Louisiana. You don't raise it in Ohio because you can't raise it profitably, because the climate don't suit it. They do raise it in Louisiana because there it is profitable. Now Douglas will tell you that is precisely the slavery question: that they do have slaves there because they are profitable, and you don't have them here because they are not profitable. If that is so, then it leads to dealing with the one precisely as with the other. Is there, then, anything in the constitution or laws of Ohio against raising sugar-cane? Have you found it necessary to put any such provision in your law? Surely not! No man desires to raise sugar-cane in Ohio; but if any man did desire to do so, you would say it was a tyrannical law that forbids his doing so; and whenever you shall agree with Douglas, whenever your minds are brought to adopt his argument, as surely you will have reached the conclusion that although slavery is not profitable in Ohio, if any man want it, it is wrong to him not to let him have it.

In this matter Judge Douglas is preparing the public mind for you of Kentucky, to make perpetual that good thing in your estimation, about which you and I differ.

In this connection let me ask your attention to another thing. I believe it is safe to assert that, five years ago, no living man had expressed the opinion that the negro had no share in the Declaration of Independence. Let me state that again: Five years ago no living man had expressed the opinion that the negro had no share in the Declaration of Independence. If there is in this large audience any man who ever knew of that opinion being put upon paper as much as five years ago, I will be obliged to him now, or at a subsequent time, to show it.

If that be true, I wish you then to note the next fact—that within the space of five years Senator Douglas, in the argument of this question, has got his entire party, so far as I know, without exception, to join in saying that the negro has no share in the Declaration of Independence. If there be now in all these United States one Douglas man that does not say this, I have been unable upon any occasion to scare him up. Now, if none of you said this five years ago, and all of you say it now, that is a matter that you Kentuckians ought to note. That is a vast change in the Northern public sentiment upon that question.

Of what tendency is that change? The tendency of that change is to bring the public mind to the conclusion that when men are spoken of, the negro is not meant; that when negroes are spoken of, brutes alone are contemplated. That change in public sentiment has already degraded the black man, in the estimation of Douglas and his followers, from the condition of a man of some sort, and assigned him to the condition of a brute. Now you Kentuckians ought to give Douglas credit for this. That is the largest possible stride that can be made in regard to the perpetuation of your good thing of slavery.

In Kentucky, perhaps,—in many of the slave States certainly,—you are trying to establish the rightfulness of slavery by reference to the Bible. You are trying to show that slavery existed in the Bible times by divine ordinance. [It did, as I prove in Chapter 10.] Now Douglas is wiser than you for your own benefit, upon that subject. Douglas knows that whenever you establish that slavery was right by the Bible, it will occur that that slavery was the slavery of the white man,—of men without reference to color,—and he knows very well that you may entertain that idea in Kentucky as much as you please, but you will never win any Northern support upon it. He makes a wiser argument for you; he makes the argument that the slavery of the black man, the slavery of the man who has a skin of a different color from your own, is right. He thereby brings to your support Northern voters who could not for a moment be brought by your own argument of the Bible-right of slavery. Will you not give him credit for that? Will you not say that in this matter he is more wisely for you than you are for yourselves?

Now, having established with his entire party this doctrine—having been entirely successful in that branch of his efforts in your behalf,—he is ready for another.

At this same meeting at Memphis, he declared that in all contests between the negro and the white man, he was for the white man, but that in all questions between the negro and the crocodile he was for the negro. He did not make that declaration accidentally at Memphis. He made it a great many times in the canvass in Illinois last year (though I don't know that it was reported in any of his speeches there; but he frequently made it). I believe he repeated it at Columbus, and I should not wonder if he repeated it here. It is, then, a deliberate way of expressing himself upon that subject. It is a matter of mature deliberation with him thus to express himself upon that point of his case. It therefore requires some deliberate attention.

The first inference seems to be that if you do not enslave the negro you are wronging the white man in some way or other; and that whoever is opposed to the negro being enslaved is, in some way or other, against the white man. Is not that a falsehood? If there was a necessary conflict between the white man and the negro, I should be for the white man as much as Judge Douglas; but I say there is no such necessary conflict. I say that there is room enough for us all to be free, and that it not only does not wrong the white man that the negro should be free, but it positively wrongs the mass of the white men that the negro should be enslaved; that *the mass of white men are really injured by the effects of slave-labor* in the vicinity of the fields of their own labor [emphasis added].

But I do not desire to dwell upon this branch of the question more than to say that this assumption of his is false, and I do hope that that fallacy will not long prevail in the minds of intelligent white men. At all events, you ought to thank Judge Douglas for it. It is for your benefit it is made.

The other branch of it is, that in a struggle between the negro and the crocodile, he is for the negro. Well, I don't know that there is any struggle between the negro and the crocodile, either. I suppose that if a crocodile (or, as we old Ohio River boatmen used to call them, alligators) should come across a white man, he would kill him if he could, and so he would a negro. But what, at last, is this proposition? I believe that it is a sort of proposition in proportion, which may be stated thus: "As the negro is to the white man, so is the crocodile to the negro; and as the negro may rightfully treat the crocodile as a beast or reptile, so the white man may rightfully treat the negro as a beast or reptile." That is really the point of all that argument of his.

Now, my brother Kentuckians, who believe in this, you ought to thank Judge Douglas for having put that in a much more taking way than any of yourselves have done.

Again, Douglas's great principle, "popular sovereignty," as he calls it, gives you by natural consequence the revival of the slave trade whenever you want it. If you are disposed to question this, listen awhile, consider awhile, what I shall advance in support of that proposition.

He says that it is the sacred right of the man who goes into the Territories to have slavery if he wants it. Grant that for argument's sake. Is it not the sacred right of the man who don't go there, equally to buy slaves in Africa, if he wants them? Can you point out the difference? The man who goes into the Territories of Kansas and Nebraska, or any other new Territory, with the sacred right of taking a slave there which belongs to him, would certainly have no more right to take one there than *I would who own no slave, but who would desire to buy one and take him there* [emphasis added].[195] You will not say—you, the friends of Judge Douglas—but that the man who does not own a slave, has an equal right to buy one and take him to the Territory as the other does?

I say that Douglas's popular sovereignty, establishing his sacred right in the people, if you please, if carried to its logical conclusion, gives equally the sacred right to the people of the States or the Territories themselves to buy slaves, wherever they can buy them cheapest; and if any man can show a distinction, I should like to hear him try it. If any man can show how the people of Kansas have a better right to slaves because they want them, than the people of Georgia have to buy them in Africa, I want him to do it. I think it cannot be done. If it is "popular sovereignty" for the people to have slaves because they want them, it is popular sovereignty for them to buy them in Africa, because they desire to do so.

I know that Douglas has recently made a little effort—not seeming to notice that he had a different theory—has made an effort to get rid of that. He has written a letter, addressed to somebody, I believe, who resides in Iowa, declaring his opposition to the repeal of the laws that prohibit the African slave-trade. He bases his opposition to such repeal upon the ground that these laws are themselves one of the compromises of the Constitution of the United States. Now it would be very interesting to see Judge Douglas, or any of his friends, turn to the Constitution of the United States and point out that compromise, to show where there is any compromise in the Constitution, or provision in the Constitution, expressed or implied, by which the administrators of that Constitution are under any obligation to repeal the African slave-trade. I know, or at least I think I know, that the framers of that Constitution did expect that the African slave-trade would be abolished at the end of twenty years, to which time their prohibition against its being abolished extended. I think there is abundant contemporaneous history to show that the framers of the Constitution expected it to be abolished. But while they so expected, they gave nothing for that expectation, and they put no provision in the Constitution requiring it should be so abolished. The migration or importation of such persons as the States shall see fit to admit shall not be prohibited, but a certain tax might be levied upon such importation. But what was to be done after that time? The Constitution is as silent about that as it is silent, personally, about myself. There is absolutely nothing in it about that subject—there is only the expectation of the framers of the Constitution that the slave-trade would be abolished at the end of that time, and they expected it would be abolished, owing to public sentiment, before that time, and they put that provision in, in order that it should not be abolished before that time, for reasons which I suppose they thought to be sound ones, but which I will not now try to enumerate before you.

But while they expected the slave-trade would be abolished at that time, they expected that the spread of slavery into the new Territories should also be restricted. It is as easy to prove that the framers of the Constitution of the United States expected that slavery should be prohibited from extending into the new Territories, as it is to prove that it was expected that the slave-trade should be abolished. Both these things were expected. One was no more expected than the other, and one was no more a compromise of the Constitution than the other. There was nothing said in the Constitution in regard to the spread of slavery into the Territories. I grant that, but there was something very important said about it by the same generation of men in the adoption of the old ordinance of '87, through the influence of which you here in Ohio, our neighbors in Indiana, we in Illinois, our neighbors in Michigan and Wisconsin, are happy, prosperous, teeming millions of free men. That generation of men, though not to the full extent members of the convention that framed the Constitution, were to some extent members of that convention, holding seats at the same time in one body and the other, so that if there was any compromise on either of these subjects, the strong evidence is that that compromise was in favor of the restriction of slavery from the new Territories.

But Douglas says that he is unalterably opposed to the repeal of those laws: because, in his view, it is a compromise of the Constitution. You Kentuckians, no doubt, are somewhat offended with that! You ought not to be! You ought to be patient! You ought to know that if he said less than that, he would lose the power of "lugging" the Northern States to your support. Really, what you would push him to do would take from him his entire power to serve you. And you ought to remember how long, by precedent. Judge Douglas holds himself obliged to stick by compromises. You ought to remember that by the time you yourselves think you are ready to inaugurate measures for the revival of the African slave-trade, that sufficient time will have arrived, by precedent, for Judge Douglas to break through that compromise. He says now nothing more strong than he said in 1849 when he declared in favor of the Missouri Compromise—that precisely four years and a quarter after he declared that compromise to be a sacred thing, which "no ruthless hand would ever dared to touch," he, himself, brought forward the measure ruthlessly to destroy it. By a mere calculation of time it will only be four years more until he is ready to take back his profession about the sacredness of the compromise abolishing the slave-trade. Precisely as soon as you are ready to have his services in that direction, by fair calculation, you may be sure of having them.

But you remember and set down to Judge Douglas's debt, or discredit, that he, last year, said the people of Territories can, in spite of the Dred Scott decision, exclude your slaves from those Territories; that he declared by " unfriendly legislation" the extension of your property into the new Territories may be cut off in the teeth of that decision of the Supreme Court of the United States.

He assumed that position at Freeport, on the 27th of August, 1858. He said that the people of the Territories can exclude slavery, in so many words. You ought, however, to bear in mind that he has never said it since. You may hunt in every speech that he has since made, and he has never used that expression once. He has never seemed to notice that he is stating his views differently from what he did then; but by some sort of accident, he has always really stated it differently. He has always since then declared that "the Constitution does not carry slavery into the Territories of the United States beyond the power of the people legally to control it, as other property." Now there is a difference in the language used upon that former occasion and in this latter day. There may or may not be a difference in the meaning, but it is worth while considering whether there is not also a difference in meaning.

What, is it to exclude? Why, it is to drive it out. It is in some way to put it out of the Territory. It is to force it across the line, or change its character, so that as property it is out of existence. But what is the controlling of it "as other property"? Is controlling it as other property the same thing as destroying it, or driving it away? I should think not. I should think the controlling of it as other property would be just about what you in Kentucky should want.

I understand the controlling of property means the controlling of it for the benefit of the owner of it. While I have no doubt the Supreme Court of the United States would say " God speed" to any of the territorial legislatures that should thus control slave property, they would sing quite a different tune if by the pretense of controlling it they were to undertake to pass laws which virtually excluded it, and that upon a very well known principle to all lawyers, that what a legislature cannot directly do, it cannot do by indirection; that as the legislature has not the power to drive slaves out, they have no power by indirection, by tax, or by imposing burdens in any way on that property, to effect the same end, and that any attempt to do so would be held by the Dred Scott court unconstitutional.

Douglas is not willing to stand by his first proposition that they can exclude it, because we have seen that that proposition amounts to nothing more nor less than the naked absurdity that you may lawfully drive out that which has a lawful right to remain. He admitted at first that the slave might be lawfully taken into the Territories under the Constitution of the United States, and yet asserted that he might be lawfully driven out. That being the proposition, it is the absurdity I have stated. He is not willing to stand in the face of that direct, naked, and impudent absurdity; he has, therefore, modified his language into that of being "controlled as other property."

The Kentuckians don't like this in Douglas! I will tell you where it will go. He now swears by the court. He was once a leading man in Illinois to break down a court because it had made a decision he did not like. But he now not only swears by the court, the courts having got to working for you, but he denounces all men that do not swear by the courts as unpatriotic, as bad citizens. When one of these acts of unfriendly legislation shall impose such heavy burdens as to, in effect, destroy property in slaves in a Territory, and show plainly enough that there can be no mistake in the purpose of the legislature to make them so burdensome, this same Supreme Court will decide that law to be unconstitutional, and he will be ready to say for your benefit, "I swear by the court; I give it up"; and while that is going on he has been getting all his men to swear by the courts, and to give it up with him. In this again he serves you faithfully, and, as I say, more wisely than you serve yourselves.

Again, I have alluded in the beginning of these remarks to the fact that Judge Douglas has made great complaint of my having expressed the opinion that this government "cannot endure permanently half slave and half free." He has complained of Seward for using different language, and declaring that there is an "irrepressible conflict" between the principles of free and slave labor. [Audience member: "He says it is not original with Seward. That is original with Lincoln."] I will attend to that immediately, sir. Since that time, [John] Hickman, of Pennsylvania, expressed the same sentiment. He has never denounced Mr. Hickman. Why? There is a little chance, notwithstanding that opinion in the mouth of Hickman, that he may yet be a Douglas man. That is the difference. It is not unpatriotic to hold that opinion, if a man is a Douglas man.

But neither I, nor Seward, nor Hickman is entitled to the enviable or unenviable distinction of having first expressed that idea. That same idea was expressed by the Richmond "Enquirer" in Virginia, in 1856, quite two years before it was expressed by the first of us. And while Douglas was pluming himself that in his conflict with my humble self, last year, he had "squelched out" that fatal heresy, as he delighted to call it, and had suggested that if he only had had a chance to be in New York and meet Seward he would have "squelched" it there also, it never occurred to him to breathe a word against [Roger A.] Pryor. I don't think that you can discover that Douglas ever talked of going to Virginia to "squelch" out that idea there. No. More than that. That same Roger A. Pryor was brought to Washington City and made the editor of the *par excellence* Douglas paper after making use of that expression which, in us, is so unpatriotic and heretical. From all this my Kentucky friends may see that this opinion is heretical in his view only when it is expressed by men suspected of a desire that the country shall all become free; and not when expressed by those fairly known to entertain the desire that the whole country shall become slave. When expressed by that class of men, it is in no wise offensive to him. In this again, my friends of Kentucky, you have Judge Douglas with you.

There is another reason why you Southern people ought to nominate Douglas at your convention at Charleston. That reason is the wonderful capacity of the man; the power he has of doing what would seem to be impossible. Let me call your attention to one of these apparently impossible things.

Douglas had three or four very distinguished men, of the most extreme antislavery views of any men in the Republican party, expressing their desire for his reelection to the Senate last year. That would, of itself, have seemed to be a little wonderful, but that wonder is heightened when we see that [Henry Alexander] Wise, of Virginia, a man exactly opposed to them, a man who believes in the divine right of slavery, was also expressing his desire that Douglas should be reelected; that another man that may be said to be kindred to Wise, Mr. [John Cabell] Breckinridge, the Vice-President, and of your own State, was also agreeing with the antislavery men in the North that Douglas ought to be reelected. Still, to heighten the wonder, a senator from Kentucky, whom I have always loved with an affection as tender and endearing as I have ever loved any man, who was opposed to the antislavery men for reasons which seemed sufficient to him, and equally opposed to Wise and Breckinridge, was writing letters into Illinois to secure the reelection of Douglas. Now that all these conflicting elements should be brought, while at daggers' points with one another, to support him, is a feat that is worthy for you to note and consider. It is quite probable that each of these classes of men thought, by the reelection of Douglas, their peculiar views would gain something: it is probable that the antislavery men thought their views would gain something; that Wise and Breckinridge thought so too, as regards their opinions; that Mr. [John Jordan] Crittenden thought that his views would gain something, although he was opposed to both these other men. It is probable that each and all of them thought that they were using Douglas, and it is yet an unsolved problem whether he was not using them all. If he was, then it is for you to consider whether that power to perform wonders is one for you lightly to throw away.

There is one other thing that I will say to you in this relation. It is but my opinion; I give it to you without a fee. It is my opinion that it is for you to take him or be defeated; and that if you do take him you may be beaten. You will surely be beaten if you do not take him. We, the Republicans and others forming the opposition of the country, intend to "stand by our guns," to be patient and firm, and in the long run to beat you whether you take him or not. We know that before we fairly beat you, we have to beat you both together. We know that "you are all of a feather," and that we have to beat you all together, and we expect to do it. We don't intend to be very impatient about it. We mean to be as deliberate and calm about it as it is possible to be, but as firm and resolved as it is possible for men to be. When we do as we say, beat you, you perhaps want to know what we will do with you.

I will tell you, so far as I am authorized to speak for the opposition, what we mean to do with you. We mean to treat you, as near as we possibly can, as [George] Washington, [Thomas] Jefferson, and [James] Madison treated you. We mean to leave you alone, and in no way to interfere with your institution; to abide by all and every compromise of the Constitution, and, in a word, coming back to the original proposition, to treat you, so far as degenerated men (if we have degenerated) may, according to the example of those noble fathers—Washington, Jefferson, and Madison. We mean to remember that you are as good as we; that there is no difference between us other than the difference of circumstances. We mean to recognize and bear in mind always that you have as good hearts in your bosoms as other people, or as we claim to have, and treat you accordingly. We mean to marry your girls when we have a chance—the white ones, I mean, and I have the honor to inform you that I once did have a chance in that way.

  I have told you what we mean to do. I want to know, now, when that thing takes place, what do you mean to do? I often hear it intimated that you mean to divide the Union whenever a Republican or anything like it is elected President of the United States. [Audience member: "That is so."] "That is so," one of them says; I wonder if he is a Kentuckian? [A voice: "He is a Douglas man."] Well, then, I want to know what you are going to do with your half of it? Are you going to split the Ohio down through, and push your half off a piece? Or are you going to keep it right alongside of us outrageous fellows? Or are you going to build up a wall some way between your country and ours, by which that movable property of yours can't come over here any more, to the danger of your losing it? Do you think you can better yourselves on that subject by leaving us here under no obligation whatever to return those specimens of your movable property that come hither? You have divided the Union because we would not do right with you, as you think, upon that subject; when we cease to be under obligations to do anything for you, how much better off do you think you will be? Will you make war upon us and kill us all? Why, gentlemen, I think you as gallant and as brave men as live; that you can fight as bravely in a good cause, man for man, as any other people living; that you have shown yourselves capable of this upon various occasions; but man for man, you are not better than we are, and there are not so many of you as there are of us. You will never make much of a hand at whipping us. If we were fewer in numbers than you, I think that you could whip us; if we were equal it would likely be a drawn battle; but being inferior in numbers, you will make nothing by attempting to master us.

  But perhaps I have addressed myself as long, or longer, to the Kentuckians than I ought to have done, inasmuch as I have said that whatever course you take, we intend in the end to beat you. I propose to address a few remarks to our friends, by way of discussing with them the best means of keeping that promise that I have in good faith made.

It may appear a little episodical for me to mention the topic of which I shall speak now. It is a favorite proposition of Douglas's that the interference of the General Government, through the ordinance of '87, or through any other act of the General Government, never has made, nor ever can make, a free State; that the ordinance of '87 did not make free States of Ohio, Indiana, or Illinois; that these States are free upon his "great principle" of popular sovereignty, because the people of those several States have chosen to make them so. At Columbus, and probably here, he undertook to compliment the people that they themselves had made the State of Ohio free, and that the ordinance of '87 was not entitled in any degree to divide the honor with him. I have no doubt that the people of the State of Ohio did make her free according to their own will and judgment; but let the facts be remembered.

In 1802, I believe, it was you who made your first constitution, with the clause prohibiting slavery, and you did it, I suppose, very nearly unanimously; but you should bear in mind that you—speaking of you as one people—that you did so unembarrassed by the actual presence of the institution amongst you; that you made it a free State, not with the embarrassment upon you of already having among you many slaves, which, if they had been here, and you had sought to make a free State, you would not know what to do with. If they had been among you, embarrassing difficulties, most probably, would have induced you to tolerate a slave Constitution instead of a free one; as, indeed, these very difficulties have constrained every people on this continent who have adopted slavery.

Pray, what was it that made you free? What kept you free? Did you not find your country free when you came to decide that Ohio should be a free State? It is important to inquire by what reason you found it so. Let us take an illustration between the States of Ohio and Kentucky. Kentucky is separated by this river Ohio, not a mile wide. A portion of Kentucky, by reason of the course of the Ohio, is further north than this portion of Ohio in which we now stand. Kentucky is entirely covered with slavery—Ohio is entirely free from it. What made that difference? Was it climate? No! A portion of Kentucky was further north than this portion of Ohio.

Was it soil? No! There is nothing in the soil of the one more favorable to slave-labor than the other. It was not climate or soil that caused one side of the line to be entirely covered with slavery and the other side free of it. What was it? Study over it. Tell us, if you can, in all the range of conjecture, if there be anything you can conceive of that made that difference, other than that there was no law of any sort keeping it out of Kentucky, while the ordinance of '87 kept it out of Ohio. If there is any other reason than this, I confess that it is wholly beyond my power to conceive of it. This, then, I offer to combat the idea that that ordinance has never made any State free.

I don't stop at this illustration. I come to the State of Indiana; and what I have said as between Kentucky and Ohio, I repeat as between Indiana and Kentucky; it is equally applicable. One additional argument is applicable also to Indiana. In her territorial condition she more than once petitioned Congress to abrogate the ordinance entirely, or at least so far as to suspend its operation for a time, in order that they should exercise the "popular sovereignty" of having slaves if they wanted them. The men then controlling the General Government, imitating the men of the Revolution, refused Indiana that privilege. And so we have the evidence that Indiana supposed she could have slaves, if it were not for that ordinance; that she besought Congress to put that barrier out of the way; that Congress refused to do so, and it all ended at last in Indiana being a free State. Tell me not then that the ordinance of '87 had nothing to do with making Indiana a free State, when we find some men chafing against and only restrained by that barrier.

Come down again to our State of Illinois. The great Northwest Territory, including Ohio, Indiana, Illinois, Michigan, and Wisconsin, was acquired first, I believe, by the British government, in part, at least, from the French. Before the establishment of our independence, it became a part of Virginia, enabling Virginia afterward to transfer it to the General Government. There were French settlements in what is now Illinois, and at the same time there were French settlements in what is now Missouri—in the tract of country that was not purchased till about 1803. In these French settlements negro slavery had existed for many years—perhaps more than a hundred, if not as much as two hundred, years—at Kaskaskia, in Illinois, and at St. Genevieve, or Cape Girardeau, perhaps, in Missouri. The number of slaves was not very great, but there was about the same number in each place. They were there when we acquired the Territory. There was no effort made to break up the relation of master and slave, and even the ordinance of '87 was not so enforced as to destroy that slavery in Illinois; nor did the ordinance apply to Missouri at all.

What I want to ask your attention to, at this point, is that Illinois and Missouri came into the Union about the same time, Illinois in the latter part of 1818, and Missouri, after a struggle, I believe, some time in 1820. They had been filling up with American people about the same period of time, their progress enabling them to come into the Union about the same. At the end of that ten years, in which they had been so preparing (for it was about that period of time), the number of slaves in Illinois had actually decreased; while in Missouri, beginning with very few, at the end of that ten years there were about ten thousand. This being so, and it being remembered that Missouri and Illinois are, to a certain extent, in the same parallel of latitude,—that the northern half of Missouri and the southern half of Illinois are in the same parallel of latitude,—so that climate would have the same effect upon one as upon the other; and that in the soil there is no material difference so far as bears upon the question of slavery being settled upon one or the other; there being none of those natural causes to produce a difference in filling them, and yet there being a broad difference in their filling up, we are led again to inquire what was the cause of that difference.

It is most natural to say that in Missouri there was no law to keep that country from filling up with slaves, while in Illinois there was the ordinance of '87. The ordinance being there, slavery decreased during that ten years—the ordinance not being in the other, it increased from a few to ten thousand. Can anybody doubt the reason of the difference?

I think all these facts most abundantly prove that my friend Judge Douglas's proposition, that the ordinance of '87, or the national restriction of slavery, never had a tendency to make a free State, is a fallacy—a proposition without the shadow or substance of truth about it.

Douglas sometimes says that all the States (and it is part of that same proposition I have been discussing) that have become free, have become so upon his "great principle"; that the State of Illinois itself came into the Union as a slave State, and that the people, upon the "great principle" of popular sovereignty, have since made it a free State. Allow me but a little while to state to you what facts there are to justify him in saying that Illinois came into the Union as a slave State.

I have mentioned to you that there were a few old French slaves there. They numbered, I think, one or two hundred. Besides that, there had been a territorial law for indenturing black persons. Under that law, in violation of the ordinance of '87, but without any enforcement of the ordinance to overthrow the system, there had been a small number of slaves introduced as indentured persons. Owing to this, the clause for the prohibition of slavery was slightly modified. Instead of running like yours, that neither slavery nor involuntary servitude, except for crime, of which the party shall have been duly convicted, should exist in the State, they said that neither slavery nor involuntary servitude should thereafter be introduced, and that the children of indentured servants should be born free; and nothing was said about the few old French slaves. Out of this fact, that the clause for prohibiting slavery was modified because of the actual presence of it, Douglas asserts again and again that Illinois came into the Union as a slave State. How far the facts sustain the conclusion that he draws, it is for intelligent and impartial men to decide. I leave it with you, with these remarks, worthy of being remembered, that that little thing, those few indentured servants being there, was of itself sufficient to modify a constitution made by a people ardently desiring to have a free constitution; showing the power of the actual presence of the institution of slavery to prevent any people, however anxious to make a free State, from making it perfectly so. I have been detaining you longer perhaps than I ought to do.

I am in some doubt whether to introduce another topic upon which I could talk awhile. [Audience cries of "Go on," and "Give us it."] It is this then—Douglas's popular sovereignty, as a principle, is simply this: If one man chooses to make a slave of another man, neither that man nor anybody else has a right to object. Apply it to government, as he seeks to apply it, and it is this: If, in a new Territory, into which a few people are beginning to enter for the purpose of making their homes, they choose to either exclude slavery from their limits, or to establish it there, however one or the other may affect the persons to be enslaved, or the infinitely greater number of persons who are afterward to inhabit that Territory, or the other members of the family of communities, of which they are but an incipient member, or the general head of the family of States as parent of all—however their action may affect one or the other of these, there is no power or right to interfere. That is Douglas's popular sovereignty applied. Now I think that there is a real popular sovereignty in the world. I think a definition of popular sovereignty, in the abstract, would be about this—that each man shall do precisely as he pleases with himself, and with all those things which exclusively concern him. Applied in government, this principle would be, that a general government shall do all those things which pertain to it, and all the local governments shall do precisely as they please in respect to those matters which exclusively concern them.

Douglas looks upon slavery as so insignificant that the people must decide that question for themselves, and yet they are not fit to decide who shall be their governor, judge, or secretary, or who shall be any of their officers. These are vast national matters, in his estimation; but the little matter in his estimation is that of planting slavery there. That is purely of local interest, which nobody should be allowed to say a word about.

Labor is the great source from which nearly all, if not all, human comforts and necessities are drawn. There is a difference in opinion about the elements of labor in society. Some men assume that there is a necessary connection between capital and labor, and that connection draws within it the whole of the labor of the community. They assume that nobody works unless capital excites them to work. They begin next to consider what is the best way. They say there are but two ways—one is to hire men and to allure them to labor by their consent; the other is to buy the men and drive them to it, and that is slavery. Having assumed that, they proceed to discuss the question of whether the laborers themselves are better off in the condition of slaves or of hired laborers, and they usually decide that they are better off in the condition of slaves.

In the first place, I say that the whole thing is a mistake. That there is a certain relation between capital and labor, I admit. That it does exist, and rightfully exists, I think is true. That men who are industrious and sober and honest in the pursuit of their own interests should after a while accumulate capital, and after that should be allowed to enjoy it in peace, and also if they should choose, when they have accumulated it, to use it to save themselves from actual labor, and hire other people to labor for them, is right. In doing so, they do not wrong the man they employ, for they find men who have not their own land to work upon, or shops to work in, and who are benefited by working for others—hired laborers, receiving their capital for it. Thus a few men that own capital hire a few others, and these establish the relation of capital and labor rightfully—a relation of which I make no complaint. But I insist that that relation, after all, does not embrace more than one eighth of the labor of the country.

[Lincoln proceeded to argue that the hired laborer, with his ability to become an employer, must have every precedence over him who labors under the inducement of force. He continued:]

I have taken upon myself, in the name of some of you, to say that we expect upon these principles to ultimately beat them [the conservatives]. In order to do so, I think we want and must have a national policy in regard to the institution of slavery that acknowledges and deals with that institution as being wrong. Whoever desires the prevention of the spread of slavery and the nationalization of that institution, yields all when he yields to any policy that either recognizes slavery as being right, or as being an indifferent thing. Nothing will make you successful but setting up a policy which shall treat the thing as being wrong. When I say this, I do not mean to say that this General Government is charged with the duty of redressing or preventing all the wrongs in the world; but I do think that it is charged with preventing and redressing all wrongs which are wrongs to itself. This government is expressly charged with the duty of providing for the general welfare. We believe that the spreading out and perpetuity of the institution of slavery impairs the general welfare. We believe—nay, we know—that that is the only thing that has ever threatened the perpetuity of the Union itself. The only thing which has ever menaced the destruction of the government under which we live, is this very thing. To repress this thing, we think, is providing for the general welfare. Our friends in Kentucky differ from us. We need not make our argument for them; but we who think it is wrong in all its relations, or in some of them at least, must decide as to our own actions, and our own course, upon our own judgment.

I say that we must not interfere with the institution of slavery in the States where it exists, because the Constitution forbids it, and the general welfare does not require us to do so. We must not withhold an efficient fugitive-slave law, because the Constitution requires us, as I understand it, not to withhold such a law. But we must prevent the outspreading of the institution, because neither the Constitution nor general welfare requires us to extend it. We must prevent the revival of the African slave-trade, and the enacting by Congress of a territorial slave-code. We must prevent each of these things being done by either congresses or courts. The people of these United States are the rightful masters of both congresses and courts, not to overthrow the Constitution, but to overthrow the men who pervert the Constitution.

To do these things we must employ instrumentalities. We must hold conventions; we must adopt platforms, if we conform to ordinary custom; we must nominate candidates; and we must carry elections. In all these things, I think that we ought to keep in view our real purpose, and in none do anything that stands adverse to our purpose. If we shall adopt a platform that fails to recognize or express our purpose, or elect a man that declares himself inimical to our purpose, we not only take nothing by our success, but we tacitly admit that we act upon no other principle than a desire to have "the loaves and fishes," by which, in the end, our apparent success is really an injury to us.

I know that it is very desirable with me, as with everybody else, that all the elements of the Opposition shall unite in the next presidential election, and in all future time. I am anxious that that should be, but there are things seriously to be considered in relation to that matter. If the terms can be arranged, I am in favor of the union. But suppose we shall take up some man, and put him upon one end or the other of the ticket, who declares himself against us in regard to the prevention of the spread of slavery, who turns up his nose and says he is tired of hearing anything more about it, who is more against us than against the enemy—what will be the issue? Why, he will get no slave States after all—he has tried that already until being beat is the rule for him. If we nominate him upon that ground, he will not carry a slave State, and not only so, but that portion of our men who are high strung upon the principle we really fight for will not go for him, and he won't get a single electoral vote anywhere, except, perhaps, in the State of Maryland. There is no use in saying to us that we are stubborn and obstinate because we won't do some such thing as this. We cannot do it. We cannot get our men to vote it. I speak by the card, that we cannot give the State of Illinois in such case by fifty thousand. We would be flatter down than the "Negro Democracy" themselves have the heart to wish to see us.

After saying this much, let me say a little on the other side. There are plenty of men in the slave States that are altogether good enough for me to be either President or Vice-President, provided they will profess their sympathy with our purpose, and will place themselves on such ground that our men, upon principle, can vote for them. There are scores of them—good men in their character for intelligence, and talent, and integrity. If such an one will place himself upon the right ground, I am for his occupying one place upon the next Republican or Opposition ticket. I will heartily go for him. But unless he does so place himself, I think it is a matter of perfect nonsense to attempt to bring about a union upon any other basis; that if a union be made, the elements will scatter so that there can be no success for such a ticket, nor anything like success. The good old maxims of the Bible are applicable, and truly applicable, to human affairs, and in this, as in other things, we may say here that he who is not for us is against us; he who gathereth not with us scattereth. I should be glad to have some of the many good, and able, and noble men of the South to place themselves where we can confer upon them the high honor of an election upon one or the other end of our ticket. It would do my soul good to do that thing. It would enable us to teach them that, inasmuch as we select one of their own number to carry out our principles, we are free from the charge that we mean more than we say.

But, my friends, I have detained you much longer than I expected to do. I believe I may allow myself the compliment to say that you have stayed and heard me with great patience, for which I return you my most sincere thanks.[196]

Again, Lincoln here is up to his old tricks, of completely misrepresenting Douglas, the Constitution, and the Southern states. He says, for instance, that slavery is Kentuckians' **"favorite institution, which you desire to have spread out and made perpetual."** Such comments are so absurd they are scarcely worthy of a reply, but a few words are in order.

Few Kentuckians were personally *for* slavery. But nearly *all* were for the Constitutional right of each state to choose whether or not to maintain, ignore, or prohibit slavery.

Lincoln also acknowledges that **"it positively wrongs the mass of the white men that the negro should be enslaved; that the mass of white men are really injured by the effects of slave-labor in the vicinity of the fields of their own labor."** No sympathy here for blacks themselves. Just whites—and their economy.[197]

At least Lincoln does not attempt to hide his racism, admitting that: **"If there was a necessary conflict between the white man and the negro, I should be for the white man . . ."**,[198] and that after his liberal party beats the conservatives: **"We mean to marry your girls when we have a chance—the white ones, I mean . . ."**

In this same address he also claims that **"the spreading out and perpetuity of the institution of slavery impairs the general welfare. We believe—nay, we know—that that is the only thing that has ever threatened the perpetuity of the Union itself. The only thing which has ever menaced the destruction of the government under which we live, is this very thing."**

But it was not slavery that threatened the Union. It was Lincoln! It was his mysterious hatred for his homeland, the South, along with his hatred of states' rights, that imperiled the Founders' voluntary Union of nation-states. Our conservative Fathers must have been turning over in their graves during Lincoln's presidency, for in four short years he undid much of the arduous labor they performed in order that we would have "a more perfect Union."

Unfortunately for we Americans, the Union of the Founding generation was not the Union of Lincoln. If it had been we today would not have a gargantuan all-powerful central government, largely subservient states, a bloated military establishment, the Internal Revenue Service (the IRS), and the intrusive Big Brother mentality that now permeates all levels of government. Are these things "American"? We think not, for Lincoln was not.

Liberal Lincoln's un-American left-leaning political stance is made all the more obvious when we consider that he was, and still is, also beloved by Marxists, who have admired and even worshiped him over the years.

In late November 1864, for example, the man who literally gave his name to Marxism, Karl Marx, wrote Lincoln a letter congratulating him on his "re-election by a large majority." The missive included Marx's sincere hope that Lincoln would "lead his country through the matchless struggle for the rescue of an enchained race and the reconstruction of a social world."[199] These two socialistic men had much in common, far more than modern day Lincoln apologists will ever admit.

As one who was an economic protectionist, mercantilist, and interventionist, who supported the ideas of corporate welfare (then called "internal improvements") and a nationalized banking system, and who sought the permanent installation of an all-powerful central government and the destruction of states' rights so that he could dominate the South economically,[200] it would be difficult, if not impossible to call Lincoln a true and traditional American. It would be more accurate to call him a dictatorial-like leader with socialistic leanings.

On February 17, 1864, speaking of a bit of political dissension among Arkansas' citizens, despot Lincoln said: **"This discord must be silenced."**[201] How would today's Americans feel if our current president made this same remark? Let us also consider the following socialistic words written out by Lincoln around July 1, 1854:

> **Government is a combination of the people of a country to effect certain objects by joint effort. The best framed and best administered governments are necessarily expensive; while by errors in frame and maladministration most of them are more onerous than they need be, and some of them very oppressive. Why, then, should we have government? Why not each**

individual take to himself the whole fruit of his labor, without having any of it taxed away, in services, corn, or money? Why not take just so much land as he can cultivate with his own hands, without buying it of any one?

The legitimate object of government is "to do for the people what needs to be done, but which they can not, by individual effort, do at all, or do so well, for themselves." There are many such things—some of them exist independently of the injustice in the world. Making and maintaining roads, bridges, and the like; providing for the helpless young and afflicted; common schools; and disposing of deceased men's property, are instances.²⁰²

Lincoln's statement that **"the legitimate object of government is to do for the people what needs to be done, but which they can not, by individual effort, do at all, or do so well, for themselves,"** opens the door for the infinite expansion of the central government and for all manner of Big Brother styled governmental intrusion on the people. This, of course, is exactly what liberals and progressives like Lincoln, as well as socialists and Marxists, have always most ardently desired.

The man who was adored by Adolf Hitler and Karl Marx is now on our penny, our five-dollar bill, the Illinois license plate, and the rock face of Mount Rushmore. God only knows where, what his fellow Yankees called, the "hideous form of Abraham Lincoln" will appear in the future.²⁰³ Is this love affair with an un-American, dictatorial, sectional, socialistic, South-hating, Constitution-loathing president right and proper? You the reader must decide.

Many of us in the South, however, agree with renowned Maryland author William Hand Browne, who, in September 1872, said:

> The whole story of Lincoln's career from beginning to end is so dreary, so wretched, so shabby, such a tissue of pitiful dodging and chicanery, so unrelieved by anything pure, noble, or dignified, that to even follow it as far as we have done, has well-nigh surpassed our limits of endurance; and when, putting all partisan feeling aside, we look back at the men who once were chosen by their countrymen to fill the places that this man has occupied—a Washington, a Jefferson, a Madison, an Adams, or later, a Webster, a Clay, or a Calhoun—men of culture and refinement, of honor, of exalted patriotism, of broad views and wise

statesmanship—and measure the distance from them to Abraham Lincoln, we sicken with shame and disgust.[204]

Nineteenth-Century Southerners concurred with such opinions, noting that the sad-faced leader was cunning, dangerous, shrewd,[205] primitive, deceitful, uncultivated, weak, contemptible, idiotic, demagogic, and heartless (that is, the very opposite of the archetypal Southern gentleman).[206] Widely known across Dixie as "the Illinois Ape,"[207] others in the Confederacy called him "a cross between a sandhill crane and an Andalusian jackass."[208] Jefferson Davis (who once turned down a request to write an article on Lincoln after his assassination),[209] referred to him simply as "nothing."[210]

From the South's point of view, such accusations were not only fair, they were correct, for Lincoln must qualify as our nation's most reckless, dishonest, emotionally disturbed, and conniving leader, a largely uneducated man who was not deemed fit to be an Illinois senator, but two years later was deemed fit to become a U.S. president; a sociopath who lived in his own dismal fantasy world, completely out of touch with both American history and the American people.

Here, for example, is what our psychologically detached president had to say on February 13, 1861, on the eve of America's bloodiest and most violent home war, and with seven Southern states having already seceded:

> I have not maintained silence from any want of real anxiety. It is a good thing that there is no more than anxiety, for there is nothing going wrong. It is a consoling circumstance that when we look out there is nothing that really hurts anybody. We entertain different views upon political questions, but nobody is suffering anything. This is a most consoling circumstance, and from it we may conclude that all we want is time, patience, and a reliance on that God who has never forsaken this people.[211]

Such statements are especially frightening when we consider that it came from the world's most powerful leader at the time.

Only a few days later, on February 15, at Pittsburgh, Pennsylvania, Lincoln made the following astonishing remark:

> Notwithstanding the troubles across the river [Lincoln points southward across the Monongahela River, and smiles], there is no crisis but an artificial one. What is there now to warrant the condition of affairs presented by our friends [i.e., Southerners] over the river? Take even their own view of the questions involved, and there is nothing to justify the course they are pursuing [i.e., secession]. I repeat, then, there is no crisis, excepting such a one as may be gotten up at any time by turbulent men aided by designing politicians. My advice to them, under such circumstances, is to keep cool.[212]

A week later Lincoln seemed even less impressed with the political upheaval and social chaos going on around him. On February 21, 1861, here is what he wrote to the Mayor of Philadelphia, Pennsylvania, Alexander Henry, and "fellow citizens of Philadelphia":

> . . . I have felt all the while justified in concluding that the crisis, the panic, the anxiety of the country at this time, is artificial. If there be those who differ with me upon this subject, they have not pointed out the substantial difficulty that exists.[213]

Not surprisingly, with comments like these, Lincoln had his critics. But his reply to them is not what we generally expect of an American president. In fact, it could have only made his opponents even more doubtful of his ability to lead the United States of America. **"I am not controlling events,"** he once said in a speech that was quoted in New York newspapers on October 10, 1864, **"but events are controlling me."**[214]

LINCOLN & SECESSION

WAS SECESSION LEGAL PRIOR TO 1861? At one time Lincoln thought so. Calling it a **"most sacred right,"** here is what he had to say on the matter on January 12, 1848, in a speech before the U.S. House of Representatives:

> Any people anywhere, being inclined and having the power, have the right to rise up, and shake off the existing government, and form a new one that suits them better. This is a most valuable, a most sacred right—a right which, we hope and believe, is to liberate the world. Nor is this right confined to cases in which the whole people of an existing government may choose to exercise it. Any portion of such people that can may revolutionize, and make their own of so much of the territory as they inhabit.[215]

As secession is one of the rights of states, it is important to note here that Lincoln also publicly declared that he was a firm believer in the **"principle of self-government"** and of states' rights. He made one such pronouncement ten years later, in a speech at Chicago, Illinois, on July 10, 1858. Refuting an accusation made by his political opponent Stephen A. Douglas, Lincoln said:

> Now in relation to his inference that I am in favor of a general consolidation of all the local institutions of the various States. I will attend to that for a little while, and try to inquire, if I can, how on earth it could be that any man could draw such an inference from anything I said.

I have said very many times in Judge Douglas's hearing that no man believed more than I in the principle of self-government; that it lies at the bottom of all my ideas of just government from beginning to end. I have denied that his use of that term applies properly. But for the thing itself I deny that any man has ever gone ahead of me in his devotion to the principle, whatever he may have done in efficiency in advocating it. I think that I have said it in your hearing—that I believe each individual is naturally entitled to do as he pleases with himself and the fruit of his labor, so far as it in no wise interferes with any other man's rights; that each community, as a State, has a right to do exactly as it pleases with all the concerns within that State that interfere with the right of no other State; and that the General Government, upon principle, has no right to interfere with anything other than that general class of things that does concern the whole. I have said that at all times. I have said as illustrations that I do not believe in the right of Illinois to interfere with the cranberry laws of Indiana, the oyster laws of Virginia, or the liquor laws of Maine. I have said these things over and over again, and I repeat them here as my sentiments.[216]

Nine years earlier, in 1849, Lincoln supported Hungary's 1848 bid for independence from Hapsburg rule. On September 12, 1849, Lincoln and several others submitted their "Resolutions of Sympathy with the Cause of Hungarian Freedom." According to Lincoln's biographers John G. Nicolay and John Hay:

> At a meeting to express sympathy with the cause of Hungarian Freedom, Dr. Todd, Thos. Lewis, Hon. A. Lincoln, and Wm. Carpenter were appointed a committee to present appropriate resolutions, which reported through Hon. A. Lincoln the following:
> Resolved, That in their present glorious struggle for liberty, the Hungarians command our highest admiration and have our warmest sympathy.
> Resolved, That they have our most ardent prayers for their speedy triumph and final success.
> Resolved, That the Government of the United States should acknowledge the independence of Hungary as a nation of freemen at the very earliest moment consistent with our amicable relations with the

government against which they are contending.

Resolved, That in the opinion of this meeting, the immediate acknowledgment of the independence of Hungary by our government is due from American freemen to their struggling brethren, to the general cause of republican liberty, and not violative of the just rights of any nation or people.[217]

It is stunning that just twelve short years later, in 1861, Lincoln would refuse to give the Southern Confederacy this same enthusiastic support.

At one time the lanky liberal even deceptively cast himself as a conservative Jeffersonian, as he writes in a letter dated April 6, 1859:

> . . . it is now no child's play to save the principles of Jefferson from total overthrow in this nation. One would state with great confidence that he could convince any sane child that the simpler propositions of Euclid are true; but nevertheless he would fail, utterly, with one who should deny the definitions and axioms. The principles of Jefferson are the definitions and axioms of free society. And yet they are denied and evaded, with no small show of success. One dashingly calls them "glittering generalities." Another bluntly calls them "self-evident lies." And others insidiously argue that they apply to "superior races." These expressions, differing in form, are identical in object and effect—the supplanting the principles of free government, and restoring those of classification, caste, and legitimacy. They would delight a convocation of crowned heads plotting against the people. They are the vanguard, the miners and sappers of returning despotism. We must repulse them, or they will subjugate us. This is a world of compensation; and he who would be no slave must consent to have no slave. Those who deny freedom to others deserve it not for themselves, and, under a just God, cannot long retain it. All honor to Jefferson—to the man who, in the concrete pressure of a struggle for national independence by a single people, had the coolness, forecast, and capacity to introduce into a merely revolutionary document an abstract truth, applicable to all men and all times, and so to embalm it there that to-day and in all coming days it shall be a rebuke and a stumbling-block to the very harbingers of reappearing tyranny and oppression.[218]

Having been nominated as the presidential candidate of the Republican (i.e., the liberal) party in the spring of 1860, Lincoln and his cohorts released "The Platform of the Republican National Convention," held in Chicago, Illinois, from May 16 to May 18. Resolution 4 reads like something from the pen of Southern conservative Thomas Jefferson himself:

> Resolved: That the maintenance inviolate of the rights of the States, and especially the right of each State to order and control its own domestic institutions according to its own judgment exclusively, is essential to that balance of power on which the perfection and endurance of our political fabric depends; and we denounce the lawless invasion by armed force of the soil of any State or Territory, no matter under what pretext, as among the gravest of crimes.[219]

On December 28, 1860, after winning his first presidential election, Lincoln personalized this clause in a letter to journalist, politician, and states' rights and free trade advocate Duff Green, as if he himself had written it:

> **I declare that the maintenance inviolate of the rights of the States, and especially the right of each State to order and control its own domestic institutions according to its own judgment exclusively, is essential to that balance of powers on which the perfection and endurance of our political fabric depend; and I denounce the lawless invasion by armed force of the soil of any State or Territory, no matter under what pretext, as the gravest of crimes.**[220]

The ultimate demagogue, Lincoln always espoused whatever ideas would curry the most votes and win him financial backing. Thus, by the time he was in the White House, only a few months later, he had by then found it politically expedient to denounce his party's Jeffersonian-like resolution concerning states' rights, while simultaneously declaring secession illegal, enabling him to plot his bloody and **"lawless invasion by armed force"** of the South.

On March 4, 1861, during his First Inaugural Address, a fuming Lincoln began referring to secession as **"the essence of anarchy"**:

> That there are persons in one section or another who

seek to destroy the Union at all events, and are glad of any pretext to do it, I will neither affirm nor deny; but if there be such, I need address no word to them. To those, however, who really love the Union may I not speak?

Before entering upon so grave a matter as the destruction of our national fabric, with all its benefits, its memories, and its hopes, would it not be wise to ascertain precisely why we do it? Will you hazard so desperate a step while there is any possibility that any portion of the ills you fly from have no real existence? Will you, while the certain ills you fly to are greater than all the real ones you fly from—will you risk the commission of so fearful a mistake?

All profess to be content in the Union if all constitutional rights can be maintained. Is it true, then, that any right, plainly written in the Constitution, has been denied? I think not. Happily the human mind is so constituted that no party can reach to the audacity of doing this. Think, if you can, of a single instance in which a plainly written provision of the Constitution has ever been denied. If by the mere force of numbers a majority should deprive a minority of any clearly written constitutional right, it might, in a moral point of view, justify revolution—certainly would if such a right were a vital one. But such is not our case. All the vital rights of minorities and of individuals are so plainly assured to them by affirmations and negations, guarantees and prohibitions, in the Constitution, that controversies never arise concerning them. But no organic law can ever be framed with a provision specifically applicable to every question which may occur in practical administration. No foresight can anticipate, nor any document of reasonable length contain, express provisions for all possible questions. Shall fugitives from labor be surrendered by national or by State authority? The Constitution does not expressly say. May Congress prohibit slavery in the Territories? The Constitution does not expressly say. Must Congress protect slavery in the Territories? The Constitution does not expressly say.

From questions of this class spring all our constitutional controversies, and we divide upon them into majorities and minorities. If the minority will not acquiesce, the majority must, or the government must cease. There is no other alternative; for continuing the government is acquiescence on one side or the other.

> If a minority in such case will secede rather than acquiesce, they make a precedent which in turn will divide and ruin them; for a minority of their own will secede from them whenever a majority refuses to be controlled by such minority. For instance, why may not any portion of a new confederacy a year or two hence arbitrarily secede again, precisely as portions of the present Union now claim to secede from it? All who cherish disunion sentiments are now being educated to the exact temper of doing this.
>
> Is there such perfect identity of interests among the States to compose a new Union, as to produce harmony only, and prevent renewed secession?
>
> Plainly, the central idea of secession is the essence of anarchy. A majority held in restraint by constitutional checks and limitations, and always changing easily with deliberate changes of popular opinions and sentiments, is the only true sovereign of a free people. Whoever rejects it does, of necessity, fly to anarchy or to despotism. Unanimity is impossible; the rule of a minority, as a permanent arrangement, is wholly inadmissible; so that, rejecting the majority principle, anarchy or despotism in some form is all that is left.[221]

Lincoln here lies and misleads throughout, first by pretending that the South wants to **"destroy the Union"** and the **"national fabric"** and that, in fact, she hates the Union. This is completely false. Southerners loved the Union and for decades had resisted secession, doing everything in their power to stay within the Union. It was the election of the South-hating sectional Lincoln, who publicly admitted that he did not like the Constitution as it was written, that caused the secession of the Southern states.

The president then speaks of the **"benefits"** the South will lose by leaving the Union and the **"risks"** she will be taking by seceding. But he did not understand that Southerners saw his election as so threatening to the Founder's Constitution and Union, that they were willing to take any risk in order to free themselves from what they saw as an emerging Northern tyranny under his dictatorial fist.

He ends this section of his address by calling secession **"anarchy,"** one that can only lead to **"despotism."** But the South was trying to avoid both by leaving the Union, while Lincoln was creating both by threatening the South with violence if she did not return!

More of Lincoln's garbled and irrational thoughts on secession soon followed, as, for example, during his "Message to Congress in Special Session," delivered on July 4, 1861:

> It might seem, at first thought, to be of little difference whether the present movement at the South be called "secession" or "rebellion." The movers, however, well understand the difference. At the beginning they knew they could never raise their treason to any respectable magnitude by any name which implies violation of law. They knew their people possessed as much of moral sense, as much of devotion to law and order, and as much pride in and reverence for the history and government of their common country as any other civilized and patriotic people. They knew they could make no advancement directly in the teeth of these strong and, noble sentiments. Accordingly, they commenced by an insidious debauching of the public mind. They invented an ingenious sophism which, if conceded, was followed by perfectly logical steps, through all the incidents, to the complete destruction of the Union. The sophism itself is that any State of the Union may consistently with the National Constitution, and therefore lawfully and peacefully, withdraw from the Union without the consent of the Union or of any other State. The little disguise that the supposed right is to be exercised only for just cause, themselves to be the sole judges of its justice, is too thin to merit any notice.
>
> With rebellion thus sugar-coated they have been drugging the public mind of their section for more than thirty years, and until at length they have brought many good men to a willingness to take up arms against the government the day after some assemblage of men have enacted the farcical pretense of taking their State out of the Union, who could have been brought to no such thing the day before.
>
> This sophism derives much, perhaps the whole, of its currency from the assumption that there is some omnipotent and sacred supremacy pertaining to a State—to each State of our Federal Union. Our States have neither more nor less power than that reserved to them in the Union by the Constitution—no one of them ever having been a State out of the Union. The original ones passed into the Union even before they cast off their

British colonial dependence; and the new ones each came into the Union directly from condition of dependence, excepting Texas. And even Texas, in its temporary independence, was never designated a State. The new ones only took the designation of States on coming into the Union while that name was first adopted for the old ones in and by the Declaration of Independence. Therein the "United Colonies" were declared to be "free and independent States"; but even then the object plainly was not to declare their independence of one another or of the Union, but directly the contrary, as their mutual pledge and their mutual action before, at the time, and afterward, abundantly show. The express plighting of faith by each and all or the original thirteen in the Articles of Confederation, two years later, that the Union shall be perpetual, is most conclusive. Having never been States either in substance or in name outside of the Union, whence this magical omnipotence of "State Rights," asserting a claim of power to lawfully destroy the Union itself? Much is said about the "sovereignty" of the States; but the word even is not in the National Constitution, nor, as is believed, in any of the State constitutions. What is "sovereignty" in the political sense of the term? Would it be far wrong to define it "a political community without a political superior"? Tested by this, no one of our States except Texas ever was a sovereignty. And even Texas gave up the character on coming into the Union; by which act she acknowledged the Constitution of the United States, and the laws and treaties of the United States made in pursuance of the Constitution, to be for her the supreme law of the land. The States have their status in the Union, and they have no other legal status. If they break from this, they can only do so against law and by revolution. The Union, and not themselves separately, procured their independence and their liberty. By conquest or purchase the Union gave each of them whatever of independence or liberty it has. The Union is older than any of the States, and, in fact, it created them as States. Originally some dependent colonies made the Union, and, in turn, the Union threw off their old dependence for them, and made them States, such as they are. Not one of them ever had a State constitution independent of the Union. Of course, it is not forgotten that all the new States framed their constitutions before they entered the

Union—nevertheless, dependent upon and preparatory to coming into the Union.

Unquestionably the States have the powers and rights reserved to them in and by the National Constitution; but among these surely are not included all conceivable powers, however mischievous or destructive, but, at most, such only as were known in the world at the time as governmental powers; and certainly a power to destroy the government itself had never been known as a governmental, as a merely administrative power. This relative matter of national power and State rights, as a principle, is no other than the principle of generality and locality. Whatever concerns the whole should be confided to the whole—to the General Government; while whatever concerns only the State should be left exclusively to the State. This is all there is of original principle about it. Whether the National Constitution in denning boundaries between the two has applied the principle with exact accuracy, is not to be questioned. We are all bound by that denning, without question.

What is now combated is the position that secession is consistent with the Constitution—is lawful and peaceful. It is not contended that there is any express law for it; and nothing should ever be implied as law which leads to unjust or absurd consequences. The nation purchased with money the countries out of which several of these States were formed. Is it just that they shall go off without leave and without refunding? The nation paid very large sums (in the aggregate, I believe, nearly a hundred millions) to relieve Florida of the aboriginal tribes. Is it just that she shall now be off without consent or without making any return? The nation is now in debt for money applied to the benefit of these so-called seceding States in common with the rest. Is it just either that creditors shall go unpaid or the remaining States pay the whole? A part of the present national debt was contracted to pay the old debts of Texas. Is it just that she shall leave and pay no part of this herself?

Again, if one State may secede, so may another; and when all have seceded, none is left to pay the debts. Is this quite just to creditors? Did we notify them of this sage view of ours when we borrowed their money? If we now recognize this doctrine by allowing the seceders to go in peace, it is difficult to see what we can do if others choose to go or to extort terms upon which they will promise to remain.

The seceders insist that our Constitution admits of secession. They have assumed to make a national constitution of their own, in which of necessity they have either discarded or retained the right of secession as they insist it exists in ours. If they have discarded it, they thereby admit that on principle it ought not to be in ours. If they have retained it by their own construction of ours, they show that to be consistent they must secede from one another whenever they shall find it the easiest way of settling their debts, or effecting any other selfish or unjust object. The principle itself is one of disintegration, and upon which no government can possibly endure.

If all the States save one should assert the power to drive that one out of the Union, it is presumed the whole class of seceder politicians would at once deny the power and denounce the act as the greatest outrage upon State rights. But suppose that precisely the same act, instead of being called "driving the one out," should be called "the seceding of the others from that one," it would be exactly what the seceders claim to do, unless, indeed, they make the point that the one, because it is a minority, may rightfully do what the others, because they are a majority, may not rightfully do. These politicians are subtle and profound on the rights of minorities. They are not partial to that power which made the Constitution and speaks from the preamble calling itself "We, the People."[222]

Lincoln insinuates that the Southern states are leaving the U.S. because it is **"the easiest way of settling their debts."** Preposterous. Even before the Battle of Fort Sumter April 12, 1861, the Confederacy repeatedly offered to pay off the debts accrued by the Southern states prior to secession. This promise was even included in the Confederate Constitution (Article 6, Section 2). President Jefferson Davis discusses this issue in his magnificent work, *The Rise and Fall of the Confederate Government*:

> The Provisional [Confederate] Constitution itself, in the second section of its sixth article, had ordained as follows :
> "The [Confederate] Government hereby instituted shall

take immediate steps for the settlement of all matters between the States forming it and their other late confederates of the United States, in relation to the public property and public debt at the time of their withdrawal from them; these States hereby declaring it to be their wish and earnest desire to adjust everything pertaining to the common property, common liabilities, and common obligations of that Union, upon the principles of right, justice, equity, and good faith."

In accordance with this requirement of the Constitution, the [Confederate] Congress, on the 15th of February—before my arrival at Montgomery [Alabama]—passed a resolution declaring "that it is the sense of this Congress that a commission of three persons be appointed by the President-elect, as early as may be convenient after his inauguration, and sent to the Government of the United States of America, for the purpose of negotiating friendly relations between that Government and the Confederate States of America, and for the settlement of all questions of disagreement between the two Governments, upon principles of right, justice, equity, and good faith."[223]

In his July 4, 1861, "Message to Congress" Lincoln conveniently ignores these facts, just as he ignored the Confederacy's offer to settle her financial obligations with the U.S.

Even though it was completely untrue, Lincoln even began telling his constituents that the secession of the Southern states would cause the **"overthrow of the government,"**[224] **"destroy the Union,"**[225] create general lawlessness and disorder,[226] and cause representative government to **"perish from the earth."**[227] No less ridiculous, on August 18, 1864, he told the 164th Ohio Regiment that **"every human right is endangered if our enemies succeed."**[228] On August 15, 1860, less than six months before the first of the Southern states seceded, he wrote to John B. Fry and said:

> The people of the South have too much of good sense and good temper to attempt the ruin of the government rather than see it administered as it was administered by the men who made it. At least so I hope and believe.[229]

Yet it was the conservative South that wanted to preserve the government of **"the men who made it."** Liberal Lincoln was the one who wanted to **"ruin"** it by squashing states' rights and rewriting the Constitution.

On January 11, 1861, President-elect Lincoln wrote a letter to J.

T. Hale claiming that **"if we surrender** [to the South], **it is the end of us and of the government."**[230] In his July 4, 1861, "Message to Congress in Special Session" he fibbed again, telling his audience that Dixie was seeking **"the early destruction of our National Union,"** and that **"the government itself will go to pieces"** if the South is allowed to depart.[231] In a July 25, 1864, letter to Abram Wakeman, Lincoln absurdly associates the **"independence of the South"** with the **"dissolution of the Union."**[232] In his September 3, 1864, "Proclamation of Thanksgiving," he urges his constituents to thank God

> for his mercy in preserving our national existence against the insurgent rebels who have been waging a cruel war against the government of the United States for its overthrow.[233]

This was all a lie, for the Confederacy had no interest whatsoever in overthrowing the U.S. government, seizing her land, or attaining dominion over her people. And while it is true that the War was **"cruel,"** it was not being waged by the South. It had been, as we will see in Chapter 7, started and waged by the North. Jefferson Davis and the South had repeatedly said: "All we ask is to be left alone."[234] But Lincoln would not listen. He was more interested in trying to trick the public into believing that the South was **"attempting to destroy the Federal Union."**[235]

A November 21, 1864, letter to a Mrs. Bixby of Boston, Massachusetts, is particularly poignant as all five of her sons perished on the battlefield fighting in Lincoln's army. The president's response is predictable, callous, and above all disinformative:

> **Dear Madam: I have been shown in the files of the War Department a statement of the Adjutant-General of Massachusetts that you are the mother of five sons who have died gloriously on the field of battle. I feel how weak and fruitless must be any words of mine which should attempt to beguile you from the grief of a loss so overwhelming. But I cannot refrain from tendering to you the consolation that may be found in the thanks of the Republic they died to save. I pray that our heavenly Father may assuage the anguish of your bereavement, and leave you only the cherished memory of the loved and lost, and the solemn pride that must be yours to have laid so costly a sacrifice upon the altar of freedom. Yours**

very sincerely and respectfully, Abraham Lincoln.[236]

While, even 150 years later, no one—not even the most diehard traditional Southerners—can feel anything but compassion for this Yankee mother, Lincoln insensitively chalks the death of her five boys up to the cost of **"saving the Republic"** by **"sacrificing themselves on the altar of freedom."**

But the Republic was never in any danger due to the secession of the Southern states, and the U.S. was in no way diminished, hampered, or injured by the formation of the Confederacy. In fact, a good argument could be made that both the U.S. and the C.S. were vastly strengthened. This is exactly what occurred when, in 1905, for example, Norway seceded from Sweden. Today these nations possess two of the most robust economies and stable governments in the world.[237]

Just as idiotic was Lincoln's insinuation that the Union was fighting for **"freedom"** while the South was fighting for dominance and tyranny. This was all a fabrication of his autocratic mind, for it was he himself who subverted the Constitution, clamped down on civil rights, threatened the liberties of the American people, and opened the door to governmental enlargement and presidential excesses and abuses of power that have lasted into the present day.[238]

Based on Lincoln's own words and actions, as this book will readily show, it is apparent that the real tragedy here is that Mrs. Bixby's sons died, not to **"preserve the Union,"**[239] but to preserve Lincoln's liberal agenda: the installation of big government in the North and the destruction of states' rights in the South.

On July 24, 1863, the Northern president referred to his soldiers as bearing the **"burden of saving our country."**[240] **"Saving"** it from what? The Union and its central government were still intact and functioning on and at all levels before, throughout, and after the conflict. In a December 27, 1864, letter to Dr. John MacLean, Lincoln foolishly asserts that **"the fate of civilization upon this continent is involved in the issue of our contest."**[241]

Such exaggerations, bizarre statements, obvious disinformation, and intentional mischaracterizations of the conflict continued up until the day Lincoln died.

Such anti-South propaganda came naturally to him, for as a former newspaper agent and journalist (for the Springfield, Illinois, *Sangamon Journal*) and a newspaper owner (of the *Illinois Staats-Anzeiger*), he was highly aware of the power of the press in shaping public opinion. Little wonder then that newspaperman Lincoln often used and manipulated both the public and the media. Not only to assist with his own political aspirations, but in aiding and abetting the creation of what is now a large corpus of spurious anti-South myths.[242] Well aware of his power over public opinion, and sounding very much like a Nazi dictator, here is how expressed it on August 21, 1858:

> . . . public sentiment is everything. With public sentiment, nothing can fail; without it, nothing can succeed. Consequently he who molds public sentiment goes deeper than he who enacts statutes or pronounces decisions. He makes statutes and decisions possible or impossible to be executed.[243]

How much Lincoln's media blitz of disinformation contributed to the North's victory over the South is impossible to know, but contribute it certainly did. Though nearly every word of it is false, the world still considers Lincoln's wartime propaganda to be "Gospel." Indeed, it is Lincoln's view of the "Civil War" that is still taught in every school, not only in America, but around the globe.

How different the outcome of the War would have been if, for instance, "Honest Abe" had not used the press to spread lies throughout Europe about the South's "rebellion," declaring that she had split from the Union to preserve slavery, that the Confederacy was not a legitimate sovereign nation, and that secession was illegal. Such fallacies delayed, and finally killed off, any hope of official European support for Dixie, in turn destroying one of the South's last great chances for victory. Such was the mind of the man Americans annually vote our "greatest president."

As for the idea of secession, this was just another piece on Lincoln's chessboard, one to be moved when, where, and how it suited him. This is why, by the winter of 1863, he had apparently forgotten (or pretended to forget) his public statements from January 12, 1848, and July 10, 1858, in which he had thoroughly supported the legality of secession. For it was on November 9, 1863, that he said: **"I have always thought the act of secession is legally nothing."**[244]

The beginning of 1864 finds Lincoln continuing his lie from November, as the following January 16 to letter to "Crosby and Nichols" illustrates:

Gentlemen: The number for this month and year of the "North American Review" was duly received, and for which please accept my thanks. Of course, I am not the most impartial judge; yet, with due allowance for this, I venture to hope that the article entitled "The President's Policy" will be of value to the country. I fear I am not quite worthy of all which is therein kindly said of me personally.

The sentence of twelve lines, commencing at the top of page 252, I could wish to be not exactly as it is. In what is there expressed, the writer has not correctly understood me. I have never had a theory that secession could absolve States or people from their obligations. Precisely the contrary is asserted in the inaugural address; and it was because of my belief in the continuation of these obligations that I was puzzled, for a time, as to denying the legal rights of those citizens who remained individually innocent of treason or rebellion. But I mean no more now than to merely call attention to this point. Yours respectfully, A. Lincoln.[245]

By the spring of 1864 Lincoln was defining the Union as **"liberty"** and the Confederacy as **"tyranny,"** the opposite of what they actually were.[246] By the summer of 1864 he was thanking his soldiers for devoting their lives to the **"salvation"** of the U.S., even though it was not the U.S. that needed saving.[247] It was the U.S. Constitution that was in danger of being lost—and that because of Lincoln himself!

Why the drastic transformation between 1848 and 1861? What changed?

Lincoln's agenda changed, along with his political ambitions. In 1848 he was content to honor the Constitution, a conservative notion. But in 1861, now president and imbued with seemingly unlimited power, his true liberal nature began to emerge, and, along with it, his insatiable urge to spend other people's money and enlarge the central government. Like all ultra liberals Lincoln now wanted to control not only the American citizenry, but more importantly the nation's finances and military. It is in the words above that we see Lincoln's dictatorial personality beginning to manifest in earnest.

Our sixteenth chief executive, of course, was wrong on all counts in his 1861 speech before Congress. As he himself stated in 1848, secession is perfectly legal, and it always has been: in 1776 it was born in the Declaration of Independence; in 1781 it was carried forward in the Articles of Confederation (Article 2); and in 1789 it was forever ensconced, though tacitly, in the U.S. Constitution (Ninth and Tenth Amendments).

As president, Lincoln chose to disregard the legality of secession because it interfered with his primary goal: to install Henry Clay's "American System" (that is, big government) in Washington, D.C. From the day he walked into the White House until the day he lost his life at Ford's Theater, Lincoln almost never referred to the Southern Confederacy as anything other than a **"rebellion,"**[248] **"sedition,"**[249] an **"illegal organization,"**[250] and an **"insurrection."**[251]

As for its individual members, he called them **"rebels,"**[252] **"disloyal citizens,"**[253] **"disloyal people,"**[254] **"insurgents,"**[255] **"our erring brethren,"**[256] **"southern disunionists,"**[257] and **"treacherous associates."**[258] The idea of secession he laughed off as a **"farcical pretense"**;[259] the Confederacy's national sovereign power, he said, was merely a **"pretended authority"**;[260] and finally he discounted the entire movement as nothing but a **"foul spirit."**[261]

It was with just such words that he publicly justified his illegal war on the South. Based on the number of people today who believe this nonsensical, wicked, and historically inaccurate anti-South propaganda, Lincoln succeeded wonderfully.[262]

Two days before he was shot, our sixteenth president was still playing his game of pretend, misrepresenting the facts, trying to force his obviously false notion (that the Confederacy was not legitimate) on the world. It must have been exhausting. On April 12, 1865, in a letter to Yankee General Godfrey Weitzel, Lincoln wrote out the very last important document of his short fifty-six year life:

> I have just seen Judge Campbell's letter to you of the 7th. He assumes, as appears to me, that I have called the insurgent legislature of Virginia together, as the rightful legislature of the State, to settle all differences with the United States. I have done no such thing. I spoke of them, not as a legislature, but as "the gentlemen who have acted as the legislature of Virginia in support of the rebellion." I did this on purpose to exclude the assumption that I was recognizing them as a rightful body. I dealt with them as men having power *de facto* to do a specific thing, to wit: "To withdraw the Virginia troops and other support from resistance to the General Government," for which, in the paper handed Judge Campbell, I promised a specific equivalent, to wit: a

remission to the people of the State, except in certain cases, of the confiscation of their property. I meant this, and no more. Inasmuch, however, as Judge Campbell misconstrues this, and is still pressing for an armistice, contrary to the explicit statement of the paper I gave him, and particularly as General [Ulysses S.] Grant has since captured the Virginia troops, so that giving a consideration for their withdrawal is no longer applicable, let my letter to you and the paper to Judge Campbell both be withdrawn, or countermanded, and he be notified of it. Do not now allow them to assemble but if any have come, allow them safe return to their homes. A. Lincoln.[263]

Lincoln displays not only a cunning ability to deceive here, he also reveals an amazing degree of ignorance of American history and law. For instance, in the following February 14, 1861, address at Steubenville, Ohio, President-elect Lincoln states that the U.S. operates on the basis of "the majority rules":

I fear that the great confidence placed in my ability is unfounded. Indeed, I am sure it is. Encompassed by vast difficulties as I am, nothing shall be wanting on my part, if sustained by God and the American people. I believe the devotion to the Constitution is equally great on both sides of the river. It is only the different understanding of that instrument that causes difficulty. The only dispute on both sides is, "What are their rights?" If the majority should not rule, who would be the judge? Where is such a judge to be found? We should all be bound by the majority of the American people; if not, then the minority must control. Would that be right? Would it be just or generous? Assuredly not. I reiterate that the majority should rule. If I adopt a wrong policy, the opportunity for condemnation will occur in four years' time. Then I can be turned out, and a better man with better views put in my place.[264]

As it happened, Lincoln *was* adopting **"a wrong policy"** here, and as a result he would be **"turned out"** four years later. Not by the voters, but by an assassin's bullet.

In *The Rise and Fall of the Confederate Government*, the far more intelligent and educated Confederate president, Jefferson Davis, corrects

Lincoln's error, or what he calls "the tyranny of an unbridled majority"[265]:

> From the earliest period, it was foreseen by the wisest of our statesmen that a danger to the perpetuity of the Union would arise from the conflicting interests of different sections, and every effort was made to secure each of these classes of interests against aggression by the other. As a proof of this, may be cited the following extract from Mr. [James] Madison's report of a speech made by himself in the Philadelphia Convention on the 30th of June, 1787:
>
>> "He admitted that every peculiar interest, whether in any class of citizens or any description of States, ought to be secured as far as possible. Wherever there is danger of attack, there ought to be given a constitutional power of defense. But he contended that the States were divided into different interests, not by their difference of size, but by other circumstances; the most material of which resulted from climate, but principally from the effects of their having or not having slaves. These two causes concurred in forming the great division of interests in the United States. It did not lie between the large and small States; it lay between the Northern and Southern; and, if any defensive power were necessary, it ought to be mutually given to these two interests."
>
> Mr. Rufus King, a distinguished member of the Convention from Massachusetts, a few days afterward, said, to the same effect: "He was fully convinced that the question concerning a difference of interests did not lie where it had hitherto been discussed, between the great and small States, but between the Southern and Eastern. For this reason he had been ready to yield something, in the proportion of representatives, for the security of the Southern. . . . He was not averse to giving them a still greater security, but did not see how it could be done."
> The wise men who formed the Constitution were not seeking to bind the States together by the material power of a majority; nor were they so blind to the influences of passion and interest as to believe that paper barriers would suffice to restrain a majority actuated by either or both of these motives. They endeavored, therefore, to prevent the conflicts inevitable from the

ascendancy of a sectional or party majority, by so distributing the powers of government that each interest might hold a check upon the other. It was believed that the compromises made with regard to representation—securing to each State an equal vote in the Senate, and in the House of Representatives giving the States a weight in proportion to their respective population, estimating the negroes as equivalent to three fifths of the same number of free whites—would have the effect of giving at an early period a majority in the House of Representatives to the South, while the North would retain the ascendancy in the Senate. Thus it was supposed that the two great sectional interests would be enabled to restrain each other within the limits of purposes and action beneficial to both.[266]

Lawyer Lincoln's ignorance of American law is also evident when he speaks of the preamble of the Constitution, "We, the people," as if these words mean that the United States of America is a single inseparable entity, with no allowance for secession.

Actually the Founding Fathers intended no such meaning, nor did the Constitution originally begin with these words.[267] In his *Notes of the Debates in the Federal Convention*, James Madison reveals the introductory text of the Preamble as it was written in the first draft of the U.S. Constitution. It read:

> We, the people of the States of New Hampshire, Massachusetts, Rhode Island and Providence Plantations, Connecticut, New York, New Jersey, Pennsylvania, Delaware, Maryland, Virginia, North Carolina, South Carolina, and Georgia, do ordain, declare and establish, the following Constitution, for the government of ourselves and our posterity.[268]

In other words, in the earliest rough outline of the Constitution the thirteen original colonies were listed individually. Why? Because each one was considered a little "nation-state," each with its own separate national rights and powers.

Why then were these individual state names dropped and replaced with the phrase "We, the people"? This question was aptly answered in 1876 by lawyer, author, and legal scholar William O. Bateman:

> The change of this expression of the organic will, to that of 'We, the people of the United States,' etc., was proposed by a sub-committee on *style*. And wherefore? Because, it could not be

foreknown, which of the States would accept and ratify the new constitution. If any *nine* of them should do so, they, at all events, *according to the last article of the instrument*, would thence become the *United States* of America. Hence the committee on style revised the language of the convention, and substituted 'the United States,' in place of 'the States of New Hampshire, Massachusetts, Rhode Island,' etc.[269]

The change in wording then came because of a simple timing issue.

What Lincoln did not understand (or pretended not to understand) was that the original states could come and go in and out of the Union as they pleased. The right to accede (enter the Union) automatically gave the opposite right, to secede (leave the Union). These rights never changed, for as the Constitution itself says:

> The powers not delegated to the United States by the Constitution, nor prohibited by it to the States, are reserved to the States respectively, or to the people.[270]

It is true, as some have argued, that despite the inclusion of this, the Tenth Amendment, the Constitution of the United States does not refer directly to the right of secession. At the same time, however, it should be pointed out that it makes no mention of any governmental power to prohibit it. Lincoln regularly disregarded this second important fact.

The real question is this: why did the Founders not make clear mention of it?

They took this very important right so for granted that they did not feel it was necessary: up until 1865 secession was the most frequently discussed political issue in both the United States and the Confederate States.[271] Thus to both the Framers and the general populace it was just another common law that was universally recognized and accepted by every American citizen.

Constitutional authority William Rawle, the Yankee author of the 1829 West Point textbook, *A View of the Constitution of the United States of America*, put it this way:

> This right [of secession] must be considered as an ingredient in the original composition of the general government, which, though not expressed, was mutually understood . . . The states, then, may wholly withdraw from the Union . . .[272]

Rawle had the full weight of our first president behind him: he was appointed U.S. District Attorney for Pennsylvania by President George Washington.

The depth of Lincoln's ignorance pertaining to secession is highlighted by the fact that even many foreigners had a far better grasp of the Founding documents than he did. In his two-volume book, *Democracy in America*, for instance, published consecutively in 1835 and 1840, French aristocrat Alexis de Tocqueville displayed a concise understanding of the legal right of secession in America:

> The [American] Union was formed by the voluntary agreement of States; and, in uniting together, they have not forfeited their nationality, nor have they been reduced to the condition of one and the same people. If one of the States chose to withdraw its name from the contract, it would be difficult to disprove its right of doing so; and the Federal Government would have no means of maintaining its claims directly either by force or by right.[273]

Lincoln was also incorrect when he says that there is no mention of state **"sovereignty"** in any of the individual state constitutions, and that because of this the states do not possess the right of secession. While the word sovereignty may not appear, secession itself *is* mentioned, for the notion of self-rule was indeed "mutually understood" by all U.S. citizens at the time.

For instance, President Jefferson Davis, named after Thomas Jefferson, and an adept student of the U.S. Constitution, noted that in addition to the Tenth Amendment, several state Constitutions openly refer to the right of secession. Virginia's Constitution, for example, affirms that:

> the powers granted under the [U.S.] Constitution, being derived from the people of the United States, may be resumed by them, whensoever the same shall be perverted to their injury or oppression, and that every power not granted thereby remains with them and at their will.[274]

The Constitutions of New York and Rhode Island also include clauses regarding secession, stating that

> the powers of government may be resumed by the people whenever it shall become necessary to their happiness.[275]

As Davis points out in *The Rise and Fall of the Confederate Government*:

> By inserting these declarations in their ordinances, Virginia, New York, and Rhode Island formally, officially, and permanently declared their interpretation of the [U.S.] Constitution as recognizing the right of secession by the resumption of their grants. By accepting the ratifications with this declaration incorporated, the other states as formally accepted the principle which it asserted.[276]

No matter how Lincoln chose to interpret the Constitution, it is patently obvious what the Founders' intentions were concerning this issue 225 years ago. In June 1816, the man who authored the Declaration of Independence, now former President Thomas Jefferson, wrote a letter to William Crawford that read in part:

> If any state in the Union will declare that it prefers separation to a continuance in the Union, I have no hesitation in saying, 'Let us separate.'[277]

According to Article 4, Section 4 of the Tenth Amendment, the only power originally granted to the national government by the people was the power to protect them against the formation of state dictatorships, foreign invasion, and internal disturbances (e.g., riots). Outside of these three obligations (basically, the defense of lives, rights, and property), all sovereign power was to remain in the hands of the people.[278] On this topic President James Madison said:

> The powers delegated by the proposed constitution to the Federal Government are few and defined; those which are to remain in the State governments are numerous and indefinite; the former will be exercised principally on external objects, as war, peace, negotiation, and foreign commerce—with which last the powers of taxation will, for the most part, be connected. The powers reserved to the several States, will extend to all the objects which, in the ordinary course of affairs, concern the lives, liberties, and properties of the people, and the internal order, improvement, and prosperity of the State.[279]

Madison is speaking here of states' rights, one of which was the right of secession. Who would dare argue with the literal "Father of the Constitution"?

Lincoln would—and did!

It was due to this very undermining of the Constitution that Lincoln was so often rightly called a "disunionist." Conservatives knew full well that if liberal Lincoln and his progressive followers ever came to power that it would split the nation in half. For they knew, as Stephen A. Douglas affirmed, that:

> Our [Founding] fathers, I say, made this government on the principle of the right of each State to do as it pleases in its own domestic affairs, subject to the Constitution, and allowed the people of each to apply to every new change of circumstances such remedy as they may see fit to improve their condition. This right they have for all time to come.[280]

Here is how Lincoln defended himself against the accusation of disunionism on August 1, 1856, in a speech at Galena, Illinois:

> **You further charge us with being disunionists. If you mean that it is our aim to dissolve the Union, I for myself answer that it is untrue; for those who act with me I answer that it is untrue. Have you heard us assert that as our aim? Do you really believe that such is our aim? Do you find it in our platform, our speeches, our conventions, or anywhere? If not, withdraw the charge.**
>
> **But you may say that though it is not our aim, it will be the result if we succeed, and that we are therefore disunionists in fact. This is a grave charge you make against us, and we certainly have a right to demand that you specify in what way we are to dissolve the Union. How are we to effect this?**
>
> **The only specification offered is volunteered by Mr. [Millard] Fillmore in his Albany speech. His charge is that if we elect a President and Vice-President both from the free States, it will dissolve the Union. This is open folly. The Constitution provides that the President and Vice-President of the United States shall be of different States; but says nothing as to the latitude and longitude of those States. In 1828 Andrew Jackson, of Tennessee, and John C. Calhoun, of South Carolina, were elected President and Vice-President, both from slave States; but no one thought of dissolving the Union then on that account. In 1840 [William Henry] Harrison, of Ohio, and [John] Tyler, of Virginia, were elected. In 1841 Harrison**

died and John Tyler succeeded to the presidency, and William R. [D.] King, of Alabama, was elected acting Vice-President by the Senate; but no one supposed that the Union was in danger. In fact, at the very time Mr. Fillmore uttered this idle charge, the state of things in the United States disproved it. Mr. [Franklin] Pierce, of New Hampshire, and Mr. [Jesse David] Bright, of Indiana, both from free States, are President and Vice-President, and the Union stands and will stand. You do not pretend that it ought to dissolve the Union; and the facts show that it won't; therefore the charge may be dismissed without further consideration.

No other specification is made, and the only one that could be made is that the restoration of the restriction of 1820, making the United States territory free territory, would dissolve the Union. Gentlemen, it will require a decided majority to pass such an act. We, the majority, being able constitutionally to do all that we purpose, would have no desire to dissolve the Union. Do you say that such restriction of slavery would be unconstitutional, and that some of the States would not submit to its enforcement? I grant you that an unconstitutional act is not a law; but I do not ask and will not take your construction of the Constitution. The Supreme Court of the United States is the tribunal to decide such a question, and we will submit to its decisions: and if you do also, there will be an end of the matter. Will you? If not, who are the disunionists—you or we? We, the majority, would not strive to dissolve the Union; and if any attempt is made, it must be by you, who so loudly stigmatize us as disunionists. But the Union, in any event, will not be dissolved. We don't want to dissolve it, and if you attempt it we won't let you. With the purse and sword, the army and navy and treasury, in our hands and at our command, you could not do it. This government would be very weak indeed if a majority with a disciplined army and navy and a well-filled treasury could not preserve itself when attacked by an unarmed, undisciplined, unorganized minority. All this talk about the dissolution of the Union is humbug, nothing but folly. We do not want to dissolve the Union; you shall not.[281]

Lincoln, of course, was dead wrong. Even if he did not want to believe it, his liberal party *was* the party of disunion, and his election—*and* the secession of the first Southern state—in 1860, would prove it.

In summary secession was legal, and Lincoln knew it. Despite this, he waged war on the legally formed Southern Confederacy. This not only makes the "Civil War" illegal, it makes it one great war crime and its instigator, President Lincoln, one of the world's great war criminals.[282]

Lincoln & The So-Called "Rebellion"

WE HAVE PROVEN THAT LINCOLN was fully aware of the legality of secession before he became president. Referring to it as a **"most valuable, a most sacred right,"** he publicly supported it throughout his early political career. In 1848 he stated before the House of Representatives that **"allowing the people to do as they please with their own business"** was **"the best sort of principle."**[283] That same year he backed Zachary Taylor for president, saying:

> We prefer a candidate who, like General Taylor, will allow the people to have their own way regardless of private opinion; . . . he would force nothing on them which they don't want . . .[284]

As late as May 17, 1859, on which day he wrote the following in a letter to Dr. Theodore Canisius, he was defending states rights—at least in the North:

> Dear Sir: Your note asking, in behalf of yourself and other German citizens, whether I am for or against the constitutional provision in regard to naturalized citizens, lately adopted by Massachusetts, and whether I am for or against a fusion of the Republicans, and other opposition elements, for the canvass of 1860, is received.
> Massachusetts is a sovereign and independent State; and it is no privilege of mine to scold her for what

she does.[285]

It was only when, now as chief executive, he saw his dream of big government slipping away with the formation of the Southern Confederacy, that he reversed his position on our American freedoms, calling secession an **"ingenious sophism"** and the defiant departure of the Southern states a **"rebellion."**

Obviously he was being duplicitous, for knowing that secession is a constitutional right how could any sane individual ever change their opinion on the matter? Is not a constitutional law that has never been amended unvarying and impermeable?

What changed was not the Constitution. It was Lincoln's hunger for power and his newly realized liberal agenda after he took the Oval Office.

It appears that one of the earliest, if not the earliest, instance in which Lincoln spoke of the seceding states as a **"rebellion"** came on July 1, 1861, during his "Message To Congress in Special Session," when he said:

> **It was decided that we have a case of rebellion . . .**[286]

He does not tell us who **"decided"** to call the legal right of secession a **"rebellion,"** but we can be sure that he played a role in the decision, if he was not the originator of the idea to begin with.

What we do know is that once he embraced the term he used it constantly, pounding his message home in every speech possible: the **"so-called Confederate government,"** Lincoln cried, is not an individual nation, and it has no right to separate from the Union. It's so-called citizens are nothing more than **"insurgents,"** the Confederacy itself a **"belligerent power"** in **"rebellion,"**[287] her states **"never having been out of the Union."**[288]

By 1863 he had fully warmed to the word "rebellion," as we see from this excerpt from his "Proclamation of Amnesty and Reconstruction," given that year on December 8:

> Whereas, in and by the Constitution of the United States, it is provided that the President "shall have power to grant reprieves and pardons for offenses against the United States, except in cases of impeachment"; and
>
> Whereas a rebellion now exists whereby the loyal State governments of several States have for a long

time been subverted, and many persons have committed, and are now guilty of, treason against the United States; and

Whereas, with reference to said rebellion and treason, laws have been enacted by Congress, declaring forfeitures and confiscation of property and liberation of slaves, all upon terms and conditions therein stated, and also declaring that the President was thereby authorized at any time thereafter, by proclamation, to extend to persons who may have participated in the existing rebellion, in any State or part thereof, pardon and amnesty, with such exceptions and at such times and on such conditions as he may deem expedient for the public welfare; and

Whereas the congressional declaration for limited and conditional pardon accords with well-established judicial exposition of the pardoning power; and

Whereas, with reference to said rebellion, the President of the United States has issued several proclamations, with provisions in regard to the liberation of slaves; and

Whereas it is now desired by some persons heretofore engaged in said rebellion to resume their allegiance to the United States, and to reinaugurate loyal State governments within and for their respective States; therefore

I, Abraham Lincoln, President of the United States, do proclaim, declare, and make known to all persons who have, directly or by implication, participated in the existing rebellion, except as hereinafter excepted, that a full pardon is hereby granted to them and each of them, with restoration of all rights of property, except as to slaves, and in property cases where rights of third parties shall have intervened, and upon the condition that every such person shall take and subscribe an oath, and thenceforward keep and maintain said oath inviolate; and which oath shall be registered for permanent preservation, and shall be of the tenor and effect following, to wit:

I, _____ do solemnly swear, in presence of almighty God, that I will henceforth faithfully support, protect, and defend the Constitution of the United States, and the union of the States thereunder; and that I will, in like manner, abide by and faithfully support all acts of Congress passed during the existing rebellion with reference to slaves, so long and so far as not repealed, modified, or held void by Congress, or by decision of the Supreme Court; and that I will, in like manner, abide by and faithfully support all proclamations of the President made during the existing rebellion having reference to slaves, so long and so far as not modified or declared void by decision of the Supreme Court. So help me God.

    The persons exempted from the benefits of the foregoing provisions are all who are, or shall have been, civil or diplomatic officers or agents of the so-called Confederate Government; all who have left judicial stations under the United States to aid the rebellion; all who are or shall have been military or naval officers of said so-called Confederate Government above the rank of colonel in the army or of lieutenant in the navy; all who left seats in the United States Congress to aid the rebellion; all who resigned commissions in the army or navy of the United States and afterward aided the rebellion; and all who have engaged in any way in treating colored persons, or white persons in charge of such, otherwise than lawfully as prisoners of war, and which persons may have been found in the United States service as soldiers, seamen, or in any other capacity.[289]

Lincoln uses the word "rebellion" eleven times in the above quote, and this is only an excerpt from just one of his hundreds of speeches.

But was it really a rebellion? Most Americans, and nearly all Southerners, at the time considered secession a legal or constitutional question, or at most a "political party question." It was thus seen as anything but an actual rebellion.[290]

Lawyer Lincoln himself knew well that it was not. But he wanted the world to think it was because it suited his agenda: to assume dictatorial powers and implement slave owner Henry Clay's "American System" (i.e., big government) at Washington. This was a socialistic liberal agenda he was so obsessed with that on February 22, 1861, he told an audience at Independence Hall, Philadelphia, Pennsylvania, that he would rather be **"assassinated on this spot"** than give up his commitment to it.[291]

Let us acknowledge here that the South did indeed "rebel." But it was not the Union she rebelled against, as Lincoln wanted the world to believe. She rebelled against Lincoln himself, against his nefarious desire to alter the Constitution and enlarge the central government. This is why the first state to secede, South Carolina, did not officially break from the Union until December 20, 1860, just weeks *after* Lincoln was elected on November 6. There would have been no secession and no Southern Confederacy had Lincoln not been chosen president of the United States.

In fact, I personally believe that it is this fact, so painful and mortifying for Lincoln, which became one of the many reasons for his irrational and illegal war against the South, beginning at Fort Sumter on April 12, 1861: in my opinion the "Civil War" was, in great part, Lincoln's personal revenge against a region that had publicly humiliated him before the world.

The truth is that it was Lincoln who rebelled by flagrantly defying the will of the people: during his first election he was voted in by only 39.8 percent (1,866,452 votes out of 4,680,193) of the ballots cast that year. His Democratic opponents, Stephen A. Douglas, John C. Breckinridge, and John Bell, received the other 60.2 percent (2,813,741 votes).[292] In other words, Lincoln received nearly one million votes less than his opponents put together,[293] making him a true minority president.[294]

Most shocking is the fact that out of the total population of the U.S. that November, only one out of every seventeen eligible whites voted for him.[295] His election was only made possible by the Electoral College,[296] and by rancorous division among the Democrats, which left the door open for Lincoln's win.[297]

Obviously, as one who received only one in seventeen votes, he did not have the support of the American people during his first four years in office, making every one of his official acts a miniature insurrection against the will of the majority. Despite this, Lincoln had the nerve to say, as he did on December 3, 1861, during his First Annual Message to Congress, that

> the insurrection is largely, if not exclusively, a war upon the first principle of popular government—the rights of the people.[298]

He was in error. In going to war against the North the South was trying to preserve the rights of the people. It was Lincoln who was trying to destroy them.

Most importantly, however, Lincoln rebelled against the

Constitution, committing so many constitutional crimes that no historian has ever been able to catalog them all, as we will discuss in our next chapter.

To 19th-Century Southerners the Constitution was second only to the Bible in sacredness. So holy was it to them that they were willing to die to preserve it. It was the election of big government, big spending liberal Lincoln, and his veiled promise to tamper with the Constitution (only one month before his inauguration),[299] that inspired the small government conservative South to take up arms against the Union. Not the Union itself.

Thus it was Lincoln's rebellion against our nation's most sacred document that caused what he called the Southern **"rebellion,"** a conflict that permanently split the nation, and in which millions were injured, killed, or left homeless. The terrible irony of this may escape most modern Northerners and New South scallywags, but it has never escaped us here in the traditional South.

It never will.[300]

Lincoln & the Constitution

WHEN ABRAHAM LINCOLN ACCEPTED HIS nomination for U.S. president in the spring of 1860, he swore that he would give **"due regard"** to states' rights and the Constitution. Here is how he phrased it in a letter to George Ashmun on May 23:

> Sir: I accept the nomination tendered me by the convention over which you presided, and of which I am formally apprised in the letter of yourself and others, acting as a committee of the convention for that purpose.
>
> The declaration of principles and sentiments which accompanies your letter meets my approval; and it shall be my care not to violate or disregard it in any part.
>
> Imploring the assistance of Divine Providence, and with due regard to the views and feelings of all who were represented in the convention—to the rights of all the States and Territories and people of the nation; to the inviolability of the Constitution; and the perpetual union, harmony, and prosperity of all—I am most happy to cooperate for the practical success of the principles declared by the convention.
>
> Your obliged friend and fellow-citizen, A. Lincoln.[301]

These words would prove to be hollow, and short-lived.

When Lincoln took the presidential oath he also made a solemn promise to obey and uphold the Constitution. Again, sadly for our nation, he did anything but.

Hints of what was to turn out to be Lincoln's burning desire to alter (i.e., enlarge) the U.S. government and his near total disregard for our nation's most hallowed document were evident early in his political career. On December 10, 1856, for instance, during an address at a Republican banquet in Chicago, he said:

> **Our government rests in public opinion. Whoever can change public opinion can change the government...**[302]

Just seven months later, on June 26, 1857, during a speech at Springfield, Illinois, Lincoln quoted President Andrew Jackson, saying cryptically,

> **...hear General Jackson:**
>
>> **"Each public officer who takes an oath to support the Constitution swears that he will support it as he understands it, and not as it is understood by others."**[303]

Just a little over a year later, on August 21, 1858, Lincoln offered the world this foreboding statement:

> **... public sentiment is everything. With public sentiment, nothing can fail; without it, nothing can succeed. Consequently he who molds public sentiment goes deeper than he who enacts statutes or pronounces decisions.**[304]

But these were mere pre-presidential intimations compared to what was to come.

After being elected president in November 1860, his words took on a more aggressive and sinister tone regarding the Constitution. In February 1861, while meeting with a Southern peace commission at Willard's Hotel in Washington, D.C., the president-elect was asked by New York businessman William E. Dodge what he was going to do to prevent war with the South. Lincoln's response is chilling, for it spells out his opinion of the Constitution that our Founding Fathers so painstakingly and lovingly created. When I get to the Oval Office, he said,

> I shall take an oath to the best of my ability to preserve, protect, and defend the Constitution. This is a great and solemn duty. With the support of the people and the assistance of the Almighty I shall undertake to perform it. I have full faith that I shall perform it. *It is not the Constitution as I would like to have it*, but as it is that is to be defended [emphasis added].[305]

Reading between the lines it is obvious that just prior to being inaugurated Lincoln was plotting to modify, and even destroy, the Constitution of George Washington, Thomas Jefferson, James Madison, George Mason, Charles Pinckney, and the other Founders. Why? Because it was largely a conservative document, one created largely by conservative Southerners like those just listed; a document that strictly limited the powers of the central government while giving the individual states almost limitless rights of self-determination (states' rights).

Lincoln, an ultra liberal who leaned strongly toward socialism, was not pleased, saying, as we saw above, that the Constitution **"is not as I would like to have it."** This is not surprising, for the Ninth and Tenth Amendments prevented him from initiating his progressive plan to enlarge the powers of both the central government and the chief executive.

But the Bill of Rights was no barrier to someone like Lincoln, a man who believed that the Constitution was subordinate to the president and that it could be bent and shaped to fit his personal whims and goals.

As usual, earlier in his career the political chameleon held the opposite view, and was fully aware of the constitutional limitations placed on the chief executive. On July 27, 1848, he gave a speech in the House of Representatives, where he quoted a February 15, 1791, letter written by Thomas Jefferson, in which our third president says:

> [Lincoln quoting Jefferson] **"It must be admitted, however, that unless the President's mind, on a view of everything which is urged for and against this bill, is tolerably clear that it is unauthorized by the Constitution,—if the pro and con hang so even as to balance his judgment,—a just respect for the wisdom of the legislature would naturally decide the balance in favor of their opinion. It is chiefly for cases where they are clearly misled by error, ambition, or interest, that the Constitution has placed a check in the negative of the President."**[306]

Lincoln then cites our twelfth president, Zachary Taylor:

> [Lincoln quoting Taylor] "**The power given by the veto is a high conservative power; but, in my opinion, should never be exercised except in cases of clear violation of the Constitution, or manifest haste and want of consideration by Congress.**"[307]

At the time Lincoln was also acutely aware of the power of the people, for in this very same speech he said:

> We . . . are in favor of making presidential elections, and the legislation of the country distinct matters; so that people can elect whom they please, and afterwards, legislate just as they please, without any hindrance, save only so much as may guard against infraction of the Constitution, undue haste, and want of consideration. . . . In leaving the people's business in their hands, we cannot be wrong. We are willing, and even anxious, to go to the people on this issue.[308]

In debating his political opponents, Lincoln then went on to attack them for violating

> the primary, the cardinal, the one great living principle of all Democratic representative—the principle that the representative is bound to carry out the known will of his constituents.[309]

A month earlier, on June 20, 1848, in another address before the House, Lincoln made this amazing comment concerning tampering with the Constitution:

> As a general rule, I think we would much better let it alone. No slight occasion should tempt us to touch it. Better not take the first step, which may lead to a habit of altering it. Better, rather, habituate ourselves to think of it as unalterable. It can scarcely be made better than it is. New provisions would introduce new difficulties, and thus create and increase appetite for further change. No, sir; let it stand as it is. New hands have never touched it. The men who made it have done their work, and have passed away. Who shall improve on what they did?[310]

Despite such conservative and constitutional views, by 1860 our sixteenth president would completely reverse his mind on the issues of the peoples' and the president's powers, becoming one of America's most liberal, criminalistic, and dictatorial leaders; a man who would not even allow his own cabinet members[311] or military officers[312] to resign if and when they chose.[313]

Lincoln's constitutional crimes are legion; probably beyond counting. Nonetheless we will discuss some of the more conspicuously reprehensible ones here. The first question we need to address is how Lincoln got away with trashing the Constitution, the very document he pledged to uphold in the following oath at his inauguration on March 4, 1861:

> **I do solemnly swear (or affirm) that I will faithfully execute the office of President of the United States, and will to the best of my ability, preserve, protect, and defend the Constitution of the United States.**[314]

The answer comes from his imagined theory known as **"military necessity."**[315]

Lincoln's belief in the idea of military necessity gave him unfettered freedom to do whatever he wanted, particularly regarding the Constitution, a conservative paper that clearly displeased him. As he said in a letter to Yankee General Benjamin F. Butler on August 9, 1864:

> **Nothing justifies the suspending of the civil by the military authority, but military necessity . . .**[316]

Lincoln's war on the South, in turn, gave him full justification for using military necessity any time he chose, since he believed that everything, including the Emancipation Proclamation, was related to the military.[317] As he himself said on July 28, 1862:

> **The truth is, that what is done and omitted about slaves is done and omitted on the same military necessity. It is a military necessity to have men and money; and we can get neither in sufficient numbers or amounts if we keep from or drive from our lines slaves coming to them.**[318]

One example of Lincoln's use of military necessity was his brazen violation of what would become the internationally recognized Geneva Conventions. According to a private September 22, 1861, letter Lincoln wrote to Orville Hickman Browning:

> **If a commanding general finds a necessity to seize the farm of a private owner for a pasture, an encampment, or a fortification, he has the right to do so, and to so hold it as long as the necessity lasts; and this is within military law, because within military necessity.**[319]

In his August 9 letter to Butler, Lincoln discards all self-restraint and regard for the Constitution, saying:

> **I now think you would better place whatever you feel is necessary to be done on this distinct ground of military necessity . . .**[320]

Such outrageous pronouncements, of course, opened the door for nearly unlimited corruption and abuses by Lincoln's soldiers. For once this door was unlocked, many of them, like Yankee war criminals Ulysses S. Grant, William T. Sherman, and Philip H. Sheridan, gladly walked right through it and never looked back.

On January 3, 1863, Lincoln himself made note of some of these abuses in a letter to Union General Samuel R. Curtis:

> **My dear Sir: I am having a good deal of trouble with Missouri matters, and I now sit down to write you particularly about it. One class of friends believe in greater severity and another in greater leniency in regard to arrests, banishments, and assessments. As usual in such cases, each questions the other's motives. On the one hand, it is insisted that Governor** [Hamilton R.] **Gamble's unionism, at most, is not better than a secondary spring of action; that hunkerism and a wish for political influence stand before unionism with him. On the other hand, it is urged that arrests, banishments, and assessments are made more for private malice, revenge, and pecuniary interest than for the public good. This morning I was told by a gentleman who I have no doubt believes what he says, that in one case of assessments for $10,000, the different persons who paid compared receipts, and found they had paid $30,000. If this be true,**

the inference is that the collecting agents pocketed the odd $20,000. And true or not in the instance, nothing but the sternest necessity can justify the making and maintaining of a system so liable to such abuses. Doubtless the necessity for the making of the system in Missouri did exist, and whether it continues for the maintenance of it is now a practical and very important question. Some days ago Governor Gamble telegraphed me, asking that the assessments outside of St. Louis County might be suspended, as they already have been within it, and this morning all the members of Congress here from Missouri but one laid a paper before me asking the same thing. Now, my belief is that Governor Gamble is an honest and true man, not less so than yourself; that you and he could confer together on this and other Missouri questions with great advantage to the public; that each knows something which the other does not; and that acting together you could about double your stock of pertinent information. May I not hope that you and he will attempt this? I could at once safely do (or you could safely do without me) whatever you and he agree upon. There is absolutely no reason why you should not agree. Yours as ever, A. Lincoln.[321]

On October 5, 1863, Lincoln was again forced to discuss the innumerable abuses that were taking place under his auspices:

> To restrain contraband intelligence and trade, a system of searches, seizures, permits, and passes had been introduced, I think, by General [John C.] Fremont. When General [Henry W.] Halleck came, he found and continued this system, and added an order, applicable to some parts of the State, to levy and collect contributions from noted rebels, to compensate losses and relieve destitution caused by the rebellion. The action of General Fremont and General Halleck, as stated, constituted a sort of system, which General [Samuel R.] Curtis found in full operation when he took command of the department. That there was a necessity for something of the sort was clear, but that it could only be justified by stern necessity, and that it was liable to great abuse in administration, was equally clear. Agents to execute it, contrary to the great prayer, were led into temptation. Some might, while others would not, resist that

temptation. It was not possible to hold any to a very strict accountability, and those yielding to the temptation would sell permits and passes to those who would pay most and most readily for them; and would seize property and collect levies in the aptest way to fill their own pockets. Money being the object, the man having money, whether loyal or disloyal, would be a victim. This practice doubtless existed to some extent, and it was a real additional evil that it could be and was plausibly charged to exist in greater extent than it did.[322]

On July 25, 1864, yet another grievance of Yankee abuse came across Lincoln's desk, and once again he responded, this time to Union General Edward Richard Sprigg Canby:

> Frequent complaints are made to me that persons endeavoring to bring in cotton in strict accordance with the trade regulations of the Treasury Department are frustrated, by seizures of district attorneys, marshals, provost-marshals, and others, on various pretenses, all looking to blackmail and spoils, one way and another. I wish, if you can find time, you would look into this matter within your department, and, finding these abuses to exist, break them up, if in your power, so that fair dealing under the regulations can proceed. The printed regulations, no doubt, are accessible to you. If you find the abuses existing, and yet beyond your power, please report to me somewhat particularly upon the facts.[323]

An interesting commentary on the outrages of some of Lincoln's soldiers was delivered to the president in the fall of 1864. Here is how he replied to it in an October 27 letter to Union General Stephen Gano Burbridge:

> It is represented to me that an officer has, by your authority, assessed and collected considerable sums of money from citizens of Allen and Barren counties, Kentucky, to compensate Union men for depredations committed upon them in the vicinity by rebels; and I am petitioned to order the money to be refunded. At most, I could not do this without hearing both sides, which, as yet, I have not. I write now to say that, in my opinion, in some extreme cases this class of proceedings becomes a

necessity; but that it is liable to—almost inseparable from—great abuses, and therefore should only be sparingly resorted to, and be conducted with great caution; that you, in your department, must be the judge of the proper localities and occasions for applying it; and that it will be well for you to see that your subordinates be at all times ready to account for every dollar, as to why collected, of whom, and how applied. Without this you will soon find some of them making assessments and collections merely to put money in their own pockets, and it will also be impossible to correct errors in future and better times.

In the case I have mentioned, such good men as Hon. J. R. Underwood and Hon. Henry Grider, though not personally interested, have appealed to me in behalf of others. So soon as you can, consistently with your other duties, I will thank you to acquaint yourself with the particulars of this case, and make any correction which may seem to be proper. Yours truly, A. Lincoln.[324]

One of the more common constitutional crimes committed against civilians by Lincoln's soldiers was the destruction of private property, a clear violation of the Geneva Conventions. Lincoln made reference to one such incident on November 21, 1864, in a letter to A. R. Wright of Louisville, Kentucky.[325] As is so often the case, Lincoln shows little sympathy or mercy, even though Mr. Wright is a fellow Kentuckian:

> Admitting that your cotton was destroyed by the Federal army, I do not suppose anything could be done for you now. Congress has appropriated no money for that class of claims, and will not, I expect, while the active war lasts. A. Lincoln.[326]

Another problem was the "illegal" seizure of Southern property by Lincoln's soldiers, as he noted in a February 12, 1865, letter to Union General John Pope:

> I understand that provost-marshals in different parts of Missouri are assuming to decide that the conditions of bonds are forfeited, and therefore are seizing and selling property to pay damages. This, if true, is both outrageous and ridiculous. Do not allow it. The courts, and not provost-marshals, are to decide such questions

unless when military necessity makes an exception.... A. Lincoln.[327]

What Lincoln does not acknowledge here, of course, is the fact that *all* seizure of Southern property was illegal under the Fourth Amendment of the U.S. Constitution!

Some of Lincoln's officers gave him particular trouble when he came to war crimes. One such officer, whose name is still cursed here in the South, is Yankee General David Hunter. The following August 3, 1864, letter was sent to Lincoln from his secretary of war, Edwin M. Stanton:

> Mr. President: This note will introduce to you Mr. Schley of Baltimore, [Maryland] who desires to appeal to [you] for the revocation of an order of General Hunter, removing some persons, citizens of Frederick, beyond his lines, and imprisoning others. This Department has no information of the reasons or proofs on which General Hunter acts, and I do not therefore feel at liberty to suspend or interfere with his action except under your direction. Yours truly, Edwin M. Stanton, Secretary of War.

Lincoln replied the same day:

> **The Secretary of War will suspend the order of General Hunter mentioned within, until further order, and direct him to send to the Department a brief report of what is known against each one proposed to be dealt with. A. Lincoln.**[328]

Another troublesome Yank officer was Benjamin F. "the Beast" Butler, widely known for his vile depredations upon the Southern people. Lincoln acknowledged the fact in a January 19, 1865, letter to Secretary of War Stanton:

> Dear Sir: You remember that from time to time appeals have been made to us by persons claiming to have attempted to come through our lines with their effects to take the benefit of the amnesty proclamation, and to have been despoiled of their effects under General Butler's administration. Some of these claims have color of merit, and may be really meritorious. Please consider whether we cannot set on foot an investigation which may advance justice in the premises. Yours truly, A.

Lincoln.[329]

Even Union General Ulysses S. Grant received a telegram from Lincoln regarding the crimes of Yankee soldiers. Dated August 14, 1864, it reads:

> **The Secretary of War and I concur that you had better confer with General** [Robert E.] **Lee, and stipulate for a mutual discontinuance of house-burning and other destruction of private property. The time and manner of conference and particulars of stipulation we leave, on our part, to your convenience and judgment. A. Lincoln.**[330]

We must note here that, contrary to what Lincoln infers, any destruction of private property perpetuated by Confederate soldiers was only done to prevent it from falling into the hands of Lincoln's illegal invaders.

The upshot of all of this is that these types of **"evils,"** as Lincoln called them, only existed because of his War, which gave rise, in his mind anyway, to his so-called "constitutional" idea of **"military necessity."** As he noted in his Final Emancipation Proclamation:

> **And upon this act, sincerely believed to be an act of justice, warranted by the Constitution upon military necessity, I invoke the considerate judgment of mankind and the gracious favor of Almighty God.**[331]

"Sincerely *believing*" and sincerely *knowing* are two different things, however, for the Constitution gives the president no such power. Indeed, it nowhere contains the phrase **"military necessity."**

Where did he get this idea from then?

Lincoln relied on Article 2, Section 2, Clause 1 of the Constitution, which assigns the president the title "commander in chief" of the armed forces.[332] He apparently broadly interpreted this to mean that he had near unlimited dictator-like war powers concerning anything related to the military. And, as we will see, in his despotic mind the word "military" would come to include nearly every aspect of everyday American life, aspects not ordinarily listed under the heading "military": free speech, voting rights, private property, civil legal procedure, medicines, the clergy, taxes, and the Post Office, just to name a few.

Lincoln's notion of "military necessity" itself also appears to have come from the Constitution, in this case Article 1, Section 9, Clause 2:

> The privilege of the writ of *habeas corpus* shall not be suspended, unless when in cases of rebellion or invasion the public safety may require it.³³³

It is an outrageous assumption to believe that suspending *habeas corpus* (a civil right that protects one from illegal imprisonment) due to a "rebellion" means that the president also has the right to dispense martial law due to "military necessity." But this is exactly what Lincoln did on September 15, 1863, when he imposed martial law in many of the Northern states and, for the first time in American history, suspended *habeas corpus* across the entire U.S. (in an attempt to silence Yankee antiwar protestors). Here are his exact words:

> **Whereas, the Constitution of the United States has ordained that the privilege of the writ of** *habeas corpus* **shall not be suspended unless when, in cases of rebellion or invasion, the public safety may require it; and whereas, a rebellion was existing on the third day of March, 1863, which rebellion is still existing; and whereas, by a statute which was approved on that day, it was enacted by the Senate and House of Representatives of the United States, in Congress assembled, that during the present insurrection the President of the United States, whenever in his judgment the public safety may require it, is authorized to suspend the privilege of the writ of** *habeas corpus* **in any case throughout the United States, or any part thereof; and whereas, in the judgment of the President, the public safety does require the privilege of the said writ shall now be suspended, throughout the United States, in the cases where, by the authority of the President of the United States, military, naval, and civil officers of the United States, or any of them, hold persons under their command, or in their custody, either as prisoners of war, spies, or aiders or abettors of the enemy, or officers, soldiers, or seamen enrolled or drafted or mustered or enlisted in, or belonging to, the land or naval forces of the United States, or as deserters therefrom, or otherwise amenable to military law, or the rules and articles of war, or the rules or regulations prescribed for the military or naval**

service by authority of the President of the United States; or for resisting a draft, or for any other offense against the military or naval service:

Now, therefore, I, Abraham Lincoln, President of the United States, do hereby proclaim and make known to all whom it may concern, that the privilege of the writ of *habeas corpus* is suspended throughout the United States in the several cases before mentioned, and that this suspension will continue throughout the duration of the said rebellion, or until this proclamation shall, by a subsequent one to be issued by the President of the United States, be modified or revoked. And I do hereby require all magistrates, attorneys, and other civil officers within the United States, and all officers and others in the military and naval service of the United States, to take distinct notice of this suspension, and to give it full effect, and all citizens of the United States to conduct and govern themselves accordingly, and in conformity with the Constitution of the United States and the laws of Congress in such cases made and provided.[334]

Lincoln, consumed with his new authoritarian powers, suspended *habeas corpus* in one state after another. One of his most bizarre proclamations in this regard came on July 5, 1864, when he slammed his iron fist down on his birth state, Kentucky:

Whereas, by a proclamation which was issued on the fifteenth day of April, 1861, the President of the United States announced and declared that the laws of the United States had been for some time past, and then were, opposed, and the execution thereof obstructed, in certain States therein mentioned, by combinations too powerful to be suppressed by the ordinary course of judicial proceedings, or by the powers vested in the marshals by law;

And whereas, immediately after the issuing of the said proclamation, the land and naval forces of the United States were put into activity to suppress the said insurrection and rebellion;

And whereas the Congress of the United States, by an act approved on the third day of March, 1863, did enact that during the said rebellion the President of the United States, whenever in his judgment the public safety may require it, is authorized to suspend the privilege of the writ of *habeas corpus* in any case throughout the United States, or in any part thereof;

And whereas the said insurrection and rebellion still continue, endangering the existence of the Constitution and government of the United States;

And whereas the military forces of the United States are now actively engaged in suppressing the said insurrection and rebellion in various parts of the States where the said rebellion has been successful in obstructing the laws and public authorities, especially in the States of Virginia and Georgia;

And whereas, on the fifteenth day of September last, the President of the United States duly issued his proclamation, wherein he declared that the privilege of the writ of *habeas corpus* should be suspended throughout the United States in the cases where, by the authority of the President of the United States, military, naval, and civil officers of the United States, or any of them, hold persons under their command or in their custody, either as prisoners of war, spies, or aiders or abettors of the enemy, or officers; soldiers, or seamen, enrolled or drafted or mustered or enlisted in, or belonging to, the land or naval forces of the United States, or as deserters therefrom, or otherwise amenable to military law or the rules and articles of war, or the rules or regulations prescribed for the military or naval services by authority of the President of the United States, or for resisting a draft, or for any other offense against the military or naval services;

And whereas many citizens of the State of Kentucky have joined the forces of the insurgents, and such insurgents have, on several occasions, entered the State of Kentucky in large force, and, not without aid and comfort furnished by disaffected and disloyal citizens of the United States residing therein, have not only disturbed the public peace, but have overborne the civil authorities and made flagrant civil war, destroying property and life in various parts of that State;

And whereas it has been made known to the President of the United States by the officers commanding the national armies, that combinations have been formed in the said State of Kentucky with a purpose of inciting rebel forces to renew the said operations of civil war within the said State, and thereby to embarrass the United States armies now operating in the said States of Virginia and Georgia, and even to endanger their safety:

Now, therefore, I, Abraham Lincoln, President of the United States, by virtue of the authority vested in me by the Constitution and laws, do hereby declare that, in my judgment, the public safety especially requires that the suspension of the privilege of the writ of *habeas corpus*, so proclaimed in the said proclamation of the fifteenth of September, 1863, be made effectual and be duly enforced in and throughout the said State of Kentucky, and that martial law be for the present established therein. I do, therefore, hereby require of the military officers in the said State that the privilege of the writ of *habeas corpus* be effectually suspended within the said State according to the aforesaid proclamation, and that martial law be established therein, to take effect from the date of this proclamation, the said suspension and establishment of martial law to continue until this proclamation shall be revoked or modified, but not beyond the period when the said rebellion shall have been suppressed or come to an end. And I do hereby require and command, as well all military officers as all civil officers and authorities existing or found within the said State of Kentucky, to take notice of this proclamation, and to give full effect to the same.

The martial law herein proclaimed, and the things in that respect herein ordered, will not be deemed or taken to interfere with the holding of lawful elections, or with the proceedings of the constitutional legislature of Kentucky, or with the administration of justice in the courts of law existing therein between the citizens of the United States in suits or proceedings which do not affect the military operations or the constituted authorities of the government of the United States.[335]

At the time this proclamation was issued, not only was Kentucky still the home of he and his wife's families and relations, but it was not even a full and official member of the Confederacy. Lincoln's justification for suspending *habeas corpus* there was because it was in **"rebellion," "embarrassing"** his armies, threatening the **"public safety,"** and **"endangering the existence of the Constitution and government of the United States."**

Unfortunately for "Honest Abe" there was no **"rebellion"** (as proven in the previous chapter) in Kentucky—or anywhere else, and thus there was no "military necessity"; and without military necessity there was no basis for riding roughshod over the Constitution or imposing martial law. Little wonder then that this particular legal shenanigan was challenged and overturned by the Supreme Court in the Constitutional landmark case *ex parte Milligan* in 1866. According to the Court's justices, the Constitution cannot be suspended in time of emergency—a ruling that it has never rescinded, even up to the present day. Thus, no less than the Supreme Court ruled Lincoln's megalomanic powers unconstitutional.[336]

Using his imaginary idea of **"military necessity,"** however, Lincoln went on to commit a litany of other crimes against the Constitution. One of the more egregious of these occurred in June of 1861, when he signed an arrest warrant for his own chief justice of the Supreme Court, Roger B. Taney. Why? Because Taney had rightly advised him that it was illegal for a U.S. president to suspend the right of *habeas corpus*.

Lincoln's actions were unconstitutional, Taney asserted, because, according to the Constitution itself (Article 1, Section 1), only Congress has the authority to suspend the writ.[337] The president, the chief justice correctly charged, was merely an administrative officer whose primary responsibility was to faithfully enforce the laws, not break them.[338] This was a factual definition of presidential powers that Lincoln never cared about, let alone practiced.

Fortunately for Taney he was never taken into custody, for the arresting officer, federal marshal Ward Hill Lamon (one of Lincoln's close friends and a former law partner),[339] gallantly refused the order.[340] But Lincoln was a man who could not bear to be questioned or challenged. Ignoring Taney's warning,[341] he simply overturned the former attorney general's opinion and went on to imprison tens of thousands of people without due process.[342]

Legal scholars are still discussing this astonishing breach of law. Why would a U.S. president seek to have his own chief justice handcuffed, booked, and jailed for trying to uphold the Constitution? By now, the answer is patently obvious.

Lincoln also advocated such unconstitutional activities as **"internal improvements,"** or what we now call "corporate welfare": first proposed by big government Federalist Alexander Hamilton in 1791,[343] internal improvements are private business projects funded by the state or central government—that is, by the taxpayer.

Lincoln entered politics, in great part, because of his interest in internal improvements. In fact, the Republican (i.e., the liberal) party platform, released in May 1860, included resolutions specifically dedicated to corporate welfare:

> 15. That appropriations by Congress for river and harbor improvements of a national character, required for the accommodation and security of an existing commerce, are authorized by the Constitution and justified by the obligation of government to protect the lives and property of its citizens.
>
> 16. That a railroad to the Pacific Ocean is imperatively demanded by the interests of the whole country; that the Federal Government ought to render immediate and efficient aid in its construction; and that, as preliminary thereto, a daily overland mail should be promptly established.[344]

With the blessing of his party, upon entering the White House in February 1861 Lincoln wasted little time in implementing this plank of Henry Clay's liberal American System. In 1862, for example, the former Illinois Central Railroad attorney[345] rammed through the "Pacific Railway Act," which gave millions of taxpayers' dollars to railroad corporations so they could construct a railroad in California, a railroad that should have been built using private investment. The South was against internal improvements because they were unconstitutional, and they were unconstitutional because government subsidies, as opposed to free market economics, always create corruption, fraud, waste, increased debt, and ultimately financial ruin.[346]

Government subsidies were so hated by the American populace that nearly every state constitution banned them. Minnesota's state constitution, for instance, declared that

> the state shall never contract any debts or works of internal improvements or be a party in carrying on such works.[347]

Lincoln, that great trampler of states' rights, cared little about state constitutions, and even less about the U.S. Constitution, which is why, early in his political career as an Illinois state legislator, he spearheaded the drive to force his state government to provide millions of dollars for internal improvement ventures. Though nearly all ended in economic catastrophe, Lincoln was proud of his efforts, efforts that helped make Illinois one of the top five states to receive federal subsidies for internal improvements up until

1860.[348]

Lincoln's friend, law partner, and eventually one of his biographers, William H. Herndon, commented on the genesis, and the disastrous results, of liberal Lincoln's obsession with internal improvements in Illinois:

> The Legislature of which Mr. Lincoln . . . became a member was one that will never be forgotten in Illinois. Its legislation in aid of the so-called internal improvement system was significantly reckless and unwise. The gigantic and stupendous operations of the scheme dazzled the eyes of nearly everybody, but in the end it rolled up a debt so enormous as to impede the otherwise marvelous progress of Illinois. The burdens imposed by this Legislature under the guise of improvements became so monumental in size it is little wonder that at intervals for years afterward the monster of repudiation often showed its hideous face above the waves of popular indignation. These attempts at a settlement of the debt brought about a condition of things which it is said led the Little Giant [Illinois Democrat Stephen A. Douglas], in one of his efforts on the stump, to suggest that "Illinois ought to be honest if she never paid a cent." However much we may regret that Lincoln took part and aided in this reckless legislation, we must not forget that his party and all his constituents gave him their united endorsement. They gave evidence of their approval of his course by two subsequent elections to the same office. It has never surprised me in the least that Lincoln fell so harmoniously in with the great system of improvement. He never had what some people call "money sense." By reason of his peculiar nature and construction he was endowed with none of the elements of a political economist. He was enthusiastic and theoretical to a certain degree; could take hold of, and wrap himself up in, a great moral question; but in dealing with the financial and commercial interests of a community or government he was equally as inadequate as he was ineffectual in managing the economy of his own household. In this respect alone I always regarded Mr. Lincoln as a weak man.
>
> One of his biographers, describing his legislative career at this time, says of him: "He was big with prospects: his real public service was just now about to begin. In the previous Legislature he had been silent, observant, studious. He had improved the opportunity so well that of all men in this new body, of equal age in the service, he was the smartest parliamentarian and cunningest 'log roller.' He was fully determined to identify himself conspicuously with the liberal legislation in contemplation, and dreamed of a fame very different from that which he actually

obtained as an anti-slavery leader. It was about this time he told his friend [Joshua F.] Speed that he aimed at the great distinction of being called the 'DeWitt Clinton of Illinois.'" [New York Governor Clinton helped push through the construction of the Erie Canal—using taxpayers' money.]

  The representatives in the Legislature from Sangamon county had been instructed by a mass convention of their constituents to vote "for a general system of internal improvements." Another convention of delegates from all the counties in the State met at Vandalia and made a similar recommendation to the members of the Legislature, specifying that it should be "commensurate with the wants of the people." Provision was made for a gridiron of railroads. The extreme points of the State, east and west, north and south, were to be brought together by thirteen hundred miles of iron rails. Every river and stream of the least importance was to be widened, deepened, and made navigable. A canal to connect the Illinois River and Lake Michigan was to be dug, and thus the great system was to be made "commensurate with the wants of the people." To effect all these great ends, a loan of twelve million dollars was authorized before the session closed. Work on all these gigantic enterprises was to begin at the earliest practicable moment; cities were to spring up everywhere; capital from abroad was to come pouring in; attracted by the glowing reports of marvelous progress and great internal wealth, people were to come swarming in by colonies, until in the end Illinois was to outstrip all the others, and herself become the Empire State of the Union.

  Lincoln served on the Committee on Finance, and zealously labored for the success of the great measures proposed, believing they would ultimately enrich the State, and redound to the glory of all who aided in their passage. In advocating these extensive and far-reaching plans he was not alone. Stephen A. Douglas, John A. McClernand, James Shields, and others prominent in the subsequent history of the State, were equally as earnest in espousing the cause of improvement, and sharing with him the glory that attended it. Next in importance came the bill to remove the seat of government from Vandalia. Springfield, of course, wanted it. So also did Alton, Decatur, Peoria, Jacksonville, and Illiopolis. But the Long Nine, by their adroitness and influence, were too much for their contestants. They made a bold fight for Springfield, intrusting the management of the bill to Lincoln. The friends of other cities fought Springfield bitterly, but under Lincoln's leadership the Long Nine contested with them every inch of the way. The struggle was warm and protracted. "Its enemies," relates one of Lincoln's colleagues, "laid it on the table twice. In those darkest hours when our bill to all appearances was beyond resuscitation, and all our opponents were jubilant over our defeat, and when friends could see no hope, Mr. Lincoln never for one moment despaired; but collecting his colleagues to his room for consultation, his practical common-sense, his thorough knowledge of human nature, then made him an overmatch for his compeers and for any man that I have ever known." The friends of the bill at last surmounted all obstacles, and only a day or two before the close of the session secured its passage by a joint vote of both houses.[349]

In a speech before the U.S. House of Representatives on June 20, 1848, Lincoln attacked those who would prohibit internal improvements, tearing apart their arguments piece by piece. Lincoln biographers Nicolay and Hay described the proceedings, citing Lincoln's words before the House:

> In Committee of the Whole on the State of the Union, on the Civil and Diplomatic Appropriation Bill:
> **Mr. Chairman: I wish at all times in no way to practise any fraud upon the House or the committee, and I also desire to do nothing which may be very disagreeable to any of the members. I therefore state in advance that my object in taking the floor is to make a speech on the general subject of internal improvements; and if I am out of order in doing so, I give the chair an opportunity of so deciding, and I will take my seat.**
> The Chair: I will not undertake to anticipate what the gentleman may say on the subject of internal improvements. He will, therefore, proceed in his remarks, and if any question of order shall be made, the chair will then decide it.
> Mr. Lincoln: **At an early day of this session the President** [James Knox Polk] **sent us what may properly be called an internal improvement veto message. The late Democratic** [i.e., conservative] **convention, which sat at Baltimore, and which nominated General** [Lewis] **Cass for the presidency, adopted a set of resolutions, now called the Democratic platform, among which is one in these words:**
>
>> "That the Constitution does not confer upon the General Government the power to commence and carry on a general system of internal

improvements."

General Cass, in his letter accepting the nomination, holds this language:

> "I have carefully read the resolutions of the Democratic National Convention, laying down the platform of our political faith, and I adhere to them as firmly as I approve them cordially."

These things, taken together, show that the question of internal improvements is now more distinctly made—has become more intense—than at any former period. The veto message and the Baltimore resolution I understand to be, in substance, the same thing; the latter being the more general statement, of which the former is the amplification—the bill of particulars. While I know there are many Democrats, on this floor and elsewhere, who disapprove that message, I understand that all who shall vote for General Cass will thereafter be counted as having approved it,— as having indorsed all its doctrines. I suppose all, or nearly all, the Democrats will vote for him. Many of them will do so not because they like his position on this question, but because they prefer him, being wrong on this, to another whom they consider farther wrong on other questions. In this way the internal improvement Democrats are to be, by a sort of forced consent, carried over and arrayed against themselves on this measure of policy. General Cass, once elected, will not trouble himself to make a constitutional argument, or perhaps any argument at all, when he shall veto a river or harbor bill; he will consider it a sufficient answer to all Democratic murmurs to point to Mr. Polk's message, and to the "Democratic Platform." This being the case, the question of improvements is verging to a final crisis; and the friends of this policy must now battle, and battle manfully, or surrender all. In this view, humble as I am, I wish to review, and contest as well as I may, the general positions of this veto message. When I say general positions, I mean to exclude from consideration so much as relates to the present embarrassed state of the treasury in consequence of the Mexican War.

Those general positions are: that internal

improvements ought not to be made by the General Government—First. Because they would overwhelm the treasury. Second. Because, while their burdens would be general, their benefits would be local and partial, involving an obnoxious inequality; and—Third. Because they would be unconstitutional. Fourth. Because the States may do enough by the levy and collection of tonnage duties; or if not—Fifth. That the Constitution may be amended. "Do nothing at all, lest you do something wrong," is the sum of these positions—is the sum of this message. And this, with the exception of what is said about constitutionality, applying as forcibly to what is said about making improvements by State authority as by the national authority; so that we must abandon the improvements of the country altogether, by any and every authority, or we must resist and repudiate the doctrines of this message. Let us attempt the latter.

The first position is, that a system of internal improvements would overwhelm the treasury. That in such a system there is a tendency to undue expansion, is not to be denied. Such tendency is founded in the nature of the subject. A member of Congress will prefer voting for a bill which contains an appropriation for his district, to voting for one which does not; and when a bill shall be expanded till every district shall be provided for, that it will be too greatly expanded is obvious. But is this any more true in Congress than in a State legislature? If a member of Congress must have an appropriation for his district, so a member of a legislature must have one for his county. And if one will overwhelm the national treasury, so the other will overwhelm the State treasury. Go where we will, the difficulty is the same. Allow it to drive us from the halls of Congress, and it will, just as easily, drive us from the State legislatures. Let us, then, grapple with it, and test its strength. Let us, judging of the future by the past, ascertain whether there may not be, in the discretion of Congress, a sufficient power to limit and restrain this expansive tendency within reasonable and proper bounds. The President himself values the evidence of the past. He tells us that at a certain point of our history more than two hundred millions of dollars had been applied for to make improvements; and this he does to prove that the treasury would be overwhelmed by such a system. Why did he not tell us how much was granted? Would not that have been better evidence? Let us turn to it, and see what it proves. In the message the President tells us that "during the four succeeding years embraced by the administration of President [John Quincy] Adams, the power not only to appropriate money, but to apply it, under the direction and authority of the General Government, as well to the construction of roads as to the improvement of harbors and rivers, was fully asserted and exercised."

This, then, was the period of greatest enormity. These, if any, must have been the days of the two hundred millions. And how much do you suppose was really expended for improvements during that four years? Two hundred millions? One hundred? Fifty? Ten? Five? No, sir; less than two millions. As shown by authentic documents, the expenditures on improvements during 1825, 1826, 1827, and 1828 amounted to one million eight hundred and seventy-nine thousand six hundred and twenty-seven dollars one cent. These four years were the period of Mr. Adams's administration, nearly and substantially. This fact shows that when the power to make improvements "was fully asserted and exercised," the Congress did keep within reasonable limits; and what has been done, it seems to me, can be done again.

Now for the second portion of the message—namely, that the burdens of improvements would be general, while their benefits would be local and partial, involving an obnoxious inequality. That there is some degree of truth in this position, I shall not deny. No commercial object of government patronage can be so exclusively general as to not be of some peculiar local advantage. The navy, as I understand it, was established, and is maintained at a great annual expense, partly to be ready for war when war shall come, and partly also, and perhaps chiefly, for the protection of our commerce on the high seas. This latter object is, for all I can see, in principle the same as internal improvements. The driving a pirate from the track of commerce on the broad ocean, and the removing a snag from its more narrow path in the Mississippi River, cannot, I think, be distinguished in principle. Each is done to save life and property, and for nothing else.

The navy, then, is the most general in its benefits of all this class of objects; and yet even the navy is of some peculiar advantage to Charleston, Baltimore, Philadelphia, New York, and Boston, beyond what it is to the interior towns of Illinois. The next most general object I can think of would be improvements on the Mississippi River and its tributaries. They touch thirteen of our States—Pennsylvania, Virginia, Kentucky, Tennessee, Mississippi, Louisiana, Arkansas, Missouri, Illinois, Indiana, Ohio, Wisconsin, and Iowa. Now I suppose it will not be denied that these thirteen States are a little more interested in improvements on that great river than are the remaining seventeen. These instances of the navy and the Mississippi River show clearly that there is something of local advantage in the most general objects. But the converse is also true. Nothing is so local as to not be of some general benefit. Take, for instance, the Illinois and Michigan Canal. Considered apart from its effects, it is perfectly local. Every inch of it is within the State of Illinois. That canal was first opened for business last April. In a very few days we were all gratified to learn, among other things, that sugar had been carried from New Orleans through this canal to Buffalo in New York. This sugar took this route, doubtless, because it was cheaper than the old route. Supposing benefit of the reduction in the cost of carriage to be shared between seller and buyer, the result is that the New Orleans merchant sold his sugar a little dearer, and the people of Buffalo sweetened their coffee a little cheaper, than before,—a benefit resulting from the canal, not to Illinois, where the canal is, but to Louisiana and New York, where it is not. In other transactions Illinois will, of course, have her share, and perhaps the larger share too, of the benefits of the canal; but this instance of the sugar clearly shows that the benefits of an improvement are by no means confined to the particular locality of the improvement itself.

  The just conclusion from all this is that if the nation refuse to make improvements of the more general kind because their benefits may be somewhat local, a State may for the same reason refuse to make an improvement of a local kind because its benefits may be somewhat general. A State may well say to the nation, "If you will do nothing for me, I will do nothing for you." Thus it is seen that if this argument of "inequality" is sufficient anywhere, it is sufficient everywhere, and puts an end to improvements altogether. I hope and believe that if both the nation and the States would, in good faith, in their respective spheres do what they could in the way of improvements, what of inequality might be produced in one place might be compensated in another, and the sum of the whole might not be very unequal.

But suppose, alter all, there should be some degree of inequality. Inequality is certainly never to be embraced for its own sake; but is every good thing to be discarded which may be inseparably connected with some degree of it? If so, we must discard all government. This Capitol is built at the public expense, for the public benefit; but does any one doubt that it is of some peculiar local advantage to the property-holders and business people of Washington? Shall we remove it for this reason? And if so, where shall we set it down, and be free from the difficulty? To make sure of our object, shall we locate it nowhere, and have Congress hereafter to hold its sessions, as the loafer lodged, "in spots about"? I make no allusion to the present President when I say there are few stronger cases in this world of "burden to the many and benefit to the few," of "inequality," than the presidency itself is by some thought to be. An honest laborer digs coal at about seventy cents a day, while the President digs abstractions at about seventy dollars a day. The coal is clearly worth more than the abstractions, and yet what a monstrous inequality in the prices! Does the President, for this reason, propose to abolish the presidency? He does not, and he ought not. The true rule, in determining to embrace or reject anything, is not whether it have any evil in it, but whether it have more of evil than of good. There are few things wholly evil or wholly good. Almost everything, especially of government policy, is an inseparable compound of the two; so that our best judgment of the preponderance between them is continually demanded. On this principle the President, his friends, and the world generally act on most subjects. Why not apply it, then, upon this question? Why, as to improvements, magnify the evil, and stoutly refuse to see any good in them?

Mr. Chairman, on the third position of the message—the constitutional question—I have not much to say. Being the man I am, and speaking where I do, I feel that in any attempt at an original constitutional argument, I should not be, and ought not to be, listened to patiently. The ablest and the best of men have gone over the whole ground long ago. I shall attempt but little more than a brief notice of what some of them have said. In relation to Mr. [Thomas] Jefferson's views, I read from Mr. Polk's veto message:

> [Lincoln quoting President Polk] "**President Jefferson, in his message to Congress in 1806, recommended an amendment of the Constitution, with a view to apply an anticipated surplus in the Treasury** "to the great purpose of the public education, roads, rivers, canals, and such other objects of public improvements as it may be thought proper to add to the constitutional enumeration of the federal powers"; and he adds: "I suppose an amendment to the Constitution, by consent of the States, necessary, because the objects now recommended are not among those enumerated in the Constitution, and to which it permits the public moneys to be applied." In 1825, he repeated in his published letters the opinion that no such power has been conferred upon Congress."

I introduce this not to controvert just now the constitutional opinion, but to show that, on the question of expediency, Mr. Jefferson's opinion was against the present President— that this opinion of Mr. Jefferson, in one branch at least, is in the hands of Mr. Polk like McFingal's gun—"bears wide and kicks the owner over."

But to the constitutional question. In 1826 Chancellor [James] Kent first published his "Commentaries" on American law. He devoted a portion of one of the lectures to the question of the authority of Congress to appropriate public moneys for internal improvements. He mentions that the subject had never been brought under judicial consideration, and proceeds to give a brief summary of the discussion it had undergone between the legislative and executive branches of the government. He shows that the legislative branch had usually been for, and the executive against, the power, till the period of Mr. J. Q. Adams's administration, at which point he considers the executive influence as withdrawn from opposition, and added to the support of the power. In 1844 the chancellor published a new edition of his "Commentaries," in which he adds some notes of what had transpired on the question since 1826. I have not time to read the original text on the notes; but the whole may be found on page 267, and the two or three following pages, of the first volume of the edition of 1844. As to what Chancellor Kent seems to consider the sum of the whole, I read from one of the notes:

> [Lincoln quoting James Kent] "**Mr. Justice Story,** in his commentaries on the Constitution of the United States, Vol. II., pp. 429-440, and again pp. 519-538, has stated at large the arguments for and against the proposition that Congress have a constitutional authority to lay taxes, and to apply the power to regulate commerce as a means directly to encourage and protect domestic manufactures; and without giving any opinion of his own on the contested doctrine, he has left the reader to draw his own conclusions. I should think, however, from the arguments as stated, that every mind which has taken no part in the discussion, and felt no prejudice or territorial bias on either side of the question, would deem the arguments in favor of the Congressional power vastly superior."

It will be seen that in this extract the power to make improvements is not directly mentioned; but by examining the context, both of Kent and Story, it will be seen that the power mentioned in the extract, and the power to make improvements, are regarded as identical. It is not to be denied that many great and good men have been against the power; but it is insisted that quite as many, as great and as good, have been for it; and it is shown that, on a full survey of the whole, Chancellor Kent was of opinion that the arguments of the latter were vastly superior. This is but the opinion of a man; but who was that man? He was one of the ablest and most learned lawyers of his age, or of any age. It is no disparagement to Mr. Polk, nor indeed to any one who devotes much time to politics, to be placed far behind Chancellor Kent as a lawyer. His attitude was most favorable to correct conclusions. He wrote coolly, and in retirement. He was struggling to rear a durable monument of fame; and he well knew that truth and thoroughly sound reasoning were the only sure foundations. Can the party opinion of a party President on a law question, as this purely is, be at all compared or set in opposition to that of such a man, in such an attitude, as Chancellor Kent? This constitutional question will probably never be better settled than it is, until it shall pass under judicial consideration; but I do think no man who is clear on the questions of expediency need feel his conscience much pricked upon this.

 Mr. Chairman, the President seems to think that enough may be done, in the way of improvements, by means of tonnage duties under State authority, with the consent of the General Government. Now I suppose this matter of tonnage duties is well enough in its own sphere. I suppose it may be efficient, and perhaps sufficient, to make slight improvements and repairs in harbors already in use and not much out of repair. But if I have any correct general idea of it, it must be wholly inefficient for any general beneficent purposes of improvement. I know very little, or rather nothing at all, of the practical matter of levying and collecting tonnage duties; but I suppose one of its principles must be to lay a duty for the improvement of any particular harbor upon the tonnage coming into that harbor; to do otherwise—to collect money in one harbor, to be expended on improvements in another—would be an extremely aggravated form of that inequality which the President so much deprecates. If I be right in this, how could we make any entirely new improvement by means of tonnage duties? How make a road, a canal, or clear a greatly obstructed river? The idea that we could involves the same absurdity as the Irish bull about the new boots. "I shall niver git 'em on," says Patrick, "till I wear 'em a day or two, and stretch 'em a little." We shall never make a canal by tonnage duties until it shall already have been made awhile, so the tonnage can get into it.

After all, the President concludes that possibly there may be some great objects of improvement which cannot be effected by tonnage duties, and which it therefore may be expedient for the General Government to take in hand. Accordingly he suggests, in case any such be discovered, the propriety of amending the Constitution. Amend it for what? If, like Mr. Jefferson, the President thought improvements expedient, but not constitutional, it would be natural enough for him to recommend such an amendment. But hear what he says in this very message:

> [Lincoln quoting President Polk] "In view of these portentous consequences, I cannot but think that this course of legislation should be arrested, even were there nothing to forbid it in the fundamental laws of our Union."[350]

For what, then, would he have the Constitution amended? With him it is a proposition to remove one impediment merely to be met by others which, in his opinion, cannot be removed,—to enable Congress to do what, in his opinion, they ought not to do if they could.

Here Mr. [Richard Kidder] Meade of Virginia inquired if Mr. Lincoln understood the President to be opposed, on grounds of expediency, to any and every improvement.

Mr. Lincoln answered: **In the very part of his message of which I am speaking, I understand him as giving some vague expression in favor of some possible objects of improvement; but in doing so I understand him to be directly on the teeth of his own arguments in other parts of it. Neither the President nor any one can possibly specify an improvement which shall not be clearly liable to one or another of the objections he has urged on the score of expediency. I have shown, and might show again, that no work—no object—can be so general as to dispense its benefits with precise equality; and this inequality is chief among the "portentous consequences" for which he declares that improvements should be arrested. No, sir. When the President intimates that something in the way of improvements may properly be done by the General Government, he is shrinking from the conclusions to which his own arguments would force him. He feels that the** improvements of this broad and goodly land are a mighty interest; and he is unwilling to confess to the people, or perhaps to himself, that he has built an argument which, when pressed to its conclusions, entirely annihilates this interest.

I have already said that no one who is satisfied of the expediency of making improvements needs be much uneasy in his conscience about its constitutionality. I wish now to submit a few remarks on the general proposition of amending the Constitution. As a general rule, I think we would much better let it alone. No slight occasion should tempt us to touch it. Better not take the first step, which may lead to a habit of altering it. Better, rather, habituate ourselves to think of it as unalterable. It can scarcely be made better than it is. New provisions would introduce new difficulties, and thus create and increase appetite for further change. No, sir; let it stand as it is. New hands have never touched it. The men who made it have done their work, and have passed away. Who shall improve on what they did?

Mr. Chairman, for the purpose of reviewing this message in the least possible time, as well as for the sake of distinctness, I have analyzed its arguments as well as I could, and reduced them to the propositions I have stated. I have now examined them in detail. I wish to detain the committee only a little while longer with some general remarks upon the subject of improvements. That the subject is a difficult one, cannot be denied. Still it is no more difficult in Congress than in the State legislatures, in the counties, or in the smallest municipal districts which anywhere exist. All can recur to instances of this difficulty in the case of county roads, bridges, and the like. One man is offended because a road passes over his land, and another is offended because it does not pass over his; one is dissatisfied because the bridge for which he is taxed crosses the river on a different road from that which leads from his house to town; another cannot bear that the county should be got in debt for these same roads and bridges; while not a few struggle hard to have roads located over their lands, and then stoutly refuse to let them be opened until they are first paid the damages. Even between the different wards and streets of towns and cities we find this same wrangling and difficulty. Now these are no other than the very difficulties against which, and out of which, the President constructs his objections of "inequality," "speculation," and "crushing the treasury." There is but a single alternative about them: they are sufficient, or they are not. If sufficient, they are sufficient out of Congress as well as in it, and there is the end. We must reject them as insufficient, or lie down and do nothing by any authority. Then, difficulty though there be, let us meet and encounter it. "Attempt the end, and never stand to doubt: nothing so hard, but search will find it out." Determine that the thing can and shall be done, and then we shall find the way. The tendency to undue expansion is unquestionably the chief difficulty.

How to do something, and still not do too much, is the desideratum. Let each contribute his mite in the way of suggestion. The late Silas Wright, in a letter to the Chicago convention, contributed his, which was worth something; and I now contribute mine, which may be worth nothing. At all events, it will mislead nobody, and therefore will do no harm. I would not borrow money. I am against an overwhelming, crushing system. Suppose that, at each session, Congress shall first determine how much money can, for that year, be spared for improvements; then apportion that sum to the most important objects. So far all is easy; but how shall we determine which are the most important? On this question comes the collision of interests. I shall be slow to acknowledge that your harbor or your river is more important than mine, and vice versa. To clear this difficulty, let us have that same statistical information which the gentleman from Ohio [Samuel Finley Vinton] suggested at the beginning of this session. In that information we shall have a stern, unbending basis of facts—a basis in no wise subject to whim, caprice, or local interest. The pre-limited amount of means will save us from doing too much, and the statistics will save us from doing what we do in wrong places. Adopt and adhere to this course, and, it seems to me, the difficulty is cleared.

One of the gentlemen from South Carolina [Robert Barnwell Rhett] very much deprecates these statistics. He particularly objects, as I understand him, to counting all the pigs and chickens in the land. I do not perceive much force in the objection. It is true that if everything be enumerated, a portion of such statistics may not be very useful to this object. Such products of the country as are to be consumed where they are produced need no roads or rivers, no means of transportation, and have no very proper connection with this subject. The surplus—that which is produced in one place to be consumed in another; the capacity of each locality for producing a greater surplus; the natural means of transportation, and their susceptibility of improvement; the hindrances, delays, and losses of life and property during transportation, and the causes of each, would be among the most valuable statistics in this connection. From these it would readily appear where a given amount of expenditure would do the most good. These statistics might be equally accessible, as they would be equally useful, to both the nation and the States. In this way, and by these means, let the nation take hold of the larger works, and the States the smaller ones; and thus, working in a meeting direction, discreetly, but steadily and firmly, what is made unequal in one place may be equalized in another, extravagance avoided, and the whole country put on that career of prosperity which shall correspond with its extent of territory, its natural resources, and the intelligence and enterprise of its people.[351]

Despite the fact that, as Thomas Jefferson pointed out, federal internal improvements are illegal because they are not listed as one of the powers of the central government in Article 4, Section 4, of the U.S. Constitution (see also the Ninth and Tenth Amendments),[352] liberal Lincoln was an ardent proponent, and active agent, of corporate welfare for the remainder of his life.

The conservative Confederacy, of course, wisely specifically prohibited internal improvements, even including the ban in the C.S. Constitution, Article 1, Section 8, Clause 3:

> The [Confederate] Congress shall have the power to regulate commerce with foreign nations, and among the several States, and with the Indian tribes; but neither this, nor any other clause contained in the Constitution, shall ever be construed to delegate the power to Congress to appropriate money for any internal improvement intended to facilitate commerce; except for the purpose of furnishing lights, beacons, and buoys, and other aids to navigation upon the coasts, and the improvement of harbors and the removing of obstructions in river navigation; in all which cases

such duties shall be laid on the navigation facilitated thereby as may be necessary to pay the costs and expenses thereof.[353]

Another one of Lincoln's constitutional crimes was initiating a naval blockade in the Southern states. Blockades are only legal during war, and international wars at that. Although he often referred to his illegal invasion of the South as a **"civil war,"**[354] Lincoln did not give any legal authority to the phrase. Instead, as we saw in Chapter 3, his official term for it was a **"rebellion."**[355]

More serious was the fact that he had inaugurated war with the Confederacy without the approval of Congress, while plainly aware that this was illicit.[356] Indeed, according to the Constitution, Article 1, Section 8, Clause 11, the president cannot declare war with or without the approval of Congress. Only Congress possesses this power.[357] Here is Lincoln's "Proclamation of Blockade," issued on April 19, 1861:

> Whereas an insurrection against the government of the United States has broken out in the States of South Carolina, Georgia, Alabama, Florida, Mississippi, Louisiana, and Texas, and the laws of the United States for the collection of the revenue cannot be effectually executed therein conformably to that provision of the Constitution which requires duties to be uniform throughout the United States:
> And whereas a combination of persons engaged in such insurrection have threatened to grant pretended letters of marque to authorize the bearers thereof to commit assaults on the lives, vessels, and property of good citizens of the country lawfully engaged in commerce on the high seas, and in waters of the United States:
> And whereas an executive proclamation has been already issued requiring the persons engaged in these disorderly proceedings to desist therefrom, calling out a militia force for the purpose of repressing the same, and convening Congress in extraordinary session to deliberate and determine thereon:
> Now, therefore, I, Abraham Lincoln, President of the United States, with a view to the same purposes before mentioned, and to the protection of the public peace, and the lives and property of quiet and orderly citizens pursuing their lawful occupations, until Congress shall have assembled and deliberated on the

said unlawful proceedings, or until the same shall have ceased, have further deemed it advisable to set on foot a blockade of the ports within the States aforesaid, in pursuance of the laws of the United States, and of the law of nations in such case provided. For this purpose a competent force will be posted so as to prevent entrance and exit of vessels from the ports aforesaid. If, therefore, with a view to violate such blockade, a vessel shall approach or shall attempt to leave either of the said ports, she will be duly warned by the commander of one of the blockading vessels, who will indorse on her register the fact and date of such warning, and if the same vessel shall again attempt to enter or leave the blockaded port, she will be captured and sent to the nearest convenient port, for such proceedings against her and her cargo, as prize, as may be deemed advisable.

And I hereby proclaim and declare that if any person, under the pretended authority of the said States, or under any other pretense, shall molest a vessel of the United States, or the persons or cargo on board of her, such person will be held amenable to the laws of the United States for the prevention and punishment of piracy.[358]

Lincoln states here that he has issued his blockade **"in pursuance of the laws of the United States, and of the law of nations in such case provided."** How so? He had to have been either completely ignorant of those laws or he knew of them but chose to ignore them. For on every level the blockade was clearly against the wartime and maritime rules of both the U.S. and the international community. The truth is that he fabricated his own wartime and maritime "laws" out of thin air, as he always did when his political aspirations were barred by rules and regulations he did not like.

As a left-wing liberal with dictatorial leanings, Lincoln had no choice but to create such imaginary laws, for the weight of the world's conservative legal system was wholly against him. Consider the following.

International law at the time stipulated that for a blockade to be legitimate every mile of coastline had to be patrolled. Knowing that this was impossible Lincoln never even attempted it, making this particular military action nothing more than a "paper blockade," and as such, unlawful.[359]

Other requirements for legality were that a blockade had to be both 100 percent effective and continuous. Lincoln's was neither.[360] Indeed, the impossibility of barricading every port, bay, inlet, channel, estuary, lagoon, and swamp along the South's 3,549 mile coastline was obvious even to Europeans who, as was to be expected, heaped scorn and ridicule upon Lincoln's preposterous plan.[361]

Adding to its ineffectiveness the blockade was often suspended at varying points along the Southern coast.[362] The result in the first year, 1861, was that the rate of Union capture of Rebel ships was only about one in ten vessels.[363] More revealingly, during the entire four years of Lincoln's War not a single blockade runner commanded by a Confederate navy officer was ever captured by the Yankee navy.[364] We would not call this "effective."

Lincoln's main problem here was the Declaration of Paris of 1856, a set of well established international maritime laws[365] that had been signed by the Confederacy in the summer of 1861, and which was binding upon the United States as a maritime nation. The edict specified that in order for a blockade to be legal, entree beyond the blockaded nation's coastline would have to be rendered completely inaccessible. In the case of the South's enormous labyrinthian coastline this was clearly not true, for it was never totally blockaded at any time during the War.[366]

Despite all of this, Lincoln had the audacity to repeatedly refer to his unlawful and ineffective blockade as a **"lawful and effective blockade,"**[367] even issuing a second "Proclamation of Blockade" on April 27, 1861, to cover Virginia and North Carolina.[368] It was using just such outrageous lies that he was able to hoodwink most of his Northern constituents, as well as much of Europe.

Lincoln's illegitimate naval barricade of Southern ports and waterways did not just hurt its intended target, however. It also had a serious and negative impact on much of Europe, which in turn severely affected the worldwide economy.

As early as October 5, 1861, just six months into Lincoln's War, Confederate European agents William L. Yancey and Pierre Rost sent a report to Richmond notifying President Davis of the effects of the blockade. According to the two men, tobacco and cotton imports had been so profoundly impeded by then that thousands of Europeans were now unemployed, textile companies were operating at half-time, and the blue-collar class as a whole was under extreme duress, particularly the laboring poor of France[369] and England, who were forced into living conditions universally described as "absolutely intolerable."[370]

Lincoln's blockade caused a literal "cotton famine" in Lancashire,

England, where its "deadly" effect resulted in massive unemployment. In 1862, as the famine was peaking in France, the cotton producers of the Lower Seine, Rouen, Dieppe, and Harve "suffered terribly," and every last cotton mill had to be closed down, the smaller ones going into bankruptcy.[371]

By the end of that year some 130,000 French men were unemployed. This means that at least 390,000 French (this number includes dependents) were immediately thrown into poverty as a result. Starvation set in, beggars overwhelmed France's cities, and filthy half-naked children were seen roaming the countryside. So widespread was the impact that at least two million Europeans were eventually negatively affected.[372]

Lincoln even acknowledged the misery he was causing all across Europe in a letter addressed to English cotton workers on January 19, 1863:

> . . . I know and deeply deplore the sufferings which the working-men at Manchester, and in all Europe, are called to endure in this crisis. It has been often and studiously represented that the attempt to overthrow this government, which was built upon the foundation of human rights, and to substitute for it one which should rest exclusively on the basis of human slavery, was likely to obtain the favor of Europe. Through the action of our disloyal citizens, the working-men of Europe have been subjected to severe trials, for the purpose of forcing their sanction to that attempt. Under the circumstances, I cannot but regard your decisive utterances upon the question as an instance of sublime Christian heroism which has not been surpassed in any age or in any country. It is indeed an energetic and reinspiring assurance of the inherent power of truth, and of the ultimate and universal triumph of justice, humanity, and freedom. I do not doubt that the sentiments you have expressed will be sustained by your great nation; and, on the other hand, I have no hesitation in assuring you that they will excite admiration, esteem, and the most reciprocal feelings of friendship among the American people. I hail this interchange of sentiment, therefore, as an augury that whatever else may happen, whatever misfortune may befall your country or my own, the peace and friendship which now exist between the two nations will be, as it shall be my desire to make them, perpetual. Abraham Lincoln.[373]

Here Lincoln claims to **"deeply deplore"** the **"sufferings"** that the **"crisis"** is causing in Britain. What he neglects to apologize for is starting the "crisis" to begin with![374] He also states that the South wanted a government that rested **"exclusively on the basis of human slavery,"** and that the North's attempt to abolish slavery **"was likely to obtain the favor of Europe."** Both statements are entirely false and an outright perversion of reality, the usual Lincolnian misrepresentation of the facts.[375]

An overt legal debacle and an international embarrassment, several U.S. justices understandably tried to stop Lincoln's illegal blockade. Their fight was in vain, however, for a majority of the Supreme Court members—no doubt out of fear of arrest and imprisonment—sided with Lincoln, and through a convoluted maze of irrational arguments, upheld his absurd theory that the **"Civil War"** was a **"domestic insurrection"** with the characteristics of an **"international war."** In essence this fabricated loophole gave the president four more years to further abuse the Constitution and the American people.[376]

As just mentioned, one of Lincoln's greatest crimes was starting a war against a foreign nation, the Confederate States of America (one of the early nicknames for the U.S.),[377] without the authorization of Congress. As Article 1, Section 8, Clause 11 of the U.S. Constitution states:

> The Congress shall have power . . . to declare war . . .[378]

Despite this implacable constitutional law, on April 15, 1861, Lincoln issued his "Proclamation Calling 75,000 Militia." It read:

> Whereas the laws of the United States have been for some time past and now are opposed, and the execution thereof obstructed, in the States of South Carolina, Georgia, Alabama, Florida, Mississippi, Louisiana, and Texas, by combinations too powerful to be suppressed by the ordinary course of judicial proceedings, or by the powers vested in the marshals by law:
> Now, therefore, I, Abraham Lincoln, President of the United States, in virtue of the power in me vested by the Constitution and the laws, have thought fit to call forth, and hereby do call forth, the militia of the several States of the Union, to the aggregate number of seventy-five thousand, in order to suppress said combinations, and to cause the laws to be duly executed. The details for this object will be immediately

communicated to the State authorities through the War Department.

I appeal to all loyal citizens to favor, facilitate, and aid this effort to maintain the honor, the integrity, and the existence of our National Union, and the perpetuity of popular government; and to redress wrongs already long enough endured.

I deem it proper to say that the first service assigned to the forces hereby called forth will probably be to repossess the forts, places, and property which have been seized from the Union; and in every event the utmost care will be observed, consistently with the objects aforesaid, to avoid any devastation, any destruction of or interference with property, or any disturbance of peaceful citizens in any part of the country.

And I hereby command the persons composing the combinations aforesaid to disperse and retire peacefully to their respective abodes within twenty days from date.

Deeming that the present condition of public affairs presents an extraordinary occasion, I do hereby, in virtue of the power in me vested by the Constitution, convene both Houses of Congress. Senators and Representatives are therefore summoned to assemble at their respective chambers, at twelve o'clock noon, on Thursday, the fourth day of July next, then and there to consider and determine such measures as, in their wisdom, the public safety and interest may seem to demand.[379]

Intentionally misinterpreting Article 2, Section 2, Clause 1 of the Constitution, where the president is named "commander in chief" of the army and navy, Lincoln has the nerve to say here that he has now declared war on the South **"in virtue of the power in me vested by the Constitution."** As we have seen, and as any student of the Constitution knows, it gives him no such power or authority. Not only that, neither the **"public safety"** or the **"public interest"** were in jeopardy, and thus there was no **"demand"** for **"measures"** to be taken.

As strict constitutionalist Judge Andrew Napolitano assures us, it was because of just such potential abuse of martial power by the president that the Founding Fathers "put the power to declare war in the article of the Constitution that enumerates the powers of the Congress and *not* in the article that enumerates the powers of the president."³⁸⁰

Lincoln's violation of this power gave tacit permission to succeeding presidents to follow in his footsteps. Sadly, as a result, American history is now replete with conspicuous examples of executive disregard of the Constitution's Article 1, Section 8, Clause 11. For example, though America has been involved in countless wars since December 1941 (the last time Congress declared war), since World War II:

- Harry Truman invaded Korea.
- Lyndon Johnson invaded Vietnam.
- Richard Nixon invaded Cambodia.
- Ronald Reagan invaded Granada.
- George H. W. Bush invaded Kuwait.
- Bill Clinton invaded Haiti.
- George W. Bush invaded Iraq and Afghanistan.
- Barack Obama invaded Libya.³⁸¹

Congress did not declare war in any of these cases. Each was, as Napolitano rightly observes, "presidentially created."

After Nixon's illegal invasion of Cambodia in 1963, Congress tried to further curb the president's power as commander-in-chief by enacting the War Powers Act. Yet, this statute itself is unconstitutional, for it allocates some of what was once an integral aspect of Congressional authority to the president.³⁸² In this way Lincoln once again greatly contributed to the disintegration of the Founders' original constitutional intentions.

Yet another violation of our nation's most famous and sacred legal document came when Lincoln reluctantly issued his Final Emancipation Proclamation on January 1, 1863. It was illegal because at the time the Constitution protected slavery both in the South and in the North: by tacitly defining slaves as "private property," it was clear that the institution could not be tampered with under the Fifth Amendment.³⁸³ Lincoln admitted as much in his First Inaugural Address on March 4, 1861:

> **Apprehension seems to exist among the people of the Southern States that by the accession of a Republican administration their property and their peace and personal security are to be endangered. There has never been any reasonable cause for such apprehension. Indeed, the most ample evidence to the contrary has all the while existed and been open to their inspection. It is**

found in nearly all the published speeches of him who now addresses you. I do but quote from one of those speeches when I declare that 'I have no purpose, directly or indirectly, to interfere with the institution of slavery in the States where it exists. I believe I have no lawful right to do so, and I have no inclination to do so.' Those who nominated and elected me did so with full knowledge that I had made this and many similar declarations, and had never recanted them.[384]

Lincoln's admission here, that he had **"no lawful right"** to emancipate Southern slaves, is extraordinary, especially considering that just twenty months later he openly broke his own promise *and* violated the Constitution by issuing his Final Emancipation Proclamation. (It is important to note here, as we will discuss in Chapter 13, that his edict did not free slaves in the North, only in the South where he had no legal authority, and then only in areas *not* occupied by Union troops. Thus not one slave was actually freed by the proclamation).[385]

As always, Lincoln used tortured logic to justify his unlawful action, as he did on April 4, 1864, in a letter to A. G. Hodges. When it came to the Emancipation Proclamation, the president wrote,

> I felt that measures, otherwise unconstitutional might become lawful by becoming indispensable to the preservation of the Constitution through the preservation of the nation. Right or wrong, I assumed this ground, and now avow it.[386]

Here Lincoln does everything but openly admit that he is a dictator, for only a dictator can **"assume ground"** and enact **"unconstitutional measures"**!

Lincoln's Reconstruction Acts were also unconstitutional, for they were active only in the states of the Confederacy, a legally formed foreign nation. To further humiliate the already prostrate South, the acts imposed involuntary abolition of slavery, the rewriting of state constitutions (to fit Lincoln's liberalistic views), and a comprehensive reformation of Dixie's political and social systems (to fit the North's),[387] items that independent Southerners naturally wanted to deal with in their own time and way. To make matters worse, Lincoln declared martial law throughout the South, stationing Yankee troops in major cities and towns, many who committed heinous crimes on the war weary Southern citizenry. As Dixie's courts were still open and functioning, all of these acts were strident violations of the Constitution.[388]

But Lincoln was not concerned. Drunk with power he went on to abuse his position and subvert the Constitution in hundreds, perhaps thousands, of other ways as well.

How did Lincoln get away with his constitutional crimes, particularly when most of them were committed right out in the public forum for all to see?

As we will explore in more detail in Chapter 17, our sixteenth president regularly used bribery, double-dealing, horse-trading, patronage, and threats to get his way. When these failed there was always arrest, deportation, imprisonment, various modes of coercion, physical violence, torture, and even murder to add to the list of possibilities. This type of thuggery prevented most pro-South Northerners (called "doughfaces"), antiwar peace advocates, and even members of his own cabinet, from speaking out against Lincoln, thus enabling him to run his criminal operations with little or no resistance.

"Honest Abe" perpetrated many of his constitutional crimes during his first few months in office, at a time when one would think he would be most unlikely to get away with such illicit behavior. In fact, he committed so many unconstitutional acts so quickly during his first year in office, that Congress did not have time to process and legalize them all. This was intentional on his part, of course, as was his ploy of delaying calling Congress into session for four months.[389] The reason? It prevented any official debate over his illegalities.[390]

When Congress finally convened in July 1861, the hurried process of legitimatizing Lincoln's lawless offences took weeks, sometimes months, to complete. By then he had already committed a host of new crimes.[391] In most cases the Northern courts ignored what Lincoln was doing, or simply supported his actions in order to avoid scandal or trouble, for Lincoln had a nasty habit of hurting people who stood in his way.[392]

It was for such crimes and indecencies that legal and constitutional scholars now maintain that the Lincoln administration was the worst period for civil liberties up until then, ranking it, in fact, as one of the worst in all of American history.[393] The Yankee myth that the North's main concern in 1861 was to "maintain the nation's civil rights as laid out in the Constitution" can now be exposed for what it is: an abject falsehood, a fact proven by the words of our most Constitution-loathing president: Abraham Lincoln.[394]

Lincoln & the Union

IN GREAT PART LINCOLN WAS able to initiate war with the South because he fooled the Northern people into believing that the Union was meant to be **"perpetual,"** and that, therefore, secession was illegal. This is so, he pleaded deceptively, because perpetuity is **"implied, if not expressed, in the fundamental law of all national governments"** (including the U.S. Constitution),[395] and more importantly, he claimed, because the Union existed before the states.[396] Since his erroneous thinking on this topic did indeed help launch his War, it is worthy of closer examination.

The United States of America began as a confederation of thirteen powerful, sovereign, individual nations with a weak central government, a Union that was subordinate to those nations, or "states," as they would later be known. Indeed, the U.S. was literally referred to as the "Confederacy" from 1781 to 1789,[397] during which time its constitution was called the "Articles of Confederation."[398]

For various reasons the Articles of Confederation, our first Constitution, were eventually found wanting, leading to the Constitutional Convention of 1787, where they were replaced by the U.S. Constitution, the one we know today. Nonetheless, despite this massive judicial and legislative overhaul, our government remained a Confederate Republic and each of the states retained all of the rights originally accorded to them as individual nation-states by the Declaration of Independence and the Articles of Confederation—and later by the U.S. Constitution, and finally the Bill of Rights (see the Ninth and Tenth Amendments).

Ever the megalomaniac and demagogue, after being elected president, dictatorial Lincoln decided that this important portion of

American history never occurred! In doing so he ignored the fact that the U.S. began as a Confederacy, which by definition means that the states are superior to the Union, the Union inferior to the states. This obviously means, in turn, that the Union *could not* exist without the states, but that the states *could* exist without the Union. For the states came first, *then* the Union, an entity that was formed by the states. This is why our nation was seen at the time not as the United States, but rather as the "States United,"[399] a vitally important distinction.

Lincoln reversed all of this by insisting, impossibly, that **"the Union created the states,"** that they were indeed the **"*United States*,"**[400] even declaring, as he did in the Gettysburg Address, that:

> Four score and seven years ago our fathers brought forth on this continent, a new nation . . .[401]

But by declaring its independence from Britain in 1776 a **"new nation"** was not **"brought forth."** What was eventually created was a confederacy made up of thirteen sovereign nations (that is, colonies or states).

Additionally, the word perpetual appears nowhere in the Declaration of Independence, the U.S. Constitution, or the Bill of Rights.[402]

Still, despite these facts, from his own twisted mind Lincoln extrapolated that, allegedly based on the Constitution, there could be no states without the Union, and that the Union was meant to be **"perpetual."** Here, on March 4, 1861, is how he phrased these silly, confused, and ultimately dangerous ideas in his First Inaugural Address:

> I hold that, in contemplation of universal law, and of the Constitution, the Union of these States is perpetual. Perpetuity is implied, if not expressed, in the fundamental law of all national governments. It is safe to assert that no government proper ever had a provision in its organic law for its own termination. Continue to execute all the express provisions of our national Constitution, and the Union will endure forever—it being impossible to destroy it, except by some action not provided for in the instrument itself.
>
> Again, if the United States be not a government proper, but an association of States in the nature of contract merely, can it, as a contract, be peaceably unmade, by less than all the parties who made it? One

party to a contract may violate it—break it, so to speak; but does it not require all to lawfully rescind it?

Descending from these general principles, we find the proposition that, in legal contemplation, the Union is perpetual, confirmed by the history of the Union itself. The Union is much older than the Constitution. It was formed in fact by the Articles of Association in 1774. It was matured and continued by the Declaration of Independence in 1776. It was further matured, and the faith of all the then thirteen States expressly plighted and engaged that it should be perpetual, by the Articles of Confederation in 1778. And, finally, in 1787, one of the declared objects for ordaining and establishing the Constitution, was '*to form a more perfect Union.*'

But if the destruction of the Union, by one, or by a part only, of the States, be lawfully possible, the Union is *less* perfect than before, the Constitution having lost the vital element of perpetuity.

It follows, from these views, that no State, upon its own mere motion, can lawfully get out of the Union; that *resolves* and *ordinances* to that effect are legally void, and that acts of violence, within any State or States, against the authority of the United States, are insurrectionary or revolutionary, according to circumstances.

I, therefore, consider that, in view of the Constitution and the laws, the Union is unbroken, and, to the extent of my ability, I shall take care, as the Constitution itself expressly enjoins upon me, that the laws of the Union be faithfully executed in all the States.[403]

The ignorance and arrogance behind these comments would not be so appalling if they had come from an illiterate 19th-Century common laborer. What makes them truly shocking is that they came from an intelligent and successful lawyer, a man who should have known better; the man who became our sixteenth president.[404]

In 1866 pro-South advocate Edward A. Pollard artfully expressed the conservative South's reaction to this liberal nonsense:

> In his message, Mr. Lincoln announced a great political discovery. It was that all former statesmen of America had lived, and written,

and labored under a great delusion: that the States, instead of having created the Union, were its *creatures*; that they obtained their sovereignty and independence from it, and never possessed either until the [Constitutional] Convention of 1787. This singular doctrine of consolidation was the natural preface to a series of measures to strengthen the Government, to enlarge the Executive power, and to conduct the war with new decision, and on a most unexpected scale of magnitude.[405]

Pollard was entirely correct. Lincoln went on to use his fictitious ideas to grow the Federal government and help justify crushing personal liberties across the country, both South and North, severely damaging civil rights, as John C. Breckinridge of Kentucky pointed out:

> The atrocious doctrine is announced by the President, and acted upon, that the States derive their power from the Federal Government, and may be suppressed on any pretence of military necessity. Everywhere the civil has given way to the military power.[406]

Lincoln's personal beliefs, that the states could not exist without the Union and that the Union was meant to be **"perpetual,"** must certainly rank as two of the most preposterous and historically inaccurate ideas ever put forth. Why? Because as any first-year American history student knows, *the Union did not exist prior to the states*. It only came afterward as a result of its creation by those states, at which point the thirteen original colonies legally and voluntary joined it.

Why then, some counter, did the Founding Fathers begin the Preamble of the U.S. Constitution with the words "We the people of the United States . . ." if they did not intend to create a nation of one people?

As we saw in Chapter 2, the answer is that these were not the original opening words of the Preamble.[407] The first draft reads:

> We, the people of the States of New Hampshire, Massachusetts, Rhode Island and Providence Plantations, Connecticut, New York, New Jersey, Pennsylvania, Delaware, Maryland, Virginia, North Carolina, South Carolina, and Georgia, do ordain, declare and establish, the following Constitution, for the government of ourselves and our posterity.[408]

Here the thirteen original nation-states are listed as individual entities.

These were only later replaced with the phrase "We the people" due to an issue of timing.[409]

With that problem settled, it is plain to see that the right to voluntarily enter a union gives one the right to voluntarily leave a union as well. This idea, being the very marrow of the rights of both accession and secession, decimates Lincoln's conviction that the Union, and by extension the Constitution, were meant to be **"perpetual."**

Eighty years earlier, in his pamphlet *Notes on the State of Virginia* (authored during the years 1781 and 1782), Thomas Jefferson wrote of the formation of America's first government by the colonies, noting that

> . . . they organized the government by the ordinance entitled a Constitution . . . . it does not say, that it shall be perpetual; that it shall be unalterable . . .[410]

Jefferson goes on to refute those who had wrongly declared that both the Constitution and the Union were meant to be everlasting:

> Not only the silence of the instrument is a proof they [i.e., the legislatures] thought it would be alterable, but their own practice also: for this very convention, meeting as a House of Delegates in General Assembly with the new Senate in the autumn of that year, passed acts of assembly in contradiction to their ordinance of government; and every assembly from that time to this has done the same. I am safe therefore in the position, that the constitution itself is alterable by the ordinary legislature. Though this opinion seems founded on the first elements of common sense, yet is the contrary maintained by some persons. First, because, say they, the conventions were vested with every power necessary to make effectual opposition to Great-Britain. But to complete this argument, they must go on, and say further, that effectual opposition could not be made to Great-Britain, without establishing a form of government perpetual and unalterable by the legislature; which is not true. An opposition which at some time or other was to come to an end, could not need a perpetual institution to carry it on: and a government, amendable as its defects should be discovered, was as likely to make effectual resistance, as one which should be unalterably wrong. Besides, the assemblies were as much vested with all powers requisite for resistance as the conventions were. If, therefore, these powers included that of modelling the form of government in the one case, they did so in the other. The assemblies then as well as the conventions may model the government; that is, they may alter the ordinance of

government.[411]

From this it is evident that, because of the right of secession, the Union was not, is not, and could not be perpetual. The same is true of the original Constitution: because of the right of legislative amendments, it was not and is not meant to be perpetual. And the Constitution now possesses twenty-seven Amendments added to it since its creation to prove it.[412] The only thing that *was* meant to be perpetual was the constitutional sovereignty of the states, the very thing that Lincoln despised and tried to destroy by illegally invading the South!

Our sixteenth president reenforced his great lie about the Union by constantly driving home the erroneous notion that the secession of the Southern states was pushing the U.S. toward certain death and destruction; that it would **"perish from the earth,"** as he put it in his infamous Gettysburg Address.[413]

When it came to this particular theme his hyperbole reached appalling heights, such as when he delivered addresses to several Ohio Regiments. The first was given to the 164th on August 18, 1864:

> Soldiers: You are about to return to your homes and your friends, after having, as I learn, performed in camp a comparatively short term of duty in this great contest. I am greatly obliged to you, and to all who have come forward at the call of their country. I wish it might be more generally and universally understood what the country is now engaged in. We have, as all will agree, a free government, where every man has a right to be equal with every other man. In this great struggle, this form of government and every form of human right is endangered if our enemies succeed. There is more involved in this contest than is realized by every one. There is involved in this struggle the question whether your children and my children shall enjoy the privileges we have enjoyed. I say this in order to impress upon you, if you are not already so impressed, that no small matter should divert us from our great purpose.
>
> There may be some inequalities in the practical application of our system. It is fair that each man shall pay taxes in exact proportion to the value of his property; but if we should wait, before collecting a tax, to adjust the taxes upon each man in exact proportion with every other man, we should never collect any tax at

all. There may be mistakes made sometimes; things may be done wrong, while the officers of the government do all they can to prevent mistakes. But I beg of you, as citizens of this great republic, not to let your minds be carried off from the great work we have before us. This struggle is too large for you to be diverted from it by any small matter. When you return to your homes, rise up to the height of a generation of men worthy of a free government, and we will carry out the great work we have commenced. I return to you my sincere thanks, soldiers, for the honor you have done me this afternoon.[414]

In this speech Lincoln pretends that the **"free government"** of the United States is under threat due to the creation of the Southern Confederacy. He ends by thanking his soldiers for the honor they have done, not to their country, but to Lincoln himself, another overt indication that the president did not truly see the conflict as a **"Civil War,"** as he disingenuously and continually referred to it,[415] but as his own personal struggle. It truly was "Lincoln's War," an illegal invasion to implement his socialistic program, the American System.

Lincoln gave a similar address to the 166th Ohio Regiment on August 22, 1864:

> Soldiers: I suppose you are going home to see your families and friends. For the services you have done in this great struggle in which we are all engaged, I present you sincere thanks for myself and the country.
>
> I almost always feel inclined, when I happen to say anything to soldiers, to impress upon them, in a few brief remarks, the importance of success in this contest. It is not merely for to-day, but for all time to come, that we should perpetuate for our children's children that great and free government which we have enjoyed all our lives. I beg you to remember this, not merely for my sake, but for yours. I happen, temporarily, to occupy this White House. I am a living witness that any one of your children may look to come here as my father's child has. It is in order that each one of you may have, through this free government which we have enjoyed, an open field and a fair chance for your industry, enterprise, and intelligence; that you may all have equal privileges in the race of life, with all its desirable human aspirations. It is

for this the struggle should be maintained, that we may not lose our birthright—not only for one, but for two or three years. The nation is worth fighting for, to secure such an inestimable jewel.[416]

Lincoln claims here that his **"inestimable jewel,"** that is, a free government wherein everyone is equal, is at the root of the War. However, here is what he said in September 1859, just a year before he was elected president:

> **Negro equality! Fudge!! How long, in the Government of a God great enough to make and maintain this universe, shall there continue [to be] knaves to vend and fools to gulp, so low a piece of demagoguism as this?**[417]

On August 21, 1858, during one of his debates with Stephen A. Douglas at Ottawa, Illinois, Lincoln not only agreed with his opponent's call for continued white supremacy, he also complained that he had been misrepresented as having promoted interracial marriage. In response, he angrily denied the charge, saying that he had never intended to **"set the niggers and white people to marry together."**[418] As if to try and put a permanent period on this sentiment, at the same debate Lincoln declared:

> **. . . this is the true complexion of all I have ever said in regard to the institution of slavery and the black race. This is the whole of it, and anything that argues me into this idea of perfect, social, and political equality with the negro, is but a specious and fantastic arrangement of words, by which a man can prove a horse chestnut to be a chestnut horse.**[419]

He also took the time to answer Douglas' charge that he was trying to establish racial equality with this remark:

> **I had no thought in the world that I was doing anything to bring about a political and social equality of the black and white races.**[420]

On October 18, 1858, from Springfield, Illinois, Lincoln wrote a letter to one J. N. Brown. Impatient with those who continually questioned and misunderstood him, the exasperated president again expanded on his racial feelings:

> I do not perceive how I can express myself, more plainly, than I have done . . . I have expressly disclaimed all intention to bring about social and political equality between the white and black races . . . I say . . . that Congress, which lays the foundations of society, should . . . be strongly opposed to the incorporation of slavery among its elements. But it does not follow that social and political equality between whites and blacks, must be incorporated . . .[421]

A third speech, this one to the 148th Ohio Regiment, came on August 31, 1864:

> I am most happy to meet you on this occasion. I understand that it has been your honorable privilege to stand, for a brief period, in the defense of your country, and that now you are on your way to your homes. I congratulate you, and those who are waiting to bid you welcome home from the war; and permit me in the name of the people to thank you for the part you have taken in this struggle for the life of the nation. You are soldiers of the republic, everywhere honored and respected. Whenever I appear before a body of soldiers, I feel tempted to talk to them of the nature of the struggle in which we are engaged. I look upon it as an attempt on the one hand to overwhelm and destroy the national existence, while on our part we are striving to maintain the government and institutions of our fathers, to enjoy them ourselves, and transmit them to our children and our children's children forever.
>
> To do this the constitutional administration of our government must be sustained, and I beg of you not to allow your minds or your hearts to be diverted from the support of all necessary measures for that purpose, by any miserable picayune arguments addressed to your pockets, or inflammatory appeals made to your passions and your prejudices.
>
> It is vain and foolish to arraign this man or that for the part he has taken or has not taken, and to hold the government responsible for his acts. In no administration can there be perfect equality of action and uniform satisfaction rendered by all.

But this government must be preserved in spite of the acts of any man or set of men. It is worthy of your every effort. Nowhere in the world is presented a government of so much liberty and equality. To the humblest and poorest amongst us are held out the highest privileges and positions. The present moment finds me at the White House, yet there is as good a chance for your children as there was for my father's.

Again I admonish you not to be turned from your stern purpose of defending our beloved country and its free institutions by any arguments urged by ambitious and designing men, but to stand fast for the Union and the old flag. Soldiers, I bid you God-speed to your homes.[422]

As always, Lincoln's speech overflows with misinformation and disinformation, purposefully laid before both his soldiers and the public to seduce and mislead.

He begins by stating that Southerners are attempting **"to overwhelm and destroy the national existence."** The South was actually trying to preserve the national existence: a *voluntary* Union comprised of all-powerful sovereign states overseeing a small weak central government. It was the North that was trying to destroy this.

Lincoln then says that he and his fellow Northerners **"are striving to maintain the government and institutions of our fathers, to enjoy them ourselves, and transmit them to our children and our children's children forever."** In truth, they were seeking the destruction of the government and institutions of the Founding Fathers, for it gave all the power and authority to the states and almost none to the central government, a liberal's worst nightmare.

Lincoln says that in order to preserve the Union, **"the constitutional administration of our government must be sustained."** Yet he consciously, and with clear intent, violated the Constitution at nearly every turn, flagrantly disregarding one article, section, clause, and amendment after another.

He goes on to pronounce the fact that **"nowhere in the world is presented a government of so much liberty and equality."** How true. But why did Lincoln boast about this, then try to undermine and restrict those liberties while blocking equal rights for African-Americans, Native-Americans, women, and other minorities?[423]

The president closes by admonishing the soldiers of the 148th **"to**

stand fast for the Union and the old flag." Yet it was he himself who was tearing apart the Union and desecrating the U.S. flag by illegally invading the Southern Confederacy.

What Lincoln called an **"inestimable jewel"**—that is, a free government based on constitutional liberties and equal rights for all—was a sham then, a euphemism to conceal the real cause of the War, as we will discover in our next chapter.[424]

Lincoln & the Cause of the War

YANKEE MYTHOLOGY HAS LONG TAUGHT us that the "Civil War" was fought over slavery, that Lincoln went into battle against the "evil South" to emancipate the slaves.

The truth, from Lincoln's own mouth, is quite the opposite. Actually, the Northern president gave several reasons for going to war with the Confederacy. None of them had anything to do with slavery, particularly *Southern* slavery, for slavery was still very much alive in the North (which still owned some 500,000[425] to 1 million working slaves),[426] as Lincoln himself acknowledged in November 1861,[427] and again on March 6, 1862, when he made reference to **"the slave States north . . . of the existing insurrection . . ."**[428]

First and foremost the conflict for Lincoln was about money. Here is how he phrased his monetary concerns on July 4, 1861, during his "Message to Congress in Special Session":

> What is now combated is the position that secession is consistent with the Constitution—is lawful and peaceful. It is not contended that there is any express law for it; and nothing should ever be implied as law which leads to unjust or absurd consequences. The nation purchased with money the countries out of which several of these States were formed. Is it just that they shall go off without leave and without refunding? The nation paid very large sums (in the aggregate, I believe, nearly a hundred millions) to relieve Florida of the aboriginal

tribes. Is it just that she shall now be off without consent or without making any return? The nation is now in debt for money applied to the benefit of these so-called seceding States in common with the rest. Is it just either that creditors shall go unpaid or the remaining States pay the whole? A part of the present national debt was contracted to pay the old debts of Texas. Is it just that she shall leave and pay no part of this herself?

Again, if one State may secede, so may another; and when all shall have seceded, none is left to pay the debts. Is this quite just to creditors? Did we notify them of this sage view of ours when we borrowed their money? If we now recognize this doctrine by allowing the seceders to go in peace, it is difficult to see what we can do if others choose to go or to extort terms upon which they will promise to remain.

The seceders insist that our Constitution admits of secession. They have assumed to make a national constitution of their own, in which of necessity they have either discarded or retained the right of secession as they insist it exists in ours. If they have discarded it, they thereby admit that on principle it ought not to be in ours. If they have retained it by their own construction of ours, they show that to be consistent they must secede from one another whenever they shall find it the easiest way of settling their debts, or effecting any other selfish or unjust object. The principle itself is one of disintegration, and upon which no government can possibly endure.[429]

During a speech he gave in Indianapolis, Indiana, on February 12, 1861, just two months before launching his War at Fort Sumter, Lincoln deflects criticisms that he is considering using **"coercion"** to **"invade"** the South. It is not an invasion, he states, as long as all the U.S. does is **"collect the duties on foreign importations"**:

> The words "coercion" and "invasion" are much used in these days, and often with some temper and hot blood. Let us make sure, if we can, that we do not misunderstand the meaning of those who use them. Let us get exact definitions of these words, not from dictionaries, but from the men themselves, who certainly deprecate the things they would represent by the use of words. What, then, is "coercion"? What is "invasion"?

> Would the marching of an army into South Carolina without the consent of her people, and with hostile intent toward them, be "invasion"? I certainly think it would; and it would be "coercion" also if the South Carolinians were forced to submit. But if the United States should merely hold and retake its own forts and other property, and collect the duties on foreign importations, or even withhold the mails from places where they were habitually violated, would any or all of these things be "invasion" or "coercion"?[430]

If there is any doubt as to Lincoln's meaning here, let us consider a meeting that Confederate Colonel John Brown Baldwin had with Lincoln shortly after he became president. It was at this time (early 1861) that Baldwin traveled from Virginia to the White House to meet with the new chief executive to confer upon the War. Why can the North not allow the South to go in peace? the Colonel asked, to which Lincoln replied:

> **If I let the South go on what will become of my tariff?**[431]

Lincoln had a similar conversation with Southern peace commissioner Alexander H. Stuart. Just prior to the War several Southern peace commissioners had an interview with the newly sworn in president in an attempt to avoid the coming bloodbath. At the meeting Stuart pleaded for time and further discussions, to which Lincoln replied impatiently:

> **If I do that** [that is, recognize the Southern Confederacy], **what will become of my revenue? I might as well shut up housekeeping at once.**[432]

On March 18, 1861, now less than three weeks before the opening of the conflict, Lincoln furiously sent off a number of notes to his cabinet members. But it was not the coming battle that concerned him. It was the **"duties"** and **"revenue."** Here, for example, is what he wrote to his Secretary of the Treasury Salmon P. Chase:

> Sir: I shall be obliged if you will inform me whether any goods, wares, and merchandise subject by law to the payment of duties, are now being imported into the United States without such duties being paid or secured according to law. And if yea, at what place or places, and for what cause, do such duties remain unpaid or

unsecured?

> I will also thank you for your opinion whether, as a matter of fact, vessels off shore could be effectively used to prevent such importations, or to enforce the payment or securing of the duties. If yea, what number and description of vessels in addition to those already in the revenue service would be requisite? Your obedient servant, A. Lincoln.[433]

Lincoln's Secretary of the Navy Gideon Welles received this message from the president:

> Sir: I shall be obliged if you will inform me what amount of naval force you could at once place at the control of the revenue service, and also whether at some distance of time you could so place an additional force, and how much? and at what time? Your obedient servant, A. Lincoln.[434]

Attorney General Edward Bates was sent this note from Lincoln, also on the same day:

> Sir: I shall be obliged if you will give me your opinion in writing whether, under the Constitution and existing laws, the executive has power to collect duties on shipboard off shore in cases where their collection in the ordinary way is by any cause rendered impracticable. This would include the question of lawful power to prevent the landing of dutiable goods unless the duties were paid. Your obedient servant, A. Lincoln.[435]

As America's bloodiest homeland military campaign was about to explode across the nation, all Lincoln could think about were **"duties"** and the **"revenue."**

Even midway through his War Lincoln could not keep himself from publicly discussing his true motivation for trying to force the South back into the Union: money. In his December 1, 1862, "Message to Congress," for instance, he angrily claims that the secession of the Southern states will lead to **"onerous trade regulations and tolls"**:

> **But there is another difficulty** [that would result from the separation of North and South]. **The great interior region,**

bounded east by the Alleghanies, north by the British dominions, west by the Rocky Mountains, and south by the line along which the culture of corn and cotton meets, and which includes part of Virginia, part of Tennessee, all of Kentucky, Ohio, Indiana, Michigan, Wisconsin, Illinois, Missouri, Kansas, Iowa, Minnesota, and the Territories of Dakota, Nebraska, and part of Colorado, already has above ten millions of people, and will have fifty millions within fifty years if not prevented by any political folly or mistake. It contains more than one third of the country owned by the United States—certainly more than one million of square miles. Once half as populous as Massachusetts already is, it would have more than seventy-five millions of people. A glance at the map shows that, territorially speaking, it is the great body of the republic. The other parts are but marginal borders to it, the magnificent region sloping west from the Rocky Mountains to the Pacific being the deepest and also the richest in undeveloped resources. In the production of provisions, grains, grasses, and all which proceed from them, this great interior region is naturally one of the most important in the world. Ascertain from the statistics the small proportion of the region which has, as yet, been brought into cultivation, and also the large and rapidly increasing amount of its products, and we shall be overwhelmed with the magnitude of the prospect presented; and yet this region has no sea-coast, touches no ocean anywhere. As part of one nation, its people now find, and may forever find, their way to Europe by New York, to South America and Africa by New Orleans, and to Asia by San Francisco. But separate our common country into two nations, as designed by the present rebellion, and every man of this great interior region is thereby cut off from some one or more of these outlets—not, perhaps, by a physical barrier, but by embarrassing and onerous trade regulations.

And this is true wherever a dividing or boundary line may be fixed. Place it between the now free and slave country, or place it south of Kentucky or north of Ohio, and still the truth remains that none south of it can trade to any port or place north of it, and none north of it can trade to any port or place south of it, except upon terms dictated by a government foreign to them. These outlets, east, west, and south, are indispensable to the well-being of the people inhabiting, and to inhabit, this vast interior region. Which of the three may be the best, is no proper question. All are better than either; and all of right belong to that people and to their successors forever. True to themselves, they will not ask where a line of separation shall be, but will vow rather that there shall be no such line. Nor are the marginal regions less interested in these communications to and through them to the great outside world. They, too, and each of them, must have access to this Egypt of the West without paying toll at the crossing of any national boundary.[436]

On September 24, 1863, when Lincoln finally lifted his illegal naval blockade from the port at Alexandria, Virginia, it was not for the benefit of the longsuffering people of Virginia. It was for the express purpose of allowing the U.S. government to once again begin **"the collection of duties on imports."**[437] This is the same man who, on June 29, 1863, told William Kellogg that **"profit controls all."**[438]

In Lincoln's case at least, no truer words were ever spoken, as the following from his December 8, 1863, Annual Message to Congress illustrates:

> The receipts during the year from all sources, including loans and the balance in the treasury at its commencement, were $901,125,674.86, and the aggregate disbursements $895,796,630.65, leaving a balance on the 1st of July, 1863, of $5,329,044.21. Of the receipts there were derived from customs $69,059,642.40; from internal revenue, $37,640,787.95; from direct tax, $1,485,103.61; from lands, $167,617.17; from miscellaneous sources, $3,046,615.35; and from loans, $776,682,361.57; making the aggregate, $901,125,674.86. Of the disbursements there were for the civil service, $23,253,922.08; for pensions and Indians, $4,216,520.79; for interest on public debt, $24,729,846.51; for the War Department, $599,298,600.83; for the Navy Department, $63,211,105.27; for payment of funded and temporary debt, $181,086,635.07; making the aggregate, $895,796,630.65, and leaving the balance of $5,329,044.21. But the payments of funded and temporary debt, having been made from moneys borrowed during the year, must be regarded as merely nominal payments, and the moneys borrowed to make them as merely nominal receipts; and their amount, $181,086,635.07,

should therefore be deducted both from receipts and disbursements. This being done, there remain as actual receipts, $720,039,039.79, and the actual disbursements, $714,709,995.58, leaving the balance as already stated.

. . . During the past fiscal year the financial condition of the Post Office Department has been one of increasing prosperity, and I am gratified in being able to state that the actual postal revenue has nearly equaled the entire expenditures; the latter amounting to $11,314,206.84, and the former to $11,163,789.59, leaving a deficiency of but $150,417.25. In 1860, the year immediately preceding the rebellion, the deficiency amounted to $5,656,705.49, the postal receipts of that year being $2 645,722.19 less than those of 1863. The decrease since 1860 in the annual amount of transportation has been only about 25 per cent., but the annual expenditure on account of the same has been reduced 35 per cent. It is manifest, therefore, that the Post Office Department may become self-sustaining in a few years even with the restoration of the whole service.[439]

Lincoln's Annual Message to Congress on December 6, 1864, contained the same economic focus:

The financial affairs of the government have been successfully administered during the last year. The legislation of the last session of Congress has beneficially affected the revenues, although sufficient time has not yet elapsed to experience the full effect of several of the provisions of the acts of Congress imposing increased taxation.

The receipts during the year, from all sources, upon the basis of warrants signed by the Secretary of the Treasury, including loans and the balance in the treasury on the first day of July, 1863, were $1,394,796,007.62, and the aggregate disbursements, upon the same basis, were $1,298,056,101.89, leaving a balance in the treasury, as shown by warrants, of $96,739,905.73.

Deduct from these amounts the amount of the principal of the public debt redeemed, and the amount of issues in substitution therefor, and the actual cash operations of the treasury were: receipts, $884,076,646.57; disbursements, $865,234,087.86, which leaves a cash balance in the treasury of $18,842,558.71.

Of the receipts, there were derived from customs, $102,316,152.99; from lands, $588,333.29; from direct taxes, $475,648.96; from internal revenue, $109,741,134.10; from miscellaneous sources, $47,511,448.10; and from loans applied to actual expenditures, including former balance, $623,443,929.13.

There were disbursed for the civil service, $27,505,599.46; for pensions and Indians, $7,517,930.97; for the War Department, $690,791,842.97; for the Navy Department, $85,733,292.77; for interest on the public debt, $53,685,421.69,—making an aggregate of $865,234,087.86, and leaving a balance in the treasury of $18,842,558.71, as before stated.

For the actual receipts and disbursements for the first quarter, and the estimated receipts and disbursements for the three remaining quarters of the current fiscal year, and the general operations of the treasury in detail, I refer you to the report of the Secretary of the Treasury. I concur with him in the opinion that the proportion of moneys required to meet the expenses consequent upon the war derived from taxation should be still further increased; and I earnestly invite your attention to this subject, to the end that there may be such additional legislation as shall be required to meet the just expectations of the Secretary.

The public debt on the first day of July last, as appears by the books of the treasury, amounted to $1,740,690,489.49. Probably, should the war continue for another year, that amount may be increased by not far from $500,000,000. Held as it is, for the most part, by our own people, it has become a substantial branch of national though private property. For obvious reasons, the more nearly this property can be distributed among all the people, the better. To favor such general distribution, greater inducements to become owners might, perhaps, with good effect, and without injury, be presented to persons of limited means. With this view, I suggest whether it might not be both competent and expedient for Congress to provide that a limited amount of some future issue of public securities might be held by any bona-fide purchaser exempt from taxation, and from seizure for debt under such restrictions and limitations as might be necessary to guard against abuse of so important a privilege. This would enable every prudent person to set aside a small annuity against a possible day of want.

        Privileges like these would render the possession of such securities, to the amount limited, most desirable to every person of small means who might be able to save enough for the purpose. The great advantage of citizens being creditors as well as debtors, with relation to the public debt, is obvious. Men readily perceive that they cannot be much oppressed by a debt which they owe to themselves.

        The public debt on the first day of July last, although somewhat exceeding the estimate of the Secretary of the Treasury made to Congress at the commencement of the last session, falls short of the estimate of that officer made in the preceding December, as to its probable amount at the beginning of this year, by the sum of $3,995,097.31. This fact exhibits a satisfactory condition and conduct of the operations of the treasury.[440]

In a December 12, 1864, letter to Union General Edward R. S. Canby, Lincoln discusses his illegal naval blockade across the South, but only in monetary terms:

> As to cotton. By the external blockade, the price is made certainly six times as great as it was. And yet the enemy gets through at least one-sixth part as much in a given period, say a year, as if there were no blockade, and receives as much for it as he would for a full crop in time of peace. The effect, in substance, is, that we give him six ordinary crops without the trouble of producing any but the first; and at the same time leave his fields and his laborers free to produce provisions. You know how this keeps up his armies at home and procures supplies from abroad. For other reasons we cannot give up the blockade, and hence it becomes immensely important to us to get the cotton away from him. Better give him guns for it than let him, as now, get both guns and ammunition for it. But even this only presents part of the public interest to get out cotton. Our finances are greatly involved in the matter. The way cotton goes now carries so much gold out of the country as to leave us paper currency only, and that so far depreciated as that for every hard dollar's worth of supplies we obtain, we contract to pay two and a half hard dollars hereafter.

This is much to be regretted; and, while I believe we can live through it, at all events it demands an earnest effort on the part of all to correct it. And if pecuniary greed can be made to aid us in such effort, let us be thankful that so much good can be got out of pecuniary greed.[441]

The lust for money, and the control and power that went along with it, was obviously always Lincoln's primary interest, which is why there can be no question that it was at the heart of his hidden purpose for waging war on the South. For money is at the root of all wars.

But such a purpose sounded too crass, even for the ordinarily crass Lincoln. Thus he had to couch the Northern Cause in more elegant terms, and in a more heroic guise. This need was ably fulfilled in the impossibly ridiculous notion that he was **"maintaining the unity and the free principles of our common country"**[442] in this **"life-and-death struggle of the nation."**[443] Or, as he put it more succinctly, the South needed to be conquered in order to **"preserve the Union."**[444]

Up to his final days Lincoln maintained that this was the only reason the North had gone to war against the South. In his last public address, for instance, he mentions slavery only once, but goes into great detail about the rebellion and secession. In fact, he states quite clearly that the **"sole object"** of the entire conflict was bringing the Confederate states back into the United States:

> We all agree that the seceded States, so called, are out of their proper practical relation with the Union, and that the sole object of the government, civil and military, in regard to those States is to again get them into that proper practical relation.[445]

Lincoln uttered these words on April 11, 1865, just three days before he was shot.

This was no last minute statement, meant to fool the public into thinking that his War was really *not* about abolishing slavery. Over a year earlier, on June 16, 1864, at a "Sanitary Fair" in Philadelphia, Pennsylvania, Lincoln said:

> We accepted this war for an object, a worthy object, and the war will end when that object is attained. Under God, I hope it never will end until that time. Speaking of the present campaign, General [Ulysses S.] **Grant is**

reported to have said, "I am going through on this line if it takes all summer." This war has taken three years; it was begun or accepted upon the line of restoring the national authority over the whole national domain, and for the American people, as far as my knowledge enables me to speak, I say we are going through on this line if it takes three years more.[446]

Dictator Lincoln states it quite clearly here that his sole object in the War is **"restoring the national authority over the whole national domain."**

In a July 23, 1864, letter to Commander Bertinatti, an Italian Envoy, Lincoln makes a nearly identical comment, asserting that in **"this unhappy fraternal war"** the United States is **"only endeavoring to save and strengthen the foundations of our national unity . . ."**[447]

Like the president of the Union, the president of the Confederacy, Jefferson Davis, was also adamant about the real cause of the War—and it was not slavery:

> The truth remains intact and incontrovertible, that the existence of African servitude was in no wise the cause of the conflict, but only an incident. In the later controversies that arose, however, its effect in operating as a lever upon the passions, prejudices, or sympathies of mankind, was so potent that it has been spread like a thick cloud over the whole horizon of historic truth.[448]

As all Southerners knew and understood, they were fighting for the right of self-determination, for freedom of choice—in the end, to do as they pleased regarding politics, taxes, railroads, exporting, and every other aspect of human society. This included slavery of course, for unlike authoritarian Northerners (who demanded that everyone think and act one way: their way), Southerners wanted the personal liberty to decide whether to own slaves or not own them.

Although Lincoln was not among them, even some Northerners recognized this simple fact. One of them, Illinois Senator Stephen A. Douglas, said the following on October 15, 1858:

> The whole South is rallying to the support of the doctrine that if the people of a Territory want slavery they have a right to have it, and if they do not want it that no power on earth can force it upon them.[449]

Tragically, after issuing his Final Emancipation Proclamation in 1863, Lincoln falsely tried to alter the character of his War from one about money and **"preserving the Union"** to one about abolition. For by January of that year it suited his agenda to disrupt slavery in the South, the very thing he had promised not to do in his First Inaugural Address.

However, few were fooled by this conspicuous political scheming: as Lincoln was a well-known anti-abolitionist, the entire North knew that the War and slavery were not connected—and it would have been extremely unhappy if it were otherwise. In speaking for nearly all Federal soldiers, Yankee General Ulysses S. Grant, an Ohio slave owner[450] and black colonizationist[451] who kept his slaves until eight months *after* the War was over,[452] is said to have once declared:

> The sole object of this war is to restore the union. Should I be convinced it has any other object, or that the government designs using its soldiers to execute the wishes of the Abolitionists, I pledge to you my honor as a man and a soldier. I would resign my commission and carry my sword to the other side.[453]

Most Northern newspapers too understood the publicly heralded foundations of the conflict. On October 8, 1861, Washington, D.C.'s *National Intelligencer* wrote:

> The existing war has no direct relation to slavery. It is a war for the restoration of the Union under the existing Constitution.[454]

Confederate soldiers were of the exact same mind. After the War, Rebel Moses Jacob Ezekiel, one of 12,000 Jews who fought for the Confederacy[455] against anti-Semites Lincoln and Grant,[456] spoke on behalf of every Southern military man, saying: we did not fight to maintain slavery. We fought for states' rights, free trade, and in defense of our families, homes, and land.[457] Confederate Colonel Joseph F. Burke declared similarly:

> It has often been said that we were fighting for the perpetuation of slavery. This was not so. We were simply fighting for our right to keep slaves if we wanted to. We were fighting for State rights—rights to be allowed to make our laws for our particular States.[458]

In 1863, in her wonderful pro-South work *My Imprisonment and the First Year of Abolition Rule at Washington*, famed Confederate female spy Rose O'Neal Greenhow wrote:

> It is not my purpose to elucidate the causes which have brought about the downfall of the American Republic. I do not pretend to the character of a publicist, or that of a philosophical historian. But as an attentive, and, I trust, impartial observer, I think I can correct some grave misconceptions of the events which have gained credence.
>
> In the first place, slavery, although the occasion, was not the producing cause of the dissolution. The cord which bound the sections together was strained beyond its strength, and, of course, snapped at the point where the fretting of the strands was greatest.
>
> The contest on the part of the North was for supreme control, especially in relation to the fiscal action of the Government. This object could not be fully attained by a mere numerical majority. A majority of States was also necessary. To secure this majority, and thus complete the political ascendency of the North, the policy of 'no more Slave States' was formally set forth.
>
> A political party was formed, whose sole principle was the exclusion of slavery from the territories. There was no moral sentiment involved in this. It did not alter the status of slavery. It made not a human being free; nor did it propose to do so. 'Sir,' said Mr. [Daniel] Webster in the Senate, 'this is not a moral question: it is a question of political power.' Lord [John] Russell has more recently corroborated this bold assertion, by saying, that 'this was a struggle on one side for supremacy, and on the other for independence.'
>
> On the other hand, the Southern States, struggling for equality, and seeking to maintain the equilibrium of the Government, insisted upon the rights of their citizens to enter and live in the new territories upon terms of equality with the men north of Mason and Dixon's line. They contended for the right of extending their social institutions, not to propagate slavery—not to make a single human being a slave that would otherwise be free—but simply to preserve the equilibrium of power between the two sections.
>
> It is true that the anti-slavery fanaticism was brought to bear; and it is also true that there followed a rancorous agitation which divided churches, rent asunder political parties, diminished and embittered the intercourse of society, and unfitted Congress for the performance of its constitutional duties, and resulted in the

estrangement of the Southern people from their Northern connection. But this estrangement was not an active or stimulating motive, and manifested itself rather in the want of any general anxiety to restrain the movement for disunion.[459]

Southern citizens were indeed keenly aware of the Confederate Cause, as it was called. Even Lincoln was forced to acknowledge this, as he did in an October 26, 1864, letter to J. R. Underwood and Henry Grider:

> A petition has been presented to me on behalf of certain citizens of Allen and Barren counties, in the State of Kentucky, assuming that certain sums of money have been assessed and collected from them by the United States military authorities to compensate certain Union citizens of the same vicinage for losses by rebel depredations, and praying that I will order the money to be refunded. The petition is accompanied by a letter of yours, which so presents the case as to induce me to make a brief response. You distinctly admit that the petitioners "sympathize with the Confederate States and regard them as warring to preserve their Constitutional and legal rights." . . .[460]

The U.S. Congress generally agreed with Greenhow, Burke, and Ezekiel as to the purpose of Lincoln's War. Shortly after the start of the conflict, on July 22, 1861, it released a declaration stating that the Union's intention for going to war with the South was not for the

> purpose of overthrowing or interfering with the rights or established institutions [i.e., slavery] of those States; but to defend and maintain the supremacy of the Constitution and to preserve the Union with all the dignity, equality, and rights of the several States unimpaired; that as soon as these objects are accomplished, the war ought to cease.[461]

On January 19, 1863, several years into his War, Lincoln wrote the following to "the working-men of Manchester, England":

> I have the honor to acknowledge the receipt of the address and resolutions which you sent me on the eve of the new year. When I came, on the 4th of March, 1861, through a free and constitutional election to preside in the Government of the United States, the country was

found at the verge of civil war. Whatever might have been the cause, or whosesoever the fault, one duty, paramount to all others, was before me, namely, to maintain and preserve at once the Constitution and the integrity of the Federal Republic. A conscientious purpose to perform this duty is the key to all the measures of administration which have been and to all which will hereafter be pursued. Under our frame of government and my official oath, I could not depart from this purpose if I would. It is not always in the power of governments to enlarge or restrict the scope of moral results which follow the policies that they may deem it necessary for the public safety from time to time to adopt.[462]

Here the president states that the purpose of the War is **"to maintain and preserve at once the Constitution and the integrity of the Federal Republic,"** and that **"this duty is the key to all the measures of administration which have been and to all which will hereafter be pursued."** Lincoln was seldom so clear and direct.

On March 10, 1862, according to Maryland Representative John Woodland Crisfield, the president privately told him, along with a group of representatives from the Border States, that he

> disclaimed any intent to injure the interests or wound the sensibilities of the slave States. On the contrary, his purpose was to protect the one and respect the other . . . that emancipation was a subject exclusively under the control of the States, and must be adopted or rejected by each for itself; that he did not claim nor had this government any right to coerce them for that purpose . . .[463]

And furthermore, Crisfield continues:

> The President said he saw and felt the force of the objection [to forcing abolition on the states]; it was a fearful responsibility, and every gentleman must do as he thought best; that he did not know how this scheme was received by the members from the free States; some of them had spoken to him and received it kindly; but for the most part they were as reserved and chary as we had been, and he could not tell how they would vote. And in reply to some expression of Mr. [William Augustus] Hall [Representative of Missouri] as to his own opinion regarding slavery, he said he did not pretend to disguise his antislavery feeling; that he thought it

was wrong, and should continue to think so; but that was not the question we had to deal with now. Slavery existed, and that, too, as well by the act of the North as of the South; and in any scheme to get rid of it, the North as well as the South was morally bound to do its full and equal share. He thought the institution wrong and ought never to have existed; but yet he recognized the rights of property which had grown out of it, and would respect those rights as fully as similar rights in any other property; that property can exist, and does legally exist. He thought such a law wrong, but the rights of property resulting must be respected; he would get rid of the odious law, not by violating the right, but by encouraging the proposition and offering inducements to give it up.[464]

On April 18, 1864, during a speech at a "Sanitary Fair" in Baltimore, Maryland, Lincoln expressed surprise that slavery had been dragged into the conflict. This was over a year after he had issued his Final Emancipation Proclamation:

> **When the war began, three years ago, neither party, nor any man, expected it would last till now. . . . Neither did any anticipate that domestic slavery would be much affected by the war.**[465]

This is one of the few times we may believe Lincoln, for, as we will recall, this is the same man who used his First Inaugural Address to declare:

> **'I have no purpose, directly or indirectly, to interfere with the institution of slavery in the States where it exists. I believe I have no lawful right to do so, and I have no inclination to do so.' Those who nominated and elected me did so with full knowledge that I had made this and many similar declarations, and had never recanted them.**[466]

As late as February 13, 1865, just two months before he died, Lincoln told his commanding officers in West Tennessee that

> **the object of the war being to restore and maintain the blessings of peace and good government, I desire you to help, and not hinder, every advance in that direction.**[467]

In an unfinished letter to Isaac M. Schermerhorn, dated September

12, 1864, Lincoln writes:

> The preservation of our Union was not the sole avowed object for which the war was commenced. It was commenced for precisely the reverse object—to destroy our Union.... It is true, however, that the administration accepted the war thus commenced for the sole avowed object of preserving our Union; and it is not true that it has since been, or will be, prosecuted by this administration for any other object. In declaring this I only declare what I can know and do know to be true, and what no other man can know to be false.
>
> In taking the various steps which have led to my present position in relation to the war, the public interest and my private interest have been perfectly parallel, because in no other way could I serve myself so well as by truly serving the Union. The whole field has been open to me where to choose. No place-hunting necessity has been upon me urging me to seek a position of antagonism to some other man, irrespective of whether such position might be favorable or unfavorable to the Union.[468]

Here once more Lincoln states emphatically that **"the administration accepted the war thus commenced for the sole avowed object of preserving our Union,"** and not **"for any other object."**

On August 15, 1864, only eight months before the end of the conflict, Lincoln gave what is without question the most definitive and explicit statement regarding its cause. And again, according to our sixteenth president, it was *not* slavery:

> My enemies pretend I am now carrying on this war for the sole purpose of abolition. So long as I am President, it shall be carried on for the sole purpose of restoring the Union.... Let my enemies prove to the country that the destruction of slavery is not necessary to a restoration of the Union. I will abide the issue.[469]

Since the presidents, the congresses, and the military officers of both the U.S.A. and the C.S.A. agreed that the War was not over slavery, indeed, asserted that it was not in any way connected to slavery, is it not now time to lay this Yankee fiction to rest once and for all?

Again, Lincoln's own words on this topic are instructive. Southern partisan Albert Taylor Bledsoe recorded the following infuriating conversation with the Yankee leader:

> When asked, as President of the United States, 'why not let the South go?' his simple, direct, and honest answer revealed one secret of the wise policy of the Washington Cabinet. 'Let the South go!' said he, **'where, then, shall we get our revenue?'** There lies the secret. The Declaration of Independence is great; the voice of all the fathers is mighty; but then they yield us no revenue. The right of self government is **'a most valuable, a most sacred right;'** but in this particular case, it gives us no revenue. Hence, this **'most valuable, this most sacred right,'** may and should shine upon every other land under heaven; but here it must 'pale its ineffectual fires,' and sink into utter insignificance and contempt in the August presence of the 'ALMIGHTY DOLLAR.'[470]

Foreigners too were acutely aware that slavery had nothing to do with Lincoln's War. In their opinion it was, as Bledsoe observed, about only one thing: "the almighty dollar." German progressive and socialist Karl Marx, no friend of the conservative, anti-socialist South (but a true friend of liberal Lincoln),[471] elucidated the sentiments of much of Europe, and certainly of London, England, where he wrote the following on October 20, 1861: the American Civil War has nothing to do with slavery; only the tariff and the Yankee's lust for power and dominance.[472]

As early as 1833 Virginian John Tyler, soon to become America's tenth president, gave the Southern people's viewpoint of the Yankee tariff:

> In plain terms . . . [it is] an unwarranted extension of the powers of the government and an appeal to the numerical majority of the North to grow rich at the expense of their section.[473]

Far earlier, in the 1820s, Southern firebrand John C. Calhoun wrote that when it came to South-North tensions, the Northern tariff was always "the great central interest, around which all the others revolved."[474] No less than Woodrow Wilson, America's twenty-eighth president, would later concur with these comments. For it was very evident, he wrote in 1892, that because of the North's increasing tariff pressures on the South,

> that she was to suffer almost in direct proportion as other sections of the country gained advantage from such legislation.[475]

No wonder Lincoln was enraged over the departure of Dixie: the tariffs amounted to 95 percent of the federal revenue, and through them the South by herself had been financing 70 percent of the cost of the central government in Washington.[476] In short, an independent South would have spelled financial doom for the North.

Lincoln was not about to let this occur. He and his Northern business associates were thick as thieves, and together they were committed to recapturing the goose that laid the golden egg: the seceded Southern states.

Lincoln had Northern financial concerns as well. He wanted and needed the support of special interest groups, most importantly, the "Wall Street Boys," robber barons, and Yankee industrialists; that is, the Northern business establishment, which had bankrolled his first (and later his second) presidential campaign using money they had made primarily from the Yankee slave trade.[477]

If the South were allowed to go her own way Northern businessmen would have been financially devastated, many even bankrupted, by Dixie's insistence on low tariffs, a *laissez-faire* economy, and a free trade system. There was also the certainty that secession would shift trade from the three great Northern ports, Boston, New York City, and Philadelphia, to the Southern ports, resulting in an economic decline of the former.[478]

Yankee abolitionist, individualist, and natural rights advocate, Lysander Spooner, saw right through Lincoln's tragicomedy, correctly referring to the president's Wall Street Boys as the "lenders of blood money." As Spooner saw it:

> . . . these lenders of blood money had, for a long series of years previous to the war, been the willing accomplices of the slave-holders in perverting the government from the purposes of liberty and justice, to the greatest of crimes. They had been such accomplices *for a purely pecuniary consideration*, to wit, a control of the markets in the South; in other words, the privilege of holding the slave-holders themselves in industrial and commercial subjection to the manufacturers and merchants of the North (who afterwards furnished the money for the [Civil] war). And these Northern merchants and manufacturers, these lenders of blood money, were willing to continue to be the accomplices of the slaveholders in the future, for the same pecuniary considerations. But the slaveholders, either doubting the fidelity of their Northern allies, or feeling themselves strong enough to keep their slaves in subjection without Northern assistance, would no longer pay the

price these Northern men demanded. And it was to enforce this price in the future—that is, to monopolize the Southern markets, to maintain their industrial and commercial control over the South—that these Northern manufacturers and merchants lent some of the profits of their former monopolies for the [Civil] war, in order to secure themselves the same, or greater, monopolies in the future. These—and not any love of liberty or justice—were the motives on which the money for the [Civil] war was lent by the North.[479]

By subduing the South and forcing her to return to the Union Lincoln was able to continue imposing high tariffs on his southern neighbors who, in turn, created huge corporate profits for Yankee businessmen (which included dozens of Northern slave traders), his biggest and most important financial backers. For not only did they fund both his campaigns, but, as is clear from Spooner's observations above, they also financed the "Civil War" itself.[480] It was a self-serving symbiotic relationship that the wily Lincoln crafted and managed with the skill and finesse of a surgeon.

Liberal Lincoln's love of anti-South tariffs manifested in a myriad of ways, no more so than in his speeches and writings. He delivered the following address to a Pittsburgh, Pennsylvania, audience on February 15, 1861:

> **It is often said that the tariff is the specialty of Pennsylvania. Assuming that direct taxation is not to be adopted, the tariff question must be as durable as the government itself.** It is a question of national housekeeping. It is to the government what replenishing the meal-tub is to the family. Ever-varying circumstances will require frequent modifications as to the amount needed and the sources of supply. So far there is little difference of opinion among the people. It is as to whether, and how far, duties on imports shall be adjusted to favor home production in the home market, that **controversy begins. One party** [i.e., the Democratic party, the conservatives of the day] **insists that such adjustment oppresses one class for the advantage of another; while the other party** [i.e., Lincoln's Republican party, the liberals of the day] **argues that, with all its incidents, in the long run all classes are benefited. In the Chicago platform there is a plank upon this subject which should be a general law to the incoming administration. We should do neither more nor less than we gave the people reason to believe**

we would when they gave us their votes. Permit me, fellow-citizens, to read the tariff plank of the Chicago platform, or rather have it read in your hearing by one who has younger eyes.

Mr. Lincoln's private secretary then read Section 12 of the Chicago platform, as follows:

> "That while providing revenue for the support of the General Government by duties upon imports, sound policy requires such an adjustment of these imposts as will encourage the development of the industrial interest of the whole country; and we commend that policy of national exchanges which secures to working-men liberal wages, to agriculture remunerating prices, to mechanics and manufacturers adequate reward for their skill, labor, and enterprise, and to the nation commercial prosperity and independence."

Mr. Lincoln resumed: **As with all general propositions, doubtless there will be shades of difference in construing this. I have by no means a thoroughly matured judgment upon this subject, especially as to details; some general ideas are about all. I have long thought it would be to our advantage to produce any necessary article at home which can be made of as good quality and with as little labor at home as abroad, at least by the difference of the carrying from abroad. In such case the carrying is demonstrably a dead loss of labor. For instance, labor being the true standard of value, is it not plain that if equal labor get a bar of railroad iron out of a mine in England, and another out of a mine in Pennsylvania, each can be laid down in a track at home cheaper than they could exchange countries, at least by the carriage? If there be a present cause why one can be both made and carried cheaper in money price than the other can be made without carrying, that cause is an unnatural and injurious one, and ought gradually, if not rapidly, to be removed. The condition of the treasury at this time would seem to render an early revision of the tariff indispensable. The Morrill [tariff] bill, now pending before Congress, may or may not become a law. I am not posted as to its particular provisions, but if they are** generally satisfactory, and the bill shall now pass, there will be an end for the present. If, however, it shall not pass, I suppose the whole subject will be one of the most pressing and important for the next Congress. [The severely anti-South Morrill Tariff was adopted by the U.S. Congress a few weeks later on March 2, 1861.] **By the Constitution, the executive may recommend measures which he may think proper, and he may veto those he thinks improper, and it is supposed that he may add to these certain indirect influences to affect the action of Congress. My political education strongly inclines me against a very free use of any of these means by the executive to control the legislation of the country. As a rule, I think it better that Congress should originate as well as perfect its measures without external bias. I therefore would rather recommend to every gentlemen who knows he is to be a member of the next Congress to take an enlarged view, and post himself thoroughly, so as to contribute his part to such an adjustment of the tariff as shall produce a sufficient revenue, and in its other bearings, so far as possible, be just and equal to all sections of the country and classes of the people.**[481]

Besides tariffs, Lincoln's war on the South benefitted the North financially in another way: Dixie's 3,549 miles of coastline, her innumerable port towns, inlets, rivers, immense fertile farmlands, abundant agricultural products, and her hardworking people, were all vital to Northern economic growth and stability. The South's major seaports alone—New Orleans, Louisiana; Mobile, Alabama; Pensacola, Florida; Fernandina, Florida; Savannah, South Carolina; Charleston, South Carolina; Wilmington, Delaware; New Bern, North Carolina; and Norfolk, Virginia—were worth untold billions of dollars to the North.

The South was so abundant in natural and manmade resources that in 1860, just prior to the start of Lincoln's War, not only was she far richer than the North,[482] but her economy was the third largest of any region or country in either Europe or the Americas.[483] As far as wealth, the Confederate States were the fourth richest nation in the world,[484] more affluent than any European country except England. Modern Italy did not reach the level of per capita income the antebellum South possessed until the beginning of World War II.[485]

Additionally, between 1840 and 1860, the per capita income of the South grew at an average annual rate of 1.7 percent, and was a third higher than in the North. This is a sustained long-term growth rate that has been achieved by few nations.[486] And though the South possessed only 30 percent of America's population, 60 percent of America's wealthiest men were Southerners, a group that owned twice as much property as moneyed Northerners.[487]

In 1860, of the 7,000 U.S. families who possessed wealth of $111,000 or more, 4,500 of them (nearly 65 percent) lived in the South, while of the richest percentile that same year, 59 percent were Southerners.[488] So wealthy was the Confederacy that if she had been allowed to develop without interference from Lincoln, she would have become one of the world's major international powers, with a standing army many times bigger than the North's[489]—and this with a far smaller population than the North.[490]

The greedy, materialistic, commercially-minded North could not ignore such riches, power, and potential. For the Southern states, in essence, were seen by Yankees as vital elements in the creation of a nationwide domestic market that was to be controlled at the North.[491]

Based on economics alone then, Lincoln was not going to allow the South to secede. For the North, the American "Civil War" was indeed a conflict built around business and finance. While modern Yankee mythologists have tried hard to obscure this fact, Lincoln knew it and so did nearly everyone else, including most foreigners. In 1862 English novelist Charles Dickens exposed the truth behind America's "War Between the States":

> The Northern onslaught upon slavery is no more than a piece of specious humbug disguised to conceal its desire for economic control of the United States. Union means so many millions a year lost to the South; secession means loss of the same millions to the North. The love of money is the root of this as many, many other evils. The quarrel between the North and South is, as it stands, solely a fiscal quarrel.[492]

The South was rich in countless resources. Therefore her "economic control" was absolutely vital to Northern interests. It is easy to see why Lincoln and his Wall Street Boys considered Dixie the ultimate monetary prize, one they could not afford to lose.[493] For money-hungry Lincoln then, war was inevitable.

Despite the facts, Lincoln worshipers continue to believe that his primary, if not only, purpose in fighting the South was to abolish slavery.

Lincoln himself, of course, is partly to blame for this. For as he did with other issues, he liked to send out mixed messages so that future generations would find it nearly impossible to uncover his crimes or establish the truth about the cause of his illegal War.

One of the chief culprits in this obfuscation policy was his "Message to Congress" on December 1, 1862, when he declared:

> Without slavery the rebellion could never have existed; without slavery it could not continue.[494]

On January 31, 1865, Lincoln gave the following rambling speech about himself, the Emancipation Proclamation, and the Thirteenth Amendment—though eerily in the third person (thus the "he" in this address is Lincoln):

> He supposed the passage through Congress of the constitutional amendment for the abolition of slavery throughout the United States was the occasion to which he was indebted for the honor of this call.
>
> The occasion was one of congratulation to the country, and to the whole world. But there is a task yet before us—to go forward and have consummated by the votes of the States that which Congress had so nobly begun yesterday. He had the honor to inform those present that Illinois had already to-day done the work. Maryland was about half through, but he felt proud that Illinois was a little ahead.
>
> He thought this measure was a very fitting if not an indispensable adjunct to the winding up of the great difficulty. He wished the reunion of all the States perfected, and so effected as to remove all causes of disturbance in the future; and, to attain this end, it was necessary that the original disturbing cause should, if possible, be rooted out. He thought all would bear him witness that he had never shrunk from doing all that he could to eradicate slavery, by issuing an emancipation proclamation. But that proclamation falls short of what the amendment will be when fully consummated. A question might be raised whether the proclamation was legally valid. It might be urged, that it only aided those that came into our lines, and that it was inoperative as to those who did not give themselves up; or that it would have no effect upon the children of slaves born hereafter;

in fact, it would be urged that it did not meet the evil. But this amendment is a king's cure-all for all evils. It winds the whole thing up. He would repeat that it was the fitting if not the indispensable adjunct to the consummation of the great game we are playing. He could not but congratulate all present—himself, the country, and the whole world—upon this great moral victory.[495]

Here the president disingenuously calls slavery **"the original disturbing cause,"** when he knew full well, as his March 4, 1861, Inaugural Address attests, that this was completely false. (However, he does acknowledge something that is actually completely true: he refers to the Final Emancipation Proclamation as an **"indispensable adjunct to the consummation"** of the War. As Lincoln would repeat endlessly throughout the remainder of his life, his Emancipation Proclamation was never about black civil rights. He always and only characterized it as a **"military necessity"**[496] meant to help **"preserve the Union"**[497] in **"the great game we are playing."**[498]

There was also his Second Inaugural Address, given March 4, 1865. Four years ago, the president said:

> One-eighth of the whole population were colored slaves, not distributed generally over the Union, but localized in the Southern part of it. These slaves constituted a peculiar and powerful interest. All knew that this interest was, somehow, the cause of the war. To strengthen, perpetuate, and extend this interest was the object for which the insurgents would rend the Union, even by war; while the government claimed no right to do more than to restrict the territorial enlargement of it.[499]

Such purposefully misleading statements were buttressed by the Republican (liberal) party platform, released on June 7 and 8, 1864. The third plank reads:

> Resolved, That as slavery was the cause, and now constitutes the strength, of this rebellion, and as it must be, always and everywhere, hostile to the principles of republican government, justice and the national safety demand its utter and complete extirpation from the soil of the republic; and that while we uphold

> and maintain the acts and proclamations by which the government, in its own defense, has aimed a death-blow at this gigantic evil, we are in favor, furthermore, of such an amendment to the Constitution, to be made by the people in conformity with its provisions, as shall terminate and forever prohibit the existence of slavery within the limits or the jurisdiction of the United States.[500]

As all educated people knew then and know now—and contrary to what Lincoln wanted the public to believe—it is more than evident that slavery was neither the **"cause"** or the **"strength"** of the Confederacy.[501] This was just more Lincolnian disinformation.

Had Lincoln changed his mind about the cause of the War over the years? As is apparent from his words on April 11, 1865, uttered a month *after* the words from his Second Inaugural Address above, obviously not. We repeat them here:

> **We all agree that the seceded States, so called, are out of their proper practical relation with the Union, and that the sole object of the government, civil and military, in regard to those States is to again get them into that proper practical relation.**[502]

The crowning demagogue, Lincoln always carefully crafted his words to fit the moment and his audience, as one of his political opponents Stephen A. Douglas would point out time and time again. This suited the devilish bureaucrat, whose ambiguous speech, obfuscationary tricks, passivity, prevarication, stall tactics, secrecy, shady back-room dealings, deception, pseudo-religiosity, opportunism, do-nothing policies, and political double-talk kept him out of prison and got him elected twice with under 50 percent of the American vote.

The president once gave away the secret behind his *modus operandi* with the following sensational and revealing remark:

> **My policy is to have no policy**.[503]

Douglas put Lincoln's stupendous talent for tricking the American people this way: "He has a fertile genius in devising language to conceal his thoughts."[504] This is, of course, why, as Douglas also once said: "Lincoln is to be voted in the south as a proslavery man, and he is to be voted for in the north as an Abolitionist . . . [for] he can trim his principles any way in any section, so as to secure votes."⁵⁰⁵

The truth of the matter is that privately, as opposed to publicly, Lincoln never once wavered on the cause of his War. Thus, in an effort to obliterate this fanciful Yankee myth (that "the conflict was over slavery") once and for all, let us close this chapter with Lincoln's own words on the topic.

In the summer of 1861, after angrily revoking an attempt by one of his officers to emancipate slaves in Missouri, Lincoln had a conversation with abolitionist Reverend Charles Edward Lester. The president expressed his impatience with Lester and other Northern abolitionists who were pushing for emancipation. Said Lincoln:

> I think [Massachusetts Senator Charles] **Sumner, and the rest of you, would upset our apple-cart altogether, if you had your way.** . . . **We didn't go into the war to put down Slavery, but to put the flag back, and to act differently at this moment, would, I have no doubt, not only weaken our cause, but smack of bad faith; for I never should have had votes enough to send me here, if the people had supposed I should try to use my power to upset Slavery. Why, the first thing you'd see, would be a mutiny in the army. No! We must wait until every other means has been exhausted. This thunderbolt will keep.**⁵⁰⁶

Amen.⁵⁰⁷

Lincoln & the Start of the War

ACCORDING TO YANKEE AND NEW South mythology, the South "fired the first shot," triggering the so-called "Civil War." But according to Lincoln's own words, and those of his associates, the North initiated the conflict by tricking the Confederacy into shooting first.

Because of the illegalities and nefariousness of this, one of the greatest coverups in American history, the amazing story of how it actually unfolded was never fully described or recorded by Lincoln, or, of course, by his authorized biographers John G. Nicolay and John Hay. Thus to explore it we must rely primarily on the testimonies of others.

On February 22, 1861, just two months before the onset of the first battle at Fort Sumter, during his address in Independence Hall, at Philadelphia, Pennsylvania, Lincoln said:

> ... in my view of the present aspect of affairs, there need be no bloodshed or war. There is no necessity for it. I am not in favor of such a course, and I may say, in advance, that there will be no bloodshed unless it be forced upon the [U.S.] Government, and then it will be compelled to act in self-defense.... I have said nothing but I what I am willing to live by and, if it be the pleasure of Almighty God, die by.[508]

Lincoln would indeed later die by these words at the hands of disgruntled Confederate sympathizer John Wilkes Booth. But that was still four years in the future.

On December 26, 1860, under growing Southern threats, Yankee Major Robert Anderson moved his Union troops onto a small island, a military post called Fort Sumter, in South Carolina's Charleston Harbor. Since the Palmetto State had already seceded from the Union, the South considered this an act of hostility, for the "Yankee fort," once the property of the U.S.A., now clearly belonged to what was soon to become the C.S.A.

Tensions built over the following months as six more Southern states joined the Confederacy, further highlighting Fort Sumter as a symbol of Northern territorial aggression. Meanwhile, toward the end of February 1861, William H. Seward, Lincoln's secretary of state, made the first of three promises that U.S. forces would evacuate Sumter[509] and that Fort Pickens (still in Union hands, and located to the south at Pensacola, Florida) would not be reenforced.[510]

On March 1, 1861, Confederate President Jefferson Davis sent his general, Pierre Gustave Toutant Beauregard (one of Anderson's former students at West Point Military Academy), to Charleston to take command of the situation. As the Creole officer strategically placed artillery around the harbor, Dixie planned to make its intentions perfectly clear: Yankee troops were now in a foreign country, enemy territory, and were to be removed from Fort Sumter and sent North. Beauregard and his men settled in and awaited Lincoln's next move.[511]

On March 4 Lincoln gave his First Inaugural Address. In it he sets up the American public for his coming skullduggery by emphasizing that he is a peacemaker, and that if war erupts, it will be entirely the South's fault:

> Physically speaking, we cannot separate. We cannot remove our respective sections from each other, nor build an impassable wall between them. A husband and wife may be divorced, and go out of the presence and beyond the reach of each other; but the different parts of our country cannot do this. . . .
> In your hands, my dissatisfied fellow countrymen, and not in mine, is the momentous issue of civil war. The government will not assail you. You can have no conflict, without being yourselves the aggressors. You have no oath registered in Heaven to destroy the government, while I shall have the most solemn one to "preserve, protect and defend" it.
> I am loth to close. We are not enemies, but friends. We must not be enemies. Though passion may have strained, it must not break our bonds of affection.

> The mystic chords of memory, stretching from every battle-field, and patriot grave, to every living heart and hearth-stone, all over this broad land, will yet swell the chorus of the Union, when again touched, as surely they will be, by the better angels of our nature.[512]

This high flown poetic rhetoric blinded most 19th-Century Northerners, as it still does, to its inner diabolical meaning.

Yet, reading them objectively from a 21st-Century perspective, Lincoln's words are actually quite clear. He says: secession is illegal; the Confederacy is *not* a lawful nation (hence his endless and annoying use of the improper and misleading term **"civil war"**);[513] secession will **"destroy the government"** (a ridiculous *and* false assertion); the U.S. government promises not to attack the South; if there is a war the Southern people will be responsible for causing it; the South may think we are sworn adversaries but I think we are affectionate comrades (an overt lie).

It is my opinion that these three paragraphs from Lincoln's First Inaugural Address betray his secret agenda to foment war and foist the blame on the South like no other evidence ever could. Indeed, on July 4, 1861, in his "Message to Congress in Special Session," this is why Lincoln was able to accuse the Confederacy of ignoring his pre-meditated warning here that: **"You can have no conflict without being yourselves the aggressors . . ."**[514]

On March 5 Anderson sent Lincoln a report stating that he would run out of provisions "in about six weeks" (that is, in forty-two days, or on April 17), and that if he was not resupplied by then he would have no option but to surrender and evacuate the fort. This pushed Lincoln into a corner from which there seemed to be no escape: if he did not resupply Anderson in time the U.S. would lose the fort and the Union would appear to be a weak and indecisive nation, one that had capitulated to the threats of a small group of upstart rebels. If he resupplied the fort, however, the Confederates would take it as an act of aggression. This could lead to a conflict of immense proportions, one neither side was truly prepared for. In either eventuality, history would hold Lincoln accountable for either humiliating the U.S. or instigating war.[515]

Reprovision or evacuate? For the moment Lincoln promised to withdraw Anderson and his men, and on March 10 this plan was "widely published."[516] But in Lincoln's mind this did not fully resolve the problem, and over the next few weeks it became the main topic of discussion at a series of cabinet meetings between he and his secretaries (the most important one taking place on March 29, 1861). It was during these meetings that Lincoln began pushing for resupplying Fort Sumter.

The majority of Lincoln's cabinet, five out of seven (a sixth was neutral), urged him instead to quickly surrender the fort: the South had claimed Sumter and it was no longer of any value to the Union anyway.[517] Why risk life and limb over it? The secretaries who intelligently voted for evacuation were Seward, Gideon Welles, Simon Cameron, Caleb B. Smith, and Edward Bates. Furthermore, these five men added, any Union vessel heading for the island would be targeted by Confederate cannon. Why gamble the lives of U.S. soldiers and the possible destruction of U.S. property for the sake of a tiny spit of land?[518]

But Lincoln held his ground, even sending out letters to his cabinet members once again strongly advising that the fort be resupplied. On March 15, 1861, Cameron responded to the president's aggressive suggestion with a letter of his own:

> In reply to the letter of inquiry addressed to me by the President, whether, 'Assuming it to be possible now to provision Fort Sumter, under all the circumstances is it wise to attempt it'? I beg leave to say that it has received the careful consideration, in the limited time I could bestow upon it, which its very grave importance demands, and that my mind has been most reluctantly forced to the conclusion that it would be unwise now to make such an attempt.
>
> In coming to this conclusion, I am free to say I am greatly influenced by the opinions of the Army officers who have expressed themselves on the subject, and who seem to concur that it is, perhaps, now impossible to succor that fort substantially, if at all, without capturing, by means of a large expedition of ships of war and troops, all the opposing batteries of South Carolina. All the officers within Fort Sumter, together with Generals [Winfield] Scott and [Joseph Gilbert] Totten, express this opinion, and it would seem to me that the President would not be justified to disregard such high authority without overruling considerations of public policy.
>
> Major Anderson, in his report of the 28th ultimo, says:
>
> > "I confess that I would not be willing to risk my reputation on an attempt to throw reinforcements into this harbor within the time for our relief rendered necessary by the limited supply of our provisions, and with a

view of holding possession of the same with a force of less than twenty thousand good and well-disciplined men."

In this opinion Major Anderson is substantially sustained by the reports of all the other officers within the fort, one of whom, Captain Seymour, speaks thus emphatically on the subject:

"It is not more than possible to supply this fort by ruse with a few men or a small amount of provisions, such is the unceasing vigilance employed to prevent it. To do so openly by vessels alone, unless they are shot proof, is virtually impossible, so numerous and powerful are the opposing batteries. No vessel can lay near the fort without being exposed to continual fire, and the harbor could, and probably would, whenever necessary, be effectually closed, as one channel has already been. A projected attack in large force would draw to this harbor all the available resources in men and material of the contiguous States. Batteries of guns of heavy calibre would be multiplied rapidly and indefinitely. At least 20,000 men, good marksmen, and trained for months past with a view to this very contingency, would be concentrated here before the attacking force could leave Northern ports. The harbor would be closed. A landing must be effected at some distance from our guns, which could give no aid. Charleston Harbor would be a Sebastopol in such a conflict, and unlimited means would probably be required to ensure success, before which time the garrison of Fort Sumter would be starved out."

General Scott, in his reply to the question addressed to him by the President, on the 12th instant, "What amount of means and of what description, in addition to those already at command, would it require to supply and re-enforce the fort"? says:

"I should need a fleet of war vessels and transports, which, in the scattered disposition of the Navy (as understood), could not be collected in less than four months; 5,000 additional regular troops and 20,000 volunteers; that is, a force sufficient to take all the batteries, both in the harbor (including Fort Moultrie) as well as in the approach or outer bay. To raise, organize, and discipline such an army (not to speak of necessary legislation by Congress, not now in session) would require from six to eight months. As a practical military question, the time for succoring Fort Sumter with any means at hand has passed away nearly a month ago. Since then a surrender under assault or from starvation has been merely a question of time."

It is true there are those, whose opinions are entitled to respectful consideration, who entertain the belief that Fort Sumter could yet be succored to a limited extent without the employment of the large army and naval forces believed to be necessary by the Army officers whose opinions I have already quoted.

Commander [James Harmon] Ward, of the Navy, an officer of acknowledged merit, a month ago believed it to be practicable to supply the fort with men and provisions to a limited extent without the employment of any very large military or naval force. He then proposed to employ four or more small steamers belonging to the Coast Survey to accomplish the purpose, and we have the opinion of General Scott that he has no doubt that Captain Ward at that time would have succeeded with his proposed expedition, but was not allowed by the late President [James Buchanan] to attempt the execution of his plan. Now it is pronounced, from the change of circumstances, impracticable by Major Anderson and all the other officers of the fort, as well as by Generals Scott and Totten, and in this opinion Commander Ward, after full consultation with the latter-named officers and the Superintendent of the Coast Survey, I understand now reluctantly concurs.

Mr. [Gustavus Vasa] Fox [a Swedish-American and former naval officer], another gentleman of experience as a seaman, who, having formerly been engaged on the Coast Survey, is familiar with the waters of the Charleston Harbor, has proposed to make the attempt to supply the fort with cutters of light draught and large dimensions, and his proposal has in a measure been approved by Commodore [Silas Horton] Stringham, but he does not suppose or propose or profess to believe that provisions for more than one or two months could be furnished at a time.

There is no doubt whatever in my mind that when Major Anderson first took possession of Fort Sumter he could have been easily supplied with men and provisions, and that when Commander Ward, with the concurrence of General Scott, a month ago proposed his expedition he would have succeeded had he been allowed to attempt it, as I think he should have been. A different state of things now, however, exists. Fort Moultrie is now rearmed and strengthened in every way; many new land batteries have been constructed; the principal channel has been obstructed; in short, the difficulty of re-enforcing the fort has been increased ten if not twenty fold.

Whatever might have been done as late as a month ago, it is too sadly evident that it cannot now be done without the sacrifice of life and treasure not at all commensurate with the object to be attained; and as the abandonment of the fort in a few weeks, sooner or later, appears to be an inevitable necessity, it seems to me that the sooner it be done the better.

The proposition presented by Mr. Fox, so sincerely entertained and ably advocated, would be entitled to my favorable consideration if, with all the light before me, and in the face of so many distinguished military authorities on the other side, I did not believe that the attempt to carry it into effect would initiate a bloody and protracted conflict. Should he succeed in relieving Fort Sumter, which is doubted by many of our most experienced soldiers and seamen, would that enable us to maintain our authority against the troops and fortifications of South Carolina?

Sumter could not now contend against these formidable adversaries, if filled with provisions and men. That fortress was intended, as her position on the map will show, rather to repel an invading foe. It is equally clear, from repeated investigations and trials, that the range of her guns is too limited to reach the city of Charleston, if that were desirable.

No practical benefit will result to the country or the Government by accepting the proposal alluded to, and I am therefore of opinion that the cause of humanity and the highest obligation to the public interest would be best promoted by adopting the counsels of those brave and experienced men whose suggestions I have laid before you.[519]

Only a few weeks earlier, in a conversation with the Supreme Court's Associate Justice John A. Campbell of Alabama, Seward himself had proposed evacuation. The same was true of noted prohibitionist Neal Dow of Maine, who, on March 13, 1861, guaranteed Lincoln that every Republican (the liberal Democrats of that time) of his state fully backed the idea of immediately giving Sumter to the South.[520]

Abolitionists, Northern members of the opposing party, and Union military brass from across the U.S. were nearly all of the same mind. Horace Greeley's newspaper, the New York *Tribune*, called on Lincoln to avoid the use of force and allow the Southern states to secede in peace, while Illinois Democrat Stephen A. Douglas said that "Anderson and his gallant band should be instantly withdrawn."[521]

On March 28, as Cameron noted above, the greatly respected Yankee General Winfield Scott had advised his president to not only evacuate Fort Sumter, but the nearby Union-held garrison Fort Pickens, as well.[522] Such action would politically benefit the U.S., Scott assured a stunned Lincoln. And, as Cameron also told him: "All the officers within Fort Sumter . . . [also] express this opinion . . ." including Anderson himself, still awaiting orders there.[523]

Anderson in particular was troubled by Lincoln's hawkish stance. Originally a slaveholder from Kentucky and thus possessing some sympathy for the South, he was understandably lukewarm about the idea of the North making war on his homeland. In a letter addressed to Lincoln's office, intercepted by Confederate soldiers, a "despondent" Anderson questioned the wisdom of resupplying the fort, then noted:

> We shall strive to do our duty, though I frankly say that my heart is not in the war which I see is to be thus commenced. That God will still avert it, and cause us to resort to pacific measures to maintain our rights, is my ardent prayer.[524]

At this point, however, not even God could prevent Lincoln from moving forward with his sinister plan.

The U.S. president—who later brazenly admitted to Congress that from the beginning he had seen the entire affair as something that would be exploited and **"used or not according to circumstances"**[525]—ignored the emotional pleas and rational suggestions of Anderson, Cameron, and the rest of his more sagacious contemporaries, most notably Scott. What kind of a president completely disregards the military advice of his general-in-chief?

In actuality Lincoln did not care what his subordinates thought about Sumter or the seceding states. For by now he was just playing for time: he had already decided what he was going to do, as his own words prove.

As early as February 22, 1861, weeks before he was even inaugurated, Lincoln was using such phrases as **"when war is inevitable."**[526] Why? Because long before the actual start of the conflict he had hatched an underhanded scheme, one in which he was determined to risk everything in order to implement his political agenda: the installation of Henry Clay's liberal American System, what we today call "big government."

With so many Southern states seceding, a war was now necessary for Lincoln's scheme to work, and Fort Sumter was to be his golden opportunity to initiate it. As he imperiously admitted years later in his Fourth Annual Message to Congress on December 6, 1864:

> [This] **is an issue which can only be tried by war, and decided by victory.**[527]

Revealingly, in this same speech Lincoln goes on to admit that his War did indeed enlarge both the central government and his presidential powers, for when questioned about what would occur if the conflict were to come to an immediate end, he winced and said:

> **The Executive power itself would be greatly diminished by the cessation of actual war.**[528]

This was clearly not part of Lincoln's long-term plans. This is why he needed to continue his War, for in the winter of 1864 states' rights in the South had not yet been completely destroyed. And he had sworn to finish what he had started, as he said on June 28, 1862, in a letter to Seward:

> **I expect to maintain this contest until successful, or till I die, or am conquered, or my term expires, or Congress or the country forsake me . . .**[529]

By his own admission this was a man determined to achieve his liberal dream of installing big government and destroying states' rights, at all costs.

As mentioned, his plan to launch war on the South had actually been set in motion even before his inauguration, when fellow party member Orville Hickman Browning[530] sent Lincoln a letter dated February 17, 1861. It read:

> In any conflict which may ensue between the government and the

seceding States, it is very important that the traitors shall be the aggressors, and that they be kept constantly and palpably in the wrong. The first attempt that is made to furnish supplies or reinforcements to Sumter will induce aggression by South Carolina, and then the government will stand justified, before the entire country, in repelling that aggression, and retaking the forts. And so it will be everywhere, and all the places now occupied by traitors can be recaptured without affording them additional material with which to inflame the public mind by representing your inaugural as containing an irritating threat.[531]

Here was Lincoln's whole plot laid out, brilliantly encapsulated in a single paragraph, before he had even been inducted into the Oval Office.

Within days, on March 4, with Browning's words still occupying his mind, Lincoln gave his First Inaugural Address. By this time seven Southern states—South Carolina, Mississippi, Florida, Alabama, Georgia, Louisiana, and Texas—had seceded and legally formed the C.S.A. (exactly one month earlier, on February 4). Yet, Lincoln acted oblivious.

In his speech he laid down the groundwork for his upcoming contrivance, emphatically asserting—bizarrely, as he often did, in the third person—that secession had not taken place; that **"the Union is unbroken"**; that the thirty-three states of the U.S., South and North, were still intact; and that it was his duty to **"administer the present government, as it came into his hands, and to transmit it, unimpaired by him, to his successor."**[532]

Lincoln insolently laid out the second part of his plot by stating that the Union **"will constitutionally defend and maintain itself." "In doing this,"** he continued,

> there needs to be no bloodshed or violence; and there shall be none, unless it be forced upon the national authority. The power confided to me will be used to hold, occupy, and possess the property and places belonging to the [U.S.] government, and to collect the duties and imposts; but beyond what may be necessary for these objects, there will be no invasion—no using of force against or among the people anywhere.[533]

Lincoln had cleverly turned the tables on the South by placing her in a position where she would have to make the first move: he would not give up Fort Sumter, but he also promised that he would not invade or be the first to initiate bloodshed.

The tinder and the flint needed to spark the fire of war that he so desperately wanted and needed were now in place. In the meantime Lincoln advised Anderson to continue to hold his ground.

On March 29 Lincoln sent the following letter to Secretary of War Cameron:

> **Sir: I desire that an expedition to move by sea be got ready to sail as early as the 6th of April next, the whole according to memorandum attached, and that you cooperate with the Secretary of the Navy for that object. Your obedient servant, A. Lincoln.**
>
> [Inclosure.]
>
> **Steamers *Pocahontas* at Norfolk, *Pawnee* at Washington, *Harriet Lane* at New York, to be under sailing orders for sea, with stores, etc., for one month. Three hundred men to be kept ready for departure from on board the receiving-ships at New York.**
>
> **Two hundred men to be ready to leave Governor's Island in New York. Supplies for twelve months for one hundred men to be put in portable shape, ready for instant shipping. A large steamer and three tugs conditionally engaged.**[534]

Lincoln was thinking far ahead here, devising all of the minute details of his sinister scheme to force war on the South, with soldiers to be supplied for a full twelve months in advance!

While all of this was going on, the "spark" needed to ignite the conflict soon appeared. Food and ammunition were regularly delivered to Anderson and his troops until April 1, when Confederate General Beauregard cut off all Yankee shipments to the island. Now it was made clear to everyone South and North: Anderson and his men would soon either have to defend the fort or surrender it. Lincoln calmly bided his time, letting nearly a week pass as pressure built.

Then on April 6, in a shocking and sudden move, Lincoln played his hand. Cunningly breaking his earlier promise to evacuate Sumter, he sent word to South Carolina's governor, Francis W. Pickens, that he would be sending ships out to reprovision the fort, and that neither the vessels or Anderson and his men were to be interfered with. If so, he would take whatever defensive action he deemed necessary, which by definition included the possibility of a full-scale assault on Confederate troops. Though it was not stated as such, Lincoln justified his reprovision plan by insinuating that Anderson and his men were starving. As we will see, this would turn out to be one of the most unscrupulous and monstrous political moves in American history.[535]

Here are Lincoln's instructions to State Department Clerk Robert S. Chew:

> Drafted By President Lincoln And Signed By The Secretary Of War. Washington, April 6, 1861.
> **Sir: You will proceed directly to Charleston, South Carolina; and if, on your arrival there, the flag of the United States shall be flying over Fort Sumter, and the fort shall not have been attacked, you will procure an interview with Governor Pickens, and read to him as follows:** "I am directed by the President of the United States to notify you to expect an attempt will be made to supply Fort Sumter with provisions only; and that, if such attempt be not resisted, no effort to throw in men, arms, or ammunition will be made without further notice, or in case of an attack upon the fort."
> **After you shall have read this to Governor Pickens, deliver to him the copy of it herein inclosed, and retain this letter yourself.**
> **But if, on your arrival at Charleston, you shall ascertain that Fort Sumter shall have been already evacuated, or surrendered by the United States force, or shall have been attacked by an opposing force, you will seek no interview with Governor Pickens, but return here forthwith.**[536]

As Lincoln had intended, these words brought forth a burst of activity. On April 8 the well supplied Federal Revenue Cutter *Harriet Lane* set off from New York Harbor,[537] on April 9 the Union steamer *Baltic* (with naval vet Gustavus Fox on board) also sailed from New York,[538] and on April 10 the Federal ship U.S.S. *Pawnee* left the docks at Hampton Roads, Virginia. Their destination? Fort Sumter, South Carolina.[539]

That same day, April 10, even with war looming, Lincoln found time to devote to his favorite cause, black colonization, meeting with an ambassador of Chiriqui, a developing coal mining region in what is today the nation of Panama. The future "Great Emancipator" was hoping to convince the visiting representative to allow freed American black slaves to be deported there.[540]

It was also on April 10 that Lincoln gave official authorization for his so-called **"relief mission,"**[541] complete with bristling ammunition-laden warships, heavily armed troops, and a battery of steamers, tugboats, and naval convoys.[542] In today's jargon Lincoln's armada was nothing less than complete overkill, far more than was needed to deliver a few boxes of food to a little garrison on an insignificant speck of sand in the middle of Charleston Harbor.

Indeed, all of this was a grand deception. Anderson and his men had not run out of supplies. The "starving garrison" story now going around was just that: Northern war propaganda, invented by Lincoln to gain support for his upcoming War. For the Yanks stationed on the tiny island were far from being out of supplies.[543] Besides Yankee deliveries, every day the kind and generous "people of Charleston sent to Sumter a boat load of food supplies, fresh meats, fowls, fruits, vegetables, etc."[544]

As we will recall, the report Anderson sent to Lincoln on March 5 stated that his supplies would last until at least April 17. And as late as 1:30 A.M., April 12, the morning of the upcoming battle, in a conversation with Beauregard's aide, Colonel James Chesnut, Jr. (the husband of diarist Mary Chesnut), Anderson admitted that his troops had several more days of provisions. We will "await the first shot, and if not battered to pieces," he told Chesnut, "we will be starved out in a few days."[545] Clearly Anderson still had plenty of food on April 10, the day Lincoln ordered his fleet to sail.

While the Confederacy desperately wanted a peaceful resolution to the building crisis, and had even sent peace commissioners to Washington, D.C. (to no avail of course, since Lincoln desperately wanted war), this latest threat by the Northern president was pushing the limits of the South's patience.[546] Still, there was one more game of Northern one-upmanship to come.

On April 11, though the Confederacy had been vehemently against initiating war, Beauregard had little choice but to demand that Anderson surrender the fort or be fired on. The U.S. officer, by now feeling like little more than a chess piece in the president's pointless war game, reluctantly refused, having been ordered by his boss to stand his ground. With Lincoln's powerful armed flotilla on its way to "resupply" the fort, the decisive moment for the South to take action was at hand.

On April 12, at 1:00 A.M. in the morning, Anderson told Chesnut that he would evacuate Sumter at noon on April 15, near the date the

Yankee major had predicted he would be "starved out." But it was already too late. The well-mannered Anderson, who, as we will recall, loved his Southern homeland, cordially shook the hands of Colonel Chesnut and the other Rebel aides, saying that he hoped to meet him again, but if not, they would see each other in the Afterlife.[547]

A few hours later, at 3:20 A.M., Lincoln's fake reinforcement fleet of warships began arriving outside the mouth of Charleston Harbor, at which time Beauregard notified Anderson that he would begin shelling in one hour. At 4:30 A.M., as Lincoln had hoped and predicted, Confederate forces opened fire,[548] lured into a web of violence, treachery, and Northern deception unknown in U.S. politics before or since.

In 1867, six years later, Southern fire-eater Edward A. Pollard wrote of the situation in his extraordinary book, *The Lost Cause*:

> The point of the [Northern] government was to devise some artifice for the relief of Fort Sumter, short of open military reinforcements, decided to be impracticable, and which would have the effect of inaugurating the war by a safe indirection and under a plausible and convenient pretence. The device was at last conceived.[549]

Lincoln's "device" having now been employed, the next day, April 13, fell like an ominous shadow on the oblivious Southern people. After nearly thirty-four hours of near constant Rebel bombardment—though with no deaths and only a few minor injuries as a result of the cannonading—Anderson surrendered Sumter to a triumphant Confederacy.[550] Inside the fort, in full view, were another four days of food and provisions, revealing, to those with eyes to see, the full import of Lincoln's duplicitous secret plot.

Also in plain sight were Lincoln's navy ships fresh from New York and Virginia, packed to the gunwales with firepower, quietly moored just offshore. Revealingly the fleet made no move to participate in the battle, despite Lincoln's earlier threats to use force if the Confederates fired on the fort.[551] He had, in fact, never intended to fight back. Another ruse. Lincoln had lied in an effort to force the South's hand. Forever after the South would be accused of "starting the Civil War." "Honest Abe's" unscrupulous ploy worked, and here was overt proof.[552]

Again, as Pollard notes:

> The battle of Sumter had been brought on by the Washington Government by a trick too dishonest and shallow to account for the

immense display of sentiment in the North that ensued. The event afforded indeed to many politicians in the North a most flimsy and false excuse for loosing passions of hate against the South that had all along been festering in the concealment of their hearts.[553]

Unfortunately, most of the South did not at first seem to notice the Yankee president's evildoing. Instead, it was happily preoccupied with winning its first victory in the first battle of America's first internal war.

In the immediate aftermath the South viewed the Battle of Fort Sumter I (there was to be a second battle at Sumter, August 17-23, 1863) as little more than a minor conflict, a colorful, harmless show of military bravado for the fascinated Victorian crowds who lined Charleston Harbor, cheering on their beloved Southern soldiers through the din of booming cannon, sheets of fire, and acrid powder smoke. The Yanks had surrendered and evacuated Fort Sumter, and had been sent packing northward. It was true after all, or so they thought: one Johnny Reb could whip three Billy Yanks in no time at all. Perhaps the War was over before it began. So it appeared to a hopeful South that day.

What the inhabitants of Dixie did not fully grasp was that they had fallen into a pitiless trap carefully laid by a deceptive Lincoln, one intended to make it look as if the South had started the conflict,[554] and one which would justify what was to come next: the North's total war on the South in order to destroy states' rights and force the Confederacy back into the Union—all so that Lincoln could install his new Northern-styled liberal big government. As a Yankee paper, Rhode Island's *Providence Daily Post*, noted so insightfully on April 13, 1861, Lincoln had, without question, used the situation at Fort Sumter as a way to open the War without looking like the instigator.[555]

As we will see shortly, Lincoln himself later admitted as much in a May 1 letter to Gustavus Fox. He made a similar dastardly comment to Orville Hickman Browning: My plan worked! The South was the first to fire at Sumter, doing more good for us than they could have imagined, he boasted.[556]

Later, realizing he might be found out, Lincoln attempted to cover his tracks by offering a number of different explanations for his actions in the Sumter crisis. But this only made things worse, for none of them corresponded with the facts, and some, like his explanation that he would have let Fort Sumter go if had he been able to reinforce Fort Pickens, was an outright lie, completely unsupported by contemporary evidence.[557]

The truth of Lincoln's villainous "card trick" manifested anyway: Browning later noted in his diary that the president never demonstrated any regret, least of all guilt, over his actions in the debacle, all which led inevitably to war,[558] just as he had planned from the start. For Lincoln knew full well that resupplying the fort would lead to violence and bloodletting.

South Carolina Governor Pickens, among many others, had told him so. Earlier Pickens had written a terse and unyielding message to Ward Hill Lamon, U.S. Marshal of the District of Columbia, that was later read by Lincoln. Written from Charleston, it warned, in part, that:

> Nothing can prevent war except the acquiescence of the President of the United States in secession, and his unalterable resolve not to attempt any reinforcement of the Southern forts. To think of [South Carolina] longer remaining in the Union is simply preposterous. We have five thousand well-armed soldiers around this city; all the States are arming with great rapidity; and this means war with all its consequences. Let your President attempt to reinforce Sumter and the tocsin of war will be sounded from every hilltop and valley in the South.[559]

On March 27, Stephen A. Hurlbut, a friend of Lincoln's, told the president that even the slightest U.S. movement toward Sumter would be received as an "act of war." Lincoln's Secretary of State, Robert Toombs, had also warned his boss of the impending disaster that would surely follow any attempts on the island. According to Toombs:

> The firing on that fort will inaugurate a civil war greater than any the world has yet seen; . . .[560] Mr. President, at this time it is suicide, murder, and you will lose every friend at the North. You will wantonly strike a hornet's nest which extends from mountains to ocean, and legions, now quiet, will swarm out and sting us to death. It is unnecessary; it puts us in the wrong; it is fatal.[561]

U.S. Secretary of State Seward said much the same thing on March 15, 1861:

> The President submits to me the following question—namely: "Assuming it to be possible to now provision Fort Sumter, under all the circumstances is it wise to attempt it?"
>
> If it were possible to peacefully provision Fort Sumter, of course I should answer that it would be both unwise and inhuman not to attempt it. But the facts of the case are known to

be that the attempt must be made with the employment of military and marine force, which would provoke combat, and probably initiate a civil war, which the government of the United States would be committed to maintain through all changes to some definite conclusion.

. . . I suppose the expedition [to reprovision Anderson and his men] successful. We have then a garrison in Fort Sumter that can defy assault for six months. What is it to do then? Is it to make war by opening its batteries and attempting to demolish defenses of the Carolinians? Can it demolish them if it tries? If it cannot, what is the advantage we shall have gained? If it can, how will it serve to check or prevent disunion?

In either case it seems to me that we will have inaugurated a civil war by our own act, without an adequate object, after which reunion will be hopeless, at least under this administration, or in any other way than by a popular disavowal both of the war and of the administration which unnecessarily commenced it. Fraternity is the element of union; war, the very element of disunion. Fraternity, if practised by this administration, will rescue the Union from all its dangers. If this administration, on the other hand, take up the sword, then an opposite party will offer the olive branch, and will, as it ought, profit by the restoration of peace and union.

I may be asked whether I would in no case, and at no time, advise force—whether I propose to give up everything. I reply—No, I would not initiate war to regain a useless and unnecessary position on the soil of the seceding States. I would not provoke war in any way now. I would resort to force to protect the collection of the revenue, because that is a necessary as well as a legitimate public object. Even then it should be only a naval force that I would employ for that necessary purpose, while I would defer military action on land until a case should arise where we would hold the defensive. In that case we should have the spirit of the country and the approval of mankind on our side. In the other, we should peril peace and union, because we had not the courage to practise prudence and moderation at the cost of temporary misapprehension. If this counsel seem to be impassive and even unpatriotic, I console myself by the reflection that it is such as Chatham gave to his country under circumstances not widely different.[562]

Only days later, on March 29, Seward wrote again to Lincoln, warning him not to go forward with his plan to send an "expedition" to relieve Fort Sumter:

> *First.* The despatch of an expedition to supply or reinforce Sumter would provoke an attack, and so involve a war at that point.
>
> The fact of preparation for such an expedition would inevitably transpire, and would therefore precipitate the war, and probably defeat the object. I do not think it wise to provoke a civil war beginning at Charleston, and in rescue of an untenable position.
>
> Therefore I advise against the expedition in every view.
>
> *Second.* I would call in Captain M. [Montgomery] C. Meigs forthwith. Aided by his counsel, I would at once, and at every cost, prepare for a war at Pensacola and Texas: to be taken, however, only as a consequence of maintaining the possessions and authority of the United States.
>
> *Third.* I would instruct Major Anderson to retire from Sumter forthwith.[563]

Secretary of the Navy Welles also promised war if Lincoln went ahead with his insane plan:

> By sending or attempting to send provisions into Sumter, will not war be precipitated? It may be impossible to escape it under any course of policy that may be pursued, but I am not prepared to advise a course that would provoke hostilities. It does not appear to me that the dignity, strength, or character of the government will be promoted by an attempt to provision Sumter in the manner proposed, even should it succeed, while a failure would be attended with untold disaster.
>
> I do not, therefore, under all the circumstances, think it wise to attempt to provision Fort Sumter. I am, very respectfully, Gideon Welles.[564]

Secretary of the Interior Smith also warned of an impending bloodbath:

> The occupation of Fort Sumter is not essential to the performance of any of the duties imposed upon the government.
>
> . . . The commencement of a civil war would be a calamity greatly to be deplored, and should be avoided if the just authority of the government may be maintained without it.
>
> . . . I therefore respectfully answer the inquiry of the President by saying that, in my opinion, it would not be wise under all the circumstances to attempt to provision Fort Sumter. I am, with respect, Your obedient servant, Caleb B. Smith.[565]

Lincoln's Attorney General Bates had this to say on the subject:

> I am most unwilling to strike—I will not say the first blow, for South Carolina has already struck that—but I am unwilling, "under all the circumstances," at this moment to do any act which may have the semblance before the world of beginning a civil war, the terrible consequences of which would, I think, find no parallel in modern times; for I am convinced that flagrant civil war in the Southern States would soon become a social war, and that could hardly fail to bring on a servile war, the horrors of which need not be dwelt upon.
>
> . . . I persuade myself that the nation will be restored to its integrity without the effusion of blood.
>
> For these reasons I am willing to evacuate Fort Sumter, rather than be an active party in the beginning of civil war.
>
> . . . Upon the whole, I do not think it wise now to attempt to provision Fort Sumter. Most respectfully submitted. Your obedient servant, Edward Bates.[566]

But far from dissuading Lincoln from trying to resupply Sumter, such words were exactly what he wanted to hear. Even many Lincoln apologists have had to hesitatingly admit that at least by April 6, Lincoln was sure that his Sumter scam would certainly lead to open hostilities, to what he persistently and wrongly called **"civil war."**[567]

Somewhere in Lincoln's seething Machiavellian brain, however, the idea of foisting violence upon the South had been percolating for at least several years before he became president. We will never know why the Kentuckian hated his own home region so intensely, unless it was simply the liberal's desire to impose his will, by coercion if necessary, on all those who disagreed with him. What we do know is that many of his antebellum words ring with threatening hyperbole, as if preparing the world for a future war between North and South.

As early as March 4, 1843, for instance, Lincoln had begun using the threatening phrase: **"A house divided against itself cannot stand."**[568] Fifteen years later, on July 17, 1858, during a speech at Springfield, Illinois, he had refined this expression, using it to purposefully antagonize the South, while openly hinting at the invasion, violence, and oppression that was to come:

> **I believe that this government cannot endure permanently half slave and half free. It will become all**

one thing or all the other.[569]

But, as always, Lincoln was wrong. As Stephen A. Douglas countered:

> Why cannot this government endure, divided into Free and Slave States as our fathers made it? When this government was established by Washington, Jefferson, Madison, Jay, Hamilton, Franklin, and the other sages and patriots of that day, it was composed of Free States and Slave States, bound together by one common Constitution. We have existed and prospered from that day to this thus divided, and have increased with a rapidity never before equalled, in wealth, the extension of territory, and all the elements of power and greatness, until we have become the first nation on the face of the globe. Why can we not thus continue to prosper? We can, if we will live up to and execute the government upon those principles upon which our fathers established it.[570]

Lincoln himself admitted in the same July 17 speech that the U.S. had already **"endured, half slave and half free, for eighty-two years"**![571] But this was just more typical Lincoln-speak: saying one thing while believing another.

On March 1, 1859, only a year and a half before being elected president, Lincoln used the following ominous language in an address to party supporters in Chicago:

> **You Republicans** [liberals] **of Illinois have deliberately taken your ground; you have heard the whole subject discussed again and again; you have stated your faith in platforms laid down in a State convention and in a national convention; you have heard and talked over and considered it until you are now all of opinion that you are on a ground of unquestionable right. All you have to do is to keep the faith, to remain steadfast to the right, to stand by your banner. Nothing should lead you to leave your guns. Stand together, ready, with match in hand. Allow nothing to turn you to the right or to the left. Remember how long you have been in setting out on the true course; how long you have been in getting your neighbors to understand and believe as you now do. Stand by your principles, stand by your guns, and victory, complete and permanent, is sure at the last.**[572]

Lincoln also enjoyed uttering a biblical-inspired phrase, one guaranteed to anger all Constitution-loving Southerners:

> He that is not for us is against us; and he that gathereth not with us scattereth.[573]

On September 17, 1859, at Cincinnati, Ohio, Lincoln spoke to an audience full of Kentuckians, to whom he offered the following ridiculous, false, and menacing words, even predicting a "civil war" that would be started, not by the North, but by the South:

> You have divided the Union because we would not do right with you, as you think, upon that subject; when we cease to be under obligations to do anything for you, how much better off do you think you will be? Will you make war upon us and kill us all? Why, gentlemen, I think you as gallant and as brave men as live; that you can fight as bravely in a good cause, man for man, as any other people living; that you have shown yourselves capable of this upon various occasions; but man for man, you are not better than we are, and there are not so many of you as there are of us. You will never make much of a hand at whipping us. If we were fewer in numbers than you, I think that you could whip us; if we were equal it would likely be a drawn battle; but being inferior in numbers, you will make nothing by attempting to master us.[574]

On February 27, 1860, at New York, he gave his notorious Cooper Union Speech, in which we find the following portentous words:

> Neither let us be slandered from our duty by false accusations against us, nor frightened from it by menaces of destruction to the government, nor of dungeons to ourselves. Let us have faith that right makes might, and in that faith let us to the end dare to do our duty as we understand it.[575]

"Right makes might" and **"do our duty."** What did these terms mean? Coming from the bellicose and traitorous Southerner-turned-Northerner, they could only mean one thing. It was phrases like these, uttered just seven months before the presidential election, that made Southerners shutter in horror.

On February 12, 1861, just prior to his inauguration, Lincoln addressed the Indiana Legislature at Indianapolis as if brandishing a sword above his head:

> Fellow-citizens of the State of Indiana: I am here to thank you much for this magnificent welcome, and still more for the generous support given by your State to that political cause which I think is the true and just cause of the whole country and the whole world. Solomon says there is "a time to keep silence," and when men wrangle by the month with no certainty that they mean the same thing, while using the same word, it perhaps were as well if they would keep silence. The words "coercion" and "invasion" are much used in these days, and often with some temper and hot blood. Let us make sure, if we can, that we do not misunderstand the meaning of those who use them. Let us get exact definitions of these words, not from dictionaries, but from the men themselves, who certainly deprecate the things they would represent by the use of words. What, then, is "coercion"? What is "invasion"? Would the marching of an army into South Carolina without the consent of her people, and with hostile intent toward them, be "invasion"? I certainly think it would; and it would be "coercion" also if the South Carolinians were forced to submit. But if the United States should merely hold and retake its own forts and other property, and collect the duties on foreign importations, or even withhold the mails from places where they were habitually violated, would any or all of these things be "invasion" or "coercion"? Do our professed lovers of the Union, but who spitefully resolve that they will resist coercion and invasion, understand that such things as these on the part of the United States would be coercion or invasion of a State? If so, their idea of means to preserve the object of their great affection would seem to be exceedingly thin and airy. If sick, the little pills of the homeopathist would be much too large for them to swallow. In their view, the Union as a family relation would seem to be no regular marriage, but rather a sort of "free-love" arrangement, to be maintained only on "passional attraction." By the way, in what consists the special sacredness of a State? I speak not of the position assigned to a State in the Union by the Constitution; for that, by the bond, we all recognize.

That position, however, a State cannot carry out of the Union with it. I speak of that assumed primary right of a State to rule all which is less than itself, and ruin all which is larger than itself. If a State and a county, in a given case, should be equal in extent of territory, and equal in number of inhabitants, in what, as a matter of principle, is the State better than the county? Would an exchange of names be an exchange of rights upon principle? On what rightful principle may a State, being not more than one fiftieth part of the nation in soil and population, break up the nation and then coerce a proportionally larger subdivision of itself in the most arbitrary way? What mysterious right to play tyrant is conferred on a district of country with its people, by merely calling it a State? Fellow-citizens, I am not asserting anything: I am merely asking questions for you to consider. And now allow me to bid you farewell.[576]

Clever devilish Lincoln is already trying to force his fantasy onto the public; namely, that it is the South which is acting tyrannical and aggressive rather than he himself. Little did he realize how well this type of treacherous double-talk would succeed in making him a national hero for hundreds of years into the future.

Or maybe he did.

One of Lincoln's favorite threats was inspired by fellow liberal, and Lincoln's future secretary of state, William H. Seward, who spoke the following words in a speech at Rochester, New York, on October 25, 1858:

> When we see before us the transactions of this day, do they not illustrate the subject of the "irrepressible conflict?" Did not our forefathers, in 1787, settle this whole question, and, by an ordinance, put at rest forever the question of freedom and slavery in the United States? Certainly they did. Did they not, in 1820, settle this conflict forever? Did they not declare that all north of 36° 30' and west of the Missouri river should be given up to freedom? Certainly they did. Was it not settled finally a third time in 1850, when Kansas and Nebraska were still saved to freedom, and all lying west of them? Was it not settled a fourth time in 1854, when it was ordained that the people of Kansas were free to choose freedom or slavery for themselves, subject to the constitution of the United States? Was it not settled for the fifth time, when the Lecompton constitution was adopted by one scratch of the pen of the President of the United States and the

Supreme Court—and this became a land of slavery? Why was not slavery settled by all these settlements? For no other reason than because the conflict was irrepressible. But you determined, in your struggle for Kansas, that she shall be forever free; and that settles the question. In New Mexico they tried to settle it in favor of slavery, but they now find it is irrepressible there. I think you will find that the whole battle has been settled in the deliverance of Kansas, and that henceforth freedom will be triumphant in all the territories in the United States.[577]

Seward's references to the slavery issue between the largely liberal North and the largely conservative South as a "battle" and as an "irrepressible conflict," were words that every South-hating Yankee warmonger could relate to, and none more so than Abraham Lincoln. As such, on March 6, 1860, at Norwich, Connecticut, he framed his entire speech around Seward's aggressive and bullying vocabulary:

> Whether we will or not, the question of slavery is the question, the all-absorbing topic, of the day. It is true that all of us—and by that I mean, not the Republican party alone, but the whole American people, here and elsewhere—all of us wish the question settled—wish it out of the way.
>
> It stands in the way and prevents the adjustment and the giving of necessary attention to other questions of national housekeeping. The people of the whole nation agree that this question ought to be settled, and yet it is not settled. And the reason is that they are not yet agreed how it shall be settled.
>
> Again and again it has been fondly hoped that it was settled, but every time it breaks out afresh and more violently than ever. It was settled, our fathers hoped, by the Missouri Compromise, but it did not stay settled. Then the compromise of 1850 was declared to be a full and final settlement of the question. The two great parties, each in national convention, adopted resolutions declaring that the settlement made by the compromises of 1850 was a finality—that it would last forever. Yet how long before it was unsettled again? It broke out again in 1854, and blazed higher and raged more furiously than ever before, and the agitation has not rested since.
>
> These repeated settlements must have some fault about them. There must be some inadequacy in their very nature to the purpose for which they were designed.

We can only speculate as to where that fault—that inadequacy is, but we may perhaps profit by past experience.

I think that one of the causes of these repeated failures is that our best and greatest men have greatly underestimated the size of this question. They have constantly brought forward small cures for great sores—plasters too small to cover the wound. This is one reason that all settlements have proved so temporary, so evanescent.

Look at the magnitude of this subject. About one sixth of the whole population of the United States are slaves. The owners of the slaves consider them property. The effect upon the minds of the owners is that of property, and nothing else—it induces them to insist upon all that will favorably affect its value as property, to demand laws and institutions and a public policy that shall increase and secure its value, and make it durable, lasting, and universal. The effect on the minds of the owners is to persuade them that there is no wrong in it.

But here in Connecticut and at the North slavery does not exist, and we see it through no such medium. To us it appears natural to think that slaves are human beings; men, not property; that some of the things, at least, stated about men in the Declaration of Independence apply to them as well as to us. We think slavery a great moral wrong; and while we do not claim the right to touch it where it exists, we wish to treat it as a wrong in the Territories where our votes will reach it. Now these two ideas, the property idea that slavery is right, and the idea that it is wrong, come into collision, and do actually produce that irrepressible conflict which Mr. Seward has been so roundly abused for mentioning. The two ideas conflict, and must conflict.

There are but two policies in regard to slavery that can be at all maintained. The first, based upon the property view that slavery is right, conforms to the idea throughout, and demands that we shall do everything for it that we ought to do if it were right. The other policy is one that squares with the idea that slavery is wrong, and it consists in doing everything that we ought to do if it is wrong. I don't mean that we ought to attack it where it exists. To me it seems that if we were to form a government anew, in view of the actual presence of slavery we should find it necessary to frame just such a government as our fathers did—giving to the slaveholder the entire control where the system was established, while we possessed the power to restrain it from going outside those limits.

Now I have spoken of a policy based upon the idea that slavery is wrong, and a policy based upon the idea that it is right. But an effort has been made for a policy that shall treat it as neither right nor wrong. Its central idea is indifference. It holds that it makes no more difference to me whether the Territories become free or slave States than whether my neighbor stocks his farm with horned cattle or puts it into tobacco. All recognize this policy, the plausible, sugar-coated name of which is "popular sovereignty."

[From Nicolay and Hay: "Mr. Lincoln showed up the fallacy of this policy at length, and then made a manly vindication of the principles of the Republican party, urging the necessity of the union of all elements to free our country from its present rule, and closed with an eloquent exhortation for each and every one to do his duty without regard to the sneers and slanders of our political opponents."][578]

Lincoln's use of the word **"collision,"** and also the phrase, **"the two ideas conflict, and must conflict,"** are revealing, for the idea of an inevitable impact, of an **"irrepressible conflict,"** existed only in Lincoln's mind. The issue *had* indeed been settled by 1860: at that time under the Constitution the states were free to choose or reject slavery, and it was no one else's business which choice a particular state made.

In addition, as we saw in Chapter 1, by 1860 the *idea* of slavery was fast dying out, and the institution itself would have become extinct on its own, probably within the next ten or twenty years. Certainly in the South, where the American abolition movement had begun in the 1700s, and where less than 6 percent owned slaves, the region was ripe for the natural abolition of slavery by then. As both Maryland Representative John Woodland Crisfield and Missouri Representative John William Noell told Lincoln on March 10, 1862, an emancipation proclamation was not even necessary in their states as

slavery was not considered a permanent institution . . . [and] natural causes were there in operation which would at no distant day extinguish it . . .[579]

But Lincoln would not leave the situation alone. Like so many liberals today, he could not bear to live in an intellectually pluralistic society. Only his views, beliefs, and opinions mattered. And everyone around him would come to embrace them as well, even if he had to use physical force.

Clearly the new president had been itching for a fight with the conservative South even before he entered the White House, and Fort Sumter would turn out to provide convenient rationalizations for his illegal military campaign against the legally formed Confederacy.

Lincoln had accomplished the near impossible: he had kept his double vow to neither give up Fort Sumter or be the first to strike. He did break one promise, however: he had pledged not to relieve the garrison. But even this was no accident, for this left the Confederates with no alternative but to fire first, while leaving Lincoln looking like an innocent pawn, one who had not forced war, but one who had had war forced upon him.

Here then was the perfect justification for invading the South.[580] For with the **"rebel attack on the U.S. flag,"** as Lincoln told Congress,

> no choice was left but to call out the war power of the Government, and so to resist force employed for its destruction by force for its preservation.[581]

Lincoln's policy toward the South in those early days, now known as "the strategy of defense," was in fact nothing more than a sly tactical maneuver meant to make it appear as if the U.S. was only interested in **"enforcing the laws"** and **"preserving the Union."** Through this skullduggery he was able to portray the South as the "guilty party," the region that had fired the first volley of the War.[582]

Even Lincoln's own official biographers, Nicolay and Hay, later admitted that:

> When the President determined on war, and with the purpose of making it appear that the South was the aggressor, he took measures . . .[583]

These "measures" began just weeks after Lincoln was elected in November 1860.

On December 21 of that year, the day after South Carolina seceded, the Yankee president wrote a "confidential" letter to Elihu B.

Washburne in which he said:

> Please present my respects to the General [Winfield Scott], and tell him, confidentially, I shall be obliged to him to be as well prepared as he can to either *hold*, or *retake*, the forts, as the case may require, at, and after the inauguration.[584]

Lincoln's meaning here is clear. He is saying: "Be prepared to retake the forts when I become president."[585] He was certainly thinking far ahead: he had not even been inaugurated yet and the War was still five months away!

On January 11, 1861, Lincoln wrote to Scott personally to thank him for sharing his strategical ideas with President Buchanan, encouraging Scott to stay in close communication:

> My dear Sir: I herewith beg leave to acknowledge the receipt of your communication of the 4th instant, inclosing (documents Nos. 1, 2, 3, 4, 5, and 6) copies of correspondence and notes of conversation with the President of the United States and the Secretary of War concerning various military movements suggested by yourself for the better protection of the government and the maintenance of public order.
>
> Permit me to renew to you the assurance of my high appreciation of the many past services you have rendered the Union, and of my deep gratification at this evidence of your present active exertions to maintain the integrity and honor of the nation.
>
> I shall be highly pleased to receive from time to time such communications from yourself as you may deem it proper to make to me. Very truly your obedient servant, A. Lincoln.[586]

On January 14, 1861, in a letter to Union General John E. Wool, Lincoln states that he is relying almost exclusively on Wool's and General Scott's military suggestions:

> My dear Sir: Many thanks for your patriotic and generous letter of the 11th instant. As to how far the military force of the government may become necessary to the preservation of the Union, and more particularly how that force can best be directed to the object, I must chiefly rely upon General Scott and yourself. It affords

me the profoundest satisfaction to know that with both of you judgment and feeling go heartily with your sense of professional and official duty to the work.

It is true that I have given but little attention to the military department of government; but, be assured, I cannot be ignorant as to who General Wool is, or what he has done. With my highest esteem and gratitude, I subscribe myself. Your obedient servant, A. Lincoln.[587]

Shrewd as he was, Lincoln cannot claim credit for coming up with the idea of tricking the Confederates; only for perpetrating the hoax.[588] Along with Orville Hickman Browning's earlier suggestion, there was also Lincoln's secretary of the navy, Gideon Welles,[589] who had calculatingly advised the president that "it is very important that the Rebels strike the first blow in the conflict."[590]

Lincoln's assistant secretary of the navy, Gustavus Fox, then took Browning's and Welles' idea and worked out the details of the plan. Writing to Montgomery Blair (soon to be Lincoln's postmaster general) on February 23, 1861, Fox said:

> I simply propose three tugs, convoyed by light-draft men-of-war. . . . The first tug to lead in empty, to open their fire.[591]

This was a no-win situation for the South: if she allowed Lincoln to "resupply" the fort, it would remain in the enemy's hands, humiliating the Confederacy. If the South attacked, she would be blamed for "starting the War." Lincoln had her right where he wanted.

Fox's tugboat plan never materialized, however, because the Rebels, having been grossly misled and lied to, went ahead and bombed and captured the fort first. But either way, the end result was still what Lincoln had intended: the South had, in Lincoln's words, **"fired upon the United States flag,"**[592] and thus now appeared to the world to be the aggressor.[593] The onus of initiating war thus came to lay with the Confederacy.

On May 1, 1861, three weeks after his foul deed at Sumter had been committed, Lincoln acknowledged his devilish connivance in a letter to Fox. While Fox was disappointed that his and Welles' scheme had not succeeded as planned, Lincoln was elated:

> My dear Sir: I sincerely regret that the failure of the late attempt to provision Fort Sumter should be the source of any annoyance to you.

The practicability of your plan was not, in fact, brought to a test. By reason of a gale, well known in advance to be possible and not improbable, the tugs, an essential part of the plan, never reached the ground; while, by an accident for which you were in no wise responsible, and possibly I to some extent was, you were deprived of a war vessel, with her men, which you deemed of great importance to the enterprise.

I most cheerfully and truly declare that the failure of the undertaking has not lowered you a particle, while the qualities you developed in the effort have greatly heightened you in my estimation.

For a daring and dangerous enterprise of a similar character you would to-day be the man of all my acquaintances whom I would select. You and I both anticipated that the cause of the country would be advanced by making the attempt to provision Fort Sumter, even if it should fail; and it is no small consolation now to feel that our anticipation is justified by the result. Very truly your friend, A. Lincoln.[594]

What "results?" The inauguration of a war he so desperately wanted.

Lincoln also states here that it was bad weather that prevented his war flotilla from entering the harbor. But this was not the reason. He had told his navy commanders, either privately or secretly, to stand down, and allow the Confederacy to shoot itself in the foot, so to speak. Thus, as Confederate army chaplain Robert Lewis Dabney so aptly observed, Lincoln's War was "conceived in duplicity, and brought forth in iniquity."[595]

As we have seen, signs of Lincoln's desire to inaugurate war on the South came long before the War itself, or even his election to the presidency. One of the many who picked up on these ominous indicators was Illinois Senator Stephen A. Douglas, who loved to get under Lincoln's skin by accusing him of being an "abolitionist." Here is what Douglas said during his seventh and final debate with Lincoln at Alton, Illinois, on October 15, 1858. Note in particular Douglas' last sentence, which he no doubt addressed directly to Lincoln's face during the debate:

> Remember that the Union was then composed of thirteen States, twelve of which were slave-holding and one free. Do you think that the one free State would have out-voted the twelve slaveholding States, and thus have secured the abolition of slavery? On the other hand, would not the twelve slave-holding States have

outvoted the one free State, and thus have fastened slavery, by a constitutional provision, on every foot of the American republic forever? You see that if this Abolition doctrine of Mr. Lincoln had prevailed when the government was made, it would have established slavery as a permanent institution, in all the States, whether they wanted it or not; and the question for us to determine in Illinois now, as one of the free States, is whether or not we are willing, having become the majority section, to enforce a doctrine on the minority which we would have resisted with our hearts' blood had it been attempted on us when we were in a minority. How has the South lost her power as the majority section in this Union, and how have the free States gained it, except under the operation of that principle which declares the right of the people of each State and each Territory to form and regulate their domestic institutions in their own way? It was under that principle that slavery was abolished in New Hampshire, Rhode Island, Connecticut, New York, New Jersey, and Pennsylvania; it was under that principle that one half of the slave-holding States became free; it was under that principle that the number of free States increased until, from being one out of twelve States, we have grown to be the majority of States of the whole Union, with the power to control the House of Representatives and Senate, and the power, consequently, to elect a President by Northern votes without the aid of a Southern State. Having obtained this power under the operation of that great principle, are you now prepared to abandon the principle, and declare that merely because we have the power you will wage a war against the Southern States and their institutions until you force them to abolish slavery everywhere?[596]

Thus, by the fall of 1858, Americans everywhere were fully aware of Lincoln's desire to wage war on the Southern states.

On July 4, 1861, in his "Message to Congress in Special Session" three years later, Lincoln himself unveiled a by now well thought out justification for his treachery, claiming that all of the forts located in the seceded states (then South Carolina, Georgia, Alabama, Mississippi, Louisiana, and Florida) **"had been seized** [by the South]**, and were held in open hostility"** to the U.S. government.[597] He ignores the plain fact that the Confederacy was a lawfully formed foreign nation and that these forts now belonged to the South. But he had to, of course, in order to keep up his charade.

The rest of this speech is filled with hyperbolic references to the South's **"hostile purpose,"** her **"warlike preparations,"** her **"hostile batteries,"** and her **"treacherous associates,"** all who **"had taken up** arms against the [U.S.] Government," all who were members of **"this illegal organization in the character of confederate states . . ."**[598]

Lincoln continues on and on, giving his fake version of the events at Fort Sumter; describing what he considers to be the misconceptions and illegalities of secession; offering his twisted and unconstitutional reasons for assuming **"extraordinary powers"** in time of a **"dangerous emergency"**; issuing his request of Congress for $400 million (about $10 billion in today's currency) to expedite his war; and finally revealing his true purpose in trying to force the South back into what the Founders had intended to be a *voluntary* union: hard cold cash and the Southern people and their nearly limitless natural resources—or what he called, in his typical unpoetic fashion, **"blood and treasure."**[599] The entire illicit invasion of the South was authorized using the equally deceptive and mangled reasoning that the Constitution provides that **"the United States shall guarantee to every State in this Union a republican form of government."**[600]

Here is Lincoln's entire speech:

> Fellow-citizens of the Senate and House of Representatives: Having been convened on an extraordinary occasion, as authorized by the Constitution, your attention is not called to any ordinary subject of legislation.
>
> At the beginning of the present presidential term, four months ago, the functions of the Federal Government were found to be generally suspended within the several States of South Carolina, Georgia, Alabama, Mississippi, Louisiana, and Florida, excepting only those of the Post-office Department.
>
> Within these States all the forts, arsenals, dockyards, customhouses, and the like, including the movable and stationary property in and about them, had been seized, and were held in open hostility to this government, excepting only Forts Pickens, Taylor, and Jefferson, on and near the Florida coast, and Fort Sumter, in Charleston Harbor, South Carolina. The forts thus seized had been put in improved condition, new ones had been built, and armed forces had been organized and were organizing, all avowedly with the same hostile purpose.
>
> The forts remaining in the possession of the Federal Government in and near these States were either besieged or menaced by warlike preparations, and

especially Fort Sumter was nearly surrounded by well-protected hostile batteries, with guns equal in quality to the best of its own, and outnumbering the latter as perhaps ten to one. A disproportionate share of the Federal muskets and rifles had somehow found their way into these States, and had been seized to be used against the government. Accumulations of the public revenue lying within them had been seized for the same object. The navy was scattered in distant seas, leaving but a very small part of it within the immediate reach of the government. Officers of the Federal army and navy had resigned in great numbers; and of those resigning a large proportion had taken up arms against the [U.S.] government. Simultaneously, and in connection with all this, the purpose to sever the Federal Union was openly avowed. In accordance with this purpose, an ordinance had been adopted in each of these States, declaring the States respectively to be separated from the National Union. A formula for instituting a combined government of these States had been promulgated; and this illegal organization, in the character of confederate States, was already invoking recognition, aid, and intervention from foreign powers.

  Finding this condition of things, and believing it to be an imperative duty upon the incoming executive to prevent, if possible, the consummation of such attempt to destroy the Federal Union, a choice of means, to that end became indispensable. This choice was made and was declared in the inaugural address. The policy chosen looked to the exhaustion of all peaceful measures before a resort to any stronger ones. It sought only to hold the public places and property not already wrested from the government, and to collect the revenue, relying for the rest on time, discussion, and the ballot-box. It promised a continuance of the mails, at government expense, to the very people who were resisting the government; and it gave repeated pledges against any disturbance to any of the people, or any of their rights. Of all that which a President might constitutionally and justifiably do in such a case, everything was forborne without which it was believed possible to keep the government on foot.

  On the 5th of March (the present incumbent's first full day in office), a letter of Major Anderson, commanding at Fort Sumter, written on the 28th of February and received at the War Department on the 4th

of March, was by that department placed in his hands. This letter expressed the professional opinion of the writer that reinforcements could not be thrown into that fort within the time for his relief, rendered necessary by the limited supply of provisions, and with a view of holding possession of the same, with a force of less than twenty thousand good and well-disciplined men. This opinion was concurred in by all the officers of his command, and their memoranda on the subject were made inclosures of Major Anderson's letter. The whole was immediately laid before Lieutenant-General [Winfield] Scott, who at once concurred with Major Anderson in opinion. On reflection, however, he took full time, consulting with other officers, both of the army and the navy, and at the end of four days came reluctantly but decidedly to the same conclusion as before. He also stated at the same time that no such sufficient force was then at the control of the government, or could be raised and brought to the ground within the time when the provisions in the fort would be exhausted. In a purely military point of view, this reduced the duty of the administration in the case to the mere matter of getting the garrison safely out of the fort.

It was believed, however, that to so abandon that position, under the circumstances, would be utterly ruinous: that the necessity under which it was to be done would not be fully understood; that by many it would be construed as a part of a voluntary policy; that at home it would discourage the friends of the Union, embolden its adversaries, and go far to insure to the latter a recognition abroad; that, in fact, it would be our national destruction consummated. This could not be allowed. Starvation was not yet upon the garrison, and ere it would be reached Fort Pickens might lie reinforced. This last would be a clear indication of policy, and would better enable the country to accept the evacuation of Fort Sumter as a military necessity. An order was at once directed to be sent for the landing of the troops from the steamship *Brooklyn* into Fort Pickens. This order could not go by land, but must take the longer and slower route by sea. The first return news from the order was received just one week before the fall of Fort Sumter. This news itself was that the officer commanding the *Sabine*, to which vessel the troops had been transferred from the Brooklyn, acting upon some *quasi* armistice of the late administration (and of the existence of which the present administration, up to the time the order was despatched, had only too vague and uncertain rumors to fix attention), had refused to land the troops. To now reinforce Fort Pickens before a crisis would be reached at Fort Sumter was impossible—rendered so by the near exhaustion of provisions in the latter-named fort. In precaution against such a conjuncture, the government had, a few days before, commenced preparing an expedition as well adapted as might be to relieve Fort Sumter, which expedition was intended to be ultimately used, or not, according to circumstances. The strongest anticipated case for using it was now presented, and it was resolved to send it forward. As had been intended in this contingency, it was also resolved to notify the governor of South Carolina [Francis W. Pickens] that he might expect an attempt would be made to provision the fort; and that, if the attempt should not be resisted, there would be no effort to throw in men, arms, or ammunition, without further notice, or in case of an attack upon the fort. This notice was accordingly given; whereupon the fort was attacked and bombarded to its fall, without even awaiting the arrival of the provisioning expedition.

It is thus seen that the assault upon and reduction of Fort Sumter was in no sense a matter of self-defense on the part of the assailants. They well knew that the garrison in the fort could by no possibility commit aggression upon them. They knew—they were expressly notified—that the giving of bread to the few brave and hungry men of the garrison was all which would on that occasion be attempted, unless themselves, by resisting so much, should provoke more. They knew that this government desired to keep the garrison in the fort, not to assail them, but merely to maintain visible possession, and thus to preserve the Union from actual and immediate dissolution—trusting, as hereinbefore stated, to time, discussion, and the ballot-box for final adjustment; and they assailed and reduced the fort for precisely the reverse object—to drive out the visible authority of the Federal Union, and thus force it to immediate dissolution. That this was their object the executive well understood; and having said to them in the inaugural address, "You can have no conflict without being yourselves the aggressors," he took pains not only to keep this declaration good, but also to keep the case so free from the power of ingenious sophistry that the world should not be able to misunderstand it. By the affair at Fort Sumter, with its surrounding circumstances, that point was reached. Then and thereby the assailants of the government began the conflict of arms, without a gun in sight or in expectancy to return their fire, save only the few in the fort sent to that harbor years before for their own protection, and still ready to give that protection in whatever was lawful. In this act, discarding all else, they have forced upon the country the distinct issue, "immediate dissolution or blood."

And this issue embraces more than the fate of these United States. It presents to the whole family of man the question whether a constitutional republic or democracy—a government of the people by the same people—can or cannot maintain its territorial integrity against its own domestic foes. It presents the question whether discontented individuals, too few in numbers to control administration according to organic law in any case, can always, upon the pretenses made in this case, or on any other pretenses, or arbitrarily without any pretense, break up their government, and thus practically put an end to free government upon the earth. It forces us to ask: "Is there, in all republics, this inherent and fatal weakness?" "Must a government, of necessity, be too strong for the liberties of its own people, or too weak to maintain its own existence?"

So viewing the issue, no choice was left but to call out the war power of the government; and so to resist force employed for its destruction, by force for its preservation.

The call was made, and the response of the country was most gratifying, surpassing in unanimity and spirit the most sanguine expectation. Yet none of the States commonly called slave States, except Delaware, gave a regiment through regular State organization. A few regiments have been organized within some others of those States by individual enterprise, and received into the government service. Of course the seceded States, so called (and to which Texas had been joined about the time of the inauguration), gave no troops to the cause of the Union. The border States, so called, were not uniform in their action, some of them being almost for the Union, while in others—as Virginia, North Carolina,

Tennessee, and Arkansas—the Union sentiment was nearly repressed and silenced. The course taken in Virginia was the most remarkable—perhaps the most important. A convention elected by the people of that State to consider this very question of disrupting the Federal Union was in session at the capital of Virginia when Fort Sumter fell. To this body the people had chosen a large majority of professed Union men. Almost immediately after the fall of Sumter, many members of that majority went over to the original disunion minority, and with them adopted an ordinance for withdrawing the State from the Union. Whether this change was wrought by their great approval of the assault upon Sumter, or their great resentment at the government's resistance to that assault, is not definitely known. Although they submitted the ordinance for ratification to a vote of the people, to be taken on a day then somewhat more than a month distant, the convention and the legislature (which was also in session at the same time and place), with leading men of the State not members of either, immediately commenced acting as if the State were already out of the Union. They pushed military preparations vigorously forward all over the State. They seized the United States armory at Harper's Ferry, and the navy-yard at Gosport, near Norfolk. They received—perhaps invited—into their State large bodies of troops, with their warlike appointments, from the so-called seceded States. They formally entered into a treaty of temporary alliance and cooperation with the so-called "Confederate States," and sent members to their congress at Montgomery. And, finally, they permitted the insurrectionary government to be transferred to their capital at Richmond.

  The people of Virginia have thus allowed this giant insurrection to make its nest within her borders; and this government has no choice left but to deal with it where it finds it. And it has the less regret as the loyal citizens have, in due form, claimed its protection. Those loyal citizens this government is bound to recognize and protect, as being Virginia.

  In the border States, so called,—in fact, the Middle States,—there are those who favor a policy which they call "armed neutrality"; that is, an arming of those States to prevent the Union forces passing one way, or the disunion the other, over their soil. This would be disunion completed. Figuratively speaking, it would be the building of an impassable wall along the line of separation—and yet not quite an impassable one, for under the guise of neutrality it would tie the hands of Union men and freely pass supplies from among them to the insurrectionists, which it could not do as an open enemy. At a stroke it would take all the trouble off the hands of secession, except only what proceeds from the external blockade. It would do for the disunionists that which, of all things, they most desire—feed them well, and give them disunion without a struggle of their own. It recognizes no fidelity to the Constitution, no obligation to maintain the Union; and while very many who have favored it are doubtless loyal citizens, it is, nevertheless, very injurious in effect.

Recurring to the action of the government, it may be stated that at first a call was made for 75,000 militia; and, rapidly following this, a proclamation was issued for closing the ports of the insurrectionary districts by proceedings in the nature of blockade. So far all was believed to be strictly legal. At this point the insurrectionists announced their purpose to enter upon the practice of privateering.

Other calls were made for volunteers to serve for three years, unless sooner discharged, and also for large additions to the regular army and navy. These measures, whether strictly legal or not, were ventured upon, under what appeared to be a popular demand and a public necessity; trusting then, as now, that Congress would readily ratify them. It is believed that nothing has been done beyond the constitutional competency of Congress.

Soon after the first call for militia, it was considered a duty to authorize the commanding general in proper cases, according to his discretion, to suspend the privilege of the writ of *habeas corpus*, or, in other words, to arrest and detain, without resort to the ordinary processes and forms of law, such individuals as he might deem dangerous to the public safety. This authority has purposely been exercised but very sparingly. Nevertheless, the legality and propriety of what has been done under it are questioned, and the attention of the country has been called to the proposition that one who has sworn to "take care that the laws be faithfully executed" should not himself violate them. Of course some consideration was given to the questions of power and propriety before this matter was acted upon. The whole of the laws which were required to be faithfully executed were being resisted and failing of execution in nearly one third of the States. Must they be allowed to finally fail of execution, even had it been perfectly clear that by the use of the means necessary to their execution some single law, made in such extreme tenderness of the citizen's liberty that, practically, it relieves more of the guilty than of the innocent, should to a very limited extent be violated? To state the question more directly, are all the laws but one to go unexecuted, and the government itself go to pieces lest that one be violated? Even in such a case, would not the official oath be broken if the government should be overthrown, when it was believed that disregarding the single law would tend to preserve it? But it was not believed that this question was presented. It was not believed that any law was violated. The provision of the Constitution that "the privilege of the writ of *habeas corpus* shall not be suspended, unless when, in cases of rebellion or invasion, the public safety may require it," is equivalent to a provision—is a provision—that such privilege may be suspended when, in case of rebellion or invasion, the public safety does require it. It was decided that we have a case of rebellion, and that the public safety does require the qualified suspension of the privilege of the writ which was authorized to be made. Now it is insisted that Congress, and not the executive, is vested with this power. But the Constitution itself is silent as to which or who is to exercise the power; and as the provision was plainly made for a dangerous emergency, it cannot be believed the framers of the instrument intended that in every case the danger should run its course until Congress could be called together, the very assembling of which might be prevented, as was intended in this case, by the rebellion.

No more extended argument is now offered, as an opinion at some length will probably be presented by the attorney-general. Whether there shall be any legislation upon the subject, and if any, what, is submitted entirely to the better judgment of Congress.

The forbearance of this government had been so extraordinary and so long continued as to lead some foreign nations to shape their action as if they supposed the early destruction of our National Union was probable. While this, on discovery, gave the executive some concern, he is now happy to say that the sovereignty and rights of the United States are now everywhere practically respected by foreign powers; and a general sympathy with the country is manifested throughout the world.

The reports of the Secretaries of the Treasury, War, and the Navy will give the information in detail deemed necessary and convenient for your deliberation and action; while the executive and all the departments will stand ready to supply omissions, or to communicate new facts considered important for you to know.

It is now recommended that you give the legal means for making this contest a short and decisive one: that you place at the control of the government for the work at least four hundred thousand men and $400,000,000. That number of men is about one tenth of those of proper ages within the regions where, apparently, all are willing to engage; and the sum is less than a twenty-third part of the money value owned by the men who seem ready to devote the whole. A debt of $600,000,000 now is a less sum per head than was the debt of our Revolution when we came out of that struggle; and the money value in the country now bears even a greater proportion to what it was then than does the population. Surely each man has as strong a motive now to preserve our liberties as each had then to establish them.

A right result at this time will be worth more to the world than ten times the men and ten times the money. The evidence reaching us from the country leaves no doubt that the material for the work is abundant, and that it needs only the hand of legislation to give it legal sanction, and the hand of the executive to give it practical shape and efficiency. One of the greatest perplexities of the government is to avoid receiving troops faster than it can provide for them. In a word, the people will save their government if the government itself will do its part only indifferently well.

It might seem, at first thought, to be of little difference whether the present movement at the South be called "secession" or "rebellion." The movers, however, well understand the difference. At the beginning they knew they could never raise their treason to any respectable magnitude by any name which implies violation of law. They knew their people possessed as much of moral sense, as much of devotion to law and order, and as much pride in and reverence for the history and government of their common country as any other civilized and patriotic people. They knew they could make no advancement directly in the teeth of these strong and noble sentiments. Accordingly, they commenced by an insidious debauching of the public mind. They invented an ingenious sophism which, if conceded, was followed by perfectly logical steps, through all the incidents, to the complete destruction of the Union. The sophism itself is that any State of the Union may consistently with the National Constitution, and therefore lawfully and peacefully, withdraw from the Union without the consent of the Union or of any other State. The little disguise that the supposed right is to be exercised only for just cause, themselves to be the sole judges of its justice, is too thin to merit any notice.

With rebellion thus sugar-coated they have been drugging the public mind of their section for more than thirty years, and until at length they have brought many good men to a willingness to take up arms against the government the day after some assemblage of men have enacted the farcical pretense of taking their State out of the Union, who could have been brought to no such thing the day before.

This sophism derives much, perhaps the whole, of its currency from the assumption that there is some omnipotent and sacred supremacy pertaining to a State—to each State of our Federal Union. Our States have neither more nor less power than that reserved to them in the Union by the Constitution—no one of them ever having been a State out of the Union. The original ones passed into the Union even before they cast off their British colonial dependence; and the new ones each came into the Union directly from a condition of dependence, excepting Texas. And even Texas, in its temporary independence, was never designated a State. The new ones only took the designation of States on coming into the Union, while that name was first adopted for the old ones in and by the Declaration of Independence. Therein the "United Colonies" were declared to be "free and independent States"; but even then the object plainly was not to declare their independence of one another or of the Union, but directly the contrary, as their mutual pledge and their mutual action before, at the time, and afterward, abundantly show. The express plighting of faith by each and all of the original thirteen in the Articles of Confederation, two years later, that the Union shall be perpetual, is most conclusive. Having never been States either in substance or in name outside of the Union, whence this magical omnipotence of "State Rights," asserting a claim of power to lawfully destroy the Union itself? Much is said about the "sovereignty" of the States; but the word even is not in the National Constitution, nor, as is believed, in any of the State constitutions. What is "sovereignty" in the political sense of the term? Would it be far wrong to define it "a political community without a political superior"? Tested by this, no one of our States except Texas ever was a sovereignty. And even Texas gave up the character on coming into the Union; by which act she acknowledged the Constitution of the United States, and the laws and treaties of the United States made in pursuance of the Constitution, to be for her the supreme law of the land. The States have their status in the Union, and they have no other legal status. If they break from this, they can only do so against law and by revolution. The Union, and not themselves separately, procured their independence and their liberty. By conquest or purchase the Union gave each of them whatever of independence or liberty it has. The Union is older than any of the States, and, in fact, it created them as States. Originally some dependent colonies made the Union, and, in turn, the Union threw off their old dependence for them, and made them States, such as they are. Not one of them ever had a State constitution independent of the Union. Of course, it is not forgotten that all the new States framed their constitutions before they entered the Union—nevertheless, dependent upon and preparatory to coming into the Union.

Unquestionably the States have the powers and rights reserved to them in and by the National Constitution; but among these surely are not included all conceivable powers, however mischievous or destructive, but, at most, such only as were known in the world at the time as governmental powers; and certainly a power to destroy the government itself had never been known as a governmental, as a merely administrative power. This relative matter of national power and State rights, as a principle, is no other than the principle of generality and locality. Whatever concerns the whole should be confided to the whole—to the General Government; while whatever concerns only the State should be left exclusively to the State. This is all there is of original principle about it. Whether the National Constitution in denning boundaries between the two has applied the principle with exact accuracy, is not to be questioned. We are all bound by that denning, without question.

What is now combated is the position that secession is consistent with the Constitution—is lawful and peaceful. It is not contended that there is any express law for it; and nothing should ever be implied as law which leads to unjust or absurd consequences. The nation purchased with money the countries out of which several of these States were formed. Is it just that they shall go off without leave and without refunding? The nation paid very large sums (in the aggregate, I believe, nearly a hundred millions) to relieve Florida of the aboriginal tribes. Is it just that she shall now be off without consent or without making any return? The nation is now in debt for money applied to the benefit of these so-called seceding States in common with the rest. Is it just either that creditors shall go unpaid or the remaining States pay the whole? A part of the present national debt was contracted to pay the old debts of Texas. Is it just that she shall leave and pay no part of this herself? Again, if one State may secede, so may another; and when all shall have seceded, none is left to pay the debts. Is this quite just to creditors? Did we notify them or this sage view of ours when we borrowed their money? If we now recognize this doctrine by allowing the seceders to go in peace, it is difficult to see what we can do if others choose to go or to extort terms upon which they will promise to remain.

The seceders insist that our Constitution admits of secession. They have assumed to make a national constitution of their own, in which of necessity they have either discarded or retained the right of secession as they insist it exists in ours. If they have discarded it, they thereby admit that on principle it ought not to be in ours. If they have retained it by their own construction of ours, they show that to be consistent they must secede from one another whenever they shall find it the easiest way of settling their debts, or effecting any other selfish or unjust object. The principle itself is one of disintegration, and upon which no government can possibly endure.

If all the States save one should assert the power to drive that one out of the Union, it is presumed the whole class of seceder politicians would at once deny the power and denounce the act as the greatest outrage upon State rights. But suppose that precisely the same act, instead of being called "driving the one out," should be called "the seceding of the others from that one," it would be exactly what the seceders claim to do, unless, indeed, they make the point that the one, because it is a minority, may rightfully do what the others, because they are a majority, may not rightfully do. These politicians are subtle and profound on the rights of minorities. They are not partial to that power which made the Constitution and speaks from the preamble calling itself "We, the People."

It may well be questioned whether there is to-day a majority of the legally qualified voters of any State, except perhaps South Carolina, in favor of disunion. There is much reason to believe that the Union men are the majority in many, if not in every other one, of the so-called seceded States. The contrary has not been demonstrated in any one of them. It is ventured to affirm this even of Virginia and Tennessee; for the result of an election held in military camps, where the bayonets are all on one side of the question voted upon, can scarcely be considered as demonstrating popular sentiment. At such an election, all that large class who are at once for the Union and against coercion would be coerced to vote against the Union.

It may be affirmed without extravagance that the free institutions we enjoy have developed the powers and improved the condition of our whole people beyond any example in the world. Of this we now have a striking and an impressive illustration. So large an army as the government has now on foot was never before known, without a soldier in it but who has taken his place there of his own free choice. But more than this, there are many single regiments whose members, one and another, possess full practical knowledge of all the arts, sciences, professions, and whatever else, whether useful or elegant, is known in the world; and there is scarcely one from which there could not be selected a President, a cabinet, a congress, and perhaps a court, abundantly competent to administer the government itself. Nor do I say this is not true also in the army of our late friends, now adversaries in this contest; but if it is, so much better the reason why the government which has conferred such benefits on both them and us should not be broken up. Whoever in any section proposes to abandon such a government would do well to consider in deference to what principle it is that he does it—what better he is likely to get in its stead—whether the substitute will give, or be intended to give, so much of good to the people? There are some foreshadowings on this subject. Our adversaries have adopted some declarations of independence in which, unlike the good old one, penned by [Thomas] Jefferson, they omit the words "all men are created equal." Why? They have adopted a temporary national constitution, in the preamble of which, unlike our good old one, signed by [George] Washington, they omit "We, the People," and substitute, "We, the deputies of the sovereign and independent States." Why? Why this deliberate pressing out of view the rights of men and the authority of the people?

This is essentially a people's contest. On the side of the Union it is a struggle for maintaining in the world that form and substance of government whose leading object is to elevate the condition of men—to lift artificial weights from all shoulders; to clear the paths of laudable pursuit for all; to afford all an unfettered start, and a fair chance in the race of life. Yielding to partial and temporary departures, from necessity, this is the leading object of the government for whose existence we contend.

I am most happy to believe that the plain people understand and appreciate this. It is worthy of note that while in this, the government's hour of trial, large numbers of those in the army and navy who have been favored with the offices have resigned and proved false to the hand which had pampered them, not one common soldier or common sailor is known to have deserted his flag.

Great honor is due to those officers who remained true, despite the example of their treacherous associates; but the greatest honor, and most important fact of all, is the unanimous firmness of the common soldiers and common sailors. To the last man, so far as known, they have successfully resisted the traitorous efforts of those whose commands, but an hour before, they obeyed as absolute law. This is the patriotic instinct of the plain people. They understand, without an argument, that the destroying of the government which was made by Washington means no good to them.

Our popular government has often been called an experiment. Two points in it our people have already settled—the successful establishing and the successful administering of it. One still remains—its successful maintenance against a formidable internal attempt to overthrow it. It is now for them to demonstrate to the world that those who can fairly carry an election can also suppress a rebellion; that ballots are the rightful and peaceful successors of bullets; and that when ballots have fairly and constitutionally decided, there can be no successful appeal back to bullets; that there can be no successful appeal, except to ballots themselves, at succeeding elections. Such will be a great lesson of peace: teaching men that what they cannot take by an election, neither can they take it by a war; teaching all the folly of being the beginners of a war.

Lest there be some uneasiness in the minds of candid men as to what is to be the course of the government toward the Southern States after the rebellion shall have been suppressed, the executive deems it proper to say it will be his purpose then, as ever, to be guided by the Constitution and the laws; and that he probably will have no different understanding of the powers and duties of the Federal Government relatively to the rights of the States and the people, under the Constitution, than that expressed in the inaugural address.

He desires to preserve the government, that it may be administered for all as it was administered by the men who made it. Loyal citizens everywhere have the right to claim this of their government, and the government has no right to withhold or neglect it. It is not perceived that in giving it there is any coercion, any conquest, or any subjugation, in any just sense of those terms.

The Constitution provides, and all the States have accepted the provision, that "the United States shall guarantee to every State in this Union a republican form of government." But if a State may lawfully go out of the Union, having done so, it may also discard the republican form of government; so that to prevent its going out is an indispensable means to the end of maintaining the guarantee mentioned; and when an end is lawful and obligatory, the indispensable means to it are also lawful and obligatory.

It was with the deepest regret that the executive found the duty of employing the war power in defense of the government forced upon him. He could but perform this duty or surrender the existence of the government. No compromise by public servants could, in this case, be a cure; not that compromises are not often proper, but that no popular government can long survive a marked precedent that those who carry an election can only save the government from immediate destruction by giving up the main point upon which the people gave the election. The people themselves, and not their servants, can safely reverse their own deliberate decisions.

As a private citizen the executive could not have consented that these institutions shall perish; much less could he, in betrayal of so vast and so sacred a trust as the free people have confided to him. He felt that he had no moral right to shrink, nor even to count the chances of his own life in what might follow. In full view of his great responsibility he has, so far, done what he has deemed his duty. You will now, according to your own judgment, perform yours. He sincerely hopes that your views and your actions may so accord with his, as to assure all faithful citizens who have been disturbed in their rights of a certain and speedy restoration to them, under the Constitution and the laws.

And having thus chosen our course, without guile and with pure purpose, let us renew our trust in God, and go forward without fear and with manly hearts. Abraham Lincoln.[601]

This speech, written in typical self-serving lawyer speak—and weirdly, often in the third person—is filled with so many falsehoods, so much misinformation and outright disinformation, that it is difficult to know where to begin.

Lincoln claims he **"exhausted all peaceful measures"** before deciding to go to war. Actually, he *ignored* all peaceful measures before deciding to go to war. Prior to, and all through the conflict, Confederate

President Davis sent peace commission after peace commission to Washington in an attempt, first to prevent any bloodshed, and afterward to halt the bloodshed. Lincoln coldly disregarded all of them, even admitting publicly that

> no attempt at negotiation with the insurgent leader could result in any good.[602]

There is also the March 3, 1865, letter, signed by Union Secretary of War Edwin M. Stanton, but written in Lincoln's hand in the third person:

> **The President wishes me to say that he wishes you to have no conference with General Lee unless it be for the capitulation of General Lee's army, or on some minor or purely military matter. He desires me to say that you are not to decide, discuss or confer upon any political questions. Such questions the President holds in his own hands, and will submit them to no military conferences or conventions. Meanwhile you are to press to the utmost your military advantages.**[603]

Such statements show that Lincoln never had any intention of meeting with Southern officers or diplomats, let alone even considering trying to settle differences and ending the War as quickly as possible.

For example, the following July 4, 1863, dispatch from Lincoln to U.S. Rear Admiral Samuel Phillips Lee (a relative of Robert E. Lee), reveals how the president typically handled the South's many attempts to meet with him in an effort to counsel for peace:

> Your despatch transmitting a note from [Confederate Vice President] **Mr. Alexander H. Stephens has been received.**
> You will not permit Mr. Stephens to proceed to Washington or to pass the blockade. He does not make known the subjects to which the communication in writing from Mr. [Jefferson] **Davis relates, which he bears and seeks to deliver in person to the President, and upon which he desires to confer. Those subjects can only be military or not military, or partly both. Whatever may be military will be readily received if offered through the well-understood military channel. Of course nothing else will be received by the President when offered, as in this case, in terms assuming the independence of the**

so-called Confederate States; and anything will be received, and carefully considered by him, when offered by any influential person or persons in terms not assuming the independence of the so-called Confederate States."[604]

We will note here not only Lincoln's unnecessarily sarcastic remarks and his complete and utter inflexibility, but also his refusal to address his Southern counterpart, the Confederacy's highest leader, as *President* Davis.

There *was* one exception to Lincoln's stubbornness concerning negotiations with the Confederacy.

On February 3, 1865, he personally met with a Rebel peace commission aboard the presidential steamer *River Queen*, anchored at Fort Monroe, at Hampton Roads (Hampton, Virginia). Here he argued and obfuscated with the Rebel diplomats for four hours, refusing to give one inch on any issue—although he did promise that the Southern states could continue to practice slavery indefinitely if they would only return to the Union[605] and pay their taxes.[606] The whole meeting on Lincoln's part was nothing but a fraud to keep up the pretense that it was not he who was prolonging the War, it was the South.

In his "Message to Congress in Special Session" on July 4, 1861, he repeats his assertion that his main interest was not in abolishing slavery, but in **"collecting the revenue"** owed to the U.S. by the Southern states.[607] Could not this issue have been settled in court, and without waging a full scale war on a legally formed nation?

He retells the "starving fort" fairy tale and puts full blame on the Rebels for launching the conflict, accusing them of **"forcing the immediate dissolution of the Federal Union"** and **"putting an end to free government upon the earth,"** both ideas which are preposterous, demonstrably false, and technically impossible.

Due to the **"rebellion"** of the **"so-called Confederate States,"** as he labeled the South disparagingly, Lincoln says he had the right to declare a **"dangerous emergency"** and **"call out the war power,"** which, in essence, he assumed gave him unlimited power. Indeed he used this imaginary power to commit a long list of war crimes, such as waging war and suspending *habeas corpus* without congressional approval, and establishing an illegal naval blockade in the South, among hundreds of other felonies. Laughingly, he believed that all of his actions were **"strictly legal,"** and that:

> These measures, whether strictly legal or not, were ventured upon, under what appeared to be a popular demand and a public necessity; trusting then, as now, that Congress would readily ratify them. It is believed that nothing has been done beyond the constitutional competency of Congress.[608]

All of this was untrue: as there was no **"popular demand"** and no **"public necessity,"** it was all unconstitutional. These should have been termed what they really were: "unpopular demand"[609] and "Lincoln's necessity." And just what was that necessity? His need to destroy the concept of states' rights across Dixie so that he could force the wealth-producing Southern states back into the Union.

Our sixteenth chief executive claims here that the Confederacy is seeking to **"overthrow"** the U.S. government, and that the South is the **"beginner of a war."** But the South had no designs on Washington, D.C. and, as we have shown in this chapter, it was Lincoln who began the conflict.

He claims that **"this is essentially a people's contest."** But it was actually essentially a Lincoln contest. He maintains that his goal is to **"preserve the government"** so that it may be **"administered for all as it was administered by the men who made it."** But the U.S. government was never in jeopardy, and the men who made it never intended for it to be forced on those who did not want it.

Lincoln states that he is struggling to

> elevate the condition of men—to lift artificial weights from all shoulders; to clear the paths of laudable pursuit for all; to afford all an unfettered start, and a fair chance in the race of life.[610]

But it was he who continually hampered the legal, civil, and social progress of blacks, and who in general lowered their condition, put artificial weights on their shoulders, obstructed their paths, fettered their start, and gave them an unfair chance in **"the race of life."**

Lincoln pronounces Southerners guilty of **"treason,"** an impossibility since the Confederate States of America were formed legally under the Constitution's Ninth and Tenth Amendments. In point of fact, it was Lincoln who was guilty of treason: in the 1840s he put U.S. forces at risk by repeatedly issuing antiwar statements about the Mexican-American

War (1846-1848). In his seventh and final senatorial debate with Lincoln on October 15, 1858, Stephen A. Douglas detailed Lincoln's treason:

> When the Mexican war was being waged, and the American army was surrounded by the enemy in Mexico, he thought the war was unconstitutional, unnecessary, and unjust. He thought it was not commenced on the right spot.
>
> When I made an incidental allusion of that kind in the joint discussion over at Charleston, some weeks ago, Lincoln, in replying, said that I, Douglas, had charged him with voting against supplies for the Mexican war, and then he reared up, full length, and swore that he never voted against the supplies,—that it was a slander,—and caught hold of [Orlando Bell] Ficklin, who sat on the stand, and said, "Here, Ficklin, tell the people that it is a lie." Well, Ficklin, who had served in Congress with him, stood up and told them all he recollected about it. It was that when George Ashmun, of Massachusetts, brought forward a resolution declaring the war unconstitutional, unnecessary, and unjust, [and] Lincoln had voted for it. "Yes," said Lincoln, "I did." Thus he confessed that he voted that the war was wrong, that our country was in the wrong, and consequently that the Mexicans were in the right; but charged that I had slandered him by saying that he voted against the supplies. I never charged him with voting against the supplies in my life, because I knew that he was not in Congress when they were voted. The war was commenced on the 13th day of May, 1846, and on that day we appropriated in Congress ten millions of dollars and fifty thousand men to prosecute it. During the same session we voted more men and more money, and at the next session we voted more men and more money, so that by the time Mr. Lincoln entered Congress we had enough men and enough money to carry on the war, and had no occasion to vote for any more. When he got into the House, being opposed to the war, and not being able to stop the supplies, because they had all gone forward, all he could do was to follow the lead of [Thomas] Corwin, and prove that the war was not begun on the right spot, and that it was unconstitutional, unnecessary, and wrong. Remember, too, that this he did after the war had been begun. It is one thing to be opposed to the declaration of a war, another and very different thing to take sides with the enemy against your own country after the war has been commenced. Our army was in Mexico at the time, many battles had been fought; our citizens, who were defending the honor of their country's flag, were surrounded by the daggers, the guns, and the poison of the enemy. Then it was that Corwin made his speech in which he declared that

the American soldiers ought to be welcomed by the Mexicans with bloody hands and hospitable graves; then it was that Ashmun and Lincoln voted in the House of Representatives that the war was unconstitutional and unjust; and Ashmun's resolution, Corwin's speech, and Lincoln's vote were sent to Mexico and read at the head of the Mexican army, to prove to them that there was a Mexican party in the Congress of the United States who were doing all in their power to aid them. That a man who takes sides with the common enemy against his own country in time of war should rejoice in a war being made on me now, is very natural. And, in my opinion, no other kind of a man would rejoice in it.[611]

In his July 4, 1861, "Message to Congress in Special Session" Lincoln goes on to say that his use of the suspension of *habeas corpus* was **"exercised but very sparingly,"** an outright fabrication: not only was he the first president to both suspend *habeas*, *and* the first to suspend it across the entire United States, but he went on to use this illegality to arbitrarily arrest (without warrants) and imprison (without charges) 38,000 Northerners (without trial)[612] for speaking out against him[613] (some for the duration of the War)[614]—sending many of them to his "government gulag," the pitifully overcrowded and unsanitary Fort Lafayette in New York Harbor, where countless innocent Northerners died horrible deaths.[615]

Lincoln also used his special message speech to spread his false doctrine about the illegality of secession. Maintaining that because **"the Union is older than any of the States,"** the states were created by the Union and therefore have no inherent sovereignty. As any student of the Constitution knows, of course, it is the opposite: the states preceded the Union and, in fact, created the Union. In the Ninth and Tenth Amendments the Founding Fathers clearly spelled out the limited powers of the central government and the nearly unlimited sovereign powers of the states.

After deceptively and wrongly insinuating that the Southern people were **"coerced"** into **"voting against the Union,"**[616] he falsely expresses **"the deepest regret"** for having to use physical force against the South in a war he himself purposefully and cunningly instigated at Fort Sumter on April 12, 1861.

The height of his artifice comes in the last paragraph of his special session speech, where he states:

> **And having thus chosen our course, without guile and with pure purpose, let us renew our trust in God, and go forward without fear and with manly hearts.**[617]

Though a self-proclaimed atheist, here Lincoln references God, then openly lies about his **"course"**—one that was far from guileless, and his **"purpose"**—one that was far from pure. Northerners and New South Southerners may consider this type of behavior **"manly,"** but not traditional Southerners.

That winter, December 3, 1861, during his First Annual Message to Congress, Lincoln restates the lie, saying:

> **The last ray of hope for preserving the Union peaceably, expired at the assault upon Fort Sumter.**[618]

The only **"assault"** that occurred was when the U.S.A. seized Fort Sumter under Lincoln's orders. The C.S.A. had no choice but to protect its property from foreign invasion.

The president ends this particular speech with the following sentence:

> **With a reliance on Providence, all the more firm and earnest, let us proceed in the great task which events have devolved upon us.**[619]

"Events" did not simply **"devolve"** upon the North. It was Lincoln himself who forced them upon both the North and the South. He was still touting the same lie six months later, when, on May 6, 1862, he told a group of Evangelical Lutherans that **"the sword"** of war was **"forced into our hands."**[620] Here is powerful evidence of a man who knew the fine art of propagandizing better than anyone else in his day.

In his May 26, 1862, "Message to Congress," Lincoln puts forth the humorous theories that the South had been planning all along to split from the Union, that her aim was to destroy the U.S. government, and that it was she who had started the **"Civil War"** at Fort Sumter:

> **To the Senate and House of Representatives: The insurrection which is yet existing in the United States and aims at the overthrow of the Federal Constitution and the Union, was clandestinely prepared during the winter of 1860 and 1861, and assumed an open organization in the form of a treasonable provisional government at Montgomery, in Alabama, on the 18th day of February, 1861. On the 12th day of April, 1861, the insurgents committed the flagrant act of civil war by the**

bombardment and capture of Fort Sumter, which cut off the hope of immediate conciliation. Immediately afterward all the roads and avenues to this city were obstructed, and the capital was put into the condition of a siege. The mails in every direction were stopped and the lines of telegraph cut off by the insurgents, and military and naval forces which had been called out by the government for the defense of Washington were prevented from reaching the city by organized and combined treasonable resistance in the State of Maryland. There was no adequate and effective organization for the public defense. Congress had indefinitely adjourned. There was no time to convene them. It became necessary for me to choose whether, using only the existing means, agencies, and processes which Congress had provided, I should let the government fall at once into ruin, or whether, availing myself of the broader powers conferred by the Constitution in cases of insurrection, I would make an effort to save it with all its blessings for the present age and for posterity.[621]

Lincoln also lies here about Congress being **"indefinitely adjourned,"** saying that **"there was no time to convene them."** As we saw in Chapter 4, he intentionally delayed calling Congress into session for four months[622] in an effort to prevent any debate over his military and constitutional crimes.[623]

On July 26, 1862, in a private letter to Reverdy Johnson, Lincoln restates his now well formulated self-delusion that the South brought the war on itself:

> My dear Sir: Yours of the 16th, by the hand of Governor [George Foster] Shepley, is received. It seems the Union feeling in Louisiana is being crushed out by the course of [Union] General [John Wolcott] Phelps. Please pardon me for believing that is a false pretense. The people of Louisiana—all intelligent people everywhere—know full well that I never had a wish to touch the foundations of their society, or any right of theirs. With perfect knowledge of this they forced a necessity upon me to send armies among them, and it is their own fault, not mine, that they are annoyed by the presence of General Phelps. They also know the remedy—know how to be

cured of General Phelps. Remove the necessity of his presence. And might it not be well for them to consider whether they have not already had time enough to do this? If they can conceive of anything worse than General Phelps within my power, would they not better be looking out for it? They very well know the way to avert all this is simply to take their place in the Union upon the old terms. If they will not do this, should they not receive harder blows rather than lighter ones? You are ready to say I apply to friends what is due only to enemies. I distrust the wisdom if not the sincerity of friends who would hold my hands while my enemies stab me. This appeal of professed friends has paralyzed me more in this struggle than any other one thing . . . . I am a patient man—always willing to forgive on the Christian terms of repentance, and also to give ample time for repentance. Still, I must save this government, if possible. What I cannot do, of course I will not do; but it may as well be understood, once for all, that I shall not surrender this game leaving any available card unplayed. Yours truly, A. Lincoln.[624]

Two years later, on September 12, 1864, Lincoln wrote the following unfinished draft of a letter to Isaac M. Schermerhorn. In it the president perpetuates his lie about who started the War, a lie that has today become a "fact," at least in *Northern* history books:

My dear Sir: Yours inviting me to attend a Union mass-meeting at Buffalo is received. Much is being said about peace, and no man desires peace more ardently than I. Still, I am yet unprepared to give up the Union for a peace which, so achieved, could not be of much duration. The preservation of our Union was not the sole avowed object for which the war was commenced. It was commenced for precisely the reverse object—to destroy our Union. The insurgents commenced it by firing upon the *Star of the West* and on Fort Sumter, and by other similar acts.[625]

Just six month later, in his Second Inaugural Address, on March 4, 1865, the Great Pretender was still trying to keep up appearances before the public. Here he had the nerve to say that both the South and the North had tried to avoid bloodshed, but one of them would *make* war rather than let the nation survive, and the other would *accept* war rather than let it perish; and the war came.[626]

The idea that the war simply **"came,"** and that this was due to the aggressive actions of those he preposterously called the Southern **"insurgents,"**[627] is absurd, and an insult to all intelligent people. Yet it was in this exact way that the South has been held criminally responsible for a war it did not begin—or want.[628]

Yes, after falling prey to Lincoln's wiles the South did let loose the first volley. But anti-South proponents should bear in mind, as President Jefferson Davis noted, that:

> He who makes the assault is not necessarily he that strikes the first blow or fires the first gun.[629]

Even as late as December 6, 1864, just months before his assassination, Lincoln was still at it, perpetuating the fraudulence he himself had perpetrated. When confronted with the question of when and how the War would finally come to an end, the president gave this deceptive reply:

> **In stating a single condition of peace, I mean simply to say, that the war will cease on the part of the government whenever it shall have ceased on the part of those who began it.**[630]

Looking back from today's perspective one wishes that cooler, more rational heads had prevailed in the halls of the Confederate government; that someone with emotional restraint in the Rebel Congress would have recognized Lincoln's boundless and amoral determination to achieve his political ends; that someone in the Confederate military would have suggested calling Lincoln's bluff, allowed him to resupply the fort, and then forced him back to the negotiation table, this time with a battery of constitutional attorneys.

But Southerners at the time, like their Northern counterparts, were products of Victorian culture, which emphasized masculine courage and honor, equated manliness with aggressiveness, sentimentalized military death, sanitized away the gore of the battlefield, and romanticized war in all its horrific glory. The aversion with which 21st-Century Americans view warfare would not manifest for another 100 years, with the televising of the

Vietnam War.

     In the spring of 1861, however, amid the razzle-dazzle of victory parades across the South, few in that region noticed or cared that Lincoln had deceptively started the War by skillfully maneuvering Dixie into firing the first shot. If the South could have only seen into the future no sane Confederate would have dared aim his cannon at the little island in Charleston Harbor on that mild April day.[631]

Lincoln & Abolition

ACCORDING TO YANKEE "HISTORY" ABRAHAM Lincoln was a dyed-in-the-wool abolitionist, one who would stop at nothing to free the slaves, welcome blacks into American society, and imbue them with full civil rights.

Lincoln's own words tell a very different story, however.

He was asked once how he felt about having abolitionists in his political party, to which he impatiently replied:

> As long as I'm not tarred with the abolitionist brush.[632]

On August 27, 1858, when he was accused of having "abolition tendencies," Lincoln angrily dismissed the entire issue as a **"bugaboo"** (i.e., an imaginary fear) and a **"melancholy theme,"** one that he had replied to so often that **"I almost turn with disgust from the discussion."**[633]

Others often commented on Lincoln's strong anti-abolitionist stance. One of these was Stephen A. Douglas, who, speaking before both Lincoln and a large Illinois audience, said:

> Whenever I allude to the Abolition doctrines, which he considers a slander to be charged with being in favor of, you all indorse them, and hurrah for them, not knowing that your candidate is ashamed to acknowledge them.[634]

Lincoln was so far from being an abolitionist that he often blocked the freeing of slaves, such as when he countermanded the emancipation proclamations of his cabinet members and military officers, including Simon

Cameron,[635] John W. Phelps,[636] John C. Frémont,[637] Jim Lane,[638] and David Hunter[639]—proving once and for all, if nothing else does, that Lincoln did not wage war against the South over slavery.[640]

Here, from May 17, 1862, for example, is Lincoln's brief order to Hunter to cease freeing slaves:

> No commanding general shall do such a thing upon my responsibility without consulting me.[641]

Two days later, on March 19, Lincoln made his countermand official by issuing a "Proclamation Revoking General Hunter's Order Of Military Emancipation." It reads:

> By The President Of The United States Of America:
> A Proclamation.
> Whereas there appears in the public prints what purports to be a proclamation of Major-General Hunter, in the words and figures following, to wit:
>
>> (General Orders No. 11.)
>> Headquarters Department Of The South,
>> Hilton Head, Port Royal, S. C., May 9, 1862.
>> The three States of Georgia, Florida, and South Carolina, comprising the military department of the South, having deliberately declared themselves no longer under the protection of the United States of America, and having taken up arms against the said United States, it became a military necessity to declare martial law. This was accordingly done on the 25th day of April, 1862. Slavery and martial law in a free country are altogether incompatible; the persons in these three States—Georgia, Florida, and South Carolina—heretofore held as slaves, are therefore declared forever free. By command of Major-General D. Hunter: Ed. W. Smith, Acting Assistant Adjutant-General.
>
> And whereas the same is producing some excitement and misunderstanding: therefore,
>
> I, Abraham Lincoln, President of the United

States, proclaim and declare that the Government of the United States had no knowledge, information, or belief of an intention on the part of General Hunter to issue such a proclamation; nor has it yet any authentic information that the document is genuine. And further, that neither General Hunter, nor any other commander or person, has been authorized by the Government of the United States to make a proclamation declaring the slaves of any State free; and that the supposed proclamation now in question, whether genuine or false, is altogether void so far as respects such a declaration.

I further make known that, whether it be competent for me, as commander-in-chief of the army and navy, to declare the slaves of any State or States free, and whether, at any time, in any case, it shall have become a necessity indispensable to the maintenance of the government to exercise such supposed power, are questions which, under my responsibility, I reserve to myself, and which I cannot feel justified in leaving to the decision of commanders in the field. These are totally different questions from those of police regulations in armies and camps.

On the sixth day of March last, by special message, I recommended to Congress the adoption of a joint resolution, to be substantially as follows:

> Resolved, That the United States ought to cooperate with any State which may adopt gradual abolishment of slavery, giving to such State pecuniary aid, to be used by such State, in its discretion, to compensate for the inconvenience, public and private, produced by such change of system.

The resolution, in the language above quoted, was adopted by large majorities in both branches of Congress, and now stands an authentic, definite, and solemn proposal of the nation to the States and people most immediately interested in the subject-matter. To the people of those States I now earnestly appeal. I do not argue—I beseech you to make arguments for yourselves. You cannot, if you would, be blind to the signs of the times. I beg of you a calm and enlarged consideration of them, ranging, if it may be, far above personal and partizan politics. This proposal makes common cause for a common object, casting no reproaches upon any. It acts not the Pharisee. The change it contemplates would come gently as the dews of heaven, not rending or wrecking anything. Will you not embrace it? So much good has not been done, by one effort, in all past time, as in the providence of God it is now your high privilege to do. May the vast future not have to lament that you have neglected it.

In witness whereof, I have hereunto set my hand and caused the seal of the United States to be affixed. Abraham Lincoln.[642]

Lincoln clearly states here that the reason he suspended Hunter's emancipation proclamation is that it was not a **"necessity indispensable to the maintenance of the government."** Not being an abolitionist, he says nothing about black civil rights.

Lincoln's countermand of Frémont's emancipation proclamation was much more complicated and difficult, for both Frémont and his wife resisted the president every step of the way. Lincoln began his attack on Frémont gently (Lincoln misspells Frémont's surname as "Fremont"):

Washington, D.C., September 2, 1861. Major-general Fremont.

My dear Sir: Two points in your proclamation of August 30 give me some anxiety:

First. Should you shoot a man, according to the proclamation, the Confederates would very certainly shoot our best men in their hands in retaliation; and so, man for man, indefinitely. It is, therefore, my order that you allow no man to be shot under the proclamation without first having my approbation or consent.

Second. I think there is great danger that the closing paragraph, in relation to the confiscation of property and the liberating slaves of traitorous owners, will alarm our Southern Union friends and turn them against us; perhaps ruin our rather fair prospect for Kentucky. Allow me, therefore, to ask that you will, as of your own motion, modify that paragraph so as to conform to the first and fourth sections of the act of Congress entitled, "An act to confiscate property used for insurrectionary purposes," approved August 6, 1861, and a copy of which act I herewith send you.

This letter is written in a spirit of caution, and not of censure. I send it by special messenger, in order that it may certainly and speedily reach you. Yours very truly, A. Lincoln.[643]

Lincoln's second dispatch to Frémont, which went out on September 11, 1861, contained stronger language:

> Sir: Yours of the 8th, in answer to mine of the 2d instant, is just received. Assuming that you, upon the ground, could better judge of the necessities of your position than I could at this distance, on seeing your proclamation of August 30 I perceived no general objection to it. The particular clause, however, in relation to the confiscation of property and the liberation of slaves appeared to me to be objectionable in its nonconformity to the act of Congress passed the 6th of last August upon the same subjects; and hence I wrote you, expressing my wish that that clause should be modified accordingly. Your answer, just received, expresses the preference on your part that I should make an open order for the modification, which I very cheerfully do. It is therefore ordered that the said clause of said proclamation be so modified, held, and construed as to conform to, and not to transcend, the provisions on the same subject contained in the act of Congress entitled, "An act to confiscate property used for insurrectionary purposes," approved August 6, 1861, and that said act be published at length with this order. Your obedient servant, A. Lincoln.[644]

Frémont's wife, Jessie Ann Benton, the daughter of famed Missouri Senator Thomas Hart Benton, not only went to the White House to confront the president, she sent several emotional notes of entreaty to him regarding her husband and his emancipation proclamation. By antagonizing the already grumpy Lincoln, however, she ended up doing more damage than good,[645] as his September 12 reply to Mrs. Frémont indicates:

> My dear Madam: Your two notes of to-day are before me. I answered the letter you bore me from General Fremont on yesterday, and not hearing from you during the day, I sent the answer to him by mail. It is not exactly correct, as you say you were told by the elder Mr. [Francis Preston]

Blair, to say that I sent [his son] Postmaster-General [Montgomery] **Blair** to St. Louis to examine into that department and report. Postmaster General Blair did go, with my approbation, to see and converse with General Fremont as a friend. I do not feel authorized to furnish you with copies of letters in my possession without the consent of the writers. No impression has been made on my mind against the honor or integrity of General Fremont, and I now enter my protest against being understood as acting in any hostility toward him. Your obedient servant, A. Lincoln.[646]

The president's anti-abolition activities did not go unnoticed by his few slavery-hating constituents. One of these was Illinois Senator Orville Hickman Browning, one of Lincoln's oldest friends. When a shocked Browning sent a letter to Lincoln questioning his countermand of Frémont's emancipation proclamation, he received this sharp response on September 22, 1861:

(Private and Confidential.) Executive Mansion, Washington, September 22,1861. Hon. O. H. Browning.
My dear Sir: Yours of the 17th is just received: and coming from you, I confess it astonishes me. That you should object to my adhering to a law which you had assisted in making and presenting to me less than a month before is odd enough. But this is a very small part. General Fremont's proclamation as to confiscation of property and the liberation of slaves is purely political and not within the range of military law or necessity. If a commanding general finds a necessity to seize the farm of a private owner for a pasture, an encampment, or a fortification, he has the right to do so, and to so hold it as long as the necessity lasts; and this is within military law, because within military necessity. But to say the farm shall no longer belong to the owner, or his heirs forever, and this as well when the farm is not needed for military purposes as when it is, is purely political, without the savor of military law about it. And the same is true of slaves. If the general needs them, he can seize them and use them; but when the need is past, it is not for him to fix their permanent future condition. That must be settled according to laws made by law-makers, and not by military proclamations. The proclamation in the point in question is simply "dictatorship." It assumes

that the general may do anything he pleases—confiscate the lands and free the slaves of loyal people, as well as of disloyal ones. And going the whole figure, I have no doubt, would be more popular with some thoughtless people than that which has been done! But I cannot assume this reckless position, nor allow others to assume it on my responsibility.

You speak of it as being the only means of saving the government. On the contrary, it is itself the surrender of the government. Can it be pretended that it is any longer the Government of the United States—any government of constitution and laws—wherein a general or a president may make permanent rules of property by proclamation? I do not say Congress might not with propriety pass a law on the point, just such as General Fremont proclaimed. I do not say I might not, as a member of Congress, vote for it. What I object to is, that I, as President, shall expressly or impliedly seize and exercise the permanent legislative functions of the government.

So much as to principle. Now as to policy. No doubt the thing was popular in some quarters, and would have been more so if it had been a general declaration of emancipation. The Kentucky legislature would not budge till that proclamation was modified: and General [Robert] Anderson telegraphed me that on the news of General Fremont having actually issued deeds of manumission, a whole company of our volunteers threw down their arms and disbanded. I was so assured as to think it probable that the very arms we had furnished Kentucky would be turned against us. I think to lose Kentucky is nearly the same as to lose the whole game. Kentucky gone, we cannot hold Missouri, nor, as I think, Maryland. These all against us, and the job on our hands is too large for us. We would as well consent to separation at once, including the surrender of this capital. On the contrary, if you will give up your restlessness for new positions, and back me manfully on the grounds upon which you and other kind friends gave me the election and have approved in my public documents, we shall go through triumphantly. You must not understand I took my course on the proclamation because of Kentucky. I took the same ground in a private letter to General Fremont before I heard from Kentucky.

You think I am inconsistent because I did not

> also forbid General Fremont to shoot men under the proclamation. I understand that part to be within military law, but I also think, and so privately wrote General Fremont, that it is impolitic in this, that our adversaries have the power, and will certainly exercise it, to shoot as many of our men as we shoot of theirs. I did not say this in the public letter, because it is a subject I prefer not to discuss in the hearing of our enemies.
>
> There has been no thought of removing General Fremont on any ground connected with his proclamation, and if there has been any wish for his removal on any ground, our mutual friend Sam. Glover can probably tell you what it was. I hope no real necessity for it exists on any ground. Your friend, as ever, A. Lincoln[647]

As usual Lincoln's words are a muddy hodgepodge of contradictions, lies, misinformation, and oddities.

He begins by insisting that Frémont's emancipation proclamation was illegitimate because it did not fall under the auspices of **"military necessity."** Like a true anti-abolitionist he makes no mention of black civil rights or the Constitutional assertion that "all men are created equal." Having an authoritarian mindset he can only think in terms of military power and political control.

Lincoln then calls Frémont's slave liberation a **"dictatorship."** Yet he himself was to become a dictatorial president, breaking nearly every constitutional law ever written, as we will see in Chapter 16.

Lincoln tells Browning that it is unlawful for Union officers to confiscate Southern farms unless it is a **"military necessity,"** and freeing slaves is not a military necessity. Yet Lincoln would go on to give his approval for this very crime as his War progressed.

Lincoln provides a stunning admission to Browning, namely that when one particular company of Kentucky Volunteers heard about Frémont's emancipation proclamation, they immediately **"threw down their arms"** and quit the army in disgust. Why? Because like 99 percent of the rest of Lincoln's military, they had not left their homes and families to fight for abolition. They had joined to **"preserve the Union."**

The Confederate Battle Flag possesses thirteen stars for the thirteen states that sided with it. But in Lincoln's letter to Browning he acknowledges what very few Americans today realize: there would have been many more stars on that flag if he had not threatened the Northern states with violence. He then names three of the many Northern and Southern states that wanted to join the Confederacy, but which he blocked: Kentucky, Missouri, and Maryland. Maryland in particular suffered extreme duress under Lincoln's autocratic rule, as we will see in Chapter 15.

The president ends his missive by stating that he has no intention of removing General Frémont from his command. Yet this is precisely what he did shortly after this letter was sent. Here is the October 24, 1861, dispatch, signed by General Winfield Scott:

> Major-General Fremont, of the United States Army, the present commander of the Western Department of the same, will, on the receipt of this order, call Major-General [David] Hunter, of the United States Volunteers, to relieve him temporarily in that command, when he (Major-General Fremont) will report to general headquarters by letter for further orders. Winfield Scott.[648]

It was all a disaster: Frémont's dismissal sparked near riots across the North, and Lincoln's nullification of his emancipation proclamation angered the Border States while creating even more hatred between abolitionists and the president.[649] (The tussle between the two men was not over yet, however: an embittered Frémont was later chosen by Republican abolitionists to run against his former boss as a presidential candidate in the 1864 election. But sadly for the nation—particularly enslaved blacks, Frémont withdrew before November.)[650]

While Frémont ended up both embarrassing Lincoln and undermining his beloved colonization plan to ship all emancipated blacks out of the U.S., the insubordinate officer's attempt to free slaves in Missouri in the summer of 1861 was a major component in altering the character of the War from one to **"preserve the Union"**[651] to one meant to force the **"extirpation of slavery."**[652]

Despite such obvious anti-abolitionist activities as the Frémont debacle, Lincoln's devoted followers continue to insist that the president was an abolitionist. Yet if he was, we must wonder why he made the following statement on October 15, 1858, at Alton, Illinois:

> **It is nothing but a miserable perversion of what I have said, to assume that I have declared Missouri, or any other Slave State, shall emancipate her slaves; I have proposed no such thing.**[653]

There is also the July 3, 1862, note from Lincoln's Secretary of War Edwin M. Stanton to Union General Benjamin F. "the Beast" Butler. Through Stanton Lincoln orders Butler to feed and shelter any "fugitive negroes" that "come to his pickets." However, the secretary continues:

> In directing this to be done, the President does not mean, at present, to settle any general rule in respect to slaves or slavery, but simply to provide for the particular case under the circumstances in which it is now presented.[654]

As these words intimate, the truth is that far from being an abolitionist Lincoln actually detested the group as a whole,[655] tried to distance himself from it, and continually spoke of abolitionists in the negative.[656] Indeed, he considered the very concept of abolition itself a pernicious influence, which is why he often made public comments on how he loathed and distrusted abolitionists—whom he derogatorily called the **"Greeley faction"** (after the staunch Yankee abolitionist leader Horace Greeley)—and considered its members a public nuisance.[657]

Lincoln was not alone in his hatred of abolitionists and what he referred to as the enormous **"unpopularity"** of their doctrines.[658] Antislavery advocates and their "accursed doctrines"—as most Yankees called them,[659] were so detested in the North that they were constantly harassed and threatened, both in the press and in the street. Attempts were made on their lives as well, with some success.

In Boston, Massachusetts, where both the American slave trade[660] and American slavery got their start,[661] and where wealthy slave owner Peter Faneuil[662] used some of the profits from slaving to bestow Faneuil Hall on the city in 1742,[663] fiery Northern abolitionist William Lloyd Garrison was attacked by a lynch mob on October 21, 1835, (possibly incited by members of the Yankee version of the Ku Klux Klan).[664] Dragged through the streets by a rope, he barely escaped with his life.[665] In order to protect him, the city had him arrested and driven off to jail in a carriage surrounded by armed guards. A few years earlier, in 1830, when Garrison spoke out against Francis Todd, a Yankee slave trader from Newburyport, Massachusetts, the outspoken abolitionist was sued, found guilty, and spent forty-nine days in prison.[666] His judge and jurors, of course, were not Southerners. They were fellow Northerners.

Bostonians were so upset with Garrison that in 1835, some 1,500 of them signed a petition to hold a public convention to discuss what to do about him, along with other antislavery advocates. On August 21, during the meeting at Faneuil Hall, Boston residents rightfully accused local abolitionists of trying to "scatter among our Southern friends firebrands, arrows, and death."[667] Garrison fired back, declaring that the title of Faneuil Hall should be changed from "the Cradle of Liberty" to "the Refuge of Slavery."[668] New Yorkers hated Garrison with the same passion New Englanders did, demanding that he and his "band of nigger minstrels" be banned from the city.[669]

In 1834 deeply entrenched Northern racism was the reason New Englanders forced the closure of Prudence Crandall's "High School for young colored Ladies and Misses" in Canterbury, Connecticut. For trying to offer blacks a free education in New England, Crandall, a Yankee Quaker and abolitionist, was harassed, arrested (three times), and imprisoned, while Northern white mobs attacked and stoned her school.[670] To try and drive her out, local shopkeepers refused to sell food to her, and her Yankee neighbors smashed her windows out and filled the school's drinking well with cow dung.[671]

When none of these attacks succeeded, they tried to burn Crandall's school to the ground. With the promise of nothing but more threats and violence in her future, she finally abandoned her dream of tutoring blacks, and moved out of state.[672] "That nigger school shall never be allowed in Canterbury, nor in any other town in this State," she had been told repeatedly by her anti-abolition neighbors in Connecticut.[673] Yankee politicians agreed. "Once open this door, and New England will become the Liberia of America," the town's elected officials bitterly proclaimed.[674]

While as late as the 1860s blacks could not safely walk the streets of Boston, Detroit, Albany, Chicago, and Cleveland after dark,[675] Northern whites who supported black equality continued to be hounded, hunted down, and even killed by other Northerners. In 1837 Maine abolitionist-publisher, Elijah P. Lovejoy, was shot to death by an anti-abolition gang in Illinois, Lincoln's (adopted) home state.[676] Lovejoy had been trying to protect his fourth printing press (his Yankee neighbors had already destroyed the three previous ones).[677] Even earlier, in 1834, a New York gang attacked and gutted the home of Yankee abolitionist Lewis Tappan, and in 1835 Connecticut abolitionist Theodore Weld was stoned by angry crowds in Ohio.[678]

No doubt anti-abolitionist Lincoln felt some empathy for these Northern mobs. Not for their murderous ways, but because he had little use for or feeling toward blacks as anything but pawns in his political games.

Thus in his 1860 autobiography[679] the "Great Emancipator" mentions nothing about abolition or even slavery,[680] though he does describe an incident in which he and a white companion were viciously attacked by seven blacks in New Orleans, who intended to rob and murder them. He and his friend **"were hurt in the melee,"** Lincoln wrote disdainfully, **"but succeeded in driving the Negroes from the boat."**[681]

That same year Lincoln ran for president on a party platform that called for upholding slavery in the South. His nomination in 1860 by fellow party members was, after all, due to the fact that as a white supremacist he was considered a "safe" candidate,[682] a trait for which he had a long and distinguished history.

As early as 1837, for example, while he was still a young member of his state's legislature, Lincoln made it a practice to send anti-abolition statements to the U.S. House of Representatives, as he did on March 3 under the title "Protest in the Illinois Legislature on the Subject of Slavery." Here an obviously irritated Lincoln wrote that when it comes to slavery,

> **the promulgation of abolition doctrines tends rather to increase than abate its evils.**[683]

His views on this topic never changed. Indeed, he never once referred to himself as an "abolitionist." Instead he called himself **"an anti-slavery man,"** as he did in an August 5, 1863, letter to Union General Nathaniel P. Banks.[684] As we are about to see, being an antislavery man is not at all the same as being an abolition man.

William H. Herndon, Lincoln's law partner and later his biographer, labored throughout his entire friendship with Lincoln trying to convert him to abolitionism. But he would not be moved. In fact, the U.S. president equated abolitionism with slavery itself, seeing both as two dangerous sides of the same coin.[685] I do not see, Lincoln warned members of the Springfield, Illinois, State House on July 16, 1852,

> **how it [slavery] could be at once eradicated without producing a greater evil even to the cause of liberty itself.**[686]

On September 15, 1858, Lincoln told his audience at Jonesboro, Illinois, that the Whig party did not get a **"good name"** until it died (after which it was replaced by the Republican party) and the public stopped associating it with **"abolitionism"**:

> I recollect in the presidential election which followed, when we had General [Winfield] Scott up for the presidency; Judge [Stephen A.] Douglas was around berating us Whigs as Abolitionists, precisely as he does to-day—not a bit of difference. I have often heard him. We could do nothing when the Old Whig party was alive that was not Abolitionism, but it has got an extremely good name since it has passed away.[687]

The plain truth is that no other Northerner, or Southerner, ever held more extreme anti-abolitionist views than Lincoln.

Naturally, in return he was heartily despised by abolitionists, who, from the very first day of his presidency, were extremely cautious of him. Why? Because he had not yet called for the immediate destruction of slavery. Toward the end of 1862, for instance, two years into his first term, anti-slave forces continued to express their unhappiness with Lincoln over his reluctance, even his refusal, to emancipate the nation's slaves.[688] In June 1863, six months *after* issuing his Final Emancipation Proclamation, Lincoln was still offering to protect slave owners.[689] And on July 4 of that year he wrote the following to Union General Robert Cumming Schenck:

> Your despatches about negro regiments are not uninteresting or unnoticed by us, but we have not been quite ready to respond. . .[690]

It was just such efforts to defend slavers, stall black enlistment, and hinder abolition that earned him the nickname the "tortoise President" from fellow Yankees.[691]

Lincoln himself once made note of the extreme pressure he was constantly under to issue an emancipation proclamation. This particular instance occurred on July 12, 1862, when, obviously uncomfortable, he begged representatives of the Border States to consider his favored plan, gradual-compensated emancipation and the subsequent deportation of freed blacks. He begins by making reference to his countermand of one of his officers' own personal emancipation proclamations:

> I am pressed with a difficulty not yet mentioned—one which threatens division among those who, united, are none too strong. An instance of it is known to you. General [David] Hunter is an honest man. He was, and I hope still is, my friend. I valued him none the less for his

> agreeing with me in the general wish that all men everywhere could be free. He proclaimed all men free within certain States, and I repudiated the proclamation. He expected more good and less harm from the measure than I could believe would follow. Yet, in repudiating it, I gave dissatisfaction, if not offense, to many whose support the country cannot afford to lose. And this is not the end of it. The pressure in this direction is still upon me, and is increasing. By conceding what I now ask, you can relieve me, and, much more, can relieve the country, in this important point.[692]

Thus, in the summer of 1862, Lincoln was considering emancipation simply to take political pressure off himself. He exhibits not a single shred of abolitionist sentiment here. Even his wish that **"all men everywhere could be free"** was merely the standard colonizationist plea, for blacks could not be deported while held in bondage, for at the time the Constitution protected slaves as "private property."[693]

In a December 29, 1862, letter to John Alexander McClernand, Lincoln admits that he had purposefully delayed emancipation:

> **After the commencement of hostilities, I struggled nearly a year and a half to get along without touching the "institution"; and when finally I conditionally determined to touch it, I gave a hundred days' fair notice of my purpose to all the States and people, within which time they could have turned it wholly aside by simply again becoming good citizens of the United States.**[694]

That Lincoln did not consider himself an abolitionist, that he in fact intentionally delineated himself from them, is clearly evidenced by numerous statements he made. One of the earliest of these occurred in a October 3, 1845, letter where he referred to **"the liberty men,"**[695] a 19th-Century term for abolitionists. If Lincoln had considered himself one of them he would have said "we Liberty men." In the same letter he says:

> If the . . . abolitionists had voted with us last fall, Mr. [Henry] **Clay would now be President . . .**[696]

Even at this early stage in his political career Lincoln is clearly setting himself apart from abolitionists.

A similar statement was made during one of his debates with Illinois

Senator Stephen A. Douglas, this one at Chicago on July 10, 1858:

> I have always hated slavery, I think, as much as any Abolitionist.[697]

Ten years earlier, in a March 22, 1848, letter to Usher F. Linder, Lincoln answered the question as to whether or not the liberal party (at the time the Republicans) had ever benefitted from associating with abolitionists. Absolutely. They helped us get the Whig candidate William Henry Harrison elected president, he replied. But, Lincoln added, we were careful not to embrace abolitionist doctrines; only the individual whose prestige induced the abolitionists to help us vote him into office.[698]

We will note here that there is a vast difference between someone who hates slavery and someone who is an abolitionist. Someone who dislikes the institution is just that: an individual who would rather that slavery disappear. This does not mean, however, that this same person also wants freed slaves to merge into mainstream society with complete civil rights.

On the other side of the coin we have the true abolitionist. This is someone who not only seeks the complete destruction of the institution, but also wants freed slaves, whatever their color or race,[699] to be completely assimilated into society, given full civil rights, and treated as equals on every level.

Based on this definition, **"anti-slavery man"** Lincoln, as he called himself,[700] did not come close to meeting the criteria of being an authentic abolitionist. Earlier in his political career he did not even care if abolition ever took place. As he himself said during the July 10, 1858, Lincoln-Douglas Debate at Chicago, where he was accused of espousing abolitionist sentiment:

> [Senator Douglas] says that I am in favor of making war by the North upon the South for the extinction of slavery; that I am also in favor of inviting (as he expresses it) the South to a war upon the North, for the purpose of nationalizing slavery. Now, it is singular enough, if you will carefully read that passage over, that I did not say that I was in favor of anything in it. I only said what I expected would take place. I made a prediction only—it may have been a foolish one, perhaps. I did not even say that I desired that slavery should be put in course of ultimate extinction.[701]

At the same debate Lincoln went on to make the following remark:

> I have said a hundred times, and I have now no inclination to take it back, that I believe there is no right and ought to be no inclination in the people of the free States to enter into the slave States and interfere with the question of slavery at all.[702]

On September 17, 1859, Lincoln made a similar comment. After my party wins at the polls in 1860, he stated to an audience largely made up of Kentuckians:

> We mean to leave you alone, and in no way to interfere with your institution; to abide by all and every compromise of the Constitution . . .[703]

Far earlier, on March 3, 1837, Lincoln, along with Dan Stone, sent a **"protest"** to the Illinois legislature **"on the subject of slavery."** It read:

> Resolutions upon the subject of domestic slavery having passed both branches of the General Assembly at its present session, the undersigned hereby protest against the passage of the same.
> They believe that the institution of slavery is founded on both injustice and bad policy, but that the promulgation of abolition doctrines tends rather to increase than abate its evils.
> They believe that the Congress of the United States has no power under the Constitution to interfere with the institution of slavery in the different States.
> They believe that the Congress of the United States has the power, under the Constitution, to abolish slavery in the District of Columbia, but that the power ought not to be exercised, unless at the request of the people of the District.
> The difference between these opinions and those contained in the said resolutions is their reason for entering this protest.[704]

Yes, Lincoln did abhor slavery. But, if like a true abolitionist, we are supposed to believe that he also wanted freed slaves to be given civil rights and live alongside Northern whites in complete racially equality, we must ask ourselves several questions. Why did he, at first, promise not to interfere with the institution? Why, as an attorney, did he defend, not slaves, but slave owners?[705] Why did he use slave labor instead of free labor to construct Federal buildings and roads in Washington, D.C.?[706] Why did it take until April 16, 1862, for the passage of the District of Columbia Emancipation Act, which, while abolishing slavery in Washington,[707] also called for the deportation of freed blacks?[708]

If he was truly an abolitionist, as Northern historians asserts, one would think that the first item on his agenda as president would have been to abolish slavery in America's capital city. Instead, he stalled and deferred month after month, until over a year passed. As he himself said in a public speech at Freeport, Illinois, on August 27, 1858, one and half years before his election:

> **I do not stand to-day pledged to the abolition of slavery in the District of Columbia.**[709]

And more importantly, as the president-elect said on December 15, 1860, just a few months prior to his inauguration:

> **I have no thought of recommending the abolition of slavery in the District of Columbia, nor the slave-trade among the slave States.**[710]

On his way from Springfield, Illinois, to his inauguration in Washington, D.C., Lincoln paused on February 27, 1861, to write a quick reply to the city's mayor, James Gabriel Berret, about his concerns of slavery being abolished there.[711] Lincoln assured Berret that under his presidency he would not allow this to happen:

> **Mr. Mayor: I thank you, and through you the municipal authorities of this city who accompany you, for this welcome. And as it is the first time in my life, since the present phase of politics has presented itself in this country, that I have said anything publicly within a region of country where the institution of slavery exists, I will take this occasion to say that I think very much of the ill feeling that has existed and still exists between the people in the section from which I came and the people here, is dependent upon a misunderstanding of one**

another. I therefore avail myself of this opportunity to assure you, Mr. Mayor, and all the gentlemen present, that I have not now, and never have had, any other than as kindly feelings toward you as to the people of my own section. I have not now, and never have had, any disposition to treat you in any respect otherwise than as my own neighbors. I have not now any purpose to withhold from you any of the benefits of the Constitution, under any circumstances, that I would not feel myself constrained to withhold from my own neighbors; and I hope, in a word, that when we shall become better acquainted—and I say it with great confidence—we shall like each other better. I thank you for the kindness of this reception.[712]

Lincoln's delay tactics in ridding Washington of slavery earned him yet another one of his many nicknames: "America's biggest slave owner." As an angry Charles Sumner stated:

Do you know who, at this moment, is the largest slaveholder in this country? It is Abraham Lincoln; for he holds all of the three thousand slaves of the District, which is more than any other person in the country holds.[713]

If Lincoln was a real abolitionist why did he delay issuing the Final Emancipation Proclamation for even longer, until January 1, 1863, two years into his presidency? Why did he at first prohibit blacks (along with Native-Americans) from serving in the U.S. military?[714] And why did he bar free blacks from entering the White House?[715]

The answer is that he was not a true abolitionist, for he did not want freed slaves to receive full civil rights *or* live in close proximity to Northern whites. In fact, as we will discuss in more detail in Chapter 12, he did not even want them to live in the U.S. after emancipation. His goal was always to end slavery, free blacks, and "ship them," as he so indelicately put it, "back to Africa." Abolition first, deportation second, this was always Lincoln's stated goal.

Here, at Peoria, Illinois, on October 16, 1854, is how the colonizationist politician described his real feelings on slavery, abolition, and American blacks:

If all earthly power were given me, I should not know what to do as to the existing institution. My first impulse would be to free all the slaves, and send them to Liberia [Africa]—to their own native land. But a moment's reflection would convince me, that whatever of high hope (as I think there is) there may be in this, in the long run, its sudden execution is impossible. If they were all landed there in a day, they would all perish in the next ten days; and there are not surplus shipping and surplus money enough in the world to carry them there in many times ten days. What then? Free them all, and keep them among us as underlings? Is it quite certain that this betters their condition? I think I would not hold one in slavery at any rate; yet the point is not clear enough to me to denounce people upon. What next? Free them, and make them politically and socially our equals? My own feelings will not admit of this; and if mine would, we well know that those of the great mass of white people will not.[716]

Many of Lincoln's soldiers certainly believed that he was not an abolitionist, and most of these seemed to think that he was actually trying to preserve slavery not the Union. One such man was Yankee Major John J. Key, who was personally thrown out of the Union military for stating this very idea. Here is Lincoln's September 26, 1862, letter to Key, in which the president describes the event:

> Sir: I am informed that in answer to the question, "Why was not the rebel army bagged immediately after the battle near Sharpsburg?" propounded to you by Major Levi C. Turner, judge-advocate, etc., you answered, "That is not the game. The object is that neither army shall get much advantage of the other, that both shall be kept in the field till they are exhausted, when we will make a compromise and save slavery." I shall be very happy if you will, within twenty-four hours from the receipt of this, prove to me by Major Turner that you did not, either literally or in substance, make the answer stated. Yours, A. Lincoln.
>
> This is indorsed as follows: Copy delivered to Major Key at 10.25 A. M., September 27, 1862. John Hay.
>
> At about eleven o'clock A. M., September 27, 1862, Major Key and Major Turner appear before me. Major Turner says: "As I remember it, the conversation was: I asked the

question why we did not bag them after the battle of Sharpsburg. Major Key's reply was, 'That was not the game; that we should tire the rebels out and ourselves. That that was the only way the Union could be preserved. We must come together fraternally, and slavery be saved.'" On cross-examination Major Turner says he has frequently heard Major Key converse in regard to the present troubles, and never heard him utter a sentiment unfavorable to the maintenance of the Union. He has never uttered anything which he (Major T.) would call disloyalty. The particular conversation detailed was a private one. A. Lincoln.

Indorsed on the above is:

In my view it is wholly inadmissible for any gentleman holding a military commission from the United States to utter such sentiments as Major Key is within proved to have done. Therefore let Major John J. Key be forthwith dismissed from the military service of the United States. A. Lincoln.[717]

Major Key, and the thousands of other Union soldiers who believed as he did, can hardly be faulted for thinking that Lincoln did not care about abolition, for the "tortoise president" himself promised not to interfere with the institution of slavery in his First Inaugural Address on March 4, 1861.[718] Would a true abolitionist make such a pledge before the American public?

If Lincoln was not an abolitionist, what then was he? In reality he was what I call an *emancipationist-racist*: a white separatist who wanted to free the slaves in order to deport them out of the U.S. as quickly as possible. This is why he seldom used such phrases as "abolish slavery," or "the abolition of slavery." Instead he would say the **"extirpation of slavery,"**[719] the **"arrest of slavery,"**[720] the **"destruction of slavery,"**[721] or the **"extinction of slavery."**[722]

Lincoln himself broke the different types of so-called "abolitionists" into four main categories, from which numerous subcategories sprang. Here is how he saw it, as noted in an October 5, 1863, letter to Charles D. Drake:

> . . . We are in civil war. In such cases there always is a main question; but in this ease that question is a perplexing compound—Union and slavery. It thus

becomes a question not of two sides merely, but of at least four sides, even among those who are for the Union, saying nothing of those who are against it. Thus, those who are for the Union with, but not without, slavery—those for it without, but not with—those for it with or without, but prefer it with—and those for it with or without, but prefer it without.

Among these again is a subdivision of those who are for gradual, but not for immediate, and those who are for immediate, but not for gradual, extinction of slavery. It is easy to conceive that all these shades of opinion, and even more, may be sincerely entertained by honest and truthful men. Yet, all being for the Union, by reason of these differences each will prefer a different way of sustaining the Union.[723]

Lincoln was among the fourth primary category, or as he referred to it, **"those who are for the Union with or without slavery, but prefer the Union without it."** This is as good a definition of an emancipationist (as opposed to an abolitionist) as any.

For Lincoln and other emancipationist-racists, slavery was objectionable, not because it violated the natural rights of enslaved humans, but because it checked economic growth and competed with white labor. In 1841 Lincoln's political idol, slave owner Henry Clay, stood before the Kentucky legislature and said:

> [there are many whites who] would import slaves 'to clear up the forests of the Green River Country' . . . . [But] [t]ake one day's ride from this capital and then go and tell them what you have seen. . . . tell them of the houses untenanted and decaying: tell them of the depopulation of the country and consequent ruin of the towns and villages: tell them the white Kentuckian has been driven out by slaves, by the unequal competition of unpaid labor: tell them that the mass of our people are uneducated: tell them that you have heard the children of the white Kentuckian crying for bread, whilst the children of the African was clothed, and fed, and laughed! And then ask them if they will have blacks to fell their forests.[724]

These were words that emancipationist-racists like Lincoln could well relate to. No wonder he considered black colonizationist and slave owner Clay his **"beau ideal of a statesman."**[725]

Indeed, this is why the Yankee president always emphasized the distinction between the Radicals of his party (then the Republicans, or liberals) and the Conservatives (then the Democrats, or traditionalists) of the opposing party. In Lincoln's day, of course, the term "Radicals" referred to abolitionists, a group he repeatedly treated as alien and odious. Take the following for example, which he wrote on October 5, 1863:

> **I do not feel justified to enter upon the broad field** [regarding] . . . **the political differences between Radicals and Conservatives. From time to time I have done and said what appeared to me proper to do and say. The public knows it all. It obliges nobody to follow me, and I trust it obliges me to follow nobody. The Radicals and Conservatives each agree with me in some things and disagree in others. I could wish both to agree with me in all things, for then they would agree with each other and would be too strong for any foe from any quarter. They, however, choose to do otherwise; and I do not question their right. I too shall do what seems to be my duty. I hold whoever commands in Missouri or elsewhere responsible to me and not to either Radicals or Conservatives.**[726]

Little wonder that authentic abolitionists, such as Massachusetts-born Lysander Spooner, excoriated Lincoln at every opportunity.[727] Here is what Spooner thought, for instance, about Lincoln's violent and unplanned emancipation. In a letter to Yankee "abolitionist" Charles Sumner, Spooner spoke eloquently of his empathy for the South's position, and of Northern hypocrisy and its relation to the Emancipation Proclamation and the U.S. Constitution:

> . . . slavery, from its first introduction into this country, to this time, has never had any legal or constitutional existence; but has been a mere abuse, tolerated by the strongest party, without any color of legality, except what was derived from false interpretations of the Constitution, and from practices, statutes, and adjudications, that were in plain conflict with the fundamental constitutional law. And these views have been virtually confessed to be true by John C. Calhoun, James M. Mason [grandson of Jeffersonian George Mason], Jefferson Davis, and many other Southern men; while such professed [Northern] advocates of liberty as Charles Sumner, Henry Wilson, William H. Seward, Salmon P. Chase, and the like, have been continually denying them.
>
> Had all those men at the North, who believed these ideas

to be true, promulgated them, as was their plain and obvious duty to do, it is reasonable to suppose that we should long since have had freedom, without shedding one drop of blood; certainly without one tithe of the blood that has now been shed; for the slaveholders would never have dared, in the face of the world, to attempt to overthrow a government that gave freedom to all, for the sake of establishing in its place one that should make slaves of those who, by the existing constitution, were free. But so long as the North, and especially so long as the professed (though hypocritical) advocates of liberty, like those named, conceded the constitutional right of property in slaves, they gave the slaveholders the full benefit of the argument that they were insulted, disturbed, and endangered in the enjoyment of their acknowledged constitutional rights; and that it was therefore necessary to their honor, security, and happiness that they should have a separate government. And this argument, conceded to them by the North, has not only given them strength and union among themselves, but has given them friends, both in the North and among foreign nations; and has cost the nation hundreds of thousands of lives, and thousands of millions of treasure.

Upon yourself, and others like you, professed friends of freedom, who, instead of promulgating what you believed to be the truth, have, for selfish purposes, denied it, and thus conceded to the slaveholders the benefit of an argument to which they had no claim,—upon your heads, more even, if possible, than upon the slaveholders themselves, (who have acted only in accordance with their associations, interests, and avowed principles as slaveholders) rests the blood of this horrible, unnecessary, and therefore guilty, war.

Your concessions, as to the pro-slavery character of the Constitution, have been such as, if true, would prove the Constitution unworthy of having one drop of blood shed in its support. They have been such as to withhold from the North all the benefit of the argument, that a war for the Constitution was a war for liberty. You have thus, to the extent of your ability, placed the North wholly in the wrong, and the South wholly in the right. And the effect of these false positions in which the North and the South have respectively been placed, not only with your consent, but, in part, by your exertions, has been to fill the land with blood.

The South could, consistently with honor, and probably would, long before this time, and without a conflict, have surrendered their slavery to the demand of the Constitution, (if that had been pressed upon them,) and to the moral sentiment of the world; while they could not with honor, or at least certainly would not, surrender anything to a confessedly unconstitutional demand, especially when coining from mere demagogues, who were so openly unprincipled as to profess the greatest moral abhorrence of slavery, and at time same time, for the sake of office, swear to support it, by swearing to support a Constitution which they declared to be its bulwark.

You, and others like you have done more, according to your abilities, to prevent the peaceful abolition of slavery, than any other men in the nation; for while honest men were explaining the true character of the constitution, as an instrument giving freedom to all, you were continually denying it, and doing your utmost (and far more than any avowed pro slavery man could do) to defeat their efforts. And it now appears that all this was done by you in violation of your own conviction of truth.

In your pretended zeal for liberty, you have been urging on the nation to the most frightful destruction of human life; but your love of liberty has never yet induced you to declare publicly, but has permitted you constantly to deny, a truth that was sufficient for, and vital to, the speedy and peaceful accomplishment of freedom. You have, with deliberate purpose, and through a series of years, betrayed the very citadel of liberty, which you were under oath to defend. And there has been, in the country, no other treason at all comparable with this.[728]

Here Spooner not only rightfully lambasts Sumner, Lincoln, Chase, and all of the other "hypocritical" Northerners for subverting the Constitution for selfish, political gain, but also for their double-dealing in regards to slavery and abolition.

Lincoln could have cared less how Spooner or any other true abolitionist felt. To all of them he repeatedly offered the same opinion regarding abolition and abolitionists, as he did on July 16, 1852, when he gave the eulogy at Henry Clay's funeral in Springfield, Illinois:

> **Those who would shiver into fragments the Union of these States, tear to tatters its now venerated Constitution, and even burn the last copy of the Bible, rather than slavery should continue a single hour, together with all their more halting sympathizers, have received, and are receiving, their just execration; and the name and opinions and influence of** [black colonizationist] **Mr.** [Henry] **Clay are fully and, as I trust, effectually and enduringly arrayed against them.**[729]

Just what Lincoln meant by saying that abolitionists have received, and are receiving, their just curse, condemnation, and punishment (i.e., **"execration"**), only he knows. What we know for sure is that our sixteenth president, according to his own words, was no abolitionist.

The upshot of all this, of course, is that slavery would have been abolished in the South much sooner had Lincoln and other Northerners not interfered with the institution to begin with.

While Lincoln saw abolition as a simple process of emancipation and deportation to Africa, back **"to their own native land,"**[730] as he harshly put it, it was far more complicated than this. In 1820 Thomas Jefferson brilliantly captured the slavery situation in America's Southland:

> We have the wolf by the ears, and we can neither hold him, nor safely let him go.[731]

But not knowing how or when to free the slaves did not mean that Southerners found slavery good or even acceptable. To the contrary, as we have seen, throughout the early decades of the U.S., much of the South's time and energy was directed almost solely on how to deal with "the wolf."

Most servant owners not only hated seeing blacks enslaved, they themselves felt enslaved by the slavery system. The onerous weight of the responsibility for caring for slaves was such that it became a universal joke in the South: it was not the slaves one need fear would run away, but their employers.

William M. Thackeray characterized slave ownership as being similar to owning an elephant when all that is needed is a horse.[732] Mary Chesnut wrote that nearly all Southerners considered slaves "a nuisance that did not pay." It is far cheaper, she noted, to simply hire someone, than to own a man whose father, mother, wife, and numerous children had to be fed, clothed, housed, nursed, and have their taxes and doctor's bills paid, throughout their entire lives, from cradle to coffin.[733]

Most Southern slave owners agreed. One of these was fire-eating, die-hard Confederate Rebel Edmund Ruffin.[734] Ruffin, like thousands of his slave owning comrades, eventually auctioned off his black servants. Not because they were poor producers. But because they were excellent consumers, making the expense of maintaining them nearly impossible.[735] The cost of owning slaves only increased as Lincoln's War progressed and massive inflation (6,000 percent)[736] spread across the South,[737] leading many Southerners to declare that it was not they who owned slaves, it was the slaves who owned them.[738]

The truth that has been suppressed by Northern historians is that antislavery sentiment was nearly universal throughout Dixie,[739] dating back, as mentioned, to at least the time of Jefferson,[740] just one of millions of Southerners and slave owners who loathed the institution with every fiber of their being. In his famous work, *Notes on the State of Virginia*, penned in 1781 and 1782, our third president writes:

> I think a change already perceptible, since the origin of the present revolution. The spirit of the master is abating, that of the slave rising from the dust, his condition mollifying, the way I hope preparing, under the auspices of heaven, for a total emancipation . . .[741]

Mississippian Jefferson Davis had believed since the very formation of the Confederacy that the end of slavery was inevitable, whether the South won the War or not.[742] This is one reason he pushed for the governmental purchase of slaves, their enlistment, and their emancipation as a reward for military service, in November 1864. Robert E. Lee also recommended enlistment and liberty for Southern slaves.[743] On March 13, 1865, Davis and Lee got their wish when the Confederate Congress authorized the "Negro Soldier Law,"[744] which allowed for the enrollment of as many as one-fourth of all Southern male slaves between the ages of 18 and 45.[745]

With the South so obviously antislavery and pro-abolition, why do Northern history books continue to tell us that Southerners were proslavery and anti-abolition? Because the truth would expose Lincoln for what he really was: a despot and a war criminal who waged an illegal and needless military campaign against the Southern Confederacy, a Constitutionally formed sovereign nation that, in 1861, was in the process of abolishing slavery within its borders.

However, in honor of all those who perished under Lincoln's autocratic rule (South and North, white and black, soldier and civilian), and in an effort to preserve authentic American history, we owe the world this much: to reveal the truth that Northern myth has for so long kept concealed. So reveal it we will.

Traditional Southern families supported the idea of self-government, asserting that the Federal government did not possess the right to appropriate their rights, their property, or their servants, by any means, especially by force. For Southerners, these were local state issues, not national ones. Thus, they only asked that they be left alone to manage their own personal and local affairs, a sentiment clearly articulated by all of the great Southern leaders, from John C. Calhoun to Jefferson Davis.[746]

Had Lincoln done just that, the South's slave owners would have eventually ended the institution in their own time and manner,[747] gradually, legally, and without violence—"by slow, sure, and imperceptible degrees," as Southerner President George Washington suggested decades earlier[748]—just as the North had allowed itself the privilege to do between the late 1700s and early 1800s.

Indeed, as early as 1787, at the Constitutional Convention in Philadelphia, Charles Pinckney of South Carolina maintained that if left to decide for themselves, the citizens of his state would eventually prohibit the slave trade—just as Virginia had already done. At the same assembly his compatriot, Virginian George Mason, said that slavery need not be interfered with in the South, for it was going extinct all on its own anyway.[749]

In postwar 1866 Yankee President James Buchanan, Lincoln's far more level-headed and intelligent predecessor, said of slavery:

> If left to the wise ordinance of a superintending Providence, which never acts rashly, it would have been gradually extinguished in our country, peacefully and without bloodshed, as has already been done throughout nearly the whole of Christendom. . . . If we would preserve the peace of the world and avoid much greater evils that we desire to destroy, we must act upon the wise principles of international law, and leave each people to decide domestic questions for themselves. Their sins are not our sins.[750]

In fact, Lincoln's War only postponed the inevitable destruction of slavery, which would have come much sooner had the nosey, arrogant, and self-righteous president simply left the South alone. As Captain Samuel A. Ashe correctly observed in 1911:

> . . . an independent South would have conformed to the ideas of the world at large. Slavery would have been abolished in a manner less hurtful to the South, naturally and peacefully, and in the meantime the South would have advanced in all the elements of prosperity.[751]

Indeed, by mid-1863 the South had already nearly reached the point of total emancipation.[752] Why not let her complete the process on her own? Why spend billions of dollars and kill untold thousands to accomplish what was already occurring naturally? And why push something on the South that the North had given itself the luxury to occur naturally in its own region, the very section of the country where slavery got its start?

At first the North acknowledged that it had instigated both slavery and the slave trade. And it fully accepted this fact as well—at least up until 1831, the year the loud, meddlesome, Radical Yankee abolitionist William Lloyd Garrison launched his antislavery gazette, *The Liberator*. Though, like Harriet Beecher Stowe, Garrison knew absolutely nothing about either the South or black servitude, he published articles in his paper condemning Southern slavery as a "crime" and Southern slave owners as "criminals." His columns brimmed with misinformation, disinformation, errors, and outright lies regarding the institution, all carefully calculated to whip the North into an anti-South frenzy.[753] Garrison did cause agitation. But not the kind that would weaken Southern slavery. Instead, he and his paper helped strengthen it, becoming one of the many embers that helped light the "Civil War."[754] How?

Though *The Liberator* was not widely influential (subscriptions never exceeded 3,000), many Southerners blamed Garrison for the Nat Turner Rebellion of 1831,[755] for his paper was read almost exclusively by radicalized free blacks. Though most were from the North (mainly from Boston, New York, and Philadelphia),[756] the paper found its way into the hands of a few Southern blacks. One of these was Turner.

On the evening of August 21, the Virginia slave led a gang of black thugs on a murderous rampage to "kill all whites." Before it was over some sixty European-Americans were dead.[757] Entire families were massacred that night, from newborn infants to senior citizens, their heads cut off while they slept.[758] Most of the decapitated victims were not only non-slave owners, they were ardent abolitionists, for Virginia had long been the center of Southern antislavery sentiment. Indeed, as we have noted, the American abolition movement got its start in Virginia.[759]

An unremorseful Turner and his racist madmen were all caught within a few weeks. Many of the mob, including their psychopathic leader, swung from the hangman's rope.[760]

But the bloody mayhem was all for naught. In fact, if Turner was trying to end slavery, he had done the worst thing possible: his "rebellion" not only did not advance the cause of blacks, it actually reversed it. For in its aftermath at least 100 blacks were killed,[761] whites passed new exceptionally harsh slave codes, and abolitionist sentiment, once strong across the entire South, was considerably dampened for decades.[762]

This was a revolutionary change in attitude for white Southerners, who had for so long viewed their black servants as "family" and free blacks as fellow citizens of Dixie. Thus, while nearly every Southerner had once been an abolitionist,[763] now the idea of emancipation was considered "too dangerous," and blacks everywhere, bonded and free, were viewed with suspicion.[764]

Between Garrison's increasingly vociferous attacks on Dixie and Turner's bloody killing spree, white Southerners had had enough. Now, instead of discussing abolition, they dug in their heels and built up a defensive wall of resentment and fear. No one, especially Yankees, would tell them what to do, not when they and their family's lives were at stake.[765]

How would the South end slavery? This was her decision. *When* would the South end slavery? It was her right to decide this for herself, as the Constitution clearly affirmed.[766]

In an 1847 speech the president of Washington College, Dr. Henry Ruffner of Virginia, spoke for the whole of the South when he commented on Dixie's defensive reaction to Northern attacks on the institution of slavery:

> . . . this unfavorable change of sentiment is due chiefly to the fanatical violence of those Northern antislavery men usually called Abolitionists. . . . They have not, by honourable means, liberated a single slave, and they never will by such a course of procedure as they have pursued. On the contrary they have created new difficulties in the way of all judicious schemes of emancipation by prejudicing the minds of slaveholders, and by compelling us to combat their false principles and rash schemes in our rear; whilst we are facing the opposition of men and the natural difficulties of the case in our front.[767]

The situation was so obvious that even some Yankees understood. One of them, William Ellery Channing, wrote the following in 1835:

> The adoption of the common system of agitation by the Abolitionists has not been justified by success. From the beginning it created alarm in the considerate and strengthened the sympathies of the free states with the slaveholder. It made converts of a few individuals but alienated multitudes.
>
> Its influence at the South has been almost wholly evil. It has stirred up bitter passions and a fierce fanaticism which have shut every ear and every heart against its arguments and persuasions.[768]

Southern defensiveness was indeed the only natural reaction to Northern pushiness when it came to slavery, as even many Northerners, like Channing, acknowledged. President Francis Wayland, of Rhode Island's Brown University (named after the New England slave trading Brown family),[769] once told Garrison that his abolitionist newspaper, *The Liberator*, would only produce rebellion in the South. "It's attitude," Wayland protested,

> to slave-owners is menacing and vindictive. The tendency of your remarks is to prejudice their minds against a cool discussion of the subject.[770]

No truer words have ever been uttered, as Lincoln would discover years later.

On March 10, 1862, Maryland Representative John Woodland Crisfield spoke with Lincoln about the president's proposition that emancipation be forced on the Old Line State in order to help end his War. According to Crisfield he replied to Lincoln that

> he did not think the people of Maryland looked upon slavery as a permanent institution; and he did not know that they would be very reluctant to give it up if provision was made to meet the loss and they could be rid of the race; but they did not like to be coerced into emancipation, either by the direct action of the government or by indirection, as through the emancipation of slaves in this District, or the confiscation of Southern property as now threatened; and he thought before they would consent to consider this proposition they would require to be informed on these points.[771]

The real question was this: why was the North striving to impose racial egalitarianism on the South when this was something that she herself would not even entertain?

On December 1, 1864, the Richmond *Sentinel* pointed out the rank hypocrisy of the Yankee. The North hates the negro, it declared, and does all it can to prevent the two races from associating. Yet, Yankees insist that Southerners treat blacks with complete equality. Thus the North does not practice what it preaches, but instead seeks to force upon Dixie that which she herself refuses to abide by. Furthermore, the South does not hate the negro, she loves the negro. No wonder the two sections came to detest one another!, the *Sentinel* concluded.[772]

Besides their constitutional rights, Southern slave owners had another dilemma to deal with: when it came to slavery, they were far more concerned about preserving their financial investment than preserving the institution. Slaves represented enormous private capital, each one being worth a small fortune: their cost was from between $25,000 and $50,000 each in today's currency. How would owners get the money back on their investment if their servants were simply freed? At about $1,500 a piece, the South's 3.5 million slaves[773] were worth $14 billion (in 1860) converted into today's money. Where was this massive compensation to come from? In 1865 Lincoln only offered the Southern states the modern equivalent of about $7 billion, some $7 billion short,[774] and even this pitiful offer was later withdrawn.

These were serious questions about a serious issue, questions that needed time and careful deliberation. And it was this very problem that primarily stalled abolition in the South, not racism or a perverse obsession with slavery. And it is why Southerners wanted to be allowed to decide for themselves when and how to emancipate their servants. This was all they asked of Lincoln.[775]

Unfortunately, he would not listen. He was far more interested in his own primary agenda: crushing states' rights in the South, installing big government in the North, deporting all blacks out of the U.S., and disseminating as much anti-South propaganda as possible, as quickly as possible.

One of his favorite pieces of anti-South propaganda was the notion that

> **every advocate of slavery naturally desires to see blasted and crushed the liberty promised the black man.**[776]

As Lincoln completely ignored the reality of the North's 500,000 to 1 million slaves, we can be sure he is speaking of *Southerners* here. But as always, Lincoln was wrong yet again.

The reality, as we have examined throughout this chapter, is that there were actually few Southerners who were what Lincoln called **"advocates of slavery."** Being America's first abolitionists, they wanted to see the institution come to an end, not continued. The issue was how and when it would come to end. Southerners naturally wanted to decide this for themselves. Having a South-hating leader from the far away North telling them how and when to emancipate their slaves was repulsive to nearly every inhabitant of Dixie.

As for Lincoln's comment that Southerners wanted to thwart the **"liberty promised the black man,"** nothing could be further from the truth. If the evidence presented in this chapter so far is not convincing enough to counter this myth, we have more.

While many Southerners, like famed Confederate General Nathan Bedford Forrest, were advocating the idea of putting their original slaves back to work on the same plantations as freedmen, while simultaneously calling for repopulating the South with new black immigrants from Africa,[777] many Northerners, like Lincoln, were publicly and enthusiastically promoting the ideas of withholding black civil rights while supporting black colonization (as we will discuss more thoroughly in Chapter 12).

With this knowledge in hand, it is more than apparent that it was not the South, but the North, who **"naturally desired to see blasted and crushed the liberty promised the black man."** This was, after all, the region where America's infamous Black Codes (laws severely limiting the movements, freedoms, and rights of blacks) first got their start,[778] where they took root,[779] where they became far harsher than anywhere else in the U.S.,[780] and where one of the greatest supporters of the Black Codes lived and worked: Abraham Lincoln.[781]

This was not a coincidence. "The Land of Lincoln," Illinois, Lincoln's adopted home state, was one of the most anti-black Jim Crow states in America at the time,[782] in large part because of Lincoln's work to restrict black civil rights there. White Illinoisans, for instance, arguably among the most racist Northerners in the 1850s and 60s, threatened to "commence a war of extermination" if blacks were given equal rights in their state.[783] It was said that Illinois' Black Codes were so stringent that the civil rights of African-Americans there were "virtually nonexistent."[784]

In 1857 Lincoln aided this white supremacist movement by asking the Illinois legislature to appropriate funds for the deportation of all blacks out of the state. Why? To help prevent one of his greatest fears: the dilution of the white race through interracial breeding.[785]

Whites from central Illinois in particular had little use for blacks, considering them, not human beings, but lowly creatures, little more than livestock "with wool on their heads."[786] Wrote one newspaper editor from the area, who could not abide the idea of free blacks moving to Illinois: We don't want any Negroes around here. Send them all to the Northeast![787]

An Illinois senator, Joseph Kitchell, was of the same mind as the rest of the whites in his state, including Lincoln. The residence of Negroes among us, he announced,

> even as servants . . . is productive of moral and political evil. . . . The natural difference between them and ourselves forbids the idea that they should ever be permitted to participate with us in the political affairs of our government.[788]

Illinoisans went on to pass countless anti-integration and anti-immigration laws in an effort to prevent blacks from settling in or even traveling through their state, with punishments ranging from whipping to being sold back into slavery at public auction.[789] In 1862 Illinois voters adopted a constitutional provision that barred the further admission of blacks into their state,[790] a Black Code that Lincoln allowed to remain on the books until 1865, the year his War finally came to an end.[791]

In 1863, as just one example, eight blacks were arrested and convicted for entering Illinois unlawfully. Of these, seven were sold back into slavery (temporarily) to pay off their fines[792]—all under Lincoln's watch.

Our sixteenth president was no abolitionist.[793]

Lincoln & Slavery

PART 1

WE HAVE ESTABLISHED THAT ABRAHAM Lincoln was not an abolitionist, but rather an emancipationist, someone who merely wanted to set slaves free. At the same time we have seen that he did indeed loathe the so-called "peculiar institution," saying:

> I have always hated slavery, I think, as much as any Abolitionist.[794]

We have seen that Lincoln often used his political position and power as a platform to rail against the idea of slavery, as he did in the following undeveloped "fragments" of proposed future speeches:

> [About July 1, 1854]
> The ant who has toiled and dragged a crumb to his nest will furiously defend the fruit of his labor against whatever robber assails him. So plain that the most dumb and stupid slave that ever toiled for a master does constantly know that he is wronged. So plain that no one, high or low, ever does mistake it, except in a plainly selfish way; for although volume upon volume is written to prove slavery a very good thing, we never hear of the man who wishes to take the good of it by being a slave himself.
>
> Most governments have been based, practically, on the denial of the equal rights of men, as I have, in part, stated them; ours began by affirming those rights. They

said, some men are too ignorant and vicious to share in government. Possibly so, said we; and, by your system, you would always keep them ignorant and vicious. We proposed to give all a chance; and we expected the weak to grow stronger, the ignorant wiser, and all better and happier together.

We made the experiment, and the fruit is before us. Look at it, think of it. Look at it in its aggregate grandeur, of extent of country, and numbers of population—of ship, and steamboat, and railroad.

[About July 1, 1854]
Equality in society alike beats inequality, whether the latter be of the British aristocratic sort or of the domestic slavery sort. We know Southern men declare that their slaves are better off than hired laborers amongst us. How little they know whereof they speak! There is no permanent class of hired laborers amongst us. Twenty-five years ago I was a hired laborer. The hired laborer of yesterday labors on his own account to-day, and will hire others to labor for him to-morrow. Advancement—improvement in condition—is the order of things in a society of equals. As labor is the common burden of our race, so the effort of some to shift their share of the burden onto the shoulders of others is the great durable curse of the race. Originally a curse for transgression upon the whole race, when, as by slavery, it is concentrated on a part only, it becomes the double-refined curse of God upon his creatures.

Free labor has the inspiration of hope; pure slavery has no hope. The power of hope upon human exertion and happiness is wonderful. The slave-master himself has a conception of it, and hence the system of tasks among slaves. The slave whom you cannot drive with the lash to break seventy-five pounds of hemp in a day, if you will task him to break a hundred, and promise him pay for all he does over, he will break you a hundred and fifty. You have substituted hope for the rod. And yet perhaps it does not occur to you that to the extent of your gain in the case, you have given up the slave system and adopted the free system of labor.

[About July 1, 1854]
If A can prove, however conclusively, that he may of right enslave B, why may not B snatch the same argument

> and prove equally that he may enslave A? You say A is white and B is black. It is color, then; the lighter having the right to enslave the darker? Take care. By this rule you are to be slave to the first man you meet with a fairer skin than your own. You do not mean color exactly? You mean the whites are intellectually the superiors of the blacks, and therefore have the right to enslave them? Take care again. By this rule you are to be slave to the first man you meet with an intellect superior to your own. But, say you, it is a question of interest, and if you make it your interest you have the right to enslave another. Very well. And if he can make it his interest he has the right to enslave you.[795]

Yes, Lincoln detested slavery, as did all thinking people at the time, including most slave owners and slave traders both North and South.

The issue we must address now is *why* Lincoln hated slavery.

According to Northern "history" it was because he was an anti-racist egalitarian; a humanitarian who detested bigotry and loved African-Americans; a compassionate politician who wanted to incorporate blacks into American society with full civil rights.

But is this the real reason Lincoln wanted to rid the U.S. of slavery? Let us allow him to speak for himself.

Just over two years before he was elected president, during a speech at Chicago, Illinois, on July 10, 1858 (in which he replied to charges made by his senatorial opponent Stephen A. Douglas), Lincoln made these remarks:

> I have said that always; Judge Douglas has heard me say it—if not quite a hundred times, at least as good as a hundred times; and when it is said that I am in favor of interfering with slavery where it exists, I know it is unwarranted by anything I have ever intended, and, as I believe, by anything I have ever said. If by any means I have ever used language which could fairly be so construed (as, however, I believe I never have), I now correct it.
>
> So much, then, for the inference that Judge Douglas draws, that I am in favor of setting the sections at war with one another. I know that I never meant any such thing, and I believe that no fair mind can infer any such thing from anything I have ever said.[796]

On September 16, 1858, Lincoln recorded the following notes for his future speeches:

> I believe . . . [that] by our form of government the States which have slavery are to retain or disuse it, at their own pleasure; and that all others—individuals, free States, and National Government—are constitutionally bound to leave them alone about it.[797]

That same year, on August 27, Lincoln used his second debate with Douglas (at Freeport, Illinois) to clarify and emphasize his positions on the various aspects of slavery, including what he would come to call his primary goal, **"the preventing of the spread and nationalization of slavery"**[798]:

> Ladies and Gentlemen: On Saturday last, Judge Douglas and myself first met in public discussion. He spoke one hour, I an hour and a half, and he replied for half an hour. The order is now reversed. I am to speak an hour, he an hour and a half, and then I am to reply for half an hour. I propose to devote myself during the first hour to the scope of what was brought within the range of his half-hour speech at Ottawa. Of course there was brought within the scope of that half-hour's speech something of his own opening speech. In the course of that opening argument Judge Douglas proposed to me seven distinct interrogatories. In my speech of an hour and a half, I attended to some other parts of his speech, and incidentally, as I thought, answered one of the interrogatories then. I then distinctly intimated to him that I would answer the rest of his interrogatories on condition only that he should agree to answer as many for me. He made no intimation at the time of the proposition, nor did he in his reply allude at all to that suggestion of mine. I do him no injustice in saying that he occupied at least half of his reply in dealing with me as though I had refused to answer his interrogatories. I now propose that I will answer any of the interrogatories, upon condition that he will answer questions from me not exceeding the same number. I give him an opportunity to respond. The judge remains silent. I now say that I will answer his interrogatories, whether he answers mine or not; and that after I have

done so, I shall propound mine to him.

  I have supposed myself, since the organization of the Republican party [then the liberal party, similar to today's Democrats] at Bloomington, in May, 1856, bound as a party man by the platforms of the party then and since. If in any interrogatories which I shall answer I go beyond the scope of what is within these platforms, it will be perceived that no one is responsible but myself. Having said this much, I will take up the judge's interrogatories as I find them printed in the Chicago "Times," and answer them *seriatim* [i.e., separately]. In order that there may be no mistake about it, I have copied the interrogatories in writing, and also my answers to them. The first one of these interrogatories is in these words:

  Question 1. "I desire to know whether Lincoln to-day stands as he did in 1854, in favor of the unconditional repeal of the fugitive-slave law?"

  Answer. I do not now, nor ever did, stand in favor of the unconditional repeal of the fugitive-slave law.

  Q. 2. "I desire him to answer whether he stands pledged to-day as he did in 1854, against the admission of any more slave States into the Union, even if the people want them?"

  A. I do not now, nor ever did, stand pledged against the admission of any more slave States into the Union.

  Q. 3. "I want to know whether he stands pledged against the admission of a new State into the Union with such a constitution as the people of that State may see fit to make?"

  A. I do not stand pledged against the admission of a new State into the Union with such a constitution as the people of that State may see fit to make.

  Q. 4. "I want to know whether he stands to-day pledged to the abolition of slavery in the District of Columbia?"

  A. I do not stand to-day pledged to the abolition of slavery in the District of Columbia.

  Q. 5. "I desire him to answer whether he stands pledged to the prohibition of the slave-trade between the different States?"

  A. I do not stand pledged to the prohibition of the slave-trade between the different States.

Q. 6. "I desire to know whether he stands pledged to prohibit slavery in all the Territories of the United States, North as well as South of the Missouri Compromise line?"

A. I am impliedly, if not expressly, pledged to a belief in the right and duty of Congress to prohibit slavery in all the United States Territories.

Q. 7. "I desire him to answer whether he is opposed to the acquisition of any new territory unless slavery is first prohibited therein?"

A. I am not generally opposed to honest acquisition of territory; and, in any given case, I would or would not oppose such acquisition, accordingly as I might think such acquisition would or would not aggravate the slavery question among ourselves.

Now, my friends, it will be perceived upon an examination of these questions and answers, that so far I have only answered that I was not pledged to this, that, or the other. The judge has not framed his interrogatories to ask me anything more than this, and I have answered in strict accordance with the interrogatories, and have answered truly that I am not pledged at all upon any of the points to which I have answered. But I am not disposed to hang upon the exact form of his interrogatory. I am really disposed to take up at least some of these questions, and state what I really think upon them.

As to the first one, in regard to the fugitive-slave law, I have never hesitated to say, and I do not now hesitate to say, that I think, under the Constitution of the United States, the people of the Southern States are entitled to a congressional fugitive-slave law. Having said that, I have had nothing to say in regard to the existing fugitive-slave law, further than that I think it should have been framed so as to be free from some of the objections that pertain to it, without lessening its efficiency. And inasmuch as we are not now in an agitation in regard to an alteration or modification of that law, I would not be the man to introduce it as a new subject of agitation upon the general question of slavery.

In regard to the other question, of whether I am pledged to the admission of any more slave States into the Union, I state to you very frankly that I would be exceedingly sorry ever to be put in a position of having to pass upon that question. I should be exceedingly glad to know that there would never be another slave State admitted into the Union; but I must add, that if slavery shall be kept out of the Territories during the territorial existence of any one given Territory, and then the people shall, having a fair chance and a clear field, when they come to adopt the Constitution, do such an extraordinary thing as to adopt a slave constitution, uninfluenced by the actual presence of the institution among them, I see no alternative, if we own the country, but to admit them into the Union.

The third interrogatory is answered by the answer to the second, it being, as I conceive, the same as the second.

The fourth one is in regard to the abolition of slavery in the District of Columbia. In relation to that, I have my mind very distinctly made up. I should be exceedingly glad to see slavery abolished in the District of Columbia. I believe that Congress possesses the constitutional power to abolish it. Yet as a member of Congress, I should not with my present views be in favor of endeavoring to abolish slavery in the District of Columbia unless it would be upon these conditions: First, that the abolition should be gradual; second, that it should be on a vote of the majority of qualified voters in the District; and third, that compensation should be made to unwilling owners. With these three conditions, I confess I would be exceedingly glad to see Congress abolish slavery in the District of Columbia, and, in the language of Henry Clay, "sweep from our capital that foul blot upon our nation."

In regard to the fifth interrogatory, I must say here that as to the question of the abolition of the slave-trade between the different States, I can truly answer, as I have, that I am pledged to nothing about it. It is a subject to which I have not given that mature consideration that would make me feel authorized to state a position so as to hold myself entirely bound by it. In other words, that question has never been prominently enough before me to induce me to investigate whether we really have the constitutional power to do it. I could investigate it if I had sufficient time to bring myself to a conclusion upon that subject, but I have not done so, and I say so frankly to you here and to Judge Douglas. I must say, however, that if I should be of opinion that Congress does possess the constitutional power to abolish the slave-trade among the different States, I should still not be in favor of the exercise of that power unless upon some conservative principle as I conceive it, akin to what I have said in relation to the abolition of slavery in the District of Columbia.

My answer as to whether I desire that slavery should be prohibited in all the Territories of the United States is full and explicit within itself, and cannot be made clearer by any comments of mine. So I suppose in regard to the question whether I am opposed to the acquisition of any more territory unless slavery is first prohibited therein, my answer is such that I could add nothing by way of illustration, or making myself better understood, than the answer which I have placed in writing.

Now in all this the judge has me, and he has me on the record. I suppose he had flattered himself that I was really entertaining one set of opinions for one place and another set for another place—that I was afraid to say at one place what I uttered at another. What I am saying here I suppose I say to a vast audience as strongly tending to Abolitionism as any audience in the State of Illinois, and I believe I am saying that which, if it would be offensive to any persons and render them enemies to myself, would be offensive to persons in this audience.

I now proceed to propound to the judge the interrogatories so far as I have framed them. I will bring forward a new instalment when I get them ready. I will bring them forward now, only reaching to number four.

The first one is:

Question 1. If the people of Kansas shall, by means entirely unobjectionable in all other respects, adopt a State constitution, and ask admission into the Union under it, before they have the requisite number of inhabitants according to the English bill,—some ninety-three thousand,—will you vote to admit them?

Q. 2. Can the people of a United States Territory, in any lawful way, against the wish of any citizen of the United States, exclude slavery from its limits prior to the formation of a State constitution?

Q. 3. If the Supreme Court of the United States shall decide that States cannot exclude slavery from their limits, are you in favor of acquiescing in, adopting, and following such decision as a rule of political action?

Q. 4. Are you in favor of acquiring additional territory, in disregard of how such acquisition may affect the nation on the slavery question?

As introductory to these interrogatories which Judge Douglas propounded to me at Ottawa, [Illinois,] he read a set of resolutions which he said Judge [Lyman] Trumbull and myself had participated in adopting, in the first Republican State convention, held at Springfield, in October, 1854. He insisted that I and Judge Trumbull, and perhaps the entire Republican [liberal] party, were responsible for the doctrines contained in the set of resolutions which he read, and I understand that it was from that set of resolutions that he deduced the interrogatories which he propounded to me, using these resolutions as a sort of authority for propounding those questions to me. Now I say here to-day that I do not answer his interrogatories because of their springing at all from that set of resolutions which he read. I answered them because Judge Douglas thought fit to ask them. I do not now, nor ever did, recognize any responsibility upon myself in that set of resolutions. When I replied to him on that occasion, I assured him that I never had anything to do with them. I repeat here to-day, that I never in any possible form had anything to do with that set of resolutions. It turns out, I believe, that those resolutions were never passed at any convention held in Springfield. It turns out that they were never passed at any convention or any public meeting that I had any part in. I believe it turns out, in addition to all this, that there was not, in the fall of 1854, any convention holding a session in Springfield calling itself a Republican State convention; yet it is true there was a convention, or assemblage of men calling themselves a convention, at Springfield, that did pass some resolutions. But so little did I really know of the proceedings of that convention, or what set of resolutions they had passed, though having a general knowledge that there had been such an assemblage of men there, that when Judge Douglas read the resolutions, I really did not know but that they had been the resolutions passed then and there. I did not question that they were the resolutions adopted. For I could not bring myself to suppose that Judge Douglas could say what he did upon this subject without knowing that it was true. I contented myself, on that occasion, with denying, as I truly could, all connection with them, not denying or affirming whether they were passed at Springfield. Now it turns out that he had got hold of some resolutions passed at some convention or public meeting in Kane County. I wish to say here, that I don't conceive that in any fair and just mind this discovery relieves me at all. I had just as much to do with the convention in Kane County as that at Springfield. I am just as much responsible for the resolutions at Kane County as those at Springfield, the amount of the responsibility being exactly nothing in either case; no more than there would be in regard to a set of resolutions passed in the moon.

I allude to this extraordinary matter in this canvass for some further purpose than anything yet advanced. Judge Douglas did not make his statement upon that occasion as matters that he believed to be true, but he stated them roundly as being true, in such form as to pledge his veracity for their truth. When the whole matter turns out as it does, and when we consider who Judge Douglas is,— that he is a distinguished senator of the United States; that he has served nearly twelve years as such; that his character is not at all limited as an ordinary senator of the United States, but that his name has become of world-wide renown,—it is most extraordinary that he should so far forget all the suggestions of justice to an adversary, or of prudence to himself, as to venture upon the assertion of that which the slightest investigation would have shown him to be wholly false. I can only account for his having done so upon the supposition that that evil genius which has attended him through his life, giving to him an apparent astonishing prosperity, such as to lead very many good men to doubt there being any advantage in virtue over vice—I say I can only account for it on the supposition that that evil genius has at last made up its mind to forsake him.

And I may add that another extraordinary feature of the judge's conduct in this canvass—made more extraordinary by this incident—is, that he is in the habit, in almost all the speeches he makes, of charging falsehood upon his adversaries, myself and others. I now ask whether he is able to find in anything that Judge

Trumbull, for instance, has said, or in anything that I have said, a justification at all compared with what we have, in this instance, for that sort of vulgarity.

I have been in the habit of charging as a matter of belief on my part, that, in the introduction of the Nebraska bill into Congress, there was a conspiracy to make slavery perpetual and national. I have arranged from time to time the evidence which establishes and proves the truth of this charge. I recurred to this charge at Ottawa. I shall not now have time to dwell upon it at very great length; but inasmuch as Judge Douglas in his reply of half an hour made some points upon me in relation to it, I propose noticing a few of them.

The judge insists that, in the first speech I made, in which I very distinctly made that charge, he thought for a good while I was in fun—that I was playful—that I was not sincere about it—and that he only grew angry and somewhat excited when he found that I insisted upon it as a matter of earnestness. He says he characterized it as a falsehood as far as I implicated his moral character in that transaction. Well, I did not know, till he presented that view, that I had implicated his moral character. He is very much in the habit, when he argues me up into a position I never thought of occupying, of very cozily saying he has no doubt Lincoln is "conscientious" in saying so. He should remember that I did not know but what he was altogether "conscientious" in that matter. I can conceive it possible for men to conspire to do a good thing, and I really find nothing in Judge Douglas's course of arguments that is contrary to or inconsistent with his belief of a conspiracy to nationalize and spread slavery as being a good and blessed thing, and so I hope he will understand that I do not at all question but that in all this matter he is entirely "conscientious."

But to draw your attention to one of the points I made in this case, beginning at the beginning. When the Nebraska bill was introduced, or a short time afterward, by an amendment, I believe, it was provided that it must be considered "the true intent and meaning of this act not to legislate slavery into any State or Territory, or to exclude it therefrom, but to leave the people thereof perfectly free to form and regulate their own domestic institutions in their own way, subject only to the Constitution of the United States." I have called his attention to the fact that when he and some others began arguing that they were giving an increased degree of liberty to the people m the Territories over and above what they formerly had on the question of slavery, a question was raised whether the law was enacted to give such unconditional liberty to the people; and to test the sincerity of this mode of argument, Mr. [Salmon Portland] Chase, of Ohio, introduced an amendment, in which he made the law—if the amendment were adopted—expressly declare that the people of the Territory should have the power to exclude slavery if they saw fit. I have asked attention also to the fact that Judge Douglas, and those who acted with him, voted that amendment down, notwithstanding it expressed exactly the thing they said was the true intent and meaning of the law. I have called attention to the fact that in subsequent times a decision of the Supreme Court has been made in which it has been declared that a Territorial Legislature has no constitutional right to exclude slavery. And I have argued and said that for men who did intend that the people of the Territory should have the right to exclude slavery absolutely and unconditionally, the voting down of Chase's amendment is wholly inexplicable. It is a puzzle—a riddle. But I have said that with men who did look forward to such a decision, or who had it in contemplation that such a decision of the Supreme Court would or might be made, the voting down of that amendment would be perfectly rational and intelligible. It would keep Congress from coming in collision with the decision when it was made. Anybody can conceive that if there was an intention or expectation that such a decision was to follow, it would not be a very desirable party attitude to get into for the Supreme Court—all or nearly all its members belonging to the same party—to decide one way, when the party in Congress had decided the other way. Hence it would be very rational for men expecting such a decision to keep the niche in that law clear for it. After pointing this out, I tell Judge Douglas that it looks to me as though here was the reason why Chase's amendment was voted down. I tell him that as he did it, and knows why he did it, if it was done for a reason different from this, he knows what that reason was, and can tell us what it was. I tell him, also, it will be vastly more satisfactory to the country for him to give some other plausible, intelligible reason why it was voted down than to stand upon his dignity and call people liars. Well, on Saturday he did make his answer, and what do you think it was? He says if I had only taken upon myself to tell the whole truth about that amendment of Chase's, no explanation would have been necessary on his part—or words to that effect. Now I say here that I am quite unconscious of having suppressed anything material to the case, and I am very frank to admit if there is any sound reason other than that which appeared to me material, it is quite fair for him to present it. What reason does he propose? That when Chase came forward with his amendment expressly authorizing the people to exclude slavery from the limits of every Territory, General [Lewis] Cass proposed to Chase, if he (Chase) would add to his amendment that the people should have the power to introduce or exclude, they would let it go.

This is substantially all of his reply. And because Chase would not do that they voted his amendment down. Well, it turns out, I believe, upon examination, that General Cass took some part in the little running debate upon that amendment, and then ran away and did not vote on it at all. Is not that the fact? So confident, as I think, was General Cass that there was a snake somewhere about, he chose to run away from the whole thing. This is an inference I draw from the fact that though he took part in the debate his name does not appear in the ayes and noes. But does Judge Douglas's reply amount to a satisfactory answer? [Cries of "Yes," "Yes," and "No," "No."] There is some little difference of opinion here. But I ask attention to a few more views bearing on the question of whether it amounts to a satisfactory answer. The men who were determined that that amendment should not get into the bill, and spoil the place where the Dred Scott decision was to come in, sought an excuse to get rid of it somewhere. One of these ways—one of these excuses—was to ask Chase to add to his proposed amendment a provision that the people might introduce slavery if they wanted to. They very well knew Chase would do no such thing—that Mr. Chase was one of the men differing from them on the broad principle of his insisting that freedom was better than slavery—a man who would not consent to enact a law penned with his own hand, by which he was made to recognize slavery on the one hand and liberty on the other as precisely equal; and when they insisted on his doing this, they very well knew they insisted on that which he would not for a moment think of doing, and that they were only bluffing him. I believe—I have not, since he made his answer, had a chance to examine the journals or "Congressional Globe," and therefore speak from memory—I believe the state of the bill at that time, according to parliamentary rules, was such that no member could propose an additional amendment to Chase's amendment. I rather think this is the truth—the judge shakes his head. Very well. I would like to know then, if they wanted Chase's amendment fixed over, why somebody else could not have offered to do it? If they wanted it amended, why did they not offer the amendment? Why did they stand there taunting and quibbling at Chase? Why did they not put it in themselves? But to put it on the other ground: suppose that there was such an amendment offered, and Chase's was an amendment to an amendment; until one is disposed of by parliamentary law, you cannot pile another on. Then all these gentlemen had to do was to vote Chase's on, and then, in the amended form in which the whole stood, add their own amendment to it if they wanted to put it in that shape. This was all they were obliged to do, and the ayes and noes show that there were thirty-six who voted it down, against ten who voted in favor of it. The thirty-six held entire sway and control. They could in some form or other have put that bill in the exact shape they wanted. If there was a rule preventing their amending it at the time, they could pass that, and then, Chase's amendment being merged, put it in the shape they wanted. They did not choose to do so, but they went into a quibble with Chase to get him to add what they knew he would not add, and because he would not, they stand upon that flimsy pretext for voting down what they argued was the meaning and intent of their own bill. They left room thereby for this Dred Scott decision, which goes very far to make slavery national throughout the United States.

I pass one or two points I have because my time will very soon expire, but I must be allowed to say that Judge Douglas recurs again, as he did upon one or two other occasions, to the enormity of Lincoln—an insignificant individual like Lincoln—upon his *ipse dixit* [i.e., an unproven assertion] **charging a conspiracy upon a** large number of members of Congress, the Supreme Court, and two Presidents, to nationalize slavery. I want to say that, in the first place, I have made no charge of this sort upon my *ipse dixit*. I have only arrayed the evidence tending to prove it, and presented it to the understanding of others, saying what I think it proves, but giving you the means of judging whether it proves it or not. This is precisely what I have done. I have not placed it upon my *ipse dixit* at all. On this occasion, I wish to recall his attention to a piece of evidence which I brought forward at Ottawa on Saturday, showing that he had made substantially the same charge against substantially the same persons, excluding his dear self from the category. I ask him to give some attention to the evidence which I brought forward, that he himself had discovered a "fatal blow being struck" against the right of the people to exclude slavery from their limits, which fatal blow he assumed as in evidence in an article in the Washington "Union," published "by authority." I ask by whose authority? He discovers a similar or identical provision in the Lecompton constitution. Made by whom? The framers of that constitution. Advocated by whom? By all the members of the party in the nation, who advocated the introduction of Kansas into the Union under the Lecompton constitution.

I have asked his attention to the evidence that he arrayed to prove that such a fatal blow was being struck, and to the facts which he brought forward in support of that charge—being identical with the one which he thinks so villainous in me. He pointed it not at a newspaper editor merely, but at the President and his cabinet, and the members of Congress advocating the Lecompton constitution, and those framing that instrument. I must again be permitted to remind him, that although my *ipse dixit* may not be as great as his, yet it somewhat reduces the force of his calling my attention to the enormity of my making a like charge against him.[799]

Clearly, as the above words make patently clear, Lincoln—though he personally detested slavery because it brought whites and blacks into close association[800]—was most interested in preventing the institution's spread outside the South, not in outright abolition. And even this was not for the welfare of Southern blacks. It was for the welfare of Northern whites. As Lincoln said on September 17, 1859, at Cincinnati, Ohio: **"the mass of white men are really injured by the effects of slave-labor."**[801] If he had been a true abolitionist he would have said: "the mass of *black* men are really injured by the effects of slave-labor."

Douglas then responded to Lincoln's remarks, falsely accusing him of being an abolitionist, but rightly accusing him of trying to undermine states' rights. Lincoln replied to Douglas a second time, vigorously denying both charges while continuing to promote his desire to stop the spread of slavery:

> The plain truth is this. At the introduction of the Nebraska policy, we [liberals] believed there was a new era being introduced in the history of the republic, which tended to the spread and perpetuation of slavery. But in our opposition to that measure we did not agree with one another in everything. The people in the north end of the State were for stronger measures of opposition than we of the central and southern portions of the State, but we were all opposed to the Nebraska doctrine. We had that one feeling and that one sentiment in common. You at the north end met in your conventions and passed your resolutions. We in the middle of the State and further south did not hold such conventions and pass the same resolutions, although we had in general a common view and a common sentiment. So that these meetings which the judge has alluded to, and the resolutions he has read from, were local, and did not spread over the whole State. We at last met together in 1856, from all parts of the State, and we agreed upon a common platform. You who held more extreme notions, either yielded those notions, or if not wholly yielding them, agreed to yield them practically, for the sake of embodying the opposition to the measures which the opposite party were pushing forward at that time. We met you then, and if there was anything yielded, it was for practical purposes. We agreed then upon a platform for the party throughout the entire State of Illinois, and now we are all bound, as a party, to that platform. And I say here to you, if any one expects of me, in the case of my election, that I will do anything not signified by our Republican platform and my answers here to-day, I tell you very frankly that person will be deceived. I do not ask for the vote of any one who supposes that I have

secret purposes or pledges that I dare not speak out. Cannot the judge be satisfied? If he fears, in the unfortunate case of my election, that my going to Washington will enable me to advocate sentiments contrary to those which I expressed when you voted for and elected me, I assure him that his fears are wholly needless and groundless. Is the judge really afraid of any such thing? I'll tell you what he is afraid of. He is afraid we'll all pull together. This is what alarms him more than anything else. For my part, I do hope that all of us, entertaining a common sentiment in opposition to what appears to us a design to nationalize and perpetuate slavery, will waive minor differences on questions which either belong to the dead past or the distant future, and all pull together in this struggle. What are your sentiments? If it be true that on the ground which I occupy—ground which I occupy as frankly and boldly as Judge Douglas does his—my views, though partly coinciding with yours, are not as perfectly in accordance with your feelings as his are, I do say to you in all candor, go for him and not for me. I hope to deal in all things fairly with Judge Douglas, and with the people of the State, in this contest. And if I should never be elected to any office, I trust I may go down with no stain of falsehood upon my reputation, notwithstanding the hard opinions Judge Douglas chooses to entertain of me.

  The judge has again addressed himself to the Abolition tendencies of a speech of mine, made at Springfield in June last. I have so often tried to answer what he is always saying on that melancholy theme, that I almost turn with disgust from the discussion—from the repetition of an answer to it. I trust that nearly all of this intelligent audience have read that speech. If you have, I may venture to leave it to you to inspect it closely, and see whether it contains any of those "bugaboos" which frighten Judge Douglas.

  The judge complains that I did not fully answer his questions. If I have the sense to comprehend and answer those questions, I have done so fairly. If it can be pointed out to me how I can more fully and fairly answer him, I will do it—but I aver I have not the sense to see how it is to be done. He says I do not declare I would in any event vote for the admission of a slave State into the Union. If I have been fairly reported, he will see that I did give an explicit answer to his interrogatories. I did not merely say that I would dislike to be put to the test; but I said clearly, if I were put to the test, and a Territory from which slavery had been excluded should present herself with a State constitution sanctioning slavery,—a most extraordinary thing and wholly unlikely to happen,—I did not see how I could avoid voting for her admission. But he refuses to understand that I said so, and he wants this audience to understand that I did not say so. Yet it will be so reported in the printed speech that he cannot help seeing it.

He says if I should vote for the admission of a slave State I would be voting for a dissolution of the Union, because I hold that the Union cannot permanently exist half slave and half free. I repeat that I do not believe this government can endure permanently half slave and half free, yet I do not admit, nor does it at all follow, that the admission of a single slave State will permanently fix the character and establish this as a universal slave nation. The judge is very happy indeed at working up these quibbles. Before leaving the subject of answering questions, I aver as my confident belief, when you come to see our speeches in print, that you will find every question which he has asked me more fairly and boldly and fully answered than he has answered those which I put to him. Is not that so? The two speeches may be placed side by side; and I will venture to leave it to impartial judges whether his questions have not been more directly and circumstantially answered than mine.

Judge Douglas says he made a charge upon the editor of the Washington "Union," alone, of entertaining a purpose to rob the States of their power to exclude slavery from their limits. I undertake to say, and I make the direct issue, that he did not make his charge against the editor of the "Union" alone. I will undertake to prove by the record here that he made that charge against more and higher dignitaries than the editor of the Washington "Union." I am quite aware that he was shirking and dodging around the form in which he put it, but I can make it manifest that he leveled his "fatal blow" against more persons than this Washington editor. Will he dodge it now by alleging that I am trying to defend Mr. [James] Buchanan against the charge? Not at all. Am I not making the same charge myself? I am trying to show that you, Judge Douglas, are a witness on my side.

I am not defending Buchanan, and I will tell Judge Douglas that in my opinion when he made that charge he had an eye farther north than he was to-day. He was then fighting against people who called him a Black Republican and an Abolitionist. It is mixed all through his speech, and it is tolerably manifest that his eye was a great deal farther north than it is to-day. The judge says that though he made this charge, [Robert] Toombs got up and declared there was not a man in the United States, except the editor of the "Union," who was in favor of the doctrines put forth in that article. And thereupon I understand that the judge withdrew the charge. Although he had taken extracts from the newspaper, and then from the Lecompton constitution, to show the existence of a conspiracy to bring about a "fatal blow," by which the States were to be deprived of the right of excluding slavery, it all went to pot as soon as Toombs got up and told him it was not true. It reminds me of the story that John Phoenix, the California railroad surveyor, tells. He says they started out from the Plaza to the Mission of Dolores. They had two ways of determining distances. One was by a chain and pins taken over the ground; the other was by a "go-it-ometer,"—an invention of his own,—a three-legged instrument, with which he computed a series of triangles between the points. At night he turned to the chain-man to ascertain what distance they had come, and found that by some mistake he had merely dragged the chain over the ground without keeping any record. By the "go-it-ometer" he found he had made ten miles. Being skeptical about this, he asked a drayman who was passing how far it was to the Plaza. The drayman replied it was just half a mile, and the surveyor put it down in his book—just as Judge Douglas says, after he had made his calculations and computations, he took Toombs's statement. I have no doubt that after Judge Douglas had made his charge, he was as easily satisfied about its truth as the surveyor was of the drayman's statement of the distance to the Plaza. Yet it is a fact that the man who put forth all that matter which Douglas deemed a "fatal blow" at State sovereignty, was elected by the Democrats as public printer.

Now, gentlemen, you may take Judge Douglas's speech of March 22, 1858, beginning about the middle of page 21, and reading to the bottom of page 24, and you will find the evidence on which I say that lie did not make his charge against the editor of the "Union" alone. I cannot stop to read it, but I will give it to the reporters. Judge Douglas said:

> "Mr. President [i.e., James Buchanan], you here find several distinct propositions advanced boldly by the Washington 'Union' editorially, and apparently authoritatively, and every man who questions any of them is denounced as an Abolitionist, a Free-soiler, a fanatic. The propositions are: first, that the primary object of all government at its original institution is the protection of persons and property; second, that the Constitution of the United States declares that the citizens of each State shall be entitled to all the privileges and immunities of citizens in the several States; and that, therefore, thirdly, all State laws, whether organic or otherwise, which prohibit the citizens of one State from settling in another with their slave property, and especially declaring it forfeited, are direct violations of the original intention of the government and Constitution of the United States; and fourth, that the emancipation of the slaves of the Northern States was a gross outrage on the rights of property, inasmuch as it was involuntarily done on the part of the owner.
>
> "Remember that this article was published in the 'Union' on the 17th of November, and on the 18th appeared the first article giving the adhesion of the 'Union' to the Lecompton constitution. It was in these words:
>
>> "'Kansas And Her Constitution.—The vexed question is settled. The problem

> is solved. The dead point of danger is passed. All serious trouble to Kansas affairs is over and gone.'

"And a column, nearly, of the same sort. Then, when you come to look into the Lecompton constitution, you find the same doctrine incorporated in it which was put forth editorially in the 'Union.' What is it?

> "'Article 7, Section 1. The right of property is before and higher than any constitutional sanction; and the right of the owner of a slave to such slave and its increase is the same and as invariable as the right of the owner of any property whatever.'

"Then in the schedule is a provision that the constitution may be amended after 1864 by a two-thirds vote.

> "'But no alteration shall be made to affect the right of property in the ownership of slaves.'

"It will be seen by these clauses in the Lecompton constitution that they are identical in spirit with this authoritative article in the Washington 'Union' of the day previous to its indorsement of this constitution.

> "When I saw that article in the 'Union' of the 17th of November, followed by the glorification of the Lecompton constitution on the 18th of November, and this clause in the constitution asserting the doctrine that a State has no right to prohibit slavery within its limits, I saw that there was a fatal blow being struck at the sovereignty of the States of this Union."

Here he [Douglas] says, "Mr. President, you here find several distinct propositions advanced boldly, and apparently authoritatively." By whose authority, Judge Douglas? Again, he says in another place, "It will be seen by these clauses in the Lecompton constitution that they are identical in spirit with this authoritative article." By whose authority? Who do you mean to say authorized the publication of these articles? He knows that the Washington "Union" is considered the organ of the administration. I demand of Judge Douglas by whose authority he meant to say those articles were published, if not by the authority of the President of the United States and his cabinet? I defy him to show whom he referred to, if not to these high functionaries in the Federal Government. More than this, he says the articles in that paper and the provisions of the Lecompton constitution are "identical," and being identical, he argues that the authors are cooperating and conspiring together. He does not use the word "conspiring," but what other construction can you put upon it? He winds up with this:

> "When I saw that article in the 'Union' of the 17th of November, followed by the glorification of the Lecompton constitution on the 18th of November, and this clause in the constitution asserting the doctrine that a State has no right to prohibit slavery within its limits, I saw that there was a fatal blow being struck at the sovereignty of the States of this Union."

I ask him if all this fuss was made over the editor

of this newspaper. It would be a terribly "fatal blow" indeed which a single man could strike, when no President, no cabinet officer, no member of Congress, was giving strength and efficiency to the movement. Out of respect to Judge Douglas's good sense I must believe he didn't manufacture his idea of the "fatal" character of that blow out of such a miserable scapegrace as he represents that editor to be. But the judge's eye is farther south now. Then, it was very peculiarly and decidedly north. His hope rested on the idea of enlisting the great "Black Republican" party, and making it the tail of his new kite. He knows he was then expecting from day to day to turn Republican and place himself at the head of our organization. He has found that these despised "Black Republicans" estimate him by a standard which he has taught them only too well. Hence he is crawling back into his old camp, and you will find him eventually installed in full fellowship among those whom he was then battling, and with whom he now pretends to be at such fearful variance. [Loud applause, and cries of "Go on, go on."] I cannot, gentlemen, my time has expired.[802]

On September 15, 1858, Lincoln entered into his third debate with Douglas. Again, Lincoln's main thrust was limiting the expansion of slavery, not abolition:

> Ladies and Gentlemen: There is very much in the principles that Judge Douglas has here enunciated that I most cordially approve, and over which I shall have no controversy with him. In so far as he has insisted that all the States have the right to do exactly as they please about all their domestic relations, including that of slavery, I agree entirely with him. He places me wrong in spite of all I can tell him, though I repeat it again and again, insisting that I have made no difference with him upon this subject. I have made a great many speeches, some of which have been printed, and it will be utterly impossible for him to find anything that I have ever put in print contrary to what I now say upon this subject I hold myself under constitutional obligations to allow the people in all the States, without interference, direct or indirect, to do exactly as they please, and I deny that I have any inclination to interfere with them, even if there were no such constitutional obligation. I can only say

again that I am placed improperly—altogether improperly, in spite of all I can say—when it is insisted that I entertain any other view or purpose in regard to that matter.

While I am upon this subject, I will make some answers briefly to certain propositions that Judge Douglas has put. He says, "Why can't this Union endure permanently, half slave and half free?" I have said that I supposed it could not, and I will try, before this new audience, to give briefly some of the reasons for entertaining that opinion. Another form of his question is, "Why can't we let it stand as our fathers placed it?" That is the exact difficulty between us. I say that Judge Douglas and his friends have changed it from the position in which our fathers originally placed it. I say, in the way our fathers originally left the slavery question, the institution was in the course of ultimate extinction, and the public mind rested in the belief that it was in the course of ultimate extinction. I say when this government was first established, it was the policy of its founders to prohibit the spread of slavery into the new Territories of the United States, where it had not existed. But Judge Douglas and his friends have broken up that policy, and placed it upon a new basis by which it is to become national and perpetual. All I have asked or desired anywhere is that it should be placed back again upon the basis that the fathers of our government originally placed it upon. I have no doubt that it would become extinct, for all time to come, if we but readopted the policy of the fathers by restricting it to the limits it has already covered—restricting it from the new Territories.

I do not wish to dwell at great length on this branch of the subject at this time, but allow me to repeat one thing that I have stated before. [Conservative Southern Congressman Preston Smith] **Brooks, the man who assaulted** [Yankee] **Senator** [Charles] **Sumner on the floor of the Senate** [in 1856],[803] **and who was complimented with dinners, and silver pitchers, and gold-headed canes, and a good many other things for that feat, in one of his speeches declared that when this government was originally established, nobody expected that the institution of slavery would last until this day.** That was but the opinion of one man, but it was such an opinion as we can never get from Judge Douglas, or anybody in favor of slavery in the North at all. You can sometimes get it from a Southern man. He said at the same time that the framers of our government did not have the knowledge that experience has taught us—that experience and the invention of the cotton-gin have taught us that the perpetuation of slavery is a necessity. He insisted, therefore, upon its being changed from the basis upon which the fathers of the government left it to the basis of its perpetuation and nationalization.

  I insist that this is the difference between Judge Douglas and myself—that Judge Douglas is helping that change along. I insist upon this government being placed where our fathers originally placed it.

  I remember Judge Douglas once said that he saw the evidences on the statute-books of Congress of a policy in the origin of government to divide slavery and freedom by a geographical line—that he saw an indisposition to maintain that policy, and therefore he set about studying up a way to settle the institution on the right basis—the basis which he thought it ought to have been placed upon at first; and in that speech he confesses that he seeks to place it, not upon the basis that the fathers placed it upon, but upon one gotten up on "original principles." When he asks me why we cannot get along with it in the attitude where our fathers placed it, he had better clear up the evidences that he has himself changed it from that basis; that he has himself been chiefly instrumental in changing the policy of the fathers. Any one who will read his speech of the 22d of last March will see that he there makes an open confession, showing that he set about fixing the institution upon an altogether different set of principles. I think I have fully answered him when he asks me why we cannot let it alone upon the basis where our fathers left it, by showing that he has himself changed the whole policy of the government in that regard.

  Now, fellow-citizens, in regard to this matter about a contract that was made between Judge Trumbull and myself, and all that long portion of Judge Douglas's speech on this subject, I wish simply to say what I have said to him before, that he cannot know whether it is true or not, and I do know that there is not a word of truth in it. And I have told him so before. I don't want any harsh language indulged in, but I do not know how to deal with this persistent insisting on a story that I know to be utterly without truth. It used to be a fashion amongst men that when a charge was made, some sort of proof was brought forward to establish it, and if no proof was found to exist, the charge was dropped. I don't know how to meet this kind of an argument. I don't want to have a fight with Judge Douglas, and I have no way of making an argument up into the consistency of a corn-cob and stopping his mouth with it. All I can do is, good-humoredly, to say that from the beginning to the end of all that story about a bargain between Judge Trumbull and myself [in which Trumbull was to abolitionize the Democratic or conservative party and Lincoln was to abolitionize the Republican or liberal party], there is not a word of truth in it. I can only ask him to show some sort of evidence of the truth of his story. He brings forward here and reads from what he contends is a speech by James H. Matheny, charging such a bargain between Trumbull and myself. My own opinion is that Matheny did do some such immoral thing as to tell a story that he knew nothing about. I believe he did. I contradicted it instantly, and it has been contradicted by Judge Trumbull, while nobody has produced any proof, because there is none. Now, whether the speech which the judge brings forward here is really the one Matheny made, I do not know, and I hope the judge will pardon me for doubting the genuineness of this document, since his production of those Springfield resolutions at Ottawa. I do not wish to dwell at any great length upon this matter. I can say nothing when a long story like this is told, except that it is not true, and demand that he who insists upon it shall produce some proof. That is all any man can do, and I leave it in that way, for I know of no other way of dealing with it.

  The judge has gone over a long account of the Old Whig and Democratic parties, and it connects itself with this charge against Trumbull and myself. He says that they agreed upon a compromise in regard to the slavery question in 1850: that in a national Democratic convention resolutions were passed to abide by that compromise as a finality upon the slavery question. He also says that the Whig party in national convention agreed to abide by and regard as a finality the compromise of 1850. I understand the judge to be altogether right about that; I understand that part of the history of the country as stated by him to be correct. I recollect that I, as a member of that party, acquiesced in that compromise. I recollect in the presidential election which followed, when we had General [Winfield] Scott up for the presidency [in 1852]; Judge Douglas was around berating us Whigs as Abolitionists, precisely as he does to-day—not a bit of difference. I have often heard him. We could do nothing when the Old Whig party was alive that was not Abolitionism, but it has got an extremely good name since it has passed away.

When that compromise was made, it did not repeal the old Missouri Compromise. It left a region of United States territory half as large as the present territory of the United States, north of the line of 36° 30', in which slavery was prohibited by act of Congress. This compromise did not repeal that one. It did not affect or propose to repeal it. But at last it became Judge Douglas's duty, as he thought (and I find no fault with him), as chairman of the Committee on Territories, to bring in a bill for the organization of a territorial government—first of one, then of two Territories north of that line. When he did so it ended in his inserting a provision substantially repealing the Missouri Compromise. That was because the compromise of 1850 had not repealed it. And now I ask why he could not have left that compromise alone? We were quiet from the agitation of the slavery question. We were making no fuss about it. All had acquiesced in the compromise measures of 1850. We never had been seriously disturbed by any Abolition agitation before that period. When he came to form governments for the Territories north of the line of 36° 30', why could he not have let that matter stand as it was standing? Was it necessary to the organization of a Territory? Not at all. Iowa lay north of the line and had been organized as a Territory, and came into the Union as a State without disturbing that compromise. There was no sort of necessity for destroying it to organize these Territories. But, gentlemen, it would take up all my time to meet all the little quibbling arguments of Judge Douglas to show that the Missouri Compromise was repealed by the compromise of 1850. My own opinion is that a careful investigation of all the arguments to sustain the position that that compromise was virtually repealed by the compromise of 1850 would show that they are the merest fallacies. I have the report that Judge Douglas first brought into Congress at the time of the introduction of the Nebraska bill, which in its original form did not repeal the Missouri Compromise, and he there expressly stated that he had forborne to do so because it had not been done by the compromise of 1850. I close this part of the discussion on my part by asking him the question again, "Why, when we had peace under the Missouri Compromise, could you not have let it alone?"

In complaining of what I said in my speech at Springfield, in which he says I accepted my nomination for the senatorship (where, by the way, he is at fault, for if he will examine it, he will find no acceptance in it), he again quotes that portion in which I said that "a house divided against itself cannot stand." Let me say a word in regard to that matter.

He tries to persuade us that there must be a variety in the different institutions of the States of the Union; that that variety necessarily proceeds from the variety of soil, climate, of the face of the country, and the difference in the natural features of the States. I agree to all that. Have these very matters ever produced any difficulty amongst us? Not at all. Have we ever had any quarrel over the fact that they have laws in Louisiana designed to regulate the commerce that springs from the production of sugar? or because we have a different class relative to the production of flour in this State? Have they produced any differences? Not at all. They are the very cements of this Union. They don't make the house a house divided against itself. They are the props that hold up the house and sustain the Union.

But has it been so with this element of slavery? Have we not always had quarrels and difficulties over it? And when will we cease to have quarrels over it? Like causes produce like effects. It is worth while to observe that we have generally had comparative peace upon the slavery question, and that there has been no cause for alarm until it was excited by the effort to spread it into new territory. Whenever it has been limited to its present bounds, and there has been no effort to spread it, there has been peace. All the trouble and convulsion has proceeded from efforts to spread it over more territory. It was thus at the date of the Missouri Compromise. It was so again with the annexation of Texas; so with the territory acquired by the Mexican war; and it is so now. Whenever there has been an effort to spread it there has been agitation and resistance. Now, I appeal to this audience (very few of whom are my political friends), as national men, whether we have reason to expect that the agitation in regard to this subject will cease while the causes that tend to reproduce agitation are actively at work? Will not the same cause that produced agitation in 1820, when the Missouri Compromise was formed,—that which produced the agitation upon the annexation of Texas, and at other times,—work out the same results always? Do you think that the nature of man will be changed—that the same causes that produced agitation at one time will not have the same effect at another?

This has been the result so far as my observation of the slavery question and my reading in history extend. What right have we then to hope that the trouble will cease, that the agitation will come to an end; until it shall either be placed back where it originally stood, and where the fathers originally placed it, or, on the other hand, until it shall entirely master all opposition? This is the view I entertain, and this is the reason why I entertained it, as Judge Douglas has read from my Springfield speech.

Now, my friends, there is one other thing that I feel under some sort of obligation to mention. Judge Douglas has here to-day—in a very rambling way, I was about saying—spoken of the platforms for which he seeks to hold me responsible. He says, "Why can't you come out and make an open avowal of principles in all places alike?" and he reads from an advertisement that he says was used to notify the people of a speech to be made by Judge Trumbull at Waterloo. In commenting on it he desires to know whether we cannot speak frankly and manfully as he and his friends do! How, I ask, do his friends speak out their own sentiments? A convention of his party in this State met on the 21st of April, at Springfield, and passed a set of resolutions which they proclaim to the country as their platform. This does constitute their platform, and it is because Judge Douglas claims it is his platform—that these are his principles and purposes—that he has a right to declare that he speaks his sentiments "frankly and manfully." On the 9th of June, Colonel John Dougherty, Governor [John] Reynolds, and others, calling themselves National Democrats, met in Springfield, and adopted a set of resolutions which are as easily understood, as plain and as definite in stating to the country and to the world what they believed in and would stand upon, as Judge Douglas's platform. Now, what is the reason that Judge Douglas is not willing that Colonel Dougherty and Governor Reynolds should stand upon their own written and printed platform as well as he upon his? Why must he look farther than their platform when he claims himself to stand by his platform?

Again, in reference to our platform: On the 16th of June the Republicans had their convention and published their platform, which is as clear and distinct as Judge Douglas's. In it they spoke their principles as plainly and as definitely to the world. What is the reason that Judge Douglas is not willing that I should stand upon that platform? Why must he go around hunting for some one who is supporting me, or has supported me at some time in his life, and who has said something at some time contrary to that platform? Does the judge regard that rule as a good one? If it turn out that the rule is a good one for me,—that I am responsible for any and every opinion that any man has expressed who is my friend,—then it is a good rule for him. I ask, is it not as good a rule for him as it is for me? In my opinion, it is not a good rule for either of us. Do you think differently, judge?

Mr. Douglas: I do not.

Mr. Lincoln: **Judge Douglas says he does not think differently. I am glad of it.** Then can he tell me why he is looking up resolutions of five or six years ago, and insisting that they were my platform, notwithstanding my protest that they are not, and never were, my platform, and my pointing out the platform of the State convention which he delights to say nominated me for the Senate? I cannot see what he means by parading these resolutions, if it is not to hold me responsible for them in some way. If he says to me here, that he does not hold the rule to be good, one way or the other, I do not comprehend how he could answer me more fully if he answered me at greater length. I will therefore put in as my answer to the resolutions that he has hunted up against me what I, as a lawyer, would call a good plea to a bad declaration. I understand that it is a maxim of law, that a poor plea may be a good plea to a bad declaration. I think that the opinions the judge brings from those who support me, yet differ from me, are a bad declaration against me, but if I can bring the same things against him, I am putting in a good plea to that kind of declaration, and now I propose to try it.

At Freeport Judge Douglas occupied a large part of his time in producing resolutions and documents of various sorts, as I understood, to make me somehow responsible for them; and I propose now doing a little of the same sort of thing for him. In 1850 a very clever gentleman by the name of Thompson Campbell, a personal friend of Judge Douglas and myself, a political friend of Judge Douglas and opponent of mine, was a candidate for Congress in the Galena district. He was interrogated as to his views on this same slavery question. I have here before me the interrogatories, and Campbell's answers to them. I will read them:

> Interrogatories.
>
> 1. Will you, if elected, vote for and cordially support a bill prohibiting slavery in the Territories of the United States?
>
> 2. Will you vote for and support a bill abolishing slavery in the District of Columbia?
>
> 3. Will you oppose the admission of any slave States which may be formed out of Texas or the Territories?
>
> 4. Will you vote for and advocate the repeal of the fugitive-slave law passed at the recent session of Congress?
>
> 5. Will you advocate and vote for the election of a Speaker of the House of Representatives who shall be willing to organize the committees of that House so as to give the free States their just influence in the business of legislation?
>
> 6. What are your views, not only as to the constitutional right of Congress to prohibit the slave-trade

between the States, but also as to the expediency of exercising that right immediately?

Campbell's Reply,

> To the first and second interrogatories, I answer unequivocally in the affirmative.
> To the third interrogatory, I reply that I am opposed to the admission of any more slave States into the Union, that may be formed out of Texan or any other territory.
> To the fourth and fifth interrogatories, I unhesitatingly answer in the affirmative.
> To the sixth interrogatory, I reply that so long as the slave States continue to treat slaves as articles or commerce, the Constitution confers power on Congress to pass laws regulating that peculiar commerce, and that the protection of human rights imperatively demands the interposition of every constitutional means to prevent this most inhuman and iniquitous traffic. T. Campbell.

I want to say here that Thompson Campbell was elected to Congress on that platform, as the Democratic candidate in the Galena District, against Martin P. Sweet.

Judge Douglas: Give me the date of the letter.

Mr. Lincoln: **The time Campbell ran was in 1850. I have not the exact date here. It was some time in 1850 that these interrogatories were put and the answer given. Campbell was elected to Congress, and served out his term. I think a second election came up before he served out his term, and he was not reelected. Whether defeated or not nominated, I do not know.** [Campbell was nominated for reelection by the Democratic party, by acclamation.] **At the end of his term his very good friend, Judge Douglas, got him a high office from President** [Franklin] **Pierce, and sent him** off to California. Is not that the fact? Just at the end of his term in Congress it appears that our mutual friend Judge Douglas got our mutual friend Campbell a good office, and sent him to California upon it. And not only so, but on the 27th of last month, when Judge Douglas and myself spoke at Freeport in joint discussion, there was his same friend Campbell, come all the way from California, to help the judge beat me; and there was poor Martin P. Sweet standing on the platform, trying to help poor me to be elected. That is true of one of Judge Douglas's friends.

So again, in that same race of 1850, there was a congressional convention assembled at Joliet, and it nominated R. S. [Richard Sheppard] Molony for Congress, and unanimously adopted the following resolution:

> Resolved, That we are uncompromisingly opposed to the extension of slavery; and while we would not make such opposition a ground of interference with the interests of the States where it exists, yet we moderately but firmly insist that it is the duty of Congress to oppose its extension into territory now free by all means compatible with the obligations of the Constitution, and with good faith to our sister States; that these principles were recognized by the ordinance of 1787, which received the sanction of Thomas Jefferson, who is acknowledged by all to be the great oracle and expounder of our faith.

Subsequently the same interrogatories were propounded to Dr. Molony which had been addressed to Campbell, as above, with the exception of the sixth, respecting the interstate slave-trade, to which Dr. Molony, the Democratic nominee for Congress, replied as follows:

> I received the interrogatories this day, and as you will see by the La Salle "Democrat" and Ottawa "Free Trader," I took at Peru on the 5th and at Ottawa

on the 7th, the affirmative side of interrogatories 1st and 2d; and in relation to the admission of any more slave States from free territory, my position taken at these meetings, as correctly reported in said papers, was emphatically and distinctly opposed to it. In relation to the admission of any more slave States from Texas, whether I shall go against it or not will depend upon the opinion that I may hereafter form of the true meaning and nature of the resolutions of annexation. If by said resolutions the honor and good faith of the nation is pledged to admit more slave States from Texas when she (Texas) may apply for admission of such State, then I should, if in Congress, vote for their admission. But if not so pledged and bound by sacred contract, then a bill for the admission of more slave States from Texas would never receive my vote.

To your fourth interrogatory I answer most decidedly in the affirmative, and for reasons set forth in my reported remarks at Ottawa last Monday.

To your fifth interrogatory I also reply in the affirmative most cordially, and that I will use my utmost exertions to secure the nomination and election of a man who will accomplish the objects of said interrogatories. I most cordially approve of the resolutions adopted at the union meeting held at Princeton on the 27th September ult. Yours, etc., R. S. Molony.

All I have to say in regard to Dr. Molony is that he was the regularly nominated Democratic candidate for Congress in his district; was elected at that time; at the end of his term was appointed to a land-office at Danville. (I never heard anything of Judge Douglas's instrumentality in this.) He held this office a considerable time, and when we were at Freeport the other day, there were handbills scattered about notifying the public that after our debate was over R. S. Molony would make a Democratic speech in favor of Judge Douglas. That is all I know of my own personal knowledge. It is added here to this resolution (and truly, I believe) that "among those who participated in the Joliet convention, and who supported its nominee, with his platform as laid down in the resolution of the convention, and in his reply as above given, we call at random the following names, all of which are recognized at this day as leading [Illinois] Democrats: Cook County — E. B. Williams, Charles McDonell, Arno Voss, Thomas Hoyne, Isaac Cook,"—I reckon we ought to except Cook,—"F. C. Sherman. Will [County] — Joel A. Matteson, S. W. Bowen. Kane [County] — B. F. Hall, G. W. Renwick, A. M. Herrington, Elijah Wilcox. McHenry [County] — W. M. Jackson, Enos W. Smith, Neil Donnelly. La Salle [County] — John Hise, William Reddick"—William Reddick—another one of Judge Douglas's friends that stood on the stand with him at Ottawa at the time the judge says my knees trembled so that I had to be carried away! The names are all here: "DuPage [County] — Nathan Allen. DeKalb [County] — Z. B. Mayo."

Here is another set of resolutions which I think are apposite to the matter in hand.

On the 28th of February of the same year, a Democratic [i.e., conservative] district convention was held at Naperville, to nominate a candidate for circuit judge. Among the delegates were Bowen and Kelly, of Will [County]; Captain Naper, H. H. Cody, Nathan Allen, of DuPage [County]; W. M. Jackson, J. M. Strode, P. W. Piatt, and Enos W. Smith, of McHenry [County]; J. Horsman and others, of Winnebago [County]. Colonel Strode presided over the convention. The following resolutions were unanimously adopted—the first on motion of P. W. Piatt, the second on motion of William M. Jackson:

> Resolved, That this convention is in favor of the Wilmot proviso, both in principle and practice, and that we know of no good reason why any person should oppose the largest

latitude in free soil, free territory, and free speech.
  Resolved, That in the opinion of this convention, the time has arrived when all men should be free, whites as well as others.

Judge Douglas: What is the date of those resolutions?

Mr. Lincoln: **I understand it was in 1850, but I do not know it. I do not state a thing and say I know it when I do not. But I have the highest belief that this is so. I know of no way to arrive at the conclusion that there is an error in it. I mean to put a case no stronger than the truth will allow. But what I was going to comment upon is an extract from a newspaper in DeKalb County, and it strikes me as being rather singular, I confess, under the circumstances. There is a Judge [Z. B.] Mayo in that county, who is a candidate for the legislature, for the purpose, if he secures his election, of helping to reelect Judge Douglas. He is the editor of a newspaper** [the DeKalb County *Sentinel*], **and in that paper I find the extract I am going to read. It is part of an editorial article in which he was electioneering as fiercely as he could for Judge Douglas and against me. It was a curious thing, I think, to be in such a paper. I will agree to that, and the judge may make the most of it:**

> [Lincoln quoting Mayo] "Our education has been such that we have ever been rather in favor of the equality of the blacks; that is, that they should enjoy all the privileges of the whites where they reside. We are aware that this is not a very popular doctrine. We have had many a confab with some who are now strong 'Republicans,' we taking the broad ground of equality and they the opposite ground.
>   "We were brought up in a State where blacks were voters, and we do not know of any inconvenience resulting from it, though perhaps it would not work so well where the blacks are more numerous. We have no

doubt of the right of the whites to guard against such an evil, if it is one. Our opinion is that it would be best for all concerned to have the colored population in a State by themselves [in this I agree with him (Lincoln's note)]; but if within the jurisdiction of the United States, we say by all means they should have the right to have their senators and their representatives in Congress, and to vote for President. With us 'worth makes the man, and want of it the fellow.' We have seen many a 'nigger' that we thought more of than some white men."

That is one of Judge Douglas's [conservative] friends. Now I do not want to leave myself in an attitude where I can be misrepresented, so I will say I do not think the judge is responsible for this article; but he is quite as responsible for it as I would be if one of my friends had said it. I think that is fair enough.

I have here also a set of resolutions passed by a Democratic [i.e., conservative] State convention in Judge Douglas's own good old State of Vermont, and that, I think, ought to be good for him too.

> Resolved, That liberty is a right inherent and inalienable in man, and that herein all men are equal.
> Resolved, That we claim no authority in the Federal Government to abolish slavery in the several States. But we do claim for it constitutional power perpetually to prohibit the introduction of slavery into territory now free, and abolish it wherever, under the jurisdiction of Congress, it exists.
> Resolved, That this power ought immediately to be exercised in prohibiting the introduction and existence of slavery in New Mexico and California, in abolishing slavery and the slave-trade in the District of Columbia,

on the high seas, and wherever else, under the Constitution, it can be reached.

Resolved, That no more slave States should be admitted into the Federal Union.

Resolved, That the government ought to return to its ancient policy, not to extend, nationalize, or encourage, but to limit, localize, and discourage slavery.

At Freeport I answered several interrogatories that had been propounded to me by Judge Douglas at the Ottawa meeting. The judge as yet not seen fit to find any fault with the position that I took in regard to those seven interrogatories, which were certainly broad enough, in all conscience, to cover the entire ground. In my answers, which have been printed, and all have had the opportunity of seeing, I take the ground that those who elect me must expect that I will do nothing which will not be in accordance with those answers. I have some right to assert that Judge Douglas has no fault to find with them. But he chooses to still try to thrust me upon different ground without paying any attention to my answers, the obtaining of which from me cost him so much trouble and concern. At the same time, I propounded four interrogatories to him, claiming it as a right that he should answer as many interrogatories for me as I did for him, and I would reserve myself for a future instalment when I got them ready. The judge, in answering me upon that occasion, put in what I suppose he intends as answers to all four of my interrogatories. The first one of these interrogatories I have before me, and it is in these words:

Question 1. If the people of Kansas shall, by means entirely unobjectionable in all other respects, adopt a State constitution, and ask admission into the Union under it, before they have the requisite number of inhabitants according to the English bill,—some ninety-three thousand,—will you vote to admit them?

As I read the judge's answer in the newspaper, and as I remember it as pronounced at the time, he does not give any answer which is equivalent to yes or no—I will or I won't. He answers at very considerable length, rather quarreling with me for asking the question, and insisting that Judge Trumbull had done something that I ought to say something about; and finally getting out such statements as induce me to infer that he means to be understood he will, in that supposed case, vote for the admission of Kansas. I only bring this forward now for the purpose of saying that, if he chooses to put a different construction upon his answer, he may do it. But if he does not, I shall from this time forward assume that he will vote for the admission of Kansas in disregard of the English bill. He has the right to remove any misunderstanding I may have. I only mention it now that I may hereafter assume this to be the true construction of his answer, if he does not now choose to correct me.

The second interrogatory that I propounded to him was this:

Question 2. Can the people of a United States Territory, in any lawful way, against the wish of any citizen of the United States, exclude slavery from its limits prior to the formation of a State constitution?

To this Judge Douglas answered that they can lawfully exclude slavery from the Territory prior to the formation of a constitution. He goes on to tell us how it can be done. As I understand him, he holds that it can be done by the territorial legislature refusing to make any enactments for the protection of slavery in the Territory, and especially by adopting unfriendly legislation to it. For the sake of clearness, I state it again: that they can exclude slavery from the Territory—first, by withholding what he assumes to be an indispensable assistance to it in the way of legislation; and, second, by unfriendly legislation. If I rightly understand him, I wish to ask your attention for a while to his position.

In the first place, the Supreme Court of the United States has decided that any congressional prohibition of slavery in the Territories is unconstitutional—they have reached this proposition as a conclusion from their former proposition, that the Constitution of the United States expressly recognizes property in slaves; and from that other constitutional provision, that no person shall be deprived of property without due process of law. Hence they reach the conclusion that as the Constitution of the United States expressly recognizes property in slaves, and prohibits any person from being deprived of property without due process of law, to pass an act of Congress by which a man who owned a slave on one side of a line would be deprived of him if he took him on the other side is depriving him of that property without due process of law. That I understand to be the decision of the Supreme Court. I understand also that Judge Douglas adheres most firmly to that decision; and the difficulty is, how is it possible for any power to exclude slavery from the Territory unless in violation of that decision? That is the difficulty.

In the Senate of the United States, in 1856, Judge Trumbull, in a speech, substantially, if not directly, put the same interrogatory to Judge Douglas, as to whether the people of a Territory had the lawful power to exclude slavery prior to the formation of a constitution? Judge Douglas then answered at considerable length, and his answer will be found in the "Congressional Globe," under the date of June 9, 1856. The judge said that whether the people could exclude slavery prior to the formation of a constitution or not was a question to be decided by the Supreme Court. He put that proposition, as will be seen by the "Congressional Globe," in a variety of forms, all running to the same thing in substance—that it was a question for the Supreme Court. I maintain that when he says, after the Supreme Court has decided the question, that the people may yet exclude slavery by any means whatever, he does virtually say that it is not a question for the Supreme Court. He shifts his ground. I appeal to you whether he did not say it was a question for the Supreme Court? Has not the Supreme Court decided that question? When he now says that the people may exclude slavery, does he not make it a question for the people? Does he not virtually shift his ground and say that it is not a question for the court, but for the people? This is a very simple proposition—a very plain and naked one. It seems to me that there is no difficulty in deciding it. In a variety of ways he said that it was a question for the Supreme Court. He did not stop then to tell us that, whatever the Supreme Court decides, the people can by withholding necessary "police regulations" keep slavery out. He did not make any such answer. I submit to you now, whether the new state of the case has not induced the judge to sheer away from his original ground. Would not this be the impression of every fair-minded man?

I hold that the proposition that slavery cannot enter a new country without police regulations is historically false. It is not true at all. I hold that the history of this country shows that the institution of slavery was originally planted upon this continent without these "police regulations" which the judge now thinks necessary for the actual establishment of it. Not only so, but is there not another fact—how came this Dred Scott decision to be made? It was made upon the case of a negro being taken and actually held in slavery in Minnesota Territory, claiming his freedom because the act of Congress prohibited his being so held there. Will the judge pretend that Dred Scott was not held there without police regulations? There is at least one matter of record as to his having been held in slavery in the Territory, not only without police regulations, but in the teeth of congressional legislation supposed to be valid at the time. This shows that there is vigor enough in slavery to plant itself in a new country even against unfriendly legislation. It takes not only law but the enforcement of law to keep it out. That is the history of this country upon the subject.

I wish to ask one other question. It being understood that the Constitution of the United States guarantees property in slaves in the Territories, if there is any infringement of the right of that property, would not the United States courts, organized for the government of the Territory, apply such remedy as might be necessary in that case? It is a maxim held by the courts, that there is no wrong without its remedy; and the courts have a remedy for whatever is acknowledged and treated as a wrong.

Again: I will ask you, my friends, if you were elected members of the legislature, what would be the first thing you would have to do before entering upon your duties? Swear to support the Constitution of the United States. Suppose you believe, as Judge Douglas does, that the Constitution of the United States guarantees to your neighbor the right to hold slaves in that Territory,—that they are his property,—how can you clear your oaths unless you give him such legislation as is necessary to enable him to enjoy that property? What do you understand by supporting the Constitution of a State, or of the United States? Is it not to give such constitutional helps to the rights established by that Constitution as may be practically needed? Can you, if you swear to support the Constitution, and believe that the Constitution establishes a right, clear your oath, without giving it support? Do you support the Constitution if, knowing or believing there is a right established under it which needs specific legislation, you withhold that legislation? Do you not violate and disregard your oath? I can conceive of nothing plainer in the world. There can be nothing in the words "support the Constitution," if you may run counter to it by refusing support to any right established under the Constitution. And what I say here will hold with still more force against the judge's doctrine of "unfriendly legislation." How could you, having sworn to support the Constitution, and believing that it guaranteed the right to hold slaves in the Territories, assist in legislation intended to defeat that right? That would be violating your own view of the Constitution. Not only so, but if you were to do so, how long would it take the courts to hold your votes unconstitutional and void? Not a moment.

Lastly I would ask—Is not Congress itself under obligation to give legislative support to any right that is established under the United States Constitution? I repeat the question—Is not Congress itself bound to give legislative support to any right that is established in the United States Constitution? A member of Congress swears to support the Constitution of the United States, and if he sees a right established by that Constitution which needs specific legislative protection, can he clear his oath without giving that protection? Let me ask you why many of us who are opposed to slavery upon principle give our acquiescence to a fugitive-slave law? Why do we hold ourselves under obligations to pass such a law, and abide by it when it is passed? Because the Constitution makes provision that the owners of slaves shall have the right to reclaim them. It gives the right to reclaim slaves, and that right is, as Judge Douglas says, a barren right, unless there is legislation that will enforce it.

The mere declaration, "No person held to service

or labor in one State under the laws thereof, escaping into another, shall in consequence of any law or regulation therein be discharged from such service or labor, but shall be delivered up on claim of the party to whom such service or labor may be due," is powerless without specific legislation to enforce it. Now, on what ground would a member of Congress who is opposed to slavery in the abstract vote for a fugitive law, as I would deem it my duty to do? Because there is a constitutional right which needs legislation to enforce it. And although it is distasteful to me, I have sworn to support the Constitution, and having so sworn, I cannot conceive that I do support it if I withhold from that right any necessary legislation to make it practical. And if that is true in regard to a fugitive-slave law, is the right to have fugitive slaves reclaimed any better fixed in the Constitution than the right to hold slaves in the Territories? For this decision is a just exposition of the Constitution, as Judge Douglas thinks. Is the one right any better than the other? Is there any man who, while a member of Congress, would give support to the one any more than the other? If I wished to refuse to give legislative support to slave property in the Territories, if a member of Congress, I could not do it, holding the view that the Constitution establishes that right. If I did it at all, it would be because I deny that this decision properly construes the Constitution. But if I acknowledge, with Judge Douglas, that this decision properly construes the Constitution, I cannot conceive that I would be less than a perjured man if I should refuse in Congress to give such protection to that property as in its nature it needed.

At the end of what I have said here I propose to give the judge my fifth interrogatory, which he may take and answer at his leisure. My fifth interrogatory is this:

If the slaveholding citizens of a United States Territory should need and demand congressional legislation for the protection of their slave property in such Territory, would you, as a member of Congress, vote for or against such legislation?

Judge Douglas: Will you repeat that? I want to answer that question.

Mr. Lincoln: **If the slaveholding citizens of a United States**

Territory should need and demand congressional legislation for the protection of their slave property in such Territory, would you, as a member of Congress, vote for or against such legislation?

I am aware that in some of the speeches Judge Douglas has made, he has spoken as if he did not know or think that the Supreme Court had decided that a territorial legislature cannot exclude slavery. Precisely what the judge would say upon the subject—whether he would say definitely that he does not understand they have so decided, or whether he would say he does understand that the court have so decided, I do not know; but I know that in his speech at Springfield he spoke of it as a thing they had not decided yet; and in his answer to me at Freeport, he spoke of it again, so far as I can comprehend it, as a thing that had not yet been decided. Now I hold that if the judge does entertain that view, I think that he is not mistaken in so far as it can be said that the court has not decided anything save the mere question of jurisdiction. I know the legal arguments that can be made—that after a court has decided that it cannot take jurisdiction in a case, it then has decided all that is before it, and that is the end of it. A plausible argument can be made in favor of that proposition, but I know that Judge Douglas has said in one of his speeches that the court went forward, like honest men as they were, and decided all the points in the case. If any points are really extra-judicially decided because not necessarily before them, then this one as to the power of the territorial legislature to exclude slavery is one of them, as also the one that the Missouri Compromise was null and void. They are both extra-judicial, or neither is, according as the court held that they had no jurisdiction in the case between the parties, because of want of capacity of one party to maintain a suit in that court. I want, if I have sufficient time, to show that the court did pass its opinion, but that is the only thing actually done in the case. If they did not decide, they showed what they were ready to decide whenever the matter was before them. What is that opinion? After having argued that Congress had no power to pass a law excluding slavery from a United States Territory, they then used language to this effect: That inasmuch as Congress itself could not exercise such

> a power, it followed as a matter of course that it could not authorize a territorial government to exercise it, for the territorial legislature can do no more than Congress could do. Thus it expressed its opinion emphatically against the power of a territorial legislature to exclude slavery, leaving us in just as little doubt on that point as upon any other point they really decided.[804]

Lincoln states here as carefully and clearly as he possibly can:

> All I have asked or desired anywhere is that it [slavery] should be placed back again upon the basis that the fathers of our government originally placed it upon. I have no doubt that it would become extinct, for all time to come, if we but readopted the policy of the fathers by restricting it to the limits it has already covered—restricting it from the new Territories.[805]

In September 1858 Lincoln scrawled out the following note for possible use in future speeches:

> I believe . . . that by our form of government the States which have slavery are to retain or disuse it, at their own pleasure; and that all others—individuals, free States, and National Government—are constitutionally bound to leave them alone about it. That our government was thus framed because of the necessity springing from the actual presence of slavery when it was formed.[806]

On October 30 that same year, as the Illinois senatorial race of 1858 was drawing to a close, Lincoln gave his final campaign speech in Springfield. In it he restated that the U.S. Constitution plainly allowed slavery, something over which he had no argument. And Congress, he again added, has no legal right to interfere with the institution.[807]

Two years later, on October 23, 1860, Lincoln, now the Republican (liberal) candidate for president, wrote a letter to William S. Speer that read:

> My dear Sir: Yours of the 13th was duly received. I appreciate your motive when you suggest the propriety of my writing for the public something disclaiming all intention to interfere with slaves or slavery in the States;

but in my judgment it would do no good. I have already done this many, many times; and it is in print, and open to all who will read. Those who will not read or heed what I have already publicly said would not read or heed a repetition of it. "If they hear not Moses and the prophets, neither will they be persuaded though one rose from the dead." Yours truly, A. Lincoln.[808]

Six months later, now president, Lincoln used his First Inaugural Address on March 4, 1861, to reconfirm his promise not to disturb slavery, adding that he had neither the right nor the desire:

> I have no purpose, directly or indirectly, to interfere with the institution of slavery in the States where it exists. I believe I have no lawful right to do so, and I have no inclination to do so.[809]

This promise was quite shocking to the average citizen of the South, the region where the American abolition movement got its start[810] (Virginia was the first state to prohibit slavery),[811] and where, in 1860, only 4.8 percent of the populace owned slaves.[812] Anti-South proponents do not want you to know these facts, but ever since Virginian Thomas Jefferson tried to end slavery in the 1700s,[813] the vast majority of Southerners had been pushing for abolition, hoping, and assuming, that one day slavery would die out.[814]

Lincoln himself too believed that the end of slavery was inevitable. According to the Yankee president the entire American populace, South and North, took for granted that the institution was doomed, as he said on July 10, 1858, at Chicago, Illinois:

> I am not, in the first place, unaware that this government has endured eighty-two years half slave and half free. I know that. I am tolerably well acquainted with the history of the country, and I know that it has endured eighty-two years half slave and half free. I believe—and that is what I meant to allude to there—I believe it has endured because during all that time, until the introduction of the Nebraska bill, the public mind did rest all the time in the belief that slavery was in course of ultimate extinction. That was what gave us the rest that we had through that period of eighty-two years; at least, so I believe. . . . I always believed that everybody was

against it, and that it was in course of ultimate extinction. [Pointing to Mr. Orville H. Browning, who stood nearby.] **Browning thought so; the great mass of the nation have rested in the belief that slavery was in course of ultimate extinction. They had reason so to believe.**

The adoption of the Constitution and its attendant history led the people to believe so, and that such was the belief of the framers of the Constitution itself. Why did those old men, about the time of the adoption of the Constitution, decree that slavery should not go into the new Territory, where it had not already gone? Why declare that within twenty years the African slave-trade, by which slaves are supplied, might be cut off by Congress? Why were all these acts? I might enumerate more of these acts—but enough. What were they but a clear indication that the framers of the Constitution intended and expected the ultimate extinction of that institution?[815]

With Lincoln promising not to tamper with slavery, and with the entire nation believing that the institution would some day come to a natural end, Northern and Southern slave owners had every right to assume that for now, at least, it would continue to be protected by the Constitution. And they were right.

This being the case, Southerners—always strong believers in states' rights, personal freedom, and self-determination—felt that slavery should be allowed in every state, including the Western Territories (vast tracks of land that would eventually be carved into America's Western states). As the Constitution applies to *all* Americans in *all* the states, this was certainly a rational assumption. The South simply believed that each state should be allowed to make up its own mind as to whether slavery was to be permitted within its borders or not.

Victorian Northerners, however, primarily liberals who were widely known in the conservative South as what we would now call meddlesome socialists, wanted the central government in Washington, D.C. to decide which states could or could not allow slavery. In particular they did not want slavery to spread into the Western Territories. Hoping that it would be restricted to the Southern states, they called themselves "restrictionists," their opponents "extensionists."[816]

Arguably the most vigorous restrictionist of all was none other than Abraham Lincoln—a man who, ridiculously, believed that the South's desire that the individual states should be allowed to decide whether to be slave-free or slavery-optional, was a vast **"conspiracy to perpetuate and nationalize slavery."**[817] In a word, the president, along with most of his Yankee constituents, was for limiting slavery not abolishing it, as he declared to an Illinois audience on August 21, 1858. I would like to keep slavery, Lincoln said,

> at the position in which our [Founding] fathers originally placed it—restricting it from the new [Western] Territories where it had not gone, and legislating to cut off its source by the abrogation of the slave-trade, thus putting the seal of legislation against its spread.[818]

Lincoln said much the same thing during his fourth debate with Douglas on September 18, 1858, at Charleston, Illinois:

> I say, then, there is no way of putting an end to the slavery agitation amongst us but to put it back upon the basis where our fathers placed it, no way but to keep it out of our new Territories—to restrict it forever to the old States where it now exists. Then the public mind will rest in the belief that it is in the course of ultimate extinction. That is one way of putting an end to the slavery agitation.[819]

All of his efforts had been focused on one thing and one thing only, he noted a month later on October 30, during his last speech of the 1858 Illinois senatorial campaign: preventing the spread of slavery into the new Western Territories.[820] This is why, on March 1, 1859, at Chicago, Illinois, Lincoln gave a speech asking his party members for

> the cooperation of all good men in that resistance to the extension of slavery upon which we all agree.[821]

Again, this time on December 13, 1860, Lincoln penned a letter to Elihu B. Washburne, that read:

> My dear Sir: Your long letter received. Prevent, as far as possible, any of our friends from demoralizing themselves and our cause by entertaining propositions for compromise of any sort on "slavery extension." There is no possible compromise upon it but which puts

us under again, and leaves all our work to do over again. Whether it be a Missouri line or Eli Thayer's popular sovereignty, it is all the same. Let either be done, and immediately filibustering and extending slavery recommences. On that point hold firm, as with a chain of steel. Yours as ever, A. Lincoln.[822]

Two days later, on December 15, 1860, Lincoln replied to a letter from North Carolinian John A. Gilmer. In it he attempts to allay the South's fears that he would either interfere with or abolish slavery:

> My dear Sir: Yours of the 10th is received. I am greatly disinclined to write a letter on the subject embraced in yours; and I would not do so, even privately as I do, were it not that I fear you might misconstrue my silence. Is it desired that I shall shift the ground upon which I have been elected? I cannot do it. You need only to acquaint yourself with that ground, and press it on the attention of the South. It is all in print and easy of access. May I be pardoned if I ask whether even you have ever attempted to procure the reading of the Republican platform, or my speeches, by the Southern people? If not, what reason have I to expect that any additional production of mine would meet a better fate? It would make me appear as if I repented for the crime of having been elected, the present peril the country is in, and the weight of responsibility on me. Do the people of the South really entertain fears that a Republican administration would, directly or indirectly, interfere with the slaves, or with them about the slaves? If they do, I wish to assure you, as once a friend, and still, I hope, not an enemy, that there is no cause for such fears. The South would be in no more danger in this respect than it was in the days of [George] Washington. I suppose, however, this does not meet the case. You think slavery is right and ought to be extended, while we think it is wrong and ought to be restricted. That, I suppose, is the rub. It certainly is the only substantial difference between us. Yours very truly, A. Lincoln.[823]

We will note here that, as he usually was, Lincoln was wrong, making assumptions about the South that were quite false: Gilmer, along with most other Southerners did not want to extend slavery. They merely wanted the states and the Western Territories to have the choice of whether to accept or reject slavery. Being a liberal, Lincoln wanted his view imposed on the nation, even if it was against the will of the majority of people.

On February 1, 1861, Lincoln wrote the following to William H. Seward:

> I say now . . . as I have all the while said, that on the territorial question—that is, the question of extending slavery under the national auspices—I am inflexible. I am for no compromise which assists or permits the extension of the institution on soil owned by the nation. And any trick by which the nation is to acquire territory, and then allow some local authority to spread slavery over it, is as obnoxious as any other. I take it that to effect some such result as this, and to put us again on the highroad to a slave empire, is the object of all these proposed compromises. I am against it. . . . Nor do I care much about New Mexico, if further extension were hedged against.[824]

Along with his restrictionist views, Lincoln here infers that the South is trying to develop itself into a **"slave empire"** through the acquisition of the Western Territories and the **"trick"** of spreading of slavery over them. Of course this is completely false (for reasons already given).

But far worse, Lincoln conveniently ignores the naked fact that, as we saw in Chapter 1, the only **"slave empire"** the U.S. has ever known was located in the North, for both the American slave trade[825] and American slavery were born there,[826] with New York City serving as the literal capital of American slavery for decades.[827]

Those wanting more proof that the North was our nation's true slave empire need only consider the following fact: far more Northerners tended to own slaves than Southerners. In the early 1700s, for example, 42 percent of New York households owned slaves, and the share of slaves in both New York and New Jersey was larger than that of North Carolina.[828] By 1690, in Perth Amboy, New Jersey, as another example, nearly every white inhabitant owned one or more black slaves. This is close to 100 percent slave ownership![829]

Contrast this with the mere 4.8 percent of Southerners who owned slaves in 1860, the year Southern slave ownership reached it zenith. In fact, going back in time, the number of Southern slave owners decreases precipitously. In 1850, for instance, of the 8,039,000 whites living in the

Southern states, only 186,551 were slave owners, a mere 2.3 percent of the total white population. Thus, 97.7 percent of Southern whites that year were non-slave owners.[830] Of these same whites, only 46,274 owned twenty or more servants (0.5 percent), only 2,500 owned thirty or more (0.03 percent), and a mere handful (0.02 percent) owned 100 or more.[831]

Based on mathematics alone it is clear then that Yankees were far more enthusiastic slavers than Southerners, and that the Northeast deserves the title I have given it: America's one and only true slave empire.

Far earlier, in an October 3, 1845, letter to William Durley, Lincoln lamented that Kentucky liberal and slave owner Henry Clay had not been made U.S. president in the 1844 election (he lost to Tennessee conservative James K. Polk), for emancipationist-colonizationist Clay, like emancipationist-colonizationist Lincoln, was also a restrictionist who wanted to halt both the spread of slavery and the acquisition of new territory by the U.S. Wrote Lincoln:

> **If the Whig abolitionists of New York had voted with us last fall, Mr. Clay would now be President, Whig principles in the ascendant, and Texas not annexed;** whereas, by the division, all that either had at stake in the contest was lost. And, indeed, it was extremely probable, beforehand, that such would be the result. As I always understood, the Liberty men [i.e., abolitionists] deprecated the annexation of Texas extremely; and this being so, why they should refuse to cast their votes [so] as to prevent it, even to me seemed wonderful. What was their process of reasoning, I can only judge from what a single one of them told me. It was this: "We are not to do evil that good may come." This general proposition is doubtless correct; but did it apply? If by your votes you could have prevented the extension, etc., of slavery would it not have been good, and not evil, so to have used your votes, even though it involved the casting of them for a slave-holder? By the fruit the tree is to be known. An evil tree cannot bring forth good fruit. If the fruit of electing Mr. Clay would have been to prevent the extension of slavery, could the act of electing have been evil?
>
> ... I hold it to be a paramount duty of us in the free States, due to the Union of the States, and perhaps to liberty itself (paradox though it may seem), to let the slavery of the other States alone; while, on the other

hand, I hold it to be equally clear that we should never knowingly lend ourselves, directly or indirectly, to prevent that slavery from dying a natural death—to find new places for it to live in, when it can no longer exist in the old.[832]

Lincoln was so obsessed with restricting slavery to the South that he claimed that his party, the Republican party, was formed for the sole purpose of preventing this very thing from happening. As he wrote in early December 1859 in a note for future speeches:

> **Purpose of the Republican organization.**—The Republican party believe there is danger that slavery will be further extended, and ultimately made national in the United States; and to prevent this incidental and final consummation, is the purpose of this organization.
>
> **Chief danger to that purpose.**—A congressional slave code for the Territories, and the revival of the African trade, and a second Dred Scott decision, are not just now the chief danger to our purpose. These will press us in due time, but they are not quite ready yet—they know that, as yet, we are too strong for them. The insidious Douglas popular sovereignty, which prepares the way for this ultimate danger, it is which just now constitutes our chief danger.[833]

Why were Northerners like Lincoln against slavery in the West and in the North, but for it in the South?

The answer is Northern white racism.

In wanting to restrict slavery as much as possible to the South Lincoln was merely following a long and venerable Yankee tradition, one that started decades before he became president.

In 1846, for example, Northern representative David Wilmot introduced his Wilmot Proviso to try and prevent the spread of slavery into Western lands acquired by the U.S. from Mexico during the Mexican-American War (1846-1848).[834] His proposition was not for the sake of blacks, however. It was solely for whites.[835]

In the winter of 1847 the Pennsylvania politician articulated the motivations behind his notorious document this way. Said Wilmot:

> I have no squeamish sensitiveness upon the subject of slavery, no

morbid sympathy for the slave. I plead the cause and the rights of white freemen. I would preserve to free white labor a fair country, a rich inheritance, where the sons of toil, of my own race and own color, can live without the disgrace which association with negro slavery brings upon free labor. I stand for the inviolability of free territory. It shall remain free, so far as my voice or vote can aid in the preservation of its free character. . . . The white laborer of the North claims your service; he demands that you stand firm to his interests and his rights, that you preserve the future homes of his children, on the distant shores of the Pacific, from the degradation and dishonor of negro servitude. Where the negro slave labors, the free white man cannot labor by his side without sharing in his degradation and disgrace.[836]

Wilmot, who once commented that he had spent much of his adult life (like Lincoln) fighting against Northern Abolitionists,[837] later remarked to a colleague:

By God, sir, men born and nursed of white women are not going to be ruled by men who were brought up on the milk of some damn Negro wench![838]

Wilmot had plenty of company, particularly among those who would one day serve under President Lincoln. In 1860, the man who was to become Lincoln's secretary of state, New Yorker William H. Seward, described the African race as a

foreign and feeble element, like the Indians, incapable of assimilation . . . it is a pitiful exotic unwisely and unnecessarily transplanted to our fields . . .[839]

Lincoln could not have agreed more with Seward and Wilmot, and in fact, according to his own statement on October 16, 1854, and again on August 24, 1855, he voted for the anti-black, pro-white Wilmot Proviso on dozens of occasions:

When I was at Washington, I voted for the Wilmot proviso as good as forty times; . . . I now do no more than oppose the extension of slavery.[840]

During the same speech Lincoln went on to say:

> Much as I hate slavery, I would consent to the extension of it rather than see the Union dissolved, just as I would consent to any great evil to avoid a greater one.⁸⁴¹

On October 1, 1856, Lincoln responded to the then raging debate on "sectionalism." But he used the occasion for his own purposes, to discuss how sectionalism affected the slavery extension issue, taking, of course, the side of the restrictionists:

> It is constantly objected to [John Charles] Fremont and [William Lewis] Dayton, that they are supported by a sectional party, who by their sectionalism endanger the national union. This objection, more than all others, causes men really opposed to slavery extension to hesitate. Practically, it is the most difficult objection we have to meet. For this reason I now propose to examine it a little more carefully than I have heretofore done, or seen it done by others. First, then, what is the question between the parties respectively represented by [James] Buchanan and Fremont? Simply this, "Shall slavery be allowed to extend into United States territories now legally free?" Buchanan says it shall, and Fremont says it shall not.
>
> That is the naked issue, and the whole of it. Lay the respective platforms side by side, and the difference between them will be found to amount to precisely that. True, each party charges upon the other designs much beyond what is involved in the issue as stated; but as these charges cannot be fully proved either way, it is probably better to reject them on both sides, and stick to the naked issue as it is clearly made up on the record.
>
> And now to restate the question, "Shall slavery be allowed to extend into United States territories now legally free?" I beg to know how one side of that question is more sectional than the other? Of course I expect to effect nothing with the man who makes the charge of sectionalism without caring whether it is just or not. But of the candid, fair man who has been puzzled with this charge, I do ask how is one side of this question more sectional than the other? I beg of him to consider well, and answer calmly.
>
> If one side be as sectional as the other, nothing is gained, as to sectionalism, by changing sides; so that each must choose sides of the question on some other

ground, as I should think, according as the one side or the other shall appear nearest right. If he shall really think slavery ought to be extended, let him go to Buchanan; if he think it ought not, let him go to Fremont.

But Fremont and Dayton are both residents of the free States, and this fact has been vaunted in high places as excessive sectionalism. While interested individuals become indignant and excited against this manifestation of sectionalism, I am very happy to know that the Constitution remains calm—keeps cool—upon the subject. It does say that President and Vice-President shall be residents of different States, but it does not say that one must live in a slave and the other in a free State.

It has been a custom to take one from a slave and the other from a free State; but the custom has not at all been uniform. In 1828 General [Andrew] Jackson and Mr. [John C.] Calhoun, both from slave States, were placed on the same ticket; and Mr. [John Quincy] Adams and Dr. [Richard] Rush, both from free States, were pitted against them. General Jackson and Mr. Calhoun were elected, and qualified and served under the election, yet the whole thing never suggested the idea of sectionalism. In 1841 the President, General [William Henry] Harrison, died, by which Mr. [John] Tyler, the Vice-President and a slave-State man, became President. Mr. [Willie Person] Mangum, another slave-State man, was placed in the vice-presidential chair, served out the term, and no fuss about it, no sectionalism thought of. In 1853 the present President [Franklin Pierce] came into office. He is a free-State man. Mr. [William Rufus DeVane] King, the new Vice-President elect, was a slave-State man : but he died without entering on the duties of his office. At first his vacancy was filled by [David Rice] Atchison, another slave-State man; but he soon resigned, and the place was supplied by [Jesse David] Bright, a free-State man. So that right now, and for the half year last past, our President and Vice-President are both actually free-State men. But it is said the friends of Fremont avow the purpose of electing him exclusively by free-State votes, and that this is unendurable sectionalism.

This statement of fact is not exactly true. With the friends of Fremont it is an expected necessity, but it is not an "avowed purpose" to elect him, if at all, principally by free-State votes; but it is with equal intensity true that Buchanan's friends expect to elect him, if at all, chiefly by slave-State votes. Here, again, the sectionalism is just as much on one side as the other.

The thing which gives most color to the charge of sectionalism, made against those who oppose the spread of slavery into free territory, is the fact that they can get no votes in the slave States, while their opponents get all, or nearly so, in the slave States, and also a large number in the free States. To state it in another way, the extensionists can get votes all over the nation, while the restrictionists can get them only in the free States.

This being the fact, why is it so? It is not because one side of the question dividing them is more sectional than the other, nor because of any difference in the mental or moral structure of the people North and South. It is because in that question the people of the South have an immediate palpable and immensely great pecuniary interest, while with the people of the North it is merely an abstract question of moral right, with only slight and remote pecuniary interest added.

The slaves of the South, at a moderate estimate, are worth a thousand millions of dollars. Let it be permanently settled that this property may extend to new territory without restraint, and it greatly enhances, perhaps quite doubles, its value at once. This immense palpable pecuniary interest on the question of extending slavery unites the Southern people as one man. But it cannot be demonstrated that the North will gain a dollar by restricting it. Moral principle is all, or nearly all, that unites us of the North. Pity't is, it is so, but this is a looser bond than pecuniary interest. Right here is the plain cause of their perfect union and our want of it. And see how it works. If a Southern man aspires to be President, they choke him down instantly, in order that the glittering prize of the presidency may be held up on Southern terms to the greedy eyes of Northern ambition. With this they tempt us and break in upon us.

The Democratic party in 1844 elected a Southern president [James Knox Polk]. Since then they have neither had a Southern candidate for election nor nomination. Their conventions of 1848, 1852 and 1856 have been struggles exclusively among Northern men, each vying to outbid the other for the Southern vote; the South standing calmly by to finally cry "Going, going, gone" to the highest bidder, and at the same time to make its power more distinctly seen, and thereby to secure a still higher bid at the next succeeding struggle.

"Actions speak louder than words" is the maxim, and if true the South now distinctly says to the North, "Give us the measures and you take the men." The total withdrawal of Southern aspirants for the presidency multiplies the number of Northern ones. These last, in competing with each other, commit themselves to the utmost verge that, through their own greediness, they have the least hope their Northern supporters will bear. Having got committed in a race of competition, necessity drives them into union to sustain themselves. Each at first secures all he can on personal attachments to him and through hopes resting on him personally. Next they unite with one another and with the perfectly banded South, to make the offensive position they have got into "a party measure." This done, large additional numbers are secured.

When the repeal of the Missouri Compromise was first proposed, at the North there was literally "nobody" in favor of it. In February, 1854, our [Illinois] legislature met in called, or extra, session. From them [Stephen Arnold] Douglas sought an indorsement of his then pending measure of repeal. In our legislature were about seventy Democrats to thirty Whigs. The former held a caucus, in which it was resolved to give Douglas the desired indorsement. Some of the members of the caucus bolted,—would not stand it,—and they now divulge the secrets. They say that the caucus fairly confessed that the repeal was wrong, and they pleaded the determination to indorse it solely on the ground that it was necessary to sustain Douglas. Here we have the direct evidence of how the Nebraska bill obtained its strength in Illinois. It was given, not in a sense of right, but in the teeth of a sense of wrong, to sustain Douglas. So Illinois was divided. So New England for [Franklin] Pierce, Michigan for [Lewis] Cass, Pennsylvania for [James] Buchanan, and all for the Democratic party.

And when by such means they have got a large portion of the Northern people into a position contrary to their own honest impulses and sense of right, they have the impudence to turn upon those who do stand firm, and call them sectional. Were it not too serious a matter, this cool impudence would be laughable, to say the least. Recurring to the question, "Shall slavery be allowed to extend into United States territory now legally free?" This is a sectional question—that is to say, it is a question in its nature calculated to divide the American people geographically. Who is to blame for that? Who can help it? Either side can help it; but how? Simply by yielding to the other side; there is no other way; in the whole range of possibility there is no other way. Then, which side shall yield? To this, again, there can be but one answer,—the side which is in the wrong. True, we differ as to which side is wrong, and we boldly say, let all who really think slavery ought to be spread into free territory, openly go over against us; there is where they rightfully belong. But why should any go who really think slavery ought not to spread? Do they really think the right ought to yield to the wrong? Are they afraid to stand by the right? Do they fear that the Constitution is too weak to sustain them in the right? Do they really think that by right surrendering to wrong the hopes of our Constitution, our Union, and our liberties can possibly be bettered?[842]

These are mighty strong words coming from a highly partisan politician who proudly and defiantly stated publicly that **"I am a northern man,"**[843] and who would soon become, quite openly and intentionally, America's first sectional president by emphasizing the many profound differences between South and North instead of their similarities![844] But he is already talking like one, particularly in his use of the anti-South phrases **"free states"** and **"slave states."**[845]

As we show in this very book, the Confederacy was never about slavery, either for or against. It was about giving the states the choice to accept or reject slavery, an inherent states' right tacitly embodied in the U.S. Constitution (Amendments Nine and Ten). This is why the correct phraseology here should be "slavery-prohibited states" (the North) and a "slavery-optional states" (the South).[846]

The gist of Lincoln's 1856 message, however, is that slavery should be restricted to the South and not allowed to spread outside it, either to the North or into the new Western Territories. What he does not say here is that the reason he is a slavery restrictionist is because he is a white racist, one who prefers living in an all-white America. But it would not be long before he would begin discussing his white supremacist thoughts in public.

On February 27, 1860, during his renowned Cooper Union Speech in New York, Lincoln states that slavery should continue to be protected under the Constitution. His only stipulation is that it should **"not be extended"** beyond where it was already permitted:

> This is all Republicans ask—all Republicans desire—in relation to slavery. As those [Founding] **fathers marked it, so let it be again marked, as an evil not to be extended, but to be tolerated and protected only because of and so far as its actual presence among us makes that toleration and protection a necessity. Let all the guaranties those fathers gave it be not grudgingly, but fully and fairly, maintained.**[847]

Lincoln then quotes one of **"those fathers,"** Thomas Jefferson, stressing his own personal beliefs pertaining to white supremacy, the emancipation and deportation of freed slaves, and the restriction of slavery to the South:[848]

> [Lincoln quoting Jefferson] **"It is still in our power to direct the process of emancipation and deportation peaceably, and in such slow degrees, as that the evil will wear off sensibly; and their places be . . . filled up by free white laborers. If, on the contrary, it is left to force itself on, human nature must shudder at the prospect held up."**[849]

Furthermore, in his own words Lincoln asserts:

> **If slavery is right, all words, acts, laws, and constitutions against it are themselves wrong, and should be silenced and swept away. If it is right, we cannot justly object to its nationality—its universality; if it is wrong, they** [Southerners] **cannot justly insist upon its extension—its enlargement. . . . Wrong as we think slavery is, we can yet afford to let it alone where it is, because that much is due to the necessity arising from its actual presence in the nation; but can we, while our votes will prevent it, allow it to spread into the national Territories, and to overrun us here in these free States?**[850]

On December 11, 1860, Lincoln wrote to William Kellogg:

> Entertain no proposition for a compromise in regard to the extension of slavery. The instant you do they have us under again; all our labor is lost, and sooner or later must be done over. . . .

Have none of it. The tug has to come, and better now than later.[851]

Here is more evidence. On December 22, 1860, Lincoln wrote an almost exact duplicate of the letter he sent to John A. Gilmer on December 20. This second version he mailed to Southerner and soon-to-be Confederate Vice President Alexander H. Stephens. What this means is that Lincoln believed very firmly in these words—and he wanted everyone to know it:

> Do the people of the South really entertain fears that a Republican administration would, directly or indirectly, interfere with the slaves, or with them about the slaves? If they do, I wish to assure you, as once a friend, and still, I hope, not an enemy, that there is no cause for such fears. The South would be in no more danger in this respect than it was in the days of Washington. I suppose, however, this does not meet the case. You think slavery is right and ought to be extended, while we think it is wrong and ought to be restricted. That, I suppose, is the rub. It certainly is the only substantial difference between us.[852]

To reemphasize, "Honest Abe," for once being completely honest, ends his letter to Stephens with this sensational remark: To extend or restrict. This is the **"only substantial difference between us."**

Just a few months later, on March 4, 1861, he would repeat the same sentiment almost word for word in his First Inaugural Address:

> One section of our country believes slavery . . . ought to be extended, while the other believes it . . . ought not . . . be extended. This is the only substantial dispute.[853]

Thus, just prior to his War, Lincoln held that the only real difference between the South's view of slavery and the North's was that the former wanted to allow it to spread (mainly into the new Western Territories), while the latter wanted to contain it where it already existed (that is, in the South). No mention of emancipation or abolition. Just limitation.

On October 16, 1854, during a speech at Peoria, Illinois, the real reason for Lincoln's opposition to both slavery and to its expansion was revealed in all of its undisguised glory. Said Lincoln:

> Whether slavery shall go into Nebraska, or other new Territories, is not a matter of exclusive concern to the people who may go there. The whole nation is interested that the best use shall be made of the Territories. *We want them for homes of free white people.* This cannot be, to any considerable extent, if slavery shall be planted within them [emphasis added].[854]

Four years later, on October 15, 1858, at Alton, Illinois, in his seventh and final joint debate with Judge Stephen A. Douglas, Lincoln reasserted his views on the matter, this time even more forcefully:

> The judge alludes very often in the course of his remarks to the exclusive right which the States have to decide the whole thing for themselves. I agree with him very readily that the different States have that right. He is but fighting a man of straw when he assumes that I am contending against the right of the States to do as they please about it. Our controversy with him is in regard to the new Territories. We agree that when the States come in as States they have the right and the power to do as they please. We have no power as citizens of the free States, or in our federal capacity as members of the Federal Union through the General Government, to disturb slavery in the States where it exists. We profess constantly that we have no more inclination than belief in the power of the government to disturb it; yet we are driven constantly to defend ourselves from the assumption that we are warring upon the rights of the States. What I insist upon is, that the new Territories shall be kept free from it while in the territorial condition. Judge Douglas assumes that we have no interest in them—that we have no right whatever to interfere. I think we have some interest. I think that as white men we have. Do we not wish for an outlet for our surplus population, if I may so express myself? Do we not feel an interest in getting to that outlet with such institutions as we would like to have prevail there? If you go to the Territory opposed to slavery, and another man comes upon the same ground with his slave, upon the assumption that the things are equal, it turns out that he has the equal right all his way, and you have no part of

it your way. If he goes in and makes it a slave Territory, and by consequence a slave State, is it not time that those who desire to have it a free State were on equal ground? Let me suggest it in a different way. How many Democrats are there about here [audience member: "A thousand"] who have left slave States and come into the free State of Illinois to get rid of the institution of slavery? [Another audience member: "A thousand and one."] I reckon there are a thousand and one. I will ask you, if the policy you are now advocating had prevailed when this country was in a territorial condition, where would you have gone to get rid of it? Where would you have found your free State or Territory to go to? And when hereafter, for any cause, the people in this place shall desire to find new homes, if they wish to be rid of the institution, where will they find the place to go to?

Now, irrespective of the moral aspect of this question as to whether there is a right or wrong in enslaving a negro, I am still in favor of our new Territories being in such a condition that white men may find a home—may find some spot where they can better their condition—where they can settle upon new soil, and better their condition in life. I am in favor of this not merely (I must say it here as I have elsewhere) for our own people who are born amongst us, but as an outlet for free white people everywhere, the world over—in which Hans, and Baptiste, and Patrick, and all other men from all the world, may find new homes and better their condition in life [emphasis added].

I have stated upon former occasions, and I may as well state again, what I understand to be the real issue of this controversy between Judge Douglas and myself. On the point of my wanting to make war between the free and the slave States, there has been no issue between us. So, too, when he assumes that I am in favor of introducing a perfect social and political equality between the white and black races. These are false issues, upon which Judge Douglas has tried to force the controversy. There is no foundation in truth for the charge that I maintain either of these propositions. The real issue in this controversy—the one pressing upon every mind—is the sentiment on the part of one class that looks upon the institution of slavery as a wrong, and of another class that does not look upon it as a wrong. The sentiment that contemplates the institution of slavery in this country as a wrong is the sentiment of the

Republican [liberal] party. It is the sentiment around which all their actions, all their arguments, circle; from which all their propositions radiate. They look upon it as being a moral, social, and political wrong; and while they contemplate it as such, they nevertheless have due regard for its actual existence among us, and the difficulties of getting rid of it in any satisfactory way, and to all the constitutional obligations thrown about it. Yet having a due regard for these, they desire a policy in regard to it that looks to its not creating any more danger. They insist that it, as far as may be, be treated as a wrong, and one of the methods of treating it as a wrong is to make provision that it shall grow no larger. They also desire a policy that looks to a peaceful end of slavery some time, as being a wrong. These are the views they entertain in regard to it, as I understand them; and all their sentiments, all their arguments and propositions, are brought within this range. I have said, and I repeat it here, that if there be a man amongst us who does not think that the institution of slavery is wrong in any one of the aspects of which I have spoken, he is misplaced, and ought not to be with us. And if there be a man amongst us who is so impatient of it as a wrong as to disregard its actual presence among us and the difficulty of getting rid of it suddenly in a satisfactory way, and to disregard the constitutional obligations thrown about it, that man is misplaced if he is on our platform. We disclaim sympathy with him in practical action. He is not placed properly with us.

On this subject of treating it as a wrong, and limiting its spread, let me say a word. Has anything ever threatened the existence of this Union save and except this very institution of slavery? What is it that we hold most dear amongst us? Our own liberty and prosperity. What has ever threatened our liberty and prosperity save and except this institution of slavery? If this is true, how do you propose to improve the condition of things by enlarging slavery—by spreading it out and making it bigger? You may have a wen or cancer upon your person, and not be able to cut it out lest you bleed to death; but surely it is no way to cure it, to engraft it and spread it over your whole body. That is no proper way of treating what you regard as a wrong. You see this peaceful way of dealing with it as a wrong—restricting the spread of it, and not allowing it to go into new countries where it has not already existed. That is the peaceful way, the old-fashioned way, the way in which the [Founding] fathers themselves set us the example.[855]

It is here that we finally uncover the reason Lincoln himself was not a slave owner like General Ulysses S. Grant and many other Yankees. It is here that we come to the very foundation of his antislavery views and of his Emancipation Proclamation. It was not so much slavery itself that bothered him. It was that the institution brought whites and blacks into close proximity with one another, the latter "degrading" and "disgracing" the former, as Lincoln's associate David Wilmot once put it.[856] As Lincoln openly avows here, he wants the new Western Territories set aside for whites, **"irrespective of the moral aspect of this question as to whether there is a right or wrong in enslaving a negro."**

Thus to keep America white (one of Lincoln's stated lifelong goals), slavery would have to be limited (restriction) and abolished (emancipation), then blacks would have to be deported to a foreign land (colonization).[857] Restriction. Emancipation. Colonization. Here is Lincoln' true plan for slavery and the black man, all clearly mapped out for the entire world to see.

Lincoln, like the black racists, black separatists, and black colonizationists who came before and after him,[858] felt a deep repugnance toward those of other races. On June 26, 1857, speaking from his own European-American point of view, he summed up his feelings on the matter:

> There is a natural disgust in the minds of nearly all white people, at the idea of an indiscriminate amalgamation of the white and black races . . .[859]

Based on Lincoln's own words and actions, it is obvious that he included himself in the category of **"nearly all white people."** (Most Southern whites did *not* feel this way, as is shown throughout this book.)[860]

Later, others in Lincoln's party would concur: America's Western Territories (soon to become the Western states) should remain as white as New England.[861] One of these members, Senator Lyman Trumbull, was certainly speaking for his good friend and neighbor Lincoln when he said publicly:

> I, for one, am very much disposed to favor the colonization of such free negroes as are willing to go in Central America. I want to have

nothing to do either with the free negro or the slave negro. We, the Republican party [Lincoln's party], are the white man's party. [Great applause] We are for free white men, and for making white labor respectable and honorable, which it never can be when negro slave labor is brought into competition with it. [Great applause]

    We wish to settle the [Western] Territories with free white men, and we are willing that this negro race should go anywhere that it can to better its condition, wishing them God speed wherever they go. We believe it is better for us that they should not be among us. I believe it will be better for them to go elsewhere.[862] . . . When we say that all men are created equal, we do not mean that every man in organized society has the same rights. We do not tolerate that in Illinois.[863]

Trumbull made great efforts to reassure the public that neither he, Lincoln, or their party advocated the idea of Negro equality. As he said at a political debate:

> I by no means assent to the doctrine that negroes are required by the Constitution of the United States to be placed on an equal footing in the States with white citizens.[864]

Both being from ultra Negrophobic Illinois—a state that even Lincoln admitted had more stringent anti-black laws than Louisiana[865]—Trumbull and Lincoln had strong feelings about blocking the spread of slavery, not only from their state, but also from the Western Territories, for Illinois itself was considered a Western state at the time.[866] On October 16, 1854, during a speech at Peoria, Illinois, for example, Lincoln could not have been more explicit:

> **Let it not be said I am contending for the establishment of political and social equality between the whites and blacks. I have already said the contrary. . . I am . . . arguing against the extension of a bad thing, which where it already exists, we must of necessity, manage as best we can.**[867]

This is precisely why liberal Lincoln had been against the Mexican-American War:[868] unable to see it for what it actually was (a land war to expand U.S. territory; i.e., an aspect of Manifest Destiny),[869] he viewed it as an intentional ploy by conservatives, in particular Southern conservatives, to spread slavery westward.[870] As he said in July 1848:

> As to the Mexican war, I still think the defensive line policy the best to terminate it. In a final treaty of peace, we shall probably be under a sort of necessity of taking some territory; but it is my desire that we shall not acquire any extending so far south as to enlarge and aggravate the distracting question of slavery.[871]

Lincoln, a liberal who, unlike conservatives, was against enlarging the territory of the still newly developing United States,[872] was dead wrong of course. But this did not stop him from pushing his white supremacist views, views he hoped to impose upon the entire North American continent.[873]

Just a few years later, Trumbull, and by extension his boss, Lincoln, noted that

> There is a very great aversion in the West—I know it to be so in my State [of Illinois]—against having free Negroes come among us. Our people want nothing to do with the Negro.[874]

Then, with the approach of the 1860 election, Trumbull, in an attempt to mollify the fears of the South, asserted that if given a chance Lincoln and his party would clearly demonstrate that they did not favor "negro equality or amalgamation."[875] While his assurances had no effect on the South (which, by November, was already heading toward becoming a separate sovereign nation), they did succeed in the North, where some 60 percent of those who voted were completely indifferent toward the institution of slavery.[876]

Lincoln, the man who desperately wanted to be all things to all people, purposefully introduced the idea of white supremacy into his party's platform that year in the hope of getting the votes of the Negrophobes and the anti-abolitionists, two groups to which he belonged and which formed the majority of the Northern population. It was widely known at the time that he had no emotional feelings concerning slavery whatsoever.[877]

Just two years earlier, in 1858, David Davis, a friend of Lincoln's, a fellow party member, and one of his political advisers, suggested to other Republican candidates that they

> emphatically disavow negro suffrage, negroes holding office, serving on the juries and the like.[878]

Lincoln agreed wholeheartedly with these sentiments and for the remainder of his life acted on Davis' suggestion.

At national conventions Lincoln's party leaders continually discussed their opposition to slavery and its extension. Not because they wanted to liberate the slaves or grant political or social equality to free blacks in the North.[879] But because they wanted, in Lincoln's own words, to maintain **"the superior position assigned to the white race."**[880] Just because the Declaration of Independence states that "all men are created equal," he wrote to James N. Brown on October 18, 1858,

> **it does not follow that social and political equality between white and black, must be incorporated, because slavery must not. The declaration does not require so.**[881]

Speaking for Lincoln, one of his party executives went before a large and approving white Yankee audience and said: it is not for negro civil liberties that we gather here today. It is to guard the civil liberties of working whites.[882]

Lincoln's party newspapers spread the same gospel, with even more conviction. The reason we are against the extension of slavery, they stated, is because we prefer whites to blacks, and because the Caucasian is superior to the African. Containing slavery in the South is the only method of protecting the North and the Western Territories from the "offensive" presence of the Negro, they maintained.[883]

No wonder so many blacks, such as civil rights leader Frederick Douglass, refused to support Lincoln in the 1860 presidential election.[884] By the middle of 1862 it was painfully clear to all enemies of slavery that one of the strongest barriers to black social progress was the Yankee's rank intolerance and bigotry,[885] and that the institution would have ended much sooner had Lincoln, the "Old Rail-splitter" from Illinois, not become president.[886]

In both Lincoln's and Trumbull's opinion, black colonization (the deportation of all blacks out of the U.S.) was the only answer to what they viewed as "America's racial problem." In reality, this "problem" stemmed primarily from the prejudices of Northern white racists like Lincoln and Trumbull, a prejudice that was on public display for all to see.

As we have seen, for Lincoln's colonization plan to work the spread of the institution of slavery would have to be restricted, then contained, and finally abolished so that the freed blacks could then be deported **"back to their native land,"** Africa, as he put it.

If there is any doubt about Lincoln's extremist views concerning limiting slavery, they are banished by the following speech he gave at Peoria, Illinois, on October 16, 1854, a response to remarks made earlier by Senator Stephen A. Douglas. This is one of Lincoln's longest and most passionate speeches, one directed upon a sole subject: confining slavery to the South so that African-Americans everywhere else could be deported:

> The repeal of the Missouri Compromise, and the propriety of its restoration, constitute the subject of what I am about to say.
>
> As I desire to present my own connected view of this subject, my remarks will not be, specifically, an answer to Judge Douglas; yet, as I proceed, the main points he has presented will arise, and will receive such respectful attention as I may be able to give them.
>
> I wish further to say, that I do not propose to question the patriotism, or to assail the motives of any man, or class of men; but rather to strictly confine myself to the naked merits of the question.
>
> I also wish to be no less than National in all the positions I may take; and whenever I take ground which others have thought, or may think, narrow, sectional and dangerous to the Union, I hope to give a reason, which will appear sufficient, at least to some, why I think differently.
>
> And, as this subject is no other, than part and parcel of the larger general question of domestic-slavery, I wish to make and to keep the distinction between the existing institution, and the extension of it, so broad, and so clear, that no honest man can misunderstand me, and no dishonest one, successfully misrepresent me.
>
> In order to [get?] a clear understanding of what the Missouri Compromise is, a short history of the preceding kindred subjects will perhaps be proper. When we established our independence, we did not own, or claim, the country to which this compromise applies. Indeed, strictly speaking, the confederacy then owned no country at all; the States respectively owned the country within their limits; and some of them owned territory beyond their strict State limits. Virginia thus owned the North-Western territory—the country out of which the principal part of Ohio, all Indiana, all Illinois, all Michigan and all Wisconsin, have since been formed. She also owned (perhaps within her then limits) what has since been formed into the State of Kentucky. North

Carolina thus owned what is now the State of Tennessee; and South Carolina and Georgia, in separate parts, owned what are now Mississippi and Alabama. Connecticut, I think, owned the little remaining part of Ohio—being the same where they now send [Joshua Reed] Giddings to Congress, and beat all creation at making cheese. These territories, together with the States themselves, constituted all the country over which the confederacy then claimed any sort of jurisdiction. We were then living under the Articles of Confederation, which were superceded by the Constitution several years afterwards. The question of ceding these territories to the general government was set on foot.

Mr. [Thomas] Jefferson, the author of the Declaration of Independence, and otherwise a chief actor in the revolution; then a delegate in Congress; afterwards twice President; who was, is, and perhaps will continue to be, the most distinguished politician of our history; a Virginian by birth and continued residence, and withal, a slave-holder; conceived the idea of taking that occasion, to prevent slavery ever going into the north-western territory. He prevailed on the Virginia Legislature to adopt his views, and to cede the territory, making the prohibition of slavery therein, a condition of the deed. Congress accepted the cession, with the condition; and in the first Ordinance (which the acts of Congress were then called) for the government of the territory, provided that slavery should never be permitted therein. This is the famed ordinance of '87 so often spoken of. Thenceforward, for sixty-one years, and until in 1848, the last scrap of this territory came into the Union as the State of Wisconsin, all parties acted in quiet obedience to this ordinance. It is now what Jefferson foresaw and intended—the happy home of teeming millions of free, white, prosperous people, and no slave amongst them.

Thus, with the author of the Declaration of Independence, the policy of prohibiting slavery in new territory originated. Thus, away back of the constitution, in the pure fresh, free breath of the revolution, the State of Virginia, and the National congress put that policy in practice. Thus through sixty odd of the best years of the republic did that policy steadily work to its great and beneficent end. And thus, in those five states, and five millions of free, enterprising people, we have before us the rich fruits of this policy

But now new light breaks upon us. Now congress declares this ought never to have been; and the like of it, must never be again. The sacred right of self government is grossly violated by it! We even find some men, who drew their first breath, and every other breath of their lives, under this very restriction, now live in dread of absolute suffocation, if they should be restricted in the "sacred right" of taking slaves to Nebraska. That perfect liberty they sigh for—the liberty of making slaves of other people—Jefferson never thought of; their own father never thought of; they never thought of themselves, a year ago. How fortunate for them, they did not sooner become sensible of their great misery! Oh, how difficult it is to treat with respect, such assaults upon all we have ever really held sacred.

But to return to history. In 1803 we purchased what was then called Louisiana, of France. It included the now states of Louisiana, Arkansas, Missouri, and Iowa; also the territory of Minnesota, and the present bone of contention, Kansas and Nebraska. Slavery already existed among the French at New Orleans; and, to some extent, at St. Louis. In 1812 Louisiana came into the Union as a slave state, without controversy. In 1818 or '19, Missouri showed signs of a wish to come in with slavery. This was resisted by northern members of Congress; and thus began the first great slavery agitation in the nation. This controversy lasted several months, and became very angry and exciting; the House of Representatives voting steadily for the prohibition of slavery in Missouri, and the Senate voting as steadily against it. Threats of breaking up the Union were freely made; and the ablest public men of the day became seriously alarmed. At length a compromise was made, in which, like all compromises, both sides yielded something. It was a law passed on the 6th day of March, 1820, providing that Missouri might come into the Union with slavery, but that in all the remaining part of the territory purchased of France, which lies north of 36 degrees and 30 minutes north latitude, slavery should never be permitted. This provision of law, is the Missouri Compromise. In excluding slavery North of the line, the same language is employed as in the Ordinance of '87. It directly applied to Iowa, Minnesota, and to the present bone of contention, Kansas and Nebraska. Whether there should or should not, be slavery south of that line, nothing was said in the law; but Arkansas constituted the principal remaining part, south of the line; and it has since been admitted as a slave state without serious controversy. More recently, Iowa, north of the line, came in as a free state without controversy. Still later, Minnesota, north of the line, had a territorial organization without controversy. Texas principally south of the line, and West of Arkansas; though originally within the purchase from France, had, in 1819, been traded off to Spain, in our treaty for the acquisition of Florida. It had thus become a part of Mexico. Mexico revolutionized and became independent of Spain. American citizens began settling rapidly, with their slaves in the southern part of Texas. Soon they revolutionized against Mexico, and established an independent government of their own, adopting a constitution, with slavery, strongly resembling the constitutions of our slave states. By still another rapid move, Texas, claiming a boundary much further West, than when we parted with her in 1819, was brought back to the United States, and admitted into the Union as a slave state. There then was little or no settlement in the northern part of Texas, a considerable portion of which lay north of the Missouri line; and in the resolutions admitting her into the Union, the Missouri restriction was expressly extended westward across her territory. This was in 1845, only nine years ago.

  Thus originated the Missouri Compromise; and thus has it been respected down to 1845. And even four years later, in 1849, our distinguished Senator, in a public address, held the following language in relation to it:

> [Lincoln quoting Douglas] "The Missouri Compromise had been in practical operation for about a quarter of a century, and had received the sanction and approbation of men of all parties in every section of the Union. It had allayed all sectional jealousies and irritations growing out of this vexed question, and harmonized and tranquilized the whole country. It had given to Henry Clay, as its prominent champion, the proud sobriquet of the

"Great Pacificator" and by that title and for that service, his political friends had repeatedly appealed to the people to rally under his standard, as a presidential candidate, as the man who had exhibited the patriotism and the power to suppress, an unholy and treasonable agitation, and preserve the Union. He was not aware that any man or any party from any section of the Union, had ever urged as an objection to Mr. Clay, that he was the great champion of the Missouri Compromise. On the contrary, the effort was made by the opponents of Mr. Clay, to prove that he was not entitled to the exclusive merit of that great patriotic measure, and that the honor was equally due to others as well as to him, for securing its adoption—that it had its origin in the hearts of all patriotic men, who desired to preserve and perpetuate the blessings of our glorious Union—an origin akin that of the constitution of the United States, conceived in the same spirit of fraternal affection, and calculated to remove forever, the only danger, which seemed to threaten, at some distant day, to sever the social bond of union. All the evidences of public opinion at that day, seemed to indicate that this Compromise had been canonized in the hearts of the American people, as a sacred thing which no ruthless hand would ever be reckless enough to disturb."

I do not read this extract to involve Judge Douglas in an inconsistency. If he afterwards thought he had been wrong, it was right for him to change. I bring this forward merely to show the high estimate placed on the Missouri Compromise by all parties up to so late as the year 1849.

But, going back a little, in point of time, our war with Mexico broke out in 1846. When Congress was about adjourning that session, President Polk asked them to place two millions of dollars under his control, to be used by him in the recess, if found practicable and expedient, in negotiating a treaty of peace with Mexico, and acquiring some part of her territory. A bill was duly got up, for the purpose, and was progressing swimmingly, in the House of Representatives, when a member by the name of David Wilmot, a democrat from Pennsylvania, moved as an amendment "Provided that in any territory thus acquired, there shall never be slavery."

This is the origin of the far-famed "Wilmot Proviso." It created a great flutter; but it stuck like wax, was voted into the bill, and the bill passed with it through the House. The Senate, however, adjourned without final action on it and so both appropriation and proviso were lost, for the time. The war continued, and at the next session, the president renewed his request for the appropriation, enlarging the amount, I think, to three million. Again came the proviso; and defeated the measure. Congress adjourned again, and the war went on. In Dec. 1847, the new congress assembled. I was in the lower House that term. The "Wilmot Proviso" or the principle of it, was constantly coming up in some shape or other, and I think I may venture to say I voted for it at least forty times; during the short term I was there. The Senate, however, held it in check, and it never became law. In the spring of 1848 a treaty of peace was made with Mexico; by which we obtained that portion of her country which now constitutes the territories of New Mexico and Utah, and the now state of California. By this treaty the Wilmot Proviso was defeated, as so far as it was intended to be, a condition of the acquisition of territory. Its friends however, were still determined to find some way to restrain slavery from getting into the new country. This new acquisition lay directly West of our old purchase from France, and extended west to the Pacific ocean—and was so situated that if the Missouri line should be extended straight West, the new country would be divided by such extended line, leaving some North and some South of it. On Judge Douglas' motion a bill, or provision of a bill, passed the Senate to so extend the Missouri line. The Proviso men in the House, including myself, voted it down, because by implication, it gave up the Southern part to slavery, while we were bent on having it all free.

In the fall of 1848 the gold mines were discovered in California. This attracted people to it with unprecedented rapidity, so that on, or soon after, the meeting of the new congress in Dec., 1849, she already had a population of nearly a hundred thousand, had called a convention, formed a state constitution, excluding slavery, and was knocking for admission into the Union. The Proviso men, of course were for letting her in, but the Senate, always true to the other side would not consent to her admission. And there California stood, kept out of the Union, because she would not let slavery into her borders. Under all the circumstances perhaps this was not wrong. There were other points of dispute, connected with the general question of slavery, which equally needed adjustment. The South clamored for a more efficient fugitive slave law. The North clamored for the abolition of a peculiar species of slave trade in the District of Columbia, in connection with which, in view from the windows of the capitol, a sort of negro-livery stable, where droves of negroes were collected, temporarily kept, and finally taken to Southern markets, precisely like droves of horses, had been openly maintained for fifty years. Utah and New Mexico needed territorial governments; and whether slavery should or should not be prohibited within them, was another question. The indefinite Western boundary of Texas was to be settled. She was received a slave state; and consequently the farther West the slavery men could push her boundary, the more slave country they secured. And the farther East the slavery opponents could thrust the boundary back, the less slave ground was secured. Thus this was just as clearly a slavery question as any of the others.

These points all needed adjustment; and they were all held up, perhaps wisely to make them help to adjust one another. The Union, now, as in 1820, was thought to be in danger; and devotion to the Union rightfully inclined men to yield somewhat, in points where nothing else could have so inclined them. A compromise was finally effected. The south got their new fugitive-slave law; and the North got California, (the far best part of our acquisition from Mexico,) as a free State. The south got a provision that New Mexico and Utah, when admitted as States, may come in with or without slavery as they may then choose; and the north got the slave-trade abolished in the District of Columbia. The north got the western boundary of Texas, thence further back eastward than the south desired; but, in turn, they gave Texas ten millions of dollars, with which to pay her old debts. This is the Compromise of 1850.

Preceding the Presidential election of 1852, each of the great political parties, democrats and whigs, met in convention, and adopted resolutions endorsing the compromise of '50; as a "finality," a final settlement, so far as these parties could make it so, of all slavery agitation. Previous to this, in 1851, the Illinois Legislature had indorsed it.

During this long period of time Nebraska had remained, substantially an uninhabited country, but now emigration to, and settlement within it began to take place. It is about one third as large as the present United States, and its importance so long overlooked, begins to come into view. The restriction of slavery by the Missouri Compromise directly applies to it; in fact, was first made, and has since been maintained, expressly for it. In 1853, a bill to give it a territorial government passed the House of Representatives, and, in the hands of Judge Douglas, failed of passing the Senate only for want of time. This bill contained no repeal of the Missouri Compromise. Indeed, when it was assailed because it did not contain such repeal, Judge Douglas defended it in its existing form. On January 4th, 1854, Judge Douglas introduces a new bill to give Nebraska territorial government. He accompanies this bill with a report, in which last, he expressly recommends that the Missouri Compromise shall neither be affirmed nor repealed.

Before long the bill is so modified as to make two territories instead of one; calling the Southern one Kansas. Also, about a month after the introduction of the bill, on the judge's own motion, it is so amended as to declare the Missouri Compromise inoperative and void; and, substantially, that the People who go and settle there may establish slavery, or exclude it, as they may see fit. In this shape the bill passed both branches of congress, and became a law.

This is the repeal of the Missouri Compromise. The foregoing history may not be precisely accurate in every particular; but I am sure it is sufficiently so, for all the uses I shall attempt to make of it, and in it, we have before us, the chief material enabling us to correctly judge whether the repeal of the Missouri Compromise is right or wrong.

I think, and shall try to show, that it is wrong; wrong in its direct effect, letting slavery into Kansas and Nebraska—and wrong in its prospective principle, allowing it to spread to every other part of the wide world, where men can be found inclined to take it.

This declared indifference, but as I must think, covert real zeal for the spread of slavery, I can not but hate. I hate it because of the monstrous injustice of slavery itself. I hate it because it deprives our republican example of its just influence in the world—enables the enemies of free institutions, with plausibility, to taunt us as hypocrites—causes the real friends of freedom to doubt our sincerity, and especially because it forces so many really good men amongst ourselves into an open war with the very fundamental principles of civil liberty—criticizing the Declaration of Independence, and insisting that there is no right principle of action but self-interest.

Before proceeding, let me say I think I have no prejudice against the Southern people. They are just what we would be in their situation. If slavery did not now exist amongst them, they would not introduce it. If it did now exist amongst us, we should not instantly give it up. This I believe of the masses north and south. Doubtless there are individuals, on both sides, who would not hold slaves under any circumstances; and others who would gladly introduce slavery anew, if it were out of existence. We know that some southern men do free their slaves, go north, and become tip-top abolitionists; while some northern ones go south, and become most cruel slave-masters.

When southern people tell us they are no more responsible for the origin of slavery than we, I acknowledge the fact. When it is said that the institution exists, and that it is very difficult to get rid of it, in any satisfactory way, I can understand and appreciate the saying. I surely will not blame them for not doing what I should not know how to do myself. If all earthly power were given me, I should not know what to do, as to the existing institution. My first impulse would be to free all the slaves, and send them to Liberia [Africa],—to their own native land. But a moment's reflection would convince me, that whatever of high hope, (as I think there is) there may be in this, in the long run, its sudden execution is impossible. If they were all landed there in a day, they would all perish in the next ten days; and there are not surplus shipping and surplus money enough in the world to carry them there in many times ten days. What then? Free them all, and keep them among us as underlings? Is it quite certain that this betters their condition? I think I would not hold one in slavery, at any rate; yet the point is not clear enough for me to denounce people upon. What next? Free them, and make them politically and socially, our equals? My own feelings will not admit of this; and if mine would, we well know that those of the great mass of white people will not. Whether this feeling accords with justice and sound judgment, is not the sole question, if indeed, it is any part of it. A universal feeling, whether well or ill-founded, can not be safely disregarded. We can not, then, make them equals. It does seem to me that systems of gradual emancipation might be adopted; but for their tardiness in this, I will not undertake to judge our brethren of the south.

When they remind us of their constitutional rights, I acknowledge them, not grudgingly, but fully, and fairly; and I would give them any legislation for the reclaiming of their fugitives, which should not, in its stringency, be more likely to carry a free man into slavery, than our ordinary criminal laws are to hang an innocent one [emphasis added].

But all this, to my judgment, furnishes no more excuse for permitting slavery to go into our own free territory, than it would for reviving the African slave trade by law. The law which forbids the bringing of slaves from Africa; and that which has so long forbid the taking them to Nebraska, can hardly be distinguished on any moral principle; and the repeal of the former could find quite as plausible excuses as that of the latter.

The arguments by which the repeal of the Missouri Compromise is sought to be justified, are these: First, that the Nebraska country needed a territorial government. Second, that in various ways, the public had repudiated it, and demanded the repeal, and therefore should not now complain of it.

And lastly, that the repeal establishes a principle, which is intrinsically right.

I will attempt an answer to each of them in its turn.

First, then, if that country was in need of a territorial organization, could it not have had it as well without as with the repeal? Iowa and Minnesota, to both of which the Missouri restriction applied, had, without its repeal, each in succession, territorial organizations. And even, the year before, a bill for Nebraska itself, was within an ace of passing, without the repealing clause, and this in the hands of the same men who are now the champions of repeal. Why no necessity then for the repeal? But still later, when this very bill was first brought in, it contained no repeal. But, say they, because the public had demanded, or rather commanded the repeal, the repeal was to accompany the organization, whenever that should occur.

Now I deny that the public ever demanded any such thing—ever repudiated the Missouri Compromise—ever commanded its repeal. I deny it, and call for the proof. It is not contended, I believe, that any such command has ever been given in express terms. It is only said that it was done in principle. The support of the Wilmot Proviso, is the first fact mentioned, to prove that the Missouri restriction was repudiated in principle, and the second is, the refusal to extend the Missouri line over the country acquired from Mexico. These are near enough alike to be treated together. The one was to exclude the chances of slavery from the whole new acquisition by the lump, and the other was to reject a division of it, by which one half was to be given up to those chances. Now whether this was a repudiation of the Missouri line, in principle , depends upon whether the Missouri law contained any principle requiring the line to be extended over the country acquired from Mexico. I contend it did not. I insist that it contained no general principle, but that it was, in every sense, specific. That its terms limit it to the country purchased from France, is undenied and undeniable. It could have no principle beyond the intention of those who made it. They did not intend to extend the line to country which they did not own. If they intended to extend it, in the event of acquiring additional territory, why did they not say so? It was just as easy to say, that "in all the country west of the Mississippi, which we now own, or may hereafter acquire there shall never be slavery," as to say, what they did say; and they would have said it if they had meant it. An intention to extend the law is not only not mentioned in the law, but is not mentioned in any contemporaneous history. Both the law itself, and the history of the times are a blank as to any principle of extension; and by neither the known rules for construing statutes and contracts, nor by common sense, can any such principle be inferred.

Another fact showing the specific character of the Missouri law—showing that it intended no more than it expressed—showing that the line was not intended as a universal dividing line between free and slave territory, present and prospective—north of which slavery could never go—is the fact that by that very law, Missouri came in as a slave state, north of the line. If that law contained any prospective principle, the whole law must be looked to in order to ascertain what the principle was. And by this rule, the south could fairly contend that inasmuch as they got one slave state north of the line at the inception of the law, they have the right to have another given them north of it occasionally—now and then in the indefinite westward extension of the line. This demonstrates the absurdity of attempting to deduce a prospective principle from the Missouri Compromise line.

When we voted for the Wilmot Proviso, we were voting to keep slavery out of the whole Mexican acquisition; and little did we think we were thereby voting, to let it into Nebraska, laying several hundred miles distant. When we voted against extending the Missouri line, little did we think we were voting to destroy the old line, then of near thirty years standing. To argue that we thus repudiated the Missouri Compromise is no less absurd than it would be to argue that because we have, so far, forborne to acquire Cuba, we have thereby, in principle, repudiated our former acquisitions, and determined to throw them out of the Union! No less absurd than it would be to say that because I may have refused to build an addition to my house, I thereby have decided to destroy the existing house! And if I catch you setting fire to my house, you will turn upon me and say I instructed you to do it! The most conclusive argument, however, that, while voting for the Wilmot Proviso, and while voting against the extension of the Missouri line, we never thought of disturbing the original Missouri Compromise, is found in the facts, that there was then, and still is, an unorganized tract of fine country, nearly as large as the state of Missouri, lying immediately west of Arkansas, and south of the Missouri Compromise line; and that we never attempted to prohibit slavery as to it. I wish particular attention to this. It adjoins the original Missouri Compromise line, by its northern boundary; and consequently is part of the country, into which, by implication, slavery was permitted to go, by that compromise. There it has lain open ever since, and there it still lies. And yet no effort has been made at any time to wrest it from the south. In all our struggles to prohibit slavery within our Mexican acquisitions, we never so much as lifted a finger to prohibit it, as to this tract. Is not this entirely conclusive that at all times, we have held the Missouri Compromise as a sacred thing; even when against ourselves, as well as when for us?

Senator Douglas sometimes says the Missouri line itself was, in principle, only an extension of the line of the ordinance of '87—that is to say, an extension of the Ohio river. I think this is weak enough on its face. I will remark, however that, as a glance at the map will show, the Missouri line is a long way farther South than the Ohio; and that if our Senator, in proposing his extension, had stuck to the principle of jogging southward, perhaps it might not have been voted down so readily.

But next it is said that the compromises of '50 and the ratification of them by both political parties, in '52, established a new principle , which required the repeal of the Missouri Compromise. This again I deny. I deny it, and demand the proof. I have already stated fully what the compromises of '50 are. The particular part of those measures, for which the virtual repeal of the Missouri compromise is sought to be inferred (for it is admitted they contain nothing about it, in express terms) is the provision in the Utah and New Mexico laws, which permits them when they seek admission into the Union as States, to come in with or without slavery as they shall then see fit. Now I insist this provision was made for Utah and New Mexico, and for no other place whatever. It had no more direct reference to Nebraska than it had to the territories of the moon. But, say they, it had reference to Nebraska, in principle. Let us see. The North consented to this provision, not because they considered it right in itself; but because they were compensated—paid for it. They, at the same time, got

California into the Union as a free State. This was far the best part of all they had struggled for by the Wilmot Proviso.

They also got the area of slavery somewhat narrowed in the settlement of the boundary of Texas. Also, they got the slave trade abolished in the District of Columbia. For all these desirable objects the North could afford to yield something; and they did yield to the South the Utah and New Mexico provision. I do not mean that the whole North, or even a majority, yielded, when the law passed; but enough yielded, when added to the vote of the South, to carry the measure. Now can it be pretended that the principle of this arrangement requires us to permit the same provision to be applied to Nebraska, without any equivalent at all? Give us another free State; press the boundary of Texas still further back, give us another step toward the destruction of slavery in the District, and you present us a similar case. But ask us not to repeat, for nothing, what you paid for in the first instance. If you wish the thing again, pay again. That is the principle of the compromises of '50, if indeed they had any principles beyond their specific terms—it was the system of equivalents.

Again, if Congress, at that time, intended that all future territories should, when admitted as States, come in with or without slavery, at their own option, why did it not say so? With such an universal provision, all know the bills could not have passed. Did they, then—could they—establish a principle contrary to their own intention? Still further, if they intended to establish the principle that wherever Congress had control, it should be left to the people to do as they thought fit with slavery why did they not authorize the people of the District of Columbia at their adoption to abolish slavery within these limits? I personally know that this has not been left undone, because it was unthought of. It was frequently spoken of by members of Congress and by citizens of Washington six years ago; and I heard no one express a doubt that a system of gradual emancipation, with compensation to owners, would meet the approbation of a large majority of the white people of the District. But without the action of Congress they could say nothing; and Congress said "no." In the measures of 1850 Congress had the subject of slavery in the District expressly in hand. If they were then establishing the principle of allowing the people to do as they please with slavery, why did they not apply the principle to that people?

Again, it is claimed that by the Resolutions of the Illinois Legislature, passed in 1851, the repeal of the Missouri compromise was demanded. This I deny also. Whatever may be worked out by a criticism of the language of those resolutions, the people have never understood them as being any more than an endorsement of the compromises of 1850; and a release of our Senators from voting for the Wilmot Proviso. The whole people are living witnesses, that this only, was their view. Finally, it is asked "If we did not mean to apply the Utah and New Mexico provision, to all future territories, what did we mean, when we, in 1852, endorsed the compromises of '50?"

For myself, I can answer this question most easily. I meant not to ask a repeal, or modification of the fugitive slave law. I meant not to ask for the abolition of slavery in the District of Columbia. I meant not to resist the admission of Utah and New Mexico, even should they ask to come in as slave States. I meant nothing about additional territories, because, as I understood, we then had no territory whose character as to slavery was not already settled. As to Nebraska, I regarded its character as being fixed, by the Missouri compromise, for thirty years—as unalterably fixed as that of my own home in Illinois. As to new acquisitions I said "sufficient unto the day is the evil thereof." When we make new acquisitions we will, as heretofore, try to manage them some how. That is my answer. That is what I meant and said; and I appeal to the people to say, each for himself, whether that was not also the universal meaning of the free States.

And now, in turn, let me ask a few questions. If by any, or all these matters, the repeal of the Missouri Compromise was commanded, why was not the command sooner obeyed? Why was the repeal omitted in the Nebraska bill of 1853? Why was it omitted in the original bill of 1854? Why, in the accompanying report, was such a repeal characterized as a departure from the course pursued in 1850? and its continued omission recommended?

I am aware Judge Douglas now argues that the subsequent express repeal is no substantial alteration of the bill. This argument seems wonderful to me. It is as if one should argue that white and black are not different.

He admits, however, that there is a literal change in the bill; and that he made the change in deference to other Senators, who would not support the bill without. This proves that those other Senators thought the change a substantial one; and that the Judge thought their opinions worth deferring to. His own opinions, therefore, seem not to rest on a very firm basis even in his own mind—and I suppose the world believes, and will continue to believe, that precisely on the substance of that change this whole agitation has arisen.

I conclude then, that the public never demanded the repeal of the Missouri compromise.

I now come to consider whether the repeal, with its avowed principle, is intrinsically right. I insist that it is not. Take the particular case. A controversy had arisen between the advocates and opponents of slavery, in relation to its establishment within the country we had purchased of France. The southern, and then best part of the purchase, was already in as a slave state. The controversy was settled by also letting Missouri in as a slave State; but with the agreement that within all the remaining part of the purchase, North of a certain line, there should never be slavery. As to what was to be done with the remaining part south of the line, nothing was said; but perhaps the fair implication was, that it should come in with slavery if it should so choose. The southern part, except a portion heretofore mentioned, afterwards did come in with slavery, as the State of Arkansas. All these many years since 1820, the Northern part had remained a wilderness. At length settlements began in it also. In due course, Iowa, came in as a free State, and Minnesota was given a territorial government, without removing the slavery restriction. Finally the sole remaining part, North of the line, Kansas and Nebraska, was to be organized; and it is proposed, and carried, to blot out the old dividing line of thirty-four years standing, and to open the whole of that country to the introduction of slavery. Now, this, to my mind, is manifestly unjust. After an angry and dangerous controversy, the parties made friends by dividing the bone of contention. The one party first appropriates her own share, beyond all power to be disturbed in the possession of it; and then seizes the share of the other party. It is as if two starving men had divided their only loaf; the one had hastily swallowed his half, and then grabbed the other half just as he was putting it to his mouth!

Let me here drop the main argument, to notice what I consider rather an inferior matter. It is argued that slavery will not go to Kansas and Nebraska, in any event. This is a palliation—a lullaby. I have some hope that it will not; but let us not be too confident. As to climate, a glance at the map shows that there are five slave States—Delaware, Maryland, Virginia, Kentucky, and Missouri—and also the District of Columbia, all north of the Missouri compromise line. The census returns of 1850 show that, within these, there are 867,276 slaves—being more than one-fourth of all the slaves in the nation.

It is not climate, then, that will keep slavery out of these territories. Is there any thing in the peculiar nature of the country? Missouri adjoins these territories, by her entire western boundary, and slavery is already within every one of her western counties. I have even heard it said that there are more slaves, in proportion to whites, in the northwestern county of Missouri, than within any county of the State. Slavery pressed entirely up to the old western boundary of the State, and when, rather recently, a part of that boundary, at the north-west was moved out a little farther west, slavery followed on quite up to the new line. Now, when the restriction is removed, what is to prevent it from going still further? Climate will not. No peculiarity of the country will—nothing in nature will. Will the disposition of the people prevent it? Those nearest the scene, are all in favor of the extension. The yankees, who are opposed to it may be more numerous; but in military phrase, the battle-field is too far from their base of operations.

But it is said, there now is no law in Nebraska on the subject of slavery; and that, in such case, taking a slave there, operates his freedom. That is good book-law; but is not the rule of actual practice. Wherever slavery is, it has been first introduced without law. The oldest laws we find concerning it, are not laws introducing it, but regulating it, as an already existing thing. A white man takes his slave to Nebraska now; who will inform the negro that he is free? Who will take him before court to test the question of his freedom? In ignorance of his legal emancipation, he is kept chopping, splitting and plowing. Others are brought, and move on in the same track. At last, if ever the time for voting comes, on the question of slavery, the institution already in fact exists in the country, and cannot well be removed. The facts of its presence, and the difficulty of its removal will carry the vote in its favor. Keep it out until a vote is taken, and a vote in favor of it, can not be got in any population of forty thousand, on earth, who have been drawn together by the ordinary motives of emigration and settlement. To get slaves into the country simultaneously with the whites, in the incipient stages of settlement, is the precise stake played for, and won in this Nebraska measure.

The question is asked us, "If slaves will go in, notwithstanding the general principle of law liberates them, why would they not equally go in against positive statute law?—go in, even if the Missouri restriction were maintained?" I answer, because it takes a much bolder man to venture in, with his property, in the latter case, than in the former—because the positive congressional enactment is known to, and respected by all, or nearly all; whereas the negative principle that no law is free law, is not much known except among lawyers. We have some experience of this practical difference. In spite of the Ordinance of '87, a few negroes were brought into Illinois, and held in a state of quasi slavery; not enough, however to carry a vote of the people in favor of the institution when they came to form a constitution. But in the adjoining Missouri country, where there was no ordinance of '87—was no restriction—they were carried ten times, nay a hundred times, as fast, and actually made a slave State. This is fact—naked fact.

Another lullaby argument is, that taking slaves to new countries does not increase their number—does not make any one slave who otherwise would be free. There is some truth in this, and I am glad of it, but it is not wholly true. The African slave trade is not yet effectually suppressed; and if we make a reasonable deduction for the white people amongst us, who are foreigners, and the descendants of foreigners, arriving here since 1808, we shall find the increase of the black population out-running that of the white, to an extent unaccountable, except by supposing that some of them too, have been coming from Africa. If this be so, the opening of new countries to the institution, increases the demand for, and augments the price of slaves, and so does, in fact, make slaves of freemen by causing them to be brought from Africa, and sold into bondage.

But, however this may be, we know the opening of new countries to slavery, tends to the perpetuation of the institution, and so does keep men in slavery who otherwise would be free. This result we do not feel like favoring, and we are under no legal obligation to suppress our feelings in this respect.

Equal justice to the south, it is said, requires us to consent to the extending of slavery to new countries. That is to say, inasmuch as you do not object to my taking my hog to Nebraska, therefore I must not object to you taking your slave. Now, I admit this is perfectly logical, if there is no difference between hogs and negroes. But while you thus require me to deny the humanity of the negro, I wish to ask whether you of the south yourselves, have ever been willing to do as much? It is kindly provided that of all those who come into the world, only a small percentage are natural tyrants. That percentage is no larger in the slave States than in the free. The great majority, south as well as north, have human sympathies, of which they can no more divest themselves than they can of their sensibility to physical pain. These sympathies in the bosoms of the southern people, manifest in many ways, their sense of the wrong of slavery, and their consciousness that, after all, there is humanity in the negro. If they deny this, let me address them a few plain questions. In 1820 you joined the north, almost unanimously, in declaring the African slave trade piracy, and in annexing to it the punishment of death. Why did you do this? If you did not feel that it was wrong, why did you join in providing that men should be hung for it? The practice was no more than bringing wild negroes from Africa, to sell to such as would buy them. But you never thought of hanging men for catching and selling wild horses, wild buffaloes or wild bears.

Again, you have amongst you, a sneaking individual, of the class of native tyrants, known as the "slave-dealer." He watches your necessities, and crawls up to buy your slave, at a speculating price. If you cannot help it, you sell to him; but if you can help it, you drive him from your door. You despise him utterly. You do not recognize him as a friend, or even as an honest man. Your children must not play with his; they may rollick freely with the little negroes, but not with the "slave-dealers" children. If you are obliged to deal with him, you try to get through the job without so much as touching him. It is common with you to join hands with the men you meet; but with the slave dealer you avoid the ceremony—instinctively shrinking from the snaky contact. If he grows rich and retires from business, you still remember him, and still keep up the ban of non-intercourse upon him and his family. Now why is this? You do not so treat the man who deals in corn, cattle or tobacco.

And yet again; there are in the United States and territories, including the District of Columbia, 433,643 free blacks. At $500 [or about $13,500 in today's currency] per head they are worth over two hundred millions of dollars [or about $5.4 billion in today's currency].[887] How comes this vast amount of property to be running about without owners? We do not see free horses or free cattle running at large. How is this? All these free blacks are the descendants of slaves, or have been slaves themselves, and they would be slaves now, but for something which has operated on their white owners, inducing them, at vast pecuniary sacrifices, to liberate them. What is that something? Is there any mistaking it? In all these cases it is your sense of justice, and human sympathy, continually telling you, that the poor negro has some natural right to himself—that those who deny it, and make mere merchandise of him, deserve kickings, contempt and death.

And now, why will you ask us to deny the humanity of the slave and estimate him only as the equal of the hog? Why ask us to do what you will not do yourselves? Why ask us to do for nothing, what two hundred million of dollars could not induce you to do?

But one great argument in the support of the repeal of the Missouri Compromise, is still to come. That argument is "the sacred right of self government." It seems our distinguished Senator has found great difficulty in getting his antagonists, even in the Senate to meet him fairly on this argument—some poet has said

"Fools rush in where angels fear to tread."

At the hazard of being thought one of the fools of this quotation, I meet that argument—I rush in, I take that bull by the horns.

I trust I understand, and truly estimate the right of self-government. My faith in the proposition that each man should do precisely as he pleases with all which is exclusively his own, lies at the foundation of the sense of justice there is in me. I extend the principles to communities of men, as well as to individuals. I so extend it, because it is politically wise, as well as naturally just; politically wise, in saving us from broils about matters which do not concern us. Here, or at Washington, I would not trouble myself with the oyster laws of Virginia, or the cranberry laws of Indiana.

The doctrine of self government is right—absolutely and eternally right—but it has no just application, as here attempted. Or perhaps I should rather say that whether it has such just application depends upon whether a negro is not or is a man. If he is not a man, why in that case, he who is a man may, as a matter of self-government, do just as he pleases with him. But if the negro is a man, is it not to that extent, a total destruction of self-government, to say that he too shall not govern himself? When the white man governs himself that is self-government; but when he governs himself, and also governs another man, that is more than self-government—that is despotism. If the negro is a man, why then my ancient faith teaches me that "all men are created equal;" and that there can be no moral right in connection with one man's making a slave of another.

Judge Douglas frequently, with bitter irony and sarcasm, paraphrases our argument by saying "The white people of Nebraska are good enough to govern themselves, but they are not good enough to govern a few miserable negroes!"

Well I doubt not that the people of Nebraska are, and will continue to be as good as the average of people elsewhere. I do not say the contrary. What I do say is, that no man is good enough to govern another man, without that other's consent. I say this is the leading principle—the sheet anchor of American republicanism. Our Declaration of Independence says: "We hold these truths to be self evident: that all men are created equal; that they are endowed by their Creator with certain inalienable rights; that among these are life, liberty and the pursuit of happiness. That to secure these rights, governments are instituted among men, deriving their just powers from the consent of the governed."

I have quoted so much at this time merely to show that according to our ancient faith, the just powers of governments are derived from the consent of the governed. Now the relation of masters and slaves is, *pro tanto* [i.e., only to that extent], a total violation of this principle. The master not only governs the slave without his consent; but he governs him by a set of rules altogether different from those which he prescribes for himself. Allow all the governed an equal voice in the government, and that, and that only is self government.

Let it not be said I am contending for the establishment of political and social equality between the whites and blacks. I have already said the contrary. I am not now combating the argument of necessity, arising from the fact that the blacks are already among us; but I am combating what is set up as moral argument for allowing them to be taken where they have never yet been—arguing against the extension of a bad thing, which where it already exists, we must of necessity, manage as we best can.

In support of his application of the doctrine of self-government, Senator Douglas has sought to bring to his aid the opinions and examples of our revolutionary fathers. I am glad he has done this. I love the sentiments of those old-time men; and shall be most happy to abide by their opinions. He shows us that when it was in contemplation for the colonies to break off from Great Britain, and set up a new government for themselves, several of the states instructed their delegates to go for the measure provided each state should be allowed to regulate its domestic concerns in its own way. I do not quote; but this in substance. This was right. I see nothing objectionable in it. I also think it probable that it had some reference to the existence of slavery amongst them. I will not deny that it had. But had it, in any reference to the carrying of slavery into new countries? That is the question; and we will let the fathers themselves answer it.

This same generation of men, and mostly the same individuals of the generation, who declared this principle—who declared independence—who fought the war of the revolution through—who afterwards made the constitution under which we still live—these same men passed the ordinance of '87, declaring that slavery should never go to the north-west territory. I have no doubt Judge Douglas thinks they were very inconsistent in this. It is a question of discrimination between them and him. But there is not an inch of ground left for his claiming that their opinions—their example—their authority—are on his side in this controversy.

Again, is not Nebraska, while a territory, a part of us? Do we not own the country? And if we surrender the control of it, do we not surrender the right of self-government? It is part of ourselves. If you say we shall not control it because it is only part, the same is true of every other part; and when all the parts are gone, what has become of the whole? What is then left of us? What use for the general government, when there is nothing left for it to govern?

But you say this question should be left to the people of Nebraska, because they are more particularly interested. If this be the rule, you must leave it to each individual to say for himself whether he will have slaves. What better moral right have thirty-one citizens of Nebraska to say, that the thirty-second shall not hold slaves, than the people of the thirty-one States have to say that slavery shall not go into the thirty-second State at all?

But if it is a sacred right for the people of Nebraska to take and hold slaves there, it is equally their sacred right to buy them where they can buy them cheapest; and that undoubtedly will be on the coast of Africa; provided you will consent to not hang them for going there to buy them. You must remove this restriction too, from the sacred right of self-government. I am aware you say that taking slaves from the States of Nebraska, does not make slaves of freemen; but the African slave-trader can say just as much. He does not catch free negroes and bring them here. He finds them already slaves in the hands of their black captors, and he honestly buys them at the rate of about a red cotton handkerchief a head. This is very cheap, and it is a great abridgement of the sacred right of self-government to hang men for engaging in this profitable trade!

Another important objection to this application of the right of self-government, is that it enables the first few, to deprive the succeeding many, of a free exercise of the right of self-government. The first few may get slavery in, and the subsequent many cannot easily get it out. How common is the remark now in the slave States—"If we were only clear of our slaves, how much better it would be for us." They are actually deprived of the privilege of governing themselves as they would, by the action of a very few, in the beginning. The same thing was true of the whole nation at the time our constitution was formed.

Whether slavery shall go into Nebraska, or other new territories, is not a matter of exclusive concern to the people who may go there. The whole nation is interested that the best use shall be made of these territories. *We want them for the homes of free white people.* This they cannot be, to any considerable extent, if slavery shall be planted within them. Slave States are places for poor white people to remove from; not to remove to. New free States are the places for poor people to go to and better their condition. For this use, the nation needs these territories [emphasis added].

Still further; there are constitutional relations between the slave and free States, which are degrading to the latter. We are under legal obligations to catch and return their runaway slaves to them—a sort of dirty, disagreeable job, which I believe, as a general rule the slave-holders will not perform for one another. Then again, in the control of the government—the management of the partnership affairs—they have greatly the advantage of us. By the constitution, each State has two Senators—each has a number of Representatives; in proportion to the number of its people—and each has a number of presidential electors, equal to the whole number of its Senators and Representatives together. But in ascertaining the number of the people, for this purpose, five slaves are counted as being equal to three whites. The slaves do not vote; they are only counted and so used, as to swell the influence of the white people's votes. The practical effect of this is more aptly shown by a comparison of the States of South Carolina and Maine. South Carolina has six representatives, and so has Maine; South Carolina has eight presidential electors, and so has Maine. This is precise equality so far; and, of course they are equal in Senators, each having two. Thus in the control of the government, the two States are equals precisely. But how are they in the number of their white people? Maine has 581,813—while South Carolina has 274,567. Maine has twice as many as South Carolina, and 32,679 over. Thus each white man in South Carolina is more than the double of any man in Maine. This is all because South Carolina, besides her free people, has 384,984 slaves. The South Carolinian has precisely the same advantage over the white man in every other free State, as well as in Maine. He is more than the double of any one of us in this crowd. The same advantage, but not to the same extent, is held by all the citizens of the slave States, over those of the free; and it is an absolute truth, without an exception, that there is no voter in any slave State, but who has more legal power in the government, than any voter in any free State. There is no instance of exact equality; and the disadvantage is against us the whole chapter through. This principle, in the aggregate, gives the slave States, in the present Congress, twenty additional representatives—being seven more than the whole majority by which they passed the Nebraska bill.

  Now all this is manifestly unfair; yet I do not mention it to complain of it, in so far as it is already settled. It is in the constitution; and I do not, for that cause, or any other cause, propose to destroy, or alter, or disregard the constitution. I stand to it, fairly, fully, and firmly.

  But when I am told I must leave it altogether to other people to say whether new partners are to be bred up and brought into the firm, on the same degrading terms against me, I respectfully demur. I insist, that whether I shall be a whole man, or only, the half of one, in comparison with others, is a question in which I am somewhat concerned; and one which no other man can have a sacred right of deciding for me. If I am wrong in this—if it really be a sacred right of self-government, in the man who shall go to Nebraska, to decide whether he will be the equal of me or the double of me, then after he shall have exercised that right, and thereby shall have reduced me to a still smaller fraction of a man than I already am, I should like for some gentleman deeply skilled in the mysteries of sacred rights, to provide himself with a microscope, and peep about, and find out, if he can, what has become of my sacred rights! They will surely be too small for detection with the naked eye.

  Finally, I insist, that if there is any thing which it is the duty of the whole people to never entrust to any hands but their own, that thing is the preservation and perpetuity, of their own liberties, and institutions. And if they shall think, as I do, that the extension of slavery endangers them, more than any, or all other causes, how recreant to themselves, if they submit the question, and with it, the fate of their country, to a mere hand-full of men, bent only on temporary self-interest. If this question of slavery extension were an insignificant one—one having no power to do harm—it might be shuffled aside in this way. But being, as it is, the great Behemoth of danger, shall the strong grip of the nation be loosened upon him, to entrust him to the hands of such feeble keepers?

I have done with this mighty argument, of self-government. Go, sacred thing! Go in peace.

But Nebraska is urged as a great Union-saving measure. Well I too, go for saving the Union. Much as I hate slavery, I would consent to the extension of it rather than see the Union dissolved, just as I would consent to any great evil, to avoid a greater one. But when I go to Union saving, I must believe, at least, that the means I employ has some adaptation to the end. To my mind, Nebraska has no such adaptation.

"It hath no relish of salvation in it."

It is an aggravation, rather, of the only one thing which ever endangers the Union. When it came upon us, all was peace and quiet. The nation was looking to the forming of new bonds of Union; and a long course of peace and prosperity seemed to lie before us. In the whole range of possibility, there scarcely appears to me to have been any thing, out of which the slavery agitation could have been revived, except the very project of repealing the Missouri compromise. Every inch of territory we owned, already had a definite settlement of the slavery question, and by which, all parties were pledged to abide. Indeed, there was no uninhabited country on the continent, which we could acquire; if we except some extreme northern regions, which are wholly out of the question. In this state of affairs the Genius of Discord himself, could scarcely have invented a way of again setting us by the ears, but by turning back and destroying the peace measures of the past. The councils of that Genius seem to have prevailed, the Missouri compromise was repealed; and here we are, in the midst of a new slavery agitation, such, I think, as we have never seen before.

Who is responsible for this? Is it those who resist the measure; or those who, causelessly, brought it forward, and pressed it through, having reason to know, and, in fact, knowing it must and would be so resisted? It could not but be expected by its author, that it would be looked upon as a measure for the extension of slavery, aggravated by a gross breach of faith. Argue as you will, and long as you will, this is the naked front and aspect, of the measure. And in this aspect, it could not but produce agitation.

Slavery is founded in the selfishness of man's nature—opposition to it in his love of justice. These principles are an eternal antagonism; and when brought into collision so fiercely, as slavery extension brings them, shocks, and throes, and convulsions must ceaselessly follow. Repeal the Missouri compromise—repeal all compromises—repeal the declaration of independence—repeal all past history, you still can not repeal human nature. It still will be the abundance of man's heart, that slavery extension is wrong; and out of the abundance of his heart, his mouth will continue to speak.

The structure, too, of the Nebraska bill is very peculiar. The people are to decide the question of slavery for themselves; but when they are to decide; or how they are to decide; or whether, when the question is once decided, it is to remain so, or is it to be subject to an indefinite succession of new trials, the law does not say, Is it to be decided by the first dozen settlers who arrive there? or is it to await the arrival of a hundred? Is it to be decided by a vote of the people? or a vote of the legislature? or, indeed by a vote of any sort? To these questions, the law gives no answer. There is a mystery about this; for when a member proposed to give the legislature express authority to exclude slavery, it was hooted down by the friends of the bill. This fact is worth remembering. Some Yankees in the east are sending emigrants to Nebraska, to exclude slavery from it; and, so far as I can judge, they expect the question to be decided by voting, in some way or other. But the Missourians are awake too. They are within a stone's throw of the contested ground. They hold meetings, and pass resolutions, in which not the slightest allusion to voting is made. They resolve that slavery already exists in the territory; that more shall go there; that they, remaining in Missouri will protect it; and that abolitionists shall be hung, or driven away. Through all this, bowie-knives and six-shooters are seen plainly enough; but never a glimpse of the ballot-box. And, really, what is to be the result of this? Each party within having numerous and determined backers without, is it not probable that the contest will come to blows, and bloodshed? Could there be a more apt invention to bring about collision and violence, on the slavery question, than this Nebraska project is? I do not charge, or believe, that such was intended by Congress; but if they had literally formed a ring, and placed champions within it to fight out the controversy, the fight could be no more likely to come off, than it is. And if this fight should begin, is it likely to take a very peaceful, Union-saving turn? Will not the first drop of blood so shed, be the real knell of the Union?

The Missouri Compromise ought to be restored. For the sake of the Union, it ought to be restored. We ought to elect a House of Representatives which will vote its restoration. If by any means, we omit to do this, what follows? Slavery may or may not be established in Nebraska. But whether it be or not, we shall have repudiated—discarded from the councils of the Nation—the spirit of compromise; for who after this will ever trust in a national compromise? The spirit of mutual concession—that spirit which first gave us the constitution, and which has thrice saved the Union—we shall have strangled and cast from us forever. And what shall we have in lieu of it? The South flushed with triumph and tempted to excesses; the North, betrayed, as they believe, brooding on wrong and burning for revenge. One side will provoke; the other resent. The one will taunt, the other defy; one aggresses, the other retaliates. Already a few in the North, defy all constitutional restraints, resist the execution of the fugitive slave law, and even menace the institution of slavery in the states where it exists.

Already a few in the South, claim the constitutional right to take to and hold slaves in the free states—demand the revival of the slave trade; and demand a treaty with Great Britain by which fugitive slaves may be reclaimed from Canada. As yet they are but few on either side. It is a grave question for the lovers of the Union, whether the final destruction of the Missouri Compromise, and with it the spirit of all compromise will or will not embolden and embitter each of these, and fatally increase the numbers of both.

But restore the compromise, and what then? We thereby restore the national faith, the national confidence, the national feeling of brotherhood. We thereby reinstate the spirit of concession and compromise—that spirit which has never failed us in past perils, and which may be safely trusted for all the future. The south ought to join in doing this. The peace of the nation is as dear to them as to us. In memories of the past and hopes of the future, they share as largely as we. It would be on their part, a great act—great in its spirit, and great in its effect. It would be worth to the nation a hundred years' purchase of peace and prosperity. And what of sacrifice would they make? They only surrender to us, what they gave us for a consideration long, long ago; what they have not now, asked for, struggled or cared for; what has been thrust upon them, not less to their own astonishment than to ours.

But it is said we cannot restore it; that though we elect every member of the lower house, the Senate is still against us. It is quite true, that of the Senators who passed the Nebraska bill, a majority of the whole Senate will retain their seats in spite of the elections of this and the next year. But if at these elections, their several constituencies shall clearly express their will against Nebraska, will these senators disregard their will? Will they neither obey, nor make room for those who will?

But even if we fail to technically restore the compromise, it is still a great point to carry a popular vote in favor of the restoration. The moral weight of such a vote can not be estimated too highly. The authors of Nebraska are not at all satisfied with the destruction of the compromise—an endorsement of this principle, they proclaim to be the great object. With them, Nebraska alone is a small matter—to establish a principle, for future use, is what they particularly desire.

That future use is to be the planting of slavery wherever in the wide world, local and unorganized opposition can not prevent it. Now if you wish to give them this endorsement—if you wish to establish this principle—do so. I shall regret it; but it is your right. On the contrary if you are opposed to the principle—intend to give it no such endorsement—let no wheedling, no sophistry, divert you from throwing a direct vote against it.

Some men, mostly whigs, who condemn the repeal of the Missouri Compromise, nevertheless hesitate to go for its restoration, lest they be thrown in company with the abolitionist. Will they allow me as an old whig to tell them good humoredly, that I think this is very silly? Stand with anybody that stands right. Stand with him while he is right and part with him when he goes wrong. Stand with the abolitionist in restoring the Missouri Compromise; and stand against him when he attempts to repeal the fugitive slave law. In the latter case you stand with the southern disunionist. What of that you are still right. In both cases you are right. In both cases you expose the dangerous extremes. In both you stand on middle ground and hold the ship level and steady. In both you are national and nothing less than national. This is good old whig ground. To desert such ground, because of any company, is to be less than a whig—less than a man—less than an American.

I particularly object to the new position which the avowed principle of this Nebraska law gives to slavery in the body politic. I object to it because it assumes that there can be moral right in the enslaving of one man by another. I object to it as a dangerous dalliance for a free people—a sad evidence that, feeling prosperity we forget right—that liberty, as a principle, we have ceased to revere. I object to it because the fathers of the republic eschewed, and rejected it. The argument of "Necessity" was the only argument they ever admitted in favor of slavery; and so far, and so far only as it carried them, did they ever go. They found the institution existing among us, which they could not help; and they cast blame upon the British King for having permitted its introduction. Before the Constitution they prohibited its introduction into the Northwestern Territory, the only country we owned then free from it. At the framing and adoption of the constitution, they forbore to so much as mention the word "slave" or "slavery" in the whole instrument. In the provision for the recovery of fugitives, the slave is spoken of as a "person held to service or labor." In that prohibiting the abolition of the African slave trade for twenty years, that trade is spoken of as "The migration or importation of such persons as any of the States now existing, shall think proper to admit," etc. These are the only provisions alluding to slavery. Thus, the thing is hid away, in the constitution, just as an afflicted man hides away a wen or a cancer, which he dares not cut out at once, lest he bleed to death; with the promise, nevertheless, that the cutting may begin at the end of a given time. Less than this our fathers could not do, and more they would not do. Necessity drove them so far, and farther, they would not go. But this is not all. The earliest Congress, under the Constitution, took the same view of slavery. They hedged and hemmed it in to the narrowest limits of necessity.

In 1794 they prohibited an outgoing slave-trade—that is, the taking of slaves from the United States to sell. In 1798, they prohibited the bringing of slaves from Africa, into the Mississippi Territory—this territory then comprising what are now the States of Mississippi and Alabama. This was ten years before they had the authority to do the same thing as to the States existing at the adoption of the constitution.

In 1800 they prohibited American citizens from trading in slaves between foreign countries—as, for instance, from Africa to Brazil.

In 1803 they passed a law in aid of one or two State laws, in restraint of the internal slave trade.

In 1807, in apparent hot haste, they passed the law, nearly a year in advance to take effect the first day of 1808—the very first day the constitution would permit—prohibiting the African slave trade by heavy pecuniary and corporal penalties.

In 1820, finding these provisions ineffectual, they declared the trade piracy, and annexed to it, the extreme penalty of death. While all this was passing in the general government, five or six of the original slave States had adopted systems of gradual emancipation; and by which the institution was rapidly becoming extinct within these limits.

Thus we see, the plain unmistakable spirit of that age, towards slavery, was hostility to the principle, and toleration, only by necessity.

But now it is to be transformed into a "sacred right." Nebraska brings it forth, places it on the high road to extension and perpetuity; and, with a pat on its back, says to it, "Go, and God speed you." Henceforth it is to be the chief jewel of the nation—the very figure-head of the ship of State. Little by little, but steadily as man's march to the grave, we have been giving up the old for the new faith. Near eighty years ago we began by declaring that all men are created equal; but now from that beginning we have run down to the other declaration, that for some men to enslave others is a "sacred right of self-government." These principles can not stand together. They are as opposite as God and mammon; and whoever holds to the one, must despise the other. When [Indiana Senator John] Pettit, in connection with his support of the Nebraska bill, called the Declaration of Independence "a self-evident lie" he only did what consistency and candor require all other Nebraska men to do. Of the forty odd Nebraska Senators who sat present and heard him, no one rebuked him. Nor am I apprized that any Nebraska newspaper, or any Nebraska orator, in the whole nation, has ever yet rebuked him. If this had been said among Marion's men, Southerners though they were, what would have become of the man who said it? If this had been said to the men who captured Andre, the man who said it, would probably have been hung sooner than Andre was. If it had been said in old Independence Hall, seventy-eight years ago, the very door-keeper would have throttled the man, and thrust him into the street.

 Let no one be deceived. The spirit of seventy-six and the spirit of Nebraska, are utter antagonisms; and the former is being rapidly displaced by the latter.

 Fellow countrymen—Americans south, as well as north, shall we make no effort to arrest this? Already the liberal party throughout the world, express the apprehension "that the one retrograde institution in America, is undermining the principles of progress, and fatally violating the noblest political system the world ever saw." This is not the taunt of enemies, but the warning of friends. Is it quite safe to disregard it—to despise it? Is there no danger to liberty itself, in discarding the earliest practice, and first precept of our ancient faith? In our greedy chase to make profit of the negro, let us beware, lest we "cancel and tear to pieces" even the white man's charter of freedom.

 Our republican robe is soiled, and trailed in the dust. Let us repurify it. Let us turn and wash it white, in the spirit, if not the blood, of the Revolution. Let us turn slavery from its claims of "moral right," back upon its existing legal rights, and its arguments of "necessity." Let us return it to the position our fathers gave it; and there let it rest in peace. Let us re-adopt the Declaration of Independence, and with it, the practices, and policy, which harmonize with it. Let north and south—let all Americans—let all lovers of liberty everywhere—join in the great and good work. If we do this, we shall not only have saved the Union; but we shall have so saved it, as to make, and to keep it, forever worthy of the saving. We shall have so saved it, that the succeeding millions of free happy people, the world over, shall rise up, and call us blessed, to the latest generations.

  At Springfield, twelve days ago, where I had spoken substantially as I have here, Judge Douglas replied to me—and as he is to reply to me here, I shall attempt to anticipate him, by noticing some of the points he made there. He commenced by stating I had assumed all the way through, that the principle of the Nebraska bill, would have the effect of extending slavery. He denied that this was intended, or that this effect would follow.

  I will not re-open the argument upon this point. That such was the intention, the world believed at the start, and will continue to believe. This was the countenance of the thing; and, both friends and enemies, instantly recognized it as such. That countenance can not now be changed by argument. You can as easily argue the color out of the negroes' skin. Like the "bloody hand" you may wash it, and wash it, the red witness of guilt still sticks, and stares horribly at you.

  Next he says that congressional intervention never prevented slavery anywhere; that it did not prevent it in the Northwestern territory, nor in Illinois; that in fact, Illinois came into the Union as a slave State; that the principle of the Nebraska bill expelled it from Illinois, from several old States, from every where.

  Now this is mere quibbling all the way through. If the ordinance of '87 did not keep slavery out of the north west territory, how happens it that the north west shore of the Ohio river is entirely free from it; while the south east shore, less than a mile distant, along nearly the whole length of the river, is entirely covered with it?

  If that ordinance did not keep it out of Illinois,

what was it that made the difference between Illinois and Missouri? They lie side by side, the Mississippi river only dividing them; while their early settlements were within the same latitude. Between 1810 and 1820 the number of slaves in Missouri increased 7,211; while in Illinois, in the same ten years, they decreased 51. This appears by the census returns. During nearly all of that ten years, both were territories—not States. During this time, the ordinance forbid slavery to go into Illinois; and nothing forbid it to go into Missouri. It did go into Missouri, and did not go into Illinois. That is the fact. Can any one doubt as to the reason of it?

But, he says, Illinois came into the Union as a slave State. Silence, perhaps, would be the best answer to this flat contradiction of the known history of the country. What are the facts upon which this bold assertion is based? When we first acquired the country, as far back as 1787, there were some slaves within it, held by the French inhabitants at Kaskaskia [a town in Illinois]. The territorial legislation, admitted a few negroes, from the slave States, as indentured servants. One year after the adoption of the first State constitution the whole number of them was—what do you think? just 117—while the aggregate free population was 55,094—about 470 to one. Upon this state of facts, the people framed their constitution prohibiting the further introduction of slavery, with a sort of guaranty to the owners of the few indentured servants, giving freedom to their children to be born thereafter, and making no mention whatever, of any supposed slave for life. Out of this small matter, the Judge manufactures his argument that Illinois came into the Union as a slave State. Let the facts be the answer to the argument.

The principles of the Nebraska bill, he says, expelled slavery from Illinois. The principle of that bill first planted it here—that is, it first came, because there was no law to prevent it—first came before we owned the country; and finding it here, and having the ordinance of '87 to prevent its increasing, our people struggled along, and finally got rid of it as best they could.

But the principle of the Nebraska bill abolished slavery in several of the old States. Well, it is true that several of the old States, in the last quarter of the last century, did adopt systems of gradual emancipation, by which the institution has finally become extinct within their limits; but it may or may not be true that the principle of the Nebraska bill was the cause that led to the adoption of these measures. It is now more than fifty years, since the last of these States adopted its system of emancipation.

If the Nebraska bill is the real author of these benevolent works, it is rather deplorable, that it has, for so long a time, ceased working all together. Is there not some reason to suspect that it was the principle of the revolution, and not the principle of the Nebraska bill, that led to emancipation in these old States? Leave it to the people of those old emancipating States, and I am quite sure they will decide, that neither that, nor any other good thing, ever did, or ever will come of the Nebraska bill.

In the course of my main argument, Judge Douglas interrupted me to say, that the principle of the Nebraska bill was very old; that it originated when God made man and placed good and evil before him, allowing him to choose for himself, being responsible for the choice he should make. At the time I thought this was merely playful; and I answered it accordingly. But in his reply to me he renewed it, as a serious argument. In seriousness then, the facts of this proposition are not true as stated. God did not place good and evil before man, telling him to make his choice. On the contrary, he did tell him there was one tree, of the fruit of which, he should not eat, upon pain of certain death. I should scarcely wish so strong a prohibition against slavery in Nebraska.

But this argument strikes me as not a little remarkable in another particular—in its strong resemblance to the old argument for the "Divine right of Kings." By the latter, the King is to do just as he pleases with his white subjects, being responsible to God alone. By the former the white man is to do just as he pleases with his black slaves, being responsible to God alone. The two things are precisely alike; and it is but natural that they should find similar arguments to sustain them.

I had argued, that the application of the principle of self-government, as contended for, would require the revival of the African slave trade—that no argument could be made in favor of a man's right to take slaves to Nebraska, which could not be equally well made in favor of his right to bring them from the coast of Africa. The Judge replied, that the constitution requires the suppression of the foreign slave trade; but does not require the prohibition of slavery in the territories. That is a mistake, in point of fact. The constitution does not require the action of Congress in either case; and it does authorize it in both. And so, there is still no difference between the cases.

In regard to what I had said, the advantage the slave States have over the free, in the matter of representation, the Judge replied that we, in the free States, count five free negroes as five white people, while in the slave States, they count five slaves as three whites only; and that the advantage, at last, was on the side of the free States.

Now, in the slave States, they count free negroes just as we do; and it so happens that besides their slaves, they have as many free negroes as we have, and thirty-three thousand over. Thus their free negroes more than balance ours; and their advantage over us, in consequence of their slaves, still remains as I stated it.

In reply to my argument, that the compromise measures of 1850, were a system of equivalents; and that the provisions of no one of them could fairly be carried to other subjects, without its corresponding equivalent being carried with it, the Judge denied out-right, that these measures had any connection with, or dependence upon, each other. This is mere desperation. If they have no connection, why are they always spoken of in connection? Why has he so spoken of them, a thousand times? Why has he constantly called them a series of measures? Why does everybody call them a compromise? Why was California kept out of the Union, six or seven months, if it was not because of its connection with the other measures? Webster's leading definition of the verb "to compromise" is "to adjust and settle a difference, by mutual agreement with concessions of claims by the parties." This conveys precisely the popular understanding of the word compromise. We knew, before the Judge told us, that these measures passed separately, and in distinct bills; and that no two of them were passed by the votes of precisely the same members. But we also know, and so does he know, that no one of them could have passed both branches of Congress but for the understanding that the others were to pass also.

Upon this understanding each got votes, which it could have got in no other way. It is this fact, that gives to the measures their true character; and it is the universal knowledge of this fact, that has given them the name of compromise so expressive of that true character.

I had asked "If in carrying the provisions of the Utah and New Mexico laws to Nebraska, you could clear away other objection, how can you leave Nebraska "perfectly free" to introduce slavery before she forms a constitution—during her territorial government?—while the Utah and New Mexico laws only authorize it when they form constitutions, and are admitted into the Union?" To this Judge Douglas answered that the Utah and New Mexico laws, also authorized it before; and to prove this, he read from one of their laws, as follows: "That the legislative power of said territory shall extend to all rightful subjects of legislation consistent with the constitution of the United States and the provisions of this act."

Now it is perceived from the reading of this, that there is nothing express upon the subject; but that the authority is sought to be implied merely, for the general provision of "all rightful subjects of legislation." In reply to this, I insist, as a legal rule of construction, as well as the plain popular view of the matter, that the express provision for Utah and New Mexico coming in with slavery if they choose, when they shall form constitutions, is an exclusion of all implied authority on the same subject—that Congress, having the subject distinctly in their minds, when they made the express provision, they therein expressed their whole meaning on that subject.

The Judge rather insinuated that I had found it convenient to forget the Washington territorial law passed in 1853. This was a division of Oregon, organizing the northern part, as the territory of Washington. He asserted that, by this act, the ordinance of '87 theretofore existing in Oregon, was repealed; that nearly all the members of Congress voted for it, beginning in the H.R. [House of Representatives], with Charles Allen of Massachusetts, and ending with Richard Yates, of Illinois; and that he could not understand how those who now oppose the Nebraska bill, so voted then, unless it was because it was then too soon after both the great political parties had ratified the compromises of 1850, and the ratification therefore too fresh, to be then repudiated.

Now I had seen the Washington act before; and I have carefully examined it since; and I aver that there is no repeal of the ordinance of '87, or of any prohibition of slavery, in it. In express terms, there is absolutely nothing in the whole law upon the subject—in fact, nothing to lead a reader to think of the subject. To my judgment, it is equally free from every thing from which such repeal can be legally implied; but however this may be, are men now to be entrapped by a legal implication, extracted from covert language, introduced perhaps, for the very purpose of entrapping them? I sincerely wish every man could read this law quite through, carefully watching every sentence, and every line, for a repeal of the ordinance of '87 or any thing equivalent to it.

Another point on the Washington act. If it was intended to be modeled after the Utah and New Mexico acts, as Judge Douglas, insists, why was it not inserted in it, as in them, that Washington was to come in with or without slavery as she may choose at the adoption of her constitution? It has no such provision in it; and I defy the ingenuity of man to give a reason for the omission, other than that it was not intended to follow the Utah and New Mexico laws in regard to the question of slavery.

The Washington act not only differs vitally from the Utah and New Mexico acts; but the Nebraska act differs vitally from both. By the latter act the people are left "perfectly free" to regulate their own domestic concerns, etc.; but in all the former, all their laws are to be submitted to Congress, and if disapproved are to be null. The Washington act goes even further; it absolutely prohibits the territorial legislature, by very strong and guarded language, from establishing banks, or borrowing money on the faith of the territory. Is this the sacred right of self-government we hear vaunted so much? No sir, the Nebraska bill finds no model in the acts of '50 or the Washington act. It finds no model in any law from Adam till today. As Phillips says of Napoleon, the Nebraska act is grand, gloomy, and peculiar; wrapped in the solitude of its own originality; without a model, and without a shadow upon the earth.

In the course of his reply, Senator Douglas remarked, in substance, that he had always considered this government was made for the white people and not for the negroes. Why, in point of mere fact, I think so too. But in this remark of the Judge, there is a significance, which I think is the key to the great mistake (if there is any such mistake) which he has made in this Nebraska measure. It shows that the Judge has no very vivid impression that the negro is a human; and consequently has no idea that there can be any moral question in legislating about him. In his view, the question of whether a new country shall be slave or free, is a matter of as utter indifference, as it is whether his neighbor shall plant his farm with tobacco, or stock it with horned cattle. Now, whether this view is right or wrong, it is very certain that the great mass of mankind take a totally different view. They consider slavery a great moral wrong; and their feelings against it, is not evanescent, but eternal. It lies at the very foundation of their sense of justice; and it cannot be trifled with. It is a great and durable element of popular action, and, I think, no statesman can safely disregard it.

Our Senator also objects that those who oppose him in this measure do not entirely agree with one another. He reminds me that in my firm adherence to the constitutional rights of the slave States, I differ widely from others who are co-operating with me in opposing the Nebraska bill; and he says it is not quite fair to oppose him in this variety of ways. He should remember that he took us by surprise—astounded us—by this measure. We were thunderstruck and stunned; and we reeled and fell in utter confusion. But we rose each fighting, grasping whatever he could first reach—a scythe—a pitchfork—a chopping axe, or a butcher's cleaver. We struck in the direction of the sound; and we are rapidly closing in upon him. He must not think to divert us from our purpose, by showing us that our drill, our dress, and our weapons, are not entirely perfect and uniform. When the storm shall be past, he shall find us still Americans; no less devoted to the continued Union and prosperity of the country than heretofore.

Finally, the Judge invokes against me, the memory of [Henry] Clay and of [Daniel] Webster. They were great men; and men of great deeds. But where have I assailed them? For what is it, that their life-long enemy, shall now make profit, by assuming to defend them against me, their life-long friend? I go against the repeal of the Missouri compromise; did they ever go for it? They went for the compromise of 1850; did I ever go against them? They were greatly devoted to the Union; to the small measure of my ability, was I ever less so? Clay and Webster were dead before this question arose; by what authority shall our Senator say they would espouse his side of it, if alive? Mr. Clay was the leading spirit in making the Missouri compromise; is it very credible that if now alive, he would take the lead in the breaking of it? The truth is that some support from whigs is now a necessity with the Judge, and for thus it is, that the names of Clay and Webster are now invoked. His old friends have deserted him in such numbers as to leave too few to live by. He came to his own, and his own received him not, and Lo! he turns unto the Gentiles.

  A word now as to the Judge's desperate assumption that the compromises of '50 had no connection with one another; that Illinois came into the Union as a slave state, and some other similar ones. This is no other than a bold denial of the history of the country. If we do not know that the Compromises of '50 were dependent on each other; if we do not know that Illinois came into the Union as a free state—we do not know any thing. If we do not know these things, we do not know that we ever had a revolutionary war, or such a chief as Washington. To deny these things is to deny our national axioms, or dogmas, at least; and it puts an end to all argument. If a man will stand up and assert, and repeat, and re-assert, that two and two do not make four, I know nothing in the power of argument that can stop him. I think I can answer the Judge so long as he sticks to the premises; but when he flies from them, I can not work an argument into the consistency of a maternal gag, and actually close his mouth with it. In such a case I can only commend him to the seventy thousand answers just in from Pennsylvania, Ohio and Indiana.[888]

Lincoln here sarcastically states that the South wants to make slavery **"the chief jewel of the nation,"** intimating that it is the foundation and bedrock, the very cornerstone, of the Confederacy.

This preposterous statement was later inadvertently buttressed by Confederate Vice President Alexander H. Stephens. Here are his exact words, uttered on March 21, 1861, during a speech at Savannah, Georgia:

> [The Confederacy's] cornerstone rests upon the great truth, that the negro is not equal to the white man; that slavery, subordination

to the superior race, is his natural and normal condition.[889]

This sentence, now one of the primary weapons in the anti-South community's arsenal, is one of the most misunderstood and intentionally misinterpreted in American history. Even Lincoln took it literally, or at least he made believe he did. So let us pause to explain it.

First, let us compare Stephens' words with those of Lincoln, delivered publicly on July 17, 1858, at Springfield, Illinois:

> My declarations upon this subject of negro slavery may be misrepresented, but cannot be misunderstood. I have said that I do not understand the Declaration [of Independence] to mean that all men were created equal in all respects. . . . Certainly the negro is not our equal in color—perhaps not in many other respects . . .[890]

A few months later, on September 18, 1858, at Charleston, Illinois, Lincoln made the following statement:

> I will say then that I am not, nor ever have been, in favor of bringing about in any way the social and political equality of the white and black races—that I am not, nor ever have been, in favor of making voters or jurors of negroes, nor of qualifying them to hold office, nor to intermarry with white people; and I will say in addition to this that there is a physical difference between the white and black races which I believe will forever forbid the two races living together on terms of social and political equality. And inasmuch as they cannot so live, while they do remain together there must be the position of superior and inferior, and I as much as any other man am in favor of having the superior position assigned to the white race.[891]

The point here is that Vice President Stephens' racism was no different than President Lincoln's. Both men were products of a 19th-Century white society that saw blacks as an **"inferior race,"** as Lincoln *always* referred to African-Americans.[892] Thus, if critics of the South wish to avoid being called hypocrites, Northerner Lincoln must be denounced just as heartily as Southerner Stephens.[893] As the "Great Emancipator" Lincoln himself said of **"nearly all white people"** living in America at the time:

> There is a natural disgust in the minds of nearly all white people, to the idea of an indiscriminate amalgamation of the white and black races . . .[894]

While the deeply held lifelong white supremacy in Lincoln's speeches is obvious for all to see, the racism displayed in Stephens' speech turns out to be far less vicious and entrenched, as a closer examination reveals.

There were indeed a few Southerners who claimed that slavery was necessary for the operation of the Confederacy, and that this was the reason the Yankee government was determined to abolish it. However, there was never a period in Southern history when more than 5 percent of Southerners owned slaves. As such, it is clear that the South did not need slavery to survive, making Stephen's claim seemingly both ludicrous and illogical. In truth, he was just repeating the words of a Yankee, Associate Justice of the U.S. Supreme Court, Henry Baldwin of Connecticut, who, 28 years earlier, in 1833, had said:

> Slavery is the Cornerstone of the [U.S.] Constitution. The foundations of the Government are laid and rest on the rights of property in slaves, and the whole structure must fall by disturbing the cornerstone.[895]

In other words, Stephens was merely pointing out the fact that "on the subject of slavery there was no essential change in the new [C.S.] Constitution from the old [the U.S. Constitution]."[896]

The reality is that the Union was no threat to Southern slavery, for not only had Lincoln promised not to interfere with it,[897] but slavery was still fully legal across the entire U.S. in 1861, the year Stephens gave his "cornerstone" speech. At the time Southern slavery was actually in more danger from the Southern abolitionist majority than the much smaller Northern abolitionist minority.

Why did some Southerners, like the Rebel vice president, make such patently absurd comments then?

Those few who declared that slavery was the "cornerstone" of the South were engaging in a clever but reckless political ploy, one used to try and agitate other Southerners in the tariff conflicts with the North.[898] There were so few slave owners in the South in the early 1860s that in an attempt to gain their support it is not surprising that the traditional political tactics of exaggeration, fear mongering, and hyperbole were sometimes employed by Confederate leaders like Stephens, just as they are still used by politicians today.

We must also consider the fact that if slavery had truly been the "cornerstone of the Confederate Constitution," not to mention the cause of the "Civil War," then the conflict would have ended with Lincoln's Final Emancipation Proclamation on January 1, 1863.[899] Instead, it dragged on for over two more bloody years, not ending until Confederate abolitionist General Robert E. Lee stacked arms at Appomattox on April 9, 1865.

Afterward, Southerner Lyon Gardiner Tyler, the son of America's tenth President, John Tyler,[900] put the matter this way:

> The emancipation of slaves [on January 1, 1863] by the late war is the best evidence that the South never fought for slavery, but *against a foreign dictation and a sectional will*. Within the Union slavery was probably secure for many years to come. The war was nothing more than the outcome of a tyranny exerted for seventy-two years by the North over vital interests of the South.[901]

In summary, it would be far more accurate to say that slavery was the cornerstone of the Union, for as we have seen, not only would New England have gone bankrupt without it,[902] it was the North's Wall Street Boys (Yankee financiers, merchants, and industrialists) who made the most money from the institution and who were thus the most interested in keeping it alive.[903]

Indeed, it was this very group, keen to put anyone into the Oval Office who would maintain the lucrative Northern slave trade and the equally lucrative business of Southern slavery, that got Lincoln elected president. For he was the only candidate who promised to do just that.[904] Later, these same backers rewarded "Honest Abe" by donating millions of dollars from their slave profits to fund his war against the South and get him reelected in 1864.[905]

In short, slavery was *not* the **"chief jewel"** of the Confederacy, nor did the South want to make it the nation's. Thus another one of Lincoln's anti-South statements goes down in smoke.

The only true thing in Lincoln's above October 16, 1854, speech at Peoria is that he detested the inequities of slavery. But all thinking people did at the time, including most Northern and Southern slave owners. So the president's feelings on this topic were nothing out of the ordinary. As we are about to see, what *was* out of the ordinary to Southerners were the reasons he wanted to stop the spread of the institution outside the South.[906]

Lincoln & Slavery

PART 2

BESIDES HIS WHITE RACIST NOTIONS and desire to live in a black-free America, there was also the issue of political power. Lincoln believed that Southern slaves artificially magnified the power and representation of the Southern states in Congress. This was due to what was called the "Three-Fifths Clause," found in Article 1, Section 2, Clause 3 of the original U.S. Constitution.[907] Concerning the control of the government, he whined in his October 16, 1854, speech at Peoria, Illinois,

> they [the South] have greatly the advantage of us. By the Constitution each State has two senators, each has a number of representatives in proportion to the number of its people, and each has a number of presidential electors equal to the whole number of its senators and representatives together. But in ascertaining the number of the people for this purpose, five slaves are counted as being equal to three whites. . . . There is no instance of exact equality; and the disadvantage is against us [Northerners] the whole chapter through. This principle, in the aggregate, gives the slave States in the present Congress twenty additional representatives, being seven more than the whole majority by which they passed the Nebraska bill.
>
> Now all this is manifestly unfair; yet I do not mention it to complain of it, in so far as it is already settled. It is in the Constitution . . .[908]

Lincoln once again here neglects to mention anything about black civil rights. Instead, he complains about the South's **"unfair"** political advantage over the North due to the Three-Fifths Clause. But what the South-hating sectional president fails to mention is that this clause was originally suggested by two Northerners: Roger Sherman of Massachusetts and James Wilson of Pennsylvania!

If the "Great Emancipator" cared so deeply about enslaved blacks, as Lincoln scholars and Northern published text books and history books have preached for generations, why then did he continually pledge his support for the Fugitive Slave Act of 1850 right up until at least 1862?[909] Under the act both the government and her citizens were obligated to return runaway slaves to their owners, with fines imposed on those who interfered.[910] On December 11, 1860, he wrote to William Kellogg, restating his stand on limiting (not abolishing) slavery and his support of the fugitive-slave clause:

> Entertain no proposition for a compromise in regard to the extension of slavery. The instant you do they have us under again: all our labor is lost, and sooner or later must be done over. [Stephen A.] **Douglas is sure to be again trying to bring in his "popular sovereignty." Have none of it. The tug has to come, and better now than later. You know I think the fugitive-slave clause of the Constitution ought to be enforced—to put it in its mildest form, ought not to be resisted.**[911]

Lincoln loved the fugitive-slave law, even promising that he would personally enforce it,[912] this despite increased public opposition to it after the publication, in 1852, of *Uncle Tom's Cabin*, a fictitious (and highly embellished) attack on slavery by Stowe[913]—a Northerner who had never seen a Southern plantation or a Southern slave.[914]

So supportive was Lincoln of the Fugitive Slave Act that he even promised to strengthen it in his First Inaugural Address on March 4, 1861.[915] What today's Lincoln apologists do not seem to realize is that if he had overturned this law, or even ignored it, he would have helped bring slavery to an end much sooner.[916] However, he stated over and over that he had no intention of doing so;[917] in fact, quite the opposite, as we just saw in his December 11, 1860, letter to Kellogg.

Two months later, on February 1, 1861, just one month before he was inaugurated, Lincoln shared his thoughts regarding both the American slave trade and the fugitive slave issue with his future secretary of state William H. Seward:

> **As to fugitive slaves, . . . slave-trade among the slave States, and whatever springs of necessity from the fact that the institution is amongst us, I care but little . . .**[918]

Lincoln's apathy toward abolition was only beginning to manifest, however. Indeed, he was about to try and fortify slavery.

Four weeks later, on February 27, 1861, the president-elect met with a Southern peace delegation in Washington, D.C. that included Charles S. Morehead and William C. Rives. In their attempt to avert war with the U.S., the Confederate envoy pleaded with Lincoln to withdraw his troops from Fort Sumter and promise the Border States that they would be safe within the Union. Lincoln replied that he would not yield on blocking the expansion of slavery into the Western Territories (as this was always his primary, and *only*, goal regarding the institution). But, he added, he would most certainly be willing to approve a constitutional amendment allowing slavery to continue indefinitely where it already existed. And he wasted no time in standing behind his promise.[919]

The proposed amendment, known as the Corwin Amendment, and which allowed slavery to continue in perpetuity (without any interference from the U.S. government), was passed by the U.S. House of Representatives the very next day (February 28, 1861), and by the U.S. Senate on March 2, 1861, two days before his presidential inauguration.[920] By this time three states had actually ratified the amendment, and certainly the rest would have as well, if given the chance. However, the act was dropped with the start of the Battle of Fort Sumter, on April 12, 1861. Had hostilities not exploded between the South and the North that spring day, what can only be called Lincoln's "proslavery amendment" would have been signed into law, and American slavery would have continued indefinitely.[921]

Thus, while Lincoln sometimes preached against slavery in public, behind closed doors he was trying to use the Constitution to make the institution "irrevocable"—permitting slavery, in fact, to persist as long as the Southern states returned to the Union, remained,[922] and paid their taxes.[923]

Two days later, in his First Inaugural Address, March 4, 1861, Lincoln reiterated his views on the subject. As he often did, he opens with an outrageous lie, in this case pretending to know nothing about the Corwin

Amendment. However, he ends by emphatically stating that he supports it:

> I understand a proposed amendment to the Constitution—which amendment, however, I have not seen—has passed Congress, to the effect that the Federal Government shall never interfere with the domestic institutions of the States, including that of persons held to service. To avoid misconstruction of what I have said, I depart from my purpose not to speak of particular amendments so far as to say that, holding such a provision to now be implied constitutional law, I have no objection to its being made express and irrevocable.[924]

In plain English Lincoln says here that he supports the idea of an amendment that would forever prohibit the U.S. government from interfering with slavery.

Lincoln certainly proved, like no one before or after him, that one can hate slavery without the slightest love for civil rights. How do we explain our sixteenth president's attitudes and behavior?

Lincoln's apathy toward civil liberties, especially regarding non-whites, was rooted in his deeply held racist beliefs, which is why, when he began to consider emancipation, it was not for the benefit of blacks. It was for the benefit of Northern whites, nearly all who, like himself, saw slavery as something that degraded whites and their culture. Whether it degraded blacks or not was another matter entirely, one that seemed to hold little concern for Lincoln, or for most other 19th-Century Yankees. As he said in a letter issued from the White House on December 14, 1863, one year *after* he issued the Final Emancipation Proclamation:

> Whom it may concern: It is my wish that Mrs. Emily T. Helm (widow of the late General B. H. [Benjamin Hardin] Helm, who fell in the Confederate service), now returning to Kentucky, may have protection of person and property, except as to slaves, of which I say nothing. A. Lincoln.[925]

There were aspects of slavery that certainly bothered Lincoln. But these were based mainly on his near complete lack of first-hand knowledge of how Southern slavery worked. An example of this ignorance can be seen in the follow "fragment" of one of his "notes for speeches" from around October 1, 1858:

The sum of pro-slavery theology seems to be this: "Slavery is not universally right, nor yet universally wrong; it is better for some people to be slaves; and, in such cases, it is the will of God that they be such."
      Certainly there is no contending against the will of God; but still there is some difficulty in ascertaining and applying it to particular cases. For instance, we will suppose the Rev. Dr. Ross has a slave named Sambo, and the question is, "Is it the will of God that Sambo shall remain a slave, or be set free?" The Almighty gives no audible answer to the question, and his revelation, the Bible, gives none—or at most none but such as admits of a squabble as to its meaning; no one thinks of asking Sambo's opinion on it. So at last it comes to this, that Dr. Ross is to decide the question; and while he considers it, he sits in the shade, with gloves on his hands, and subsists on the bread that Sambo is earning in the burning sun. If he decides that God wills Sambo to continue a slave, he thereby retains his own comfortable position; but if he decides that God wills Sambo to be free, he thereby has to walk out of the shade, throw off his gloves, and delve for his own bread. Will Dr. Ross be actuated by the perfect impartiality which has ever been considered most favorable to correct decisions?[926]

      To begin with, both God and the Bible *do* give an answer to slavery question; but Lincoln, a self-professed "infidel" and "scoffer of Christianity," would not know this since he rarely if ever cracked open the Good Book.

      The answer Holy Scripture gives is that slavery is an acceptable, even divinely sanctioned, institution. Indeed, there is not a single antislavery statement between the books of Genesis and Revelation.

      The Old Testament (or Torah) is completely silent on the evils of slavery. Instead it offers many examples of both the backhanded approval of slavery and its full sanction by God.[927] Indeed, the institution was openly practiced by the early Hebrews throughout their era, with one of the more famous of them, Joseph, shown being sold into slavery by his own brothers.[928]

      In the book of Genesis one may read of the idea that Africans bore the "mark of Cain," a people cursed by Noah to be the "servants of servants," meaning the "lowest of slaves."[929] Also known as the "curse of Ham" (actually the curse of Ham's son, Canaan, and his descendants), early Americans, like the Mormons, construed these passages to mean that

Africans had inherited the "affliction" of black skin and a life of servitude under white rule.[930]

The Old Testament authors describe the origins of the "African curse" this way:

> And Ham, the father of Canaan, saw the nakedness of his father, and told his two brethren without. And Shem and Japheth took a garment, and laid it upon both their shoulders, and went backward, and covered the nakedness of their father; and their faces were backward, and they saw not their father's nakedness. And Noah awoke from his wine, and knew what his younger son had done unto him. And he said, Cursed be Canaan; a servant of servants shall he be unto his brethren. And he said, Blessed be the LORD God of Shem; and Canaan shall be his servant. God shall enlarge Japheth, and he shall dwell in the tents of Shem; and Canaan shall be his servant.[931]

In the New Testament we find a similar situation. Both Jesus, Christianity's founder, and Saint Paul, Christianity's greatest apostle, mention servitude and slavery numerous times without ever speaking out against them.[932] In the Epistle of Philemon, for example, Paul returns a runaway (white) slave named Onesimus to his master Philemon, with no comment about the injustices or evils of slavery,[933] hardly the action of an abolitionist. Rather it is the action of a law-abiding proslavery advocate, as Paul's own words to the slaves at Colossae (located in what is now southeast Turkey) testifies:

> Servants, obey in all things your masters according to the flesh; not with eyeservice, as menpleasers; but in singleness of heart, fearing God.[934]

Paul tolerated slavery in part because of his mystical belief that merely being a Christian obliterated the social, ethnic, and even gender lines that separate people from one another. Wrote Paul:

> There is neither Jew nor Greek, there is neither bond nor free, there is neither male nor female: for ye are all one in Christ Jesus.[935]

Saint Peter agreed with Paul on the topic of slavery and even issued the same command for slaves to be obedient to their owners, again without condemnation of the institution. Wrote Peter:

> Servants, be subject to your masters with all fear; not only to the good and gentle, but also to the froward.[936]

Again, there is no unequivocal admonition against slavery anywhere in the New Testament. Jesus himself demands that one who desires to be his chief disciple should be the slave of all,[937] and later, after Jesus' resurrection, the apostles are called "slaves of the Lord."[938] In today's totalitarian environment of political correctness, how many Christians would be willing to publicly refer themselves as "slaves of the Lord"?

Why did neither Jesus or his apostles denounce slavery? Slavery was so accepted, so integral to their society, that even the very idea of abolition would have caused widespread violence, resulting in massive social disorder and financial upheaval. Abolition in this particular situation would not have agreed with the teachings of Jesus,[939] who commanded blind obedience of the laws of the land.[940]

Not surprisingly the early Christian Church allowed slavery through upholding the laws of feudalism (a type of palliated slavery). Why? Again, because the Bible makes no mention of serfdom or feudalism.[941] Since both were legal, and because of Jesus' commandment regarding civil law, the Church backed away from the entire issue.

Many of the Church Fathers went much further than this. Both Saint Gregory of Nazianzus and Saint Augustine, for instance, saw the institution as a consequence of Original Sin and the Fall of Man, while Saint Thomas Aquinas taught that slavery was a punishment from God.[942]

Obviously Lincoln did not know his Bible or his Christian history, no doubt because he spent all his time reading atheist authors like Thomas Paine and Voltaire.[943]

Lincoln was also incorrect in intimating that Southern slave owners lounged in the shade sipping Mint Juleps from gloved hands while their black chattel broke their backs in the **"burning sun."**

To begin with, the Northern image of the indolent and insolent "lords of the lash" is a complete myth. Many, if not most, slave owners worked side by side with their servants, hoeing fields, planting seeds, harvesting crops, repairing farm equipment, and nursing livestock.[944] Thus, when Lincoln' War came, it was only natural that white masters and black servants would fight side by side on the battlefield.[945] For unlike in the Old North, where segregation was "almost universal" before 1860,[946] there was literally no segregation in the Old South.[947]

Second, *all* Southern servants were protected by a myriad of laws as well as civil, social, and human rights:[948] not only could they chose their own work schedule and workload,[949] but they were also free to marry and bear children, build their own homes, plant their own gardens, own their own livestock, clothes, and furniture, and farm their own parcels of land. Indeed, a number of ex-servants reported that nearly all slaves at one time owned property, and that most loved nothing more than amassing amass wealth, property, and belongings.[950]

We have numerous records of black servants owning property, hogs, horses, cows, jewelry, buggies, and wagons, and whose personal products included corn, rice, fowl, beehives, peanuts, fodder, syrup, hay, mules, butter, sugar, tea, and sheep, among hundreds of other items. Many black servants became wealthy selling their goods, had excellent credit, and owned more land than whites living in the same area.[951]

While slaves possessed numerous rights and tremendous freedom, slave owners were subject to strict laws concerning the treatment of their servants. This is not surprising. Southerners as a whole hated unmerciful slave owners and the use of the whip was widely regarded as unneeded and indefensible.[952] Many masters themselves voluntarily and permanently banned the whip from their farms and plantations.[953]

As such, the violence, unethical treatment, and immorality portrayed between black slaves and their masters and mistresses by Lincoln, and in wildly inaccurate novels like *Uncle Tom's Cabin*, was not only rare, but was a punishable crime in the South.[954] In fact, by the early 1800s *all* Southern states had passed anti-cruelty laws that provided fines, imprisonment, and even execution for those who mistreated their servants, and more than one sadistic slaver died at the wrong end of a lawman's bullet.[955]

In some Southern states, Louisiana, for example, it was illegal to divide up slave families. But even where it was lawful, the practice was so heavily frowned upon by most Southerners that it rarely occurred.[956] Furthermore, the few restrictive laws that applied to slaves were unevenly or rarely enforced. The result? Most Southern servants lived a life of considerable freedom, personal independence, and self-reliance, one far from the nasty, brutish existence portrayed by Lincoln and South-hating writers like Harriet Beecher Stowe.[957]

Jefferson Davis told the truth, one that no anti-South proponent wants to hear, when he commented on the alleged "cruelty" of servant owners. On Southern plantations, the Confederate president affirmed, inhumane treatment "probably exists to a smaller extent than in any other relation of labor to capital" in the world.[958]

So much for Lincoln's jaundiced view of Southern slavery.

Besides his liberal drive to establish big government in Washington, Lincoln's desire to restrict slavery to the South (then emancipate slaves everywhere else and deport them out of the country) was perhaps his primary goal prior to becoming president. In fact, during his seven 1858 debates with Stephen A. Douglas, Lincoln spoke about almost nothing else. Thus the Lincoln-Douglas Debates would be more appropriately called the "Lincoln-Douglas Debates on the Restriction and Expansion of Slavery."

Even when he was not deliberating with Douglas on stage, Lincoln was thinking about it. What follows, for example, are notes Lincoln wrote out for use in possible future debates and speeches:

> [About October 1, 1858] **At Freeport I propounded four distinct interrogations to Judge Douglas, all which he assumed to answer. I say he assumed to answer them: for he did not very distinctly answer any of them.**
>
> To the first, which is in these words, "If the people of Kansas shall, by means entirely unobjectionable in all other respects, adopt a State constitution, and ask admission into the Union under it, before they have the requisite number of inhabitants according to the English bill,—some ninety-three thousand,—will you vote to admit them?" the judge did not answer "Yes" or "No," "I would" or "I would not," nor did he answer in any other such distinct way. But he did so answer that I infer he would vote for the admission of Kansas in the supposed case stated in the interrogatory—that, other objections out of the way, he would vote to admit Kansas before she had the requisite population according to the English bill. I mention this now to elicit an assurance that I correctly understood the judge on this point.
>
> To my second interrogatory, which is in these words, "Can the people of a United States Territory, in any lawful way, against the wish of any citizen of the United States, exclude slavery from their limits, prior to the formation of a State constitution?" the judge answers that they can, and he proceeds to show how they can exclude it. The how, as he gives it, is by withholding friendly legislation and adopting unfriendly legislation. As he thinks, the people still can, by doing nothing to

help slavery and by a little unfriendly leaning against it, exclude it from their limits. This is his position. This position and the Dred Scott decision are absolutely inconsistent. The judge furiously indorses the Dred Scott decision; and that decision holds that the United States Constitution guarantees to the citizens of the United States the right to hold slaves in the Territories, and that neither Congress nor a territorial legislature can destroy or abridge that right. In the teeth of this, where can the judge find room for his unfriendly legislation against their right? The members of a territorial legislature are sworn to support the Constitution of the United States. How dare they legislate unfriendlily to a right guaranteed by that Constitution? And if they should, how quickly would the courts hold their work to be unconstitutional and void? But doubtless the judge's chief reliance to sustain his proposition that the people can exclude slavery, is based upon non-action—upon withholding friendly legislation. But can members of a territorial legislature, having sworn to support the United States Constitution, conscientiously withhold necessary legislative protection to a right guaranteed by that Constitution?

Again, will not the courts, without territorial legislation, find a remedy for the evasion of a right guaranteed by the United States Constitution? It is a maxim of the courts that "there is no right without a remedy." But, as a matter of fact, non-action, both legislative and judicial, will not exclude slavery from any place. It is of record that Dred Scott and his family were held in actual slavery in Kansas without any friendly legislation or judicial assistance. It is well known that other negroes were held in actual slavery at the military post in Kansas under precisely the same circumstances. This was not only done without any friendly legislation, but in direct disregard of the congressional prohibition,—the Missouri Compromise,—then supposed to be valid, thus showing that it requires positive law to be both made and executed to keep actual slavery out of any Territory where any owner chooses to take it. Slavery having actually gone into a Territory to some extent, without local legislation in its favor, and against congressional prohibition, how much more will it go there now that by a judicial decision that congressional prohibition is swept away, and the constitutional guaranty of property declared to apply to slavery in the Territories.

But this is not all. Slavery was originally planted on this continent without the aid of friendly legislation. History proves this. After it was actually in existence to a sufficient extent to become, in some sort, a public interest, it began to receive legislative attention, but not before. How futile, then, is the proposition that the people of a Territory can exclude slavery by simply not legislating in its favor. Learned disputants use what they call the *argumentum ad hominem*—a course of argument which does not intrinsically reach the issue, but merely turns the adversary against himself. There are at least two arguments of this sort which may easily be turned against Judge Douglas's proposition that the people of a Territory can lawfully exclude slavery from their limits prior to forming a State constitution. In his report of the 12th of March, 1856, on page 28, Judge Douglas says: "The sovereignty of a Territory remains in abeyance, suspended in the United States, in trust for the people, until they shall be admitted into the Union as a State." If so,—if they have no active living sovereignty,—how can they readily enact the judge's unfriendly legislation to slavery?

But in 1856, on the floor of the Senate, Judge Trumbull asked Judge Douglas the direct question, "Can the people of a Territory exclude slavery prior to forming a State constitution?"—and Judge Douglas answered, "That is a question for the Supreme Court." I think he made the same answer to the same question more than once. But now, when the Supreme Court has decided that the people of a Territory cannot so exclude slavery, Judge Douglas shifts his ground, saying the people can exclude it, and thus virtually saying it is not a question for the Supreme Court.

I am aware Judge Douglas avoids admitting in direct terms that the Supreme Court have decided against the power of the people of a Territory to exclude slavery. He also avoids saying directly that they have not so decided; but he labors to leave the impression that he thinks they have not so decided. For instance, in his Springfield speech of July 17, 1858, Judge Douglas, speaking of me, says: "He infers that it [the court] would decide that the territorial legislatures could not prohibit slavery. I will not stop to inquire whether the courts will carry the decision that far or not." The court has already carried the decision exactly that far, and I must say I think Judge Douglas very well knows it has. After stating that Congress cannot prohibit slavery in the Territories, the court adds: "And if Congress itself cannot do this, if it be beyond the powers conferred on the Federal Government, it will be admitted, we presume, that it could not authorize a territorial government to exercise them; it could confer no power on any local government, established by its authority, to violate the provisions of the Constitution."

Can any mortal man misunderstand this language? Does not Judge Douglas equivocate when he pretends not to know that the Supreme Court has decided that the people of a Territory cannot exclude slavery prior to forming a State constitution?

My third interrogatory to the judge is in these words: "If the Supreme Court of the United States shall decide that States cannot exclude slavery from their limits, are you in favor of acquiescing in, adopting, and following such decision as a rule of political action?" To this question the judge gives no answer whatever. He disposes of it by an attempt to ridicule the idea that the Supreme Court will ever make such a decision. When Judge Douglas is drawn up to a distinct point, there is significance in all he says, and in all he omits to say. In this case he will not, on the one hand, face the people and declare he will support such decision when made, nor on the other will he trammel himself by saying he will not support it.

Now I propose to show, in the teeth of Judge Douglas's ridicule, that such a decision does logically and necessarily follow the Dred Scott decision. In that case the court holds that Congress can legislate for the Territories in some respects, and in others it cannot; that it cannot prohibit slavery in the Territories, because to do so would infringe the "right of property" guaranteed to the citizen by the fifth amendment to the Constitution, which provides that "no person shall be deprived of life, liberty, or property without due process of law." Unquestionably there is such a guaranty in the Constitution, whether or not the court rightfully apply it in this case. I propose to show, beyond the power of quibble, that that guaranty applies with all the force, if not more, to States than it does to Territories. The answers to two questions fix the whole thing: to whom is this guaranty given? and against whom does it protect those to whom it is given? The guaranty makes no distinction between persons in the States and those in the Territories; it is given to persons in the States certainly as much as, if not more than, to those in the Territories. "No person," under the shadow of the Constitution, "shall be deprived of life, liberty, or property without due process of law."

Against whom does this guaranty protect the rights of property? Not against Congress alone, but against the world—against State constitutions and laws, as well as against acts of Congress. The United States Constitution is the supreme law of the land; this guaranty of property is expressly given in that Constitution, in that supreme law; and no State constitution or law can override it. It is not a case where power over the subject is reserved to the States, because it is not expressly given to the General Government; it is a case where the guaranty is expressly given to the individual citizen, in and by the organic law of the General Government; and the duty of maintaining that guaranty is imposed upon that General Government, overriding all obstacles.

The following is the article of the Constitution containing the guaranty of property upon which the Dred Scott decision is based:

> Article V. No person shall be held to answer for a capital or otherwise infamous crime, unless on a presentment or indictment by a grand jury, except in cases arising in the land or naval forces, or in the militia when in actual service, in time of war or public danger; nor shall any person be subject for the same offense to be twice put in jeopardy of life or limb; nor shall be compelled, in any criminal case, to be a witness against himself, nor be deprived of life, liberty, or property without due process of law; nor shall private property be taken for public use without just compensation.

Suppose, now, a provision in a State constitution

should negative all the above propositions, declaring directly or substantially that "any person may be deprived of life, liberty, or property without due process of law," a direct contradiction—collision—would be pronounced between the United States Constitution and such State constitution. And can there be any doubt but that which is declared to be the supreme law would prevail over the other to the extent of the collision? Such State constitution would be unconstitutional.

There is no escape from this conclusion but in one way, and that is to deny that the Supreme Court, in the Dred Scott case, properly applies this constitutional guaranty of property. The Constitution itself impliedly admits that a person may be deprived of property by "due process of law," and the Republicans hold that if there be a law of Congress or territorial legislature telling the slaveholder in advance that he shall not bring his slave into the Territory upon pain of forfeiture, and he still will bring him, he will be deprived of his property in such slave by "due process of law." And the same would be true in the case of taking a slave into a State against a State constitution or law prohibiting slavery.[959]

Another "fragment" of Lincoln's "notes for speeches" includes the following rambling thoughts, in which he puts forth the irrational and completely unfounded notion that conservatives (at the time the Democrats) wanted to **"nationalize slavery."** They wanted to do nothing of the kind. They simply wanted people, that is, the states, to have a choice as to whether to legalize slavery and own slaves or prohibit slavery and ban the owning of slaves.

Lincoln's lies, hyperbole, and exaggeration regarding this topic were meant to sway the public to his side, in the hopes that someday slavery would be eliminated from America so that blacks themselves could one day be eliminated from America, the ultimate goal of all black colonizationists like Lincoln:

> [From about October 1, 1858] . . . When Douglas ascribes such to me, he does so, not by argument, but by mere burlesques on the art and name of argument—by such fantastic arrangements of words as prove "horse-chestnuts to be chestnut horses." In the main I shall trust an intelligent community to learn my objects and aims from what I say and do myself, rather than from

what Judge Douglas may say of me. But I must not leave the judge just yet. When he has burlesqued me into a position which I never thought of assuming myself, he will, in the most benevolent and patronizing manner imaginable, compliment me by saying "he has no doubt I am perfectly conscientious in it." I thank him for that word "conscientious." It turns my attention to the wonderful evidences of conscience he manifests. When he assumes to be the first discoverer and sole advocate of the right of a people to govern themselves, he is conscientious. When he affects to understand that a man, putting a hundred slaves through under the lash, is simply governing himself, he is more conscientious. When he affects not to know that the Dred Scott decision forbids a territorial legislature to exclude slavery, he is most conscientious. When, as in his last Springfield speech, he declares that I say, unless I shall play my batteries successfully, so as to abolish slavery in every one of the States, the Union shall be dissolved, he is absolutely bursting with conscience. It is nothing that I have never said any such thing. With some men it might make a difference; but consciences differ in different individuals. Judge Douglas has a greater conscience than most men. It corresponds with his other points of greatness. Judge Douglas amuses himself by saying I wish to go into the Senate on my qualifications as a prophet. He says he has known some other prophets, and does not think very well of them. Well, others of us have also known some prophets. We know one who nearly five years ago prophesied that the 'Nebraska bill' would put an end to slavery agitation in next to no time—one who has renewed that prophecy at least as often as quarter-yearly ever since; and still the prophecy has not been fulfilled. That one might very well go out of the Senate on his qualifications as a false prophet.

Allow me now, in my own way, to state with what aims and objects I did enter upon this campaign. I claim no extraordinary exemption from personal ambition. That I like preferment as well as the average of men may be admitted. But I protest I have not entered upon this hard contest solely, or even chiefly, for a merely personal object. I clearly see, as I think, a powerful plot to make slavery universal and perpetual in this nation. The effort to carry that plot through will be persistent and long continued, extending far beyond the senatorial term for which Judge Douglas and I are just now struggling. I enter upon the contest to contribute my humble and temporary mite in opposition to that effort.

At the Republican [i.e., liberal] State convention at Springfield I made a speech. That speech has been considered the opening of the canvass on my part. In it I arranged a string of incontestable facts which, I think, prove the existence of a conspiracy to nationalize slavery. The evidence was circumstantial only; but nevertheless it seemed inconsistent with every hypothesis, save that of the existence of such conspiracy. I believe the facts can be explained to-day on no other hypothesis. Judge Douglas can so explain them if any one can. From warp to woof his handiwork is everywhere woven in.

At New York he finds this speech of mine, and devises his plan of assault upon it. At Chicago he develops that plan. Passing over, unnoticed, the obvious purport of the whole speech, he cooks up two or three issues upon points not discussed by me at all, and then authoritatively announces that these are to be the issues of the campaign. Next evening I answer, assuring him that he misunderstands me—that he takes issues which I have not tendered. In good faith I try to set him right. If he really has misunderstood my meaning, I give him language that can no longer be misunderstood. He will have none of it. At Bloomington, six days later, he speaks again, and perverts me even worse than before. He seems to have grown confident and jubilant, in the belief that he has entirely diverted me from my purpose of fixing a conspiracy upon him and his co-workers. Next day he speaks again at Springfield, pursuing the same course, with increased confidence and recklessness of assertion. At night of that day I speak again. I tell him that as he has carefully read my speech making the charge of conspiracy, and has twice spoken of the speech without noticing the charge, upon his own tacit admission I renew the charge against him. I call him, and take a default upon him. At Clinton, ten days after, he comes in with a plea. The substance of that plea is that he never passed a word with Chief Justice Taney as to what his decision was to be in the Dred Scott case; that I ought to know that he who affirms what he does not know to be true falsifies as much as he who affirms what he does know to be false; and that he would pronounce the whole charge of conspiracy a falsehood, were it not for his own self-respect!

Now I demur to this plea. Waiving objection that it was not filed till after default, I demur to it on the merits. I say it does not meet the case. What if he did not pass a word with Chief Justice Taney? Could he not have as distinct an understanding, and play his part just as well, without directly passing a word with Taney, as with it? But suppose we construe this part of the plea more broadly than he puts it himself—suppose we construe it, as in an answer in chancery, to be a denial of all knowledge, information, or belief of such conspiracy. Still I have the right to prove the conspiracy, even against his answer; and there is much more than the evidence of two witnesses to prove it by. Grant that he has no knowledge, information, or belief of such conspiracy, and what of it? That does not disturb the facts in evidence. It only makes him the dupe, instead of a principal, of conspirators.

What if a man may not affirm a proposition without knowing it to be true? I have not affirmed that a conspiracy does exist. I have only stated the evidence, and affirmed my belief in its existence. If Judge Douglas shall assert that I do not believe what I say, then he affirms what he cannot know to be true, and falls within the condemnation of his own rule.

Would it not be much better for him to meet the evidence, and show, if he can, that I have no good reason to believe the charge? Would not this be far more satisfactory than merely vociferating an intimation that he may be provoked to call somebody a liar?

So far as I know, he denies no fact which I have alleged. Without now repeating all those facts, I recall attention to only a few of them. A provision of the Nebraska bill, penned by Judge Douglas, is in these words:

> [Lincoln quoting Douglas] **It being the true intent and meaning of this act not to legislate slavery into any Territory or State, nor exclude it therefrom, but to leave the people thereof perfectly free to form and regulate their domestic institutions in their own way, subject**

only to the Constitution of the United States.

In support of this the argument, evidently prepared in advance, went forth: "Why not let the people of a Territory have or exclude slavery, just as they choose? Have they any less sense or less patriotism when they settle in the Territories than when they lived in the States?"

Now the question occurs: Did Judge Douglas, even then, intend that the people of a Territory should have the power to exclude slavery? If he did, why did he vote against an amendment expressly declaring they might exclude it? With men who then knew and intended that a Supreme Court decision should soon follow, declaring that the people of a Territory could not exclude slavery, voting down such an amendment was perfectly rational. But with men not expecting or desiring such a decision, and really wishing the people to have such power, voting down such an amendment, to my mind, is wholly inexplicable.

That such an amendment was voted down by the friends of the bill, including Judge Douglas, is a recorded fact of the case. There was some real reason for so voting it down. What that reason was, Judge Douglas can tell. I believe that reason was to keep the way clear for a court decision, then expected to come, and which has since come, in the case of Dred Scott. If there was any other reason for voting down that amendment, Judge Douglas knows of it and can tell it? Again, in the before-quoted part of the Nebraska bill, what means the provision that the people of the "State" shall be left perfectly free, subject only to the Constitution? Congress was not therein legislating for, or about, States or the people of States. In that bill the provision about the people of "States" is the odd half of something, the other half of which was not yet quite ready for exhibition. What is that other half to be? Another Supreme Court decision, declaring that the people of a State cannot exclude slavery, is exactly fitted to be that other half. As the power of the people of the Territories and of the States is cozily set down in the Nebraska bill as being the same: so the constitutional limitations on that power will then be judicially held to be precisely the same in both Territories and States—that is, that the Constitution permits neither a Territory nor a State to exclude slavery. With persons looking forward to such additional decision, the inserting a provision about States in the Nebraska bill was perfectly rational; but to persons not looking for such decision it was a puzzle. There was a real reason for inserting such provision. Judge Douglas inserted it, and therefore knows, and can tell, what that real reason was.

Judge Douglas's present course by no means lessens my belief in the existence of a purpose to make slavery alike lawful in all the States. This can be done by a Supreme Court decision holding that the United States Constitution forbids a State to exclude slavery; and probably it can be done in no other way. The idea of forcing slavery into a free State, or out of a slave State, at the point of the bayonet, is alike nonsensical. Slavery can only become extinct by being restricted to its present limits, and dwindling out. It can only become national by a Supreme Court decision. To such a decision, when it comes, Judge Douglas is fully committed. Such a decision acquiesced in by the people effects the whole object. Bearing this in mind, look at what Judge Douglas is doing every day. For the first sixty-five years under the United States Constitution, the practice of government had been to exclude slavery from the new free Territories. About the end of that period Congress, by the Nebraska bill, resolved to abandon this practice; and this was rapidly succeeded by a Supreme Court decision holding the practice to have always been unconstitutional. Some of us refuse to obey this decision as a political rule. Forthwith Judge Douglas espouses the decision, and denounces all opposition to it in no measured terms. He adheres to it with extraordinary tenacity; and under rather extraordinary circumstances. He espouses it not on any opinion of his that it is right within itself. On this he forbears to commit himself. He espouses it exclusively on the ground of its binding authority on all citizens—a ground which commits him as fully to the next decision as to this. I point out to him that Mr. [Thomas] Jefferson and General [Andrew] Jackson were both against him on the binding political authority of Supreme Court decisions. No response. I might as well preach Christianity to a grizzly bear as to preach Jefferson and Jackson to him.

I tell him I have often heard him denounce the

Supreme Court decision in favor of a national bank. He denies the accuracy of my recollection—which seems strange to me, but I let it pass.

I remind him that he, even now, indorses the Cincinnati platform, which declares that Congress has no constitutional power to charter a bank; and that in the teeth of a Supreme Court decision that Congress has such power. This he cannot deny; and so he remembers to forget it.

I remind him of a piece of Illinois history about Supreme Court decisions—of a time when the Supreme Court of Illinois, consisting of four judges, because of one decision made, and one expected to be made, were overwhelmed by the adding of five new judges to their number; that he, Judge Douglas, took a leading part in that onslaught, ending in his sitting down on the bench as one of the five added judges. I suggest to him that as to his questions how far judges have to be catechized in advance, when appointed under such circumstances, and how far a court, so constituted, is prostituted beneath the contempt of all men, no man is better posted to answer than he, having once been entirely through the mill himself.

Still no response, except "Hurrah for the Dred Scott decision!" These things warrant me in saying that Judge Douglas adheres to the Dred Scott decision under rather extraordinary circumstances—circumstances suggesting the question, "Why does he adhere to it so pertinaciously? Why does he thus belie his whole past life? Why, with a long record more marked for hostility to judicial decisions than almost any living man, does he cling to this with a devotion that nothing can baffle?" In this age, and this country, public sentiment is everything. With it, nothing can fail; against it, nothing can succeed. Whoever molds public sentiment goes deeper than he who enacts statutes or pronounces judicial decisions. He makes possible the enforcement of them, else impossible.

Judge Douglas is a man of large influence. His bare opinion goes far to fix the opinions of others. Besides this, thousands hang their hopes upon forcing their opinions to agree with his. It is a party necessity with them to say they agree with him, and there is danger they will repeat the saying till they really come to believe it. Others dread, and shrink from, his denunciations, his sarcasms, and his ingenious misrepresentations. The susceptible young hear lessons from him, such as their fathers never heard when they were young.

If, by all these means, he shall succeed in molding public sentiment to a perfect accordance with his own; in bringing all men to indorse all court decisions, without caring to know whether they are right or wrong; in bringing all tongues to as perfect a silence as his own, as to there being any wrong in slavery; in bringing all to declare, with him, that they care not whether slavery be voted down or voted up; that if any people want slaves they have a right to have them; that negroes are not men; have no part in the Declaration of Independence; that there is no moral question about slavery; that liberty and slavery are perfectly consistent—indeed, necessary accompaniments; that for a strong man to declare himself the superior of a weak one, and thereupon enslave the weak one, is the very essence of liberty, the most sacred right of self-government; when, I say, public sentiment shall be brought to all this, in the name of Heaven what barrier will be left against slavery being made lawful everywhere? Can you find one word of his opposed to it? Can you not find many strongly favoring it? If for his life, for his eternal salvation, he was solely striving for that end, could he find any means so well adapted to reach the end?

If our presidential election, by a mere plurality, and of doubtful significance, brought one Supreme Court decision that no power can exclude slavery from a Territory, how much more shall a public sentiment, in exact accordance with the sentiments of Judge Douglas, bring another that no power can exclude it from a State?

And then, the negro being doomed, and damned, and forgotten, to everlasting bondage, is the white man quite certain that the tyrant demon will not turn upon him too.[960]

Lincoln was evidently quite busy around the beginning of October 1858, formulating ideas for speeches to help convince the masses that slavery ought to be restricted to the South, then extinguished so that blacks could then legally be thrown out of the country. To do this, however, states' rights would have to be squashed, particularly in Dixie, one of the future dictator's most cherished dreams.

Because his opponents, the Democrats (conservatives), were for states' rights, liberal Lincoln had to convince the public that the Federal (central) government's power trumped that of the individual states, one of the most anti-constitutional, *and* un-constitutional, concepts ever put forth by an American politician. Why? Because it contravenes the all-important Ninth and Tenth Amendments, wherein the powers of the individual states and the Federal government are established.

Here from the same period is another "fragment" of thoughts for his future addresses, outlining some of Lincoln's politically blasphemous notions:

> [Around October 1, 1858] **From time to time, ever since the Chicago "Times" and "Illinois State Register" declared their opposition to the Lecompton constitution, and it began to be understood that Judge Douglas was also opposed to it, I have been accosted by friends of his with the question, "What do you think now?" Since the delivery of his speech in the Senate, the question has been varied a little. "Have you read Douglas's speech?" "Yes." "Well, what do you think of it?" In every instance the question is accompanied with an anxious inquiring stare, which asks, quite as plainly as words could, "Can't you go for Douglas now?" Like boys who have set a bird-trap, they are watching to see if the birds are picking at the bait and likely to go under.**
>
> **I think, then, Judge Douglas knows that the Republicans** [liberals] **wish Kansas to be a free State** [i.e., to have no choice in whether to permit slavery or not]**. He knows that they know, if the question be fairly submitted to a vote of the people of Kansas, it will be a free State; and he would not object at all if, by drawing their attention to this particular fact, and himself becoming vociferous for such fair vote, they should be induced to drop their own organization fall into rank behind him, and form a great free-State Democratic party.**
>
> **But before Republicans do this, I think they ought to require a few questions to be answered on the other side. If they so fall in with Judge Douglas, and Kansas shall be secured as a free State, there then remaining no cause of difference between him and the regular Democracy, will not the Republicans stand ready, haltered and harnessed, to be handed over by him to the regular Democracy, to filibuster indefinitely for additional slave territory,—to carry slavery into all the**

States, as well as Territories, under the Dred Scott decision, construed and enlarged from time to time, according to the demands of the regular slave Democracy,—and to assist in reviving the African slave-trade in order that all may buy negroes where they can be bought cheapest, as a clear incident of that "sacred right of property," now held in some quarters to be above all constitutions?

By so falling in, will we not be committed to or at least compromitted with, the Nebraska policy? If so, we should remember that Kansas is saved, not by that policy or its authors, but in spite of both—by an effort that cannot be kept up in future cases.

Did Judge Douglas help any to get a free-State majority into Kansas? Not a bit of it—the exact contrary. Does he now express any wish that Kansas, or any other place, shall be free? Nothing like it. He tells us, in this very speech, expected to be so palatable to Republicans, that he cares not whether slavery is voted down or voted up. His whole effort is devoted to clearing the ring; and giving slavery and freedom a fair fight. With one who considers slavery just as good as freedom, this is perfectly natural and consistent. But have Republicans any sympathy with such a view? They think slavery is wrong; and that, like every other wrong which some men will commit if left alone, it ought to be prohibited by law. They consider it not only morally wrong, but a "deadly poison" in a government like ours, professedly based on the equality of men. Upon this radical difference of opinion with Judge Douglas, the Republican party was organized. There is all the difference between him and them now that there ever was. He will not say that he has changed; have you?

Again, we ought to be informed as to Judge Douglas's present opinion as to the inclination of Republicans to marry with negroes. By his Springfield speech we know what it was last June; and by his resolution dropped at Jacksonville in September we know what it was then. Perhaps we have something even later in a Chicago speech, in which the danger of being "stunk out of church" was descanted upon. But what is his opinion on the point now? There is, or will be, a sure sign to judge by. If this charge shall be silently dropped by the judge and his friends, if no more resolutions on the subject shall be passed in Douglas Democratic meetings and conventions, it will be safe to swear that he is courting. Our "witching smile" has "caught his youthful fancy"; and henceforth Cuffy and he are rival beaux for our gushing affections.

We also ought to insist on knowing what the judge now thinks on "Sectionalism." Last year he thought it was a "clincher" against us on the question of Sectionalism, that we could get no support in the slave States, and could not be allowed to speak, or even breathe, south of the Ohio River. In vain did we appeal to the justice of our principles. He would have it that the treatment we received was conclusive evidence that we deserved it. He and his friends would bring speakers from the slave States to their meetings and conventions in the free States, and parade about, arm in arm with them, breathing in every gesture and tone, "How we national apples do swim!" Let him cast about for this particular evidence of his own nationality now. Why, just now, he and [John C.] Fremont would make the closest race imaginable in the Southern States.

In the present aspect of affairs what ought the Republicans to do? I think they ought not to oppose any measure merely because Judge Douglas proposes it. Whether the Lecompton constitution should be accepted or rejected is a question upon which, in the minds of men not committed to any of its antecedents, and controlled only by the Federal Constitution, by republican principles, and by a sound morality, it seems to me there could not be two opinions. It should be throttled and killed as hastily and as heartily as a rabid dog. What those should do who are committed to all its antecedents is their business, not ours. If, therefore, Judge Douglas's bill secures a fair vote to the people of Kansas, without contrivance to commit any one farther, I think Republican members of Congress ought to support it. They can do so without any inconsistency. They believe Congress ought to prohibit slavery wherever it can be done without violation of the Constitution or of good faith. And having seen the noses counted, and actually knowing that a majority of the people of Kansas are against slavery, passing an act to secure them a fair vote is little else than prohibiting slavery in Kansas by act of Congress.

Congress cannot dictate a constitution to a new State. All it can do at that point is to secure the people a fair chance to form one for themselves, and then to accept or reject it when they ask admission into the Union. As I understand, Republicans claim no more than this. But they do claim that Congress can and ought to keep slavery out of a Territory, up to the time of its people forming a State constitution; and they should now be careful to not stultify themselves to any extent on that point.

I am glad Judge Douglas has, at last, distinctly told us that he cares not whether slavery be voted down or voted up. Not so much that this is any news to me; nor yet that it may be slightly new to some of that class of his friends who delight to say that they "are as much opposed to slavery as anybody." I am glad because it affords such a true and excellent definition of the Nebraska policy itself. That policy, honestly administered, is exactly that. It seeks to bring the people of the nation to not care anything about slavery. This is Nebraskaism in its abstract purity—in its very best dress.

Now, I take it, nearly everybody does care something about slavery—is either for it or against it; and that the statesmanship of a measure which conforms to the sentiments of nobody might well be doubted in advance.

But Nebraskaism did not originate as a piece of statesmanship. General [Lewis] Cass, in 1848, invented it, as a political manoeuver, to secure himself the Democratic nomination for the presidency. It served its purpose then, and sunk out of sight. Six years later Judge Douglas fished it up, and glozed it over with what he called, and still persists in calling, "sacred rights of self-government."

Well, I, too, believe in self-government as I understand it; but I do not understand that the privilege one man takes of making a slave of another, or holding him as such, is any part of "self-government." To call it so is, to my mind, simply absurd and ridiculous. I am for the people of the whole nation doing just as they please in all matters which concern the whole nation; for those of each part doing just as they choose in all matters which concern no other part; and for each individual doing just as he chooses in all matters which concern nobody else. This is the principle. Of course I am content with any exception which the Constitution, or the actually existing state of things, makes a necessity.

But neither the principle nor the exception will admit the indefinite spread and perpetuity of human slavery.

I think the true magnitude of the slavery element in this nation is scarcely appreciated by any one. Four years ago the Nebraska policy was adopted, professedly, to drive the agitation of the subject into the Territories, and out of every other place, and especially out of Congress.

When Mr. [James] Buchanan accepted the presidential nomination, he felicitated himself with the belief that the whole thing would be quieted and forgotten in about six weeks. In his inaugural, and in his [Benjamin Douglas] Silliman letter, at their respective dates, he was just not quite in reach of the same happy consummation. And now, in his first annual message, he urges the acceptance of the Lecompton constitution (not quite satisfactory to him) on the sole ground of getting this little unimportant matter out of the way.

Meanwhile, in those four years, there has really been more angry agitation of this subject, both in and out of Congress, than ever before. And just now it is perplexing the mighty ones as no subject ever did before. Nor is it confined to politics alone. Presbyterian assemblies, Methodist conferences, Unitarian gatherings, and single churches to an indefinite extent, are wrangling, and cracking, and going to pieces on the same question. Why, Kansas is neither the whole nor a tithe of the real question.

A house divided against itself cannot stand.

I believe the government cannot endure permanently half slave and half free. I expressed this belief a year ago; and subsequent developments have but confirmed me. I do not expect the Union to be dissolved. I do not expect the house to fall; but I do expect it will cease to be divided. It will become all one thing or all the other. Either the opponents of slavery will arrest the further spread of it, and put it in course of ultimate extinction; or its advocates will push it forward till it shall become alike lawful in all the States, old as well as new. Do you doubt it? Study the Dred Scott decision, and then see how little even now remains to be done. That decision may be reduced to three points. The first is that a negro cannot be a citizen. That point is made in order to deprive the negro, in every possible event, of the benefit of that provision of the United States Constitution which declares that "the citizens of each State shall be entitled to all privileges and immunities of citizens in the several States."

The second point is that the United States Constitution protects slavery, as property, in all the United States territories, and that neither Congress, nor the people of the Territories, nor any other power, can prohibit it at any time prior to the formation of State constitutions.

This point is made in order that the Territories may safely be filled up with slaves, before the formation of State constitutions, thereby to embarrass the free-State sentiment, and enhance the chances of slave constitutions being adopted.

The third point decided is that the voluntary bringing of Dred Scott into Illinois by his master, and holding him here a long time as a slave, did not operate his emancipation—did not make him free.

This point is made, not to be pressed immediately; but if acquiesced in for a while, then to sustain the logical conclusion that what Dred Scott's master might lawfully do with Dred in the free State of Illinois, every other master may lawfully do with any other one or one hundred slaves in llinois? or in any other free State. Auxiliary to all this, and working hand in hand with it, the Nebraska doctrine is to educate and mold public opinion to "not care whether slavery is voted up or voted down." At least Northern public opinion must cease to care anything about it. Southern public opinion may, without offense, continue to care as much as it pleases.

Welcome or unwelcome, agreeable or disagreeable, whether this shall be an entire slave nation is the issue before us. Every incident—every little shifting of scenes or of actors—only clears away the intervening trash, compacts and consolidates the opposing hosts, and brings them more and more distinctly face to face. The conflict will be a severe one; and it will be fought through by those who do care for the result, and not by those who do not care—by those who are for, and those who are against, a legalized national slavery. The combined charge of Nebraskaism and Dred-Scottism must be repulsed and rolled back.

> The deceitful cloak of "self-government," wherewith "the sum of all villanies" seeks to protect and adorn itself, must be torn from its hateful carcass. That burlesque upon judicial decisions, and slander and profanation upon the honored names and sacred history of republican America, must be overruled and expunged from the books of authority.
> To give the victory to the right, not bloody bullets, but peaceful ballots only are necessary. Thanks to our good old Constitution, and organization under it, these alone are necessary. It only needs that every right thinking man shall go to the polls, and without fear or prejudice vote as he thinks.[961]

Clothing himself as an abolitionist when, by his own repeated admission, he clearly was not,[962] shows the depths to which Lincoln was willing to stoop to accomplish his racist colonization plan, as we will explore more fully in Chapter 12.

To better understand liberal Lincoln's unconstitutional and highly divisive sectional opinions, let us now look at him from the conservative viewpoint of the day. This was embodied in Lincoln's political opponent during the 1858 Illinois senate race, Stephen A. Douglas. What follows are Douglas' opening remarks at the pair's fifth debate on October 7, 1858, at Galesburg, Illinois:

> Ladies and Gentlemen: Four years ago I appeared before the people of Knox County for the purpose of defending my political action upon the compromise measures of 1850 and the passage of the Kansas-Nebraska bill. Those of you before me who were present then will remember that I vindicated myself for supporting those two measures by the fact that they rested upon the great fundamental principle that the people of each State and each Territory of this Union have the right, and ought to be permitted to exercise the right, of regulating their own domestic concerns in their own way, subject to no other limitation or restriction than that which the Constitution of the United States imposes upon them. I then called upon the people of Illinois to decide whether that principle of self-government was right or wrong. If it was and is right, then the compromise measures of 1850 were right, and, consequently, the Kansas and Nebraska bill, based upon the same principle, must necessarily have been right.
> The Kansas and Nebraska bill declared, in so many words, that it was the true intent and meaning of the act not to

legislate slavery into any State or Territory, nor to exclude it therefrom, but to leave the people thereof perfectly free to form and regulate their domestic institutions in their own way, subject only to the Constitution of the United States. For the last four years I have devoted all my energies, in private and public, to commend that principle to the American people. Whatever else may be said in condemnation or support of my political course, I apprehend that no honest man will doubt the fidelity with which under all circumstances I have stood by it.

During the last year a question arose in the Congress of the United States whether or not that principle would be violated by the admission of Kansas into the Union under the Lecompton constitution. In my opinion, the attempt to force Kansas in under that constitution was a gross violation of the principle enunciated in the compromise measures of 1850, and the Kansas and Nebraska bill of 1854, and therefore I led off in the fight against the Lecompton constitution, and conducted it until the effort to carry that constitution through Congress was abandoned. And I can appeal to all men, friends and foes, Democrats and Republicans, Northern men and Southern men, that during the whole of that fight I carried the banner of popular sovereignty [essentially the idea of states' right] aloft, and never allowed it to trail in the dust, or lowered my flag until victory perched upon our arms. When the Lecompton constitution was defeated, the question arose in the minds of those who had advocated it what they should next, resort to in order to carry out their views. They devised a measure known as the English bill, and granted a general amnesty and political pardon to all men who had fought against the Lecompton constitution, provided they would support that bill. I for one did not choose to accept the pardon, or to avail myself of the amnesty granted on that condition. The fact that the supporters of Lecompton were willing to forgive all differences of opinion at that time, in the event those who opposed it favored the English bill, was an admission that they did not think that opposition to Lecompton impaired a man's standing in the Democratic [i.e., conservative] party. Now the question arises: What was that English bill which certain men are now attempting to make a test of political orthodoxy in this country? It provided, in substance, that the Lecompton constitution should be sent back to the people of Kansas for their adoption or rejection, at an election which was held in August last, and in case they refused admission under it, that Kansas should be kept out of the Union until she had 93,420 inhabitants.

I was in favor of sending the constitution back in order to enable the people to say whether or not it was their act and deed, and embodied their will; but the other proposition, that if they refused to come into the Union under it, they should be kept out until they had double or treble the population they then had, I never would sanction by my vote. The reason why I could not sanction it is to be found in the fact that by the English bill, if the people of Kansas had only agreed to become a slaveholding State under the Lecompton constitution, they could have done so with 35,000 people, but if they insisted on being a free State, as they had a right to do, then they were to be punished by being kept out of the Union until they had nearly three times that population. I then said in my place in the Senate, as I now say to you, that whenever Kansas has population enough for a slave State she has population enough for a free State. I have never yet given a vote, and I never intend to record one, making an odious and unjust distinction between the different States of this Union. I hold it to be a fundamental principle in our republican form of government that all the States of this Union, old and new, free and slave, stand on an exact equality. Equality among the different States is a cardinal principle on which all our institutions rest. Wherever, therefore, you make a discrimination, saying to a slave State that it shall be admitted with 35,000 inhabitants, and to a free State that it shall not be admitted until it has 93,000 or 100,000 inhabitants, you are throwing the whole weight of the Federal Government into the scale in favor of one class of States against the other. Nor would I on the other hand any sooner sanction the doctrine that a free State could be admitted into the Union with 35,000 people, while a slave State was kept out until it had 93,000. I have always declared in the Senate my willingness, and I am willing now, to adopt the rule that no Territory shall ever become a State until it has the requisite population for a member of Congress, according to the then existing ratio. But while I have always been, and am now, willing to adopt that general rule, I was not willing and would not consent to make an exception of Kansas, as a punishment for her obstinacy in demanding the right to do as she pleased in the formation of her constitution. It is proper that I should remark here that my opposition to the Lecompton constitution did not rest upon the peculiar position taken by Kansas on the subject of slavery. I held then, and hold now, that if the people of Kansas want a slave State, it is their right to make one and be received into the Union under it; if, on the contrary, they want a free State, it is their right to have it, and no man should ever oppose their admission because they ask it under the one or the other. I hold to that great principle of self-government which asserts the right of every people to decide for themselves the nature and character of the domestic institutions and fundamental law under which they are to live.

The effort has been, and is now being, made in this State by certain postmasters and other federal office-holders, to make a test of faith on the support of the English bill. These men are now making speeches all over the State against me and in favor of Lincoln, either directly or indirectly, because I would not sanction a discrimination between slave and free States by voting for the English bill. But while that bill is made a test in Illinois for the purpose of breaking up the Democratic organization in this State, how is it in the other States? Go to Indiana, and there you find that [William Hayden] English himself, the author of the English bill, who is a candidate for reelection to Congress, has been forced by public opinion to abandon his own darling project, and to give a promise that he will vote for the admission of Kansas at once, whenever she forms a constitution in pursuance of law, and ratifies it by a majority vote of her people. Not only is this the case with English himself, but I am informed that every Democratic candidate for Congress in Indiana takes the same ground. Pass to Ohio, and there you find that [William Slocum] Groesbeck, and [George Hunt] Pendleton, and [Samuel Sullivan] Cox, and all the other anti-Lecompton men who stood shoulder to shoulder with me against the Lecompton constitution, but voted for the English bill, now repudiate it and take the same ground that I do on that question. So it is with the Joneses and others of Pennsylvania, and so it is with every other Lecompton Democrat in the free States.

They now abandon even the English bill, and come back to the true platform which I proclaimed at the time in the Senate, and upon which the Democracy of Illinois now stand. And yet, notwithstanding the fact that every Lecompton and anti-Lecompton Democrat in the free States has abandoned the English bill, you are told that it is to be made a test upon me, while the power and patronage of the government are all exerted to elect men to Congress in the other States who occupy the same position with reference to it that I do. It seems that my political offense consists in the fact that I did not first vote for the English bill, and thus pledge myself to keep Kansas out of the Union until she has a population of 93,420, and then return home, violate that pledge, repudiate the bill, and take the opposite ground. If I had done this, perhaps the administration would now be advocating my reelection, as it is that of the others who have pursued this course. I did not choose to give that pledge, for the reason that I did not intend to carry out that principle. I never will consent, for the sake of conciliating the frowns of power, to pledge myself to do that which I do not intend to perform. I now submit the question to you, as my constituency, whether I was not right—first, in resisting the adoption of the Lecompton constitution; and secondly, in resisting the English bill. I repeat that I opposed the Lecompton constitution because it was not the act and deed of the people of Kansas, and did not embody their will. I denied the right of any power on earth, under our system of government, to force a constitution on an unwilling people. There was a time when some men could pretend to believe that the Lecompton constitution embodied the will of the people of Kansas, but that time has passed. The question was referred to the people of Kansas under the English bill last August, and then, at a fair election, they rejected the Lecompton constitution by a vote of from eight to ten against it to one in its favor. Since it has been voted down by so overwhelming a majority, no man can pretend that it was the act and deed of that people. I submit the question to you, whether or not, if it had not been for me, that constitution would have been crammed down the throats of the people of Kansas against their consent. While at least ninety-nine out of every hundred people here present agree that I was right in defeating that project, yet my enemies use the fact that I did defeat it by doing right, to break me down and put another man in the United States Senate in my place. The very men who acknowledge that I was right in defeating Lecompton now form an alliance with federal office-holders, professed Lecompton men, to defeat me because I did right.

My political opponent, Mr. Lincoln, has no hope on earth, and has never dreamed that he had a chance of success, were it not for the aid that he is receiving from federal office-holders, who are using their influence and the patronage of the government against me in revenge for my having defeated the Lecompton constitution. What do you Republicans [liberals] think of a political organization that will try to make an unholy and unnatural combination with its professed foes to beat a man merely because he has done right? You know such is the fact with regard to your own party. You know that the ax of decapitation is suspended over every man in office in Illinois, and the terror of proscription is threatened every Democrat [conservative] by the present administration, unless he supports the Republican ticket in preference to my Democratic associates and myself. I could find an instance in the postmaster of the city of Galesburg, and in every other postmaster in this vicinity, all of whom have been stricken down simply because they discharged the duties of their offices honestly, and supported the regular Democratic ticket in this State in the right. The Republican party is availing itself of every unworthy means in the present contest to carry the election, because its leaders know that if they let this chance slip they will never have another, and their hopes of making this a Republican State will be blasted forever.

Now, let me ask you whether the country has any interest in sustaining this organization known as the Republican party. That party is unlike all other political organizations in this country. All other parties have been national in their character—have avowed their principles alike in the slave and free States, in Kentucky as well as Illinois, in Louisiana as well as in Massachusetts. Such was the case with the Old Whig party, and such was and is the case with the Democratic party. Whigs and Democrats could proclaim their principles boldly and fearlessly in the North and in the South, in the East and in the West, wherever the Constitution ruled and the American flag waved over American soil.

But now you have a sectional organization, a party which appeals to the Northern section of the Union against the Southern, a party which appeals to Northern passion, Northern pride, Northern ambition, and Northern prejudices, against Southern people, the Southern States, and Southern institutions. The leaders of that party hope that they will be able to unite the Northern States in one great sectional party, and inasmuch as the North is the stronger section, that they will thus be enabled to outvote, conquer, govern, and control the South. Hence you find that they now make speeches advocating principles and measures which cannot be defended in any slave-holding State of this Union. Is there a Republican residing in Galesburg who can travel into Kentucky, and carry his principles with him across the Ohio? What Republican from Massachusetts can visit the Old Dominion [Virginia] without leaving his principles behind him when he crosses Mason's and Dixon's line? Permit me to say to you in perfect good humor, but in all sincerity, that no political creed is sound which cannot be proclaimed fearlessly in every State of this Union where the Federal Constitution is the supreme law of the land. Not only is this Republican party unable to proclaim its principles alike in the North and in the South, in the free States and in the slave States, but it cannot even proclaim them in the same forms and give them the same strength and meaning in all parts of the same State. My friend Lincoln finds it extremely difficult to manage a debate in the central part of the State, where there is a mixture of men from the North and the South. In the extreme northern part of Illinois he can proclaim as bold and radical Abolitionism as ever [Joshua R.] Giddings, [Elijah P.] Lovejoy, or [William Lloyd] Garrison enunciated; but when he gets down a little further south he claims that he is an old-line Whig, a disciple of Henry Clay, and declares that he still adheres to the old-line Whig creed, and has nothing whatever to do with Abolitionism, or negro equality, or negro citizenship. I once before hinted this of

Mr. Lincoln in a public speech, and at Charleston he defied me to show that there was any difference between his speeches in the north and in the south, and that they were not in strict harmony. I will now call your attention to two of them, and you can then say whether you would be apt to believe that the same man ever uttered both. In a speech in reply to me at Chicago in July last, Mr. Lincoln, in speaking of the equality of the negro with the white man, used the following language:

> [Douglas quoting Lincoln] **I should like to know if, taking this old Declaration of Independence, which declares that all men are equal upon principle, and making exceptions to it, where will it stop? If one man says it does not mean a negro, why may not another man say it does not mean another man? If the Declaration is not the truth, let us get the statute-book in which we find it and tear it out. Who is so bold as to do it? If it is not true, let us tear it out.**

You find that Mr. Lincoln there proposed that if the doctrine of the Declaration of Independence, declaring all men to be born equal, did not include the negro and put him on an equality with the white man, that we should take the statute-book and tear it out. He there took the ground that the negro race is included in the Declaration of Independence as the equal of the white race, and that there could be no such thing as a distinction in the races, making one superior and the other inferior. I read now from the same speech:

> **My friends** [he says], **I have detained you about as long as I desire to do, and I have only to say let us discard all this quibbling about this man and the other man—this race and that race and the other race being inferior, and therefore they must be placed in an inferior position, discarding our standard that we have left us. Let us discard all these things, and unite as one people throughout this land, until we shall once more stand up declaring that all men are created equal.**

[Audience: "That's right," etc.]

  Yes, I have no doubt that you think it is right, but the Lincoln men down in Coles, Tazewell, and Sangamon counties do not think it is right. In the conclusion of the same speech, talking to the Chicago Abolitionists, he said: **"I leave you, hoping that the lamp of liberty will burn in your bosoms until there shall no longer be a doubt that all men are created free and equal."** [Audience: "Good, good!"] Well, you say good to that, and you are going to vote for Lincoln because he holds that doctrine. I will not blame you for supporting him on that ground, but I will show you, in immediate contrast with that doctrine, what Mr. Lincoln said down in Egypt [Illinois] in order to get votes in that locality where they do not hold to such a doctrine. In a joint discussion between Mr. Lincoln and myself, at Charleston, I think, on the 18th of last month, Mr. Lincoln, referring to this subject, used the following language:

> **I will say, then, that I am not nor ever have been in favor of bringing about in any way the social and political equality of the white and black races; that I am not nor ever have been in favor of making voters of the free negroes, or jurors, or qualifying them to hold office, or having them to marry with white people. I will say in addition, that there is a physical difference between the white and black races, which, I suppose, will forever forbid the two races living together upon terms of social and political equality, and inasmuch as they cannot so live, that while they do remain together, there must be the position of superior and inferior, that I as much as any other man am in favor of the superior position being assigned to the white man.**

[Audience: "Good for Lincoln!"]

  Fellow-citizens, here you find men hurrahing for Lincoln, and saying that he did right when in one part of the State he stood up for negro equality, and in another part, for political effect, discarded the doctrine, and declared that there always must be a superior and inferior race. Abolitionists up north are expected and required to vote for Lincoln because he goes for the equality of the races, holding that by the Declaration of Independence the white man and the negro were created equal, and endowed by the divine law with that equality, and down south he tells the Old Whigs, the Kentuckians, Virginians, and Tennesseeans that there is a physical difference in the races, making one superior and the other inferior, and that he is in favor of maintaining the superiority of the white race over the negro.

Now, how can you reconcile those two positions of Mr. Lincoln? He is to be voted for in the south as a pro-slavery man, and he is to be voted for in the north as an Abolitionist. Up here he thinks it is all nonsense to talk about a difference between the races, and says that we must **"discard all quibbling about this race and that race and the other race being inferior, and therefore they must be placed in an inferior position."** Down south he makes this "quibble" about this race and that race and the other race being inferior as the creed of his party, and declares that the negro can never be elevated to the position of the white man. You find that his political meetings are called by different names in different counties in the State. Here they are called Republican meetings, but in old Tazewell, where Lincoln made a speech last Tuesday, he did not address a Republican meeting, but "a grand rally of the Lincoln men." There are very few Republicans there, because Tazewell County is filled with old Virginians and Kentuckians, all of whom are Whigs or Democrats, and if Mr. Lincoln had called an Abolition or Republican meeting there, he would not get many votes. Go down into Egypt, and you will find that he and his party are operating under an alias there, which his friend [Lyman] Trumbull has given them, in order that they may cheat the people. When I was down in Monroe County a few weeks ago addressing the people, I saw handbills posted announcing that Mr. Trumbull was going to speak in behalf of Lincoln, and what do you think the name of his party was there? Why, the "Free Democracy." Mr. Trumbull and Mr. Jehu Baker were announced to address the Free Democracy of Monroe County, and the bill was signed "Many Free Democrats." The reason that Mr. Lincoln and his party adopted the name of "Free Democracy" down there was because Monroe County has always been an old-fashioned Democratic [conservative] county, and hence it was necessary to make the people believe that they were Democrats, sympathized with them, and were fighting for Lincoln as Democrats. Come up to Springfield, where Lincoln now lives and always has lived, and you find that the convention of his party which assembled to nominate candidates for the legislature, who are expected to vote for him if elected, dare not adopt the name of Republican [liberal], but assembled under the title of "All opposed to the Democracy." Thus you find that Mr. Lincoln's creed cannot travel through even one half of the counties of this State, but that it changes its hues, and becomes lighter and lighter as it travels from the extreme north, until it is nearly white when it reaches the extreme south end of the State. I ask you, my friends, why cannot Republicans avow their principles alike everywhere? I would despise myself if I thought that I was procuring your votes by concealing my opinions, and by avowing one set of principles in one part of the State, and a different set in another part.

If I do not truly and honorably represent your feelings and principles, then I ought not to be your senator; and I will never conceal my opinions, or modify or change them a hair's-breadth, in order to get votes. I tell you that this Chicago doctrine of Lincoln's—declaring that the negro and the white man are made equal by the Declaration of Independence and by Divine Providence—is a monstrous heresy. The signers of the Declaration of Independence never dreamed of the negro when they were writing that document. They referred to white men, to men of European birth and European descent, when they declared the equality of all men. I see a gentleman there in the crowd shaking his head. Let me remind him that when Thomas Jefferson wrote that document he was the owner, and so continued until his death, of a large number of slaves. Did he intend to say in that Declaration that his negro slaves, which he held and treated as property, were created his equals by divine law, and that he was violating the law of God every day of his life by holding them as slaves? It must be borne in mind that when that Declaration was put forth, every one of the thirteen colonies were slaveholding colonies, and every man who signed that instrument represented a slaveholding constituency. Recollect, also, that no one of them emancipated his slaves, much less put them on an equality with himself, after he signed the Declaration. On the contrary, they all continued to hold their negroes as slaves during the Revolutionary War. Now, do you believe—are you willing to have it said—that every man who signed the Declaration of Independence declared the negro his equal and then was hypocrite enough to continue to hold him as a slave, in violation of what he believed to be the divine law? And yet when you say that the Declaration of Independence includes the negro, you charge the signers of it with hypocrisy.

I say to you frankly, that in my opinion this government was made by our fathers on the white basis. It was made by white men for the benefit of white men and their posterity forever, and was intended to be administered by white men in all time to come. But while I hold that under our Constitution and political system the negro is not a citizen, cannot be a citizen, and ought not to be a citizen, it does not follow by any means that he should be a slave. On the contrary, it does follow that the negro as an inferior race ought to possess every right, every privilege, every immunity which he can safely exercise consistent with the safety of the society in which he lives. Humanity requires, and Christianity commands, that you shall extend to every inferior being, and every dependent being, all the privileges, immunities, and advantages which can be granted to them consistent with the safety of society. If you ask me the nature and extent of these privileges, I answer that that is a question which the people of each State must decide for themselves. Illinois has decided that question for herself. We have said that in this State the negro shall not be a slave, nor shall he be a citizen. Kentucky holds a different doctrine. New York holds one different from either, and Maine one different from all. Virginia, in her policy on this question, differs in many respects from the others, and so on, until there are hardly two States whose policy is exactly alike in regard to the relation of the white man and the negro. Nor can you reconcile them and make them alike. Each State must do as it pleases. Illinois had as much right to adopt the policy which we have on that subject as Kentucky had to adopt a different policy. The great principle of this government is that each State has the right to do as it pleases on all these questions, and no other State or power on earth has the right to interfere with us, or complain of us merely because our system differs from theirs. In the compromise measures of 1850, Mr. Clay declared that this great principle ought to exist in the Territories as well as in the States, and I reasserted his doctrine in the Kansas and Nebraska bill in 1854.

  But Mr. Lincoln cannot be made to understand, and those who are determined to vote for him, no matter whether he is a proslavery man in the south and a negro-equality advocate in the north, cannot be made to understand, how it is that in a Territory the people can do as they please on the slavery question under the Dred Scott decision. Let us see whether I cannot explain it to the satisfaction of all impartial men. Chief Justice [Roger B.] Taney has said, in his opinion in the Dred Scott case, that a negro slave, being property, stands on an equal footing with other property, and that the owner may carry them into United States territory the same as he does other property. Suppose any two of you neighbors shall conclude to go to Kansas, one carrying $100,000 worth of negro slaves and the other $100,000 worth of mixed merchandise, including quantities of liquors. You both agree that under that decision you may carry your property to Kansas, but when you get it there, the merchant who is possessed of the liquors is met by the Maine liquor law, which prohibits the sale or use of his property, and the owner of the slaves is met by equally unfriendly legislation, which makes his property worthless after he gets it there. What is the right to carry your property into the Territory worth to either, when unfriendly legislation in the Territory renders it worthless after you get it there? The slaveholder, when he gets his slaves there, finds that there is no local law to protect him in holding them, no slave code, no police regulation maintaining and supporting him in his right, and he discovers at once that the absence of such friendly legislation excludes his property from the Territory just as irresistibly as if there was a positive constitutional prohibition excluding it.

Thus you find it is with any kind of property in a Territory; it depends for its protection on the local and municipal law. If the people of a Territory want slavery, they make friendly legislation to introduce it, but if they do not want it, they withhold all protection from it, and then it cannot exist there. Such was the view taken on the subject by different Southern men when the Nebraska bill passed. See the speech of Mr. [James Lawrence] Orr, of South Carolina, the present Speaker of the House of Representatives of Congress, made at that time, and there you will find this whole doctrine argued out at full length. Read the speeches of other Southern congressmen, senators, and representatives, made in 1854, and you will find that they took the same view of the subject as Mr. Orr—that slavery could never be forced on a people who did not want it. I hold that in this country there is no power on the face of the globe that can force any institution on an unwilling people. The great fundamental principle of our government is that the people of each State and each Territory shall be left perfectly free to decide for themselves what shall be the nature and character of their institutions. When this government was made, it was based on that principle. At the time of its formation there were twelve slaveholding States, and one free State, in this Union. Suppose this doctrine of Mr. Lincoln and the Republicans, of uniformity of laws of all the States on the subject of slavery, had prevailed; suppose Mr. Lincoln himself had been a member of the convention which framed the Constitution, and that he had risen in that August body, and, addressing the Father of his Country, had said as he did at Springfield:

> A house divided against itself cannot stand. I believe this government cannot endure permanently half slave

and half free. I do not expect the Union to be dissolved—I do not expect the house to fall, but I do expect it will cease to be divided. It will become all one thing, or all the other.

What do you think would have been the result? Suppose he had made that convention believe that doctrine, and they had acted upon it, what do you think would have been the result? Do you believe that one free State would have outvoted the twelve slaveholding States, and thus abolished slavery? On the contrary, would not the twelve slaveholding States have outvoted the one free State, and under his doctrine have fastened slavery by an irrevocable constitutional provision upon every inch of the American republic? Thus you see that the doctrine he now advocates, if proclaimed at the beginning of the government, would have established slavery everywhere throughout the American continent; and are you willing, now that we have the majority section, to exercise a power which we never would have submitted to when we were in the minority? If the Southern States had attempted to control our institutions, and make the States all slave when they had the power, I ask would you have submitted to it? If you would not, are you willing, now that we have become the strongest under that great principle of self-government that allows each State to do as it pleases, to attempt to control the Southern institutions? Then, my friends, I say to you that there is but one path of peace in this republic; and that is to administer this government as our fathers made it, divided into free and slave States, allowing each State to decide for itself whether it wants slavery or not. If Illinois will settle the slavery question for herself, and mind her own business and let her neighbors alone, we will be at peace with Kentucky, and every other Southern State. If every other State in the Union will do the same, there will be peace between the North and South, and in the whole Union.[963]

Douglas does an excellent job of exposing one of Lincoln's most diabolical traits: his demagogic hypocrisy and public pandering, which allowed him to pose as whatever kind of candidate his audience wanted, without the slightest bit of guilt or embarrassment. Or as Douglas puts it, Lincoln, ever the political chameleon, could simultaneously pretend to be a "proslavery man in the south and a negro-equality advocate in the north."

Here is liberal Lincoln's reply to conservative Douglas' speech at their fifth debate on October 7, 1858, at Galesburg, Illinois:

My Fellow-citizens: A very large portion of the speech which Judge Douglas has addressed to you has previously been delivered and put in print. I do not mean that for a hit upon the judge at all. If I had not been interrupted, I was going to say that such an answer as I was able to make to a very large portion of it, had already been more than once made and published. There has been an opportunity afforded to the public to see our respective views upon the topics discussed in a large portion of the speech which he has just delivered. I make these remarks for the purpose of excusing myself for not passing over the entire ground that the judge has traversed. I, however, desire to take up some of the points that he has attended to, and ask your attention to them, and I shall follow him backward upon some notes which I have taken, reversing the order by beginning where he concluded.

The judge has alluded to the Declaration of Independence, and insisted that negroes are not included in that Declaration; and that it is, a slander upon the framers of that instrument to suppose that negroes were meant therein; and he asks you: Is it possible to believe that Mr. [Thomas] Jefferson, who penned the immortal paper, could have supposed himself applying the language of that instrument to the negro race, and yet held a portion of that race in slavery? Would he not at once have freed them? I only have to remark upon this part of the judge's speech (and that, too, very briefly, for I shall not detain myself, or you, upon that point for any great length of time), that I believe the entire records of the world, from the date of the Declaration of Independence up to within three years ago, may be searched in vain for one single affirmation, from one single man, that the negro was not included in the Declaration of Independence; I think I may defy Judge Douglas to show that he ever said so, that [George] Washington ever said so, that any president ever said so, that any member of Congress ever said so, or that any living man upon the whole earth ever said so, until the necessities of the present policy of the Democratic party, in regard to slavery, had to invent that affirmation. And I will remind Judge Douglas and this audience that while Mr. Jefferson was the owner of slaves, as undoubtedly he was, in speaking upon this very subject, he used the strong language that "he trembled for his country when he remembered that God was just"; and I will offer the highest premium in my power to Judge Douglas if he will show that he, in all his life, ever uttered a sentiment at all akin to that of Jefferson.

The next thing to which I will ask your attention is the judge's comments upon the fact, as he assumes it to be, that we cannot call our public meetings as Republican meetings; and he instances Tazewell County as one of the places where the friends of Lincoln have called a public meeting and have not dared to name it a Republican meeting. He instances Monroe County as another where Judge Trumbull and Jehu Baker addressed the persons whom the judge assumes to be the friends of Lincoln, calling them the "Free Democracy." I have the honor to inform Judge Douglas that he spoke in that very county of Tazewell last Saturday, and I was there on Tuesday last, and when he spoke there he spoke under a call not venturing to use the word "Democrat." [Turning to Judge Douglas.] What think you of this?

So, again, there is another thing to which I would ask the judge's attention upon this subject. In the contest of 1856 his party delighted to call themselves together as the "National Democracy," but now, if there should be a notice put up anywhere for a meeting of the "National Democracy," Judge Douglas and his friends would not come. They would not suppose themselves invited. They would understand that it was a call for those hateful postmasters whom he talks about.

Now a few words in regard to these extracts from speeches of mine which Judge Douglas has read to you, and which he supposes are in very great contrast to each other. Those speeches have been before the public for a considerable time, and if they have any inconsistency in them, if there is any conflict in them, the public have been able to detect it. When the judge says, in speaking on this subject, that I make speeches of one sort for the people of the northern end of the State, and of a different sort for the southern people, he assumes that I do not understand that my speeches will be put in print and read north and south. I knew all the while that the speech that I made at Chicago and the one I made at Jonesboro and the one at Charleston would all be put in print, and all the reading and intelligent men in the community would see them and know all about my opinions; and I have not supposed, and do not now suppose, that there is any conflict whatever between them. But the judge will have it that if we do not confess that there is a sort of inequality between the white and black races which justifies us in making them slaves, we must, then, insist that there is a degree of equality that requires us to make them our wives. Now, I have all the while taken a broad distinction in regard to that matter; and that is all there is in these different speeches which he arrays here, and the entire reading of either of the speeches will show that that distinction was made. Perhaps by taking two parts of the same speech he could have got up as much of a conflict as the one he has found. I have all the while maintained that in so far as it should be insisted that there was an equality between the white and black races that should produce a perfect social and political equality, it was an impossibility. This you have seen in my printed speeches, and with it I have said that in their right to "life, liberty, and the pursuit of happiness," as proclaimed in that old Declaration, the inferior races are our equals. And these declarations I have constantly made in reference to the abstract moral question, to contemplate and consider when we are legislating about any new country which is not already cursed with the actual presence of the evil—slavery. I have never manifested any impatience with the necessities that spring from the actual presence of black people amongst us, and the actual existence of slavery amongst us where it does already exist; but I have insisted that, in legislating for new countries where it does not exist, there is no just rule other than that of moral and abstract right. With reference to those new countries, those maxims as to the right of a people to "life, liberty, and the pursuit of happiness" were the just rules to be constantly referred to. There is no misunderstanding this, except by men interested to misunderstand it. I take it that I have to address an intelligent and reading community who will peruse what I say, weigh it, and then judge whether I advance improper or unsound views, or whether I advance hypocritical and deceptive and contrary views in different portions of the country. I believe myself to be guilty of no such thing as the latter, though, of course, I cannot claim that I am entirely free from all error in the opinions I advance.

The judge has also detained us awhile in regard

to the distinction between his party and our party. His he assumes to be a national [conservative] party—ours a sectional [liberal] one. He does this in asking the question whether this country has any interest in the maintenance of the Republican party? He assumes that our party is altogether sectional—that the party to which he adheres is national; and the argument is that no party can be a rightful party—can be based upon rightful principles—unless it can announce its principles everywhere. I presume that Judge Douglas could not go into Russia and announce the doctrine of our national Democracy; he could not denounce the doctrine of kings and emperors and monarchies in Russia; and it may be true of this country, that in some places we may not be able to proclaim a doctrine as clearly true as the truth of Democracy, because there is a section so directly opposed to it that they will not tolerate us in doing so. Is it the true test of the soundness of a doctrine, that in some places people won't let you proclaim it? Is that the way to test the truth of any doctrine? Why, I understand that at one time the people of Chicago would not let Judge Douglas preach a certain favorite doctrine of his. I commend to his consideration the question, whether he takes that as a test of the unsoundness of what he wanted to preach.

There is another thing to which I wish to ask attention for a little while on this occasion. What has always been the evidence brought forward to prove that the Republican party is a sectional party? The main one was that in the Southern portion of the Union the people did not let the Republicans proclaim their doctrines amongst them. That has been the main evidence brought forward—that they had no supporters, or substantially none, in the slave States. The South have not taken hold of our principles as we announce them; nor does Judge Douglas now grapple with those principles. We have a Republican State platform, laid down in Springfield in June last, stating our position all the way through the questions before the country. We are now far advanced in this canvass. Judge Douglas and I have made perhaps forty speeches apiece, and we have now for the fifth time met face to face in debate, and up to this day I have not found either Judge Douglas or any friend of his taking hold of the Republican platform or laying his finger upon anything in it that is wrong. I ask you all to recollect that. Judge Douglas turns away from the platform of principles to the fact that he can find people somewhere who will not allow us to announce those principles. If he had great confidence that our principles were wrong, he would take hold of them and demonstrate them to be wrong. But he does not do so. The only evidence he has of their being wrong is in the fact that there are people who won't allow us to preach them. I ask again is that the way to test the soundness of a doctrine?

I ask his attention also to the fact that by the rule of nationality he is himself fast becoming sectional. I ask his attention to the fact that his speeches would not go as current now south of the Ohio River as they have formerly gone there. I ask his attention to the fact that he felicitates himself to-day that all the Democrats of the free States are agreeing with him, while he omits to tell us that the Democrats of any slave State agree with him. If he has not thought of this, I commend to his consideration the evidence in his own declaration, on this day, of his becoming sectional too. I see it rapidly approaching. Whatever may be the result of this ephemeral contest between Judge Douglas and myself, I see the day rapidly approaching when his pill of sectionalism, which he has been thrusting down the throats of Republicans for years past, will be crowded down his own throat.

Now in regard to what Judge Douglas said (in the beginning of his speech) about the compromise of 1850 containing the principle of the Nebraska bill; although I have often presented my views upon that subject, yet as I have not done so in this canvass, I will, if you please, detain you a little with them. I have always maintained so far as I was able that there was nothing of the principle of the Nebraska bill in the compromise of 1850 at all—nothing whatever. Where can you find the principle of the Nebraska bill in that compromise? If anywhere, in the two pieces of the compromise organizing the Territories of New Mexico and Utah. It was expressly provided in these two acts that, when they came to be admitted into the Union, they should be admitted with or without slavery, as they should choose, by their own constitutions. Nothing was said in either of those acts as to what was to be done in relation to slavery during the territorial existence of those Territories, while Henry Clay constantly made the declaration (Judge

Douglas recognizing him as a leader) that, in his opinion, the old Mexican laws would control that question during the territorial existence, and that these old Mexican laws excluded slavery. How can that be used as a principle for declaring that during the territorial existence, as well as at the time of framing the constitution, the people, if you please, might have slaves if they wanted them? I am not discussing the question whether it is right or wrong; but how are the New Mexican and Utah laws patterns for the Nebraska bill? I maintain that the organization of Utah and New Mexico did not establish a general principle at all. It had no feature establishing a general principle. The acts to which I have referred were a part of a general system of compromises. They did not lay down what was proposed as a regular policy for the Territories; only an agreement in this particular case to do in that way, because other things were done that were to be a compensation for it. They were allowed to come in in that shape, because in another way it was paid for—considering that as a part of that system of measures called the compromise of 1850, which finally included half a dozen acts. It included the admission of California as a free State, which was kept out of the Union for half a year because it had formed a free constitution. It included the settlement of the boundary of Texas, which had been undefined before, which was in itself a slavery question; for if you pushed the line further west, you made Texas larger, and made more slave Territory; while if you drew the line toward the east, you narrowed the boundary and diminished the domain of slavery, and by so much increased free Territory. It included the abolition of the slave-trade in the District of Columbia. It included the passage of a new fugitive-slave law. All these things were put together, and though passed in separate acts, were nevertheless in legislation (as the speeches at the time will show) made to depend upon each other. Each got votes, with the understanding that the other measures were to pass, and by this system of compromise, in that series of measures, those two bills—the New Mexico and Utah bills—were passed; and I say for that reason they could not be taken as models, framed upon their own intrinsic principle, for all future Territories. And I have the evidence of this in the fact that Judge Douglas, a year afterward, or more than a year afterward perhaps, when he first introduced bills for the purpose of framing new Territories, did not attempt to follow these bills of New Mexico and Utah; and even when he introduced this Nebraska bill, I think you will discover that he did not exactly follow them. But I do not wish to dwell at great length upon this branch of the discussion. My own opinion is that a thorough investigation will show most plainly that the New Mexico and Utah bills were part of a system of compromise, and not designed as patterns for future territorial legislation, and that this Nebraska bill did not follow them as a pattern at all.

The judge tells us, in proceeding, that he is opposed to making any odious distinctions between free and slave States. I am altogether unaware that the Republicans are in favor of making any odious distinctions between the free and slave States. But there still is a difference, I think, between Judge Douglas and the Republicans in this. I suppose that the real difference between Judge Douglas and his friends and the Republicans, on the contrary, is that the judge is not in favor of making any difference between slavery and liberty—that he is in favor of eradicating, of pressing out of view, the questions of preference in this country for free or slave institutions; and consequently every sentiment he utters discards the idea that there is any wrong in slavery. Everything that emanates from him or his coadjutors in their course of policy carefully excludes the thought that there is anything wrong in slavery. All their arguments, if you will consider them, will be seen to exclude the thought that there is anything whatever wrong in slavery. If you will take the judge's speeches, and select the short and pointed sentences expressed by him,—as his declaration that he "don't care whether slavery is voted up or down,"—you will see at once that this is perfectly logical, if you do not admit that slavery is wrong. If you do admit that it is wrong, Judge Douglas cannot logically say he don't care whether a wrong is voted up or voted down. Judge Douglas declares that if any community wants slavery they have a right to have it. He can say that logically, if he says that there is no wrong in slavery; but if you admit that there is a wrong in it, he cannot logically say that anybody has a right to do wrong. He insists that, upon the score of equality, the owners of slaves and owners of property—of horses and every other sort of property—should be alike, and hold them alike in a new Territory. That is perfectly logical, if the two species of property are alike, and are equally founded in right. But if you admit that one of them is wrong, you cannot institute any equality between right and wrong. And from this difference of sentiment—the belief on the part of one that the institution is wrong, and a policy springing from that belief which looks to the arrest of the enlargement of that wrong; and this other sentiment, that it is not wrong, and a policy sprung from that sentiment which will tolerate no idea of preventing that wrong from growing larger, and looks to there never being an end of it through all the existence of things—arises the real difference between Judge Douglas and his friends on the one hand, and the Republicans on the other. Now, I confess myself as belonging to that class in the country who contemplate slavery as a moral, social, and political evil, having due regard for its actual existence amongst us, and the difficulties of getting rid of it in any satisfactory way, and to all the constitutional obligations which have been thrown about it; but who, nevertheless, desire a policy that looks to the prevention of it as a wrong, and looks hopefully to the time when as a wrong it may come to an end.

Judge Douglas has again, for, I believe, the fifth time, if not the seventh, in my presence, reiterated his charge of a conspiracy or combination between the National Democrats and Republicans. What evidence Judge Douglas has upon this subject I know not, inasmuch as he never favors us with any. I have said upon a former occasion, and I do not choose to suppress it now, that I have no objection to the division in the judge's party. He got it up himself. It was all his and their work. He had, I think, a great deal more to do with the steps that led to the Lecompton constitution than Mr. Buchanan had; though at last, when they reached it, they quarreled over it, and their friends divided upon it. I am very free to confess to Judge Douglas that I have no objection to the division; but I defy the judge to show any evidence that I have in any way promoted that division, unless he insists on being a witness himself in merely saying so. I can give all fair friends of Judge Douglas here to understand exactly the view that Republicans take in regard to that division. Don't you remember how two years ago the opponents of the Democratic party were divided between [John C.]

Fremont and [Millard] Fillmore? I guess you do. Any Democrat who remembers that division will remember also that he was at the time very glad of it, and then he will be able to see all there is between the National Democrats and the Republicans. What we now think of the two divisions of Democrats, you then thought of the Fremont and Fillmore divisions. That is all there is of it.

But if the judge continues to put forward the declaration that there is an unholy, unnatural alliance between the Republicans and the National Democrats, I now want to enter my protest against receiving him as an entirely competent witness upon that subject. I want to call to the judge's attention an attack he made upon me in the first one of these debates, at Ottawa, on the 21st of August. In order to fix extreme Abolitionism upon me, Judge Douglas read a set of resolutions which he declared had been passed by a Republican State convention, in October, 1854, at Springfield, Illinois, and he declared I had taken part in that convention. It turned out that although a few men calling themselves an anti-Nebraska State convention had sat at Springfield about that time, yet neither did I take any part in it, nor did it pass the resolutions or any such resolutions as Judge Douglas read. So apparent had it become that the resolutions which he read had not been passed at Springfield at all, nor by any State convention in which I had taken part, that seven days afterward, at Freeport, Judge Douglas declared that he had been misled by Charles H. Lanphier, editor of the "State Register," and Thomas L. Harris, member of Congress in that district, and he promised in that speech that when he went to Springfield he would investigate the matter. Since then Judge Douglas has been to Springfield, and I presume has made the investigation; but a month has passed since he has been there, and so far as I know, he has made no report of the result of his investigation. I have waited as I think a sufficient time for the report of that investigation, and I have some curiosity to see and hear it. A fraud, an absolute forgery, was committed, and the perpetration of it was traced to the three—Lanphier, Harris, and Douglas. Whether it can be narrowed in any way, so as to exonerate any one of them, is what Judge Douglas's report would probably show.

It is true that the set of resolutions read by Judge Douglas were published in the Illinois "State Register" on the 16th of October, 1854, as being the resolutions of an anti-Nebraska convention which had sat in that same month of October, at Springfield. But it is also true that the publication in the "Register" was a forgery then, and the question is still behind, which of the three, if not all of them, committed that forgery? The idea that it was done by mistake is absurd. The article in the Illinois "State Register" contains part of the real proceedings of that Springfield convention, showing that the writer of the article had the real proceedings before him, and purposely threw out the genuine resolutions passed by the convention, and fraudulently substituted the others. Lanphier then, as now, was the editor of the "Register," so that there seems to be but little room for his escape. But then it is to be borne in mind that Lanphier had less interest in the object of that forgery than either of the other two. The main object of that forgery at that time was to beat [Richard] Yates and elect [Thomas Langrell] Harris to Congress, and that object was known to be exceedingly dear to Judge Douglas at that time. Harris and Douglas were both in Springfield when the convention was in session, and although they both left before the fraud appeared in the "Register," subsequent events show that they have both had their eyes fixed upon that convention.

The fraud having been apparently successful upon that occasion, both Harris and Douglas have more than once since then been attempting to put it to new uses. As the fisherman's wife, whose drowned husband was brought home with his body full of eels, said when she was asked what was to be done with him, "Take the eels out and set him again," so Harris and Douglas have shown a disposition to take the eels out of that stale fraud by which they gained Harris's election, and set the fraud again more than once. On the 9th of July, 1856, Douglas attempted a repetition of it upon [Lyman] Trumbull on the floor of the Senate of the United States, as will appear from the appendix to the "Congressional Globe" of that date. On the 9th of August, Harris attempted it again upon [Jesse Olds] Norton in the House of Representatives, as will appear by the same document—the appendix to the "Congressional Globe" of that date. On the 21st of August last, all three—Lanphier, Douglas, and Harris—reattempted it upon me at Ottawa [Illinois]. It has been clung to and played out again and again as an exceedingly high trump by this blessed trio. And now that it has been discovered publicly to be a fraud, we find that Judge Douglas manifests no surprise at it at all. He makes no complaint of Lanphier, who must have known it to be a fraud from the beginning. He, Lanphier, and Harris are just as cozy now, and just as active in the concoction of new schemes as they were before the general discovery of this fraud. Now all this is very natural if they are all alike guilty in that fraud, and it is very unnatural if any one of them is innocent. Lanphier perhaps insists that the rule of honor among thieves does not quite require him to take all upon himself, and consequently my friend Judge Douglas finds it difficult to make a satisfactory report upon his investigation. But meanwhile the three are agreed that each is "a most honorable man."

Judge Douglas requires an indorsement of his truth and honor by a reelection to the United States Senate, and he makes and reports against me and against Judge Trumbull, day after day, charges which we know to be utterly untrue, without for a moment seeming to think that this one unexplained fraud, which he promised to investigate, will be the least drawback to his claim to belief. Harris ditto. He asks a reelection to the lower House of Congress without seeming to remember at all that he is involved in this dishonorable fraud! The Illinois "State Register," edited by Lanphier, then, as now, the central organ of both Harris and Douglas, continues to din the public ear with these assertions without seeming to suspect that they are at all lacking in title to belief.

After all, the question still recurs upon us, how did that fraud originally get into the "State Register"? Lanphier then, as now, was the editor of that paper. Lanphier knows. Lanphier cannot be ignorant of how and by whom it was originally concocted. Can he be induced to tell, or if he has told, can Judge Douglas be induced to tell how it originally was concocted? It may be true that Lanphier insists that the two men for whose benefit it was originally devised shall at least bear their share of it! How that is, I do not know, and while it remains unexplained, I hope to be pardoned if I insist that the mere fact of Judge Douglas making charges against Trumbull and myself is not quite sufficient evidence to establish them!

While we were at Freeport, in one of these joint discussions, I answered certain interrogatories which Judge Douglas had propounded to me, and there in turn propounded some to him, which he in a sort of way answered. The third one of these interrogatories I have with me, and wish now to make some comments upon it. It was in these words: "If the Supreme Court of the United States shall decide that States cannot exclude slavery from their limits; are you in favor of acquiescing in, adopting, and following such decision as a rule of political action?"

To this interrogatory Judge Douglas made no answer in any just sense of the word. He contented himself with sneering at the thought that it was possible for the Supreme Court ever to make such a decision. He sneered at me for propounding the interrogatory. I had not propounded it without some reflection, and I wish now to address to this audience some remarks upon it.

In the second clause of the sixth article, I believe it is, of the Constitution of the United States, we find the following language: "This Constitution and the laws of the United States which shall be made in pursuance thereof, and all treaties made, or which shall be made, under the authority of the United States, shall be the supreme law of the land; and the judges in every State shall be bound thereby, anything in the constitution or laws of any State to the contrary notwithstanding."

The essence of the Dred Scott case is compressed into the sentence which I will now read: "Now, as we have already said in an earlier part of this opinion, upon a different point, the right of property in a slave is distinctly and expressly affirmed in the Constitution." I repeat it, "the right of property in a slave is distinctly and expressly affirmed in the Constitution"! What is it to be "affirmed" in the Constitution? Made firm in the Constitution—so made that it cannot be separated from the Constitution without breaking the Constitution—durable as the Constitution, and part of the Constitution? Now, remembering the provision of the Constitution which I have read, affirming that that instrument is the supreme law of the land; that the judges of every State shall be bound by it, any law or constitution of any State to the contrary notwithstanding; that the right of property in a slave is affirmed in that Constitution, is made, formed into, and cannot be separated from it without breaking it; durable as the instrument, part of the instrument,—what follows as a short and even syllogistic argument from it? I think it follows, and I submit to the consideration of men capable of arguing, whether as I state it, in syllogistic form, the argument has any fault in it?

Nothing in the constitution or laws of any State can destroy a right distinctly and expressly affirmed in the Constitution of the United States.

The right of property in a slave is distinctly and expressly affirmed in the Constitution of the United States.

Therefore, nothing in the constitution or laws of any State can destroy the right of property in a slave.

I believe that no fault can be pointed out in that argument; assuming the truth of the premises, the conclusion, so far as I have capacity at all to understand it, follows inevitably. There is a fault in it, as I think, but the fault is not in the reasoning; the falsehood, in fact, is a fault in the premises. I believe that the right of property in a slave is not distinctly and expressly affirmed in the Constitution, and Judge Douglas thinks it is. I believe that the Supreme Court and the advocates of that decision may search in vain for the place in the Constitution where the right of property in a slave is distinctly and expressly affirmed. I say, therefore, that I think one of the premises is not true in fact. But it is true with Judge Douglas. It is true with the Supreme Court who pronounced it. They are estopped from denying it, and being estopped from denying it, the conclusion follows that the Constitution of the United States, being the supreme law, no constitution or law can interfere with it. It being affirmed in the decision that the right of property in a slave is distinctly and expressly affirmed in the Constitution, the conclusion inevitably follows that no State law or constitution can destroy that right. I then say to Judge Douglas, and to all others, that I think it will take a better answer than a sneer to show that those who have said that the right of property in a slave is distinctly and expressly affirmed in the Constitution are not prepared to show that no constitution or law can destroy that right. I say I believe it will take a far better argument than a mere sneer to show to the minds of intelligent men that whoever has so said is not prepared, whenever public sentiment is so far advanced as to justify it, to say the other.

This is but an opinion, and the opinion of one very humble man; but it is my opinion that the Dred Scott decision, as it is, never would have been made in its present form if the party that made it had not been sustained previously by the elections. My own opinion is that the new Dred Scott decision, deciding against the right of the people of the States to exclude slavery, will never be made if that party is not sustained by the elections. I believe, further, that it is just as sure to be made as to-morrow is to come, if that party shall be sustained. I have said upon a former occasion, and I repeat it now, that the course of argument that Judge Douglas makes use of upon this subject (I charge not his motives in this) is preparing the public mind for that new Dred Scott decision. I have asked him again to point out to me the reasons for his first adherence to the Dred Scott decision as it is. I have turned his attention to the fact that General [Andrew] Jackson differed with him in regard to the political obligation of a Supreme Court decision. I have asked his attention to the fact that [Thomas] Jefferson differed with him in regard to the political obligation of a Supreme Court decision. Jefferson said that "judges are as honest as other men, and not more so." And he said, substantially, that whenever a free people should give up in absolute submission to any department of government, retaining for themselves no appeal from it, their liberties were gone. I have asked his attention to the fact that the Cincinnati platform, upon which he says he stands, disregards a time-honored decision of the Supreme Court, in defying the power of Congress to establish a national bank. I have asked his attention to the fact that he himself was one of the most active instruments at one time in breaking down the Supreme Court of the State of Illinois, because it had made a decision distasteful to him—a struggle ending in the remarkable circumstance of his sitting down as one of the new judges who were to overslaugh that decision, getting his title of judge in that very way.

So far in this controversy I can get no answer at all from Judge Douglas upon these subjects. Not one can I get from him, except that he swells himself up and says: "All of us who stand by the decision of the Supreme Court are the friends of the Constitution; all you fellows that dare question it in any way are the enemies of the

Constitution." Now in this very devoted adherence to this decision, in opposition to all the great political leaders whom he has recognized as leaders—in opposition to his former self and history, there is something very marked. And the manner in which he adheres to it—not as being right upon the merits, as he conceives (because he did not discuss that at all), but as being absolutely obligatory upon every one simply because of the source from whence it comes—as that which no man can gainsay, whatever it may be—this is another marked feature of his adherence to that decision. It marks it in this respect, that it commits him to the next decision, whenever it comes, as being as obligatory as this one, since he does not investigate it, and won't inquire whether this opinion is right or wrong. So he takes the next one without inquiring whether it is right or wrong. He teaches men this doctrine, and in so doing prepares the public mind to take the next decision when it comes without any inquiry. In this I think I argue fairly (without questioning motives at all) that Judge Douglas is most ingeniously and powerfully preparing the public mind to take that decision when it comes; and not only so, but he is doing it in various other ways. In these general maxims about liberty—in his assertions that he "don't care whether slavery is voted up or voted down"; that "whoever wants slavery has a right to have it"; that "upon principles of equality it should be allowed to go everywhere"; and that "there is no inconsistency between free and slave institutions"—in this he is also preparing (whether purposely or not) the way for making the institution of slavery national. I repeat again, for I wish no misunderstanding, that I do not charge that he means it so; but I call upon your minds to inquire, if you were going to get the best instrument you could, and then set it to work in the most ingenious way, to prepare the public mind for this movement, operating in the free States, where there is now an abhorrence of the institution of slavery, could you find an instrument so capable of doing it as Judge Douglas, or one employed in so apt a way to do it?

I have said once before, and I will repeat it now, that Mr. Clay, when he was once answering an objection to the Colonization Society, that it had a tendency to the ultimate emancipation of the slaves, said that "those who would repress all tendencies to liberty and ultimate emancipation must do more than put down the benevolent efforts of the Colonization Society—they must go back to the era of our liberty and independence, and muzzle the cannon that thunders its annual joyous return—they must blot out the moral lights around us—they must penetrate the human soul, and eradicate the light of reason and the love of liberty"! And I do think—I repeat, though I said it on a former occasion—that Judge Douglas, and whoever, like him, teaches that the negro has no share, humble though it may be, in the Declaration of Independence, is going back to the era of our liberty and independence, and, so far as in him lies, muzzling the cannon that thunders its annual joyous return; that he is blowing out the moral lights around us, when he contends that whoever wants slaves has a right to hold them; that he is penetrating, so far as lies in his power, the human soul, and eradicating the light of reason and the love of liberty, when he is in every possible way preparing the public mind, by his vast influence, for making the institution of slavery perpetual and national.

There is, my friends, only one other point to which I will call your attention for the remaining time that I have left me, and perhaps I shall not occupy the entire time that I have, as that one point may not take me clear through it.

Among the interrogatories that Judge Douglas propounded to me at Freeport, there was one in about this language: "Are you opposed to the acquisition of any further territory to the United States, unless slavery shall first be prohibited therein?" I answered as I thought, in this way, that I am not generally opposed to the acquisition of additional territory, and that I would support a proposition for the acquisition of additional territory, according as my supporting it was or was not calculated to aggravate this slavery question amongst us. I then proposed to Judge Douglas another interrogatory, which was correlative to that: "Are you in favor of acquiring additional territory in disregard of how it may affect us upon the slavery question?" Judge Douglas answered—that is, in his own way he answered it. I believe that, although he took a good many words to answer it, it was little more fully answered than any other. The substance of his answer was that this country would continue to expand—that it would need additional territory—that it was as absurd to suppose that we could continue upon our present territory, enlarging in population as we are, as it would be to hoop a boy twelve years of age, and expect him to grow to man's size without bursting the hoops. I believe it was something like that. Consequently he was in favor of the acquisition of further territory, as fast as we might need it, in disregard of how it might affect the slavery question. I do not say this as giving his exact language, but he said so substantially, and he would leave the question of slavery where the territory was acquired, to be settled by the people of the acquired territory. [Audience member: "That's the doctrine."] **Maybe it is; let us consider that for a while.** This will probably, in the run of things, become one of the concrete manifestations of this slavery question. If Judge Douglas's policy upon this question succeeds and gets fairly settled down until all opposition is crushed out, the next thing will be a grab for the territory of poor Mexico, an invasion of the rich lands of South America, then the adjoining islands will follow, each one of which promises additional slave-fields. And this question is to be left to the people of those countries for settlement. When we shall get Mexico, I don't know whether the judge will be in favor of the Mexican people that we get with it settling that question for themselves and all others; because we know the judge has a great horror for mongrels, and I understand that the people of Mexico are most decidedly a race of mongrels. I understand that there is not more than one person there out of eight who is a pure white, and I suppose from the judge's previous declaration that when we get Mexico, or any considerable portion of it, he will be in favor of these mongrels settling the question, which would bring him somewhat into collision with his horror of an inferior race.

It is to be remembered, though, that this power of acquiring additional territory is a power confided to the President and Senate of the United States. It is a power not under the control of the representatives of the people any further than they, the President and the Senate, can be considered the representatives of the people. Let me illustrate that by a case we have in our history. When we acquired the territory from Mexico in the Mexican war, the House of Representatives, composed of the immediate representatives of the people, all the time insisted that the territory thus to be acquired should be brought in upon condition that slavery should be forever prohibited therein, upon the terms and in the language that slavery had been prohibited from coming into this country. That was insisted upon constantly, and never failed to call forth an assurance that any territory thus acquired should have that prohibition in it, so far as the House of Representatives was concerned. But at last the President and Senate acquired the territory without asking the House of Representatives anything about it, and took it without that prohibition. They have the power of acquiring territory without the immediate representatives of the people being called upon to say anything about it, thus furnishing a very apt and powerful means of bringing new territory into the Union, and, when it is once brought into the country, involving us anew in this slavery agitation. It is therefore, as I think, a very important question for the consideration of the American people, whether the policy of bringing in additional territory, without considering at all how it will operate upon the safety of the Union in reference to this one great disturbing element in our national politics, shall be adopted as the policy of the country. You will bear in mind that it is to be acquired, according to the judge's view, as fast as it is needed, and the indefinite part of this proposition is that we have only Judge Douglas and his class of men to decide how fast it is needed. We have no clear and certain way of determining or demonstrating how fast territory is needed by the necessities of the country. Whoever wants to go out filibustering, then, thinks that more territory is needed. Whoever wants wider slave-fields feels sure that some additional territory is needed as slave territory. Then it is as easy to show the necessity of additional slave territory as it is to assert anything that is incapable of absolute demonstration. Whatever motive a man or a set of men may have for making annexation of property or territory, it is very easy to assert, but much less easy to disprove, that it is necessary for the wants of the country.

And now it only remains for me to say that I think it is a very grave question for the people of this Union to consider whether, in view of the fact that this slavery question has been the only one that has ever endangered our republican institutions—the only one that has ever threatened or menaced a dissolution of the Union—that has ever disturbed us in such a way as to make us fear for the perpetuity of our liberty—in view of these facts, I think it is an exceedingly interesting and important question for this people to consider whether we shall engage in the policy of acquiring additional territory, discarding altogether from our consideration, while obtaining new territory, the question how it may affect us in regard to this the only endangering element to our liberties and national greatness. The judge's view has been expressed. I, in my answer to his question, have expressed mine. I think it will become an important and practical question. Our views are before the public. I am willing and anxious that they should consider them fully—that they should turn it about and consider the importance of the question, and arrive at a just conclusion as to whether it is or is not wise in the people of this Union, in the acquisition of new territory, to consider whether it will add to the disturbance that is existing among us—whether it will add to the one only danger that has ever threatened the perpetuity of the Union or our own liberties. I think it is extremely important that they shall decide, and rightly decide, that question before entering upon that policy.

And now, my friends, having said the little I wish to say upon this head, whether I have occupied the whole of the remnant of my time or not, I believe I could not enter upon any new topic so as to treat it fully without transcending my time, which I would not for a moment think of doing. I give way to Judge Douglas.[964]

From Douglas' opening remarks we learn that he was willing to live with or without slavery, for he knew full well that it was the state government's choice to decide, not the federal government's. Douglas was also ready to accept blacks, free or enslaved, as part of American society.

From Lincoln's reply, however, we learn that *he was not willing to live with slavery because he was not willing to live with blacks*. Like the majority of liberals today he wanted to impose his views on everyone, strip the states of their constitutional rights, and enlarge and strengthen the federal government. He also believed that through the **"benevolent efforts of the** [Northern founded American] **Colonization Society,"** his favorite organization (and one in which he worked as a manager),[965] he could deport as many African-Americans out of the U.S. as he wanted.

Here is Douglas' reply to Lincoln's left-wing radicalism, or as the judge rightly calls them, "revolutionary principles":

> Gentlemen: The highest compliment you can pay me during the brief half-hour that I have to conclude is by observing a strict silence. I desire to be heard rather than to be applauded.
>
> The first criticism that Mr. Lincoln makes on my speech was that it was in substance what I have said everywhere else in the State where I have addressed the people. I wish I could say the same of his speech. Why, the reason I complain of him is because he makes one speech north and another south. Because he has one set of sentiments for the Abolition counties, and another set for the counties opposed to Abolitionism. My point of complaint against him is that I cannot induce him to hold up the same standard, to carry the same flag in all parts of the State. He does not pretend, and no other man will, that I have one set of principles for Galesburg and another for Charleston. He does not pretend that I hold to one doctrine in Chicago and an opposite one in Jonesboro. I have proved that he has a different set of principles for each of these localities. All I asked of him was that he should deliver the speech that he has made here to-day in Coles County instead of in old Knox. It would have settled the question between us in that doubtful county. Here I understand him to reaffirm the doctrine of negro equality, and to assert that by the Declaration of Independence the negro is declared equal to the white man. He tells you to-day that the negro was included in the Declaration of Independence when it asserted that all men were created equal. [Audience: "We believe it."] Very well.
>
> Mr. Lincoln asserts to-day, as he did at Chicago, that the negro was included in that clause of the Declaration of Independence which says that all men were created equal, and endowed by the Creator with certain inalienable rights, among which are life, liberty, and the pursuit of happiness. If the negro was made his equal and mine, if that equality was established by divine law, and was the negro's inalienable right, how came he to say at Charleston to the Kentuckians residing in that section of our State, that the negro was physically inferior to the white man, belonged to an inferior race, and he was for keeping him always in that inferior condition. I wish you to bear these things in mind. At Charleston he said that the negro belonged to an inferior race, and that he was for keeping him in that inferior condition. There he gave the people to understand that there was no moral question involved, because the inferiority being established, it was only a question of degree and not a question of right; here, to-day, instead

of making it a question of degree, he makes it a moral question, says that it is a great crime to hold the negro in that inferior condition. [Audience member: "He's right."] Is he right now, or was he right in Charleston? [Audience member: "Both."] He is right then, sir, in your estimation, not because he is consistent, but because he can trim his principles any way in any section, so as to secure votes. All I desire of him is that he will declare the same principles in the south that he does in the north.

But did you notice how he answered my position that a man should hold the same doctrines throughout the length and breadth of this republic? He said, **"Would Judge Douglas go to Russia and proclaim the same principles he does here?"** I would remind him that Russia is not under the American Constitution. If Russia was a part of the American republic, under our Federal Constitution, and was sworn to support the Constitution, I would maintain the same doctrine in Russia that I do in Illinois. The slaveholding States are governed by the same Federal Constitution as ourselves, and hence a man's principles, in order to be in harmony with the Constitution, must be the same in the South as they are in the North, the same in the free States as they are in the slave States. Whenever a man advocates one set of principles in one section, and another set in another section, his opinions are in violation of the spirit of the Constitution which he has sworn to support. When Mr. Lincoln went to Congress in 1847, and, laying his hand upon the Holy Evangelists, made a solemn vow in the presence of high Heaven that he would be faithful to the Constitution—what did he mean? the Constitution as he expounds it in Galesburg, or the Constitution as he expounds it in Charleston.

Mr. Lincoln has devoted considerable time to the circumstance that at Ottawa I read a series of resolutions as having been adopted at Springfield, in this State, on the 4th or 5th of October, 1854, which happened not to have been adopted there. He has used hard names; has dared to talk about fraud, about forgery, and has insinuated that there was a conspiracy between Mr. Lanphier, Mr. Harris, and myself to perpetrate a forgery. Now, bear in mind that he does not deny that these resolutions were adopted in a majority of all the Republican counties of this State in that year: he does not deny that they were declared to be the platform of this Republican party in the first congressional district, in the second, in the third, and in many counties of the fourth, and that they thus became the platform of his party in a majority of the counties upon which he now relies for support; he does not deny the truthfulness of the resolutions, but takes exception to the spot on which they were adopted. He takes to himself great merit because he thinks they were not adopted on the right spot for me to use them against him, just as he was very severe in Congress upon the government of his country, when he thought that he had discovered that the Mexican war was not begun in the right spot, and was therefore unjust. He tries very hard to make out that there is something very extraordinary in the place where the thing was done, and not in the thing itself. I never believed before that Abraham Lincoln would be guilty of what he has done this day in regard to those resolutions. In the first place, the moment it was intimated to me that they had been adopted at Aurora and Rockford instead of Springfield, I did not wait for him to call my attention to the fact, but led off and explained in my first meeting after the Ottawa debate, what the mistake was and how it had been made. I supposed that for an honest man, conscious of his own rectitude, that explanation would be sufficient. I did not wait for him, after the mistake was made, to call my attention to it, but frankly explained it at once as an honest man would. I also gave the authority on which I had stated that these resolutions were adopted by the Springfield Republican convention; that I had seen them quoted by Major Harris in a debate in Congress, as having been adopted by the first Republican State convention in Illinois, and that I had written to him and asked him for the authority as to the time and place of their adoption; that Major Harris being extremely ill Charles H. Lanphier had written to me for him that they were adopted at Springfield, on the 5th of October, 1854, and had sent me a copy of the Springfield paper containing them. I read them from the newspaper just as Mr. Lincoln reads the proceedings of meetings held years ago from the newspapers. After giving that explanation, I did not think there was an honest man in the State of Illinois who doubted that I had been led into the error, if it was such, innocently, in the way I detailed; and I will now say that I do not now believe that there is an honest man on the face of the globe who will not regard with abhorrence and disgust Mr. Lincoln's insinuations of my complicity in that forgery, if it was a forgery. Does Mr. Lincoln wish to push these things to the point of personal difficulties here? I commenced this contest by treating him courteously and kindly; I always spoke of him in words of respect, and in return he has sought, and is now seeking, to divert public attention from the enormity of his revolutionary principles by impeaching men's sincerity and integrity, and inviting personal quarrels.

    I desired to conduct this contest with him like a gentleman, but I spurn the insinuation of complicity and fraud made upon the simple circumstance of an editor of a newspaper having made a mistake as to the place where a thing was done, but not as to the thing itself. These resolutions were the platform of this Republican [liberal] party of Mr. Lincoln's of that year. They were adopted in a majority of the Republican counties in the State; and when I asked him at Ottawa whether they formed the platform upon which he stood, he did not answer, and I could not get an answer out of him. He then thought, as I thought, that those resolutions were adopted at the Springfield convention, but excused himself by saying that he was not there when they were adopted, but had gone to Tazewell court in order to avoid being present at the convention. He saw them published as having been adopted at Springfield, and so did I, and he knew that if there was a mistake in regard to them, that I had nothing under heaven to do with it. Besides, you find that in all these northern counties where the Republican candidates are running pledged to him, that the conventions which nominated them adopted that identical platform. One cardinal point in that platform which he shrinks from is this—that there shall be no more slave States admitted into the Union, even if the people want them. [Elijah P.] Lovejoy stands pledged against the admission of any more slave States. [Audience: "Right; so do we."] So do you, you say. [John F.] Farnsworth stands pledged against the admission of any more slave States. [Elihu B.] Washburne stands pledged the same way. The candidate for the legislature who is running on Lincoln's ticket in Henderson and Warren stands committed by his vote in the legislature to the same thing, and I am informed, but do not know of the fact, that your candidate here is also so pledged. [Audience: "Hurrah for him! Good!"] Now, you Republicans [liberals] all hurrah for him, and for the doctrine of "no more slave States," and yet Lincoln tells you that his conscience will not permit him to sanction that doctrine, and complains because the resolutions I read at Ottawa made him, as a member of the party, responsible for sanctioning the doctrine of no more slave States. You are one way, you confess, and he is or pretends to be the other, and yet you are both governed by principle in supporting one another. If it be true, as I have shown it is, that the whole Republican party in the northern part of the State stands committed to the doctrine of no more slave States, and that this same doctrine is repudiated by the Republicans in the other part of the State, I wonder whether Mr. Lincoln and his party do not present the case which he cited from the Scriptures, of a house divided against itself which cannot stand! I desire to know what are Mr. Lincoln's principles and the principles of his party. I hold, and the [conservative] party with which I am identified holds; that the people of each State, old and new, have the right to decide the slavery question for themselves, and when I used the remark that I did not care whether slavery was voted up or down, I used it in the connection that I was for allowing Kansas to do just as she pleased on the slavery question. I said that I did not care whether they voted slavery up or down, because they had the right to do as they pleased on the question, and therefore my action would not be controlled by any such consideration. Why cannot Abraham Lincoln, and the [liberal] party with which he acts, speak out their principles so that they may be understood? Why do they claim to be one thing in one part of the State and another in the other part? Whenever I allude to the Abolition doctrines, which he considers a slander to be charged with being in favor of, you all indorse them, and hurrah for them, not knowing that your candidate is ashamed to acknowledge them.

   I have a few words to say upon the Dred Scott decision, which has troubled the brain of Mr. Lincoln so much. He insists that that decision would carry slavery into the free States, notwithstanding that the decision says directly the opposite; and goes into a long argument to make you believe that I am in favor of, and would sanction, the doctrine that would allow slaves to be brought here and held as slaves contrary to our constitution and laws. Mr. Lincoln knew better when he asserted this; he knew that one newspaper, and so far as is within my knowledge but one, ever asserted that doctrine, and that I was the first man in either House of Congress that read that article in debate, and denounced it on the floor of the Senate as revolutionary [i.e., progressive]. When the Washington "Union," on the 17th of last November, published an article to that effect, I branded it at once, and denounced it, and hence the "Union" has been pursuing me ever since. Mr. [Robert] Toombs, of Georgia, replied to me, and said that there was not a man in any of the slave States south of the Potomac River that held any such doctrine. Mr. Lincoln knows that there is not a member of the Supreme Court who holds that doctrine; he knows that every one of them, as shown by their opinions, holds the reverse. Why this attempt, then, to bring the Supreme Court into disrepute among the people? It looks as if there was an effort being made to destroy public confidence in the highest judicial tribunal on earth. Suppose he succeeds in destroying public confidence in the court, so that the people will not respect its decisions, but will feel at liberty to disregard them, and resist the laws of the land, what will he have gained? He will have changed the government from one of laws into that of a mob, in which the strong arm of violence will be substituted for the decisions of the courts of justice. He complains because I did not go into an argument reviewing Chief Justice Taney's opinion, and the other opinions of the different judges, to determine whether their reasoning is right or wrong on the questions of law. What use would that be? He wants to take an appeal from the Supreme Court to this meeting to determine whether the questions of law were decided properly. He is going to appeal from the Supreme Court of the United States to every town meeting, in the hope that he can excite a prejudice against that court, and on the wave of that prejudice ride into the Senate of the United States, when he could not get there on his own principles, or his own merits. Suppose he should succeed in getting into the Senate of the United States, what then will he have to do with the decision of the Supreme Court in the Dred Scott case? Can he reverse that decision when he gets there? Can he act upon it? Has the Senate any right to reverse it or revise it? He will not pretend that it has. Then why drag the matter into this contest, unless for the purpose of making a false issue, by which he can divert public attention from the real issue.

He has cited General [Andrew] Jackson in justification of the war he is making on the decision of the court. Mr. Lincoln misunderstands the history of the country if he believes there is any parallel in the two cases. It is true that the Supreme Court once decided that if a bank of the United States was a necessary fiscal agent of the government it was constitutional, and if not, that it was unconstitutional, and also, that whether or not it was necessary for that purpose was a political question for Congress, and not a judicial one for the courts to determine. Hence the court would not determine the bank unconstitutional. Jackson respected the decision, obeyed the law, executed it, and carried it into effect during its existence; but after the charter of the bank expired, and a proposition was made to create a new bank, General Jackson said: "It is unnecessary and improper, and therefore I am against it on constitutional grounds as well as those of expediency." Is Congress bound to pass every act that is constitutional? Why, there are a thousand things that are constitutional, but yet are inexpedient and unnecessary, and you surely would not vote for them merely because you had the right to? And because General Jackson would not do a thing which he had a right to do, but did not deem expedient or proper, Mr. Lincoln is going to justify himself in doing that which he has no right to do. I ask him whether he is not bound to respect and obey the decisions of the Supreme Court as well as I? The Constitution has created that court to decide all constitutional questions in the last resort, and when such decisions have been made they become the law of the land, and you, and he, and myself, and every other good citizen are bound by them. Yet he argues that I am bound by their decisions, and he is not. He says that their decisions are binding on Democrats [conservatives], but not on Republicans [liberals]. Are not Republicans bound by the laws of the land as well as Democrats? And when the court has fixed the construction of the Constitution on the validity of a given law, is not their decision binding upon Republicans as well as upon Democrats? Is it possible that you Republicans have the right to raise your mobs and oppose the laws or the land and the constituted authorities, and yet hold us Democrats bound to obey them? My time is within half a minute of expiring, and all I have to say is that I stand by the laws of the land. I stand by the Constitution as our fathers made it, by the laws as they are enacted, and by the decisions of the court upon all points within their jurisdiction as they are pronounced by the highest tribunal on earth; and any man who resists these must resort to mob-law and violence to overturn the government of laws.[966]

Again, Douglas succeeds admirably in uncovering Lincoln's hypocrisy, double-dealing, forked-tongue declarations, provocative sectionalism, false charges, insane prevarications, overt racism, political trickery, inconsistencies, evasiveness, absurd and cruel slanders, obfuscation, personal attacks, and radical anti-states' rights and anti-Constitution views. Yet stunningly, Lincoln seemed completely unfazed at being caught in his own web of lies, even when Douglas made statements like the following directly to Lincoln's face:

> Whenever a man advocates one set of principles in one section, and another set in another section, his opinions are in violation of the spirit of the Constitution which he has sworn to support. When Mr. Lincoln went to Congress in 1847, and, laying his hand upon the Holy Evangelists, made a solemn vow in the presence of high Heaven that he would be faithful to the Constitution—what did he mean? the Constitution as he expounds it in Galesburg, or the Constitution as he expounds it in Charleston.[967]

Douglas here also reveals Lincoln's perverse desire to undermine the Supreme Court, and change "the government from one of laws into that of a mob, in which the strong arm of violence will be substituted for the decisions of the courts of justice." Little did Douglas realize that this was exactly what Lincoln would actually do after becoming president and launching his illegal war against the South!

In particular Douglas detested Lincoln's rank sectionalism, which pitted the various regions of the nation against one another, mainly South against North. What was the point of this? Lincoln was only making an already combustible situation worse. Douglas, like conservatives today, wanted there to be tranquil relations between the states. This was, after all, one of the purposes behind the conservative idea of states' rights to begin with: each state was to be in control of the business and issues within its own borders; all other states were off limits, a constitutional attempt to promote harmonious relations between the individual states. As conservative Douglas said on October 13, 1858, during their sixth joint debate at Quincy, Illinois:

> If each state will only agree to mind its own business, and let its neighbors alone, there will be peace forever between us. . . . I repeat that the principle is the right of each State, each Territory, to decide this slavery question for itself, to have slavery or not, as it chooses, and it does not become Mr. Lincoln, or anybody else, to tell the people of Kentucky that they have no consciences, that they are living in a state of iniquity, and that they are cherishing an institution to their bosoms in violation of the law of God. Better for him to adopt the doctrine of "Judge not, lest ye shall be judged." Let him perform his own duty at home, and he will have a better fate in the future. I think there are objects of charity enough in the free States to excite the sympathies and open the pockets of all the benevolence we have amongst us, without going abroad in search of- negroes, of whose condition we know nothing. We have enough objects of charity at home, and it is our duty to take care of our own poor, and our own suffering, before we go abroad to intermeddle with other people's business.[968]

Lincoln obviously completely disagreed with this point of view. How else to explain the clear and antagonistic sectionalism in his speeches, his constant interference in the South's affairs, and the fact that he inaugurated an illegal and unnecessary war against the Confederacy just two years later?

At this same debate, Douglas, who was for working to peacefully resolve differences between South and North, once again attacked Lincoln's overt sectionalism and duplicity:

> Mr. Lincoln complains that, in my speech the other day at Galesburg, I read an extract from a speech delivered by him at Chicago, and then another from his speech at Charleston, and compared them, thus showing the people that he had one set of principles in one part of the State and another in the other part. And how does he answer that charge? Why, he quotes from his Charleston speech as I quoted from it, and then quotes another extract from a speech which he made at another place, which he

says is the same as the extract from his speech at Charleston; but he does not quote the extract from his Chicago speech, upon which I convicted him of double-dealing. I quoted from his Chicago speech to prove that he held one set of principles up north among the Abolitionists, and from his Charleston speech to prove that he held another set down at Charleston and in southern Illinois. In his answer to this charge, he ignores entirely his Chicago speech, and merely argues that he said the same thing which he said at Charleston at another place. If he did, it follows that he has twice, instead of once, held one creed in one part of the State, and a different creed in another part. Up at Chicago, in the opening of the campaign, he reviewed my reception speech, and undertook to answer my argument attacking his favorite doctrine of negro equality. I had shown that it was a falsification of the Declaration of Independence to pretend that that instrument applied to and included negroes in the clause declaring that all men are created equal. What was Lincoln's reply? I will read from his Chicago speech, and the one which he did not quote, and dare not quote, in this part of the State. He said:

> I should like to know if, taking this old Declaration of Independence, which declares that all men are equal upon principle, and making exceptions to it, where will it stop? If one man says it does not mean a negro, why may not another man say it does not mean another man? If that declaration is not the truth, let us get this statute-book in which we find it and tear it out.

There you find that Mr. Lincoln told the Abolitionists of Chicago that if the Declaration of Independence did not declare that the negro was created by the Almighty the equal of the white man, that you ought to take that instrument and tear out the clause which says that all men are created equal. But let me call your attention to another part of the same speech. You know that in his Charleston speech, an extract from which he has read, he declared that the negro belongs to an inferior race, is physically inferior to the white man, and should always be kept in an inferior position. I will now read to you what he said at Chicago on that point. In concluding his speech at that place, he remarked:

> My friends, I have detained you about as long as I desire to do, and I have only

> to say, let us discard all this quibbling about this man and the other man—this race and that race and the other race being inferior, and therefore they must be placed in an inferior position, discarding our standard that we have left us. Let us discard all these things, and unite as one people throughout this land until we shall once more stand up declaring that all men are created equal.

Thus you see that when addressing the Chicago Abolitionists he declared that all distinctions of race must be discarded and blotted out, because the negro stood on an equal footing with the white man; that if one man said the Declaration of Independence did not mean a negro when it declared all men created equal, that another man would say that it did not mean another man; and hence we ought to discard all difference between the negro race and all other races, and declare them all created equal. Did old [Joshua R.] Giddings, when he came down among you four years ago, preach more radical Abolitionism than this? Did [Elijah P.] Lovejoy, or Lloyd Garrison, or Wendell Phillips, or Fred Douglass, ever take higher Abolition grounds than that? Lincoln told you that I had charged him with getting up these personal attacks to conceal the enormity of his principles, and then commenced talking about something else, omitting to quote this part of his Chicago speech which contained the enormity of his principles to which I alluded. He knew that I alluded to his negro-equality doctrines when I spoke of the enormity of his principles, yet he did not find it convenient to answer on that point. Having shown you what he said in his Chicago speech in reference to negroes being created equal to white men, and about discarding all distinctions between the two races, I will again read to you what he said at Charleston:

> I will say, then, that I am not, nor ever have been, in favor of bringing about in any way the social and political equality of the white and black races; that I am not, nor ever have been, in favor of making voters of the free negroes, or jurors, or qualifying them to hold office, or having them to marry with white people. I will say, in

> addition, that there is a physical difference between the white and black races which, I suppose, will forever forbid the two races living together upon terms of social and political equality; and inasmuch as they cannot so live, while they do remain together, there must be the position of superior and inferior, and I, as much as any other man, am in favor of the superior position being assigned to the white man.

[Audience member: "That's the doctrine."]

Mr. Douglas: Yes, sir. that is good doctrine; but Mr. Lincoln is afraid to advocate it in the latitude of Chicago, where he hopes to get his votes. It is good doctrine in the anti-Abolition counties for him, and his Chicago speech is good doctrine in the Abolition counties. I assert, on the authority of these two speeches of Mr. Lincoln, that he holds one set of principles in the Abolition counties, and a different and contradictory set in the other counties. I do not question that he said at Ottawa what he quoted, but that only convicts him further, by proving that he has twice contradicted himself instead of once. Let me ask him why he cannot avow his principles the same in the north as in the south—the same in every county, if he has a conviction that they are just? But I forgot—he would not be a Republican if his principles would apply alike to every part of the country. The [liberal] party to which he belongs is bounded and limited by geographical lines. With their principles they cannot even cross the Mississippi River on your ferry-boats. They cannot cross over the Ohio into Kentucky. Lincoln himself cannot visit the land of his fathers, the scenes of his childhood, the graves of his ancestors, and carry his Abolition principles, as he declared them at Chicago, with him.

  This Republican organization appeals to the North against the South; it appeals to Northern passion, Northern prejudice, and Northern ambition, against Southern people, Southern States, and Southern institutions, and its only hope of success is by that appeal. Mr. Lincoln goes on to justify himself in making a war upon slavery upon the ground that Frank Blair and Gratz Brown did not succeed in their warfare upon the institutions in Missouri. Frank Blair was elected to Congress, in 1856, from the State of Missouri, as a Buchanan Democrat, and he turned Fremonter after the people elected him, thus belonging to one party before his election, and another afterward. What right, then, had he to expect, after having thus cheated his constituency, that they would support him at another election? Mr. Lincoln thinks that it is his duty to preach a crusade in the free States against slavery, because it is a crime, as he believes, and ought to be extinguished, and because the people of the slave States will never abolish it. How is he going to abolish it? Down in the southern part of the State he takes the ground openly that he will not interfere with slavery where it exists, and says that he is not now and never was in favor of interfering with slavery where it exists in the States. Well, if he is not in favor of that, how does he expect to bring slavery into a course of ultimate extinction? How can he extinguish it in Kentucky, in Virginia, in all the slave States, by his policy, if he will not pursue a policy which will interfere with it in the States where it exists? In his speech at Springfield before the Abolition or Republican convention, he declared his hostility to any more slave States in this language:

> Under the operation of that policy the agitation has not only not ceased, but has constantly augmented. In my opinion it will not cease until a crisis shall have been reached and passed. "A house divided against itself cannot stand." I believe this government cannot endure permanently half slave and half free. I do not expect the Union to be dissolved,—I do not expect the house to fall,—but I do expect it will cease to be divided. It will become all one thing, or all the other. Either the opponents of slavery will arrest the further spread of it, and place it where the public mind shall rest in the belief that it is in the course of ultimate extinction, or its advocates will push it forward till it shall become alike lawful in all the States—old as well as new, North as well as South.

Mr. Lincoln there told his Abolition friends that this government could not endure permanently divided into free and slave States as our fathers made it, and that it must become all free or all slave; otherwise, that the government could not exist. How then does Lincoln propose to save the Union, unless by compelling all the States to become free, so that the house shall not be divided against itself? He intends making them all free; he will preserve the Union in that way; and yet he is not going to interfere with slavery anywhere it now exists. How is he going to bring it about? Why, he will agitate; he will induce the North to agitate until the South shall be worried out, and forced to abolish slavery. Let us examine the policy by which that is to be done. He first tells you that he would prohibit slavery everywhere in the Territories. He would thus confine slavery within its present limits. When he thus gets it confined, and surrounded, so that it cannot spread, the natural laws of increase will go on until the negroes will be so plenty that they cannot live on the soil. He will hem them in until starvation seizes them, and by starving them to death he will put slavery in the course of ultimate extinction. If he is not going to interfere with slavery in the States, but intends to interfere and prohibit it in the Territories, and thus smother slavery out, it naturally follows that he can extinguish it only by extinguishing the negro race; for his policy would drive them to starvation. This is the humane and Christian remedy that he proposes for the great crime of slavery.[969]

Ever the wily politician, Lincoln, of course, denied all of Douglas' charges, particularly the one accusing him of sectionalism. But as the following document testifies, Lincoln was without question the most sectional individual to ever grace the Oval Office. Here, now president, Lincoln issues his August 16, 1861, "Proclamation Forbidding Intercourse With Rebel States," driving home one of his central messages, that the South was a hostile, alien, and uppity society, one that needed to be isolated, annihilated, then punished:

> **Whereas on the fifteenth day of April, eighteen hundred and sixty-one, the President of the United States, in view of an insurrection against the laws, Constitution, and government of the United States which had broken out within the States of South Carolina, Georgia, Alabama, Florida, Mississippi, Louisiana, and Texas, and in pursuance of the provisions of the act entitled "An act to provide for calling forth the militia to execute the laws of the Union, suppress insurrections, and repel invasions, and to repeal the act now in force for that purpose," approved February twenty-eighth, seventeen hundred and ninety-five, did call forth the militia to suppress said insurrection, and to cause the laws of the Union to be**

duly executed, and the insurgents have failed to disperse by the time directed by the President; and whereas, such insurrection has since broken out and yet exists within the States of Virginia, North Carolina, Tennessee, and Arkansas; and whereas, the insurgents in all the said States claim to act under the authority thereof, and such claim is not disclaimed or repudiated by the persons exercising the functions of government in such State or States, or in the part or parts thereof in which such combinations exist, nor has such insurrection been suppressed by said States:

Now, therefore, I, Abraham Lincoln, President of the United States, in pursuance of an act of Congress approved July thirteen, eighteen hundred and sixty-one, do hereby declare that the inhabitants of the said States of Georgia, South Carolina, Virginia, North Carolina, Tennessee, Alabama, Louisiana, Texas, Arkansas, Mississippi, and Florida (except the inhabitants of that part of the State of Virginia lying west of the Alleghany Mountains, and of such other parts of that State, and the other States hereinbefore named, as may maintain a loyal adhesion to the Union and the Constitution, or may be from time to time occupied and controlled by forces of the United States engaged in the dispersion of said insurgents), are in a state of insurrection against the United States, and that all commercial intercourse between the same and the inhabitants thereof, with the exceptions aforesaid, and the citizens of other States and other parts of the United States, is unlawful, and will remain unlawful until such insurrection shall cease or has been suppressed; that all goods and chattels, wares and merchandise, coming from any of said States, with the exceptions aforesaid, into other parts of the United States, without the special license and permission of the President, through the Secretary of the Treasury, or proceeding to any of said States, with the exceptions aforesaid, by land or water, together with the vessel or vehicle conveying the same, or conveying persons to or from said States, with said exceptions, will be forfeited to the United States; and that from and after fifteen days from the issuing of this proclamation all ships and vessels belonging in whole or in part to any citizen or inhabitant of any of said States, with, said exceptions, found at sea, or in any port of the United States, will be forfeited to the United States; and I hereby enjoin upon all district attorneys, marshals, and officers of the revenue and or the military and naval forces of the United States to be vigilant in the execution of said act, and in the enforcement of the penalties and forfeitures imposed or declared by it; leaving any party who may think himself aggrieved thereby to his application to the Secretary of the Treasury for the remission of any penalty or forfeiture, which the said secretary is authorized by law to grant if, in his judgment, the special circumstances of any case shall require such remission.[970]

Such words makes Lincoln's rejection of the accusation of sectionalism hollow and meaningless.

While Douglas hounded Lincoln for his guilefulness and sectionalism, in debate after debate Lincoln kept steadfastly to his main theme: limiting, not abolishing, slavery, as he emphasized in his opening remarks at the same October 13, 1858, debate at Quincy, Illinois:

> We have in this nation the element of domestic slavery. It is a matter of absolute certainty that it is a disturbing element. It is the opinion of all the great men who have expressed an opinion upon it, that it is a dangerous element. We keep up a controversy in regard to it. That controversy necessarily springs from difference of opinion, and if we can learn exactly—can reduce to the lowest element—what that difference of opinion is, we perhaps shall be better prepared for discussing the different systems of policy that we would propose in regard to that disturbing element. I suggest that the difference of opinion, reduced to its lowest terms, is no other than the difference between the men who think slavery a wrong and those who do not think it wrong. The Republican party think it wrong—we think it is a moral, a social, and a political wrong. We think it is a wrong not confining itself merely to the persons or the States where it exists, but that it is a wrong which in its tendency, to say the least, affects the existence of the whole nation. Because we think it wrong, we propose a course of policy that shall deal with it as a wrong. We deal with it as with any other wrong, in so far as we can prevent its growing any larger, and so deal with it that in the run of time there may be some promise of an end to it. We have a due regard to the actual presence of it amongst us, and the difficulties of getting rid of it in any

satisfactory way, and all the constitutional obligations thrown about it. I suppose that in reference both to its actual existence in the nation, and to our constitutional obligations, we have no right at all to disturb it in the States where it exists, and we profess that we have no more inclination to disturb it than we have the right to do it. We go further than that: we don't propose to disturb it where, in one instance, we think the Constitution would permit us. We think the Constitution would permit us to disturb it in the District of Columbia. Still we do not propose to do that, unless it should be in terms which I don't suppose the nation is very likely soon to agree to—the terms of making the emancipation gradual and compensating the unwilling owners. Where we suppose we have the constitutional right, we restrain ourselves in reference to the actual existence of the institution and the difficulties thrown about it. We also oppose it as an evil so far as it seeks to spread itself. We insist on the policy that shall restrict it to its present limits. We don't suppose that in doing this we violate anything due to the actual presence of the institution, or anything due to the constitutional guaranties thrown around it.[971]

After Douglas' scathing and deadly accurate reply to this deceitful nonsense, Lincoln made the following rejoinder, again sticking to his object of restricting not eliminating slavery:

> ... when the fathers of the government cut off the source of slavery by the abolition of the slave-trade [in 1808], and adopted a system of restricting it from the new Territories where it had not existed, I maintain that they placed it where they understood, and all sensible men understood, it was in the course of ultimate extinction; and when Judge Douglas asks me why it cannot continue as our fathers made it, I ask him why he and his friends could not let it remain as our fathers made it?
>
> It is precisely all I ask of him in relation to the institution of slavery, that it shall be placed upon the basis that our fathers placed it upon. Mr. [Preston Smith] Brooks, of South Carolina, once said, and truly said, that when this government was established, no one expected the institution of slavery to last until this day; and that the men who formed this government were wiser and

better than the men of these days; but the men of these days had experience which the fathers had not, and that experience had taught them the invention of the cotton-gin, and this had made the perpetuation of the institution of slavery a necessity in this country. Judge Douglas could not let it stand upon the basis where our fathers placed it, but removed it, and put it upon the cotton-gin basis. It is a question, therefore, for him and his friends to answer—why they could not let it remain where the fathers of the government originally placed it.[972]

While, as Lincoln states here, he was happy to tolerate slavery as long as it was limited to the South, it was quite another matter when it came to the foreign slave trade (which is different than slavery). He wanted to put an end to it as soon as possible, and for one very good reason: by bringing in a constant new supply of African slaves it undermined his black deportation plan.

As the South never engaged in foreign slave trading, Lincoln's efforts were all focused in the North, mainly cities like Boston, Providence, Baltimore, and Philadelphia, and of course New York City, the very epicenter of the American slave trade.

As hard evidence we have the case of Northerner Captain Nathaniel Gordon of New York, the only person ever tried, convicted, and executed for slaving: on February 21, 1862, he was put to death by Lincoln's personal order.[973] The February 4th missive reads:

> Whereas it appears that at a term of the Circuit Court of the United States of America for the southern district of New York, held in the month of November, A. D. 1861, Nathaniel Gordon was indicted and convicted for being engaged in the slave-trade, and was by the said court sentenced to be put to death by hanging by the neck on Friday the 7th day of February, A. D. 1862;
>
> And whereas a large number of respectable citizens have earnestly besought me to commute the said sentence of the said Nathaniel Gordon to a term of imprisonment for life, which application I have felt it to be my duty to refuse;
>
> And whereas it has seemed to me probable that the unsuccessful application made for the commutation of his sentence may have prevented the said Nathaniel

Gordon from making the necessary preparation for the awful change which awaits him:

Now, therefore, be it known that I, Abraham Lincoln, President of the United States of America, have granted and do hereby grant unto him, the said Nathaniel Gordon, a respite of the above-recited sentence until Friday, the 21st day of February, A. D. 1862, between the hours of twelve o'clock at noon and three o'clock in the afternoon of the said day, when the said sentence shall be executed.

In granting this respite it becomes my painful duty to admonish the prisoner that, relinquishing all expectation of pardon by human authority, he refer himself alone to the mercy of the common God and Father of all men.[974]

More evidence of the Northern slave trade comes from the fact that the last American slave ship to be captured by the U.S. government was a Northern one: the *Nightingale*, also from New York, confiscated on April 21, 1861. At the time of its seizure, this vessel, from the so-called "abolitionist North," had nearly 1,000 manacled Africans on board.[975] It was doing "business as usual" up until the first few weeks of the "Civil War."[976] Lincoln refers to Captain Gordon, along with the *Nightingale* and several other seized Yankee slave ships, in his First Annual Message to Congress:

The execution of the laws for the suppression of the African slave-trade has been confided to the Department of the Interior. It is a subject of gratulation that the efforts which have been made for the suppression of this inhuman traffic have been recently attended with unusual success. Five vessels being fitted out for the slave-trade have been seized and condemned. Two mates of vessels engaged in the trade, and one person in equipping a vessel as a slaver, have been convicted and subjected to the penalty of fine and imprisonment, and one captain, taken with a cargo of Africans on board his vessel, has been convicted of the highest grade of offense under our laws, the punishment of which is death.[977]

Despite Lincoln's white racist hatred of slavery, and contrary to the lies of Yankee myth, he did not blame the South for the institution, for the South had nothing to do with the origins of our nation's system of servitude. Knowing, like every other American at the time, that slavery got its start in the North (in Massachusetts in 1641, to be exact),[978] Lincoln could say, as he did on August 21, 1858, at Ottawa, Illinois:

> . . . I think I have no prejudice against the Southern people. They are just what we would be in their situation. If slavery did not now exist among them, they would not introduce it. If it did now exist among us, we should not instantly give it up. This I believe of the masses North and South. Doubtless there are individuals on both sides who would not hold slaves under any circumstances, and others who would gladly introduce slavery anew if it were out of existence. We know that some Southern men do free their slaves, go North and become tip-top Abolitionists, while some Northern ones go South and become most cruel slave-masters.
>
> When Southern people tell us they are no more responsible for the origin of slavery than we are, I acknowledge the fact. When it is said that the institution exists, and that it is very difficult to get rid of it in any satisfactory way, I can understand and appreciate the saying. I surely will not blame them for not doing what I should not know how to do myself.[979]

Sadly, the warm empathy displayed here for the Southland would not last much longer. In fact, within two years it would suit his political purposes and ambitions to turn Dixie into the Devil incarnate; full justification, at least in his mind, for waging full scale warfare on what he tenderly refers to as the **"Southern people,"** literally his own kind.[980]

LINCOLN, AFRICAN-AMERICANS, & WHITE RACISM

W E ARE SO USED TO hearing Abraham Lincoln described as the "Great Emancipator," the "best friend of the black man," and America's most celebrated "civil rights leader," that it is difficult to think of him as the opposite; namely, as a white racist, white supremacist, white separatist, and black colonizationist, one who blocked the progress of black civil rights at nearly every turn.

Yet, we know this is true because this is how Lincoln depicts himself in his own words. It is only the fabricated mountain of Lincolnian mythology, some 16,000 books penned by his adoring but unenlightened devotees, that has prevented the real Lincoln from becoming known to the general public.

Let us bypass all of these myopic apologetics and this unacademic silliness and let Lincoln speak for himself.

The president's true feelings toward African-Americans were evident early on, such as when, as a young lawyer, he could have defended slaves, but instead chose to defend slave owners.[981] But it is his actual words we are most interested in.

One of the earliest public statements Lincoln made concerning his beliefs about white supremacy came on June 13, 1836, when he made an announcement declaring his political views in the local paper, the Illinois *Sangamo Journal*:

> To the Editor of the "Journal": In your paper of last Saturday I see a communication, over the signature of "Many Voters," in which the candidates who are announced in the "Journal" are called upon to "show their hands." Agreed. Here's mine.
> I go for all sharing the privileges of the government who assist in bearing its burdens. Consequently, I go for admitting all whites to the right of suffrage who pay taxes or bear arms . . .[982]

Though blacks, enslaved and free, certainly **"bore the burden"** of helping settle, develop, and maintain the United States through their many contributions, Lincoln did not feel they deserved to **"share the privileges"** of its government.

Another early example of his feelings about the two races came on October 16, 1854, during a speech at Peoria, Illinois. Speaking on the topic of emancipating blacks slaves, he asked:

> What next? Free them, and make them politically and socially our equals. My own feelings will not admit of this, and if mine would, we well know that those of the great mass of whites will not. Whether this feeling accords with justice and sound judgment is not the sole question, if indeed it is any part of it. A universal feeling, whether well or ill founded, cannot be safely disregarded. We cannot then make them equals.[983]

During the same speech Lincoln went on to say:

> Let it not be said I am contending for the establishment of political and social equality between the whites and blacks. I have already said the contrary.[984]

Four years later, on July 10, 1858, at Chicago, Illinois, Lincoln gave a speech in which he replied to accusations made by his senatorial opponent Democrat Stephen A. Douglas. Among his responses was the following:

> We were often—more than once at least—in the course of Judge Douglas's speech last night reminded that this government was made for white men—that he believed it was made for white men. Well, that is putting it into a shape in which no one wants to deny it; but the judge

then goes into his passion for drawing inferences that are not warranted. I protest, now and forever, against that counterfeit logic which presumes that because I do not want a negro woman for a slave, I do necessarily want her for a wife. My understanding is that I need not have her for either; but, as God made us separate, we can leave one another alone, and do one another much good thereby. There are white men enough to marry all the white women, and enough black men to marry all the black women, and in God's name let them be so married. The judge regales us with the terrible enormities that take place by the mixture of races: that the inferior race bears the superior down. Why, judge, if we do not let them get together in the Territories, they won't mix there. [An audience member: "Three cheers for Lincoln!" The cheers were given with a hearty good will.] **I should say at least that that is a self-evident truth.**[985]

Besides confirming his private belief that the U.S. government was **"made for white men,"** Lincoln also espouses here one of the primary ideas held by today's Ku Klux Klan; namely, that since God made the races separate and distinct, Man should not attempt to mix them, for **"the inferior race** [blacks] **bears the superior** [whites] **down."** Lincoln's opinion here is that because blacks are "inferior" to whites, the two races should not mix socially, and certainly not physically, for this would only degrade, demean, debase, diminish, and devalue white society.

On July 17, 1858, at Springfield, Illinois, Lincoln expressed his opinion that the Declaration of Independence's statement, "all men are created equal," was not meant to be taken literally, particularly in regards to African-Americans:

> My declarations upon this subject of negro slavery may be misrepresented, but cannot be misunderstood. I have said that I do not understand the Declaration to mean that all men were created equal in all respects. They are not our equal in color; but I suppose that it does mean to declare that all men are equal in some respects; they are equal in their right to "life, liberty, and the pursuit of happiness." Certainly the negro is not our equal in color—perhaps not in many other respects . . .[986]

When it came to the aesthetics of skin color, Lincoln clearly preferred his own.

On August 21, 1858, during his first of seven debates with Douglas at Ottawa, Illinois, Lincoln made the following remarks:

> Now, gentlemen, I don't want to read at any great length, but this is the true complexion of all I have ever said in regard to the institution of slavery and the black race. This is the whole of it, and anything that argues me into his idea of perfect social and political equality with the negro is but a specious and fantastic arrangement of words, by which a man can prove a horse-chestnut to be a chestnut horse. I will say here, while upon this subject, that I have no purpose, either directly or indirectly, to interfere with the institution of slavery in the States where it exists. I believe I have no lawful right to do so, and I have no inclination to do so. I have no purpose to introduce political and social equality between the white and the black races. There is a physical difference between the two, which, in my judgment, will probably forever forbid their living together upon the footing of perfect equality; and inasmuch as it becomes a necessity that there must be a difference, I, as well as Judge Douglas, am in favor of the race to which I belong having the superior position. I have never said anything to the contrary, but I hold that, notwithstanding all this, there is no reason in the world why the negro is not entitled to all the natural rights enumerated in the Declaration of Independence—the right to life, liberty, and the pursuit of happiness. I hold that he is as much entitled to these as the white man. I agree with Judge Douglas he is not my equal in many respects—certainly not in color, perhaps not in moral or intellectual endowment. But in the right to eat the bread, without the leave of anybody else, which his own hand earns, he is my equal and the equal of Judge Douglas, and the equal of every living man.[987]

At Alton, Illinois, during his seventh and final senatorial debate with Douglas on October 15, 1858, Lincoln said:

> Now I have upon all occasions declared as strongly as Judge Douglas against the disposition to interfere with the existing institution of slavery. You hear me read it from the same speech from which he takes garbled

extracts for the purpose of proving upon me a disposition to interfere with the institution of slavery, and establish a perfect social and political equality between negroes and white people.

Allow me, while upon this subject, briefly to present one other extract from a speech of mine, made more than a year ago, at Springfield, in discussing this very same question, soon after Judge Douglas took his ground that negroes were not included in the Declaration of Independence:

> [Lincoln quoting himself] I think the authors of that notable instrument intended to include all men, but they did not intend to declare all men equal in all respects. They did not mean to say that all men were equal in color, size, intellect, moral development, or social capacity. They defined with tolerable distinctness in what respects they did consider all men created equal—equal in certain inalienable rights, among which are life, liberty, and the pursuit of happiness. This they said, and this they meant. They did not mean to assert the obvious untruth, that all were then actually enjoying that equality, nor yet that they were about to confer it immediately upon them. In fact, they had no power to confer such a boon. They meant simply to declare the right, so that the enforcement of it might follow as fast as circumstances should permit.
>
> They meant to set up a standard maxim for free society which should be familiar to all and revered by all—constantly looked to, constantly labored for, and even, though never perfectly attained, constantly approximated; and thereby constantly spreading and deepening its influence and augmenting the happiness and value of life to all people, of all colors, everywhere.

There, again, are the sentiments I have expressed in regard to the Declaration of Independence upon a former occasion—sentiments which have been put in print and read wherever anybody cared to know what so humble an individual as myself chose to say in regard to it.

At Galesburg the other day, I said, in answer to Judge Douglas, that three years ago there never had been a man, so far as I knew or believed, in the whole world, who had said that the Declaration of Independence did not include negroes in the term "all men." I reassert it to-day. I assert that Judge Douglas and all his friends may search the whole records of the country, and it will be a matter of great astonishment to me if they shall be able to find that one human being three years ago had ever uttered the astounding sentiment that the term "all men" in the Declaration did not include the negro. Do not let me be misunderstood. I know that more than three years ago there were men who, finding this assertion constantly in the way of their schemes to bring about the ascendancy and perpetuation of slavery, denied the truth of it. I know that Mr. [John C.] Calhoun and all the politicians of his school denied the truth of the Declaration. I know that it ran along in the mouth of some Southern men for a period of years, ending at last in that shameful though rather forcible declaration of [John] Pettit of Indiana, upon the floor of the United States Senate, that the Declaration of Independence was in that respect "a self-evident lie," rather than a self-evident truth. But I say, with a perfect knowledge of all this hawking at the Declaration without directly attacking it, that three years ago there never had lived a man who had ventured to assail it in the sneaking way of pretending to believe it and then asserting it did not include the negro. I believe the first man who ever said it was Chief Justice Taney in the Dred Scott case, and the next to him was our friend, Stephen A. Douglas. And now it has become the catchword of the entire party. I would like to call upon his friends everywhere to consider how they have come in so short a time to view this matter in a way so entirely different from their former belief; to ask whether they are not being borne along by an irresistible current—whither, they know not.

In answer to my proposition at Galesburg last week, I see that some man in Chicago has got up a letter addressed to the Chicago "Times," to show, as he professes, that somebody had said so before; and he signs himself "An Old-Line Whig," if I remember correctly. In the first place I would say he was not an old-line Whig. I am somewhat acquainted with old-line Whigs. I was with the old-line Whigs from the origin to the end of that party; I became pretty well acquainted with them, and I know they always had some sense, whatever else you could ascribe to them. I know there never was one who had not more sense than to try to show by the evidence he produces that some man had, prior to the time I named, said that negroes were not included in the term "all men" in the Declaration of Independence. What is the evidence he produces? I will bring forward his evidence, and let you see what he offers by way of showing that somebody more than three years ago had said negroes were not included in the Declaration. He brings forward part of a speech from Henry Clay—the part of the speech of Henry Clay which I used to bring forward to prove precisely the contrary. I guess we are surrounded to some extent to-day by the old friends of Mr. Clay, and they will be glad to hear anything from that authority. While he was in Indiana a man presented a petition to liberate his negroes, and he (Mr. Clay) made a speech in answer to it, which I suppose he carefully wrote himself and caused to be published. I have before me an extract from that speech which constitutes the evidence this pretended "Old-Line Whig" at Chicago brought forward to show that Mr. Clay didn't suppose the negro was included in the Declaration of Independence. Hear what Mr. Clay said:

> [Lincoln quoting Clay] And what is the foundation of this appeal to me in Indiana, to liberate the slaves under my care in Kentucky? It is a general declaration in the act announcing to the world the independence of the thirteen American colonies, that all men are created equal. Now, as an abstract principle, there is no doubt of the truth of that declaration; and it is desirable, in the original construction of society, and in organized societies, to keep it in view as a great fundamental

principle. But then I apprehend that in no society that ever did exist, or ever shall be formed, was or can the equality asserted among the members of the human race be practically enforced and carried out. There are portions, large portions,—women, minors, insane, culprits, transient sojourners,—that will always probably remain subject to the government of another portion of the community.

That declaration, whatever may be the extent of its import, was made by the delegations of the thirteen States. In most of them slavery existed, and had long existed, and was established by law. It was introduced and forced upon the colonies by the paramount law of England. Do you believe that in making that declaration the States that concurred in it intended that it should be tortured into a virtual emancipation of all the slaves within their respective limits? Would Virginia and other Southern States have ever united in a declaration which was to be interpreted into an abolition of slavery among them? Did any one of the thirteen colonies entertain such a design or expectation? To impute such a secret and unavowed purpose would be to charge a political fraud upon the noblest band of patriots that ever assembled in council—a fraud upon the confederacy of the Revolution—a fraud upon the union of those States whose constitution not only recognized the lawfulness of slavery, but permitted the importation of slaves from Africa until the year 1808.

This is the entire quotation brought forward to prove that somebody previous to three years ago had said the negro was not included in the term "all men" in the Declaration. How does it do so? In what way has it a tendency to prove that? Mr. Clay says it is true as an abstract principle that all men are created equal, but that we cannot practically apply it in all cases. He illustrates this by bringing forward the cases of females, minors, and insane persons, with whom it cannot be enforced; but he says that it is true as an abstract principle in the organization of society as well as in organized society, and it should be kept in view as a fundamental principle. Let me read a few words more before I add some comments of my own. Mr. Clay says a little further on:

> [Lincoln quoting Clay] I desire no concealment of my opinions in regard to the institution of slavery. I look upon it as a great evil, and deeply lament that we have derived it from the parent government, and from our ancestors. I wish every slave in the United States was in the country of his ancestors. But here they are, and the question is, how can they be best dealt with? If a state of nature existed, and we were about to lay the foundations of society, no man would be more strongly opposed than I should be, to incorporating the institution of slavery among its elements.

Now, here in this same book—in this same speech—in this same extract brought forward to prove that Mr. Clay held that the negro was not included in the Declaration of Independence—we find no such statement on his part, but instead the declaration that it is a great fundamental truth, which should be constantly kept in view in the organization of society and in societies already organized. But if I say a word about it; if I attempt, as Mr. Clay said all good men ought to do, to keep it in view; if, in this "organized society," I ask to have the public eye turned upon it; if I ask, in relation to the organization of new Territories, that the public eye should be turned upon it,—forthwith I am vilified as you hear me to-day. What have I done that I have not the license of Henry Clay's illustrious example here in doing? Have I done aught that I have not his authority for, while maintaining that in organizing new Territories and societies, this fundamental principle should be regarded, and in organized society holding it up to the public view and recognizing what he recognized as the great principle of free government?

And when this new principle—this new proposition that no human being ever thought of three years ago—is brought forward, I combat it as having an evil tendency, if not an evil design. I combat it as having a tendency to dehumanize the negro—to take away from him the right of ever striving to be a man. I combat it as being one of the thousand things constantly done in these days to prepare the public mind to make property, and nothing but property, of the negro in all the States in this Union.

But there is a point that I wish, before leaving this part of the discussion, to ask attention to. . . . The principle upon which I have insisted in this canvass, is in relation to laying the foundations of new societies. I have never sought to apply these principles to the old States for the purpose of abolishing slavery in those States. It is nothing but a miserable perversion of what I have said, to assume that I have declared Missouri, or any other slave State, shall emancipate her slaves. I have proposed no such thing. But when Mr. Clay says that in laying the foundations of societies in our Territories where it does not exist, he would be opposed to the introduction of slavery as an element, I insist that we have his warrant—his license for insisting upon the exclusion of that element which he declared in such strong and emphatic language was most hateful to him.[988]

Earlier, at Charleston, Illinois, during his fourth debate with Douglas on September 18, 1858, Lincoln said the following:

While I was at the hotel to-day, an elderly gentleman called upon me to know whether I was really in favor of producing a perfect equality between the negroes and white people. While I had not proposed to myself on this occasion to say much on that subject, yet as the question was asked me I thought I would occupy perhaps five minutes in saying something in regard to it. I will say then that I am not, nor ever have been, in favor of bringing about in any way the social and political equality of the white and black races—that I am not, nor ever have been, in favor of making voters or jurors of negroes, nor of qualifying them to hold office, nor to intermarry with white people; and I will say in addition to this that there is a physical difference between the white and black races which I believe will forever forbid the two races living together on terms of social and political equality. And inasmuch as they cannot so live, while they do remain together there must be the position of superior and inferior, and I as much as any other man am in favor of having the superior position assigned to the white race. I say upon this occasion I do not perceive that because the white man is to have the superior position the negro should be denied everything. I do not understand that because I do not want a negro woman for a slave I must necessarily want her for a wife. My understanding is that I can just let her alone. I am now in my fiftieth year, and I certainly never have had a black woman for either a slave or a wife. So it seems to me quite possible for us to get along without making either slaves or wives of negroes. I will add to this that I have never seen, to my knowledge, a man, woman, or child who was in favor of producing a perfect equality, social and political, between negroes and white men. I recollect of but one distinguished instance that I ever heard of so frequently as to be entirely satisfied of its correctness, and that is the case of Judge Douglas's old friend Colonel Richard M. Johnson. I will also add to the remarks I have made (for I am not going to enter at large upon this subject), that I have never had the least apprehension that I or my friends would marry negroes if there was no law to keep them from it; but as Judge Douglas and his friends seem to be in great apprehension that they might, if there were no law to keep them from it, I give him the most solemn pledge that I will to the very last stand by the law of this State, which forbids the marrying of white people with negroes. I will add one further word, which is this: that I do not understand that there is any place where an alteration of the social and political relations of the negro and the white man can be made except in the State legislature—not in the Congress of the United States; and as I do not really apprehend the approach of any such thing myself, and as Judge Douglas seems to be in constant horror that some such danger is rapidly approaching, I propose, as the best means to prevent it, that the judge be kept at home and placed in the State legislature to fight the measure. I do not propose dwelling longer at this time on the subject.[989]

In Lincoln's mind he had good reason for wanting to prevent blacks from voting, sitting on juries, holding political office, or marrying whites.[990] Since, according to him, whites are the superior race and blacks the inferior, the mixing of the two could only lead to that most dreaded of all the racist's fears, what Victorian whites called "amalgamation"; that is, the interbreeding and intermarriage of the two races. Said Lincoln on June 26, 1857, in his famous Dred Scott Speech at Springfield, Illinois:

> There is a natural disgust in the minds of nearly all white people, to the idea of an indiscriminate amalgamation of the white and black races; . . . Now I protest against that counterfeit logic which concludes that, because I do not want a black woman for a slave I must necessarily want her for a wife. I need not have her for either, I can just leave alone. In some respects she certainly is not my equal; but in her natural right the bread she earns with her own hands without asking leave of any one else, she is my equal, and the equal of all others.[991]

During this same address Lincoln gives perhaps the primary reason he is against slavery to begin with: it brings the two races into close contact, potentially causing the "mixing of blood" through intimate contact:

> But Judge Douglas is especially horrified at the thought of the mixing of blood by the white and black races. Agreed for once—a thousand times agreed. There are white men enough to marry all the white women, and black men enough to marry all the black women; and so let them be married. On this point we fully agree with the judge, and when he shall show that his policy is better adapted to prevent amalgamation than ours, we shall drop ours and adopt his. Let us see. In 1850 there were in the United States 405,751 mulattos. Very few of these are the offspring of whites and free blacks; nearly all have sprung from black slaves and white masters. A separation of the races is the only perfect preventive of amalgamation; but as an immediate separation is impossible, the next best thing is to keep them apart where they are not already together. If white and black people never get together in Kansas, they will never mix

blood in Kansas. That is at least one self-evident truth. A few free colored persons may get into the free States, in any event; but their number is too insignificant to amount to much in the way of mixing blood. In 1850 there were in the free States 56,649 mulattos; but for the most part they were not born there—they came from the slave States, ready made up. In the same year the slave States had 348,874 mulattos, all of home production. The proportion of free mulattos to free blacks—the only colored classes in the free States—is much greater in the slave than in the free States. It is worthy of note, too, that among the free States those which make the colored man the nearest equal to the white have proportionably the fewest mulattos, the least of amalgamation. In New Hampshire, the State which goes farthest toward equality between the races, there are just 184 mulattos, while there are in Virginia—how many do you think?—79,775, being 23,126 more than in all the free States together.

    These statistics show that slavery is the greatest source of amalgamation, and next to it, not the elevation, but the degradation of the free blacks. Yet Judge Douglas dreads the slightest restraints on the spread of slavery, and the slightest human recognition of the negro, as tending horribly to amalgamation.

    The very Dred Scott case affords a strong test as to which party most favors amalgamation, the Republicans or the dear Union-saving Democracy. Dred Scott, his wife, and two daughters were all involved in the suit. We desired the court to have held that they were citizens so far at least as to entitle them to a hearing as to whether they were free or not; and then, also, that they were in fact and in law really free. Could we have had our way, the chances of these black girls ever mixing their blood with that of white people would have been diminished at least to the extent that it could not have been without their consent. But Judge Douglas is delighted to have them decided to be slaves, and not human enough to have a hearing, even if they were free, and thus left subject to the forced concubinage of their masters, and liable to become the mothers of mulattos in spite of themselves: the very state of case that produces nine tenths of all the mulattos—all the mixing of blood in the nation.

    Of course, I state this case as an illustration only, not meaning to say or intimate that the master of Dred

Scott and his family, or any more than a percentage of masters generally, are inclined to exercise this particular power which they hold over their female slaves.

I have said that the separation of the races is the only perfect preventive of amalgamation. I have no right to say all the members of the Republican party are in favor of this, nor to say that as a party they are in favor or it. There is nothing in their platform directly on the subject. But I can say a very large proportion of its members are for it, and that the chief plank in their platform—opposition to the spread of slavery—is most favorable to that separation.[992]

Lincoln goes on to discuss the deportation ("colonization") of all freed blacks, his ideal solution to the "race problem":

> Such separation, if ever effected at all, must be effected by colonization; and no political party, as such, is now doing anything directly for colonization. Party operations at present only favor or retard colonization incidentally. The enterprise is a difficult one; but "where there is a will there is a way," and what colonization needs most is a hearty will. Will springs from the two elements of moral sense and self-interest. Let us be brought to believe it is morally right, and at the same time favorable to, or at least not against, our interest to transfer the African to his native clime, and we shall find a way to do it, however great the task may be. The children of Israel, to such numbers as to include four hundred thousand fighting men, went out of Egyptian bondage in a body.
>
> How differently the respective courses of the Democratic and Republican parties incidentally bear on the question of forming a will—a public sentiment—for colonization, is easy to see.[993]

For Lincoln emancipating then deporting freed African-Americans was as easy as blocking black civil rights. As he stated in September 1859, just a year before he was elected president:

> Negro equality! Fudge!! How long, in the Government of a God great enough to make and maintain this universe, shall there continue [to be] knaves to vend and fools to gulp, so low a piece of demagoguism as this?[994]

Lincoln's adopted home state of Illinois, arguably the most racist state at the time, was in full agreement with him. Illinoisans passed countless anti-integration and anti-immigration laws to prevent blacks from settling in or even traveling through their state, with punishments ranging from whipping to being sold back into slavery at public auction.[995] In 1862 Illinois voters adopted a constitutional provision that barred the further admission of blacks into their state,[996] a Black Code that Lincoln allowed to remain on the books until 1865, the year his War finally came to an end.[997]

In 1863, for example, eight blacks were arrested and convicted for entering Illinois unlawfully. Of these, seven were sold back into slavery (temporarily) to pay off their fines[998]—all under Lincoln's watch, the same man who had at one time been a manager of the Illinois chapter of the American Colonization Society (ACS).[999]

Black Illinois residents complained bitterly of their treatment. One of these, John Jones, a wealthy African-American living in Chicago, sent the following message to Governor Richard Yates. We, the colored people of Illinois, it began, are highly displeased with the degradation we are suffering under in our State. Though we were born here, we are viewed as strangers. A black man cannot even buy a burial plot in Chicago for himself. The hatred toward us all comes from the anti-Negro laws passed by the whites of Illinois.[1000]

Lincoln ignored Jones' complaint. Why?

As his own words have made clear, Lincoln detested the presence of blacks in America, thought nothing of using the "n" word,[1001] constantly referred to them as the **"inferior race,"**[1002] and held that they should not be allowed to vote, sit on juries, hold political office, or intermarry with whites.[1003] **"We cannot make them equals,"** he consistently maintained both privately and publicly.[1004]

During his August 21, 1858, debate with Douglas at Ottawa, Illinois, Lincoln not only agreed with his opponent's call for continued white supremacy, he also complained that he had been misrepresented as having promoted interracial marriage. In response, he angrily denied the charge, saying that he had never intended to **"set the niggers and white people to marry together."**[1005]

During this same debate Lincoln touched on the topic of nationalizing slavery. As we have seen, he was not against slavery. As a white separatist he was merely against it spreading outside the South. To assuage the fears of his supporters in the audience, he assured them that not even war could extend slavery beyond the borders of the Southern states.

As he put it:

> In the first place, what is necessary to make the institution national? Not war. There is no danger that the people of Kentucky will shoulder their muskets, and, with a young nigger stuck on every bayonet, march into Illinois and force them upon us. There is no danger of our going over there and making war upon them.[1006]

Sometime, perhaps in the summer of 1861, liberal U.S. Congressman James Mitchell Ashley recorded the following conversation with Lincoln, in which they discussed so-called "Reconstruction":

> After an unusually long and warm discussion one morning on this subject, I rose to go, quite dissatisfied with the result of my interview and exhibiting a little more feeling than I ought, when the President called out, and said: **"Ashley, that was a great speech you made out in Ohio the other day."** I turned, and, I fear with some irritation in both manner and voice, said: "I have made no speech anywhere, Mr. President, and have not been out of Washington." He laughed and said: **"Well, I see Nasby says that in consequence of one speech made by Jim Ashley, four hundred thousand niggers moved into Wood County last week, and it must have taken a great speech to do that."** Of course I joined in the laugh, and then Mr. Lincoln, in his kindly manner, said: **"Come up soon, Ashley, and we will take up reconstruction again."**[1007]

The following fragment of one of Lincoln's speeches, from September 8, 1858, at Paris, Illinois, reveals that the soon-to-be president was very comfortable using the "n" word, whether coming from his own lips, or quoting someone else:

> Let us inquire what Judge [Stephen A.] Douglas really invented when he introduced the Nebraska Bill. He called it popular sovereignty. What does that mean? It means the sovereignty of the people over their own affairs—in other words, the right of the people to govern themselves. Did Judge Douglas invent this? Not quite. The idea of popular sovereignty was floating about several ages before the author of the Nebraska Bill was born—indeed, before Columbus set foot on this continent. In the year 1776 it took form in the noble

words which you are all familiar with: "We hold these truths to be self-evident, that all men are created equal," etc. Was not this the origin of popular sovereignty as applied to the American people? Here we are told that governments are instituted among men deriving their just powers from the consent of the governed. If that is not popular sovereignty, then I have no conception of the meaning of words. If Judge Douglas did not invent this kind of popular sovereignty, let us pursue the inquiry and find out what kind he did invent. Was it the right of emigrants to Kansas and Nebraska to govern themselves, and a lot of "niggers," too, if they wanted them? Clearly this was no invention of his, because General [Lewis] Cass put forth the same doctrine in 1848 in his so-called Nicholson letter, six years before Douglas thought of such a thing. Then what was it that the "Little Giant" invented? It never occurred to General Cass to call his discovery by the odd name of popular sovereignty. He had not the face to say that the right of the people to govern "niggers" was the right of the people to govern themselves. His notions of the fitness of things were not moulded to the brazenness of calling the right to put a hundred "niggers" through under the lash in Nebraska a "sacred" right of self-government. And here I submit to you was Judge Douglas's discovery, and the whole of it: He discovered that the right to breed and flog negroes in Nebraska was popular sovereignty.[1008]

In a conversation that Yankee lawyer Edward L. Pierce once had with Lincoln, he reported that the president unashamedly referred to blacks as **"niggers"** rather than as Negroes.[1009]

We should not be surprised at such language. After all, this is the same man who referred to Mexicans as **"greasers,"**[1010] **"mongrels,"**[1011] and also inevitably as an **"inferior race."**[1012] What is surprising is that Lincoln continues to be lovingly referred to as a "humanitarian," an "egalitarian," the "true friend of the black man," and the "Great Emancipator."

Sometimes Lincoln's racism was somewhat obscured, such as in the following unfinished, August 6, 1864, draft of a letter to an unidentified person in Pennsylvania. As was so often the case, bizarrely, Lincoln here writes in the third person:

> The President has received yours of yesterday and is kindly paying attention to it. As it is my business to assist him whenever I can, I will thank you to inform me, for his use, whether you are either a white man or black man, because in either case you cannot be regarded as an entirely impartial judge. It may be that you belong to a third or fourth class of yellow or red men, in which case the impartiality of your judgment would be more apparent.[1013]

What such words meant to Lincoln is anyone's guess. What they tell us, however, is that our sixteenth president, like most liberals today, was extremely, if not obsessively, race conscious.[1014]

The truth that you will never read in books by Lincoln apologists, Lincoln worshipers, or pro-North/anti-South proponents is that it was Lincoln who was the main barrier against the abolition of slavery, against the granting of full civil rights to blacks, and against the incorporation of blacks into mainstream white America. All, in fact, came only *after* Lincoln died on April 15, 1865.

Throughout his political career, for example, Lincoln was repeatedly challenged as to whether he was in favor of "negro citizenship," and he repeatedly gave the same answer, as he did at Charleston, Illinois, on September 18, 1858, in a rebuttal to Stephen A. Douglas:

> Judge Douglas has said to you that he has not been able to get from me an answer to the question whether I am in favor of negro citizenship. So far as I know, the judge never asked me the question before. He shall have no occasion to ever ask it again, for I tell him very frankly that I am not in favor of negro citizenship. This furnishes me an occasion for saying a few words upon the subject. I mentioned in a certain speech of mine, which has been printed, that the Supreme Court had decided that a negro could not possibly be made a citizen, and without saying what was my ground of complaint in regard to that, or whether I had any ground of complaint, Judge Douglas has from that thing manufactured nearly everything that he ever says about my disposition to produce an equality between the negroes and the white people. If any one will read my speech, he will find I mentioned that as one of the points decided in the course of the Supreme Court opinions, but I did not state what objection I had to it. But Judge Douglas tells the people what my objection

was when I did not tell them myself. Now my opinion is that the different States have the power to make a negro a citizen under the Constitution of the United States, if they choose. The Dred Scott decision decides that they have not that power. If the State of Illinois had that power, I should be opposed to the exercise of it. That is all I have to say about it.[1015]

The reader must now ask himself or herself: are these the words of someone who deserves the title the "Great Emancipator"?[1016]

Lincoln, Black Colonization, & White Separatism

I F ABRAHAM LINCOLN IS SUPPOSED to have been the "voice of American racial harmony," we are entitled to wonder why, on July 17, 1858, he made the following statement:

> When our government was established, we had the institution of slavery among us. We were in a certain sense compelled to tolerate its existence. It was a sort of necessity. We had gone through our struggle, and secured our own independence. The framers of the Constitution found the institution of slavery amongst their other institutions at the time. They found that by an effort to eradicate it, they might lose much of what they had already gained. They were obliged to bow to the necessity. They gave power to Congress to abolish the slave-trade at the end of twenty years. They also prohibited slavery in the Territories where it did not exist. They did what they could and yielded to necessity for the rest. I also yield to all which follows from that necessity. What I would most desire would be the separation of the white and black races.[1017]

Lincoln's yearning to live in a white-only America, known to modern blacks as "Abraham Lincoln's white dream,"[1018] was something close to the heart of nearly every white Northerner. This "dream" dated back to the very origins of our nation at which time Yankees enthusiastically supported the idea of American apartheid: the geographical separation of the races.

The problem was not blacks, of course. It was white racism: the belief that the "superior" Caucasian race is sullied by contact with the "inferior" black and brown races.

This is the reason most white Northerners were lukewarm toward, or even completely against, abolition: they were afraid that Southern emancipation would send millions of African-Americans northward to intermix with their children, dilute and corrupt the white race, endanger racial purity, threaten prosperity, lower moral standards, scare off visitors and tourists, discourage new business, spread diseases, drive down property values, instigate a massive crime wave, thwart colonization, promote abolitionist doctrines, "Africanize" the white North, and worst of all, take away jobs from whites.[1019]

Boston-born inventor, statesman, Founding Father, slave owner, and white supremacist Benjamin Franklin[1020] could have been speaking for the vast majority of Yankees and Northerners when he voted to prohibit slavery while at the same time complaining about the problem of disappearing whites in the face of an ever increasing black population.[1021] Slaves, Franklin wrote, have

> blackened half [of] America. . . why should we . . . [continue to] darken its people? Why increase the sons of Africa by planting them in America, where we have so fair an opportunity, by excluding all blacks and tawneys [pure Africans and mulattoes], of increasing the lovely white . . . ? I am partial to the complexion of my country . . .[1022]

The widely respected New Englander summed up the essential problem as he saw it: Black slaves depreciate the white families who own them.[1023] This was a notion accepted in nearly every home throughout the North during the 17th, 18th, and 19th Centuries.

Yes, Negrophobia was alive and well across Yankeedom from America's earliest days to the "Civil War," and beyond.[1024]

Like Franklin, Lincoln too was obsessed with the idea that freed Southern slaves would overrun the North and dilute and corrupt the white race. After all, like other Northerners, he had grown accustomed to living in a largely black-free region—and he wanted to keep it that way.

For Northerners, keeping slavery in the South was an ideal form of race control: not only did it prevent blacks from emigrating northward, but with African-Americans far removed from Yankee society the question of racial equality need never be confronted. Thus, the North's Free-Soil party was not about free land, as Yankee myth teaches.[1025] It was about keeping Northern and Western soil free of blacks,[1026] a people clearly despised by most Yankees at the time, as Lincoln himself intimated.

On September 8, 1858, during a speech at Clinton, Illinois, Lincoln responded to accusations that he and his party favored racial equality, a serious taboo in the North at the time:

> And now let me say a few words in regard to [Stephen A.] Douglas's great hobby of negro equality. He thinks—he says at least—that the Republican [liberal] party is in favor of allowing whites and blacks to intermarry, and that a man can't be a good Republican unless he is willing to elevate black men to office and to associate with them on terms of perfect equality. He knows that we advocate no such doctrines as those . . .[1027]

That issue settled, a year later, on September 16, 1859, in a speech at Columbus, Ohio, Lincoln voiced his concerns about the expansion of slavery. If the institution is allowed to spread across the U.S., he said fearfully:

> They will be ready for Jeff Davis and [Alexander H.] Stephens and other leaders of that company, to sound the bugle for the revival of the slave-trade, for the second Dred Scott decision, for the flood of slavery to be poured over the Free States [the North], while we shall be here tied down and helpless, and run over like sheep.[1028]

Earlier, in 1838, Lincoln's political idol, slave owner Henry Clay,[1029] articulated his dread of the situation as well:

> I am no friend of slavery. The Searcher of all hearts knows that every pulsation of mine beats high and strong in the cause of civil liberty. Wherever it is safe and practicable, I desire to see every portion of the human family in the enjoyment of it. But I prefer the liberty of my own country to that of any other people, and the liberty of my own race to that of any other race. The liberty of the descendants of Africa in the United States is incompatible with the liberty and safety of the European descendants. Their slavery forms

an exception—an exception resulting from a stern and inexorable necessity—to the general liberty in the United States. We did not originate, nor are we responsible for, this necessity. Their liberty, if it were possible, could only be established by violating the incontestable powers of the states and subverting the Union; and beneath the ruins of the Union would be buried, sooner or later, the liberty of both races.[1030]

The Boston *Post* joined in the antiblack paranoia. If you liberate the slaves, it declared, the North's poorhouses will soon overflow with them.[1031]

It was for these very reasons that Yankees were reluctant to extend civil rights to blacks: any improvement in their condition in the North, so they believed, would surely lead to an unwanted massive migration of Southern blacks into their region. Thus, even after Lincoln's War, many Northern and Western states were still turning down constitutional amendments that would have authorized black suffrage. Such states included Connecticut, Michigan, Kansas, Wisconsin, Ohio, and Missouri. As late as 1868, black men were still refused the vote in nearly every Northern state.[1032]

Some from Lincoln's party, trying to stem the panic and reassure fearful Northern whites, turned the situation around, claiming hopefully that a Southern emancipation would actually create a "mass migration" of Northern blacks *southward* into Dixie. No one believed this, of course, and the North-wide scare continued. After issuing his Emancipation Proclamation, Lincoln then tried following a "containment" policy, a method by which he could keep freed slaves "hemmed in," as Douglas put it, across the South.[1033] But this, like his emancipation itself, turned out to be nothing more than a transparent political maneuver meant to garner support and votes for his reelection.[1034]

In reality, the racist dread Lincoln and his Northern constituents felt concerning a "great horde of blacks swarming Northward" was imaginary. Southern blacks were mainly poor rural farmers, with no love of big city lights and industry, and no money to move long distances. More importantly, they adored their homeland Dixie, with its soothing weather, friendly people, spacious crop lands, and its bountiful mountains, rivers, and forests. Yankee soldiers stationed in the South admitted as much. One of them, Charles Nordhoff, noted sourly in March 1863 that despite the fact that, if they desired, *all* Southern blacks were allowed official passes to move North, less than twelve applications had been submitted to his office since the start of the War. This was over a span of two years.[1035]

Southern blacks who had either been forcibly taken North or who had gone North voluntarily during the War usually regretted the move. Even free Northern blacks felt an affinity with the South that they never had for their own region. Thus, when they worked, especially on steamers that journeyed South, they could often be heard singing the beloved traditional Southern tune, *Dixie*:[1036]

> O, I wish I was in the land of cotton
> Old times there are not forgotten
> Look away! Look away!
> Look away! Dixie Land
>
> In Dixie Land where I was born in
> Early on one frosty mornin'
> Look away! Look away!
> Look away! Dixie Land
>
> O, I wish I was in Dixie!
> Hooray! Hooray!
> In Dixie Land I'll take my stand
> To live and die in Dixie
> Away, away,
> Away down south in Dixie![1037]

Clearly, Lincoln and his white supremacist friends at the North were in no danger of a **"flood"** of freed Southern blacks running over them **"like sheep,"** as he put it.

But this fact did not put a stop to their fears. Their ignorance of Southern blacks and Southern society in general made them blind to what all Southerners, whatever their race, knew instinctively: by 1860 the South was the birthplace and homeland of most of America's blacks, and they were not about to leave and head North; not even if they were freed by a Yankee president.

Lincoln's fear of living among blacks prevented him from grasping even this elementary fact. What was he to do? For Negrophobic Northerners like Lincoln the only "solution" to this dilemma was colonization, the deportation of any and all blacks who would voluntarily leave the U.S.[1038] As he stated emphatically in a September 17, 1859, speech regarding slavery and Africa:

. . . I would . . . own no slave, but . . . would desire to buy

one and take him there.[1039]

Here for once Lincoln had the full backing of the rest of his cabinet, not to mention the majority of his Northern constituents. Indeed, most Northerners were repulsed by the idea of racial integration, and instead at every opportunity pushed for colonization and forced expulsion—or at the very least, social proscription.[1040]

Thus for Lincoln, emancipation, colonization, and white supremacy (or rather black insubordination), became the only logical solutions to the nation's racial woes.[1041] This is why, in the summer of 1861, when runaway Southern slaves started to appear in Yankee military camps, citizens all across the North began promoting the idea of black deportation harder than ever.[1042]

On July 16, 1852, Lincoln summed up the quintessential "problem" of slavery and emancipation like this:

> **I think no wise man has perceived . . . how it could be at once eradicated without producing a greater evil even to the cause of human liberty itself.**[1043]

According to Lincoln then, for most Northern whites abolition was worse than slavery itself.

The famed emancipationist-racist Hinton Rowan Helper, one of Lincoln's most passionate supporters, put the matter this way:

> [America will only have peace after the] country shall have been thoroughly cleansed of the vulgar and disgusting negroes and their next of kin . . .[1044]

Helper's anti-black book, *The Impending Crisis of the South*—which contained statements such as "we do not believe in the unity of the races"[1045]—was heartily endorsed by Lincoln[1046] (who even mentioned Helper and his book in his speeches),[1047] and in 1860 it was used as a campaign document by his party.[1048] Concerning blacks, a people that Helper described as a "God-forsaken race" and Lincoln called an **"inferior race,"**[1049] the two men agreed on numerous points. These included white separatism, along with prohibitions against voting, sitting on juries, and interracial marriage.[1050] For his efforts on Lincoln's behalf Helper was rewarded with a South American consulate.[1051]

We will note here that while liberal Northerner Lincoln was

reading and avidly promoting Helper's white supremacist book, conservative Southerners were not only burning it,[1052] but also punishing whites who circulated it, owned it, or read it.[1053] Indeed, after pouring over its pages, Lincoln's only major criticisms of *The Impending Crisis of the South* were that it called for *immediate* emancipation and that it referred to proslavery slaveholders as "criminals."[1054] Lincoln was vehemently against both of these ideas.

Lincoln's postmaster general, lawyer Montgomery Blair, agreed with Lincoln and Helper, insisting that the forced deportation of Negroes was vital, for after emancipation:

> It would be necessary to rid the country of its black population, and some place must be found for them.[1055]

Lincoln's secretary of state, William H. Seward, too had a copy of Helper's book. Of it he said:

> I have read the *Impending Crisis of the South* with great attention. It seems to me a work of great merit; rich yet accurate in statistical information, and logical in analysis.[1056]

In case his own views on race, white labor, and colonization were not clear to everyone, Lincoln continued to emphasize them time and time again: he was thoroughly committed to white supremacy,[1057] even if it meant allowing slavery to continue. One of his most notable declarations in this regard occurred in New York on February 27, 1860, during his renowned Cooper Union Speech, where he stated that he held the view of slavery of Thomas Jefferson and the other Founding Fathers. Said Lincoln:

> **This is all Republicans ask—all Republicans desire—in relation to slavery. As those fathers marked it, so let it be again marked, as an evil not to be extended, but to be tolerated and protected only because of and so far as its actual presence among us makes that toleration and protection a necessity. Let all the guaranties those fathers gave it be not grudgingly, but fully and fairly, maintained.**[1058]

Lincoln then quoted Jefferson himself, stressing his personal beliefs pertaining to white supremacy:[1059]

> "It is still in our power to direct the process of emancipation and deportation peaceably, and in such slow degrees, as that the evil will wear off sensibly; and their places be . . . filled up by free white laborers. If, on the contrary, it is left to force itself on, human nature must shudder at the prospect held up."[1060]

Over time, Lincoln, a dyed-in-the-wool white separatist, became literally obsessed with the idea of apartheid, which is one reason why, when he was a member of the Illinois legislature, he asked for funds to expel all free blacks from his state, or what he termed **"the troublesome presence of the free negroes."**[1061] This was also the reason he became a manager of the Illinois chapter of the American Colonization Society (ACS)[1062]—at one time headed by his "beau ideal,"[1063] slaver Henry Clay.[1064]

The ACS was founded in 1816 in Washington, D.C., by a Northerner, New Jerseyan Reverend Robert Finley.[1065] Among its early leaders, officers, and supporters were such famed Yankees as New England statesman Daniel Webster (after whom the town of Webster, Massachusetts, was named), New Yorker William H. Seward (Lincoln's secretary of state, and the man after whom the city of Seward, Alaska, and the Seward Peninsula were named), and Marylander Francis Scott Key (author of the U.S. National Anthem, *The Star-Spangled Banner*).[1066]

The nation's largest and most enthusiastic chapter was in Boston, Massachusetts, where antislavery and anti-black sentiment were at their highest in the nation. As we have seen, the two were not mutually exclusive in New England,[1067] the birthplace of both the American slave trade[1068] and American slavery.[1069]

The stated mission of the ACS was the preservation of white culture through the deportation of all American blacks, both free and emancipated, out of the U.S. The African colony of Liberia was created by the ACS in 1822 for this very purpose: to "liberate" America from blacks, hence its name.[1070]

As we saw in the previous chapter, on June 26, 1857, at Springfield, Illinois, ACS member Lincoln lectured his Northern audience on the many benefits of "a separation of the races":

> **Judge** [Stephen] **Douglas is especially horrified at the thought of the mixing of blood by the white and black races: agreed for once—a thousand times agreed. There are white men enough to marry all the white women, and**

black men enough to marry all the black women; and so let them be married. . . . A separation of the races is the only perfect preventive of amalgamation; but as an immediate separation is impossible the next best thing is to keep them apart where they are not already together. If white and black people never get together in Kansas, they will never mix blood in Kansas. That is at least one self-evident truth. A few free colored persons may get into the free States, in any event; but their number is too insignificant to amount to much in the way of mixing blood. . . . In 1850 there were in the United States 405,751 mulattoes. Very few of these are the offspring of whites and *free* blacks; nearly all have sprung from the black *slaves* and white masters. These statistics show that slavery is the greatest source of amalgamation.[1071]

By "amalgamation," Lincoln was referring to one of white Northerners' most monumental fears: miscegenation (i.e., interracial mixing, cohabitation, or marriage), something fairly common and much more widely accepted in the South. Indeed, the word miscegenation was coined by Northerners in the early 1860s. Why? Anti-Lincoln Yankees wanted to play up on the Northern trepidation of "race-mixing," which they believed would be the certain result of any kind of Southern emancipation program.[1072]

But these men misunderstood Lincoln, for prior to reluctantly issuing his Final Emancipation Proclamation on January 1, 1863, he was on their side.

In his July 6, 1852, eulogy to his lifelong icon Henry Clay, for example, Lincoln managed to bring up the topics of miscegenation and colonization, noting that the former could be allayed, even prevented, in the North by the latter. Let us now look at the words of **"that truly national man whose life and death we now commemorate and lament,"** Lincoln said at Clay's funeral:

> I quote from a speech of Mr. Clay delivered before the American Colonization Society in 1827:
>
>> [Lincoln quoting Clay] "We are reproached with doing mischief by the agitation of this question. The society goes into no household to disturb its domestic tranquillity. It addresses itself to no

slaves to weaken their obligations of obedience. It seeks to affect no man's property. It neither has the power nor the will to affect the property of any one contrary to his consent. The execution of its scheme would augment instead of diminishing the value of property left behind. The society, composed of free men, concerns itself only with the free. Collateral consequences we are not responsible for. It is not this society which has produced the great moral revolution which the age exhibits. What would they who thus reproach us have done? If they would repress all tendencies toward liberty and ultimate emancipation, they must do more than put down the benevolent efforts of society. They must go back to the era of our liberty and independence, and muzzle the cannon which thunders its annual joyous return. They must renew the slave-trade, with all its train of atrocities. They must suppress the workings of British philanthropy, seeking to meliorate the condition of the unfortunate West Indian slave. They must arrest the career of South American deliverance from thraldom. They must blow out the moral light around us and extinguish that greatest torch of all which America presents to a benighted world—pointing the way to their rights, their liberties, and their happiness. And when they have achieved all those purposes their work will be yet incomplete. They must penetrate the human soul, and eradicate the light of reason and the love of liberty. Then, and not till then, when universal darkness and despair prevail, can you perpetuate slavery and repress all sympathy and all humane and benevolent efforts among free men in behalf of the unhappy portion of our race doomed to bondage."

The American Colonization Society was organized in 1816. Mr. Clay, though not its projector [i.e., founder], was one of its earliest members; and he died, as for many preceding years he had been, its president. It was one of the most cherished objects of his direct care and consideration, and the association of his name with it has probably been its very greatest collateral support. He considered it no demerit in the society that it tended, to relieve the slaveholders from the troublesome presence of the free negroes; but this was far from being its whole merit in his estimation. In the same speech from which we have quoted he [Clay] says:

> "There is a moral fitness in the idea of returning to Africa her children, whose ancestors have been torn from her by the ruthless hand of fraud and violence. Transplanted in a foreign land, they will carry back to their native soil the rich fruits of religion, civilization, law, and liberty. May it not be one of the great designs of the Ruler of the universe, whose ways are often inscrutable by short-sighted mortals, thus to transform an original crime into a signal blessing to that most unfortunate portion of the globe?"

This suggestion of the possible ultimate redemption of the African race and African continent was made twenty-five years ago. Every succeeding year has added strength to the hope of its realization. May it indeed be realized. Pharaoh's country was cursed with plagues, and his hosts were lost in the Red Sea, for striving to retain a captive people who had already served them more than four hundred years. May like disasters never befall us! If, as the friends of colonization hope, the present and coming generations of our countrymen shall by any means succeed in freeing our land from the dangerous presence of slavery, and at the same time in restoring a captive people to their long-lost fatherland with bright prospects for the future, and this too so gradually that neither races nor individuals shall have suffered by the change, it will indeed be a *glorious consummation* [emphasis added]. And if to such a consummation the efforts of Mr. Clay shall have contributed, it will be what he most ardently wished, and none of his labors will have been more valuable to his country and his kind.

But Henry Clay is dead. His long and eventful life is closed. Our country is prosperous and powerful; but could it have been quite all it has been, and is, and is to be, without Henry Clay? Such a man the times have demanded, and such in the providence of God was given us. But he is gone. Let us strive to deserve, as far as mortals may, the continued care of Divine Providence, trusting that in future national emergencies He will not fail to provide us the instruments of safety and security.[1073]

Amazingly, the man who uttered these words—that the success of deporting all blacks out of the U.S. would be a **"glorious consummation"**—is still referred to as "the great friend of the black man" by the very people who should know better: scholars, professors, teachers, educators, librarians, writers, museum directors, historic house directors, Civil War site directors, school administrators, tour guides, and researchers.

Nine years on, now president of the United States, Lincoln was just as zealous about black colonization. In his First Annual Message to Congress on December 3, 1861, he once again took the opportunity to promote the idea of deporting blacks, in this case, free blacks:

> Under and by virtue of the act of Congress entitled "An act to confiscate property used for insurrectionary purposes," approved August 6, 1861, the legal claims of certain persons to the labor and service of certain other persons have become forfeited; and numbers of the latter, thus liberated, are already dependent on the United States, and must be provided for in some way. Besides this, it is not impossible that some of the States will pass similar enactments for their own benefit respectively, and by operation of which persons of the same class will be thrown upon them for disposal. In such case I recommend that Congress provide for accepting such persons from such States, according to some mode of valuation, in lieu, *pro tanto*, of direct taxes,

or upon some other plan to be agreed on with such States respectively; that such persons, on such acceptance by the General Government, be at once deemed free; and that, in any event, steps be taken for colonizing both classes (or the one first mentioned, if the other shall not be brought into existence) at some place or places in a climate congenial to them. It might be well to consider, too, whether the free colored people already in the United States could not, so far as individuals may desire, be included in such colonization.

To carry out the plan of colonization may involve the acquiring of territory, and also the appropriation of money beyond that to be expended in the territorial acquisition. Having practised the acquisition of territory for nearly sixty years, the question of constitutional power to do so is no longer an open one with us. The power was questioned at first by Mr. [Thomas] Jefferson, who, however, in the purchase of Louisiana, yielded his scruples on the plea of great expediency. If it be said that the only legitimate object of acquiring territory is to furnish homes for white men, this measure effects that object; for the emigration of colored men leaves additional room for white men remaining or coming here. Mr. Jefferson, however, placed the importance of procuring Louisiana more on political and commercial grounds than on providing room for population.

On this whole proposition, including the appropriation of money with the acquisition of territory, does not the expediency amount to absolute necessity—that without which the government itself cannot be perpetuated?[1074]

Lincoln here proposes to Congress that the U.S. **"liberate"** the slaves, purchase new lands to put them on, then deport them there as soon as possible. As a result of this speech, in 1861 and 1862, Congress had $600,000 (about $15 million in today's currency) set aside to aid Lincoln's colonization proposal.[1075]

Five months later, on April 16, 1862, Lincoln helped push through the District of Columbia Emancipation Act, or as it was technically known: "An Act for the Release of Certain Persons held to Service or Labor in the District of Columbia." Both slaves and abolitionists rejoiced that Lincoln finally relented, banning slavery in the nation's capital. Up until then the president had been decidedly against shutting down America's largest slave mart,[1076] one located in full view of Northern members of Congress, who walked by it each day without so much as wincing.[1077] We will recall that only months before his inauguration Lincoln had testified to the fact that:

> **I have no thought of recommending the abolition of slavery in the District of Columbia, nor the slave-trade among the slave States.**[1078]

The shouts of joy and praise lasted only momentarily however. For when the entire act was read, abolitionists and black civil rights leaders were horrified to realize that it did not just call for the destruction of slavery in the District. It called for the deportation of all those who were freed by the act as well. Lincoln had craftily worded the bill so that both abolitionists, and colonizationists like himself, would benefit: the slaves would be liberated, then immediately sent out of the U.S. and settled in a foreign country, as he intimated in his April 16, "Message to Congress."[1079]

Here is the exact wording of Lincoln's Emancipation Proclamation for the District of Washington, D.C.:

> **An Act for the Release of certain Persons held to Service or Labor in the District of Columbia. "All persons held to service or labor within the District of Columbia by reason of African descent are hereby discharged and freed of and from all claim to such service or labor; and from and after the passage of this act neither slavery nor involuntary servitude, except for crime, whereof the party shall be duly convicted, shall hereafter exist in said District."** All loyal persons holding claims against persons discharged by this act may, within 90 days from its passage, but not thereafter, present such claims in writing to the commissioners hereinafter mentioned. Three commissioners shall be appointed, residents of the District of Columbia, any two of whom shall have power to act, to investigate the validity and appraise and apportion the value in money of such claims; but the entire sum so appraised and apportioned shall not exceed in the aggregate an amount equal to $300 for each person shown to have been so held by lawful claim; and no claim shall be allowed for any slave or slaves brought into said District after the passage of this act, nor for any claimed by persons who have in any manner aided or

sustained the rebellion against the Government of the United States. The commissioners shall within nine months deposit a full and final report of their proceedings and awards with the Secretary of the Treasury, who shall cause the amounts apportioned to be paid from the Treasury of the United States, except in the case of conflicting claims, in which 60 days are allowed for filing a bill in equity. $1,000,000 are appropriated for the purposes of this act, and $100,000 for the colonization of such free persons of African descent now residing in said District, or liberated by this act, as may desire to emigrate to the Republics of Hayti [Haiti] or Liberia, or such other country beyond the limits of the United States as the President may determine, at a rate not exceeding $100 for each emigrant. (April 16, 1862.)[1080]

The same day a gloating Lincoln sent a letter to the Senate and the House of Representatives concerning the District of Columbia Emancipation Act. It read, in part:

> I am gratified that the two principles of compensation and colonization are both recognized and practically applied in the act.[1081]

A few months later, on July 11, 1862, Lincoln addressed an "appeal" to representatives of the Border States concerning gradual and compensated emancipation. After spending several minutes explaining how his plan would help bring a speedy end to his War, he says:

> Room in South America for colonization can be obtained cheaply and in abundance, and when numbers shall be large enough to be company and encouragement for one another, the freed people will not be so reluctant to go.[1082]

This statement was made just three months before he issued his Preliminary Emancipation Proclamation on September 22, 1862.

Five months later, in his Second Annual Message to Congress on December 1, 1862, he elaborated his position on the issue:

> Applications have been made to me by many free Americans of African descent to favor their emigration,

with a view to such colonization as was contemplated in recent acts of Congress. Other parties at home and abroad—some from interested motives, others upon patriotic considerations, and still others influenced by philanthropic sentiments—have suggested similar measures; while, on the other hand, several of the Spanish-American republics have protested against the sending of such colonies to their respective territories. Under these circumstances, I have declined to move any such colony to any state without first obtaining the consent of its government, with an agreement on its part to receive and protect such emigrants in all the rights of freemen; and I have at the same time offered to the several states situated within the tropics, or having colonies there, to negotiate with them, subject to the advice and consent of the Senate, to favor the voluntary emigration of persons of that class to their respective territories, upon conditions which shall be equal, just, and humane. Liberia and Hayti [Haiti] are as yet the only countries to which colonists of African descent from here could go with certainty of being received and adopted as citizens; and I regret to say such persons contemplating colonization do not seem so willing to migrate to those countries as to some others, nor so willing as I think their interest demands. I believe, however, opinion among them in this respect is improving; and that ere long there will be an augmented and considerable migration to both these countries from the United States.[1083]

These thoughts were voiced just one month before he issued his Final Emancipation Proclamation on January 1, 1863.

Amazingly, Lincoln states here that he was at one time considering shipping freed American blacks to foreign nations without those governments' permission. But now, because of the resistance to this idea, he would try to get their **"consent"** first. He also admits that most nations did not want America's freedmen and women, *and* that most freedmen and women did not want to be forced from their homeland (the latter reality which he completely ignored). He ends the above paragraph with the incredible statement that he believes that a **"considerable"** number of liberated blacks will soon be leaving the U.S. for Liberia and Haiti—a belief that never came close to becoming a reality.

In order to ram his "white dream" of a black-free America through Congress as quickly as possible, Lincoln has by now come up with his own black deportation plan, one based on a three-article amendment to the Constitution.[1084] In this same speech he outlines them as follows.

The first article proposed compensating slave owners for the loss of their slaves if they emancipated them by the year 1900.[1085] The second article stated that all slaves liberated under this resolution would be "**forever free.**"[1086] The third article read:

> Congress may appropriate money and otherwise provide for colonizing free colored persons, with their own consent, at anyplace or places without the United States.[1087]

Lincoln goes on to explain this particular clause in more detail:

> The third article relates to the future of the freed people. It does not oblige, but merely authorizes, Congress to aid in colonizing such as may consent. This ought not to be regarded as objectionable, on the one hand or on the other, insomuch as it comes to nothing unless by the mutual consent of the people to be deported, and the American voters through their representatives in Congress.
>
> I cannot make it better known than it already is, that I strongly favor colonization.[1088]

The president then addresses the fears of white Northerners about the universal Yankee horror of a flood of freed Southern blacks migrating North, where they would allegedly compete with whites for jobs. Again, the solution is colonization:

> And yet I wish to say there is an objection urged against free colored persons remaining in the country which is largely imaginary, if not sometimes malicious.
>
> It is insisted that their presence would injure and displace white labor and white laborers. If there ever could be a proper time for mere catch arguments, that time surely is not now. In times like the present, men should utter nothing for which they would not willingly be responsible through time and in eternity. Is it true, then, that colored people can displace any more white labor by being free than by remaining slaves? If they stay in their old places, they jostle no white laborers; if they leave their old places, they leave them

open to white laborers. Logically, there is neither more nor less of it. Emancipation, even without deportation, would probably enhance the wages of white labor, and very surely would not reduce them. Thus, the customary amount of labor would still have to be performed; the freed people would surely not do more than their old proportion of it, and very probably for a time would do less, leaving an increased part to white laborers, bringing their labor into greater demand, and consequently enhancing the wages of it. With deportation, even to a limited extent, enhanced wages to white labor is mathematically certain. Labor is like any other commodity in the market—increase the demand for it, and you increase the price of it. Reduce the supply of black labor by colonizing the black laborer out of the country, and by precisely so much you increase the demand for, and wages of, white labor.

But it is dreaded that the freed people will swarm forth and cover the whole land? Are they not already in the land? Will liberation make them any more numerous? Equally distributed among the whites of the whole country, and there would be but one colored to seven whites. Could the one in any way greatly disturb the seven? There are many communities now having more than one free colored person to seven whites, and this without any apparent consciousness of evil from it. The District of Columbia, and the States of Maryland and Delaware, are all in this condition. The District has more than one free colored to six whites; and yet in its frequent petitions to Congress I believe it has never presented the presence of free colored persons as one of its grievances. But why should emancipation south send the free people north? People of any color seldom run unless there be something to run from. Heretofore colored people, to some extent, have fled north from bondage; and now, perhaps, from both bondage and destitution. But if gradual emancipation and deportation be adopted, they will have neither to flee from. Their old masters will give them wages at least until new laborers can be procured; and the freedmen, in turn, will gladly give their labor for the wages till new homes can be found for them in congenial climes and with people of their own blood and race. This proposition can be trusted on the mutual interests involved. And, in any event, cannot the North decide for itself whether to receive them?

Again, as practice proves more than theory, in any case, has there been any irruption of colored people northward because of the abolishment of slavery in this District last spring?

What I have said of the proportion of free colored persons to the whites in the District is from the census of 1860, having no reference to persons called contrabands, nor to those made free by the act of Congress abolishing slavery here.

The plan consisting of these articles is recommended, not but that a restoration of the national authority would be accepted without its adoption.

Nor will the war, nor proceedings under the proclamation of September 22, 1862, be stayed because of the recommendation of this plan. Its timely adoption, I doubt not, would bring restoration, and thereby stay both.[1089]

Lincoln was so adamant about expatriating American blacks that he was willing to settle them almost anyplace—as long as it was, as he said, **"without the United States."** This included Europe, Latin America, or the Caribbean, or anywhere else they would be accepted. As such, he funded experimental colonies in what are now Panama and Belize, as well as in Haiti. All failed miserably, with death rates of over 50 percent in some cases.[1090] The situation eventually became so horrendous that many of Lincoln's deported blacks begged to be allowed back into the U.S.

One of the more severe of these cases occurred on the Island of Vache, located off the coast of Haiti. On February 1, 1864, Lincoln was forced to deliver the following order to his secretary of war, Edwin M. Stanton:

> Sir: You are directed to have a transport (either a steam or sailing vessel, as may be deemed proper by the Quartermaster-General) sent to the colored colony established by the United States at the Island of Vache, on the coast of San Domingo, to bring back to this country such of the colonists there as desire to return. You will have the transport furnished with suitable supplies for that purpose, and detail an officer of the Quartermaster's department, who, under special instructions to be given, shall have charge of the business. The colonists will be brought to Washington unless otherwise hereafter

directed, and be employed and provided for at the camps for colored persons around that city.

Those only will be brought from the island who desire to return, and their effects will be brought with them. Abraham Lincoln.[1091]

As an obviously disappointed Lincoln inadvertently admits here, over a year after issuing his fake and illegal Emancipation Proclamation, "freed" blacks in America's capital city still had not been welcomed by the president—or apparently by any other whites. Instead, all were relegated to the foul and seedy **"camps for colored persons"** then situated around Washington, D.C., just as the whites of Concord, Massachusetts, had done with their "freed" slaves only a few years earlier.[1092]

Despite such disastrous and costly attempts at "freeing" the U.S. of blacks, Lincoln always maintained a special interest in Liberia, no doubt because he was a manager in the Illinois Chapter of the American Colonization Society, whose members had founded the African colony in 1822.[1093]

In public speeches on both October 16, 1854, and again on August 21, 1858, Lincoln told his supportive Yankee audiences that his remedy for America's "racial problem" would be to first emancipate all enslaved blacks, then send them back to Africa, **"to their own native land"**:

> If all earthly power were given me, I should not know what to do as to the existing institution. My first impulse would be to free all the slaves, and send them to Liberia, to their own native land. But a moment's reflection would convince me that whatever of high hope (as I think there is) there may be in this in the long run, its sudden execution is impossible. If they were all landed there in a day, they would all perish in the next ten days; and there are not surplus shipping and surplus money enough to carry them there in many times ten days. What then? Free them all, and keep them among us as underlings? Is it quite certain that this betters their condition? I think I would not hold one in slavery at any rate, yet the point is not clear enough for me to denounce people upon. What next? Free them, and make them politically and socially our equals. My own feelings will not admit of this, and if mine would, we well know that those of the great mass of whites will not. Whether this feeling accords with justice and sound judgment is not

the sole question, if indeed it is any part of it. A universal feeling, whether well or ill founded, cannot be safely disregarded. We cannot then make them equals.[1094]

Lincoln's words are revealing here, for he had not been asked what he would do with blacks after they were freed. Only what he intended to do about slavery.[1095] Consumed with the idea of colonization, he himself added the comment about deporting them to Liberia.

On December 6, 1864, during his Annual Message to Congress, Lincoln brings up the topic of Liberia yet again, this time making reference to the many freed American blacks he had already sent there:

> Official correspondence has been freely opened with Liberia, and it gives us a pleasing view of social and political progress in that republic. It may be expected to derive new vigor from American influence, improved by the rapid disappearance of slavery in the United States.[1096]

In other words, Lincoln felt that Liberia would grow in political power and population only as newly freed slaves were deported there from the U.S.

Besides working hand-in-hand with the Yankee-founded ACS, white separatist Lincoln labored for years on his own personal emancipation-colonization plan, one that contained five clauses. The fifth stated that all emancipated blacks were to be shipped out of the U.S. and settled on foreign soil. For a variety of reasons, noted below, neither Congress, the border states, or most African-Americans themselves, ever showed the slightest bit of interest in this racist scheme.[1097]

Nonetheless, Lincoln went on promoting it and, as we have seen, even included it in his Preliminary Emancipation Proclamation. In honor of his indefatigable efforts to rid the nation of African-Americans, one of Lincoln's senators, Samuel Clarke Pomeroy of Kansas,[1098] came up with the idea of naming a black colony in Latin America, "Linconia."[1099]

Was this authentic abolitionism? Certainly not, and anti-abolitionist Lincoln knew it. Still, for him there was no shame in it, which is why he never tried to hide it. Most of his military officers were not true abolitionists either. Some, like Lincoln's favorite commander, Ulysses S. Grant, went so far as to say that: "I never was an abolitionist, not even what could be called anti-slavery."[1100] Hence, after the issuance of Lincoln's Emancipation Proclamation Grant could happily write that white Americans were still "just as free to avoid the social intimacy with the blacks as ever they were . . ."[1101]

None of this should appall us. While Northerner Grant and his wife Julia Boggs Dent were ardent slave owners before, during, and after the War,[1102] Lincoln's days as a lawyer included defending not slaves, but slave owners.[1103] He even participated in a case that involved the selling of black slaves, a case for which he was well paid.[1104]

Lincoln was no radical. He was in the mainstream of American thought at the time, particularly *Northern* thought, for this is the region where racism was at its worst. As French aristocrat Alexis de Tocqueville wrote in the early 1830s after visiting America:

> Whosoever has inhabited the United States must have perceived that in those parts of the Union in which the negroes are no longer slaves, they have in nowise drawn nearer to the whites. On the contrary, the prejudice of the race appears to be stronger in the States which have abolished slavery than in those where it still exists; and nowhere is it so intolerant as in those States where servitude never has been known.
>
> It is true that in the North of the Union marriages may be legally contracted between negroes and whites; but public opinion would stigmatize a man who should connect himself with a negress as infamous, and it would be difficult to meet with a single instance of such a union. The electoral franchise has been conferred upon the negroes in almost all the States in which slavery has been abolished; but if they come forward to vote, their lives are in danger. If oppressed, they may bring an action at law, but they will find none but whites among their judges; and although they may legally serve as jurors, prejudice repulses them from that office. The same schools do not receive the child of the black and of the European. In the theatres, gold can not procure a seat for the servile race beside their former masters; in the hospitals they lie apart; and although they are allowed to invoke the same Divinity as the whites, it must be at a different altar, and in their own churches with their own clergy. The gates of Heaven are not closed against these unhappy beings; but their inferiority is continued to the very confines of the other world; when the negro is defunct, his bones are cast aside, and the distinction of condition prevails even in the equality of death. The [Northern] negro is free, but he can share neither the rights, nor the pleasures, nor the labour, nor the afflictions, nor the tomb of him whose equal he has been declared to be; and he can not meet him upon fair terms in life or in death.
>
> In the South, where slavery still exists, the negroes are

less carefully kept apart; they sometimes share the labour and the recreations of the whites; the whites consent to intermix with them to a certain extent, and although the legislation treats them more harshly, the habits of the [Southern] people are more tolerant and compassionate. In the South the master is not afraid to raise his slave to his own standing, because he knows that he can in a moment reduce him to the dust at pleasure. In the North the white no longer distinctly perceives the barrier which separates him from the degraded race, and he shuns the negro with the more pertinacity, since he fears lest they should some day be confounded together.

Among the Americans of the South, Nature sometimes reasserts her rights, and restores a transient equality between the blacks and the whites; but in the North pride restrains the most imperious of human passions. The American of the Northern States would perhaps allow the negress to share his licentious pleasures if the laws of his country did not declare that she may aspire to be the legitimate partner of his bed; but he recoils with horror from her who might become his wife.

Thus it is, in the United States, that the prejudice which repels the negroes seems to increase in proportion as they are emancipated, and inequality is sanctioned by the manners while it is effaced from the laws of the country. But if the relative position of the two races which inhabit the United States is such as I have described, it may be asked why the Americans have abolished slavery in the North of the Union, why they maintain it in the South, and why they aggravate its hardships there? The answer is easily given. It is not for the good of the negroes, but for that of the whites, that measures are taken to abolish slavery in the United States.[1105]

In the 1840s English writer James Silk Buckingham wrote that "the prejudice of colour is not nearly so strong in the South as in the North."[1106] Here is how Robert Young Hayne, a South Carolina senator, described the treatment of those few Southern blacks who fled to the North:

> . . . there does not exist on the face of the whole earth, a population so poor, so wretched, so vile, so loathsome, so utterly destitute of all the comforts, conveniences, and decencies of life, as the unfortunate blacks of Philadelphia, and New York and Boston. Liberty has been to them the greatest of calamities, the heaviest of curses. Sir, I have had some opportunities of making comparison between the condition of the free negroes of the North, and the slaves of the South, and the comparison has left not only an

indelible impression of the superior advantages of the latter, but has gone far to reconcile me to slavery itself. Never have I felt so forcibly that touching description, 'the foxes have holes, and the birds of the air have nests, but the Son of Man hath not where to lay his head,' as when I have seen this unhappy race, naked and houseless, almost starving in the streets, and abandoned by all the world. Sir, I have seen, in the neighborhood of one of the most moral, religious and refined cities of the North, a family of free blacks driven to the caves of the rocks, and there obtaining a precarious subsistence from charity and plunder.[1107]

Only a few years later, in 1835, Virginian James Madison met with English author Harriet Martineau and regaled her with stories about how the Northern states erected numerous barriers in an attempt to thwart Negro emigration.[1108] During the conversation our fourth president

mentioned the astonishment of some strangers, who had an idea that slaves were always whipped all day long, at seeing his negroes go to church one Sunday. They were gayly dressed, the women in brightly-coloured calicoes; and, when a sprinkling of rain came, up went a dozen umbrellas. The astonished strangers veered round to the conclusion that slaves were very happy . . .[1109]

In 1841, after traveling through Philadelphia, an English Quaker, Joseph Sturge, met with former Illinois Governor Edward Coles. Writes Sturge:

In the course of conversation, the Governor spoke of the prejudice against colour prevailing here as much stronger than in the slave States [the South]. I may add, from my own observation, and much concurring testimony, that Philadelphia appears to be the metropolis of this odious prejudice, and that there is probably no city in the known world, where dislike, amounting to hatred of the coloured population, prevails more than in the city of brotherly love![1110]

After a visit to New York City, English writer Edward Dicey recorded his observations concerning Yankee racism and Northern blacks. In the North, Dicey noted:

Everywhere and at all seasons the coloured people form a separate community. In the public streets you hardly ever see a coloured person in company with a white, except in the capacity of servant. . . . On board the river steamboats, the commonest and homeliest of working [white] men has a right to dine, and does dine, at the public meals; but, for coloured passengers, there is always a separate table. At the great [Northern] hotels there is, as with us [in England], a servants' table, but the coloured servants are not allowed to dine in common with the white. At the inns, in the barbers' shops, on board the steamers, and in most hotels, the servants are more often than not coloured people. . . . White [Northern] servants will not associate with black on terms of equality. . . . I hardly ever remember seeing a black employed as shopman, or placed in any post of responsibility. As a rule, the blacks you meet in the Free [i.e., Northern] States are shabbily, if not squalidly dressed; and, as far as I could learn, the instances of black men having made money by trade in the North, are very few in number.[1111]

On August 15, 1862, a black Massachusetts justice of the peace, John S. Rock, made the following remarks about white racism there. According to Rock, the Bay State did not compare favorably with Southern states, such as South Carolina:

> The masses seem to think that we [blacks] are oppressed only in the South. This is a mistake; we are oppressed everywhere in this slavery-cursed land. Massachusetts has a great name, and deserves much credit for what she has done, but the position of the colored people in Massachusetts is far from being an enviable one. While colored men have many rights, they have few privileges here. . . . The educated colored man meets, on the one hand, the embittered prejudices of the whites. And on the other the jealousies of his own race. . . . You can hardly imagine the humiliation and contempt a colored lad must feel by graduating the first in his class, and then being rejected everywhere else because of his color.
>
> No where in the United States is the colored man of talent appreciated. Even in Boston, which has a great reputation for being anti-slavery, he has no field for his talent. Some persons think that, because we have the right of suffrage [in Massachusetts] . . . there is less prejudice here than there is farther South. In some respects this is true, and in others it is not true. We are colonized in Boston. It is five times as difficult to get a house in a good location in Boston as it is in Philadelphia, and it is ten times more difficult for a colored mechanic to get employment than in Charleston [South Carolina]. . . . if we don't like that state of things, there is an appropriation to colonize us.[1112]

It was this very Northern white racism that prevented a proposed constitutional amendment that would have abolished slavery throughout the U.S. from being passed by the Yankee House of Representatives in 1864.[1113] Indeed, American slavery would not be officially extinguished until the ratification of the Thirteenth Amendment on December 6, 1865, eight months *after* Lincoln's death.[1114]

Modern Americans today who believe that their early leaders intended the nation to be a "Melting Pot," a rainbow of various races, colors, and cultures, are of course grossly mistaken. Lincoln is the most obvious example of just one of millions of Northerners who devoted their entire lives to creating what Southern President Woodrow Wilson saw, in reality, as the "Unmelted Pot,"[1115] a nation of geographically separated races—created in great part by Lincoln himself. The fictions that the "Great Emancipator" was a civil rights activist, and that he inaugurated his War to end slavery in order to merge blacks into mainstream American society, can now finally be put out to pasture.

While strangely today's anti-South pro-Lincoln crowd refuses to acknowledge any of these well established facts, they have an even more difficult time accepting that our sixteenth president's unrelenting lobbying for colonization continued up until the very last day of his life. Actually, he never stopped thinking or talking about this subject,[1116] and there is no record of him ever renouncing his obsession with it.[1117]

Yet, for as long and as hard as he pitched his colonization program, it never officially made it past his Preliminary Emancipation Proclamation: Lincoln's cabinet removed all references to black deportation before he issued his final draft (on January 1, 1863)—the version best known to the public—because they feared it would alienate the Radicals in their party, that is, the abolitionists, whose votes would be needed in the president's 1864 reelection campaign.

Let us now bring the entire transcript of this suppressed Yankee document, the Preliminary Emancipation Proclamation, out of the shadows and into the light of the public forum:

September 22, 1862.—Preliminary Emancipation Proclamation. By The President Of The United States Of America:

A Proclamation.

I Abraham Lincoln, President of the United States of

America, and commander-in-chief of the army and navy thereof, do hereby proclaim and declare that hereafter, as heretofore, the war will be prosecuted for the object of practically restoring the constitutional relation between the United States and each of the States, and the people thereof, in which States that relation is or may be suspended or disturbed.

That it is my purpose, upon the next meeting of Congress, to again recommend the adoption of a practical measure tendering pecuniary aid to the free acceptance or rejection of all slave States, so called, the people whereof may not then be in rebellion against the United States, and which States may then have voluntarily adopted, or thereafter may voluntarily adopt, immediate or gradual abolishment of slavery within their respective limits; and that the effort to colonize persons of African descent with their consent upon this continent or elsewhere, with the previously obtained consent of the governments existing there, will be continued.

That on the first day of January, in the year of our Lord one thousand eight hundred and sixty-three, all persons held as slaves within any State or designated part of a State the people whereof shall then be in rebellion against the United States, shall be then, thenceforward, and forever free; and the Executive Government of the United States, including the military and naval authority thereof, will recognize and maintain the freedom of such persons, and will do no act or acts to repress such persons, or any of them, in any efforts they may make for their actual freedom.

That the Executive will, on the first day of January aforesaid, by proclamation designate the States and parts of States, if any, in which the people thereof, respectively, shall then be in rebellion against the United States; and the fact that any State, or the people thereof, shall on that day be in good faith represented in the Congress of the United States by members chosen thereto at elections wherein a majority of the qualified voters of such State shall have participated, shall, in the absence of strong countervailing testimony, be deemed conclusive evidence that such State, and the people thereof, are not then in rebellion against the United States.

That attention is hereby called to an act of Congress entitled "An act to make an additional article of war," approved March 13, 1862, and which act is in the words and figure following:

Be it enacted by the Senate and House of Representatives of the United States of America in Congress assembled, That hereafter the following shall be promulgated as an additional article of war, for the government of the army of the United States, and shall be obeyed and observed as such:

Article—. All officers or persons in the military or naval service of the United States are prohibited from employing any of the forces under their respective commands for the purpose of returning fugitives from service or labor who may have escaped from any persons to whom such service or labor is claimed to be due; and any officer who shall be found guilty by a court martial of violating this article shall be dismissed from the service.

Sec. 2. And be it further enacted, That this act shall take effect from and after its passage.

Also to the ninth and tenth sections of an act entitled "An act to suppress insurrection, to punish treason and rebellion, to seize and confiscate property of rebels, and for other purposes," approved July 17, 1862, and which sections are in the words and figures following:

Sec. 9. And be it further enacted, That all slaves of persons who shall hereafter be engaged in rebellion against the Government of the United States, or who shall in any way give aid or comfort thereto, escaping from such persons and taking refuge within the lines of the army; and all slaves captured from such persons or deserted by them, and coming under the control of the Government of the United States; and all slaves of such persons found on [or] being within any place occupied by rebel forces and afterwards occupied by the forces of the United States, shall be deemed captives of war, and shall be forever free of their servitude, and not again held as slaves.

Sec. 10. And be it further enacted, That no slave escaping into any State, Territory, or the District of Columbia, from any other State, shall be delivered up, or in any way impeded or hindered of his liberty, except for crime, or some offense against the laws, unless the person claiming said fugitive shall first make oath that the person to whom the labor or service of such fugitive is alleged to be due is his lawful owner, and has not borne arms against the United States in the present rebellion; nor in any way given aid and comfort thereto; and no person engaged in the military or naval service of the United States shall, under any pretense whatever, assume to decide on the validity of the claim of any person to the service or labor of any other person, or surrender up any such person to the claimant, on pain of being dismissed from the service.

And I do hereby enjoin upon and order all persons engaged in the military and naval service of the United States to observe, obey, and enforce, within their respective spheres of service, the act and sections above recited.

And the Executive will in due time recommend that all citizens of the United States who shall have remained loyal thereto throughout the rebellion shall (upon the restoration of the constitutional relation between the United States and their respective States and people, if that relation shall have been suspended or disturbed) be compensated for all losses by acts of the United States, including the loss of slaves.

In witness whereof, I have hereunto set my hand and caused the seal of the United States to be affixed.

Done at the city of Washington, this twenty-second day of September, in the year of our Lord one thousand eight hundred and sixty-two, and of the independence of the United States the eighty-seventh. Abraham Lincoln.[1118]

Let us reemphasize: this, the *Preliminary* Emancipation Proclamation, is the version Lincoln wanted to issue, not the *Final* Emancipation Proclamation, the one now known so well by the public.

We will note here that the nation's initial reaction to his September 22 edict was not at all what Lincoln expected, as he noted dejectedly in a September 28, 1862, letter to Vice President Hannibal Hamlin:

My Dear Sir: Your kind letter of the 25th is just received. It is known to some that while I hope something from the proclamation, my expectations are not as sanguine [i.e., optimistic] as are those of some friends. The time for its effect southward has not come; but northward the effect should be instantaneous.

It is six days old, and while commendation in newspapers and by distinguished individuals is all that a vain man could wish, the stocks have declined, and troops come forward more slowly than ever. This, looked soberly in the face, is not very satisfactory. We have fewer troops in the field at the end of six days than we had at the beginning—the attrition among the old outnumbering the addition by the new. The North responds to the proclamation sufficiently in breath; but breath alone kills no rebels.

I wish I could write more cheerfully; nor do I thank you the less for the kindness of your letter. Yours very truly, A. Lincoln.[1119]

As Lincoln himself stated, emancipation first, colonization second. Just like Henry Clay, this was always his plan for blacks.[1120] Had he lived, there is no question that he would have done everything in his power to fulfill the second phase concerning black deportation. Thus it was, in great part, John Wilkes Booth who truly and finally freed American blacks, not Abraham Lincoln. For the stark reality is that African-Americans would have never been completely free while Lincoln was alive.[1121]

After his death in April 1865 Lincoln's entire mad colonization scheme was tossed out, due mainly to the enormous costs and logistical complications that would have been involved. Nearly everyone seemed to be aware of these obstacles except Lincoln. Just as odd, while he was alive he seemed completely oblivious of the bold fact that whites and blacks could indeed live together harmoniously, even affectionately. One hundred largely quiet years of Southern slavery, whatever one thought of it at the time, had proven this for all who had eyes to see.[1122] But Lincoln did not view blacks and whites as equals, therefore he could not perceive what was obvious to nearly everyone else, particularly Southerners.

There was something else that Lincoln and other Northern supporters of colonization completely ignored: the feelings of blacks themselves. Most, who now rightly considered themselves Americans, not Africans, refused to leave the only homeland they had ever known.[1123] Why, many blacks must have wondered, was the President of the United States, the veritable "Great Emancipator," pushing for colonization when all this did was reinforce slavery?[1124] Why indeed.

Today we know the answer to this question because we have access to many of Lincoln's documents, letters, and assorted papers, items that were not readily available to the public in the 1860s. All clearly show that Lincoln was a white supremacist who cared little about black civil rights and was against any mixing of the two races.[1125]

Let us compare America's sixteenth president to one of the Confederacy's greatest officers, General Thomas "Stonewall" Jackson, who founded an all-black Sunday school class, then donated $50 (today's equivalent of about $1,300) to the group to buy books.[1126]

Or consider the Confederacy's first and only president, Jefferson Davis: while Lincoln was plotting the exile of all blacks from America's shores, Davis and his wife Varina (Howell) adopted a young black boy, Jim Limber, who they raised as their own in the Confederate White House.[1127] During the War they always treated their black servants equitably and with the greatest respect, as part of their family in fact. After Lee's surrender, during the Davis family's escape southward, their coachman was a "faithful" free black.[1128] Later, after the War, the one-time Rebel president and his wife sold their plantation, Brierfield, to a former slave.[1129] Davis even spoke once of a time when he led "negroes against a lawless body of armed white men . . .,"[1130] something we can be sure that white separatist Lincoln never did. For, as we will see, it was "Honest Abe" himself who ordered that all Union troops be segregated.[1131]

Who then, we must now ask, was the authentic "Great Emancipator"? It is true that Lincoln wanted to end slavery. But this was primarily so he could deport all blacks out of the country. Davis too wanted to abolish the institution. However, he was against colonization. Instead, Davis wanted freed blacks to remain in the South, where they would continue to help build and maintain the region, just as they had since the late 1500s.[1132]

What Lincoln never understood, and what is completely unknown to the average American today, is that the apartheid he so desperately craved is actually another form of slavery (in this case one known as "collective slavery"), which is exactly how apartheid is defined by Anti-Slavery International, the world's oldest international human rights organization.[1133] Thus, it must go down as one of American history's greatest ironies that Lincoln is credited with ending chattel slavery, yet he actually spent his entire adult life promoting another form of the institution, collective slavery, one just as potentially onerous, degrading, and exploitative.

In great contrast to white separatist and black colonizationist Lincoln were most white Southerners, who, like Jefferson Davis, overwhelmingly preferred that blacks remain in America. Why?

Not only did they consider black Southerners their friends and "family members" in many cases,[1134] but many Southern whites also believed that blacks were better workers than whites, and they wanted to be able to hire their trusted laborers back after emancipation.

After the War, one of these, Southern hero and Confederate General Nathan Bedford Forrest (the only man in either the Confederate or Union army to rise from private to lieutenant general),[1135] even lobbied to repopulate and resettle the South, not only with freed blacks, but also with new African immigrants.[1136] Of his Southern black brothers and sisters Forrest said:

> They are the best laborers we have ever had in the South. . . . there is no need for a war of the races. I want to see the whole country prosper.[1137]

One would have to search long and hard to find an example of a Yankee officer, or any Northerner for that matter, expressing similar sentiments. Lincoln's postbellum plan to deport all blacks out of the U.S., and Dixie's desire to import additional blacks into the U.S., were just two more of the many differences between South and North.

On August 14, 1862, almost a year-and-a-half into his war, Lincoln requested that a group of blacks meet with him at the White House. They were the first free African-Americans to ever enter those hallowed halls. But the event was not something that many would want recorded in the pages of American history.[1138] The fact that the five black men were hand-picked by Reverend James Mitchell, Lincoln's commissioner of *emigration*, hints at the enormous social fiasco Lincoln was about to create, surely the worst to ever occur inside the White House.

None of the Negroes who were hurriedly ushered into the president's office that day were well-known. In fact, four of them were lowly "contrabands" (captured Southern slaves), as Lincoln and other Northerners derogatorily referred to them.[1139] The awe-struck, passive group had been selected purposefully to avoid a "scene." For as it turns out, Lincoln wanted a captive uneducated audience who would sit and listen to a racist monologue on the advantages of black deportation (colonization), not engage him in an intellectual debate about slavery.[1140]

As the colored delegation sat in stunned silence, Lincoln removed a crumbled up piece of paper from inside his large stovepipe hat. On it was a speech, written in hastily scrawled words. In his thin high voice, Lincoln began to read aloud to the men gathered before him. What follows is an exact chronicle of the scene from Lincoln's personal friends and official biographers, John G. Nicolay and John Hay:

> August 14, 1862. — Address On Colonization To A Deputation Of Colored Men.
>
> Washington, Thursday, August 14, 1862.
>
> This afternoon the President of the United States gave an audience to a committee of colored men at the White House. They were introduced by Rev. J. Mitchell, Commissioner of Emigration. E. M. Thomas, the chairman, remarked that they were there by invitation to hear what the Executive had to say to them.
> Having all been seated, the President, after a few preliminary observations, informed them that a sum of money had been appropriated by Congress, and placed at his disposition, for the purpose of aiding the colonization in some country of the people, or a portion of them, of African descent, thereby making it his duty, as it had for a long time been his inclination, to favor that cause. **And why, he asked, should the people of your race be colonized, and where? Why should they leave this country? This is, perhaps, the first question for proper consideration. You and we are different races. We have between us a broader difference than exists between almost any other two races. Whether it is right or wrong I need not discuss; but this physical difference is a great disadvantage to us both, as I think. Your race suffer very greatly, many of them, by living among us, while ours suffer from your presence. In a word, we suffer on each side. If this is admitted, it affords a reason, at least, why we should be separated. You here are freemen, I suppose?**
>
> A voice: Yes, sir.
>
> The President: **Perhaps you have long been free, or all your lives. Your race is suffering, in my judgment, the greatest wrong inflicted on any people. But even when you cease to be slaves, you are yet far removed from being placed on an equality with the white race. You are cut off from**

many of the advantages which the other race enjoys. The aspiration of men is to enjoy equality with the best when free, but on this broad continent not a single man of your race is made the equal of a single man of ours. Go where you are treated the best, and the ban is still upon you. I do not propose to discuss this, but to present it as a fact with which we have to deal. I cannot alter it if I would. It is a fact about which we all think and feel alike, I and you. We look to our condition. Owing to the existence of the two races on this continent, I need not recount to you the effects upon white men, growing out of the institution of slavery.

I believe in its general evil effects on the white race. See our present condition—the country engaged in war—our white men cutting one another's throats—none knowing how far it will extend—and then consider what we know to be the truth. But for your race among us there could not be war, although many men engaged on either side do not care for you one way or the other. Nevertheless, I repeat, without the institution of slavery, and the colored race as a basis, the war could not have an existence. It is better for us both, therefore, to be separated. I know that there are free men among you who, even if they could better their condition, are not as much inclined to go out of the country as those who, being slaves, could obtain their freedom on this condition. I suppose one of the principal difficulties in the way of colonization is that the free colored man cannot see that his comfort would be advanced by it. You may believe that you can live in Washington, or elsewhere in the United States, the remainder of your life as easily, perhaps more so, than you can in any foreign country; and hence you may come to the conclusion that you have nothing to do with the idea of going to a foreign country.

This is (I speak in no unkind sense) an extremely selfish view of the case. You ought to do something to help those who are not so fortunate as yourselves. There is an unwillingness on the part of our people, harsh as it may be, for you free colored people to remain with us. Now, if you could give a start to the white people, you would open a wide door for many to be made free. If we deal with those who are not free at the beginning, and whose intellects are clouded by slavery, we have very poor material to start with. If intelligent colored men, such as are before me, would move in this matter, much might be accomplished. It is exceedingly important that we have men at the beginning capable of thinking as white men, and not those who have been systematically oppressed. There is much to encourage you. For the sake of your race you should sacrifice something of your present comfort for the purpose of being as grand in that respect as the white people. It is a cheering thought throughout life, that something can be done to ameliorate the condition of those who have been subject to the hard usages of the world. It is difficult to make a man miserable while he feels he is worthy of himself and claims kindred to the great God who made him. In the American Revolutionary war sacrifices were made by men engaged in it, but they were cheered by the future. General Washington himself endured greater physical hardships than if he had remained a British subject, yet he was a happy man because he was engaged in benefiting his race, in doing something for the children of his neighbors, having none of his own.

The colony of Liberia has been in existence a long time. In a certain sense it is a success. The old President of Liberia, [Joseph Jenkins] Roberts, has just been with me—the first time I ever saw him. He says they have within the bounds of that colony between three and four hundred thousand people, or more than in some of our old States, such as Rhode Island or Delaware, or in some of our newer States, and less than in some of our larger ones. They are not all American colonists or their descendants. Something less than 12,000 have been sent thither from this country. Many of the original settlers have died; yet, like people elsewhere, their offspring outnumber those deceased. The question is, if the colored people are persuaded to go anywhere, why not there?

One reason for unwillingness to do so is that some of you would rather remain within reach of the country of your nativity. I do not know how much attachment you may have toward our race. It does not strike me that you have the greatest reason to love them. But still you are attached to them, at all events.

The place I am thinking about for a colony is in Central America. It is nearer to us than Liberia—not much more than one fourth as far as Liberia, and within seven days' run by steamers. Unlike Liberia, it is a great line of travel—it is a highway. The country is a very excellent one for any people, and with great natural resources and advantages, and especially because of the similarity of climate with your native soil, thus being suited to your physical condition. The particular place I have in view is to be a great highway from the Atlantic or Caribbean Sea to the Pacific Ocean, and this particular place has all the advantages for a colony. On both sides there are harbors—among the finest in the world. Again, there is evidence of very rich coal-mines. A certain amount of coal is valuable in any country. Why I attach so much importance to coal is, it will afford an opportunity to the inhabitants for immediate employment till they get ready to settle permanently in their homes. If you take colonists where there is no good landing, there is a bad show; and so where there is nothing to cultivate and of which to make a farm. But if something is started so that you can get your daily bread as soon as you reach there, it is a great advantage. Coal land is the best thing I know of with which to commence an enterprise.

  To return—you have been talked to upon this subject, and told that a speculation is intended by gentlemen who have an interest in the country, including the coal-mines. We have been mistaken all our lives if we do not know whites, as well as blacks, look to their self-interest. Unless among those deficient of intellect, everybody you trade with makes something. You meet with these things here and everywhere. If such persons have what will be an advantage to them, the question is, whether it cannot be made of advantage to you? You are intelligent, and know that success does not so much depend on external help as on self-reliance. Much, therefore, depends upon yourselves. As to the coal-mines, I think I see the means available for your self-reliance. I shall, if I get a sufficient number of you engaged, have provision made that you shall not be wronged. If you will engage in the enterprise, I will spend some of the money intrusted to me. I am not sure you will succeed. The government may lose the money, but we cannot succeed unless we try; and we think, with care, we can succeed. The political affairs in Central America are not in quite as satisfactory a condition as I wish. There are contending factions in that quarter; but, it is true, all the factions are agreed alike on the subject of colonization, and want it, and are more generous than we are here.

To your colored race they have no objection. I would endeavor to have you made the equals, and have the best assurance that you should be, the equals of the best.

The practical thing I want to ascertain is, whether I can get a number of able-bodied men, with their wives and children, who are willing to go when I present evidence of encouragement and protection. Could I get a hundred tolerably intelligent men, with their wives and children, and able to "cut their own fodder," so to speak? Can I have fifty? If I could find twenty-five able-bodied men, with a mixture of women and children,—good things in the family relation, I think,— I could make a successful commencement. I want you to let me know whether this can be done or not. This is the practical part of my wish to see you. These are subjects of very great importance—worthy of a month's study, instead of a speech delivered in an hour. I ask you, then, to consider seriously, not pertaining to yourselves merely, nor for your race and ours for the present time, but as one of the things, if successfully managed, for the good of mankind—not confined to the present generation, but as

From age to age descends the lay
To millions yet to be,
Till far its echoes roll away Into eternity.

The above is merely given as the substance of the President's remarks.

The chairman of the delegation briefly replied that they would hold a consultation, and in a short time give an answer.

The President said: **Take your full time—no hurry at all.**

The delegation then withdrew.[1141]

The black committee did take its **"full time."** Lincoln waited and waited, but did not receive an immediate answer to his question concerning how many African-Americans would allow themselves to be shipped to Central America, or **"back to Africa."** Unbeknownst to the "Great Emancipator," there was good reason for this: the five black delegates were in a state of humiliation, confusion, anger, and shock, and needed time to formulate a response.

A few days later their reply finally arrived at the White House. The missive was brief and to the point. Furious, the black committee members scolded Lincoln for campaigning for the deportation of America's colored people. They then asked him to please mind his own business![1142]

Lincoln must have scratched his head in bewilderment. He never grasped what every black and nearly every white Southerner understood instinctively: if America was ever to rid herself of color prejudice, Lincoln's black colonization plans were certainly not the "solution." In fact, it was obvious to nearly everyone that the deportation of blacks would only aggravate the problem;[1143] obvious to everyone, that is, except Lincoln. But then again, he was never truly interested in working toward a racist-free, color-blind society.

When educated black leaders heard about the White House conference they were enraged. Easily seeing through the charade, Frederick Douglass, the prominent abolitionist, former Northern slave, and Lincoln's confidant, publicly denounced the president for his white racial pride, disdain for blacks, and rank dishonesty.[1144] Furthermore, wrote a fuming Douglass in his newspaper:

> The tone of frankness and benevolence which he assumes in his speech to the colored committee is too thin a mask not to be seen through. The genuine spark of humanity is missing in it. It expresses merely the desire to get rid of them . . .[1145]

A New Jersey newspaper printed the response of an exasperated black citizen. In lambasting the "meddlesome, impudent" president, he asked Lincoln to remember that in God's eyes there is only one race on earth: the human race.[1146] But being an atheist[1147] Lincoln never understood, or believed, this simple but powerful truth.

Black people across the country were indeed disgusted after learning what Lincoln had told the committee at the Executive Mansion, for by 1862 nearly all blacks in both the U.S. and the C.S. were native-born Americans. Most were fourth and fifth generation Americans[1148]—some were as much as sixth and seventh generation Americans, or more (blacks, for example, were in the area now known as Virginia by 1526).[1149] A great many whites, however, were not more than first, second, or third generation Americans. In light of this, which race was more American, the white or the black one? blacks rightly asked. After all by 1860, 99 percent of all blacks were native born Americans, a larger percentage than for whites.[1150]

We already know how Lincoln would have answered this question. The fact remained that the vast majority of African-Americans had no intention of taking the president up on his offer to be shipped to a foreign land, for it meant leaving behind their loved ones (both black and white), their homes and farms, and their family cemeteries, filled with ancestors dating back to the early 1600s, and in some cases, even beyond.

Angered about Lincoln's endless and insensitive promotion of colonization, blacks from Long Island, New York, put their foot down, stating publicly:

> This is our native country; we have as strong attachment naturally to our native hills, valleys, plains, luxuriant forests, flowing streams, mighty rivers and lofty mountains, as any other people.[1151]

Taking a spiritual approach, a group of black men from Pennsylvania wrote up "An Appeal From the Colored Men of Philadelphia to the President of the United States." It read:

> We can find nothing in the religion of our Lord and Master teaching us that color is the standard by which He judges His creatures, either in this life or in the life to come. . . . We ask, that by the standard of justice and humanity we may be weighed, and that men shall not longer be measured by their stature or color.[1152]

On August 28, 1862, just two weeks after Lincoln's racial debacle at the White House, African-American Robert Purvis spoke for nearly all American blacks in an open letter to the president:

> The children of the black man have enriched the soil by their tears, and sweat, and blood. Sir, we were born here, and here we choose to remain. For twenty years we were goaded and harassed by systematic efforts to make us colonize. We were coaxed and mobbed, and mobbed and coaxed, but we refused to budge. We planted ourselves upon our inalienable rights, and were proof against all the efforts that were made to expatriate us. For the last fifteen years we have enjoyed comparative quiet. Now again the malign project is broached, and again, as before, in the name of humanity are we invited to leave.
>
> In God's name what good do you expect to accomplish

by such a course? If you will not let our brethren in bonds go free, if you will not let us, as did our fathers, share in the privileges of the government, if you will not let us even help fight the battles of the country, in Heaven's name, at least, *let us alone*. Is that too great a boon to ask of your magnanimity?

I elect to stay on the soil on which I was born, and on the plot of ground which I have fairly bought and honestly paid for. Don't advise me to leave, and don't add insult to injury by telling me it's for my own good; of that I am to be the judge. It is in vain that you talk to me about the 'two races,' and their 'mutual antagonism.' In the matter of rights there is but one race, and that is the *human* race. 'God has made of one blood all nations to dwell on all the face of the earth' [Acts 17:26]. And it is not true that there is a mutual antagonism between the white and colored people of this community. You may antagonize us, but we do not antagonize you. You may hate us, but we do not hate you.[1153]

All of these "appeals" were forwarded directly to the President. If he ever read any of them, no one would have known. For despite them he continued to pursue his plan to deport all blacks out of the U.S. as vigorously as ever.

Lincoln's March 12, 1864, "Message to the Senate," for example, was devoted solely to the idea of ridding the U.S. of its black citizens:

> **To the Senate of the United States: In obedience to the resolution of the Senate of the 28th of January last, I communicate herewith a report, with accompanying papers from the Secretary of the Interior, showing what portion of the appropriations for the colonization of persons of African descent has been expended, and the several steps which have been taken for the execution of the acts of Congress on that subject. Abraham Lincoln.**[1154]

On December 6, 1864, during his Fourth Annual Message to Congress, Lincoln brought up Liberia again. This time it was to suggest stopping the slave trade there. Not to abolish the evils of slavery, but so that no more African slaves would be sent to the U.S. After all, Liberia was the very country that he wanted to deport American blacks to. He then asserts, as we will recall, that Liberia will **"derive new vigor from American influence."** Not from ending slavery there, but from the influx of thousands of deported African-Americans he planned on sending to the colony. Said Lincoln:

> Official correspondence has been freely opened with Liberia, and it gives us a pleasing view of social and political progress in that republic. It may be expected to derive new vigor from American influence, improved by the rapid disappearance of slavery in the United States.
>
> I solicit your authority to furnish to the republic a gunboat, at moderate cost, to be reimbursed to the United States by instalments. Such a vessel is needed for the safety of that State against the native African races, and in Liberian hands it would be more effective in arresting the African slave-trade than a squadron in our own hands. The possession of the least organized naval force would stimulate a generous ambition in the republic, and the confidence which we should manifest by furnishing it would win forbearance and favor toward the colony from all civilized nations.[1155]

Lincoln apologists and loyalists like to pretend that the president's racism and grotesque obsession with black colonization softened, and even disappeared, as time passed, particularly during his War. But this is not true. In fact, he was ardently discussing the issue right up until the day he died.

According to the memoirs of Yankee Union General Benjamin F. "the Beast" Butler (like Lincoln, also despised in the South for war crimes against humanity), in early April 1865 the president invited him to the White House to discuss his latest deportation plans to ship blacks out of the country.[1156] This was just days before Lincoln was killed by John Wilkes Booth, a disillusioned Confederate supporter from Maryland.

Of his last meeting with Lincoln in April, Butler writes:

> A conversation was held between us after the negotiations had failed at Hampton Roads [February 3, 1865], and in the course of the conversation he said to me: —
> "But what shall we do with the negroes after they are free? I can hardly believe that the South and North can live in peace, unless we can get rid of the negroes. Certainly they cannot if we don't get rid of the negroes whom we have armed and disciplined and who have fought with us, to the amount, I believe of some one hundred and fifty thousand men. I believe that it would

be better to export them all to some fertile country with a good climate, which they could have to themselves.

"You have been a staunch friend of the race from the time you first advised me to enlist them at New Orleans. You have had a good deal of experience in moving bodies of men by water,—your movement up the James was a magnificent one. Now we shall have no use for our very large navy; what, then, are our difficulties in sending all the blacks away?"[1157]

Butler responded by discussing his own idea of how to **"send all the blacks away."** The solution was simple: settle a colony for them in the Isthmus of Darien (modern Panama). To this Lincoln agreed, replying: **"There is meat in that, General Butler; there is meat in that."**[1158]

These words, so intently focused on the deportation of American blacks, were among the last ever spoken by our sixteenth president.[1159]

Lincoln & the Emancipation Proclamation

ACCORDING TO YANKEE AND NEW South "history," there is only one Emancipation Proclamation. Actually Lincoln wrote four Emancipation Proclamations: two drafts, a "preliminary" version, and a "final" version. Let us take these one by one. Here is the first:

> July 22, 1862.— Emancipation Proclamation As First Submitted To The Cabinet.
> In pursuance of the sixth section of the act of Congress entitled "An act to suppress insurrection and to punish treason and rebellion, to seize and confiscate property of rebels, and for other purposes," approved July 17, 1862, and which act and the joint resolution explanatory thereof are herewith published, I, Abraham Lincoln, President of the United States, do hereby proclaim to and warn all persons within the contemplation of said sixth section to cease participating in, aiding, countenancing, or abetting the existing rebellion, or any rebellion, against the Government of the United States, and to return to their proper allegiance to the United States, on pain of the forfeitures and seizures as within and by said sixth section provided.
> And I hereby make known that it is my purpose, upon the next meeting of Congress, to again recommend the adoption of a practical measure for tendering

pecuniary aid to the free choice or rejection of any and all States which may then be recognizing and practically sustaining the authority of the United States, and which may then have voluntarily adopted, or thereafter may voluntarily adopt, gradual abolishment of slavery within such State or States; that the object is to practically restore, thenceforward to be maintained, the constitutional relation between the General Government and each and all the States wherein that relation is now suspended or disturbed; and that for this object the war, as it has been, will be prosecuted. And as a fit and necessary military measure for effecting this object, I, as commander-in-chief of the army and navy of the United States, do order and declare that on the first day of January, in the year of our Lord one thousand eight hundred and sixty-three, all persons held as slaves within any State or States wherein the constitutional authority of the United States shall not then be practically recognized, submitted to, and maintained, shall then, thenceforward, and forever be free.[1160]

Here is the second version:

September 22, 1862. — Preliminary Emancipation Proclamation. By The President Of The United States Of America: A Proclamation.

I Abraham Lincoln, President of the United States of America, and commander-in-chief of the army and navy thereof, do hereby proclaim and declare that hereafter, as heretofore, the war will be prosecuted for the object of practically restoring the constitutional relation between the United States and each of the States, and the people thereof, in which States that relation is or may be suspended or disturbed.

That it is my purpose, upon the next meeting of Congress, to again recommend the adoption of a practical measure tendering pecuniary aid to the free acceptance or rejection of all slave States, so called, the people whereof may not then be in rebellion against the United States, and which States may then have voluntarily adopted, or thereafter may voluntarily adopt, immediate or gradual abolishment of slavery within their respective limits; and that the effort to colonize persons of African descent with their consent upon this continent or elsewhere, with the previously obtained consent of the governments existing there, will be continued.

That on the first day of January, in the year of our Lord one thousand eight hundred and sixty-three, all persons held as slaves within any State or designated part of a State the people whereof shall then be in rebellion against the United States, shall be then, thenceforward, and forever free; and the Executive Government of the United States, including the military and naval authority thereof, will recognize and maintain the freedom of such persons, and will do no act or acts to repress such persons, or any of them, in any efforts they may make for their actual freedom.

That the Executive will, on the first day of January aforesaid, by proclamation designate the States and parts of States, if any, in which the people thereof, respectively, shall then be in rebellion against the United States; and the fact that any State, or the people thereof, shall on that day be in good faith represented in the Congress of the United States by members chosen thereto at elections wherein a majority of the qualified voters of such State shall have participated, shall, in the absence of strong countervailing testimony, be deemed conclusive evidence that such State, and the people thereof, are not then in rebellion against the United States.

That attention is hereby called to an act of Congress entitled "An act to make an additional article of war," approved March 13, 1862, and which act is in the words and figure following:

Be it enacted by the Senate and House of Representatives of the United States of America in Congress assembled, That hereafter the following shall be promulgated as an additional article of war, for the government of the army of the United States, and shall be obeyed and observed as such:

Article—. All officers or persons in the military or naval service of the United States are prohibited from employing any of the forces under their respective commands for the purpose of returning fugitives from service or labor who may have escaped from any persons to whom such service or labor is claimed to be due; and any officer who shall be found guilty by a court martial of violating this article shall be dismissed from the service.

Sec. 2. And be it further enacted, That this act shall take effect from and after its passage.

Also to the ninth and tenth sections of an act entitled "An act to suppress insurrection, to punish treason and rebellion, to seize and confiscate property of rebels, and for other purposes," approved July 17, 1862, and which sections are in the words and figures following:

Sec. 9. And be it further enacted, That all slaves of persons who shall hereafter be engaged in rebellion against the Government of the United States, or who shall in any way give aid or comfort thereto, escaping from such persons and taking refuge within the lines of the army; and all slaves captured from such persons or deserted by them, and coming under the control of the Government of the United States; and all slaves of such persons found on [or] being within any place occupied by rebel forces and afterwards occupied by the forces of the United States, shall be deemed captives of war, and shall be forever free of their servitude, and not again held as slaves.

Sec. 10. And be it further enacted, That no slave escaping into any State, Territory, or the District of Columbia, from any other State, shall be delivered up, or in any way impeded or hindered of his liberty, except for crime, or some offense against the laws, unless the person claiming said fugitive shall first make oath that the person to whom the labor or service of such fugitive is alleged to be due is his lawful owner, and has not borne arms against the United States in the present rebellion; nor in any way given aid and comfort thereto; and no person engaged in the military or naval service of the United States shall, under any pretense whatever, assume to decide on the validity of the claim of any person to the service or labor of any other person, or surrender up any such person to the claimant, on pain of being dismissed from the service.

And I do hereby enjoin upon and order all persons engaged in the military and naval service of the United States to observe, obey, and enforce, within their respective spheres of service, the act and sections above recited.

And the Executive will in due time recommend that all citizens of the United States who shall have remained loyal thereto throughout the rebellion shall (upon the restoration of the constitutional relation between the United States and their respective States and people, if that relation shall have been suspended or disturbed) be compensated for all losses by acts of the United States, including the loss of slaves.

In witness whereof, I have hereunto set my hand and caused the seal of the United States to be affixed.

Done at the city of Washington, this twenty-second day of September, in the year of our Lord one thousand eight hundred and sixty-two, and of the independence of the United States the eighty-seventh. Abraham Lincoln.[1161]

We now list the third version of the Emancipation Proclamation:

December 30, 1862.—Draft Of The Emancipation Proclamation Of January 1, 1863, As Submitted To The Cabinet For Final Revision.

Now therefore, I, Abraham Lincoln, President of the United States, by virtue of the power in me vested as commander-in-chief of the army and navy of the United States, in time of actual armed rebellion against the authority and government of the United States, and as a proper and necessary war measure for suppressing said rebellion, do on this first day of January, in the year of our Lord one thousand eight hundred and sixty-three, and in accordance with my intention so to do, publicly proclaimed for one hundred days as aforesaid, order and designate as the States and parts of States in which the people thereof respectively are this day in rebellion against the United States, the following, to wit: Arkansas, Texas, Louisiana (except the parishes of

Mississippi, Alabama, Florida, Georgia, South Carolina, North Carolina, and Virginia (except the forty-eight counties designated as West Virginia, and also the counties of [unfinished]

And by virtue of the power, and for the purpose

aforesaid, I do order and declare that all persons held as slaves within said designated States and parts of States are, and henceforward forever shall be, free; and that the Executive Government of the United States, including the military and naval authorities thereof, will recognize and maintain the freedom of said persons, and will do no act or acts to repress said persons, or any of them, in any suitable efforts they may make for their actual freedom; and I hereby appeal to the people so declared to be free to abstain from all disorder, tumult, and violence, unless in necessary self-defense; and in all cases, when allowed, to labor faithfully for wages.

And I further declare and make known that such persons of suitable condition will be received into the armed service of the United States to garrison and defend forts, positions, stations, and other places, and to man vessels of all sorts in said service.[1162]

We come now to the fourth and last version, known specifically as the Final Emancipation Proclamation:

January 1, 1863.— Final Emancipation Proclamation.
By The President Of The United States Of America:
A Proclamation.

Whereas, on the twenty-second day of September, in the year of our Lord one thousand eight hundred and sixty-two, a proclamation was issued by the President of the United States, containing, among other things, the following, to wit:

"That on the first day of January, in the year of our Lord one thousand eight hundred and sixty-three, all persons held as slaves within any State, or designated part of a State, the people whereof shall then be in rebellion against the United States, shall be then, thenceforward, and forever free; and the Executive Government of the United States, including the military and naval authority thereof, will recognize and maintain the freedom of such persons, and will do no act or acts to repress such persons, or any of them, in any efforts they may make for their actual freedom.

"That the Executive will, on the first day of January aforesaid, by proclamation, designate the States and parts of States, if any, in which the people thereof respectively shall then be in rebellion against the United

States; and the fact that any State, or the people thereof, shall on that day be in good faith represented in the Congress of the United States by members chosen thereto at elections wherein a majority of the qualified voters of such State shall have participated, shall in the absence of strong countervailing testimony be deemed conclusive evidence that such State and the people thereof are not then in rebellion against the United States."

Now, therefore, I, Abraham Lincoln, President of the United States, by virtue of the power in me vested as commander-in-chief of the army and navy of the United States, in time of actual armed rebellion against the authority and government of the United States, and as a fit and necessary war measure for suppressing said rebellion, do, on this first day of January, in the year of our Lord one thousand eight hundred and sixty-three, and in accordance with my purpose so to do, publicly proclaimed for the full period of 100 days from the day first above mentioned, order and designate as the States and parts of States wherein the people thereof, respectively, are this day in rebellion against the United States, the following, to wit:

Arkansas, Texas, Louisiana (except the parishes of St. Bernard, Plaquemines, Jefferson, St. John, St. Charles, St. James, Ascension, Assumption, Terre Bonne, Lafourche, St. Mary, St. Martin, and Orleans, including the city of New Orleans), Mississippi, Alabama, Florida, Georgia, South Carolina, North Carolina, and Virginia (except the forty-eight counties designated as West Virginia, and also the counties of Berkeley, Accomac, Northampton, Elizabeth City, York, Princess Ann, and Norfolk, including the cities of Norfolk and Portsmouth), and which excepted parts are for the present left precisely as if this proclamation were not issued.

And by virtue of the power and for the purpose aforesaid, I do order and declare that all persons held as slaves within said designated States and parts of States are, and henceforward shall be, free; and that the Executive Government of the United States, including the military and naval authorities thereof, will recognize and maintain the freedom of said persons.

And I hereby enjoin upon the people so declared to be free to abstain from all violence, unless in necessary self-defense; and I recommend to them that, in all cases when allowed, they labor faithfully for reasonable wages.

And I further declare and make known that such persons of suitable condition will be received into the armed service of the United States to garrison forts, positions, stations, and other places, and to man vessels of all sorts in said service.

And upon this act, sincerely believed to be an act of justice, warranted by the Constitution upon military necessity, I invoke the considerate judgment of mankind and the gracious favor of Almighty God.

In witness whereof, I have hereunto set my hand, and caused the seal of the United States to be affixed.

Done at the city of Washington, this first day of January, in the year of our Lord one thousand eight hundred and sixty-three, and of the independence of the United States of America the eighty-seventh.
Abraham Lincoln[1163]

Most of the world is wholly unaware of the first three versions of Lincoln's Emancipation Proclamation, while the fourth and final version, the one widely known, is generally misunderstood because it has been translated for the public by biased Lincoln apologists and devotees. In the process the president's words have been reinterpreted and twisted to agree with a liberal, usually anti-South, mainstream political and social agenda. Our history books and textbooks are thus filled with both misinformation and disinformation concerning the several Emancipation Proclamations, and the true intention and meaning behind these documents has been lost.

As the first version is an unfinished draft of the second, and the third version is an unfinished draft of the fourth, our focus will be specifically on the second and fourth: the Preliminary Emancipation Proclamation and the Final Emancipation Proclamation respectively.

We saw in the previous chapter that the Preliminary Emancipation Proclamation is basically a document asking Congress to allow for the liberation of Southern slaves and their deportation out of the country, or as Lincoln put it, to recommend

> that the effort to colonize persons of African descent with their consent upon this continent or elsewhere, with the previously obtained consent of the governments existing there, will be continued.[1164]

This section was struck from the Final Emancipation Proclamation by

Lincoln's cabinet for fear that it would alienate the Radicals (i.e., the abolitionists) in his party.

The Final Emancipation Proclamation then was not the version that Lincoln wanted. It was the version forced on him. And yet this is the one that is now known to the world. How differently Lincoln would be seen today if his cabinet had approved his Preliminary Emancipation Proclamation and the final version had never been created!

While the Final Emancipation Proclamation was a watered down version of Lincoln's true and original words, it did contain many other elements that were vital to his planned destruction and so-called "Reconstruction" (i.e., northernization) of the South. Let us examine this document in more detail, and strip away the Yankee/New South mythology surrounding it. Only then can we extract the real Lincoln from the tomb of his suppressed writings.

We will begin by asking this question: was the issuance of the Final Emancipation Proclamation legal?

Plainly it was not. Lincoln's edict was only active in the Confederacy, which had been a constitutionally formed independent nation for over two years by January 1, 1863. The leader of one country cannot decide the laws of another. Thus, because it violates both international law and the U.S. Constitution, the military-based Emancipation Proclamation was illegal, and its author, Abraham Lincoln, a war criminal.

While not admitting he was a war criminal, Lincoln did openly confess that his proclamation was illicit.[1165] In a September 2, 1863, letter to his secretary of the treasury, Salmon P. Chase, he states that:

> **The original proclamation has no constitutional or legal justification, except as a military measure.**[1166]

A year earlier, on September 13, 1862, he told a group of abolitionist ministers that it was pointless to issue a proclamation of emancipation, for it would **"necessarily be inoperative, like the Pope's bull against the comet."**[1167] Why would it have been **"inoperative"**? Because it would have been rendered ineffective against the Constitution (the **"comet"**), making it unlawful.

In his December 8, 1863, "Message to Congress," Lincoln once again acknowledges the illegality of his proclamation, even admitting that it was only done as a **"military measure"**:

> According to our political system, as a matter of civil administration, the General Government had no lawful power to effect emancipation in any State, and for a long time it had been hoped that the rebellion could be suppressed without resorting to it as a military measure.[1168]

In an April 5, 1864, letter to Mrs. Horace Mann, *written over a year after issuing the Final Emancipation Proclamation*, Lincoln once again admits that he did not have the authority to free the slaves. Instead, as he so often does, he conveniently passes the buck to the Almighty:

> Madam: The petition of persons under eighteen, praying that I would free all slave children, and the heading of which petition it appears you wrote, was handed me a few days since by Senator [Charles] Sumner. Please tell these little people I am very glad their young hearts are so full of just and generous sympathy, and that, while I have not the power to grant all they ask, I trust they will remember that God has, and that, as it seems, he wills to do it. Yours truly, A. Lincoln.[1169]

It is with just such deceptive words that Lincoln has hidden the true purpose of the Final Emancipation Proclamation from the world for generations.

What then was its true purpose?

Yankee and New South historians tell us that it enabled an egalitarian Lincoln to grant blacks full civil rights and incorporate them into American society. However, as we will see, Lincoln was no egalitarian, and he issued his most famous edict for a number of reasons—not one of them having to do with civil liberties.

On February 6, 1864, for example, a year after his final proclamation was published, he hinted at the actual motivation behind it when he gave the following "Account of the Emancipation Proclamation" to artist Francis Bicknell Carpenter:

> Things had gone from bad to worse until I felt that we had reached the end of our rope on the plan of operations we had been pursuing [that is, to quickly and efficiently crush the South]—that we had played our last card and must change our tactics, or lose the game. I determined on the Emancipation Proclamation, and . . . called a Cabinet meeting upon the subject. This was the

last of July or the first part of the month of August, 1862. [The exact date was July 22, 1862].[1170]

Lincoln makes no mention here of black civil rights; there are no humanitarian gestures, no great sweeping oratory on the evils of slavery. Just banal talk of military **"tactics"** and a political **"game"** he was determined to win. The underlying message here is obvious: for Lincoln, "freeing the slaves" had nothing to do with slavery itself and everything to do with politics.

Lincoln's verbal account of the idea of his Emancipation Proclamation to Carpenter continues:

> . . . All were present excepting Mr. [Montgomery] **Blair, the Postmaster-General, who was absent at the opening of the discussion, but came in subsequently. I said to the Cabinet that I had resolved upon this step, and had not called them together to ask their advice, but to lay the subject-matter of a proclamation before them, suggestions as to which would be in order after they had heard it read. Mr.** [Owen] **Lovejoy was in error when he informed you that it excited no comment excepting on the part of Secretary** [William H.] **Seward. Various suggestions were offered. Secretary** [Salmon P.] **Chase wished the language stronger in reference to the arming of the blacks.**
>
> **Mr. Blair, after he came in, deprecated the policy on the ground that it would cost the administration the fall elections. Nothing, however, was offered that I had not already fully anticipated and settled in my own mind, until Secretary Seward spoke. He said in substance, 'Mr. President, I approve of the proclamation, but I question the expediency of its issue at this juncture. The depression of the public mind, consequent upon our repeated reverses, is so great that I fear the effect of so important a step. It may be viewed as the last measure of an exhausted government, a cry for help; the government stretching forth its hands to Ethiopia, instead of Ethiopia stretching forth her hands to the government.' His idea . . . was that it would be considered our last shriek on the retreat.** [This was his precise expression.] **'Now,' continued Mr. Seward, 'while I approve the measure, I suggest, sir, that you postpone its issue until you can give it to the country supported by**

> military success, instead of issuing it, as would be the case now, upon the greatest disasters of the war.' The wisdom of the view of the Secretary of State struck me with very great force. It was an aspect of the case that, in all my thought upon the subject, I had entirely overlooked. The result was that I put the draft of the proclamation aside, as you do your sketch for a picture, waiting for a victory.
>
> From time to time I added or changed a line, touching it up here and there, anxiously watching the progress of events. Well, the next news we had was of [General John] **Pope's disaster at** [Second] **Bull Run** [the Battle of Second Manassas to Southerners]. Things looked darker than ever. Finally came the week of the battle of **Antietam** [the Battle of Sharpsburg to Southerners]. I determined to wait no longer. The news came, I think, on Wednesday, that the advantage was on our side. I was then staying at the Soldier's Home [three miles out of Washington]. Here I finished writing the second draft of the preliminary proclamation; came up on Saturday; called the Cabinet together to hear it, and it was published on the following Monday.[1171]

Lincoln here states that not only was his decision to issue the Preliminary Emancipation Proclamation on September 22, 1862, due to politics, but also because of a single military action in Maryland: the Battle of Antietam on September 17. Again, no mention of blacks, abolition, slavery, or civil rights.

Is it really possible that the Emancipation Proclamation had nothing to do with black civil rights? Absolutely, and we have more of Lincoln's own thoughts and words to prove it.

On March 26, 1864, he explained to a group of Kentuckians why he issued his most famous document. Here he reveals the practical thinking and illegal maneuvering that went on behind the scenes, none of it having anything to do with the rights, feelings, or needs of enslaved African-Americans:

> I felt that measures, otherwise unconstitutional might become lawful by becoming indispensable to the preservation of the Constitution through the preservation of the nation. Right or wrong, I assumed this ground, and now avow it. I could not feel that, to the best of my ability, I had even tried to preserve the Constitution, if, to preserve slavery, or any minor matter,

I should permit the wreck of government, country, and Constitution altogether. When, early in the war, General [John C.] Frémont attempted military emancipation, I forbade it, because I did not then think it an indispensable necessity. When, a little later, General [Simon] Cameron, then Secretary of War, suggested the arming of the blacks, I objected, because I did not yet think it an indispensable necessity. When, still later, General [David] Hunter attempted military emancipation, I again forbade it, because I did not yet think the indispensable necessity had come. When, in March and May and July, 1862, I made earnest and successive appeals to the border States to favor compensated emancipation, I believed the indispensable necessity for military emancipation and arming the blacks would come, unless averted by that measure. They declined the proposition; and I was, in my best judgment, driven to the alternative of either surrendering the Union, and with it the Constitution, or of laying strong hand upon the colored element. I chose the latter. In choosing it, I hoped for greater gain than loss; but of this, I was not entirely confident. More than a year of trial now shows no loss by it in our foreign relations, none in our home popular sentiment, none in our white military force,—no loss by it anyhow or anywhere. On the contrary, it shows a gain of quite a hundred and thirty thousand soldiers, seamen, and laborers. These are palpable facts, about which, as facts, there can be no caviling. We have the men and we could not have had them without the measure.[1172]

Once when asked to defend his plan to free black slaves merely to enlist them in his armies, Lincoln replied:

> . . . no human power can subdue this rebellion without the use of the emancipation policy and every other policy calculated to weaken the moral and physical forces of the rebellion.[1173]

As Lincoln clearly states over and over again, the Union needed more soldiers, and his Emancipation Proclamation provided them—period, end of story. Thus, the issuance of the Preliminary Emancipation Proclamation immediately following the Battle of Sharpsburg (Antietam) was no accident.

The Final version, however, speaks much more clearly of Lincoln's three other main intentions:

1. End slavery in order to
2. Foment slave insurrection in the South and
3. Inaugurate black enlistment

Let us discuss these one at a time.

Lincoln begins his edict by allegedly emancipating the slaves. On closer examination, however, he does nothing of the kind. The following areas are where Lincoln's proclamation stipulates that slavery must come to an immediate halt:

> **Arkansas, Texas, Louisiana (except the parishes of St. Bernard, Plaquemines, Jefferson, St. John, St. Charles, St. James, Ascension, Assumption, Terre Bonne, Lafourche, St. Mary, St. Martin, and Orleans, including the city of New Orleans), Mississippi, Alabama, Florida, Georgia, South Carolina, North Carolina, and Virginia (except the forty-eight counties designated as West Virginia, and also the counties of Berkeley, Accomac, Northampton, Elizabeth City, York, Princess Ann, and Norfolk, including the cities of Norfolk and Portsmouth), and which excepted parts are for the present left precisely as if this proclamation were not issued.**[1174]

Note that *all* of the areas designated for abolition are in the Confederacy, a separate and constitutionally formed nation where Lincoln had not the slightest bit of authority.

Just as importantly he exempts a number of regions in the South, such as many parishes in Louisiana, which were by then occupied by Yankee troops. Also noticeable by its absence is Tennessee. Why did Lincoln not list it? Because the Volunteer State was largely under Yankee domination by January 1863 (the state's capital city, Nashville, had been captured a year earlier on February 23, 1862),[1175] and was well on her way to being forced back into the Union.[1176] Indeed, the last state to secede (on June 8, 1861),[1177] after the War Tennessee would be the first Confederate state to be reunionized (on July 24, 1866).[1178] In other words, according to Lincoln's own words, *slavery was allowed to continue in areas that were now under the control of the Union.*

Finally, the president completely ignores slavery in the North, even saying that these parts are **"for the present left precisely as if this proclamation were not issued."** In this way Northern slave owners (such as General Ulysses S. Grant),[1179] who owned a total of between 500,000 to 1 million slaves at the time,[1180] were allowed to continue to practice the Yankees' "peculiar institution" all the way up until the ratification of the Thirteenth Amendment on December 6, 1865, eight months after Lincoln died.[1181]

In plain English, Lincoln freed slaves where he could not (in the South), while not freeing slaves where he could (in the North). Or as Lincoln's own secretary of state, a frustrated William H. Seward put it, the Final Emancipation Proclamation is an empty, meaningless document, one

> that emancipates the slaves where we cannot reach them and holds them in bondage where we can set them free.[1182]

Thus, not a single American slave was actually freed by the Emancipation Proclamation, an act issued, by Lincoln's own admission, solely out of **"military necessity"**![1183] Why then do Lincolnians continue to refer to his edict as "America's most important *abolitionist* document"?

The second primary reason Lincoln issued his decree was to try and instigate slave rebellions across the South. Such insurrections, he hoped, would turn servant against master, resulting in political anarchy, social chaos, and lawless violence. In Lincoln's distorted, inhumane, and criminal way of thinking, slaves murdering their owners was thought to be an efficient way of crushing the South and bringing the War to a speedy end.

Since this aspect of his final proclamation is routinely and completely ignored by Northern and New South historians, let us present it again for clarification:

> . . . the Executive Government of the United States, including the military and naval authority thereof, will recognize and maintain the freedom of such persons, and will do no act or acts to repress such persons, or any of them, in any efforts they may make for their actual freedom.[1184]

Lincoln here is ordering his soldiers to allow Southern slaves to use **"any efforts"** they deem appropriate to attain **"their actual freedom."** Since he does not list which efforts are allowed and which are not, it is obvious that he was giving permission to slaves to break any law they wished in order to gain their liberty.

 Unfortunately for Lincoln and fortunately for the South, there was not a single slave rebellion in the Confederacy after he issued his Emancipation Proclamation, as even the Northern president himself was forced to grudgingly admit on December 8, 1863, nearly a year later:

> **No servile insurrection, or** [even] **tendency to violence or cruelty, has marked the measures of emancipation and arming of blacks.**[1185]

 In fact there were no so-called **"servile insurrections"** during the entire War.[1186] Yankee and New South historians like to tell us that this is because Southern blacks, being "uneducated" and "demoralized" by centuries of subjugation, were so scared and confused that they had become utterly passive by January 1, 1863.

 We do not accept such racist nonsense, however. Most Southern slaves, far from being uneducated and demoralized, were bright, savvy, talented individuals, who married, had children, owned their own homes and businesses, farmed their own fields, sold their own products, had time off to hunt, fish, and picnic, celebrated their own holidays, and attended their own churches.

 Imbued with numerous civil, legal, and social rights, many had enormous power and freedom, such as those who were managers of their owners' entire plantations. Fed, clothed, sheltered, and doctored by their masters from cradle to grave, they did not share the daily stresses and concerns of free blacks, who, like free whites, were always in danger of joblessness, starvation, and homelessness. Thus, while we acknowledge that Southern slaves would have rather been (and should have been) completely free, at the same time it is not true that they were dumb, passive, oppressed, helpless, illiterate creatures, as Yankee mythology teaches.

 What then were the real reasons Southern slaves did not rise up and kill their owners after being "freed" by Lincoln? There were four: 1) the Southern black's mistrust of white supremacist Lincoln and the racist Northern people; 2) his undying love for his Southern homeland; 3) his belief in the Southern Cause (i.e., self-determination); and 4) his certain knowledge that slavery was soon coming to an end, whether the Confederacy won the War or not.

 Little wonder then that 95 percent of all Southern black servants chose to remain in their Southern homeland after "emancipation,"[1187] on their masters' plantations, where safety and certainty reigned.[1188] Evidence for this comes from the Underground Railroad. Though it functioned throughout most of the War, only about 4,000 total (just 1,000 Southern slaves a year) out of 3.5 million availed themselves of it—a mere 0.11 percent of the total.[1189] The rest voluntarily stayed at home, defending both their owners' farms, and the owners themselves, from marauding Yanks.[1190]

What occurred at the Confederate home of Sarah Morgan's parents was the norm, not the exception, as Northern textbooks insists. On the day of Jubilee (emancipation) in New Orleans, Louisiana, her family's slaves were (illegally) "set free" by arrogant Yankee officers, who ordered the servants to leave with them. All refused, however. One servant named Margret, snapped back at the Union soldiers: "I don't want to be any free-er than I is now—I'll stay with my mistress." Another one of the Morgan's servants, a black man, was tossed a musket and commanded to join the Federal army, to which he replied: "I am only a slave, but I am a secesh [i.e., secession] nigger, and won't fight in such a damned crew!"[1191]

It was this same loyal stay-at-home group—representing 95 percent of all Southern blacks (a group even recognized by Lincoln)[1192]—that eventually inspired the concept of sharecropping: as nearly all slaves refused to leave their plantations after emancipation, postwar owners simply subdivided their land into small plots and turned them over to their new freedmen and freedwomen. This saved blacks from having to seek employment elsewhere (or worse, try and raise money to buy their own land), while it saved plantation owners the trouble of having to find new employees.[1193]

There was something far deeper going on here than just mere practicality, however.

Former slaves quite rightly considered themselves true Americans and true Southerners. After all, by 1860, 99 percent of all blacks were native-born Americans, a larger percentage than for whites.[1194] Educator and former Southern servant Booker T. Washington eloquently spoke for the 95 percent of Southern blacks who remained in Dixie after Lincoln's emancipation, when he wrote:

> I was born in the South, I have lived and labored in the South, and I expect to die and be buried in the South.[1195]

On September 29, 1865, just five months after Lincoln's War came to an end at Appomattox, North Carolina blacks held a "Negro Convention" that issued the following declaration:

> Born upon the same soil and brought up in an intimacy of relationship unknown in any other state of society, we have formed attachments for the white race which must be as enduring as life, and we can conceive of no reason that our God-bestowed freedom should now sever the kindly ties which have so long united us. . .
>
> We acknowledge with gratitude that there are those among former slave masters who have promptly conceded our freedom and have manifested a just and humane disposition towards their former slaves. . .
>
> Though associated with many memories of suffering, as well as of enjoyment, we have always loved our homes, and dreaded, as the worst of evils, a forcible separation from them. Now that freedom and a new career are before us, we love this land and people more than ever before. Here we have toiled and suffered; our parents, wives, and children are buried here; and in this land we will remain, unless forcibly driven away.[1196]

So strong was their attachment to Dixie that as late as the 1880s, a generation after the "Civil War," 90 percent of all Southern blacks still lived in the plantation belts of the Deep South.[1197]

Naturally the North conveniently glosses over these facts, and instead focuses on its own anti-South Yankee mythology.

We now come to the third and final primary purpose of the Emancipation Proclamation: black enlistment.

As Lincoln was no humanitarian, and was completely unconcerned about racial equality for blacks,[1198] why would he want to enroll them in his army? Indeed, when he started his War in 1861, though many Northern blacks turned out at recruiting offices to sign up, they were "thanked for their troubles and sent home." On August 6, 1862, for instance, Lincoln's War Department sent the following brusque message to Edward Salomon, the governor of Wisconsin: "The President declines to receive Indians or negroes as troops."[1199]

Obviously, at the time, Lincoln had no intention whatsoever of using blacks in his military,[1200] and neither did any of the governors of the Northern states.[1201] The president later admitted as much, saying, on April 18, 1864:

> **At the beginning of the war, and for some time, the use of colored troops was not contemplated; and how the**

change of purpose was wrought, I will not now take time to explain.¹²⁰²

When Lincoln states that **"the use of colored troops was not contemplated,"** what he is really saying is that due to entrenched Northern white racism—including his own, neither he, his cabinet, or most of his military officers wanted African-Americans in the army for fear that their presence would degrade what Lincoln referred to as the **"superior race,"** that is, whites.¹²⁰³ Or, as he indecorously put it on July 10, 1858, at Chicago, Illinois, **"the inferior race bears the superior down."**¹²⁰⁴

What changed Lincoln's mind then?

In great part it was the issue of manpower.

Two years into his War white enlistments were down and his all-white army was sharply dwindling in numbers¹²⁰⁵ due to disease, wounds, desertion, defection, and death, as Lincoln himself acknowledged.¹²⁰⁶ The Union desertion rate alone was so high that countless individuals were arrested and executed, as Yankee General Benjamin F. Butler noted in an April 12, 1864, to Lincoln:

> Large numbers of the New Hampshire substitutes have deserted from Yorktown yesterday and to-day, some have gone to the enemy, some are lurking in swamps, and some are attempting to get to Baltimore; they are from the regiments lately at Point Lookout, which I have had to remove from there because I found them colluding with the prisoners and escaping, three having seized a boat and carried off five prisoners. Those that we catch are being tried by Court Martial, and believe it will be necessary to execute quite a number of them.¹²⁰⁷

Butler is speaking here of just one small group in the Spring of 1864. There were tens of thousands of other cases of Union desertion. Indeed, most authorities agree that some 200,000 Yanks deserted during the War, about 4,166 soldiers a week.¹²⁰⁸ Lincoln needed to fill these 200,000 positions one way or another.

Thus, though he was still against enlisting blacks in the U.S. Army, thinking them inferior to whites,¹²⁰⁹ he eventually gave in to military expediency, for it was obvious by then that their numbers would eventually be needed by the Union in order to subdue the South.¹²¹⁰

On July 3, 1862, in a dispatch to his Northern governors (begging for more soldiers), Lincoln callously commented on his army's losses:

> I should not want the half of 300,000 new troops if I could have them now. If I had 50,000 additional troops here now, I believe I could substantially close the war in two weeks. But time is everything, and if I get 50,000 new men in a month, I shall have lost 20,000 old ones during the same month, having gained only 30,000, with the difference between old and new troops still against me. The quicker you send, the fewer you will have to send. Time is everything. Please act in view of this. The enemy having given up Corinth, it is not wonderful that he is thereby enabled to check us for a time at Richmond. Yours truly, A. Lincoln.[1211]

There was also the inevitable racist motivation. As Lincoln later asserted:

> I thought that whatever negroes could be got to do as soldiers, leaves just so much less for white soldiers to do in saving the Union.[1212]

"Whatever negroes could be got to do," of course, included taking Confederate steel and dying for Lincoln's cause, purportedly **"preserving the Union."** (As this book makes patently clear, liberal Lincoln actually destroyed the voluntary Union envisioned and created by the Founding Fathers, turning individual allegiance from the state to the nation, one whose capital in Washington, D.C. became the head of an all-powerful, monolithic empire—conservative Jefferson's worst nightmare.)[1213]

Lincoln's problem was that slaves could not be made soldiers as long as they were considered "property."[1214] The resolution to this difficulty was the Emancipation Proclamation,[1215] which is why Lincoln later admitted that without his 200,000 additional black soldiers the North would not have won the war.[1216] Keep the **"physical force"** provided by the black Union soldier, said Lincoln on September 12, 1864,

> and you can save the Union. Throw it away, and the Union goes with it.[1217]

It was this need, to replace lost white soldiers, that prompted Lincoln to include the following clause near the end of his Final Emancipation Proclamation:

> And I further declare and make known that such persons of suitable condition will be received into the armed service of the United States to garrison forts, positions, stations, and other places, and to man vessels of all sorts in said service.[1218]

We will note from the wording that Lincoln did not intend for his new black recruits to be armed soldiers. Instead Lincoln says that they will be assigned simple guard duty of **"forts, positions, stations, and other places, and to man vessels of all sorts in said service."**

If there is any doubt that Lincoln issued the Emancipation Proclamation primarily for military purposes, we need only carefully examine the wording of the following dispatch sent by the president to Yankee General Ulysses S. Grant on August 9, 1863:

> . . . General [Lorenzo] Thomas has gone again to the Mississippi Valley, with the view of raising colored troops. I have no reason to doubt that you are doing what you reasonably can upon the same subject. I believe *it is a resource which if vigorously applied now will soon close the contest. It works doubly, weakening the enemy and strengthening us. We were not fully ripe for it, until the river was opened. Now, I think at least one hundred thousand can and ought to be rapidly organized along its shores, relieving all white troops to serve elsewhere.* Mr. [Charles Anderson] Dana understands you as believing that the emancipation proclamation has helped some in your military operations. I am very glad if this is so [emphasis added].[1219]

During his December 8, 1863 "Message to Congress," Lincoln once again admits in no uncertain terms that his Final Emancipation Proclamation had been for the sole (or main) purpose of enlisting freed blacks:

> The preliminary emancipation proclamation, issued in September, was running its assigned period to the beginning of the new year. A month later the final proclamation came, including the announcement that colored men of suitable condition would be received into the war service. The policy of emancipation, and of employing black soldiers, gave to the future a new aspect, about which hope, and fear, and doubt contended in uncertain conflict.[1220]

Following the issuance of his racist proclamation on January 1, 1863, Lincoln wasted no time in implementing its military aspects, as the following example illustrates. Written to Union General John Adams Dix on January 14, 1863, it reads:

> My dear Sir: The proclamation has been issued. We were not succeeding—at best were progressing too slowly—without it. Now that we have it, and bear all the disadvantages of it (as we do bear some in certain quarters), we must also take some benefit from it, if practicable. I therefore will thank you for your well-considered opinion whether Fortress Monroe and Yorktown, one or both, could not, in whole or in part, be garrisoned by colored troops, leaving the white forces now necessary at those places to be employed elsewhere. Yours very truly, A. Lincoln.[1221]

Shortly thereafter Lincoln began desperately pushing for the formation of black U.S. troops, though up until then he had been completely against allowing African-Americans into the military, even as common slave-like laborers! Here is how he approached Tennessee's Governor Andrew Johnson on March 26, 1863:

> My dear Sir: I am told you have at least thought of raising a negro military force. In my opinion the country now needs no specific thing so much as some man of your ability and position to go to this work. When I speak of your position, I mean that of an eminent citizen of a slave State and himself a slaveholder. The colored population is the great available and yet unavailed of force for restoring the Union. The bare sight of fifty thousand armed and drilled black soldiers upon the banks of the Mississippi would end the rebellion at once; and who doubts that we can present that sight if we but take hold in earnest? If you have been thinking of it, please do not dismiss the thought. Yours very truly, A. Lincoln.[1222]

Why did Lincoln want to place 50,000 black soldiers **"upon the banks of the Mississippi"**? That body of water was the concern of the U.S. navy, not the U.S. army.

The reality is they were to be sent there, not to serve as actual combatants, but merely to replace white "grunt" soldiers whose terms of service were expiring.¹²²³ They were then to take over the grunts' jobs loading and unloading ships and guarding the Union storehouses and garrisons situated along the river.

A few days later, on March 29, Lincoln said as much to Yankee General Nathaniel P. Banks:

> My dear Sir: Hon. Daniel Ullman, with a commission of a brigadier-general and two or three hundred other gentlemen as officers, goes to your department and reports to you, for the purpose of raising a colored brigade. To now avail ourselves of this element of force is very important, if not indispensable. I therefore will thank you to help General Ullman forward with his undertaking as much and as rapidly as you can; and also to carry the general object beyond his particular organization if you find it practicable. The necessity of this is palpable if, as I understand, you are now unable to effect anything with your present force; and which force is soon to be greatly diminished by the expiration of terms of service, as well as by ordinary causes. I shall be very glad if you will take hold of the matter in earnest. You will receive from the War Department a regular order upon this subject. Yours truly, A. Lincoln.¹²²⁴

Again, no mention of recruiting blacks out of concern for racial equality or black civil rights.

Why did Lincoln restrict blacks to simple garrison duty, while refusing to train and arm them as legitimate soldiers? In part because he did not think them intelligent enough to handle the army's expensive weapons without losing them. He also believed that most enlisted Southern blacks would simply return to the Confederacy as soon as possible, taking their guns with them, further strengthening Dixie's military.

On September 13, 1862, Lincoln addressed a group of clergymen who were trying to get the hesitant anti-abolitionist leader to issue the Emancipation Proclamation. He had been stalling it since the day he got into office, nearly two years earlier. And he was not ready to do so yet, he replied, though by issuing it

> . . . some additional strength would be added in that way to the war, and then, unquestionably, it would weaken the rebels by drawing off their laborers, which is of great importance; but I am not so sure we could do much with

the blacks. If we were to arm them, I fear that in a few weeks the arms would be in the hands of the rebels; and, indeed, thus far we have not had arms enough to equip our white troops. I will mention another thing, though it meet only your scorn and contempt. There are fifty thousand bayonets in the Union armies from the border slave States. It would be a serious matter if, in consequence of a proclamation such as you desire, they should go over to the rebels.[1225]

As a result of Lincoln's racism his black soldiers would not be armed until much later in the War, and then only after much prodding from infuriated abolitionists.

As it turns out, there were moments when Lincoln came to regret his decision to enlist and arm blacks. For it led to a number of illegalities, including crimes against innocent non-combatants, disorderly conduct, violence, and even the murder of his own white officers, as the following dispatches to Union General Robert Cumming Schenck illustrate:

> Executive Mansion, Washington, October 21, 1863. 2.45 P. M. Major-general Schenck, Baltimore, Maryland:
> A delegation is here saying that our armed colored troops are at many, if not all, the landings on the Patuxent River, and by their presence with arms in their hands are frightening quiet people and producing great confusion. Have they been sent there by any order, and if so, for what reason? A. Lincoln.[1226]
>
> October 22, 1863.—Telegram To General R. C. Schenck. Executive Mansion, Washington, October 22, 1863. 1.30 P. M. Major-general Schenck, Baltimore, Maryland:
> Please come over here. The fact of one of our officers being killed on the Patuxent is a specimen of what I would avoid. It seems to me we could send white men to recruit better than to send negroes and thus inaugurate homicides on *punctilio*. Please come over. A. Lincoln.[1227]

Here, Lincoln's racism emerges once again. In fact, it was this very mistrust of African-Americans that prompted him to segregate his black units[1228] and order them to be officered by whites.[1229]

As it turns out then, Lincoln's desire, reluctant as it was, to enlist

African-Americans was for the benefit of whites not blacks. He confirms this very thing in the Emancipation Proclamation itself. Here he clearly refers to it, not as a "civil rights measure," or as a "civil liberties necessity," but rather as a **"*war* measure"** and as a **"*military* necessity."** It is obvious that for Lincoln the issue of slavery was only relevant if it could influence the outcome of his War in some way.

In a private July 28, 1862, letter to Cuthbert Bullitt of New Orleans, Louisiana, Lincoln is completely transparent (for once) about why he issued the first draft of his Preliminary Emancipation Proclamation a week earlier on July 22:

> Mr. [Thomas J.] Durant complains that in various ways the relation of master and slave is disturbed by the presence of our army, and he considers it particularly vexatious that this, in part, is done under cover of an act of Congress, while constitutional guaranties are suspended on the plea of military necessity. The truth is, that what is done and omitted about slaves is done and omitted on the same military necessity. It is a military necessity to have men and money; and we can get neither in sufficient numbers or amounts if we keep from or drive from our lines slaves coming to them. Mr. Durant cannot be ignorant of the pressure in this direction, nor of my efforts to hold it within bounds till he and such as he shall have time to help themselves.[1230]

Nothing about black civil rights here.

Shedding further light on this is an exchange that took place between New York abolitionist Horace Greeley and Illinois anti-abolitionist Lincoln in the summer of 1862.

Greeley was one of Lincoln's greatest critics,[1231] a bitter contest that culminated on August 19 when the antislavery advocate published an open letter to the president in his newspaper, the *Tribune*, assaulting Lincoln's abysmal civil rights record and accusing him of prolonging the war by refusing to abolish slavery. Greeley's missive, entitled "The Prayer of Twenty Millions," reveals how the Northern people actually felt about the "Great Emancipator" at the time. The truth is quite different from what we have been misled to think. Wrote Greeley:

> The Prayer Of Twenty Millions.
> To Abraham Lincoln, President of the United States:

Dear Sir:—I do not intrude to tell you—for you must know already—that a great proportion of those who triumphed in your election, and of all who desire the unqualified suppression, of the rebellion now desolating our country, are sorely disappointed and deeply pained by the policy you seem to be pursuing with regard to the slaves of the rebels. I write only to set succinctly and unmistakably before you what we require, what we think we have a right to expect, and of what we complain.

I. We require of you, as the first servant of the Republic, charged especially and preeminently with this duty, that you Execute The LAWS. Most emphatically do we demand that such laws as have been recently enacted, which therefore may fairly be presumed, to embody the present will and to be dictated by the present needs of the Republic, and which, after due consideration, have received your personal sanction, shall by you be carried into full effect, and that you publicly and decisively instruct your subordinates that such laws exist, that they are binding on all functionaries and citizens, and that they are to be obeyed to the letter.

II. We think you are strangely and disastrously remiss in the discharge of your official and imperative duty with regard to the emancipation provisions of the new Confiscation Act. Those provisions were designed to fight slavery with liberty. They prescribe that men loyal to the Union, and willing to shed their blood in her behalf, shall no longer be held, with the nation's consent, in bondage to persistent, malignant traitors, who for twenty years have been plotting, and for sixteen months have been fighting to divide and destroy our country. Why these traitors should be treated with tenderness by you, to the prejudices of the dearest rights of loyal men, we cannot conceive.

III. We think you are unduly influenced by the councils, the representations, the menaces, of certain fossil politicians hailing from the border States. Knowing well that the heartily, unconditionally loyal portion of the white citizens of those States do not expect nor desire that slavery shall be upheld to the prejudice of the Union—(for the truth of which we appeal not only to every Republican residing in those States, but to such eminent loyalists as H. Winter Davis, Parson Brownlow, the Union Central Committee of Baltimore, and to the Nashville Union)—we ask you to consider that slavery is everywhere the inciting cause and sustaining base of treason: the most slaveholding sections of Maryland and Delaware being this day, though under the Union flag, in full sympathy with the rebellion, while the free labor portions of Tennessee and of Texas, though writhing under the bloody heel of treason, are unconquerably loyal to the Union. So emphatically is this the case, that a most intelligent Union banker of Baltimore recently avowed his confident belief that a majority of the present Legislature of Maryland, though elected as and still professing to be Unionists, are at heart desirous of the triumph of the Jeff Davis conspiracy; and when asked how they could be won back to loyalty, replied: "Only by the complete abolition of slavery." It seems to us the most obvious truth, that whatever strengthens or fortifies slavery in the border States strengthens also treason, and drives home the wedge intended to divide the Union. Had you, from the first, refused to recognize in those States, as here, any other than unconditional loyalty—that which stands for the Union, whatever may become of slavery—those States would have been, and would be, far more helpful and less troublesome to the defenders of the Union than they have been, or now are.

IV. We think timid counsels in such a crisis calculated to prove perilous, and probably disastrous. It is the duty of a government so wantonly, wickedly assailed by rebellion as ours has been, to oppose force to force in a defiant, dauntless spirit. It cannot afford to temporize with traitors, nor with semi-traitors. It must not bribe them to behave themselves, nor make them fair promises in the hope of disarming their causeless hostility. Representing a brave and high-spirited people, it can afford to forfeit any thing else better than its own self-respect, or their admiring confidence. For our government even to seek, after war has been made on it, to dispel the affected apprehensions of armed traitors that their cherished privileges may be assailed by it, is to invite insult and encourage hopes of its own downfall. The rush to arms of Ohio, Indiana, Illinois, is the true answer at once to the rebel raids of John [Hunt] Morgan and the traitorous sophistries of Beriah Magoffin.

V. We complain that the Union cause has suffered, and is now suffering immensely, from mistaken deference to rebel slavery. Had you, sir, in your inaugural address, unmistakeably given notice that, in case the rebellion, already commenced, were persisted in, and your efforts to preserve the Union and enforce the laws should be resisted by armed force, you would recognize no loyal person as rightfully held in slavery by a traitor, we believe the rebellion would therein have received a staggering, if not a fatal blow. At that moment, according to the returns of the most recent elections, the Unionists were a large majority of the voters of the slave States. But they were composed in good part of the aged, the feeble, the wealthy, the timid—the young, the reckless, the aspiring, the adventurous, had already been largely lured by the gamblers, and negro-traders, the politicians by trade and the conspirators by instinct, into the toils of treason. Had you then proclaimed that rebellion would strike the shackles from the slaves of every traitor, the wealthy and the cautious would have been supplied with a powerful inducement to remain loyal. As it was, every coward in the South soon became a traitor from fear; for loyalty was perilous, while treason seemed comparatively safe. Hence the boasted unanimity of the South—a unanimity based on rebel terrorism and the fact that immunity and safety were found on that side, danger and probably death on ours. The rebels, from the first, have been eager to confiscate, imprison, scourge and kill; we have fought with wolves with the devices of sheep. The result is just what might have been expected. Tens of thousands are fighting in the rebel ranks to-day, whose original bias and natural leaning would have led them into ours.

VI. We complain that the Confiscation Act which you approved is habitually disregarded by your generals, and that no word of rebuke for them from you has yet reached the public ear. [John C.] Fremont's proclamation and [David] Hunter's order favoring emancipation were promptly annulled by you; while [Henry W.] Halleck's Number Three, forbidding fugitives from slavery to rebels to come within his lines—an order as unmilitary as inhuman, and which received the hearty approbation of every traitor in America—with scores of like tendency, have never provoked even your remonstrance. We complain that the officers of your armies have habitually repelled, rather than invited the approach of slaves who would have gladly taken the risks of escaping from their rebel masters to our camps, bringing intelligence often of inestimable value to the Union cause. We complain that those who have escaped to us, avowing a willingness to do for us whatever might be required, have been brutally and madly repulsed, and often surrendered to be scourged, maimed, and tortured by the ruffian traitors who pretend to own them. We complain that a large portion of our regular army officers, with many of the volunteers, evince far more solicitude to uphold slavery than to put down the rebellion. And finally, we complain that you, Mr. President, elected as a Republican, knowing well what an abomination slavery is, and how emphatically it is the core and essence of this atrocious rebellion, seem never to interfere with these atrocities, and never give a direction to your military subordinates, which does not appear to have been conceived in the interest of slavery rather than of freedom.

VII. Let me call your attention to the recent tragedy in New Orleans, whereof the facts are obtained entirely through pro-slavery channels. A considerable body of resolute, ablebodied men, held in slavery by two rebel sugar-planters in defiance of the Confiscation Act which you have approved, left plantations thirty miles distant and made their way to the great mart of the south-west, which they knew to be in the undisputed possession of the Union forces. They made their way safely and quietly through thirty miles of rebel territory, expecting to find freedom under the folds of our flag. Whether they had or had not heard of the passage of the Confiscation Act, they reasoned logically that we could not kill them for deserting the service of their life-long oppressors, who had through treason become our implacable enemies. They came to us for liberty and protection, for which they were willing to render their best services; they met with hostility, captivity and murder. The barking of the base curs of slavery in this quarter deceives no one—not even themselves. They say, indeed, that the negroes had no right to appear in New Orleans armed, (with their implements of daily labor in the cane-field;) but no one doubts that they would gladly have laid these down if assured that they should be free. They were set upon and maimed, captured and killed, because they sought the benefit of that act of Congress which they may not specifically have heard of, but which was none the less the law of the land—which they had a clear *right* to the benefit of—which it was somebody's duty to publish far and wide, in order that so many as possible should be impelled to desist from serving rebels and the rebellion, and come over to the side of the Union. They sought their liberty in strict accordance with the laws of the land—they were butchered or reenslaved for doing so by the help of Union soldiers enlisted to fight against slaveholding treason. It was *somebody's* fault that they were so murdered—if others shall hereafter suffer in like manner, in default of explicit and public direction to your generals that they are to recognize and obey the Confiscation Act, the world will lay the blame on *you*. Whether you will choose to hear it through future history and at the bar of God, I will not judge. I can only hope.

   VIII. On the face of this wide earth, Mr. President, there is not one disinterested, determined, intelligent champion of the Union cause who does not feel that all attempts to put down the rebellion, and at the same time uphold its inciting cause are preposterous and futile—that the rebellion, if crushed out tomorrow, would be renewed within a year if slavery were left in full vigor—that army officers who remain this day devoted to slavery can at best be but half-way loyal to the Union—and that every hour of deference to slavery is an hour of added and deepened peril to the Union. I appeal to the testimony of your embassadors in Europe. It is freely at your service, not at mine. Ask them to tell you candidly whether the subserviency of your policy to the slaveholding, slavery-upholding interest, is not the perplexity, the despair of statesmen of all parties, and be admonished by the general answer!

  IX. I close as I began, with the statement that what an immense majority of the loyal millions of your country require of you is a frank, declared, unqualified, ungrudging execution of the laws of the land, more especially of the Confiscation Act. That act gives freedom to the slaves of rebels coming within our lines, or whom those lines may at any time inclose —we ask you to render it due obedience by publicly requiring your subordinates to recognize and obey it. The rebels are everywhere using the late anti-negro riots in the North, as they have long used your officers' treatment of negroes in the South, to convince the slaves that they have nothing to hope from a Union success—that we mean in that case to sell them into a bitter bondage to defray the cost of the war. Let them impress this as a truth on the great mass of their ignorant and credulous bondmen, and the Union will never be restored—never. We cannot conquer ten millions of people united in solid phalanx against us, powerfully aided by northern sympathizers and European allies. We must have scouts, guides, spies, cooks, teamsters, diggers and choppers from the blacks of the South, whether we allow them to fight for us or not or whether we shall be baffled and repelled. As one of the millions who would gladly have avoided this struggle at any sacrifice but that of principle and honor, but who now feels that the triumph of the Union is indispensable not only to the existence of our country but to the well-being of mankind, I entreat you to render a hearty and unequivocal obedience to the laws of the land. Yours, Horace Greeley. August, 19, 1862.[1232]

Four days later, on August 22, a haughty Lincoln responded to the celebrated antislavery advocate's withering public attack with one of his own:

>Executive Mansion, Washington, August 22, 1862. Hon. Horace Greeley:
> Dear Sir: I have just read yours of the 19th instant, addressed to myself through the New York "Tribune." If there be in it any statements or assumptions of fact which I may know to be erroneous, I do not, now and here, controvert them. If there be any inferences which I may believe to be falsely drawn, I do not, now and here, argue against them. If there be perceptible in it an impatient dictatorial tone, I waive it in deference to an old friend whose heart I have always supposed to be right.
> As to the policy I "seem to be pursuing," as you

say, I have not meant to leave any one in doubt.

  I would save the Union. I would save it in the shortest way under the Constitution. The sooner the national authority can be restored the nearer the Union will be "the Union as it was." If there be those who would not save the Union unless they could at the same time save slavery, I do not agree with them. If there be those who would not save the Union unless they could at the same time destroy slavery, I do not agree with them. My paramount object is to save the Union, and not either to save or destroy slavery. If I could save the Union without freeing any slave, I would do it; and if I could save it by freeing all the slaves, I would do it; and if I could do it by freeing some and leaving others alone, I would also do that. What I do about slavery and the colored race, I do because I believe it helps to save this Union, and what I forbear, I forbear because I do not believe it would help to save the Union. I shall do less whenever I shall believe what I am doing hurts the cause, and I shall do more whenever I believe doing more will help the cause. I shall try to correct errors when shown to be errors, and I shall adopt new views so fast as they shall appear to be true views.

  I have here stated my purpose according to my official duty; and I intend no modification of my oft-expressed personal wish that all men everywhere could be free. Yours, A. Lincoln.[1233]

It is obvious from Lincoln's letter to Greeley alone that neither the Preliminary Emancipation Proclamation (issued only a few weeks later) and his Final Emancipation Proclamation (issued only a few months later) were abolitionary documents, that their intent was to destroy slavery and free America's slaves. The intent, as we can see now, was anything but.

Being America's craftiest and most self-interested president, however, we can assume that besides ending slavery so that Southern blacks would kill their owners and join the Union army, Lincoln issued the Emancipation proclamation for a number of other less vital reasons as well. And in fact he did.

Tragically for posterity, all have been suppressed by pro-North, anti-South proponents in an effort to hide Lincoln's duplicity and crimes. Since we cannot truly understand Lincoln or U.S. history without a thorough knowledge of *all* of Lincoln's actions and thoughts, let us look at these secondary reasons now.

The fourth reason: Winning the support of Europe, by then a vigorously antislavery region, was paramount to Lincoln. He believed that issuing the Emancipation Proclamation would prove to Europeans once and for all that his illegal War was not merely about greed, ego, power, and money (which it was).

But this particular ploy failed, as most of Europe, in particular England and France, never believed that the object of the War was to abolish slavery, which is why they sided with the Confederacy to begin with. The true objective, Europeans held, was domination and acquisition on the part of the North and self-determination on the part of the South (Europe was correct). As the London *Times* put it on November 7, 1861:

> . . . the contest is really for empire on the side of the North, and for independence on that of the South, and in this respect we recognize an exact analogy between the North and the Government of George III, and the South and the [original] Thirteen Revolted Provinces. These opinions . . . are the general opinions of the English nation.[1234]

The idea that the War was over slavery was known to be an outrageous lie because of Lincoln himself.[1235] During his first Inaugural Address, March 4, 1861, Lincoln clearly and emphatically promised not to disturb the system of slavery. Even if he did, the president affirmed, it would be illegal.[1236]

The text of Lincoln's First Inaugural Address, widely published in newspapers across Europe, was eagerly read by millions. It said, in part[1237]:

> **Apprehension seems to exist among the people of the Southern States that by the accession of a Republican administration their property and their peace and personal security are to be endangered. There has never been any reasonable cause for such apprehension. Indeed, the most ample evidence to the contrary has all the while existed and been open to their inspection. It is found in nearly all the published speeches of him who now addresses you. I do but quote from one of those speeches when I declare that 'I have no purpose, directly or indirectly, to interfere with the institution of slavery in the States where it exists. I believe I have no lawful right to do so, and I have no inclination to do so.' Those who nominated and elected me did so with full**

knowledge that I had made this and many similar declarations, and had never recanted them.[1238]

Lincoln conceded that his proclamation was political not racial when he called it a **"civil necessity,"**[1239] one he hoped would **"prevent the Radicals** [i.e., the abolitionists] **from openly embarrassing the government in the conduct of the war."**[1240] No wonder Lincoln's attempt to win abolitionist European support via the proclamation miscarried.

There was a fifth reason Lincoln issued the Emancipation Proclamation, one, unlike the first three reasons, that was not spelled out in that document: the need to procure votes for the 1864 election.

Halfway through his War Lincoln's "approval ratings" (along with re-enlistments) were plunging rapidly, causing dismay and fear throughout his party.[1241] Lincoln, always struggling with melancholia (depression),[1242] wrote a memorandum to his cabinet stating that **"it seems exceedingly probable that this Administration will not be re-elected."**[1243]

According to Lincoln, freeing Southern slaves and enrolling them in the U.S. Army at the beginning of 1863, however, added some 100,000 new soldiers.[1244] These, along with about 100,000 Northern blacks, gave him a total of 205,000 new recruits (186,000 blacks joined the U.S. army; about 19,000 enlisted in the U.S. navy),[1245] an enormous pool of fresh potential Republican voters for the upcoming 1864 election. Lincoln then sent out "directives" to his commanders in the field strongly suggesting that they allow their soldiers to **"go home to vote at the State election."** His order to Yankee General William T. Sherman in September 1864, for example, read:

> Any thing you can safely do to let your soldiers, or any part of them, go home to vote at the State election, will be greatly in point.[1246]

Lincoln's **"point"** was well understood.

As a result, tens of thousands of Yankee soldiers were furloughed "just in time to return home and vote." Lincoln would not have been reelected in 1864 without the army vote, one only made possible by his politically motivated enlistment of 100,000 thousand Northern blacks and 100,000 emancipated Southern blacks.[1247]

A sixth reason for issuing the Emancipation Proclamation can be found in Lincoln's March 6, 1862, "Message to Congress Recommending

Compensated Emancipation." Here, Lincoln wisely proposed paying slave owners for the loss of the value of their servants upon being freed. But as was so often the case with our sixteenth president, this was not for the benefit of black slaves. It was for his own political benefit:

> **The Federal Government would find its highest interest in such a measure, as one of the most efficient means of self-preservation.** The leaders of the existing insurrection entertain the hope that this government will ultimately be forced to acknowledge the independence of some part of the disaffected region, and that all the slave States north of such part will then say, "The Union for which we have struggled being already gone, we now choose to go with the Southern section." To deprive them of this hope substantially ends the rebellion; and the initiation of emancipation completely deprives them of it as to all the States initiating it. The point is not that all the States tolerating slavery would very soon, if at all, initiate emancipation; but that while the offer is equally made to all, the more Northern shall, by such initiation, make it certain to the more Southern that in no event will the former ever join the latter in their proposed confederacy.[1248]

In other words, Lincoln believed that illegally freeing the South's 3.5 million black servants would help prevent more states from joining the Confederacy.

What he did not seem to grasp was that the Confederacy was not formed around the institution of slavery. It was founded on the Constitutional guarantee of states' rights!

We will note here that Lincoln's proposition to gradually free the slaves, then financially compensate their owners, was one of the few humane and rational ideas he ever entertained, particularly in relation to Southern whites and blacks. At one time he even advocated that **"education of young blacks should be included in the plan."**[1249] For promoting such opinions, we in the South can for once commend Lincoln.

Sadly, however, the Radicals in his party (i.e., the abolitionists) consistently ignored or rejected his ideas, and he himself eventually gave up on them,[1250] allowing himself to be pressured into accepting the disastrous concept of immediate emancipation.[1251]

Worse, after his death these same abolitionists, the Radicals, tossed his idea of gradual-compensated emancipation out the window completely, asserting that Southern slave owners did not deserve to be repaid for anything, let alone for giving up their "black chattel"—this from the very people who sold the South these slaves to begin with!

Added to the many reasons, both major and minor, that Lincoln issued the Emancipation Proclamation, we have an overabundance of evidence reenforcing the fact that the decree was not motivated by any desire to bestow legitimate civil rights on African-Americans. It was purely for the benefit of European-Americans.

For example, prior to being elected president, Lincoln showed an acceptance of the Fugitive Slave Act that infuriated Northern abolitionists,[1252] as he revealed in a June 9, 1859, letter to Ohio Governor Salmon P. Chase, soon to become his secretary of the treasury:

> **Please pardon the liberty I take in addressing you, as I now do. It appears by the papers that the late Republican State Convention of Ohio adopted a Platform, of which the following is one plank, "A repeal of the atrocious Fugitive Slave Law."**
>
> **This is already damaging us here. I have no doubt that if that plank be even introduced into the next Republican National Convention, it will explode it. Once introduced, its supporters and it's opponents will quarrel irreconcilably. The latter believe the U.S. constitution declares a fugitive slave "shall be delivered up"; and they look upon the above plank as dictated by the spirit which declares a fugitive slave "shall not be delivered up."**
>
> **I enter upon no argument one way or the other; but I assure you the cause of Republicanism is hopeless in Illinois, if it be in any way made responsible for that plank. I hope you can, and will, contribute something to relieve us from it.[1253]**

Lincoln disregarded and delayed the emancipation ideas of others, in part, because he had his own emancipation plan, one that he relentlessly embraced until the last day of his life. Because of his premature death, however, this plan was never initiated: the abolitionists in his party believed it was too generous, and replaced it with their own far more severe scheme. Thus, Lincoln's is little known today.

The president's emancipation plan was comprised of five-parts:

1) Lincoln held that slavery was a domestic concern and that therefore the states themselves must take whatever action they deemed necessary on the issue.

2) Slave owners must be compensated if their slaves are freed.

3) This compensation should come from the Federal government in the form of grants-in-aid bonds to the states.

4) The abolition of slavery must occur gradually, so as to allow whites, blacks, and society itself, time to adjust; the states, in fact, would have until the year 1900 to free their last slave.

5) All freed blacks must be deported and settled outside the U.S., though this must be done on a voluntary basis.

Not surprisingly, no one liked every aspect of this plan, and it never got off the ground. But Lincoln never gave up promoting it.[1254]

He also blocked the extension of slavery into the new Western territories for several reasons, none of them out of concern for blacks.

First, he prohibited it because it would have artificially magnified the congressional power of the opposing party, the Democrats.[1255]

Second, as we have seen, Lincoln opposed the spread of slavery into the new Western territories, not because he was against the institution, but because he did not want whites in those areas to have to live among blacks or compete with blacks for jobs. As he noted in a speech on October 16, 1854:

> Whether slavery shall go into Nebraska, or other new Territories, is not a matter of exclusive concern to the people who may go there. The whole nation is interested that the best use shall be made of the Territories. *We want them for homes of free white people.* This cannot be, to any considerable extent, if slavery shall be planted within them [emphasis added].[1256]

On this topic Lincoln had the "almost unanimous" support of the

North, whose inhabitants agreed with the President that the territories should remain as white as New England.[1257] If there is any doubt as to Lincoln's stand on the matter, one of his own friends and senators, Lyman Trumbull, referred to their Republican party as "the white man's party."[1258]

More than once Lincoln suggested that he might not issue any proclamation to free the slaves.[1259] Even after it was issued, originally, by his own orders, the Emancipation Proclamation was supposed to be temporary, not permanent; he said it would cease when the South (or individual states) surrendered.[1260] He then offered the Confederacy **"liberal terms on . . . substantial and collateral points."**[1261] What were these points?

At least one of them was allowing any Southern state returning to the Union to continue practicing slavery within its borders. Lincoln demanded only one thing: slaves who were already free could not be reenslaved, for eventually he wanted to be able to deport them to Liberia. As for those still under slavery, he said he would leave their fate to their individual state governments,[1262] a states' right he had been defending for many years prior to the War.[1263]

In essence, in the summer and fall of 1864, complete and full emancipation was not absolutely necessary to Lincoln if a Confederate state would simply surrender peacefully, rejoin the Union,[1264] and pay its taxes.[1265]

Seward confirmed this, stating that the effect of the Emancipation Proclamation and other "war measures" would end with the fighting. Thus it is patently clear then that Lincoln originally intended that the institution of slavery would be reestablished after the South's defeat, or if and when it capitulated.[1266]

Further evidence of this is supplied by Lincoln's "Ten Percent Plan," issued in December 1863.[1267] Here a Confederate state could be "readmitted" to the Union if just 10 percent of its citizens took an oath of allegiance to the U.S. Afterward that state could reestablish slavery if it so desired.[1268] On June 9, 1864, Lincoln made reference to his Ten Percent Plan in his "Reply to the Committee Notifying President Lincoln of his Renomination":

> I will say now . . . I approve the declaration in favor of so amending the Constitution as to prohibit slavery throughout the nation. When the people in revolt [that is, in the Confederacy], **with a hundred days of explicit notice that *they could within those days resume their allegiance***

without the overthrow of their institution, and that they could not so resume it afterward, elected to stand out, such amendment of the Constitution as now proposed became a fitting and necessary conclusion to the final success of the Union cause [emphasis added].[1269]

In 1864, according to Confederate Secretary of State Judah Benjamin, far from demanding complete and immediate abolition, Lincoln let it be known that he was willing to let the issue of slavery be decided on by a general vote in both the South and the North.[1270]

On August 24 of that year, Lincoln drafted the following unsent and unused instructions to Henry Jarvis Raymond of the *New York Times*:

> **Sir: You will proceed forthwith and obtain, if possible, a conference for peace with Honorable Jefferson Davis, or any person by him authorized for that purpose. You will address him in entirely respectful terms, at all events, and in any that may be indispensable to secure the conference. At said conference you will propose, on behalf of this government, that upon the restoration of the Union and the national authority, the war shall cease at once, all remaining questions to be left for adjustment by peaceful modes. If this be accepted, hostilities to cease at once. If it be not accepted, you will then request to be informed what terms, if any, embracing the restoration of the Union would be accepted. If any such be presented you in answer, you will forthwith report the same to this government, and await further instructions. If the presentation of any terms embracing the restoration of the Union be declined, you will then request to be informed what terms of peace would be accepted; and, on receiving any answer, report the same to this government, and await further instructions.**[1271]

Lincoln states unwaveringly here that as long as the Southern states rejoin the Union they can continue slavery; or as he put it more obliquely, **"upon restoration of the union . . . all remaining questions [are] to be left for adjustment by peaceful modes."** Where is the evidence here that Lincoln was an abolitionist?

The president eventually even went so far as to suggest that former slaves be **"subject to apprenticeship"**[1272] after emancipation, even though apprenticeship is clearly just another form of slavery. As Webster defines it: "one bound by indenture to serve another for a prescribed period."[1273]

Though, by his own admission, he was constantly bombarded by abolitionists to **"drop the suggestion about apprenticeship for freed-people,"**[1274] he never did. Here is how Lincoln phrased his idea in November 1861:

> Draft Of A Proposed Bill For Compensated Abolishment In Delaware.
>
> Be it enacted by the State of Delaware that on condition the United States of America will, at the present session of Congress, engage by law to pay, and thereafter faithfully pay, to the said State of Delaware, in the six per cent, bonds of said United States, the sum of seven hundred and nineteen thousand and two hundred dollars in thirty-one equal annual instalments, there shall be neither slavery nor involuntary servitude at any time after the first day of January in the year of our Lord one thousand eight hundred and ninety-three, within the said State of Delaware, except in the punishment of crime, whereof the party shall have been duly convicted; nor, except in the punishment of crime as aforesaid, shall any person who shall be born after the passage of this act, nor any person above the age of thirty-five years, be held in slavery or to involuntary servitude within said State of Delaware at any time after the passage of this act.
>
> And be it further enacted that said State shall in good faith prevent, as far as possible, the carrying of any person out of said State into involuntary servitude beyond the limits of said State at any time after the passage of this act.
>
> And be it further enacted that said State may make provision of apprenticeship, not to extend beyond the age of twenty-one years for males nor eighteen for females, for all minors whose mothers were not free at the respective births of such minors.
>
> On reflection I like No. 2 the better. By it the nation would pay the State $23,200 per annum for thirty-one years, and
>
> All born after the passage of the act would be born free, and
>
> All slaves above the age of thirty-five years would become free on the passage of the act, and
>
> All others would become free on arriving at the

> age of thirty-five years, until January, 1893, when
>> All remaining of all ages would become free, subject to apprenticeship for minors born of slave mothers up to the respective ages of twenty-one and eighteen.
>> If the State would desire to have the money sooner, let the bill be altered only in fixing the time of final emancipation earlier and making the annual instalments correspondingly fewer in number, by which they would also be correspondingly larger in amount. For instance, strike out "1893" and insert "1872," and strike out "thirty-one" annual instalments and insert "ten" annual instalments. The instalments would then be $71,920 instead of $23,200 as now. In all other particulars let the bill stand precisely as it is.[1275]

Lincoln not only recommends replacing one form of slavery (servitude) with another (apprenticeship), but he also advises that all duly convicted criminals be enslaved, giving plenty of time, until at least 1893, for all traces of slavery to be swept clean.

He made similar statements in a letter to Yankee General John Alexander McClernand, like Lincoln, a Kentuckian who hated abolitionists.[1276] McClernand had written to the president on December 29, 1862, requesting that he work harder toward establishing immediate peace with the South, and also to ask about Lincoln's "purpose to enslave or exterminate the whites of the South." Lincoln replied to McClernand about a week later on January 8, 1863:

> My dear Sir: Your interesting communication by the hand of Major [Walter B.] Scates is received. I never did ask more, nor ever was willing to accept less, than for all the States, and the people thereof, to take and hold their places and their rights in the Union, under the Constitution of the United States. For this alone have I felt authorized to struggle, and I seek neither more nor less now. Still, to use a coarse but an expressive figure, "broken eggs cannot be mended." I have issued the Emancipation Proclamation, and I cannot retract it. After the commencement of hostilities, I struggled nearly a year and a half to get along without touching the "institution"; and when finally I conditionally determined to touch it, I gave a hundred days' fair notice of my purpose to all the States and people, within which

time they could have turned it wholly aside by simply again becoming good citizens of the United States.
  They chose to disregard it, and I made the peremptory proclamation on what appeared to me to be a military necessity. And being made, it must stand. As to the States not included in it, of course they can have their rights in the Union as of old. Even the people of the States included, if they choose, need not to be hurt by it. Let them adopt systems of apprenticeship for the colored people, conforming substantially to the most approved plans of gradual emancipation; and with the aid they can have from the General Government they may be nearly as well off, in this respect, as if the present trouble had not occurred, and much better off than they can possibly be if the contest continues persistently.
  As to any dread of my having a "purpose to enslave or exterminate the whites of the South," I can scarcely believe that such dread exists. It is too absurd. I believe you can be my personal witness that no man is less to be dreaded for undue severity in any case.
  If the friends you mention really wish to have peace upon the old terms, they should act at once. Every day makes the case more difficult.
  They can so act with entire safety, so far as I am concerned.
  I think you had better not make this letter public; but you may rely confidently on my standing by whatever I have said in it. Please write me if anything more comes to light. Yours very truly, A. Lincoln.[1277]

Here Lincoln not only refutes the charge that he is seeking to kill off or enslave Southern whites, but he also

- notes that he would allow the Southern states to retain slavery if they would just once again become **"good citizens of the United States."**
- reasserts his position that he only issued the Emancipation Proclamation as, not a civil rights necessity, but as a **"military necessity"** (mentioned in the document itself).
- repeats his suggestion that Southern slaves (he carefully avoids the mention of *Northern* slaves) should be freed then reenslaved as **"apprentices."**

As always, we see that he is in no hurry to either end slavery or make blacks equal citizens. In fact, he shows no interest whatsoever in civil rights of any kind for African-Americans, bonded or free.

Even before becoming president Lincoln made similar comments, such as the following from his February 27, 1860, Cooper Union Speech:

> **If the Republicans** [i.e., Lincoln's party, the liberals], **who think slavery is wrong, get possession of the General Government, we may not root out the evil at once, but may at least prevent its extension.**[1278]

The president backed up such views with numerous other statements. On August 17, 1864, for instance, he responded to an attack charging him with demanding complete emancipation in all Southern states. This was incorrect, as he pointed out in a letter to Charles D. Robinson:

> **My dear Sir: Your letter of the seventh was placed in my hand yesterday by** [Wisconsin] **Governor** [Alexander] **Randall. To me it seems plain that saying reunion and abandonment of slavery would be considered, if offered, is not saying that nothing else or less would be considered, if offered. But I will not stand upon the mere construction of language. It is true, as you remind me, that in the Greeley letter of 1862 I said: "If I could save the Union without freeing any slave I would do it; and if I could save it by freeing all the slaves I would do it; and if I could save it by freeing some and leaving others alone I would also do that." I continued in the same letter as follows: "What I do about slavery and the colored race, I do because I believe it helps to save the Union; and what I forbear, I forbear because I do not believe it would help to save the Union. I shall do less whenever I shall believe what I am doing hurts the cause; and I shall do more whenever I shall believe doing more will help the cause."**
>
> **All this I said in the utmost sincerity; and I am as true to the whole of it now as when I first said it. When I afterward proclaimed emancipation, and employed colored soldiers, I only followed the declaration just quoted from the Greeley letter that "I shall do more whenever I shall believe doing more will help the cause." The way these measures were to help the cause was not to be by magic or miracles, but by inducing the colored**

people to come bodily over from the rebel side to ours. On this point, nearly a year ago, in a letter to Mr. [James C.] Conkling, made public at once, I wrote as follows: "But negroes, like other people, act upon motives. Why should they do anything for us if we will do nothing for them? If they stake their lives for us they must be prompted by the strongest motive — even the promise of freedom. And the promise being made, must be kept." I am sure you will not, on due reflection, say that the promise being made must be broken at the first opportunity. I am sure you would not desire me to say, or to leave an inference, that I am ready, whenever convenient, to join in reenslaving those who shall have served us in consideration of our promise. As matter of morals, could such treachery by any possibility escape the curses of heaven, or of any good man? As matter of policy, to announce such a purpose would ruin the Union cause itself. All recruiting of colored men would instantly cease, and all colored men now in our service would instantly desert us. And rightfully, too. Why should they give their lives for us, with full notice of our purpose to betray them? Drive back to the support of the rebellion the physical force which the colored people now give and promise us, and neither the present, nor any coming, administration can save the Union. Take from us and give to the enemy the hundred and thirty, forty, or fifty thousand colored persons now serving us as soldiers, seamen, and laborers, and we cannot longer maintain the contest. The party who could elect a President on a War and Slavery Restoration platform would, of necessity, lose the colored force; and that force being lost, would be as powerless to save the Union as to do any other impossible thing.

It is not a question of sentiment or taste, but one of physical force, which may be measured and estimated, as horse-power and steampower are measured and estimated. And, by measurement, it is more than we can lose and live. Nor can we, by discarding it, get a white force in place of it. There is a witness in every white man's bosom that he would rather go to the war having the negro to help him than to help the enemy against him. It is not the giving of one class for another—it is simply giving a large force to the enemy for nothing in return. In addition to what I have said, allow me to remind you that no one, having control of the rebel armies, or, in fact, having any influence whatever in the rebellion, has offered, or intimated, a willingness to a restoration of the Union, in any event, or on any condition whatever. Let it be constantly borne in mind that no such offer has been made or intimated. Shall we be weak enough to allow the enemy to distract us with an abstract question which he himself refuses to present as a practical one? In the Conkling letter before mentioned, I said: "Whenever you shall have conquered all resistance to the Union, if I shall urge you to continue fighting, it will be an apt time then to declare that you will not fight to free negroes." I repeat this now. If Jefferson Davis wishes for himself, or for the benefit of his friends at the North, to know what I would do if he were to offer peace and reunion, saying nothing about slavery, let him try me.[1279]

Again, nothing here about black civil rights. What *is* on display in this letter is an open-minded malleability on the topic of emancipation, as shown particularly at the beginning and end of the document.

As late as February 3, 1865, only two months before his death, Lincoln was still of the same mind. On this day he attended a peace conference on board the presidential steamer *River Queen*, anchored at Fort Monroe, at Hampton Roads (Hampton, Virginia). A Southern committee, headed by Confederate Vice President Alexander Hamilton Stephens, had come to the Yankee garrison to negotiate for peace.

As with all of the Confederate peace commissions, the Hampton Roads Peace Conference accomplished nothing, Lincoln being unwilling to yield or compromise on any important, or even minor, points. His single demand was always simple, bluntly stated, and completely one-sided, as he noted on December 6, 1864, during his Fourth Annual Message to Congress:

> They can, at any moment, have peace simply by laying down their arms and submitting to the national authority under the Constitution.[1280]

(That the U.S. government had no **"national authority"** over the C.S. government, and that the Confederacy had its own Constitution, were facts completely ignored by Lincoln.)

No one should have been surprised at Lincoln's rigidity. Here are his stipulations for ending the War, which he laid out to Seward on January 31, 1865:

> You will proceed to Fortress Monroe, Virginia, there to meet and informally confer with [Confederate] Messrs. [Alexander H.] **Stevens**, [Robert M. T.] **Hunter, and** [John A.] **Campbell**, on the basis of my letter to F. [Francis] P. Blair, Esq., of January 18, 1865, a copy of which you have. You will make known to them that three things are indispensable—to wit:
> 1. The restoration of the national authority throughout all the States.
> 2. No receding by the executive of the United States on the slavery question from the petition assumed thereon in the late annual message to Congress, and in preceding documents.
> 3. No cessation of hostilities short of an end of the war, and the disbanding of all forces hostile to the government.
>
> You will inform them that all propositions of theirs, not inconsistent with the above, will be considered and passed upon in a spirit of sincere liberality. You will hear all they may choose to say and report it to me. You will not assume to definitely consummate anything. Yours, etc., Abraham Lincoln.[1281]

Despite his complete inflexibility at Hampton Roads, the conference did reveal one thing: Lincoln's true feelings about slavery at the time.

Stephens asked him about the Emancipation Proclamation. "Would it be held to emancipate the whole, or only those who had, at the time the war ended, become actually free under it?" Stephens recollected later that Lincoln's

> own opinion was, that as the Proclamation was a *war measure*, and would have effect only from its being an exercise of the war power, as soon as the war ceased, it would be inoperative for the future. It would be held to apply only to such slaves as had come under its operation while it was in active exercise.[1282]

Because Lincoln would not allow the Hampton Roads meeting to be recorded, and because his own account is full of omissions, obfuscation, and disinformation,[1283] we must rely on the Confederate version of events. What follows is the full transcript of the above mentioned portion of the conference, as narrated by Confederate Vice President Stephens. As mentioned, attending the meeting were Lincoln and his secretary of state, William H. Seward, and Confederates Stephens, Senator Robert M. T. Hunter, and Assistant Secretary of War John A. Campbell:

> I asked Mr. Lincoln what would be the status of that portion of the Slave population in the Confederate States, which had not then become free under his Proclamation; or in other words, what effect that Proclamation would have upon the entire Black population? Would it be held to emancipate the whole, or only those who had, at the time the war ended, become actually free under it?
> Mr. Lincoln said, that was a judicial question. How the Courts would decide it, he did not know, and could give no answer. His own opinion was, that as the Proclamation was a war measure, and would have effect only from its being an exercise of the war power, as soon as the war ceased, it would be inoperative for the future. It would be held to apply only to such slaves as had come under its operation while it was in active exercise. This was his individual opinion, but the Courts might decide the other way, and hold that it effectually emancipated all the slaves in the States to which it applied at the time. So far as he was concerned, he should leave it to the Courts to decide. He never would change or modify the terms of the Proclamation in the slightest particular. Mr. Seward said there were only about two hundred thousand slaves, who, up to that time, had come under the actual operation of the Proclamation, and who were then in the enjoyment of their freedom under it; so, if the war should then cease, the status of much the larger portion of the slaves would be subject to judicial construction. Mr. Lincoln sustained Mr. Seward as to the number of slaves who were then in the actual enjoyment of their freedom under the Proclamation. Mr. Seward also said, it might be proper to state to us, that Congress, a day or two before, had proposed a Constitutional Amendment [that is, the Thirteenth Amendment][1284] for the immediate abolition of slavery throughout the United States, which he produced and read to us from a newspaper. He said this was done as a war measure. If the war were then to cease, it would probably not be adopted by a number of States, sufficient to make it a part of the Constitution; but presented the case in such light as clearly showed his object to be, to impress upon the minds of the Commissioners that, if the war should not cease, this, as a war measure, would be adopted by a sufficient number of States to become a part of the Constitution, and without saying it in direct

words, left the inference very clearly to be perceived by the Commissioners that his opinion was, if the Confederate States would then abandon the war, they could of themselves defeat this amendment, by voting it down as members of the Union. The whole number of States, it was said, being thirty-six, any ten of them could defeat this proposed amendment [the Thirteenth].

I inquired how this matter could be adjusted, without some understanding as to what position the Confederate States would occupy towards the others, if they were then to abandon the war. Would they be admitted to representation in Congress?

Mr. Lincoln very promptly replied, that his own individual opinion was, they ought to be. He also thought they would be; but he could not enter into any stipulation upon the subject. His own opinion was, that when the resistance ceased and the National Authority was recognized, the States would be immediately restored to their practical relations to the Union. This was a form of expression repeatedly used by him during the conversation, in speaking of the restoration of the Union. He spoke of it as a **"restoration of the States to their practical relations to the Union."**

Upon my urging the importance of some understanding on this point, even in case the Confederate States should entertain the proposition of a return to the Union, he persisted in asserting that he could not enter into any agreement upon this subject, or upon any other matters of that sort, with parties in arms against the Government.

Mr. Hunter interposed, and in illustration of the propriety of the Executive entering into agreements with persons in arms against the acknowledged rightful public authority, referred to repeated instances of this character between Charles I, of England, and the people in arms against him.

Mr. Lincoln in reply to this said: **I do not profess to be posted in history. On all such matters I will turn you over to Seward. All I distinctly recollect about the case of Charles I, is, that he lost his head in the end.**

This was the familiar manner in which Mr. Lincoln, throughout the conversation, spoke of and to Mr. Seward. In the same familiar manner he addressed me throughout, as was his custom with all his intimate acquaintances when in Congress.

I insisted that if he could, as a war measure, issue his Proclamation for Emancipation, which he did not venture to justify under the Constitution on any other grounds, he could certainly, as a like war measure, or as a measure for putting an end to the war rather, enter into some stipulation on this subject.

He then went into a prolonged course of remarks about

the Proclamation. He said it was not his intention in the beginning to interfere with Slavery in the States; that he never would have done it, if he had not been compelled by necessity to do it, to maintain the Union; that the subject presented many difficult and perplexing questions to him; that he had hesitated for some time, and had resorted to this measure, only when driven to it by public necessity; that he had been in favor of the General Government prohibiting the extension of Slavery into the Territories, but did not think that that Government possessed power over the subject in the States, except as a war measure; and that he had always himself been in favor of emancipation, but not immediate emancipation, even by the States. Many evils attending this appeared to him.

After pausing for some time, his head rather bent down, as if in deep reflection, while all were silent, he rose up and used these words, almost, if not, quite identical:

> 'Stephens, if I were in Georgia, and entertained the sentiments I do—though, I suppose, I should not be permitted to stay there long with them; but if I resided in Georgia, with my present sentiments, I'll tell you what I would do, if I were in your place: I would go home and get the Governor of the State to call the Legislature together, and get them to recall all the State troops from the war; elect Senators and Members to Congress, and ratify this Constitutional Amendment [the Thirteenth] prospectively, so as to take effect—say in five years. Such a ratification would be valid in my opinion. I have looked into the subject, and think such a prospective ratification would be valid. Whatever may have been the views of your people before the war, they must be convinced now, that Slavery is doomed. It cannot last long in any event, and the best course, it seems to me, for your public men to pursue, would be to adopt such a policy as will avoid, as far as possible, the evils of immediate emancipation. This would be my course, if I were in

your place.'

> Mr. Seward also indulged in remarks at considerable length on the progress of the Anti-Slavery sentiment of the country, and stated that what he had thought would require forty or fifty years of agitation to accomplish, would certainly be attained in a much shorter time.
> Judge Campbell inquired of Mr. Seward if he thought, that agitation upon the subject of the political relations between the two races would cease upon the emancipation of the Blacks—the point to which heretofore it had been entirely confined.
> Mr. Seward replied, perhaps not, or possibly not.
> Other matters were then talked over relating to the evils of immediate emancipation, if that policy should be pressed, especially the sufferings which would necessarily attend the old and the infirm, as well as the women and children, who were unable to support themselves. These were fully admitted by Mr. Lincoln, but in reference to them, in that event, he illustrated all he could say by telling the anecdote, which has been published in the papers, about the Illinois farmer and his hogs.[1285] The conversation then took another turn.[1286]

Here we have evidence that Lincoln was not the "champion of the Thirteenth Amendment," as pro-North historians always present him, but rather someone who was lukewarm on the subject, even advising the Confederacy on how to postpone and even "defeat" it.

Like the true anti-abolitionist that he was, Lincoln routinely prevented U.S. officials and military officers possessed of abolitionist leanings, such as socialist John Charles Frémont,[1287] Simon Cameron,[1288] and David Hunter,[1289] from freeing Southern slaves,[1290] actions for which he was angrily denounced by antislavery advocates.[1291]

The primary reason Lincoln delayed issuing the Emancipation Proclamation, of course, was that the War was never about slavery. As he said repeatedly to the Radicals (abolitionists) in his party: **"We didn't go into the war to put down slavery . . ."**[1292] When he finally did issue it, it was against his own wishes, and then only for the reasons we have discussed in this chapter.[1293] For this lassitude he was severely criticized by abolitionists such as Wendell Phillips—soon to become the president of the Anti-Slavery Society, who angrily denounced him as "the slavehound of Illinois."[1294]

So unmistakably clear was Lincoln's procrastination toward emancipation that some of the more vociferous antislavery groups saw it as a sign of traitorousness. Lincoln, they complained, is not only a Southerner by birth, he has a brother-in-law (Confederate Captain Nathaniel Dawson) who fights for the Confederacy.[1295] Obviously, his sympathies lie with the South and with slavery, for he could end the War tomorrow if he would only go after the slave owners, they cried.[1296]

Lincoln's hesitation to emancipate America's slaves was more than evident in a letter he penned on September 13, 1862, in reply "To A Committee From The Religious Denominations Of Chicago, Asking The President To Issue A Proclamation Of Emancipation." The letter really should have been called "The Emancipation Proclamation: My Many Excuses for Blocking It and Delaying Its Issuance." Wrote Lincoln:

> The subject presented in the memorial is one upon which I have thought much for weeks past, and I may even say for months. I am approached with the most opposite opinions and advice, and that by religious men who are equally certain that they represent the divine will. I am sure that either the one or the other class is mistaken in that belief, and perhaps in some respects both. I hope it will not be irreverent for me to say that if it is probable that God would reveal his will to others on a point so connected with my duty, it might be supposed he would reveal it directly to me; for, unless I am more deceived in myself than I often am, it is my earnest desire to know the will of Providence in this matter. And if I can learn what it is, I will do it. These are not, however, the days of miracles, and I suppose it will be granted that I am not to expect a direct revelation. I must study the plain physical facts of the case, ascertain what is possible, and learn what appears to be wise and right.
>
> The subject is difficult, and good men do not agree. For instance, the other day four gentlemen of standing and intelligence from New York called as a delegation on business connected with the war; but, before leaving, two of them earnestly beset me to proclaim general emancipation, upon which the other two at once attacked them. You know also that the last session of Congress had a decided majority of antislavery men, yet they could not unite on this policy. And the same is true of the religious people. Why, the rebel soldiers are praying with a great deal more earnestness, I fear, than our own troops, and expecting God to favor their side; for one of our soldiers who had been taken

prisoner told Senator Wilson a few days since that he met with nothing so discouraging as the evident sincerity of those he was among in their prayers. But we will talk over the merits of the case.

    What good would a proclamation of emancipation from me do, especially as we are now situated? I do not want to issue a document that the whole world will see must necessarily be inoperative, like the Pope's bull against the comet. Would my word free the slaves, when I cannot even enforce the Constitution in the rebel States? Is there a single court, or magistrate, or individual that would be influenced by it there? And what reason is there to think it would have any greater effect upon the slaves than the late law of Congress, which I approved, and which offers protection and freedom to the slaves of rebel masters who come within our lines? Yet I cannot learn that that law has caused a single slave to come over to us. And suppose they could be induced by a proclamation of freedom from me to throw themselves upon us, what should we do with them? How can we feed and care for such a multitude? General [Benjamin F.] Butler wrote me a few days since that he was issuing more rations to the slaves who have rushed to him than to all the white troops under his command. They eat, and that is all; though it is true General Butler is feeding the whites also by the thousand, for it nearly amounts to a famine there. If, now, the pressure of the war should call off our forces from New Orleans to defend some other point, what is to prevent the masters from reducing the blacks to slavery again? For I am told that whenever the rebels take any black prisoners, free or slave, they immediately auction them off. They did so with those they took from a boat that was aground in the Tennessee River a few days ago. And then I am very ungenerously attacked for it! For instance, when, after the late battles at and near Bull Run, an expedition went out from Washington under a flag of truce to bury the dead and bring in the wounded, and the rebels seized the blacks who went along to help, and sent them into slavery, Horace Greeley said in his paper that the government would probably do nothing about it. What could I do?

    Now, then, tell me, if you please, what possible result of good would follow the issuing of such a proclamation as you desire? Understand, I raise no objections against it on legal or constitutional grounds; for, as commander-in-chief of the army and navy, in time of war I suppose I have a right to take any measure which may best subdue the enemy; nor do I urge objections of a moral nature, in view of possible consequences of insurrection and massacre at the South. I view this matter as a practical war measure, to be decided on according to the advantages or disadvantages it may offer to the suppression of the rebellion.

  I admit that slavery is the root of the rebellion, or at least its *sine qua non*. The ambition of politicians may have instigated them to act, but they would have been impotent without slavery as their instrument. I will also concede that emancipation would help us in Europe, and convince them that we are incited by something more than ambition. I grant, further, that it would help somewhat at the North, though not so much, I fear, as you and those you represent imagine. Still, some additional strength would be added in that way to the war, and then, unquestionably, it would weaken the rebels by drawing off their laborers, which is of great importance; but I am not so sure we could do much with the blacks. If we were to arm them, I fear that in a few weeks the arms would be in the hands of the rebels; and, indeed, thus far we have not had arms enough to equip our white troops. I will mention another thing, though it meet only your scorn and contempt. There are fifty thousand bayonets in the Union armies from the border slave States. It would be a serious matter if, in consequence of a proclamation such as you desire, they should go over to the rebels. I do not think they all would—not so many, indeed, as a year ago, or as six months ago—not so many to-day as yesterday. Every day increases their Union feeling. They are also getting their pride enlisted, and want to beat the rebels. Let me say one thing more: I think you should admit that we already have an important principle to rally and unite the people, in the fact that constitutional government is at stake. This is a fundamental idea going down about as deep as anything.

  Do not misunderstand me because I have mentioned these objections. They indicate the difficulties that have thus far prevented my action in some such way as you desire. I have not decided against a proclamation of liberty to the slaves, but hold the matter under advisement; and I can assure you that the subject is on my mind, by day and night, more than any other. Whatever shall appear to be God's will, I will do. I trust that in the freedom with which I have canvassed your views I have not in any respect injured your feelings.[1297]

Even earlier, on March 1, 1859, Lincoln said to a large Chicago audience:

> I do not wish to be misunderstood upon this subject of slavery in this country. I suppose it may long exist; and perhaps the best way for it to come to an end peaceably is for it to exist for a length of time.[1298]

More proof of Lincoln's lack of sentiment towards African-Americans comes from the manner in which he issued the Emancipation Proclamation: in January 1863, and again in December 1865, the U.S., under both Lincoln's Emancipation Proclamation and his pet project the Thirteenth Amendment respectively, abolished slavery suddenly, illegally, and violently.[1299] And all of this occurred without restitution to owners, even though compensation (buying every Southern slave from their owners at market value and then freeing them) would have cost the nation ten times less than what it cost to go to war[1300]—a fact that even the money-obsessed president himself once alluded to.[1301]

In short, Lincoln had no organized plan to admit freed blacks into American society as equal citizens;[1302] nothing to help the elderly, the ill, or orphaned blacks who could not work and who had previously been under the lifelong care of their owners;[1303] no education, no loans or grants, no job training, no housing, to ease freedmen and freedwomen into the world of capitalism, competition, and a free, highly skilled, and often hostile labor force. Lincoln did not even offer them any legal protection.[1304] All were merely "liberated" to roam the streets and make their way as best they could; or as Lincoln flippantly styled it, to "root, pig, or perish."[1305]

It is true that Lincoln had promised freed Southern blacks "forty acres and a mule." But as with most of the North's other pledges to blacks, this one too turned out to be a lie:[1306] there were no mules,[1307] only deprivation, starvation, and vagrancy.[1308] And Lincoln's so-called "black land giveaways" were only meant to be temporary[1309]—and most of those that were issued ultimately went to rich white Northerners,[1310] railroads, land speculators, and lumber companies.[1311] After the reality sank in, all hope of free land for blacks evaporated.[1312] (Lincoln and the U.S. Congress did eventually create the Bureau of Refugees, Freedmen, and Abandoned Lands. But this was in March 1865,[1313] over two years after the Emancipation Proclamation—too late to mitigate the myriad of problems caused by sudden and violent abolition in January 1863.)

Black civil rights leader W. E. B. Du Bois summed up Lincoln's emancipation "plan" this way: former slaves are now free to do whatever they want with the nothing they never had to begin with.[1314] Thomas Hall, an ex-slave, saw it this way:

> Lincoln got the praise for freeing us, but did he do it? He give us freedom without giving us any chance to live to ourselves and we still had to depend on the Southern white man for work, food, and clothing, and he held us through our necessity and want in a state of servitude but little better than slavery. Lincoln done but little for the negro race and from a living standpoint nothing.[1315]

White Southerners too were appalled at Lincoln's inhumanity. An incredulous General Robert E. Lee posed a rhetorical query to the Yankee president:

> What will you do with the freed people? That is a serious question today. Unless some humane course, based on wisdom and Christian principles, is adopted, you do them a great injustice in setting them free.[1316]

Lee was correct, of course. Under Lincoln's "root, pig, or perish" emancipation plan, blacks who as servants had lived quality lives equal to and often superior to many whites and most free blacks, now found themselves living out in the open or in makeshift tents, begging for food and work. Disease, homelessness, starvation, beggary, poverty, prostitution, and thievery now became the lot of untold millions of former black servants.

Lincoln's unplanned emancipation affected former white and black slave owners just as severely. Many, who had invested millions of dollars in their servants, found themselves bankrupt and without labor of any kind. Crops died in the ground, fields went fallow, farms were deserted, sold, or foreclosed. Besides his illegal naval blockade, the ruthless bombing of Southern cities, and the unprovoked murder of thousands of Southern civilians, Lincoln's "emancipation" must be counted among the most destructive of his assaults on the South.

      The problem was not due to Southern slaves being liberated. It was that they were set free without any aid to either the slave or the slave owner. In this way, economically and racially, Lincoln's "emancipation" set the South back decades, making a mockery of his so-called "Reconstruction" program.[1317] In fact, many areas, especially those that lost schools, universities, and libraries due to Yankee atrocities, are still recovering in the 21st Century.[1318]

      Based on Lincoln's own words, and actions then, calling him the "Great Emancipator" is obviously a misnomer, for it is impossible to square this title with his words and actions. In regards to his freeing America's black slaves it would be far more accurate to refer to him as the "Great Procrastinator."[1319]

Lincoln & His War on the South

PRIOR TO HIS WAR LINCOLN evinced a surprising empathy for the South and her inhabitants, as he noted on August 21, 1858, at Ottawa, Illinois:

> . . . I think I have no prejudice against the Southern people. They are just what we would be in their situation. . . . When Southern people tell us they are no more responsible for the origin of slavery than we are, I acknowledge the fact. When it is said that the institution exists, and that it is very difficult to get rid of it in any satisfactory way, I can understand and appreciate the saying. I surely will not blame them for not doing what I should not know how to do myself.[1320]

We have seen that at one time Lincoln also supported the right of secession, calling it **"a most valuable, a most sacred right."**[1321] On August 21, 1858, he even denied planning to go to war with the South:

> **When I made my speech at Springfield, of which the judge** [Stephen A. Douglas] **complains, and from which he quotes, I really was not thinking of the things which he ascribes to me at all. I had no thought in the world that I was doing anything to bring about a war between the free and slave States. I had no thought in the world that I was doing anything to bring about a political and social equality of the black and white races.**[1322]

Yet after the secession of South Carolina (December 20, 1860), Mississippi (January 9, 1861), Florida (January 10), Alabama (January 11), Georgia (January 19), Louisiana (January 26), and Texas (February 1), and the formation of the provisional Confederate government (February 9), Lincoln's attitude toward the South turned decidedly ugly.

This change was much in evidence, for example, in his famous Cooper Union Speech, given at New York on February 27, 1860. The address, which brims with vitriol, sarcasm, indignation, and malevolence, presents the president-elect with a golden opportunity to begin spreading lies, slander, misinformation, and disinformation about the South and the newly formed Confederacy:

> And now, if they would listen,—as I suppose they will not,—I would address a few words to the Southern people.
>
> I would say to them: You consider yourselves a reasonable and a just people; and I consider that in the general qualities of reason and justice you are not inferior to any other people. Still, when you speak of us Republicans [that is, liberals], you do so only to denounce us as reptiles, or, at the best, as no better than outlaws. You will grant a hearing to pirates or murderers, but nothing like it to "Black Republicans" [white Republicans who advocated black equality]. In all your contentions with one another, each of you deems an unconditional condemnation of "Black Republicanism" as the first thing to be attended to. Indeed, such condemnation of us seems to be an indispensable prerequisite—license, so to speak—among you to be admitted or permitted to speak at all. Now can you or not be prevailed upon to pause and to consider whether this is quite just to us, or even to yourselves? Bring forward your charges and specifications, and then be patient long enough to hear us deny or justify.
>
> You say we are sectional. We deny it. That makes an issue; and the burden of proof is upon you. You produce your proof; and what is it? Why, that our party has no existence in your section—gets no votes in your section. The fact is substantially true; but does it prove the issue? If it does, then in case we should, without change of principle, begin to get votes in your section, we should thereby cease, to be sectional. You cannot escape this conclusion; and yet, are you willing to

abide by it? If you are, you will probably soon find that we have ceased to be sectional, for we shall get votes in your section this very year. You will then begin to discover, as the truth plainly is, that your proof does not touch the issue. The fact that we get no votes in your section is a fact of your making, and not of ours. And if there be fault in that fact, that fault is primarily yours, and remains so until you show that we repel you by some wrong principle or practice. If we do repel you by any wrong principle or practice, the fault is ours; but this brings you to where you ought to have started—to a discussion of the right or wrong of our principle. If our principle, put in practice, would wrong your section for the benefit of ours, or for any other object, then our principle, and we with it, are sectional, and are justly opposed and denounced as such. Meet us, then, on the question of whether our principle, put in practice, would wrong your section; and so meet us as if it were possible that something may be said on our side. Do you accept the challenge? No! Then you really believe that the principle which "our fathers who framed the government under which we live" thought so clearly right as to adopt it, and indorse it again and again, upon their official oaths, is in fact so clearly wrong as to demand your condemnation without a moment's consideration.

Some of you delight to flaunt in our faces the warning against sectional parties given by [George] Washington in his Farewell Address. Less than eight years before Washington gave that warning, he had, as President of the United States, approved and signed an act of Congress enforcing the prohibition of slavery in the Northwestern Territory, which act embodied the policy of the government upon that subject up to and at the very moment he penned that warning; and about one year after he penned it, he wrote Lafayette that he considered that prohibition a wise measure, expressing in the same connection his hope that we should at some time have a confederacy of free States.

Bearing this in mind, and seeing that sectionalism has since arisen upon this same subject, is that warning a weapon in your hands against us, or in our hands against you? Could Washington himself speak, would he cast the blame of that sectionalism upon us, who sustain his policy, or upon you, who repudiate it? We respect that warning of Washington, and we commend it to you, together with his example pointing to the right application of it.

But you say you are conservative—eminently conservative—while we are revolutionary, destructive, or something of the sort. What is conservatism? Is it not adherence to the old and tried against the new and untried? We stick to, contend for, the identical old policy on the point in controversy which was adopted by "our fathers who framed the government under which we live"; while you with one accord reject, and scout, and spit upon that old policy, and insist upon substituting something new. True, you disagree among yourselves as to what that substitute shall be. You are divided on new propositions and plans, but you are unanimous in rejecting and denouncing the old policy of the fathers. Some of you are for reviving the foreign slave-trade; some for a congressional slave code for the Territories; some for Congress forbidding the Territories to prohibit slavery within their limits; some for maintaining slavery in the Territories through the judiciary; some for the "gur-reat pur-rinciple" that "if one man would enslave another, no third man should object," fantastically called "popular sovereignty"; but never a man among you is in favor of Federal prohibition of slavery in Federal Territories, according to the practice of "our fathers who framed the government under which we live." Not one of all your various plans can show a precedent or an advocate in the century within which our government originated. Consider, then, whether your claim of conservatism for yourselves, and your charge of destructiveness against us, are based on the most clear and stable foundations.

Again, you say we have made the slavery question more prominent than it formerly was. We deny it. We admit that it is more prominent, but we deny that we made it so. It was not we, but you, who discarded the old policy of the fathers. We resisted, and still resist, your innovation; and thence comes the greater prominence of the question. Would you have that question reduced to its former proportions? Go back to that old policy. What has been will be again, under the same conditions. If you would have the peace of the old times, readopt the precepts and policy of the old times.

You charge that we stir up insurrections among your slaves. We deny it; and what is your proof?

Harper's Ferry! John Brown!! John Brown was no Republican; and you have failed to implicate a single Republican in his Harper's Ferry enterprise. If any member of our party is guilty in that matter, you know it, or you do not know it. If you do know it, you are inexcusable for not designating the man and proving the fact. If you do not know it, you are inexcusable for asserting it, and especially for persisting in the assertion after you have tried and failed to make the proof. You need not be told that persisting in a charge which one does not know to be true, is simply malicious slander.

Some of you admit that no Republican designedly aided or encouraged the Harper's Ferry affair, but still insist that our doctrines and declarations necessarily lead to such results. We do not believe it. We know we hold no doctrine, and make no declaration, which were not held to and made by "our fathers who framed the government under which we live." You never dealt fairly by us in relation to this affair. When it occurred, some important State elections were near at hand, and you were in evident glee with the belief that, by charging the blame upon us, you could get an advantage of us in those elections. The elections came, and your expectations were not quite fulfilled. Every Republican man knew that, as to himself at least, your charge was a slander, and he was not much inclined by it to cast his vote in your favor. Republican doctrines and declarations are accompanied with a continual protest against any interference whatever with your slaves, or with you about your slaves. Surely, this does not encourage them to revolt. True, we do, in common with "our fathers who framed the government under which we live," declare our belief that slavery is wrong; but the slaves do not hear us declare even this. For anything we say or do, the slaves would scarcely know there is a Republican party. I believe they would not, in fact, generally know it but for your misrepresentations of us in their hearing. In your political contests among yourselves, each faction charges the other with sympathy with Black Republicanism; and then, to give point to the charge, defines Black Republicanism to simply be insurrection, blood, and thunder among the slaves.

Slave insurrections are no more common now than they were before the Republican party was organized. What induced the Southampton insurrection, twenty-eight years ago, in which at least three times as many lives were lost as at Harper's Ferry? You can scarcely stretch your very elastic fancy to the conclusion that Southampton was "got up by Black Republicanism." In the present state of things in the United States, I do not think a general, or even a very extensive, slave insurrection is possible. The indispensable concert of action cannot be attained. The slaves have no means of rapid communication; nor can incendiary freemen, black or white, supply it. The explosive materials are everywhere in parcels; but there neither are, nor can be supplied, the indispensable connecting trains.

Much is said by Southern people about the affection of slaves for their masters and mistresses; and a part of it, at least, is true. A plot for an uprising could scarcely be devised and communicated to twenty individuals before some one of them, to save the life of a favorite master or mistress, would divulge it. This is the rule; and the slave revolution in Hayti [Haiti] was not an exception to it, but a case occurring under peculiar circumstances. The gunpowder plot of British history, though not connected with slaves, was more in point. In that case, only about twenty were admitted to the secret; and yet one of them, in his anxiety to save a friend, betrayed the plot to that friend, and, by consequence, averted the calamity. Occasional poisonings from the kitchen, and open or stealthy assassinations in the field, and local revolts extending to a score or so, will continue to occur as the natural results of slavery; but no general insurrection of slaves, as I think, can happen in this country for a long time. Whoever much fears, or much hopes, for such an event, will be alike disappointed.

In the language of Mr. [Thomas] Jefferson, uttered many years ago, "It is still in our power to direct the process of emancipation and deportation peaceably, and in such slow degrees, as that the evil will wear off insensibly; and their places be, *pari passu*, filled up by free white laborers. If, on the contrary, it is left to force itself on, human nature must shudder at the prospect held up."

Mr. Jefferson did not mean to say, nor do I, that the power of emancipation is in the Federal Government. He spoke of Virginia; and, as to the power of emancipation, I speak of the slaveholding States only. The Federal Government, however, as we insist, has the power of restraining the extension of the institution—the power to insure that a slave insurrection shall never occur on any American soil which is now free from slavery.

John Brown's effort was peculiar. It was not a slave insurrection. It was an attempt by white men to get up a revolt among slaves, in which the slaves refused to participate. In fact, it was so absurd that the slaves, with all their ignorance, saw plainly enough it could not succeed. That affair, in its philosophy, corresponds with the many attempts, related in history, at the assassination of kings and emperors. An enthusiast broods over the oppression of a people till he fancies himself commissioned by Heaven to liberate them. He ventures the attempt, which ends in little else than his own execution. [Felice] Orsini's attempt on Louis Napoleon [Bonaparte], and John Brown's attempt at Harper's Ferry, were, in their philosophy, precisely the same. The eagerness to cast blame on old England in the one case, and on New England in the other, does not disprove the sameness of the two things.

And how much would it avail you, if you could, by the use of John Brown, [Hinton R.] Helper's Book, and the like, break up the Republican organization? Human action can be modified to some extent, but human nature cannot be changed. There is a judgment and a feeling against slavery in this nation, which cast at least a million and a half of votes. You cannot destroy that judgment and feeling—that sentiment—by breaking up the political organization which rallies around it. You can scarcely scatter and disperse an army which has been formed into order in the face of your heaviest fire; but if you could, how much would you gain by forcing the sentiment which created it out of the peaceful channel of the ballot-box into some other channel? What would that other channel probably be? Would the number of John Browns be lessened or enlarged by the operation?

But you will break up the Union rather than submit to a denial of your constitutional rights.

That has a somewhat reckless sound; but it would be palliated, if not fully justified, were we proposing, by the mere force of numbers, to deprive you of some right plainly written down in the Constitution. But we are proposing no such thing.

When you make these declarations you have a

specific and well-understood allusion to an assumed constitutional right of yours to take slaves into the Federal Territories, and to hold them there as property. But no such right is specifically written in the Constitution. That instrument is literally silent about any such right. We, on the contrary, deny that such a right has any existence in the Constitution, even by implication.

Your purpose, then, plainly stated, is that you will destroy the government, unless you be allowed to construe and force the Constitution as you please, on all points in dispute between you and us. You will rule or ruin in all events.

This, plainly stated, is your language. Perhaps you will say the Supreme Court has decided the disputed constitutional question in your favor. Not quite so. But waiving the lawyer's distinction between dictum and decision, the court has decided the question for you in a sort of way. The court has substantially said, it is your constitutional right to take slaves into the Federal Territories, and to hold them there as property. When I say the decision was made in a sort of way, I mean it was made in a divided court, by a bare majority of the judges, and they not quite agreeing with one another in the reasons for making it; that it is so made as that its avowed supporters disagree with one another about its meaning, and that it was mainly based upon a mistaken statement of fact—the statement in the opinion that "the right of property in a slave is distinctly and expressly affirmed in the Constitution."

An inspection of the Constitution will show that the right of property in a slave is not "distinctly and expressly affirmed" in it. Bear in mind, the judges do not pledge their judicial opinion that such right is impliedly affirmed in the Constitution; but they pledge their veracity that it is "distinctly and expressly" affirmed there—"distinctly," that is, not mingled with anything else—"expressly," that is, in words meaning just that, without the aid of any inference, and susceptible of no other meaning.

If they had only pledged their judicial opinion that such right is affirmed in the instrument by implication, it would be open to others to show that neither the word "slave" nor "slavery" is to be found in the Constitution, nor the word "property" even, in any connection with language alluding to the things slave, or slavery; and that wherever in that instrument the slave is alluded to, he is called a "person"; and wherever his master's legal right in relation to him is alluded to, it is spoken of as "service or labor which may be due"—as a debt payable in service or labor. Also it would be open to show, by contemporaneous history, that this mode of alluding to slaves and slavery, instead of speaking of them, was employed on purpose to exclude from the Constitution the idea that there could be property in man.

To show all this is easy and certain.

When this obvious mistake of the judges shall be brought to their notice, is it not reasonable to expect that they will withdraw the mistaken statement, and reconsider the conclusion based upon it?

And then it is to be remembered that "our fathers who framed the government under which we live"—the men who made the Constitution—decided this same constitutional question in our favor long ago: decided it without division among themselves when making the decision; without division among themselves about the meaning of it after it was made, and, so far as any evidence is left, without basing it upon any mistaken statement of facts.

Under all these circumstances, do you really feel yourselves justified to break up this government unless such a court decision as yours is shall be at once submitted to as a conclusive and final rule of political action? But you will not abide the election of a Republican president! In that supposed event, you say, you will destroy the Union; and then, you say, the great crime of having destroyed it will be upon us! That is cool. A highwayman holds a pistol to my ear, and mutters through his teeth, "Stand and deliver, or I shall kill you, and then you will be a murderer!"

To be sure, what the robber demanded of me—my money—was my own; and I had a clear right to keep it; but it was no more my own than my vote is my own; and the threat of death to me, to extort my money, and the threat of destruction to the Union, to extort my vote, can scarcely be distinguished in principle.[1323]

Few political speeches have been filled with as much biliousness, falsehood, exaggeration, fraud, hyperbole, and outright deceit regarding the Southern Confederacy as this one. For example, while Lincoln denies that he is **"sectional,"** objective historians label him the first and most openly sectional president in American history.[1324] Why? Because for years prior to becoming president he constantly railed against the South in the most threatening manner, always highlighting the differences between South and North instead of their similarities.

Lincoln also paints the entire South as a massive slave holding region in which every citizen is an ardent proslavery slave owner. As we have seen, however, the 1860 Census shows that only 4.8 percent (or less) of Southerners owned slaves on the eve of his War.[1325] As he usually did, the president later reversed his opinion on this topic, saying on December 3, 1861, that:

> In most of the southern states, a majority of the whole people of all colors are neither slaves nor masters . . .[1326]

While those involved in the so-called **"slave breeding"** business Lincoln ignorantly speaks of[1327] were virtually nonexistent (there was no such profession in the Old South),[1328] those he calls **"slave traders"** actually made up a tiny fraction of the Southern population, contrary to popular Yankee myth. In part, Lincoln acknowledged this fact in a August 24, 1855, letter to Joshua F. Speed:

> The slave-breeders and slave-traders are a small, odious, and detested class among you; and yet in politics they dictate the course of all of you, and are as completely your masters as you are the master of your own negroes.[1329]

Later, when it suited his political agenda, Lincoln unfairly, inaccurately, absurdly, and maliciously portrayed the entire South as a slave trading, slave owning, slave breeding region.

This type of flip-flopping and deception was typical of Lincoln's duplicitous double-talk and political chicanery, which is why speeches like the one at the Cooper Union only fanned the flames of sectionalism (in both the South and the North), further enraged Southerners, and drove the age-old wedge between the two regions even deeper. While Lincoln pretends to be a peacemaker here, trying to bring the two sides together, he is actually laying the groundwork for the bloody conflict he would instigate within two short months (as discussed in Chapter 7).

The president-elect did manage to convey two important truths in this particular speech, however: 1) he was an enthusiastic advocate of shipping all blacks out of the country ("colonization"), and 2) he was not interested in abolishing slavery, only preventing its spread into the new Western Territories.

Whatever shred of good will Lincoln pretended to possess toward Dixie, even that had disappeared by April 15, 1861, the day he issued his proclamation calling for 75,000 Union troops and an invasion of the South.[1330] Four years later, according to the estimates of *Southern* historians, with the War now ended, some 2 million Southerners lay dead, the nation was bankrupt, race relations across Dixie had been poisoned, and the South and North were now divided by an emotional scar that will never completely heal.[1331]

Despite this, in his Second Inaugural Address, on March 4, 1865, Lincoln had the unmitigated gall to say:

> **With malice toward none; with charity for all; with firmness in the right, as God gives us to see the right, let us strive on to finish the work we are in; to bind up the nation's wounds; to care for him who shall have borne the battle, and for his widow, and his orphan—to do all which may achieve and cherish a just and lasting peace among ourselves, and with all nations.**[1332]

Even worse, in the same speech Lincoln takes absolutely no responsibility for the conflict that he created. Instead, he blames his War on God, even stating that it is the Almighty's decision as to whether the War will continue or end:

> **The Almighty has his own purposes. "Woe unto the world because of offenses! For it must needs be that offenses come; but woe to that man by whom the offense cometh." If we shall suppose that American slavery is one of those offenses which, in the providence of God, must needs come, but which, having continued through his appointed time, he now wills to remove, and that he gives to both North and South this terrible war, as the woe due to those by whom the offense came, shall we discern therein any departure from those divine attributes which the believers in a living God always**

ascribe to him? Fondly do we hope—fervently do we pray—that this mighty scourge of war may speedily pass away. Yet, if God wills that it continue until all the wealth piled by the bondman's two hundred and fifty years of unrequited toil shall be sunk, and until every drop of blood drawn with the lash shall be paid by another drawn with the sword, as was said three thousand years ago, so still it must be said, "The judgments of the Lord are true and righteous altogether."[1333]

This brings us to one of Lincoln's most famous speeches, the Gettysburg Address, where he insidiously promotes his overriding message that the South, by seceding, threatened to obliterate the U.S. government. Even though this is an impossibility, and of course it never came close to occurring, the dishonest beauty of his words has brainwashed six generations of Americans against the South.

The Gettysburg Address was delivered at the dedication of the cemetery at Gettysburg, Pennsylvania, November 19, 1863. It reads:

> Fourscore and seven years ago our fathers brought forth on this continent a new nation, conceived in liberty, and dedicated to the proposition that all men are created equal.
> Now we are engaged in a great civil war, testing whether that nation, or any nation so conceived and so dedicated, can long endure. We are met on a great battle-field of that war. We have come to dedicate a portion of that field as a final resting-place for those who here gave their lives that that nation might live. It is altogether fitting and proper that we should do this.
> But, in a larger sense, we cannot dedicate—we cannot consecrate—we cannot hallow—this ground. The brave men, living and dead, who struggled here, have consecrated it, far above our poor power to add or detract. The world will little note nor long remember what we say here, but it can never forget what they did here. It is for us, the living, rather, to be dedicated here to the unfinished work which they who fought here have thus far so nobly advanced. It is rather for us to be here dedicated to the great task remaining before us—that from these honored dead we take increased devotion to that cause for which they gave the last full measure of

devotion—that we here highly resolve that these dead shall not have died in vain; that this nation, under God, shall have a new birth of freedom; and that government of the people, by the people, for the people, shall not perish from the earth.[1334]

The Gettysburg Address must go down in history as one of the most faithless, cynical, erroneous, and cruelly ironic speeches ever uttered, for in it atheist Lincoln promises to uphold the Constitution, when in fact he did the opposite. He blames the South for the War, when it was a conflict that he not only wanted but that he also nefariously instigated. Finally he praises America's true political heritage. Yet two years later, on April 9, 1865, at Appomattox,[1335] he overturned it, then caused it to **"perish from the earth."** What was that political heritage? It was our original Jeffersonian Confederate Republic, a constitutional government "of the people, by the people, for the people."[1336]

Here is what Maryland journalist H. L. Mencken had to say about Lincoln's most famous declamation: the Gettysburg Address is understandably celebrated for its poetry, beauty, and eloquence. But this is all that can be said for it. In truth, it is a nonsensical piece of bombast. If we approach it objectively, Lincoln is saying that those Northern soldiers who were blown to pieces at the Pennsylvania town in early July 1863, gave up their lives so that "government of the people, by the people, for the people, shall not perish from the earth." Actually, Mencken goes on to say, nothing could be further from the truth. Lincoln's armies fought against free government, while the Southern Rebels fought for it, for the right of the people to determine their own destinies.[1337]

British journalist Alistair Cooke agreed, calling Lincoln's Gettysburg Address a classic work of oratory of highly questionable reasoning.[1338] How true.

I myself consider it political theater of the most mendacious, divisive, pathetic, and incendiary kind. Yet incredibly, this speech has been lauded by thousands of scholars, authors, and academicians, with hundreds of books being entirely and worshipfully devoted to it.[1339]

In early Fall of 1864 Lincoln was accused of planning to "ruin the government" if he lost the election in November. Here, on October 19, 1864, is how he responded to the charge:

> **Something said by the Secretary of State** [William H. Seward], **in his recent speech at Auburn, has been**

construed by some into a threat that if I shall be beaten at the election I will, between then and the end of my constitutional term, do what I may be able to ruin the government. Others regard the fact that the Chicago Convention adjourned, not *sine die* [i.e., indefinitely] but to meet again, if called to do so by a particular individual, as the intimation of a purpose that if their nominee shall be elected he will at once seize control of the government. I hope the good people will permit themselves to suffer no uneasiness on either point.

I am struggling to maintain the government, not to overthrow it. I am struggling, especially, to prevent others from overthrowing it. I therefore say that if I shall live I shall remain President until the 4th of next March; and that whoever shall be constitutionally elected therefor, in November, shall be duly installed as President on the 4th of March; and that, in the interval, I shall do my utmost that whoever is to hold the helm for the next voyage shall start with the best possible chance to save the ship.

This is due to the people both on principle and under the Constitution. Their will, constitutionally expressed, is the ultimate law for all. If they should deliberately resolve to have immediate peace, even at the loss of their country and their liberty, I know not the power or the right to resist them. It is their own business, and they must do as they please with their own. I believe, however, they are still resolved to preserve their country and their liberty; and in this, in office or out of it, I am resolved to stand by them.

I may add that in this purpose—to save the country and its liberties—no classes of people seem so nearly unanimous as the soldiers in the field and the sailors afloat. Do they not have the hardest of it? Who should quail when they do not? God bless the soldiers and seamen, with all their brave commanders.[1340]

The accusation that Lincoln would "ruin the government" if he lost his bid for reelection is revealing in and of itself, particularly since the claim came not from Southerners, but from Northerners. Antebellum Southerners had been well aware of what was coming if Lincoln were to be elected in 1860, which is precisely why the Southern states began to secede only weeks after his victory in November of that year.

Despite the fears of many Northerners in the Fall of 1864, the reality is that by then Lincoln had already ruined the U.S. government, the one installed by the Founding Fathers to be "of the people, by the people, for the people." Yet in this speech he attempts to distract and mislead the public by saying that he is trying to **"save the country and its liberties,"** that **"I am struggling to maintain the government, not to overthrow it. I am struggling, especially, to prevent others from overthrowing it."**

Contrary to these overt lies, the Southern states were not trying to **"overthrow"** the U.S. government. Prior to the War they were trying to preserve it. Then when they saw that Lincoln was determined to destroy it they seceded and wrote out their own Constitution, one that *did* maintain the Founders' original government and its inherent liberties: a confederate republic,[1341] or the "Confederacy" as the U.S. was known from 1781 to 1789.[1342] This is precisely why the South called its newly independent league of states the "Confederacy."

Using beguiling words, as he did in the Gettysburg Address, Lincoln has been able to fool the world into thinking that the South started the War and that God continued it in order to violently punish the "wicked South." And so it is still wrongly believed by the majority of people to this day.

But what of Lincoln's role? As the paragraphs above alone show, he never took an ounce of responsibility for any of it. This despite the plain fact that it was he who both launched and maintained the War, all the while ignoring Jefferson Davis' many offers of compromise, the journeys of numerous Confederate peace commissions to Washington,[1343] the desperate pleas of the Southern people, and even the antiwar appeals of much of the Northern populace, including individuals like Ohio Congressman Clement Laird Vallandigham.

What was Lincoln's response to such citizens? The unlawful suspension of *habeas corpus*,[1344] their unlawful arrest, their unlawful trial (if they were lucky) in a military court, and their unlawful deportation.[1345] Lincoln did not even try to hide this particular constitutional violation, as the following example—an unsent June 20, 1864, letter to Union General Samuel Peter Heintzelman and Ohio Governor John Brough—reveals:

> **Both of you have official responsibility as to the United States military in Ohio, and generally—one in organizing and furnishing, the other in directing, commanding, and forwarding. Consult together freely, watch Vallandigham and others closely, and upon discovering**

any palpable injury or imminent danger to the military proceeding from him, them, or any of them, arrest all implicated; otherwise do not arrest without further order. Meanwhile report the signs to me from time to time. Yours truly, A. Lincoln.[1346]

This was Lincoln's response to antiwar sentiment.

Indeed, from the first to the last day of his War Lincoln never once offered a single compromise that could have realistically led to cessation of the conflict. Those that were offered, and there were many, all came from the South. Every last one was rejected by Lincoln, who was hellbent on continuing the War, *and* "punishing" the South, for as long as possible.[1347]

Yet while in public Lincoln seemed to be cold, unbending, and efficient when it came to inflicting pain, misery, and death on Dixie, his private words revealed a man who was in deep anguish internally. Not for waging an illegal and unnecessary war on Dixie and the subsequent deaths of hundreds of thousands of innocent people. But because of the hatred and scorn heaped on him by his cabinet, military officers, and many of his Yankee constituents, over his utter ineptitude in the White House. As he once told his associate Ward Hill Lamon:

> **I wish I had never been born! I would rather be dead than as President thus abused in the house of my friends.**[1348]

Unfortunately for Lincoln the Grim Reaper was not ready to visit him yet. Instead, the president went on to commit one atrocity after another in his bid to subjugate the South and install big government at Washington.

Lincoln greatly underestimated the South's traditionalism and strict constitutionalism when it came to secession, war, and the trampling of states' rights. On February 2, 1848, Alexander H. Stephens, future vice president of the Southern Confederacy, spoke before the U.S. House of Representatives. The focus of his address was the Mexican-American War (1846-1848): why was the U.S. meddling in Mexico's affairs? Why not leave her alone? Why wage war on our neighbor simply to acquire another acre of dirt?, he asked rightfully.

But Stephens could have just as easily been addressing the North in regard to the American South thirteen years later:

> The honor of this country does not and cannot require us to force and compel the people of any other to sell theirs. I have, I trust, as high a regard for national honor as any man. It is the brightest gem in the chaplet of a nation's glory; and there is nothing of which I am prouder than the high character for honor this country has acquired throughout the civilized world—that code of honor which was established by [George] Washington and the men of the Revolution, and which rests upon truth, justice, and honesty, which, is the offspring of virtue and integrity, and which is seen in the length and breadth of our land, in all the evidences of art and civilization and moral advancement, and every thing that tends to elevate, dignify, and ennoble man. This is the honor of my admiration, and it is made of 'sterner,' purer, nobler 'stuff' than that aggressive and degrading, yea, odious principle now avowed of waging a war against a neighboring people to compel them to sell their country. Who is here so base as to be willing, under any circumstances, to sell his country? For myself, I can only say, if the last funeral pile of liberty were lighted, I would mount it and expire in its flames before I would be coerced by any power, however great and strong, to sell or surrender the land of my home, the place of my nativity, and the graves of my sires! Sir, the principle is not only dishonorable, but infamous. As the representative upon this floor of a highminded and honorable constituency, I repeat, that the principle of waging war against a neighboring people to compel them to sell their country, is not only dishonorable, but disgraceful and infamous. What, shall it be said that American honor aims at nothing higher than land—than the ground on which we tread? Do we look no higher in our aspirations for honor, than do the soulless brutes? Shall we disavow the similitude of our Maker, and disgrace the very name of man? Tell it not to the world. Let not such an aspersion and reproach rest upon our name. I have heard of nations whose honor could be satisfied with gold—that glittering dust, which is so precious in the eyes, of some—but never did I expect to live to see the day when the Executive of this country should announce that our honor was such a loathsome, beastly thing, that it could not be satisfied with any achievements in arms, however brilliant and glorious, but must feed on earth—gross, vile, dirt!—and require even a prostrate foe to be robbed of mountain rocks and desert plains![1349]

Lincoln must have either heard or read Stephens' speech, and agreed with it. For he too was against the Mexican-American War.[1350] Yet it was for a very different reason. As we have seen, Lincoln believed that Southerners and conservatives wanted Mexican land for the sole purpose of extending and planting slavery there.¹³⁵¹ He preferred, as he said many times, that any newly acquired Western lands should be used solely for the benefit of **"white people."**¹³⁵² Such views would help him justify, to himself anyway, his own illicit war on the Southern Confederacy just over a decade later.

To maintain support for his War Lincoln went to extraordinary lengths, even often and openly lying to his constituency, as he did during his Fourth Annual Message to Congress on December 6, 1864:

> **The important fact remains demonstrated that we have more men now than we had when the war began; that we are not exhausted, nor in process of exhaustion; that we are gaining strength, and may, if need be, maintain the contest indefinitely. This as to men. Material resources are now more complete and abundant than ever.**
>
> **The national resources, then, are unexhausted, and, as we believe, inexhaustible. . . .**¹³⁵³

Here Lincoln was engaging in his usual hyperbolic rhetoric. The North may indeed have had three times the men, money, and supplies,¹³⁵⁴ but it was not **"inexhaustible"** and it could not maintain the contest **"indefinitely."** As his most important and most knowledgeable military officer, General Ulysses S. Grant, said in his 1885 *Memoirs*:

> I think that [Confederate General Nathan Bedford Forrest's protraction] . . . policy was the best one that could have been pursued by the whole South—protract the war, which was all that was necessary to enable them to gain recognition in the end. The North was already growing weary . . .¹³⁵⁵ Anything that could have prolonged the war a year beyond the time that it did finally close, would probably have exhausted the North to such an extent that they might then have abandoned the contest and agreed to separation.¹³⁵⁶

LINCOLN & HIS WAR ON THE NORTH

MOST AMERICANS BELIEVE THAT LINCOLN waged the so-called "Civil War" only on the South. Few realize, however, that he also used all manner of violence on his own Northern constituents. This was necessary, in Lincoln's mind, because a huge percentage of the Northern populace was against him.

To control the people of his region, silence his critics, maintain support for his war, and assure his reelection in 1864, Lincoln stooped to an all time low, engaging in felonious behavior that has never been witnessed in a U.S. president before or since (a fact for which we can all be eternally grateful). In the process he became the greatest political criminal in American history.

Lincoln' war on the North began with his using private vigilante gangs[1357] to arbitrarily arrest (without warrants) and imprison (without charges) 38,000 Northerners (without trial)[1358] for standing up to him at the pulpit and in the press.[1359] In many cases these unfortunate victims remained in their cells until the War ended.[1360] He had a great number of these individuals shipped to his infamous "government gulag," Fort Lafayette in New York Harbor, a hellish prison where an untold number of innocent Northerners died due to unsanitary conditions.[1361]

Lincoln went on to illegally suspend *habeas corpus* for the first time in American history[1362]—and all across the U.S.;[1363] impose martial law,[1364] under whose military courts those arrested for **"treason"** (that is, for advocating peace and recognition of the Confederacy)[1365] were illegally tried;[1366] introduce forced conscription;[1367] expand the army; order emergency spending;[1368] violate the concept of the separation of powers; give away 270 million acres of public lands (under the 1862 Homestead Act);[1369] and spend $2 million ($50 million in today's currency), *all* without constitutional authority or congressional approval.

In order to silence his critics and prevent the truth about his lies and crimes from coming out, Lincoln, in fact, shut down entire Northern states. One of these was Maryland, where he gave his generals permission to both suspend *habeas corpus* and bomb her cities into rubble.[1370] President Jefferson Davis describes Lincoln's outrageous crimes here:

> A military force, under the authority of the Government of the United States, occupied the city of Baltimore at a time when no invasion of the State was threatened, and when there had been no application of the Legislature, or of the Executive, for protection against domestic violence, which circumstances alone could give a constitutional authority for this organized military force to occupy the state. The commanding [Union] general, [Robert C.] Schenck, soon issued an order, of which the following is an extract:
>
>> Martial law is declared and hereby established in the city and county of Baltimore, and in all the counties of the Western Shore of Maryland. The commanding General gives assurance that this suspension of civil government within the limits defined shall not extend beyond the necessities of the occasion. All the civil courts, tribunals, and political functionaries of State, county, or city authority, are to continue in the discharge of their duties as in times of peace, only in no way interfering with the exercise of the predominant power assumed and asserted by the military authority.
>
> It will be noticed that this military force of the Government of the United States had no constitutional permission to come into Maryland and exercise authority; that the commanding General says that the civil government of the State is suspended within certain limits; that this suspension will be continued according to the necessities of the occasion; that the courts and political functionaries may discharge their duties, only in no way interfering with the exercise of the predominant military power. Now, where were the 'just powers' of the State government at this time? They

were suspended in a part of the State, says the commanding General, and for so long a time as the military authority may judge the necessities of the occasion to require, and that the courts and political functionaries may discharge their duties while recognizing the supremacy of the military power. Thus was the State government subjugated.

A further subversion of the [Maryland] State government was now commenced by an invasion and denial of some of the unalienable rights of the citizens, for the security of which that government was instituted. The Constitution of the United States says:

> No person shall be deprived of life, liberty, or property, without due process of law.
> The right of the people to be secure in their persons, houses, papers, and effects, against unreasonable searches and seizures, shall not be violated.
> Excessive bail shall not be required, nor excessive fines imposed, nor cruel and unusual punishments inflicted.
> Congress shall make no law abridging the freedom of speech or of the press.

The Declaration of Independence says:

> That they are endowed by their Creator with certain unalienable rights; that among these are life, liberty, and the pursuit of happiness; that, to secure these rights, governments are instituted among men.

Immediately upon the issue of the order of the commanding General, the arrests of [Maryland's] citizens commenced by provost marshals. The family residence of a lady was forced open; she was seized, put on board of a steamer, and sent to the Confederate States. A man was arrested for being 'disloyal' to the United States Government, and held for examination. Another was charged with interfering with the enrollment; he was held for further examination. Another, charged with being 'disloyal' to the United States Government, took the oath of allegiance, and was released. A woman charged with the attempt to resist the enrollment, was arrested and subsequently released. A man, on a charge of 'disloyalty,' took the oath, and was released. Another, charged with having given improper information to enrolling officers, was released on furnishing the information. Another, charged with having [gun] powder in his possession, was released on taking the oath of allegiance. Two others, charged with abuse of the negroes laboring on the fortifications, were held for examination. Another, charged with rendering assistance to wounded Confederate soldiers, and expressing treasonable sentiments, took the oath of allegiance and was released. Another, charged with being a soldier in the Confederate army and paroled, was ordered to be sent across the lines. A man, charged with treasonable language, was ordered to be sent across the lines. Two others, charged with aiding Confederate soldiers, took the oath of allegiance and were discharged. Another, charged with receiving letters from Confederates for the purpose of delivery, took the oath of allegiance and was discharged. Another, charged with expressing treasonable sentiments, was held for examination. Two charged with cheering for Jefferson Davis, took the oath and were released.

    One case more must be stated. On May 25, 1861, John Merryman, a most respectable citizen of the State, residing in Baltimore County, was seized in his bed by an armed force and imprisoned in Fort McHenry. He petitioned the Chief Justice of the United States [Roger B. Taney] that a writ of *habeas corpus* might be issued, which was granted. The officer upon whom it was served [Ward Hill Lamon] declined to obey the writ. An attachment was issued against the officer. The marshal was refused admittance to the fort to serve it.

    . . . During the month of July arrests were made of 361 persons, on charges like the above mentioned by the military authority. Of this number, 317 took the oath of allegiance to the Government of the United States and were released; 5 were sent to Fort McHenry, 3 to Washington for the action of the authorities there, 11 to the North, 6 across the lines, and 19 were held for further examination.

    On September 11, 1863, one of the city newspapers published the poem entitled 'The Southern Cross.' The publishers and editor were immediately arrested, not allowed communication with any person whatever, and on the same day sent across the lines, with the understanding that they should not return during the war. On July 2d an order was issued which forbade the citizens of Baltimore City and County to keep arms unless they were enrolled as volunteer companies. The Fifty-first Regiment of Massachusetts Volunteers was placed at the disposal of General Erastus B. Tyler, assisted by the provost marshal and the chief of police. The soldiers, in concert with the police, formed into parties of three or four, and were soon diligently engaged in searching houses. Large wagons were provided, and muskets, carbines, rifles, revolvers of all kinds, sabers, bayonets, swords, and bird and ducking guns in considerable quantities were gathered. The Constitution of the United States says:

> The right of the people to keep and bear arms shall not be infringed.

A further subversion of the State government of Maryland was next made by a direct interference with the elections. An election was to be held in the State for members of the Legislature and members of Congress on November 3, 1863. The commanding General, on October 27th issued an order to all marshals and military officers to cause their direct interference with the voters. The Governor [Augustus] (Bradford) applied to the President of the United States to have the order revoked, and protested against any person who offered to vote being put to any test not found in the laws of Maryland. President Lincoln declined to interfere with the order, except in one less important point. The Governor issued a proclamation on the day preceding the election, which the military commander endeavored to suppress, and issued an order charging that the tendency of the proclamation was to invite and suggest disturbance. One or more regiments of soldiers were sent out and distributed among several of the counties to attend the places of election, in defiance of the known laws of the State prohibiting their presence. Military officers and provost marshals were ordered to arrest voters guilty, in their opinion, of certain offenses, and to menace judges of election with the power of the army in case this order was not respected. But perhaps the forcible language of the Governor to the Legislature will furnish the most undeniable statement of the facts. He says:

> ... These abuses present a humiliating record, such as I had never supposed we should be called upon to read in any State, still less in a loyal one like this. Unless it be, indeed, a fallacy to suppose that any rights whatever remain to such a State, or that any line whatever marks the limit of Federal power, a bolder stride across that line that power never made, even in a rebel State, than it did in Maryland on the 3d of last November. A part of the army, which a generous people had supplied for a very different purpose, was on

> that day engaged in stifling the freedom of election in a faithful State, intimidating its sworn officers, violating the constitutional rights of its loyal citizens, and obstructing the usual channels of communication between them and their Executive.
>
> The result was the election of a majority of members of the Legislature in favor of a State Constitutional Convention. The acts necessary for this object were passed. At the election of delegates the military authority again interfered in order to secure a majority in favor of immediate and unconditional emancipation. The so-called Convention assembled and drafted a so-called Constitution, in which the twenty-third article of the Bill of Rights prohibited the existence of slavery in the State, and said, 'All persons held to service or labor as slaves are hereby declared free.'
> . . . Thus was the State government [of Maryland] subjugated and made an instrument of destruction to the people; thus were their rights ruthlessly violated, and property millions of dollars in value annihilated.[1371]

Famed Southern General Robert E. Lee was so upset by Lincoln's persecution, oppression, and overthrow of the citizens of Maryland that he personally offered his services and those of his army in an effort to free them. On September 8, 1862, he dispatched a letter "to the people of Maryland." It read:

> It is right that you should know the purpose that brought the army under my command within the limits of your State, so far as that purpose concerns yourselves. The people of the Confederate States have long watched with the deepest sympathy the wrongs and outrages that have been inflicted upon the citizens of a commonwealth allied to the States of the South by the strongest social, political, and commercial ties. They have seen with profound indignation their sister State deprived of every right and reduced to the condition of a conquered province. Under the pretense of supporting the Constitution, but in violation of its most valuable provisions, your citizens have been arrested and imprisoned upon no charge and contrary to all forms of law. The faithful and manly protest against this outrage made by the venerable and illustrious Marylander, to whom in better days no citizen appealed for right in vain, was treated with scorn and contempt; the government of your chief city has been usurped by armed strangers; your legislature has been dissolved by the

unlawful arrest of its members; freedom of the press and of speech has been suppressed; words have been declared offenses by an arbitrary decree of the Federal Executive, and citizens ordered to be tried by a military commission for what they may dare to speak. Believing that the people of Maryland possessed a spirit too lofty to submit to such a government, the people of the South have long wished to aid you in throwing off this foreign yoke, to enable you again to enjoy the inalienable rights of freemen, and restore independence and sovereignty to your State. In obedience to this wish, our army has come among you, and is prepared to assist you with the power of its arms in regaining the rights of which you have been despoiled.

This, citizens of Maryland, is our mission, so far as you are concerned. No constraint upon your free will is intended; no intimidation will be allowed within the limits of this army, at least. Marylanders shall once more enjoy their ancient freedom of thought and speech. We know no enemies among you, and will protect all, of every opinion. It is for you to decide your destiny freely and without constraint. This army will respect your choice, whatever it may be; and while the Southern people will rejoice to welcome you to your natural position among them, they will only welcome you when you come of your own free will.[1372]

Lincoln, of course, pretended that none of this occurred. Not only did he never tell the truth, he spread the opposite story; namely that the South tried to force Maryland to become part of the Confederacy! As he put it in his First Annual Message to Congress on December 3, 1861:

The [Southern] **insurgents confidently claimed a strong support from north of Mason and Dixon's line; and the friends of the Union were not free from apprehension on the point. This, however, was soon settled definitely, and on the right side. South of the line, noble little Delaware led off right from the first. Maryland was made to seem against the Union. Our soldiers were assaulted, bridges were burned, and railroads torn up within her limits, and we were many days, at one time, without the ability to bring a single regiment over her soil to the capital. Now her bridges and railroads are repaired and open to the government; she already gives seven regiments to the cause of the Union and none to the enemy; and her people, at a regular election, have sustained the Union by a larger majority and a larger aggregate vote than they ever before gave to any candidate or any question.**[1373]

Lincoln fails to mention several important facts here: Maryland did not **"seem"** to be against the Union, she *was* against the Union. Proof comes from his own statement, that Yankee soldiers in the Old Line State were attacked, bridges were burned, and railroads torn up. Why? Because Marylanders believed in states' rights and wanted nothing to do with the anti-South president or his War on Dixie. As for the reason Marylanders finally **"sustained the Union"** by a larger majority than ever before, this was only because Lincoln imposed martial law over the state, threw its entire legislature into prison, and threatened its citizens with violence. Marylanders had no choice but to **"sustain the Union."**

As the year 1864 drew to a close Maryland began preparing its new state constitution for ratification. This was not a voluntarily move. Upon the earlier imposition of martial law across the state, Lincoln had had the original state constitution trashed and a new one drawn up according to his own personal dictates. One of these was the involuntary **"extinction of slavery"** across the state, so that he could draft young freed black men and deport the rest back **"to their native land"** (Africa) as quickly as possible.[1374] On October 10, 1864, Lincoln made note of his (illegal) action in a letter to Henry W. Hoffman:

> My dear Sir: A convention of Maryland has framed a new constitution for the State; a public meeting is called for this evening at Baltimore to aid in securing its ratification by the people, and you ask a word from me for the occasion. I presume the only feature of the instrument about which there is serious controversy is that which provides for the extinction of slavery. It needs not to be a secret, and I presume it is no secret, that I wish success to this provision. I desire it on every consideration. I wish all men to be free. I wish the material prosperity of the already free, which I feel sure the extinction of slavery would bring. I wish to see in process of disappearing that only thing which ever could bring this nation to civil war. I attempt no argument. Argument upon the question is already exhausted by the abler, better informed, and more immediately interested sons of Maryland herself. I only add that I shall be gratified exceedingly if the good people of the State shall, by their votes, ratify the new constitution. Yours truly, A. Lincoln.[1375]

That Marylanders were entering into their new state constitution *unwillingly* is clear from Lincoln's final sentence.

Still he could not contain his glee over the subjugation of the Old Line State, as he put it in his Fourth Annual Message to Congress on December 6, 1864:

> **Important movements have ... occurred during the year to the effect of molding society for durability in the Union. Although short of complete success, it is much in the right direction that 12,000 citizens in each of the States of Arkansas and Louisiana have organized loyal State governments, with free constitutions, and are earnestly struggling to maintain and administer them. The movements in the same direction, more extensive though less definite, in Missouri, Kentucky, and Tennessee, should not be overlooked. But Maryland presents the example of complete success. Maryland is secure to liberty and Union for all the future. The genius of rebellion will no more claim Maryland. Like another foul spirit, being driven out, it may seek to tear her, but it will woo her no more.**[1376]

Maryland would only be **"wooed by the South no more"** if Lincoln could maintain martial law over the state!

Even as the freedom-loving spirit of Maryland was slowly being suffocated under the boot heel of Yankee military bondage, a host of other Northern states were falling prey to Lincoln's reign of terror, including one of his greatest supporters and financial backers: the great slave trading capital of New York. Since he never acknowledged his crimes against the Empire State, we will once again turn to one of our best eyewitnesses, President Jefferson Davis. Wrote the former Confederate leader:

> Now follows the humiliating spectacle of the subjugation of the State government of New York—the "Empire" State, as she calls herself—where, with all her men and treasures, it might have been supposed that some stanch defenders of constitutional liberty would have sprung up. On the contrary, under the pretext of "preserving the Union," her deluded children aided to destroy the Constitution on which the Union was founded, and put forth all their strength to exalt the Government of the United States to supremacy. Thus the States were brought to a condition of subjugation, and their governments subverted from the protection of the rights for which they were instituted. These unalienable

rights of the people were left without a protector or a shield before the crushing hand of the usurper; the sovereignty of the people was set aside, and in its place arose the sovereignty of the Government of the United States. With the foundation undermined, the superstructure subverted, the ends for which the Great Republic was organized entirely lost to sight, and the true balance of the system destroyed, unless the dormant virtue and love for their inherited rights shall arouse the citizens to a vigorous effort to restore the republican institutions and powers of the States, the emperors and kings of the earth have only to await calmly the lapse of time to behold a fulfillment of their evil prophecies in regard to the "Great Republic" of the world.

To show how the laws were disregarded, and how despotically the personal liberty of the citizen was invaded, let this example bear witness: The Secretary of State at Washington, William H. Seward, a favored son of the State of New York, would "ring a little bell," which brought to him a messenger, to whom was given a secret order to arrest and confine in Fort Lafayette a person designated. This order was sent by telegraph to the United States Marshal of the district in which would be found the person who was to be arrested. The arrest being forcibly made by the marshal with armed attendants without even the form of a warrant, the prisoner without the knowledge of any charge against him was conveyed to Fort Hamilton and turned over to the commandant. An aid with a guard of soldiers then conveyed him in a boat to Fort Lafayette and delivered him to the keeper in charge, who gave a receipt for the prisoner. He was then divested of any weapons, money, valuables, or papers in his possession. His baggage was opened and searched. A soldier then took him in charge to the designated quarter, which was a portion of one of the casemates for guns, lighted only from the port-hole, and occupied by seven or eight other prisoners. All were subjected to prison fare. Some were citizens of New York, and the others of different States. This manner of imprisonment was subsequently put under the direction of the Secretary of War, and continued at intervals until the close of the war.

In the brief period between July 1 and October 19, 1861, the Secretary of State, William H. Seward, made such diligent use of his "little bell," that one hundred and seventy-five of the most respectable citizens of the country were consigned to imprisonment in this Fort Lafayette, a strong fortress in the lower part of the harbor of New York. A decent regard for the memory of the friend of Washington, and for the services rendered to the colonies in their struggle for independence, might have led Mr. Seward to select for such base uses some other place than that which bore the honored name of Lafayette.

The American citizen has always, like the ancient Roman, felt that his personal liberty was secure. He supposed himself to be surrounded with numerous paper safeguards, which, together with the love of justice and respect for law, common to his fellow-citizens, would be sufficient for his protection against any usurper. These now proved to be as weak as the paper upon which they were written. What were these supposed safeguards? There was the Constitution of the State of New York, an instrument for the protection and government of the people. It had received the consent of the people of the State who were governed by it, and therefore its powers were "just powers." Its first object was to protect the unalienable rights of its citizens, relative to which it contains various provisions in its Bill of Rights: its declarations respecting personal liberty; its regulations to secure and enforce the great writ of freemen, the *habeas corpus*; the powers granted to the courts which it created; the Legislature; the Executive, in whose hands was placed the richest purse and the strongest sword of the sovereign States to protect the rights of its citizens.

Further safeguards were placed in the Constitution of the United States. These were designed to restrain that Government from any invasion of the citizen's personal liberty. They are as follows:

> "The right of the people to be secure in their persons . . . shall not be violated, and no warrant shall issue but upon probable cause, supported by oath, or affirmation, and particularly describing . . . the persons to be seized."[1377]

Again:

> "No person shall . . . be deprived of life, liberty, or property, without due process of law."[1378]

Again:

> "No person shall be held to answer for a capital or otherwise infamous crime, unless on a presentment or indictment of a grand jury."[1379]

Again:

"In all criminal prosecutions the accused shall enjoy the right to a speedy and public trial, by an impartial jury of the State and district wherein the crime shall have been committed, and to be informed of the nature and cause of the accusation; to be confronted with the witnesses against him; to have compulsory process for obtaining witnesses in his favor, and to have the assistance of counsel for his defense."[1380]

Among the enumerated powers of Congress is the following clause:

"The privilege of the writ of *habeas corpus* shall not be suspended, unless when in cases of rebellion or invasion the public safety may require."[1381]

This clause first forbids the suspension of the writ absolutely. A single exception is then made by the words "unless the public safety may require." A condition is attached to this exception which still further limits it, by the words "in cases of rebellion or invasion." There is still another and far more sweeping limitation attached to this clause. The writ must be suspended by an act of Congress, which can be passed only when Congress is in session. This suspension must be positive and absolute by Congress, not indefinite and dependent on any future contingency. For the acts of Congress are not absolute powers, if between enactment and enforcement they can be set aside by a contingency, unless such contingency was attached in the clause of the grant creating the power. But in these words of the Constitution there is no contingency expressed. Congress alone by positive enactment can suspend the writ of *habeas corpus*. It can not authorize the President to suspend its force, nor has he any authority under the Constitution to do it. Neither can Congress make an intermittent suspension of the force of the writ; but it must be absolute under the specific condition.

It is evident that the citizen of New York was abundantly provided with the safeguards of personal liberty; yet they all proved to be of no avail to secure and enforce his right in the hour of trial. A few instances will afford an illustration of the facts. Mr. Pierce Butler was suspected of corresponding with persons in the Confederate States. He was arrested in Philadelphia on August 19, 1861, by order of Simon Cameron, then Secretary of War, without process of law and without any assigned cause. His trunks and drawers, wardrobe, and entire apartments were searched, and his private papers taken by the marshal and his four assistants. His office was also examined, and his books and papers taken, and within an hour he was on his way to Fort Lafayette with an armed guard. After five weeks of detention he was liberated. No reason was given for his discharge any more than for his arrest. As Mr. Cameron was about to sail as Minister to Russia, in January ensuing, he was arrested for assault and battery and false imprisonment, at the suit of Mr. Butler. The case was brought to the knowledge of the President of the United States, and on April 18, 1862, the Secretary of State, Seward, replied as follows:

> "The communication has been submitted to the President, and I am directed by him to say in reply that he avows the proceeding of Mr. Cameron referred to as one taken by him when Secretary of War, under the President's directions, and deemed necessary for the prompt suppression of the existing rebellion."

The writ of *habeas corpus* was issued by some of the State courts, directing the officer in command at the fort to bring some one or other of the prisoners into court for an investigation of the cause and authority for his detention. But no attention was given to these writs by the officer. Neither did the Governor of the State make any effort to enforce the processes of the courts. He, perhaps, expected that his efforts might be resisted by an overpowering force. But expectations, of whatsoever nature, do not justify or excuse the neglect of a positive duty. It is through such weaknesses that the liberties of mankind have been too often lost.

Thus the Constitution, the laws, the courts, the Executive of the State of New York, were subverted, turned aside from the end for which they were instituted, and all the specific arrangements were of no avail to secure this guaranteed right of its citizens. Probably every one of the prisoners was entirely innocent of any act whatever that was criminal under the laws, either of the State or of the United States.

In opinion they were opposed to the military proceedings of the Government of the United States; and these opinions they had expressed, which liberty is a part of the birthright of freemen. Indeed, Judge [Samuel] Nelson, of the Supreme Court of the United States, in the Circuit of New York, in an opinion delivered about this time, thus expressed himself:

"Words, oral, written, or printed, however treasonable, seditious, or criminal of themselves, do not constitute an overt act of treason within the definition of the crime. When spoken, written, or printed, in relation to an act or acts which, if committed with a treasonable design, might constitute such overt act, they are admissible as evidence, tending to characterize it and show the intent with which the act was committed."

Finally, the prison in New York Harbor became so full that many prisoners were sent to Fort Warren in the harbor of Boston. At this time the Government of the United States used the Old Capitol at Washington, Fort McHenry of Baltimore, Fort Lafayette at New York, and Fort Warren at Boston, for the confinement of those whom the usurper designated as "state prisoners." Still further to relieve the fullness of the prisons, two men, John A. Dix, of the army, and Edwards Pierrepont, of civil life, were sent to investigate the cases of the prisoners, and release some who were willing to take an "oath of allegiance." Next it was made a condition precedent to an investigation that the said oath should be taken by the prisoner. As an instance, this proposal was made to two persons named Flanders, citizens of the interior of New York. The oath was as follows:

"I do solemnly swear that I will support, protect, and defend the Constitution and Government of the United States against all enemies, whether domestic or foreign, and that I will bear true faith, allegiance, and loyalty to the same, any ordinance, resolution, or law of any State Convention, or Legislature, to the contrary notwithstanding; and, further, that I do this with a full determination, pledge, and purpose, without any mental reservation or evasion whatsoever; and, further, that I will well and faithfully perform all the duties which may be required of me by law."

These persons declined to take the prescribed oath. The reasons which they gave for this refusal furnish painful evidence of the extreme subjugation of the government of the State of New York, and its silent submission to the arbitrary and unconstitutional acts of the Government of the United States, even at the sacrifice of the most sacred rights of freemen. They said:

> "We have been guilty of no offense against the laws of our country, but have simply exercised our constitutional rights as free citizens in the open and manly expression of our opinions upon public affairs. We have been placed here without legal charges, or, indeed, any charges whatsoever being made against us, and upon no legal process, but upon an arbitrary and illegal order of the Hon. William H. Seward, Secretary of State of the United States. Every moment of our detention here is a denial of our most sacred rights. We are entitled to and hereby demand an unconditional discharge; and, while we could cheerfully take the oath prescribed by the Constitution of the United States, because we are, always have been, and ever intend to be loyal to that instrument (though at the same time protesting against the right of the Government to impose even such oath upon us as the condition of our discharge), we can not consent to take the oath now required of us, because we hold no office of any kind under the Government of the United States, and it is an oath unknown to and unauthorized by the Constitution, and commits us to the support of the Government though it may be acting in direct conflict with the Constitution, and deprives us of the right of freely discussing, and by peaceful and constitutional methods opposing its measures—a right which is sacred to freedom, and which no American citizen should voluntarily surrender. That such is the interpretation put upon this oath by the Government, and such its intended effect is plainly demonstrated by the fact that it is dictated to us as a condition of our release from an imprisonment inflicted upon us for no other cause than that we have exercised the above-specified constitutional rights."

One important fact which illustrates the flagrant outrage

committed on all these prisoners should not be omitted. The Constitution of the United States declares as follows:

> "In all criminal prosecutions, the accused shall enjoy the right . . . to have the assistance of counsel for his defense."

On December 3, 1861, the commanding officer at Fort Lafayette came to the prisoners' quarters, and read a document, of which the following is a copy:

> *"To the political prisoners in Fort Lafayette:*
> "I am instructed by the Secretary of State to inform you that the Department of State of the United States will not recognize any one as an attorney for political prisoners, and will look with distrust upon all applications for release through such channels; and that such applications will be regarded as additional reasons for declining to release the prisoners.
> "And, further, that if such prisoners wish to make any communication to the Government, they are at liberty to make it directly to the State Department. Seth C. Hawley."

Space will not permit me further to notice the instances of this immense class of cases. In almost every Northern State the victims of this violence were to be found. That there was no just cause for these invasions of the rights of the States, and of the citizens, was demonstrated in the most decisive manner. At this time (November 4, 1862) the friends of the Administration of the United States Government were decisively defeated at the elections. On November 22d ensuing, the War Department issued an order releasing all except prisoners of war. The order was muffled up in a phraseology suited to hide from the observation of the people that the result of the elections had stricken home to the sensibilities of the usurpers. It said:

> "Ordered—1. That all persons now in military custody, who have been arrested for discouraging volunteer enlistments, opposing the draft,[1382] or for otherwise giving aid and comfort to the enemy, in States where the

draft has been made or the quota of volunteers and militia has been furnished, shall be discharged from further military restraint."

Thus these arrests were for a short period suspended, and then vigorously renewed.

Many of these persons who had been illegally seized and imprisoned now commenced suits for damages. This led to another step on the part of the Government of the United States, by which the judiciary of the State was entirely subverted and deprived of all jurisdiction in these cases. Congress passed an act on March 3, 1863, which provided that any order of the President of the United States, or arrest made under his authority, when pleaded, should be a defense, in all courts, to any action or prosecution for any search, seizure, arrest, or imprisonment made, done, or committed, or any acts omitted to be done, under or by virtue of such order, or under color of any law of Congress. The act further provided that all actions against officers and others for torts in arrests might be removed for trial to the next Circuit Court of the United States held in the district, and said:

> "It shall then be the duty of the State court to accept the surety and proceed no further in the cause or prosecution, and the bail that shall have been originally taken shall be discharged."

It will be noticed that by the terms of this act the case could be removed to the Circuit Court when the defendant "filed a petition stating the facts verified by affidavit." Thus the jurisdiction of all the courts of the State of New York was made to terminate and cease upon the simple word of the defendant accompanied by an affidavit. But these courts were instituted by the consent of the governed, for the protection of the personal freedom of the citizen; yet in the cases brought before them they ordered the removal on the ground that they involved the question of the constitutionality of an act of Congress, over which the courts of the United States had a jurisdiction. The absurdity of this plea is manifest; for it is founded on the presumption that the question, whether, under authority from the President of the United States, any one, without intervention of the judicial tribunals, can incarcerate a citizen, is a question which can be treated as constituting a case arising under the Constitution of the United States. Any statute authorizing such acts is palpably void, and not entitled to be a ground for a hearing under an appeal.

The subjugation of the government of the State of New

York was made in another section of the same act of Congress of March 3, 1863. It declares:

> "That, during the present rebellion, the President of the United States, whenever in his judgment the public safety may require it, is authorized to suspend the privilege of the writ of *habeas corpus* in any case throughout the United States, or any part thereof."

Let us turn to the words of the Constitution of the United States which are contained in the grant of powers to Congress:

> "The privilege of the writ of *habeas corpus* shall not be suspended, unless when in cases of rebellion or invasion the public safety may require it."

It will be seen that two facts are required to exist before the Congress of the United States can suspend the privilege of this writ. Congress must, therefore, determine the existence of these facts before it has power constitutionally to act. If it finds either fact to exist and not the other, it has no power to suspend the privilege of the writ. There must be rebellion, and the public safety must require the suspension. When Congress finds these facts to exist, it can enact the suspension. It is the judgment of Congress alone that can determine that the public safety requires the suspension. This can not be delegated to the judgment of any other department of the Government. Therefore, when Congress tells the President, in the abovementioned act, that he is authorized to suspend the privilege of this writ whenever, in his judgment, the public safety may require it, then that body undertakes to do that for which it has no authority in the Constitution. The States delegated the power solely to Congress; an act to transfer the trust to any other depository could rightfully have no force whatever.

Now, the State of New York, in which this writ was thus suspended by the Government of the United States, was one of the Northern States and a most ardent advocate of the Union. It had contributed more men and money to support the Government of the United States than any other State, and than some whole sections of States. Peace reigned throughout all its borders. Yet, in this quiet and "loyal" State, whose people had given so freely to aid the Government of the United States, a claim was now set up to the right to nullify the rights and immunities of every citizen, by that Government which had already nullified the powers of every court in the State. This was done by the declaration of the President that "the public safety" required the suspension of the privilege of the writ of *habeas corpus*.

The act of Congress was passed on March 3, 1863, and on September 15th the President [Lincoln] issued his proclamation, and, referring to the authority claimed to have been granted by the act, he proceeded to say:

> "Whereas, In the judgment of the President, the public safety does require that the privilege of said writ shall now be suspended throughout the United States, in cases where, by the authority of the President of the United States, military, naval, and civil officers of the United States, or either of them, hold persons under their custody, either as prisoners of war, spies, or aiders or abettors of the enemy, or officers, soldiers, or seamen, enrolled, drafted, or mustered, or enlisted in, or belonging to, the land or naval forces of the United States, or as deserters therefrom, or otherwise amenable to military law, or to the rules or articles of war, or the rules and regulations prescribed for military and naval service by the authority of the President of the United States, or for resisting a draft, or for any other offense against the military or naval service: Therefore I do hereby proclaim and make known that the privilege of the writ of *habeas corpus* is suspended throughout the United States in the several cases before mentioned throughout the duration of said rebellion."[1383]

No autocrat ever issued an edict more destructive of the natural right to personal liberty. Not only was the State government of New York deprived of the power to fulfill its obligations to protect and preserve this right of its citizens, but every State government of the Northern States was in like manner subverted. The only distinction known among the citizens was that established by the Government of the United States in answer to the question applied to each one, "Is he loyal or disloyal?" The only test of loyalty was based on submission, and, as usual in such cases, the most abject in spirit were the most loyal to the usurper. All those liberties of conduct and action which stamp the true freeman everywhere throughout the world disappeared; and the suppressed voice, the apprehensive look, and the cautious movements were substituted for the free speech, the open brow, and fearless tread which had characterized the American.

Another step in the subjugation of the government of the State of New York was made by the domination over it of the military power of the Government of the United States. This took place in a time of peace in the State, when the courts were all open and the civil administration of affairs was unobstructed. On July 30, 1863, the United States commanding General of that department addressed a letter to Governor [Horatio] Seymour, saying:

> "As the draft under the act of Congress of March 3, 1863, for enrolling and calling out the national forces, will probably be resumed in this city (New York) at an early day, I am desirous of knowing whether the military power of the State may be relied on to enforce the execution of the law, in case of forcible resistance to it. I am very anxious there should be perfect harmony of action between the Federal Government and that of the State of New York; and if, under your authority to see the laws faithfully executed, I can feel assured that the act referred to will be enforced, I need not ask the War Department to put at my disposal, for the purpose, troops in the service of the United States."

Governor Seymour replied on August 3d:

> "I have this day sent to the President of the United States a communication in relation to the draft in this State. I believe his answer will relieve you and me from the painful questions growing out of an armed enforcement of the conscription law in this patriotic State, which has contributed so largely and freely to the

support of the national cause during the existing war."

On August 8th General Dix writes again:

"It is my duty, as commanding officer of the troops in the service of the United States in this department, if called on by the enrolling officers, to aid them in resisting forcible opposition to the execution of the law; and it is from an earnest desire to avoid the necessity of employing for the purpose any of my forces, which have been placed here to garrison the forts and protect the public property, that I wished to see the draft enforced by the military power of the State, in case of armed or organized resistance to it. . . . I designed, if your cooperation could not be relied on, to ask the General Government for a force which should be adequate to insure the execution of the law and to meet any emergency growing out of it."

Meantime Governor Seymour received no answer to his letter to the President. He had asked for a suspension of the draft, on the ground that the enrollments in the city were excessive as compared with other portions of the State, and that due credit was not given for the past. He therefore replied to General Dix, saying:

"As you state in your letter that it is your duty to enforce the act of Congress, and, as you apprehend its provisions may excite popular resistance, it is proposed you should know the position which will be held by the State authorities. Of course, under no circumstances, can they perform duties expressly confided to others, nor can they undertake to relieve others from their proper responsibilities. But there can be no violations of good order, or riotous proceedings, no disturbances of the public peace, which are not infractions of the laws of the State; and those laws will be enforced under all circumstances. I shall take care that all the executive officers of this State perform their duties vigorously and thoroughly, and, if need be, the military power will be called into requisition. As you are an officer of the General Government, and not of the State, it does not become me to make suggestions to you with regard to your action under a law of Congress. You will, of course, be governed by your instructions and your own views of duty."

On August 18th General Dix thus wrote to the Governor:

"Not having received an answer from you, I applied to the Secretary of War on the 14th inst. for a force adequate to the object. The call was promptly responded to, and I shall be ready to meet all opposition to the draft."

The force sent by the Secretary of War, to keep the peace and subjugate the sovereignty of the people, amounted to forty-two regiments and two batteries. There was no occasion for the exertion of their powers, but the wrong to the State of New York was none the less gross.

Again, the subjugation of the government of the State of New York by the domination of the military power was made still more manifest by another act on the part of the Government of the United States. A spurious proclamation, seeming to have been issued by the President [Lincoln], calling for four hundred thousand men, by a fraudulent imposition appeared in two papers of New York City (the "Journal of Commerce" and the "World") on the morning of May 18, 1864. It was immediately contradicted by the authorities at Washington, and orders were issued, under which the offices of these papers were entered by armed men, the property of the owners seized, the premises held by force for several days, and the publications suspended. At the same time the office of the independent telegraph line was occupied by a military force in the name of the Government of the United States. The operators were taken into custody, and the proprietors of the newspapers were ordered to be arrested and imprisoned. But these orders were suspended.

Governor Seymour immediately instructed the District Attorney to proceed against the offenders, saying:

"In the month of July last, when New York was a scene of violence, I gave warning that 'the laws of the State must be enforced, its peace and order maintained, and the property of its citizens protected at every hazard.' The laws were enforced at a fearful cost of blood and life. The declaration I then made was not intended merely for that occasion, or against any class of men. It is one of an enduring character, to be asserted at all times, and against all conditions of citizens without favor or distinction. Unless all are made to bow to the law, it will be respected by none. Unless all are made secure in their rights of person and property, none can be protected."

An investigation was made by one of the city judges, and warrants were issued for the arrest of Major-General Dix and several of his officers. They voluntarily appeared by counsel on July 6th, and the argument was set down for the 9th. On that day the counsel for the defense said:

"Since this warrant was issued, the President of the United States has issued another order to General Dix, which directs him that, while this civil war lasts, he 'must not relieve himself from his command, or be deprived of his liberty to obey any order of a military nature which the President of the United States directs him to execute.'"

The result of the arguments was that the officers were held to await the action of the grand jury, who, however, took no action on the charges. The guilty person was arrested in two or three days after the appearance of the proclamation, and imprisoned in Fort Lafayette; the newspaper and telegraph offices were restored to the owners, and the publications resumed. But the government of New York never obtained any indemnification of these losses by its citizens.

Another subversion of the State government was brought about by the military interference on the part of the Government of the United States with the State election. This was in 1864, when President Lincoln and General [George B.] McClellan were the candidates for the Presidency of the United States. As usual, in all these cases, proceedings to work up a pretended necessity for interference on the part of the United States Government were commenced by the appearance of a grandiloquent proclamation from the commanding General, Dix, telling what horrible designs, there was reason to believe, the agents of the Confederate States in Canada had prepared to be executed on election-day, by an invasion of voters from Canada to colonize different points. Therefore, to avert these dreadful dangers and arrest the guilty parties, it was necessary that provost-marshals, sustained by a military force, should be present with authority at the polls. At the same time the State Department issued a dispatch, saying:

> "Information has been received from the British provinces to the effect that there is a conspiracy on foot to set fire to the principal cities in the Northern States on the day of the Presidential election."

Thus was created an apparent necessity for the military force to be very active on the day of election. Governor Seymour issued a proclamation, saying:

> "There is no reason to doubt that the coming election will be conducted with the usual quiet and order."

Major-General [Benjamin F.] Butler was sent to take command in the city, and seven thousand additional men were placed in the forts of the harbor, and proclamations were issued, threatening, by the United States Government, the severest punishment upon every person who might attempt improperly to vote at the election in the State of New York.

The State Legislature, at its previous session, had passed an act to provide for the vote of the soldiers in the field, to be taken previous to the day of election. Agents were appointed by the State government, to the localities where the soldiers were stationed, to receive the votes. The informers of the United States Government immediately brought charges of fraud against some of these agents, and they were seized by the military authorities, sent to Washington, cast into prison, and held to be tried by a military commission. The Governor of New York immediately appointed Amasa J. Parker and two other most respectable citizens as commissioners, to proceed to Washington in behalf of the State and investigate the difficulties. They informed the Governor that several hundred ballots, which had been seized, were given up, and that they visited the principal agent of the State of New York in his prison, through the permission of Edwin M. Stanton, Secretary of War. They reported thus:

"The undersigned availed themselves of the permit granted them to visit Colonel North, M. M. Jones, and Levi Cohn. They found them in the 'Carroll Prison,' in close confinement. They then learned that Messrs. North and Cohn had been confined together in one room, and had not been permitted to leave it for a moment during the four days they had been prisoners, even for the purposes of answering the calls of nature. They had been supplied with meager and coarse prison-rations, to be eaten in their room, where they constantly breathed the foul atmosphere arising from the standing odor. They had no vessel out of which to drink water, except the one furnished them for the purpose of urination. They had but one chair, and had slept three of the nights of their confinement upon a sack of straw upon the floor. They had not been permitted to see a newspaper, and were ignorant of the cause of their arrest. All communication between them and the outer world had been denied them, and no friend had been allowed to see them. The undersigned complained to the acting superintendent, who seemed humanely disposed, but justified his course by the prison rules and the instructions of his superiors."

The commissioners further say:

"From the best investigation the undersigned have been able to make, though there may have been irregularities, they have found no evidence that any frauds, either against any elector or the elective franchise, have been committed by any person connected with the New York agency."

The commissioners then addressed a communication to the Secretary of War. A few extracts from this communication will show how utter was the subversion of the authority of the government of the State of New York. They say:

"They, North, Cohn, and Jones, were not in

the military or naval service of the United States, and by no law of which we are aware were they subject to the martial and military laws of the United States, or to the orders of the War Department. . . . The charges, so far as we can learn, are not for the violation of any law of the United States, but relate to acts purporting to have been done under the law of the State of New York concerning elections, and making provisions for soldiers voting in that State; it being claimed that certain irregularities have intervened which give reason to suspect that frauds and forgeries are intended, and may be consummated. These suspected and anticipated frauds have respect solely to the election laws of the State of New York, and the action of the Government in making the arrest is claimed to be justified upon the ground that, unless thus prevented, frauds will be perpetrated against the ballot-box at the approaching election in the State of New York. We beg leave, in behalf of the State, respectfully to protest against this jurisdiction, assumed as well over the alleged offense as over the persons of the accused, who are citizens of the State, in its employ, and entitled to its protection. The proper business of the State agency is greatly interfered with by the arrest and detention of the agents, and the State is deprived of its proper jurisdiction over its agents and citizens, over offenses against its laws, and over its own ballot-box and the exercise of the elective franchise within its limits."

The demands made by the State of New York through these commissioners were refused. The persons arrested were finally tried before a military commission, clearly without jurisdiction, in violation of their personal rights, and in usurpation of the just powers of the State. They were, however, acquitted and discharged, glad to get off no worse.

The proposed limits will not permit me further to present the details relative to the subjugation of the State government of New York by the Government of the United States. Neither can space be spared to relate the details of the subjugation of the government of each Northern State. In many the events were similar to those in New York; in others they arose under dissimilar circumstances; but, in all, the sovereignty of the people was entirely disregarded, and the operation of the institutions which had been established for the protection of their rights was suspended, or nullified, by a military force of the Government of the United States. Only such events, therefore, can be stated as serve to show how universal and how complete was the work done by the United States Government to secure a recognition of its supremacy, over not only acts but even words, from every citizen. All were its subjects; the "loyal," as some were called, were its friends, and could be trusted; the "disloyal" were its disaffected subjects, and must be watched by spies and informers, and, if necessary, put in prison to secure their passive submission.

A military domination was established in all of the Northern States, under the pretext of securing the arrest of deserters from the army. This was accomplished on September 24, 1862, by the appointment of a Provost-Marshal-General of the War Department at Washington, and in each State one or more special provost-marshals, who were required to report to and receive instructions from the Provost-Marshal-General. It was made the duty of the special marshals—

> "To arrest all deserters, whether regulars, volunteers, or militia, and send them to the nearest military commander or military post, where they can be cared for and sent to their respective regiments; to arrest, upon the warrant of the Judge Advocate, all disloyal persons subject to arrest under the orders of the War Department; to inquire into and report treasonable practices, seize stolen or embezzled property of the Government, detect spies of the enemy, and perform such other duties as may be enjoined on them by the War Department."

To enable these marshals to perform their duties efficiently, they were authorized to call on any available military force within their respective districts, or else to employ the assistance of citizens, constables, sheriffs, or police officers, so far as might be necessary. No trial was allowed to any person thus arrested except before a military commission consisting of military officers designated for the purpose; the prosecutor was the Judge Advocate, and the punishments were exemplary, unusual, and too often such as were unknown to the laws. The State governments within whose domains the courts were open, the civil institutions in quiet operation, and the transactions of peaceful life uniform and constant, were powerless to protect their citizens in their unalienable rights of freedom of speech and personal liberty, and the mandates of their courts were treated with contempt. In utter disregard of the principles of civil liberty, a military control was established in every Northern State, the declarations of rights in their Constitutions were violated, their laws nullified, and the authority of their governments subverted by an absolute and direct usurpation on the part of the Government of the United States.[1384]

Of Lincoln's usurious behavior toward his own people, Richmond's newspaper, *The Southern Illustrated News*, wrote that Lincoln would not permit any opposition toward himself or his War. Those who engaged in such anti-Union activity were considered traitors and thrown in prison. The original U.S. Constitution, the editor noted, had been trampled into the mud, with the United States herself becoming a "military despotism" as restrictive, oppressive, and aggressively authoritarian as anything ever seen, even in Russia.[1385]

Lincoln admitted, in so many words, that his **"measures"** were unlawful; but then defended them in his typically obscure way, as he did July 4, 1861, in a message to Congress:

> **These measures, whether strictly legal or not, were ventured upon, under what appeared to be a popular demand and a public necessity; trusting then, as now, that Congress would readily ratify them.**[1386]

There was no **"popular demand"** or **"public necessity,"** of course, for the president to break the law and void the Constitution. These were **"demands"** and **"necessities"** he fabricated, then placed upon himself. And Congress had no choice but to ratify them, for as Lincoln had repeatedly demonstrated, those who stood in his way would be swiftly arrested and imprisoned—or worse.[1387]

Naturally, part of the financial burden for Lincoln's War fell on the backs of the long-suffering Northern people. Toiling under Lincoln's increased tariffs and taxes, and a new personal income tax (the first),[1388] Northerners saw prices increase nearly 120 percent between 1860 and 1865. Meanwhile, during the same period, money wages only increased 50 percent, while the real wages of Northern workers actually declined a staggering 30 percent. It was not until 1878, thirteen years after Lincoln's death, that the economy began to return to normal.[1389]

As his first term progressed, crime boss Lincoln showed an almost unlimited capacity for committing outrages against the American people and their Constitution. The criminal-minded president, who William H. Herndon (Lincoln's law partner and biographer) once described as a man who "cared little for simple facts, rules and methods,"[1390] went on to invade sitting courts, disrupt their proceedings, and threaten, intimidate, and even arrest judges.[1391] He also aggressively recruited thousands of foreigners into the U.S. army (of questionable legality);[1392] deported Northern politicians, such as Ohio Congressman Vallandigham, for advocating peace;[1393] and, as Davis mentioned, curbed the press, closing down over 300 Northern newspapers for printing antiwar articles.[1394] Under Lincoln's direct orders, some printing presses were actually confiscated or destroyed and the papers' editors were jailed.[1395]

The following is a partial list of the hundreds of papers Lincoln suppressed and shut down:

The *Chicago Daily Times* (Illinois)
The *Christian Observer* (Pennsylvania)
The *Day-Book* (New York)
The *Democrat* (New Hampshire)
The *Farmer* (Maine)
The *Freeman's Journal* (New York)
The *Herald* (Missouri)
The *Journal* (Missouri)
The *Journal of Commerce* (New York)
The *Missourian* (Missouri)
The *Morning News* (New York)
The *New York World* (New York)
The *Philadelphia Evening Journal* (Pennsylvania)
The *Republican Watchman* (Pennsylvania)
The *Sentinel* (Connecticut)[1396]

As always, the owners of these newspapers were imprisoned without legal representation or trial, a gross violation of both constitutional law and American civil rights.

For those who doubt the validity of this charge, let us examine Lincoln's own words. No better evidence can be found than in a May 18,

1864, letter Lincoln wrote to Union General John A. Dix:

> Whereas there has been wickedly and traitorously printed and published this morning in the New York "World" and New York "Journal of Commerce," newspapers printed and published in the city of New York, a false and spurious proclamation, purporting to be signed by the President and to be countersigned by the Secretary of State, which publication is of a treasonable nature designed to give aid and comfort to the enemies of the United States and to the rebels now at war against the government, and their aiders and abettors: you are therefore hereby commanded forthwith to arrest and imprison, in any fort or military prison in your command, the editors, proprietors, and publishers of the aforesaid newspapers, and all such persons as, after public notice has been given of the falsehood of said publication, print and publish the same with intent to give aid and comfort to the enemy; and you will hold the persons so arrested in close custody until they can be brought to trial before a military commission for their offense. You will also take possession, by military force, of the printing establishments of the New York "World" and "Journal of Commerce," and hold the same until further orders, and prevent any further publication therefrom.[1397]

That Lincoln's actions were a flagrant infringement of the First Amendment's guarantee of "freedom of speech, or of the press,"[1398] and of the Fourth Amendment's guarantee against "unreasonable searches and seizures,"[1399] never troubled him. Indeed, he continued to heartily commend those in the Union who stood by the North's **"free government and the rights of humanity"**![1400] Strangely, to this day such outright lies and unconstitutional misdeeds do not seem to trouble his devotees either.

Not even Lincoln's own relations were safe from his dictatorial reach. On August 8, 1864, he sent the following letter to Union General Stephen Gano Burbridge:

> Last December Mrs. Emily T. Helm, half-sister of Mrs. Lincoln, and widow of the rebel general, Ben Hardin Helm, stopped here on her way from Georgia to Kentucky, and I gave her a paper, as I remember, to protect her against the mere fact of her being General

Helm's widow. I hear a rumor to-day that you recently sought to arrest her, but were prevented by her presenting the paper from me. I do not intend to protect her against the consequences of disloyal words or acts, spoken or done by her since her return to Kentucky, and if the paper given her by me can be construed to give her protection for such words or acts, it is hereby revoked *pro tanto* [i.e., only to that extent]. **Deal with her for current conduct just as you would with any other. A. Lincoln.**[1401]

It bears repeating that every one of the victims of these particular crimes, those he illegally harassed, arrested, and jailed, were Northerners or citizens of Southern states remaining in the Union, Lincoln's own constituents; and all this against the advice and counsel of many of his top administrators, well respected Yankees like Salmon P. Chase, David Davis, and Stephen J. Field. We can hardly be surprised then at how Lincoln treated Southerners during this same period.

Here, for example, is how he typically handled the heartbreaking suffering of the Southern people. The letter is addressed to Yankee General Edward R. S. Canby and is dated September 21, 1864:

> **General Baily** [Joseph Bailey] **of Rapides Parish, Louisiana, is vouched to me as entirely trustworthy, and appeals to me in behalf of the people in his region, who he says are mostly Union people, and are in great destitution—almost absolute starvation.** He says their condition is greatly aggravated by [Union] General [Nathaniel P.] **Banks's expedition up Red River, last spring, in reliance upon which they mostly took the oath of allegiance.**
>
> Of course what General Baily asks is permission to carry provisions to them.
>
> This I will not give without your consent, but I will thank you to hear and consider their case, and do for them the best you can, consistently with the interests of the public service. Yours truly, A. Lincoln.[1402]

Lincoln's cavalier attitude is all the more repulsive when we consider that it was he himself, along with his illegally invading officers, who were directly responsible for driving the citizens of Louisiana into **"destitution"** and **"absolute starvation."**

The case of Clement Laird Vallandigham, in particular, reveals the depth of Lincoln's malevolence and madness, as well as the lengths he was willing to go in order to silence his critics. What was it that the Ohio politician, head of the peace party and the Order of the Sons of Liberty, said that upset Lincoln so greatly?

The following excerpt from a speech given by Vallandigham on July 10, 1861, in the U.S. House of Representatives, provides the answer. In particular the Northern Congressman targeted President Lincoln's "usurpations and infractions" regarding the Constitution and the War:

> Sir, however much necessity—the tyrant's plea—may be urged in extenuation of the usurpations and infractions of the President in regard to public liberty, there can be no such apology or defence for his invasions of private right. What overruling necessity required the violation of the sanctity of private property and private confidence? What great public danger demanded the arrest and imprisonment, without trial by common law, of one single private citizen, for an act done weeks before, openly, and by authority of his State? If guilty of treason, was not the judicial power ample enough and strong enough for his conviction and punishment? What, then, was needed in his case, but the precedent under which other men, in other places, might become the victims of executive suspicion and displeasure?
>
> As to the pretence, sir, that the President has the Constitutional right to suspend the writ of *habeas corpus*, I will not waste time in arguing it. The case is as plain as words can make it. It is a legislative power; it is found only in the legislative article; it belongs to Congress only to do it. Subordinate officers have disobeyed it: General [James] Wilkinson disobeyed it, but he sent his prisoners on for judicial trial; General [Andrew] Jackson disobeyed it, and was reprimanded by James Madison; but no President, nobody but Congress, ever before assumed the right to suspend it. And, sir, that other pretence of necessity, I repeat, cannot be allowed. It had no existence in fact. The Constitution cannot be preserved by violating it. It is an offence to the intelligence of this House, and of the country, to pretend that all this, and the other gross and multiplied infractions of the Constitution and usurpations of power were done by the President and his advisers out of pure love and devotion to the Constitution. But if so, sir, then they have but one step further to take, and declare, in the language of Sir Boyle Roche, in the Irish House of Commons, that such is the depth of their attachment to it, that they are prepared to give up, not merely a part, but the whole of the Constitution, *to preserve the remainder*. And yet, if indeed this

pretext of necessity be well founded, then let me say, that a cause which demands the sacrifice of the Constitution and of the dearest securities of property, liberty, and life, cannot be just; certainly it is not worth the sacrifice.

Sir, I am obliged to pass by, for want of time, other grave and dangerous infractions and usurpations of the President since the 4th of March. I only allude casually to the quartering of soldiers in private houses without the consent of the owners, and without any manner having been prescribed by law; to the subversion in a part, at least, of Maryland of her own State Government and of the authorities under it; to the censorship over the telegraph, and the infringement, repeatedly, in one or more of the States, of the right of the people to keep and to bear arms for their defence. But if all these things, I ask, have been done in the first two months after the commencement of this war, and by men not military chieftains, and unused to arbitrary power, what may we not expect to see in three years, and by the successful heroes of the fight? Sir, the power and rights of the States and the people, and of their Representatives, have been usurped; the sanctity of the private house and of private property has been invaded; and the liberty of the person wantonly and wickedly stricken down; free speech, too, has been repeatedly denied; and all this under the plea of necessity. Sir, the right of petition will follow next—nay, it has already been shaken; the freedom of the press will soon fall after it; and let me whisper in your ear, that there will be few to mourn over its loss, unless, indeed, its ancient high and honorable character shall be rescued and redeemed from its present reckless mendacity and degradation. Freedom of religion will yield too, at last, amid the exultant shouts of millions, who have seen its holy temples defiled, and its white robes of a former innocency trampled now under the polluting hoofs of an ambitious and faithless or fanatical clergy. Meantime national banks, bankrupt laws, a vast and permanent public debt, high tariffs, heavy direct taxation, enormous expenditure, gigantic and stupendous peculation, anarchy first, and a strong government afterwards—no more State lines, no more State governments, but a consolidated monarchy or vast centralized military despotism must all follow in the history of the future, as in the history of the past they have, centuries ago, been written. Sir, I have said nothing, and have time to say nothing now, of the immense indebtedness and the vast expenditures which have already accrued, nor of the folly and mismanagement of the war so far, nor of the atrocious and shameless peculations and frauds which have disgraced it in the State governments and the Federal Government from the beginning. The avenging hour for all these will come hereafter . . .[1403]

It was for publicly stating such sentiments that Lincoln had Vallandigham, a Northerner, arrested in the early morning hours by nearly seventy armed Yankee soldiers and tossed into a military prison. He was convicted and tried (without legal representation) by a military court comprised of a panel of eight army officers,[1404] then exiled out of the country.[1405] Here is Lincoln's May 19, 1863, order to General Ambrose Everett Burnside as it came through General Edward R. S. Canby:

> Commanding Department of the Ohio, Cincinnati, Ohio: Sir: The President directs that without delay you send C. L. Vallandigham under secure guard to the headquarters of [Union] General [William Starke] Rosecrans, to be put by him beyond our military lines; and in case of his return within our lines, he be arrested and kept in close custody for the term specified in his sentence. By order of the President: Ed. R. S. Canby, Brigadier-General.[1406]

As usual, all of this was unconstitutional, illegal, and unnecessary, and many of his cabinet members knew it, as even Lincoln himself later acknowledged.[1407] But he had no compunctions about such acts, as long as he was reelected and won his War.[1408] As he said defensively in a June 12, 1863, letter to New Yorker Erastus Corning:

> [Vallandigham] **was not arrested because he was damaging the political prospects of the administration or the personal interests of the commanding general, but because he was damaging the army, upon the existence and vigor of which the life of the nation depends. He was warring upon the military, and this gave the military constitutional jurisdiction to lay hands upon him.** [1409]

Contrary to Lincoln's statement, it is obvious that Vallandigham was not **"warring upon the military."** He was warring upon Lincoln himself, jeopardizing his chances of reelection and winning his illegal war on the South. This is the *real* reason the president had Vallandigham arrested and deported.

Had he listened to the Ohio attorney instead of throwing him out of the country, the disaster that became the "Civil War," the War for Southern Independence, could have been avoided, or at least shortened, and thousands of lives spared.

Vallandigham had summed up the essential belief of lovers of liberty everywhere, South and North: "The Constitution as it is, the Union as it was."[1410] This statement, the height of rationality, was in full accordance with Jeffersonianism (powerful sovereign states, weak central government), and Southerners admired Vallandigham for expressing it. Sadly for America, rationality was not among the attributes possessed by Lincoln, one of the most virulent anti-Jeffersonian liberals to have ever graced the halls of the U.S. government.

By such tactics as the military subjugation of Northern states and the arrest and deportation of Northern citizens who disagreed with him, America's sixteenth president virtually assured himself a win in the 1864 election, for not only could he now count on 180,000 extra votes from the free and freed blacks he had grudgingly allowed to enlist (nonmilitary blacks were still not allowed to vote and no blacks had full civil rights yet),[1411] but he ordered all Union soldiers to be furloughed at election time (late October to early November 1864), with the unwritten directive—verbally handed down by his officers in the field—that they were to vote for him. This admonition was aided along by an army slogan that was soon making the rounds among Yankee troops: Soldiers, you fight for the Union. Now vote for the Union![1412]

It was patently clear to everyone, particularly to an elated Lincoln, that without the soldiers' vote he would not have won the 1864 election.[1413]

Lincoln & His War Crimes

ONE OF THE GREATEST FABRICATIONS of Northern propagandists was nicknaming Lincoln "Honest Abe." Like nearly everything else that has been invented about him, this too was meant to portray a man too ethical to even lie, let alone inaugurate an illegal war and commit heinous war crimes. But start an illegal war and commit heinous war crimes he did, so many of them that no one has ever been able to catalog them all. I have been studying Lincoln for decades and still continue to come across new atrocities that he perpetrated in the name of **"preserving the Union."**

As such, it would be far more appropriate to call Lincoln "Dishonest Abe," for he not only lied repeatedly, but we have indisputable proof that he committed a truly dazzling number of well chronicled constitutional, civil, political, ethical, social, religious, spiritual, and moral felonies and misdemeanors.

These would include everything from calling himself a **"military hero"** in the Black Hawk War (**"I fought, bled, and came away,"** he fibbed to the House of Representatives on July 27, 1848)[1414]—even though he actually never saw a single day of combat[1415] or even a single Indian in that conflict,[1416] to launching the largest and most bloody conflict on U.S. soil without congressional approval, violating Article 1, Section 8, Clause 11 of the U.S. Constitution, which states that only Congress can formally declare war.[1417]

What follows is a highly abbreviated list of our sixteenth president's many atrocities. Lincoln is patently and evidentially guilty of:

- Subverting (and perverting) the Constitution[1418]
- Arresting and deporting Yankee antiwar advocates, like Ohio Congressman Vallandigham, who, though a civilian, was illegally tried by a military court[1419]
- Arbitrarily arresting and trying (by military commission) civilian draft resistors and others suspected of "disloyalty"[1420]
- Seizing rail and telegraph lines leading to the capital[1421]
- Suppressing and shutting down over 300 hundred pro-peace Northern newspapers, and arresting their owners[1422]
- Censoring telegraph communications[1423]
- Torturing both Northern soldiers (accused of desertion) and Northern citizens (accused of espousing antiwar sentiment, which Lincoln referred to as **"treason"**);[1424] the preferred methods were "violent cold water torture" and being suspended by handcuffed wrists[1425]
- Prohibiting former Confederates and supporters of the Confederacy from voting in the 1864 election, thereby helping to guarantee that he would be reelected[1426]
- Using spies, detectives, **"secret agents,"**[1427] fraud, and bribery to insure his reelection in 1864, resulting in "the foulest corruptions," said to have been obvious at every level of his party[1428]
- Forcing foreigners (i.e., citizens of the Confederate States of America) to take an oath of allegiance to the United States of America, or face arrest and imprisonment.[1429]
- Illegally suspending the writ of *habeas corpus* across the entire U.S.,[1430] and for the first time in U.S. history[1431]
- Assuming the extraordinary right of **"extraordinary powers"**[1432] (unconstitutional and therefore illegal)[1433]
- Prohibiting the emancipation of slaves by his cabinet members and Union military officers, such as General John. C. Frémont,[1434] General David Hunter,[1435] John W. Phelps,[1436] Jim Lane,[1437] and General Simon Cameron[1438] (which proves once and for all, if nothing else does, that Lincoln did not wage war against the South over slavery)[1439]
- Unlawfully ordering a naval blockade of Southern ports (unlawful because Lincoln never recognized the Confederacy as a separate nation and war had not yet been officially declared)[1440]
- Completely removing every inhabitant living in certain counties, **"en masse,"** as Lincoln put it, in the Southern states[1441]
- **"Checking"** (i.e., arresting) clergymen who had **"become dangerous**

to the public interest" (i.e., who contradicted Lincoln)[1442]
- Declaring all medicines contraband of war (which helped kill countless thousands of Southerners, both soldiers and civilians, not to mention thousands of Yankee soldiers held in Confederate prisons)[1443]
- Threatening war on any nation, particularly England and France, if they in any way supported, aided, or recognized the Confederacy—not necessarily illegal but highly unethical, as the U.S. herself had long insisted on the right to assist "belligerent" nations, for example, in 1793, 1841, and 1855 (as recently as the 1860s, Lincoln's Secretary of State Seward had declared that the U.S. be allowed to sell arms to Mexico, which was then at war with France. Such facts, however, did not suit Lincoln's purposes, so he chose not to remind the world of them)[1444]
- Proclaiming Confederate privateersmen **"insurgents"**[1445] and **"pirates,"**[1446] subject to the death penalty[1447] (privateering, that is, working on an armed privately-owned vessel, was and is a legal profession)[1448]
- Intimidating judges[1449]
- Closing the post office in an effort to prevent anti-Lincoln, antiwar mail from being sent or delivered[1450]
- Forcing all Federal employees to contribute 5 percent of their annual income to his 1864 re-election campaign[1451]
- Refusing to exchange military prisoners with the Confederacy (which contributed to the unnecessary deaths of thousands of soldiers, both Rebel and Yankee)[1452]
- Defying the U.S. Supreme Court[1453]
- Instituting the largest number of military drafts in U.S. history[1454]
- Fabricating heretofore unknown offices, such as **"military governor,"** in conquered Southern states[1455]
- Using the U.S. military to prevent Northern state legislatures from meeting[1456]
- Shutting down the governments of entire Northern states and arresting members of their state legislatures (usually for suspicion of advocating peace with the South); one of the more notable of these, as we have seen, was the state of Maryland, which originally had hoped to join the Confederacy[1457]
- Establishing U.S. military rule in a foreign nation (the C.S.A.), and even within states still part of the Union (such as Missouri)[1458]

- Inaugurating America's first federal monetary monopoly[1459]
- Imprisoning some 38,000 to 50,000 Northern civilians (men, women, and children),[1460] without trial, many for as long as four years (the duration of the War)[1461]
- Incarcerating civilians, like Rebel Vice President Alexander H. Stephens, in military prisons[1462]
- Levying the first personal income tax, launching what would later become the Internal Revenue Service (IRS)[1463]
- Preventing governmental debate over secession[1464]
- Ordering the first and only mass execution (and that of his own citizens) by a president in U.S. history[1465]
- Changing the meaning of the term the U.S. from plural (i.e., "United States") to singular ("United State")[1466]
- Establishing provisional courts in conquered Southern states[1467] (this was illegal because Dixie's own civilian courts remained open during the War)[1468]
- Illegally creating the state of West Virginia from the state of Virginia[1469] (Lincoln encouraged the western area of Virginia to secede while he was at war with the South because she had seceded)[1470]
- Rigging Northern elections to skew the outcome in his favor[1471]
- Bribing voters, soldiers, and fellow politicians to vote for his party[1472]

Lincoln also signed an order for the arrest of the Supreme Court's Chief Justice Roger B. Taney, simply because Taney had correctly told him that suspending *habeas corpus* was unconstitutional and therefore illegal.[1473]

Though not exactly illegal, Lincoln also put a stop to the tremendous economic growth of the 1850s, forced the nation into a hyperinflationary state, and terminated the vital connection between the currency and precious metals.[1474]

One of his more unethical moves came at the beginning of his war, when he prohibited Jews from serving as military chaplains. By his order, only ordained Christian ministers were allowed to fill the positions.[1475] In 1861, for instance, the 5th Pennsylvania Cavalry appointed a rabbi to be its chaplain. When Lincoln found out about it the Jewish clergyman was forced to resign.[1476]

In a February 14, 1862, announcement, Lincoln's Secretary of War Edwin M. Stanton describes a few of Lincoln's crimes, though from the North's point of view; that is, as inherent powers of a president during "cases of insurrection":

In this emergency the President felt it his duty to employ with energy the extraordinary powers which the Constitution confides to him in cases of insurrection. He called into the field such military and naval forces, unauthorized by the existing laws, as seemed necessary. He directed measures to prevent the use of the post-office for treasonable correspondence. He subjected passengers to and from foreign countries to new passport regulations, and he instituted a blockade, suspended the writ of *habeas corpus* in various places, and caused persons who were represented to him as being or about to engage in disloyal or treasonable practices to be arrested by special civil as well as military agencies, and detained in military custody, when necessary, to prevent them and deter others from such practices. Examinations of such cases were instituted, and some of the persons so arrested have been discharged from time to time, under circumstances or upon conditions compatible, as was thought, with the public safety.[1477]

Lincoln claims here, through Stanton, that the "Constitution confides to him . . . extraordinary powers . . . in cases of insurrection." Constitutional scholars and Southern historians have thoroughly searched that document for any evidence to support this claim, and found nothing. The word "extraordinary," for example, only appears once in the Constitution (Article 2, Section 3), and in connection with the president it only gives him the ability to "take care that the laws be faithfully executed." Which laws? Specifically those of the United States of the America.[1478] But the Confederate States of America was a separate constitutionally formed nation at the time, one over which Lincoln had no authority whatsoever. Also contrary to Lincoln's claims, he did not have the authority to, as he put it, **"suppress insurrection."**[1479] According to the Constitution, Article 1, Section 8, Clause 15, only Congress has this power.[1480]

Lincoln later tried to justify his staggering criminal, bigoted, and anti-American activities with the following bizarre declaration, sounding more like a delusional demented dictator than a U.S. president:

> I felt that measures otherwise unconstitutional might become lawful by becoming indispensable to the preservation of the Constitution through the preservation of the nation. Right or wrong, I assumed this ground and I now avow it.[1481]

Believing that he was "preserving" the Constitution when in fact he was destroying it reveals the true depth of Lincoln's twisted thinking. Unsurprisingly, as we saw in Chapter 4, objective constitutional and legal scholars now refer to the Lincoln administration as the lowest period for civil liberties up to that time. Some actually rank it as one of the worst in all of American history.[1482]

Lincoln's order to mass execute thirty-nine Native-Americans is particularly egregious. While it is true that a number of Indians had committed heinous crimes against European-American families, at the root of their attacks was their frustration over Lincoln's lies and broken promises; or as Lincoln himself phrased it, the **"failure of treaty obligations"** on the part of the U.S. government.[1483] The president commented on the horrendous situation in his Second Annual Message To Congress on December 1, 1862:

> In the month of August last the Sioux Indians in Minnesota attacked the settlements in their vicinity with extreme ferocity, killing indiscriminately men, women, and children. This attack was wholly unexpected, and therefore no means of defense had been provided. It is estimated that not less than eight hundred persons were killed by the Indians, and a large amount of property was destroyed. How this outbreak was induced is not definitely known, and suspicions, which may be unjust, need not to be stated. Information was received by the Indian bureau, from different sources, about the time hostilities were commenced, that a simultaneous attack was to be made upon the white settlements by all the tribes between the Mississippi River and the Rocky Mountains. The State of Minnesota has suffered great injury from this Indian war. A large portion of her territory nas been depopulated, and a severe loss has been sustained by the destruction of property. The people of that State manifest much anxiety for the removal of the tribes beyond the limits of the State as a guarantee against future hostilities. The Commissioner of Indian Affairs will furnish full details. I submit for your especial consideration whether our Indian system shall not be remodeled. Many wise and good men have impressed me with the belief that this can be profitably done.[1484]

Lincoln's solution to this particular **"Indian war,"** of course, was to execute the trouble makers and "remove" the rest to reservations on unwanted land further west.

What is truly shocking about this story is that Lincoln was prepared to execute as many as 300 Indians, as he noted in a November 10, 1862, telegram to Union General John Pope (a collateral descendent of George Washington)[1485]:

> Your despatch giving the names of 300 Indians condemned to death is received. Please forward as soon as possible the full and complete record of their convictions; and if the record does not fully indicate the more guilty and influential of the culprits, please have a careful statement made on these points and forwarded to me. Send all by mail. A. Lincoln.[1486]

This was followed a month later by Lincoln's "Message to the Senate," on December 11, 1862, in which he discussed his final verdict on the case:

> To the Senate of the United States: In compliance with your resolution of December 5, 1862, requesting the President "to furnish the Senate with all information in his possession touching the late Indian barbarities in the State of Minnesota, and also the evidence in his possession upon which some of the principal actors and head men were tried and condemned to death," I have the honor to state that, on receipt of said resolution, I transmitted the same to the Secretary of the Interior, accompanied by a note, a copy of which is herewith inclosed, marked A, and in response to which I received, through that department, a letter of the Commissioner of Indian Affairs, a copy of which is herewith inclosed, marked B.
>   I further state that on the eighth day of November last I received a long telegraphic despatch from Major-General [John] Pope, at St. Paul, Minnesota, simply announcing the names of the persons sentenced to be hanged. I immediately telegraphed to have transcripts of the records in all the cases forwarded to me, which transcripts, however, did not reach me until two or three days before the present meeting of Congress. Meantime I received, through telegraphic despatches and otherwise, appeals in behalf of the condemned—appeals for their execution—and

expressions of opinion as to the proper policy in regard to them and to the Indians generally in that vicinity, none of which, as I understand, falls within the scope of your inquiry. After the arrival of the transcripts of records, but before I had sufficient opportunity to examine them, I received a joint letter from one of the senators and two of the representatives from Minnesota, which contains some statements of fact not found in the records of the trials, and for which reason I herewith transmit a copy, marked C. I also, for the same reason, inclose a printed memorial of the citizens of St. Paul, addressed to me, and forwarded with the letter aforesaid.

Anxious to not act with so much clemency as to encourage another outbreak on the one hand, nor with so much severity as to be real cruelty on the other, I caused a careful examination of the records of trials to be made, in view of first ordering the execution of such as had been proved guilty of violating females. Contrary to my expectation, only two of this class were found. I then directed a further examination and a classification of all who were proven to have participated in massacres, as distinguished from participation in battles. This class numbered forty, and included the two convicted of female violation. One of the number is strongly recommended, by the commission which tried them, for commutation to ten years' imprisonment. I have ordered the other thirty-nine to be executed on Friday, the 19th instant. The order was despatched from here on Monday, the 8th instant, by a messenger to General [Henry Hastings] Sibley, and a copy of which order is herewith transmitted, marked D.[1487]

It was thus that Lincoln became the first and only president in U.S. history to order a mass execution of his own citizens.[1488]

Unfortunately for the thirty-nine Native-Americans who were killed by Lincoln's order, their guilt was never proven beyond a reasonable doubt. Additionally, it was later shown that Lincoln would have preferred to have executed all 300 Indians (under pressure from white Minnesotans—whose votes he knew he would need in the 1864 election). He only refrained from doing so because he feared that such an act would prompt humanitarian Europe to come to the aid of the South, a desire she had clearly expressed since the start of the War.[1489]

The military draft, another dictatorial move made by Lincoln, caused particular aggravation across the North, especially in New York. The state's governor, Horatio Seymour, sent one letter after another to the president pleading to have the conscription act suspended or altered in his state, but to no avail.[1490] Despite the act's unconstitutionality, warmonger Lincoln would not listen, either to Seymour or to reason. As a result, violence exploded throughout the North, with some of the worst public disturbances taking place in New York City.[1491]

It was between July 12 and July 16, 1863, that 50,000 whites rioted in the Big Apple against Lincoln's military draft. But because this occurred in the racist North, tellingly, the mobs did not vent their anger on Lincoln or the government. They targeted blacks, who they harassed, beat, and even lynched, in great numbers over four terrible days in what Northern authors still deceitfully call the "New York Draft Riots."[1492]

In fact, these were largely Northern anti-Negro riots, using Lincoln's new conscription policy as an excuse to intimidate Northern blacks.[1493] Even black women and children were hunted down and murdered by white Yankee mobs, after which their corpses were set on fire in the streets. For those who believe that these particular blacks just happened to be in the wrong place at the wrong time, there is the fact that white abolitionists were also tracked down, viciously attacked, and had their property looted and torched.[1494] A little black girl, who was found hiding under a bed (she was being cared for by Catholic priests at the time), was summarily dragged out and killed.[1495]

Before it was all over, as many as 500 people, mostly blacks, lay dead.[1496] Even the Colored Orphan Asylum was targeted, pillaged, and then torched.[1497] Days later the bodies of African-Americans could still be seen hanging from lampposts and trees, all the work of white New Yorkers.[1498]

We must ask here that if this violence was truly about Lincoln's draft, as Northern historians maintain, why were blacks specifically selected as the focus of white rage?

A Northern newspaper, the *Christian Recorder*, raised the same issue:

> These rioters of New York could not be satisfied with their resistance of the draft and doing all the damage they could against the government and those of the white citizens who are friends to the administration, but must wheel upon the colored people, killing and beating every one whom they could see and catch, and destroying their property. . . . A gloom of infamy and shame will hang over New York for centuries.[1499]

After the bloodbath subsided, Lincoln responded in his usual apathetic way, with no comment. Even when he was advised to appoint a commission to conduct an inquiry into the horrendous incident, he stonily refused, saying:

> **Better let the dirt alone,—at least for the present. One rebellion at a time is about as much as we can conveniently handle.**[1500]

While the cold-blooded murder of hundreds of blacks by Northern whites did not seem to phase the president, he *was* concerned about how his constituents viewed about his military draft. Thus, on August 17, 1863, he wrote out the following never issued or published explanation entitled "Opinion of the Draft":

> **It is at all times proper that misunderstanding between the public and the public servant should be avoided; and this is far more important now than in times of peace and tranquillity. I therefore address you without searching for a precedent upon which to do so. Some of you are sincerely devoted to the republican institutions and territorial integrity of our country, and yet are opposed to what is called the draft, or conscription.**
>
> **At the beginning of the war, and ever since, a variety of motives, pressing, some in one direction and some in the other, would be presented to the mind of each man physically fit for a soldier, upon the combined effect of which motives he would, or would not, voluntarily enter the service. Among these motives would be patriotism, political bias, ambition, personal courage, love of adventure, want of employment, and convenience, or the opposites of some of these.**
>
> **We already have, and have had in the service, as appears, substantially all that can be obtained upon this voluntary weighing of motives. And yet we must somehow obtain more, or relinquish the original object of the contest, together with all the blood and treasure already expended in the effort to secure it. To meet this necessity the law for the draft has been enacted. You who do not wish to be soldiers do not like this law. This is natural; nor does it imply want of patriotism. Nothing can be so just and necessary as to make us like it if it is disagreeable to us. We are prone, too, to find false**

arguments with which to excuse ourselves for opposing such disagreeable things. In this case, those who desire the rebellion to succeed, and others who seek reward in a different way, are very active in accommodating us with this class of arguments. They tell us the law is unconstitutional. It is the first instance, I believe, in which the power of Congress to do a thing has ever been questioned in a case when the power is given by the Constitution in express terms. Whether a power can be implied when it is not expressed has often been the subject of controversy; but this is the first case in which the degree of effrontery has been ventured upon of denying a power which is plainly and distinctly written down in the Constitution. The Constitution declares that "The Congress shall have power . . . to raise and support armies; but no appropriation of money to that use shall be for a longer term than two years." The whole scope of the conscription act is "to raise and support armies." There is nothing else in it. It makes no appropriation of money, and hence the money clause just quoted is not touched by it.

The case simply is, the Constitution provides that the Congress shall have power to raise and support armies; and by this act the Congress has exercised to raise and support armies. This is the whole of it. It is a law made in literal pursuance of this part of the United States Constitution; and another part of the same Constitution declares that "this Constitution, and the laws made in pursuance thereof, . . . shall be the supreme law of the land, and the judges in every State shall be bound thereby, anything in the constitution or laws of any State to the contrary notwithstanding." Do you admit that the power is given to raise and support armies, and yet insist that by this act Congress has not exercised the power in a constitutional mode?—has not done the thing in the right way? Who is to judge of this? The Constitution gives Congress the power, but it does not prescribe the mode, or expressly declare who shall prescribe it. In such case Congress must prescribe the mode, or relinquish the power. There is no alternative. Congress could not exercise the power to do the thing if it had not the power of providing a way to do it, when no way is provided by the Constitution for doing it. In fact, Congress would not have the power to raise and support armies, if even by the Constitution it were left to the option of any other or others to give or withhold the only mode of doing it. If the Constitution had prescribed a mode, Congress could and must follow that mode; but, as it is, the mode necessarily goes to Congress, with the power expressly given. The power is given fully, completely, unconditionally. It is not a power to raise armies if State authorities consent; nor if the men to compose the armies are entirely willing; but it is a power to raise and support armies given to Congress by the Constitution, without an "if."

It is clear that a constitutional law may not be expedient or proper. Such would be a law to raise armies when no armies were needed. But this is not such. The republican institutions and territorial integrity of our country cannot be maintained without the further raising and supporting of armies. There can be no army without men. Men can be had only voluntarily or involuntarily. We have ceased to obtain them voluntarily, and to obtain them involuntarily is the draft—the conscription. If you dispute the fact, and declare that men can still be had voluntarily in sufficient numbers, prove the assertion by yourselves volunteering in such numbers, and I shall gladly give up the draft. Or, if not a sufficient number, but any one of you will volunteer, he for his single self will escape all the horrors of the draft, and will thereby do only what each one of at least a million of his manly brethren have already done. Their toil and blood have been given as much for you as for themselves. Shall it all be lost rather than that you, too, will bear your part?

I do not say that all who would avoid serving in the war are unpatriotic; but I do think every patriot should willingly take his chance under a law made with great care, in order to secure entire fairness. This law was considered, discussed, modified, and amended by Congress at great length, and with much labor; and was finally passed by both branches, with a near approach to unanimity. At last, it may not be exactly such as any one man out of Congress, or even in Congress, would have made it. It has been said, and I believe truly, that the Constitution itself is not altogether such as any one of its framers would have preferred. It was the joint work of all, and certainly the better that it was so.

Much complaint is made of that provision of the conscription law which allows a drafted man to substitute three hundred dollars for himself; while, as I believe, none is made of that provision which allows him to substitute another man for himself. Nor is the three hundred dollar provision objected to for unconstitutionality; but for inequality, for favoring the rich against the poor. The substitution of men is the provision, if any, which favors the rich to the exclusion of the poor. But this, being a provision in accordance with an old and well-known practice in the raising of armies, is not objected to. There would have been great objection if that provision had been omitted. And yet, being in, the money provision really modifies the inequality which the other introduces. It allows men to escape the service who are too poor to escape but for it. Without the money provision, competition among the more wealthy might, and probably would, raise the price of substitutes above three hundred dollars, thus leaving the man who could raise only three hundred dollars no escape from personal service. True, by the law as it is, the man who cannot raise so much as three hundred dollars, nor obtain a personal substitute for less, cannot escape; but he can come quite as near escaping as he could if the money provision were not in the law. To put it another way: is an unobjectionable law which allows only the man to escape who can pay a thousand dollars made objectionable by adding a provision that any one may escape who can pay the smaller sum of three hundred dollars? This is the exact difference at this point between the present law and all former draft laws. It is true that by this law a somewhat larger number will escape than could under a law allowing personal substitutes only; but each additional man thus escaping will be a poorer man than could have escaped by the law in the other form. The money provision enlarges the class of exempts from actual service simply by admitting poorer men into it. How then can the money provision be a wrong to the poor man? The inequality complained of pertains in greater degree to the substitution of men, and is really modified and lessened by the money provision. The inequality could only be perfectly cured by sweeping both provisions away. This, being a great innovation, would probably leave the law more distasteful than it now is. The principle of the draft, which simply is involuntary or enforced service, is not new. It has been practised in all ages of the world. It was well-known to the framers of our Constitution as one of the modes of raising armies, at the time they placed in that instrument the provision that "the Congress shall have power to raise and support armies." It had been used just before in establishing our independence, and it was also used under the Constitution in 1812. Wherein is the peculiar hardship now? Shall we shrink from the necessary means to maintain our free government, which our grandfathers employed to establish it and our own fathers have already employed once to maintain it? Are we degenerate? Has the manhood of our race run out?

Again, a law may be both constitutional and expedient, and yet may be administered in an unjust and unfair way. This law belongs to a class, which class is composed of those laws whose object is to distribute burdens or benefits on the principle of equality. No one of these laws can ever be practically administered with that exactness which can be conceived of in the mind. A tax law, the principle of which is that each owner shall pay in proportion to the value of his property, will be a dead letter, if no one can be compelled to pay until it can be shown that every other one will pay in precisely the same proportion, according to value; nay, even, it will be a dead letter if no one can be compelled to pay until it is certain that every other one will pay at all—even in unequal proportion. Again, the United States House of Representatives is constituted on the principle that each member is sent by the same number of people that each other one is sent by; and yet, in practice, no two of the whole number, much less the whole number, are ever sent by precisely the same number of constituents. The districts cannot be made precisely equal in population at first, and if they could, they would become unequal in a single day, and much more so in the ten years which the districts, once made, are to continue. They cannot be remodeled every day; nor, without too much expense and labor, even every year.

This sort of difficulty applies in full force to the practical administration of the draft law. In fact, the difficulty is greater in the case of the draft law. First, it starts with all the inequality of the congressional districts; but these are based on entire population, while the draft is based upon those only who are fit for soldiers, and such may not bear the same proportion to the whole in one district that they do in another. Again, the facts must be ascertained and credit given for the unequal numbers of soldiers which have already gone from the several districts. In all these points errors will occur in spite of the utmost fidelity. The government is bound to administer the law with such an approach to exactness as is usual in analogous cases, and as entire good faith and fidelity will reach. If so great departures as to be inconsistent with such good faith and fidelity, or great departures occurring in any way, be pointed out, they shall be corrected; and any agent shown to have caused such departures intentionally shall be dismissed.

With these views, and on these principles, I feel bound to tell you it is my purpose to see the draft law faithfully executed.[1501]

As usual Lincoln felt free to bend, twist, and reinterpret the Constitution to his own liking, even against the will of the people. Yet his own arguments reveal his draft acts to be unconstitutional and therefore illegal.

Always his own worst enemy, he issued another "Order For a Draft" on February 1, 1864. It reads:

Ordered, That a draft for five hundred thousand (500,000) men, to serve for three years or during the war, be made on the tenth (10th) day of March next, for the military service of the United States, crediting and deducting therefrom so many as may have been enlisted or drafted into the service prior to the first (1st) day of March, and not before credited. Abraham Lincoln.[1502]

Southerners were not the only ones who noticed Lincoln's criminal mind and activity. Shrewd Northerners too could not help but observe the countless felonies emanating from the White House. One of these was Yankee businessman and politician Erastus Corning, who fired off a letter to the president, lambasting him for his unconstitutional affairs. The letter was formulated during a Democratic meeting at Albany, New York, on May 16, 1863, where the group, headed by Corning, set forth a list of resolutions protesting Lincoln's actions:

May 19, 1863, To His Excellency the President of the United States:

The undersigned, officers of a public meeting held in the city of Albany the 16th day of May instant, herewith transmit to your

Excellency a copy of the resolutions adopted at the said meeting, and respectfully request your earnest consideration of them. They deem it proper on their personal responsibility to state that the meeting was one of the most respectable as to numbers and character, and one of the most earnest in support of the Union, ever held in this city. Yours, with great regard, ERASTUS CORNING, President. Vice-Presidents—Eli Perry, Peter Gansevoort, Peter Monteath, Samuel W. Gibbs, John Niblock, H. W. McClellan, Lemuel W. Rodgers, William Seymour, Jeremiah Osborn, William S. Paddock, J. B. Sanders, Edward Mulcahy, D. V. N. Radcliff. Secretaries—William A. Rice, Edward Newcomb, R. W. Peckham, Jr., M. A. Nolan, John R. Nessle, and others.

The resolutions were as follows:

Resolved, That the Democrats of New York point to their uniform course of action during the two years of civil war through which we have passed, to the alacrity which they have evinced in filling the ranks of the army, to their contributions and sacrifices, as the evidence of their patriotism and devotion to the cause, of our imperilled country. Never in the history of civil wars has a Government been sustained with such ample resources of means and men, as the people have voluntarily placed in the hands of this Administration.

Resolved, That as Democrats, we are determined to maintain this patriotic attitude, and, despite of adverse and disheartening circumstances, to devote all our energies to sustain the cause of the Union, to secure peace through victory, and to bring about the restoration of all the States under the safeguards of the Constitution.

Resolved, That while we will not consent to be misrepresented upon these points, we are determined not to be misunderstood in regard to others not less essential. We demand that the Administration shall be true to the Constitution, shall recognize and maintain the rights of the States and the liberties of the citizen, shall everywhere outside of the lines of necessary military occupation and the scenes of insurrection, exert all its powers to maintain the supremacy of the civil over military law.

Resolved, That in view of these principles we denounce the recent assumption of a military commander to seize and try a citizen of Ohio, Clement L. Vallandigham, for no other reason than words addressed to a public meeting, in criticism of the course of the Administration, and in condemnation of the military orders of that general.

Resolved, That this assumption of power by a military

tribunal, if successfully asserted, not only abrogates the right of the people to assemble and discuss the affairs of Government, the liberty of speech and of the press, the right of trial by jury, the law of evidence, and the privilege of *habeas corpus*, but it strikes a fatal blow at the supremacy of law, and the authority of the State and Federal Constitutions.

Resolved, That the Constitution of the United States—the supreme law of the land—has defined the crime of treason against the United States to consist "only in levying war against them, or adhering to their enemies, giving them aid and comfort;" and has provided that "no person shall be convicted of treason, unless on the testimony of two witnesses to the same overt act, or on confession in open court." And it further provides that "no person shall be held to answer for a capital or otherwise infamous crime, unless on a presentment or indictment of a grand jury; except in cases arising in the land and naval forces, or in the militia, when in actual service in time of war or public danger;" and further, that "in all criminal prosecutions, the accused shall enjoy the right of a speedy and public trial, by an impartial jury of the State and district wherein the crime was committed."

Resolved, That these safeguards of the rights of the citizen against the pretensions of arbitrary power, were intended more especially for his protection in times of civil commotion. They were secured substantially to the English people, after years of protracted civil war, and were adopted into our own Constitution at the close of the Revolution. They have stood the test of seventy-six years of trial under our republican system, under circumstances which show that while they constitute the foundation of all free government, they are the elements of the enduring stability of the republic.

Resolved, That in adopting the language of Daniel Webster, we declare, "it is the ancient and undoubted prerogative of this people to canvass public measures and the merits of public men. It is a 'homebred right,' a fireside privilege. It has been enjoyed in every house, cottage, and cabin in the nation. It is as undoubted as the right of breathing the air or walking on the earth. Belonging to private life as a right, it belongs to public life as a duty, and it is the last duty which those whose representatives we are shall find us to abandon. Aiming at all times to be courteous and temperate in its use, except when the right itself is questioned, we shall place ourselves on the extreme boundary of our own right, and bid defiance to any arm that would move us from our ground. This high constitutional privilege we shall defend and exercise in all places; in time of peace, in time of war, and at all times. Living, we shall assert it; and should we leave no other inheritance to our children, by the blessing of God we will leave them the inheritance of free principles and the example of a manly, independent, and constitutional defence of them."

Resolved, That in the election of [New York] Gov. [Horatio] Seymour, the people of this State, by an emphatic majority, declared their condemnation of the system of arbitrary arrests, and their determination to stand by the Constitution. That the revival of this lawless system can have but one result, to divide and distract the North, and destroy its confidence in the purposes of the Administration. That we deprecate it as an element of confusion at home, of weakness to our armies in the field, and as calculated to lower the estimate of American character and magnify the apparent peril of our cause abroad. And that, regarding the blow struck at a citizen of Ohio as aimed at the rights of every citizen of the North, we denounce it as against the spirit of our laws and Constitution, and most earnestly call upon the President of the United States to reverse the action of the military tribunal which has passed a "cruel and unusual punishment" upon the party arrested, prohibited in terms by the Constitution, and to restore him to the liberty of which he has been deprived.

Resolved, That the president, vice-presidents, and secretary of this meeting be requested to transmit a copy of these resolutions to his Excellency the President of the United States, with the assurance of this meeting of their hearty and earnest desire to support the Government in every constitutional and lawful measure to suppress the existing rebellion.[1503]

A month later, on June 12, 1863, Lincoln took up his pen and replied in his predictable defensive manner. It is one of the most perspicuous examples of muddled thinking, brazen self-deception, self-serving declarations, Constitution-ignorant ramblings, ridiculous assumptions, and erroneous conclusions ever recorded:

> Gentlemen: Your letter of May 19, inclosing the resolutions of a public meeting held at Albany, New York, on the 16th of the same month, was received several days ago.
> The resolutions, as I understand them, are resolvable into two propositions—first, the expression of a purpose to sustain the cause of the Union, to secure peace through victory, and to support the administration in every constitutional and lawful measure to suppress the rebellion; and, secondly, a declaration of censure upon the administration for supposed unconstitutional

action, such as the making of military arrests. And from the two propositions a third is deduced, which is that the gentlemen composing the meeting are resolved on doing their part to maintain our common government and country, despite the folly or wickedness, as they may conceive, of any administration. This position is eminently patriotic, and as such I thank the meeting, and congratulate the nation for it. My own purpose is the same; so that the meeting and myself have a common object, and can have no difference, except in the choice of means or measures for effecting that object.

And here I ought to close this paper, and would close it, if there were no apprehension that more injurious consequences than any merely personal to myself might follow the censures systematically cast upon me for doing what, in my view of duty, I could not forbear. The resolutions promise to support me in every constitutional and lawful measure to suppress the rebellion; and I have not knowingly employed, nor shall knowingly employ, any other. But the meeting, by their resolutions, assert and argue that certain military arrests, and proceedings following them, for which I am ultimately responsible, are unconstitutional. I think they are not. The resolutions quote from the Constitution the definition of treason, and also the limiting safeguards and guarantees therein provided for the citizen on trials for treason, and on his being held to answer for capital or otherwise infamous crimes, and in criminal prosecutions his right to a speedy and public trial by an impartial jury. They proceed to resolve "that these safeguards of the rights of the citizen against the pretensions of arbitrary power were intended more especially for his protection in times of civil commotion." And, apparently to demonstrate the proposition, the resolutions proceed: "They were secured substantially to the English people after years of protracted civil war, and were adopted into our Constitution at the close of the revolution." Would not the demonstration have been better if it could have been truly said that these safeguards had been adopted and applied during the civil wars and during our revolution, instead of after the one and at the close of the other? I, too, am devotedly for them after civil war, and before civil war, and at all times, "except when, in cases of rebellion or invasion, the public safety may require" their suspension. The resolutions proceed to tell us that these safeguards "have stood the test of seventy-six years of trial under our republican system, under circumstances which show that while they constitute the foundation of all free government, they are the elements of the enduring stability of the republic." No one denies that they have so stood the test up to the beginning of the present rebellion, if we except a certain occurrence at New Orleans hereafter to be mentioned; nor does any one question that they will stand the same test much longer after the rebellion closes. But these provisions of the Constitution have no application to the case we have in hand, because the arrests complained of were not made for treason—that is, not for the treason defined in the Constitution, and upon the conviction of which the punishment is death—nor yet were they made to hold persons to answer for any capital or otherwise infamous crimes; nor were the proceedings following, in any constitutional or legal sense, "criminal prosecutions." The arrests were made on totally different grounds, and the proceedings following accorded with the grounds of the arrests. Let us consider the real case with which we are dealing, and apply to it the parts of the Constitution plainly made for such cases.

Prior to my installation here it had been inculcated that any State had a lawful right to secede from the national Union, and that it would be expedient to exercise the right whenever the devotees of the doctrine should fail to elect a president to their own liking. I was elected contrary to their liking; and, accordingly, so far as it was legally possible, they had taken seven States out of the Union, had seized many of the United States forts, and had fired upon the United States flag, all before I was inaugurated, and, of course, before I had done any official act whatever. The rebellion thus begun soon ran into the present civil war; and, in certain respects, it began on very unequal terms between the parties. The insurgents had been preparing for it more than thirty years, while the government had taken no steps to resist them. The former had carefully considered all the means which could be turned to their account. It undoubtedly was a well-pondered reliance with them that in their own unrestricted effort to destroy Union, Constitution, and law, all together, the government would, in great degree, be restrained by the same Constitution and law from arresting their progress.

Their sympathizers pervaded all departments of the government and nearly all communities of the people. From this material, under cover of "liberty of speech," "liberty of the press," and *habeas corpus*," they hoped to keep on foot amongst us a most efficient corps of spies, informers, suppliers, and aiders and abettors of their cause in a thousand ways. They knew that in times such as they were inaugurating, by the Constitution itself the "*habeas corpus*" might be suspended; but they also knew they had friends who would make a question as to who was to suspend it; meanwhile their spies and others might remain at large to help on their cause. Or if, as has happened, the Executive should suspend the writ without ruinous waste of time, instances of arresting innocent persons might occur, as are always likely to occur in such cases; and then a clamor could be raised in regard to this, which might be at least of some service to the insurgent cause. It needed no very keen perception to discover this part of the enemy's program, so soon as by open hostilities their machinery was fairly put in motion. Yet, thoroughly imbued with a reverence for the guaranteed rights of individuals, I was slow to adopt the strong measures which by degrees I have been forced to regard as being within the exceptions of the Constitution, and as indispensable to the public safety. Nothing is better known to history than that courts of justice are utterly incompetent to such cases. Civil courts are organized chiefly for trials of individuals, or, at most, a few individuals acting in concert—and this in quiet times, and on charges of crimes well defined in the law. Even in times of peace bands of horse-thieves and robbers frequently grow too numerous and powerful for the ordinary courts of justice. But what comparison, in numbers, have such bands ever borne to the insurgent sympathizers even in many of the loyal States? Again, a jury too frequently has at least one member more ready to hang the panel than to hang the traitor. And yet again, he who dissuades one man from volunteering, or induces one soldier to desert, weakens the Union cause as much as he who kills a Union soldier in battle. Yet this dissuasion or inducement may be so conducted as to be no defined crime of which any civil court would take cognizance.

Ours is a case of rebellion—so called by the resolutions before me—in fact, a clear, flagrant, and gigantic case of rebellion; and the provision of the Constitution that "the privilege of the writ of *habeas corpus* shall not be suspended unless when, in cases of rebellion or invasion, the public safety may require it," is the provision which specially applies to our present case. This provision plainly attests the understanding of those who made the Constitution that ordinary courts of justice are inadequate to "cases of rebellion"—attests their purpose that, in such cases, men may be held in custody whom the courts, acting on ordinary rules, would discharge. *Habeas corpus* does not discharge men who are proved to be guilty of defined crime; and its suspension is allowed by the Constitution on purpose that men may be arrested and held who cannot be proved to be guilty of defined crime, "when, in cases of rebellion or invasion, the public safety may require it."

This is precisely our present case—a case of rebellion wherein the public safety does require the suspension. Indeed, arrests by process of courts and arrests in cases of rebellion do not proceed altogether upon the same basis. The former is directed at the small percentage of ordinary and continuous perpetration of crime, while the latter is directed at sudden and extensive uprisings against the government, which, at most, will succeed or fail in no great length of time. In the latter case arrests are made not so much for what has been done, as for what probably would be done. The latter is more for the preventive and less for the vindictive than the former. In such cases the purposes of men are much more easily understood than in cases of ordinary crime. The man who stands by and says nothing when the peril of his government is discussed, cannot be misunderstood. If not hindered, he is sure to help the enemy; much more if he talks ambiguously—talks for his country with "buts," and "ifs" and "ands." Of how little value the constitutional provision I have quoted will be rendered if arrests shall never be made until defined crimes shall have been committed, may be illustrated by a few notable examples: General John C. Breckinridge, General Robert E. Lee, General Joseph E. Johnston, General John B. Magruder, General William B. Preston, General Simon B. Buckner, and Commodore Franklin Buchanan, now occupying the very highest places in the rebel war service, were all within the power of the government since the rebellion began, and were nearly as well known to be traitors then as now. Unquestionably if we had seized and held them, the insurgent cause would be much weaker. But no one of them had then committed any crime defined in the law. Every one of them, if arrested, would have been discharged on *habeas corpus* were the writ allowed to operate. In view of these and similar cases, I think the time not unlikely to come when I shall be blamed for having made too few arrests rather than too many.

By the third resolution the meeting indicate their opinion that military arrests may be constitutional in localities where rebellion actually exists, but that such arrests are unconstitutional in localities where rebellion or insurrection does not actually exist. They insist that such arrests shall not be made "outside of the lines of necessary military occupation and the scenes of insurrection." Inasmuch, however, as the Constitution itself makes no such distinction, I am unable to believe that there is any such constitutional distinction. I concede that the class of arrests complained of can be constitutional only when, in cases of rebellion or invasion, the public safety may require them; and I insist that in such cases they are constitutional wherever the public safety does require them, as well in places to which they may prevent the rebellion extending, as in those where it may be already prevailing; as well where they may restrain mischievous interference with the raising and supplying of armies to suppress the rebellion, as where the rebellion may actually be; as well where they may restrain the enticing men out of the army, as where they would prevent mutiny in the army; equally constitutional at all places where they will conduce to the public safety, as against the dangers of rebellion or invasion. Take the particular case mentioned by the meeting. It is asserted in substance, that Mr. Vallandigham was, by a military commander, seized and tried "for no other reason than words addressed to a public meeting in criticism of the course of the administration, and in condemnation of the military orders of the general." Now, if there be no mistake about this, if this assertion is the truth and the whole truth, if there was no other reason for the arrest, then I concede that the arrest was wrong. But the arrest, as I understand, was made for a very different reason. Mr. Vallandigham avows his hostility to the war on the part of the Union; and his arrest was made because he was laboring, with some effect, to prevent the raising of troops, to encourage desertions from the army, and to leave the rebellion without an adequate military force to suppress it. He was not arrested because he was damaging the political prospects of the administration or the personal interests or the commanding general, but because he was damaging the army, upon the existence and vigor of which the life of the nation depends. He was warring upon the military, and this gave the military constitutional jurisdiction to lay hands upon him. If Mr. Vallandigham was not damaging the military power of the country, then his arrest was made on mistake of fact, which I would be glad to correct on reasonably satisfactory evidence.

I understand the meeting whose resolutions I am considering to be in favor of suppressing the rebellion by military force—by armies. Long experience has shown that armies cannot be maintained unless desertion shall be punished by the severe penalty of death. The case requires, and the law and the Constitution sanction, this punishment. Must I shoot a simple-minded soldier boy who deserts, while I must not touch a hair of a wily agitator who induces him to desert? This is none the less injurious when effected by getting a father, or brother, or friend into a public meeting, and there working upon his feelings till he is persuaded to write the soldier boy that he is fighting in a bad cause, for a wicked administration of a contemptible government, too weak to arrest and punish him if he shall desert. I think that, in such a case, to silence the agitator and save the boy is not only constitutional, but withal a great mercy.

If I be wrong on this question of constitutional power, my error lies in believing that certain proceedings are constitutional when, in cases of rebellion or invasion, the public safety requires them, which would not be constitutional when, in absence of rebellion or invasion, the public safety does not require them: in other words, that the Constitution is not in its application in all respects the same in cases of rebellion or invasion involving the public safety, as it is in times of profound peace and public security. The Constitution itself makes the distinction, and I can no more be persuaded that the government can constitutionally take no strong measures in time of rebellion, because it can be shown that the same could not be lawfully taken in time of peace, than I can be persuaded that a particular drug is not good medicine for a sick man because it can be shown to not be good food for a well one. Nor am I able to appreciate the danger apprehended by the meeting, that the American people will by means of military arrests during the rebellion lose the right of public discussion, the liberty of speech and the press, the law of evidence, trial by jury, and *habeas corpus* throughout the indefinite peaceful future which I trust lies before them, any more than I am able to believe that a man could contract so strong an appetite for emetics during temporary illness as to persist in feeding upon them during the remainder of his healthful life.

In giving the resolutions that earnest consideration which you request of me, I cannot overlook the fact that the meeting speak as "Democrats." Nor can I, with full respect for their known intelligence, and the fairly presumed deliberation with which they prepared their resolutions, be permitted to suppose that this occurred by accident, or in any way other than that they preferred to designate themselves "Democrats" rather than "American citizens." In this time of national peril I would have preferred to meet you upon a level one step higher than any party platform, because I am sure that from such more elevated position we could do better battle for the country we all love than we possibly can from those lower ones where, from the force of habit, the prejudices of the past, and selfish hopes of the future, we are sure to expend much or our ingenuity and strength in finding fault with and aiming blows at each other. But since you have denied me this, I will yet be thankful for the country's sake that not all Democrats have done so. He on whose discretionary judgment Mr. Vallandigham was arrested and tried is a Democrat, having no old party affinity with me, and the judge who rejected the constitutional view expressed in these resolutions, by refusing to discharge Mr. Vallandigham on *habeas corpus*, is a Democrat of better days than these, having received his judicial mantle at the hands of President [Andrew] Jackson. And still more, of all those Democrats who are nobly exposing their lives and shedding their blood on the battle-field, I have learned that many approve the course taken with Mr. Vallandigham, while I have not heard of a single one condemning it. I cannot assert that there are none such. And the name of President Jackson recalls an instance of pertinent history. After the battle of New Orleans, and while the fact that the treaty of peace had been concluded was well known in the city, but before official knowledge of it had arrived, General Jackson still maintained martial or military law. Now that it could be said the war was over, the clamor against martial law, which had existed from the first, grew more furious. Among other things, a Mr. [Louis] Louaillier published a denunciatory newspaper article. General Jackson arrested him. A lawyer by the name of Morel procured the United States Judge Hall to order a writ of *habeas corpus* to release Mr. Louaillier. General Jackson arrested both the lawyer and the judge. A Mr. Hollander ventured to say of some part of the matter that "it was a dirty trick." General Jackson arrested him. When the officer undertook to serve the writ of *habeas corpus*, General Jackson took it from him, and sent him away with a copy. Holding the judge in custody a few days, the general sent him beyond the limits of his encampment, and set him at liberty with an order to remain till the ratification of peace should be regularly announced, or until the British should have left the southern coast. A day or two more elapsed, the ratification of the treaty of peace was regularly announced, and the judge and others were fully liberated. A few days more, and the judge called General Jackson into court and fined him $1000 for having arrested him and the others named. The general paid the fine, and then the matter rested for nearly thirty years, when Congress refunded principal and interest. The late Senator [Stephen A.] Douglas, then in the House of Representatives, took a leading part in the debates in which the constitutional question was much discussed. I am not prepared to say whom the journals would show to have voted for the measure.

It may be remarked—first, that we had the same Constitution then as now; secondly, that we then had a case of invasion, and now we have a case of rebellion; and, thirdly, that the permanent right of the people to public discussion, the liberty of speech and of the press, the trial by jury, the law of evidence, and the *habeas corpus*, suffered no detriment whatever by that conduct of General Jackson, or its subsequent approval by the

American Congress.

And yet, let me say that, in my own discretion, I do not know whether I would have ordered the arrest of Mr. Vallandigham. While I cannot shift the responsibility from myself, I hold that, as a general rule, the commander in the field is the better judge of the necessity in any particular case. Of course I must practise a general directory and revisory power in the matter.

One of the resolutions expresses the opinion of the meeting that arbitrary arrests will have the effect to divide and distract those who should be united in suppressing the rebellion, and I am specifically called on to discharge Mr. Vallandigham. I regard this as, at least, a fair appeal to me on the expediency of exercising a constitutional power which I think exists. In response to such appeal I have to say, it gave me pain when I learned that Mr. Vallandigham had been arrested (that is, I was pained that there should have seemed to be a necessity for arresting him), and that it will afford me great pleasure to discharge him so soon as I can by any means believe the public safety will not suffer by it.

I further say that, as the war progresses, it appears to me, opinion and action, which were in great confusion at first, take shape and fall into more regular channels, so that the necessity for strong dealing with them gradually decreases. I have every reason to desire that it should cease altogether, and far from the least is my regard for the opinions and wishes of those who, like the meeting at Albany, declare their purpose to sustain the government in every constitutional and lawful measure to suppress the rebellion. Still, I must continue to do so much as may seem to be required by the public safety. A. Lincoln.[1504]

In defense of his usurious crimes the president uses the constitutional term **"public safety"** thirteen times in this letter alone, openly maintaining that the Confederacy was somehow threatening it. However, it must be clear to my readers by now that it was not the South but Lincoln who was putting the public's welfare in jeopardy!

Since we detailed the reasons Lincoln's arrest and deportation of Vallandigham were unlawful in Chapter 15, there is no need to cover this ground again. What we will cover were the ensuing communications between liberal Lincoln and Erastus Corning and the conservative Ohio

Constitutionalists,[1505] as these are illustrative of the president's criminal mind at work.

On June 26, 1863, the Ohio Democratic State Convention wrote back to Lincoln:

> To his Excellency the President of The United States :
>
> The undersigned, having been appointed a committee, under the authority of the resolutions of the State Convention held at the city of Columbus, Ohio, on the 11th instant, to communicate with you on the subject of the arrest and banishment of Clement L. Vallandigham, most respectfully submit the following as the resolutions of that Convention bearing upon the subject of this communication, and ask of your Excellency their earnest consideration. And they deem it proper to state that the Convention was one in which all parts of the State were represented, one of the most respectable as to numbers and character, and one the most earnest and sincere in support of the Constitution and the Union, ever held in that State:
>
> > Resolved, That the will of the people is the foundation of all free government; that, to give effect to this free will, free thought, free speech, and a free press are absolutely indispensable. Without free discussion there is no certainty of sound judgment: without sound judgment there can be no wise government.
> >
> > 2. That it is an inherent and constitutional right of the people to discuss all measures of their Government, and to approve or disapprove, as to their best judgment seems right. That they have a like right to propose and advocate that policy which in their judgment is best, and to argue and vote against whatever policy seems to them to violate the Constitution, to impair their liberties, or to be detrimental to their welfare.
> >
> > 3. That these and all other rights guaranteed to them by their Constitutions are their rights in time of war as well as in time of peace, and of far more value and necessity in war than in peace, for in peace liberty, security, and property are seldom endangered; in war they are ever in peril.
> >
> > 4. That we now say to all whom it may concern, not by way of threat, but calmly and firmly, that we will not surrender these rights, nor submit to their forcible violation. We will obey the laws ourselves, and all others must obey them.
> >
> > 11. That Ohio will adhere to the Constitution and the Union as the best—it may be the last—hope of popular freedom, and for all wrongs which may have been committed, or evils which may exist, will seek redress, under the Constitution and within the

Union, by the peaceful but powerful agency of the suffrages of a free people.

14. That we will earnestly support every constitutional measure tending to preserve the Union of the States. No men have a greater interest in its preservation than we have, none desire it more; there are none who will make greater sacrifices or endure more than we will to accomplish that end. We are, as we ever have been, the devoted friends of the Constitution and the Union, and we have no sympathy with the enemies of either.

15. That the arrest, imprisonment, pretended trial, and actual banishment of Clement L. Vallandigham, a citizen of the State of Ohio, not belonging to the land or naval force of the United States, nor to the militia in actual service, by alleged military authority, for no other pretended crime than that of uttering words of legitimate criticism upon the conduct of the Administration in power, and of appealing to the ballot-box for a change of policy— said arrest and military trial taking place where the courts of law are open and unobstructed, and for no act done within the sphere of active military operations in carrying on the war—we regard as a palpable violation of the following provisions of the Constitution of the United States:

1. "Congress shall make no law abridging the freedom of speech or of the press, or the right of the people peaceably to assemble and to petition the Government for a redress of grievances."

2. "The right of the people to be secure in their persons, houses, papers, and effects, against unreasonable searches and seizures, shall not be violated; and no warrants shall issue but upon probable cause, supported by oath or affirmation, and particularly describing the place to be searched and the persons or things to be seized."

3. "No person shall be held to answer for a capital or otherwise infamous crime, unless on a presentment or indictment of a grand jury, except in cases arising in the land or naval forces, or in the militia, when in actual service in time of war or public danger."

4. "In all criminal prosecutions, the accused shall enjoy the right to a speedy and public trial, by an impartial jury of the State and district wherein the crime shall have been committed, which district shall have been previously ascertained by law."

And we furthermore denounce said arrest, trial, and banishment as a direct insult offered to the sovereignty of the people of Ohio, by whose organic law it is declared that no person shall be transported out of the State for any offence committed within the same.

16. That Clement L. Vallandigham was, at the time of his arrest, a prominent candidate for nomination by the Democratic party of Ohio for the office of Governor of the State; that the Democratic party was fully competent to decide whether he is a fit man for that nomination, and that the attempt to deprive them of that right, by his arrest and banishment, was an unmerited imputation upon their intelligence and loyalty, as well as a violation of the Constitution.

17. That we respectfully, but most earnestly, call upon the President of the United States to restore Clement L. Vallandigham to his home in Ohio, and that a committee of one from each Congressional district of the State, to be selected by the presiding officer of this Convention, is hereby appointed to present this application to the President.

The undersigned, in the discharge of the duty assigned them, do not think it necessary to reiterate the facts connected with the arrest, trial, and banishment of Mr. Vallandigham— they are well known to the President, and are of public history—nor to enlarge upon the positions taken by the Convention, nor to recapitulate the constitutional provisions which it is believed have been contravened; they have been stated at length, and with clearness, in the resolutions which have been recited. The undersigned content themselves with brief reference to other suggestions pertinent to the subject.

They do not call upon your Excellency as suppliants, praying the revocation of the order banishing Mr. Vallandigham as a favor; but, by the authority of a Convention representing a majority of the citizens of the State of Ohio, they respectfully ask it as a right due to an American citizen, in whose personal injury the sovereignty and dignity of the people of Ohio, as a free State, have been offended. And this duty they perform the more cordially from the consideration that, at a time of great national emergency, pregnant with danger to our Federal Union, it is all important that the true friends of the Constitution and the Union, however they may differ as to the mode of administering the Government, and the measures most likely to be successful in the maintenance of the Constitution and the restoration of the Union, should not be thrown into conflict with each other.

The arrest, unusual trial, and banishment of Mr. Vallandigham have created wide-spread and alarming disaffection among the people of the State, not only endangering the harmony of the friends of the Constitution and the Union, and tending to disturb the peace and tranquillity of the State, but also impairing that confidence in the fidelity of your Administration to the great landmarks of free government essential to a peaceful and successful enforcement of the laws in Ohio.

You are reported to have used in a public communication on this subject, the following language:

> "It gave me pain when I learned that Mr. Vallandigham had been arrested—that is, I was pained that there should have seemed to be a necessity for arresting him; and that it will afford me great pleasure to discharge him, so soon as I can by any means believe the public safety will not suffer by it."

The undersigned assure your Excellency, from our own personal knowledge of the feelings of the people of Ohio, that the public safety will be far more endangered by continuing Mr. Vallandigham in exile than by releasing him. It may be true that persons differing from him in political views may be found in Ohio, and elsewhere, who will express a different opinion. But they are certainly mistaken.

Mr. Vallandigham may differ with the President, and even with some of his own political party, as to the true and most effectual means of maintaining the Constitution and restoring the Union; but this difference of opinion does not prove him to be unfaithful to his duties as an American citizen. If a man, devotedly attached to the Constitution and the Union, conscientiously believes that, from the inherent nature of the Federal compact, the war, in the present condition of things in this country, cannot be used as a means of restoring the Union; or that a war to subjugate a part of the States, or a war to revolutionize the social system in a part of the States, could not restore, but would inevitably result in the final destruction of both the Constitution and the Union, is he not to be allowed the right of an American citizen to appeal to the judgment of the people for a change of policy by the constitutional remedy of the ballot-box?

During the war with Mexico many of the political opponents of the Administration then in power thought it their duty to oppose and denounce the war, and to urge before the people of the country that it was unjust and prosecuted for unholy purposes. With equal reason it might have been said of them that their discussions before the people were calculated to discourage enlistments, "to prevent the raising of troops," and to induce desertions from the army, and leave the Government without an adequate military force to carry on the war.

If the freedom of speech and of the press are to be suspended in time of war, then the essential element of popular government to effect a change of policy in the constitutional mode is at an end. The freedom of speech and of the press is indispensable, and necessarily incident to the nature of popular government itself if any inconvenience or evils arise from its exercise, they are unavoidable.

On this subject you [Lincoln] are reported to have said further:

> "It is asserted, in substance, that Mr. Vallandigham was, by a military commander, seized and tried 'for no other reason than words addressed to a public meeting in criticism of the course of the Administration, and in condemnation of the military order of the general.' Now, if there be no mistake about this, if there was no other reason for the arrest, then I concede that the arrest was wrong. But the arrest, I understand, was made for a very different reason. Mr. Vallandigham avows his hostility to the war on the part of the Union, and his arrest was made because he was laboring, with some effect, to prevent the raising of troops, to encourage desertions from the army, and to leave the rebellion without an adequate military force to suppress it. He was not arrested because he was damaging the political prospects of the Administration or the personal interests of the commanding general, but because he was damaging the army, upon the existence and vigor of which the life of the nation depends. He was warring upon the military, and this gave the military constitutional jurisdiction to lay hands upon him. If Mr. Vallandigham was not damaging the military power of the country, then his arrest was made on mistake of facts, which I would be glad to correct on

reasonable satisfactory evidence."

In answer to this permit us to say, first, that neither the charge nor the specifications in support of the charge on which Mr. Vallandigham was tried impute to him the act of either laboring to prevent the raising of troops or to encourage desertions from the army. Secondly, no evidence on the trial was offered with a view to support, or even tended to support, any such charge. In what instance, and by what act, did he either discourage enlistments or encourage desertion in the army? Who is the man who was discouraged from enlisting, and who encouraged to desert, by any act of Mr. Vallandigham? If it be assumed that perchance some person might have been discouraged from enlisting, or that some person might have been encouraged to desert, on account of hearing Mr. Vallandigham's views as to the policy of the war as a means of restoring the Union, would that have laid the foundation for his conviction and banishment? If so, upon the same grounds every political opponent of the Mexican war might have been convicted and banished from the country.

When gentlemen of high standing and extensive influence, including your Excellency, opposed, in the discussions before the people, the policy of the Mexican war, were they "warring upon the military," and did this "give the military constitutional jurisdiction to lay hands upon" them? And, finally, the charge in the specifications upon which Mr. Vallandigham was tried entitled him to a trial before the civil tribunals according to the express provisions of the late acts of Congress, approved by yourself July 17, 1862, and March 3, 1863, which were manifestly designed to supersede all necessity or pretext for arbitrary military arrests.

The undersigned are unable to agree with you in the opinion you have expressed that the Constitution is different in time of insurrection or invasion from what it is in time of peace and public security. The Constitution provides for no limitation upon or exceptions to the guarantees of personal liberty, except as to the writ of *habeas corpus*. Has the President, at the time of invasion or insurrection, the right to engraft limitations or exceptions upon these constitutional guarantees whenever, in his judgment, the public safety requires it?

True it is, the article of the Constitution which defines the various powers delegated to Congress declares that "the privilege of the writ of *habeas corpus* shall not be suspended unless when, in cases of rebellion or invasion, the public safety may require it." But this qualification or limitation upon this restriction upon the powers of Congress has no reference to or connection with the other constitutional guarantees of personal liberty. Expunge from the Constitution this limitation upon the power of Congress to suspend the writ of *habeas corpus* and yet the other guarantees of personal liberty would remain unchanged.

Although a man might not have a constitutional right to have an immediate investigation made as to the legality of his arrest upon *habeas corpus*, yet his "right to a speedy and public trial by an impartial jury of the State and district wherein the crime shall have been committed'" will not be altered; neither will his right to the exemption from "cruel and unusual punishment;" nor his right to be secure in his person, houses, papers, and effects, against unreasonable seizures and searches; nor his right not to be deprived of life, liberty, or property, without due process of law; nor his right not to be held to answer for a capital or otherwise infamous offence, unless on presentment or indictment of a grand jury, be in anywise changed.

And certainly the restriction upon the power of Congress to suspend the writ of *habeas corpus*, in time of insurrection or invasion, could not affect the guaranty that the freedom of speech and of the press shall not be abridged. It is sometimes urged that the proceedings in the civil tribunals are too tardy and ineffective for cases arising in times of insurrection or invasion. It is a full reply to this to say that arrests by civil process may be equally as expeditious and effective as arrests by military orders.

True, a summary trial and punishment are not allowed in the civil courts. But if the offender be under arrest and imprisoned, and not entitled to a discharge on writ of *habeas corpus* before trial, what more can be required for the purposes of the Government? The idea that all the constitutional guarantees of personal liberty are suspended throughout the country at a time of insurrection or invasion in any part of it places us upon a sea of uncertainty, and subjects the life, liberty, and property of every citizen to the mere will of a military commander, or what he may say that he considers the public safety requires. Does your Excellency wish to have it understood that you hold that the rights of every man throughout this vast country are subject to be annulled whenever you may say that you consider the public safety requires it, in time of invasion or insurrection ?

You are further reported as having said that the constitutional guarantees of personal liberty have "no application to the present case we have in hand, because the arrests complained of were not made for treason—that is, not for the treason defined in the Constitution, and upon the conviction of which the punishment is death—nor yet were they made to hold persons to answer for capital or otherwise infamous crimes; nor were the proceedings following in any constitutional or legal sense 'criminal prosecutions.' The arrests were made on totally different grounds, and the proceedings following accorded with the grounds of the arrests," &c.

The conclusion to be drawn from this position of your Excellency is, that where a man is liable to "a criminal prosecution," or is charged with a crime known to the laws of the land, he is clothed with all the constitutional guarantees for his safety and security from wrong and injustice; but that, where he is not liable to "a criminal prosecution," or charged with any crime known to the laws, if the President or any military commander shall say that he considers that the public safety requires it, this man may be put outside of the pale of the constitutional guarantees, and arrested without charge of crime, imprisoned without knowing what for, and any length of time, or be tried before a court-martial and sentenced to any kind of punishment, unknown to the laws of the land, which the President or the military commander may see proper to impose.

Did the Constitution intend to throw the shield of its securities around the man liable to be charged with treason as defined by it, and yet leave the man not liable to any such charge unprotected by the safeguards of personal liberty and personal security? Can a man not in the military or naval service, nor within the field of the operations of the army, be arrested and imprisoned without any law of the land to authorize it? Can a man thus, in civil life, be punished without any law defining the offence and describing the punishment? If the President or a court-martial may prescribe one kind of punishment unauthorized by law, why not any other kind? Banishment is an unusual punishment, and unknown to our laws. If the President has the right to prescribe the punishment of banishment, why not that of death and confiscation of property? If the President has the right to change the punishment prescribed by the court-martial from imprisonment to banishment, why not from imprisonment to torture upon the rack or execution upon the gibbet?

If an indefinable kind of constructive treason is to be introduced and engrafted upon the Constitution, unknown to the laws of the land and subject to the will of the President whenever an insurrection or invasion shall occur in any part of this vast country, what safety or security will be left for the liberties of the people?

The constructive treasons that gave the friends of freedom so many years of toil and trouble in England were inconsiderable compared to this. The precedents which you make will become a part of the Constitution for your successors, if sanctioned and acquiesced in by the people now.

The people of Ohio are willing to co-operate zealously with you in every effort warranted by the Constitution to restore the Union of the States, but they cannot consent to abandon those fundamental principles of civil liberty which are essential to their existence as a free people.

In their name we ask that, by a revocation of the order of his banishment, Mr. Vallandigham may be restored to the enjoyment of those rights of which they believe he has been unconstitutionally deprived.

We have the honor to be respectfully, yours, &c.

M. BIRCHARD, Chairman, 19th Dist.
DAVID A. HOUK, Secretary, 3rd Dist.
GEO. BLISS, 14th Dist.
T. W. BARTLEY, 8th Dist.
W. J. GORDON, 18th Dist.
JOHN O'NEILL, 13th Dist.
C. A. WHITE, 6th Dist.
W. E. FINCK, 12th Dist.
ALEXANDER LONG, 2nd Dist.
J. W. WHITE, 16th Dist.
JAS. R. MORRIS, 15th Dist.
GEO. S. CONVERSE, 7th Dist.
WARREN P. NOBLE, 9th Dist.
GEO. H. PENDLETON, 1st Dist.
W. A. HUTCHINS, 11th Dist.
ABNER L. BACKUS, 10th Dist.
J. F. McKINNEY, 4th Dist.
F. C. LeBLOND, 5th Dist.
LOUIS SHAEFER, 17th Dist.[1506]

On June 29, 1863, Lincoln responded:

> **Gentlemen:** The resolutions of the Ohio Democratic State Convention, which you present me, together with your introductory and closing remarks, being in position and argument mainly the same as the resolutions of the Democratic meeting at Albany, New York, I refer you to my response to the latter as meet in preparing your remarks, and I desire no more than that it be used with accuracy. In a single reading of your remarks, I only discovered one inaccuracy in matter which I suppose you took from that paper. It is where you say, "The

undersigned are unable to agree with you in the opinion you have expressed that the Constitution is different in time of insurrection or invasion from what it is in time of peace and public security."

A recurrence to the paper will show you that I have not expressed the opinion you suppose. I expressed the opinion that the Constitution is different in its application in cases of rebellion or invasion, involving the public safety, from what it is in times of profound peace and public security; and this opinion I adhere to, simply because by the Constitution itself things may be done in the one case which may not be done in the other.

I dislike to waste a word on a merely personal point, but I must respectfully assure you that you will find yourselves at fault should you ever seek for evidence to prove your assumption that I "opposed in discussions before the people the policy of the Mexican war."[1507]

You say: "Expunge from the Constitution this limitation upon the power of Congress to suspend the writ of *habeas corpus*, and yet the other guarantees of personal liberty would remain unchanged." Doubtless if this clause of the Constitution, improperly called, as I think, a limitation upon the power of Congress, were expunged, the other guarantees would remain the same; but the question is, not how those guarantees would stand with that clause out of the Constitution, but how they stand with that clause remaining in it, in case of rebellion or invasion, involving the public safety. If the liberty could be indulged in expunging that clause, letter and spirit, I really think the constitutional argument would be with you.

My general view on this question was stated in the Albany response, and hence I do not state it now. I only add that, as seems to me, the benefit of the writ of *habeas corpus* is the great means through which the guarantees of personal liberty are conserved and made available in the last resort; and corroborative of this view is the fact that Mr. Vallandigham, in the very case in question, under the advice of able lawyers, saw not where else to go but to the *habeas corpus*. But by the Constitution the benefit of the writ of *habeas corpus* itself may be suspended, when, in case of rebellion or invasion, the public safety may require it.

You ask, in substance, whether I really claim that I may override all the guaranteed rights of individuals, on the plea of conserving the public safety—when I may choose to say the public safety requires it. This question, divested of the phraseology calculated to represent me as straggling for an arbitrary personal prerogative, is either simply a question who shall decide, or an affirmation that nobody shall decide, what the public safety does require in cases of rebellion or invasion. The Constitution contemplates the question as likely to occur for decision, but it does not expressly declare who is to decide it. By necessary implication, when rebellion or invasion comes, the decision is to be made, from time to time; and I think the man whom, for the time, the people have, under the Constitution, made the Commander-in-Chief of their Army and Navy, is the man who holds the power and bears the responsibility of making it. If he uses the power justly, the same people will probably justify him; if he abuses it, he is in their hands, to be dealt with by all the modes they have reserved to themselves in the Constitution.

The earnestness with which you insist that persons can only, in times of rebellion, be lawfully dealt with, in accordance with the rules for criminal trials and punishments in times of peace, induces me to add a word to what I said on that point in the Albany response. You claim that men may, if they choose, embarrass those whose duty it is to combat a giant rebellion and then be dealt with only in turn as if there were no rebellion. The Constitution itself rejects this view. The military arrests and detentions which have been made, including those of Mr. Vallandigham, which are not different in principle from the other, have been for prevention, and not for punishment—as injunctions to stay injury, as proceedings to keep the peace—and hence, like proceedings in such cases and for like reasons, they have not been accompanied with indictments, or trials by juries, nor in a single case by any punishment whatever beyond what is purely incidental to the prevention. The original sentence of imprisonment in Mr. Vallandigham's case was to prevent injury to the military service only, and the modification of it was made as a less disagreeable mode to him of securing the same prevention.

I am unable to perceive an insult to Ohio in the case of Mr. Vallandigham. Quite surely nothing of this sort was or is intended. I was wholly unaware that Mr. Vallandigham was, at the time of his arrest, a candidate for the Democratic nomination for Governor, until so informed by your reading to me the resolutions of the Convention. I am grateful to the State of Ohio for many things, especially for the brave soldiers and officers she has given in the present national trial to the armies of the Union.

You claim as I understand, that according to my own position in the Albany response, Mr. Vallandigham should be released; and this because, as you claim, he has not damaged the military service by discouraging enlistments, encouraging desertions, or otherwise; and that if he had, he should be turned over to the civil authorities under the recent acts of Congress. I certainly do not know that Mr. Vallandigham has specifically and by direct language advised against enlistments, and in favor of desertion and resistance to drafting. We all know that combinations, armed in some instances, to resist the arrest of deserters, began several months ago; that more recently the like has appeared in resistance to the enrollment preparatory to a draft; and that quite a number of assassinations have occurred from the same animus. These had to be met by military force, and this again has led to bloodshed and death. And now, under a sense of responsibility more weighty and enduring than any which is merely official, I solemnly declare my belief that this hindrance of the military, including maiming and murder, is due to the course in which Mr. Vallandigham has been engaged, in a greater degree than to any other cause; and it is due to him personally in a greater degree than to any other man.

These things have been notorious, known to all, and of course known to Mr. Vallandigham. Perhaps I would not be wrong to say they originated with his especial friends and adherents. With perfect knowledge of them he has frequently, if not constantly, made speeches in Congress and before popular assemblies; and if it can be shown that, with these things staring him in the face, he has ever uttered a word of rebuke or counsel against them, it will be a fact greatly in his favor with me, and one of which, as yet, I am totally ignorant. When it is known that the whole burden of his speeches has been to stir up men against the prosecution of the war, and that in the midst of resistance to it he has not been known in any instance to counsel against such resistance, it is next to impossible to repel the inference that he has counselled directly in favor of it.

With all this before their eyes, the Convention you represent have nominated Mr. Vallandigham for Governor of Ohio, and both they and you have declared the purpose to sustain the National Union by all constitutional means. But, of course, they and you, in common, reserve to yourselves to decide what are constitutional means, and, unlike the Albany meeting, you omit to state or intimate that, in your opinion, an army is a constitutional means of saving the Union against a rebellion, or even to intimate that you are conscious of an existing rebellion being in progress with the avowed object of destroying that very Union. At the same time, your nominee for Governor, in whose behalf you appeal, is known to you and to the world to declare against the use of an army to suppress the rebellion. Your own attitude, therefore, encourages desertion, resistance to the draft, and the like, because it teaches those who incline to desert and to escape the draft to believe it is your purpose to protect them and to hope that you will become strong enough to do so.

After a short personal intercourse with you, gentlemen of the committee, I cannot say I think you desire this effect to follow your attitude; but I assure you that both friends and enemies of the Union look upon it in this light. It is a substantial hope, and by consequence a real strength to the enemy. It is a false hope, and one which you would willingly dispel. I will make the way exceedingly easy. I send you duplicates of this letter, in order that you, or a majority, may, if you choose, endorse your names upon one of them, and return it thus endorsed to me, with the understanding that those signing are hereby committed to the following propositions, and to nothing else:

1. That there is now a rebellion in the United States, the object and tendency of which is to destroy the National Union; and that, in your opinion, an army and navy are constitutional means for suppressing that rebellion.

2. That no one of you will do anything which, in his own judgment, will tend to hinder the increase or favor the decrease or lessen the efficiency of the army and navy, while engaged in the effort to suppress that rebellion; and

3. That each of you will, in his sphere, do all he

can to have the officers, soldiers, and seamen of the army and navy, while engaged in the effort to suppress the rebellion, paid, fed, clad, and otherwise well provided for and supported.

And with the further understanding that upon receiving the letter and names thus endorsed, I will cause them to be published, which publication shall be, within itself, a revocation of the order in relation to Mr. Vallandigham.

It will not escape observation that I consent to the release of Mr. Vallandigham upon terms not embracing any pledge from him or from others as to what he will or will not do. I do this because he is not present to speak for himself, or to authorize others to speak for him; and hence I shall expect that on returning he would not put himself practically in antagonism with his friends. But I do it chiefly because I thereby prevail on other influential gentlemen of Ohio to so define their position as to be of immense value to the army—thus more than compensating for the consequences of any mistake allowing Mr. Vallandigham to return, so that, on the whole, the public safety will not have suffered by it. Still, in regard to Mr. Vallandigham and all others, I must hereafter, as heretofore, do so much as the public service may seem to require.

I have the honor to be, respectfully, yours, &c. A. LINCOLN.[1508]

On July 1, 1863, the Ohio committee replied to the Yankee leader once again:

To his Excellency the President of The Unites States:
Sir: Your answer to the application of the undersigned for a revocation of the order of banishment of Clement L. Vallandigham requires a reply, which they proceed with as little delay as possible to make.

They are not able to appreciate the force of the distinction you make between the Constitution and the application of the Constitution, whereby you assume that powers are delegated to the President at the time of invasion or insurrection, in derogation of the plain language of the Constitution. The inherent provisions of the Constitution remaining the same in time of insurrection or invasion as in time of peace, the President can have no more right to disregard their positive and imperative requirements at the former time than at the latter. Because some things may be done by the terms of the Constitution at the time of invasion or insurrection which would not be required by the occasion in time of peace, you assume that any thing whatever, even though not expressed by the Constitution, may be done on the occasion of insurrection or invasion, which the President may choose to say is required by the public safety. In plainer terms, because the writ of *habeas corpus* may be suspended at time of invasion or insurrection, you infer that all other provisions of the Constitution having in view the protection of the life, liberty, and property of the citizen, may be in like manner suspended.

The provision relating to the writ of *habeas corpus* being contained in the first part of the Constitution, the purpose of which is to define the powers delegated to Congress, has no connection in language with the Declaration of Rights, as guarantees of personal liberty, contained in the additional and amendatory articles, and inasmuch as the provision relating to *habeas corpus* expressly provides for its suspension, and the other provisions alluded to do not provide for any such thing, the legal conclusion is that the suspension of the later [latter?] is unauthorized. The provision for the writ of *habeas corpus* is merely intended to furnish a summary remedy, and not the means whereby personal security is conserved in the final resort; while the other provisions are guarantees of personal rights, the suspension of which puts an end to all pretence of free government. It is true Mr. Vallandigham applied for a writ of *habeas corpus* as a summary remedy against oppression. But the denial of this did not take away his right to a speedy public trial by an impartial jury, or deprive him of his other rights as an American citizen. Your assumption of the right to suspend all the constitutional guarantees of personal liberty, and even of the freedom of speech and of the press, because the summary remedy of *habeas corpus* may be suspended, is at once startling and alarming to all persons desirous of preserving free government in this country.

The inquiry of the undersigned, whether "you hold the rights of every man throughout this vast country, in time of invasion or insurrection, are subject to be annulled whenever you may say that you consider the public safety requires it?" was a plain question, undisguised by circumlocution, and intended simply to elicit information. Your affirmative answer to this question throws a shade upon the fondest anticipations of the framers of the Constitution, who flattered themselves that they had provided safeguards against the dangers which have ever beset and overthrown free government in other ages and countries. Your answer is not to be disguised by the phraseology that the question "is simply a question who shall decide, or an affirmation that nobody shall decide, what the public safety does require in case of rebellion or invasion." Our Government was designed to be a Government of law, settled and defined, and not of the arbitrary will of a single man. As a safeguard, the powers were delegated to the legislative, executive, and judicial branches of the Government, and each made co-ordinate with the others, and supreme within its sphere, and thus a mutual check upon each other in case of abuse of power.

It has been the boast of the American people that they had a written Constitution, not only expressly defining, but also limiting the powers of the Government, and providing effectual safeguards for personal liberty, security, and property. And, to make the matter more positive and explicit, it was provided by the amendatory articles nine and ten that "the enumeration in the Constitution of certain rights shall not be construed to deny or disparage others retained by the people," and that "the powers not delegated to the United States by the Constitution, nor prohibited by it to the States, are reserved to the States respectively or to the people." With this care and precaution on the part of our forefathers who framed our institutions, it was not to be expected that, at so early a day as this, a claim of the President to arbitrary power, limited only by his conception of the requirements of the public safety, would have been asserted. In derogation of the constitutional provisions making the President strictly an executive officer, and vesting all the delegated legislative powers in Congress, your position, as we understand it, would make your will the rule of action, and your declaration of the requirements of the public safety the law of the land. Our inquiry was not, therefore, "simply a question who shall decide, or the affirmation that nobody shall decide, what the public safety requires." Our Government is a Government of law, and it is the law-making power which ascertains what the public safety requires, and prescribes the rule of action; and the duty of the President is simply to execute the laws thus enacted, and not to make or annul laws. If any exigency shall arise, the President has the power to convene Congress at any time to provide for it; so that the plea of necessity furnishes no reasonable pretext for any assumption of legislative power.

For a moment contemplate the consequences of such a claim to power. Not only would the dominion of the President be absolute over the rights of individuals, but equally so over the other departments of the Government. If he should claim that the public safety required it, he could arrest and imprison a judge for the conscientious discharge of his duties, paralyze the judicial power, or supercede it by the substitution of courts-martial, subject to his own will, throughout the whole country. If any one of the States, even far removed from the rebellion, should not sustain his plan for prosecuting the war, he could, on the plea of public safety, annul and set at defiance the State laws and authorities, arrest and imprison the Governor of the State or the members of the Legislature, while in the faithful discharge of their duties, or he could absolutely control the action, either of Congress or of the Supreme Court, by arresting and imprisoning its members, and upon the same ground he could suspend the elective franchise, postpone the elections, and declare the perpetuity of his high prerogative. And neither the power of impeachment nor the elections of the people could be made available against such concentration of power.

Surely it is not necessary to subvert free government in this country in order to put down the rebellion; and it cannot be done under the pretence of putting down the rebellion. Indeed, it is plain that your Administration has been weakened, and greatly weakened, by the assumption of power not delegated in the Constitution.

In your answer you say to us : **"You claim that men may, if they choose, embarrass those whose duty it is to combat a giant rebellion and then be dealt with in terms as if there were no rebellion."** You will find yourself in fault, if your will search our communication to you for any such idea. The undersigned believe that the Constitution and laws of the land, properly administered, furnish ample power to put down an insurrection without the assumption of powers not granted. And if existing legislation be inadequate, it is the duty of Congress to consider what further legislation is necessary, and to make suitable provision by law.

You claim that the military arrests made by your Administration are merely preventive remedies, **"as injunctions to stay injury, or proceedings to keep the peace, and not for punishment."** The ordinary preventive remedies alluded to are authorized by established law, but the preventive proceedings you institute have their authority merely in the will of the Executive or that of officers subordinate to his authority. And in this proceeding a discretion seems to be exercised as to whether the prisoner shall be allowed a trial or even be permitted to know the nature of the complaint alleged against him, or the name of his accuser. If the proceedings be merely preventive, why not allow the prisoner the benefit of a bond to keep the peace? But if no offence has been committed, why was Mr. Vallandigham tried, convicted, and sentenced by a court-martial? And why the actual punishment by imprisonment or banishment, without the opportunity of obtaining his liberty in the mode usual in preventive remedies, and yet say it is not for punishment?

You still place Mr. Vallandigham's conviction and banishment upon the ground that he had damaged the military service by discouraging enlistments and encouraging desertions, &c., and yet you have not even pretended to controvert our position that he was not charged with, tried, or convicted for any such offence before the court-martial.

In answer to our position that Mr. Vallandigham was entitled to a trial in the civil tribunals, by virtue of the late acts of Congress you say: **"I certainly do not know that Mr. Vallandigham has specifically and by direct language advised against enlistments and in favor of desertions and resistance to drafting,"** &c., and yet, in a subsequent part of your answer, after speaking of certain disturbances which are alleged to have occurred in resistance of the arrest of deserters and of the enrollment preparatory to the draft, and which you attribute mainly to the course Mr. Vallandigham has pursued, you say that he has made speeches against the war in the midst of resistance to it; that **"he has never been known, in any instance, to counsel against such resistance;"** and that **"it is next to impossible to repel the inference that he has counselled directly in favor of it."** Permit us to say that your information is most grievously at fault.

The undersigned have been in the habit of hearing Mr. Vallandigham speak before popular assemblages, and they appeal with confidence to every truthful person who has ever heard him for the accuracy of the declaration, that he has never made a speech before the people of Ohio in which he has not counselled submission and obedience to the laws and the Constitution, and advised the peaceful remedies of the judicial tribunals and of the ballot-box for the redress of grievances and for the evils which afflict our bleeding and suffering country. And, were it not foreign to the purposes of this communication, we would undertake to establish to the satisfaction of any candid person that the disturbances among the people to which you allude, in opposition to the arrest of deserters and the draft, have been occasioned mainly by the measures, policy, and conduct of your Administration, and the course of its political friends. But if the circumstantial evidence exists, to which you allude, which makes **"it next to impossible to repel the inference that Mr. Vallandigham has counselled directly in favor"** of this resistance, and that the same has been mainly attributable to his conduct, why was he not turned over to the civil authorities to be tried under the late acts of Congress? If there be any foundation in fact for your statements implicating him in resistance to the constituted authorities, he is liable to such prosecution. And we now demand, as a mere act of justice to him, an investigation of this matter before a jury of his country; and respectfully insist that fairness requires either that you retract these charges which you make against him, or that you revoke your order of banishment and allow him the opportunity of an investigation before an impartial jury.

The committee do not deem it necessary to repel at length the imputation that the attitude of themselves or of the Democratic party in Ohio **"encourage desertions, resistance to the draft, and the like."** Suggestions of that kind are not unusual weapons in our ordinary political contests. They rise readily in the minds of politicians heated with the excitement of partisan strife. During the two years in which the Democratic party of Ohio has been constrained to oppose the policy of the Administration, and to stand up in defence of the Constitution and of personal rights, this charge has been repeatedly made. It has fallen harmless, however, at the feet of those whom it was intended to injure. The committee believe it will do so again. If it were proper to do so in this paper, they might suggest that the measures of the Administration, and its changes of policy in the prosecution of the war, have been the fruitful sources of discouraging enlistments and inducing desertions, and furnish a reason for the undeniable fact that the first call for volunteers was answered by very many more than were demanded, and that the next call for soldiers will probably be responded to by drafted men alone.

The observation of the President in this connection, that neither the Convention in its resolutions, nor the committee in its communication, intimate that they **"are conscious of an existing rebellion being in progress with tie avowed object of destroying the Union,"** needs, perhaps, no reply. The Democratic party of Ohio has felt so keenly the condition of the country, and been so stricken to the heart by the misfortunes and sorrows which have befallen it, that they hardly deemed it necessary by solemn resolution, when their very State exhibited everywhere the sad evidences of war, to remind the President that they were aware of its existence.

In the conclusion of your communication you propose that, if a majority of the committee shall affix their signatures to a duplicate copy of it, which you have furnished, they shall stand committed to three propositions, therein at length set forth, that he will publish the names thus signed, and that this publication shall operate as a revocation of the order of banishment. The committee cannot refrain from the expression of their surprise that the

President should make the fate of Mr. Vallandigham depend upon the opinion of this committee upon these propositions. If the arrest and banishment were legal, and were deserved; if the President exercised a power clearly delegated, under circumstances which warranted its exercise, the order ought not to be revoked, merely because the committee hold, or express, opinions accordant with those of the President. If the arrest and banishment were not legal, or were not deserved by Mr. Vallandigham, then surely he is entitled to an immediate and unconditional discharge.

The people of Ohio were not so deeply moved by the action of the President merely because they were concerned for the personal safety and convenience of Mr. Vallandigham, but because they saw in his arrest and banishment an attack upon their own personal rights; and they attach value to his discharge chiefly as it will indicate an abandonment of the claim to the power of such arrest and banishment. However just the undersigned might regard the principles contained in the several propositions submitted by the President, or how much soever they might, under other circumstance, feel inclined to indorse the sentiments contained therein, yet they assure him that they have not been authorized to enter into any bargains, terms, contracts, or conditions with the President of the United States to procure the release of Mr. Vallandigham. The opinions of the undersigned touching the questions involved in these propositions are well known, have been many times publicly expressed, and are sufficiently manifested in the resolutions of the convention which they represent, and they cannot suppose that the President expects that they will seek the discharge of Mr. Vallandigham by a pledge implying not only an imputation upon their own sincerity and fidelity as citizens of the United States, and also carrying with it by implication a concession of the legality of his arrest, trial, and banishment, against which they and the convention they represent have solemnly protested. And, while they have asked the revocation of the order of banishment not as a favor, but as a right due to the people of Ohio, and with a view to avoid the possibility of conflict or disturbance of the public tranquillity, they do not do this, nor does Mr. Vallandigham desire it, at any sacrifice of their dignity and self-respect.

The idea that such a pledge as that asked from the undersigned would secure the public safety sufficiently to compensate for any mistake of the President in discharging Mr. Vallandigham is, in their opinion, a mere evasion of the grave questions involved in this discussion, and of a direct answer to their demand. And this is made especially apparent by the fact that this pledge is asked in a communication which concludes with an intimation of a disposition on the part of the President to repeat the acts complained of. The undersigned, therefore, having fully discharged the duty enjoined upon them, leave the responsibility with the President.

M. BIRCHARD, Chairman, 19th Dist.
DAVID A. HOUK, Secretary, 3rd Dist.
GEO. BLISS, 14th Dist.
T. W. BARTLEY, 8th Dist.
W. J. GORDON, 18th Dist.
JOHN O'NEILL, 13th Dist.
C. A. WHITE, 6th Dist.
W. E. FINCK, 12th Dist.
ALEXANDER LONG, 2nd Dist.
J. W. WHITE, 16th Dist.
JAS. R. MORRIS, 15th Dist.
GEO. S. CONVERSE, 7th Dist.
WARREN P. NOBLE, 9th Dist.
GEO. H. PENDLETON, 1st Dist.
W. A. HUTCHINS, 11th Dist.
ABNER L. BACKUS, 10th Dist.
J. F. McKINNEY, 4th Dist.
F. C. LeBLOND, 5th Dist.
LOUIS SHAEFER, 17th Dist.[1509]

Vallandigham himself, of course, had plenty to say about Lincoln's numerous constitutional violations and of his illegal treatment by the president. On June 15, 1864, the Ohio politician returned to his home state, where he addressed the Democratic Convention in the town of Hamilton:

> Men Of Ohio: To-day I am again in your midst and upon the soil of my native State. To-day I am once more within the district which for ten years extended to me the highest confidence, and three times honored me as its Representative in the Congress of the United States. I was accused of no crime against the Constitution or laws, and guilty of none. But whenever and wherever thus charged upon due process of law, I am now here ready to answer before any civil court of competent jurisdiction, to a jury of my countrymen, and in the meantime to give bail in any sum which any judge or court, State or Federal, may affix, and you, the 186,000 Democrats of Ohio, I offer as my sureties.
>
> Never for one hour have I remained in exile because I recognized any obligation of obedience to the unconstitutional and

arbitrary edict. Neither did personal fear ever restrain me. And to-day I return of my own act and pleasure, because it is my constitutional and legal right to return. Only by an exertion of arbitrary power, itself against the Constitution and law, and consummated by military force, I was abducted from my home and forced into banishment. The assertion or insinuation of the President that I was arrested **"because laboring, with some effect, to prevent the raising of troops, and to encourage desertions from the army,"** and was responsible for numerous acts of resistance to the draft and to the arrest of deserters, causing **"assassination, maiming, and murder,"** or that at any time, in any way, I had disobeyed or foiled to counsel obedience to the lawful authority, or even to the semblance of law, is absolutely false.

  I appeal for the proof to every speech I ever made upon those questions, and to the very record of the mock Military Commission by the trial and sentence of which I was outraged. No; the sole offence then laid to my charge was words of criticism of the public policy of the Administration, addressed to open and public political meetings of my fellow-citizens of Ohio, lawfully and peaceably assembled. And to-day, my only "crime" is, that in the way which they call treason, worship I the Constitution of my fathers. But for now more than one year, no public man has been arrested, and no newspaper suppressed within the States adhering still to the Union, for the expression of political opinion; while hundreds, in public assembly and through the press, have, with a license and violence in which I never indulged, criticised and condemned the acts and policies of the [Lincoln] Administration, and denounced the war, maintaining even the propriety and necessity of the recognition of southern independence.

  Indorsed by nearly two hundred thousand freemen of the Democratic [i.e., conservative] party of my native State at the late elections, and still with the sympathy and support of millions more, I do not mean any longer to be the only man of that party who is to be the victim of arbitrary power. If Abraham Lincoln seeks my life, let him so declare; but he shall not again restrain me of my personal liberty except upon "due process of law." The unconstitutional and monstrous "Order 38," under which alone I was arrested thirteen months ago, was defied and spit upon at your State convention of 1863, by the gallant gentleman who bore the standard as your candidate for Lieutenant Governor, and by every Democratic press and public speaker ever since. It is dead. From the first it was against the Constitution and laws, and without validity; and all proceedings under it were and are utterly null and void and of no effect.

The indignant voice of condemnation long since went forth from the vast majority of the people and presses of America and from all free countries in Europe with entire unanimity. And more recently, too, the "platform" of an earnest, numerous, and most formidable Convention of the sincere Republicans [i.e., liberals], and still further, the emphatic letter of acceptance by the candidate of that Convention, Gen. John C. Fremont, the first candidate also of the Republican party for the Presidency eight years ago, upon the rallying cry of "Free speech and a free Press," give renewed hope that at last the reign of arbitrary power is about to be brought to an end in the United States. It is neither just nor fit, therefore, that the wrongs inflicted under "Order 38," and the other edicts and acts of such power, should be any longer endured—certainly not by me alone.

But every ordinary means of redress has first been exhausted; yet either by the direct agency of the Administration and its subordinates, or through its influence or intimidation, or because of want of jurisdiction in the civil courts which no American in former times conceived to be possible here, all have failed. Counsel applied in my behalf to an unjust judge for the writ of *habeas corpus*. It was denied; and now the privilege of that writ is suspended by act of Congress and Executive order in every State. The Democratic Convention of Ohio, one year ago, by a resolution formally presented through a committee of your best and ablest men in person, at Washington, demanded of the President, in behalf of a very large minority of the people, a revocation of the edict of banishment.

Pretending that the public safety then required it, he refused; saying, at the same time, that **"it would afford him pleasure to comply as soon as he could by any means be made to believe that the public safety would not suffer by it."** One year has elapsed, yet this hollow pretence is still tacitly asserted, and to-day I am here to prove it unfounded in fact. I appealed to the Supreme Court of the United States; and because Congress had never conferred jurisdiction in behalf of a citizen tried by a tribunal unknown for such purpose, to the laws, and expressly forbidden by the Constitution, it was powerless to redress the wrong. The time has, therefore, arrived, when it becomes me as a citizen of Ohio and of the United States, to demand, and, by my own act, to vindicate the rights, liberties, and privileges which I never forfeited, but of which, for so many months, I have been deprived.

Wherefore, men of Ohio, I am again in your midst to-day. I owe duties to the State, and am here to discharge them. I have rights as a citizen, and am here to assert them; a wife, and child, and home, and would enjoy all the pleasures which are implied in those cheerful words. But I am here for peace, not disturbance; for quiet not convulsion; for order and law, not anarchy. Let no man of the Democratic party begin any act of violence or disorder; but let none shrink from any responsibility, however urgent, if forced upon him. Careful of the rights of others, let him see to it that he fully and fearlessly exacts his own. Subject to rightful authority in all things, let him submit to excess or usurpation in nothing. Obedient to the Constitution and law, let him demand and have the full measure of protection which law and Constitution secure to him.

Men of Ohio: You have already vindicated your right to hear; it is now my duty to assert my right to speak. Wherefore, as to the sole offence for which I was arrested, imprisoned, and banished—free speech in criticism and condemnation of the Administration—an Administration fitly described in a recent public paper by one of its early supporters, "marked at home by disregard of constitutional rights, by its violation of personal liberty and the liberty of the press, and, as its crowning shame, by its abandonment of the right of asylum, a right especially dear to all free nations abroad," I repeat it here to-day, and will again and yet again so long as I live, or the Constitution and our present form of Government shall survive.

The words then spoken and the appeal at that time made, and now enforced by one year more of taxation and debt, and of blood and disaster, entreating the people to change the public servants and their policy, not by force, but peaceably, through the ballot, I now and here reiterate in their utmost extent, and with all their significancy I repeat them, one and all, in no spirit of challenge or bravado, but as earnest, sober, solemn truth and warning to the people.

Upon another subject allow me here a word:

A powerful, widely-spread and very dangerous secret, oath-bound combination among the friends of the [Lincoln] Administration, known as the "Loyal Union League," exists in every State, yet the very men who control it charge persistently upon the members of the Democratic party, that they have organized—especially in the North West—the "Order of Knights of the Golden Circle," or some other secret society, treasonable or "disloyal" in its character, affiliated with the South, and for the purpose of armed resistance to the Federal and State Governments. Whether any such ever existed I do not know; but the charge that organizations of that sort, or having any such purpose, do now exist among members of that party in Ohio or other non-slaveholding States, is totally and positively false.

That lawful political or party associations have been established, having, as their object, the organizing and strengthening of the Democratic party, and its success in the coming Presidential election, and designed as a countermovement to the so-called "Union Leagues," and, therefore secret in their proceedings, is very probable, and however objectionable hitherto, and in ordinary times, I recognise to the fullest extent, not the lawfulness only, but the propriety and necessity of such organizations—for "when bad men combine good men must associate." But they are no conspiracy against the Government, and their members are not conspirators, but patriots; men not leagued together for the overthrow of the Constitution or the laws, and still less, of liberty, but firmly united for the preservation and support of these great objects.

There is indeed, a "conspiracy" very powerful, very ancient, and I trust that before long I may add, strongly consolidated also, upon sound principles, and destined yet to be triumphant—a conspiracy known as the Democratic [conservative] party, the present object of which is the overthrow of the Administration in November next, not by force but through the ballot-box, the election of a President who shall be true to his oath, to Liberty and the Constitution. This is the sole conspiracy of which I know anything; and I am proud to be one of the conspirators. If any other exist, looking to unlawful armed resistance to the Federal State authorities anywhere, in the exercise of their legal and constitutional rights, I admonish all persons concerned that the act is treason, and the penalty death.

But I warn also the men in power that there is a vast multitude, a host whom they cannot number, bound together by the strongest and holiest ties, to defend, by whatever means the exigencies of the times shall demand, their natural and constitutional rights as freemen, at all hazards and to the last extremity.

Three years have now passed, men of Ohio, and the great issue—constitutional liberty and free popular governments—is still before you. To you I again commit it, confident that in this, the time of their greatest peril, you will be found worthy of the ancestors who for so many ages, in England and America, on the field, in prison, and upon the scaffold, defended them against tyrants and usurpers, whether is councils or in arms.[1510]

To this day in the South Clement Laird Vallandigham is held as a hero of sorts. For to his lasting credit he was not only an arch foe of the South's greatest enemy, the monarchical Northern leader he referred to as

"King Lincoln," he was also a strict constitutionalist and a champion of states' rights, one who correctly held that the Southern states had every legal right to secede, and that they should have been allowed to do so in peace. At one time the Ohio conservative even promoted the idea of the secession of his state if Lincoln did not let the South go. As Vallandigham himself often said of Lincoln's idea of an involuntary Union held together by force and threat of violence: If this is the United States Lincoln desires, "I do not want to belong to it."[1511]

While as a conservative Vallandigham's loathing of liberal Lincoln was understandable, what many are unaware of—thanks to the always energetic efforts of Lincoln scholars to suppress the truth—is that Lincoln was also disliked and distrusted by many members of his own party. One of these was James C. Conkling, an Illinois Republican (liberal), attorney, and politician.

Conkling had sent Lincoln a letter criticizing the War and the obvious illegality of his Emancipation Proclamation. As we saw in Chapter 13, it was unlawful because the leader of one nation (in this case the U.S.A.) has no legal authority to enact laws in another nation (in this case the C.S.A.). Conkling's letter kindly included an invitation to the president to address a meeting of fellow Republicans and explain his illicit behavior.

Shortly thereafter Lincoln replied to the Illinois politician in his now famous "Conkling letter," a Lincolnian document much beloved by liberals, progressives, socialists, and Constitution haters in general. Dated August 26, 1863, it reads:

> My dear Sir: Your letter inviting me to attend a mass-meeting of unconditional Union men, to be held at the capital of Illinois on the 3d day of September, has been received. It would be very agreeable to me to thus meet my old friends at my own home, but I cannot just now be absent from here so long as a visit there would require.
> The meeting is to be of all those who maintain unconditional devotion to the Union; and I am sure my old political friends will thank me for tendering, as I do, the nation's gratitude to those and other noble men whom no partizan malice or partizan hope can make false to the nation's life.
> There are those who are dissatisfied with me. To such I would say: You desire peace, and you blame me that we do not have it. But how can we attain it? There

are but three conceivable ways: First, to suppress the rebellion by force of arms. This I am trying to do. Are you for it? If you are, so far we are agreed. If you are not for it, a second way is to give up the Union. I am against this. Are you for it? If you are, you should say so plainly. If you are not for force, nor yet for dissolution, there only remains some imaginable compromise. I do not believe any compromise embracing the maintenance of the Union is now possible. All I learn leads to a directly opposite belief. The strength of the rebellion is its military, its army. That army dominates all the country and all the people within its range. Any offer of terms made by any man or men within that range, in opposition to that army, is simply nothing for the present, because such man or men have no power whatever to enforce their side of a compromise, if one were made with them.

To illustrate: Suppose refugees from the South and peace men of the North get together in convention, and frame and proclaim a compromise embracing a restoration of the Union. In what way can that compromise be used to keep [Confederate General Robert E.] Lee's army out of Pennsylvania? [Union General George G.] Meade's army can keep Lee's army out of Pennsylvania, and, I think, can ultimately drive it out of existence. But no paper compromise to which the controllers of Lee's army are not agreed can at all affect that army. In an effort at such compromise we should waste time which the enemy would improve to our disadvantage; and that would be all. A compromise, to be effective, must be made either with those who control the rebel army, or with the people first liberated from the domination of that army by the success of our own army. Now, allow me to assure you that no word or intimation from that rebel army, or from any of the men controlling it, in relation to any peace compromise, has ever come to my knowledge or belief. All charges and insinuations to the contrary are deceptive and groundless. And I promise you that if any such proposition shall hereafter come, it shall not be rejected and kept a secret from you. I freely acknowledge myself the servant of the people, according to the bond of service—the United States Constitution—and that, as such, I am responsible to them.

But to be plain. You are dissatisfied with me about the negro. Quite likely there is a difference of opinion between you and myself upon that subject. I certainly wish that all men could be free, while I suppose you do not. Yet, I have neither adopted nor proposed any measure which is not consistent with even your view, provided you are for the Union. I suggested compensated emancipation, to which you replied you wished not to be taxed to buy negroes. But I had not asked you to be taxed to buy negroes, except in such way as to save you from greater taxation to save the Union exclusively by other means.

You dislike the emancipation proclamation, and perhaps would have it retracted. You say it is unconstitutional. I think differently. I think the Constitution invests its commander-in-chief with the law of war in time of war. The most that can be said—if so much—is that slaves are property. Is there—has there ever been—any question that by the law of war, property, both of enemies and friends, may be taken when needed? And is it not needed whenever taking it helps us, or hurts the enemy? Armies, the world over, destroy enemies' property when they cannot use it; and even destroy their own to keep it from the enemy. Civilized belligerents do all in their power to help themselves or hurt the enemy, except a few things regarded as barbarous or cruel. Among the exceptions are the massacre of vanquished foes and non-combatants, male and female.

But the proclamation, as law, either is valid or is not valid. If it is not valid, it needs no retraction. If it is valid, it cannot be retracted any more than the dead can be brought to life. Some of you profess to think its retraction would operate favorably for the Union. Why better after the retraction than before the issue? There was more than a year and a half of trial to suppress the rebellion before the proclamation issued; the last one hundred days of which passed under an explicit notice that it was coming, unless averted by those in revolt returning to their allegiance. The war has certainly progressed as favorably for us since the issue of the proclamation as before. I know, as fully as one can know the opinions of others, that some of the commanders of our armies in the field, who have given us our most important successes, believe the emancipation policy and the use of the colored troops constitute the heaviest blow yet dealt to the rebellion, and that at least one of these important successes could not have been achieved when it was but for the aid of black soldiers. Among the commanders holding these views are some who have never had any affinity with what is called Abolitionism, or with Republican party politics, but who hold them purely as military opinions. I submit these opinions as being entitled to some weight against the objections often urged that emancipation and arming the blacks are unwise as military measures, aud were not adopted as such in good faith.

You say you will not fight to free negroes. Some of them seem willing to fight for you; but no matter. Fight you, then, exclusively, to save the Union. I issued the proclamation on purpose to aid you in saving the Union. Whenever you shall have conquered all resistance to the Union, if I shall urge you to continue fighting, it will be an apt time then for you to declare you will not fight to free negroes.

I thought that in your struggle for the Union, to whatever extent the negroes should cease helping the enemy, to that extent it weakened the enemy in his resistance to you. Do you think differently? I thought that whatever negroes can be got to do as soldiers, leaves just so much less for white soldiers to do in saving the Union. Does it appear otherwise to you? But negroes, like other people, act upon motives. Why should they do anything for us if we will do nothing for them? If they stake their lives for us they must be prompted by the strongest motive, even the promise of freedom. And the promise, being made, must be kept.

The signs look better. The Father of Waters again goes unvexed to the sea. Thanks to the great Northwest for it. Nor yet wholly to them. Three hundred miles up they met New England, Empire, Keystone, and Jersey, hewing their way right and left. The sunny South, too, in more colors than one, also lent a hand. On the spot, their part of the history was jotted down in black and white. The job was a great national one, and let none be banned who bore an honorable part in it. And while those who have cleared the great river may well be proud, even that is not all. It is hard to say that anything has been more bravely and well done than at Antietam, Murfreesboro, Gettysburg, and on many fields of lesser note. Nor must Uncle Sam's web-feet be forgotten. At all the watery margins they have been present. Not only on the deep sea, the broad bay, and the rapid river, but also up the narrow, muddy bayou, and wherever the ground was a little damp, they have been and made their tracks. Thanks to all: for the great republic—for the principle it lives by and keeps alive—for man's vast future—thanks to all.

Peace does not appear so distant as it did. I hope it will come soon, and come to stay; and so come as to be worth the keeping in all future time. It will then have been proved that among free men there can be no successful appeal from the ballot to the bullet, and that they who take such appeal are sure to lose their case and pay the cost. And then there will be some black men who can remember that with silent tongue, and clenched teeth, and steady eye, and well-poised bayonet, they have helped mankind on to this great consummation, while I fear there will be some white ones unable to forget that with malignant heart and deceitful speech they strove to hinder it.

Still, let us not be over-sanguine of a speedy final triumph. Let us be quite sober. Let us diligently apply the means, never doubting that a just God, in his own good time, will give us the rightful result. Yours very truly, A. Lincoln.[1512]

Once again Lincoln's words here brim with misinformation, disinformation, lies, deception, a dictator's hatred of states' rights, and an appalling ignorance of the Constitution.

He begins by stating that he is striving for **"peace."** But how will he attain this? He believes it will come by illegally invading the South with some 2 million soldiers! Since he tricked the South into firing the first shot at Fort Sumter, it is obvious that he is the one who wanted war, making his alleged desire for **"peace"** all the more absurd.

He then declares that the **"strength of the Rebellion is its military."** Only a monarch or autocrat would think such a thing. As every traditional Southerner knew then and knows today, the Confederacy's strength was in her people, in her communities, in her culture, and in her churches.

Lincoln asserts that he is a **"servant of the people"** and calls the Constitution his **"bond of service."** As "King Abraham" he was anything but a servant of the people. Instead, he saw the masses as his loyal subjects, malleable automatons who existed merely to pay their taxes, support his socialistic Big Brother policies, and keep him in office. As for the Constitution being his **"bond of service,"** it is clear that he possessed neither a true understanding or any respect for that document, as his hundreds of crimes duly attest.

The president maintains here that **"the use of colored troops is the heaviest blow yet dealt to the rebellion,"** a piece of political hyperbole that is destroyed by the facts: only half of his 200,000 black soldiers came from the South (and many of these, as we are about to see, did not enroll voluntarily, but were forced into the Union military at gunpoint). The South, on the other hand, had between 300,000 and 1 million black soldiers[1513] (depending on how one defines a "soldier").[1514]

Lincoln also used the Conkling letter to reemphasize the fact that he did not issue the Emancipation Proclamation for blacks, but **"to aid in saving the Union."** This was a statement he made continually throughout his political career, but his devotees either ignore it or suppress it.

Finally, he says here that he issued the Emancipation Proclamation and then enlisted blacks so that they could perform duties that whites did not want to do. As the edict itself states, this work amounted to little more than guard duty, or as he put it, blacks were to be received into the Yankee military for only one purpose: **"to garrison forts, positions, stations and other places . . ."** Indeed, he would not allow his African-American soldiers to be armed and trained until later in the War, and this only after much pressure from abolitionists and black civil rights leaders.

The only factual statement in Lincoln's letter to Conkling is Conkling's own comment that he, like the majority of Northern whites, did not want to fight to end slavery or give blacks full civil rights, a sentiment shared by most of Lincoln's servicemen as well. Speaking for nearly all Federal officers, Yankee General Ulysses S. Grant, for example, an Ohio slave owner[1515] and colonizationist[1516] who kept his slaves until eight months *after* the War was over,[1517] is said to have once declared:

> The sole object of this war is to restore the union. Should I be convinced it has any other object, or that the government designs using its soldiers to execute the wishes of the Abolitionists, I pledge to you my honor as a man and a soldier. I would resign my commission and carry my sword to the other side.[1518]

Still, the War, whatever cause the Yankee president wished to invent for initiating it, had to be carried to its completion in order to achieve his socialistic agenda: the installation of an omnipotent, dictatorial, Big

Brother, big spending, big government in the North that would totally control the American economy and military. Since he felt he could not accomplish this without the Southern states, Lincoln had to fabricate the bogus ideas that secession was illegal and that the Union was being destroyed by the existence of the Confederacy. This, he believed, justified his invasion of the South, even giving him the right as president to declare war.

But as always, Lincoln knew very well that legally he was in the wrong, that he did not have the constitutional authority to inaugurate War on a foreign nation. In order to achieve his goals, of course, he had to pretend otherwise. Still, the official record has chronicled his pre-presidential knowledge of Constitutional principles and law in this area.

For example, there is Lincoln's February 15, 1848, anti-Mexican War letter to his friend William H. Herndon, penned twelve years before he became our sixteenth chief executive:

> Dear William: Your letter of the 29th January was received last night. Being exclusively a constitutional argument, I wish to submit some reflections upon it in the same spirit of kindness that I know actuates you. Let me first state what I understand to be your position. It is that if it shall become necessary to repel invasion, the President may, without violation of the Constitution, cross the line and invade the territory of another country, and that whether such necessity exists in any given case the President is the sole judge.
>
> Before going further consider well whether this is or is not your position. If it is, it is a position that neither the President himself, nor any friend of his, so far as I know, has ever taken. Their only positions are—first, that the soil was ours when the hostilities commenced; and second, that whether it was rightfully ours or not, Congress had annexed it, and the President for that reason was bound to defend it; both of which are as clearly proved to be false in fact as you can prove that your house is mine. The soil was not ours, and Congress did not annex or attempt to annex it. But to return to your position. Allow the President to invade a neighboring nation whenever he shall deem it necessary to repel an invasion, and you allow him to do so whenever he may choose to say he deems it necessary for such purpose, and you allow him to make war at pleasure. Study to see if you can fix any limit to his power in this respect, after having given him so much as

you propose. If to-day he should choose to say he thinks it necessary to invade Canada to prevent the British from invading us, how could you stop him? You may say to him, "I see no probability of the British invading us"; but he will say to you, "Be silent; I see it, if you don't."

The provision of the Constitution giving the war-making power to Congress was dictated, as I understand it, by the following reasons: Kings had always been involving and impoverishing their people in wars, pretending generally, if not always, that the good of the people was the object. This our convention understood to be the most oppressive of all kingly oppressions, and they resolved to so frame the Constitution that no one man should hold the power of bringing this oppression upon us. But your view destroys the whole matter, and places our President where kings have always stood. Write soon again. Yours truly, A. Lincoln.[1519]

Lincoln, the demagogues' demagogue, discarded this very accurate view of presidential powers when it became inconvenient. We know the exact date this occurred: November 6, 1860, the day he was elected president of the United States, the day the Southern states began planning to legally secede. From that day forward Lincoln's lies began to quickly mount, one atop the other, bringing to mind Sir Walter Scott's famous dictum:

> O, what a tangled web we weave, when first we practice to deceive![1520]

In order to utilize his newly discovered dictatorial powers, deceptive Lincoln had to manufacture the idea that the Confederacy was not legitimate, which is why from the very beginning he nearly always referred to it publicly and derogatorily as the **"so-called Confederacy."**

Behind closed doors, however, he knew full well that it was a legally formed foreign nation. Indeed, it is this very fact makes Lincoln a war criminal: if secession was truly unlawful, then the Confederacy itself would have been unlawful, and Lincoln would have had every right to try and coerce her back into the Union.

It is this reality that has forced the North into its present uncomfortable position: justification must be found for the "Civil War" in order for Lincoln to be exonerated and the slaughter of 3 million Americans excused. The effort to achieve this has resulted in what I call the "Great Yankee Coverup": the suppression of the Truth, replaced by Northern anti-South myths and fairy tales that paint Dixie and her people in the worst light possible in order to justify Lincoln's actions.

Yet, before his War Lincoln himself was well aware that his own native homeland, the South, was not the evil monster portrayed by many Northerners. Being from a lower class and underprivileged Kentucky family, he well understood that the South was made up primarily of poor farmers and soft-hearted, defenseless country folk. He knew full well too that if the tables had been turned and it was the North that had been openly practicing slavery at the time, its citizens would have done exactly what the South's had.[1521]

Thus during the August 21, 1858, Ottawa, Illinois, debate between himself and Stephen A. Douglas, Lincoln made this remarkable statement:

> . . . I think I have no prejudice against the Southern people. They are just what we would be in their situation. If slavery did not now exist among them, they would not introduce it. If it did now exist among us, we should not instantly give it up. This I believe of the masses north and south. . . .
> When southern people tell us they are no more responsible for the origin of slavery than we, I acknowledge the fact. . . . I surely will not blame them for not doing what I should not know how to do myself.[1522]

On December 29, 1860, president-elect Lincoln wrote the following in a letter to William Cullen Bryant:

> I promise you that I shall unselfishly try to deal fairly with all men and all shades of opinion among our friends.[1523]

We will note that he does not actually promise to **"deal fairly with all men and all shades of opinion."** He merely promises that he will **"try"** to do so, a difference wide enough to drive a tractor through. Also, his pledge only extends to his **"friends"**; that is, those who agree with his liberal philosophy on all issues. This, of course, excluded nearly everyone who lived south of the Mason-Dixon Line!

Despite these seemingly tender sentiments, three years later Lincoln used what he ludicrously called his **"better angel"**[1524] to viciously and illegitimately invade the South, using a scorched earth policy of total war to destroy her infrastructure, and burn her homes, shops, towns, schools, churches, hospitals, libraries, and universities to the ground, killing nearly two million (one million Southern whites and one million Southern blacks) of her people in the process. Horribly, most of these were non-combatants, as almost all civilian deaths during the War occurred in the South.[1525]

Lincoln's unyielding total war policy was actually embedded into his party's 1864 platform. The second plank reads:

> Resolved, That we approve the determination of the government of the United States not to compromise with rebels, or to offer them any terms of peace, except such as may be based upon an unconditional surrender of their hostility and a return to their just allegiance to the Constitution and laws of the United States, and that we call upon the government to maintain this position, and to prosecute the war with the utmost possible vigor to the complete suppression of the rebellion, in full reliance upon the self-sacrificing patriotism, the heroic valor, and the undying devotion of the American people to their country and its free institutions.[1526]

It was just such inflexible Yankee hatred of the South that helped ignite the first embers of the War to begin with.

It is obvious that by June 1864, when the above Republican platform was released, Lincoln and his cohorts still had not learned their lesson (that the Constitution is the basis of American government) or repented of their sins (lies, slanders, and high crimes and misdemeanors). Neither had they yet realized the desperate need to end, as soon as possible, the terrible violence they had launched at Fort Sumter three years earlier.

And so Lincoln's illegal and needless War raged on.

In my Tennessee hometown alone, some 1,750 Confederate men and boys were slaughtered by Lincoln's invaders on a single afternoon in the Fall of 1864 in one of the goriest and most senseless battles of his War. Cut down like wheat before the scythe, as one eyewitness described the horrific scene,[1527] many a brave Southern soldier died within sight of his own home, as parents, wives, and children raged and sobbed in disbelief at Lincoln's bewildering aggression. Another 4,500 Rebels were wounded and maimed that day in one of the darkest and bloodiest chapters in American history: the Battle of Franklin II.[1528] Confederate soldier Sam Watkins, who was on the Franklin battlefield that day, called it "the blackest page" of the entire

War, and "the finishing stroke to the independence of the Southern Confederacy."¹⁵²⁹

In 1864 my own third great-grandfather, Confederate cavalryman Elias Jent, Sr., who served in the 1ˢᵗ Regiment of the 13ᵗʰ Kentucky Cavalry (known as "Caudill's Army"), was unlawfully executed by Yankee soldiers while at home in Kentucky on furlough. Elias thus became one of the conservatively estimated 329,000 Confederate soldiers who died needlessly due to Lincoln's illegitimate warmongering.

Tragically, Elias' wife, Rachel Cornett, my third great-grandmother, was also murdered. The unarmed gentle farming couple had been visiting relatives in Perry County, Kentucky, when they were discovered by marauding Union soldiers. Ignoring the heart-rending screams and futile entreaties of kin, the pitiless Yankee wretches dragged Elias and Rachel unceremoniously into the yard and, at gunpoint, hanged them side-by-side from a large tree in front of family, friends, and neighbors. No reason was given and no punishment was ever meted out. This was typical Lincolnian military procedure, and our family still holds "Honest Abe" directly responsible for Elias and Rachel's deaths.

In 1863 it was this very type of behavior that inspired Confederates, like Sergeant Edwin Fay, to avow: even if peace is ever made with the North, if I live another 100 years I will murder every single Yankee I come across. As long as I can kill him without much risk, I will.¹⁵³⁰

Indeed, for their crimes, the name Lincoln, along with those of hundreds of other Yankee war criminals, among them William T. Sherman, Philip H. Sheridan, Benjamin F. Butler, Edward Hatch, David Hunter,¹⁵³¹ John Pope, Ulysses S. Grant (who Lysander Spooner called "the chief murderer of the war"),¹⁵³² and Robert Huston Milroy, will never be forgotten in Dixie.¹⁵³³ All bragged of the destruction they wreaked on the South.¹⁵³⁴ Entire Southern cities disappeared under the commands of these and numerous other Northern officers.

One of them, Sherman—who was deemed "unstable and mentally deranged" even by other Yankees¹⁵³⁵—gave an order to his men that their "destruction be so thorough that not a rail or tie can be used again,"¹⁵³⁶ then boasted that many of the towns he and his troops marched through would not be found on future maps. On March 7, 1864, he reported on one of these, Meridian, Mississippi, saying:

> For five days 10,000 men worked hard and with a will in that work of destruction, with axes, crowbars, sledges, clawbars, and with

fire, and I have no hesitation in pronouncing the work as well done. Meridian, with its depots, store-houses, arsenal, hospitals, offices, hotels, and cantonments, no longer exists.[1537]

Such arrogant pronouncements were standard procedure for flinty Yankees like Ohio-born Sherman.[1538]

The town was later rebuilt. But to this day, the only evidence that many of the places he obliterated were once thriving communities are small stone markers.

After leveling Meridian Sherman robbed, burned, and bombed his way through the rest of the Magnolia state, cutting, as he bragged, "a swath of desolation fifty miles broad across the state of Mississippi, which the present generation will not forget."[1539] In Savannah, Georgia, he callously admitted that 80 percent of the devastation he had caused was "simple waste and destruction."[1540]

In late December 1864, after subduing and occupying the city, a cocky Sherman sent a telegram to Lincoln, offering the defeated town to the president as a Christmas present.[1541] It read:

> SAVANNAH, GEORGIA, December 22, 1864.
> To His Excellency President Lincoln, Washington, D.C.:
> I beg to present you as a Christmas-gift the city of Savannah, with one hundred and fifty heavy guns and plenty of ammunition, also about twenty-five thousand bales of cotton.
> W. T. Sherman, Major-General.[1542]

Lincoln's reply to this missive deserves special mention since it reveals his complicity in Sherman's war crimes:

> **My Dear General Sherman: Many, many thanks for your Christmas gift, the capture of Savannah.**
>
> **When you were about to leave Atlanta for the Atlantic coast, I was anxious, if not fearful; but feeling that you were the better judge, and remembering that 'nothing risked, nothing gained,' I did not interfere. Now, the undertaking being a success, the honor is all yours; for I believe that none of us went further than to acquiesce.**
>
> **And taking the work of General [George H.] Thomas into the count, as it should be taken, it is indeed a great success. Not only does it afford the obvious and immediate military advantages; but in showing to the**

world that your army could be divided, putting the stronger part to an important new service, and yet leaving enough to vanquish the old opposing forces of the whole,—[Confederate General John Bell] Hood's army,—it brings those who sat in darkness to see a great light. But what next?
       I suppose it will be safe if I leave General Grant and yourself to decide.
       Please make my grateful acknowledgments to your whole army—officers and men.
Yours very truly, A. Lincoln.[1543]

On rare occasions Lincoln's soldiers "kindly" first allowed Southern women and children to select a few important items to be saved and carried out into the street before attacking their home. Then as the horrified family looked on, their house was ransacked and pillaged, jewelry and other valuables pocketed, paintings sliced to ribbons with bayonets, pianos hammered to pieces, windows smashed out with rifle butts, doors violently ripped off their hinges, bookcases pulled down, beds overturned, and furniture broken apart. The dwelling was then set afire, instantly rendering the family homeless refugees.[1544]

Lincoln was well aware of such acts of violence, as is evident in the following letter sent to Union General Joseph Jones Reynolds on January 20, 1864:

> It would appear by the accompanying papers that Mrs. Mary E. Morton is the owner, independently of her husband, of a certain building, premises, and furniture, which she, with her children, has been occupying and using peaceably during the war until recently, when the Provost-Marshal has, in the name of the United States Government, seized the whole of said property, and ejected her from it. It also appears by her statement to me that her husband went off in the rebellion at the beginning, wherein he still remains.
>   It would seem that this seizure has not been made for any military object, as for a place of storage, a hospital, or the like, because this would not have required the seizure of the furniture, and especially not the return of furniture previously taken away.
>   The seizure must have been on some claim of confiscation, a matter of which the courts, and not the provost-marshals or other military officers, are to judge.

In this very case would probably be the questions, "Is either the husband or wife a traitor?" "Does the property belong to the husband or to the wife?" "Is the property of the wife confiscable for the treason of the husband?" and other similar questions, all which it is ridiculous for a provost-marshal to assume to decide.

The true rule for the military is to seize such property as is needed for military uses and reasons, and let the rest alone. Cotton and other staple articles of commerce are seizable for military reasons. Dwelling-houses and furniture are seldom so. If Mrs. Morton is playing traitor to the extent of practical injury, seize her, but leave her house to the courts. Please revise and adjust this case upon these principles. Yours, etc., A. Lincoln.[1545]

What was the point of such actions, of seizing the homes of innocent non-combatants? It was all both illegal and cruel. Nonetheless, Sherman and his men laughed when the Southern women whose homes they were destroying would "cry aloud for mercy." Such scenes were never witnessed in any Northern towns or cities.[1546]

Admitting that he pilfered some $20 million from Southern banks and citizens, and bragging that he had destroyed $100 million worth of private property, Sherman then declared that the enormous number of Southerners he and his men had killed was "a beautiful sight," for the quicker more of them died, the sooner the War would end.[1547]

At Atlanta, Georgia, Sherman illegally forced the deportation of thousands of citizens, then attempted to bomb the town into gravel. Razing most of the private homes there, by the time the heartless Yankee general departed, 90 percent of the city was literally nonexistent. Lincoln's troops robbed girls and women of their trinkets, and even vandalized Southern cemeteries, digging up corpses for their jewelry.[1548] So lightly did Sherman and his men take such crimes upon the Southern citizenry that they humorously referred to it as "treasure-seeking," enjoyable "excitements of the march."[1549]

Beloved family pets, mainly dogs and cats, were shot on the spot, along with any other type of animal, such as horses, pigs, hogs, geese, and cattle, that could not be carried off.[1550] In one typical case, one of Lincoln's soldiers saw some Southern children playing with a frisky young greyhound. Walking over to the startled children, he grabbed the puppy and cruelly pummeled its brains out in front of them.[1551]

Those Atlantans who were not beaten, arrested, or killed, fled into the mountains. Those civilians unlucky enough to be left behind faced a demonic force of unparalleled evil, as J. Clarence Stonebraker noted:

> At one place Sherman took four hundred factory girls and sent them north of the Ohio River, away from home and friends. Such things are inhuman, and one's blood is made to boil to even relate them.
>
> All the white inhabitants were made to leave the city without regard to age or condition. All who would not take Lincoln's oath were sent South to famish.
>
> Such a stream of men, women and children with their all in their hands, could be seen wending their way from the desolated city. [Rebel General John Bell] Hood retorted against this cruelty, but Sherman said, 'War is cruelty! This year we will take your property, and next year your lives!'[1552]

In their wake the Yanks often left nothing but thousands of solitary, charred chimney stacks, known as "Sherman's sentinels," and miles of grotesquely twisted railroad track, known as "Sherman's neckties," to indicate their fearful progress.[1553] Steel-toed boots aided the Yanks in their destruction, enabling them to kick down the strongest doors and break open the toughest locks.[1554]

Following in Sherman's path were the "bummers": great mobs of criminals, felons, outlaws, refugees, prostitutes, and stevedores, picking through the spoils of devastation, preying on the Southern victims of the general's wrath.[1555] Finally, rounding up this motley menagerie, were trailing throngs of newly freed blacks, homeless, hungry, and confused. The South could not help them now, and Sherman, a lifelong racist, was certainly not going to.[1556]

As the North's soldiers moved across Dixie terrorizing her inhabitants and leveling her cities, untold thousands of defenseless girls and women, both white and black, free and bonded, were threatened, intimidated, beaten, maimed, wounded, tortured, raped, and killed.[1557] Age was no barrier to the battle-hardened Yankee interlopers. All were considered fair game, including innocent children and fragile seniors.[1558]

Confederate General Jubal Early followed Yankee General David Hunter through the Shenandoah Valley, the "Breadbasket of the Confederacy,"[1559] and so became just one of millions of eyewitnesses to the outrages perpetuated under the auspices of President Lincoln. In his book,

A Memoir of the Last Year of the War for Independence in the Confederate States of America, Early describes what he saw:

> The scenes on Hunter's route from Lynchburg [Virginia] had been truly heart-rending. Houses had been burned, and helpless women and children left without shelter. The country had been stripped of provisions and many families left without a morsel to eat. Furniture and bedding had been cut to pieces, and old men and women and children robbed of all the clothing they had except that on their backs. Ladies trunks had been rifled and their dresses torn to pieces in mere wantonness. Even the negro girls had lost their little finery. We now had renewed evidences of the outrages committed by Hunter's orders in burning and plundering private houses. We saw the ruins of a number of houses to which the torch had been applied by his orders. At Lexington he had burned the Military Institute, with all of its contents, including its library and scientific apparatus; and Washington College had been plundered and the statue of Washington stolen. The residence of Ex-Governor [John] Letcher at that place had been burned by orders, and but a few minutes given Mrs. Letcher and her family to leave the house. In the same county a most excellent Christian gentleman, a Mr. Creigh, had been hung, because, on a former occasion he had killed a straggling and marauding Federal soldier while in the act of insulting and outraging the ladies of his family. These are but some of the outrages committed by Hunter or his orders, and I will not insult the memory of the ancient barbarians of the North by calling them "acts of Vandalism." If those old barbarians were savage and cruel, they at least had the manliness and daring of rude soldiers, with occasional traits of magnanimity. Hunter's deeds were those of a malignant and cowardly fanatic, who was better qualified to make war upon helpless women and children than upon armed soldiers.[1560]

Blacks, the very people Lincoln's troops were allegedly invading the South to "liberate," were particularly targeted by white Union soldiers. The following field dispatch (dated December 30, 1864) from Union General Rufus Saxton to U.S. Secretary of War Edwin M. Stanton, offers a glimpse into the violent, sordid, crime-infested world created by "mob boss" Lincoln. Reporting from his post at Beaufort, South Carolina, the appalled Yankee Saxton writes:

> I found the prejudice of color and race here in full force, and the general feeling of the army of occupation was unfriendly to the

blacks. It was manifested in various forms of personal insult and abuse, in depredations on their plantations, stealing and destroying their crops and domestic animals, and robbing them of their money.

The [Negro] women were held as the legitimate prey of lust, and as they had been taught it was a crime to resist a white man they had not learned to dare to defend their chastity.

Licentiousness was widespread . . . in the [Northern] army of occupation. Among our [Union] officers and soldiers there were many honorable exceptions to this, but the influence of too many was demoralizing to the negro, and has greatly hindered the efforts for their improvement and elevation. There was a general disposition among the soldiers and civilian speculators here to defraud the negroes in their private traffic, to take the commodities which they offered for sale by force, or to pay for them in worthless money.

At one time these practices were so frequent and notorious that the negroes would not bring their produce to market for fear of being plundered. Other occurrences have tended to cool the enthusiastic joy with which the coming of the Yankees was welcomed.[1561]

Under such treatment, "freed" Southern blacks often had difficulty discerning the difference between "working for nothing as a slave and working for the same wages under the Yankee . . ."[1562]

In 1862 an eyewitness living on Hilton Head Island, South Carolina, reported that the occupying white Northern soldiers there spoke horribly to the blacks, using the most insulting words, while in Norfolk, Virginia, a freed black woman wrote of seeing other blacks being abused "in every possible way" by Union men. Yankee crimes in the Palmetto State included the destruction of property, pillage, assault and battery, and even rape, against innocent black females who had fled to them, believing them to be liberators. The woman forlornly penned: it looks like I'm Master Lincoln's slave from now on.[1563]

Master Lincoln and his War unleashed tremendous violence and bloodshed in all of the Southern states, but nowhere more so than Missouri, as even the president admitted in the following February 20, 1865, letter to the state's governor, Thomas Clement Fletcher:

> It seems that there is now no organized military force of the enemy in Missouri, and yet that destruction of property and life is rampant everywhere. Is not the cure

for this within easy reach of the people themselves? It cannot but be that every man not naturally a robber or cut-throat would gladly put an end to this state of things. A large majority in every locality must feel alike upon this subject; and if so, they only need to reach an understanding, one with another. Each leaving all others alone solves the problem; and surely each would do this but for his apprehension that others will not leave him alone. Cannot this mischievous distrust be removed? Let neighborhood meetings be everywhere called and held, of all entertaining a sincere purpose for mutual security in the future, whatever they may heretofore have thought, said, or done about the war, or about anything else. Let all such meet, and, waiving all else, pledge each to cease harassing others, and to make common cause against whoever persists in making, aiding, or encouraging further disturbance. The practical means they will best know how to adopt and apply. At such meetings old friendships will cross the memory, and honor and Christian charity will come in to help.

Please consider whether it may not be well to suggest this to the now afflicted people of Missouri. Yours truly, A Lincoln.[1564]

Lincoln refuses to concede that because he is the one responsible for launching the bloodshed to begin with, that the **"cure"** cannot come from the **"now afflicted people of Missouri."** It must come from him, in the form of immediately terminating his War and allowing the South to go in peace. Instead he believes that if Missourians would only **"reach an understanding,"** then **"Christian charity"** will magically appear, and peace will once again return.

Is Lincoln here being hopelessly naive, stupid, or duplicitous? Whichever it was, this is a frightening scenario, for clearly he was not the type of individual that should have been put in charge of leading a nation. We will recall that he had been deemed unqualified to be an Illinois senator only a few years earlier!

While all of these horrors were transpiring around him, our sixteenth president was indulging in pointless frivolities, such as attending theater, balls,[1565] and parties,[1566] commenting on **"pretty ladies"** visiting the White House,[1567] thanking his followers for sending him presents (like **"Mackinaw salmon trout"**),[1568] and discussing the intricacies of Shakespeare, as the following August 17, 1863, letter to James H. Hackett reveals:

> My dear Sir: Months ago I should have acknowledged the receipt of your book and accompanying kind note; and I now have to beg your pardon for not having done so.
> For one of my age I have seen very little of the drama. The first presentation of *Falstaff* I ever saw was yours here, last winter or spring. Perhaps the best compliment I can pay is to say, as I truly can, I am very anxious to see it again. Some of Shakspere's plays I have never read; while others I have gone over perhaps as frequently as any unprofessional reader. Among the latter are "Lear," "Richard III.," "Henry VIII.," "Hamlet," and especially "Macbeth." I think nothing equals "Macbeth." It is wonderful.
> Unlike you gentlemen of the profession, I think the soliloquy in "Hamlet" commencing "Oh, my offense is rank," surpasses that commencing "To be or not to be." But pardon this small attempt at criticism. I should like to hear you pronounce the opening speech of Richard III. Will you not soon visit Washington again? If you do, please call and let me make your personal acquaintance. Yours truly, A. Lincoln.[1569]

In fairness Lincoln did take the occasional moment to send dispatches to his men on the battlefield, ordering them to leave specific Southern citizens alone (as long as they pledged his odious and illegal anti-South "U.S. Oath of Allegiance"). In some cases he was a little late, however, as in the following "Permit" issued on December 21, 1863:

> Mr. and Mrs. Craig, of Arkansas, whose plantation, situated upon the Mississippi River a few miles below Helena, has been desolated during the present war, propose returning to reoccupy and cultivate said plantation; and it is my wish that they be permitted to do so, and that the United States military forces in that vicinity will not molest them or allow them to be molested, so long as the said Mr. and Mrs. Craig shall demean themselves as peaceful loyal citizens of the United States. Abraham Lincoln.[1570]

While Lincoln sometimes lapsed into such moments of compassion,[1571] this was not his normal temperament. He knew all too perfectly his well-earned reputation as a homicidal savage, which is why, a few days later, on January 7, 1864, he commuted one of his soldiers' death sentence to hard labor for the duration of the War. This was, as he put it, not done due to **"any merit in the case,"** but **"to evade the butchering business lately."**[1572] This is the same **"butchering business"** he himself had instigated at Fort Sumter just 1,000 days before.

Was Lincoln truly this shallow, superficial, and callous? Obviously!

But what about the barbaric, cruel, and pathetic stories of his soldiers? How can any of these be true? They are not in our history books.

We know about these crimes because both eyewitness accounts and Federal field orders instructing the purposeful harassment, arrest, imprisonment, and even killing of noncombatants still survive. Naturally, anti-South historians disregard or suppress these accounts. Yet they exist for all to see.

One of these is the North's own 158-volume work entitled, the *Official Records of the War of the Rebellion*, better known to historians and scholars as simply the OR.[1573] On October 29, 1864, for example, at Rome, Georgia, the OR tells us that Sherman sent out an order to a subordinate officer that read:

> Cannot you send over about Fairmount and Adairsville, burn ten or twelve houses of known secessionists, kill a few at random, and let them know that it will be repeated every time a train is fired on from Resaca to Kingston?[1574]

Note that besides ordering the killing of civilians (at the time an offence punishable by hanging), Sherman also ordered the destruction of private property, a war crime under the Geneva Convention of 1863.

During Sherman's twenty-six day "March to the Sea"[1575] as he and his men approached South Carolina (the first Southern state to proudly secede from the Union), the dastardly Northern officer revealed their real motivation, one that had nothing to do with Lincoln's fraudulent goal of **"preserving the Union"**:

> The truth is, the whole army is burning with an insatiable desire to wreak vengeance upon South Carolina. I almost tremble at her fate, but feel that she deserves all that seems to be in store for her.[1576]

South Carolina's "fate" was later described by Reverend Dr. John

Bachman of Charleston:

> When Sherman's army came sweeping through Carolina, leaving a broad track of desolation for hundreds of miles, whose steps were accompanied with fire, and sword, and blood . . . I happened to be at Cash's Depot, six miles from Cheraw. The owner was a widow, Mrs. Ellerbe, seventy-one years of age. Her son, Colonel Cash, was absent. I witnessed the barbarities inflicted on the aged, the widow, and young and delicate females. [Yankee] [o]fficers, high in command, were engaged tearing from the ladies their watches, their ear and wedding rings, the daguerreotypes [a type of early photograph] of those they loved and cherished. A lady of delicacy and refinement, a personal friend, was compelled to strip before them, that they might find concealed watches and other valuables under her dress. A system of torture was practiced toward the weak, unarmed, and defenseless, which as far as I know and believe, was universal throughout the whole course of that invading army. Before they arrived at a plantation, they inquired the names of the most faithful and trustworthy family servants; these were immediately seized, pistols were presented at their heads; with the most terrific curses, they were threatened to be shot if they did not assist them in finding buried treasures. If this did not succeed, they were tied up and cruelly beaten. Several poor creatures died under the infliction. The last resort was that of hanging, and the officers and men of the triumphant army of General Sherman were engaged in erecting gallows and hanging up these faithful and devoted servants. They were strung up until life was nearly extinct, when they were let down, suffered to rest awhile, then threatened and hung up again. It is not surprising that some should have been left hanging so long that they were taken down dead. Coolly and deliberately these hardened men proceeded on their way, as if they had perpetrated no crime, and as if the God of heaven would not pursue them with his vengeance. But it was not alone the poor blacks to whom they professed to come as liberators that were thus subjected to torture and death. Gentlemen of high character, pure and honorable and gray-headed, unconnected with the military, were dragged from their fields or their beds, and subjected to this process of threats, beating, and hanging. Along the whole track of Sherman's army, traces remain of the cruelty and inhumanity practiced on the aged and the defenseless. Some of those who were hung up died under the rope, while their cruel murderers have not only been left unreproached and unhung, but have been hailed as heroes and patriots. The list of those martyrs whom the cupidity of the officers and men of Sherman's army sacrificed to their thirst for gold and silver, is large and most revolting.[1577]

On March 5, 1865, Mary Chesnut recorded the following in her diary:

> Sherman's men had burned the convent. . . . Men were rolling tar barrels and lighting torches to fling on the house when the nuns came. Columbia is but dust and ashes, burned to the ground. Men, women, and children are left there, houseless, homeless, without a particle of food—reduced to picking up corn that was left by Sherman's horses on picket grounds and parching it to stay their hunger.[1578]

Many Northerners too were horrified by Sherman's actions. One of them happened to be a Yankee officer, General Don Carlos Buell.[1579] After resigning from the military over the issue, he said:

> I believe that the policy and means with which the war was being prosecuted were discreditable to the nation and a stain upon civilization.[1580]

A number of formally pro-Northern newspapers were equally disturbed by the inhumane policies of Sherman and Sheridan (the Yankee demon who killed my cousin, Southern hero Jeb Stuart). In 1864, a Washington, D.C. paper asked the villainous pair the following question: what prompted you to drive children, women, and the aged from their burning homes, out into the streets to freeze, starve, and die? Was all the misery and suffering you heaped upon the Southern people merely to liberate Southern slaves, a race who was far more content before you arrived than after you left?[1581]

Yankee news reporter Sidney Andrews visited Dixie in the winter of 1865. In his book chronicling the journey, *The South Since the War*, Andrews wrote:

> The 'Shermanizing process,' as an ex Rebel colonel jocosely called it, has been complete everywhere. To simply say that the people hate that officer is to put a fact in very mild terms. [The highly detested General Benjamin 'the Beast'] Butler is, in their estimation an angel, when compared to Sherman. They charge the latter with the entire work and waste of the war so far as their State is concerned,— even claim that Columbia was burned by his express orders. They pronounce his spirit 'infernal,' 'atrocious,' 'cowardly,' 'devilish,' and would unquestionably use stronger terms if they were to be had. I have been told by dozens of men

that he [Sherman] couldn't walk up the main street of Columbia in the daytime without being shot; and three different gentlemen, residing in different parts of the State, declare that Wade Hampton expresses a purpose to shoot him at sight whenever and wherever he meets him. Whatever else the South Carolina mothers forget, they do not seem likely in this generation to forget to teach their children to hate Sherman.[1582]

Another Yankee, General Carl Schurz, no friend of the South, also journeyed through Dixie in 1865, and recorded this observation:

> My travels in the interior took me to the track of Sherman's march, which, in South Carolina at least, looked for many miles like a broad black streak of ruin and desolation—the fences all gone; lonesome smoke stacks, surrounded by dark heaps of ashes and cinders, marking the spots where human habitations had stood; the fields along the road wildly overgrown by weeds, with here and there a sickly looking patch of cotton or corn cultivated by negro squatters. In the city of Columbia, the political capital of the State, I found a thin fringe of houses encircling a confused mass of charred ruins of dwellings and business buildings, which had been destroyed by a sweeping conflagration.[1583]

In all, Sherman's "March to the Sea" inflicted some $100,000,000 of damage on Georgia alone,[1584] almost two billion dollars in today's currency. It was for this remorseless devastation that Henry C. Work's ode to Sherman, "Marching Through Georgia," became the most detested song in Dixie,[1585] and Sherman himself became the most hated man across the South, for a time even more so than Lincoln.[1586]

The two had much in common and were thick as thieves, which is why Lincoln took a moment during his Annual Message to Congress on December 6, 1864, to heap accolades upon the savage Yankee officer:

> **The most remarkable feature in the military operations of the year is General Sherman's attempted march of three hundred miles, directly through the insurgent region. It tends to show a great increase of our relative strength, that our general-in-chief should feel able to confront and hold in check every active force of the enemy, and yet to detach a well-appointed large army to move on such an expedition.**[1587]

Lincoln's "Response to a Serenade" from the same day contained similar sentiments:

> Friends and Fellow-citizens: I believe I shall never be old enough to speak without embarrassment when I have nothing to talk about. I have no good news to tell you, and yet I have no bad news to tell. We have talked of elections until there is nothing more to say about them. The most interesting news we now have is from Sherman. We all know where he went in, but I can't tell where he will come out. I will now close by proposing three cheers for General Sherman and his army.[1588]

Yankee war criminal General Philip H. Sheridan was no less barbaric and unfeeling than Lincoln and Sherman.[1589] During the Union's Shenandoah Valley Campaign, Sheridan personally approved the torching of barns and crops[1590] (an inhumane tactic Lincoln admiringly referred to as **"pretty hot work"**),[1591] after which he and his men left the region a blackened wasteland, pillaging, burning, and murdering as they went. Sheridan then joked that "a crow could not fly over it without carrying his rations with him."[1592] Civilians who opposed him were hanged on the spot.[1593] In October 1864, Sheridan boasted to Grant:

> I have destroyed over 2,000 barns, filled with wheat, hay, and farming implements; over 70 mills, filled with flour and wheat; have driven in front of the army over 4,000 head of stock, and have killed and issued to the troops not less than 3,000 sheep. . . . all the houses within an area of five miles were burned.[1594]

Sheridan's soldiers bragged that "we stripped the Valley to the bare earth; when we got through there weren't enough crumbs left to feed a pigeon." Sheridan himself—a man who, for "some light entertainment," would often burn every fifth house[1595]—pronounced his "scorched earth" approach to warfare a "humanitarian" policy, since he believed that Southerners would give in rather than die of starvation.[1596]

He was wrong.

A Confederate officer who survived the Shenandoah Holocaust described the scene this way:

> I rode down the Valley with the advance after Sheridan's retreating cavalry beneath great columns of smoke which almost shut out the

sun by day, and in the red glare of bonfires which, all across the Valley, poured out flames and sparks heavenward and crackled mockingly in the night air; and I saw mothers and maidens tearing their hair and shrieking to Heaven in their fright and despair, and little children, voiceless and tearless in their pitiable terror.[1597]

Grant, who was soon to become America's second worst president, was no better than Sheridan or Sherman. In several letters to Sheridan, dated August 16, 1864, he ordered the wanton destruction of private property (adding theft to the crime), the murder of Rebel soldiers "without trial," and the hostage taking, military arrest, and imprisonment of noncombatants (civilians), all illegal. One of these dispatches has been preserved in the *Official Records*. Grant writes:

> The families of most of [Confederate Colonel John S.] Mosby's men are known, and can be collected. I think they should be taken and kept at Fort McHenry or some secure place, as hostages for the good conduct of Mosby and his men. Where any of Mosby's men are caught hang them without trial.
> . . . If you can possibly spare a division of cavalry, send them through Loudoun County [Virginia], to destroy and carry off the crops, animals, negroes, and all men under fifty years of age capable of bearing arms. In this way you will get many of Mosby's men. All male citizens under fifty can fairly be held as prisoners of war, and not as citizen prisoners.[1598]

Just weeks before, on August 5, 1864, Grant had written to General Hunter:

> In pushing up the Shenandoah Valley, where it is expected you will have to go first or last, it is desirable that nothing should be left to invite the enemy to return. Take all provisions, forage, and stock wanted for the use of your command; such as cannot be consumed destroy.[1599]

In an official report, dated March 25, 1862, Union commander General Henry W. Halleck made this confession from his headquarters at St. Louis, Missouri, to Lincoln's Secretary of War Stanton:

> It cannot be denied that some of our volunteer regiments have behaved very badly, plundering to an enormous extent. I have done everything in my power to prevent this and to punish the

guilty. Many of the regimental officers are very bad men and participate in this plunder.[1600]

As a direct result of Lincoln's "badly behaved" soldiers, by the end of the conflict some 500,000 Southern farms and plantations had gone bankrupt, become insolvent, or were ruined, real property value had plummeted 30 percent, and between 10 and 25 percent of the South's inhabitants were dead.[1601] Most of her cities were desolate, the total assessed property evaluation of the Southern states had decreased by 43 percent, and two-thirds of her railroads were gone. All of this was a direct result of Lincoln's order to invade the South. In Mississippi alone, one-third of the state's white men had been killed or were disabled.[1602]

Did Lincoln know about all of this and actually sanction it? Of course. Not only had he personally issued military orders that violated the Geneva Convention,[1603] but he also personally approved his officers' illegalities, such as, for example, Sherman's plan to level Georgia to the ground,[1604] as well as the red-head's total war and scorched earth policies.[1605] Just as General Lee took his orders directly from President Davis, Sherman, Grant, Sheridan, and the rest took their orders directly from Lincoln.[1606]

Why else would "Honest Abe" repeatedly dine with,[1607] recognize, reward, and promote men like Grant and Sherman?[1608] Here, for example, is a September 3, 1864, thank you note to Sherman:

> The national thanks are tendered by the President to Major-General William T. Sherman, and the gallant officers and soldiers of his command before Atlanta, for the distinguished ability, courage, and perseverance displayed in the campaign in Georgia, which, under divine favor, has resulted in the capture of Atlanta. The marches, battles, sieges, and other military operations that have signalized the campaign must render it famous in the annals of war, and have entitled those who have participated therein to the applause and thanks of the nation. Abraham Lincoln, President of the United States.[1609]

Not only had Lincoln been in constant telegraph contact with both Sherman and Grant throughout the War, but on March 28, 1865, he excitedly met with them at City Point, Virginia, to hear about their **"achievements"** and congratulate them on their work in person.[1610] Only a few months earlier, on August 17, 1864, he had sent a telegram to Grant in the field that read:

> I have seen your despatch expressing your unwillingness to break your hold where you are. Neither am I willing. Hold on with a bulldog grip, and chew and choke as much as possible.[1611]

What Lincoln meant by these words would have been clear to every Southerner. They were certainly well understood by Grant, for he acted on them to the letter, and usually in the most vicious manner.

Lincoln could not wait to repay Grant for his crimes against the South with a commission, making him lieutenant general, assigned to command the U.S. armies:

> March 9, 1864.—The nation's appreciation of what you have done, and its reliance upon you for what remains to do, in the existing great struggle, are now presented with this commission, constituting you lieutenant-general in the Army of the United States.
> With this high honor devolves upon you also a corresponding responsibility. As the country herein trusts you, so, under God, it will sustain you. I scarcely need add, that with what I here speak for the nation, goes my own hearty personal concurrence.[1612]

> March 10, 1864.— Order Assigning U. S. Grant To The Command of the Armies of the United States.
> Executive Mansion, Washington, D. C., March 10, 1864. Under the authority of an act of Congress to revive the grade of lieutenant-general in the United States Army, approved February 29, 1864, Lieutenant-General Ulysses S. Grant, United States Army, is assigned to the command of the Armies of the United States. Abraham Lincoln.[1613]

The close relationship between the two men, and both Lincoln's toleration and approval of Grant's actions, can be seen in the following letter, written by Lincoln to Grant on April 30, 1864:

> Not expecting to see you again before the spring campaign opens, I wish to express in this way my entire

satisfaction with what you have done up to this time, so far as I understand it. The particulars of your plans I neither know nor seek to know. You are vigilant and self-reliant; and, pleased with this, I wish not to obtrude any constraints or restraints upon you. While I am very anxious that any great disaster or capture of our men in great numbers shall be avoided, I know these points are less likely to escape your attention than they would be mine. If there is anything wanting which is within my power to give, do not fail to let me know it. And now, with a brave army and a just cause, may God sustain you. Yours very truly, A. Lincoln.[1614]

On September 20, 1864, Lincoln sent Yankee war criminal Philip H. Sheridan a similar congratulatory letter:

Have just heard of your great victory. God bless you all, officers and men. Strongly inclined to come up and see you. A. Lincoln.[1615]

Another letter of thanks to Sheridan followed a month later, this one on October 22, 1864:

With great pleasure I tender to you and your brave army the thanks of the nation, and my own personal admiration and gratitude, for the month's operations in the Shenandoah Valley; and especially for the splendid work of October 19, 1864 [at the Battle of Cedar Creek, Virginia]. Your obedient servant, Abraham Lincoln.[1616]

Here again we see presidential culpability and complicity connected with some of the War's most heinous atrocities. Lincoln called these a **"splendid work."**

While he completely ignored the monstrous deeds of Grant, Sherman, Sheridan, and those of his other more famous generals, Lincoln chose instead to target Yankee officers who committed relatively harmless crimes in comparison. One of these was General Stephen Gano Burbridge (then stationed at Lexington, Kentucky), to whom the president sent the following telegram on November 10, 1864:

I have just received a telegram from Governor [Thomas Elliott] **Bramlette** saying: "General John B. Houston, a loyal man and prominent citizen, was arrested, and, yesterday, started off by General Burbridge, to be sent beyond our lines by way of Catlettsburg, for no other offense than opposition to your reelection," and I have answered him as follows below, of which please take notice and report to me. A. Lincoln.

To Governor Bramlette: Yours of yesterday received. I can scarcely believe that General John B. Houston has been arrested "for no other offense than opposition to my reelection"; for, if that had been deemed sufficient cause of arrest, I should have heard of more than one arrest in Kentucky on election day. If, however, General Houston has been arrested for no other cause than opposition to my reelection, General Burbridge will discharge him at once, I [am] sending him a copy of this as an order to that effect. A. Lincoln.[1617]

Lincoln, of course, had to occasionally issue public countermands like this one in order to distance himself from the possible subsequent charge of perpetuating war crimes. The fact is, as Bramlette's letter proves—and as we will see in our next chapter—that countless citizens were arrested for speaking out against Lincoln, for promoting peace with the South, for giving antiwar speeches, and for printing antiwar articles. Many were also imprisoned and tortured, and even murdered. Only one person had the power to sanction such criminal activities. And he was sitting in the Oval Office.

The warmongering secretive president was particularly delighted with Sherman's destructive March to the Sea, seeing it as the most noteworthy military operation of 1864. As he said in his Fourth Annual Message to Congress on December 6, 1864:

> The most remarkable feature in the military operations of the year is General Sherman's attempted march of three hundred miles, directly through the insurgent region. It tends to show a great increase of our relative strength, that our general-in-chief should feel able to confront and hold in check every active force of the enemy, and yet to detach a well-appointed large army to move on such an expedition.[1618]

Just a few months earlier Lincoln had weakly attempted to

acknowledge the insane destruction his War was wreaking. But only in the North. He had no concern whatsoever about how the conflict was effecting the South and never once sympathized with or apologized to the Southern people for venting his wrath on their fair land. On June 16, 1864, during his speech at a "Sanitary Fair" in Philadelphia, Pennsylvania, the president said:

> War, at the best, is terrible, and this war of ours, in its magnitude and in its duration, is one of the most terrible. It has deranged business, totally in many localities, and partially in all localities. It has destroyed property and ruined homes; it has produced a national debt and taxation unprecedented, at least in this country; it has carried mourning to almost every home, until it can almost be said that the "heavens are hung in black."[1619]

The heavens were indeed **"hung with black,"** placed there by the sorrowful Southern survivors of Lincoln's War on Dixie; the region where the Northern invasion took place, where the War was mainly fought, and where 99 percent of the damage was done. And the instigator of this gory slaughter had the nerve to complain that it was hurting the North!

Behind his fake public lamentations over the awful conflict that he himself had started, Lincoln's own personal war crimes continued unabated. While he committed many of these felonies in the public eye, others were perpetrated in more subtle ways quite unseen by the masses, such as when he worked "anonymously" through those around him.

One of those closest to Lincoln was his chief of staff at the time, General Henry W. Halleck. It was Halleck who, in daily contact with the president, wrote the following to Sherman on December 18, 1864:

> Should you capture Charleston, I hope that by some accident the place may be destroyed, and if a little salt should be sown upon its site it may prevent the growth of future crops of nullification and secession.[1620]

The dispatch was from Halleck. But the "message" was from Lincoln.

The official public stamp of approval for committing war crimes came from the U.S. Congress, which gave Grant, Sheridan, and Sherman the "Thanks of Congress" for achieving "significant victories" during the War (Sherman received at least two).[1621] These "significant victories," of course, were often the result of scorched-earth, total war policies that included larceny, wide destruction of civilian property, rape, maiming, torture, and the mass murder of Southern noncombatants.

Of the war crimes of Lincoln's commanders, the Honorable Judge George L. Christian states,

> we know . . . that these officers would not have dared to thus violate [the rules of civilized warfare] . . . unless these violations had been known by them to be sanctioned by their official head, Mr. Lincoln, from whom they received their appointments and commissions, and whose duty it was to prevent such violations and outrages.
>
> . . . Who alone had any semblance of authority to give this permission to Sherman and who gave it? There can be but one answer—Abraham Lincoln, the then President of the United States. Will the people of the South lick the hand that thus smote their fathers, their mothers, their brethren and their sisters by now singing paeans of glory to his name and fame?
>
> . . . We charge, and without the fear of successful contradiction, that Mr. Lincoln, as the head of the Federal Government, and the Commander-in-Chief of its armies, was directly responsible for the outrages committed by his subordinates; and that the future and unprejudiced historian will so hold him responsible. We verily believe.
>
> But this is not all. Mr. Lincoln was [also] directly responsible for all the sorrows, sufferings and deaths of prisoners on both sides during the war.[1622]

While today many Northerners and New South scallywags continue to lamely deny Lincoln's role as a war criminal, 19th-Century Northerners had the gall to fabricate numerous horror stories about Southern soldiers: that they made goblets of Yankee skulls and ladies' necklaces from Yankee teeth (never happened);[1623] that they "took scalps for trophies" (never happened);[1624] that black Northern soldiers were routinely and intentionally beaten, shot, and burned, as was alleged to have occurred at the Battle of Fort Pillow (never happened);[1625] and that Union prisoners were purposefully "starved, frozen, and killed off" (most of the Yanks who perished in Southern prisons died because of Lincoln's war-long refusal to exchange prisoners,[1626] and also due to lack of food, medicines, and clothing caused by his illegal naval blockade).[1627]

In reality, it was Lincoln's troops who committed the vast preponderance of war crimes. One of General Nathan Bedford Forrest's officers, Lieutenant Colonel W. M. Reed, wrote out the following report on March 21, 1864. It concerns various outrages committed by Yankee Colonel Fielding Hurst against both Rebel soldiers and innocent Southern civilians. Hurst had been sent by another Yankee war criminal, General William Sooy Smith, to "grub up" West Tennessee:

> [Confederate] Private Silas Hodges, a scout, acting under orders from Colonel Tansil, states that he saw the body of [Confederate] Lieutenant Dodds very soon after his murder, and that it was most horribly mutilated, the face having been skinned, the nose cut off, the under jaw disjointed, the privates cut off, and the body otherwise barbarously lacerated and most wantonly injured, and that his death was brought about by the most inhuman process of torture.
>
> . . . On or about the 5th February, 1864, Private Martin, Company—, Wilson's regiment Tennessee volunteers, was captured by [the] same command and was shot to death and the rights of sepulture forbidden while the command remained, some four days. Mr. Lee Doroughty, a citizen of McNairy County, Tenn, a youth about sixteen years of age, deformed and almost helpless, was arrested and wantonly murdered by [the] same command about 1st January, 1864.[1628]

A complete compilation of these types of Yankee atrocities would fill volumes. Lincoln was aware of nearly all of them and directly, or more often indirectly (to legally protect himself), sanctioned them.[1629]

Lincoln not only knew about and sanctioned his men's criminal activities, he constantly encouraged them by giving vague orders that allowed them total leeway in making decisions. The following August 9, 1864, letter to Yankee General Benjamin F. Butler provides an example:

> Coming to the question itself, the military occupancy of Norfolk is a necessity with us. If you, as department commander, find the cleansing of the city necessary to prevent pestilence in your army; streetlights and a fire-department necessary to prevent assassinations and incendiarism among your men and stores; wharfage necessary to land and ship men and supplies; a large pauperism, badly conducted at a needlessly large expense to the government; and find also that these things, or any of them, are not reasonably well attended to by the civil government, you rightfully may and must take them into your own hands. But you should do so on

your own avowed judgment of a military necessity, and not seem to admit that there is no such necessity by taking a vote of the people on the question.

Nothing justifies the suspending of the civil by the military authority, but military necessity; and of the existence of that necessity, the military commander, and not a popular vote, is to decide. And whatever is not within such necessity should be left undisturbed.[1630]

What exactly is **"military necessity"** and what is not? That answer Lincoln left to the discretion of his officers, many of them, like the insolent, brutish, violent, South-hating Butler (known in Dixie as "the Beast"), who had already proven themselves poor judges, incapable of self restraint on or off the battlefield. Little wonder there were so many outrages committed by the North against both the Southern people and the Northern people.

If there is any doubt as to Lincoln's knowledge and involvement in such illicit activities, consider the case of one of his generals, John B. Turchin. Turchin was rightfully ousted from the Yankee army by his superiors for burning down the town of Athens, Alabama, in 1862. However, Lincoln reversed the order, restored Turchin to his command, and even gave him a promotion.[1631]

Why did Lincoln push his officers to win at any cost, even to the point of destroying entire cities and savagely murdering thousands of innocent Southern men, women, and children?

Politics of course.

The upcoming 1864 election weighed heavily on Lincoln's mind throughout 1863 and early 1864. He felt that victories in the field would mean a victory at the polls. And he was correct. Sherman's and Sheridan's many successes during the period gave the president a 10 percent margin that November, all he needed to be reelected.[1632]

Long before this, on July 20, 1861, Jefferson Davis had spoken out against Lincoln's war crimes, condemning him for destroying "private residences in peaceful rural retreats," and for the "outrages [rapes] committed on defenseless [Southern] females by [Yankee] soldiers."[1633] In bringing nationwide attention to Lincoln's crimes Davis made special note of the following:

> In this war, rapine is the rule; private houses, in beautiful rural retreats, are bombarded and burnt; grain crops in the field are

consumed by the torch, and, when the torch is not convenient, careful labour is bestowed to render complete destruction of every article of use or ornament remaining in private dwellings, after their inhabitants have fled from the outrages of brute soldiery.[1634]

In essence, as Davis correctly observed several years before Sherman's infamous and deliberate campaign of destruction—known innocuously by Northerners as his "March to the Sea"[1635]—Lincoln was already

> waging an indiscriminate war upon . . . all, with a savage ferocity unknown to modern civilization.[1636]

Lincoln himself was aware of the horrors and hazards of the War he had created, which is why he did his best to keep his own military-age son, Robert Todd Lincoln, off the front lines. On January 19, 1865, in a letter to General Ulysses S. Grant, Lincoln wrote:

> **Please read and answer this letter as though I was not President, but only a friend. My son, now in his twenty-second year, having graduated at Harvard, wishes to see something of the war before it ends. I do not wish to put him in the ranks, nor yet to give him a commission, to which those who have already served long are better entitled and better qualified to hold. Could he, without embarrassment to you or detriment to the service, go into your military family with some nominal rank, I, and not the public, furnishing his necessary means? If no, say so without the least hesitation, because I am as anxious and as deeply interested that you shall not be encumbered as you can be yourself. Yours truly, A. Lincoln.**[1637]

This was a personal letter. In other words, he did not want the world to know that he **"did not wish to put his son in the** [active combat] **ranks."** But his own flesh and blood should have been treated like any other Northern recruit. That he secretly desired otherwise is just another indicator that he was a deceptive and hypocritical man who thought nothing of saying one thing in public and quite the opposite in private.

Meanwhile, as Lincoln's War advanced across the South and thousands were being arrested, imprisoned, tortured, killed, or simply turned into homeless refugees, Lincoln and his money-obsessed Yankee constituents carried on with business as usual, in some cases acting as if nothing were amiss. On June 13, 1862, for example, only days after the Union killed dozens of Confederates at the Battle of Chattanooga I (the Battle of Lookout Mountain to Yanks), Lincoln sent a "Message to the House of Representatives" concerning **"enlarging the locks of the Erie and Oswego canals."**[1638]

A few days later, on June 23, Lincoln issued a "Message to the Senate," in which he discussed **"an act to repeal that part of an act of Congress which prohibits the circulation of banknotes of a less denomination than five dollars in the District of Columbia."**[1639] On October 5, 1863, he was focused on

> the construction of a railroad and telegraph line from the Missouri River to the Pacific Ocean . . . to secure the [U.S.] government the use of the same for postal, military, and other purposes . . .[1640]

Unable to stop thinking about money or the Union's great monetary loss due to the seceded Southern states, on July 1, 1862, Lincoln released a "Proclamation Concerning Taxes in Rebellious States." It reads:

> Whereas, in and by the second section of an act of Congress passed on the seventh day of June, A. D. 1862, entitled "An act for the collection of direct taxes in insurrectionary districts within the United States, and for other purposes," it is made the duty of the President to declare, on or before the first day of July then next following, by his proclamation, in what States and parts of States insurrection exists:
>
> Now, therefore, be it known that I, Abraham Lincoln, President of the United States of America, do hereby declare and proclaim that the States of South Carolina, Florida, Georgia, Alabama, Louisiana, Texas, Mississippi, Arkansas, Tennessee, North Carolina, and the State of Virginia (except the following counties: Hancock, Brooke, Ohio, Marshall Wetzel, Marion, Monongalia, Preston, Taylor, Pleasants, Tyler, Ritchie, Doddridge, Harrison, Wood, Jackson, Wirt, Roane, Calhoun, Gilmer, Barbour, Tucker, Lewis, Braxton, Upshur, Randolph, Mason, Putnam, Kanawha, Clay, Nicholas, Cabell, Wayne, Boone, Logan, Wyoming, Webster, Fayette, and Raleigh),

are now in insurrection and rebellion, and by reason thereof the civil authority of the United States is obstructed so that the provisions of the "Act to provide increased revenue from imports, to pay the interest on the public debt, and for other purposes," approved August fifth, eighteen hundred and sixty-one, cannot be peaceably executed; and that the taxes legally chargeable upon real estate, under the act last aforesaid, lying within the States and parts of States as aforesaid, together with a penalty of fifty per centum of said taxes, shall be a lien upon the tracts or lots of the same, severally charged, till paid.[1641]

Lincoln's mad focus on money in the midst of supreme mindless violence is not surprising when we consider the fact that **"collecting the revenue"** was one of the primary reasons the commercial-minded Yank gave for starting his War to begin with. Is this something we have fabricated in order to tarnish Lincoln's name? Hardly. He himself said so on numerous occasions, both publicly and privately.[1642]

Lincoln & His Presidential Elections

IF HE WAS TRULY A racial bigot and, as we have seen, a morally bankrupt politician, an anarchical dictator, and a ruthless war criminal, how is it that he was elected twice to our highest office, each time with less than 50 percent of the American vote? In an effort to uncover the real Lincoln, let us examine these two elections more closely.

In his first election in 1860 Lincoln lost the popular vote by a large margin. In fact, he received only 39.8 percent (1,866,452 votes out of 4,680,193) of the ballots cast that year, while his Democratic opponents, Stephen A. Douglas, John C. Breckinridge, and John Bell, received 60.2 percent (2,813,741 votes). In short, as we discussed in Chapter 3, Lincoln received just about one million votes less than his opponents combined.[1643] With only one out of every seventeen eligible whites voting for him that November out of the total U.S. population,[1644] he is the very definition of a minority president.[1645]

This fact was borne out by Lincoln himself: during his February 1861 train ride from Springfield, Illinois, to Washington, D.C. for his inauguration, the president-elect made a number of speeches in the towns he passed through. No doubt to his own horror, he discovered that the majority of individuals who made up his crowds were not supporters. They were detractors who had voted for someone else! On February 21, in front of the New Jersey Senate, for example, Lincoln noted sourly:

> I learn that this body is composed of a majority of gentlemen who, in the exercise of their best judgment in the choice of a chief magistrate, did not think I was the man.[1646]

A similar incident occurred later the same day in front of the New Jersey Assembly, where Lincoln tried to make the best of a bad situation:

> I understand myself to be received here by the representatives of the people of New Jersey, a majority of whom differ in opinion from those with whom I have acted. This manifestation is therefore to be regarded by me as expressing their devotion to the Union, the Constitution, and the liberties of the people.[1647]

Even when he finally arrived at Washington, D.C., Lincoln was forced to note publicly that he was now primarily among Southern enemies, as he stated on February 28 at a musical affair held there in his honor:

> My Friends: I suppose that I may take this as a compliment paid to me, and as such please accept my thanks for it. I have reached this city of Washington under circumstances considerably differing from those under which any other man has ever reached it. I am here for the purpose of taking an official position amongst the people, almost all of whom were politically opposed to me, and are yet opposed to me, as I suppose.
>
> I propose no lengthy address to you. I only propose to say, as I did on yesterday, when your worthy mayor and board of aldermen called upon me, that I thought much of the ill feeling that has existed between you and the people of your surroundings and that people from among whom I came, has depended, and now depends, upon a misunderstanding.
>
> I hope that, if things shall go along as prosperously as I believe we all desire they may, I may have it in my power to remove something of this misunderstanding; that I may be enabled to convince you, and the people of your section of the country [i.e., the South], that we regard you as in all things our equals, and in all things entitled to the same respect and the same treatment that we claim for ourselves; that we are in no wise disposed, if it were in our power, to oppress you, to

deprive you of any of your rights under the Constitution of the United States, or even narrowly to split hairs with you in regard to these rights, but are determined to give you, as far as lies in our hands, all your rights under the Constitution—not grudgingly, but fully and fairly. I hope that, by thus dealing with you, we will become better acquainted, and be better friends.[1648]

Yes, even in the nation's capital city the new president-elect found himself swimming in a sea of not friends and supporters, but mainly critics and adversaries.

With less than one in seventeen whites giving him their vote, how could Lincoln have possibly won then? The answer is via the Electoral College, though even this was by a narrow margin: of the 303 electoral votes available, Lincoln received 180—all from non-Southern states—a mere twenty-eight votes above the 152 needed to win. With the Democrats (Victorian conservatives) in disarray, Lincoln then was only able to claim the 1860 election because of a four-way split.[1649]

The division came, in great part, when Democrat William Lowndes Yancey, and most of the delegates from the other Southern states, walked out of the 1860 Democratic Convention in Charleston. This seemingly insignificant act caused a rift in the Democratic party that scattered the vote, opening the door for Lincoln's election.[1650] Without this "little miracle" Lincoln would have had no chance of winning at all that year.

In the 1864 election, helped along considerably by Confederate General John Bell Hood's disastrous loss at the Battle of Atlanta (July 22, 1864),[1651] Lincoln pulled out all the stops in an effort to get reelected, lowering himself to criminal behavior unheard of by any American president before or since. His reelection illegalities succeeded and he was handed a second term.

Though Lincoln won both the popular and the electoral votes in 1864, this, his second victory, was nothing to brag about. Not only did he use countless tricks and crimes to insure the outcome, but none of the Southern states voted in the U.S. elections that year (for Lincoln a loss of eighty potential electoral votes). They were now part of a separate, sovereign, and foreign nation: the Confederate States of America, an entity that Lincoln, dwelling as he did in a megalomaniacal fantasy world, refused to recognize. For example, when Confederate President Jefferson Davis once correctly referred to the C.S.A. and the U.S.A. as "the two countries,"[1652] Lincoln ignorantly corrected him, calling them **"our one** common country."[1653]

Of the Northerners and Westerners who voted in the 1864 U.S. election only 55 percent (2,218,388 individuals of 4,031,887) thought Lincoln deserved a second chance. A full 45 percent (1,813,499 individuals), nearly half, voted for Lincoln's main opposition, George B. McClellan, whose party platform and vice presidential running mate, George Hunt Pendleton, were antiwar and openly condemned Lincoln for flagrantly curbing civil liberties. Lincoln won then by a mere 400,000 votes,[1654] and many of these were illicitly obtained, as we are about to see.

In 1864, as in 1860, all of Lincoln's electoral votes came from non-Southern states (except for West Virginia, which Lincoln had illegally created for this very purpose).[1655] Yet, if only 38,111 people, a mere 1 percent of Northerners and Westerners, had changed their votes in specific regions, Lincoln would have forfeited even the electoral vote, and McClellan's peace party would have won.[1656] If the South had also voted, it is, of course, a dead certainty that Lincoln would have lost that year.[1657]

Looking at both the 1860 and 1864 elections, it is apparent that Lincoln did not have the mandate of the American people. How then did he manage to win the Electoral College two times in a row?

In the first presidential election on November 6, 1860, though the Confederacy had not yet been formed, ten of the Southern states did not even bother putting Lincoln on their ballots, considering him too perfidious to run the nation. In fact, that year all of his popular votes and all of his electoral ones came from Northern or Western states: he did not receive a single popular vote in the South.[1658] Thus the only people who voted in his first election were those most likely to cast their ballot for Lincoln to begin with. And *all* of these were white taxpaying males (non-taxpaying males, women, free blacks, black slaves, and Native-Americans were not allowed to vote—just as Lincoln preferred).[1659]

Those white taxpaying Northern males who did vote in 1860 sided in great numbers with Lincoln. The most important segment of this group were his Wall Street Boys: Yankee financiers, merchants, and industrialists,[1660] all keen to put anyone into the Oval Office who would maintain the lucrative Northern slave trade. The candidate who promised to do just this was Abraham Lincoln.[1661] Later, these same backers rewarded him by donating millions of dollars from their slave profits to fund his war against the South.[1662]

Furthermore, there can be little question that bribery, lying, horse-trading, patronage, and cheating took place on Lincoln's behalf during the

1860 election, and that prime administrative positions and other political favors were swapped for votes. In May, at the National Republican Convention, Lincoln's campaign manager, David Davis, interfered with the printing presses so that a ballot could not be taken, had fake tickets made in order to fill seats, then pledged other nominees their choice of governmental posts if they would support Lincoln.[1663]

On February 4, 1861, in a letter to Thurlow Weed, Lincoln tried to dispel rumors about his horse-trading:

> Dear Sir: I have both your letter to myself and that to Judge Davis, in relation to a certain gentleman in your State claiming to dispense patronage in my name, and also to be authorized to use my name to advance the chances of Mr. [Horace] Greeley for an election to the United States Senate.
>
> It is very strange that such things should be said by any one. The gentleman you mention did speak to me of Mr. Greeley in connection with the senatorial election, and I replied in terms of kindness toward Mr. Greeley, which I really feel, but always with an expressed protest that my name must not be used in the senatorial election in favor of, or against, any one. Any other representation of me is a misrepresentation.
>
> As to the matter of dispensing patronage, it perhaps will surprise you to learn that I have information that you claim to have my authority to arrange that matter in New York. I do not believe that you have so claimed; but still so some men say. On that subject you know all I have said to you is "Justice to all," and I have said nothing more-particular to any one. I say this to reassure you that I have not changed my position. In the hope, however, that you will not use my name in the matter, I am Yours truly, A. Lincoln.[1664]

Later, on October 22, 1864, he sent off an angry letter to "William B. Campbell and others," saying **"I decline to interfere in any way with any presidential election."**[1665]

Such denials did nothing to stop the gossip, and the certain knowledge that Lincoln was engaging in political dirty tricks, however.

For example, Lincoln's future secretary of war, Simon Cameron, only endorsed the Illinois rail-splitter because he was pledged a cabinet position (Cameron would go on to allow administration-wide corruption regarding the approval of military contracts).[1666] Then there was Lincoln's secretary of the interior, Caleb B. Smith, also promised a post; this time in exchange for delivering the Indiana delegation.[1667] Lincoln also appointed countless numbers of political backers to high-ranking military posts, many of them, to the chagrin of Yankee soldiers, who had no military experience.[1668] The list goes on and on.

All of this could have only occurred under Lincoln's supervision,[1669] for his convention managers later admitted that they had promised "anything and everything" to anyone who would vote for him.[1670] (Lincoln would pay for this double-dealing: his sordid campaign promises necessitated appointing a myriad of individuals with opposing viewpoints, a split cabinet that he was forced to do battle with throughout his entire first term.)[1671]

A similar pattern emerged prior to the 1864 election, for once word got out that Lincoln was willing to do anything for a vote requests for various political positions and favors again began pouring in. Some of these, while not serious, point to a policy of illicit patronage behind the scenes. An example comes from Illinois Senator Burton Chauncey Cook who, in the Spring of 1864, said that the Lincoln-hating Radicals, that is the abolitionists in the Republican (liberal) party,

> had intimated to him that they would even promise to vote for Lincoln in the Convention for the promise of an admission to seats.[1672]

Despite the egregious cheating, lying, and horse-trading that went on that year, Lincoln pretended he was genuinely surprised upon learning of his nomination for a second term. He had little choice. It was either that or be found out. And so his June 9, 1864, "Reply to the Committee Notifying President Lincoln of his Renomination" contained the following fatuous words:

> **Mr. Chairman and Gentlemen of the Committee: I will neither conceal my gratification nor restrain the expression of my gratitude that the Union people, through their convention, in their continued effort to save and advance the nation, have deemed me not unworthy to remain in my present position. I know no reason to doubt that I shall accept the nomination tendered . . .**[1673]

Of the 1860 presidential election, Judge George L. Christian of Richmond, Virginia, writes that Lincoln

> was only nominated by means of a corrupt bargain entered into between his representatives and those of Simon Cameron, of Pennsylvania, and Caleb B. Smith, of Indiana, by which Cabinet positions were pledged both to Cameron and to Smith in consideration for the votes controlled by them, in the [1860 Chicago] convention, and which pledges Lincoln fulfilled, and, in that way made himself a party to these corrupt bargains.
>
> He was nominated purely as the sectional candidate of a sectional party, and not only received no votes in several of the Southern States, but he failed to get a popular majority of the section which nominated and elected him, and received nearly one million votes less than a popular majority of the vote of the country.[1674]

How true. As Stephen A. Douglas said to the audience during his final debate with Lincoln on October 15, 1858:

> Why should we thus allow a sectional party [i.e., Lincoln's liberal Republican party] to agitate this country, to array the North against the South, and convert us into enemies instead of friends, merely that a few ambitious men may ride into power on a sectional hobby? How long is it since these ambitious Northern men wished for a sectional organization? Did any one of them dream of a sectional party as long as the North was the weaker section and the South the stronger? Then all were opposed to sectional parties. But the moment the North obtained the majority in the House and Senate by the admission of California, and could elect a President without the aid of Southern votes, that moment ambitious Northern men formed a scheme to excite the North against the South, and make the people be governed in their votes by geographical lines, thinking that the North, being the stronger section, would outvote the South, and consequently they, the leaders, would ride into office on a sectional hobby.[1675]

We will note here that Lincoln lost the Illinois senate race with Douglas in November 1858. Yet this same man was considered good enough to be president of the U.S. a mere two years later! Oh, the many mysteries of the Yankee mind.

During his first term in office Lincoln had more on his sectional mind than just destroying states' rights in Dixie and then Northernizing her.

He was desperate to get reelected. Thus between 1861 and 1864 he took time away from his War to make sure his political opponents did not gain an edge over him.

One of the first things he did was issue the Emancipation Proclamation, certainly the most overtly cynical campaign strategy ever devised by a U.S. government official. Maddening to Southern and Northern abolitionists alike was the fact that even after emancipation, Lincoln favored forcing the South to give blacks the vote while he and the Northern states refused to offer them the same privilege.[1676]

To help guarantee that the soldiers would return home in time to vote for him, Lincoln stooped to an all-time low, establishing what we now call "Thanksgiving Day."[1677]

While today we think of this holiday as one connected to the Pilgrims' peaceful autumnal thanksgiving meal with Native-Americans in 1621, its inventor had no such quaint romantic notions. For politically-minded Lincoln it was to be a day of holy gratitude for the North's most recent military triumphs, or as he styled them, the **"Almighty God's signal and effective victories"** over the South.

As such, his first "Proclamation of Thanksgiving," issued on July 15, 1863, declared that the holiday would be observed on August 6. The document reads:

> **It has pleased Almighty God to hearken to the supplications and prayers of an afflicted people, and to vouchsafe to the army and the navy of the United States, victories on land and on the sea, so signal and so effective as to furnish reasonable grounds for augmented confidence that the Union of these States will be maintained, their constitution preserved, and their peace and prosperity permanently restored. But these victories have been accorded not without sacrifices of life, limb, health and liberty incurred by brave, loyal and patriotic citizens. Domestic affliction in every part of the country follows in the train of these fearful bereavements. It is meet and right to recognize and confess the presence of the Almighty Father and the power of His Hand equally in these triumphs and in these sorrows.**
>
> **Now, therefore, be it known that I do set apart Thursday, the 6th day of August next, to be observed as a day for national thanksgiving, praise, and prayer, and I invite the people of the United states to assemble on that occasion in their customary places of worship, and, in the**

forms approved by their own consciences, render the homage due to the Divine Majesty for the wonderful things he has done in the nation's behalf, and invoke the influence of his Holy Spirit to subdue the anger which has produced and so long sustained a needless and cruel rebellion, to change the hearts of the insurgents, to guide the counsels of the government with wisdom adequate to so great a national emergency, and to visit with tender care and consolation throughout the length and breadth of our land all those who, through the vicissitudes of marches, voyages, battles, and sieges have been brought to suffer in mind, body, or estate, and finally to lead the whole nation through the paths of repentance and submission to the Divine Will back to the perfect enjoyment of union and fraternal peace.

In witness whereof, I have hereunto set my hand and caused the seal of the United States to be affixed.

Done at the city of Washington, this fifteenth day of July, in the year of our Lord one thousand eight hundred and sixty-three, and of the independence of the United States of America the eighty-eighth. Abraham Lincoln.[1678]

After deceptively calling the War he himself inaugurated against the South a **"needless and cruel rebellion,"** Lincoln goes on to establish what would become America's popular Thanksgiving Day holiday.

His mid-War motivation was apparently to appear religious, patriotic, and compassionate, a naked attempt to shore up support from an increasingly despondent, hostile, and apathetic Northern populace. No doubt many lukewarm antiwar proponents were persuaded to side with him after hearing this, his latest political and military ploy.

However, as the 1864 election loomed ever closer, Lincoln conjured up a new and even more self-serving purpose for observing a day of thanksgiving.

On October 3, 1863, and again on October 20, 1864—this time only a few weeks before election day—Lincoln issued new, updated proclamations announcing that subsequently Thanksgiving Day would be observed on the last Thursday of each November.[1679] The October 3 announcement reads:

> The year that is drawing toward its close has been filled with the blessings of fruitful fields and healthful skies. To

these bounties, which are so constantly enjoyed that we are prone to forget the source from which they come, others have been added, which are of so extraordinary a nature that they cannot fail to penetrate and soften the heart which is habitually insensible to the ever-watchful providence of almighty God.

In the midst of a civil war of unequaled magnitude and severity, which has sometimes seemed to foreign states to invite and provoke their aggressions, peace has been preserved with all nations, order has been maintained, the laws have been respected and obeyed, and harmony has prevailed everywhere, except in the theater of military conflict; while that theater has been greatly contracted by the advancing armies and navies of the Union.

Needful diversions of wealth and of strength from the fields of peaceful industry to the national defense have not arrested the plow, the shuttle, or the ship; the ax has enlarged the borders of our settlements, and the mines, as well of iron and coal as of the precious metals, have yielded even more abundantly than heretofore. Population has steadily increased, notwithstanding the waste that has been made in the camp, the siege, and the battle-field, and the country, rejoicing in the consciousness of augmented strength and vigor, is permitted to expect continuance of years with large increase of freedom.

No human counsel hath devised, nor hath any mortal hand worked out these great things. They are the gracious gifts of the most high God, who, while dealing with us in anger for our sins, hath nevertheless remembered mercy.

It has seemed to me fit and proper that they should be solemnly, reverently, and gratefully acknowledged as with one heart and one voice by the whole American people. I do, therefore, invite my fellow-citizens in every part of the United States, and also those who are at sea and those who are sojourning in foreign lands, to set apart and observe the last Thursday of November next as a day of thanksgiving and praise to our beneficent Father who dwelleth in the heavens. And I recommend to them that, while offering up the ascriptions justly due to him for such singular deliverances and blessings, they do also, with humble penitence for our national perverseness and disobedience, commend to his tender care all those who have become widows, orphans, mourners, or sufferers in the lamentable civil strife in which we are unavoidably engaged, and fervently implore the interposition of the almighty hand to heal the wounds of the nation, and to restore it, as soon as may be consistent with the Divine purposes, to the full enjoyment of peace, harmony, tranquillity, and union.

In testimony whereof, I have hereunto set my hand, and caused the seal of the United States to be affixed.

Done at the city of Washington, this third day of October, in the year of our Lord one thousand eight hundred and sixty-three, and of the independence of the United States the eighty-eighth. Abraham Lincoln.[1680]

Lincoln's anti-South propaganda was in full evidence here: he uses this, his second Thanksgiving Proclamation, as an opportunity to, once again, knowingly and falsely call his War a **"civil war,"** then refers to Southerners as **"perverse"** and **"disobedient"** for acting on the Constitutional right of secession.

Though unnecessary due to the issuance of the October 3, 1863 decree, Lincoln released another "Proclamation of Thanksgiving" on October 20, 1864:

> It has pleased almighty God to prolong our national life another year, defending us with his guardian care against unfriendly designs from abroad, and vouchsafing to us in his mercy many and signal victories over the enemy, who is of our own household. It has also pleased our heavenly Father to favor as well our citizens in their homes as our soldiers in their camps, and our sailors on the rivers and seas, with unusual health. He has largely augmented our free population by emancipation and by immigration, while he has opened to us new sources of wealth, and has crowned the labor of our working-men in every department of industry with abundant rewards. Moreover, he has been pleased to animate and inspire our minds and hearts with fortitude, courage, and resolution sufficient for the great trial of civil war into which we have been brought by our adherence as a nation to the cause of freedom and humanity, and to afford to us reasonable hopes of an ultimate and happy

deliverance from all our dangers and afflictions.

Now, therefore, I, Abraham Lincoln, President of the United States, do hereby appoint and set apart the last Thursday of November next as a day which I desire to be observed by all my fellow-citizens, wherever they may then be, as a day of thanksgiving and praise to almighty God, the beneficent Creator and Ruler of the universe. And I do further recommend to my fellow-citizens aforesaid, that on that occasion they do reverently humble themselves in the dust, and from thence offer up penitent and fervent prayers and supplications to the great Disposer of events for a return of the inestimable blessings of peace, union, and harmony throughout the land which it has pleased him to assign as a dwelling-place for ourselves and for our posterity throughout all generations.

In testimony whereof, I have hereunto set my hand and caused the seal of the United States to be affixed.

Done at the city of Washington, this twentieth day of October, in the year of our Lord one thousand eight hundred and sixty-four, and of the independence of the United States the eighty-ninth. Abraham Lincoln.[1681]

As they come from a self-declared atheist, the numerous religious sentiments that permeate this document ring quite hollow.

The real question is, why did Lincoln change the date of August 6, the date in his original Thanksgiving Proclamation, to the last Thursday in November?

This so-called act of **"thanksgiving and praise to our beneficent Father"** gave the Union military an excuse to send its soldiers "home for the holidays" in late October and early November, just in time for the November elections (for in most Northern states it was illegal, according to Lincoln himself, for soldiers **"to vote away from their homes"**).[1682] Naturally, grateful Yankee soldiers went to the polls in huge numbers to vote overwhelmingly for the man who had granted them this holiday respite, this unexpected opportunity to get away from the cold, hunger, filth, dangers, and general horror of the battlefield.[1683]

Lincoln helped along his guileful plot by sending out "letters of encouragement," such as the following example, written to Yankee General William T. Sherman on September 19, 1864:

> The State election of Indiana occurs on the 11th of October, and the loss of it, to the friends of the government, would go far losing the whole Union cause. The bad effect upon the November election, and especially the giving the State government to those who will oppose the war in every possible way, are too much to risk, if it can possibly be avoided. The draft proceeds, notwithstanding its strong tendency to lose us the State. Indiana is the only important State, voting in October, whose soldiers cannot vote in the field. Anything you can safely do to let her soldiers, or any part of them, go home and vote at the State election will be greatly in point. They need not remain for the Presidential election, but may return to you at once. This is in no sense an order, but is merely intended to impress you with the importance, to the army itself, of your doing all you safely can, yourself being the judge of what you can safely do. Yours truly, A. Lincoln.[1684]

Sherman got the **"point,"** and complied, of course, as did numerous other Union officers.

In the fall of 1864, for example, Grant furloughed 15,000 of his troops just in time to return home and vote.[1685] But only those who supported liberal Lincoln. Those who did not were mysteriously "unable" to secure furloughs. Still, conservative-minded Yankee soldiers had ample opportunity to change their minds: as most Union troops were by then permitted to vote in the field, Lincoln sent party canvassers right out to the front of the lines, persuading many a fence-sitter to vote **"on the right side,"** a not so cryptic phrase whose meaning was readily deciphered by every one of the president's accomplices.[1686]

In the majority of cases, however, soldiers were simply not allowed to vote against him. As the South had already painfully learned, when all else failed, Lincoln never hesitated to fall back on his favorite methods of governing: intimidation, threats, and even violent coercion.[1687] As he wrote slyly to Arkansas Governor Isaac Murphy in a March 12, 1864, telegram:

> I am not appointing officers for Arkansas now, and I will try to remember your request. Do your best to get out the largest vote possible, and of course as much of it as possible on the right side. A. Lincoln.[1688]

To make sure his hidden message was received *and* understood, that same day he also telegrammed William Meade Fishback at Fort Smith, Arkansas[1689]:

> I know not that any change of departmental lines is likely to be made in Arkansas; but if done, it will be for purely military reasons, to which the good people there can have no just cause of objection. Get out the largest vote you can, and the largest part of it on the right side that is possible. A. Lincoln.[1690]

On April 27, 1864, Lincoln sent a follow-up letter to Governor Murphy, thanking him for getting the vote **"nearly all the right way,"** and offering him mafia-style **"protection"** in return:

> I am much gratified to learn that you got out so large a vote, so nearly all the right way, at the late election; and not less so that your State government, including the legislature, is organized and in good working order. Whatever I can I will do to protect you; meanwhile you must do your utmost to protect yourselves. Present my greeting to all. A. Lincoln.[1691]

While Lincoln's Republican (liberal) agents were assisting in gathering votes in the field, Democratic (conservative) agents who did the same were discouraged, and sometimes even arrested and imprisoned. More sinister still was Lincoln's practice of throwing out the votes of Democratic soldiers as "defective." At other times he replaced such ballots with Republican ones. On numerous other occasions he refused to count Democratic votes at all.[1692]

Though today we celebrate Thanksgiving Day to give thanks for "divine goodness," we still observe it on the last Thursday of November, betraying its authentic roots in the political shenanigans of America's most exploitive, crafty, and politically astute chief executive.

Lincoln's militarily controlled clamp down on civil rights assured a victory in the 1864 election in various other ways as well. He illegally banned the eleven states of the Confederacy from participating that year, allegedly because they were now an independent nation.[1693] This was illegal because, according to Lincoln himself, the Confederacy was not a legitimate foreign country, it was still part of the Union.

Indeed, for the rest of his life he never publicly recognized the Confederacy as anything other than eleven states **"in rebellion"** against the

U.S.A.—even though, as Jefferson Davis pointed out privately, Lincoln was obviously fully aware that the C.S.A. was a separate nation, otherwise he would not have called up troops, enacted General Winfield Scott's Anaconda Plan, and blockaded the South—all which would have been unlawful otherwise.[1694] Yet Lincoln must have desperately wanted Dixie's eighty electoral votes. Why then did he block the Southern states from the 1864 U.S. election?

For the same reason he did everything: political expediency. Why risk the embarrassment of allowing states to participate in the North's political process that he knew would never vote for him? The overt hypocrisy of his position never seemed to bother him.

Lincoln need not have taken time to bar the South from the 1864 U.S. election, however. She would not have accepted an invitation from him anyway. For since February 8, 1861, the eleven states of the Confederacy (and provisional Confederate governments in Missouri and Kentucky) had been operating as a legitimate, independent country, one preoccupied with setting up her own government.[1695]

We have now looked at just some of the crimes Lincoln committed in order to secure the *popular* votes he needed to get reelected. His attempts to specifically insure extra *electoral* votes for the '64 election were no less underhanded.

On June 20, 1863, for example, he generated five additional electoral votes for himself by illegally creating the thirty-fifth state, West Virginia[1696] (it is unlawful for a section of a state to secede from the parent state without the parent state's approval). This he did by pushing the region that would become West Virginia, to secede from Virginia at a time when he had pronounced the secession of the Southern states unlawful.[1697] Again, his double standard did not concern him.

Here is how Lincoln justified this particular criminal act:

> December 31, 1862. President's Opinion On The Admission Of West Virginia Into The Union.
> The consent of the legislature of Virginia is constitutionally necessary to the bill for the admission of West Virginia becoming a law. A body claiming to be such legislature has given its consent. We cannot well deny that it is such, unless we do so upon the outside knowledge that the body was chosen at elections in which a majority of the qualified voters of Virginia did not participate. But it is a universal practice in the

popular elections in all these States to give no legal consideration whatever to those who do not choose to vote, as against the effect of the votes of those who do choose to vote. Hence it is not the qualified voters, but the qualified voters who choose to vote, that constitute the political power of the State. Much less than to non-voters should any consideration be given to those who did not vote in this case, because it is also matter of outside knowledge that they were not merely neglectful of their rights under and duty to this government, but were also engaged in open rebellion against it. Doubtless among these non-voters were some Union men whose voices were smothered by the more numerous secessionists; but we know too little of their number to assign them any appreciable value. Can this government stand, if it indulges constitutional constructions by which men in open rebellion against it are to be accounted, man for man, the equals of those who maintain their loyalty to it? Are they to be accounted even better citizens, and more worthy of consideration, than those who merely neglect to vote? If so, their treason against the Constitution enhances their constitutional value. Without braving these absurd conclusions, we cannot deny that the body which consents to the admission of West Virginia is the legislature of Virginia. I do not think the plural form of the words "legislatures" and "States" in the phrase of the Constitution "without the consent of the legislatures of the States concerned," etc., has any reference to the new State concerned. That plural form sprang from the contemplation of two or more old States contributing to form a new one. The idea that the new State was in danger of being admitted without its own consent was not provided against, because it was not thought of, as I conceive. It is said, the devil takes care of his own. Much more should a good spirit—the spirit of the Constitution and the Union—take care of its own. I think it cannot do less and live.

But is the admission into the Union of West Virginia expedient? This, in my general view, is more a question for Congress than for the Executive. Still I do not evade it. More than on anything else, it depends on whether the admission or rejection of the new State would, under all the circumstances, tend the more strongly to the restoration of the national authority throughout the Union. That which helps most in this direction is the most expedient at this time. Doubtless those in remaining Virginia would return to the Union, so to speak, less reluctantly without the division of the old State than with it; but I think we could not save as much in this quarter by rejecting the new State, as we should lose by it in West Virginia. We can scarcely dispense with the aid of West Virginia in this struggle; much less can we afford to have her against us, in Congress and in the field. Her brave and good men regard her admission into the Union as a matter of life and death. They have been true to the Union under very severe trials. We have so acted as to justify their hopes, and we cannot fully retain their confidence and cooperation if we seem to break faith with them. In fact, they could not do so much for us, if they would. Again, the admission of the new State turns that much slave soil to free, and thus is a certain and irrevocable encroachment upon the cause of the rebellion. The division of a State is dreaded as a precedent. But a measure made expedient by a war is no precedent for times of peace. It is said that the admission of West Virginia is secession, and tolerated only because it is our secession. Well, if we call it by that name, there is still difference enough between secession against, the Constitution and secession in favor of the Constitution. I believe the admission of West Virginia into the Union is expedient.[1698]

The secession of so-called "West Virginia" was unconstitutional because it was a clear violation of the U.S. Constitution's Article 4, Section 3, and Lincoln knew it, which explains his cantankerous defensiveness over the issue. Indeed, because he could not bring himself to admit his wrongdoing publicly, he here resorts to his usual method of tortured logic, irrational rantings, incomprehensible double-talk, and twisted interpretations of the Constitution.

However, he gives himself away in the very first paragraph when he concedes that **"a body *claiming* to be such legislature has given its consent"** (emphasis added) to admit West Virginia as a state. The fact is that the Virginia legislature never officially authorized the secession of her Western region.[1699] Under the U.S. Constitution the **"body"** claiming to represent West Virginia was not authorized to do so, hence the entire affair was a political charade, one cunningly calculated to benefit Lincoln at the polls in November 1864.

On April 20, 1863, the president issued his "Proclamation Admitting West Virginia into the Union." It read:

> Whereas, by the act of Congress approved the thirty-first day of December last, the State of West Virginia was declared to be one of the United States of America, and was admitted into the Union on an equal footing with the original States in all respects whatever, upon the condition that certain changes should be duly made in the proposed constitution for that State:
>
> And whereas, proof of a compliance with that condition, as required by the second section of the act aforesaid, has been submitted to me:
>
> Now, therefore, be it known that I, Abraham Lincoln, President of the United States, do hereby, in pursuance of the act of Congress aforesaid, declare and proclaim that the said act shall take effect and be in force from and after sixty days from the date hereof.[1700]

There was no **"proof of compliance,"** however, for the proper Virginia officials never offered any. As a result of Lincoln's political treachery, to this day West Virginia is not a constitutionally formed state, nor is it a legal part of the Union, except as the western portion of the state of Virginia.

Shortly thereafter, Lincoln insidiously admitted the thirty-sixth state, Nevada, on October 31, a mere week before election day, November 8, 1864. Since this was, at the very least, shady and unethical, as usual he felt compelled to defend his crime by asserting that it had been **"completed in conformity with law,"**[1701] the typical Lincolnian strategy used to baffle his critics, veil the facts, and stall for time. Here is his duplicitous "Proclamation Admitting Nevada Into the Union," dated October 31:

> Whereas the Congress of the United States passed an act, which was approved on the twenty-first day of March last; entitled "An act to enable the people of Nevada to form a constitution and State government, and for the admission of such State into the Union on an equal footing with the original States";
>
> And whereas the said constitution and State government have been formed, pursuant to the conditions prescribed by the fifth section of the act of

> Congress aforesaid, and the certificate required by the said act, and also a copy of the constitution and ordinances, have been submitted to the President of the United States:
>
> Now, therefore, be it known that I, Abraham Lincoln, President of the United States, in accordance with the duty imposed upon me by the Act of Congress aforesaid, do hereby declare and proclaim that the said State of Nevada is admitted into the Union on an equal footing with the original States.[1702]

Like West Virginia, a "Union" state, the hurried last minute admission of Nevada raised Lincoln's electoral votes even higher, in this case by two (it would have been three, but one Nevada elector did not vote). While this latter action was not unlawful, it was not exactly proper,[1703] for he and his party had tampered with the government's Electoral College. We will note here that along with West Virginia and Nevada, the state of Kansas was created under Lincoln's auspices for the same reason as well.[1704]

In light of such facts, could any sane person consider either Lincoln's 1860 or his 1864 victories fair and ethical?

The truth is that Lincoln won both of his elections with less than 50 percent of the American vote, and many of the votes he did win were accrued through underhanded backroom deals, and outright jobbery, bribery, graft, and dupery.

Still, Lincolnites, his modern day followers, continue to defiantly and proudly refer to him as "Honest Abe," while annually voting him "America's greatest president."[1705]

Lincoln & His Black Soldiers

WE HAVE SEEN THAT LINCOLN was not an abolitionist, but rather an emancipationist-colonizationist ("free 'em up and ship 'em out"), and that he was not against slavery because it hurt blacks, but because it hurt whites—which is why he was against the spread of slavery. We have also seen that he delayed issuing the Emancipation Proclamation for as long as possible, and that even when he did it was not for the benefit of blacks, but for the benefit of whites.

It should come as no surprise then to learn that Lincoln barred the military enlistment of blacks for the first two years of his presidency, and that, when he was finally convinced (under enormous pressure) to enroll them, he saw them as mere military chess pieces in his war upon the South. Of course, as discussed earlier, this was one of the four primary reasons he pushed through the Emancipation Proclamation to begin with.

Overt evidence of his plans for the South's African-American servants came shortly after the Final Emancipation Proclamation was issued on January 1, 1863, an edict in which he openly called for "freed" blacks to be enrolled, not as soldiers, but as ordinary slave-like laborers. Subsequently, in a March 26, letter to Tennessee Governor Andrew Johnson, Lincoln wrote:

> My dear Sir: I am told you have at least thought of raising a negro military force. In my opinion the country now needs no specific thing so much as some man of your ability and position to go to this work. When I speak of

> your position, I mean that of an eminent citizen of a slave State and himself a slaveholder. The colored population is the great available and yet unavailed of force for restoring the Union. The bare sight of fifty thousand armed and drilled black soldiers upon the banks of the Mississippi would end the rebellion at once; and who doubts that we can present that sight if we but take hold in earnest? If you have been thinking of it, please do not dismiss the thought.[1706]

The idea of using blacks as slave-like military laborers rather than as armed soldiers had been in Lincoln's mind all along, as he noted earlier on July 17, 1862, to the House of Representatives:

> . . . I am ready to say now, I think it is proper for our military commanders to employ as laborers as many persons of African descent as can be used to advantage.[1707]

A few days later Lincoln issued an order "Authorizing Employment of Contrabands," the North's disparaging term for black Southern servants (this demeaning word was never used in the South). Clause 2 reads:

> That military and navy commanders shall employ as laborers, within and from said States, so many persons of African descent as can be advantageously used for military or naval purposes, giving them reasonable wages for their labor.[1708]

We will note here that the president does not state that **"contrabands"** should be paid the same wage as whites, but rather a **"reasonable wage,"** a nebulous phrase that left the door wide open for massive corruption—which is exactly what occurred.

This was helped along by Lincoln's own racism: after promising equal pay,[1709] Lincoln's order (via the Militia Act of July 17, 1862)[1710] that black soldiers receive half the pay of white soldiers[1711] infuriated both blacks and abolitionists.[1712] This was a **"necessary concession"** to white Northern racism,[1713] Lincoln explained to a stunned and understandably fuming Frederick Douglass in the summer of 1863.[1714]

In reality, many of Lincoln's black soldiers were *never* paid. Former slave Susie King Taylor wrote:

I was the wife of one of those men who did not get a penny for eighteen months for their services, only their rations and clothing.[1715]

The racism behind Lincoln's treatment of his African-American soldiers is almost unbelievable to us today. Let us consider a June 24, 1864, letter he wrote to his attorney general, Edward Bates:

> **Sir: By authority of the Constitution, and moved thereto by the fourth section of the act of Congress, entitled "An act making appropriations for the support of the army for the year ending the thirtieth of June, eighteen hundred and sixty-five, and for other purposes, approved June 15, 1864," I require your opinion in writing as to what pay, bounty, and clothing are allowed by law to persons of color who were free on the nineteenth day of April, 1861, and who have been enlisted and mustered into the military service of the United States between the month of December, 1862, and the sixteenth of June, 1864.**
>
> **Please answer as you would do, on my requirement, if the act of June 15, 1864, had not been passed, and I will so use your opinion as to satisfy that act. Your obedient servant, A. Lincoln.**[1716]

Why did Lincoln even question what **"pay, bounty, and clothing"** was allowed for his black soldiers? Why did he not automatically give them the same pay, bounty, and clothing as his white soldiers? The answer by now should be obvious.

There was also the issue of white recruitment: Lincoln and his cabinet feared that granting equal pay to black soldiers would discourage Northern whites from enlisting,[1717] most who did not want to fight next to blacks anyway, however noble the Union cause.[1718]

Adding fuel to the fire, black Yankee officers, those rare few that existed,[1719] were paid the same as white Yankee privates.[1720] (We will note here that when the Confederacy also officially enlisted blacks, on March 23, 1863, they were immediately integrated and given equal pay and equal treatment with white soldiers.)[1721]

Resistance by white Union soldiers to black officers was so severe that even Lincoln's 100 black commissioned officers,[1722] representing just 0.005 percent of the entire Union military of 2,000,000 men, ultimately had to be replaced by whites.[1723] General Nathaniel P. Banks discusses this topic in an official field report dated February 12, 1863. Speaking of the Union's all-black 1st, 2nd, and 3rd Louisiana Native Guards (infantry), Banks writes:

> The three regiments first named have ten companies each; their field and staff officers are white men, but they have negro company officers, whom I am replacing, as vacancies occur, by white ones, being entirely satisfied that the appointment of colored officers is detrimental to the service.
>
> It converts what, with judicious management and good officers, is capable of much usefulness into a source of constant embarrassment and annoyance. It demoralizes both the white troops and the negroes. The officers of the Fourth Regiment will be white men.[1724]

Though blacks seem to have been more readily accepted into Lincoln's navy than in his army, as noted, they were still confronted by rank bigotry from all sides. At the start of Yankee black enlistment, for instance, African-American sailors were not allowed to rise above the lowest rank, known as "Boy."[1725]

When Governor John A. Andrew of Massachusetts went to Lincoln to ask that he be allowed to grant qualified blacks military commissions, the president said absolutely not. As usual, the reason he gave for this decision was that the racist Northern public would not accept them.[1726] However, this was only partially true, for Lincoln himself would also not accept black officers.

It is worthy of comment here that unlike Lincoln's black soldiers—most who were violently forced into service, Southern blacks were only recruited voluntarily, "with their own consent."[1727] And while Lincoln's black soldiers served as *freed*men, Confederate black soldiers served as *free*men, an enormous difference in wording and meaning to all concerned.[1728] All except for Lincoln, that is.

Though he made many promises to his black soldiers regarding the inequality of their pay, Lincoln did little or nothing to fulfill them, and full and equal pay was not granted to black Yankee soldiers until *after* the War. The money involved was so small that there is only one way to explain the procrastination: Northern white racism.[1729] Just as a fish rots from the head down, that racism, of course, started at the top—with the president.

Lincoln was certainly his own worst enemy in this regard, for though he desperately needed blacks to join, most refused the "offer." Even

Frederick Douglass, who constantly encouraged other blacks to become soldiers, had little success at this game. After he gave a recruitment speech before a black audience in New York City, for example, only one man came forward. Insulted, Douglass told the crowd that he felt sorry for them, insinuating that they were cowards. But it was not cowardice. It was Lincoln's racist military policies that made many blacks think twice about enlisting. A man named Robert Johnson stood up, faced Douglass, and said of "the Negroes of New York":

> If the [U.S.] government wanted their services, let it guarantee to them all the rights of citizens and soldiers, and, instead of one man, he would insure them 5,000 men in twenty days.[1730]

Johnson was entirely correct. But guaranteeing black soldiers full civil rights was something that neither Lincoln, his cabinet, nor most of his white officers were prepared to do, which is precisely why most African-Americans had to be physically forced into Yankee military service.

Douglass himself eventually conceded that the trouble lay not with blacks or cowardice, but with Lincoln and his racism. Why should Negroes enlist when the U.S. military is so prejudiced against them?, he once asked the president rhetorically.[1731]

It is little wonder then that most Southern blacks not only refused to leave their homes and plantations, they also refused to enroll voluntarily in Lincoln's army. What was Lincoln's response? He had them enlisted involuntarily. Those who resisted were usually shot or bayoneted on the spot, without trial. Then when black soldiers later rebelled against the abuse of white Yankee soldiers, they were whipped.[1732] Those who deserted were mercilessly tracked through the wilderness by Northern bounty hunters and their hound dogs.[1733]

After being taken at gunpoint from the peace and safety of their farms and plantations, to the filth, hardships, and dangers of life on the battlefield,[1734] at least 50 percent of these reluctant black soldiers died alone in muddy ditches fighting for the Yanks against their own native homeland: the South.[1735]

Both white and black Union soldiers mistreated Southern slaves who remained loyal to Dixie, entering their homes, shooting bullets through their walls, overturning furniture, and stealing various personal items.[1736] A Northerner visiting South Carolina told how Southern blacks were trailed like wild animals, then mercilessly ripped from their homes and families by

Yankee recruiters.[1737]

The Yankees' own *Official Records* reveal what most Northerners and scallywags will still not admit. In December 1864 a disgusted Yankee officer, General Rufus Saxton, reported on Lincoln's racist and often violent "recruiting tactics." Southern blacks, Saxton said,

> were hunted to their hiding places by armed parties of their own people, and, if found, compelled to enlist. This conscription order is still in force. Men have been seized and forced to enlist who had large families of young children dependent upon them for support and fine crops of cotton and corn nearly ready for harvest, without an opportunity of making provision for the one or securing the other.
>
> Three [black] boys, one only fourteen years of age, were seized in a field where they were at work and sent to a regiment serving in a distant part of the department without the knowledge or consent of their parents.
>
> A [black] man on his way to enlist as a volunteer was stopped by a recruiting party. He told them where he was going and was passing on when he was again ordered to halt. He did not stop and was shot dead, and was left where he fell. It is supposed the [Union] soldiers desired to bring him in and get the bounty offered for bringing in recruits.
>
> Another [black] man who had a wife and family was shot as he was entering a boat to fish, on the pretense that he was a deserter. He fell in the water and was left. His wound, though very severe, was not mortal. An employee [black] in the [U.S.] Quartermasters Department was taken, and without being allowed to communicate with the quartermaster or settle his accounts or provide for his family, was taken to Hilton Head and enrolled, although he had a certificate of exemption from the military service from a medical officer.
>
> I protested against the order of the major-general commanding (General [possibly Robert Sanford] Foster) and sent him reports of these proceedings, but had no power to prevent them. The order has never to my knowledge been revoked.[1738]

Of Lincoln's "shot-gun policy" of coercive black enlistment it was said that it always succeeded in getting the conscript.[1739]

What the president did not seem to grasp, however, was that the very definition of "recruitment" insinuates *voluntary* military service, for the opposite is "conscription": *compulsory* military service. Thus, many of Lincoln's so-called black "recruits" were actually more akin to prisoners of war than enlisted soldiers. Yet, he still counted them as legitimate servicemen, which, of course, greatly over exaggerated the number of "black Union soldiers" in the U.S. armed services.

Speaking before the Confederate Congress on December 7, 1863, President Jefferson Davis commented on the Yankees' conduct toward Southern blacks; or as he put it, the "unrelenting warfare [that has] been waged by these pretended friends of human rights and liberties against the unfortunate negroes":

> Wherever the enemy have been able to gain access, they have forced into the ranks of their army every able-bodied [black] man that they could seize, and have either left the aged, the women, and the children to perish by starvation, or have gathered them into camps, where they have been wasted by a frightful mortality. Without clothing or shelter, often without food, incapable, without supervision, of taking the most ordinary precaution against disease, these helpless dependents, accustomed to have their wants supplied by the foresight of their masters, are being rapidly exterminated wherever brought in contact with the [Yankee] invaders. By the Northern man, on whose deep rooted prejudices no kindly restraining influence is exercised, they are treated with aversion and neglect. There is little hazard in predicting that, in all localities where the enemy have gained a temporary foothold, the negroes, who under our care increased six fold in number since their importation into the colonies of Great Britain, will have been reduced by mortality during the war to not more than one half their previous number.
>
> Information on this subject is derived not only from our own observation and from the reports of the negroes who succeeded in escaping from the enemy, but full confirmation is afforded by statements published in the Northern journals, humane persons engaged in making appeals to the charitable for aid in preventing the ravages of disease, exposure, and starvation among the negro women and children who are crowded into [Union] encampments.[1740]

After their violent forced enlistment, most Southern blacks fled from Lincoln's armies at their first opportunity,[1741] back to the comfort, warmth, security, and domesticity of their homes in the South.[1742] The Yankee top brass was not amused. While stationed at Camden, South Carolina, one of Sherman's officers, Lieutenant Thomas J. Myers, wrote to his wife on February 26, 1865:

The damned [Southern] niggers, as a general rule, preferred to stay at home, particularly when they found out that we [Yanks] only wanted the able bodied men (and to tell you the truth the youngest and best looking women).[1743]

In October 1862 a Northern reporter for the New York *Tribune* visited Union troops in North Carolina and wrote the following report on the condition of black Yankee soldiers. The situation of the miserable lowly Negroes, he said,

> is such as should excite the sympathy of every Christian man. I am sorry to say that they are treated with great sternness and severity amounting to positive cruelty, by our own soldiers who seem to regard them as hardly better than beasts. Not a few of our [Union] officers conduct themselves in the most unfeeling manner toward these unfortunate creatures . . .[1744]

Lincoln was fully aware of what was going on, as is clear from his April 4, 1864, letter to Union General William S. Rosecrans:

> . . . it is complained that the enlistment of negroes is not conducted in as orderly a manner and with as little collateral provocation as it might be. So far you have got along in the Department of the Missouri rather better than I dared to hope, and I congratulate you and myself upon it.[1745]

While the acknowledgment is understated and intentionally vague (to protect himself from post-war legal problems), it is there nonetheless. Lincoln even offers Rosecrans his tacit approval for his **"provocative"** black enlistment program.

Another example of this sort of thing came in a June 13, 1864, letter to Union General Lorenzo Thomas, then stationed at Louisville, Kentucky:

> **Complaint is made to me that in the vicinity of Henderson, our militia are seizing negroes and carrying them off without their own consent, and according to no rules whatever, except those of absolute violence. I wish you would look into this and inform me, and see that the making soldiers of negroes is done according to the rules you are acting upon, so that unnecessary provocation**

and irritation be avoided. A. Lincoln.[1746]

Why would Thomas' soldiers be violently forcing Southern blacks into the Yankee army unless an order had come from above? The man above Thomas was Grant, and the man above Grant was Lincoln. And it was Lincoln who, on July 21, 1863, wrote the following letter to Secretary of War Stanton:

> My dear Sir: I desire that a renewed and vigorous effort be made to raise colored forces along the shores of the Mississippi. Please consult the general-in-chief, and if it is perceived that any acceleration of the matter can be effected, let it be done. I think the evidence is nearly conclusive that General [Lorenzo] Thomas is one of the best (if not the very best) instruments for this service. Yours truly, A. Lincoln.[1747]

A few weeks later, on August 9, 1863, Thomas is now in Mississippi illegally **"raising colored troops,"** whereupon Lincoln sends Grant the following letter:

> A word upon another subject. General Thomas has gone again to the Mississippi Valley, with the view of raising colored troops. I have no reason to doubt that you are doing what you reasonably can upon the same subject. I believe it is a resource which if vigorously applied now will soon close the contest.[1748]

The trail up the chain of command is incontrovertible: Thomas, Grant, Lincoln.

Despite the prejudice, violence, and criminal activity going on under the president's nose, his black involuntary enlistment program continued, as did his deceitful public admonitions against the practice. Here is another example, from a February 7, 1865, letter to Union Lieutenant Colonel Glenn at Henderson, Kentucky:

> Complaint is made to me that you are forcing negroes into the military service, and even torturing them—riding them on rails and the like—to extort their consent. I hope this may be a mistake. The like must not be done by you, or any one under you. You must not force negroes any more than white men. Answer me on

this. A. Lincoln.[1749]

It is clear from this missive that whites were also undergoing involuntarily enlistment into the U.S. military—which included various forms of torture. According to Lincoln, blacks were not to undergo anything that whites were not. What does this mean exactly? Only Lincoln himself could possibly provide the answer. But now knowing what we do of him, would anyone believe him whatever his reply?

Naturally, Lincoln's black soldiers were extremely displeased with the entire situation, and many protested. At least eighteen of those who did were charged with "mutiny," and executed by hanging or firing squad. Amazingly, these executions went on even after Lincoln's death and his war had ended. As late as December 1, 1865, for example, six black privates accused of mutiny (i.e., for objecting to Lincoln's racist pay scale) were rounded up and killed by musketry at Fernandina, Florida. This was a full year-and-a-half after the U.S. Congress authorized retroactive equal pay for black soldiers in June 1864.[1750]

Other indignities courtesy of the "Great Emancipator": not only were his African-American soldiers denied the bounties,[1751] pensions, bonuses, and support for dependents accorded to whites,[1752] they were also given inferior or obsolete weapons, some completely unworkable.[1753]

Lincoln's black soldiers were even refused equal medical care. According to the president's rules, medical supplies and medical attention were to go first to injured European-American soldiers. As a result, of the 178,975 black soldiers in Lincoln's three million-man army, 35,130 died of sickness and disease alone, a staggeringly high percentage (20 percent). As if this type of Northern prejudice was not enough, Lincoln made sure that most black units were stationed in out-of-the-way sectors, and that their white officers were those judged unfit for service in more vital departments.[1754] One wonders how long it took black Yankee soldiers to finally realize that it was Lincoln who was their enemy, not the South.

The truth is that while today Lincoln is called "the black man's greatest friend" by the uninformed, during his political life he spent every spare minute plotting to deport all Americans of African descent out of the country. Virtually ignoring them, he never even commented on, let alone thanked, blacks for the many amazing architectural, linguistic, artistic, sartorial, choreographic, culinary, and musical contributions they had made to American culture up to that time.[1755] In the 1800s, for example, blacks comprised 80 percent of the South's artisan class,[1756] meaning that the vast majority of Dixie's buildings and her works of art were created by blacks. No notice was given of this amazing achievement by Lincoln, nor of the fact that, as we have seen, black *Northern* slaves built most of the governmental buildings in Washington, D.C., including both the White House and the U.S. Capitol.[1757]

Actually, Lincoln's own words show that he knew literally nothing about freed blacks, in either the North or the South. He did not know what they thought or believed or how they lived, worked, and fought. On February 15, 1864, for instance, he wrote the following to one of his more controversial generals, Daniel Edgar Sickles:

> Please . . . learn what you can as to the colored people; how they get along as soldiers, as laborers in our service, on leased plantations, and as hired laborers with their old masters, if there be such cases. Also learn what you can as to the colored people within the rebel lines.[1758]

Moreover, tens of thousands of African-Americans were maimed and killed fighting for the Union, all without a single public word of praise or gratitude from Lincoln.[1759] Instead, he underpaid and exploited the 180,000 black soldiers in his armies, then allowed their wives and children to remain enslaved for nearly the entire duration of his war. In Kentucky, as just one example, Lincoln did not free the wives and children of the state's 22,000 black Union soldiers until March 3, 1865, just one month before the War ended.[1760] Little wonder that some 14,887 black Yanks, or over 8 percent of their total number, "went over the hill" (that is, deserted).[1761]

Lincoln did come close, on one occasion, to at least acknowledging black war service. But it was not self-motivated. He had to be pushed into it by blacks themselves. Even then, his acknowledgment was not specific. It was haphazardly mentioned in a personal letter pertaining to black suffrage.

In the winter of 1863 a group of New Orleans freemen asked Yankee General Nathaniel P. Banks for permission to vote. Banks rejected their request. They then went to Lincoln. He completely ignored them, of course. But on March 13, 1864, the day after meeting with two blacks (Arnold Bertonneau and Jean Baptiste Roudanez) who urged the president to sign legislation authorizing black suffrage,[1762] he sent a rather apathetic letter to Michael Hahn, the newly installed "Reconstruction" governor of Louisiana:

My dear Sir: I congratulate you on having fixed your name in history as the first free-State governor of Louisiana. Now you are about to have a convention, which, among other things, will probably define the elective franchise. I barely suggest for your private consideration, whether some of the colored people may not be let in—as for instance, the very intelligent, and especially those who have fought gallantly in our ranks. They would probably help, in some trying time to come, to keep the jewel of liberty within the family of freedom. But this is only a suggestion, not to the public, but to you alone.[1763]

This private mail was far from any kind of public declaration supporting black enfranchisement, and in fact he shows no interest at all in allowing *all* blacks to vote. Instead, he prefers that only **"the very intelligent"** from among those who served in the Union military be given the right. Since he was no doubt referring to black officers, this would have been a small number indeed, for there were never more than 100 who held commissions in the entire Union army of 2,000,000 men.[1764]

There are two points to be made here: 1) just one year before the War ended, Lincoln had the opportunity to endorse universal black suffrage, or at least suggest it. He chose to do neither. 2) He steadfastly refused to publicly acknowledge the military service of his black soldiers.[1765]

At least in this one area Lincoln was consistent: during a speech at Columbus, Ohio, on September 16, 1859, a year before he was elected president, he publicly denounced the idea of black suffrage:

> **Fellow-citizens of the State of Ohio:** I cannot fail to remember that I appear for the first time before an audience in this now great State—an audience that is accustomed to hear such speakers as [Thomas] **Corwin**, and [Salmon Portland] **Chase**, and [Benjamin Franklin] **Wade**, and many other renowned men; and remembering this, I feel that it will be well for you, as for me, that you should not raise your expectations to that standard to which you would have been justified in raising them had one of these distinguished men appeared before you. You would perhaps be only preparing a disappointment for yourselves, and, as a consequence of your disappointment, mortification to me. I hope, therefore, that you will commence with very moderate

expectations; and perhaps, if you will give me your attention, I shall be able to interest you to a moderate degree.

Appearing here for the first time in my life, I have been somewhat embarrassed for a topic by way of introduction to my speech; but I have been relieved from that embarrassment by an introduction which the "Ohio Statesman" newspaper gave me this morning. In this paper I have read an article in which, among other statements, I find the following:

> "In debating with Senator [Stephen A.] Douglas during the memorable contest last fall, Mr. Lincoln declared in favor of negro suffrage, and attempted to defend that vile conception against the Little Giant."

I mention this now, at the opening of my remarks, for the purpose of making three comments upon it. The first I have already announced—it furnished me an introductory topic; the second is to show that the gentleman is mistaken; thirdly, to give him an opportunity to correct it.

In the first place, in regard to this matter being a mistake. I have found that it is not entirely safe, when one is misrepresented under his very nose, to allow the misrepresentation to go uncontradicted. I therefore propose, here at the outset, not only to say that this is a misrepresentation, but to show conclusively that it is so; and you will bear with me while I read a couple of extracts from that very "memorable" debate with Judge Douglas last year, to which this newspaper refers. In the first pitched battle which Senator Douglas and myself had, at the town of Ottawa, I used the language which I will now read. Having been previously reading an extract, I continued as follows:

> Now, gentlemen, I don't want to read at any greater length, but this is the true complexion of all I have ever said in regard to the institution of slavery and the black race. This is the whole of it, and anything that argues me into his idea of perfect social and political

equality with the negro is but a specious and fantastic arrangement of words, by which a man can prove a horse-chestnut to be a chestnut horse. I will say here, while upon this subject, that I have no purpose either directly or indirectly to interfere with the institution of slavery in the States where it exists. I believe I have no lawful right to do so, and I have no inclination to do so. I have no purpose to introduce political and social equality between the white and the black races. There is a physical difference between the two which, in my judgment, will probably forever forbid their living together upon the footing of perfect equality, and inasmuch as it becomes a necessity that there must be a difference, I, as well as Judge Douglas, am in favor of the race to which I belong having the superior position. I have never said anything to the contrary, but I hold that, notwithstanding all this, there is no reason in the world why the negro is not entitled to all the natural rights enumerated in the Declaration of Independence, the right to life, liberty, and the pursuit of happiness. I hold that he is as much entitled to these as the white man. I agree with Judge Douglas, he is not my equal in many respects—certainly not in color, perhaps not in moral or intellectual endowments. But in the right to eat the bread, without leave of anybody else, which his own hand earns, he is my equal, and the equal of Judge Douglas, and the equal of every living man.

Upon a subsequent occasion, when the reason for making a statement like this recurred, I said:

While I was at the hotel to-day an

elderly gentleman called upon me to know whether I was really in favor of producing a perfect equality between the negroes and white people. While I had not proposed to myself on this occasion to say much on that subject, yet as the question was asked me I thought I would occupy perhaps five minutes in saying something in regard to it. I will say, then, that I am not, nor ever have been, in favor of bringing about in any way the social and political equality of the white and the black races—that I am not, nor ever have been, in favor of making voters or jurors of negroes, nor of qualifying them to hold office, nor to intermarry with white people; and I will say in addition to this, that there is a physical difference between the white and the black races, which, I believe, will forever forbid the two races living together on terms of social and political equality. And inasmuch as they cannot so live, while they do remain together there must be the position of superior and inferior, and I, as much as any other man, am in favor of having the superior position assigned to the white race. I say upon this occasion I do not perceive that because the white man is to have the superior position, the negro should be denied everything. I do not understand that because I do not want a negro woman for a slave, I must necessarily want her for a wife. My understanding is that I can just let her alone. I am now in my fiftieth year; and I certainly never have had a black woman for either a slave or a wife. So it seems to me quite possible for us to get along without making either slaves or wives of negroes. I will add to this, that I have never seen to my knowledge a man, woman, or child who was in favor of producing a perfect equality, social and political, between negroes and white men. I recollect or but one distinguished instance that I ever heard of so frequently as to be entirely satisfied of its correctness—and that is the case of Judge Douglas's old friend, Colonel Richard H. Johnson. I will also add to the remarks I have made (for I am not going to enter at large upon this subject), that I have never had the least apprehension that I or my friends would marry negroes, if there was no law to keep them from it; but as Judge Douglas and his friends seem to be in great apprehension that they might, if there were no law to keep them from it, I give him the most solemn pledge that I will to the very last stand by the law of the State, which forbids the marrying of white people with negroes.

There, my friends, you have briefly what I have, upon former occasions, said upon the subject to which this newspaper, to the extent of its ability, has drawn the public attention. In it you not only perceive, as a probability, that in that contest I did not at any time say I was in favor of negro suffrage; but the absolute proof that twice—once substantially and once expressly—I declared against it. Having shown you this, there remains but a word of comment upon that newspaper article. It is this: that I presume the editor of that paper is an honest and truth-loving man, and that he will be greatly obliged to me for furnishing him thus early an opportunity to correct the misrepresentation he has made, before it has run so long that malicious people can call him a liar.[1766]

So much for Lincoln's reputed desire to give American blacks the right to vote.

On another occasion, in early 1864, Lincoln mentions his "colored" soldiers in this fashion:

. . . these people who have so heroically vindicated their

manhood on the battle-field, where, in assisting to save the life of the Republic, they have demonstrated in blood their right to the ballot, which is but the humane protection of the flag they have so fearlessly defended. . . . The restoration of the Rebel States to the Union must rest upon the principle of civil and political equality of both races; and it must be sealed by general amnesty.[1767]

But once again these sentiments were confined to a private letter, not meant for the public.[1768] And once again no mention is made of universal black suffrage. The right to vote is only for those blacks who served in the military, Lincoln reasserts.

Finally, he states here that restoring the Southern states to the Union will require **"civil and political equality of both races,"** something he never established—and never showed any interest in establishing—in the North. Thanks in great part to Lincoln, **"these people,"** as he dispassionately referred to Northern blacks, would have to wait another 100 years for full civil rights.[1769]

On April 11, 1865, three days before he was shot by Northerner John Wilkes Booth, Lincoln was still standing in the way of giving blacks the vote. It was on this day that the president gave his last public speech. In it he deflected Yankee criticism that he still had not granted blacks total civil rights, obfuscating and wavering, finally deferring the entire issue to future generations. I know it is unsatisfactory to some, Lincoln told his audience,

> that the elective franchise is not [yet] **given to the colored man. I would myself prefer that it were now conferred on the very intelligent, and on those who serve our cause as soldiers.**[1770]

Bizarrely, pro-Lincoln historians and scholars consider this the first time a U.S. president "endorsed black suffrage."[1771] But was **"conferring"** it only on the **"very intelligent"** and also **"soldiers"** really an endorsement? Hardly. It was just more typical Lincolnian politics—muddling, trickery, delay tactics, and word twisting—from the North's most masterful spin doctor.

It is patently clear that in the end it was not the South but Lincoln who stood in the way of not only true America-wide emancipation, but the black vote and black citizenship as well. Indeed, all three only came *after* his death: universal abolition did not occur until December 1865,[1772] universal

Negro citizenship was not instituted until 1868, and universal Negro suffrage did not come until 1870.[1773]

That the Yankee president saw his black military men as little more than slave-like laborers and cannon fodder is evident from the following letter dated September 12, 1864. Here a fuming Lincoln responds to the brilliant suggestion that a temporary cease-fire be issued, an effort to halt the massive bloodshed and give both South and North time to work toward a peaceful resolution. Lincoln will have none of it. Not because it would give the South an advantage. But because he thinks that it would deprive his armies of the physical help of the black man, whose numbers he needed to win his War:

> An armistice—a cessation of hostilities—is the end of the struggle, and the insurgents would be in peaceable possession of all that has been struggled for. Any different policy in regard to the colored man deprives us of his help, and this is more than we can bear. We cannot spare the hundred and forty or fifty thousand now serving us as soldiers, seamen, and laborers. This is not a question of sentiment or taste, but one of physical force, which may be measured and estimated as horse-power and steam-power are measured and estimated. Keep it, and you can save the Union. Throw it away, and the Union goes with it. Nor is it possible for any administration to retain the service of these people with the express or implied understanding that, upon the first convenient occasion, they are to be reenslaved. It cannot be, and it ought not to be.[1774]

Lincoln, of course, did not want freed African-Americans reenslaved because this interfered with his colonization plan, which, as we saw in Chapter 12, was to deport as many freedmen and women out of the country as possible.

No better description of how Lincoln saw his black soldiers can be found than in a curious and little-known document entitled: "Interview with John T. Mills." It is dated August 15, 1864:

> "Mr. President," said [Wisconsin] Governor [Alexander] Randall, "why can't you seek seclusion, and play hermit for a fortnight? It would reinvigorate you."
>
> **"Ah,"** said the President, **"two or three weeks would do me no good. I cannot fly from my**

thoughts—my solicitude for this great country follows me wherever I go. I do not think it is personal vanity or ambition, though I am not free from these infirmities, but I cannot but feel that the weal or woe of this great nation will be decided in November. There is no program offered by any wing of the Democratic [i.e., conservative] party but that must result in the permanent destruction of the Union."

"But, Mr. President, General [George B.] McClellan is in favor of crushing out this rebellion by force. He will be the Chicago candidate."

"Sir, the slightest knowledge of arithmetic will prove to any man that the rebel armies cannot be destroyed by Democratic strategy. It would sacrifice all the white men of the North to do it. There are now in the service of the United States nearly 150,000 ablebodied colored men, most of them under arms, defending and acquiring Union territory. The Democratic [conservative] strategy demands that these forces be disbanded, and that the masters be conciliated by restoring them to slavery. The black men who now assist Union prisoners to escape are to be converted into our enemies, in the vain hope of gaining the good-will of their masters. We shall have to fight two nations instead of one.

"You cannot conciliate the South if you guarantee to them ultimate success; and the experience of the present war proves their success is inevitable if you fling the compulsory labor of millions of black men into their side of the scale. Will you give our enemies such military advantages as insure success, and then depend on coaxing, flattery, and concession to get them back into the Union? Abandon all the posts now garrisoned by black men, take 150,000 men from our side and put them in the battle-field or corn-field against us, and we would be compelled to abandon the war in three weeks.

"We have to hold territory in inclement and sickly places; where are the Democrats to do this? It was a free fight, and the field was open to the war Democrats to put down this rebellion by fighting against both master and slave, long before the present policy was inaugurated.

"There have been men base enough to propose to me to return to slavery the black warriors of Port Hudson and Olustee, and thus win the respect of the masters they fought. Should I do so, I should deserve to be damned in time and eternity. Come what will, I will keep my faith with friend and foe. My enemies pretend I am now carrying on this war for the sole purpose of abolition. So long as I am President, it shall be carried on for the sole purpose of restoring the Union. But no human power can subdue this rebellion without the use of the emancipation policy, and every other policy calculated to weaken the moral and physical forces of the rebellion.

"Freedom has given us 150,000 men, raised on Southern soil. It will give us more yet. Just so much it has subtracted from the enemy, and, instead of alienating the South, there are now evidences of a fraternal feeling growing up between our men and the rank and file of the rebel soldiers. Let my enemies prove to the country that the destruction of slavery is not necessary to a restoration of the Union. I will abide the issue."[1775]

There are a number of startling admissions here, first and foremost being Lincoln's acknowledgment that he freed the slaves, not out of compassion, abolitionist sentiment, or to grant them equal rights, but strictly for the purpose of **"military advantage."** As he states:

> . . . no human power can subdue this rebellion without the use of the emancipation policy, and every other policy calculated to weaken the moral and physical forces of the rebellion.[1776]

He goes on to refute one of the modern North's favorite pieces of anti-South propaganda by firmly and clearly declaring:

> **My enemies pretend I am now carrying on this war for the sole purpose of abolition. So long as I am President, it shall be carried on for the sole purpose of restoring the Union. . . . Let my enemies prove to the country that the destruction of slavery is not necessary to a restoration of the Union. I will abide the issue.**[1777]

Another apt expression of Lincoln's true feelings toward his "sable-colored" combatants comes from an unfinished, August 17, 1864, draft of a letter to Charles D. Robinson. As we have detailed this missive in Chapter 13, we need only repeat the salient portion here:

> When I . . . proclaimed emancipation, and employed colored soldiers, I only followed the declaration . . . from . . . [my Horace] Greeley letter that "I shall do more whenever I shall believe doing more will help the cause." . . . It is not a question of sentiment or taste, but one of physical force, which may be measured and estimated, as horse-power and steampower are measured and estimated. And, by measurement, it is more than we can lose and live. Nor can we, by discarding it, get a white force in place of it. . . . I repeat this now. If Jefferson Davis wishes for himself, or for the benefit of his friends at the North, to know what I would do if he were to offer peace and reunion, saying nothing about slavery, let him try me.[1778]

Lincoln's racist ideas, beliefs, and policies—along with his apathy toward non-whites in general—continued to affect his black soldiers even after he was gone. Not only were blacks not allowed at his funeral,[1779] for example, but in May 1865 General Grant and his Northern compatriots planned to hold what they termed the "Grand Review," a gargantuan, two-day victory celebration in Washington that included a parade down Pennsylvania Avenue. All of Lincoln's armies were invited, except one: the United States Colored Troops (USCT). Why?

The reason was simple enough: Grant and Sherman did not want black soldiers associated with their white soldiers.[1780] Sherman, who threatened to pull his troops from the parade if black soldiers were allowed to march, had once said:

> A nigger as such is a most excellent fellow, but he is not fit to marry, associate, or vote with me or mine.[1781]

Does this appall us? Not with what we know about Yankee racism as seen in Chapters 11 and 12. After all, Lincoln himself, the North's favorite president, repeatedly and publicly stated that he would not marry a woman outside his own race.[1782]

But here is something that should appall us: according to slavery studies, in the Americas at least 75 percent of the total value of American products traded in the Atlantic area during the 17th and 18th Centuries were produced by black slaves. Furthermore, the colonization of America itself was carried out largely by forced African labor.[1783] In other words, Lincoln was seeking to deport all those of African descent out of the very country their people had largely helped found and construct.

Thus while Davis and the South were improvising plans to integrate blacks into Southern society, Lincoln and the North were plotting their expatriation "back to Africa." The sociopolitical chasm between South and North was indeed truly deep and wide.

This is especially noticeable in an unusually cold-hearted address Lincoln gave to the 140th Indiana Regiment on March 17, 1865, just a few weeks before his death:

> There are but few views or aspects of this great war upon which I have not said or written something whereby my own opinions might be known. But there is one—the recent attempt of our erring brethren, as they are sometimes called, to employ the negro to fight for them. I have neither written nor made a speech on that subject, because that was their business, not mine, and if I had a wish upon the subject, I had not the power to introduce it, or make it effective. The great question with them was whether the negro, being put into the army, will fight for them. I do not know, and therefore cannot decide. They ought to know better than me. I have in my lifetime heard many arguments why the negroes ought to be slaves; but if they fight for those who would keep them in slavery, it will be a better argument than any I have yet heard. He who will fight for that, ought to be a slave. They have concluded, at last, to take one out of four of the slaves and put them in the army, and that one out of the four who will fight to keep the others in slavery, ought to be a slave himself, unless he is killed in a fight. While I have often said that all men ought to be free, yet would I allow those colored persons to be slaves who want to be, and next to them those white people who argue in favor of making other people slaves. I am in favor of giving an appointment to such white men to try it on for these slaves.... We must now see the bottom of the enemy's resources. They will stand out as long as they can, and if the negro will fight for them they must allow him to fight. They have drawn upon their last branch of resources, and we can now see the bottom. I am glad to see the end so near at hand. I have said now more than I intended, and will therefore bid you good-by.[1784]

Among the many bizarre comments and erroneous assumptions in the above words, one in particular stands out. Lincoln says that he does not believe blacks will fight for **"those who would keep them in slavery,"** saying smugly that any black **"who will fight to keep the others in slavery, ought to be a slave himself, unless he is killed in a fight."**

Like anti-South proponents today, Lincoln believed, or pretended to believe that African-Americans would have had no reason to fight for the Southern Cause. But he was dead wrong in this, as he was in so many other areas. Southern historians have established that as many as 300,000 loyal Southern blacks (nearly 200,000 free and 100,000 bonded)[1785] picked up arms and fought against Lincoln,[1786] 33 percent more than the nearly 200,000 that fought for him.[1787] At least 3,000 Louisiana blacks alone officially served under the Confederate flag.[1788] A full 25 percent of the Confederacy's Ordnance Department was black.[1789] These numbers are more impressive when we consider that Southern blacks were exempt from the draft: though thousands were impressed into service, many times that volunteered.[1790]

We will note here that few of these brave black men will be found in the official muster rolls of the Confederate record. We know of them mainly through county histories, genealogical histories, obituaries, grave markers and memorials, period newspapers, photographs,[1791] personal letters, logbooks, diaries, journals, plantation books, postwar reunion notes, and most importantly, pension applications.[1792]

Among the known loyal Southern African-Americans who fought for the Confederacy and states' rights were Jacques Esclavon, Gabriel Grappe, Charles Lutz, Jean Baptiste Pierre-August, Levin Graham, Peter Vertrees, and Lufray Pierre-August,[1793] Henry Love, Hiram Kendael, Joe Warren, Dan Humphreys, George Briggs, Hardin Blackwell, Lewis McConnell, Daniel Robinson, and Fielding Rennolds,[1794] just a few of untold thousands. Most are unnamed and so are destined to be forever unknown. At least 30,000 alone served as faithful body servants to their white Confederate masters.[1795] Many of these men, though merely servants, carried their own weapons, firing whenever possible on the invading Yankees.

All told, the numbers of Confederate blacks were overwhelming. Even anti-South historians have been forced to admit that a "puzzling" number of Southern blacks were ready and willing to fight against Lincoln, the North, and the "damned buckram abolitionists,"[1796] many blacks even going so far as to buy Confederate bonds,[1797] donate money, food, and livestock, sew uniforms, sponsor auctions and bake sales, hold balls, fairs, and parties, and sell off property and anything else that might help advance the Confederate Cause.[1798]

In the summer of 1861 Thomas "Blind Tom" Wiggins, a popular and talented black musician from Georgia, gave free concerts for the Confederate ill and injured. One Memphis black who volunteered to fight Lincoln offered to outfit himself at his own expense. His only stipulation was that his family and home be protected while he was away. Just weeks after Sumter, sixty blacks in Richmond, Virginia, showed up carrying a Confederate flag, requesting to be enlisted. In Nashville, a group of blacks formed a well-trained company, then offered their services to the Confederate government. Though they had no weapons or uniforms, two all-black companies drilled at Fort Smith, Arkansas, in preparation for being called up.[1799]

Some of the largest groups of Southern blacks who wished to serve their country, the C.S.A., came from New Orleans. Voicing their eagerness "to take arms at a moment's notice and fight shoulder to shoulder with other citizens," thousands of coloreds, mulattos, and Creoles formed themselves into well drilled, well dressed regiments known as the famous "Native Guards." One spoke for all when he told a white officer:

> General, we come of a fighting race. Our fathers were brought here [as] slaves because they were captured in war, and in hand to hand fights, too. We are willing to fight. Pardon me, General, but the only cowardly blood we have got in our veins is the white blood.[1800]

From every corner of the new Confederacy were heard accounts of both free and enslaved blacks who were anxious to contribute in some way to the new nation.[1801] One impromptu poll found that 60 out of 72 Southern slaves (nearly 84 percent) were ready and willing to take up arms in defense of the homes of both their own families and those of their owners, to fight until their last breath against the Yankee foe.[1802]

Known for their Yankee-centric view of the world, most white Northerners like Lincoln never understood this type of sentiment, not even when it was a Northern black who evinced sympathy for the South. In October 1861, John Jones, a black New Yorker, stood before a huge crowd and gave a speech in which he articulated his undying support for the Confederacy. He was promptly arrested and silenced by New York authorities, after which he was labeled mad, fit only for the lunatic asylum.[1803]

British soldier Colonel Arthur J. Fremantle, a member of Her Majesty's Coldstream Guards, happened to be in Pennsylvania in the summer of 1863, when he made note of the following incident shortly after the Battle of Gettysburg:

> I saw a most laughable spectacle this afternoon—viz., a [Southern] negro dressed in full Yankee uniform, with a rifle at full cock, leading along a barefooted white man, with whom he had evidently changed clothes. [Confederate] General [James] Longstreet stopped the pair, and asked the black man what it meant. He replied, 'The two [Rebel] soldiers in charge of this here Yank have got drunk, so for fear he should escape I have took care of him, and brought him through that little town.' The consequential manner of the negro, and the supreme contempt with which he spoke to his prisoner, were most amusing. This little episode of a Southern slave leading a white Yankee soldier through a Northern village, *alone and of his own accord*, would not have been gratifying to an abolitionist.[1804]

Patriotism, having no color barrier, was the primary motivation behind the thousands of Southern blacks who "gined up" to go off and fight for "Jeff Davis." They could hate slavery, but still love the South and their white "families."[1805] Lincoln himself was not even intellectually capable of making this obvious and elementary distinction.

In May 1861 several blacks were seen marching stoically along with a Confederate military company in Virginia. One of them stopped to tell a white onlooker that if "ole Lincoln" tries to send his boys into "Varginny," he would raise a regiment of Negroes as fast as greased lightnin', for it's the South, not the North, who is the true friend of the black man.[1806]

On February 4, 1862, the Virginia legislature passed a bill to enroll all of the state's free Negroes for service in the Confederate army. Earlier, on November 23, 1861, a seven-mile long line of Confederate soldiers was marched through the streets of New Orleans. Among them was a regiment of 1,400 free black volunteers.[1807]

In 1905 Walter Lynwood Fleming wrote:

> The free negro population [of Alabama], though less than 3000 in number, were devoted supporters of the Confederacy, and nearly all free black men were engaged in some way in the Confederate service. Some entered the service as substitutes, others as cooks, teamsters, and musicians. In Mobile they asked to be enlisted as

soldiers under white officers. The skillful artisans usually stayed at home at the urgent request of the whites, who needed their work, but, nevertheless, they contributed. All accounts agree that they never avoided payment of the tax-in-kind, and other contributions.[1808]

When my cousin Rebel General Richard Taylor, the son of former U.S. President Zachary Taylor, met up with some black Confederate troops in Mobile, Alabama, in late 1864, he found them hard at work on fortifications. When the conversation turned to the African-American war effort, one of the black soldiers told Taylor:

> If you will give us guns we will fight for these works, too. We would rather fight for our own white folks than for strangers.[1809]

When James Chesnut, Jr. spoke to his black servants about enlisting in the Confederate military, his wife Mary noted that nearly all were keen to enlist and fight.[1810] They were happy, the famed diarist said, to fight for the Confederacy if Mr. Chesnut would only give them arms and in return grant them land and their freedom.[1811]

Confederate Secretary of State Judah Benjamin had a similar experience. One day his slaves came to him and declared:

> Master, set us free, and we will fight for you. We had rather fight for you than for the Yankees.[1812]

On July 4, 1861, one of the many thousands of slaves who joined the Confederate army, Thomas A. Phelps, wrote home to his mother from Virginia, saying:

> I take this opportunity of writing to you to let you know that I am well and doing well, and I hope that this letter will find you as well as I am now in Yorktown. I will leave at 4 o'clock p. m. today for a scout about the woods for the Yankees. . . . We are looking out for a fight on the 5th of July by the 5th Regiment Louisiana volunteers. Give my love to Mistress and Master Jim Phelps, and to all of them in New Orleans. You must excuse this bad writing. I am writing in a hurry; have not time to write. I am about to leave for the Mill. So good by all. No more at present.
> Your devoted son, THOMAS A PHELPS
> P. S. — Good by to the white folks until I kill a Yankee.[1813]

On December 22, 1861, New York troops were attacked near Newmarket Bridge, Virginia, by a Confederate force of 700 armed blacks. Six of the African-American Rebels were killed, but, it was said, these could easily be replaced from an endless supply of highly zealous blacks.[1814]

Eventually there were so many black Confederates on the battlefield that Northern soldiers, most who were overtly racist, were completely dumbstruck at the sight. General Stonewall Jackson's army alone contained some 3,000 black soldiers, an image that froze Yankees in their tracks in fear, and revulsion.[1815]

On September 10, 1862, a Union doctor caught sight of Jackson's troops and recorded the following entry in his diary:

> At four o'clock this morning the Rebel army began to move from our town, Jackson's force taking the advance. The movement continued until eight o'clock P.M., occupying sixteen hours. The most liberal calculation could not give them more than 64,000 men. Over 3,000 Negroes must be included in the number. These were clad in all kinds of uniforms, not only in cast-off or captured United States uniforms, but in coats with Southern buttons, State buttons, etc. These were shabby, but not shabbier or seedier than those worn by white men in the rebel ranks. Most of the negroes had arms, rifles, muskets, sabres, bowie-knives, dirks, etc. They were supplied, in many instances, with knapsacks, haversacks, canteens, etc., and they were manifestly an integral portion of the Southern Confederacy Army. They were seen riding on horses and mules, driving wagons, riding on caissons, in ambulances, with the staff of generals and promiscuously mixed up with all the rebel horde.[1816]

The free blacks of Mobile, Alabama, were mostly slave owners who, one white citizen said, "are as true to the South as the pure white race."[1817] In 1861 none of them had done service in the Confederate army yet, but all were chomping at the bit to do so. By 1862 they had organized and were helping to defend their city against Lincoln's invaders.[1818]

Lincoln not only doubted that Southern blacks would fight for the Confederacy, he vastly underestimated the numbers that did fight. Actually, when raw percentages are taken into account, far more blacks served in the Confederacy than in the Union: the Union possessed about three million soldiers. Of these about 200,000 were black, 6 percent of the total. The Confederacy had about one million soldiers.[1819] As mentioned, of these an estimated 300,000 were black,[1820] 30 percent of the total—24 percent more than fought for Lincoln.

And these numbers are conservative if we use the definition of a "private soldier" as determined by German-American Union General, August Valentine Kautz, in 1864:

> In the fullest sense, any man in the military service who receives pay, whether sworn in or not, is a soldier, because he is subject to military law. Under this general head, laborers, teamsters, sutlers, chaplains, etc., are soldiers.[1821]

As most of the 3.5 million black servants living in the South at the time of Lincoln's War remained loyal to Confederacy, and as at least 500,000 to one million of these either worked in or fought in the Rebel army and navy in some capacity, Kautz's definition raises the percentage of Southern blacks who defended the Confederacy as literal soldiers to as many as 50 percent of the total Confederate soldier population! If accurate, 80 percent more blacks fought for the Confederacy than for the Union.[1822]

While Northerners have always prided themselves in erecting monuments to white racists, black colonizationists, and anti-Semites like Lincoln, Grant, and Sherman (the latter who founded the theory of "modern warfare"),[1823] in the South you are more likely to see monuments like the one in Fort Mill, South Carolina, whose inscription reads:

> Dedicated to the faithful Slaves, who, loyal to a sacred trust, toiled for the support of our army with matchless devotion and sterling fidelity, guarding our defenseless homes, women and children during the struggle for the principles of our Confederate States of America.[1824]

While "doubting Thomas" Lincoln arrogantly and ignorantly believed that any black who fought for the Confederacy deserved to be a slave, he did see one benefit of blacks serving in the Southern armed forces. But it was not something that profited blacks. It was something that profited himself. As he asserted in his address to the 140th Indiana Regiment on March 17, 1865:

> I will say one thing in regard to the negroes being employed to fight for them [the Confederates]. I do know he cannot fight and stay at home and make bread too. And as one is about as important as the other to them, I don't care which they do. I am rather in favor of having

them try them as soldiers. They lack one vote of doing that, and I wish I could send my vote over the river so that I might cast it in favor of allowing the negro to fight. But they cannot fight and work both.[1825]

Is this attitude surprising? By now it should not be. This is the same man who, on October 16, 1854, said the following:

In the course of his reply, Senator Douglas remarked, in substance, that he had always considered this government was made for the white people and not for the negroes. Why, in point of mere fact, I think so too.[1826]

LINCOLN & RELIGION

ENTIRE BOOKS HAVE BEEN WRITTEN on Lincoln's alleged "virtues,"[1827] "morality,"[1828] "spirituality,"[1829] and "faith."[1830] But was he really a virtuous, moral, spiritual, and faith-filled man? Some have even gone so far as to regard him as a Bible-loving Christian,[1831] reverently citing the many examples of his scripture-quoting.[1832] But was he really a sincere and devout student of the Good Book?

He certainly liked to sprinkle references to God and Christianity throughout his speeches, like he did in his First Inaugural Address on March 4, 1861:

> Intelligence, patriotism, Christianity, and a firm reliance on Him, who has never yet forsaken this favored land, are still competent to adjust, in the best way, all our present difficulty.[1833]

His personal letters are also filled with remarks about God, Christianity, church, and faith. On May 14, 1864, for instance, he sent off the following "Reply to a Methodist Delegation":

> Gentlemen: In response to your address, allow me to attest the accuracy of its historical statements, indorse the sentiments it expresses, and thank you in the nation's name for the sure promise it gives.
>
> Nobly sustained as the government has been by all the churches, I would utter nothing which might in the least appear invidious against any. Yet without this it may fairly be said that the Methodist Episcopal Church, not less devoted than the best, is by its greater numbers

the most important of all. It is no fault in others that the Methodist Church sends more soldiers to the field, more nurses to the hospital, and more prayers to heaven than any. God bless the Methodist Church. Bless all the churches, and blessed be God, who, in this our great trial, giveth us the churches.[1834]

Another example is his missive to a Quaker named Mrs. Eliza P. Gurney, written September 4, 1864:

> My esteemed Friend: I have not forgotten—probably never shall forget—the very impressive occasion when yourself and friends visited me on a Sabbath forenoon two years ago. Nor has your kind letter, written nearly a year later, ever been forgotten. In all it has been your purpose to strengthen my reliance on God. I am much indebted to the good Christian people of the country for their constant prayers and consolations; and to no one of them more than to yourself. The purposes of the Almighty are perfect, and must prevail, though we erring mortals may fail to accurately perceive them in advance. We hoped for a happy termination of this terrible war long before this; but God knows best, and has ruled otherwise. We shall yet acknowledge his wisdom, and our own error therein. Meanwhile we must work earnestly in the best lights he gives us, trusting that so working still conduces to the great ends he ordains. Surely he intends some great good to follow this mighty convulsion, which no mortal could make, and no mortal could stay. Your people, the Friends, have had, and are having, a very great trial. On principle and faith opposed to both war and oppression, they can only practically oppose oppression by war. In this hard dilemma some have chosen one horn, and some the other. For those appealing to me on conscientious grounds, I have done, and shall do, the best I could and can, in my own conscience, under my oath to the law. That you believe this I doubt not; and, believing it, I shall still receive for our country and myself your earnest prayers to our Father in heaven. Your sincere friend, A. Lincoln.[1835]

From this letter we see that Mrs. Gurney had earlier felt compelled to send Lincoln an urgent admonition to "strengthen" his "reliance on God." What made this Quaker woman feel so passionately about Lincoln's spiritual life?

While today the world is quite ignorant of the fact thanks to its suppression by loyal Lincoln scholars, it was quite well-known in the president's day that he was completely apathetic toward all things religious. Indeed, his "Christian" persona was nothing but a mask, one that he carefully put on for public performances and removed in private when it was not needed. On December 3, 1864, Lincoln grossly understated his spiritual background this way: **"I am not much of a judge of religion . . ."**[1836]

Thus, though he liked to pass himself off as a "good Christian," he was actually a skeptic, a humanist, and—as his friends and family knew him—an "infidel," one who opposed organized religion, told impious stories,[1837] denounced his wife's spiritualism,[1838] never prayed, never attended church, never joined any religious faith or denomination,[1839] never opened a Bible, never mentioned Jesus, and was well-known for his lack of belief in the divinity of Christ, Christian salvation, the sanctity of the Bible, and even in God himself. Lincoln even once declared Jesus a "bastard" while asserting that the Bible's miracles went against the laws of Nature.[1840] In fact, our sixteenth president, who often criticized fellow politicians for mixing theology and politics, and who enjoyed arguing against the Bible in public,[1841] much preferred reading the works of atheists like Thomas Paine and Voltaire over the works of religionists.[1842]

Lincoln once authored an essay demonstrating that, far from being inspired, the Bible was actually **"uninspired"** and historically inaccurate,[1843] and in Illinois in the mid 1830s he wrote "a little book on infidelity."[1844] Allegedly Lincoln was saved from eternal disgrace by one Samuel Hill, his employer at the time, who—knowing it would certainly ruin the author's future—ripped the manuscript from young Abe's hands and hurled it into a burning stove.[1845] If this book had survived we can be sure that Lincoln would not be worshiped as the Christ-like canonized figure he is today!

Since, like his early employer, Lincoln's followers have hidden or destroyed nearly all traces of the president's own atheistic admissions, we must turn to the words of others for evidence.

His close friend Ward Hill Lamon, for example, writes of Lincoln's "burnt book," that the future president, being "thoroughly familiar" with atheistic thought,

> felt an itching to write [on the subject]. He did write, and the result was a 'little book.' It was probably merely an extended

essay, but it was ambitiously spoken of as a 'book' by himself and by the persons who were made acquainted with its contents. In this book he intended to demonstrate:

> 'First, that the Bible was not God's revelation; and
> 'Secondly, that Jesus was not the Son of God.'[1846]

The book, Lamon continues,

> was an attack upon the whole grounds of Christianity and especially was it an attack upon the idea that Jesus was the Christ the true and only begotten Son of God as the Christian world contends.[1847]

William H. Herndon, Lincoln's law partner, friend, and biographer, a man who knew the secretive president better than anyone, had this to say on the topic of Lincoln's "spiritual life":

> As to Mr. Lincoln's religious views he was, in short, an infidel, ... He did not believe that Jesus was God, nor the Son of God,—[he] was a fatalist, denied the freedom of the will. Mr. Lincoln told me *a thousand times* that he did not believe the Bible was the revelation of God, as the Christian world contends. . . . *I assert this on my own knowledge and on my veracity.* Judge Logan, John T. Stuart, James H. Matheny, and others, will tell you the truth. I say they will confirm what I say, with this exception,—they all make it blacker than I remember it. Joshua F. Speed of Louisville, I think, will tell you the same thing.[1848]

In another source Herndon says:

> Lincoln was a deep-grounded infidel. He disliked and despised churches. He never entered a church except to scoff and ridicule. On coming from a church he would mimic the preacher. Before running for any office, he wrote a book against Christianity and the Bible. He showed it to some of his friends and read extracts. A man named Hill was greatly shocked and urged Lincoln not to publish it; urged it would kill him politically. Hill got this book in his hands, opened the stove door, and it went up in flames and ashes. After that Lincoln became more discreet, and when running for office often used words and phrases to make it appear that he was a Christian. He never changed on this subject; he lived and died a deep-grounded infidel.[1849]

In an 1870 letter to Lamon, Herndon writes:

> In New Salem [Illinois] Mr. Lincoln lived with a class of men, moved with them, had his being with them. They were scoffers of religion, made loud protests against the followers of Christianity. They declared that Jesus was an illegitimate child. On all occasions that offered they debated on the various forms of Christianity. They riddled old divines, and not infrequently made those very divines skeptics by their logic; made them disbelievers as bad as themselves. In 1835 Lincoln wrote a book on infidelity and intended to have it published. The book was an attack on the idea that Jesus was Christ. Lincoln read the book to his friend Hill. Hill tried to persuade him not to publish it. Lincoln said it should be published. Hill, believing that if the book was published it would kill Lincoln forever as a politician, seized it and thrust it in the stove. It went up in smoke and ashes before Lincoln could get it out. When Mr. Lincoln was candidate for the Legislature he was accused of being an infidel, and of having said that Jesus was an illegitimate child. He never denied it, never flinched from his views on religion. In 1854 he made me erase the name of God from a speech I was about to make. He [himself] did this to one of his friends in Washington City. In the year 1847 Mr. Lincoln ran for Congress against the Rev. Peter Cartright. He was accused of being an infidel; he never denied it. He knew it could and would be proved on him. I know when he left Springfield for Washington he had undergone no change in his opinion on religion. He held many of the Christian ideas in abhorrence. He held that God could not forgive sinners. The idea that Mr. Lincoln carried a Bible in his bosom or in his boots to draw on his opponent is ridiculous.[1850]

John T. Stuart, mentioned above by Herndon, wrote:

> I knew Mr. Lincoln when he first came here, and for years afterwards. He was an avowed and open infidel, sometimes bordered on atheism. I have often and often heard Lincoln and one W. D. Herndon, who was a freethinker, talk over this subject. Lincoln went further against Christian beliefs and doctrines and principles than any man I ever heard: he shocked me. I don't remember the exact line of his argument: suppose it was against the inherent defects, so called, of the Bible, and on grounds of reason. Lincoln always denied that Jesus was the Christ of God,—denied that Jesus was the Son of God, as understood and maintained by the Christian Church. The Rev. Dr. Smith, who wrote a letter, tried to convert Lincoln from infidelity so late as 1858, and couldn't do

it.[1851]

In a letter to Herndon, James H. Matheny (also mentioned above) writes:

> I knew Mr. Lincoln as early as 1834-5; know he was an infidel. He and W. D. Herndon used to talk infidelity in the clerk's office in this city, about the years 1837-40. Lincoln attacked the Bible and the New Testament on two grounds: first, from the inherent or apparent contradictions under its lids; second, from the grounds of reason. Sometimes he ridiculed the Bible and New Testament, sometimes seemed to scoff it, though I shall not use that word in its full and literal sense. I never heard that Lincoln changed his views, though [I was] his personal and political friend from 1834 to 1860. Sometimes Lincoln bordered on atheism. He went far that way, and often shocked me. I was then a young man, and believed what my good mother told me. Stuart & Lincoln's office was in what was called Hoffman's Row, on North Fifth Street, near the public square. It was in the same building as the clerk's office, and on the same floor. Lincoln would come into the clerk's office, where I and some young men—Evan Butler, Newton Francis, and others—were writing or staying, and would bring the Bible with him; would read a chapter; argue against it. Lincoln then had a smattering of geology, if I recollect it. Lincoln often, if not wholly, was an atheist; at least, bordered on it. Lincoln was enthusiastic in his infidelity. As he grew older, he grew more discreet, didn't talk much before strangers about his religion; but to friends, close and bosom ones, he was always open and avowed, fair and honest; but to strangers, he held them off from policy. Lincoln used to quote [Scottish poet Robert] Burns. Burns helped Lincoln to be an infidel, as I think; at least, he found in Burns a like thinker and feeler. Lincoln quoted *Tam O'Shanter*. 'What send one to heaven and ten to hell!' etc.
>
> From what I know of Mr. Lincoln and his views of Christianity, and from what I know as honest and well-founded rumor; from what I have heard his best friends say and regret for years; from what he never denied when accused, and from what Lincoln has hinted and intimated, to say no more,—he did write a little book on infidelity at or near New Salem, in Menard County, [Illinois,] about the year 1834 or 1835. I have stated these things to you often. Judge Logan, John T. Stuart, yourself, know what I know, and some of you more.
>
> Mr. Herndon, you insist on knowing something which you know I possess, and got as a secret, and that is about Lincoln's little book on infidelity. Mr. Lincoln *did* tell me that he *did write a*

little book on infidelity. This statement I have avoided heretofore; but, as you strongly insist upon it,—probably to defend yourself against charges of misrepresentations,—I give it you as I got it from Lincoln's mouth.[1852]

Lincoln, the man who wanted to be all things to all people, did not like being accused of atheism, or "infidelity," as he called it, and he fought earnestly against the charge, particularly in the early part of his political career when it was most obvious and most well-known. When the accusation began appearing regularly in the newspapers, Lincoln exploded, firing off refutations, none of them convincing, like the letter to the editor of the Illinois *Gazette* on August 11, 1846, in which he reluctantly admitted that he was not a member of any Christian Church.[1853]

Lincoln was launching rebuttals even earlier, however, such as his March 26, 1843, letter to Martin M. Morris of Petersburg, Illinois, a fellow Whig (the liberal party of the day) who was interested in nominating Lincoln as a candidate for Congress. Many, Morris noted, opposed the lanky progressive due to his atheism, to which Lincoln replied testily:

> **Friend Morris: Your letter of the 23d was received on yesterday morning, and for which (instead of an excuse, which you thought proper to ask) I tender you my sincere thanks. It is truly gratifying to me to learn that while the people of Sangamon** [County, Illinois] **have cast me off, my old friends of Menard** [County, Illinois]**, who have known me longest and best, stick to me. It would astonish, if not amuse, the older citizens to learn that I (a stranger, friendless, uneducated, penniless boy, working on a flatboat at ten dollars per month) have been put down here as the candidate of pride, wealth, and aristocratic family distinction. Yet so, chiefly, it was. There was, too, the strangest combination of church influence against me. Baker is a Campbellite; and therefore, as I suppose, with few exceptions got all that church. My wife has some relations in the Presbyterian churches, and some with the Episcopal churches; and therefore, wherever it would tell, I was set down as either the one or the other, while it was everywhere contended that no Christian ought to go for me, because I belonged to no church, was suspected of being a deist, and had talked about fighting a duel** [with James A. Shields]**. With all these things, Baker, of course, had nothing to do. Nor do I complain of them. As to his own church going**

for him, I think that was right enough, and as to the influences I have spoken of in the other, though they were very strong, it would be grossly untrue and unjust to charge that they acted upon them in a body, or were very near so. I only mean that those influences levied a tax of a considerable per cent, upon my strength throughout the religious controversy. But enough of this.[1854]

As a majority of Lincoln's associates said they could prove he was an "infidel,"[1855] few believed such defenses, particularly when his own friends and admirers contradicted him on the issue. One of these was Lamon, who wrote:

> Mr. Lincoln was never a member of any church, nor did he believe in the inspiration of the Scriptures in the sense understood by evangelical Christians. . . . Overwhelming testimony out of many mouths, and none stronger than out of his own, place these facts beyond controversy. . . . When he went to church at all, he went to mock, and came away to mimic.[1856]

Lincoln's own wife Mary, who admitted that her husband had never committed himself to any conventional faith,[1857] said the following of his "religiosity":

> Mr. Lincoln had no hope and no faith in the usual acceptance of those words.[1858]

An interesting incident in Lincoln's life sheds light on his so-called "faith." One Sunday, while he was a candidate for Congress, he showed up in church, no doubt to canvass for votes. At one point in his sermon the minister said to the congregation: "All who wish to go to Heaven, please stand up." Everyone in the chapel promptly got to their feet, except one: Abraham Lincoln. The surprised clergyman turned to the towering ill-dressed rustic and asked: "Mr. Lincoln, where do you wish to go?" **"I wish to go to Congress,"** he replied snidely.[1859] Regular churchgoers were not amused. And neither was the local clergy. Twenty out of the twenty-three ministers, as well as "a very large majority" of the prominent members of the churches in his hometown of Springfield, Illinois, later opposed him for president.[1860]

Lincoln provided plenty of ammunition for his critics on this topic, such as the admission he made in a May 7, 1837, letter to Mary Owens in which he said:

> I've never been to church yet, nor probably shall not be soon. I stay away because I am conscious I should not know how to behave myself.[1861]

Lincoln was so hostile toward religion, and in particular Christianity, and so arrogantly intolerant of preachers, priests, and evangelists, that he did not trust himself to be in their presence for fear of making a public spectacle.

Lincoln's own remarks have condemned him for all time as an atheist, or at the very least, a non-believing skeptic and agnostic. He was certainly not a follower of the Prince of Peace. **"I am not a Christian,"** he once told Newton Bateman, the Superintendent of Public Instruction for the state of Illinois.[1862] During the period when Lincoln was considering fighting the above mentioned duel with James A. Shields, his friends intervened saying that such violence was against the Bible and the teachings of Jesus. Lincoln snapped back: **"The Bible is not my book, nor Christianity my profession."**[1863]

This statement was later reenforced by Lincoln's own words and actions. Where, for example, is the Christianity in the following "Order of Retaliation," issued by President Lincoln on July 30, 1863, midway through his War:

> It is the duty of every government to give protection to its citizens of whatever class, color, or condition, and especially to those who are duly organized as soldiers in the public service. The law of nations, and the usages and customs of war, as carried on by civilized powers, permit no distinction as to color in the treatment of prisoners of war as public enemies. To sell or enslave any captured person on account of his color, and for no offense against the laws of war, is a relapse into barbarism and a crime against the civilization of the age.
>
> The government of the United States will give the same protection to all its soldiers, and if the enemy shall sell or enslave any one because of his color, the offense shall be punished by retaliation upon the enemy's prisoners in our possession.
>
> It is therefore ordered that for every soldier of the United States killed in violation of the laws of war, a rebel soldier shall be executed; and for every one

enslaved by the enemy or sold into slavery, a rebel soldier shall be placed at hard labor on the public works, and continued at such labor until the other shall be released and receive the treatment due to a prisoner of war. Abraham Lincoln.[1864]

Do Christian principles—such as Saint Peter's admonition to be merciful and compassionate towards others,[1865] or Jesus' commandment to love our enemies[1866]—not apply during warfare? Only if you are not a Christian to begin with.

Knowing what we do now of Lincoln's true feelings about religion generally and Christianity specifically, we read the following with new eyes, a letter in which the height of his religious hypocrisy is fully revealed. Dated May 30, 1864, it is addressed to **"Dr. Ide and Others"**:

> In response to the preamble and resolutions of the American Baptist Home Mission Society, which you did me the honor to present, I can only thank you for thus adding to the effective and almost unanimous support which the Christian communities are so zealously giving to the country and to liberty. Indeed, it is difficult to conceive how it could be otherwise with any one professing Christianity, or even having ordinary perceptions of right and wrong. To read in the Bible, as the word of God himself, that "In the sweat of thy face shalt thou eat bread," and to preach therefrom that, "In the sweat of other men's faces shalt thou eat bread," to my mind can scarcely be reconciled with honest sincerity. When brought to my final reckoning, may I have to answer for robbing no man of his goods; yet more tolerable even this, than for robbing one of himself and all that was his. When, a year or two ago, those professedly holy men of the South met in the semblance of prayer and devotion, and, in the name of him who said, "As ye would all men should do unto you, do ye even so unto them," appealed to the Christian world to aid them in doing to a whole race of men as they would have no man do unto themselves, to my thinking they contemned and insulted God and his church far more than did Satan when he tempted the Saviour with the kingdoms of the earth. The devil's attempt was no more false, and far less hypocritical. But let me forbear, remembering it is also written, "Judge not lest ye be

judged." A. Lincoln.[1867]

There are numerous falsehoods and outrageous defamations in this epistle. However, at this point in our study of the president's suppressed, misinterpreted, and forgotten writings and speeches we need not belabor the point. All are by now obvious.

At times, when it was thought that Lincoln was not displaying enough public religiosity, he was goaded forward by his own political compatriots in Congress, who had to "request" that he issue things like proclamations for "A Day of Prayer," as the following example from July 7, 1864, illustrates:

> Whereas the Senate and House of Representatives, at their last session, adopted a concurrent resolution, which was approved on the second day of July instant, and which was in the words following, namely:
> That the President of the United States be requested to appoint a day for humiliation and prayer by the people of the United States; that he request his constitutional advisers at the head of the executive departments to unite with him as chief magistrate of the nation, at the city of Washington, and the members of Congress, and all magistrates, all civil, military, and naval officers, all soldiers, sailors, and marines, with all loyal and law-abiding people, to convene at their usual places of worship, or wherever they may be; to confess and to repent of their manifold sins; to implore the compassion and forgiveness of the Almighty, that, if consistent with his will, the existing rebellion may be speedily suppressed, and the supremacy of the Constitution and laws of the United States may be established throughout all the States; to implore him, as the supreme ruler of the world; not to destroy us as a people, nor suffer us to be destroyed by the hostility or the connivance of other nations, or by obstinate adhesion to our own counsels which may be in conflict with his eternal purposes, and to implore him to enlighten the mind of the nation to know and do his will, humbly believing that it is in accordance with his will that our place should be maintained as a united people among the family of nations; to implore him to grant to our armed defenders and the masses of the people that courage, power of resistance, and endurance necessary to secure that result;

to implore him in his infinite goodness to soften the hearts, enlighten the minds, and quicken the consciences of those in rebellion, that they may lay down their arms and speedily return to their allegiance to the United States, that they may not be utterly destroyed, that the effusion of blood may be stayed, and that unity and fraternity may be restored, and peace established throughout all our borders:

Now, therefore, I, Abraham Lincoln, President of the United States, cordially concurring with the Congress of the United States in the penitential and pious sentiments expressed in the aforesaid resolutions, and heartily approving of the devotional design and purpose thereof, do hereby appoint the first Thursday of August next to be observed by the people of the United States as a day of national humiliation and prayer.

I do hereby further invite and request the heads of the executive departments of this government, together with all legislators, all judges and magistrates, and all other persons exercising authority in the land, whether civil, military, or naval, and all soldiers, seamen, and marines in the national service, and all the other loyal and law-abiding people of the United States, to assemble in their preferred places of public worship on that day, and there and then to render to the almighty and merciful Ruler of the universe such homages and such confessions, and to offer to him such supplications, as the Congress of the United States have, in their aforesaid resolution, so solemnly; so earnestly, and so reverently recommended.[1868]

The rank hypocrisy in this document leaves one speechless.

As late as 1862 Lincoln was still openly denouncing religion, and in particular Christianity. That year Judge Wakefield had written Lincoln, inquiring as to whether he had accepted Christianity yet, to which the Yankee president replied:

> My earlier views of the unsoundness of the Christian scheme of salvation and the human origin of the scriptures have become clearer and stronger with advancing years and I see no reason for thinking I shall ever change them.[1869]

Around the same time, *Manford's Magazine* quoted Lincoln as saying:

> **It will not do to investigate the subject of religion too closely, as it is apt to lead to Infidelity** [atheism].[1870]

Religiosity has long been one of the major differences between South and North. Nowhere is this more apparent than in the political leaders of both sections. President Jefferson Davis, for example, proclaimed far more days of fasting and prayer than Lincoln,[1871] and while the U.S. Constitution is curiously lacking the word God, the C.S. Constitution not only mentions him, but refers to him as "Almighty God."[1872]

Widely known as an "open scoffer of Christianity,"[1873] Lincoln, the man who bragged that he had once written "a little book on infidelity"[1874] and that he belonged to no church, admitted that he embraced an atheistic concept called the "Doctrine of Necessity."[1875] According to this antireligious belief, said Lincoln,

> **the human mind is impelled to action, or held at rest by some power, over which the mind itself has no control.**[1876]

No definition of atheism has ever been more aptly or concisely expressed.

If Lincoln was a religious man, a philanthropist, and a devout Christian, as the members of his cult claim, one is allowed to wonder why he consistently blocked black civil rights while refusing to protect the rights of other minorities, such as women, Native-Americans, Latin-Americans, and children. Lincoln's own friend, black civil rights leader Frederick Douglass, explained it this way: the president was missing "the genuine spark of humanity."[1877]

But Lincoln's intolerance extended to other minorities, ethnicities, and religious groups as well. One of these was the Jew.

Based on numerous complaints about "illicit trade" among Jews in the Western theater of operations, on December 17, 1862, General Grant issued his ill-famed General Order No. 11.[1878] It read:

> The Jews, as a class violating every regulation of trade established by the Treasury Department and also department orders, are hereby expelled from the department within twenty-four hours from the receipt of this order. Post commanders will see that all of this class of people be furnished passes and required to leave, and

any one returning after such notification will be arrested and held in confinement until an opportunity occurs of sending them out as prisoners, unless furnished with permit from headquarters. No passes will be given these people to visit headquarters for the purpose of making personal application for trade permits. By order of Maj. Gen. U. S. Grant.[1879]

Bear in mind that this was no insignificant military edict. When Grant says, "All of this class of people," he meant exactly that. *All* Southern Jewish men, women, and children, were to vacate large areas of the South occupied at the time by Union soldiers—and within just one day. The heartless order applied not only to transient Jewish peddlers, but to everyday, law-abiding Confederate Jewish townspeople, living in homes they and their Southern ancestors had inhabited for generations.[1880] In essence, it turned every Southern Jew into a criminal.

Grant's order would be truly shocking were it not for the already well-known anti-Semitism of a great many of the Northern people.[1881] Indeed this is why, for the first year of the War, Lincoln (and the U.S. Congress) prohibited Jews from serving as army and navy chaplains;[1882] it is why August Belmont, the American agent for the British Rothschilds (a family of distinguished Jewish investors and bankers), was unfairly accused of aiding and abetting the Confederacy;[1883] it is why Grant referred to Jews as "an intolerable nuisance"; and it is why he once ordered Yankee railroad conductors to prevent Jews from traveling south of Jackson, Mississippi.[1884]

Though Grant's General Order No. 11 understandably offended thousands of Jewish soldiers and citizens across both the North and the South, the ban remained in effect until January 3, 1863, when Jewish Kentuckian, Caesar J. Kaskel, went directly to Lincoln to protest it. The president's general-in-chief at the time, Henry W. Halleck, revoked Grant's order the next day. Then, a few weeks later (on January 21),[1885] Halleck sent Grant the following feeble note explaining Lincoln's actions:

> It may be proper to give you some explanation of the revocation of your order expelling all Jews from your department. The President has no objection to your expelling traitors and Jew peddlers, which, I suppose, was the object of your order; but, as it in terms proscribed an entire religious class, some of whom are fighting in our ranks, the President deemed it necessary to revoke it.[1886]

Lincoln definitely had no love for "Jew peddlers."

One wonders how many displaced, innocent Jewish families lost everything in this forced expulsion from their homes, or how long Lincoln would have allowed Grant's ban to stand had Kaskel not paid a visit to the White House.

The order certainly raised no eyebrows among Lincoln's cabinet or party members. In fact, Congressman Elihu B. Washburne of Illinois expressed approval of Grant's order to Lincoln himself. Afterward, he paid a visit to Halleck, who told Representative Washburne that if Grant had only inserted the word "peddler" after the word "Jew," it would have been "all right," and that "no exception would have been taken" by anyone.[1887]

Despite Lincoln's overt bigotry, atheism, and even anti-Christian behavior, he could put on a sanctimonious mask at a moment's notice, and even pen words like the following, again, to Mrs. Eliza P. Gurney; this time on September 28, 1862:

> I am glad of this interview, and glad to know that I have your sympathy and prayers. We are indeed going through a great trial—a fiery trial. In the very responsible position in which I happen to be placed, being a humble instrument in the hands of our Heavenly Father, as I am, and as we all are, to work out his great purposes, I have desired that all my works and acts may be according to his will, and that it might be so, I have sought his aid; but if, after endeavoring to do my best in the light which he affords me, I find my efforts fail, I must believe that for some purpose unknown to me, he wills it otherwise. If I had had my way, this war would never have been commenced. If I had been allowed my way, this war would have been ended before this; but we find it still continues, and we must believe that he permits it for some wise purpose of his own, mysterious and unknown to us; and though with our limited understandings we may not be able to comprehend it, yet we cannot but believe that he who made the world still governs it.[1888]

We will note here that Lincoln does not capitalize the words "he" or "his" when referring to God.

In his November 15, 1862, **"Order for Sabbath Observance,"** fake Christian President Abraham Lincoln tried to imitate the authentic spirituality of a real Christian president, George Washington:

> The President, commander-in-chief of the army and navy, desires and enjoins the orderly observance of the Sabbath by the officers and men in the military and naval service. The importance for man and beast of the prescribed weekly rest, the sacred rights of Christian soldiers and sailors, a becoming deference to the best sentiment of a Christian people, and a due regard for the Divine will, demand that Sunday labor in the army and navy be reduced to the measure of strict necessity. The discipline and character of the national forces should not suffer, nor the cause they defend be imperiled, by the profanation of the day or name of the Most High. "At this time of public distress"—adopting the words of Washington in 1776—"men may find enough to do in the service of God and their country without abandoning themselves to vice and immorality." The first general order issued by the Father of his Country after the Declaration of Independence indicates the spirit in which our institutions were founded and should ever be defended. "The general hopes and trusts that every officer and man will endeavor to live and act as becomes a Christian soldier, defending the dearest rights and liberties of his country." Abraham Lincoln.[1889]

Such pronouncements coming from an admitted atheist and anti-Christian must have been stunning to those who knew him best.

On September 7, 1864, Lincoln replied to a "Committee of Colored People" from Baltimore, who had unthinkingly given the president a Bible:

> This occasion would seem fitting for a lengthy response to the address which you have just made. I would make one if prepared; but I am not. I would promise to respond in writing had not experience taught me that business will not allow me to do so. I can only now say, as I have often before said, it has always been a sentiment with me that all mankind should be free. So far as able, within my sphere, I have always acted as I believe to be right and just; and I have done all I could for the good of mankind generally. In letters and documents sent from this office I have expressed myself better than I now can. In regard to this great book, I have but to say, it is the best gift God has given to man.
>
> All the good Saviour gave to the world was

communicated through this book. But for it we could not know right from wrong. All things most desirable for man's welfare, here and hereafter, are to be found portrayed in it. To you I return my most sincere thanks for the very elegant copy of the great Book of God which you present.[1890]

Had this black committee known that Lincoln was not a Christian, and that he had long ridiculed the Bible, calling it **"uninspired,"** a fiction, and historically flawed, even referring to Jesus as a **"bastard,"** they might have thought twice before giving him a copy. But words like those above helped conceal the real Lincoln from the public in his day, just as they continue to in the 21st Century.

One of the few times Lincoln mentioned the Supreme Being in earnest was when his trick of faulting the South for starting the War was rejected by most Americans. To save face, he then tried to avoid taking the responsibility for both instigating it and maintaining it by blaming the entire fiasco on the Almighty. In his Second Inaugural Address, on March 4, 1865, one month before Lee surrendered at Appomattox, Virginia, Lincoln said that God

> gives to both North and South this terrible war . . . Fondly do we hope—fervently do we pray—that this mighty scourge of war may speedily pass away. Yet, if God wills that it continue . . . so still it must be said, 'The judgments of the Lord are true and righteous altogether.'[1891]

Lincoln uttered something similar a few years earlier on September 30, 1862, in a "Meditation on the Divine Will":

> The will of God prevails. In great contests each party claims to act in accordance with the will of God. Both may be, and one must be, wrong. God cannot be for and against the same thing at the same time. In the present civil war it is quite possible that God's purpose is something different from the purpose of either party; and yet the human instrumentalities, working just as they do, are of the best adaptation to effect his purpose. I am almost ready to say that this is probably true; that God wills this contest, and wills that it shall not end yet. By his mere great power on the minds of the now contestants, he could have either saved or destroyed the

Union without a human contest. Yet the contest began. And, having begun, he could give the final victory to either side any day. Yet the contest proceeds.[1892]

Few agnostics or atheists have been able to combine politics and religion so advantageously—and so ominously.[1893]

Lincoln & Reconstruction

L INCOLN'S IDEA OF SO-CALLED "RECONSTRUCTION," in my opinion as a Southerner, would be more accurately termed "Deconstruction." For it called for the complete Northernization of the South by destroying states' rights, and thoroughly modernizing and industrializing her. Naturally this is not something the citizens of this old-fashioned, traditional, leisurely, agricultural region wanted. So the South was forced to rebel a second time, making Reconstruction (1865 to 1877) a twelve-year continuation of the hellacious War itself.

Reconstruction under Lincoln actually began several years before the War ended. On December 8, 1863, he issued his "Proclamation of Amnesty and Reconstruction." It read:

> Whereas, in and by the Constitution of the United States, it is provided that the President "shall have power to grant reprieves and pardons for offenses against the United States, except in cases of impeachment"; and
> Whereas a rebellion now exists whereby the loyal State governments of several States have for a long time been subverted, and many persons have committed, and are now guilty of, treason against the United States; and
> Whereas, with reference to said rebellion and treason, laws have been enacted by Congress, declaring forfeitures and confiscation of property and liberation of slaves, all upon terms and conditions therein stated, and also declaring that the President was thereby authorized

at any time thereafter, by proclamation, to extend to persons who may have participated in the existing rebellion, in any State or part thereof, pardon and amnesty, with such exceptions and at such times and on such conditions as he may deem expedient for the public welfare; and

Whereas the congressional declaration for limited and conditional pardon accords with well-established judicial exposition of the pardoning power; and

Whereas, with reference to said rebellion, the President of the United States has issued several proclamations, with provisions in regard to the liberation of slaves; and

Whereas it is now desired by some persons heretofore engaged in said rebellion to resume their allegiance to the United States, and to reinaugurate loyal State governments within and for their respective States; therefore

I, Abraham Lincoln, President of the United States, do proclaim, declare, and make known to all persons who have, directly or by implication, participated in the existing rebellion, except as hereinafter excepted, that a full pardon is hereby granted to them and each of them, with restoration of all rights of property, except as to slaves, and in property cases where rights of third parties shall have intervened, and upon the condition that every such person shall take and subscribe an oath, and thenceforward keep and maintain said oath inviolate; and which oath shall be registered for permanent preservation, and shall be of the tenor and effect following, to wit:

> I, _____, do solemnly swear, in presence of almighty God, that I will henceforth faithfully support, protect, and defend the Constitution of the United States, and the union of the States thereunder: and that I will, in like manner, abide by and faithfully support all acts of Congress passed during the existing rebellion with reference to slaves, so long and so far as not repealed, modified, or held void by Congress, or by decision of the

Supreme Court; and that I will, in like manner, abide by and faithfully support all proclamations of the President made during the existing rebellion having reference to slaves, so long and so far as not modified or declared void by decision of the Supreme Court. So help me God.

The persons exempted from the benefits of the foregoing provisions are all who are, or shall have been, civil or diplomatic officers or agents of the so-called Confederate Government; all who have left judicial stations under the United States to aid the rebellion; all who are or shall have been military or naval officers of said so-called Confederate Government above the rank of colonel in the army or of lieutenant in the navy; all who left seats in the United States Congress to aid the rebellion; all who resigned commissions in the army or navy of the United States and afterward aided the rebellion; and all who have engaged in any way in treating colored persons, or white persons in charge of such, otherwise than lawfully as prisoners of war, and which persons may have been found in the United States service as soldiers, seamen, or in any other capacity.

And I do further proclaim, declare, and make known that whenever, in any of the States of Arkansas, Texas, Louisiana, Mississippi, Tennessee, Alabama, Georgia, Florida, South Carolina, and North Carolina, a number of persons, not less than one tenth in number of the votes cast in such State at the presidential election of the year of our Lord one thousand eight hundred and sixty, each having taken the oath aforesaid and not having since violated it, and being a qualified voter by the election law of the State existing immediately before the so-called act of secession, and excluding all others, shall reestablish a State government which shall be republican, and in no wise contravening said oath, such shall be recognized as the true government of the State, and the State shall receive thereunder the benefits of the constitutional provision which declares that "the United States shall guaranty to every State in this Union a republican form of government, and shall protect each of them against invasion; and, on application of the legislature, or the executive (when the legislature cannot be convened), against domestic violence."

And I do further proclaim, declare, and make known, that any provision which may be adopted by such State government in relation to the freed people of such State, which shall recognize and declare their permanent freedom, provide for their education, and which may yet be consistent as a temporary arrangement with their present condition as a laboring, landless, and homeless class, will not be objected to by the national executive.

And it is suggested as not improper that, in constructing a loyal State government in any State; the name of the State, the boundary, the subdivisions, the constitution, and the general code of laws, as before the rebellion, be maintained, subject only to the modifications made necessary by the conditions hereinbefore stated, and such others, if any, not contravening said conditions, and which may be deemed expedient by those framing the new State government.

To avoid misunderstanding, it may be proper to say that this proclamation, so far as it relates to State governments, has no reference to States wherein loyal State governments have all the while been maintained.

And, for the same reason, it may be proper to further say, that whether members sent to Congress from any State shall be admitted to seats, constitutionally rests exclusively with the respective houses, and not to any extent with the executive. And still further, that this proclamation is intended to present the people of the States wherein the national authority has been suspended, and loyal State governments have been subverted, a mode in and by which the national authority and loyal State governments may be reestablished within said States, or in any of them; and while the mode presented is the best the executive can suggest, with his present impressions, it must not be understood that no other possible mode would be acceptable.

Given under my hand at the city of Washington, the eighth day of December, in the year of our Lord one thousand eight hundred and sixty-three, and of the independence of the United States of America the eighty-eighth. Abraham Lincoln.[1894]

There are a number of astonishing pronouncements in this edict that have gone largely unnoticed by the world.

As usual Lincoln reinterprets the Constitution to fit his own tyrannical agenda, and thus far overreaches his limited authority. He begins by audaciously quoting Article 2, Section 2, Clause 1 of the Constitution, saying that he has the **"power to grant reprieves and pardons for offences against the United States."** But what **"offence"** had Southerners made against the U.S. that they needed to be **"reprieved"** and **"pardoned,"** particularly by a foreign leader? The fact is that the Confederacy had become a Constitutionally and legally formed separate nation several months before the War began. Thus Lincoln had no authority over any state that had joined it.

He goes on to call the Confederacy a mere **"rebellion,"** asserting that her state governments had been **"subverted,"** and that her inhabitants had committed **"treason"** against the United States. Yet it is impossible for citizens of one nation to commit treason against another. And what Lincoln calls the subversion of the South's state governments was merely the legal transition of those governments from the U.S.A. to the C.S.A.

Lincoln brags about the many illegal laws he has enacted in the Confederacy, such as allowing himself the right to confiscate the property of anyone participating in the **"existing rebellion."** Since this included nearly every man, woman, and child in the South, he was giving himself virtually unlimited power to evict the occupants of all Southern homes and steal their personal property, which included Southern servants—or as Lincoln incorrectly calls them, **"slaves."**[1895]

The megalomaniac president then offers a **"full pardon"** from the so-called charge of **"treason"** **"upon the condition"** that everyone involved in the **"rebellion"** take an oath of allegiance, promising to **"faithfully support, protect, and defend the Constitution of the United States"** (which he himself did not support, protect, or defend), and **"the union of the States"** (which, because it was intended by the Founders to be voluntary, he himself was in the process of destroying). Lincoln's oath then asks the Southern victims of this unlawful coercion to swear they will submit to **"all proclamations of the President,"** an impossibility since he was not their president!

All of this was for the purported purpose of protecting the **"public welfare."** As such a subjective term has no inherent objective meaning, "King Abraham" decides here that he will be the final arbitrator of its definition.

He then introduces his infamous Ten Percent Plan, an idea so seemingly un-Lincolnian that it has been all but totally suppressed in mainstream Lincoln biographies. Here a Confederate state could be "readmitted" to the Union if just 10 percent of its citizens took his oath. Afterward, that state could reestablish slavery if it so desired,[1896] for any and all acts connected to slavery, Lincoln noted coldly, were **"war measures,"** subject to the modification or nullification of the Supreme Court.[1897] In other words, as long as a Confederate state reunionized he cared little about its individual laws and institutions.

Astonishingly, for a iron-fisted, dictatorial, socialistic leader, Lincoln ends his Reconstruction proclamation with this generous and open-minded statement:

> . . . while the mode presented is the best the executive can suggest, with his present impressions, it must not be understood that no other possible mode would be acceptable.[1898]

This is almost identical to the words he wrote to one of his generals, Nathaniel Prentiss Banks, on January 31, 1864:

> . . . I tell you that you are at liberty to adopt any rule which shall admit to vote any unquestionably loyal free-state men . . .[1899]

On August 17, 1864, Lincoln penned similar words to Charles D. Robinson:

> To me it seems plain that saying reunion and abandonment of slavery would be considered, if offered, is not saying that nothing else or less would be considered, if offered. . . . If Jefferson Davis wishes for himself, or for the benefit of his friends at the North, to know what I would do if he were to offer peace and reunion, saying nothing about slavery, let him try me.[1900]

Two days after Lee's "surrender" at Appomattox, in his last public address on April 11, 1865, Lincoln again displayed a willingness to work with his Southern enemies, saying:

> In the annual message of December, 1863, and in the accompanying proclamation, I presented a plan of reconstruction, as the phrase goes, which I promised, if

adopted by any State, should be acceptable to and sustained by the executive government of the nation. I distinctly stated that this was not the only plan which might possibly be acceptable . . .[1901]

To his credit, in the areas of emancipation, reunion, and reconstruction, Lincoln seems to displays an incredible receptiveness to ideas beside his own. This same sentiment was on display in a July 9, 1864, letter to abolitionist Horace Greeley:

> Dear Sir: Your letter of the 7th, with inclosures, received.
> If you can find any person, anywhere, professing to have any proposition of Jefferson Davis in writing, for peace, embracing the restoration of the Union and abandonment of slavery, whatever else it embraces, say to him he may come to me with you; and that if he really brings such proposition, he shall at the least have safe conduct with the paper (and without publicity, if he chooses) to the point where you shall have met him. The same if there be two or more persons. Yours truly, A. Lincoln.[1902]

Again, this time on July 18, 1864, Lincoln seemingly holds out his hand to the South:

> To whom it may concern: Any proposition which embraces the restoration of peace, the integrity of the whole Union, and the abandonment of slavery, and which comes by and with an authority that can control the armies now at war against the United States, will be received and considered by the executive government of the United States, and will be met by liberal terms on other substantial and collateral points, and the bearer or bearers thereof shall have safe conduct both ways. Abraham Lincoln.[1903]

Lincoln cultists have long proclaimed these to be examples of the president's open mind and heart toward the Southern people. In reality, such offers turned out to be just another Lincolnian political tactic. For when he was actually approached with reasonable diplomatic **"propositions"** from the Confederate side, such as at the Hampton Roads Peace Conference on February 3, 1865, he flatly and coldly turned them down.

Concerning Reconstruction specifically, in the same April 11 speech Lincoln came close—in his own uniquely diabolical way—to acknowledging that his plans to "reunionize" the South were illegal, saying that:

> **Unlike a case of war between independent nations, there is no authorized organ** [i.e., agency] **for us to treat** [i.e., work] **with.**[1904]

Lincoln pretends here that the Confederacy is not an **"independent nation,"** and that therefore there is no formal department through which he can work to begin the process of rebuilding the nation he practically destroyed.

But the Confederacy *was* an independent nation, and a legally and constitutionally formed one at that. And there *was* an **"authorized organ"** for him to work with. It was called the Confederate government. The only problem was that due to Lincoln's troops overtaking Richmond, Virginia, President Jefferson Davis and his cabinet had been forced to evacuate the Confederate capital nine days earlier (on April 2, 1865).[1905] Despite this, there were many others Lincoln could have **"treated with,"** such as General Lee.

The truth of the matter is that behind Lincoln's so-called "Reconstruction" lay a truly sinister and inhumane motivation: as if four years of shooting, burning, bombing, pillaging, robbing, raping, and murder across the South was not enough, Reconstruction was to be further punishment for Dixie's audacity to break from the Union. Yankee Radicals Thaddeus Stevens of Vermont and Charles Sumner of Massachusetts led the way in doling out a vindictive, punitory justice against Dixie, all in an attempt to crush the South's political power and ensconce the North as sovereign ruler over the entire Union.[1906]

As part of their "punishment, repentance, and regeneration" program[1907] Northern Radicals intended to confiscate Southern plantations and estates, divide them up, and portion them out to landless blacks, mainly former servants.[1908] Also, all Southern white males were to be involuntarily enrolled by Federal marshals, then forced to pledge their allegiance to the Union.[1909] One can only imagine the fear, horror, and disgust these types of Northern policies had on the white people of the South. Naturally, most Southern blacks were revolted by them as well.

Lincoln, of course, made things even worse by referring to

reconstructed states as **"free-States,"**[1910] likening them now to the **"free States"** of the Union.[1911] Allegedly, he believed (or pretended to believe) that he was **"freeing"** the seceded states from **"tyranny,"** as he called the voluntarily and constitutionally formed Confederacy, by violently forcing them back into the **"liberty"** of the Union.[1912] Here was a concept near and dear to the heart of every dictator. Yet it was one that struck nearly all Southerners with revulsion and dread, for Lincoln had proven for all the world to see that true freedom could never exist on any speck of ground over which he had any authority.

The awful concept of "Reconstruction" inevitably later led, in 1886, to the creation of the phrase the "New South," coined by Georgia newspaperman Henry W. Grady.[1913] According to Grady and other scallywags, in opposition to the "bad" Old South, the "good" New South denoted a "reconciled" South, one made pliable by war and now ready for Northern settlement and investment; that is, for remodeling it into a political, social, and economic facsimile of the North.[1914]

Yankee Radical Thaddeus Stevens arrogantly called it the "Conquered Province" policy: the entire South was to be confiscated to pay for the costs of the War (that Lincoln started),[1915] and the Confederate states themselves would only be "readmitted" to the Union if they had been "redeemed";[1916] that is, thoroughly cleansed of their states' rights movements and "rebellious attitudes."[1917] Said Stevens in 1865 before the U.S. House of Representatives:

> The whole fabric of southern society must be changed and never can it be done if this opportunity is lost. . . . If the South is ever to be made a safe republic let her lands be cultivated by the toil of the owners or the free labor of intelligent citizens. This must be done even though it drive her nobility into exile. If they go, all the better.[1918]

Who but a 19th-Century Yankee could presume to say such things to a constitutionally formed foreign country, particularly one that now lay prostrate and bleeding?

That the Conquered Province policy was much on Lincoln's mind during the War as well is evidenced by a brazen comment he made to Interior Department official, T. J. Barnett: the entire South needs to be obliterated and replaced with new businessmen and new ideas, Lincoln told the civil servant.[1919]

On April 11, 1865, two days after Lee's "surrender," Lincoln made a similar comment to the public. How would he go about healing the "prostrate South?", he was asked:

> We simply must begin with, and mold from, disorganized and discordant elements.[1920]

The key word here is **"mold."** Lincoln means exactly what he says: the Old South would have to be destroyed, then molded—that is, Northernized—into the "New South."

In 1863 South-hating Yankee Henry Ward Beecher declared that winning the War would allow the North to spread "New England ideas" across poor uncultured Dixie. Such ideas included abolitionism, Fourierism,[1921] free-loveism,[1922] "and the whole brood of Yankeeisms." According to Beecher, culturally Northernizing the South would secure a victory more complete than physical violence (the bloody path Lincoln had chosen).[1923]

The Radicals in Lincoln's party, those men formerly known simply as abolitionists,[1924] agreed, asserting that before there could be reconciliation between the two regions the Southern states "must first be drastically remade."[1925] The South would have no say in the matter of her future destiny, of course; not with interfering, prying, bossy, intolerant, bigoted, self-righteous Northerners like Lincoln at the helm.

Here, for example, is how he spoke to the South on July 8, 1864, in a document he called: "Proclamation Concerning A Bill to Guarantee To Certain States, Whose Governments Have Been Usurped Or Overthrown, A Republican Form Of Government, And Concerning Reconstruction":

> **By The President Of The United States Of America: A Proclamation.**
>
> Whereas, at the late session, Congress passed a bill to "guarantee to certain States, whose governments have been usurped or overthrown, a republican form of government," a copy of which is hereunto annexed;
>
> And whereas the said bill was presented to the President of the United States for his approval less than one hour before the *sine die* adjournment of said session, and was not signed by him;
>
> And whereas the said bill contains, among other things, a plan for restoring the States in rebellion to their proper practical relation in the Union, which plan expresses the sense of Congress upon that subject, and

which plan it is now thought fit to lay before the people for their consideration:

> Now, therefore, I, Abraham Lincoln, President of the United States, do proclaim, declare, and make known, that, while I am (as I was in December last, when by proclamation I propounded a plan for restoration) unprepared, by a formal approval of this bill, to be inflexibly committed to any single plan of restoration; and, while I am also unprepared to declare that the free-State constitutions and governments already adopted and installed in Arkansas and Louisiana shall be set aside and held for nought, thereby repelling and discouraging the loyal citizens who have set up the same as to further effort, or to declare a constitutional competency in Congress to abolish slavery in States, but am at the same time sincerely hoping and expecting that a constitutional amendment abolishing slavery throughout the nation may be adopted, nevertheless I am fully satisfied with the system for restoration contained in the bill as one very proper plan for the loyal people of any State choosing to adopt it, and that I am, and at all times shall be, prepared to give the executive aid and assistance to any such people, so soon as the military resistance to the United States shall have been suppressed in any such State, and the people thereof shall have sufficiently returned to their obedience to the Constitution and the laws of the United States, in which cases military governors will be appointed, with directions to proceed according to the bill.[1926]

Here an arrogant Lincoln states that his goals are to force the Southern states back into **"their proper practical relation in the Union,"** abolish slavery in each state, **"suppress"** all **"military resistance to the United States,"** and finally appoint **"military governors"** over each conquered Southern state.

There is not one clause in the U.S. Constitution that gives Lincoln any of these powers over a foreign nation. Yet he assumed them anyway, and it was upon this unconstitutional soil that both his War and his Reconstruction program were planted.

Even the Yankee president's death did nothing to halt or even slow down Reconstruction. In fact, it only became more severe afterward when Northern Radicals took over. The horrors of the twelve-year Reconstruction period between 1865 and 1877 have been well documented by other traditional Southern historians, so we need not detail them here.

Lincoln's hellacious program to Northernize the South only finally terminated with the election of Ohioan, Rutherford Birchard Hayes, to the presidency in 1876. In the spring of 1877, under the Compromise of 1877, the sagacious Hayes mercifully put an end to the martial madness Lincoln had inaugurated almost two decades earlier.[1927] America's nineteenth president was certainly the answer to many a Southerner's prayers. But by this time even most white Northerners had come to believe that Reconstruction was wrong, that it was a failure, and that it was time to put a stop to it.[1928]

Hayes agreed. In his First Inaugural Address, March 5, 1887, he said:

> Let me assure my countrymen of the Southern States that it is my earnest desire to regard and promote their truest interests, the interests of the white and of the colored people, both and equally, and to put forth my best efforts in behalf of a civil policy which will forever wipe out in our political affairs the color line, and the distinction between North and South, to the end that we may have, not merely a united North or a united South, but a united country.[1929]

Sticking to his pledge, on April 10, 1877, Hayes pulled all U.S. troops out of South Carolina.[1930] On April 24, 1877, he withdrew them from Louisiana, as well, sounding the death knell for the carpetbag regime,[1931] along with Lincoln's ridiculous, illegal, and insulting plan to Northernize the South.[1932] Hayes then halted the enforcement of the much hated, anti-South Fourteenth[1933] and Fifteenth Amendments,[1934] and appointed ex-Confederates to various administrative posts.[1935]

In September he toured Dixie, promising reconciliation, solidarity, and *genuine* reconstruction (as opposed to Lincoln's fake "reconstruction") through a policy of pacification. Finally, despite opposition within his own party, Hayes made government appointments based on merit rather than on party loyalty and political patronage.[1936]

All of this was refreshingly un-Lincoln-like; especially considering the fact that Hayes, as a Yankee officer under General John C. Frémont, had fought for Lincoln and the Union.[1937]

One of Hayes' Supreme Court appointments, William B. Woods of Georgia (the first Southerner appointed to the Court since Lincoln's War), spoke for the majority by wisely calling for an end to government efforts to combat the South's social aid organization, the KKK.[1938]

After nearly sixteen years to the day (April 12, 1861 to April 10, 1877)—during which time the South was subjected to an illegal invasion and the social and political upheaval and unnecessary bloodshed that went along with it—Southerners began to retake control of their region.[1939] Jubilation was felt in every home across Dixie: while the crusading, intolerant North's campaign of imposing its will on the South would continue into the present day, Lincoln's "Reconstruction" program at least had utterly failed in its twelve-year attempt to turn the agricultural South into an exact image of the industrial North.

Trying to Northernize Dixie was "a fool's errand," as Ohio carpetbagger, Albion W. Tourgee, later observed:

> The North and the South are simply convenient names for two distinct, hostile, and irreconcilable ideas,—two civilizations they are sometimes called, especially at the South. At the North there is somewhat more of intellectual arrogance; and we are apt to speak of the one as civilization, and of the other as a species of barbarism. These two must always be in conflict until the one prevails, and the other falls. To uproot the one, and plant the other in its stead, is not the work of a moment or a day. That was our mistake. We [Yankees] tried to superimpose the civilization, the idea of the North, upon the South at a moment's warning. We presumed, that, by the suppression of rebellion, the Southern white man had become identical with the Caucasian of the North in thought and sentiment; and that the slave, by emancipation, had become a saint and a Solomon at once. So we tried to build up communities there which should be identical in thought, sentiment, growth, and development, with those of the North. It was A FOOL'S ERRAND.[1940]

With his Reconstruction plan having gone down to an inglorious death, the absurd, unnecessary, wasteful, counterproductive, and unlawful conflict Lincoln had underhandedly initiated a decade and a half earlier at Fort Sumter was finally over.

But the Union was not preserved because of the War, and slavery would have died out in the South without the War. So what was the point of the tremendous bloodshed, devastation, and nationwide suffering? Why did the man who was so vehemently against warring with Mexicans,[1941] a people he despised as an **"inferior race,"**[1942] believe that it was good and necessary to go to war with the American South, the land of his birth,[1943] and the home to a people he claimed to love?[1944] We will leave the answers to these questions to those who adore Lincoln.

Despite Hayes' good will, much of the Northern populace was not as forgiving: his decency toward the South lost him the support of his own party in the North.[1945] Not only that, the Confederate flags captured by Yanks during Lincoln's War were not returned to the South until the year 1905—due to Northern indignation.[1946] And it was not until a full 128 years later, in 1976, that a man from the deep South was again elected president of the United States, the first, in fact, since Zachary Taylor in 1848.

That man was Jimmy Carter. In 1978 the liberal American president from Plains, Georgia,[1947] courageously restored U.S. citizenship to the conservative Confederate President Jefferson Davis,[1948] a status that had been illegally stripped from the former Rebel leader by Lincoln himself.[1949]

The year 1877 thus marked the end of what I call the "Southern Holocaust," a sixteen-year period (four of it under "Civil War," twelve of it under "Reconstruction") in which the South had endured invasion, destruction, degradation, and death at the hands of an aggressive and lawless Northern leader.

Conservatively counting Southern and Northern military deaths (650,000),[1950] Southern white civilian deaths (1 million), Southern black civilian deaths (1 million), and those who perished from disease due to the War (350,000), at least 3 million people died so that Lincoln could realize his liberal dream of big government.[1951] This was 10 percent of the total population of America—about 30 million—at the time. Correlated in terms of America's population today (300 million), this would be the equivalent of 30 million deaths in 2011.

To put this in even better perspective, imagine if tomorrow a Southern leader launched a war against the North that killed every citizen of the states of New York and New Jersey? Or one that killed all the inhabitants of New England (Massachusetts, New Hampshire, Vermont, Rhode Island, Maine, and Connecticut), plus everyone living in Pennsylvania, Delaware, and Washington, D.C.? What kind of South-North conflict could ever justify this kind of mass bloodshed? None.

Yet today the majority of Americans continue to worship a Northern president who committed this exact atrocity on the South, a Yankee leader who once said:

The strongest bond of human sympathy, outside of the

family relation, should be one uniting all working people, of all nations, and tongues, and kindreds.[1952]

This is the same man who, one month before he launched his War, claimed that the **"better angels of our nature"** would seal the **"bonds of affection"** between South and North.[1953]

If Lincoln honestly believed in universal **"human sympathy,"** or if he himself truly possessed a **"better angel,"** one would never know it based on his words and actions. It would be more accurate to say that he had a "better devil," for only Satan himself could have done what Lincoln did between 1861 and 1865.

In his July 25, 1864, letter to Abram Wakeman, Lincoln spoke of his War, the conflict still erroneously known in the North and in the New South as the "Civil War," this way:

> The issue is a mighty one, for all people, and all times; and whoever aids the right will be appreciated and remembered.[1954]

The **"right"** Lincoln speaks of here is, of course, none other than himself.

But he was wrong, as wrong as can be.

Lovers of liberty, strict constitutionalists, true conservatives, Jeffersonians, libertarians, Tea Partyists, and traditional Southerners do not **"appreciate"** or **"remember"** Lincoln—or any of his Yankee sycophants (such as Grant and Sherman)—with fondness or thanksgiving. We only **"appreciate"** and **"remember"** them as enemies of freedom, of the people, of the United States, and of the Constitution. We **"appreciate"** and **"remember"** them as thugs, criminals, rapists, racists, and murderers. We **"appreciate"** and **"remember"** them only as destroyers of the American Dream, the American Way, and the voluntary American Union created by our Founding Fathers, with its small weak central government and its all-powerful sovereign states.

This is not how Lincoln wanted to be remembered. But it is how he is remembered to this day by at least half of the United States, and by many thousands of enlightened souls around the world. For he is condemned, tried, and sentenced by his own words, there for all to see, read, ponder, and consider, as this very book has shown.

In a February 14, 1860, letter to Oliver P. Hall, Jacob N. Fullinwider, and William F. Correll, America's most evasive, guileful, and hypocritical president can be found once again fighting the charge of ambiguous double-talking. His typical defensive response includes the following statement, one that epitomizes his entire political career:

> ... **I meant all I said, and did not mean anything I did not say** ...[1955]

Why does this comment so perfectly characterize demagogic Lincoln? Because he always said one thing while meaning another, carefully sculpting his words to fit his particular audience. Thus, what he is actually expressing here is this:

> I did not mean all I said, and meant many things I did not say.

At last, despite 150 years of his followers' best efforts to prevent it, the real Abraham Lincoln has been revealed—in his own words.[1956]

EPITAPH

. . . if the cause espoused by Mr. Lincoln had not been deemed successful, and if the 'assassin's bullet' had not contributed so greatly to immortalize him, his name would be now bandied about as only that of an ordinary, coarse, secretive, cunning man and wily politician, and one of the greatest tyrants of any age.

HONORABLE JUDGE GEORGE LLEWELLYN CHRISTIAN
RICHMOND, VIRGINIA, OCTOBER 29, 1909

APPENDIX A

PHOTOS OF LINCOLN, HIS VICE PRESIDENTS, CABINET, & MILITARY CHIEFS

Abraham Lincoln (1809-1865) of Kentucky, sixteenth president of the United States.

President Lincoln (center), with his official biographers John George Nicolay (1832-1901) of Bavaria (left), and John Hay (1838-1905) of Indiana (right).

Hannibal Hamlin (1809-1891) of Maine, Lincoln's first vice president.

Andrew Johnson (1808-1875) of North Carolina, Lincoln's second vice president.

William Henry Seward (1801-1872) of New York, Lincoln's secretary of state.

Salmon Portland Chase (1808-1873) of New Hampshire, Lincoln's first secretary of the treasury.

William Pitt Fessenden (1806-1869) of New Hampshire, Lincoln's second secretary of the treasury.

Hugh McCulloch (1808-1895) of Maine, Lincoln's third secretary of the treasury.

Simon Cameron (1799-1889) of Pennsylvania, Lincoln's first secretary of war.

Edwin McMasters Stanton (1814-1869) of Ohio, Lincoln's second secretary of war.

Edward Bates (1793-1869) of Virginia, Lincoln's first attorney general.

James Speed (1812-1887) of Kentucky, Lincoln's second attorney general.

Gideon Welles (1802-1878) of Connecticut, Lincoln's secretary of the navy.

Montgomery Blair (1813-1883) of Kentucky, Lincoln's first postmaster general.

William Dennison (1815-1882) of Ohio, Lincoln's second postmaster general.

Caleb Blood Smith (1808-1864) of Massachusetts, Lincoln's first secretary of the interior.

John Palmer Usher (1816-1889) of New York, Lincoln's second secretary of the interior.

Winfield Scott (1786-1866) of Virginia, Lincoln's first general-in-chief of the U.S. Army.

George Brinton McClellan (1826-1885) of Pennsylvania, Lincoln's second general-in-chief of the U.S. Army.

Henry Wager Halleck (1815-1872) of New York, Lincoln's third general-in-chief of the U.S. Army.

Ulysses S. Grant (1822-1885) of Ohio, Lincoln's fourth general-in-chief of the U.S. Army.

APPENDIX B

U.S. PRESIDENTS WHO INFLUENCED LINCOLN & HIS POLICIES

NOTE: The two major political parties were reversed during the Civil War (i.e., the Democrats were Conservatives and the Republicans were Liberals). They would not become the parties we know today until 1896.

Key: number order, name, dates served, general political stance

1. George Washington (1789-1797): Liberal.
2. John Adams (1797-1801): Liberal.
3. Thomas Jefferson (1801-1809): Conservative.
4. James Madison (1809-1817): Conservative.
5. James Monroe (1817-1825): Conservative.
6. John Quincy Adams (1825-1829): Conservative.
7. Andrew Jackson (1829-1837): Conservative.
8. Martin Van Buren (1837-1841): Conservative.
9. William Henry Harrison (1841): Liberal.
10. John Tyler (1841-1845): Liberal.
11. James Knox Polk (1845-1849): Conservative.
12. Zachary Taylor (1849-1850): Liberal.
13. Millard Fillmore (1850-1853): Liberal.
14. Franklin Pierce (1853-1857): Conservative.
15. James Buchanan (1857-1861): Conservative.
16. ABRAHAM LINCOLN (1861-1865): Pro-big government Liberal, extreme anti-states' rights advocate, started "Civil War," inaugurated "Reconstruction," tainted race relations, failed to end slavery or preserve the Union, left permanent emotional scar between South and North that is overt and painful to this day.
17. Andrew Johnson (1865-1869): Liberal.
18. Ulysses S. Grant (1869-1877): Liberal.
19. Rutherford Birchard Hayes (1877-1881): Liberal.[1957]

Appendix C

CHRONOLOGY OF THE LINCOLN-DOUGLAS DEBATES

The all-important Lincoln-Douglas Debates took place in the following order:

First Debate at Ottawa, Illinois, August 21, 1858

Second Debate at Freeport, Illinois, August 27, 1858

Third Debate at Jonesboro, Illinois, September 15, 1858

Fourth Debate at Charleston, Illinois, September 18, 1858

Fifth Debate at Galesburg, Illinois, October 7, 1858

Sixth Debate at Quincy, Illinois, October 13, 1858

Seventh Debate at Alton, Illinois, October 15, 1858

NOTES

1. Lincoln also obviously had no love for the Declaration of Independence and its emphasis on the right of secession, another important document written by a conservative Southern Founding Father: Thomas Jefferson of Virginia.
2. Nicolay and Hay, ALCW, Vol. 1, p. 126.
3. "The Dr. John K. Lattimer Collection of Lincolniana," *Historical Americana*, November 20, 2008, Dallas, TX, p. 23.
4. Current, LNK, p. 58.
5. Remsburg, pp. 220-221.
6. Lamon, LAL, p. 488.
7. W. B. Garrison, LNOK, pp. 265-267.
8. Woods, p. 47.
9. Grissom, pp. 149-150.
10. Nicolay and Hay, ALCW, Vol. 1, p. 606.
11. See Nicolay and Hay, ALCW, Vol. 1, pp. 606-607.
12. Nicolay and Hay, ALCW, Vol. 2, p. 423.
13. Hacker, p. 582.
14. Lincoln himself acknowledged this. See e.g., Nicolay and Hay, ALCW, Vol. 1, p. 627.
15. See e.g., Pollard, LC, p. 178; J. H. Franklin, pp. 101, 111, 130, 149.
16. Nicolay and Hay, ALCW, Vol. 1, p. 532.
17. Nicolay and Hay, ALCW, Vol. 1, p. 541.
18. Ellis, AS, p. 5; DeGregorio, s.v. "Abraham Lincoln."
19. Faust, s.v. "Lincoln, Abraham." So uneducated is the public about Lincoln that, incredibly, annual polls place him above even the Founding Presidents: George Washington, the "Father of our nation"; Thomas Jefferson, the "Father of the Declaration of Independence"; and James Madison, the "Father of the U.S. Constitution."
20. Christian, p. 7.
21. Davenport, p. 25.
22. Lewis, p. 325. To this day Lincoln's parentage, indeed much of his ancestry, is still in question. His father is certainly not known for sure. Some even believe Lincoln and Confederate President Jefferson Davis were brothers. Both were born in Kentucky within 100 miles of each other, and within one year of each other. They are also similar in height, body type, and overall appearance. For more on this topic, see e.g., W. B. Garrison, LNOK, pp. 5-13.
23. See e.g., Guelzo, ALRP, passim.
24. Shenkman and Reiger, p. 105.
25. Christian, pp. 2, 7.

26. Tyler, PH, p. 10.
27. A. Cooke, ACA, p. 216.
28. *U.S. Grant: Warrior*, PBS, January 10, 2011.
29. See e.g., Oates, AL, p. 17.
30. See e.g., Tagg, passim.
31. Nicolay and Hay, ALCW, Vol. 1, p. 644.
32. W. B. Garrison, LNOK, pp. 5-13.
33. Nicolay and Hay, ALCW, Vol. 1, p. 648.
34. DeGregorio, s.v. "Abraham Lincoln."
35. Nicolay and Hay, ALCW, Vol. 1, p. 533. Lincoln said the same thing to Samuel Galloway in a July 28, 1859, letter. Nicolay and Hay, ALCW, Vol. 1, p. 538.
36. Villard, Vol. 1, p. 96.
37. For the dates and places of the Lincoln-Douglas Debates, see Appendix C.
38. Nicolay and Hay, ALCW, Vol. 1, p. 522.
39. Nicolay and Hay, ALCW, Vol. 2, pp. 531-532.
40. Nicolay and Hay, ALCW, Vol. 1, pp. 596-597.
41. Nicolay and Hay, ALCW, Vol. 1, p. 634.
42. Nicolay and Hay, ALCW, Vol. 1, p. 684.
43. Nicolay and Hay, ALCW, Vol. 1, p. 685.
44. Nicolay and Hay, ALCW, Vol. 1, p. 687.
45. Nicolay and Hay, ALCW, Vol. 1, p. 19.
46. Nicolay and Hay, ALCW, Vol. 2, p. 435.
47. Lamon, RAL, pp. 189-190.
48. Sherman, Vol. 2, p. 466 (1892 ed.).
49. The pseudonym of Charles Farrar Browne, a popular 19th-Century humorist and writer from Maine.
50. For more on this obscene incident see Seabrook, AL, pp. 470-471.
51. Rice, RAL, p. 352.
52. *The Congressional Globe*, 37th Congress, 3rd Session, pp. 549, 550.
53. Guelzo, p. 90; Nye, p. 169.
54. Minor, p. 49; DeGregorio, s.v. "Abraham Lincoln"; Beschloss, p. 113; K. C. Davis, p. 219; Flood, p. 37; D. H. Donald, L, p. 319.
55. Beveridge, p. 405.
56. Julian, p. 241-242.
57. *House Documents*, p. 92.
58. Nicolay and Hay, ALCW, Vol. 1, p. 691.
59. For more on the tyranny of liberalism, see Levin, pp. 2-6, passim.
60. Nicolay and Hay, ALCW, Vol. 2, p. 440.
61. Nicolay and Hay, ALCW, Vol. 1, p. 226.

62. Nicolay and Hay, ALCW, Vol. 2, p. 53.
63. Nicolay and Hay, ALCW, Vol. 2, p. 70.
64. Nicolay and Hay, ALCW, Vol. 2, p. 79.
65. Nicolay and Hay, ALCW, Vol. 2, p. 126.
66. Hickey, pp. 217-218.
67. Hickey, p. 219.
68. Hickey, p. 224.
69. Nicolay and Hay, ALCW, Vol. 1, pp. 517-518.
70. See Jensen, NN and AC, passim.
71. See Seabrook, C101, passim.
72. See Hitler, Vol. 2, pp. 830-831.
73. See DiLorenzo, LU, pp. 81-84.
74. Douglas was nicknamed the "Little Giant" due to his small stature and large intellect.
75. Lincoln is referring here to the Northwest Ordinance of 1787, which created what was called the "Northwest Territory." The act also stipulated that existing states would not expand in size, but instead new ones would be created in the West. Most significantly, to black colonizationist Lincoln, slavery was banned in the newly formed Northwest Territory (what we now call the "Midwestern states"), which included Michigan, Indiana, Illinois, Wisconsin, Ohio, and parts of Minnesota.
76. See Seabrook, C101, passim; Seabrook, AL, pp. 41-43.
77. Lincoln is speaking here of the momentous changeover that began at the Constitutional Convention at Philadelphia, Pennsylvania, in 1787, when debate on the Articles of Confederation eventually led to the creation of the U.S. Constitution. See Collier and Collier, passim.
78. Nicolay and Hay, ALCW, Vol. 1, pp. 540-557.
79. Nicolay and Hay, ALCW, Vol. 2, pp. 260-261.
80. Stampp, pp. 408-418; E. M. Thomas, p. 15; Fogel, pp. 73-76. See also Fogel and Engerman, pp. 38-106, 158-257.
81. Napolitano, p. xvi.
82. Locke's philosophy of natural rights is based on the belief that people, as "natural beings," have basic inalienable rights pertaining to "life, liberty, and property," that cannot be blocked, withheld, or renounced by society or government.
83. Locke, p. 163.
84. McCabe, p. 138.
85. C. Adams, p. 129; E. M. Thomas, p. 242.
86. Fogel, p. 412.
87. Simpson, p. 79.

88. E. M. Thomas, p. 242.
89. Nicolay and Hay, ALCW, Vol. 1, p. 197.
90. Kennedy, p. 91.
91. Cash, p. 63.
92. G. H. Moore, pp. 5, 11, 17-19.
93. K. C. Davis, p. 9; Wilson and Ferris, s.v. "Miscegenation."
94. Norwood, pp. 27-30.
95. Meltzer, Vol. 2, p. 139. Also see Cartmell, p. 26. The 120-ton *Desire* was built at Marblehead, Massachusetts, in 1636. Norwood, p. 31.
96. McManus, BBN, pp. 9, 10, 11.
97. Bowen, p. 217.
98. McManus, BBN, pp. 6-7.
99. For more on the topic of slavery in Rhode Island, as well as in other New England states, see Website: www.boston.com/bostonglobe/ideas/articles/2010/09/26/new_englands_hidden_history/?page=1.
100. Nicolay and Hay, ALCW, Vol. 1, p. 619.
101. Eaton, HSC, p. 93.
102. Hinkle, p. 125.
103. For the Northern white population in 1860, see Current, CWSB, p. 46.
104. Rutherford, FA, p. 38; Wallechinsky, Wallace, and Wallace, p. 11; Woods, p. 67.
105. McElroy, p. 357.
106. Nicolay and Hay, ALCW, Vol. 2, p. 259.
107. McManus, BBN, pp. 6-7.
108. Manegold, pp. 132-134.
109. K. C. Davis, pp. 20, 23.
110. Meltzer, Vol. 2, pp. 145, 148; C. Johnson, pp. 125-126.
111. The Royall's original home and slave quarters have been turned into a museum located in Medford, MA. See Website: www.royallhouse.org.
112. See Lemire, passim. For more on the topic of slavery in Brookline, MA, see Website: www.boston.com/bostonglobe/ideas/articles/2010/09/26/new_englands_hidden_history/?page=1.
113. Farrow, Lang, and Frank, pp. 179-191.
114. Nye, pp. 30, 49.
115. W. B. Garrison, LNOK, p. 186.
116. J. M. McPherson, NCW, pp. 78-79.
117. Smelser, DR, p. 44.
118. McManus, BBN, p. 183.

119. Garraty and McCaughey, p. 146.
120. Douglass, NLFD, p. 116.
121. K. C. Davis, p. 7.
122. M. M. Smith, p. 25.
123. Garraty, p. 77.
124. C. Johnson, p. 125.
125. Hacker, pp. 19, 25.
126. "America Live," FOX News, October 25, 2010. For early evidence of Rhode Island's official full name, "Rhode Island and Providence Plantations," see Article 1 of *The Treaty With Great Britain*, the famous secession contract between England's King George III and America's original thirteen colonies, signed at Paris, France, November 30, 1782. J. Williams, p. 365; Rouse, pp. 78-79. Rhode Island's true official name was also mentioned in the first draft of the Preamble to the U.S. Constitution, written about August 1787. J. B. Scott, pp. 84-85. See also pp. 86-87.
127. Rosenbaum and Brinkley, s.v. "Slavery."
128. Spooner, NT, No. 6, p. 54.
129. McKissack and McKissack, p. 3.
130. McManus, BBN, pp. 16, 17.
131. Farrow, Lang, and Frank, pp. 4-5.
132. Hacker, p. 525.
133. Ellis, FB, p. 103.
134. Farrow, Lang, and Frank, p. xxvii.
135. Buckley, p. 103.
136. "Who Do You Think You Are?", February 4, 2011, NBC.
137. Farrow, Lang, and Frank, pp. 82-90.
138. Website: http://afgen.com/popula.html.
139. K. C. Davis, p. 24.
140. Lott, pp. 6-7.
141. Nye, p. 27.
142. For an illuminating African-American view of Alex Haley's *Roots*, see the following two Websites:
1) www.jewishworldreview.com/cols/crouch020602.asp.
2) www.jewishworldreview.com/cols/crouch011802.asp.
143. Adams and Sanders, p. 144; Nye, p. 54; Buckley, p. 61.
144. Adams and Sanders, pp. 272, 281.
145. De Angelis, p. 49.
146. W. Wilson, DR, p. 125.
147. Nicolay and Hay, ALCW, Vol. 1, p. 185.
148. Green, W, p. 180.

149. De Angelis, pp. 12-18; Lott, p. 65; J. J. Holland, passim.
150. De Angelis, p. 49.
151. Lott, pp. 61, 64.
152. Green, W, pp. 180-181.
153. Green, W, p. 181.
154. Green, W, p. 182.
155. Leech, p. 291.
156. Green, W, p. 186.
157. Leech, p. 292.
158. Leech, p. 292. Many other Northern cities have had areas called "Nigger Hill" as well, such as Boston, Massachusetts. See e.g., Bartlett, WP, p. 8; Furnas, p. 515.
159. Nicolay and Hay, ALCW, Vol. 1, p. 659.
160. Shotwell, p. 436.
161. Cromwell, pp. 121-122.
162. Though earlier in his presidency Lincoln had promised that he would never interfere with slavery in Washington, D.C., as usual, when it benefitted him he changed his mind. In this case, he needed the abolitionist vote for his upcoming bid for reelection. Additionally, freeing Washington's slaves allowed him to press Congress harder for black deportation and colonization.
163. J. C. Perry, p. 191. This did not end segregation, of course. If anything it exasperated the problem of Northern white racism. Indeed, total integration was not achieved in Washington, D.C. until 1956. See Weintraub, p. 147.
164. *The National Almanac* (1863), p. 250.
165. Nicolay and Hay, ALCW, Vol. 2, p. 144.
166. Lincoln and the abolitionists, Caucasian Washingtonians declared, were determined to make the city "a hell on earth for the white man." Leech, pp. 295, 298.
167. Buckley, p. 86; Leech, p. 298.
168. Truth, p. 254. See also McKissack and McKissack, pp. 142, 143, 144.
169. Lott, p. 64.
170. Website: www.usatoday.com/news/washington/2007-09-01-dcdemographics_N.htm.
171. Website: http://afgen.com/popula.html. Some of these blacks, of course, came north to look for jobs during World War II. Nonetheless, a large number of them descend from Northern, not Southern, slaves.
172. Lott, pp. 35-60.
173. J. C. Miller, p. 146.
174. Pollard, LC, p. 126.
175. Ashe, p. 10.

176. Denney, p. 25.
177. Stonebraker, p. 46.
178. F. Moore, Vol. 2, p. 323.
179. E. McPherson, PHUSAGR, p. 93.
180. Simpson, p. 78.
181. Foote, Vol. 1, p. 537. For Lincoln's letter to Captain Gordon confirming his sentence to be hanged, see Nicolay and Hay, ALCW, Vol. 2, pp. 121-122.
182. Farrow, Lang, and Frank, pp. 131-132.
183. Kennedy, pp. 104-105.
184. Stonebraker, p. 81.
185. C. Johnson, p. 107.
186. Rutland, p. 35.
187. DeGregorio, s.v. "Thomas Jefferson."
188. Nicolay and Hay, ALCW, Vol. 2, p. 6.
189. Faust, s.v. "slavery."
190. See Stampp, p. 271; Meltzer, Vol. 2, pp. 247-248; C. Johnson, pp. 126-128; Rosenbaum and Brinkley, s.v. "Slave Trade"; Durden, p. 288.
191. In 1862, an old law, the 1842 Treaty of Washington, was revived and strengthened, requiring U.S. and British ships to search and detain any vessel suspected of trading in slaves. This and only this finally put an effective end to Yankee slave trading. J. C. Miller, pp. 146-147.
192. Meltzer, Vol. 2, p. 247.
193. Burns, Peltason, Cronin, Magleby, and O'Brien, p. 151.
194. Spooner, NT, No. 6, p. 54.
195. Lincoln is speaking here of black colonization, the deportation of all blacks out of the U.S., one of his lifelong and most ardent goals, as we will discuss in Chapter 12.
196. Nicolay and Hay, ALCW, Vol. 1, pp. 558-576.
197. Lincoln said much the same thing during his infamous Cooper Union Speech on February 27, 1860: **"Slavery is wrong in its effect upon white people and free labor. It is the only thing that threatens the Union."** Nicolay and Hay, ALCW, Vol. 1, p. 613.
198. Again, he used a similar expression in his Cooper Union Speech: **"The proposition that there is a struggle between the white man and the negro contains a falsehood. There is no struggle. If there was, I should be for the white man."** Nicolay and Hay, ALCW, Vol. 1, p. 614.
199. For Marx's letter, and the White House's reply, see Schlüter, pp. 188-193.
200. For more on these topics, see DiLorenzo, LU, pp. 66, 171-179; DiLorenzo, RL, pp. 54, 59, 68.
201. Nicolay and Hay, ALCW, Vol. 2, p. 484.

202. Nicolay and Hay, ALCW, Vol. 1, p. 178.
203. *The Congressional Globe*, 37th Congress, 3rd Session, pp. 549, 550.
204. *The Southern Magazine*, Vol. 11, July to December 1872, p. 374.
205. W. B. Garrison, CWC, p. 215.
206. M. Davis, p. 63.
207. Pollard, LC, p. 101.
208. M. Davis, p. 67.
209. Cooper, JDA, p. 691.
210. M. Davis, p. 61.
211. Nicolay and Hay, ALCW, Vol. 1, p. 677.
212. Nicolay and Hay, ALCW, Vol. 1, p. 678.
213. Nicolay and Hay, ALCW, Vol. 1, p. 690.
214. *House Documents*, p. 91. See also Nicolay and Hay, ALCW, Vol. 2, p. 509.
215. Nicolay and Hay, ALCW, Vol. 1, p. 105.
216. Nicolay and Hay, ALCW, Vol. 1, pp. 253-254.
217. Nicolay and Hay, ALCW, Vol. 1 pp. 158-159.
218. Nicolay and Hay, ALCW, Vol. 1, p. 533.
219. Nicolay and Hay, ALCW, Vol. 1, p. 636.
220. Nicolay and Hay, ALCW, Vol. 1, pp. 661-662.
221. Nicolay and Hay, ALCW, Vol. 1, pp. 4-5.
222. Nicolay and Hay, ALCW, Vol. 1, pp. 61-63.
223. J. Davis, RFCG, Vol. 1, p. 244.
224. Nicolay and Hay, ALCW, Vol. 2, p. 499.
225. Nicolay and Hay, ALCW, Vol. 2, pp. 4, 62, 93.
226. Nicolay and Hay, ALCW, Vol. 2, p. 5.
227. Nicolay and Hay, ALCW, Vol. 2, p. 439. See also p. 5.
228. Nicolay and Hay, ALCW, Vol. 2, p. 566.
229. Nicolay and Hay, ALCW, Vol. 1, p. 648.
230. Nicolay and Hay, ALCW, Vol. 1, p. 664.
231. Nicolay and Hay, ALCW, Vol. 2, p. 60.
232. Nicolay and Hay, ALCW, Vol. 2, p. 553.
233. Nicolay and Hay, ALCW, Vol. 2, p. 571.
234. Kettell, p. 84.
235. Nicolay and Hay, ALCW, Vol. 2, p. 55.
236. Nicolay and Hay, ALCW, Vol. 2, p. 600.
237. DiLorenzo, RL, p. 117.
238. President Obama, for example, has added some 100,000 bureaucrats to the central government since he took office. "Hannity," FOX News, September 22, 2010. Additionally, according to conservatives, under Obama: "Big government is getting even bigger. For the first time since the Great Depression the

government is handing out more money to households than it's collecting in tax revenue." "Lou Dobbs Tonight," FOX Business News, April 20, 2011.
239. Nicolay and Hay, ALCW, Vol. 2, p. 57.
240. Nicolay and Hay, ALCW, Vol. 2, p. 375.
241. Nicolay and Hay, ALCW, Vol. 2, p. 622.
242. Mitgang, pp. 8-12, 205. The *Sangamon Journal* (later the *Illinois Journal*) is sometimes written *Sangamo Journal*. See Mitgang, p. 11. The two words are white American translations of the Algonquian word *saginawa*, meaning "river's mouth." The *Sangamo*, or the *Sangamon*, later came to refer to Illinois' once vast prairie lands. Faragher, pp. 74-75.
243. Nicolay and Hay, ALCW, Vol. 1, p. 298.
244. Nicolay and Hay, ALCW, Vol. 2, p. 437.
245. Nicolay and Hay, ALCW, Vol. 2, p. 470.
246. Nicolay and Hay, ALCW, Vol. 2, p. 513.
247. Nicolay and Hay, ALCW, Vol. 2, p. 538.
248. Nicolay and Hay, ALCW, Vol. 2, p. 70.
249. Nicolay and Hay, ALCW, Vol. 2, p. 143.
250. Nicolay and Hay, ALCW, Vol. 2, p. 55.
251. Nicolay and Hay, ALCW, Vol. 2, p. 66.
252. Nicolay and Hay, ALCW, Vol. 2, p. 239.
253. Nicolay and Hay, ALCW, Vol. 2, p. 94.
254. Nicolay and Hay, ALCW, Vol. 2, p. 498.
255. Nicolay and Hay, ALCW, Vol. 2, p. 103.
256. Nicolay and Hay, ALCW, Vol. 2, p. 662.
257. Nicolay and Hay, ALCW, Vol. 1, p. 202.
258. Nicolay and Hay, ALCW, Vol. 1, p. 65.
259. Nicolay and Hay, ALCW, Vol. 2, p. 61.
260. Nicolay and Hay, ALCW, Vol. 2, p. 35.
261. Nicolay and Hay, ALCW, Vol. 2, p. 612.
262. There is at least one known instance in which Lincoln called the Confederacy just that, without his usual belittling preface, the "so-called" Confederacy. It almost seems like an oversight on his part; or perhaps he was tired. Or perhaps by then he was actually starting to accept the fact that the Southern states were a separate and sovereign nation. Whatever the real reason, Lincoln's mention of "the Confederacy" occurred in an August 9, 1864, letter to Horace Greeley. See Nicolay and Hay, ALCW, Vol. 2, pp. 559-560.
263. Nicolay and Hay, ALCW, Vol. 2, p. 676.
264. Nicolay and Hay, ALCW, Vol. 1, p. 677.
265. J. Davis, RFCG, Vol. 1, p. 485.
266. J. Davis, RFCG, Vol. 1, p. 186.

267. See Stonebraker, pp. 67-68.
268. J. B. Scott, pp. 84-85. See also pp. 86-87.
269. Bateman, p. 179.
270. Desty, p. 272. See also Website: www.tenthamendmentcenter.com.
271. Smelser, DR, p. 78.
272. Rawle, pp. 296, 297, 305.
273. Tocqueville, Vol. 2, p. 426.
274. J. Davis, RFCG, Vol. 1, p. 173.
275. J. Davis, RFCG, Vol. 2, p. 623.
276. J. Davis, RFCG, Vol. 1, p. 173.
277. Randolph, p. 284.
278. Findlay and Findlay, pp. 168-169. See also, pp. 215-217.
279. Greeley, HSSER, p. 17.
280. Nicolay and Hay, ALCW, Vol. 1, p. 517.
281. Nicolay and Hay, ALCW, Vol. 1, pp. 220-221.
282. For a full discussion on Southern secession, see Seabrook, AWAITBLA, passim.
283. Nicolay and Hay, ALCW, Vol. 1, p. 137.
284. Nicolay and Hay, ALCW, Vol. 1, p. 138.
285. Nicolay and Hay, ALCW, Vol. 1, p. 534.
286. Nicolay and Hay, ALCW, Vol. 2, p. 60.
287. See e.g., Nicolay and Hay, ALCW, Vol. 2, pp. 70, 261, 327, 606.
288. Nicolay and Hay, ALCW, Vol. 2, p. 674.
289. Nicolay and Hay, ALCW, Vol. 2, pp. 442-443.
290. Stephenson, ALU, p. 116.
291. Nicolay and Hay, ALCW, Vol. 1, p. 691. The world had no way of knowing then that four years later Lincoln would pay for his anti-South liberalism in this exact manner.
292. Garraty and McCaughey, p. 241.
293. Hacker, p. 580.
294. Garraty and McCaughey, p. 241.
295. W. B. Garrison, CWTFB, p. 145.
296. Hacker, p. 580.
297. E. M. Thomas, p. 49.
298. Nicolay and Hay, ALCW, Vol. 2, p. 104.
299. Coffin, p. 235.
300. For a full discussion on the truth of Lincoln's War, see Seabrook, LW, passim.
301. Nicolay and Hay, ALCW, Vol. 1, p. 635.
302. Nicolay and Hay, ALCW, Vol. 1, p. 225.

303. Nicolay and Hay, ALCW, Vol. 1, p. 229.
304. Nicolay and Hay, ALCW, Vol. 1, p. 298.
305. Coffin, p. 235. Lincoln devotee President Barack Hussein Obama recently made a similar statement, calling the U.S. Constitution "an imperfect document." "Glenn Beck," FOX News, September, 17, 2009 (Constitution Day, 222nd anniversary).
306. Nicolay and Hay, ALCW, Vol. 1, p. 136.
307. Nicolay and Hay, ALCW, Vol. 1, p. 136.
308. Nicolay and Hay, ALCW, Vol. 1, p. 139.
309. Nicolay and Hay, ALCW, Vol. 1, p. 140.
310. Nicolay and Hay, ALCW, Vol. 1, p. 129.
311. See e.g., Nicolay and Hay, ALCW, Vol. 2, p. 282.
312. See e.g., Nicolay and Hay, ALCW, Vol. 2, pp. 295-296, 406.
313. See e.g., Nicolay and Hay, ALCW, Vol. 2, p. 548.
314. The presidential oath is taken in accordance with Article 2, Section 1, Clause 8 of the U.S. Constitution. Findlay and Findlay, p. 124.
315. Nicolay and Hay, ALCW, Vol. 2, p. 216.
316. Nicolay and Hay, ALCW, Vol. 2, p. 620.
317. In his Final Emancipation Proclamation Lincoln clearly states that he issued the edict, not for black civil rights, but as a **"war measure,"** one based on **"military necessity."** As we will learn later, these two phrases were nothing more than a euphemism for "needing more soldiers and more votes." As such, the Emancipation Proclamation is glaring in its total lack of any reference to black civil rights. See Nicolay and Hay, ALCW, Vol. 2, pp. 287-288.
318. Nicolay and Hay, ALCW, Vol. 2, p. 216.
319. Nicolay and Hay, ALCW, Vol. 2, p. 81.
320. Nicolay and Hay, ALCW, Vol. 2, p. 621.
321. Nicolay and Hay, ALCW, Vol. 2, pp. 291-292.
322. Nicolay and Hay, ALCW, Vol. 2, p. 421.
323. Nicolay and Hay, ALCW, Vol. 2, pp. 553-554.
324. Nicolay and Hay, ALCW, Vol. 2, p. 591.
325. As I descend from the Wrights of Kentucky, I am almost certainly related to this unfortunate individual.
326. Nicolay and Hay, ALCW, Vol. 2, p. 600.
327. Nicolay and Hay, ALCW, Vol. 2, p. 651.
328. Nicolay and Hay, ALCW, Vol. 2, p. 557.
329. Nicolay and Hay, ALCW, Vol. 2, pp. 629-630.
330. Nicolay and Hay, ALCW, Vol. 2, p. 561.
331. Nicolay and Hay, ALCW, Vol. 2, p. 288.
332. Findlay and Findlay, p. 126.

333. Findlay and Findlay, p. 94.
334. Nicolay and Hay, ALCW, Vol. 2, pp. 406-407.
335. Nicolay and Hay, ALCW, Vol. 2, pp. 541-543.
336. K. L. Hall, s.v. "Milligan, Ex parte."
337. Findlay and Findlay, p. 14.
338. K. L. Hall, s.v. "Civil War."
339. Christian, pp. 4-5.
340. See C. Adams, pp. 48-49.
341. Rosenbaum and Brinkley, s.v. "Merryman, Ex Parte."
342. DiLorenzo, LU, pp. 92-96.
343. Lind, p. 31.
344. Nicolay and Hay, ALCW, Vol. 1, p. 637.
345. Starr, pp. 57-72.
346. DiLorenzo, RL, pp. 245-248.
347. Rich and Farnham, p. 857.
348. Malone, p. 22.
349. Herndon and Weik, Vol. 1, pp. 165-168.
350. This is from Polk's "Special Message on Internal Improvements," given before the House of Representatives on December 15, 1847. See Jenkins, p. 342.
351. Nicolay and Hay, ALCW, Vol. 1, pp. 122-131.
352. See Findlay and Findlay, pp. 168, 212-217.
353. Moore, Vol. 2, p. 323.
354. See e.g., Nicolay and Hay, ALCW, Vol. 2, p. 420.
355. K. L. Hall, s.v. "Lincoln, Abraham."
356. Lincoln was a hypocrite in this, just as he was regarding so many other issues. According to Lincoln's official political biography (issued in June 1860), he was against the Mexican-American War (1846-1848) because "it was unconstitutional, because the power of levying war is vested in Congress, and not in the President." Nicolay and Hay, ALCW, Vol. 1, p. 643.
357. Even if the president believes that military force is necessary to protect American interests, he still cannot declare war. Congress must meet first in order to declare "that a state of war exists." Findlay and Findlay, pp. 84-85.
358. Nicolay and Hay, ALCW, Vol. 2, p. 35.
359. E. M. Thomas, p. 175.
360. Katcher, CWSB, p. 42.
361. Faust, s.v. "blockade."
362. Eaton, HSC, p. 71.
363. J. S. Bowman, ECW, s.v. "Blockade."
364. Faust, s.v. "blockade runners"; Lang, pp. 189, 190.

365. R. S. Phillips, s.v. "Declaration of Paris."
366. Owsley, KCD, pp. 224, 428, 432, 286.
367. Nicolay and Hay, ALCW, Vol. 2, p. 606.
368. Nicolay and Hay, ALCW, Vol. 2, pp. 38-39.
369. Eaton, HSC, p. 81.
370. ORN, Ser. 2, Vol. 3, p. 393.
371. Owsley, KCD, pp. 275, 302, 152.
372. Owsley, KCD, pp. 152-153.
373. Nicolay and Hay, ALCW, Vol. 2, p. 302.
374. For more on the Anglo-American cotton trade, and Lincoln's role in interrupting it, see McHenry, passim.
375. Seabrook, EYWTACWW, pp. 86-89, 191-192.
376. K. L. Hall, s.v. "Prize Cases."
377. Seabrook, C101, passim.
378. Findlay and Findlay, pp. 64, 84.
379. Nicolay and Hay, ALCW, Vol. 2, p. 34.
380. "Freedom Watch," FOX Business News, March 24, 2010.
381. In a speech to the American people on March 28, 2011, President Obama asserted that his action was legitimate because Libya was threatening U.S. "interests and values." There is nothing in the Constitution, however, that gives the chief executive the power to militarily invade a foreign country without the approval of Congress if that nation is threatening U.S. "interests and values." See Findlay and Findlay, pp. 84-85. Obama's Lincolnesque illegality is even more surprising when we recall that he made the following statement during his 2007 presidential campaign: "The president does not have the power under the Constitution to unilaterally authorize a military attack in a situation that does not involve stopping an actual or imminent threat to the nation." Website: www.hannity.com/show/2011/03/23.
382. "Freedom Watch," FOX Business News, March 24, 2010.
383. Slaves were not called "slaves" in the original Constitution. They were referred to as "other persons" (as in Article 1, Section 2, Clause 3), or as a "person held to service or labor" (as in Article 4, Section 2, Clause 3). See Findlay and Findlay, pp. 20-23, 164-165, 204-205.
384. Nicolay and Hay, ALCW, Vol. 2, p. 1.
385. See Nicolay and Hay, ALCW, Vol. 2, p. 288.
386. Nicolay and Hay, ALCW, Vol. 2, p. 508.
387. K. L. Hall, s.v. "Reconstruction."
388. Rosenbaum and Brinkley, s.v. "McCardle, Ex Parte."
389. Burns and Peltason, p. 437.
390. Christian, p. 14; Hacker, p. 581.

391. Hacker, p. 581.
392. C. Adams, pp. 39, 41.
393. Neely, p. 53.
394. For a fuller discussion on Lincoln, and Liberals in general, and the U.S. Constitution, see Seabrook, LW, passim; Seabrook, C101, passim; Seabrook, ALWALJDWAC, passim; Seabrook, AWAITBLA, passim.
395. Nicolay and Hay, ALCW, Vol. 2, p. 3.
396. See e.g., Nicolay and Hay, ALCW, Vol. 2, p. 62.
397. Like nearly all other presidents, statesmen, and politicians before him, Lincoln too often referred to pre-Civil War America as the "Confederacy." See e.g., Nicolay and Hay, ALCW, Vol. 1, pp. 168, 181, 611, 616, 628, 691.
398. See Jensen, NN and AC, passim.
399. Henry, SC, pp. 12-13.
400. Ashe, p. 21.
401. Rouse, p. 320.
402. The word perpetual does appear in the Articles of Declaration. However, this document was replaced by the U.S. Constitution, which, tellingly, omits the word.
403. Nicolay and Hay, ALCW, Vol. 2, p. 3.
404. Strangely, and deceitfully, Lincoln once said of himself: **"I am not an accomplished lawyer."** Nicolay and Hay, ALCW, Vol. 1, p. 162.
405. Pollard, LC, p. 175.
406. Pollard, LC, p. 181.
407. See Stonebraker, pp. 67-68.
408. J. B. Scott, pp. 84-85. See also pp. 86-87.
409. Bateman, p. 179.
410. Bergh, Vol. 1, p. 167.
411. Bergh, Vol. 1, pp. 167-168. See also Foley, p. 912.
412. The twenty-seven amendments to the Constitution are: (Bill of Rights, first ten Amendments) First Amendment: freedom of religion, press, expression, assembly, petition (1791); Second Amendment: right to bear arms (1791); Third Amendment: quartering of soldiers (1791); Fourth Amendment: search and seizure (1791); Fifth Amendment: grand jury, double jeopardy, self-incrimination, due process (1791); Sixth Amendment: criminal prosecutions, jury trial, right to confront and to counsel (1791); Seventh Amendment: common law suits, trial by jury in civil cases (1791); Eighth Amendment: excessive bail or fines, cruel and unusual punishment (1791); Ninth Amendment: non-enumerated rights, construction of Constitution (1791); Tenth Amendment: states' rights (rights reserved to states), i.e., powers of the states and people (1791); Eleventh Amendment: suits against a state, judicial limits (1795); Twelfth Amendment: election of president and vice president

(1804); Thirteenth Amendment: abolition of slavery (1865); Fourteenth Amendment: privileges and immunities, due process, equal protection, apportionment of representatives, Civil War disqualification and debt (1868); Fifteenth Amendment: rights not to be denied on account of race (1870); Sixteenth Amendment: status of income tax clarified (1913); Seventeenth Amendment: senators elected by popular vote (1913); Eighteenth Amendment: Prohibition, liquor abolished (1919); Nineteenth Amendment: women given the vote (1920); Twentieth Amendment: presidential term and succession (1933); Twenty-First Amendment: Eighteenth Amendment repealed (1933); Twenty-Second Amendment: two-term limit on president (1951); Twenty-Third Amendment: presidential vote for District of Columbia (1961); Twenty-Fourth Amendment: poll taxes barred (1964); Twenty-Fifth Amendment: presidential disability and succession (1967); Twenty-Sixth Amendment: voting age set to eighteen years (1971); Twenty-Seventh Amendment: compensation of members of Congress (1992). See K. L. Hall, s.v. "Constitutional Amendments."
413. Nicolay and Hay, ALCW, Vol. 2, p. 439. See also p. 5.
414. Nicolay and Hay, ALCW, Vol. 2, p. 566.
415. See e.g., Nicolay and Hay, ALCW, Vol. 2, p. 610.
416. Nicolay and Hay, ALCW, Vol. 2, p. 567.
417. U.S. gov. Website: www.nps.gov/gett/forteachers/upload/7%20Lincoln%20on%20Race.pdf.
418. Nicolay and Hay, ALCW, Vol. 1, p. 292.
419. Bryan, p. 291.
420. Lincoln and Douglas, p. 95.
421. Nicolay and Hay, ALCW, Vol. 5, pp. 87, 89.
422. Nicolay and Hay, ALCW, Vol. 2, p. 570.
423. See Seabrook, AL, pp. 315-317.
424. For more on Lincoln and the Union, see Seabrook, AL, passim; Seabrook, L, passim; Seabrook, LW, passim; Seabrook, CFF, passim; Seabrook, C101, passim; Seabrook, ALWALJDWAC, passim; Seabrook, AWAITBLA, passim; Seabrook, EYWTATCWIW, passim.
425. Eaton, HSC, p. 93.
426. Hinkle, p. 125.
427. Nicolay and Hay, ALCW, Vol. 2, p. 91.
428. Nicolay and Hay, ALCW, Vol. 2, p. 129.
429. Nicolay and Hay, ALCW, Vol. 2, p. 63.
430. Nicolay and Hay, ALCW, Vol. 1, p. 673.
431. Hayden, pp. 545-546.
432. Christian, p. 14; Hayden, p. 546.
433. Nicolay and Hay, ALCW, Vol. 2, p. 24.
434. Nicolay and Hay, ALCW, Vol. 2, pp. 24-25.

435. Nicolay and Hay, ALCW, Vol. 2, p. 25.
436. Nicolay and Hay, ALCW, Vol. 2, pp. 269-270.
437. Nicolay and Hay, ALCW, Vol. 2, p. 412.
438. Nicolay and Hay, ALCW, Vol. 2, p. 358.
439. Nicolay and Hay, ALCW, Vol. 2, pp. 448-449, 451.
440. Nicolay and Hay, ALCW, Vol. 2, pp. 607-609.
441. Nicolay and Hay, ALCW, Vol. 2, p. 616.
442. Nicolay and Hay, ALCW, Vol. 2, p. 382.
443. Nicolay and Hay, ALCW, Vol. 2, p. 387.
444. Nicolay and Hay, ALCW, Vol. 2, p. 57.
445. Nicolay and Hay, ALCW, Vol. 2, p. 674.
446. Nicolay and Hay, ALCW, Vol. 2, p. 534.
447. Nicolay and Hay, ALCW, Vol. 2, p. 552.
448. J. Davis, RFCG, Vol. 1, p. 80.
449. Nicolay and Hay, ALCW, Vol. 1, p. 495.
450. Hinkle, p. 125.
451. Adams and Sanders, pp. 215-216.
452. Grant did not free his slaves until he was forced to by the ratification of the Thirteenth Amendment on December 6, 1865, eight months after Lincoln's War ended. Rutherford, FA, p. 38; Wallechinsky, Wallace, and Wallace, p. 11; Woods, p. 67. See also McElroy, p. 357.
453. Meriwether, p. 219; Stonebraker, p. 70.
454. Rhodes, Vol. 3, p. 476.
455. Rosen, p. 161.
456. Seabrook, AL, pp. 476-478; Simmons, s.v. "General Order, Number Eleven"; Horwitz, p. 204.
457. Ferris and Greenberg, p. 114.
458. Parker, p. 343.
459. Greenhow, pp. 324-326.
460. Nicolay and Hay, ALCW, Vol. 2, p. 590.
461. E. McPherson, PHUSAPR, p. 16.
462. Nicolay and Hay, ALCW, Vol. 2, pp. 301-302.
463. Nicolay and Hay, ALCW, Vol. 2, p. 133.
464. Nicolay and Hay, ALCW, Vol. 2, p. 135.
465. Nicolay and Hay, ALCW, Vol. 2, pp. 512-513.
466. Nicolay and Hay, ALCW, Vol. 2, p. 1.
467. Nicolay and Hay, ALCW, Vol. 2, pp. 651-652.
468. Nicolay and Hay, ALCW, Vol. 2, pp. 575-576.
469. Nicolay and Hay, ALCW, Vol. 2, p. 562.
470. Bledsoe, IDT, pp. 143-144.

471. In late November 1864, Marx wrote Lincoln a letter congratulating him on his "re-election by a large majority." The missive included Marx's sincere hope that Lincoln would "lead his country through the matchless struggle for the rescue of an enchained race and the reconstruction of a social world." The two socialistic men had much in common, far more than most modern day Lincoln apologists are prepared to admit. For Marx's letter, and the White House's reply, see Schlüter, pp. 188-193.
472. Thornton and Ekelund, p. 103; C. Adams, p. 79.
473. Tyler, LTT, Vol. 3, p. 28.
474. Anonymous, p. 32.
475. W. Wilson, DR, pp. 49-50.
476. Crocker, pp. 20, 31.
477. Curti, Thorpe, and Baker, p. 572; Rosenbaum and Brinkley, s.v. "Slavery."
478. C. Adams, p. 25.
479. Spooner, NT, No. 6, p. 54.
480. Also see Pollard, LC, p. 154.
481. Nicolay and Hay, ALCW, Vol. 1, pp. 678-679.
482. Pollard, LC, pp. 131-132.
483. Kennedy and Kennedy, SWR, p. 21.
484. Fogel, p. 87.
485. Fogel and Engerman, p. 249.
486. Fogel, pp. 87-88. Sadly, Lincoln's War destroyed much of the South's wealth. As just one example, it took Dixie another 100 years (into the 1960s) to reduce her income gap to the level she had enjoyed in 1860. Fogel, p. 89.
487. Current, TC, s.v. "Plantation."
488. Fogel, p. 436.
489. Fogel, pp. 414-415.
490. Collier and Collier, p. 71.
491. Hacker, p. 593.
492. "American Disunion," Charles Dickens, *All the Year Round*, December 21, 1861, p. 299.
493. Ashe, p. 24.
494. Nicolay and Hay, ALCW, Vol. 2, p. 271.
495. Nicolay and Hay, ALCW, Vol. 2, pp. 633-634.
496. Nicolay and Hay, ALCW, Vol. 2, p. 216.
497. Nicolay and Hay, ALCW, Vol. 2, p. 57.
498. Nicolay and Hay, ALCW, Vol. 2, p. 634.
499. Nicolay and Hay, ALCW, Vol. 2, p. 657.
500. Nicolay and Hay, ALCW, Vol. 2, p. 529.
501. For more on this topic, see Seabrook, EYWTACWW, pp, 86-89.

502. Nicolay and Hay, ALCW, Vol. 2, p. 674.
503. Nicolay and Hay, ALAH, Vol. 4, p. 76.
504. Nicolay and Hay, ALCW, Vol. 1, p. 468.
505. Nicolay and Hay, ALCW, Vol. 1, pp. 433, 451.
506. Lester, pp. 359-360.
507. For more on Lincoln and his War, see Seabrook LW, passim; Seabrook, AL, passim; Seabrook, L, passim; Seabrook, LW, passim; Seabrook, ALWALJDWAC, passim; Seabrook, AWAITBLA, passim; Seabrook, EYWTATCWIW, passim.
508. Nicolay and Hay, ALCW, Vol. 1, p. 691.
509. Winston Groom, "A Shot in the Dark," *America's Civil War*, March 2011, p. 32.
510. E. M. Thomas, p. 81; Pollard, LC, p. 108.
511. LeVert, s.v. "Fort Sumter."
512. Nicolay and Hay, ALCW, Vol. 2, pp. 6, 7.
513. See e.g., Nicolay and Hay, ALCW, Vol. 2, p. 610.
514. Nicolay and Hay, ALCW, Vol. 2, p. 57.
515. J. M. McPherson, BCF, pp. 267-268.
516. Sandburg, SOL, p. 20.
517. Henry, SC, p. 30; J. M. McPherson, ACW, p. 21.
518. W. B. Garrison, LNOK, p. 81.
519. Crawford, pp. 354-357.
520. Eaton, HSC, p. 34.
521. Rhodes, HUS, Vol. 3, p. 333.
522. ORA, Ser. 1, Vol. 1, pp. 200-201; D. H. Donald, L., pp. 287, 288.
523. ORA, Ser. 1, Vol. 1, pp. 196, 197.
524. Crawford, p. 385.
525. Nicolay and Hay, ALCW, Vol. 2, p. 57.
526. Nicolay and Hay, ALCW, Vol. 1, p. 692.
527. Nicolay and Hay, ALCW, Vol. 2, p. 614.
528. Nicolay and Hay, ALCW, Vol. 2, p. 615.
529. Nicolay and Hay, ALCW, Vol. 2, p. 191.
530. Browning had earlier successfully defended the individuals accused of the jailhouse murder of Joseph Smith, former Mason, polygamist, and founder of the pseudo-Christian faith known as the LDS, or Mormons.
531. "The Abraham Lincoln Papers," Library of Congress, Series 1, General Correspondence, 1833-1916. Orville H. Browning to Abraham Lincoln, Sunday, February 17, 1861.
532. Nicolay and Hay, ALCW, Vol. 2, pp. 3, 7.
533. Nicolay and Hay, ALCW, Vol. 2, pp. 3-4.

534. Nicolay and Hay, ALCW, Vol. 2, pp. 25-26.
535. Nicolay and Hay, CWAL, Vol. 6, p. 241.
536. Nicolay and Hay, ALCW, Vol. 2, p. 32.
537. Denney, p. 33.
538. Long and Long, p. 55.
539. Denney, p. 34.
540. Long and Long, p. 55.
541. *Proceedings of the New York State Historical Association*, Vol. 72, 1974, p. 134.
542. J. M. McPherson, BCF, p. 271.
543. Tilley, FHLO, pp. 38-47.
544. Meriwether, p. 263.
545. ORA, Ser. 1, Vol. 1, pp. 13-14, 18.
546. L. Johnson, p. 77.
547. Eaton, HSC, p. 37.
548. Faust, s.v. "Fort Sumter, S.C."
549. Pollard, LC, p. 108.
550. Civil War Society, CWB, s.v. "Fort Sumter."
551. Winston Groom, "A Shot in the Dark," *America's Civil War*, March 2011, p. 34.
552. See W. B. Garrison, CWTFB, p. 101; C. Adams, pp. 202-203; Grissom, pp. 103, 108-109; Pollard, LC, p. 108.
553. Pollard, LC, pp. 111-112.
554. Winston Groom, "A Shot in the Dark," *America's Civil War*, March 2011, p. 32.
555. Denson, p. 268.
556. R. C. White, p. 408.
557. D. H. Donald, L, pp. 292, 293.
558. D. H. Donald, L, p. 293.
559. D. W. Howe, p. 590.
560. Crawford, p. 421.
561. Stovall, p. 226.
562. Baker, Vol. 5, pp. 606, 608-609. See also Nicolay and Hay, ALCW, Vol. 2, pp. 11, 14.
563. Nicolay and Hay, ALCW, Vol. 2, p. 26.
564. Nicolay and Hay, ALCW, Vol. 2, p. 18.
565. Nicolay and Hay, ALCW, Vol. 2, pp. 19, 20.
566. Nicolay and Hay, ALCW, Vol. 2, p. 22.
567. D. H. Donald, L, p. 292.
568. Nicolay and Hay, ALCW, Vol. 1, p. 77.
569. Lincoln and Douglas, p. 74.

570. Lincoln and Douglas, pp. 186-187.
571. Lincoln and Douglas, p. 74.
572. Nicolay and Hay, ALCW, Vol. 1, p. 532.
573. Nicolay and Hay, ALCW, Vol. 1, p. 594. See the biblical passage Mark 9:40, King James Version.
574. Nicolay and Hay, ALCW, Vol. 1, pp. 569-570.
575. Nicolay and Hay, ALCW, Vol. 1, p. 616.
576. Nicolay and Hay, ALCW, Vol. 1, pp. 673-674.
577. Baker, Vol. 4, pp. 389-390. For the full speech, see pp. 289-302.
578. Nicolay and Hay, ALCW, Vol. 1, pp. 630-631.
579. Nicolay and Hay, ALCW, Vol. 2, pp. 133-134.
580. Foote, Vol. 1, p. 47.
581. J. Davis, RFCG, Vol. 1, pp. 323-324.
582. Eaton, HSC, p. 37.
583. Ashe, p. 56.
584. Tilley, LTC, p. 105; Oates, AF, p. 106.
585. Norwood, p. 353.
586. Nicolay and Hay, ALCW, Vol. 1, p. 664.
587. Nicolay and Hay, ALCW, Vol. 1, p. 666.
588. Harwell, p. 344.
589. Grissom, p. 108.
590. Scharf, pp. 129-130; Tilley, FHLO, p. 50.
591. ORA, Ser. 1, Vol. 4, pp. 224-225.
592. Nicolay and Hay, ALCW, Vol. 2, p. 346.
593. Tilley, FHLO, pp. 50-51.
594. Nicolay and Hay, ALCW, Vol. 2, p. 41. See also Fox, Vol. 1, p. 44.
595. *Southern Historical Society Papers*, Vol. 1, January to June, 1876, p. 455.
596. Nicolay and Hay, ALCW, Vol. 1, p. 488.
597. Nicolay and Hay, ALCW, Vol. 2, p. 55.
598. Nicolay and Hay, ALCW, Vol. 2, pp. 55, 64.
599. See e.g., Nicolay and Hay, ALCW, Vol. 2, pp. 270, 388.
600. Nicolay and Hay, ALCW, Vol. 2, p. 65.
601. Nicolay and Hay, ALCW, Vol. 2, pp. 55-66.
602. Nicolay and Hay, ALCW, Vol. 2, p. 614.
603. Snider, p. 378.
604. Nicolay and Hay, ALCW, Vol. 2, p. 364.
605. Nicolay and Hay, ALCW, Vol. 2, p. 296.
606. Nicolay and Hay, ALAH, Vol. 10, p. 123.
607. Nicolay and Hay, ALCW, Vol. 2, p. 56.
608. Nicolay and Hay, ALCW, Vol. 2, p. 59.

609. As we will see in Chapter 17, Lincoln was elected president both times with far less than 50 percent of the American vote.
610. Nicolay and Hay, ALCW, Vol. 2, p. 64.
611. Nicolay and Hay, ALCW, Vol. 1, pp. 513-514.
612. Grissom, p. 155.
613. Rutland, p. 226.
614. Neely, pp. 113-116.
615. Dilorenzo, LU, p. 168.
616. The decision to leave the Union was made by a majority of the legislators in all of the Southern states that joined the Confederacy. The idea that these men, or their constituents, were somehow physically **"coerced,"** as Lincoln puts it, is simply ludicrous.
617. Nicolay and Hay, ALCW, Vol. 2, p. 66.
618. Nicolay and Hay, ALCW, Vol. 2, p. 103.
619. Nicolay and Hay, ALCW, Vol. 2, p. 106.
620. Nicolay and Hay, ALCW, Vol. 2, p. 148.
621. Nicolay and Hay, ALCW, Vol. 2, pp. 163-164.
622. Burns and Peltason, p. 437.
623. Christian, p. 14; Hacker, p. 581.
624. Nicolay and Hay, ALCW, Vol. 2, pp. 214-215.
625. Nicolay and Hay, ALCW, Vol. 2, p. 575.
626. W. Wilson, HAP, Vol. 9, p. 137.
627. Nicolay and Hay, ALCW, Vol. 2, p. 103.
628. Durden, p. 191.
629. J. Davis, RFCG, Vol. 1, p. 292.
630. Nicolay and Hay, ALCW, Vol. 2, p. 615.
631. For more on the Fort Sumter incident from the South's perspective, see "Lincoln and Fort Sumter," by Charles W. Ramsdell, *Journal of Southern History*, Vol. 3, 1937, pp. 259-288.
632. C. Adams, p. 135; DiLorenzo, GC, p. 255; Johannsen, p. 55.
633. Nicolay and Hay, ALCW, Vol. 1, p. 331.
634. Nicolay and Hay, ALCW, Vol. 1, p. 454.
635. D. H. Donald, L, p. 363; Leech, p. 155.
636. Quarles, pp. 115-116.
637. Leech, p. 151; Black, p. 165. As we will see, Lincoln later stripped Frémont of his command for freeing slaves in his assigned military area. K. C. Davis, p. 439.
638. Quarles, pp. 113-114.
639. Black, p. 165; Wiley, SN, pp. 296-298; Leech, pp. 305-306.
640. Lincoln admitted that he nullified the emancipation proclamations of these

men because, as he put it, there was no **"indispensable necessity."** Nicolay and Hay, ALCW, Vol. 2, p. 508. The nation's 4.5 million slaves (1 million in the North and 3.5 million in the South) at the time must have wondered what he meant by this.

641. Nicolay and Hay, ALCW, Vol. 2, p. 154.
642. Nicolay and Hay, ALCW, Vol. 2, pp. 155-156.
643. Nicolay and Hay, ALCW, Vol. 2, p. 77.
644. Nicolay and Hay, ALCW, Vol. 2, pp. 78-79.
645. Boatner, s.v. "Frémont, John Charles."
646. Nicolay and Hay, ALCW, Vol. 2, p. 79.
647. Nicolay and Hay, ALCW, Vol. 2, pp. 80-82.
648. Nicolay and Hay, ALCW, Vol. 2, p. 86. The aging Scott retired from active service only days later. Lincoln replaced him with Union General George B. McClellan. Nicolay and Hay, ALCW, Vol. 2, pp. 87-88.
649. Simmons, s.v. "Frémont, John Charles."
650. From the African-American point of view, the 1864 election of abolitionist Frémont would have been much preferred to that of the anti-abolitionist Lincoln. However, such was not to be. Under pressure from fellow Republican party members he renounced his candidacy a few months before the election, grudgingly supporting Lincoln. LeVert, s.v. "Frémont, John Charles."
651. Nicolay and Hay, ALCW, Vol. 2, p. 57.
652. Nicolay and Hay, ALCW, Vol. 2, p. 586. See also Faust, s.v. "Frémont's Emancipation Proclamation."
653. Lincoln and Douglas, p. 268.
654. Nicolay and Hay, ALCW, Vol. 2, pp. 198-199.
655. Quarles, p. 68.
656. Hacker, p. 580.
657. Nicolay and Hay, ALCW, Vol. 2, p. 135.
658. See e.g., Nicolay and Hay, ALCW, Vol. 2, p. 527.
659. Litwack, NS, p. 85.
660. Seabrook, EYWTACWW, pp. 77-80.
661. Seabrook, EYWTACWW, p. 81.
662. Hinkle, p. 111.
663. Meltzer, Vol. 2, p. 147; Farrow, Lang, and Frank, p. 54.
664. New England's version of the KKK was founded in the early 1800s, decades before the original Southern KKK was formed in 1865. Melish, p. 165. One of its later secret splinter groups, The Order of the Star Spangled Banner, was founded in Boston, Massachusetts, in 1849, sixteen years before the rise of the original Southern KKK. The Southern KKK adopted numerous "traditions" from the New England "KKK", including many of its secret codes, rituals, signals,

identification methods, and handclasps. The Order of the Star Spangled Banner, an anti-immigrant, anti-Catholic political group, eventually evolved into the Know-Nothings, or American Party, as it was also known. Wade p. 39. The organization, which was most popular in New England, eventually dissolved, and in 1860 a majority of its members joined the political party they were most comfortable with, a party of intolerance and bigotry. The man this party nominated for president of the United States that year campaigned on a platform of white supremacy. His name was Abraham Lincoln.

665. Fogel, pp. 271-272; Farrow, Lang, and Frank, p. 32.
666. Nye, pp. 27-29, 86-87.
667. Oates, AF, p. 39.
668. Hawthorne, Schouler, and Andrews, Vol. 5, p. 217.
669. Wilder, p. 85.
670. C. Adams, pp. 130-131.
671. Nye, p. 63.
672. Buckley, p. 62.
673. G. W. Williams, HNRA, Vol. 2, p. 151.
674. Garrison and Garrison, Vol. 1, p. 323.
675. Quarles, pp. 237-238.
676. Furnas, pp. 521-522.
677. Buckley, p. 62.
678. Fogel, p. 271.
679. Lincoln's "memoirs," entitled *The Autobiography of Abraham Lincoln*, were nothing more than carefully cherry-picked materials taken from John G. Nicolay and John Hay's mammoth, twelve-volume compendium, *Complete Works of Abraham Lincoln*. The purpose of the autobiography was for use as a "popular campaign biography," to be handed out to potential political supporters for the 1860 presidential election.
680. Current, LNK, p. 217.
681. Lincoln, p. 11.
682. Litwack, NS, p. 276.
683. Nicolay and Hay, ALCW, Vol. 1, p. 15.
684. Nicolay and Hay, ALCW, Vol. 2, p. 380.
685. Stephenson, p. 69.
686. Nicolay and Hay, ALCW, Vol. 1, p. 174.
687. Nicolay and Hay, ALCW, Vol. 1, p. 349.
688. McKissack and McKissack, pp. 134, 135.
689. See e.g., Nicolay and Hay, ALCW, Vol. 2, p. 357.
690. See e.g., Nicolay and Hay, ALCW, Vol. 2, p. 365.
691. W. Phillips, p. 456.

692. Nicolay and Hay, ALCW, Vol. 2, p. 205.
693. Findlay and Findlay, pp. 20-23, 164-165, 204-205.
694. Nicolay and Hay, ALCW, Vol. 2, p. 296.
695. Nicolay and Hay, CWAL, Vol. 1, p. 275.
696. Nicolay and Hay, CWAL, Vol. 1, pp. 275-276.
697. Nicolay and Hay, ALCW, Vol. 1, p. 252.
698. Hertz, ALNP, Vol. 1, p. 29.
699. The first known slaves in the world were white: Mesopotamians, Egyptians, Greeks, and Romans. White slavery continues to be practiced throughout the world to this day, including in the U.S.A. See Meltzer, Vol. 1, pp. 9-201; Nye, p. 46; Jordan and Walsh, passim; Hildreth, passim; Baepler, passim. Early Germans and early Celts also engaged in white slavery. K. C. Davis, p. 5.
700. Nicolay and Hay, ALCW, Vol. 2, p. 380.
701. Nicolay and Hay, ALCW, Vol. 1, p. 252.
702. Nicolay and Hay, ALCW, Vol. 1, p. 252.
703. Nicolay and Hay, ALCW, Vol. 1, p. 569.
704. Nicolay and Hay, ALCW, Vol. 1, p. 15.
705. Current, LNK, p. 218-219; W. B. Garrison, LNOK, pp. 35-37; Greenberg and Waugh, p. 355.
706. The "Great Emancipator" used black slaves to build the White House, the U.S. Capitol, and numerous other Federal buildings in the city, along with many of her city streets. De Angelis, pp. 12-18; Lott, p. 65; J. J. Holland, passim.
707. J. C. Perry, p. 191.
708. *The National Almanac* (1863), p. 250. See also Nicolay and Hay, ALCW, Vol. 2, pp. 144-145.
709. Nicolay and Hay, ALCW, Vol. 1, p. 306.
710. Nicolay and Hay, ALCW, Vol. 1, p. 659.
711. Berret later refused to take Lincoln's needless, spiteful, absurd, and illegal anti-South "Oath of Allegiance" to the United States, for which Lincoln had him arrested for "sedition" and sent to a military prison (illegal because Berret was a private citizen). This is just one example of how Lincoln treated those who supported him: Berret had served on Lincoln's inaugural committee.
712. Nicolay and Hay, ALCW, Vol. 1, p. 694.
713. Shotwell, p. 436.
714. Cornish, p. 73; D. Brown, pp. 179-180; ORA, Ser. 3, Vol. 1, p. 184.
715. Buckley, p. 65. See also Greenberg and Waugh, pp. 351-358.
716. Nicolay and Hay, ALCW, Vol. 1, p. 288.
717. Nicolay and Hay, ALCW, Vol. 2, p. 241. Key, of course, sent an angry letter to Lincoln correctly blasting him for his unconstitutional dismissal. Here is Lincoln's dry, authoritarian, and predictable reply: **"I am really sorry for**

the pain the case gives you; but I do not see how, consistently with duty, I can change it. Yours, etc., A. Lincoln." Nicolay and Hay, ALCW, Vol. 2, p. 242.
718. Nicolay and Hay, ALCW, Vol. 2, p. 1.
719. Nicolay and Hay, ALCW, Vol. 2, p. 586.
720. Nicolay and Hay, ALCW, Vol. 2, p. 605.
721. Nicolay and Hay, ALCW, Vol. 1, p. 190.
722. Nicolay and Hay, ALCW, Vol. 2, p. 420.
723. Nicolay and Hay, ALCW, Vol. 2, p. 420.
724. Greeley, WCMC, pp. 73-74.
725. Nicolay and Hay, ALCW, Vol. 1, p. 299.
726. Nicolay and Hay, ALCW, Vol. 2, pp. 422-423.
727. W. B. Garrison, CWC, p. 97; DiLorenzo, LU, pp. 52-61.
728. Website: www.lysanderspooner.org/sumner.htm.
729. Nicolay and Hay, ALCW, Vol. 1, p. 174; Stephenson, p. 70. Like Lincoln, Clay was a member and a leader in the American Colonization Society, a racist organization founded by Yankees, whose stated mission was the deportation of all freed blacks in order to make America white "from coast to coast."
730. Nicolay and Hay, ALCW, Vol. 1, p. 288.
731. Foley, pp. 811-812.
732. Thackeray, p. 127.
733. Chesnut, DD, p. 387.
734. Ruffin, a professional agriculturist who pioneered crop rotation and who is said to have been the person who fired the opening shot of Lincoln's War (at the Battle of Fort Sumter), committed suicide after Lee's surrender rather than live in ignoble humiliation under a Yankee dictatorship. To this day Ruffin is honored as an archetypal, unreconstructed Confederate hero among traditional Southerners, one typifying Dixie's age-old love of personal liberty, states' rights, Constitutionalism, and political independence.
735. Channing, p. 128.
736. W. B. Garrison, CWTFB, p. 164. By January 1, 1864, a gold dollar in the South was worth $20 in Confederate notes. E. M. Thomas, p. 197.
737. Wiley, SN, pp. 94-96.
738. Stampp, p. 314.
739. Weintraub, p. 54.
740. Ellis, AS, p. 102.
741. Jefferson, NSV, p. 171.
742. Crocker, p. 10.
743. Wiley, SN, p. 121.
744. Lanning, p. 55.

745. L. Johnson, pp. 178-179.
746. Coit, p. 452.
747. Crocker, p. 333.
748. Ellis, FB, p. 113.
749. Collier and Collier, p. 231.
750. J. Buchanan, Vol. 12, pp. 51, 52.
751. Ashe, p. 58.
752. E. M. Thomas, p. 242.
753. Simpson, pp. 79-80.
754. Ironically, though he was partly responsible for inflaming already existing sectional animosities, Garrison himself believed that allowing the South to secede peacefully was preferable to war between the two regions. W. B. Garrison, LNOK, p. 144.
755. Garrison was already detested by Southerners for having publicly burned a copy of the Constitution on the Fourth of July. Not only that, he had called the beloved document an "agreement with Hell" (because it protected slavery). Buckley, p. 61; Grissom, p. 127; Woods, p. 44; Nivola and Rosenbloom, p. 510.
756. Furnas, p. 408; Nye, pp. 49, 52, 134; Rosenbaum and Brinkley, s.v. "Liberator, The." Garrison's paper had only fifty white readers, most of them from Boston, almost all of them personal friends. Nye, p. 55.
757. Stampp, pp. 132-134.
758. Blassingame, pp. 129-131.
759. Kennedy, p. 91.
760. For the complete *true* story of the Nat Turner Rebellion, see T. R. Gray, passim.
761. J. S. Bowman, CWDD, s.v. "August 1831."
762. Rosenbaum and Brinkley, s.v. "Slave Revolts."
763. Simpson, p. 85.
764. Stonebraker, p. 250.
765. Garraty, p. 302.
766. Simpson, pp. 80-81.
767. Munford, pp. 52-53.
768. Munford, p. 53.
769. C. Johnson, pp. 125-126; Meltzer, Vol. 2, pp. 145, 148.
770. Garrison and Garrison, Vol. 1, p. 243.
771. Nicolay and Hay, ALCW, Vol. 2, p. 134.
772. Durden, pp. 123-124.
773. Cooper, JDA, p. 378; Quarles, p. xiii; Stephenson, ALU, p. 168.
774. Nicolay and Hay, ALCW, Vol. 2, pp. 635-636.

775. Hacker, p. 19.
776. Nicolay and Hay, ALCW, Vol. 2, p. 597.
777. Seabrook, ARB, p. 223.
778. Kennedy, p. 219.
779. Fogel and Engerman, p. 136.
780. C. Adams, p. 132.
781. See DiLorenzo, RL, pp. 257-258; DiLorenzo, LU, pp. 27-28.
782. See e.g., Litwack, NS, pp. 70-72.
783. Woodard, p. 15.
784. Nye, p. 49.
785. Berwanger, p. 4-5.
786. DeCaro, p. 17.
787. Berwanger, p. 30. Illinois was considered a "Western" state at the time.
788. N. D. Harris, pp. 233-234.
789. Litwack, NS, p. 70.
790. W. B. Garrison, CWTFB, p. 179.
791. Litwack, NS, p. 71.
792. J. M. McPherson, NCW, p. 252.
793. For more on Lincoln, abolition, and slavery, see Seabrook, AL, passim; Seabrook, EYWTAASIW, passim; Seabrook, EYWTAAAIW, passim; Seabrook, L, passim; Seabrook, TUAL, passim; Seabrook, TGI, passim; Seabrook, S101, passim; Seabrook, AWAITBLA, passim; Seabrook, EYWTATCWIW, passim.
794. Nicolay and Hay, ALCW, Vol. 1, p. 252.
795. Nicolay and Hay, ALCW, Vol. 1, pp. 178-179.
796. Nicolay and Hay, ALCW, Vol. 1, p. 253.
797. Nicolay and Hay, ALCW, Vol. 1, p. 369.
798. Nicolay and Hay, ALCW, Vol, 1, p. 534.
799. Nicolay and Hay, ALCW, Vol. 1, pp. 305-313.
800. Nicolay and Hay, ALCW, Vol. 1, p. 231.
801. Nicolay and Hay, ALCW, Vol. 1, p. 564.
802. Nicolay and Hay, ALCW, Vol. 1, pp. 330-335.
803. Sumner was not an innocent victim, as Lincoln wrongly implies. He had repeatedly insulted the South, as well of one of Brooks' relatives (Senator Andrew Pickens Butler), in the Senate (both Brooks and Butler are cousins of mine). In the minds of most Southerners Sumner only got what was rightfully coming to him, and Brooks is still considered a hero here in the South. Not for trying to silence an abolitionist, as Northern historians pretend, but for putting an ornery, interfering, and annoying Yankee in his place and teaching him some manners.
804. Nicolay and Hay, ALCW, Vol. 1, pp. 346-360.

805. Nicolay and Hay, ALCW, Vol. 1, p. 347.
806. Nicolay and Hay, ALCW, Vol. 1, p. 369.
807. Basler, ALSW, p. 480.
808. Nicolay and Hay, ALCW, Vol. 1, p. 652.
809. Nicolay and Hay, ALCW, Vol. 2, p. 508.
810. Kennedy, p. 91.
811. Seabrook, TQJD, p. 68.
812. M. M. Smith, pp. 4-5.
813. See e.g., Jefferson's antislavery views in his rough draft of the Declaration of Independence, written in 1776. Foley, p. 970.
814. Seabrook, AL, pp. 187-239.
815. Nicolay and Hay, ALCW, Vol. 1, pp. 252-253.
816. See Nicolay and Hay, CWAL, Vol. 2, p. 303.
817. Nicolay and Hay, ALCW, Vol. 1, p. 273. In light of the fact that 95.2 percent of Southerners did not own slaves (in 1860), and that nearly all these were abolitionists, Lincoln's fear of a Southern right-wing conspiracy to nationalize slavery is completely absurd.
818. Nicolay and Hay, ALCW, Vol. 1, p. 290.
819. Nicolay and Hay, ALCW, Vol. 1, p. 408.
820. Basler, ALSW, pp. 480-481.
821. Nicolay and Hay, ALCW, Vol. 1, p. 528.
822. Nicolay and Hay, ALCW, Vol. 1, p. 658.
823. Nicolay and Hay, ALCW, Vol. 1, p. 658.
824. Nicolay and Hay, ALCW, Vol. 1, pp. 668-669.
825. Meltzer, Vol. 2, p. 139; Cartmell, p. 26; Norwood, p. 31.
826. G. H. Moore, pp. 5, 11, 17-19.
827. McManus, BBN, pp. 16, 17; McKissack and McKissack, p. 3; Farrow, Lang, and Frank, pp. 14-25.
828. Fogel, pp. 203-204.
829. McManus, BBN, p. 5.
830. For the number of Southern whites in 1850, see Wilson and Ferris, s.v. "Plantations"; Bradley, p. 33. For the number of slave owners in 1850, see Helper, ICS, p. 148. How the total number of slave owners was arrived at: while "official" records state that there were 347,525 slave owners in the South in 1850, this is a gross error. Professor James D. B. DeBow, famed publisher and statistician, and Superintendent of the Census at the time, stated that this number wrongly includes slave hirers, a profession entirely different than that of a slave owner. Additionally, when slaveholders owned slaves in different states, or moved the same ones from state to state, they were erroneously counted more than once. Adjusting for these mistakes, we find the following: from

347,525 we must subtract 158,974 (the number of Southern slave-hirers) and 2,000 (the number of slave owners who were entered more than once). Thus the total number of slave owners in the South in 1850 was 186,551. See Helper, ICS, pp. 146-148.
831. Wilson and Ferris, s.v. "Plantations"; Bradley, p. 33.
832. Nicolay and Hay, CWAL, Vol. 1, p. 275-277.
833. Nicolay and Hay, ALCW, Vol. 1, pp. 585-586.
834. Rosenbaum and Brinkley, s.v. "Wilmot Proviso."
835. Weintraub, p. 64.
836. *Appendix to the Congressional Globe*, 29th Congress, 2nd Session, February 8, 1847, p. 317.
837. Ransom, p. 97.
838. Klinkner and Smith, p. 42.
839. Baker, Vol. 4, p. 317.
840. Nicolay and Hay, ALCW, Vol. 1, pp. 184, 218.
841. Nicolay and Hay, ALCW, Vol. 1, p. 199.
842. Nicolay and Hay, ALCW, Vol. 1, pp. 221-224.
843. Nicolay and Hay, ALCW, Vol. 1, p. 138.
844. C. Adams, p. 89.
845. Lincoln also incorrectly used the Yankee anti-South terms **"slave Constitution"** and **"free Constitution."** There were no such things. See e.g., Nicolay and Hay, ALCW, Vol. 1, pp. 570, 573.
846. See Seabrook, LW, passim.
847. Nicolay and Hay, ALCW, Vol. 1, p. 605.
848. C. Adams, p. 159.
849. Nicolay and Hay, ALCW, Vol. 1, p. 608. Jefferson's words are from his autobiography, written in 1821, when he was seventy-seven years old. See Foley, p. 816.
850. Nicolay and Hay, ALCW, Vol. 1, p. 612.
851. Nicolay and Hay, ALCW, Vol. 1, pp. 657-658.
852. Nicolay and Hay, ALCW, Vol. 1, p. 661.
853. Nicolay and Hay, ALCW, Vol. 2, p. 268.
854. Nicolay and Hay, ALCW, Vol. 1, p. 197.
855. Nicolay and Hay, ALCW, Vol. 1, pp. 507-509.
856. *Appendix to the Congressional Globe*, 29th Congress, 2nd Session, February 8, 1847, p. 317.
857. Catton, Vol. 1, p. 86.
858. America's history of black racism and black racial separatism is nearly as long as that of whites. Black racism toward Caucasians was particularly strong during the 1800s: many African-Americans at this time were revolted by the

sight of white skin, a vestige of the native African belief that "only black skin is beautiful." Blassingame, p. 25. Early American black nationalism, some of which grew out of a revulsion toward white racism, was expedited by a black Massachusetts Quaker named Paul Cuffe, who financed the emigration of nearly forty other blacks to Sierra Leone in 1815. Garraty and McCaughey, p. 145. In 1877 a number of blacks actually sought out the American Colonization Society (a Northern white supremacist organization to which Lincoln belonged), asking for help in resettling them in Liberia. Adams and Sanders, p. 228. In the 1920s a black-sponsored "Back to Africa" movement emerged. Its founder, Jamaican-born black nationalist Marcus Garvey, promoted the ideas of black pride, economic independence from whites, and the establishment of a black-only state in Africa. Unfortunately for supporters of the Back to Africa movement, Garvey was later convicted of fraud, imprisoned, and eventually deported. Rosenbaum, s.v. "Garvey, Marcus Moziah." Even earlier, in the 19th Century, African-American abolitionist Martin Delany advocated a separation of the races, with an emphasis on black separatism specifically. Rosenbaum, s.v. "Delaney, Martin Robinson." Delany and Garvey were not the first, nor the last, American blacks to push for black separatism. The idea continues today among numerous African-American groups, many with extreme racist ideologies (that whites are an "inferior race," for example). Rosenbaum and Brinkley, s.v. "Back to Africa"; "Colonization." Some of these groups are quite well-known, with former members even inhabiting the halls of the U.S. Congress—all without the slightest protest we should add (quite unlike what occurred when European-American rights advocate David Duke became a Louisiana state representative). Like Lincoln and most other 19th-Century white Northerners, the majority of today's black racists are against interracial marriage and for racial separation.

859. Nicolay and Hay, ALCW, Vol. 1, p. 231.

860. Lincoln was referring to "nearly all *Northern* white people." He repeatedly demonstrated that he knew almost nothing about how Southern whites felt toward blacks.

861. See DiLorenzo, LU, p. 101.

862. Trumbull, p. 13.

863. *The Congressional Globe*, 36th Congress, 1st Session, p. 58; Carey, p. 181.

864. F. L. Riley, PMHS, Vol. 6, p. 233.

865. **"A very fair proportion of the people of Louisiana,"** Lincoln stated on November 14, 1864, **"have inaugurated a new state government, making an excellent new constitution—better for the poor black man than we have in Illinois."** Nicolay and Hay, ALCW, Vol. 2, p. 597.

866. Lincoln himself was often referred to, not as a Southerner or a Northerner, but as a "Westerner."

867. Nicolay and Hay, ALCW, Vol. 1, p. 196.

868. Basler, ALSW, pp. 382-383.
869. Rosenbaum, s.v. "Mexican War." See also Buckley, p. 67.
870. DeGregorio, s.v. "James K. Polk."
871. Nicolay and Hay, ALCW, Vol. 1, p. 134. This paragraph is from what Nicolay and Hay called a "fragment" of a paper written by Lincoln "as being what he thought General [Zachary] Taylor ought to say." The statement was for Taylor, but it reflected Lincoln's thinking. (Whig Lincoln was a supporter of Taylor, the Whigs' presidential candidate, for the upcoming election on November 7, 1848. Taylor won over Democrat (then the conservative party) Lewis Cass and Free Soiler Martin Van Buren with nearly 50 percent of the American vote, becoming our twelfth president.)
872. On January 11, 1861, Lincoln wrote to J. T. Hale: **"There is in my judgement but one compromise which would really settle the slavery question, and that would be a prohibition against acquiring any more territory."** Nicolay and Hay, ALCW, Vol. 1, p. 664.
873. The idea of white American, even world, domination (Manifest Destiny) was nothing new to Lincoln, the racist dictator who used violence to control the Northern states and force a sovereign nation (the Confederacy) into a Union which by then it had come to abhor. No doubt he would have agreed with William H. Seward, his secretary of state who, in 1867, said: "Give me fifty, forty, thirty more years of life, and I will engage to give you the possession of the American continent and the control of the world." Farrar, p. 113.
874. *The American Annual Cyclopedia*, 1862, Vol. 2, p. 351.
875. Current, LNK, p. 86.
876. Cooper, JDA, p. 705.
877. Hacker, p. 580.
878. N. A. Hamilton, p. 113; Foner, FSFLFM, p. 265.
879. Fogel, pp. 386-387.
880. Nicolay and Hay, ALCW, Vol. 1, pp. 370, 539.
881. Nicolay and Hay, ALCW, Vol. 5, p. 89.
882. Mandel, p. 149.
883. Berwanger, p. 135.
884. Barney, p. 124. Instead, Douglass and many other Northern blacks supported Gerrit Smith that year, the presidential candidate of the abolitionist party, known by anti-abolitionist Lincoln as the "Radicals."
885. J. M. McPherson, NCW, p. 69.
886. Quarles, p. 130.
887. Lincoln here vastly underestimates the average price of a healthy productive slave, which was between $1,500 to $2,000 a piece, or between $40,000 and $50,000 into today's currency.
888. Nicolay and Hay, ALCW, Vol. 1, pp. 181-209.

889. F. Moore, Vol. 1, p. 45.
890. Nicolay and Hay, ALCW, Vol. 1, p. 272.
891. Nicolay and Hay, ALCW, Vol. 1, p. 539.
892. See e.g., Nicolay and Hay, ALCW, Vol. 1, pp. 257, 259, 449, 469.
893. Kennedy, pp. 191, 233.
894. Nicolay and Hay, ALCW, Vol. 1, p. 231.
895. Seabrook, CFF, pp. 159-161.
896. Seabrook, CFF, p. 161.
897. Nicolay and Hay, ALCW, Vol. 2, p. 1.
898. C. Adams, p. 4.
899. Parker, p. 343.
900. To his great credit, Virginian John Tyler (1790-1862), America's tenth president, was the only man of that office, former or future, to either join the Confederacy or serve in the Confederate government. Though he did not fight in Lincoln's "Civil War" (being too old at the time), he served as a member of the Provisional Congress of the Confederacy. He was later elected to the Confederate House of Representatives, but passed away before taking his seat. Tyler was an example of the overt anti-South bias that has long permeated the U.S. government: because of his devotion to the Confederate Cause, Northerners in his day regarded him as a traitor, his death in 1862 was ignored in Washington, and an official U.S. memorial was not placed over his grave until 1915, fifty-three years after he died. DeGregorio, s.v. "John Tyler." In total, six men who would become U.S. presidents fought in the War for Southern Independence; unfortunately for history, all got it wrong by siding with Lincoln and the North: Benjamin Harrison, James A. Garfield, Ulysses S. Grant, Rutherford B. Hayes, Chester A. Arthur, and William McKinley.
901. Tyler, LTT, Vol. 2, p. 567.
902. McManus, BBN, pp. 6-7.
903. C. Adams, pp. 4, 58.
904. Nicolay and Hay, ALCW, Vol. 2, p. 1.
905. See Spooner, NT, No. 6, p. 54; Graham, BM, passim.
906. For more on Lincoln, abolition, and slavery, see Seabrook, AL, passim; Seabrook, EYWTAASIW, passim; Seabrook, EYWTAAAIW, passim; Seabrook, L, passim; Seabrook, TUAL, passim; Seabrook, TGI, passim; Seabrook, S101, passim; Seabrook, AWAITBLA, passim; Seabrook, EYWTATCWIW, passim.
907. See Findlay and Findlay, pp. 20-23.
908. Nicolay and Hay, ALCW, Vol. 1, pp. 197-198.
909. Daugherty, p. 122.
910. K. L. Hall, s.v. "Fugitive Slaves."
911. Nicolay and Hay, ALCW, Vol. 1, pp. 657-658.

912. L. Johnson, p. 54.
913. K. L. Hall, s.v. "Fugitive Slaves."
914. Seabrook, AL, pp. 149-153.
915. Nicolay and Hay, ALCW, Vol. 2, pp. 1-2.
916. DiLorenzo, RL, p. 21.
917. See e.g., Nicolay and Hay, ALCW, Vol. 1, p. 574.
918. Nicolay and Hay, ALCW, Vol. 1, p. 669.
919. M. Davis, p. 49.
920. DiLorenzo, LU, p. 24.
921. Beard and Beard, Vol. 2, p. 65.
922. Nicolay and Hay, ALCW, Vol. 2, p. 296.
923. Nicolay and Hay, ALAH, Vol. 10, p. 123. See also, DiLorenzo, LU, p. 25.
924. Nicolay and Hay, ALCW, Vol. 2, p. 6.
925. Nicolay and Hay, ALCW, Vol. 2, p. 458.
926. Nicolay and Hay, ALCW, Vol. 1, pp. 413-414.
927. See, e.g., Exodus 21:26-27; Proverbs 29:19.
928. Genesis 37:26-28.
929. Genesis 4:1-15; 9:25. See Metzger and Coogan, s.v. "Slavery and the Bible."
930. The pseudo-Christian, non-Bible based, Mason-inspired denomination, the Mormons, or the members of the Church of Jesus Christ of Latter-Day Saints (LDS), have long embraced a belief in the "mark of Cain," though understandably this fact has been largely kept from the general public. As such, early Mormon laws did not prohibit slavery. Rather they sanctioned them. Mormon leader Brigham Young, for example, not only welcomed white slave owners into the church, he settled the Salt Lake Valley area in Utah using Mormon slave owners and their slaves. And in 1852, as the first territorial governor of Utah, Young asked the legislature to legalize slavery, making it the only territory west of the Missouri River and north of the Missouri Compromise line to allow the institution. B. H. Johnson, p. 140; Olson, p. 148. Mormons—who refuse to exhibit crosses or crucifixes anywhere inside or outside their churches—once held that blacks would continue to be an "inferior race" in the "Next World." Not surprisingly, blacks, being of the "lineage of Cain," were not allowed to join the Mormon priesthood or participate in Temple ordinances until 1978, 148 years after the church's founding in 1830 by Yankee polygamist and former Mason, Joseph Smith. The change only came after decades of severe criticism, condemnation, and charges of racism from around the world. Little wonder that in the early 1900s the Utah branch of the new KKK (as separate from the original KKK) flourished with the membership of Mormon ministers. Wade, p. 143. Despite the Church's modern 1978 concession, the belief in the "Curse of Ham" survives among some individual Mormons and Mormon groups. But this is not

the Church's only politically incorrect dogma. Mainstream Latter-Day Saints still embrace beliefs in both a Father-God and a Mother-Goddess (as well as a "plurality" of other deities), the secret ritual of baptism for the dead (condemned in 1 Cor. 15:29 by St. Paul as a Pagan practice), the belief that Jesus and Satan are brothers, the posthumous attainment of self-godhood (in order to rule other planets after earthly death), and the continuance of male polygamy after death—a tenant particularly distressing to many female LDS members. For more on these topics from an LDS perspective see the Church's publication: *Encyclopedia of Mormonism*, by Daniel H. Ludlow; s.v. "Cain," "Race, Racism," "Blacks," "Priesthood," "Mother in Heaven," "Godhood," "Baptism for the Dead," passim. For a non-Mormon Christian view of the LDS Church see: *Mormonism Unmasked*, by R. Philip Roberts.

931. Genesis 9:22-27.
932. See for example, Matthew 8:5-13; Matthew 10:24-25; Luke 12:47; Ephesians 6:5; I Timothy 6:1; Titus 2:9-10.
933. Philemon 1:1-25.
934. Colossians 3:22.
935. Galatians 3:28.
936. 1 Peter 2:18.
937. Matthew 20:27; Mark 10:44.
938. Acts 4:29; 16:17; Galatians 1:10.
939. T. C. Butler, s.v. "Slave/servant."
940. See e.g., Mark 12:14-17.
941. Walker, s.v. "Slavery."
942. Cross and Livingstone, s.v. "Slavery."
943. Oates, AL, p. 53.
944. Garraty and McCaughey, p. 27; Stampp, p. 35; Rosenbaum and Brinkley, s.v. "Slavery"; Wiley, SN, p. 65.
945. Barrow, Segars, and Rosenburg, BC, passim.
946. Rosenbaum and Brinkley, s.v. "Jim Crow Laws."
947. C. Johnson, pp. 206-207.
948. Stampp, p. 192.
949. Blassingame, pp. 180, 182.
950. M. M. Smith, p. 182.
951. M. M. Smith, pp. 175-179.
952. Stampp, pp. 178, 179.
953. Fogel and Engerman, p. 146.
954. Fox-Genovese, p. 360.
955. Stampp, pp. 219-222.
956. U. B. Phillips, p. 493.

957. Brinkley, p. 323.
958. *Appendix to the Congressional Globe*, 31st Congress, 1st Session, 1850, Vol. 23, Part 1, p. 150.
959. Nicolay and Hay, ALCW, Vol. 1, pp. 414-417.
960. Nicolay and Hay, ALCW, Vol. 1, pp. 417-422.
961. Nicolay and Hay, ALCW, Vol. 1, pp. 422-427.
962. See e.g., C. Adams, p. 135; DiLorenzo, GC, p. 255; Johannsen, p. 55.
963. Nicolay and Hay, ALCW, Vol. 1, pp. 427-437.
964. Nicolay and Hay, ALCW, Vol. 1, pp. 437-450.
965. W. B. Garrison, LNOK, p. 186; DiLorenzo, LU, p. 28.
966. Nicolay and Hay, ALCW, Vol. 1, pp. 450-455.
967. Nicolay and Hay, ALCW, Vol. 1, pp. 451-452.
968. Nicolay and Hay, ALCW, Vol. 1, pp. 478, 479.
969. Nicolay and Hay, ALCW, Vol. 1, pp. 468-472.
970. Nicolay and Hay, ALCW, Vol. 2, pp. 75-76.
971. Nicolay and Hay, ALCW, Vol. 1, pp. 462-463.
972. Nicolay and Hay, ALCW, Vol. 1, p. 480.
973. Foote, Vol. 1, p. 537.
974. Nicolay and Hay, ALCW, Vol. 2, pp. 121-122.
975. Farrow, Lang, and Frank, pp. 131-132.
976. Kennedy, pp. 104-105.
977. Nicolay and Hay, ALCW, Vol. 2, p. 101.
978. G. H. Moore, pp. 5, 11, 17-19.
979. Nicolay and Hay, ALCW, Vol. 1, pp. 186-187. Lincoln makes a number of outlandish statements here, false stereotypes, such as insinuating that all the abolitionists lived in the North and that all Southern slave owners were cruel. There is not a single authentic historical record anywhere that supports such views. In reality, there were very few true abolitionists in the North (i.e., individuals who favored both emancipation and full black civil rights), while of the 4.8 percent of Southerners who actually owned slaves, cruel masters were extremely rare. For more on these topics see my books *Everything You Were Taught About the Civil War Is Wrong, Ask A Southerner!*; *Abraham Lincoln: The Southern View*; *A Rebel Born: A Defense of Nathan Bedford Forrest*; *The McGavocks of Carnton Plantation*; and *Nathan Bedford Forrest: Southern Hero, American Patriot*.
980. For more on Lincoln, abolition, and slavery, see Seabrook, AL, passim; Seabrook, EYWTAASIW, passim; Seabrook, EYWTAAAIW, passim; Seabrook, L, passim; Seabrook, TUAL, passim; Seabrook, TGI, passim; Seabrook, S101, passim; Seabrook, AWAITBLA, passim; Seabrook, EYWTATCWIW, passim.
981. Greenberg and Waugh, p. 355; W. B. Garrison, LNOK, pp. 35-37; Current, LNK, p. 218-219.

982. Nicolay and Hay, ALCW, Vol. 1, p. 7.
983. Nicolay and Hay, ALCW, Vol. 1, p. 187.
984. Nicolay and Hay, ALCW, Vol. 1, p. 196.
985. Nicolay and Hay, ALCW, Vol. 1, p. 257.
986. Nicolay and Hay, ALCW, Vol. 1, p. 272.
987. Nicolay and Hay, ALCW, Vol. 1, p. 289.
988. Nicolay and Hay, CWAL, Vol. 5, pp. 35-44.
989. Nicolay and Hay, ALCW, Vol. 1, pp. 369-370.
990. On numerous occasions Lincoln stated that he would never marry a black woman. See e.g., Nicolay and Hay, ALCW, Vol. 1, p. 569.
991. Nicolay and Hay, ALCW, Vol. 1, pp. 231-232.
992. Nicolay and Hay, ALCW, Vol. 1, pp. 234-235.
993. Nicolay and Hay, ALCW, Vol. 1, p. 235.
994. U. S. gov. Website: www.nps.gov/gett/forteachers/upload/7%20Lincoln%20on%20Race.pdf.
995. Litwack, NS, p. 70.
996. W. B. Garrison, CWTFB, p. 179.
997. Litwack, NS, p. 71.
998. J. M. McPherson, NCW, p. 252.
999. W. B. Garrison, LNOK, p. 186; DiLorenzo, LU, p. 28.
1000. *Anglo-African*, January 14, 1865.
1001. See Nicolay and Hay, CWAL, Vol. 11, pp. 105-106; Nicolay and Hay, ALCW, Vol. 1, p. 483; Holzer, pp. 22-23, 67, 318, 361; Basler, ALSW, pp. 450, 458, 473.
1002. See e.g., Nicolay and Hay, ALCW, Vol. 1, pp. 257, 259, 449, 469.
1003. L. Johnson, p. 54.
1004. Nicolay and Hay, ALCW, Vol. 1, p. 288.
1005. Nicolay and Hay, ALCW, Vol. 1, p. 292.
1006. Nicolay and Hay, ALCW, Vol. 1, p. 298.
1007. Arnett, p. 758.
1008. Nicolay and Hay, CWAL, Vol. 11, pp. 105-106.
1009. Fehrenbacher and Fehrenbacher, p. 539. Pierce mentions this conversation (though not Lincoln's use of the "n" word) in an *Atlantic Monthly* article entitled "The Freedman of Port Royal," Volume 12, September 1863, pp. 296-297. Lincoln refers to Pierce in a letter to Salmon P. Chase on February 15, 1862. See Basler, CWAL, p. 132.
1010. See e.g., Nicolay and Hay, ALCW, Vol. 1, p. 524; Neely, p. 213.
1011. See e.g., Nicolay and Hay, ALCW, Vol. 1, p. 449.
1012. See e.g., Nicolay and Hay, ALCW, Vol. 1, p. 449.
1013. Nicolay and Hay, ALCW, Vol. 1, p. 559.

1014. Contrary to the liberal myth, conservatives of all races are much more apt to be color blind—or at the least, uninterested—in the matter of race, than liberals. This is because conservatives tend to base their value judgements on character rather than on skin color.

1015. Nicolay and Hay, ALCW, Vol. 1, pp. 406-407.

1016. For more on Lincoln and African-Americans, see Seabrook, AL, passim; Seabrook, EYWTAASIW, passim; Seabrook, EYWTAAAATCWIW, passim; Seabrook, L, passim; Seabrook, TUAL, passim; Seabrook, TGI, passim; Seabrook, S101, passim.

1017. Nicolay and Hay, ALCW, Vol. 1, p. 273.

1018. See Bennett, passim. See also DiLorenzo, LU, pp. 28, 49.

1019. Litwack, NS, pp. 113-152; Quarles, pp. 235-238; Garraty and McCaughey, p. 254.

1020. See Adams and Sanders, pp. 25-29.

1021. See Goodman, pp. 332, 333, 334, 336.

1022. B. Franklin, Vol. 2, p. 234.

1023. Hacker, p. 112.

1024. L. Johnson, p. 129.

1025. Ransom, p. 173.

1026. DiLorenzo, LU, p. 101.

1027. Nicolay and Hay, CWAL, Vol. 3, p. 354.

1028. Nicolay and Hay, ALCW, Vol. 1, p. 556.

1029. Nicolay and Hay, ALCW, Vol. 1, p. 299.

1030. Schurz, Vol. 2, pp. 166-167.

1031. Quarles, p. 235.

1032. Bailyn, Dallek, Davis, Donald, Thomas, and Wood, p. 29. Another minority, American women, black and white, would not be allowed to vote until 1920, thanks in great part to Lincoln.

1033. Nicolay and Hay, ALCW, Vol. 1, p. 241.

1034. Garraty and McCaughey, p. 254.

1035. Quarles, p. 235.

1036. Harwell, pp. 27-28.

1037. Lincoln could not always ignore, or hide, his Southern blood. When the song *Dixie* was first played for him he said: **"Now that is one of the best tunes I have ever heard."** C. Johnson, p. 53.

1038. Catton, Vol. 1, p. 86.

1039. Nicolay and Hay, ALCW, Vol. 1, p. 564.

1040. Litwack, NS, p. 64.

1041. Rosenbaum and Brinkley, s.v. "Lincoln and Douglas."

1042. J. M. McPherson, NCW, p. 77.

1043. Nicolay and Hay, ALCW, Vol. 1, p. 174.
1044. Helper, NQC, p. 281.
1045. Helper, ICS, p. 184.
1046. H. C. Bailey, p. 195; Ashe, p. 59.
1047. See e.g., Nicolay and Hay, ALCW, Vol. 1, p. 609.
1048. Ashe, p. 15.
1049. See e.g., Nicolay and Hay, ALCW, Vol. 1, pp. 257, 259, 449, 469.
1050. H. C. Bailey, pp. 139, 141.
1051. Hacker, p. 542.
1052. Katcher, BA, p. 24.
1053. W. S. Powell, p. 128.
1054. H. C. Bailey, p. 59.
1055. Welles, Vol. 1, p. 152.
1056. W. C. Fowler, p. 205.
1057. L. Johnson, p. 54; DeGregorio, s.v. "Abraham Lincoln."
1058. Nicolay and Hay, ALCW, Vol. 1, p. 605.
1059. C. Adams, p. 159.
1060. Nicolay and Hay, ALCW, Vol. 1, p. 608. Jefferson's words are from his autobiography, written in 1821, when he was seventy-seven years old. See Foley, p. 816.
1061. Nicolay and Hay, ALCW, Vol. 1, p. 175.
1062. W. B. Garrison, LNOK, p. 186; DiLorenzo, LU, p. 28.
1063. Nicolay and Hay, ALCW, Vol. 1, p. 299.
1064. W. B. Garrison, LNOK, p. 186; DiLorenzo, LU, p. 28.
1065. Fogel, p. 252.
1066. Website: www.slavenorth.com/colonize.htm.
1067. Nye, p. 20.
1068. Meltzer, Vol. 2, p. 139; Cartmell, p. 26; Norwood, p. 31.
1069. G. H. Moore, pp. 5, 11, 17-19.
1070. Some 12,000 to 15,000 American blacks were eventually deported to Liberia, many of them under Lincoln. But their "liberation" was short-lived: conditions were so despicable that hundreds died before they could find a way back to the U.S. To this day, the descendants of these 19th-Century inhabitants are still called "Americo-Liberians," and make up 10 percent of the nation's population. This group is to be contrasted with the other 90 percent, the native, indigenous population of Africans, with whom they share ongoing rivalries and disputes in this, Africa's oldest black republic. Rosenbaum, s.v. "Liberia"; Nye, p. 17; Brunner, s.v. "Liberia."
1071. Nicolay and Hay, ALCW, Vol. 1, p. 234. Actually, Lincoln was wrong: later scientific studies, such as those done by Edward Byron Reuter, revealed that

the percentage of mulattos went up only *after* slavery ended. Reuter, pp. 120-122. Thus there was almost no connection between slavery and "amalgamation" (race mixing), as Lincoln derogatorily referred to it. See Fogel and Engerman, pp. 130-136.
1072. Wilson and Ferris, s.v. "Miscegenation."
1073. Nicolay and Hay, ALCW, Vol. 1, pp. 175-176.
1074. Nicolay and Hay, ALCW, Vol. 2, pp. 102-103.
1075. Nicolay and Hay, ALAH, Vol. 6, p. 356. See also pp. 357-358.
1076. De Angelis, p. 49.
1077. W. Wilson, DR, p. 125.
1078. Nicolay and Hay, ALCW, Vol. 1, p. 659. Lincoln made this statement in a "strictly confidential" letter to North Carolinian John A. Gilmer, on December 15, 1860. The president-elect was interested in appointing Gilmer secretary of the treasury. Desperate to have a Southerner in his cabinet, in his letter Lincoln laid out his position on slavery, hoping to allay any fears Gilmer might have about the future of the institution. Gilmer saw through it and the ploy failed. New Englander Salmon P. Chase became Lincoln's first secretary of the treasury.
1079. Nicolay and Hay, ALCW, Vol. 2, pp. 144-145.
1080. *The National Almanac* (1863), p. 250.
1081. Nicolay and Hay, ALCW, Vol. 2, p. 144.
1082. Nicolay and Hay, ALCW, Vol. 2, p. 205.
1083. Nicolay and Hay, ALCW, Vol. 2, pp. 262-263.
1084. Cornish, p. 95.
1085. Nicolay and Hay, ALCW, Vol. 2, p. 270.
1086. Nicolay and Hay, ALCW, Vol. 2, p. 271.
1087. Nicolay and Hay, ALCW, Vol. 2, p. 271.
1088. Nicolay and Hay, ALCW, Vol. 2, p. 274.
1089. Nicolay and Hay, ALCW, Vol. 2, p. 274.
1090. C. Johnson, p. 182.
1091. Nicolay and Hay, ALCW, Vol. 2, p. 477.
1092. Lemire, passim.
1093. W. B. Garrison, LNOK, p. 186; DiLorenzo, LU, p. 28.
1094. Nicolay and Hay, ALCW, Vol. 1, pp. 187, 288.
1095. See Holzer, p. 49.
1096. Nicolay and Hay, ALCW, Vol. 2, p. 605.
1097. Current, LNK, pp. 221-222.
1098. Pomeroy, though a Kansas politician, was born in Massachusetts, birthplace of both the American slave trade and American slavery. He died in the Bay State in 1891 and is buried at Forest Hills Cemetery, in Boston.
1099. DiLorenzo, RL, p. 18.

1100. Foote, Vol. 2, p. 638. Grant uttered this remark in a letter to Elihu B. Washburne, August 30, 1863.
1101. U. S. Grant, Vol. 1, p. 215.
1102. Rutherford, FA, p. 38; Wallechinsky, Wallace, and Wallace, p. 11; Woods, p. 67.
1103. DiLorenzo, RL, pp. 15-16.
1104. Manning, p. 26.
1105. Tocqueville, Vol. 1, pp. 383-385.
1106. Buckingham, Vol. 2, p. 112.
1107. Hawthorne, Vol. 2, pp. 109-110.
1108. Peterson, JM, p. 377.
1109. Martineau, Vol. 2, pp. 7-8.
1110. Sturge, p. 40.
1111. Dicey, Vol. 1, pp. 70-72.
1112. *The Liberator*, August 15, 1862.
1113. See Nicolay and Hay, ALCW, Vol. 2, p. 612.
1114. Findlay and Findlay, p. 164.
1115. Wade, p. 148.
1116. W. P. Pickett, p. 317.
1117. C. Johnson, p.182.
1118. Nicolay and Hay, ALCW, Vol. 2, pp. 237-238.
1119. Nicolay and Hay, ALCW, Vol. 2, pp. 242-243. Lincoln's letter to Hamlin concerned the Preliminary Emancipation Proclamation issued on September 22, 1862. The Final Emancipation Proclamation, issued on January 1, 1863, had much the same effect: nothing happened.
1120. Basler, ALWS, p. 471.
1121. W. P. Pickett, pp. 328, 330. Lincoln's death in April 1865, at Booth's hands, allowed the Radicals (abolitionists) in his party to take over the government, after which they pushed through the Thirteenth Amendment in December 1865. It was this bill, not Lincoln's Emancipation Proclamation, that finally ended slavery across the entire U.S. In this sense then, Booth was the "Great Emancipator," not Lincoln.
1122. M. Perry, p. 49.
1123. Most white Northern abolitionists and colonizationists only finally abandoned their belief in black colonization when they realized that 99 percent of all African-Americans were not interested in it. Rosenbaum and Brinkley, s.v. "Colonization."
1124. Rosenbaum and Brinkley, s.v. "Colonization."
1125. L. Johnson, p. 54.
1126. Gragg, pp. 218-220.

1127. After the War, as the Davises were fleeing, Union troops caught up with them in Georgia and tore the screaming, sobbing boy away from his adoptive mother Varina. The Davis family was never able to find out what became of little Jim Limber, the beloved son who they had raised and educated as their own. Even after his death, Lincoln's devotees, propagandists, and mythographers continued to suppress the truth about the South, for had the public known about Jefferson Davis' black son, Lincoln's assault on Dixie would not have seemed so righteous. See C. Johnson, pp. 187-188.
1128. J. Davis, RFCG, Vol. 2, p. 701.
1129. Shenkman and Reiger, p. 124.
1130. J. Davis, RFCG, Vol. 1, p. 518.
1131. Barrow, Segars, and Rosenburg, BC, p. 4; Mullen, p. 31; L. Johnson, p. 134.
1132. Meltzer, Vol. 2, p. 127.
1133. Drescher and Engerman, p. 165.
1134. See e.g., Wiley, SN, pp. 64-66; Barrow, Segars, and Rosenburg, BC, pp. 4, 155-156; Fox-Genovese, pp. 133-134; Wiley, LJR, p. 328; Golay, p. 25; Olmsted, CK, Vol. 1, p. 39.
1135. Strain, p. 52.
1136. Hurst, p. 330.
1137. Seabrook, NBF, p. 67.
1138. Hacker, p. 584.
1139. See e.g., Nicolay and Hay, ALCW, Vol. 2, p. 126.
1140. Quarles, pp. 146-147.
1141. Nicolay and Hay, ALCW, Vol. 2, pp. 222-225.
1142. R. L. Riley, p. 109.
1143. Quarles, p. 148.
1144. Oates, AL, p. 103. See also Janessa Hoyte, "Taking Another Look at Abraham Lincoln," *The Crisis*, November/December 2000, pp. 52-54.
1145. *Douglass' Monthly*, September, 1862, Vol. 5, pp. 707-708.
1146. See the *National Anti-Slavery Standard*, September 6, 1862.
1147. See Seabrook, AL, pp. 478-485; Remsburg, passim; Christian, p. 7; Meriwether, pp. 54-55; Oates, AL, pp. 5, 40, 53; Current, LNK, pp. 58, 60-61; Kane, p. 163; *Southern Review*, January 1873, Vol. 12, No. 25, p. 364; Lamon, LAL, pp. 488, 489, 493; W. B. Garrison, LNOK, p. 265; Barton, p. 146; DeGregorio, s.v. "Abraham Lincoln."
1148. Fogel, pp. 31-32; Remsburg, passim.
1149. Meltzer, Vol. 2, p. 127.
1150. Fogel and Engerman, pp. 23-24. Contrary to Northern mythology, of the South's 3.5 million black servants, only 14 percent (or about 500,000

individuals) were brought from Africa by Yankees between the settling of Jamestown, Virginia, and 1861. The other 3 million (86 percent), all American-born, were the result of natural reproduction. Garraty and McCaughey, p. 214.
1151. Blight, p. 141.
1152. *An Appeal*, pp. 4, 7-8.
1153. W. W. Brown, pp. 258-259.
1154. Nicolay and Hay, ALCW, Vol. 2, p. 495.
1155. Nicolay and Hay, ALCW, Vol. 2, p. 605.
1156. B. F. Butler, p. 903. See also W. P. Pickett, p. 326; M. Davis, pp. 147-148; Adams and Sanders, p. 192.
1157. B. F. Butler, p. 903. See also W. P. Pickett, pp. 326-327.
1158. B. F. Butler, p. 907.
1159. For more on Lincoln, black colonization, and white separatism, see Seabrook, AL, passim; Seabrook, EYWTAASIW, passim; Seabrook, EYWTAAAATCWIW, passim; Seabrook, L, passim; Seabrook, TUAL, passim; Seabrook, TGI, passim; Seabrook, S101, passim.
1160. Nicolay and Hay, Vol. 2, p. 213.
1161. Nicolay and Hay, ALCW, Vol. 2, pp. 237-238.
1162. Nicolay and Hay, ALCW, Vol. 2, p. 285.
1163. Nicolay and Hay, ALCW, Vol. 2, pp. 287-288.
1164. Nicolay and Hay, ALCW, Vol. 2, p. 237.
1165. D. H. Donald, LR, p. 203.
1166. Nicolay and Hay, ALCW, Vol. 2, pp. 402-403.
1167. Nicolay and Hay, ALCW, Vol. 2, p. 234.
1168. Nicolay and Hay, ALCW, Vol. 2, p. 453.
1169. Nicolay and Hay, ALCW, Vol. 2, p. 509.
1170. Coffin, pp. 330-331; Nicolay and Hay, ALCW, Vol. 2, p. 479.
1171. Nicolay and Hay, ALCW, Vol. 2, pp. 479-480.
1172. Nicolay and Hay, ALCW, Vol. 2, pp. 508-509.
1173. Nicolay and Hay, ALCW, Vol. 2, p. 562.
1174. Nicolay and Hay, ALCW, Vol. 2, p. 288.
1175. R. L. Mode, p. 31.
1176. According to a September 11, 1863, letter from Lincoln to Tennessee Governor Andrew Johnson: **"All of Tennessee is now clear of armed insurrectionists."** Nicolay and Hay, ALCW, Vol. 2, p. 405.
1177. Cromie, p. 248.
1178. It was Tennessean Andrew Johnson, acting as military governor of that state from 1862 to 1864, who persuaded Lincoln to leave Tennessee out of the Final Emancipation Proclamation, which essentially allowed slavery to continue in the state unhindered. DeGregorio, s.v. "Andrew Johnson."

1179. Wallechinsky, Wallace, and Wallace, p. 11; Woods, p. 67.
1180. See Eaton, HSC, p. 93; Hinkle, p. 125.
1181. Kane, s.v. "Abraham Lincoln."
1182. Piatt, p. 150.
1183. Nicolay and Hay, ALCW, Vol. 2, p. 288.
1184. Nicolay and Hay, ALCW, Vol. 2, p. 287.
1185. Nicolay and Hay, ALCW, Vol. 2, p. 454.
1186. Pollard, SHW, Vol. 1, p. 364.
1187. Gragg, p. 88.
1188. Current, LNK, p. 228.
1189. Rosenbaum and Brinkley, s.v. "Underground Railroad."
1190. Gragg, pp. 191-192.
1191. Dawson, pp. 211-212.
1192. See e.g., Nicolay and Hay, ALCW, Vol. 2, pp. 473-474.
1193. White, Foscue, and McKnight, p. 212. We will note that there were also white sharecroppers. Wilson and Ferris, s.v. "Plantations."
1194. Fogel and Engerman, pp. 23-24.
1195. Scott and Stowe, p. 321. Dr. Washington's "expectation" was fulfilled. He was buried in Tuskegee, Alabama, on November 17, 1915.
1196. S. Andrews, pp. 128-129, 130.
1197. Cooper, JDA, p. 690.
1198. D. H. Donald, LR, p. 203.
1199. ORA, Ser. 3, Vol. 2, p. 314.
1200. See ORA, Ser. 3, Vol. 1, p. 133.
1201. Mullen, p. 19. As noted above, racist Lincoln at first also prohibited Native-Americans from serving in the U.S. Army, even though many volunteered. D. Brown, p. 179.
1202. Nicolay and Hay, ALCW, Vol. 2, p. 513.
1203. See e.g., Nicolay and Hay, ALCW, Vol. 1, p. 539.
1204. Nicolay and Hay, ALCW, Vol. 1, p. 257.
1205. Mullen, p. 19.
1206. See e.g., Nicolay and Hay, ALCW, Vol. 2, pp. 192-193.
1207. Marshall, Vol. 4, pp. 63-64.
1208. Alotta, p. 188; Wiley, LBY, p. 407; Zinn, p. 232.
1209. L. Johnson, p. 131.
1210. Mullen, pp. 19-21.
1211. Nicolay and Hay, ALCW, Vol. 2, p. 198.
1212. Nicolay and Hay, ALCW, Vol. 2, p. 398.
1213. DiLorenzo, LU, pp. 138, 139, 147, 159.
1214. W. B. Garrison, LNOK, pp. 174-177.

1215. L. Johnson, p. 133.
1216. Mullen, p. 22.
1217. Nicolay and Hay, ALCW, Vol. 2, p. 576.
1218. Nicolay and Hay, ALCW, Vol. 2, p. 288.
1219. Nicolay and Hay, ALCW, Vol. 2, p. 384.
1220. Nicolay and Hay, ALCW, Vol. 2, p. 453.
1221. Nicolay and Hay, ALCW, Vol. 2, p. 298.
1222. Nicolay and Hay, ALCW, Vol. 2, p. 318.
1223. A grunt is a low-ranking soldier, typically an infantryman, who performs routine often repugnant work or heavy labor.
1224. Nicolay and Hay, ALCW, Vol. 2, pp. 318-319.
1225. Nicolay and Hay, ALCW, Vol. 2, p. 235. Lincoln had a right to be worried. In thousands of cases this is precisely what happened.
1226. Nicolay and Hay, ALCW, Vol. 2, p. 428.
1227. Nicolay and Hay, ALCW, Vol. 2, p. 428.
1228. Barrow, Segars, and Rosenburg, BC, p. 4; Mullen, p. 31.
1229. L. Johnson, p. 134.
1230. Nicolay and Hay, ALCW, Vol. 2, pp. 215-216.
1231. Nicolay and Hay, ALAH, Vol. 9, p. 184.
1232. Brockett, pp. 308-315. We will note here that *everything* Greeley says in his letter to Lincoln concerning the South is false. Since it is outside the scope of this book to address all of these falsehoods and slanders, I direct the reader to my books that do: *Everything You Were Taught About the Civil War Is Wrong, Ask A Southerner!*; *A Rebel Born: A Defense of Nathan Bedford Forrest*; *Abraham Lincoln: The Southern View*; and *The McGavocks of Carnton Plantation: A Southern History*.
1233. Nicolay and Hay, ALCW, Vol. 2, pp. 227-228.
1234. Rhodes, Vol. 3, p. 545.
1235. Owsley, KCD, pp. 187-191.
1236. Pollard, SHW, Vol. 2, pp. 372-373; Woods, 66.
1237. As a reminder: the Republicans of Lincoln's day were what we would now call Democrats (liberals), while the Democrats of that time period were what we would today refer to as Republicans (conservatives).
1238. Nicolay and Hay, ALCW, Vol. 2, p. 1.
1239. L. Johnson, p. 131.
1240. Rice, RAL, p. 533.
1241. Mullen, p. 19.
1242. W. B. Garrison, LNOK, pp. 229-230.
1243. Tarbell, Vol. 2, p. 201.
1244. Nicolay and Hay, ALCW, Vol. 2, p. 454.
1245. Greenberg and Waugh, p. xi.

1246. McClure, AL, p. 83.
1247. D. H. Donald, LR, p. 80; Simmons, s.v. "Lincoln, Abraham."
1248. Nicolay and Hay, ALCW, Vol. 2, p. 129.
1249. Nicolay and Hay, ALCW, Vol. 2, p. 380.
1250. See e.g., E. L. Jordan, p. 295.
1251. See e.g., Nicolay and Hay, ALCW, Vol. 2, p. 492.
1252. See e.g., Nicolay and Hay, ALCW, Vol. 1, p. 574.
1253. Website: http://teachingamericanhistory.org/library/index.asp?document=1028.
1254. Current, LNK, pp. 221-222. See also Delbanco, pp. 260-263.
1255. DiLorenzo, RL, pp. 23-34.
1256. Nicolay and Hay, ALCW, Vol. 1, p. 197.
1257. See DiLorenzo, LU, p. 101.
1258. *The Congressional Globe*, 36th Congress, 1st Session, p. 58; Carey, p. 181.
1259. Current, LNK, p. 225.
1260. W. B. Garrison, LNOK, p. 181.
1261. Nicolay and Hay, ALCW, Vol. 2, p. 550.
1262. Current, LNK, p. 245.
1263. Litwack, NS, p. 277.
1264. Nicolay and Hay, ALCW, Vol. 2, p. 296; Current, LNK, pp. 239-240.
1265. Nicolay and Hay, ALAH, Vol. 10, p. 123; DiLorenzo, LU, pp. 24, 25.
1266. L. Johnson, p. 141.
1267. W. S. Powell, p. 144.
1268. See Current, LNK, pp. 223, 239, 240, 241.
1269. Nicolay and Hay, ALCW, Vol. 2, p. 529.
1270. Harwell, p. 307.
1271. Nicolay and Hay, ALCW, Vol. 2, p. 568.
1272. Nicolay and Hay, ALCW, Vol. 2, p. 91.
1273. Mish, s.v. "apprentice."
1274. Nicolay and Hay, ALCW, Vol. 2, p. 673.
1275. Nicolay and Hay, ALCW, Vol. 2, p. 91.
1276. Warner, s.v. "John Alexander McClernand."
1277. Nicolay and Hay, ALCW, Vol. 2, p. 296.
1278. Nicolay and Hay, ALCW, Vol. 1, p. 614.
1279. Nicolay and Hay, ALCW, Vol. 2, pp. 563-564.
1280. Nicolay and Hay, ALCW, Vol. 2, p. 614.
1281. Nicolay and Hay, ALCW, Vol. 2, p. 633.
1282. Nicolay and Hay, ALAH, Vol. 10, p. 123.
1283. See Nicolay and Hay, ALCW, Vol. 2, pp. 650-651. For the complete official view from Lincoln and the North's perspective, see pp. 639-651.

1284. [Stephens' footnote concerning what would become the Thirteenth Amendment] Be it Resolved by the Senate and House of Representatives of the United States in Congress assembled: That the following article be proposed to the Legislatures of the several States, as an amendment to the Constitution of the United States, which, when ratified by three-fourths of said Legislatures, shall be valid to all intents and purposes, as a part of said Constitution, namely: Article XIII. Section 1. Neither slavery nor involuntary servitude, except as a punishment for crime, whereof the party shall have been duly convicted, shall exist within the United States, or any place subject to their jurisdiction. Section 2. Congress shall have power to enforce this article by appropriate legislation.

1285. The "anecdote" Stephens refers to is as follows: "An Illinois farmer was congratulating himself with a neighbor upon a great discovery he had made, by which he would economize much time and labor in gathering and taking care of the food crop for his hogs, as well as trouble in looking after and feeding them during the winter. 'What is it?' said the neighbor. 'Why, it is,' said the farmer, 'to plant plenty of potatoes, and when they are mature, without either digging or housing them, turn the hogs in the field and let them get their own food as they want it.' 'But,' said the neighbor, 'how will they do when the winter corn and the ground is hard frozen ?' 'Well,' said the farmer, 'let 'em root!' Stephens, Vol. 2, p. 615. This story, related by Lincoln to the group at the Hampton Roads Conference, was his way of explaining how he handled the fact that he had freed millions of slaves without job training, education, housing, loans, or grants. "Let them root, pig, or perish," Lincoln explained. See also Stephens, RAHS, pp. 83, 137.

1286. Stephens, Vol. 2, pp. 610-615.

1287. L. Johnson, p. 129; C. Adams, pp. 134-135; Foote, Vol. 1, pp. 95-97.

1288. Foote, Vol. 1, pp. 242-243.

1289. W. B. Garrison, LNOK, 136-141; Foote, Vol. 1, p. 535.

1290. Katcher, CWSB, p. 158.

1291. Neely, p. 35.

1292. Lester, pp. 359-360.

1293. W. B. Garrison, LNOK, p. 192.

1294. McGehee, p. 81; Meriwether, p. 159.

1295. Dawson was related to Lincoln through marriage: Dawson's wife, Elodie Todd, was the half-sister of Lincoln's wife Mary Todd, making Elodie Lincoln's sister-in-law. Dawson then, was Lincoln's brother-in-law.

1296. D. H. Donald, LR, pp. 19-20.

1297. Nicolay and Hay, ALCW, Vol. 2, pp. 234-236.

1298. Nicolay and Hay, ALCW, Vol. 1, p. 531.

1299. Fogel, p. 207.

1300. In other words, it cost Americans ten times more to fight and kill each other for four years than if they would have simply ended slavery (more proof that Lincoln's War was not over slavery). Rutland, p. 226. See also C. Johnson, p. 200.

1301. On March 9, 1862, Lincoln wrote to Henry Jarvis Raymond: **"Have you noticed the facts that less than one half day's cost of this war would pay for all the slaves in Delaware at $400 per head—that eighty-seven days' cost of this war would pay for all in Delaware, Maryland, District of Columbia, Kentucky, and Missouri at the same price? Were those States to take the step, do you doubt that it would shorten the war more than eighty-seven days, and thus be an actual saving of expense?"** Nicolay and Hay, ALCW, Vol. 2, p. 132. See also pp. 137-138.

1302. Rosenbaum and Brinkley, s.v. "Lincoln and Douglas."

1303. Thornton and Ekelund, p. 96.

1304. Haggard, p. 90.

1305. Stephens, RAHS, pp. 83, 137; Stephens, CV, Vol. 2, p. 615.

1306. Mullen, p. 33; Rosenbaum and Brinkley, s.v. "Forty Acres and a Mule."

1307. J. H. Franklin, p. 37.

1308. Grissom, p. 162.

1309. Foner, R, pp. 70-71.

1310. Thornton and Ekelund, p. 96.

1311. K. C. Davis, p. 427.

1312. Bailyn, Dallek, Davis, Donald, Thomas, and Wood, p. 16.

1313. K. C. Davis, p. 426.

1314. Buckley, p. 116.

1315. Web: www.archives.gov/nae/news/featured-programs/lincoln/080920Lincoln02 Transcript.pdf.

1316. Page, p. 38.

1317. C. Adams, pp. 139-140.

1318. At Columbia, South Carolina, for example, Sherman and his henchmen torched the once beautiful city, and along with it, "some of the finest private libraries in the South." S. Andrews, p. 35. One of the more conspicuous schools destroyed by Lincoln's soldiers was the University of Alabama, which Yankee troops mercilessly and needlessly burned to the ground on the eve of the end of the War in April 1865. Along with the destruction of the school was her enormous library, filled with rare one-of-a-kind books, now forever lost to history. C. Johnson, p. 157.

1319. For more on Lincoln and the Emancipation Proclamation, see Seabrook, AL, passim; Seabrook, EYWTAASIW, passim; Seabrook, EYWTAAAATCWIW, passim; Seabrook, L, passim; Seabrook, TUAL, passim;

Seabrook, TGI, passim; Seabrook, S101, passim.
1320. Nicolay and Hay, ALCW, Vol. 1, pp. 186-187.
1321. Nicolay and Hay, ALCW, Vol. 1, p. 105.
1322. Nicolay and Hay, ALCW, Vol. 1, p. 291.
1323. Nicolay and Hay, ALCW, Vol. 1, pp. 605-611.
1324. C. Adams, p. 89.
1325. M. M. Smith, pp. 4-5.
1326. Nicolay and Hay, ALCW, Vol. 1, p. 581.
1327. Nicolay and Hay, CWAL, Vol. 11, p. 106.
1328. Fogel and Engerman, pp. 78-86.
1329. Nicolay and Hay, ALCW, Vol. 1, p. 218.
1330. Nicolay and Hay, ALCW, Vol. 2, p. 34.
1331. Timothy D. Manning, Sr., personal correspondence. Some Southern historians, like Manning, estimate that Lincoln's War took the lives of as many as 1 million Northerners and 2 million Southerners. These figures include all races and both noncombatants and black slaves, men, women, and children. Additionally, it is important to note that nearly *all* civilian deaths occurred in the South. While the exact Southern death toll is not known, and will never be known, Jefferson Davis estimated that Lincoln killed at least half of the South's Negro population, or about 1,750,000 black men, women, and children, free and bonded. See F. Moore, pp. 278-279. You will never find this statistic in any pro-North, anti-South book.
1332. Nicolay and Hay, ALCW, Vol. 2, p. 657.
1333. Nicolay and Hay, ALCW, Vol. 2, p. 657.
1334. Nicolay and Hay, ALCW, Vol. 2, p. 439.
1335. See Napolitano, p. 8.
1336. Thornton and Ekelund, pp. 98-99.
1337. C. Adams, pp. 198-199; Woods, p. 75.
1338. A. Cooke, ACA, p. 214. Contrary to Northern mythology, Lincoln's Gettysburg Address was not received with rapt attention, constant cheers, tear swollen eyes, and thunderous applause. Lincoln's own reaction to its reception tells it all: **". . . that speech fell on the audience like a wet blanket. I am distressed about it."** Lamon, RAL, p. 173. **"It is a flat failure and the people are disappointed,"** Lincoln told his friend Ward Hill Lamon. Christian, p. 27. Victorian Americans, of course, had not yet been blinded by the anti-South movement's postwar political deification of Lincoln. Instead, at the time most saw him simply as what he really was: a demagogic rhetorician reciting vacuous nonsense.
1339. One writer has gone so far as to name his book, *Lincoln's Gettysburg Address: Echoes of the Bible and Book of Common Prayer*. This despite the fact that, as we will see, Lincoln was an unwavering anti-Christian and a devout atheist who despised

the Bible and never prayed.
1340. Nicolay and Hay, ALCW, Vol. 2, pp. 586-587.
1341. See Stephens, CV, Vol. 1, pp. 504-505.
1342. See Jensen, NN, passim; AC, passim.
1343. W. B. Garrison, CWTFB, p. 109.
1344. See e.g., Nicolay and Hay, ALCW, Vol. 2, pp. 39, 85.
1345. DiLorenzo, RL, pp. 132, 134-142, 150, 151.
1346. Nicolay and Hay, ALCW, Vol. 2, p. 535.
1347. Pollard, LC, p. 93.
1348. Meriwether, p. 9.
1349. Stephens, SMS, p. 14.
1350. Basler, ALSW, pp. 382-383.
1351. DeGregorio, s.v. "James K. Polk."
1352. Nicolay and Hay, ALCW, Vol. 1, pp. 197, 508.
1353. Nicolay and Hay, ALCW, Vol. 2, p. 614.
1354. Rosenbaum and Brinkley, s.v. "Civil War"; Weintraub, p. 70; Eaton, p. 94.
1355. U. S. Grant, Vol. 2, p. 345.
1356. U. S. Grant, Vol. 2, p. 167. For more on Lincoln and his War, see Seabrook, LW, passim.
1357. L. Johnson, p. 124.
1358. Grissom, p. 155.
1359. Rutland, p. 226.
1360. Neely, pp. 113-116.
1361. Dilorenzo, LU, p. 168.
1362. Burns and Peltason, p. 192.
1363. Nicolay and Hay, ALCW, Vol. 2, pp. 541-542.
1364. L. Johnson, pp. 124-125.
1365. See e.g., Nicolay and Hay, ALCW, Vol. 2, p. 521.
1366. Hacker, p. 586.
1367. Mirabello, p. 164.
1368. A. Cooke, ACA, p. 216.
1369. Napolitano, p. 75.
1370. See e.g., Nicolay and Hay, ALCW, Vol. 2, p. 38.
1371. J. Davis, RFCG, Vol. 2, pp. 460-468. For more on Lincoln's illegal subjugation of Maryland, see Pollard, LC, pp. 123-125.
1372. ORA, Ser. 1, Vol. 19, Pt. 2, pp. 601-602.
1373. Nicolay and Hay, ALCW, Vol. 2, p. 103.
1374. Nicolay and Hay, ALCW, Vol. 1, pp. 187, 288.
1375. Nicolay and Hay, ALCW, Vol. 2, p. 584.

1376. Nicolay and Hay, ALCW, Vol. 2, p. 612.
1377. Article 4, amendment. [Davis' footnote.]
1378. Article 5, amendment. [Davis' footnote.]
1379. Article 5, amendment. [Davis' footnote.]
1380. Article 6, amendment. [Davis' footnote.]
1381. Article 1, Section 9. [Davis' footnote.]
1382. The first act of Congress providing for an enrollment and draft was passed on March 3, 1363, three and a half months later than this order. [Davis' footnote.]
1383. See Nicolay and Hay, ALCW, Vol. 2, p. 407.
1384. J. Davis, RFCG, Vol. 2, pp. 477-496.
1385. Harwell, p. 137; Commager and Bruun, p. 581.
1386. Nicolay and Hay, ALCW, Vol. 2, p. 59.
1387. D. H. Donald, WNWCW, p. 87.
1388. Lincoln imposed the nation's first income tax under the Revenue Act of 1861, lessening the distance the Founders had purposefully created between the central government and the American people. Napolitano, p. 74. Now, every April 15, Americans can thank Lincoln for creating the department that would become the IRS.
1389. Hacker, p. 585.
1390. Rubenzer and Faschingbauer, p. 224.
1391. L. Johnson, p. 125.
1392. See Nicolay and Hay, ALCW, Vol. 2, pp. 333-334. Lincoln once admitted that foreigners were vital to his war effort, saying: **"I regard our emigrants as one of the principle replenishing streams which are appointed by Providence to repair the ravages of internal war, and its wastes of national strength and health."** Nicolay and Hay, ALCW, Vol. 2, p. 607.
1393. Napolitano, p. 69.
1394. L. Johnson, p. 125.
1395. D. H. Donald, WNWCW, p. 87.
1396. C. Adams, p. 43.
1397. Nicolay and Hay, ALCW, Vol. 2, pp. 523-524.
1398. Findlay and Findlay, pp. 196-197.
1399. Findlay and Findlay, pp. 202-203.
1400. Nicolay and Hay, ALCW, Vol. 2, p. 595.
1401. Nicolay and Hay, ALCW, Vol. 2, p. 559.
1402. Nicolay and Hay, ALCW, Vol. 2, pp. 578-579.
1403. Vallandigham, pp. 320-322.
1404. Grissom, p. 154.

1405. Shenkman and Reiger, pp. 129-130; DiLorenzo, LU, p. 163.
1406. Nicolay and Hay, ALCW, Vol. 2, p. 338.
1407. Nicolay and Hay, ALCW, Vol. 2, p. 342.
1408. K. L. Hall, s.v. "Lincoln, Abraham."
1409. Nicolay and Hay, ALCW, Vol. 2, p. 349.
1410. Curti, Thorpe, and Baker, p. 553.
1411. Nye, p. 184.
1412. Daugherty, p. 214.
1413. Hesseltine, pp. 381, 382, 384. See also D. H. Donald, LR, p. 80; Simmons, s.v. "Lincoln, Abraham." For more on Lincoln and his War, see Seabrook, LW, passim.
1414. Nicolay and Hay, ALCW, Vol. 1, p. 142.
1415. Woodworth, p. xi; Zinn, p. 129.
1416. C. Johnson, pp. 119-120. Lincoln later **"painfully"** admitted that he was **"not a military man."** Nicolay and Hay, ALCW, Vol. 2, p. 218.
1417. Findlay and Findlay, pp. 84-85.
1418. Crocker, p. 59.
1419. Scruggs, p. 24; Napolitano, p. 69.
1420. Neely, pp. 172-175.
1421. Tatalovich and Daynes, p. 322.
1422. L. Johnson, p. 125. See e.g., Nicolay and Hay, ALCW, Vol. 2, p. 416.
1423. DiLorenzo, LU, p. 52.
1424. See e.g., Nicolay and Hay, ALCW, Vol. 2, p. 521.
1425. Neely, pp. 109-112.
1426. See e.g., Nicolay and Hay, ALCW, Vol. 2, p. 417.
1427. See e.g., Nicolay and Hay, ALCW, Vol. 2, pp. 486, 489-490.
1428. Mitgang, p. 402; D. H. Donald, L, p. 385.
1429. Nicolay and Hay, ALCW, Vol. 2, pp. 442-444.
1430. Nicolay and Hay, ALCW, Vol. 2, pp. 541-542.
1431. Burns and Peltason, p. 192. For other examples of Lincoln's suspension of *habeas corpus*, see Nicolay and Hay, ALCW, Vol. 2, pp. 39, 54, 85, 93, 239, 406-407.
1432. See Nicolay and Hay, ALCW, Vol. 2, pp. 60, 124. Lincoln believed, without proof, that during civil disruption the president possessed certain powers not available to him during times of peace. As he himself said: **"I *think* the Constitution invests its Commander-in-Chief with the law of war in time of war"** [emphasis added]. Nicolay and Hay, ALCW, Vol. 2, p. 397.
1433. Christian, p. 13.
1434. Leech, p. 151; Black, p. 165. As we will recall, Lincoln later stripped Frémont of his command for freeing slaves in his assigned military area. K. C.

Davis, p. 439.

1435. Black, p. 165; Wiley, SN, pp. 296-298; Leech, pp. 305-306.

1436. Quarles, pp. 115-116.

1437. Quarles, pp. 113-114.

1438. D. H. Donald, L, p. 363; Leech, p. 155.

1439. Lincoln admitted that he nullified the emancipation proclamations of his officers because, as he put it, there was no **"indispensable necessity."** Nicolay and Hay, ALCW, Vol. 2, p. 508. The nation's 4 million slaves (North and South) must have wondered what he meant by this.

1440. W. B. Garrison, CWC, p. 13; Findlay and Findlay, pp. 84-85; C. Adams, p. 39; Owsley, pp. 79-80, 229-267; K. L. Hall, s.v. "Lincoln, Abraham"; "Civil War."

1441. Nicolay and Hay, ALCW, Vol. 2, p. 416.

1442. Nicolay and Hay, ALCW, Vol. 2, pp. 464, 491.

1443. Tyler, PH, pp. 13-14; Bailyn, Dallek, Davis, Donald, Thomas, and Wood, p. 5; Grissom, pp. 126-127; C. Adams, p. 57.

1444. Owsley, pp. 405, 401-412. For an example of Lincoln's and Seward's war threats against England, see Nicolay and Hay, ALCW, Vol. 2, pp. 48-51.

1445. Nicolay and Hay, ALCW, Vol. 2, p. 146.

1446. See Nicolay and Hay, ALCW, Vol. 2, p. 95.

1447. Gragg, p. 73; Tyler, PH, pp. 13-14.

1448. Mish, s.v. "privateer."

1449. J. Davis, RFCG, Vol. 2, pp. 460-468.

1450. Tatalovich and Daynes, p. 322.

1451. W. B. Garrison, LNOK, p. 281.

1452. C. Adams, p. 57, pp. 208-209; Grissom, pp. 126-127.

1453. Burns and Peltason, p. 437.

1454. D. H. Donald, L, pp. 429, 450, 489, 510, 539.

1455. See e.g., Nicolay and Hay, Vol. 2, pp. 131, 175, 243, 408, 498, 588, 589, 628.

1456. "Freedom Watch," FOX Business News, March 24, 2010.

1457. J. Davis, RFCG, Vol. 2, pp. 460-468. For more on Lincoln's illegal subjugation of Maryland, see Pollard, LC, pp. 123-125.

1458. See e.g., Nicolay and Hay, ALCW, Vol. 2, p. 416.

1459. DiLorenzo, LU, p. 137.

1460. Lott, p. 158.

1461. Neely, pp. 113-114.

1462. Stephens, RAHS, pp. 356-357, passim.

1463. Hacker, p. 584; Napolitano, p. 74.

1464. Christian, p. 14; Hacker, p. 581.

1465. Nicolay and Hay, ALCW, Vol. 2, p. 267; D. H. Donald, L, 392-395; W. B. Garrison, CWTFB, p. 62; C. Adams, p. 210.

1466. DiLorenzo, LU, pp. 75, 89, 90.

1467. Lincoln lied to the American public, telling them that the courts in *all* of the Confederate states had been **"suppressed,"** giving him alleged justification for imposing military rule and committing countless other crimes in the South. See Nicolay and Hay, ALCW, Vol. 2, p. 99. Actually, the courts in the Southern states remained open throughout the War. Any that were **"suppressed"** were suppressed by Lincoln himself. For an example of Lincoln's illegal establishment of a provisional court in a foreign country, in this case, the Confederate States of America, see Nicolay and Hay, ALCW, Vol. 2, pp. 248-249.

1468. E. M. Thomas, p. 152.

1469. Lincoln knew this was unconstitutional, which is why he brought the issue up with his cabinet members on December 23, 1862. Nicolay and Hay, ALCW, Vol. 2, p. 283.

1470. It is illegal for a section of a state to secede from the parent state without the parent's state's approval. Virginia never authorized the secession of West Virginia. C. Adams, p. 58. See also W. B. Garrison, LNOK, pp. 193-197; D. H. Donald, L, pp. 300-301, 405; DiLorenzo, RL, pp. 148-149.

1471. L. Johnson, pp. 123-124; Horn, IE, p. 217; DiLorenzo, LU, p. 52; Simpson, p. 62.

1472. W. B. Garrison, ACW, pp. 194-195; DeGregorio, s.v. "Abraham Lincoln"; D. H. Donald, L, p. 249.

1473. K. L. Hall, s.v. "Civil War"; Christian, pp. 4-5; C. Adams, pp. 48-49; Rosenbaum and Brinkley, s.v. "Merryman, Ex Parte"; DiLorenzo, LU, pp. 92-96.

1474. Denson, p. 8.

1475. See e.g., Nicolay and Hay, ALCW, Vol. 2, p. 106.

1476. Katcher, CWSB, pp. 176-177.

1477. Nicolay and Hay, ALCW, Vol. 2, p. 124.

1478. Findlay and Findlay, p. 136.

1479. See Nicolay and Hay, ALCW, Vol. 2, pp. 209, 213, 214, 238, 253, 333.

1480. Findlay and Findlay, p. 88.

1481. Ingersoll, p. 22; Nicolay and Hay, ALCW, Vol. 2, p. 508.

1482. Neely, p. 53.

1483. Nicolay and Hay, ALCW, Vol. 2, p. 240.

1484. Nicolay and Hay, ALCW, Vol. 2, p. 267.

1485. Warner, GB, s.v. "John Pope."

1486. Nicolay and Hay, ALCW, Vol. 2, p. 252.

1487. Nicolay and Hay, ALCW, Vol. 2, pp. 279-280.

1488. C. Adams, p. 210; W. B. Garrison, CWTFB, p. 62; D. H. Donald, L, 392-395.
1489. DiLorenzo, RL, pp. 157-158.
1490. See Nicolay and Hay, ALCW, Vol. 2, pp. 381-382.
1491. J. S. Bowman, ECW, s.v. "New York Draft Riots."
1492. DiLorenzo, RL, pp. 43-45; K. C. Davis, pp. 315-316.
1493. Crocker, p. 62.
1494. Simmons, p. 75.
1495. Buckley, p. 102.
1496. Hacker, p. 586.
1497. Buckley, p. 102.
1498. Quarles, p. 239.
1499. *Christian Recorder*, July 18, 1863. The "gloom of infamy and shame" from this incident did not "hang over New York for centuries," as this writer predicted. Most New Yorkers are still completely unaware of the fact that their town was the center of the early American slave trade, and that it is today the nation's largest, wealthiest, and most powerful city mainly because of slavery. Even fewer seem to know about the so-called "New York Draft Riots" of 1863, and the terrible racial slaughter that took place.
1500. Gilmore, p. 199.
1501. Nicolay and Hay, ALCW, Vol. 2, p. 388-391.
1502. Nicolay and Hay, ALCW, Vol. 2, pp. 477-478.
1503. *The American Annual Cyclopedia*, 1863, Vol. 3, pp. 799-800.
1504. Nicolay and Hay, ALCW, Vol. 2, pp. 345-352.
1505. As has been pointed out throughout this book, though Corning and his associates were Democrats, these were the equivalents of today's Republicans (i.e., they were small government conservatives). Conversely, Lincoln's Republican party was identical to today's Democratic party (i.e., they were big government liberals).
1506. E. McPherson, PHUSAGR, pp. 167-170.
1507. Actually Lincoln was very much against the Mexican War (see e.g., Basler, ALSW, pp. 382-383), and being a liberal—and thus one who is likely to believe in freedom of speech only for himself—it is not surprising that he wanted to censor those (mainly conservatives) who were in favor of the conflict.
1508. E. McPherson, PHUSAGR, pp. 170-172.
1509. E. McPherson, PHUSAGR, pp. 172-175.
1510. E. McPherson, PHUSAGR, pp. 175-176.
1511. *The Outlook*, Vol. 59, May 7 to August 27, 1898, p. 116 (New York, NY). Vallandigham's story was incorporated into the fictional anti-South tale *The Man Without a Country*, penned by Yankee clergyman and author Edward Everett Hale

of Roxbury, Massachusetts. The pro-Lincoln, pro-Union short story first appeared in the December 1863 issue of *The Atlantic*.
1512. Nicolay and Hay, ALCW, Vol. 2, pp. 396-399.
1513. See Seabrook, EYWTACWW, pp. 157-158. Also see, Barrow, Segars, and Rosenburg, BC, p. 97; *The United Daughters of the Confederacy Magazine*, Vols. 54-55, 1991, p. 32; Hinkle, p. 106.
1514. See Kautz, p. 11.
1515. Hinkle, p. 125.
1516. Adams and Sanders, pp. 215-216.
1517. As we will recall, Grant did not free his slaves until he was forced to by the ratification of the Thirteenth Amendment on December 6, 1865, eight months after Lincoln's War ended. Rutherford, FA, p. 38; Wallechinsky, Wallace, and Wallace, p. 11; Woods, p. 67. See also, McElroy, p. 357.
1518. Meriwether, p. 219; Stonebraker, p. 70.
1519. Nicolay and Hay, ALCW, Vol. 1, pp. 111-112.
1520. Norris, p. 165.
1521. As we have seen throughout this book, Northerners *were* practicing slavery, right up to and even during Lincoln's War—a fact that has been wickedly hidden from the public for a century and a half. That many Yankees found it difficult to give up their "peculiar institution" is not surprising: it was practiced in the North far longer than in the South, for the North was the cradle of both the American slave trade and American slavery.
1522. Nicolay and Hay, ALCW, Vol. 1, p. 288.
1523. Nicolay and Hay, ALCW, Vol. 1, p. 662.
1524. That is, the good side of his nature, as opposed to the evil one. See Nicolay and Hay, ALCW, Vol. 2, p. 7.
1525. J. M. McPherson, ACW, p. 9.
1526. Nicolay and Hay, ALCW, Vol. 2, p. 530.
1527. Logsdon, EBF, p. 36.
1528. McDonough and Connelly, p. 157.
1529. Watkins, p, 209.
1530. Fay, p. 12; C. Adams, p. 149.
1531. Hunter alone was responsible for destroying millions of dollars of Southern property in Virginia's beautiful Shenandoah Valley. His destruction included torching the town of Lexington, tearing up miles of railroad, razing factories, mills, and private residences, and burning down the Virginia Military Institute. What military advantage there was in burning down our schools is still a mystery here in the South. It was obviously just plain cruelty, both unnecessary and illegal. For more on Hunter's crimes see below, and also Gragg, pp. 88-89.
1532. DiLorenzo, LU, p. 58.
1533. Many Southerners consider *all* Yankee officers to have been war criminals.

See Christian, p. 15.
1534. Ashe, p. 57.
1535. Warner, GB, s.v. "William Tecumseh 'Cump' Sherman."
1536. ORA, Ser. 1, Vol. 38, Pt. 5, p. 688.
1537. ORA, Ser. 1, Vol. 32, Pt. 1, p. 176.
1538. See Montgomery, p. 490.
1539. ORA, Ser. 1, Vol. 32, Pt. 2, p. 498.
1540. ORA, Ser. 1, Vol. 44, p. 13.
1541. Civil War Society, CWB, s.v. "Sherman's March to the Sea."
1542. Sherman, Vol. 2, p. 231 (1891 ed.).
1543. Nicolay and Hay, ALCW, Vol. 2, p. 622.
1544. See Gragg, pp. 90-93, 175-192.
1545. Nicolay and Hay, ALCW, Vol. 2, pp. 471-472.
1546. Critics here may point to Confederate General Jubal Early's burning of Chambersburg, Pennsylvania. See Warner, GG, s.v. "Jubal Anderson Early." But this was not wantonly savage in the manner of Northern soldiers. Early had merely requested a levy of $500,000 from the town's citizens for damages made against the South, particularly for the burning of thousands of homes and farms in the Shenandoah Valley. When this was refused, he understandably set fire to the city. Simmons, s.v. "Early, Jubal Anderson"; C. Johnson, p. 160; E. M. Thomas, p. 276.
1547. Napolitano, p. 73.
1548. Gragg, pp. 177-181.
1549. J. Davis, RFCG, Vol. 2, p. 634.
1550. Hurmence, pp. 99-102; J. Davis, RFCG, Vol. 2, p. 716.
1551. Gragg, pp. 182-183, 188.
1552. Stonebraker, pp. 170-171.
1553. Gragg, pp. 169-175, 239.
1554. Gragg, p. 189.
1555. Wiley, LBY, p. 203.
1556. M. Perry, p. 223.
1557. See e.g., J. Davis, RFCG, Vol. 2, pp. 632-633; C. Johnson, p. 157; Lott, pp. 158-159; L. Johnson, p. 188; Grissom, pp. 115-116; Christian, p. 15.
1558. Gragg, pp. 192-196.
1559. W. B. Garrison, CWTFB, p. 170.
1560. Early, p. 48.
1561. ORA, Ser. 3, Vol. 4, p. 1029.
1562. Knox, p. 317.
1563. Channing, p. 131; Jimerson, p. 81; J. D. Fowler, p. 317.
1564. Nicolay and Hay, ALCW, Vol. 2, pp. 653-654.

1565. See e.g., Nicolay and Hay, ALCW, Vol. 2, p. 658.
1566. M. Davis, p. 68.
1567. Nicolay and Hay, ALCW, Vol. 2, p. 416.
1568. Nicolay and Hay, ALCW, Vol. 2, p. 635.
1569. Nicolay and Hay, ALCW, Vol. 2, pp. 392-393.
1570. Nicolay and Hay, ALCW, Vol. 2, p. 463.
1571. See e.g., Lincoln's January 24, 1865, letter to Union General Grenville Mellen Dodge. Nicolay and Hay, ALCW, Vol. 2, p. 630.
1572. Nicolay and Hay, ALCW, Vol. 2, p. 468.
1573. The OR is actually divided into the "Official Records of the Union and Confederate Armies" (ORA) and the "Official Records of the Union and Confederate Navies" (ORN).
1574. ORA, Ser. 1, Vol. 39, Pt. 3, p. 494.
1575. Sherman's March to the Sea lasted from November 15 to December 10, 1864. W. B. Garrison, CWTFB, p. 248.
1576. Sherman, Vol. 2, pp. 227-228 (1891 ed.).
1577. Letter dated September 14, 1865. J. Davis, RFCG, Vol. 2, pp. 710-711.
1578. Chesnut, DD, p. 358.
1579. Warner, GB, s.v. "Don Carlos Buell."
1580. Grimsley, p. 182.
1581. C. Adams, p. 117.
1582. S. Andrews, p. 31.
1583. Bancroft and Dunning, Vol. 3, p. 167.
1584. W. B. Garrison, CWTFB, p. 162.
1585. W. B. Garrison, CWTFB, p. 75.
1586. J. S. Bowman, ECW, s.v. "Sherman, William Tecumseh."
1587. Nicolay and Hay, ALCW, Vol. 2, p. 612.
1588. Nicolay and Hay, ALCW, Vol. 2, p. 615.
1589. Sheridan's restrictive, cruel, and overly severe policies continued even after the War. Finally, during "Reconstruction," President Andrew Johnson was forced to remove him from his post as commander of the Fifth Military District after only six months. Warner, GB, s.v. "Philip Henry Sheridan."
1590. J. C. Bradford, p. 90.
1591. Nicolay and Hay, ALCW, Vol. 2, p. 666.
1592. C. T. Brady, p. 408.
1593. E. M. Thomas, p. 284.
1594. ORA, Ser. 1, Vol. 43, Pt. 2, p. 308.
1595. Grissom, p. 116.
1596. W. B. Garrison, CWTFB, p. 211.
1597. Douglas, p. 315; Catton, Vol. 3, p. 343.

1598. ORA, Ser. 1, Vol. 18, Pt. 1, p. 811.
1599. ORA, Ser. 1, Vol. 34, Pt. 1, p. 26.
1600. ORA, Ser. 1, Vol. 8, p. 642.
1601. Cartmell, p. 16.
1602. Bailyn, Dallek, Davis, Donald, Thomas, and Wood, pp. 8, 15.
1603. Christian, p. 16.
1604. Civil War Society, CWB, s.v. "Sherman's March to the Sea."
1605. Oates, AL, p. 136.
1606. Christian, p. 18.
1607. See e.g., Nicolay and Hay, ALCW, Vol. 2, p. 494.
1608. See e.g., Nicolay and Hay, ALCW, Vol. 2, pp. 457, 461, 493, 533, 555, 573.
1609. Nicolay and Hay, ALCW, Vol. 2, p. 572. Interestingly, though an atheist, Lincoln ascribes the North's victory over the city of Atlanta, Georgia, to **"divine favor,"** not Sherman's military acumen. One wonders what the crusty red-headed general thought about this remark.
1610. Denney, p. 551. See also Nicolay and Hay, ALCW, Vol. 2, p. 556.
1611. Nicolay and Hay, ALCW, Vol. 2, p. 563. See also p. 536.
1612. Nicolay and Hay, ALCW, Vol. 2, p. 493.
1613. Nicolay and Hay, ALCW, Vol. 2, p. 494.
1614. Nicolay and Hay, ALCW, Vol. 2, p. 517.
1615. Nicolay and Hay, ALCW, Vol. 2, p. 578. Lincoln is probably referring to the Battle of Winchester, Virginia (September 19, 1864), or the Battle of Opequon Creek, as it is known to Yankees.
1616. Nicolay and Hay, ALCW, Vol. 2, p. 589.
1617. Nicolay and Hay, ALCW, Vol. 2, p. 596.
1618. Nicolay and Hay, ALCW, Vol. 2, p. 612.
1619. Nicolay and Hay, ALCW, Vol. 2, pp. 533-534.
1620. ORA, Ser. 1, Vol. 44, p. 741.
1621. J. S. Bowman, ECW, s.v. "Thanks of Congress."
1622. Christian, pp. 15, 17, 20.
1623. Bailyn, Dallek, Davis, Donald, Thomas, and Wood, p. 5.
1624. Christian, p. 30.
1625. See my books, *Nathan Bedford Forrest: Southern Hero, American Patriot*, and *A Rebel Born: A Defense of Nathan Bedford Forrest*.
1626. C. Adams, pp. 208-209.
1627. Bailyn, Dallek, Davis, Donald, Thomas, and Wood, p. 5.
1628. ORA, Ser. 1, Vol. 32, Pt. 1, pp. 118-119.
1629. Christian, pp. 15-20.
1630. Nicolay and Hay, ALCW, Vol. 2, pp. 620-621.

1631. Grissom, pp. 117-118.
1632. Grissom, p. 117.
1633. Current, TC, s.v. "Lincoln, Abraham."
1634. Stephens, CV, Vol. 2, p. 466; McElroy, p. 319.
1635. Hacker, p. 588.
1636. Richardson, Vol. 1, p. 119.
1637. Nicolay and Hay, ALCW, Vol. 2, p. 630.
1638. Nicolay and Hay, ALCW, Vol. 2, p. 180.
1639. Nicolay and Hay, ALCW, Vol. 2, p. 186.
1640. Nicolay and Hay, ALCW, Vol. 2, p. 423.
1641. Nicolay and Hay, ALCW, Vol. 2, p. 195.
1642. See e.g., Bledsoe, IDT, pp. 143-144; Christian, p. 14; Nicolay and Hay, ALCW, Vol. 2, p. 56. For more on Lincoln and his criminal activities, see Seabrook, AL, passim; Seabrook, CFF, passim.
1643. Hacker, p. 580.
1644. W. B. Garrison, CWTFB, p. 145.
1645. Garraty and McCaughey, p. 241.
1646. Nicolay and Hay, ALCW, Vol. 1, p. 688.
1647. Nicolay and Hay, ALCW, Vol. 1, p. 688.
1648. Nicolay and Hay, ALCW, Vol. 1, pp. 694-695.
1649. Hacker, p. 580.
1650. E. M. Thomas, p. 49.
1651. See Woodworth, p. 290; Lytle, pp. 271-272; N. Bradford, p. 490; Sword, CLH, pp. 33-35; Groom, pp. 49-54; J. M. McPherson, NCW, pp. 305-306; Warner, GG, s.v. "John Bell Hood." In Margaret Mitchell's powerful and factual Confederate epic, *Gone With the Wind*, Southern belle Scarlett O'Hara angrily denounces Hood, saying: He effectively abandoned Atlanta, and allowed the Yanks to overwhelm us, with only teenaged boys, prisoners, and volunteers left to defend the city. Mitchell, p. 475. Hood's incompetence at Atlanta that July boasted Lincoln's sagging approval ratings, helping to assure the unscrupulous president a second victory at the polls in November.
1652. Nicolay and Hay, ALCW, Vol. 2, p. 640.
1653. Nicolay and Hay, ALCW, Vol. 2, pp. 632, 641.
1654. Hacker, p. 589.
1655. C. Adams, p. 58; W. B. Garrison, LNOK, pp. 193-197.
1656. L. Johnson, p. 127.
1657. D. H. Donald, LR, p. 65.
1658. Hacker, p. 580.
1659. W. B. Garrison, CWTFB, p. 145.
1660. Burns, Peltason, Cronin, Magleby, and O'Brien, p. 151.

1661. Nicolay and Hay, ALCW, Vol. 2, p. 1.
1662. See Spooner, NT, No. 6, p. 54.
1663. W. B. Garrison, ACW, pp. 194-195.
1664. Nicolay and Hay, ALCW, Vol. 1, p. 669.
1665. Nicolay and Hay, ALCW, Vol. 2, p. 589.
1666. DeGregorio, s.v. "Abraham Lincoln."
1667. D. H. Donald, L, p. 249; DeGregorio, s.v. "Abraham Lincoln."
1668. Wood, pp. 47, 237.
1669. Current, LNK, p. 200.
1670. W. B. Garrison, p. LNOK, p. 75.
1671. Simmons, s.v. "Lincoln, Abraham."
1672. Nicolay and Hay, ALCW, Vol. 2, p. 528.
1673. Nicolay and Hay, ALCW, Vol. 2, p. 529.
1674. Christian, p. 25.
1675. Nicolay and Hay, ALCW, Vol. 1, p. 496.
1676. Nye, p. 185.
1677. See Basler, ALSW, p. 729.
1678. Nicolay and Hay, ALCW, Vol. 2, p. 370.
1679. D. H. Donald, L, p. 471.
1680. Nicolay and Hay, ALCW, Vol. 2, pp. 417-418.
1681. Nicolay and Hay, ALCW, Vol. 2, p. 587.
1682. Nicolay and Hay, ALCW, Vol. 2, p. 614.
1683. W. B. Garrison, LNOK, p. 214.
1684. Nicolay and Hay, ALCW, Vol. 2, pp. 577-578.
1685. ORA, Ser. 1, Vol. 45, Pt. 1, p. 1034.
1686. D. H. Donald, WNWCW, pp. 87, 89-90.
1687. Ashe, p. 60.
1688. Nicolay and Hay, ALCW, Vol. 2, p. 495.
1689. Fishback was the author of the pro-South Fishback Amendment, which prohibited legislature from paying fraudulent bonds issued by Lincoln's party during so-called "Reconstruction" (this was just another transparent attempt by liberal Northerners, carpetbaggers, and scallywags to punish the South economically). Fishback was elected governor of Arkansas in 1892. He passed away February 9, 1903.
1690. Nicolay and Hay, ALCW, Vol. 2, p. 495.
1691. Nicolay and Hay, ALCW, Vol. 2, p. 515.
1692. L. Johnson, p. 126.
1693. W. B. Garrison, LNOK, p. 215.
1694. Hansen, pp. 58-59; K. L. Hall, s.v. "Lincoln, Abraham." Lincoln's unlawful acts stirred up a number of serious court cases. See K. L. Hall, s.v.

"Prize Cases."
1695. Denney, p. 25.
1696. W. C. Davis, HD, pp. 79-80.
1697. W. B. Garrison, LNOK, pp. 193-197.
1698. Nicolay and Hay, ALCW, Vol. 2, pp. 285-287.
1699. C. Adams, p. 58.
1700. Nicolay and Hay, ALCW, Vol. 2, p. 326.
1701. Nicolay and Hay, ALCW, Vol. 2, p. 610.
1702. Nicolay and Hay, ALCW, Vol. 2, p. 592.
1703. D. H. Donald, LR, p. 79.
1704. Napolitano, pp. 69-70.
1705. For more on Lincoln and the 1860 and 1865 elections, see Seabrook, AL, passim.
1706. Nicolay and Hay, ALCW, Vol. 2, p. 318.
1707. Nicolay and Hay, ALCW, Vol. 2, p. 211.
1708. Nicolay and Hay, ALCW, Vol. 2, p. 212.
1709. ORA, Ser. 3, Vol. 3, p. 252.
1710. Cornish, p. 46.
1711. Wiley, SN, pp. 322-323; Mullen, p. 25.
1712. See Cornish, pp. 181-196.
1713. Douglass, LTFD, p. 303.
1714. Barney, pp. 146-147.
1715. S. K. Taylor, p. 51.
1716. Nicolay and Hay, ALCW, Vol. 2, p. 536.
1717. Quarles, pp. 200-201.
1718. P. Smith, p. 308.
1719. Though 5,000 white Union officers eventually commanded all-black troops, only "about one hundred" blacks ever held Union officer commissions during Lincoln's War, and this despite the apathy, protests, and even outright opposition of Lincoln and his War Department. Cornish, pp. 214-215.
1720. Alotta, p. 27. Lincoln paid his black soldiers $7 a month; he paid his white soldiers $13 a month. Quarles, p. 200.
1721. E. M. Thomas, p. 297.
1722. Cornish, p. 214.
1723. Wiley, LBY, p. 313; J. M. McPherson, NCW, pp. 238-239.
1724. ORA, Ser. 3, Vol. 3, p. 46.
1725. Buckley, p. 83.
1726. Pearson, Vol. 2, pp. 70-74.
1727. See W. C. Davis, JDMH, p. 599; Quarles, p. 279; Durden, pp. 203, 269, 272.

1728. E. M. Thomas, pp. 296-297.
1729. See Cornish, pp. 184, 192, 195.
1730. *The Liberator*, May 22, 1863.
1731. *Douglass' Monthly*, March, 1863, Vol. 5, p. 802.
1732. Wiley, SN, pp. 241, 309-310, 317.
1733. L. Johnson, p. 134.
1734. L. Johnson, p. 134.
1735. Pollard, SHW, Vol. 2, pp. 196-198.
1736. Henry, ATSF, p. 248.
1737. L. Johnson, p. 134.
1738. ORA, Ser. 3, Vol. 4, p. 1029.
1739. J. M. McPherson, NCW, p. 170.
1740. F. Moore, pp. 278-279.
1741. Wiley, SN, pp. 12-14.
1742. Gragg, p. 85.
1743. Dean, p. 83.
1744. *Charlotte Daily Bulletin*, November 13, 1862.
1745. Nicolay and Hay, ALCW, Vol. 2, p. 507.
1746. Nicolay and Hay, ALCW, Vol. 2, pp. 532-533.
1747. Nicolay and Hay, ALCW, Vol. 2, p. 372.
1748. Nicolay and Hay, ALCW, Vol. 2, p. 384.
1749. Nicolay and Hay, ALCW, Vol. 2, 637.
1750. Alotta, pp. 26-28.
1751. Leech, p. 312.
1752. Current, TC, s.v. "African Americans in the Confederacy."
1753. Quarles, pp. 204-205.
1754. Cartmell, pp. 144, 145.
1755. Faust, s.v. "slavery." For examples of black contributions to American culture, see Wilson and Ferris, s.v. "Black life." See also M. M. Smith, p. 30.
1756. Fogel, p. 157.
1757. De Angelis, pp. 12-18; Lott, p. 65.
1758. Nicolay and Hay, ALCW, Vol. 2, pp. 482-483.
1759. See e.g., D. H. Donald, L, p. 471.
1760. J. Davis, RFCG, Vol. 2, pp. 472-473.
1761. Cornish, p. 289.
1762. Foner, R, p. 49.
1763. Nicolay and Hay, ALCW, Vol. 2, p. 496.
1764. Due to Northern white racism, even these few black officers, just 0.005 percent of the total Union soldier population, were eventually replaced by Caucasians. Cornish, p. 214.

1765. See e.g., D. H. Donald, L, p. 471.
1766. Nicolay and Hay, ALCW, Vol. 1, pp. 538-540.
1767. Nicolay and Hay, ALCW, Vol. 11, pp. 130-131.
1768. The letter, probably written sometime between January and February 1864, was addressed to General James Wadsworth. Nicolay and Hay, Lincoln's official biographers, added a cryptic remark to it: "Given by F. B. Carpenter." Nicolay and Hay, ALCW, Vol. 11, p. 130.
1769. Confederate general and Southern hero Robert E. Lee also used the clinical phrase "these people." But not for African-Americans, as Lincoln did. Lee used it for Yankees. See e.g., T. C. Johnson, pp. 499-500.
1770. Nicolay and Hay, ALCW, Vol. 2, p. 674.
1771. Foner, R, p. 74.
1772. Kane, s.v. "Abraham Lincoln"; Findlay and Findlay, p. 164.
1773. Kinder and Hilgemann, Vol. 2, p. 117.
1774. Nicolay and Hay, ALCW, Vol. 2, p. 576.
1775. Nicolay and Hay, ALCW, Vol. 2, p. 561-562.
1776. Nicolay and Hay, ALCW, Vol. 2, p. 562.
1777. Nicolay and Hay, ALCW, Vol. 2, p. 562.
1778. Nicolay and Hay, ALCW, Vol. 2, pp. 563-565.
1779. Seabrook, ARB, p. 12.
1780. C. Johnson, pp. 166-167.
1781. Flood, p. 400; Kennett, p. 107; C. Johnson, p. 167.
1782. See e.g., Nicolay and Hay, ALCW, Vol. 1, p. 569.
1783. Drescher and Engerman, p. 109.
1784. Lapsley, Vol. 7, pp. 337-338.
1785. There were some 182,000 free blacks in the eleven states of the Confederacy (Quarles, p. 35), nearly all who sided with Dixie. In addition, most traditional Southern historians believe that between 100,000 and 300,000 Southern slaves fought for Dixie. See following footnote.
1786. Barrow, Segars, and Rosenburg, BC, p. 97; *The United Daughters of the Confederacy Magazine*, Vols. 54-55, 1991, p. 32. Though the exact number is not known, estimates of the number of Southern blacks who fought for the Confederacy range from 30,000 to 93,000, from 100,000 to 300,000. See e.g., Hinkle, p. 106; R. M. Brown, p. xiv; Shenkman and Reiger, p. 106. I have chosen to go with the largest figure for reasons that will be discussed shortly. Skewing the already confusing figures were the thousands of blacks who posed as whites (presumably the lighter skinned blacks), eager to join the Confederate army or navy. See e.g., E. L. Jordan, p. 217. Since these particular men were never counted, the number 300,000 is no doubt quite conservative.
1787. Interestingly, 300,000 is the same number of blacks authorized for enlistment by the Confederate Congress' General Ordinance No. 14, issued in

March 1865. Greenberg and Waugh, p. 395.
1788. Greenberg and Waugh, pp. 362, 385.
1789. Barrow, Segars, and Rosenburg, BC, p. 7.
1790. E. M. Thomas, p. 236.
1791. Segars and Barrow, BSCA, p. ii.
1792. Barrow, Segars, and Rosenburg, BC, p. 111.
1793. *Civil War Book of Lists*, pp. 169-170.
1794. Segars and Barrow, BSCA, pp. 48, 99, 142, 200, 221.
1795. Barrow, Segars, and Rosenburg, BC, p. 71.
1796. Helper, NQC, p. 206.
1797. L. Johnson, p. 180.
1798. Quarles, p. 37; Greenberg and Waugh, pp. 372-373.
1799. Quarles, pp. 37-38.
1800. B. F. Butler, p. 498.
1801. W. C. Davis, LA, p. 142.
1802. L. Johnson, p. 181.
1803. E. L. Jordan, p. 372.
1804. Fremantle, p. 281.
1805. Quarles, pp. 39, 50.
1806. E. L. Jordan, p. 216.
1807. Greeley, AC, Vol. 2, p. 522.
1808. Fleming, p. 208.
1809. R. Taylor, p. 210.
1810. Foote, Vol. 3, p. 755.
1811. Chesnut, DD, p. 147.
1812. Lubbock, p. 561.
1813. Wallcut, p. 20.
1814. E. L. Jordan, p. 222.
1815. Hinkle, p. 106.
1816. L. H. Steiner, pp. 19-20.
1817. ORA, Ser. 4, Vol. 1, p. 1088.
1818. Greenberg and Waugh, p. 394.
1819. The exact number of Yanks and Rebels, by some estimates, was 2,898,304 of the former, 1,234,000 of the latter. Livermore, p. 63. Also see Katcher, CWSB, p. 46.
1820. Barrow, Segars, and Rosenburg, BC, p. 97; *The United Daughters of the Confederacy Magazine*, Vols. 54-55, 1991, p. 32.
1821. Kautz, p. 11. Using Kautz' definition of a "private soldier," some 2 million Southerners fought in the Confederacy: 1 million whites and perhaps as many as 1 million blacks. (These numbers do not include the other three "races,"

yellow, brown, and red, that sided with and fought for the Confederacy. See C. Johnson, pp. 169-197.)

1822. Using Kautz' definition and these numbers, 200,000 blacks fought for the Union, 1,000,000 blacks for the Confederacy. Thus, 80 percent more blacks wore Rebel gray than wore Yankee blue.

1823. Sherman's theory of modern warfare included waging "total destruction" upon the civilian population, as thousands of innocent Southern men, women, and children were to discover. Warner, GB, s.v. "William Tecumseh 'Cump' Sherman."

1824. C. A. Evans, Vol. 5, p. 911.

1825. Lapsley, Vol. 7, pp. 337-338.

1826. Nicolay and Hay, Vol. 1, p. 208. For more on Lincoln and his African-American Union soldiers, see Seabrook, AL, passim; Seabrook, EYWTAASIW, passim; Seabrook, EYWTAAAATCWIW, passim; Seabrook, L, passim; Seabrook, TUAL, passim; Seabrook, TGI, passim; Seabrook, S101, passim.

1827. See e.g., W. L. Miller, passim.

1828. See e.g., Morel, passim.

1829. See e.g., Freiling, passim.

1830. See e.g., J. L. Wheeler, passim.

1831. See e.g., Burkhimer, passim.

1832. See e.g., Ostergard, passim.

1833. Nicolay and Hay, ALCW, Vol. 2, p. 7.

1834. Nicolay and Hay, ALCW, Vol. 2, p. 522.

1835. Nicolay and Hay, ALCW, Vol. 2, pp. 573-574.

1836. Nicolay and Hay, ALCW, Vol. 2, p. 603.

1837. Oates, AL, pp. 5, 40; Current, LNK, p. 60.

1838. Mary, despondent over her young son Willie's death (on February 20, 1862), held at least eight known seances at the White House in an attempt to contact her boy on the Other Side. Her atheist husband, however, would have none of it: Mr. Lincoln pronounced all of Mary's spiritualist efforts horse feathers and flapdoodle—this despite the fact that, according to Mary herself, Willie punctually appeared to her at the foot of her bed night after night. D. H. Donald, L, p. 427.

1839. Kane, p. 163.

1840. *Southern Review*, January 1873, Vol. 12, No. 25, p. 364.

1841. Current, LNK, pp. 58, 61.

1842. Oates, AL, p. 53.

1843. Current, LNK, p. 58.

1844. Lamon, LAL, p. 488.

1845. W. B. Garrison, LNOK, p. 265.

1846. Barton, p. 146.
1847. Lamon, LAL, p, 493.
1848. Lamon, LAL, p. 489.
1849. Christian, p. 7.
1850. Meriwether, pp. 54-55.
1851. Lamon, LAL, p. 488.
1852. Lamon, LAL, pp. 487-488.
1853. Zall, p. 71.
1854. Nicolay and Hay, ALCW, Vol. 1, pp. 79-80.
1855. Basler, ALSW, pp. 188-189.
1856. Lamon, LAL, pp. 486, 487.
1857. Current, LNK, p. 65.
1858. Lamon, LAL, p. 489.
1859. Ashe, p. 62.
1860. Minor, p. 25.
1861. Nicolay and Hay, ALCW, Vol. 1, p. 16.
1862. J. G. Holland, p. 236.
1863. Remsburg, p. 292.
1864. Nicolay and Hay, ALCW, Vol. 2, p. 378.
1865. 1 Peter 3:8.
1866. Matthew 5:44.
1867. Nicolay and Hay, ALCW, Vol. 2, p. 526.
1868. Nicolay and Hay, ALCW, Vol. 2, pp. 543-544.
1869. Remsburg, p. 292.
1870. Remsburg, p. 296.
1871. Wiley, LBY, p. 359.
1872. Lang, pp. 215, 216.
1873. DeGregorio, s.v. "Abraham Lincoln."
1874. Lamon, LAL, p. 488.
1875. The word similarity between this, Lincoln's "Doctrine of Necessity," and his political theory of "military necessity," is intriguing. Someday a psychological study might be performed to try and establish why Lincoln seemed so drawn to "necessity," an unusual word he sprinkled hundreds of times throughout his speeches and writings.
1876. D. H. Donald, L, p. 49; Guelzo, p. 32; DeGregorio, s.v. "Abraham Lincoln."
1877. *Douglass' Monthly*, September 1862, Vol. 5, pp. 707-708.
1878. Neely, p. 108.
1879. ORA, Ser. 1, Vol. 17, Pt. 2, p. 424.
1880. Simmons, s.v. "General Order, Number Eleven;" Shenkman and Reiger,

p. 84.
1881. Neely, p. 107.
1882. As we have seen, in 1861, for example, when Lincoln discovered that a rabbi had been made chaplain of the 5th Pennsylvania Cavalry, he forced him to renounce his office. As per Lincoln's orders only ordained Christian ministers could function in the capacity of chaplain. Katcher, CWSB, pp. 176-177.
1883. K. C. Davis, p. 273; Neely, p. 109.
1884. Horwitz, p. 204.
1885. J. S. Bowman, CWDD, s.v. "21 January 1863."
1886. ORA, Ser. 1, Vol. 24, Pt. 1, p. 9.
1887. Neely, pp. 108-109.
1888. Nicolay and Hay, ALCW, Vol. 2, p. 243.
1889. Nicolay and Hay, ALCW, Vol. 2, p. 254.
1890. Nicolay and Hay, ALCW, Vol. 2, p. 574.
1891. Nicolay and Hay, ALCW, Vol. 2, p. 657.
1892. Nicolay and Hay, ALCW, Vol. 2, pp. 243-244.
1893. For more on Lincoln and his views on religion, see Seabrook, AL, passim.
1894. Nicolay and Hay, ALCW, Vol. 2, pp. 442-444.
1895. Authentic slavery was never practiced in the South. Only servitude. Those who say different are only perpetuating anti-South propaganda and Yankee mythology. For more on the differences between genuine slavery and genuine servitude, see Seabrook, AL, pp. 137-153.
1896. See Current, LNK, pp. 223, 239, 240, 241.
1897. Haggard, p. 90.
1898. Nicolay and Hay, ALCW, Vol. 2, p. 444.
1899. Nicolay and Hay, ALCW, Vol. 2, p. 477.
1900. Nicolay and Hay, ALCW, Vol. 2, pp. 563-564.
1901. Nicolay and Hay, ALCW, Vol. 2, p. 673.
1902. Nicolay and Hay, ALCW, Vol. 2, p. 546.
1903. Nicolay and Hay, ALCW, Vol. 2, p. 550.
1904. Nicolay and Hay, ALCW, Vol. 2, p. 672.
1905. Denney, p. 553.
1906. DeGregorio, s.v. "Andrew Johnson."
1907. L. Johnson, p. 191.
1908. Hacker, p. 583.
1909. Hacker, p. 589.
1910. See e.g., Nicolay and Hay, ALCW, Vol. 2, pp. 466, 469, 475, 477, 496, 545, 598, 599, 674.
1911. See e.g., Nicolay and Hay, ALCW, Vol. 2, pp. 13, 29, 90, 135.
1912. Nicolay and Hay, ALCW, Vol. 2, p. 513.

1913. A gifted speaker who was known as the "Spokesman for the New South," naturally, Grady was far more popular in the North than in the South. Rosenbaum and Brinkley, s.v. "New South."
1914. Simpson, pp. 193-194.
1915. Chodes, p. 98; P. M. Roberts, p. 226.
1916. J. H. Franklin, p. 196.
1917. Hacker, p. 589.
1918. *"Reconstruction": Speech of the Hon. Thaddeus Stevens*, p. 7. Delivered at Lancaster, Pennsylvania, September 7, 1865.
1919. Catton, Vol. 2, p. 443.
1920. Nicolay and Hay, ALCW, Vol. 2, p. 672.
1921. A type of communism promoted by French socialist Charles Fourier.
1922. In essence, the belief in intimate relations without marriage.
1923. Durden, p. 112.
1924. Hacker, p. 582.
1925. DiLorenzo, LU, p. 38; Current, LNK, p. 254.
1926. Nicolay and Hay, ALCW, Vol. 2, p. 545.
1927. P. M. Roberts, p. 229; L. Johnson, p. 267.
1928. Cooper, JDA, p. 676.
1929. C. R. Williams, Vol. 2, p. 13.
1930. J. H. Franklin, p. 216.
1931. Weintraub, p. 76
1932. Kane, p.217.
1933. In essence the Fourteenth Amendment was an attempt by liberals to supersede the Tenth Amendment, the part of the Bill of Rights that guarantees states' rights. W. S. Powell, p. 145. For more on why the Fourteenth Amendment was condemned across Dixie, see L. Johnson, pp. 241-242; Woods, pp. 86-90; Findlay and Findlay, pp. 228-235; DiLorenzo, RL, pp. 207-208, 211.
1934. Bradley, p. 138. At the time the Fifteenth Amendment was passed, Radical Yankee liberal Thaddeus Stevens said revealingly: "I shall vote for this not because of any constitutional right, but because we have the power." Stonebraker, p. 76.
1935. Rosenbaum, s.v. "Hayes, Rutherford Birchard."
1936. Parry, s.v. "Hayes, Rutherford B."
1937. J. S. Bowman, ECW, s.v. "Hayes, Rutherford Birchard."
1938. DeGregorio, s.v. "Rutherford B. Hayes."
1939. Southerners had not stood idly by while the North imposed "Reconstruction" upon them, of course. Besides forming the self-protective social aid organization known as the KKK, during Johnson's short time in office alone the Confederacy's vice president, four Confederate generals, five

Confederate colonels, six Confederate cabinet officers, and fifty-eight Confederate congressmen were sent to the Thirty-ninth Congress, elected by a loyal Southern populace. Former Confederates, most of them still "unpardoned," also took control of the state governments, even proudly wearing their Rebel uniforms to work (though it was against the law to do so), while Confederate flags were sold openly in the streets (also a crime under Yankee rules). See J. H. Franklin, pp. 43-44, 53.

1940. Tourgee, p. 300.
1941. I am speaking here of the Mexican-American War, 1846-1848.
1942. Lincoln and Douglas, p. 221; Holzer, pp. 266-267; Neely, p. 213.
1943. Lincoln was born on February 12, 1809, in Hardin (now Larue) Co., Kentucky.
1944. In his First Inaugural Address, Lincoln lied to the South, saying: **"We are not enemies, but friends."** Nicolay and Hay, ALCW, Vol. 2, p. 7. However, in the same speech, in reference to Southern forts occupied by Yankee troops, he turned around and declared that: **"The power confided to me will be used to hold, occupy, and possess the property and places belonging to the** [U.S.] **Government . . ."** Pollard, LC, p. 104. As was so often the case, in the same breath Lincoln was both contradictory and hypocritical, pacific and aggressive.
1945. K. C. Davis, p. 441.
1946. W. B. Garrison, CWTFB, p. 123.
1947. Historical note: President Carter's great-grandfather, Littleberry Walker Carter, proudly fought for the Confederacy in the War for Southern Independence.
1948. K. C. Davis, p. 438.
1949. DeGregorio, s.v. "Abraham Lincoln."
1950. Zinn, p. 232. This is the standard Yankee figure, which means it is woefully underestimated.
1951. Timothy D. Manning, Sr., personal correspondence. As mentioned earlier, President Jefferson Davis believed that Lincoln was responsible for killing at least half of the South's Negro population, which would be about 1,750,000 black men, women, and children. See F. Moore, pp. 278-279.
1952. Nicolay and Hay, ALCW, Vol. 2, p. 503.
1953. Nicolay and Hay, ALCW, Vol. 2, p. 7.
1954. Nicolay and Hay, ALCW, Vol. 2, p. 553.
1955. Tracy, p. 133.
1956. For more on Lincoln and Reconstruction, see Seabrook, AL, passim; Seabrook, NBFATKKK, passim.
1957. See Seabrook, ALWALJDWAC, passim.

BIBLIOGRAPHY

Note: My pro-South readers are to be advised that the majority of the books listed here are anti-South in nature (some extremely so), and were written primarily by liberal elitist, socialist, communist, and Marxist authors who loathe the South, and typically the United States and the U.S. Constitution as well. Despite this, as a scholar I find these titles indispensable, for *an honest evaluation of Lincoln's War is not possible without studying both the Southern and the Northern versions*—an attitude, unfortunately, completely lacking among pro-North historians (who read and study only their own ahistorical version). Still, it must be said that the material contained in these often mean-spirited works is largely the result of a century and a half of Yankee myth, falsehoods, cherry-picking, slander, sophistry, editorializing, anti-South propaganda, outright lies, and junk research, as modern pro-North writers merely copy one another's errors without ever looking at the original 19th-Century sources. This type of literature, filled as it is with both misinformation and disinformation, is called "scholarly" and "objective" by pro-North advocates. In the process, the mistakes and lies in these fact-free, fault-ridden, South-shaming, historically inaccurate works have been magnified over the years, and the North's version of the "Civil War" has come to be accepted as the only legitimate one. Indeed, it is now the only one known by most people. That over 95 percent of the titles in my bibliography fall into the anti-South category is simply a reflection of the enormous power and influence that the pro-North movement—our nation's cultural ruling class—has long held over America's education system, libraries, publishing houses, and media (paper and electronic). My books serve as a small rampart against the overwhelming tide of anti-South Fascists, Liberals, cultural Marxists, and political elites, all who are working hard to obliterate Southern culture and guarantee that you will never learn the Truth about Lincoln and his War on the Constitution and the American people.

Abbott, John Stevens Cabot. *The Life of General Ulysses S. Grant*. Boston, MA: B. B. Russell, 1868.

Adams, Charles. *When in the Course of Human Events: Arguing the Case for Southern Secession*. Lanham, MD: Rowman and Littlefield, 2000.

Adams, Francis D., and Barry Sanders. *Alienable Rights: The Exclusion of African Americans in a White Man's Land, 1619-2000*. 2003. New York, NY: Perennial, 2004 ed.

Adams, Henry (ed.). *Documents Relating to New-England Federalism, 1800-1815*. Boston, MA: Little, Brown, and Co., 1877.

Adams, Nehemiah, Rev. *A South-side View of Slavery: Three Months at the South, in 1854*. Boston, MA: T. R. Marvin, 1855.

Alexander, William T. *History of the Colored Race in America*. Kansas City, MO: Palmetto Publishing, 1887.

Alotta, Robert I. *Civil War Justice: Union Army Executions Under Lincoln.* Shippensburg, PA: White Mane, 1989.
An Appeal From the Colored Men of Philadelphia to the President of the United States. Philadelphia, PA, 1862.
Anastaplo, George. *Abraham Lincoln: A Constitutional Biography.* Lanham, MD: Rowman and Littlefield, 1999.
Anderson, John Q. (ed.). *Brokenburn: The Journal of Kate Stone, 1861-1868.* 1955. Baton Rouge, LA: Louisiana State University Press, 1995 ed.
Andrews, Elisha Benjamin. *The United States in Our Own Time: A History From Reconstruction to Expansion.* 1895. New York, NY: Charles Scribner's Sons, 1903 ed.
Andrews, Sidney. *The South Since the War: As Shown by Fourteen Weeks of Travel and Observation.* Boston, MA: Ticknor and Fields, 1866.
Angle, Paul M. (ed.). *The Complete Lincoln-Douglas Debates of 1858.* Chicago, IL: University of Chicago Press, 1991.
Annunzio, Frank (chairman). *The Capitol: A Pictorial History of the Capitol and of the Congress.* Washington, D.C.: U.S. Joint Committee on Printing, 1983.
Anonymous. *Life of John C. Calhoun: Presenting a Condensed History of Political Events, From 1811 to 1843.* New York, NY: Harper and Brothers, 1843.
Appleman, Roy Edgar (ed.). *Abraham Lincoln: From His Own Words and Contemporary Accounts.* Washington, D.C.: U.S. Department of the Interior, National Park Service, 1942.
Arnett, Benjamin William (ed.). *Duplicate Copy of the Souvenir From the Afro-American League of Tennessee to Honorable James M. Ashley of Ohio.* Philadelphia, PA: A. M. E. Church, 1894.
Arnold, Isaac Newton. *The History of Abraham Lincoln, and the Overthrow of Slavery.* Chicago, IL: Clarke and Co., 1866.
Aron, Stephen. *American Confluence: The Missouri Frontier from Borderland to Border State.* Bloomington, IN: Indiana University Press, 2009.
Ashdown Paul, and Edward Caudill. *The Myth of Nathan Bedford Forrest.* 2005. Lanham, MD: Rowman and Littlefield, 2006 ed.
Ashe, Captain Samuel A'Court. *A Southern View of the Invasion of the Southern States and War of 1861-1865.* 1935. Crawfordville, GA: Ruffin Flag Co., 1938 ed.
Ashworth, John. *Slavery, Capitalism, and Politics in the Antebellum Republic.*

2 vols. New York, NY: Cambridge University Press, 2007.
Astor, Gerald. *The Right to Fight: A History of African Americans in the Military*. Cambridge, MA: Da Capo, 2001.
Baepler, Paul (ed.). *White Slaves, African Masters: An Anthology of American Barbary Captivity Narratives*. Chicago, IL: University of Chicago Press, 1999.
Bailey, Anne C. *African Voices of the Atlantic Slave Trade: Beyond the Silence and the Shame*. Boston, MA: Beacon Press, 2005.
Bailey, Hugh C. *Hinton Rowan Helper: Abolitionist-Racist*. Tuscaloosa, AL: University of Alabama Press, 1965.
Bailyn, Bernard, Robert Dallek, David Brion Davis, David Herbert Donald, John L. Thomas, and Gordon S. Wood. *The Great Republic: A History of the American People*. 1977. Lexington, MA: D. C. Heath and Co., 1992 ed.
Baker, George E. (ed.). *The Works of William H. Seward*. 5 vols. 1861. Boston, MA: Houghton, Mifflin and Co., 1888 ed.
Baker, Jean H. *Mary Todd Lincoln: A Biography*. New York, NY: W. W. Norton and Co., 1989.
Ballagh, James Curtis. *White Servitude in the Colony of Virginia: A Study of the System of Indentured Servitude in the American Colonies*. Whitefish, MT: Kessinger Publishing, 2004.
Bancroft, Frederic. *The Life of William H. Seward*. 2 vols. New York, NY: Harper and Brothers, 1900.
———. *Slave-Trading in the Old South*. Baltimore, MD: J. H. Furst, 1931.
Bancroft, Frederic, and William A. Dunning (eds.). *The Reminiscences of Carl Schurz*. 3 vols. New York, NY: McClure Co., 1909.
Barnes, Gilbert H., and Dwight L. Dumond (eds.). *Letters of Theodore Dwight Weld, Angelina Grimké Weld and Sarah Grimké, 1822-1844*. 2 vols. New York, NY: D. Appleton-Century Co., 1934.
Barney, William L. *Flawed Victory: A New Perspective on the Civil War*. New York, NY: Praeger Publishers, 1975.
Barrow, Charles Kelly, J. H. Segars, and R. B. Rosenburg (eds.). *Black Confederates*. 1995. Gretna, LA: Pelican Publishing Co., 2001 ed.
———. *Forgotten Confederates: An Anthology About Black Southerners*. Saint Petersburg, FL: Southern Heritage Press, 1997.
Bartlett, Irving H. *John C. Calhoun: A Biography*. New York, NY: W. W. Norton, 1994.

———. *Wendell Phillips: Brahmin Radical*. Boston, MA: Beacon Press, 1961.
Barton, William E. *The Soul of Abraham Lincoln*. New York, NY: George H. Doran, 1920.
Basler, Roy Prentice (ed.). *Abraham Lincoln: His Speeches and Writings*. 1946. New York, NY: Da Capo Press, 2001 ed.
——— (ed.). *The Collected Works of Abraham Lincoln*. 9 vols. New Brunswick, NJ: Rutgers University Press, 1953.
Bateman, William O. *Political and Constitutional Law of the United States of America*. St. Louis, MO: G. I. Jones and Co., 1876.
Baxter, Maurice G. *Henry Clay and the American System*. Lexington, KY: University Press of Kentucky, 2004.
Beard, Charles A., and Birl E. Schultz. *Documents on the State-Wide Initiative, Referendum and Recall*. New York, NY: Macmillan, 1912.
Beard, Charles A., and Mary R. Beard. *The Rise of American Civilization*. 1927. New York, NY: MacMillan, 1930 ed.
Beck, Glenn. *Glenn Beck's Common Sense: The Case Against an Out-of-Control Government, Inspired by Thomas Paine*. New York, NY: Threshold, 2009.
Belz, Herman. *Abraham Lincoln, Constitutionalism, and Equal Rights in the Civil War Era*. Bronx, NY: Fordham University Press, 1997.
Bennett, Lerone. *Forced into Glory: Abraham Lincoln's White Dream*. Chicago, IL: Johnson Publishing Co., 2000.
Benton, Thomas Hart. *Thirty Years View; or A History of the Working of the American Government for Thirty Years, From 1820 to 1850*. 2 vols. New York, NY: D. Appleton and Co., 1854.
Bergh, Albert Ellery (ed.). *The Writings of Thomas Jefferson*. 20 vols. Washington, D.C.: Thomas Jefferson Memorial Association of the U.S., 1905.
Bernhard, Winfred E. A. (ed.). *Political Parties in American History* (Vol. 1, 1789-1828). New York, NY: G. P. Putnams' Sons, 1973.
Berry, Stephen William. *House of Abraham: Lincoln and the Todds, A Family Divided by War*. New York, NY: Houghton Mifflin, 2007.
Berry, Wendell. *The Unsettling of America: Culture and Agriculture*. San Francisco, CA: Sierra Club Books, 1996.
Berwanger, Eugene H. *The Frontier Against Slavery: Western Anti-Negro Prejudice and the Slavery Extension Controversy*. 1967. Urbana, IL: University of Illinois Press, 1971 ed.

Beschloss, Michael R. *Presidential Courage: Brave Leaders and How They Changed America, 1789-1989*. New York, NY: Simon and Schuster, 2007.

Beveridge, Albert Jeremiah. *Abraham Lincoln: 1809-1858*. 2 vols. Boston, MA: Houghton Mifflin, 1928.

Black, Chauncey F. *Essays and Speeches of Jeremiah S. Black*. New York, NY: D. Appleton and Co., 1886.

Black, Robert W., Col. *Cavalry Raids of the Civil War*. Mechanicsburg, PA: Stackpole, 2004.

Blackerby, Hubert R. *Blacks in Blue and Gray*. New Orleans, LA: Portals Press, 1979.

Blair, William A., and Karen Fisher Younger (eds.). *Lincoln's Proclamation: Emancipation Reconsidered*. Chapel Hill, NC: University of North Carolina Press, 2009.

Blassingame, John W. *The Slave Community: Plantation Life in the Antebellum South*. 1972. New York, NY: Oxford University Press, 1974 ed.

Bledsoe, Albert Taylor. *An Essay on Liberty and Slavery*. Philadelphia, PA: J. B. Lippincott and Co., 1856.

——. *A Theodicy; or a Vindication of the Divine Glory, as Manifested in the Constitution and Government of the Moral World*. New York, NY: Carlton and Porter, 1856.

——. *Is Davis a Traitor; or Was Secession a Constitutional Right Previous to the War of 1861?* Richmond, VA: Hermitage Press, 1907.

Blee, Kathleen M. *Women of the Klan: Racism and Gender in the 1920s*. 1991. Berkeley, CA: University of California Press, 1992 ed.

Blight, David W. *Frederick Douglass' Civil War: Keeping Faith in Jubilee*. 1989. Baton Rouge, LA: Louisiana State University Press, 1991 ed.

Bliss, William Dwight Porter (ed.). *The Encyclopedia of Social Reform*. New York, NY: Funk and Wagnalls, 1897.

Boatner, Mark Mayo. *The Civil War Dictionary*. 1959. New York, NY: David McKay Co., 1988 ed.

Bode, Carl, and Malcolm Cowley (eds.). *The Portable Emerson*. 1941. Harmondsworth, UK: Penguin, 1981 ed.

Boorstin, Daniel J. *The Discoverers: A History of Man's Search to Know His World and Himself*. 1983. New York, NY: Vintage, 1985 ed.

Boritt, Gabor S. *Lincoln and the Economics of the America Dream*. Urbana, IL: University of Illinois Press, 1994.

———. (ed.) *Lincoln's Generals*. New York, NY: Oxford University Press, 1995.

———. *The Gettysburg Gospel: The Lincoln Speech That Nobody Knows*. New York, NY: Simon and Schuster, 2006.

Bowen, Catherine Drinker. *John Adams and the American Revolution*. 1949. New York, NY: Grosset and Dunlap, 1977 ed.

Bowers, John. *Chickamauga and Chattanooga: The Battles that Doomed the Confederacy*. New York, NY: HarperCollins, 1994.

Bowman, John S. (ed.). *The Civil War Day by Day: An Illustrated Almanac of America's Bloodiest War*. 1989. New York, NY: Dorset Press, 1990 ed.

———. *Encyclopedia of the Civil War* (ed.). 1992. North Dighton, MA: JG Press, 2001 ed.

Bowman, Virginia McDaniel. *Historic Williamson County: Old Homes and Sites*. 1971. Franklin, TN: Territorial Press, 1989 ed.

Bradford, James C. (ed.). *Atlas of American Military History*. New York, NY: Oxford University Press, 2003.

Bradford, Ned (ed.). *Battles and Leaders of the Civil War*. 1-vol. ed. New York, NY: Appleton-Century-Crofts, 1956.

Bradley, Michael R. *Nathan Bedford Forrest's Escort and Staff*. Gretna, LA: Pelican Publishing Co., 2006.

Brady, Cyrus Townsend. *Three Daughters of the Confederacy*. New York, NY: G. W. Dillingham, 1905.

Brady, James S. (ed.). *Ronald Reagan: A Man True to His Word - A Portrait of the 40th President of the United States In His Own Words*. Washington D.C.: National Federation of Republican Women, 1984.

Brent, Linda. *The Deeper Wrong; or Incidents in the Life of a Slave Girl, Written by Herself*. London, UK: W. Tweedie, 1862.

Brinkley, Alan. *The Unfinished Nation: A Concise History of the American People*. 1993. Boston, MA: McGraw-Hill, 2000 ed.

Brockett, Linus Pierpont. *The Life and Times of Abraham Lincoln, Sixteenth President of the United States*. Philadelphia, PA: Bradley and Co., 1865.

Brooks, Gertrude Zeth. *First Ladies of the White House*. Chicago, IL: Charles Hallberg and Co., 1969.

Brooksher, William R., and David K. Snider. *Glory at a Gallop: Tales of the Confederate Cavalry*. 1993. Gretna, LA: Pelican Publishing Co.,

2002 ed.

Brown, Dee. *Bury My Heart at Wounded Knee: An Indian History of the American West*. 1970. New York, NY: Owl Books, 1991 ed.

Brown, Rita Mae. *High Hearts*. New York, NY: Bantam, 1987.

Brown, William Wells. *The Black Man: His Antecedents, His Genius, and His Achievements*. New York, NY: Thomas Hamilton, 1863.

Browne, Ray B., and Lawrence A. Kreiser, Jr. *The Civil War and Reconstruction*. Westport, CT: Greenwood Publishing, 2003.

Bruce, Philip Alexander. *The Plantation Negro As a Freeman*. New York, NY: G. P. Putnam's Sons, 1889.

Brunner, Borgna (ed.). *The Time Almanac* (1999 ed.). Boston, MA: Information Please, 1998.

Bryan, William Jennings. *The Commoner Condensed*. New York, NY: Abbey Press, 1902.

Buchanan, James. *The Works of James Buchanan*. 12 vols. Philadelphia, PA: J. B. Lippincott Co., 1911.

Buchanan, Patrick J. *A Republic, Not an Empire: Reclaiming America's Destiny*. Washington, D.C.: Regenry, 1999.

Buckingham, James Silk. *The Slave States of America*. 2 vols. London, UK: Fisher, Son, and Co., 1842.

Buckley, Gail. *American Patriots: The Story of Blacks in the Military From the Revolution to Desert Storm*. New York, NY: Random House, 2001.

Bultman, Bethany. *Redneck Heaven: Portrait of a Vanishing Culture*. New York, NY: Bantam, 1996.

Burkhimer, Michael. *Lincoln's Christianity*. Yardley, PA: Westholme, 2007.

Burlingame, Michael. *The Inner World of Abraham Lincoln*. Champaign, IL: University of Illinois Press, 1997.

Burns, James MacGregor, and Jack Walter Peltason. *Government by the People: The Dynamics of American National, State, and Local Government*. 1952. Englewood Cliffs, NJ: Prentice-Hall, 1964 ed.

Burns, James MacGregor, Jack Walter Peltason, Thomas E. Cronin, David B. Magleby, and David M. O'Brien. *Government by the People* (National Version). 1952. Upper Saddle River, NJ: Prentice Hall, 2001-2002 ed.

Burton, Orville Vernon. *The Age of Lincoln*. New York, NY: Hill and Wang, 2007.

Burton, Robert. *The Anatomy of Melancholy*. 3 vols. 1621. London, UK: George Bell and Sons, 1896 ed.

Bushnell, Horace. *The Census and Slavery, Thanksgiving Discourse, Delivered in the Chapel at Clifton Springs, New York, November 29, 1860*. Hartford, CT: L. E. Hunt, 1860.

Butler, Benjamin Franklin. *Butler's Book (Autobiography and Personal Reminiscences of Major-General Benjamin F. Butler: A Review of His Legal, Political, and Military Career)*. Boston, MA: A. M. Thayer and Co., 1892.

Butler, Lindley S., and Alan D. Watson (eds.). *The North Carolina Experience: An Interpretive and Documentary History*. Chapel Hill, NC: University of North Carolina Press, 1984.

Butler, Trent C. (ed.). *Holman Bible Dictionary*. Nashville, TN: Holman Bible Publishers, 1991.

Calvert, Thomas H. *The Federal Statutes Annotated*. 10 vols. Northport, NY: Edward Thompson, 1905.

Cannon, Devereaux D., Jr. *The Flags of the Confederacy: An Illustrated History*. Memphis, TN: St. Luke's Press, 1988.

Carey, Matthew, Jr. (ed.). *The Democratic Speaker's Hand-Book*. Cincinnati, OH: Miami Print and Publishing Co., 1868.

Carlton, Frank Tracy. *Organized Labor in America*. New York, NY: D. Appleton and Co., 1920.

Carnahan, Burrus M. *Lincoln on Trial: Southern Civilians and the Law of War*. Lexington, KY: University Press of Kentucky, 2010.

Carpenter, Stephen D. *Logic of History: Five Hundred Political Texts, Being Concentrated Extracts of Abolitionism*. Madison, WI: published by author, 1864.

Cartmell, Donald. *Civil War 101*. New York, NY: Gramercy, 2001.

Carwardine, Richard. *Lincoln: A Life of Purpose and Power*. New York, NY: Vintage, 2006.

Cash, W. J. *The Mind of the South*. 1941. New York, NY: Vintage, 1969 ed.

Catton, Bruce. *The Coming Fury* (Vol. 1). 1961. New York, NY: Washington Square Press, 1967 ed.

——. *Terrible Swift Sword* (Vol. 2). 1963. New York, NY: Pocket Books, 1967 ed.

——. *A Stillness at Appomattox* (Vol. 3). 1953. New York, NY: Pocket Books, 1966 ed.

Celeste, Sister Mary. *The Old World's Gifts to the New*. 1932. Long Prairie, MN: Neumann Press, 1999 ed.

Chadwick, Bruce. *The Two American Presidents: A Dual Biography of Abraham Lincoln and Jefferson Davis*. New York, NY: Citadel, 1999.

Chambers, Robert (ed.). *The Book of Days: A Miscellany of Popular Antiquities in Connection with the Calender*. 2 vols. London, UK: W. & R. Chambers, 1883.

Channing, Steven A. *Confederate Ordeal: The Southern Home Front*. 1984. Morristown, NJ: Time-Life Books, 1989 ed.

Chernow, Ron. *Alexander Hamilton*. New York, NY: Penguin, 2004.

Chesnut, Mary. *A Diary From Dixie: As Written by Mary Boykin Chesnut, Wife of James Chesnut, Jr., United States Senator from South Carolina, 1859-1861, and afterward an Aide to Jefferson Davis and a Brigadier-General in the Confederate Army*. (Isabella D. Martin and Myrta Lockett Avary, eds.). New York, NY: D. Appleton and Co., 1905 ed.

——. *Mary Chesnut's Civil War*. 1860-1865 (Woodward, Comer Vann, ed.). New Haven, CT: Yale University Press, 1981 ed.

Chodes, John. *Destroying the Republic: Jabez Curry and the Re-Education of the Old South*. New York, NY: Algora, 2005.

Christian, George Llewellyn. *Abraham Lincoln: An Address Delivered Before R. E. Lee Camp, No. 1 Confederate Veterans at Richmond, VA, October 29, 1909*. Richmond, VA: L. H. Jenkins, 1909.

——. *A Capitol Disaster: A Chapter of Reconstruction in Virginia*. Richmond, VA: self-published, 1915.

——. *Confederate Memories and Experiences*. Richmond, VA: self-published, 1915.

Cimprich, John. *Fort Pillow, a Civil War Massacre, and Public Memory*. Baton Rouge, LA: Louisiana State University Press, 2005.

Cisco, Walter Brian. *War Crimes Against Southern Civilians*. Gretna, LA: Pelican Publishing Co., 2007.

Civil War Book of Lists. 1993. Edison, NJ: Castle Books, 2004 ed.

Civil War Society, The. *Civil War Battles: An Illustrated Encyclopedia*. 1997. New York, NY: Gramercy, 1999 ed.

——. *The Civil War Society's Encyclopedia of the Civil War*. New York, NY: Wings Books, 1997.

Clark, L. Pierce. *Lincoln: A Psycho-Biography*. New York, NY: Charles Scribner's Sons, 1933.

Clarke, James W. *The Lineaments of Wrath: Race, Violent Crime, and*

American Culture. 1998. New Brunswick, NJ: Transaction, 2001 ed.
Cluskey, Michael W. (ed.). *The Political Text-Book, or Encyclopedia.* Philadelphia, PA: Jas. B. Smith, 1859 ed.
Cmiel, Kenneth. *Democratic Eloquence: The Fight Over Popular Speech in Nineteenth-Century America.* Berkeley, CA: University of California Press, 1990.
Coe, Joseph. *The True American.* Concord, NH: I. S. Boyd, 1840.
Coffin, Charles Carleton. *Abraham Lincoln.* New York, NY: Harper and Brothers, 1893.
Coit, Margaret L. *John C. Calhoun: American Portrait.* Boston, MA: Sentry, 1950.
Collier, Christopher, and James Lincoln Collier. *Decision in Philadelphia: The Constitutional Convention of 1787.* 1986. New York, NY: Ballantine, 1987 ed.
Collins, Elizabeth. *Memories of the Southern States.* Taunton, UK: J. Barnicott, 1865.
Collins, John A. (ed.). *The Anti-Slavery Picknick: A Collection of Speeches, Poems, Dialogues and Songs Intended for Use in Schools and Anti-Slavery Meetings.* Boston, MA: H. W. Williams, 1842.
Commager, Henry Steele, and Erik Bruun (eds.). *The Civil War Archive: The History of the Civil War in Documents.* 1950. New York, NY: Black Dog and Leventhal, 1973 ed.
Conner, Frank. *The South Under Siege, 1830-2000: A History of the Relations Between the North and the South.* Newnan, GA: Collards Publishing Co., 2002.
Conway, Moncure Daniel. *Testimonies Concerning Slavery.* London, UK: Chapman and Hall, 1865.
Cooke, Alistair. *Alistair Cooke's America.* 1973. New York, NY: Alfred A. Knopf, 1984 ed.
Cooke, John Esten. *A Life of General Robert E. Lee.* New York, NY: D. Appleton and Co., 1871.
Cooley, Henry S. *A Study of Slavery in New Jersey.* Baltimore, MD: Johns Hopkins University Press, 1896.
Cooper, William J., Jr. *Jefferson Davis, American.* New York, NY: Vintage, 2000.
——. (ed.). *Jefferson Davis: The Essential Writings.* New York, NY: Random House, 2003.

Cornish, Dudley Taylor. *The Sable Arm: Black Troops in the Union Army, 1861-1865*. 1956. Lawrence, KS: University Press of Kansas, 1987 ed.

Coulter, Ann. *Guilty: Liberal "Victims" and Their Assault on America*. New York, NY: Three Rivers Press, 2009.

Cox, Hank H. *Lincoln and the Sioux Uprising of 1862*. Nashville, TN: Cumberland House, 2005.

Cox, LaWanda. *Lincoln and Black Freedom: A Study in Presidential Leadership*. Columbia, SC: University of South Carolina Press, 1994.

Crallé, Richard Kenner. (ed.). *The Works of John C. Calhoun*. 6 vols. New York: NY: D. Appleton and Co., 1853-1888.

Craven, John J. *Prison Life of Jefferson Davis*. New York: NY: Carelton, 1866.

Crawford, Samuel Wylie. *The Genesis of the Civil War: The Story of Sumter, 1860-1861*. New York, NY: Charles L. Webster and Co., 1887.

Crocker, H. W., III. *The Politically Incorrect Guide to the Civil War*. Washington, D.C.: Regnery, 2008.

Cromie, Alice Hamilton. *A Tour Guide to the Civil War: The Complete State-by-State Guide to Battlegrounds, Landmarks, Museums, Relics, and Sites*. 1964. Nashville, TN: Rutledge Hill Press, 1990 ed.

Cromwell, John Wesley. *The Negro in American History: Men and Women Eminent in the Evolution of the American of African Descent*. Washington, D.C.: American Negro Academy, 1914.

Cross, F. L., and F. A. Livingston (eds.). *The Oxford Dictionary of the Christian Church*. 1957. London, UK: Oxford University Press, 1974 ed.

Crutchfield, James A. *Franklin: A Photographic Recollection*. 2 vols. Franklin, TN: Canaday Enterprises, 1996.

Crutchfield, James A., and Robert Holladay. *Franklin: Tennessee's Handsomest Town*. Franklin, TN: Hillsboro Press, 1999.

Cummins, Joseph. *Anything For a Vote: Dirty Tricks, Cheap Shots, and October Surprises in U.S. Presidential Campaigns*. Philadelphia, PA: Quirk, 2007.

Current, Richard N. *The Lincoln Nobody Knows*. 1958. New York, NY: Hill and Wang, 1963 ed.

———. (ed.) T*he Confederacy (Information Now Encyclopedia)*. 1993. New York, NY: Macmillan, 1998 ed.

Curry, Leonard P. *Blueprint for Modern America: Nonmilitary Legislation of*

the First Civil War Congress. Nashville, TN: Vanderbilt University Press, 1968.
Curti, Merle, Willard Thorpe, and Carlos Baker (eds.). *American Issues: The Social Record*. 1941. Chicago, IL: J. B. Lippincott, 1960 ed.
Curtin, Philip D. *The Atlantic Slave Trade: A Census*. Madison, WI: The University of Wisconsin Press, 1969.
———. *The Rise and Fall of the Plantation Complex: Essays in Atlantic History*. 1990. Cambridge, UK: Cambridge University Press, 1999 ed.
Curtis, George Ticknor. *Life of James Buchanan: Fifteenth President of the United States*. 2 vols. New York, NY: Harper and Brothers, 1883.
Curtis, William Eleroy. *Abraham Lincoln*. Philadelphia, PA: J. B. Lippincott Co., 1902.
Cushman, Horatio Bardwell. *History of the Choctaw, Chickasaw and Natchez Indians*. Greenville, TX: Headlight Printing House, 1899.
Custer, George Armstrong. *Wild Life on the Plains and Horrors of Indian Warfare*. St. Louis, MO: Excelsior Publishing, 1891.
Dabney, Robert Lewis. *A Defense of Virginia and the South*. Dahlonega, GA: Confederate Reprint Co., 1999.
Daniel, John M. *The Richmond Examiner During the War*. New York, NY: John M. Daniel, 1868.
Daniel, John W. *Life and Reminiscences of Jefferson Davis by Distinguished Men of His Time*. Baltimore, MD: R. H. Woodward, and Co., 1890.
Darwin, Charles. *On the Origin of Species By Means of Natural Selection*. London, UK: John Murray, 1866.
Daugherty, James. *Abraham Lincoln*. 1943. New York, NY: Scholastic Book Services, 1966 ed.
Davidson, Basil. *The African Slave Trade*. 1961. Boston, MA: Back Bay Books, 1980 ed.
Davis, Jefferson. *The Rise and Fall of the Confederate Government*. 2 vols. New York, NY: D. Appleton and Co., 1881.
———. *A Short History of the Confederate States of America*. New York, NY: Belford, 1890.
Davis, Kenneth C. *Don't Know Much About the Civil War: Everything You Need to Know About America's Greatest Conflict But Never Learned*. 1996. New York, NY: HarperCollins, 1997 ed.
Davis, Michael. *The Image of Lincoln in the South*. Knoxville, TN: University of Tennessee Press, 1971.

Davis, Varina. *Jefferson Davis: Ex-President of the Confederate States of America - A Memoir by His Wife.* 2 vols. New York, NY: Belford Co., 1890.

Davis, William C. *Jefferson Davis: The Man and His Hour.* New York, NY: HarperCollins, 1991.

——. *An Honorable Defeat: The Last Days of the Confederate Government.* New York, NY: Harcourt, 2001.

——. *Look Away: A History of the Confederate States of America.* 2002. New York, NY: Free Press, 2003 ed.

Davenport, Robert R. *Roots of the Rich and Famous: Real Cases of Unlikely Lineage.* Dallas, TX: Taylor Publishing Co., 1998.

Dawson, Sarah Morgan. *A Confederate Girl's Diary.* London, UK: William Heinemann, 1913.

Dean, Henry Clay. *Crimes of the Civil War, and Curse of the Funding System.* Baltimore, MD: William T. Smithson, 1869.

De Angelis, Gina. *It Happened in Washington, D.C.* Guilford, CT: Globe Pequot Press, 2004.

DeCaro, Louis A., Jr. *Fire From the Midst of You: A Religious Life of John Brown.* New York, NY: New York University Press, 2002.

Deems, Edward Mark. *Holy-Days and Holidays: A Treasury of Historical Material, Sermons in Full and Brief, Suggestive Thoughts, and Poetry.* New York, NY: Funk and Wagnalls, 1902.

De Forest, John William. *A Volunteer's Adventures: A Union Captain's Record of the Civil War.* 1946. North Haven, CT: Archon, 1970 ed.

DeGregorio, William A. *The Complete Book of U.S. Presidents.* 1984. New York, NY: Barricade, 1993 ed.

Delbanco, Andrew. *The Portable Abraham Lincoln.* New York, NY: Penguin, 1992.

Deloria, Vine, Jr. *Custer Died for Your Sins: An Indian Manifesto.* 1969. New York, NY: Avon, 1973 ed.

Denney, Robert E. *The Civil War Years: A Day-by-Day Chronicle of the Life of a Nation.* 1992. New York, NY: Sterling Publishing, 1994 ed.

Denson, John V. (ed.). *Reassessing the Presidency: The Rise of the Executive State and the Decline of Freedom.* Auburn, AL: Mises Institute, 2001.

Derosa, Marshall L. *The Confederate Constitution of 1861: An Inquiry into American Constitutionalism.* Columbia, MO: University of Missouri Press, 1991.

Desty, Robert. *The Constitution of the United States*. San Francisco, CA: Sumner Whitney and Co., 1881.

Diamond, Jared. *Guns, Germs, and Steel: The Fate of Human Societies*. 1997. New York, NY: W. W. Norton, 1999 ed.

Dicey, Edward. *Six Months in the Federal States*. 2 vols. London, UK: Macmillan and Co., 1863.

DiLorenzo, Thomas J. "The Great Centralizer: Abraham Lincoln and the War Between the States." *The Independent Review*, Vol. 3, No. 2, Fall 1998, pp. 243-271.

——. *The Real Lincoln: A New Look at Abraham Lincoln, His Agenda, and an Unnecessary War*. Three Rivers, MI: Three Rivers Press, 2003.

——. *Lincoln Unmasked: What You're Not Supposed to Know About Dishonest Abe*. New York, NY: Crown Forum, 2006.

——. *Hamilton's Curse: How Jefferson's Archenemy Betrayed the American Revolution—and What It Means for America Today*. New York, NY: Crown Forum, 2008.

DiLorenzo, Thomas J., and Joseph A. Morris. *Abraham Lincoln: Friend or Foe of Freedom?* Chicago, IL: Heartland Institute, 2008.

Dinkins, James. *1861 to 1865: Personal Recollections and Experiences in the Confederate Army, by an "Old Johnnie"*. Cincinnati, OH: Robert Clarke, 1897.

Doddridge, Joseph. *Notes on the Settlement and Indian Wars of the Western Parts of Virginia and Pennsylvania, From 1763 to 1783, Inclusive*. Albany, NY: Joel Munsell, 1876.

Dodge, Daniel Kilham. *Abraham Lincoln: Master of Words*. New York, NY: D. Appleton and Co., 1924.

Donald, David Herbert. *Lincoln Reconsidered: Essays on the Civil War Era*. 1947. New York, NY: Vintage Press, 1989 ed.

——. (ed.). *Why the North Won the Civil War*. 1960. New York, NY: Collier, 1962 ed.

——. *Lincoln*. New York, NY: Simon and Schuster, 1995.

Douglas, Henry Kyd. *I Rode With Stonewall: The War Experiences of the Youngest Member of Jackson's Staff*. 1940. Chapel Hill, NC: University of North Carolina Press, 1968 ed.

Douglass, Frederick. *Narrative of the Life of Frederick Douglass: An American Slave*. 1845. New York, NY: Signet, 1997 ed.

——. *The Life and Times of Frederick Douglass, From 1817 to 1882*. London, UK: Christian Age Office, 1882.

Drescher, Seymour, and Stanley L. Engerman (eds.). *A Historical Guide to World Slavery*. New York, NY: Oxford University Press, 1998.

Du Bois, William Edward Burghardt. *Darkwater: Voices From Within the Veil*. New York, NY: Harcourt, Brace and Howe, 1920.

DuBose, John Witherspoon. *General Joseph Wheeler and the Army of Tennessee*. New York, NY: Neale Publishing Co., 1912.

Duff, Mountstuart E. Grant. *Notes From a Diary, 1851-1872*. 2 vols. London, UK: John Murray, 1897.

Duke, Basil W. *Reminiscences of General Basil W. Duke, C.S.A.* New York, NY: Doubleday, Page and Co., 1911.

Dunbar, Rowland (ed.). *Jefferson Davis, Constitutionalist: His Letters, Papers, and Speeches*. 10 vols. Jackson, MS: Mississippi Department of Archives and History, 1923.

Durden, Robert F. *The Gray and the Black: The Confederate Debate on Emancipation*. Baton Rouge, LA: Louisiana State University Press, 1972.

Early, Jubal A. *A Memoir of the Last Year of the War for Independence in the Confederate States of America*. Lynchburg, VA: Charles W. Button, 1867.

Eaton, Clement. *A History of the Southern Confederacy*. 1945. New York, NY: Free Press, 1966 ed.

——. *Jefferson Davis*. New York, NY: Free Press, 1977.

Eaton, John, and Ethel Osgood Mason. *Grant, Lincoln and the Freedmen: Reminiscences of the Civil War, With Special Reference to the Work of the Contrabands and Freedmen of the Mississippi Valley*. New York, NY: Longmans, Green, and Co., 1907.

Edmonds, Franklin Spencer. *Ulysses S. Grant*. Philadelphia, PA: George W. Jacobs and Co., 1915.

Egerton, Douglas R. *Year of Meteors: Stephen Douglas, Abraham Lincoln, and the Election that Brought on the Civil War*. New York, NY: Bloomsbury Press, 2010.

Elliot, Jonathan. *The Debates in the Several State Conventions on the Adoption of the Federal Constitution, As Recommended by the General Convention at Philadelphia in 1787*. 5 vols. Philadelphia, PA: J. B. Lippincott, 1891.

Elliott, E. N. *Cotton is King, and Pro-Slavery Arguments: Comprising the Writings of Hammond, Harper, Christy, Stringfellow, Hodge, Bledsoe, and Cartwright, on this Important Subject*. Augusta, GA: Pritchard,

Abbott and Loomis, 1860.

Ellis, Joseph J. *American Sphinx: The Character of Thomas Jefferson.* 1996. New York, NY: Vintage, 1998 ed.

——. *Founding Brothers: The Revolutionary Generation.* 2000. New York, NY: Vintage, 2002 ed.

Eltis, David. *The Rise of African Slavery in the Americas.* Cambridge, UK: Cambridge University Press, 2000.

Emerson, Bettie Alder Calhoun. *Historic Southern Monuments: Representative Memorials of the Heroic Dead of the Southern Confederacy.* New York, NY: Neale Publishing Co., 1911.

Emerson, Ralph Waldo. *The Complete Works of Ralph Waldo Emerson.* 12 vols. 1878. Boston, MA: Houghton, Mifflin and Co., 1904 ed.

——. *Journals of Ralph Waldo Emerson.* 10 vols. Edward Waldo Emerson and Waldo Emerson Forbes, eds. Boston, MA: Houghton, Mifflin and Co., 1910.

——. *The Journals and Miscellaneous Notebooks of Ralph Waldo Emerson.* 16 vols. Cambridge, MA: Belknap Press, 1975.

Emison, John Avery. *Lincoln Über Alles: Dictatorship Comes to America.* Gretna, LA: Pelican Publishing Co., 2009.

Encyclopedia Britannica: A New Survey of Universal Knowledge. 1768. Chicago, IL/London, UK: Encyclopedia Britannica, 1955 ed.

Epstein, Daniel Mark. *The Lincolns: Portrait of a Marriage.* New York, NY: Ballantine, 2008.

——. *Lincoln's Men: The President and His Private Secretaries.* New York, NY: HarperCollins, 2009.

Escott, Paul D. (ed.). *North Carolinians in the Era of the Civil War and Reconstruction.* Chapel Hill, NC: University of North Carolina Press, 2008.

——. *"What Shall We Do with the Negro?": Lincoln, White Racism, and Civil War America.* Charlottesville, VA: University of Virginia Press, 2009.

Essah, Patience. *A House Divided: Slavery and Emancipation in Delaware, 1638-1865.* Charlottesville, VA: University Press of Virginia, 1996.

Etulain, Richard W. (Ed.). *Lincoln Looks West: From the Mississippi to the Pacific.* Carbondale, IL: Southern Illinois University Press, 2010.

Evans, Clement Anselm (ed.). *Confederate Military History: A Library of Confederate States History, in Twelve Volumes, Written By Distinguished Men of the South.* 12 vols. Atlanta, GA: Confederate Publishing

Co., 1899.

Evans, Eli N. *Judah P. Benjamin: The Jewish Confederate.* 1988. New York, NY: Free Press, 1989 ed.

Evans, Lawrence B. (ed.). *Writings of George Washington.* New York, NY: G. P. Putnam's Sons, 1908.

Faragher, John Mack. *Sugar Creek: Life on the Illinois Prairie.* New Haven, CT: Yale University Press, 1986.

Farrar, Victor John. *The Annexation of Russian America to the United States.* Washington D.C.: W. F. Roberts, 1937.

Farrow, Anne, Joel Lang, and Jennifer Frank. *Complicity: How the North Promoted, Prolonged, and Profited From Slavery.* New York, NY: Ballantine, 2005.

Faulkner, William. *The Unvanquished.* 1934. New York, NY: Vintage, 1966 ed.

Faust, Patricia L. (ed.). *Historical Times Illustrated Encyclopedia of the Civil War.* New York, NY: Harper and Row, 1986.

Fay, Edwin Hedge. *This Infernal War: The Confederate Letters of Edwin H. Fay.* Austin, TX: University of Texas Press, 1958.

Fehrenbacher, Don E. (ed.). *Abraham Lincoln: A Documentary Portrait Through His Speeches and Writings.* New York, NY: Signet, 1964.

———. *Lincoln in Text and Context: Collected Essays.* Stanford, CA: Stanford University press, 1987.

———. (ed.) *Abraham Lincoln: Speeches and Writings, 1859-1865.* New York, NY: Library of America, 1989.

———. *The Slaveholding Republic: An Account of the United States Government's Relations to Slavery.* New York, NY: Oxford University Press, 2002.

Fehrenbacher, Don E., and Virginia Fehrenbacher (eds). *Recollected Works of Abraham Lincoln.* Stanford, CA: Stanford University Press, 1996.

Ferris, Marcie Cohen, and Mark I. Greenberg (eds.). *Jewish Roots in Southern Soil: A New History.* Waltham, MA: Brandeis University Press, 2006.

Fields, Annie (ed.) *Life and Letters of Harriet Beecher Stowe.* Cambridge, MA: Riverside Press, 1897.

Findlay, Bruce, and Esther Findlay. *Your Rugged Constitution: How America's House of Freedom is Planned and Built.* 1950. Stanford, CA: Stanford University Press, 1951 ed.

Finkelman, Paul. *Dred Scott v. Sanford: A Brief History With Documents*. Boston, MA: Bedford Books, 1997.
Fite, Emerson David. *Social and Industrial Conditions in the North During the Civil War*. New York, NY: Macmillan, 1910.
——. *The Presidential Election of 1860*. New York, NY: MacMillan, 1911.
Fleming, Walter Lynwood. *Civil War and Reconstruction in Alabama*. New York, NY: Macmillan, 1905.
Flood, Charles Bracelen. *1864: Lincoln At the Gates of History*. New York, NY: Simon and Schuster, 2009.
Fogel, Robert William. *Without Consent or Contract: The Rise and Fall of American Slavery*. New York, NY: W. W. Norton, 1989.
Fogel, Robert William, and Stanley L. Engerman. *Time On the Cross: The Economics of American Negro Slavery*. Boston, MA: Little, Brown, and Co., 1974.
Foley, John P. (ed.). *The Jeffersonian Cyclopedia*. New York, NY: Funk and Wagnalls, 1900.
Foner, Eric. *Free Soil, Free Labor, Free Men: The Ideology of the Republican Party Before the Civil War*. New York, NY: Oxford University Press, 1970.
——. *Reconstruction: America's Unfinished Revolution, 1863-1877*. 1988. New York, NY: Harper and Row, 1989 ed.
Foote, Shelby. *The Civil War: A Narrative, Fort Sumter to Perryville, Vol. 1*. 1958. New York, NY: Vintage, 1986 ed.
——. *The Civil War: A Narrative, Fredericksburg to Meridian, Vol. 2*. 1963. New York, NY: Vintage, 1986 ed.
——. *The Civil War: A Narrative, Red River to Appomattox, Vol. 3*. 1974. New York, NY: Vintage, 1986 ed.
Ford, Paul Leicester (ed.). *The Works of Thomas Jefferson*. 12 vols. New York, NY: G. P. Putnam's Sons, 1904.
Ford, Worthington Chauncey (ed.). *A Cycle of Adams Letters*. 2 vols. Boston, MA: Houghton Mifflin, 1920.
Forman, S. E. *The Life and Writings of Thomas Jefferson*. Indianapolis, IN: Bowen-Merrill, 1900.
Fornieri, Joseph (ed.). *The Language of Liberty: The Political Speeches and Writings of Abraham Lincoln*. Washington, D.C.: Regnery, 2009.
Förster, Stig, and Jörg Nagler (eds.). *On the Road to Total War: The American Civil War and the German Wars of Unification, 1861-1871*. 1997. Cambridge, UK: Cambridge University Press, 2002 ed.

Foster, John W. *A Century of American Diplomacy*. Boston, MA: Houghton, Mifflin and Co., 1901.

Fowler, John D. *The Confederate Experience Reader: Selected Documents and Essays*. New York, NY: Routledge, 2007.

Fowler, William Chauncey. *The Sectional Controversy; or Passages in the Political History of the United States, Including the Causes of the War Between the Sections*. New York, NY: Charles Scribner, 1864.

Fox, Gustavus Vasa. *Confidential Correspondence of Gustavus Vasa Fox, Assistant Secretary of the Navy, 1861-1865*. 2 vols. 1918. New York, NY: Naval History Society, 1920 ed.

Fox-Genovese, Elizabeth. *Within the Plantation Household: Black and White Women of the Old South (Gender and American Culture)*. Chapel Hill, NC: University of North Carolina Press, 1988.

Franklin, Benjamin. *The Complete Works of Benjamin Franklin*. 10 vols. New York, NY: G. P. Putnam's Sons, 1887.

Franklin, John Hope. *Reconstruction After the Civil War*. Chicago, IL: University of Chicago Press, 1961.

Fredrickson, George M. *The Black Image in the White Mind: The Debate on Afro-American Character and Destiny, 1817-1914*. New York, NY: Harper and Row, 1971.

———. *Big Enough to Be Inconsistent: Abraham Lincoln Confronts Slavery and Race*. Cambridge, MA: Harvard University Press, 2008.

Freiling, Thomas. *Walking With Lincoln: Spiritual Strength From America's Favorite President*. Grand Rapids, MI: Revell, 2009.

Fremantle, Arthur James. *Three Months in the Southern States, April-June, 1863*. New York, NY: John Bradburn, 1864.

Friedman, Saul S. *Jews and the American Slave Trade*. New Brunswick, NJ: Transaction, 2000.

Furguson, Ernest B. *Freedom Rising: Washington in the Civil War*. 2004. New York, NY: Vintage, 2005 ed.

Furnas, J. C. *The Americans: A Social History of the United States, 1587-1914*. New York, NY: G. P. Putnam's Sons, 1969.

Galenson, David W. *White Servitude in Colonial America*. New York, NY: Cambridge University Press, 1981.

Garland, Hugh A. *The Life of John Randolph of Roanoke*. New York, NY: D. Appleton and Co., 1874.

Garraty, John A. (ed.). *Historical Viewpoints: Notable Articles From American Heritage, Vol. One to 1877*. 1970. New York, NY: Harper and

Row, 1979 ed.
Garraty, John A., and Robert A. McCaughey. *A Short History of the American Nation*. 1966. New York, NY: HarperCollins, 1989 ed.
Garrison, Webb B. *Civil War Trivia and Fact Book*. Nashville, TN: Rutledge Hill Press, 1992.
——. *The Lincoln No One Knows: The Mysterious Man Who Ran the Civil War*. Nashville, TN: Rutledge Hill Press, 1993.
——. *Civil War Curiosities: Strange Stories, Oddities, Events, and Coincidences*. Nashville, TN: Rutledge Hill Press, 1994.
——. *The Amazing Civil War*. Nashville, TN: Rutledge Hill Press, 1998.
Garrison, Wendell Phillips, and Francis Jackson Garrison. *William Lloyd Garrison, 1805-1879*. 4 vols. New York, NY: Century Co., 1889.
Garrison, William Lloyd. *Thoughts on African Colonization*. Boston, MA: Garrison and Knapp, 1832.
Gates, Henry Louis, Jr. (ed.) *The Classic Slave Narratives*. New York, NY: Mentor, 1987.
Gates, Henry Louis, Jr., and Donald Yacovone (eds). *Lincoln on Race and Slavery*. Princeton, NJ: Princeton University Press, 2009.
Genovese, Eugene D. *Roll, Jordan, Roll: The World the Slaves Made*. New York, NY: Pantheon, 1974.
Gerster, Patrick, and Nicholas Cords (eds.). *Myth and Southern History*. 2 vols. 1974. Champaign, IL: University of Illinois Press, 1989 ed.
Gienapp, William E. *Abraham Lincoln and Civil War America: A Biography*. Oxford, UK: Oxford University Press, 2002.
Gilmore, James Roberts. *Personal Recollections of Abraham Lincoln and the Civil War*. Boston, MA: L. C. Page and Co., 1898.
Golay, Michael. *A Ruined Land: The End of the Civil War*. New York, NY: John Wiley and Sons, 1999.
Gordon, Armistead Churchill. *Figures From American History: Jefferson Davis*. New York, NY: Charles Scribner's Sons, 1918.
Gower, Herschel, and Jack Allen (eds.). *Pen and Sword: The Life and Journals of Randal W. McGavock*. Nashville, TN: Tennessee Historical Commission, 1959.
Gragg, Rod. *The Illustrated Confederate Reader: Extraordinary Eyewitness Accounts by the Civil War's Southern Soldiers and Civilians*. New York, NY: Gramercy Books, 1989.

Graham, John Remington. *A Constitutional History of Secession*. Gretna, LA: Pelican Publishing Co., 2003.

——. *Blood Money: The Civil War and the Federal Reserve*. Gretna, LA: Pelican Publishing Co., 2006.

Grant, Arthur James. *Greece in the Age of Pericles*. London, UK: John Murray, 1893.

Grant, Ulysses Simpson. *Personal Memoirs of U. S. Grant*. 2 vols. 1885-1886. New York, NY: Charles L. Webster and Co., 1886.

Gray, Robert, Rev. (compiler). *The McGavock Family: A Genealogical History of James McGavock and His Descendants, from 1760 to 1903*. Richmond, VA: W. E. Jones, 1903.

Gray, Thomas R. *The Confessions of Nat Turner: The Leader of the Late Insurrection in Southampton, Virginia*. Richmond, VA: Thomas R. Gray, 1831.

Greeley, Horace (ed.). *The Writings of Cassius Marcellus Clay*. New York, NY: Harper and Brothers, 1848.

——. *A History of the Struggle for Slavery Extension or Restriction in the United States From the Declaration of Independence to the Present Day*. New York, NY: Dix, Edwards and Co., 1856.

——. *The American Conflict: A History of the Great Rebellion in the United States, 1861-1865*. 2 vols. Hartford, CT: O. D. Case and Co., 1867.

Green, Constance McLaughlin. *Eli Whitney and the Birth of American Technology*. Boston, MA: Little, Brown, and Co., 1956.

——. *Washington: A History of the Capital, 1800-1950*. 1962. Princeton, NJ: Princeton University Press, 1976 ed.

Greenberg, Martin H., and Charles G. Waugh (eds.). *The Price of Freedom: Slavery and the Civil War—Vol. 1, The Demise of Slavery*. Nashville, TN: Cumberland House, 2000.

Greene, Lorenzo Johnston. *The Negro in Colonial New England, 1620-1776*. New York, NY: Columbia University Press, 1942.

Greenhow, Rose O'Neal. *My Imprisonment and the First Year of Abolition Rule at Washington*. London, UK: Richard Bentley, 1863.

Grimsley, Mark. *The Hard Hand of War: Union Military Policy Toward Southern Civilians, 1861-1865*. 1995. Cambridge, UK: Cambridge University Press, 1997 ed.

Grissom, Michael Andrew. *Southern By the Grace of God*. 1988. Gretna, LA: Pelican Publishing Co., 1995 ed.

Groom, Winston. *Shrouds of Glory - From Atlanta to Nashville: The Last Great Campaign of the Civil War*. New York, NY: Grove Press, 1995.

Guelzo, Allen C. *Abraham Lincoln: Redeemer President*. Cambridge, UK: William B. Eerdmans, 1999.

——. *Abraham Lincoln As a Man of Ideas*. Carbondale, IL: Southern Illinois University Press, 2009.

Gwatkin, H. M., and J. P. Whitney (eds.). *The Cambridge Medieval History, Vol. 2: The Rise of the Saracens and the Foundation of the Western Empire*. New York, NY: Macmillan, 1913.

Hacker, Louis Morton. *The Shaping of the American Tradition*. New York, NY: Columbia University Press, 1947.

Haggard, Dixie Ray (ed.). *African Americans in the Nineteenth Century: People and Perspectives*. Santa Barbara, CA: ABC-Clio, 2010.

Hall, B. C., and C. T. Wood. *The South: A Two-step Odyssey on the Backroads of the Enchanted Land*. New York, NY: Touchstone, 1996.

Hall, Kermit L. (ed.). *The Oxford Companion to the Supreme Court of the United States*. New York, NY: Oxford University Press, 1992.

Hamblin, Ken. *Pick a Better Country: An Unassuming Colored Guy Speaks His Mind About America*. New York, NY: Touchstone, 1997.

Hamilton, Alexander, James Madison, and John Jay. *The Federalist Papers*. New York, NY: Signet Classics, 2003.

Hamilton, Neil A. *Rebels and Renegades: A Chronology of Social and Political Dissent in the United States*. New York, NY: Routledge, 2002.

Hanchett, William. *Out of the Wilderness: The Life of Abraham Lincoln*. Urbana, IL: University of Illinois Press, 1994.

Hannity, Sean. *Let Freedom Ring: Winning the War of Liberty Over Liberalism*. New York, NY: HarperCollins, 2002.

Hansen, Harry. *The Civil War: A History*. 1961. Harmondsworth, UK: Mentor, 1991 ed.

Harding, Samuel Bannister. *The Contest Over the Ratification of the Federal Constitution in the State of Massachusetts*. New York, NY: Longmans, Green, and Co., 1896.

Harper, William, James Henry Hammond, William Gilmore Simms, and Thomas Roderick Dew. *The Pro-Slavery Argument, As Maintained by the Most Distinguished Writers of the Southern States*. Charleston, SC: Walker, Richards and Co., 1852.

Harrell, David Edwin, Jr., Edwin S. Gaustad, John B. Boles, Sally

Foreman Griffith, Randall M. Miller, and Randall B. Woods. *Unto a Good Land: A History of the American People*. Grand Rapids, MI: William B. Eerdmans, 2005.

Harris, Joel Chandler. *Stories of Georgia*. New York, NY: American Book Co., 1896.

Harris, Norman Dwight. *The History of Negro Servitude in Illinois*. Chicago, IL: A. C. McClurg and Co., 1904.

Harris, William C. *Lincoln's Rise to the Presidency*. Lawrence, KS: University Press of Kansas, 2007.

Harrison, Peleg D. *The Stars and Stripes and Other American Flags*. 1906. Boston, MA: Little, Brown, and Co., 1908 ed.

Hartzell, Josiah. *The Genesis of the Republican Party*. Canton, OH: n.p., 1890.

Harwell, Richard B. (ed.). *The Confederate Reader: How the South Saw the War*. 1957. Mineola, NY: Dover, 1989 ed.

Hattaway, Herman, and Archer Jones. *How the North Won: A Military History of the Civil War*. 1983. Champaign, IL: University of Illinois Press, 1991 ed.

Hawthorne, Julian (ed.). *Orations of American Orators*. 2 vols. New York, NY: Colonial Press, 1900.

Hawthorne, Julian, James Schouler, and Elisha Benjamin Andrews. *United States, From the Discovery of the North American Continent Up to the Present Time*. 9 vols. New York, NY: Co-operative Publication Society, 1894.

Hayden, Horace Edwin. *Virginia Genealogies: A Genealogy of the Glassell Family of Scotland and Virginia*. 1885. Wilkes-Barre, PA: N.P., 1891 ed.

Haygood, Atticus G. *Our Brother in Black: His Freedom and His Future*. Nashville, TN: M. E. Church, 1896.

Hedrick, Joan D. (ed.). *The Oxford Harriet Beecher Stowe Reader*. New York, NY: Oxford University Press, 1999.

Heidler, David S., and Jeanne T. Heidler. *Henry Clay: The Essential American*. New York, NY: Random House, 2010.

Helper, Hinton Rowan. *The Impending Crisis of the South: How to Meet It*. New York, NY: A. B. Burdick, 1860.

——. *Compendium of the Impending Crisis of the South*. New York, NY: A. B. Burdick, 1860.

——. *Nojoque: A Question for a Continent*. New York, NY: George W.

Carleton, 1867.

———. *The Negroes in Negroland: The Negroes in America; and Negroes Generally*. New York, NY: George W. Carlton, 1868.

———. *Oddments of Andean Diplomacy and Other Oddments*. St. Louis, MO: W. S. Bryan, 1879.

Henderson, George Francis Robert. *Stonewall Jackson and the American Civil War*. 2 vols. London, UK: Longmans, Green, and Co., 1919.

Henry, Robert Selph (ed.). *The Story of the Confederacy*. 1931. New York, NY: Konecky and Konecky, 1999 ed.

———. *As They Saw Forrest: Some Recollections and Comments of Contemporaries*. 1956. Wilmington, NC: Broadfoot Publishing Co., 1991 ed.

———. *First with the Most: Forrest*. New York, NY: Konecky and Konecky, 1992.

Henson, Josiah. *Father Henson's Story of His Own Life*. Boston, MA: John P. Jewett and Co., 1858.

Herndon, William H., and Jesse W. Weik. *Abraham Lincoln: The True Story of a Great Life*. 2 vols. New York, NY: D. Appleton and Co., 1892.

Hertz, Emanuel. *Abraham Lincoln: A New Portrait*. 2 Vols. New York, NY: H. Liveright, 1931.

———. *The Hidden Lincoln*. New York, NY: Blue Ribbon Works, 1940.

Hervey, Anthony. *Why I Wave the Confederate Flag, Written By a Black Man: The End of Niggerism and the Welfare State*. Oxford, UK: Trafford Publishing, 2006.

Hesseltine, William B. *Lincoln and the War Governors*. New York, NY: Alfred A. Knopf, 1948.

Hey, David. *The Oxford Guide to Family History*. Oxford, UK: Oxford University Press, 1993.

Hickey, William. *The Constitution of the United States*. Philadelphia, PA: T. K. and P. G. Collins, 1853.

Highsmith, Carol M. and Ted Landphair. *Civil War Battlefields and Landmarks: A Photographic Tour*. New York, NY: Random House, 2003.

Hildreth, Richard. *The White Slave: Another Picture of Slave Life in America*. Boston, MA: Adamant Media Corp., 2001.

Hinkle, Don. *Embattled Banner: A Reasonable Defense of the Confederate Battle Flag*. Paducah, KY: Turner Publishing Co., 1997.

Hitler, Adolf. *Mein Kampf*. 2 vols. 1925, 1926. New York: NY: Reynal and Hitchcock, 1941 English translation ed.

Hoffman, Michael A., II. *They Were White and They Were Slaves: The Untold History of the Enslavement of Whites in Early America.* Dresden, NY: Wiswell Ruffin House, 1993.

Hofstadter, Richard. *The American Political Tradition, and the Men Who Made It.* New York, NY: Alfred A. Knopf, 1948.

Holland, Jesse J. *Black Men Built the Capitol: Discovering African-American History in and Around Washington, D.C.* Guilford, CT: The Globe Pequot Press, 2007.

Holland, Josiah Gilbert. *The Life of Abraham Lincoln.* Springfield, MA: Gurdon Bill, 1866.

Holland, Rupert Sargent (ed.). *Letters and Diary of Laura M. Towne: Written From the Sea Islands of South Carolina, 1862-1884.* Cambridge, MA: Riverside Press, 1912.

Holzer, Harold (ed.). *The Lincoln-Douglas Debates: The First Complete, Unexpurgated Text.* 1993. Bronx, NY: Fordham University Press, 2004 ed.

Hood, John Bell. *Advance and Retreat: Personal Experiences in the United States and Confederate States Armies.* New Orleans, LA: G. T. Beauregard, 1880.

Horn, Stanley F. *Invisible Empire: The Story of the Ku Klux Klan, 1866-1871.* 1939. Montclair, NJ: Patterson Smith, 1969 ed.

——. *The Decisive Battle of Nashville.* 1956. Baton Rouge, LA: Louisiana State University Press, 1991 ed.

Horwitz, Tony. *Confederates in the Attic: Dispatches From the Unfinished Civil War.* 1998. New York, NY: Vintage, 1999 ed.

House Documents, 64th Congress, 1st Session, December 6, 1915, to September 8, 1916, Vol. 145. Washington, D.C.: Government Printing Office, 1916.

Howe, Daniel Wait. *Political History of Secession.* New York, NY: G. P. Putnam's Sons, 1914.

Howe, Henry. *Historical Collections of Virginia.* Charleston, SC: William R. Babcock, 1852.

Howe, M. A. DeWolfe (ed.). *Home Letters of General Sherman.* New York, NY: Charles Scribner's Sons, 1909.

Hubbard, John Milton. *Notes of a Private.* St. Louis, MO: Nixon-Jones, 1911.

Hunt, John Gabriel (ed.). *The Essential Abraham Lincoln.* Avenel, NJ:

Portland House, 1993.

Hurmence, Belinda (ed.). *Before Freedom, When I Can Just Remember: Twenty-seven Oral Histories of Former South Carolina Slaves.* 1989. Winston-Salem, NC: John F. Blair, 2002 ed.

Hurst, Jack. *Nathan Bedford Forrest: A Biography.* 1993. New York, NY: Vintage, 1994 ed.

Ingersoll, Thomas G., and Robert E. O'Connor. *Politics and Structure: Essential of American National Government.* North Scituate, MA: Duxbury Press, 1979.

Isaacson, Walter (ed.). *Profiles in Leadership: Historians on the Elusive Quality of Greatness.* New York, NY: W. W. Norton and Co., 2010.

Jaffa, Harry V. *Crisis of the House Divided: An Interpretation of the Issues in the Lincoln-Douglas Debates.* 1959. Chicago, IL: University of Chicago Press, 2009 ed.

Jahoda, Gloria. *The Trail of Tears: The Story of the American Indian Removals, 1813-1855.* 1975. New York, NY: Wings Book, 1995 ed.

Jaquette, Henrietta Stratton (ed.). *South After Gettysburg: Letters of Cornelia Hancock, 1863-1868.* Philadelphia, PA: University of Pennsylvania Press, 1937.

Jefferson, Thomas. *Notes on the State of Virginia.* Boston, MA: H. Sprague, 1802.

——. *Thomas Jefferson's Farm Book.* (Edwin Morris Betts, ed.). Charlottesville, VA: Thomas Jefferson Memorial Foundation, 1999.

Jenkins, John S. *The Life of James Knox Polk, Late President of the United States.* Auburn, NY: James M. Alden, 1850.

Jensen, Merrill. *The New Nation: A History of the United States During the Confederation, 1781-1789.* New York, NY: Vintage, 1950.

——. *The Articles of Confederation: An Interpretation of the Social-Constitutional History of the American Revolution, 1774-1781.* Madison, WI: University of Wisconsin Press, 1959.

Jimerson, Randall C. *The Private Civil War: Popular Thought During the Sectional Conflict.* Baton Rouge, LA: Louisiana State University Press, 1988.

Johannsen, Robert Walter. *Lincoln, the South, and Slavery: The Political Dimension.* Baton Rouge, LA: Louisiana State University Press, 1991.

Johnson, Adam Rankin. *The Partisan Rangers of the Confederate States Army.*

Louisville, KY: George G. Fetter, 1904.
Johnson, Benjamin Heber. *Making of the American West: People and Perspectives.* Santa Barbara, CA: ABC-Clio, 2007.
Johnson, Clint. *The Politically Incorrect Guide to the South (and Why It Will Rise Again).* Washington, D.C.: Regnery, 2006.
Johnson, Ludwell H. *North Against South: The American Iliad, 1848-1877.* 1978. Columbia, SC: Foundation for American Education, 1993 ed.
Johnson, Michael, and James L. Roark. *Black Masters: A Free Family of Color in the Old South.* New York, NY: W.W. Norton, 1984.
Johnson, Oliver. *William Lloyd Garrison and His Times.* 1879. Boston, MA: Houghton Mifflin and Co., 1881 ed.
Johnson, Robert Underwood (ed.). *Battles and Leaders of the Civil War.* 4 vols. New York, NY: The Century Co., 1884-1888.
Johnson, Thomas Cary. *The Life and Letters of Robert Lewis Dabney.* Richmond, VA: Presbyterian Committee of Publication, 1903.
Jones, Howard. *Abraham Lincoln and a New Birth of Freedom: The Union and Slavery in the Diplomacy of the Civil War.* Lincoln, NE: University of Nebraska Press, 1999.
Jones, John Beauchamp. *A Rebel War Clerk's Diary at the Confederate States Capital.* 2 vols. in 1. Philadelphia, PA: J. B. Lippincott and Co., 1866.
Jones, John William. *Personal Reminiscences, Anecdotes, and Letters of Gen. Robert E. Lee.* New York, NY: D. Appleton and Co., 1874.
Jones, Wilmer L. *Generals in Blue and Gray.* 2 vols. Westport, CT: Praeger, 2004.
Jordan, Don, and Michael Walsh. *White Cargo: The Forgotten History of Britain's White Slaves in America.* New York, NY: New York University Press, 2008.
Jordan, Ervin L. *Black Confederates and Afro-Yankees in Civil War Virginia.* Charlottesville, VA: University Press of Virginia, 1995.
Jordan, Thomas, and John P. Pryor. *The Campaigns of General Nathan Bedford Forrest and of Forrest's Cavalry.* New Orleans, LA: Blelock and Co., 1868.
Julian, George Washington. *Speeches on Political Questions.* New York, NY: Hurd and Houghton, 1872.
Kane, Joseph Nathan. *Facts About the Presidents: A Compilation of Biographical and Historical Data.* 1959. New York, NY: Ace,

1976 ed.

Katcher, Philip. *The Civil War Source Book*. 1992. New York, NY: Facts on File, 1995 ed.

———. *Brassey's Almanac: The American Civil War*. London, UK: Brassey's, 2003.

Kautz, August Valentine. *Customs of Service for Non-Commissioned Officers and Soldiers (as Derived from Law and Regulations and Practised in the Army of the United States)*. Philadelphia, PA: J. B. Lippincott and Co., 1864.

Keckley, Elizabeth. *Behind the Scenes, or Thirty Years a Slave, and Four Years in the White House*. New York, NY: G. W. Carlton and Co., 1868.

Kelly, Alfred H., Winfred A. Harbison, and Herman Belz. *The American Constitution: Its Origins and Development* (Vol. 2). 1965. New York, NY: W.W. Norton, 1991 ed.

Keneally, Thomas. *Abraham Lincoln*. New York, NY: Viking, 2003.

Kennedy, James Ronald, and Walter Donald Kennedy. *The South Was Right!* Gretna, LA: Pelican Publishing Co., 1994.

———. *Why Not Freedom!: America's Revolt Against Big Government*. Gretna, LA: Pelican Publishing Co., 2005.

———. *Nullifying Tyranny: Creating Moral Communities in an Immoral Society*. Gretna, LA: Pelican Publishing Co., 2010.

Kennedy, Walter Donald. *Myths of American Slavery*. Gretna, LA: Pelican Publishing Co., 2003.

Kennett, Lee B. *Sherman: A Soldier's Life*. 2001. New York, NY: HarperCollins, 2002 ed.

Kettell, Thomas Prentice. *History of the Great Rebellion*. Hartford, CT: L. Stebbins, 1865.

Kinder, Hermann, and Werner Hilgemann. *The Anchor Atlas of World History: From the French Revolution to the American Bicentennial*. 2 vols. Garden City, NY: Anchor, 1978.

King, Charles R. (ed.). *The Life and Correspondence of Rufus King*. 6 vols. New York, NY: G. P. Putnam's Sons, 1897.

King, Edward. *The Great South: A Record of Journeys*. Hartford, CT: American Publishing Co., 1875.

Kinshasa, Kwando Mbiassi. *Black Resistance to the Ku Klux Klan in the Wake of the Civil War*. Jefferson, NC: McFarland and Co., 2006.

Kirkland, Edward Chase. *The Peacemakers of 1864*. New York, NY:

Macmillan, 1927.

Klingaman, William K. *Abraham Lincoln and the Road to Emancipation, 1861-1865*. 2001. New York, NY: Penguin, 2002 ed.

Knox, Thomas Wallace. *Camp-Fire and Cotton-Field: Southern Adventure in Time of War - Life With the Union Armies, and Residence on a Louisiana Plantation*. New York, NY: Blelock and Co., 1865.

Koger, Larry. *Black Slaveowners: Free Black Slave Masters in South Carolina, 1790-1860*. Columbia, SC: University of South Carolina Press, 1995.

Kunhardt, Philip B., Peter W. Kunhardt, and Peter W. Kunhardt, Jr. *Looking for Lincoln: The Making of an American Icon*. New York, NY: Borzoi, 2008.

Lamb, Brian, and Susan Swain (eds.). *Abraham Lincoln: Great American Historians on Our Sixteenth President*. New York, NY: PublicAffairs, 2010.

Lamon, Ward Hill. *The Life of Abraham Lincoln: From His Birth to His Inauguration as President*. Boston, MA: James R. Osgood and Co., 1872.

——. *Recollections of Abraham Lincoln: 1847-1865*. Chicago, IL: A. C. McClurg and Co., 1895.

Lang, J. Stephen. *The Complete Book of Confederate Trivia*. Shippensburg, PA: Burd Street Press, 1996.

Lanning, Michael Lee. *The African-American Soldier: From Crispus Attucks to Colin Powell*. 1997. New York, NY: Citadel Press, 2004 ed.

Lapsley, Arthur Brooks (ed.). *The Writings of Abraham Lincoln*. 8 vols. New York, NY: The Lamb Publishing Co., 1906.

Lawrence, William. *Life of Amos A. Lawrence*. Boston, MA: Houghton, Mifflin, and Co., 1899.

Leech, Margaret. *Reveille in Washington, 1860-1865*. 1941. Alexandria, VA: Time-Life Books, 1980 ed.

Lee, Robert E., Jr. *Recollections and Letters of General Robert E. Lee*. New York, NY: Doubleday, Page and Co., 1904.

Lehrman, Lewis E. *Lincoln at Peoria: The Turning Point*. Mechanicsburg, PA: Stackpole, 2008.

Lemay, J. A. Leo, and P. M. Zall (eds.). *Benjamin Franklin's Autobiography: An Authoritative Text, Backgrounds, Criticism*. 1791. New York, NY: W. W. Norton and Co., 1986 ed.

Lemire, Elise. *Black Walden: Slavery and Its Aftermath in Concord,*

  Massachusetts. Philadelphia, PA: University of Pennsylvania Press, 2009.
Lester, Charles Edwards. *Life and Public Services of Charles Sumner*. New York, NY: U.S. Publishing Co., 1874.
Lester, John C., and D. L. Wilson. *Ku Klux Klan: Its Origin, Growth, and Disbandment*. 1884. New York, NY: Neale Publishing, 1905 ed.
Lewis, Lloyd. *Myths After Lincoln*. 1929. New York, NY: The Press of the Reader's Club, 1941 ed.
LeVert, Suzanne (ed.). *The Civil War Society's Encyclopedia of the Civil War*. New York, NY: Wings Books, 1997.
Levin, Mark R. *Liberty and Tyranny: A Conservative Manifesto*. New York, NY: Threshold, 2009.
Lincoln, Abraham. *The Autobiography of Abraham Lincoln* (selected from the *Complete Works of Abraham Lincoln*, 1894, by John G. Nicolay and John Hay). New York, NY: Francis D. Tandy Co., 1905.
Lincoln, Abraham, and Stephen A. Douglas. *Political Debates Between Abraham Lincoln and Stephen A. Douglas*. Cleveland, OH: Burrows Brothers Co., 1894.
Lind, Michael (ed.). *Hamilton's Republic: Readings in the American Democratic Nationalist Tradition*. New York, NY: Free Press, 1997.
Littell, Eliakim (ed.). The Living Age. Seventh Series, Vol. 30. Boston, MA: The Living Age Co., 1906.
Litwack, Leon F. *North of Slavery: The Negro in the Free States, 1790-1860*. Chicago, IL: University of Chicago Press, 1961.
——. *Been in the Storm So Long: The Aftermath of Slavery*. New York, NY: Vintage, 1980.
Livermore, Thomas L. *Numbers and Losses in the Civil War in America, 1861-65*. 1900. Carlisle, PA: John Kallmann, 1996 ed.
Livingstone, William. *Livingstone's History of the Republican Party*. 2 vols. Detroit, MI: William Livingstone, 1900.
Locke, John. *Two Treatises of Government* (Mark Goldie, ed.). 1924. London, UK: Everyman, 1998 ed.
Lodge, Henry Cabot (ed.). *The Works of Alexander Hamilton*. 12 vols. New York, NY: G. P. Putnam's Sons, 1904.
Logan, John Alexander. *The Great Conspiracy: Its Origin and History*. New York, NY: A. R. Hart, 1886.
Logsdon, David R. (ed.). *Eyewitnesses at the Battle of Franklin*. 1988.

Nashville, TN: Kettle Mills Press, 2000 ed.

———. *Tennessee Antebellum Trail Guidebook*. Nashville, TN: Kettle Mills Press, 1995.

Long, David E. *The Jewel of Liberty: Abraham Lincoln's Re-election and the End of Slavery*. Mechanicsburg, PA: Stackpole, 2008.

Long, Everette Beach, and Barbara Long. *The Civil War Day by Day: An Almanac, 1861-1865*. 1971. New York, NY: Da Capo Press, 1985 ed.

Lonn, Ella. *Foreigners in the Confederacy*. 1940. Chapel Hill, NC: University of North Carolina Press, 2002 ed.

Lott, Stanley K. *The Truth About American Slavery*. 2004. Clearwater, SC: Eastern Digital Resources, 2005 ed.

Lowry, Don. *Dark and Cruel War: The Decisive Months of the Civil War, September-December 1864*. New York, NY: Hippocrene, 1993.

Lubbock, Francis Richard. *Six Decades in Texas, or Memoirs of Francis Richard Lubbock, Governor of Texas in War-Time, 1861-1863*. 1899. Austin, TX: Ben C. Jones, 1900 ed.

Ludlow, Daniel H. (ed.). *Encyclopedia of Mormonism: The History, Scripture, Doctrine, and Procedure of the Church of Jesus Christ of Latter-Day Saints*. New York, NY: Macmillan, 1992.

Lytle, Andrew Nelson. *Bedford Forrest and His Critter Company*. New York, NY: G. P. Putnam's Sons, 1931.

MacDonald, William. *Select Documents Illustrative of the History of the United States 1776-1861*. New York, NY: Macmillan, 1897.

Mackay, Charles. *Life and Liberty in America, or Sketches of a Tour in the United States and Canada in 1857-58*. New York, NY: Harper and Brothers, 1859.

Madison, James. *Letters and Other Writings of James Madison, Fourth President of the United States*. 4 vols. Philadelphia, PA: J. B. Lippincott and Co., 1865.

Maihafer, Harry J. *War of Words: Abraham Lincoln and the Civil War Press*. Dulles, VA: Brassey's, 2001.

Main, Jackson Turner. *The Anti-Federalists: Critics of the Constitution, 1781-1788*. 1961. New York, NY: W. W. Norton and Co., 1974 ed.

Malone, Laurence J. *Opening the West: Federal Internal Improvements Before 1860*. Westport, CT: Greenwood Press, 1998.

Mandel, Bernard. *Labor, Free and Slave: Workingmen and the Anti-Slavery Movement in the United States*. New York, NY: Associated

Authors, 1955.
Manegold, Catherine S. *The Forgotten History of Slavery in the North*. Princeton, NJ: Princeton University Press, 2010.
Manning, Timothy D., Sr. (ed.) *Lincoln Reconsidered: Conference Reader*. High Point, NC: Heritage Foundation Press, 2006.
Marshall, Jessie Ames. *Private and Official Correspondence of General Benjamin F. Butler During the Period of the Civil War*. 5 vols. Norwood, MA: The Plimpton Press, 1917.
Marten, James. *The Children's Civil War*. Chapel Hill, NC: University of North Carolina Press, 1998.
Martin, Iain C. *The Quotable American Civil War*. Guilford, CT: Lyons Press, 2008.
Martineau, Harriet. *Retrospect of Western Travel*. 3 vols. London, UK: Saunders and Otley, 1838.
Martinez, James Michael. *Carpetbaggers, Cavalry, and the Ku Klux Klan: Exposing the Invisible Empire During Reconstruction*. Lanham, MD: Rowman and Littlefield, 2007.
Martinez, Susan B. *The Psychic Life of Abraham Lincoln*. Franklin Lakes, NJ: New Page Books, 2009.
Masur, Louis P. *The Real War Will Never Get In the Books: Selections From Writers During the Civil War*. New York, NY: Oxford University Press, 1993.
Mathes, Capt. J. Harvey. *General Forrest*. New York, NY: D. Appleton and Co., 1902.
Maury, Dabney Herndon. *Recollections of a Virginian in the Mexican, Indian, and Civil Wars*. New York, NY: Charles Scribner's Sons, 1894.
Mayer, David N. *The Constitutional Thought of Thomas Jefferson*. Charlottesville, VA: University of Virginia Press, 1995.
Mayer, Henry. *All on Fire: William Lloyd Garrison and the Abolition of Slavery*. New York, NY: St. Martin's Press, 1998.
McAfee, Ward M. *Citizen Lincoln*. Hauppauge, NY: Nova History Publications, 2004.
McCabe, James Dabney. *Our Martyred President: The Life and Public Services of Gen. James A. Garfield, Twentieth President of the United States*. Philadelphia, PA: National Publishing Co., 1881.
McClintock, Russell. *Lincoln and the Decision for War: The Northern Response to Secession*. Chapel Hill, NC: University of North Carolina Press, 2008.

McClure, Alexander Kelly. *Abraham Lincoln and Men of War-Times: Some Personal Recollections of War and Politics During the Lincoln Administration*. Philadelphia, PA: Times Publishing Co., 1892.

——. *Our Presidents and How We Make Them*. New York, NY: Harper and Brothers, 1900.

McCullough, David. *John Adams*. New York, NY: Touchstone, 2001.

McDonald, Forrest. *States' Rights and the Union: Imperium in Imperio, 1776-1876*. Lawrence, KS: University Press of Kansas, 2000.

McDonough, James Lee, and Thomas L. Connelly. *Five Tragic Hours: The Battle of Franklin*. 1983. Knoxville, TN: University of Tennessee Press, 2001 ed.

McElroy, Robert. *Jefferson Davis: The Unreal and the Real*. 1937. New York, NY: Smithmark, 1995 ed.

McFeely, William S. *Yankee Stepfather: General O. O. Howard and the Freedmen - The Story of a Civil War Promise to Former Slaves Made—and Broken*. 1968. New York, NY: W. W. Norton, 1994.

McGehee, Jacob Owen. *Causes That Led to the War Between the States*. Atlanta, GA: A. B. Caldwell, 1915.

McGuire, Hunter, and George L. Christian. *The Confederate Cause and Conduct in the War Between the States*. Richmond, VA: L. H. Jenkins, 1907.

McHenry, George. *The Cotton Trade: Its Bearing Upon the Prosperity of Great Britain and Commerce of the American Republics, Considered in Connection with the System of Negro Slavery in the Confederate States*. London, UK: Saunders, Otley, and Co., 1863.

McIlwaine, Shields. *Memphis Down in Dixie*. New York, NY: E. P. Dutton, 1848.

McKissack, Patricia C., and Frederick McKissack. *Sojourner Truth: Ain't I a Woman?* New York: NY: Scholastic, 1992.

McManus, Edgar J. *A History of Negro Slavery in New York*. Syracuse, NY: Syracuse University Press, 1966.

——. *Black Bondage in the North*. Syracuse, NY: Syracuse University Press, 1973.

McMaster, John Bach. *Our House Divided: A History of the People of the United States During Lincoln's Administration*. 1927. New York, NY: Premier, 1961 ed.

McPherson, Edward. *The Political History of the United States of America,*

During the Great Rebellion (From November 6, 1860, to July 4, 1864). Washington, D.C.: Philp and Solomons, 1864.

——. *The Political History of the United States of America, During the Period of Reconstruction, (From April 15, 1865, to July 15, 1870,) Including a Classified Summary of the Legislation of the Thirty-ninth, Fortieth, and Forty-first Congresses*. Washington, D.C.: Solomons and Chapman, 1875.

McPherson, James M. *The Struggle for Equality: Abolitionists and the Negro in the Civil War and Reconstruction*. 1964. Princeton, NJ: Princeton University Press, 1992 ed.

——. *The Negro's Civil War: How American Negroes Felt and Acted During the War for the Union*. 1965. Chicago, IL: University of Illinois Press, 1982 ed.

——. *Battle Cry of Freedom: The Civil War Era*. Oxford, UK: Oxford University Press, 2003.

——. *The Atlas of the Civil War*. Philadelphia, PA: Courage Books, 2005.

McPherson, James M., and the staff of the *New York Times*. *The Most Fearful Ordeal: Original Coverage of the Civil War by Writers and Reporters of the New York Times*. New York, NY: St. Martin's Press, 2004.

McWhiney, Grady, and Judith Lee Hallock. *Braxton Bragg and Confederate Defeat*. 2 vols. Tuscaloosa, AL: University of Alabama Press, 1991.

McWhiney, Grady, and Perry D. Jamieson. *Attack and Die: Civil War Military Tactics and the Southern Heritage*. Tuscaloosa, AL: University of Alabama Press, 1982.

Melish, Joanne Pope. *Disowning Slavery: Gradual Emancipation and 'Race' in New England 1780-1860*. Ithaca, NY: Cornell University Press, 1998.

Meltzer, Milton. *Slavery: A World History*. 2 vols. in 1. 1971. New York, NY: Da Capo Press, 1993 ed.

Meriwether, Elizabeth Avery. *Facts and Falsehoods Concerning the War on the South, 1861-1865*. (Originally written under the pseudonym "George Edmonds.") Memphis, TN: A. R. Taylor, 1904.

Merry, Robert W. *A Country of Vast Designs: James K. Polk, the Mexican War and the Conquest of the American Continent*. New York, NY: Simon and Schuster, 2009.

Message of the President of the United States and Accompanying Documents to the Two Houses of Congress at the Commencement of the Third Session of the

40th Congress. Washington, D.C.: Government Printing Office, 1868.
Metzger, Bruce M., and Michael D. Coogan (eds.). *The Oxford Companion to the Bible.* New York, NY: Oxford University Press, 1993.
Miller, Francis Trevelyan. *Portrait Life of Lincoln.* Springfield, MA: Patriot Publishing Co., 1910.
Miller, John Chester. *The Wolf By the Ears: Thomas Jefferson and Slavery.* 1977. Charlottesville, VA: University Press of Virginia, 1994 ed.
Miller, Marion Mills (ed.). *Great Debates in American History.* 14 vols. New York, NY: Current Literature, 1913.
Miller, Nathan. *Star-Spangled Men: America's Ten Worst Presidents.* New York, NY: Touchstone, 1998.
Miller, William Lee. *Lincoln's Virtues: An Ethical Biography.* New York, NY: Vintage, 2003.
Min, Pyong Gap (ed.). *Encyclopedia of Racism in the United States.* 3 vols. Westport, CT: Greenwood Press, 2005.
Minor, Charles Landon Carter. *The Real Lincoln: From the Testimony of His Contemporaries.* Richmond, VA: Everett Waddey Co., 1904.
Mirabello, Mark. *Handbook for Rebels and Outlaws.* Oxford, UK: Mandrake of Oxford, 2009.
Mish, Frederick C. (ed.). *Webster's Ninth New Collegiate Dictionary.* 1984. Springfield, MA: Merriam-Webster.
Mitchell, Margaret. *Gone With the Wind.* 1936. New York, NY: Avon, 1973 ed.
Mitgang, Herbert (ed.). *Lincoln As They Saw Him.* 1956. New York, NY: Collier, 1962 ed.
Mode, Peter George. *Source Book and Bibliographical Guide for American Church History.* Menasha, WI: Collegiate Press, 1921.
Mode, Robert L. (ed.). *Nashville: Its Character in a Changing America.* Nashville, TN: Vanderbilt University, 1981.
Montgomery, David Henry. *The Student's American History.* 1897. Boston, MA: Ginn and Co., 1905 ed.
Moore, Frank (ed.). *The Rebellion Record: A Diary of American Events.* 12 vols. New York, NY: G. P. Putnam, 1861.
Moore, George Henry. *Notes on the History of Slavery in Massachusetts.* New York, NY: D. Appleton and Co., 1866.
Moorhead, James H. *American Apocalypse: Yankee Protestants and the Civil War, 1860-1869.* New Haven, CT: Yale University Press, 1971.

Morel, Lucas E. *Lincoln's Sacred Effort: Defining Religion's Role in American Self-Government*. Lanham, MD: Lexington Books, 2000.

Morris, Benjamin Franklin (ed.). *The Life of Thomas Morris: Pioneer and Long a Legislator of Ohio, and U.S. Senator from 1833 to 1839*. Cincinnati, OH: Moore, Wilstach, Keys and Overend, 1856.

Morris, Roy, Jr. *The Long Pursuit: Abraham Lincoln's Thirty-Year Struggle with Stephen Douglas for the Heart and Soul of America*. New York, NY: HarperCollins, 2008.

Morris, Thomas D. *Free Men All: The Personal Liberty Laws of the North, 1780-1861*. Baltimore, MD: John Hopkins University Press, 1974.

Morton, John Watson. *The Artillery of Nathan Bedford Forrest's Cavalry*. Nashville, TN: The M. E. Church, 1909.

Moses, John. *Illinois: Historical and Statistical, Comprising the Essential Facts of Its Planting and Growth as a Province, County, Territory, and State* (Vol. 2). Chicago, IL: Fergus Printing Co., 1892.

Mullen, Robert W. *Blacks in America's Wars: The Shift in Attitudes From the Revolutionary War to Vietnam*. 1973. New York, NY: Pathfinder, 1991 ed.

Munford, Beverly Bland. *Virginia's Attitude Toward Slavery and Secession*. 1909. Richmond, VA: L. H. Jenkins, 1914 ed.

Murphy, Jim. *A Savage Thunder: Antietam and the Bloody Road to Freedom*. New York, NY: Margaret K. McElderry, 2009.

Napolitano, Andrew P. *The Constitution in Exile: How the Federal Government has Seized Power by Rewriting the Supreme Law of the Land*. Nashville, TN: Nelson Current, 2006.

Neely, Mark E., Jr. *The Fate of Liberty: Abraham Lincoln and Civil Liberties*. New York, NY: Oxford University Press, 1991.

Neilson, William Allan (ed.). *Webster's Biographical Dictionary*. Springfield, MA: G. and C. Merriam Co., 1943.

Neufeldt, Victoria (ed.). *Webster's New World Dictionary of American English* (3rd college ed.). 1970. New York, NY: Prentice Hall, 1994 ed.

Nevins, Allan. *The Evening Post: A Century of Journalism*. New York, NY: Boni and Liveright, 1922.

Nicolay, John G., and John Hay (eds.). *Abraham Lincoln: A History*. 10 vols. New York, NY: The Century Co., 1890.

——. *Complete Works of Abraham Lincoln*. 12 vols. 1894. New York, NY: Francis D. Tandy Co., 1905 ed.

———. *Abraham Lincoln: Complete Works.* 12 vols. 1894. New York, NY: The Century Co., 1907 ed.

Nivola, Pietro S., and David H. Rosenbloom (eds.). *Classic Readings in American Politics.* New York, NY: St. Martin's Press, 1986.

Norris, Mary Harriot (ed.). *Sir Walter Scott's Marmion.* Boston, MA: Leach, Shewell, and Sanborn, 1891.

Norwood, Thomas Manson. *A True Vindication of the South.* Savannah, GA: Citizens and Southern Bank, 1917.

Nye, Russel B. *William Lloyd Garrison and the Humanitarian Reformers.* Boston, MA: Little, Brown and Co., 1955.

Oakes, James. *The Radical and the Republican: Frederick Douglass, Abraham Lincoln, and the Triumph of Antislavery Politics.* New York, NY: W. W. Norton, 2008.

Oates, Stephen B. *Abraham Lincoln: The Man Behind the Myths.* New York, NY: Meridian, 1984.

———. *The Approaching Fury: Voices of the Storm, 1820-1861.* New York, NY: Harper Perennial, 1998.

O'Brien, Cormac. *Secret Lives of the U.S. Presidents: What Your Teachers Never Told You About the Men of the White House.* Philadelphia, PA: Quirk, 2004.

———. *Secret Lives of the Civil War: What Your teachers Never Told You About the War Between the States.* Philadelphia, PA: Quirk, 2007.

Oglesby, Thaddeus K. *Some Truths of History: A Vindication of the South Against the Encyclopedia Britannica and Other Maligners.* Atlanta, GA: Byrd Printing, 1903.

Olmsted, Frederick Law. *A Journey in the Seaboard Slave States, With Remarks on Their Economy.* New York, NY: Dix and Edwards, 1856.

———. *A Journey Through Texas; or a Saddle-Trip on the Western Frontier.* New York, NY: Dix and Edwards, 1857.

———. *A Journey in the Back Country.* New York, NY: Mason Brothers, 1860.

———. *The Cotton Kingdom: A Traveler's Observations on Cotton and Slavery in the American Slave States.* 2 vols. London, UK: Sampson Low, Son, and Co., 1862.

Olson, Ted (ed.). *CrossRoads: A Southern Culture Annual.* Macon, GA: Mercer University Press, 2004.

ORA (full title: *The War of the Rebellion: A Compilation of the Official Records of the Union and Confederate Armies*). 70 vols. Washington, DC: Government Printing Office, 1880.

ORN (full title: *Official Records of the Union and Confederate Navies in the War of the Rebellion*). 30 vols. Washington, DC: Government Printing Office, 1894.

Ostergard, Philip L. *The Inspired Wisdom of Abraham Lincoln: How Faith Shaped an American President and Changed the Course of a Nation.* Carol Stream, IL: Tyndale House, 2008.

Owsley, Frank Lawrence. *King Cotton Diplomacy: Foreign Relations of the Confederate States of America.* 1931. Chicago, IL: University of Chicago Press, 1959 ed.

Page, Thomas Nelson. *Robert E. Lee, Man and Soldier.* New York, NY: Charles Scribner's Sons, 1911.

Palin, Sarah. *Going Rogue: An American Life.* New York, NY: HarperCollins, 2009.

Paludan, Phillip Shaw. *The Presidency of Abraham Lincoln.* Lawrence, KS: University Press of Kansas, 1994.

Parker, Bowdoin S. (ed.). *What One Grand Army Post Has Accomplished: History of Edward W. Kinsley Post, No. 113.* Norwood, MA: Norwood Press, 1913.

Parry, Melanie (ed.). *Chambers Biographical Dictionary.* 1897. Edinburgh, Scotland: Chambers Harrap, 1998 ed.

Patrick, Rembert W. *Jefferson Davis and His Cabinet.* Baton Rouge, LA: Louisiana State University Press, 1944.

Paul, Ron. *The Revolution: A Manifesto.* New York, NY: Grand Central Publishing, 2008.

Pearson, Henry Greenleaf. *The Life of John A. Andrew, Governor of Massachusetts, 1861-1865.* 2 vols. Boston, MA: Houghton, Mifflin and Co., 1904.

Perkins, Henry C. *Northern Editorials on Secession.* 2 vols. D. Appleton and Co., 1942.

Perry, James M. *Touched With Fire: Five Presidents and the Civil War Battles That Made Them.* New York, NY: Public Affairs, 2003.

Perry, John C. *Myths and Realities of American Slavery: The True History of Slavery in America.* Shippenburg, PA: Burd Street Press, 2002.

Perry, Mark. *Lift Up Thy Voice: The Grimké Family's Journey From Slaveholders to Civil Rights Leaders.* New York, NY: Penguin, 2001.

Peter, Laurence J., and Raymond Hull *The Peter Principle: Why Things*

Always Go Wrong. New York, NY: William Morrow and Co., 1969.

Peterson, Merrill D. (ed.). *James Madison, A Biography in His Own Words.* (First published posthumously in 1840.) New York, NY: Harper and Row, 1974 ed.

——. (ed.). *Thomas Jefferson: Writings, Autobiography, A Summary View of the Rights of British America, Notes on the State of Virginia, Public Papers, Addresses, Messages and Replies, Miscellany, Letters.* New York, NY: Literary Classics, 1984.

——. *Lincoln in American Memory.* New York, NY: Oxford University Press, 1994.

Peterson, Paul R. *Quantrill of Missouri: The Making of a Guerilla Warrior, The Man, the Myth, the Soldier.* Nashville, TN: Cumberland House, 2003.

Phillips, Michael. *White Metropolis: Race, Ethnicity, and Religion in Dallas, 1841-2001.* Austin, TX: University of Texas Press, 2006.

Phillips, Robert S. (ed.). *Funk and Wagnalls New Encyclopedia.* 1971. New York, NY: Funk and Wagnalls, 1979 ed.

Phillips, Ulrich Bonnell. *American Negro Slavery: A Survey of the Supply, Employment and Control of Negro Labor as Determined by the Plantation Régime.* New York, NY: D. Appleton and Co., 1929.

Phillips, Wendell. *Speeches, Letters, and Lectures.* Boston, MA: Lee and Shepard, 1894.

Piatt, Donn. *Memories of the Men Who Saved the Union.* New York, NY: Belford, Clarke, and Co., 1887.

Piatt, Donn, and Henry V. Boynton. *General George H. Thomas: A Critical Biography.* Cincinnati, OH: Robert Clarke and Co., 1893.

Pickett, George E. *The Heart of a Soldier: As Revealed in the Intimate Letters of General George E. Pickett, CSA.* 1908. New York, NY: Seth Moyle, 1913 ed.

Pickett, William Passmore. *The Negro Problem: Abraham Lincoln's Solution.* New York, NY: G. P. Putnam's Sons, 1909.

Pike, James Shepherd. *The Prostrate State: South Carolina Under Negro Government.* New York, NY: D. Appleton and Co., 1874.

Pinsker, Matthew. *Lincoln's Sanctuary: Abraham Lincoln and the Soldiers' Home.* Oxford, UK: Oxford University Press, 2003.

Pollard, Edward A. *Southern History of the War.* 2 vols. in 1. New York, NY: Charles B. Richardson, 1866.

———. *The Lost Cause*. 1867. Chicago, IL: E. B. Treat, 1890 ed.
———. *The Lost Cause Regained*. New York, NY: G. W. Carlton and Co., 1868.
———. *Life of Jefferson Davis, With a Secret History of the Southern Confederacy, Gathered "Behind the Scenes in Richmond."* Philadelphia, PA: National Publishing Co., 1869.
Post, Lydia Minturn (ed.). *Soldiers' Letters, From Camp, Battlefield and Prison*. New York, NY: Bunce and Huntington, 1865.
Potter, David M. *The Impending Crisis: 1848-1861*. New York, NY: Harper and Row, 1976.
Powell, Edward Payson. *Nullification and Secession in the United States: A History of the Six Attempts During the First Century of the Republic*. New York, NY: G. P. Putnam's Sons, 1897.
Powell, William S. *North Carolina: A History*. 1977. Chapel Hill, NC: University of North Carolina Press, 1988 ed.
Pratt, Harry E. *Concerning Mr. Lincoln: As He Appeared to Letter Writers of His Time*. Springfield, IL: The Abraham Lincoln Association, 1944.
Pritchard, Russ A., Jr. *Civil War Weapons and Equipment*. Guilford, CT: Lyons Press, 2003.
Putnam, Samuel Porter. *400 Years of Free Thought*. New York, NY: Truth Seeker Co., 1894.
Quarles, Benjamin. *The Negro in the Civil War*. 1953. Cambridge, MA: Da Capo Press, 1988 ed.
———. *Lincoln and the Negro*. 1962. Cambridge, MA: Da Capo Press, 1990 ed.
Quintero, José Agustín, Ambrosio José Gonzales, and Loreta Janeta Velazquez (Phillip Thomas Tucker, ed.). *Cubans in the Confederacy*. Jefferson, NC: McFarland and Co., 2002.
Rable, George C. *The Confederate Republic: A Revolution Against Politics*. Chapel Hill, NC: University of North Carolina Press, 1994.
Ramage, James A. *Rebel Raider: The Life of General John Hunt Morgan*. Lexington, KY: University Press of Kentucky, 1986.
Randall, James Garfield. *Lincoln: The Liberal Statesman*. New York, NY: Dodd, Mead and Co., 1947.
Randall, James Garfield, and Richard N. Current. *Lincoln the President: Last Full Measure*. 1955. Urbana, IL: University of Illinois Press, 2000 ed.
Randolph, Thomas Jefferson (ed.). *Memoir, Correspondence, and*

Miscellanies, from the Papers of Thomas Jefferson. 4 vols. Charlottesville, VA: F. Carr and Co., 1829.

Ransom, Roger L. *Conflict and Compromise: The Political Economy of Slavery, Emancipation, and the American Civil War.* Cambridge, UK: Cambridge University Press, 1989.

Rawle, William. *A View of the Constitution of the United States of America.* Philadelphia, PA: Philip H. Nicklin, 1829.

Rayner, B. L. *Sketches of the Life, Writings, and Opinions of Thomas Jefferson.* New York, NY: Alfred Francis and William Boardman, 1832.

Reaney, P. H., and R. M. Wilson. *A Dictionary of English Surnames.* 1958. Oxford, UK: Oxford University Press, 1997 ed.

Reid, Richard M. *Freedom for Themselves: North Carolina's Black Soldiers in the Era of the Civil War.* Chapel Hill, NC: University of North Carolina Press, 2008.

Remsburg, John B. *Abraham Lincoln: Was He a Christian?* New York, NY: The Truth Seeker Co., 1893.

Reports of Committees of the Senate of the United States (for the Thirty-eighth Congress). Washington, D.C.: Government Printing Office, 1864.

Report of the Joint Committee on Reconstruction (at the First Session, Thirty-ninth Congress). Washington, D.C.: Government Printing Office, 1866.

Reports of Committees of the Senate of the United States (for the Second Session of the Forty-second Congress). Washington, D.C.: Government Printing Office, 1872.

Report of the Joint Select Committee to Inquire into the Condition of Affairs in the Late Insurrectionary States. Washington, D.C.: Government Printing Office, 1872.

Reuter, Edward Byron. *The Mulatto in the United States.* Boston, MA: Gorham Press, 1918.

Rhodes, James Ford. *History of the United States from the Compromise of 1850 to the Final Restoration of Home Rule at the South in 1877.* 7 vols. 1895. New York, NY: Macmillan Co., 1907 ed.

Rice, Allen Thorndike (ed.). *The North American Review*, Vol. 227. New York, NY: D. Appleton and Co., 1879.

———. *Reminiscences of Abraham Lincoln, by Distinguished Men of His Time.* New York, NY: North American Review, 1888.

Rich, Burdett A., and Henry P. Farnham (eds.). *Lawyers' Reports,*

Annotated (Book 22). Rochester, NY: The Lawyers' Co-Operative Publishing, Co., 1894.
Richardson, James Daniel (ed.). *A Compilation of the Messages and Papers of the Confederacy*. 2 vols. Nashville, TN: United States Publishing Co., 1905.
Richardson, John Anderson. *Richardson's Defense of the South*. Atlanta, GA: A. B. Caldwell, 1914.
Ridley, Bromfield Lewis. *Battles and Sketches of the Army of Tennessee*. Mexico, MO: Missouri Printing and Publishing Co., 1906.
Riley, Franklin Lafayette (ed.). *Publications of the Mississippi Historical Society*. Oxford, MS: The Mississippi Historical Society, 1902.
——. *General Robert E. Lee After Appomattox*. New York, NY: MacMillan Co., 1922.
Riley, Russell Lowell. *The Presidency and the Politics of Racial Inequality*. New York, NY: Columbia University Press, 1999.
Rives, John (ed.). *Abridgement of the Debates of Congress: From 1789 to 1856* (Vol. 13). New York, NY: D. Appleton and Co., 1860.
Roberts, Paul M. *United States History: Review Text*. 1966. New York, NY: Amsco School Publications, 1970 ed.
Roberts, R. Philip. *Mormonism Unmasked: Confronting the Contradictions Between Mormon Beliefs and True Christianity*. Nashville, TN: Broadman and Holman, 1998.
Robertson, James I., Jr. *Soldiers Blue and Gray*. 1988. Columbia, SC: University of South Carolina Press, 1998 ed.
Rockwell, Llewellyn H., Jr. "Genesis of the Civil War." Website: www.lewrockwell.com/rockwell/civilwar.html.
Rogers, Joel Augustus. *Africa's Gift to America: The Afro-American in the Making and Saving of the United States*. St. Petersburg, FL: Helga M. Rogers, 1961.
——. *The Ku Klux Spirit*. 1923. Baltimore, MD: Black Classic Press, 1980 ed.
Rosen, Robert N. *The Jewish Confederates*. Columbia, SC: University of South Carolina Press, 2000.
Rosenbaum, Robert A. (ed). *The New American Desk Encyclopedia*. 1977. New York, NY: Signet, 1989 ed.
Rosenbaum, Robert A., and Douglas Brinkley (eds.). *The Penguin Encyclopedia of American History*. New York, NY: Viking, 2003.
Rothschild, Alonzo. *"Honest Abe": A Study in Integrity Based on the Early Life*

of Abraham Lincoln. Boston, MA: Houghton Mifflin Co., 1917.

Rouse, Adelaide Louise (ed.). *National Documents: State Papers So Arranged as to Illustrate the Growth of Our Country From 1606 to the Present Day.* New York, NY: Unit Book Publishing Co., 1906.

Rowland, Dunbar (ed.). *Jefferson Davis, Constitutionalist: His Letters, Papers, and Speeches.* 10 vols. Jackson, MS: Mississippi Department of Archives and History, 1923.

Rozwenc, Edwin Charles (ed.). *The Causes of the American Civil War.* 1961. Lexington, MA: D. C. Heath and Co., 1972 ed.

Rubenzer, Steven J., and Thomas R. Faschingbauer. *Personality, Character, and Leadership in the White House: Psychologists Assess the Presidents.* Dulles, VA: Brassey's, 2004.

Ruffin, Edmund. *The Diary of Edmund Ruffin: Toward Independence: October 1856-April 1861.* Baton Rouge, LA: Louisiana State University Press, 1972.

Rutherford, Mildred Lewis. *Four Addresses.* Birmingham, AL: The Mildred Rutherford Historical Circle, 1916.

——. *A True Estimate of Abraham Lincoln and Vindication of the South.* N.p., n.d.

——. *Truths of History: A Historical Perspective of the Civil War From the Southern Viewpoint.* Confederate Reprint Co., 1920.

——. *The South Must Have Her Rightful Place In History.* Athens, GA, 1923.

Rutland, Robert Allen. *The Birth of the Bill of Rights, 1776-1791.* 1955. Boston, MA: Northeastern University Press, 1991 ed.

Sachsman, David B., S. Kittrell Rushing, and Roy Morris, Jr. (eds.). *Words at War: The Civil War and American Journalism.* West Lafayette, IN: Purdue University Press, 2008.

Salley, Alexander Samuel, Jr. *South Carolina Troops in Confederate Service.* 2 vols. Columbia, SC: R. L. Bryan, 1913 and 1914.

Salzberger, Ronald P., and Mary C. Turck (eds.). *Reparations For Slavery: A Reader.* Lanham, MD: Rowman and Littlefield, 2004.

Samuel, Bunford. *Secession and Constitutional Liberty.* 2 vols. New York, NY: Neale Publishing, 1920.

Sancho, Ignatius. *Letters of the Late Ignatius Sancho, an African.* 1782. New York, NY: Cosimo Classics, 2005 ed.

Sandburg, Carl. *Abraham Lincoln: The War Years.* 4 vols. New York, NY: Harcourt, Brace and World, 1939.

——. *Storm Over the Land: A Profile of the Civil War.* 1939. Old Saybrook,

CT: Konecky and Konecky, 1942 ed.
Sargent, F. W. *England, the United States, and the Southern Confederacy*. London, UK: Sampson Low, Son, and Co., 1863.
Scharf, John Thomas. *History of the Confederate Navy, From Its Organization to the Surrender of Its Last Vessel*. Albany, NY: Joseph McDonough, 1894.
Schauffler, Robert Haven. *Our American Holidays: Lincoln's Birthday - A Comprehensive View of Lincoln as Given in the Most Noteworthy Essays, Orations and Poems, in Fiction and in Lincoln's Own Writings*. 1909. New York, NY: Moffat, Yard and Co., 1916 ed.
Schlüter, Herman. *Lincoln, Labor and Slavery: A Chapter from the Social History of America*. New York, NY: Socialist Literature Co., 1913.
Schurz, Carl. *Life of Henry Clay*. 2 vols. 1887. Boston, MA: Houghton, Mifflin and Co., 1899 ed.
Schwartz, Barry. *Abraham Lincoln and the Forge of National Memory*. Chicago, IL: University of Chicago Press, 2000.
Scott, Emmett J., and Lyman Beecher Stowe. *Booker T. Washington: Builder of a Civilization*. Garden City, NY: Doubleday, Page, and Co., 1916.
Scott, James Brown. *James Madison's Notes of Debates in the Federal Convention of 1787, and Their Relation to a More Perfect Society of Nations*. New York, NY: Oxford University Press, 1918.
Scruggs, *The Un-Civil War: Truths Your Teacher Never Told You*. Hendersonville, NC: Tribune Papers, 2007.
Seabrook, Lochlainn. *Carnton Plantation Ghost Stories: True Tales of the Unexplained from Tennessee's Most Haunted Civil War House!* 2005. Franklin, TN, 2016 ed.
——. *Nathan Bedford Forrest: Southern Hero, American Patriot*. 2007. Franklin, TN, 2010 ed.
——. *Abraham Lincoln: The Southern View*. 2007. Franklin, TN: Sea Raven Press, 2013 ed.
——. *The McGavocks of Carnton Plantation: A Southern History - Celebrating One of Dixie's Most Noble Confederate Families and Their Tennessee Home*. 2008. Franklin, TN, 2011ed.
——. *A Rebel Born: A Defense of Nathan Bedford Forrest*. 2010. Franklin, TN: Sea Raven Press, 2011 ed.
——. *A Rebel Born: The Screenplay* (for the film). 2011. Franklin, TN: Sea Raven Press.

———. *Everything You Were Taught About the Civil War is Wrong, Ask a Southerner!* 2010. Franklin, TN: Sea Raven Press, revised 2014 ed.

———. *The Quotable Jefferson Davis: Selections From the Writings and Speeches of the Confederacy's First President.* Franklin, TN: Sea Raven Press, 2011.

———. *The Quotable Robert E. Lee: Selections From the Writings and Speeches of the South's Most Beloved Civil War General.* Franklin, TN: Sea Raven Press, 2011 Sesquicentennial Civil War Edition.

———. *The Unquotable Abraham Lincoln: The President's Quotes They Don't Want You To Know!* Franklin, TN: Sea Raven Press, 2011.

———. *Honest Jeff and Dishonest Abe: A Southern Children's Guide to the Civil War.* Franklin, TN: Sea Raven Press, 2012.

———. *Encyclopedia of the Battle of Franklin - A Comprehensive Guide to the Conflict that Changed the Civil War.* Franklin, TN: Sea Raven Press, 2012.

———. *The Quotable Nathan Bedford Forrest: Selections From the Writings and Speeches of the Confederacy's Most Brilliant Cavalryman.* Spring Hill, TN: Sea Raven Press, 2012.

———. *Forrest! 99 Reasons to Love Nathan Bedford Forrest.* Spring Hill, TN: Sea Raven Press, 2012.

———. *Give 'Em Hell Boys! The Complete Military Correspondence of Nathan Bedford Forrest.* Spring Hill, TN: Sea Raven Press, 2012.

———. *The Constitution of the Confederate States of America Explained: A Clause-by-Clause Study of the South's Magna Carta.* Spring Hill, TN: Sea Raven Press, 2012 Sesquicentennial Civil War Edition.

———. *The Great Impersonator: 99 Reasons to Dislike Abraham Lincoln.* Spring Hill, TN: Sea Raven Press, 2012.

———. *The Old Rebel: Robert E. Lee As He Was Seen By His Contemporaries.* Spring Hill, TN: Sea Raven Press, 2012 Sesquicentennial Civil War Edition.

———. *The Quotable Stonewall Jackson: Selections From the Writings and Speeches of the South's Most Famous General.* Spring Hill, TN: Sea Raven Press, 2012 Sesquicentennial Civil War Edition.

———. *Saddle, Sword, and Gun: A Biography of Nathan Bedford Forrest for Teens.* Spring Hill, TN: Sea Raven Press, 2013.

———. *The Alexander H. Stephens Reader: Excerpts From the Works of a Confederate Founding Father.* Spring Hill, TN: Sea Raven Press,

2013.

———. *The Quotable Alexander H. Stephens: Selections From the Writings and Speeches of the Confederacy's First Vice President.* Spring Hill, TN: Sea Raven Press, 2013 Sesquicentennial Civil War Edition.

———. *Give This Book to a Yankee! A Southern Guide to the Civil War for Northerners.* Spring Hill, TN: Sea Raven Press, 2014.

———. *The Articles of Confederation Explained: A Clause-by-Clause Study of America's First Constitution.* Spring Hill, TN: Sea Raven Press, 2014.

———. *Confederate Blood and Treasure: An Interview With Lochlainn Seabrook.* Spring Hill, TN: Sea Raven Press, 2015.

———. *Nathan Bedford Forrest and the Battle of Fort Pillow: Yankee Myth, Confederate Fact.* Spring Hill, TN: Sea Raven Press, 2015.

———. *Everything You Were Taught About American Slavery War is Wrong, Ask a Southerner!* Spring Hill, TN: Sea Raven Press, 2015.

———. *Confederacy 101: Amazing Facts You Never Knew About America's Oldest Political Tradition.* Spring Hill, TN: Sea Raven Press, 2015.

———. *The Great Yankee Coverup: What the North Doesn't Want You to Know About Lincoln's War!* Spring Hill, TN: Sea Raven Press, 2015.

———. *Slavery 101: Amazing Facts You Never Knew About America's "Peculiar Institution."* Spring Hill, TN: Sea Raven Press, 2015.

———. *Confederate Flag Facts: What Every American Should Know About Dixie's Southern Cross.* Spring Hill, TN: Sea Raven Press, 2016.

———. *Nathan Bedford Forrest and the Ku Klux Klan: Yankee Myth, Confederate Fact.* Spring Hill, TN: Sea Raven Press, 2016.

———. *Seabrook's Bible Dictionary of Traditional and Mystical Christian Doctrines.* Spring Hill, TN: Sea Raven Press, 2016.

———. *Everything You Were Taught About African-Americans and the Civil War is Wrong, Ask a Southerner!* Spring Hill, TN: Sea Raven Press, 2016.

———. *Nathan Bedford Forrest and African-Americans: Yankee Myth, Confederate Fact.* Spring Hill, TN: Sea Raven Press, 2016.

———. *Women in Gray: A Tribute to the Ladies Who Supported the Southern Confederacy.* Spring Hill, TN: Sea Raven Press, 2016.

———. *Lincoln's War: The Real Cause, the Real Winner, the Real Loser.* Spring Hill, TN: Sea Raven Press, 2016.

———. *The Unholy Crusade: Lincoln's Legacy of Destruction in the American South.* Spring Hill, TN: Sea Raven Press, 2017.

———. *Abraham Lincoln Was a Liberal, Jefferson Davis Was a Conservative: The*

Missing Key to Understanding the American Civil War. Spring Hill, TN: Sea Raven Press, 2017.

———. *All We Ask is to be Let Alone: The Southern Secession Fact Book.* Spring Hill, TN: Sea Raven Press, 2017.

———. *The Ultimate Civil War Quiz Book: How Much Do You Really Know About America's Most Misunderstood Conflict?* Spring Hill, TN: Sea Raven Press, 2017.

Segal, Charles M. (ed.). *Conversations with Lincoln.* 1961. New Brunswick, NJ: Transaction, 2002 ed.

Segars, J. H., and Charles Kelly Barrow. *Black Southerners in Confederate Armies: A Collection of Historical Accounts.* Atlanta, GA: Southern Lion Books, 2001.

Seligmann, Herbert J. *The Negro Faces America.* New York, NY: Harper and Brothers, 1920.

Semmes, Admiral Ralph. *Service Afloat, or the Remarkable Career of the Confederate Cruisers Sumter and Alabama During the War Between the States.* London, UK: Sampson Low, Marston, Searle, and Rivington, 1887.

Sewall, Samuel. *Diary of Samuel Sewall.* 3 vols. Boston, MA: The Society, 1879.

Sewell, Richard H. *John P. Hale and the Politics of Abolition.* Cambridge, MA: Harvard University Press, 1965.

Shenk, Joshua Wolf. *Lincoln's Melancholy: How Depression Challenged a President and Fueled His Greatness.* New York, NY: Houghton Mifflin, 2005.

Shenkman, Richard, and Kurt Edward Reiger. *One-Night Stands with American History: Odd, Amusing, and Little-Known Incidents.* 1980. New York, NY: Perennial, 2003 ed.

Sherman, William Tecumseh. *Memoirs of General William T. Sherman.* 2 vols. 1875. New York, NY: D. Appleton and Co., 1891 ed.

———. *Memoirs of Gen. W. T. Sherman.* 2 vols. 1875. New York, NY: Charles L. Webster and Co., 1892 ed.

Shillington, Kevin. *History of Africa.* 1989. New York, NY: St. Martin's Press, 1994 ed.

Shorto, Russell. *Thomas Jefferson and the American Ideal.* Hauppauge, NY: Barron's, 1987.

Shotwell, Walter G. *Life of Charles Sumner.* New York, NY: Thomas Y. Crowell and Co., 1910.

Siepel, Kevin H. *Rebel: The Life and Times of John Singleton Mosby*. New York, NY: St. Martin's Press, 1983.

Simkins, Francis Butler. *A History of the South*. New York, NY: Random House, 1972.

Simmons, Henry E. *A Concise Encyclopedia of the Civil War*. New York, NY: Bonanza Books, 1965.

Simon, James F. *Lincoln and Chief Justice Taney: Slavery, Secession, and the President's War Powers*. New York, NY: Simon and Schuster, 2006.

Simon, Paul. *Lincoln's Preparation for Greatness: The Illinois Legislative Years*. 1965. Chicago, IL: University of Illinois Press, 1971 ed.

Simpson, Lewis P. (ed.). *I'll Take My Stand: The South and the Agrarian Tradition*. 1930. Baton Rouge, LA: University of Louisiana Press, 1977 ed.

Slotkin, Richard. *No Quarter: The Battle of the Crater, 1864*. New York, NY: Random House, 2009.

Smelser, Marshall. *American Colonial and Revolutionary History*. 1950. New York, NY: Barnes and Noble, 1966 ed.

——. *The Democratic Republic, 1801-1815*. New York, NY: Harper and Row, 1968.

Smith, Hedrick. *Reagan: The Man, The President*. Oxford, UK: Pergamon Press, 1980.

Smith, Jean Edward. *Grant*. New York, NY: Touchstone, 2001.

Smith, John David (ed.). *Black Soldiers in Blue: African American Troops in the Civil War Era*. Chapel Hill, NC: University of North Carolina Press, 2002.

Smith, Joseph. *The Pearl of Great Price*. Salt Lake City, UT: George Q. Cannon and Sons, 1891.

Smith, Mark M. (ed.). *The Old South*. Oxford, UK: Blackwell Publishers, 2001.

Smith, Page. *Trial by Fire: A People's History of the Civil War and Reconstruction*. New York, NY: McGraw-Hill, 1982.

Smith, Philip D., Jr. *Tartan for Me!: Suggested Tartan for 13,695 Scottish, Scotch-Irish, Irish and North American Names with Lists of Clan, Family, and District Tartans*. Bruceton, WV: Scotpress, 1990.

Smucker, Samuel M. *The Life and Times of Thomas Jefferson*. Philadelphia, PA: J. W. Bradley, 1859.

Snider, Denton J. *Lincoln at Richmond: A Dramatic Epos of the Civil War*. St. Louis, MO: Sigma, 1914.

Sobel, Robert (ed.). *Biographical Directory of the United States Executive Branch, 1774-1898*. Westport, CT: Greenwood Press, 1990.

Sorrel, Gilbert Moxley. *Recollections of a Confederate Staff Officer*. New York, NY: Neale Publishing Co., 1905.

Spaeth, Harold J., and Edward Conrad Smith. *The Constitution of the United States*. 1936. New York, NY: HarperCollins, 1991 ed.

Spence, James. *On the Recognition of the Southern Confederation*. Ithaca, NY: Cornell University Library, 1862.

Spooner, Lysander. *No Treason* (only Numbers 1, 2, and 6 were published). Boston, MA: Lysander Spooner, 1867-1870.

Stampp, Kenneth M. *The Peculiar Institution: Slavery in the Antebellum South*. New York, NY: Vintage, 1956.

Stanford, Peter Thomas. *The Tragedy of the Negro in America*. Boston, MA: published by author, 1898.

Stanton, Elizabeth Cady, Susan B. Anthony, and Matilda Joslyn Gage (eds.). *History of Woman Suffrage*. 2 vols. New York, NY: Fowler and Wells, 1881.

Starr, John W., Jr. *Lincoln and the Railroads: A Biographical Study*. New York, NY: Dodd, Mead and Co., 1927.

Staudenraus, P. J. *The African Colonization Movement, 1816-1865*. New York, NY: Columbia University Press, 1961.

Stebbins, Rufus Phineas. *An Historical Address Delivered At the Centennial Celebration of the Incorporation of the Town of Wilbraham, June 15, 1863*. Boston, MA: George C. Rand and Avery, 1864.

Stedman, Edmund Clarence, and Ellen Mackay Hutchinson (eds.). *A Library of American Literature From the Earliest Settlement to the Present Time*. 10 vols. New York, NY: Charles L. Webster and Co., 1888.

Steel, Samuel Augustus. *The South Was Right*. Columbia, SC: R. L. Bryan Co., 1914.

Steele, Joel Dorman, and Esther Baker Steele. *Barnes' Popular History of the United States of America*. New York, NY: A. S. Barnes and Co., 1904.

Steele, Shelby. *White Guilt: How Blacks and Whites Together Destroyed the Promise of the Civil Rights Era*. New York, NY: Harper Perennial, 2007.

Steers, Edward, Jr. *Lincoln Legends: Myths, Hoaxes, and Confabulations Associated With Our Greatest President*. Lexington, KY: University

Press of Kentucky, 2007.

Stein, Ben, and Phil DeMuth. *How To Ruin the United States of America*. Carlsbad, CA: New Beginnings Press, 2008.

Steiner, Bernard. *The History of Slavery in Connecticut*. Baltimore, MD: Johns Hopkins University Press, 1893.

Steiner, Lewis Henry. *Report of Lewis H. Steiner: Inspector of the Sanitary Commission, Containing a Diary Kept During the Rebel Occupation of Frederick, MD, September, 1862*. New York, NY: Anson D. F. Randolph, 1862.

Stephens, Alexander Hamilton. *Speech of Mr. Stephens, of Georgia, on the War and Taxation*. Washington, D.C.: J & G. Gideon, 1848.

——. *A Constitutional View of the Late War Between the States; Its Causes, Character, Conduct and Results*. 2 vols. Philadelphia, PA: National Publishing, Co., 1870.

——. *Recollections of Alexander H. Stephens: His Diary Kept When a Prisoner at Fort Warren, Boston Harbour, 1865*. New York, NY: Doubleday, Page, and Co., 1910.

Stephenson, Nathaniel Wright. *Abraham Lincoln and the Union: A Chronicle of the Embattled North*. New Haven, CT: Yale University Press, 1918.

——. *Lincoln: An Account of His Personal Life, Especially of Its Springs of Action as Revealed and Deepened by the Ordeal of War*. Indianapolis, IN: Bobbs-Merrill, 1922.

Sterling, Dorothy (ed.). *Speak Out in Thunder Tones: Letters and Other Writings by Black Northerners, 1787-1865*. 1973. Cambridge, MA: Da Capo, 1998 ed.

Stern, Philip Van Doren (ed.). *The Life and Writings of Abraham Lincoln*. 1940. New York, NY: Modern Library, 2000 ed.

Stoddard, William O. *Inside the White House in War Times: Memoirs and Reports of Lincoln's Secretary*. Lincoln, NE: University of Nebraska Press, 2000.

Stonebraker, J. Clarence. *The Unwritten South: Cause, Progress and Results of the Civil War - Relics of Hidden Truth After Forty Years*. Seventh ed., n.p., 1908.

Stovall, Pleasant A. *Robert Toombs: Statesman, Speaker, Soldier, Sage*. New York, NY: Cassell Publishing, 1892.

Strain, John Paul. *Witness to the Civil War: The Art of John Paul Strain*. Philadelphia, PA: Courage, 2002.

Strode, Hudson. *Jefferson Davis: American Patriot*. 3 vols. New York, NY: Harcourt, Brace and World, 1955, 1959, 1964.

Strozier, Charles B. *Lincoln's Quest for Union: A Psychological Portrait*. Philadelphia, PA: Paul Dry Books, 2001.

Sturge, Joseph. *A Visit to the United States in 1841*. London, UK: Hamilton, Adams, and Co., 1842.

Summers, Mark W. *The Plundering Generation: Corruption and the Crisis of the Union, 1849-1861*. New York, NY: Oxford University Press, 1988.

Sumner, Charles. *The Crime Against Kansas: The Apologies for the Crime - The True Remedy*. Boston, MA: John P. Jewett, 1856.

Swanson, James L. *Bloody Crimes: The Chase for Jefferson Davis and the Death Pageant for Lincoln's Corpse*. New York, NY: HarperCollins, 2010.

Swint, Henry L. (ed.) *Dear Ones at Home: Letters From Contraband Camps*. Nashville, TN: Vanderbilt University Press, 1966.

Sword, Wiley. *The Confederacy's Last Hurrah: Spring Hill, Franklin, and Nashville*. New York, NY: HarperCollins, 1992.

——. *Southern Invincibility: A History of the Confederate Heart*. New York, NY: St. Martin's Press, 1999.

Tagg, Larry. *The Unpopular Mr. Lincoln: The Story of America's Most Reviled President*. New York, NY: Savas Beatie, 2009.

Tarbell, Ida Minerva. *The Life of Abraham Lincoln*. 4 vols. New York, NY: Lincoln History Society, 1895-1900.

Tatalovich, Raymond, and Byron W. Daynes. *Presidential Power in the United States*. Monterey, CA: Brooks/Cole, 1984.

Taylor, Richard. *Destruction and Reconstruction: Personal Experiences of the Late War in the United States*. New York, NY: D. Appleton, 1879.

Taylor, Susie King. *Reminiscences of My Life in Camp With the 33rd United States Colored Troops Late 1st S. C. Volunteers*. Boston, MA: Susie King Taylor, 1902.

Taylor, Walter Herron. *General Lee: His Campaigns in Virginia, 1861-1865, With Personal Reminiscences*. Norfolk, VA: Nusbaum Book and News Co., 1906.

Tenney, William Jewett. *The Military and Naval History of the Rebellion in the United States*. New York, NY: D. Appleton and Co., 1865.

Terkel, Studs. *Hard Times: An Oral History of the Great Depression*. New York, NY: Avon, 1970.

Testimony Taken By the Joint Select Committee to Inquire Into the Condition of

Affairs in the Late Insurrectionary States. 13 vols. Washington, D.C.: Government Printing Office, 1872.

Thackeray, William Makepeace. *Roundabout Papers*. Boston, MA: Estes and Lauriat, 1883.

Thatcher, Marshall P. *A Hundred Battles in the West: St. Louis to Atlanta, 1861-1865*. Detroit, MI: Marshall P. Thatcher, 1884.

The American Annual Cyclopedia and Register of Important Events of the Year 1861. New York, NY: D. Appleton and Co., 1868.

The American Annual Cyclopedia and Register of Important Events of the Year 1862. New York, NY: D. Appleton and Co., 1869.

The American Annual Cyclopedia and Register of Important Events of the Year 1863. New York, NY: D. Appleton and Co., 1864.

The Congressional Globe, Containing Sketches of the Debates and Proceedings of the First Session of the Twenty-Eighth Congress (Vol. 13). Washington, D.C.: The Globe, 1844.

The Great Issue to be Decided in November Next: Shall the Constitution and the Union Stand or Fall, Shall Sectionalism Triumph? Washington, D.C.: National Democratic Executive Committee, 1860.

The National Almanac and Annual Record for the Year 1863. Philadelphia, PA: George W. Childs, 1863.

The Oxford English Dictionary. Compact edition, 2 vols. 1928. Oxford, UK: Oxford University Press, 1979 ed.

The Quarterly Review (Vol. 111). London, UK: John Murray, 1862.

Thomas, Emory M. *The Confederate Nation: 1861-1865*. New York, NY: Harper and Row, 1979.

Thomas, Gabriel. *An Account of Pennsylvania and West New Jersey*. 1698. Cleveland, OH: Burrows Brothers Co., 1903 ed.

Thompson, Frank Charles (ed.). *The Thompson Chain Reference Bible* (King James Version). 1908. Indianapolis, IN: B. B. Kirkbride Bible Co., 1964 ed.

Thompson, Neal. *Driving With the Devil: Southern Moonshine, Detroit Wheels, and the Birth of NASCAR*. Three Rivers, MI: Three Rivers Press, 2006.

Thompson, Robert Means, and Richard Wainwright (eds.). *Confidential Correspondence of Gustavus Vasa Fox, Assistant Secretary of the Navy, 1861-1865*. 2 vols. 1918. New York, NY: Naval History Society, 1920 ed.

Thorndike, Rachel Sherman (ed.). *The Sherman Letters*. New York, NY:

Charles Scribner's Sons, 1894.
Thornton, Brian. *101 Things You Didn't Know About Lincoln: Loves and Losses, Political Power Plays, White House Hauntings*. Avon, MA: Adams Media, 2006.
Thornton, Gordon. *The Southern Nation: The New Rise of the Old South*. Gretna, LA: Pelican Publishing Co., 2000.
Thornton, John. *Africa and Africans in the Making of the Atlantic World, 1400-1800*. 1992. Cambridge, UK: Cambridge University Press, 1999 ed.
Thornton, Mark, and Robert B. Ekelund, Jr. *Tariffs, Blockades, and Inflation: The Economics of the Civil War*. Wilmington, DE: Scholarly Resources, 2004.
Tilley, John Shipley. *Lincoln Takes Command*. 1941. Nashville, TN: Bill Coats Limited, 1991 ed.
———. *Facts the Historians Leave Out: A Confederate Primer*. 1951. Nashville, TN: Bill Coats Limited, 1999 ed.
Tocqueville, Alexis de. *Democracy in America*. 2 vols. 1836. New York, NY: D. Appleton and Co., 1904 ed.
Tourgee, Albion W. *A Fool's Errand By One of the Fools*. London, UK: George Routledge and Sons, 1883.
Tracy, Gilbert A. (ed.). *Uncollected Letters of Abraham Lincoln*. Boston, MA: Houghton Mifflin Co., 1917.
Traupman, John C. *The New College Latin and English Dictionary*. 1966. New York, NY: Bantam, 1988 ed.
Trumbull, Lyman. *Speech of Honorable Lyman Trumbull, of Illinois, at a Mass Meeting in Chicago, August 7, 1858*. Washington, D.C.: Buell and Blanchard, 1858.
Truth, Sojourner. *Sojourner Truth's Narrative and Book of Life*. 1850. Battle Creek, MI: Sojourner Truth, 1881 ed.
Tucker, St. George. *On the State of Slavery in Virginia, in View of the Constitution of the United States, With Selected Writings*. Indianapolis, IN: Liberty Fund, 1999.
Turner, Edward Raymond. *The Negro in Pennsylvania, Slavery, Servitude, Freedom, 1639-1861*. Washington, D.C.: American Historical Association, 1911.
Tyler, Lyon Gardiner. *The Gray Book: A Confederate Catechism*. Columbia, TN: Gray Book Committee, SCV, 1935.
———. *The Letters and Times of the Tylers*. 3 vols. Williamsburg, VA: N.P.,

1896.

———. *Propaganda in History*. Richmond, VA: Richmond Press, 1920.

Upshur, Abel Parker. *A Brief Enquiry Into the True Nature and Character of Our Federal Government*. Philadelphia, PA: John Campbell, 1863.

Vallandigham, Clement Laird. *Speeches, Arguments, Addresses, and Letters of Clement L. Vallandigham*. New York, NY: J. Walter and Co., 1864.

Vanauken, Sheldon. *The Glittering Illusion: English Sympathy for the Southern Confederacy*. Washington, D.C.: Regnery, 1989.

Van Buren, G. M. *Abraham Lincoln's Pen and Voice: Being a Complete Compilation of His Letters, Civil, Political, and Military*. Cincinnati, OH: Robert Clarke and Co., 1890.

Ver Steeg, Clarence Lester, and Richard Hofstadter. *A People and a Nation*. New York, NY: Harper and Row, 1977.

Villard, Henry. *Memoirs of Henry Villard, Journalist and Financier, 1835-1900*. 2 vols. Boston, MA: Houghton, Mifflin and Co., 1904.

Voegeli, Victor Jacque. *Free But Not Equal: The Midwest and the Negro During the Civil War*. Chicago, IL: University of Chicago Press, 1967.

Wade, Wyn Craig. *The Fiery Cross: The Ku Klux Klan in America*. 1987. New York, NY: Touchstone, 1988 ed.

Walker, Barbara G. *The Woman's Encyclopedia of Myths and Secrets*. New York, NY: Harper and Row, 1983.

Wallcut, R. F. (pub.). *Southern Hatred of the American Government, the People of the North, and Free Institutions*. Boston, MA: R. F. Wallcut, 1862.

Wallechinsky, David, Irving Wallace, and Amy Wallace. *The People's Almanac Presents The Book of Lists*. New York, NY: Morrow, 1977.

Walsh, George. *"Those Damn Horse Soldiers": True Tales of the Civil War Cavalry*. New York, NY: Forge, 2006.

Ward, John William. *Andrew Jackson: Symbol for an Age*. 1953. Oxford, UK: Oxford University Press, 1973 ed.

Waring, George Edward, Jr. *Whip and Spur*. New York, NY: Doubleday and McClure, 1897.

Warner, Ezra J. *Generals in Gray: Lives of the Confederate Commanders*. 1959. Baton Rouge, LA: Louisiana State University Press, 1989 ed.

———. *Generals in Blue: Lives of the Union Commanders*. 1964. Baton Rouge, LA: Louisiana State University Press, 2006 ed.

Warren, Robert Penn. *Who Speaks for the Negro?* New York, NY: Random House, 1965.

Waugh, John C. *Reelecting Lincoln: The Battle for the 1864 Presidency.* Cambridge, MA: Da Capo Press, 1997.

———. *Lincoln and McClellan: The Troubled Partnership Between a President and His General.* New York, NY: Palgrave Macmillan, 2010.

Washington, Booker T. *Up From Slavery: An Autobiography.* 1901. Garden City, NY: Doubleday, Page and Co., 1919 ed.

Washington, Henry Augustine. *The Writings of Thomas Jefferson.* 9 vols. New York, NY: H. W. Derby, 1861.

Watkins, Samuel Rush. *"Company Aytch," Maury Grays, First Tennessee Regiment; or, A Side Show of the Big Show.* 1882. Chattanooga, TN: Times Printing Co., 1900 ed.

Watson, Harry L. *Andrew Jackson vs. Henry Clay: Democracy and Development in Antebellum America.* New York, NY: St. Martin's Press, 1998.

Watts, Peter. *A Dictionary of the Old West.* 1977. New York, NY: Promontory Press, 1987 ed.

Waugh, John C. *Surviving the Confederacy: Rebellion, Ruin, and Recovery - Roger and Sara Pryor During the Civil War.* New York, NY: Harcourt, 2002.

Weber, Jennifer L. *Copperheads: The Rise and Fall of Lincoln's Opponents in the North.* New York, NY: Oxford University Press, 2006.

Weintraub, Max. *The Blue Book of American History.* New York, NY: Regents Publishing Co., 1960.

Welles, Gideon. *Diary of Gideon Welles, Secretary of the Navy Under Lincoln and Johnson* (Vol. 1). Boston, MA: Houghton Mifflin, 1911.

Wheeler, Joe L. *Abraham Lincoln, a Man of Faith and Courage: Stories of Our Most Admired President.* New York, NY: Howard Books, 2008.

Wheeler, Tom. *Mr. Lincoln's T-Mails: How Abraham Lincoln Used the Telegraph to Win the Civil War.* New York, NY: HarperCollins, 2008.

White, Charles Langdon, Edwin Jay Foscue, and Tom Lee McKnight. *Regional Geography of Anglo-America.* 1943. Englewood Cliffs, NJ: Prentice-Hall, 1985 ed.

White, Henry Alexander. *Robert E. Lee and the Southern Confederacy, 1807-1870.* New York, NY: G. P. Putnam's Sons, 1897.

White, Reginald Cedric. *A. Lincoln: A Biography.* New York, NY: Random House, 2009.

White, Ronald C., Jr. *The Eloquent President: A Portrait of Lincoln Through His Words*. New York, NY: Random House, 2006.

Whitman, Walt. *Leaves of Grass*. 1855. New York, NY: Modern Library, 1921 ed.

——. *Complete Prose Works*. Boston, MA: Small, Maynard, and Co., 1901.

Wilbur, Henry Watson. *President Lincoln's Attitude Towards Slavery and Emancipation: With a Review of Events Before and Since the Civil War*. Philadelphia, PA: W. H. Jenkins, 1914.

Wilder, Craig Steven. *A Covenant With Color: Race and Social Power in Brooklyn*. New York, NY: Columbia University Press, 2000.

Wiley, Bell Irvin. *Southern Negroes: 1861-1865*. 1938. New Haven, CT: Yale University Press, 1969 ed.

——. *The Life of Johnny Reb: The Common Soldier of the Confederacy*. 1943. Baton Rouge, LA: Louisiana State University Press, 1978 ed.

——. *The Plain People of the Confederacy*. 1943. Columbia, SC: University of South Carolina, 2000 ed.

——. *The Life of Billy Yank: The Common Soldier of the Union*. 1952. Baton Rouge, LA: Louisiana State University Press, 2001 ed.

Wilkens, J. Steven. *America: The First 350 Years*. Monroe, LA: Covenant Publications, 1998.

Williams, Charles Richard. *The Life of Rutherford Birchard Hayes, Nineteenth President of the United States*. 2 vols. Boston, MA: Houghton Mifflin Co., 1914.

Williams, George Washington. *History of the Negro Race in America: From 1619 to 1880, Negroes as Slaves, as Soldiers, and as Citizens*. New York, NY: G. P. Putnam's Sons, 1885.

——. *A History of the Negro Troops in the War of the Rebellion 1861-1865*. New York, NY: Harper and Brothers, 1888.

Williams, James. *The South Vindicated*. London, UK: Longman, Green, Longman, Roberts, and Green, 1862.

Williams, William H. *Slavery and Freedom in Delaware, 1639-1865*. Wilmington, DE: Scholarly Resources, 1996.

Wills, Brian Steel. *The Confederacy's Greatest Cavalryman: Nathan Bedford Forrest*. Lawrence, KS: University Press of Kansas, 1992.

Wills, Gary. *Lincoln At Gettysburg: The Words that Remade America*. New York, NY: Touchstone, 1992.

Wilson, Charles Reagan, and William Ferris. *Encyclopedia of Southern Culture* (Vol. 1). New York, NY: Anchor, 1989.

Wilson, Clyde N. *Why the South Will Survive: Fifteen Southerners Look at Their Region a Half Century After I'll Take My Stand*. Athens, GA: University of Georgia Press, 1981.

———. (ed.) *The Essential Calhoun: Selections From Writings, Speeches, and Letters*. New Brunswick, NJ: Transaction Publishers, 1991.

———. *A Defender of Southern Conservatism: M.E. Bradford and His Achievements*. Columbia, MO: University of Missouri Press, 1999.

———. *From Union to Empire: Essays in the Jeffersonian Tradition*. Columbia, SC: The Foundation for American Education, 2003.

———. *Defending Dixie: Essays in Southern History and Culture*. Columbia, SC: The Foundation for American Education, 2005.

Wilson, Douglas L. *Honor's Voice: The Transformation of Abraham Lincoln*. New York, NY: Vintage, 1998.

———. *Lincoln's Sword: The Presidency and the Power of Words*. New York, NY: Vintage, 2006.

Wilson, Henry. *History of the Rise and Fall of the Slave Power in America*. 3 vols. Boston, MA: James R. Osgood and Co., 1877.

Wilson, Joseph Thomas. *The Black Phalanx: A History of the Negro Soldiers of the United States in the Wars of 1775-1812, 1861-'65*. Hartford, CT: American Publishing Co., 1890.

Wilson, Woodrow. *Division and Reunion: 1829-1889*. 1893. New York, NY: Longmans, Green, and Co., 1908 ed.

———. *A History of the American People*. 5 vols. 1902. New York, NY: Harper and Brothers, 1918 ed.

Wood, W. J. *Civil War Generalship: The Art of Command*. 1997. New York, NY: Da Capo Press, 2000 ed.

Woodard, Komozi. *A Nation Within a Nation: Amiri Baraka (LeRoi Jones) and Black Power Politics*. Chapel Hill, NC: University of North Carolina Press, 1999.

Woodburn, James Albert. *The Life of Thaddeus Stevens*. Indianapolis, IN: Bobbs-Merrill, 1913.

Woods, Thomas E., Jr. *The Politically Incorrect Guide to American History*. Washington, D.C.: Regnery, 2004.

Woodson, Carter G. (ed.). *The Journal of Negro History* (Vol. 4). Lancaster, PA: Association for the Study of Negro Life and History, 1919.

Woodward, William E. *Meet General Grant*. 1928. New York, NY: Liveright Publishing, 1946 ed.

Woodworth, Steven E. *Jefferson Davis and His Generals: The Failure of Confederate Command in the West.* Lawrence, KS: University Press of Kansas, 1990.

Wright, John D. *The Language of the Civil War.* Westport, CT: Oryx, 2001.

Wyeth, John Allan. *Life of General Nathan Bedford Forrest.* 1899. New York, NY: Harper and Brothers, 1908 ed.

Young, John Russell. *Around the World With General Grant.* 2 vols. New York, NY: American News Co., 1879.

Zaehner, R. C. (ed.) *Encyclopedia of the World's Religions.* 1959. New York, NY: Barnes and Noble, 1997 ed.

Zall, Paul M. (ed.). *Lincoln on Lincoln.* Lexington, KY: University Press of Kentucky, 1999.

Zavodnyik, Peter. *The Age of Strict Construction: A History of the Growth of Federal Power, 1789-1861.* Washington, D.C.: Catholic University of America Press, 2007.

Zinn, Howard. *A People's History of the United States: 1492-Present.* 1980. New York, NY: HarperCollins, 1995.

LINCOLN'S TRUE LEGACY

Our sixteenth president did not preserve the Union or abolish slavery. But he did manage to leave thousands of Southern cities in rubble, their citizens homeless refugees. This 1865 photo of what was once the beautiful town of Richmond, Virginia, reveals Lincoln's true legacy, one for which he will always be remembered here in Dixie: greediness, aggressiveness, arrogance, incompetence, and ignorance. For more on this topic, see my book *The Unholy Crusade: Lincoln's Legacy of Destruction in the American South*.

INDEX

abolition, 6, 7, 58, 59, 64, 65, 69, 71, 72, 176, 183, 200, 201, 203, 205, 241, 245, 246, 273, 278, 280, 282-285, 287-290, 292, 296-298, 300, 301, 303, 305, 310, 312, 313, 320, 322, 328, 332, 351, 365, 379, 387, 402, 415, 418, 422, 451, 461, 475, 479, 484-486, 490, 493, 501, 511, 514, 518, 526, 566, 568, 581, 585, 590, 592, 600, 608, 786, 789, 946, 957, 972

abolition movement, 65, 241, 300, 351

abolition of slavery, 71, 176, 183, 241, 245, 289, 292, 296, 310, 312, 313, 387, 501, 511, 526, 581, 590, 600, 957

abolitionism, 284, 285, 313, 332, 448, 464, 475, 484, 533, 718, 826, 933

abolitionist sentiment, 286, 287, 300, 789

abolitionists, 16, 72, 200, 215, 223, 273, 281-283, 285-287, 294, 296, 300, 301, 303, 332, 353, 356, 358, 371, 381, 400, 450, 451, 483, 484, 493, 525, 526, 533, 538, 542, 563, 578, 588, 589, 593, 594, 603, 671, 720, 756, 758, 771, 792, 826, 959

Abraham Lincoln: The Southern View (Seabrook), 11

Abraham Lincoln's white dream, 513, 929

abuses, 118, 142-145, 632, 700

Account of the Emancipation Proclamation, Lincoln's, 564

ACS, 508, 520, 533

Adams, John, 64, 103, 855

Adams, John Quincy, 159, 162, 360, 855

Adams, Shelby L., 1046

Afghanistan, 175

Africa, 2, 7, 37, 38, 48, 57, 58, 64, 65, 67-74, 85-87, 99, 187, 193, 199, 281, 290, 291, 293, 297, 304, 308, 352, 357, 358, 369, 372, 373, 381, 382, 390, 391, 395, 402, 403, 407, 408, 413, 420, 421, 438, 474, 491, 492, 494, 496, 501, 507, 508, 512, 514, 515, 517, 520, 523, 526-528, 532, 533, 539, 542, 544, 545, 549, 551-553, 556, 562, 566, 573, 576, 578, 579, 589, 596, 607, 635, 671, 720, 770-774, 779, 780, 786, 787, 790-792, 795, 796, 798, 926, 928, 936, 937, 941, 945, 947, 950, 954, 967, 968, 971-974, 978

African Methodist Episcopal Church, 72

African servitude, 199

African slave trade, 382, 390, 391, 402, 403, 937

African slave-trade, 37, 38, 48, 57, 58, 85-87, 99, 352, 438, 553
African slavery, 37, 941
African-American war effort, 795
Africanization, of European-American culture, 514
African-American servants, 770
African-Americans, 2, 7, 68, 69, 71, 73, 187, 304, 308, 369, 373, 413, 474, 494, 496, 507, 512, 514, 515, 533, 542, 544, 549, 551, 552, 566, 573, 576, 578, 579, 589, 596, 607, 671, 774, 780, 786, 787, 792, 971
Age of Enlightenment, 63
Alabama, 20, 116, 129, 169, 173, 210, 222, 225, 246, 247, 268, 374, 403, 487, 488, 559, 561, 568, 571, 609, 611, 747, 749, 794-796, 819, 928, 943, 959, 972, 1047
Alaska, 520
Albany, New York, 283, 677, 680, 698
Alexandria, Virginia, 194
Algerines, the, 35
Allen, Charles, 409
Allen, Nathan, 340
Alton, Illinois, 35, 245, 281, 366, 497, 856
amalgamation, 369, 371, 414, 505-507, 521
Amendment, 175
Amendment, Fifteenth, 828
Amendment, Fourteenth, 828
Amendment, Fourth, 146, 657
Amendment, Ninth, 63, 121, 139, 168, 178, 265, 267, 363, 437
Amendment, Tenth, 63, 121, 125, 127, 139, 168, 178, 265, 267, 363, 437
Amendment, Thirteenth, 212, 569, 600-603, 607
America, 2, 4, 7-9, 11-15, 17-19, 23, 24, 26, 28, 31, 33, 34, 36, 37, 40, 44, 57, 62-71, 73, 74, 95, 102-105, 108, 116, 118-122, 124-126, 132, 134, 135, 141, 147, 148, 153, 162, 169, 172, 173, 175, 177-182, 184, 187, 192, 193, 199, 201, 206, 210, 211, 214, 216, 217, 221, 224, 227-230, 239, 241, 246, 265-267, 271, 273, 274, 280-283, 289, 290, 292, 296-298, 300, 303, 304, 308, 351, 352, 355-357, 363, 369-373, 376, 377, 393, 402-405, 411, 413, 415-418, 420, 429, 437, 443, 444, 448, 455, 472-474, 476, 491-494, 496, 500, 507, 508, 510-518, 520-523, 526-529, 531-535, 538-540, 542-544, 547-554, 556, 557, 560, 562, 564, 566, 569, 571-573, 576, 578, 579, 582, 585, 589, 593, 596, 604, 607, 609, 616, 619-622, 625, 626, 628, 638, 642,

647, 655, 656, 662, 664, 666-668, 670, 671, 680, 687, 689, 692, 693, 704, 705, 712, 714, 720-724, 730, 739, 745, 749, 751, 753, 754, 758-760, 764, 768-770, 772-774, 779, 780, 785-787, 790, 792, 795-798, 808, 811, 812, 815, 820, 826, 828-831, 926-964, 966-984, 1042-1044, 1048, 1049
American abolition movement, 65, 241, 300, 351
American apartheid, 63, 514
American Baptist Home Mission Society, 808
American Colonization Society, 67, 296, 369, 508, 520, 521, 523, 532
American Party, 282
American Revolutionary War, 547
American slavery, 2, 65, 69, 73, 282, 355, 418, 520, 533, 538, 620, 723, 943, 953, 956, 963, 971, 1049
American System, 31, 121, 134, 153, 184, 224, 929
An Appeal From the Colored Men of Philadelphia, 551
Anaconda Plan, 765
anarchy, 111, 569, 660, 713
Anderson, Loni, 1046
Anderson, Robert, 217-219, 221-223, 226-229, 232, 233, 248, 249, 279
Andrew, John A., 773
Andrews, Sidney, 736, 737
Anglo-African, 508
Annapolis, Maryland, 69
Annual Message to Congress, Lincoln's, 194, 195, 224, 533, 737
anti-Semitism, and Lincoln, 200, 666, 812
Antietam, Maryland, 718
Antigua, 67
antiwar sentiment, 148, 177, 265, 624, 625, 656, 664, 665, 743, 754, 759
anti-abolitionists, 371
Anti-Slavery International, 543
anti-South propaganda, 11, 73, 118, 121, 303, 761, 789, 821, 926
anti-South proponents, 271, 351, 511, 585, 792
apartheid, 63, 514, 520, 543
Appomattox, North Carolina, 571
Appomattox, Virginia, 815
apportionment of representatives, 183
apprenticeship, 592-595
Aquinas, Saint Thomas, 422
Arkansas, 160, 375, 376, 385, 388, 488, 559, 561, 568, 636, 733, 749, 763, 764, 793, 819, 827

Army of Tennessee, 940, 967
Arthur, King, 1044
Articles of Confederation, 2, 19, 50, 51, 113, 121, 178, 180, 257, 374, 951, 971
articles of war, 148, 150, 646
Ashe, Samuel A., 299
Ashley, James M., 509
Ashmun, George, 137, 266, 267
Asia, 72, 193, 369, 372, 514, 781, 829
Astor, John Jacob, and slavery, 69
Atchison, David R., 360
atheism, 803-805, 811, 813
Athens, Alabama, 747
Atkins, Chet, 1046
Atlanta, Georgia, 726, 728, 740
Atlantic slave trade, 928, 937
attorneys, 144, 149, 271, 489
Augustine, Saint, 422
Authorizing Employment of Contrabands, Lincoln's, 771
Bachman, John, 735
Back to Africa movement, 369
Backus, Abner L., 698, 710
Bailey, Joseph, 658
Baker, Jehu, 451, 457
Baldwin, Henry, 414
Baldwin, John B., 191
Baltimore, Maryland, 32, 69, 204, 491, 578, 629, 814
Banks, Nathaniel P., 284, 577, 658, 773, 780, 822
baptism, 421
Barnett, T. J., 825, 826
Bartley, T. W., 698, 710
Bateman, Newton, 807
Bateman, William O., 124
Bates, Edward, 62, 192, 219, 234, 772, 843
Battle of Antietam, 566, 567, 718
Battle of Atlanta, 753
Battle of Chattanooga I, 749
Battle of Fort Pillow, 2, 745, 971
Battle of Fort Sumter, 216, 244, 793
Battle of Franklin II, 724
Battle of Gettysburg, 718, 794

Battle of Lookout Mountain, 749
Battle of Murfreesboro, 718
Battle of New Orleans, 688
Battle of Opequon Creek, 742
Battle of Second Bull Run, 566
Battle of Second Manassas, 566
Battle of Sharpsburg, 291, 292, 566, 567
Battle of the Crater, 973
Battle of Winchester, 742
Beaufort, South Carolina, 730
Beauregard, P. G. T., 217, 226, 228
Beauregard, Pierre G. T., 1045
Beck, Glenn, 139
Beecher, Henry Ward, 826
Beecher, Lyman, 67
beggary, 608
Belcher, Jonathan, 66
Belchers, New England slaving family, 67
Bell, John, 135, 751
Belmont, August, 812
Benjamin, Judah, 23, 592, 795
Benton, Jessie A., 277
Benton, Thomas H., 277
Berks County, Pennsylvania, 26
Bernstein, Leonard, 1046
Berret, James G., 289
Bertinatti, Commander, 199
Bertonneau, Arnold, 780
Beveridge, Albert J., 30
Bible, 2, 13, 83, 100, 136, 296, 420-422, 622, 799, 801-804, 807, 808, 814, 815, 933, 960, 971, 977, 1043, 1044
Big Brother, 11, 102, 103, 720, 721
big government, 11, 15, 16, 31, 33, 62, 118, 121, 132, 134, 136, 152, 224, 230, 303, 424, 625, 690, 721, 830, 855, 953
Bill of Rights, 19, 139, 178, 179, 183, 633, 638, 828, 968
Billy Yank, 981
Birchard, M., 698, 710
Bixby, Mrs., 117, 118
black citizenship, 786
black civil rights, 68, 141, 213, 276, 280, 304, 417, 493, 494, 507, 526, 543, 565, 566, 577, 579, 598, 608, 720, 811

Black Codes, 68, 71, 304
black colonization, 7, 68, 85, 227, 304, 372, 513, 524, 542, 550, 553, 554
black colonizationists, 369, 429, 797
black commissioned officers, 772
black committee, at the White House, 544
black Confederate soldiers, 792, 793, 796, 797
black Confederate troops, 795
black Confederates, 796, 928, 952
black deportation, 72, 491, 518, 529, 538, 542, 544
black enlistment, 285, 568, 572, 773, 775, 777
black equality, 283
Black Hawk War, 27, 663
black labor, 530
black land giveaways, 607
black leaders, 550
black men, 321, 496, 505, 515, 516, 521, 537, 544, 551, 620, 635, 719, 788, 792, 794, 830, 950
black nationalism, 369
black officers, 772, 773, 781
black racism, 369
black racists, 369
Black Republicanism, 78, 324, 611, 614, 615
Black Republicans, 328, 611
black separatism, 369
black separatists, 369
black servitude, 300
black slave owners, 608
black soldiers, 7, 574-576, 578, 718, 720, 770-774, 779-781, 787, 790, 795, 796, 966, 973
black soldiers, under Lincoln, 779
black soldiers' children, enslaved by Lincoln, 780
black soldiers' wives, enslaved by Lincoln, 780
black suffrage, 516, 758, 780, 781, 786
black troops, 772, 936
black Yankee officers, 772
blacks, 37, 62, 63, 65, 67-73, 85, 101, 186, 265, 273, 281, 283-286, 289, 290, 293, 296, 297, 300-305, 308, 320, 341, 357, 369, 370, 372, 392, 394, 413, 417, 419, 421, 429, 436, 474, 495, 496, 505-508, 510, 511, 513-518, 520, 521, 524, 528, 529, 531-538, 542-544, 548, 550-554, 564-567, 570-573, 575, 577-579, 584, 585, 587, 588, 590, 596, 605-608, 620,

662, 671, 672, 718, 720, 724, 729-731, 735, 754, 758, 770-776, 778-781, 785, 786, 790-794, 796, 797, 824, 930, 932, 961, 974
blacks, number of that fought for Confederacy, 796
Blackwell, Hardin, 792
Blair, Francis P., 278, 599
Blair, Frank, 485
Blair, Montgomery, 244, 278, 519, 565, 847
Bledsoe, Albert Taylor, 206
Blind Tom, 793
Bliss, George, 698, 710
Bolling, Edith, 1046
Bonaparte, Louis Napoleon, 616
bondage, 72, 286, 391, 436, 507, 523, 530, 569, 580, 584, 636, 958
bondservants, 65
Boone, Daniel, 1045
Boone, Pat, 1046
Booth, John Wilkes, 542, 553, 786
Boston Post, 516
Boston, Massachusetts, 16, 65, 67, 68, 71, 117, 160, 207, 282, 283, 300, 491, 514, 520, 535, 537, 641
Bostonians, 282
Bowen, S. W., 340
Boxer, Barbara, 16
Bradford, Augustus, 632
Bramlette, Thomas E., 742, 743
Brazil, 403
Breckinridge, John C., 90, 135, 181, 684, 751, 1045
Brierfield, 543
Briggs, George, 792
Bright, Jesse D., 129, 360
Bristol County, Massachusetts, 65
Britain, 40, 68, 173, 179, 182, 394, 400, 776, 958
British dominions, 193
Brooke, Edward W., 1046
Brookline, Massachusetts, 67
Brooks, Preston S., 329, 490, 1045
Brough, John, 624
Brown University, connected to slavery, 67, 302
Brown, Gratz, 485
Brown, J. N., 185

Brown, James N., 372
Brown, John, 614, 616
Brown, William, 932
Browne, Willam H., 103
Browning, Eliza Caldwell, 29
Browning, Mrs. Orville H., 29
Browning, Orville H., 142, 224, 225, 230, 231, 244, 278, 280, 352
Brownlow, Parson, 580
Browns, New England slaving family, 67
Bryant, William C., 723
Buchanan, Franklin, 684
Buchanan, James, 221, 243, 299, 323, 325, 327, 359, 360, 362, 441, 485, 855
Buchanan, Patrick J., 1046
Buckingham, James S., 535
Buckner, Simon B., 684
Buell, Don Carlos, 736
Buford, Abraham, 1045
Bullitt, Cuthbert, 579
bummers, 729
Burbridge, Stephen G., 144, 657, 742
Burke, Joseph F., 200, 202
Burns, Robert, 804
Burnside, Ambrose E., 661
Bush, George H. W., 175
Bush, George W., 175
Butler, Andrew P., 1045
Butler, Benjamin F., 141, 142, 146, 282, 553, 554, 573, 605, 651, 725, 736, 746, 747
Butler, Evan, 804
Butler, Pierce, 639
C.S.A., 205, 217, 225, 268, 665, 715, 753, 765, 793, 821, 940
Cabots, New England slaving family, 67
Cain, of the Bible, 420
Calhoun, John C., 103, 128, 206, 294, 299, 360, 499
California, 73, 153, 324, 338, 342, 378, 379, 386, 408, 461, 757, 930, 935
Cambodia, 175
Camden, South Carolina, 776
Cameron, Simon, 219-223, 226, 274, 567, 603, 639, 640, 664, 755, 757, 842
Campbell, John A., 222, 599, 600, 603
Campbell, Joseph, 1043

Campbell, Judge, 121
Campbell, Thompson, 336-338
Campbell, William B., 755
Canaan, of the Bible, 420, 421
Canada, 18, 43, 400, 651, 722, 936, 956
Canby, Edward R. S., 144, 197, 658, 661
Canisius, Theodore, 131
Canterbury, Connecticut, 283
capitalism, 607, 927
Caribbean Sea, 548
Carnton Plantation, 2, 493, 584, 969
Carpenter, Francis B., 564, 565
Carpenter, William, 107
carpetbag rule, 828
carpetbaggers, 764, 957
Carroll Prison, 652
Carson, Martha, 1046
Carter, Jimmy, 830
Carter, Theodrick, 1045
Cartright, Peter, 803
Cash, Johnny, 1046
Cass, Lewis, 156, 157, 318, 362, 440, 510
casualty rate, of black Union soldiers, 779
Caucasians, 369, 781
Caudill, Benjamin E., 1044
Caudill's Army, 725, 1045
Celtic Warfare (Hill), 1047
Celts, 287
Central America, 369, 547-549
central government, 15, 31, 34, 62, 102, 103, 118, 120, 135, 139, 168, 178, 187, 207, 224, 267, 352, 655, 662, 831
Chambersburg, Pennsylvania, 728
Champlains, New England slaving family, 67
Channing, William Ellery, 67, 301
chaplains, 666, 797, 812
Charles I, 601
Charleston Harbor, 217, 220, 221, 228-230, 247, 272
Charleston, Illinois, 353, 413, 503, 511, 856
Charleston, South Carolina, 210, 227
Chase, Salmon P., 191, 294, 296, 317-319, 563, 565, 589, 658, 781, 839
chattel slavery, 543

Cheairs, Nathaniel F., 1045
Chesnut, James, Jr., 228, 229, 795
Chesnut, Mary, 228, 297, 736, 795, 1045
Chew, Robert S., 227
Chicago Convention Committee, 28
Chicago Daily Times, 656
Chicago, Illinois, 73, 77, 106, 109, 138, 283, 308, 351, 353, 495, 508, 573
Chickasaw, 937
chickens, 167
children, 73, 96, 172, 183, 184, 186, 187, 212, 293, 297, 358, 391, 392, 406, 423, 507, 514, 523, 547, 549, 551, 564, 570, 572, 603, 620, 636, 666, 668, 671, 680, 724, 727-730, 736, 737, 739, 747, 775, 776, 780, 797, 811, 812, 830, 1047
Choctaw, 937
Christ, 2, 24, 421, 801-803, 956, 1047
Christ Our Hope Reformed Episcopal Church, 1047
Christian Observer, 656
Christian Recorder, 671
Christian, George L., 745, 757, 833
Christianity, 2, 35, 420, 434, 453, 799, 802-804, 807, 808, 810, 811, 932, 967
Christians, 13, 23, 422, 806
Christmas, 2, 726
Church of Jesus Christ of Latter-Day Saints, 421, 956
Cincinnati, Ohio, 70, 76, 236, 321, 661
citizenship, 448, 511, 786, 787, 830
City Point, Virginia, 740
civil rights, 63, 64, 68, 118, 141, 177, 181, 213, 273, 276, 280, 287, 289, 290, 304, 308, 372, 417, 419, 493, 494, 507, 511, 516, 526, 538, 543, 564-566, 577, 579, 589, 595, 596, 598, 608, 656, 662, 720, 764, 774, 786, 811, 963, 974
Civil War, 2, 11, 18, 70, 150, 152, 169, 178, 183, 184, 203, 206, 216, 217, 229-234, 268, 292, 300, 415, 492, 493, 514, 524, 572, 584, 621, 635, 650, 661, 664, 678, 679, 681, 682, 726, 740, 760, 761, 792, 815, 830, 831, 855, 927-953, 955-960, 962, 963, 965-973, 975, 978-983, 1043, 1044, 1046, 1048, 1049
Civil War disqualification and debt, 183
civilian deaths, Southern, 724
Clark, William, 1045
Clay, Cassius M., 293

Clay, Henry, 31, 35, 61, 103, 121, 134, 153, 224, 296, 312, 356, 376, 377, 411, 448, 453, 460, 470, 500, 502, 503, 515, 520-524, 542
clergymen, 67, 577, 664
Cleveland, Ohio, 283
Clinton, DeWitt, 155
Clinton, Hillary, 16
Clinton, Illinois, 515
Clinton, William "Bill", 175
Coast Survey, 221
Cody, H. H., 340
Cohn, Levi, 652
Coldstream Guards, 794
Coles, Edward, 536
collective slavery, 543
Colonial Period, 69
colonization, 7, 67, 68, 72, 85, 227, 281, 296, 304, 369, 372, 443, 470, 471, 474, 507, 508, 513, 514, 517-521, 523-525, 527-529, 532, 533, 538, 539, 542-546, 549-554, 620, 787, 790, 945, 974
colonization of America, 790
colonization, black, Lincoln's plan for, 518
colonizationists, 72, 369, 429, 526, 542, 797
Colorado, 193
Colossae, Turkey, 421
Columbia, South Carolina, 609, 736
Columbus, Christopher, 509
Columbus, Ohio, 17, 37, 73, 515, 690, 781
Combs, Bertram T., 1046
Committee of Colored People, 814
common law suits, 183
compensated emancipation, 285, 527, 567, 588, 589, 717
compensation of members of Congress, 183
Compromise of 1850, 45, 239, 331-333, 380, 411, 460, 461, 966
Compromise of 1877, 828
Concord, Massachusetts, 67, 532
Confederacy, 2, 11, 19, 36, 50, 73, 74, 104, 108, 111, 115, 117-121, 130, 132, 135, 151, 168, 169, 171, 176, 178, 179, 184, 188, 189, 199, 200, 211, 214, 216-218, 228-230, 242, 244-246, 264, 265, 267, 281, 298, 363, 371, 373, 374, 412, 414, 415, 482, 501, 563, 568, 570, 577, 586, 588, 591, 598, 603, 604, 611, 612, 619, 624, 625, 627, 628, 634, 664, 665, 689, 720-722, 725, 729, 754, 764, 765, 772, 779,

792-797, 812, 821, 824, 825, 830, 931, 933, 936, 940, 941, 949, 956, 965, 967, 969, 971, 979-981, 1043-1046
Confederate army, 245, 631, 792, 794-796, 934, 939, 1048
Confederate Battle Flag, 280, 949, 1045
Confederate bonds, 792
Confederate Cause, 202, 415, 793, 958
Confederate Congress, 298, 776
Confederate Constitution, 74, 115, 168, 415, 938
Confederate flag, 2, 73, 792, 793, 949, 971, 1049
Confederate government, 115
Confederate Jews, 200
Confederate military, 271, 794, 795, 941
Confederate navy, 171, 969
Confederate States of America, 2, 4, 36, 116, 173, 265, 664, 666, 667, 730, 753, 797, 937, 938, 940, 963, 970, 1043
Confederate troops, 227, 795
Confederate veterans, 934, 1043
Confederate White House, 543
confederation, 2, 19, 49-51, 113, 121, 178, 180, 257, 374, 951, 971, 974
Confiscation Act, 580, 582-584
conformity, 81, 149, 214, 277, 768
Congress, 4, 27, 30, 36, 37, 45-51, 55, 56, 59, 70, 72, 74, 94, 99, 103, 110, 112, 116, 117, 120, 132-135, 140, 143, 145, 148, 149, 152, 153, 158, 159, 161-163, 165-169, 173-175, 177, 183, 186, 189, 192, 194-197, 201, 202, 209, 210, 212, 218, 221, 223-225, 242, 246, 247, 252-254, 260, 264-269, 271, 275-277, 279, 288, 298, 311-313, 316, 317, 320, 328, 330, 332, 333, 336-339, 342, 345-350, 352, 358, 369, 370, 374, 375, 377-380, 386, 397, 400, 403, 408-410, 415, 416, 419, 424, 425, 427-429, 433-435, 439-442, 444-446, 454, 456, 464-466, 469, 476, 477, 479-481, 485, 488, 492, 504, 513, 524-531, 533, 539, 540, 545, 552, 555-557, 561-563, 575, 579, 583, 587, 591, 593, 598-602, 604, 605, 608, 612, 613, 627, 630, 632, 634, 636, 639, 643-649, 655, 659, 663, 667-669, 673, 674, 676, 688, 689, 691, 695, 696, 699, 701, 704-707, 710, 712, 721, 722, 737, 741, 743, 744, 749, 766-769, 772, 776, 779, 803, 805, 806, 809, 810, 812, 817-820, 826, 827, 829, 927, 937, 950, 959, 960, 966, 967, 977, 1047
Congress of the Confederation, 49-51
Congressional Globe, 319, 345, 465

Conkling letter, 598, 715, 720
Conkling, James C., 597, 598, 715, 720
Connecticut, 65, 66, 124, 181, 239, 240, 246, 283, 374, 414, 516, 656, 830, 846, 975
Conquered Province policy, 825
conservatism, 613, 982
conservatives, 15-17, 63, 101, 118, 128, 208, 294, 370, 371, 429, 436, 481, 511, 586, 626, 690, 699, 753, 831, 855, 1044
consolidation, 106, 181
Constitution Day, 139
Constitution of the Confederate States, 2, 970
Constitutional Convention of 1787, 178, 299, 935
constitutional law, 132, 173, 280, 294, 419, 656, 674, 929
Constitutionalism, 297, 625, 929, 938
construction of Constitution, 183
contraband, 143, 665, 976
contraband camps, 976
contrabands, 531, 771, 940
Converse, George S., 698, 710
Cook, Burton C., 756
Cook, Isaac, 340
Cooke, Alistair, 622
cooks, 431, 584, 794
Cooper Union Speech, 15, 101, 236, 363, 519, 596, 611, 619
Cornett, Rachel, 725
Corning, Erastus, 661, 677-680
Correll, William F., 831
Corwin Amendment, 418
Corwin, Thomas, 266, 781
cotton, 69, 144, 145, 171-173, 193, 197, 330, 395, 491, 517, 726, 728, 737, 775, 940, 954, 958, 962, 963
coverers, 930
cows, 20, 423
Cox, Samuel S., 446
Cracker Outlaw (Lovell), 1048
Crandall, Prudence, 283
Crawford, Cindy, 1046
Crawford, William, 127
Creek, 742, 942, 978
Creoles, 793
Crete, 108, 472

criminal prosecutions, 183, 639, 643, 679, 681, 682, 691, 697
criminals, 71, 130, 142, 300, 519, 594, 725, 729, 831
Crisfield, John W., 203, 241, 302
Crittenden, John J., 91
Crockett, Davy, 1045
Crow, Jim, 304
Crowninshield Island, 67
Crowninshields, New England slaving family, 67
cruel and unusual punishment, 183, 696
Cruise, Tom, 1046
Cuba, 384, 965
Curtis, Samuel R., 142, 143
Cyrus, Billy R., 1046
Cyrus, Miley, 1046
Dabney, Robert Lewis, 245
Dana, Charles A., 575
Davis, David, 371, 658, 755
Davis, H. Winter, 580
Davis, Jefferson, 9, 14, 17, 59, 104, 115-117, 122-124, 126, 127, 171, 199, 217, 263, 264, 271, 294, 298, 299, 423, 515, 543, 544, 581, 592, 598, 624, 629-631, 633, 636-656, 740, 747, 748, 753, 765, 776, 790, 791, 794, 811, 822-824, 830, 1043, 1045
Davis, John W., 33
Davis, Varina (Howell), 543
Dawson, Nathaniel, 604
Day of Prayer, Lincoln's, 809
Dayton, William L., 359, 360
Dean, Howard, 16
death, 2, 12, 27, 54, 74, 118, 183, 198, 214, 231, 271, 283, 368, 391, 392, 403, 407, 415, 421, 452, 487, 491, 492, 521, 531, 534, 538, 542, 543, 573, 582, 588, 589, 598, 618, 620, 625, 656, 665, 669, 686, 697, 701, 714, 734, 735, 746, 767, 779, 786, 791, 801, 827-830, 976, 1044
Declaration of Independence, 11, 31, 60, 82, 113, 120, 127, 178-180, 206, 240, 256, 351, 372, 374, 381, 393, 404, 405, 436, 449, 451, 452, 456, 471, 475, 483, 484, 498-500, 630, 783, 814, 946
Declaration of Paris, 171
Deep South, 572, 830
defection, 573

DeKalb County Sentinel, 341
Delaware, 30, 124, 181, 210, 251, 530, 547, 580, 593, 607, 634, 830, 941, 981
demagoguism, 185, 507
Democracy in America (Tocqueville), 126
Democratic party, 59, 208, 337, 361, 362, 437, 448, 456, 463, 690, 692, 708, 713, 714, 753
Dennison, William, 848
Dent, Julia Boggs, 534
deportation, 72, 85, 177, 285, 289, 290, 296, 297, 304, 364, 372, 491, 507, 517-520, 526, 529, 530, 538, 542, 544, 550, 553, 554, 562, 615, 624, 662, 689, 728
depression, 118, 565, 587, 972, 976
desertion, 573, 664, 686, 695, 701, 702
desertion rates, Yankee, 573
despotism, 108, 111, 393, 660
Detroit, Michigan, 73, 283
DeWolfs, New England slave trading family, 67
diaries, 792
Dicey, Edward, 536
Dickens, Charles, 211
Dilorenzo, Thomas J., 20
disease, 573, 608, 776, 779, 830
District of Columbia Emancipation Act, 72, 289, 525, 527
disunion, 111, 130, 202, 211, 232, 252, 253, 259
Dix, John A., 576, 641, 648-650, 657
Dixie, 11, 18, 23, 29, 104, 117, 119, 207, 211, 217, 230, 265, 272, 298, 301, 302, 304, 436, 493, 516, 517, 543, 571, 572, 620, 625, 635, 723, 725, 729, 736, 737, 744, 747, 757, 774, 792, 824, 826, 828, 829, 934, 947, 958, 982, 984
Dixie (song), 517
Doctrine of Necessity, Lincoln's, 811
Dodd, Christopher, 16
Dodge, Grenville M., 733
Dodge, William E., 138
Donnelly, Neil, 340
Doroughty, Lee, 746
double jeopardy, 183
Dougherty, John, 334, 335
doughfaces, 177
Douglas, Stephen A., 25, 35-49, 51-53, 55, 57-60, 62, 63, 76, 78, 79, 81, 82,

   84, 85, 87-90, 92, 93, 95-97, 101, 106, 107, 128, 135,
   154, 155, 185, 199, 214, 223, 235, 245, 246, 266, 281,
   285, 287, 308, 309, 311-319, 321, 322, 324, 327-330,
   332-348, 353, 357, 362, 366, 367, 373, 376-378, 380, 385,
   387, 392-395, 405-411, 417, 424, 426, 427, 429, 431-440,
   443, 444, 446-452, 454-466, 468-479, 481-483, 485, 487,
   489, 490, 495, 497, 499, 503-506, 508, 509, 511, 515,
   520, 532, 610, 688, 723, 751, 757, 782, 783, 785, 798,
   856

Douglass, Frederick, 68, 372, 484, 550, 771, 774, 811
Douglass' Monthly, 550, 774, 811
Dow, Neal, 222
Drake, Charles D., 292
Dred Scott case, 56, 429, 431, 453, 467, 480, 499, 506
Dred Scott Speech, Lincoln's, 505
Dred-Scottism, 442
Du Bois, W. E. B., 608
due process, 55, 152, 183, 345, 427-429, 630, 638, 696, 710
Durant, Thomas J., 579
Durley, William, 356
Duvall, Robert, 1046
Earl of Oxford, 1044
Early, Jubal, 729, 730
economics, 153, 211, 930, 943, 978, 1047
Edward I, King, 1044
Egyptians, 287
election of 1860, 371, 751, 754, 757
election of 1864, 662, 753, 759
election of 1876, 828
election of 1976, 830
election of president and vice president, 183
Electoral College, 135, 753, 754, 769
Ellerys, New England slaving family, 67
Emancipation Proclamation, 7, 30, 69, 72, 141, 147, 175, 176, 200, 204,
   212, 213, 241, 276-278, 280, 281, 285, 290, 294, 369,
   415, 419, 516, 521, 526-528, 532, 533, 538, 541, 542,
   555, 556, 559, 560, 562-570, 572, 574, 575, 577, 579,
   585-587, 589, 591, 594, 595, 599, 603, 604, 607, 609,
   715, 717, 720, 758, 770
Emerson, Ralph Waldo, 67
empire, 16, 19, 155, 355, 356, 586, 636, 718, 932, 947, 950, 957, 982

England, 26, 65-68, 171, 172, 206, 209, 210, 282, 283, 302, 362, 369, 415, 501, 520, 586, 591, 601, 616, 665, 697, 714, 718, 826, 830, 926, 946, 959, 969, 1045
English Bill, 313, 343, 344, 424, 444-447
English, William H., 446
Episcopal Church, 72, 799, 1047
equal protection, 183
equal rights, 187, 188, 304, 306, 789, 929
Esclavon, Jacques, 792
Essex County, Massachusetts, 65
Ethiopia, 565
Euclid, 52, 108
Europe, 2, 30, 36, 64, 119, 171-173, 193, 206, 210, 300, 369, 452, 515, 531, 534, 583, 584, 586, 587, 589, 606, 668, 670, 712, 779, 1044
European Enlightenment, 64
European support, 119, 587
Europeans, 171, 172, 586
European-Americans, 300, 589
Evangelical Lutherans, 268
Evarts, Jeremiah, 67
Everett, Edward, 32
Ex parte Milligan, 152
excessive bail or fines, 183
execution of black soldiers, by Lincoln, 779
expansion of slavery, 328, 418, 424, 515
extensionists, 352
extraordinary powers, 664
Ezekiel, Moses Jacob, 200, 202
Fairfield County, Connecticut, 66
Fall of Man, 422
Faneuil Hall, 67, 282, 283
Faneuil, Peter, 282
Faneuils, New England slaving family, 67
Farewell Address, George Washington's, 33, 34
farmers, 516, 723
Farnsworth, John F., 478
Farragut, David G., 66
Fay, Edwin, 725
federal government, 63, 75, 126, 127, 153, 181, 247, 261, 298, 327, 342, 419, 427, 437, 445, 474, 588, 590, 615, 647, 660, 745,

961, 979
Federal Union, 112, 117, 248, 250, 252, 256, 343, 366, 692
Federalism, 926
Federalists, 19, 956
Feinstein, Dianne, 16
Fell, Jesse W., 26
felons, 729
Fernandina, Florida, 210, 779
Fessenden, William P., 840
feudalism, 422
Ficklin, Orlando B., 266
Field, Stephen J., 658
Fillmore, Millard, 128, 129, 464, 855
Final Emancipation Proclamation, 141, 147, 175, 176, 200, 204, 213, 285, 290, 415, 419, 521, 528, 541, 542, 560, 562-564, 568, 569, 574, 575, 585, 770
financiers, 75, 415, 754
Finck, W. E., 698, 710
Finley, Robert, 520
fire-eater, 229
First Annual Message to Congress, Lincoln's, 135, 268, 492, 524, 634
First Inaugural Address, Hayes', 828
First Inaugural Address, Lincoln's, 109, 175, 176, 179, 200, 217, 225, 292, 351, 365, 417, 418, 586, 799
Fishback Amendment, 764
Fishback, William M., 764
Fleming, Walter L., 794
Fletcher, Thomas C., 731
Florida, 8, 10, 114, 169, 173, 189, 210, 217, 225, 246, 247, 258, 274, 376, 487, 488, 559, 561, 568, 611, 749, 779, 819, 1048
Florida State University, 1048
Foner, Eric, 102
Foote, Shelby, 1043
Forbes, Christopher, 1046
forced African labor, 790
forced enlistment, 776
Ford's Theater, 121
foreign alliances, 34
Forrest, Nathan B., 1043, 1045
Forrest, Nathan Bedford, 304, 544, 627, 745
Fort Hamilton, 637

Fort Jefferson, 247
Fort Lafayette, 267, 628, 637, 640, 641, 643, 650
Fort McHenry, 33, 631, 641, 739
Fort Mill, 797
Fort Monroe, 264, 598
Fort Moultrie, 221, 222
Fort Pickens, 217, 223, 230, 249, 250
Fort Smith, 764, 793
Fort Sumter, 115, 135, 190, 216, 217, 219-225, 227, 229-234, 242, 244, 245, 247-252, 267-270, 272, 297, 418, 719, 724, 734, 829, 943
Fort Taylor, 247
Fort Warren, 641, 975
forty acres and a mule, 607
Foster, Robert Sanford, 775
Founders, 46, 125, 139, 247, 329, 655, 821
Founding documents, 126
Founding Fathers, 64, 124, 138, 174, 181, 187, 267, 519, 574, 624, 831
Founding Generation, 102
Fourierism, 826
Fourth Annual Message to Congress, Lincoln's, 552, 598, 627, 636, 743
Fox, Gustavus, 222, 244
Fox, Gustavus V., 221, 227, 230, 244
France, 68, 171, 172, 375, 376, 378, 383, 388, 586, 665
Francis, Newton, 804
Frank, Barney, 17
Franklin, Benjamin, 235, 514
Franklin, Tennessee, 14, 724
free blacks, 68, 71, 290, 300, 301, 304, 372, 392, 505, 506, 520, 521, 524, 536, 570, 608, 754, 792, 796
free labor, 63, 101, 289, 307, 358, 580, 825, 943
free trade, 109, 200, 207
free trade system, 207
Freedman's Village, 73
freedmen, 304, 528, 530, 571, 607, 608, 773, 787, 940, 958
freedom of religion, 183, 660
freedom of speech, 32, 630, 655, 691, 694, 696, 699, 704
freedom of the press, 634, 660
freedwomen, 571, 607
Freeman's Journal, 656
Freeport, Illinois, 289, 309, 856

free-loveism, 826
Free-Soil party, 515
Fremantle, Arthur J., 794
Frémont, John C., 143, 274, 276-281, 359, 360, 439, 464, 485, 567, 582, 603, 664, 712, 828
Fry, John B., 116
Fugitive Slave Act, 70, 417, 589
Fugitive Slave Law, 379, 387, 400, 402, 589
Fullinwider, Jacob N., 831
Galena, Illinois, 128
Galesburg, Illinois, 443, 455, 856
Gamble, Hamilton R., 62, 63, 142, 143
Gansevoort, Peter, 678
Gardner, Isabella Stewart, 67
Gardners, New England slaving family, 67
Garrison, William Lloyd, 30, 64, 67, 70, 282, 283, 300-302, 448, 484
Gayheart, Rebecca, 1046
General Order No. 11, 811, 812
Genesis, book of, 420
Geneva Conventions, 142, 145, 734, 740
George III, 36
Georgia, 57, 58, 68, 85, 124, 150, 151, 169, 173, 181, 225, 246, 247, 274, 374, 412, 479, 487, 488, 543, 559, 561, 568, 602, 611, 657, 726, 728, 734, 737, 740, 749, 793, 819, 825, 828, 830, 948, 975, 982
Germans, 287
Germany, 36
Gettysburg Address, 179, 183, 621, 622, 624
Gettysburg, Pennsylvania, 718
Gibbs, Samuel W., 678
Giddings, Joshua R., 374, 448, 484
Gilmer, John A., 354, 365
Gist, States R., 1045
Glenn, Colonel, 778
Glover, Samuel, 280
God, 10, 13, 45, 64, 88, 103, 104, 108, 117, 122, 133, 134, 147, 185, 187, 198, 216, 223, 262, 267, 268, 276, 307, 358, 370, 404, 407, 420-422, 452, 457, 482, 492, 496, 507, 524, 547, 562, 564, 572, 583, 604, 620-624, 680, 719, 735, 741, 742, 758, 760-762, 799-803, 808, 811, 813-815, 818, 819, 946

gold, 2, 3, 197, 297, 329, 379, 534, 735, 1043
Gordon, George W., 1045
Gordon, Nathaniel, 74, 75, 491, 492
Gordon, W. J., 698, 710
Governor's Island, 226
Gracie, Archibald, and slavery, 69
Grady, Henry W., 825
Graham, Levin, 792
Granada, 175
grand jury, 183, 428, 638, 650, 679, 691, 696
Grand Review, U.S., 790
Grant, Ulysses S., 24, 122, 142, 147, 198, 200, 369, 533, 534, 569, 575, 627, 720, 725, 727, 738-742, 744, 748, 763, 778, 790, 797, 811-813, 831, 854, 855
Grappe, Gabriel, 792
Graves, Robert, 1043
Great Britain, 40, 68, 394, 400, 776, 958
Great Emancipator, 12, 609
Great Procrastinator, 12, 609
Great Yankee Coverup, 723
Greeks, 287
Greeley faction, the, 282
Greeley, Horace, 121, 223, 282, 579-585, 596, 605, 755, 790, 823
Green, Duff, 109
Greenhow, Rose O'Neal, 201, 202
Gregory, Saint, of Nazianzus, 422
Grider, Henry, 145, 202
Griffith, Andy, 1046
Grimsley, Elizabeth Todd, 13
Groesbeck, William S., 446
Guaraldi, Vince, 1046
Gurney, Eliza P., 800, 813
habeas corpus, 32, 148-152, 253, 254, 264, 267, 624, 628, 629, 631, 638-640, 645, 646, 659, 664, 666, 667, 679, 683-685, 687, 688, 695, 696, 699, 704, 712
Hackett, James H., 29, 732
Hahn, Michael, 780
Haiti, 72, 175, 531
Hale, Edward E., 715
Hale, J. T., 117
Haley, Alex, 69

Hall, B. F., 340
Hall, Oliver P., 831
Hall, Thomas, 608
Hall, William A., 203
Halleck, Henry W., 143, 582, 739, 744, 812, 813, 853
Ham, of the Bible, 420
Hamilton, Alexander, 19, 152, 235
Hamlin, Hannibal, 541, 835
Hampton Roads Peace Conference, 264, 553, 598-600, 823
Hampton, Virginia, 598
Hampton, Wade, 737
handclasps, 282
Hanks family, 26
Hanks, Nancy, 23, 26
Hanks, Tom, 23
Hapsburg rule, 107
Hardee, William J., 1048
Hardee's Corps, 1048
Harding, William G., 1045
Hardy, R. M., 1048
Harney, William S., 32
Harper's Ferry, 252, 614-616
Harper's Ferry affair, 614
Harper's Magazine, 39, 48
Harris, Thomas L., 464, 465, 476, 477
Harrison, William H., 128, 287, 360, 855
Hartford County, Connecticut, 66
Harvard Law School, 67
Harvard University, 67, 748, 944, 972
Hatch, Edward, 725
Hawley, Seth C., 643
Hay, John, 13, 107, 156, 216, 241, 242, 291, 545, 834
Hayes, Rutherford B., 828, 830, 855
Hayne, Robert Young, 535
Hebrews, early, 420
Heintzelman, Samuel P., 624
Helm, Benjamin H., 419, 657
Helm, Emily T., 419, 657, 658
Helper, Hinton R., 518, 519, 616
Henderson, Kentucky, 778
Henry, Alexander, 105

Henry, Patrick, 19
Herndon, W. D., 803, 804
Herndon, William H., 154-156, 284, 656, 721, 802-804
Herrington, A. M., 340
Hickman, John, 42, 89
Hill, J. Michael, 8, 11, 18-20, 1047
Hill, Samuel, 13, 801, 803
Hilton Head Island, South Carolina, 731
Hilton Head, South Carolina, 775
Hise, John, 340
Hitler, Adolf, 13, 36, 103
Hodges, A. G., 176
Hodges, Silas, 746
Hoffman, Henry W., 635
Hoffman's Row, 804
hogs, 391, 423, 603, 728
homelessness, 570, 608, 727
Homestead Act, 629
Hood, John B., 1045
Hood, John Bell, 727, 729, 753
Horsman, J., 340
Houk, David A., 698, 710
House of Representatives, 32, 106, 124, 131, 139, 148, 156, 165, 246, 247, 267, 268, 284, 336, 375, 378, 380, 400, 415, 418, 454, 465, 472, 473, 527, 538, 540, 557, 600, 625, 659, 663, 676, 688, 771, 809, 825
Houston, John B., 742
Howell, Varina, 543
Hoyne, Thomas, 340
Humphreys, Dan, 792
Hungary, 107, 108
hunkerism, 142
Hunt, John, 950
Hunter, David, 146, 274-276, 281, 285, 567, 582, 603, 664, 725, 729, 730, 739
Hunter, Robert M. T., 599-601
Hurlbut, Stephen A., 231
Hurst, Fielding, 746
Hutchins, W. A., 698, 710
Ide, Dr., 808
Illinois, 5, 14, 16, 24, 26, 27, 32, 35, 49, 50, 60, 73, 76, 81, 83, 86, 89, 90,

93-96, 100, 103, 104, 106, 107, 109, 118, 119, 128, 138, 153-155, 160, 185, 193, 199, 212, 223, 234, 235, 245, 246, 273, 278, 281, 283, 284, 286, 288-290, 296, 304, 305, 308, 309, 313, 321, 350, 351, 353, 362, 365-367, 370, 372, 373, 380, 387, 390, 405, 406, 409, 412, 413, 416, 435, 442, 443, 446-448, 453, 455, 464-466, 469, 476, 477, 482, 483, 489, 493-497, 503, 505, 508, 509, 511, 512, 515, 520, 532, 536, 573, 579, 581, 589, 603, 610, 656, 715, 723, 732, 751, 755-757, 801, 805-807, 813, 856, 929, 930, 932, 941, 942, 945, 947, 948, 959, 961, 965, 973, 978

Illinois and Michigan Canal, 160
Illinois Ape, 104
Illinois Central Railroad, 153
Illinois Journal, 119
Illinois Staats-Anzeiger, 118
Illinois State Register, 437
Illinoisans, 304, 305, 508
income tax, 183, 655, 666
Independence Hall, 134, 216, 404
Indiana, 27, 30, 31, 49-51, 86, 93, 94, 107, 129, 160, 190, 193, 237, 373, 393, 412, 446, 499, 500, 581, 756, 757, 763, 791, 797, 834, 927, 943, 975, 977, 978, 982
Indiana Regiment, 140th, 791, 797
Indianapolis, Indiana, 190
Indians, 26, 194, 196, 358, 572, 668-670, 937
Industrial Revolution, 64
industrialists, 75, 207, 415, 754
inferior races, 451, 453, 458, 472, 475, 483, 496, 508, 510, 518, 573, 829
inflation, 297, 978
integration, 72, 305, 508, 518, 772
internal improvements, 102, 152-159, 162, 165, 168, 956
internal revenue, 102, 194, 196, 666
International Law, 170, 299, 563
interracial marriage, 185, 369, 508, 518
Interview with John T. Mills, Lincoln's, 787
involuntary enlistment, of blacks into U.S. military, 774
Iowa, 85, 160, 193, 332, 375, 376, 383, 388
Iraq, 175
Ireland, 2
Irish, 164, 659, 973, 1043

Irish House of Commons, 659
Irrepressible Conflict, 240
irrepressible conflict, the, myth, 89
IRS, the, 102, 666
Isabella Stewart Gardner Museum, 67
Iscariot, Judas, 23
Island of Vache, 531
Israel, 507
Israel, Benjamin, 202
Israel, Moses Jacob, 202
Italy, 210
Jackson, Andrew, 128, 138, 360, 434, 469, 480, 659, 687, 688, 855, 1045
Jackson, Henry R., 1045
Jackson, Stonewall, 1045
Jackson, Thomas Stonewall, 543, 796
Jackson, William M., 340
James, Frank, 1045
James, Jesse, 1045
Jamestown, Virginia, 551, 1045
Japheth, of the Bible, 421
Jay, John, 235
Jefferson, Thomas, 16, 19, 44, 45, 49, 65, 75, 91, 103, 108, 109, 126, 127, 139, 162, 165, 168, 182, 235, 260, 297, 298, 338, 351, 364, 374, 375, 434, 452, 456, 469, 519, 525, 574, 615, 855, 1045
Jeffersonian Confederate Republic, 622
Jeffersonianism, 108, 109, 662, 1046
Jent, Elias, Sr., 725, 1045
Jesus, 2, 13, 23, 421, 422, 801-803, 807, 815, 956, 1044
Jew peddlers, 812
Jim Crow states, 304
John, Elton, 1046
Johnny Reb, 230, 981
Johnson, Andrew, 576, 770, 837, 855
Johnson, Lyndon B., 175
Johnson, Reverdy, 269
Johnson, Richard H., 785
Johnson, Richard M., 504
Johnson, Robert, 774
Johnston, Joseph E., 684
Jones, John, 508, 793, 952

Jones, M. M., 652
Joseph, of the Bible, 420
Journal of Commerce, 649, 656, 657
journals, 319, 688, 776, 792, 941, 945, 1047
Jubilee, day of (emancipation), 571
Judd, Ashley, 1046
Judd, Naomi, 1046
Judd, Wynonna, 1046
judicial limits, 183
Julian, George W., 31
jury trial, 183
just powers, 393, 394, 510, 629, 638, 653
Kansas, 35, 44, 45, 85, 193, 238, 239, 313, 320, 326, 343, 344, 375, 380, 381, 388, 389, 424, 425, 437-439, 441, 443-447, 453, 454, 479, 505, 506, 510, 516, 521, 533, 769, 926, 936, 948, 958, 963, 976, 981, 983
Kansas-Nebraska act, 45
Kaskel, Caesar J., 812, 813
Kautz, August V., 797
Kellogg, William, 194, 364, 417
Kendael, Hiram, 792
Kent, James, 162, 163
Kentucky, 23, 26, 27, 78, 82, 83, 88, 90, 93, 94, 99, 144, 145, 149-151, 160, 181, 193, 202, 223, 276, 279-281, 293, 356, 373, 389, 419, 448, 453, 455, 482, 485, 486, 500, 509, 607, 636, 657, 658, 723, 725, 742, 743, 765, 777, 778, 780, 829, 834, 845, 847, 929, 933, 965, 975, 983, 1043-1046
Keough, Riley, 1046
Kerry, John, 16
Key, Francis Scott, 520
Key, John J., 291, 292
Killen, Alabama, 1047
King Abraham, 719, 821
King, Rufus, 123
King, William R. D., 129, 360
Kings, New York, 69
Kinte, Kunta, 69
Kitchell, Joseph, 304
KKK, 282, 421, 829
Korea, 175
Ku Klux Klan, 2, 282, 496, 950, 953, 955, 957, 971, 979

Ku Klux Klan, New England version, 282
Kuwait, 175
La Salle Democrat, 338
laborers, 97, 98, 197, 307, 364, 520, 529, 530, 544, 567, 576, 577, 597,
    606, 615, 770, 771, 780, 787, 797
Lafayette, Marquis de la, 612
laissez-faire economy, 207
Lake Champlain, 67
Lamon, Ward H., 152, 231, 625, 631, 801-803, 806
Lancaster, Pennsylvania, 825
Land of Lincoln, the, 304
Lane, Jim, 274, 664
Lanphier, Charles H., 464-466, 476, 477
larceny, 745
Latin America, 531, 533
Latin-Americans, 811
League of the South, 1047
LeBlond, F. C., 698, 710
Lecompton Constitution, 238, 320, 324-327, 437, 439, 441, 444-447, 463
Lee, Fitzhugh, 1045
Lee, Robert E., 9, 147, 263, 298, 415, 608, 633, 634, 684, 716, 740, 815,
    822, 824, 825, 1045
Lee, Samuel P., 263
Lee, Stephen D., 1045
Lee, William H. F., 1045
Leesburg, Florida, 10, 1048
Lehman Brothers, and slavery, 69
Lester, Charles Edward, 215
Letcher, John, 730
Lewis, Meriwether, 1045
Lewis, Thomas, 107
Lexington, Kentucky, 742
liberal Northerners, 764
liberalism, 32, 134, 947, 1043
liberals, 15-17, 31, 103, 120, 177, 208, 242, 294, 352, 474, 511, 586, 662,
    690, 715, 828, 855, 926, 1044
Liberia, 72, 283, 291, 369, 381, 520, 527, 528, 532, 533, 547, 552, 553, 591
libertarians, 831
liberty, 10, 17, 34, 42, 61, 64, 75, 80, 107, 108, 113, 146, 187, 199, 207,
    208, 254, 257, 284, 286, 294-298, 303, 304, 317, 318,
    342, 356, 368, 375, 393, 402, 404, 405, 427-429, 436,

450, 458, 470, 471, 475, 479, 496-498, 515, 516, 518,
522, 523, 535, 541, 558, 570, 580, 583, 589, 606, 621,
623, 626, 630, 636-640, 643, 646, 650, 655, 659-661, 679,
680, 687, 688, 690, 695-699, 704, 705, 707, 711, 713,
714, 758, 781, 783, 808, 822, 831, 930, 943, 947, 955,
956, 961, 968, 978, 1046
Libya, 175
Limber, Jim, 543
Lincoln apologists, 102, 206, 234, 417, 511, 553, 562
Lincoln scholars, 12, 417, 715, 801
Lincoln, Abraham, 8, 9, 11-17, 19, 20, 23-33, 35, 36, 38, 40-52, 54-58,
60-66, 68-91, 93-112, 115-122, 124-129, 131-139,
141-145, 147-162, 164-166, 168-171, 173, 174, 176-192,
194-200, 202-205, 207-220, 222-235, 238-251, 253-293,
296-299, 302-304, 306, 308-320, 322, 323, 325, 327-332,
334-338, 340-348, 350-359, 361-373, 375-379, 381, 382,
384-387, 389-397, 399-410, 412-420, 422, 423, 425-429,
431, 432, 434-439, 441-443, 446-451, 453-455, 457-478,
480-483, 485-497, 499-501, 503-511, 513-516, 518-521,
525-533, 538, 540-553, 555-571, 573-579, 582, 584-592,
594-601, 603-608, 610-617, 619-622, 624-626, 628, 629,
632-636, 640, 646, 648-650, 655-677, 680-683, 685, 686,
688, 689, 692-695, 698-703, 705-707, 709-712, 715-720,
722-734, 737-743, 745-749, 752-757, 759, 760, 762-794,
796-815, 817-821, 823-831, 833, 834, 855, 856, 984
Lincoln, Abraham (Lincoln's grandfather), 26, 27
Lincoln, Enoch, 26
Lincoln, Levi, 26
Lincoln, Mary (Todd), 25, 66, 657, 801, 806
Lincoln, Mordecai, 26
Lincoln, Robert Todd, 13, 748
Lincoln, Solomon, 27
Lincoln, Thomas, 27
Lincoln-Douglas Debates, 266, 353, 443, 495, 497, 503, 508, 723, 757, 856
Lincolnian mythology, 9, 494
Lincolnology (Seabrook), 9, 12, 14, 19
Lincoln-Douglas Debates, 7, 25, 424, 856
Lincoln's War, 2, 12, 14, 69, 74, 75, 136, 141, 171, 200, 202, 206, 210,
211, 245, 297, 299, 516, 571, 572, 607, 620, 655, 720,
744, 745, 747, 748, 772, 797, 828, 830, 926, 971, 1045,
1049

Linconia, 533
Linder, Usher F., 287
liquor abolished, 183
livestock, 304, 422, 423, 793
Locke, John, 64
Lodge, Henry Cabot, Jr., 67
Lodge, Henry Cabot, Sr., 67
logbooks, 792
London Times, 586
London, England, 206
Long Island, New York, 551
Long Nine, the, 155
Long, Alexander, 698, 710
Longstreet, James, 794, 1045
Los Angeles, California, 73
Lost Cause, 229, 965
Louaillier, Louis, 688
Louisiana, 81, 160, 169, 173, 210, 225, 246, 247, 269, 333, 369, 370, 375, 423, 448, 487, 488, 525, 559, 561, 568, 571, 579, 611, 636, 658, 749, 773, 780, 781, 792, 795, 819, 827, 828, 927, 930, 934, 940, 950, 951, 954, 963, 968, 973, 979, 981
Louisiana Native Guards, 773
Louisville, Kentucky, 145, 777
Love, Henry, 792
Lovejoy, Elijah P., 283, 448, 478, 484
Lovejoy, Owen, 565
Loveless, Patty, 1046
Lovell, Robert, 8-10, 1048
Lowell, James R., 10
Lutz, Charles, 792
Lynchburg, Virginia, 730
Mackinaw salmon trout, 732
MacLean, John, 118
Madison, James, 11, 91, 103, 123, 124, 127, 139, 235, 536, 659, 855
Magoffin, Beriah, 581
Magruder, John B., 684
maiming, 701, 711, 745
Maine, 30, 107, 222, 283, 396, 397, 453, 454, 656, 830, 835, 841
Malbones, New England slaving family, 67
Manchester, England, 172, 202

Manford's Magazine, 811
Mangum, Willie P., 360
Manigault, Arthur M., 1045
Manigault, Joseph, 1045
Mann, Mrs. Horace, 564
Marblehead, Massachusetts, 65
March to the Sea, Sherman's, 734, 736-738, 743, 748
Marching Through Georgia (Work), 737
marshals, 44, 144, 145, 149, 173, 489, 630, 632, 651, 654, 727, 824
martial law, 148, 151, 152, 176, 274, 628, 629, 635, 636, 688
Martineau, Harriet, 536
Marvin, Lee, 1046
Marx, Karl, 102, 103, 206
Maryland, 32, 69, 100, 103, 124, 181, 203, 204, 212, 241, 269, 279, 281, 302, 389, 530, 553, 566, 578, 580, 581, 607, 622, 629, 632-636, 660, 665
Mason County, Illinois, 27
Mason, George, 65, 75, 139, 294, 299
Mason, James M., 294
Mason, Jeremiah, 67
Mason-Dixon Line, 201, 448, 634, 723
Massachusetts, 65-68, 71, 117, 123-125, 131, 181, 193, 266, 282, 294, 369, 409, 417, 448, 493, 520, 532, 533, 537, 631, 715, 773, 824, 830, 848, 947, 955, 960, 963
Matheny, James H., 331, 802, 804, 805
Matteson, Joel A., 340
Maury, Abram P., 1045
Mayo, Z. B., 340, 341
McClellan, George B., 30, 650, 754, 788, 852
McClellan, H. W., 678
McClernand, John A., 155, 286, 594
McConnell, Lewis, 792
McCulloch, Hugh, 841
McDonell, Charles, 340
McGavock family, 298
McGavock, Caroline E., 1045
McGavock, David H., 1045
McGavock, Emily, 1045
McGavock, Francis, 1045
McGavock, James R., 1045
McGavock, John W., 1045

McGavock, Lysander, 1045
McGavock, Randal, 356
McGavock, Randal W., 1045
McGavocks, 2, 493, 584, 969
McGraw, Tim, 1046
McKinney, J. F., 698, 710
Meade, George G., 716
Meade, Richard K., 165
Meditation on the Divine Will, Lincoln's, 815
Meigs, Montgomery C., 233
Mein Kampf (Hitler), 36
melancholia, 587
Melchizedek, 23
Melting Pot, U.S. as a, 538
Memoir of the Last Year of the War for Independence, A (Early), 730
Memphis, Tennessee, 83, 793
Menard County, Illinois, 27
Mencken, H. L., 622
merchants, 65, 75, 207, 208, 415, 754
Meridian, Mississippi, 725
Meriwether, Elizabeth A., 1045
Meriwether, Minor, 1045
Merryman, John, 631
Mesopotamians, 287
Message Recommending Compensated Emancipation, Lincoln's, 587
Message to Congress in Special Session, Lincoln's, 112, 117, 132, 189, 218, 246, 264, 267
Message to Congress, Lincoln's, 192, 212, 268, 526, 563, 575
Message to the House of Representatives, Lincoln's, 749
Message to the Senate, Lincoln's, 552, 669, 749
Methodist Church, 800
Mexicans, 266, 267, 510, 829
Mexican-American War, 169, 266, 357, 370, 625, 626, 829
Mexico, 239, 266, 267, 342, 355, 357, 376-379, 383, 385-387, 409, 410, 460-462, 472, 665, 693, 967
Michigan, 49, 50, 73, 86, 94, 155, 160, 193, 362, 373, 516
Middle Tennessee, 1046
military despotism, 660
military draft, 670-672
military forces, 150, 733
military measure, 556, 563, 564

military necessity, 141, 142, 146-148, 152, 181, 249, 274, 278, 280, 562, 579, 595, 747
Militia Act of July 17, 1862, Lincoln's, 771
Milligan, Ex parte, 152
Mills, John T., 787
Milroy, Robert H., 725
Minnesota, 49, 153, 193, 346, 375, 376, 383, 388, 668-670
miscegenation, 521
Mission of Dolores, 324
Mississippi, 65, 159, 160, 169, 173, 225, 246, 247, 298, 374, 383, 403, 406, 485, 487, 488, 559, 561, 568, 575, 576, 611, 668, 725, 726, 733, 740, 749, 771, 778, 812, 819, 940, 941, 967, 968
Mississippi River, 159, 160, 406, 485, 668, 733
Missouri, 27, 32, 49, 62, 70, 87, 95, 142, 143, 145, 160, 193, 215, 238, 239, 241, 277, 279, 281, 294, 311, 332-334, 349, 354, 362, 373, 375-378, 380-385, 387-390, 392, 398-402, 406, 411, 412, 421, 425, 485, 503, 516, 607, 636, 656, 665, 731, 732, 739, 749, 765, 777, 927, 938, 964, 967, 982
Missouri Compromise, 27, 49, 239, 311, 332-334, 349, 362, 373, 375-377, 380-382, 384, 385, 387-389, 392, 398, 400-402, 411, 412, 421, 425
Missouri River, 238, 421, 749
Mitchell, James, 544
Mobile, Alabama, 210, 795, 796
Molony, Richard S., 338, 339
monarchy, 660
Monongahela River, 105
Monroe, James, 855
Monteath, Peter, 678
Montgomery, Alabama, 116
monument, Southern, to black Confederate soldiers, 797
Morehead, Charles S., 418
Morgan, John H., 581, 1045
Morgan, Pierpont, and slavery, 69
Morgan, Sarah, 571
Mormon groups, 421
Mormon laws, 421
Mormon ministers, 421
Mormon priesthood, 421
Mormon slave owners, 421

Mormons, 224, 420, 421
Morning News, 656
Morrill Tariff, 209, 210
Morris, James R., 698, 710
Morris, Martin M., 805
Morton, John W., 1045
Morton, Mary E., 727, 728
Mosby, John S., 739, 1045
Moses, of the Bible, 351
Mount Rushmore, 103
mulattoes, 521
Mulcahy, Edward, 678
murderers, 611, 735, 831
Murfreesboro, Tennessee, 718
Murphy, Isaac, 763, 764
musicians, 794
My Imprisonment (Greenhow), 201
Myers, Thomas J., 776
Myth, the Lincoln, 20
Naper, Captain, 340
Napolitano, Andrew, 174, 175
Narragansett, Rhode Island, 66
Nashville Union, 580
Nashville, Tennessee, 3, 568, 793
Nat Turner Rebellion, 300
national debt, 114, 190, 258, 744
national government, 127, 951
National Intelligencer, 200
National Park Service, 927
National Republican Convention, 1860, 755
National Socialist German Workers Party, 36
nationalism, 369
nationalized banking system, 102
nation-states, 101, 178, 181
Native Guards, 773
Native-American slave owners, 64
Native-Americans, 65, 187, 290, 572, 668, 670, 754, 758, 811
natural law, 64
natural rights, 31, 64, 75, 207, 293, 497, 783
natural selection, 937
naval blockade, 32, 169, 194, 197, 264, 608, 664, 745

naval forces, 148-150, 221, 269, 428, 489, 646, 667, 679, 691
Nazis, 36
Nebraska, 45, 85, 193, 238, 316, 321, 333, 351, 362, 366, 375, 380-391, 393, 395-407, 409-411, 416, 432-434, 438, 440-444, 453, 454, 460-462, 464, 465, 509, 510, 590, 952, 975
Nebraska Bill, 316, 333, 351, 362, 387, 397, 399, 401, 404-407, 409-411, 416, 432-434, 443, 444, 453, 454, 460-462, 509
Nebraskaism, 440, 442
Negro, 37, 45, 55, 59-61, 82-84, 94, 101, 185, 285, 302, 346, 358, 367, 369-372, 379, 389, 391-393, 404, 411-413, 436, 441, 442, 448-453, 455, 456, 471, 475, 476, 483, 484, 487, 496, 497, 499-504, 506-508, 511, 512, 515, 534-536, 576, 581, 584, 597, 608, 620, 671, 716, 730, 731, 737, 770, 773, 776, 782-785, 787, 791, 794, 798, 830, 929, 932, 936, 941, 943, 946, 948, 955, 958, 959, 964, 965, 972, 974, 978-982
Negro Convention, 571
Negro Democracy, 100
Negro Soldier Law, Confederate, 298
negro-worshipers, 60
Negroes, 60, 74, 82, 124, 284, 304, 369-371, 379, 390, 391, 393, 395, 406, 408, 410, 413, 425, 436, 438, 450, 452, 456, 482-484, 487, 498-500, 503, 504, 510, 511, 518-520, 523, 534-536, 544, 553, 572, 574, 578, 583, 584, 597, 598, 619, 631, 717, 718, 731, 739, 773, 774, 776-778, 784, 785, 791, 794, 796-798, 949, 959, 981
Negrophobia, 514
Nelson, Samuel, 640
Nessle, John R., 678
Nevada, 768, 769
New Bedford, Massachusetts, 68
New Bern, North Carolina, 210
New England, 26, 65-68, 282, 283, 302, 362, 369, 415, 520, 591, 616, 718, 830, 946, 959
New England ideas, 826
New Englanders, 283
New Hampshire, 65, 124, 125, 129, 181, 246, 506, 573, 656, 830, 839, 840
New Haven, Connecticut, 66
New Jersey, 69, 124, 181, 246, 355, 520, 550, 751, 752, 830, 935, 977
New London County, Connecticut, 66
New Mexico, 239, 342, 355, 378, 379, 385-387, 409, 410, 460-462

New Orleans, Louisiana, 571, 579, 780, 793, 794
New South, 12, 23, 65, 136, 216, 268, 555, 563, 564, 569, 570, 745, 825, 831
New South Southerners, 268
New Testament, 2, 421, 422, 804
New World, 961
New York, 24, 28, 31, 40, 68, 69, 73, 74, 77, 90, 105, 124, 126, 127, 138, 160, 181, 193, 207, 223, 226-229, 236, 238, 246, 267, 283, 300, 355, 356, 363, 431, 453, 491, 492, 519, 535, 536, 551, 579, 584, 592, 604, 611, 628, 636-641, 644-647, 649-654, 656, 657, 671, 677, 678, 680, 698, 715, 755, 774, 777, 793, 796, 830, 838, 850, 853, 926-969, 972-983
New York City, New York, 68, 69, 73, 207, 300, 491, 535, 536
New York Draft Riots, 671
New York Harbor, 227, 267, 628, 641
New York Tribune, 223, 579, 584, 777
New York World, 649, 656, 657
Newburyport, Massachusetts, 282
Newcomb, Edward, 678
Newport County, Rhode Island, 66
Niblock, John, 678
Nicolay, John G., 13, 107, 156, 216, 241, 242, 545, 834
Nigger Hill, Washington, D.C, 71
Nightingale, the, 74
Nixon, Richard M., 175
Noah, of the Bible, 420
Noble, Warren P., 698, 710
Noell, John W., 241
Nolan, M. A., 678
non-enumerated rights, 183
Nordhoff, Charles, 516
Norfolk, Virginia, 210, 731
North, 2, 5, 7, 11-13, 23, 24, 42, 61, 63-69, 73-76, 80, 81, 90, 93, 117, 118, 124, 131, 135, 155, 171, 175, 176, 181, 187, 189, 191-193, 198, 200, 201, 204, 206-208, 210, 211, 214, 216, 217, 223, 225, 226, 230, 231, 234, 236, 238-240, 251, 268, 270, 274, 281, 282, 287, 294, 295, 298-300, 302-304, 308, 311, 321, 324, 328, 330, 332, 351, 354, 355, 357, 358, 361-363, 371-376, 378-381, 384-386, 388, 389, 391, 394, 400, 404, 405, 414, 415, 417, 418, 421, 422, 448, 449, 451-453, 455, 457, 475, 476, 481-483, 485-488,

491-493, 511, 514-518, 521, 526, 529, 530, 534-537, 542, 544, 553, 559, 561, 568, 569, 571, 572, 574, 584-586, 588, 591, 592, 598, 603, 606, 619, 620, 625, 627, 628, 631, 634, 652, 661, 664, 671, 680, 713, 716, 721-723, 725, 729, 730, 744, 747, 749, 757, 777, 780, 786-788, 790-792, 794, 804, 811, 812, 815, 819, 822, 824-826, 828-831, 837, 855, 926, 930, 931, 933, 935, 938, 939, 941-944, 948, 951, 952, 955-958, 961, 965, 966, 971, 973, 975, 979, 980, 982, 1044, 1046, 1048
North American Review, 966
North Carolina, 124, 171, 181, 210, 251, 355, 374, 488, 559, 561, 568, 571, 749, 777, 819, 837, 930, 933, 939, 941, 944, 956, 957, 965, 966, 973, 982, 1044, 1048
North, Colonel, 652
Northern abolitionists, 215, 358, 542, 589, 758
Northern blacks, 372, 516, 517, 536, 572, 587, 671, 786
Northern business establishment, 75, 207
Northern businessmen, 73, 207
Northern Cause, 198
Northern historians, 289, 298, 329, 671
Northern history, 270, 298
Northern merchants, 75, 207
Northern myth, 71, 298
Northern mythology, 551, 622
Northern newspapers, 200, 656, 664, 736
Northern ports, 73, 207, 220
Northern prejudice, 485, 779
Northern racism, 283, 771
Northern slave owners, 569
Northern slavery, 68, 70, 73-75, 200, 720
Northern states, 87, 148, 281, 325, 371, 448, 535, 536, 572, 629, 636, 645, 646, 651, 654, 662, 665, 758, 762
Northern textbooks, 571
Northern whites, 71, 283, 289, 290, 321, 419, 516, 518, 672, 720, 772
Northerners, 2, 8, 15, 16, 31, 35, 66, 67, 75, 136, 177, 187, 199, 211, 218, 267, 268, 282, 283, 296, 297, 302, 304, 352, 355, 357, 369, 415, 417, 514, 517, 518, 521, 529, 538, 544, 607, 620, 623, 628, 655, 658, 677, 723, 736, 745, 748, 754, 764, 775, 793, 797, 826, 828, 971, 975
northernization, 31, 563, 817
Northwest Ordinance of 1787, 49-51, 58, 86, 93-96, 374, 375, 385, 390,

394, 405, 406, 409, 410
Northwest Territory, 49, 50, 94
Norton, Jesse O., 465
Norway, 118
Norwich, Connecticut, 239
Notes of the Debates in the Federal Convention (Madison), 124
Notes on the State of Virginia (Jefferson), 182, 298
Nugent, Ted, 1046
nullification, 281, 744, 822, 965
nurses, 800
Oath of Allegiance, 33, 591, 630, 631, 658, 664, 821
Obama, Barack H., 17, 139, 175
Official Records of the War of the Rebellion, 734, 739, 775
Ohio, 17, 37, 49-51, 60, 61, 70, 73, 76, 81, 82, 84, 86, 92-94, 116, 122, 128, 160, 167, 183, 184, 186, 193, 200, 236, 283, 317, 321, 373, 385, 405, 412, 439, 446, 448, 460, 485, 509, 515, 516, 581, 589, 624, 656, 659, 661, 664, 678, 680, 689-693, 698, 700-703, 707-715, 720, 726, 729, 749, 781, 828, 829, 843, 848, 854, 927, 961
Ohio Democratic State Convention, 690, 698
Ohio Regiment, 148th, 186, 187
Ohio Regiment, 164th, 116, 183
Ohio Regiment, 166th, 184
Ohio River, 49, 81, 84, 385, 405, 439, 460, 729
Ohio Statesman, 782
Old North, 422
Old South, 2, 423, 619, 825, 826, 928, 934, 944, 952, 973, 978
Old Testament, 420, 421
Onesimus, of the Bible, 421
Opinion of the Draft, Lincoln's, 672
Order For a Draft, Lincoln's, 677
Order for Sabbath Observance, Lincoln's, 813
Order of Knights of the Golden Circle, 713
Order of Retaliation, Lincoln's, 807
Order of the Sons of Liberty, 659
Oregon, 409
Original Sin, 422
Orr, James L., 454
Orsini, Felice, 616
Osborn, Jeremiah, 678
Ottawa Free Trader, 338

Ottawa, Illinois, 185, 493, 497, 508, 610, 723, 856
outlaws, 611, 729, 960
Owens, Mary, 807
Owsley, Frank Lawrence, 74
O'Neill, John, 698, 710
Pacific Ocean, 153, 548, 749
Pacific Railway Act, 153
Paddock, William S., 678
Paine, Thomas, 422, 801
Palin, Sarah, 17
Panama, 227, 531, 554
Paris, France, 68
Paris, Illinois, 509
Parker, Amasa J., 651
Parton, Dolly, 1046
patronage, 159, 177, 446, 447, 754-756, 828
Patuxent River, 578
Paul, Ron, 17
Paul, Saint, 421
Payne, Daniel A., 72
peace advocates, 177
peace party, 659, 754
Peckham, R. W., Jr., 678
peculiar institution, 974
Pelosi, Nancy, 16
Pendleton, George H., 446, 698, 710, 754
Pennsylvania, 26, 42, 51, 69, 73, 89, 104, 105, 124, 126, 134, 181, 198, 208,
    209, 216, 246, 357, 362, 378, 412, 417, 446, 510, 551,
    621, 622, 656, 666, 716, 728, 744, 757, 790, 794, 812,
    825, 830, 842, 852, 939, 951, 955, 977, 978
Pennsylvania Cavalry, 5th, 666
Pensacola, Florida, 210, 217
pension applications, 792
Peoria, Illinois, 290, 365, 370, 373, 416, 495
Pepperell, Massachusetts, 67
Pepperells, New England slaving family, 67
Perry County, Kentucky, 725
Perry, Eli, 678
Perry, Sydney, 8, 9
personal letters, 792, 799
Personal Memoirs of U. S. Grant (Grant), 627

Perth Amboy, New Jersey, 355
Peter, Saint, 421, 808
Petersburg, Illinois, 805
Pettit, John, 404, 499
Pettus, Edmund W., 1045
Phelps, John W., 269, 274, 664
Phelps, Thomas A., 795
Philadelphia Convention, 123
Philadelphia Evening Journal, 656
Philadelphia, Pennsylvania, 51, 69, 73, 105, 134, 198, 207, 216, 299, 300, 491, 535, 536, 744
Philemon, Epistle of, 421
Philemon, of the Bible, 421
Phillips, Wendell, 29, 484, 603
Phoenix, John, 324
Piatt, Don, 30
Piatt, P. W., 340
Pickens, Francis W., 226, 227, 231, 250
Pierce, Edward L., 510
Pierce, Franklin, 129, 337, 360, 362, 855
Pierce, William, 65
Pierre-August, Jean Baptiste, 792
Pierre-August, Lufray, 792
Pierrepont, Edwards, 641
Pillow, Gideon J., 1045
Pinckney, Charles, 139, 299
pineapple, symbol, and slavery, 66
Pittsburgh, Pennsylvania, 104, 208
Plains, Georgia, 830
plantation, 2, 417, 493, 543, 571, 572, 584, 733, 735, 792, 930, 932, 937, 944, 954, 964, 969
plantation belts, 572
plantation books, 792
plantations, 67, 68, 124, 181, 304, 423, 424, 570, 571, 582, 731, 740, 774, 780, 824
Platform of the Republican National Convention, 109
Plymouth County, Massachusetts, 66
political correctness, 422
politically correct, 9
Polk, James K., 156-158, 162, 164-166, 356, 361, 378, 855, 1045
Polk, Leonidas, 1045

Polk, Lucius E., 1045
poll taxes, 183
Pollard, Edward A., 180, 229
Pomeroy, Samuel C., 533
Pope, John, 145, 566, 669, 725
Pope, the, 563
popular sovereignty, 38, 39, 42, 43, 46-49, 52, 54, 56-58, 60-62, 65, 76, 85, 93, 96, 97, 354, 357, 417, 444, 509, 510
postwar reunion notes, 792
Potomac River, 70, 479
Potter, Charles Francis, 24
Poughkeepsie, New York, 28
poverty, 172, 608
powers of the states and people, 183
Preliminary Emancipation Proclamation, 527, 533, 538, 541, 542, 556, 562, 563, 566, 567, 575, 579, 585
preserving the Union, 198, 200, 242, 268, 574, 636, 663, 734
presidential disability and succession, 183
presidential term and succession, 183
presidential vote for District of Columbia, 183
Presley, Elvis, 1046
Presley, Lisa Marie, 1046
Preston, William B., 684
private soldier, defined, 797
privileges and immunities, 183, 325, 442
Proclamation Admitting Nevada Into the Union, Lincoln's, 768
Proclamation Admitting West Virginia into the Union, Lincoln's, 768
Proclamation Calling 75,000 Militia, Lincoln's, 173
Proclamation Concerning Taxes in Rebellious States, Lincoln's, 749
Proclamation Forbidding Intercourse With Rebel States, Lincoln's, 487
Proclamation of Amnesty and Reconstruction, Lincoln's, 132, 817
Proclamation of Blockade, Lincoln's, 169-171
Proclamation of Thanksgiving, Lincoln's, 117, 758-761
proslavery amendment, Lincoln's, 418
prostitutes, 729
prostitution, 2, 608
Providence Daily Post, 230
Providence Plantations, 68, 124, 181
Providence, Rhode Island, 491
provost-marshals, 144, 145, 651, 654, 727
pro-North historians, 603, 926

Pryor, Roger A., 90
public necessity, 253, 265, 602, 655
public opinion, 58-61, 80, 81, 119, 138, 377, 442, 446, 534
Puritans, 65
Purvis, Robert, 551
Quakerism, 800
Quakers, 26
quartering of soldiers, 183, 660
Queens, New York, 69
Quincy, Illinois, 482, 489, 856
race problem, Lincoln's solution to the, 507
racism, 7, 68, 72, 101, 283, 303, 357, 369, 413, 414, 421, 481, 494, 510, 514, 534, 536-538, 553, 578, 771-774, 781, 790, 930, 941, 960
racism, in the North, 534, 535
racist military policies, Lincoln's, 774
Radcliff, D. V. N., 678
Radicals, 15, 294, 538, 542, 563, 587, 588, 603, 756, 824, 826, 827
Randall, Alexander, 596, 787
Randolph, Edmund J., 51, 1045
Randolph, George W., 1045
Rangel, Charles, 16
rape, 729, 731, 745, 747, 824
rape of black females, by Yankee soldiers, 731
rape of white females, by Yankee soldiers, 729
rapists, 831
Ravensdale, Cassidy, 18
Rawle, William, 125
Raymond, Henry J., 592
Reagan, Ronald, 17, 175, 1046
Rebels, 117, 143, 144, 218, 244, 264, 292, 540, 542, 555, 558, 577, 578, 580, 582-584, 605, 606, 622, 657, 724, 796, 947, 960
Reconstruction, 7, 102, 132, 176, 206, 509, 817, 822-824, 827-829, 832, 927, 932, 934, 941, 943, 944, 957, 959, 966, 973, 976
Reconstruction Acts, 176
Reddick, William, 340
Reed, W. M., 746
refugees, 608, 716, 727, 729, 748, 984
refugees, Southern, 727
Reid, Harry, 16
Rennolds, Fielding, 792

Renwick, G. W., 340
Reply to a Delegation from the National Union League, Lincoln's, 25
Reply to a Methodist Delegation, Lincoln's, 799
Republican National Convention, 109, 589
Republican Party, 16, 17, 38, 39, 57, 90, 208, 239, 241, 281, 284, 310, 357, 370, 438, 447, 448, 459, 476, 478, 489, 507, 591, 614, 690, 712, 718, 943, 948, 955, 1048
Republican party platform, 1864, 213
Republican Watchman, 656
republicanism, 393, 589, 614, 615
Resolutions of Sympathy with the Cause of Hungarian Freedom, 107
Response to a Serenade, Lincoln's, 738
restrictionists, 352
reunion, 212, 232, 596, 598, 790, 792, 822, 823, 982
Revenue Act of 1861, 655
Revolutionary War, 412, 452, 547, 961
Reynolds, Burt, 1046
Reynolds, John, 334, 335
Reynolds, Joseph J., 727
Rhett, Robert B., 167
Rhode Island, 66-68, 124-127, 181, 246, 547, 830
Rice, William A., 678
Richardson, John, 967
Richmond Examiner, 937
Richmond Sentinel, 302
Richmond, New York, 69
Richmond, Virginia, 757, 793, 824, 833, 984
right to bear arms, 183
right to confront and to counsel, 183
rights not to be denied on account of race, 183
rights reserved to states, 183
rituals, 282
River Queen, 264, 598
Rives, William C., 418
robber barons, 75, 207
Robbins, Hargus, 1046
Robert the Bruce, King, 1044
Roberts, Joseph J., 547
Robertson, George, 66
Robinson, Charles D., 596, 789, 822
Robinson, Daniel, 792

Robinsons, New England slaving family, 67
Roche, Sir Boyle, 659
Rochester, New York, 238
Rock, John S., 537
Rockingham County, New Hampshire, 65
Rocky Mountains, 193, 668
Rodgers, Lemuel W., 678
Rome, Georgia, 734
Roosevelt, Franklin D., 17
root, pig, or perish emancipation plan, Lincoln's, 607, 608
Roots (Haley), 69
Rosecrans, William S., 661, 777
Rost, Pierre, 171
Rothschilds, the, 812
Roudanez, Jean Baptiste, 780
Royall family crest, 67
Royalls, New England slaving family, 67
Rucker, Edmund W., 1045
Ruffin, Edmund, 297
Ruffner, Henry, 301
rum, 20, 306, 545, 738
Rush, Richard, 360
Russell, John, 201
Russia, 459, 476, 640, 655, 942
Salem, Massachusetts, 65
Salomon, Edward, 572
San Domingo, 531
Sanders, J. B., 678
Sangamo Journal, 119, 494
Sangamo, the, 119
Sangamon Journal, 118, 119
Sangamon, Illinois, 27
Sangamon, the, 119
Saulsbury, Willard, 30
Savannah, South Carolina, 210
Saxton, Rufus, 730, 775
scallywags, 136, 745, 764, 775, 825
Scars and Stripes, 73
Scates, Walter B., 594
Schenck, Robert C., 285, 578, 629, 630
Schermerhorn, Isaac M., 204, 270

Schley, Mr., 146
school administrators, 524
Schurz, Carl, 737
Scotland, 948, 963, 1044
Scott, Dred, 38, 48, 53-56, 59-61, 87, 88, 318, 319, 346, 357, 425, 427-431, 433, 435, 441, 453, 467, 469, 479, 480, 499, 506, 507, 512, 515
Scott, George C., 1046
Scott, Walter, 722
Scott, Winfield, 66, 219-223, 243, 249, 281, 285, 332, 765, 851
Scruggs, Earl, 1046
SCV, 978
Seabrook, John L., 1045
Seabrook, Lochlainn, 9, 19, 20, 1043, 1045, 1046, 1049
search and seizure, 183
secession, 2, 7, 11, 19, 68, 106, 109, 111, 112, 114-116, 118-121, 124-127, 130-132, 134, 135, 178, 182, 183, 189, 190, 192, 198, 207, 211, 218, 225, 231, 247, 253, 258, 267, 610, 611, 625, 666, 715, 721, 722, 744, 761, 765, 767, 819, 926, 930, 946, 950, 957, 961, 963, 965, 968, 972, 973, 1049
secession, legal right of established, 126
Second Annual Message to Congress, Lincoln's, 527, 668
Second Inaugural Address, Lincoln's, 213, 270, 620, 815
sectionalism, 359-361, 439, 448, 459, 460, 481, 482, 487, 489, 611, 612, 619, 977
Seger, Bob, 1046
segregation, 68, 72, 422, 423
self-incrimination, 183
self-government, 34, 298, 443, 445, 455, 961
senators elected by popular vote, 183
separation of powers, 629
serfdom, 422
servant, 30, 154, 192, 226, 233, 234, 243, 244, 277, 278, 297, 421-423, 537, 569, 571, 580, 672, 716, 719, 742, 772, 825
servants, 65, 73, 74, 96, 262, 297, 298, 301, 303, 305, 356, 406, 420-423, 537, 543, 551, 570, 571, 588, 608, 713, 735, 770, 771, 792, 795, 797, 824
servants, expense of keeping, 297
servitude, 64, 96, 199, 300, 358, 421, 492, 526, 534, 540, 558, 593, 594, 600, 608, 821, 928, 944, 948, 978
Seward Peninsula, 520

Seward, Alaska, 520
Seward, William H., 40, 42, 77, 89, 217, 219, 222, 224, 231-233, 238-240, 294, 355, 358, 418, 519, 520, 565, 569, 591, 599, 600, 603, 622, 637, 640, 642, 665, 838
Seymour, Captain, 220
Seymour, Horatio, 69, 647, 649, 651, 671, 680
Seymour, William, 678
Shaefer, Louis, 698, 710
Shakespeare, William, 732, 733
sharecropping, 571
Shem, of the Bible, 421
Shenandoah Holocaust, 738
Shenandoah Valley, 725, 728, 729, 738, 739, 742
Shenandoah Valley Campaign, 738
Shepley, George F., 269
Sheridan, Philip H., 142, 725, 736, 738-740, 742, 744, 747
Sherman, F. C., 340
Sherman, Roger, 417
Sherman, William T., 29, 142, 587, 725, 726, 728, 729, 734-740, 742-745, 747, 748, 762, 763, 776, 790, 797, 831
Sherman's neckties, 729
Sherman's sentinels, 729
Shields, James A., 155, 805, 807
Sibley, Henry H., 670
Sickles, Daniel E., 780
Sierra Leone, 369
Silliman, Benjamin D., 441
Sioux, 668, 936
Skaggs, Ricky, 1046
slave breeding, 619
slave insurrection, 568, 615, 616
slave labor, 68, 81, 89, 289, 370
Slave Narratives, 945
slave pens, 70
slavery, 2, 7-9, 11, 12, 17, 35, 37-51, 53-83, 85-88, 90, 93-101, 110, 119, 129, 155, 172, 173, 175, 176, 183, 185, 186, 189, 198-201, 203-206, 211-215, 238-241, 245, 246, 264, 274, 275, 278, 281-285, 287-303, 305-314, 316-324, 327-334, 336, 338, 342-376, 378-391, 394-396, 398-403, 405-422, 424-427, 429-434, 436-442, 444, 445, 451, 453-456, 458, 460-463, 467, 469-474, 478, 479, 482, 485-487, 489-493,

496-499, 501-503, 505, 506, 508, 511, 513-515, 517-523, 525, 526, 531-539, 542-544, 546, 550, 552, 553, 556, 565, 566, 568, 570, 579-583, 585, 586, 588, 590-600, 602-608, 610, 612-616, 618, 620, 627, 633, 635, 664, 671, 720, 723, 770, 782, 783, 788-792, 794, 808, 821-823, 827, 829, 855, 926, 927, 929, 930, 933, 935, 940-947, 951-964, 966, 968, 969, 971, 973-975, 978, 980, 981, 984, 1044, 1049
slavery question, 35, 40, 44, 51, 81, 311, 314, 329, 331-334, 336, 371, 379, 398, 400, 420, 453, 455, 461, 471-473, 478, 479, 482, 599, 613
slavery-optional state, 363
slavery-prohibited state, 363
slaves, 35, 48, 51, 53, 55, 57, 58, 64-66, 68-75, 81, 82, 85, 87-89, 93-98, 123, 133, 134, 141, 175, 176, 189, 199, 200, 207, 212, 213, 215, 228, 240, 241, 273-282, 285-293, 295, 297, 298, 302-304, 306, 307, 325, 326, 337, 344-348, 350-356, 361, 364, 365, 372, 375, 376, 381, 382, 389-392, 394-397, 400, 403, 406-408, 414-421, 423-425, 429, 430, 436, 442, 452-454, 456, 458, 461, 462, 470, 471, 479, 491, 493-495, 500, 501, 503-507, 514, 516, 518, 521, 522, 525, 526, 529, 532-536, 539-541, 544-546, 552, 556-562, 564, 567-572, 574, 579, 580, 582, 584, 585, 587-593, 595, 596, 599, 600, 603-609, 613-620, 633, 664, 717, 720, 736, 754, 774, 780, 784, 789-793, 795, 797, 817-819, 928, 945, 950-952, 958, 981
slaves of the Lord, 422
slaves, and home ownership, 423
slaves, and personal wealth, 423
slaves, and property ownership, 423
slaves, wealthy, 423
Smith, Caleb B., 219, 233, 756, 757, 848
Smith, Edward W., 274
Smith, Enos W., 340
Smith, John, 973
Smith, William Sooy, 746
Smithsonian Institution, 70
socialism, 139
Soldier's Home, Washington, D.C., 566
Solomon, of the Bible, 237, 829
Sons of Confederate Veterans, 1043
Sorley Boy McDonnell and the Rise of Clan Ian Mor (Hill), 1047

South, 2, 3, 5, 7, 8, 10-12, 19, 23, 24, 31, 37, 42, 47, 49, 50, 59, 64, 65, 67, 68, 73-75, 100-103, 109, 111, 112, 116-119, 121, 124, 128, 134-136, 138, 141, 146, 153, 155, 167, 169, 173-178, 180, 181, 183, 187, 190-193, 197-202, 204, 206-208, 210, 211, 214, 216-219, 222-231, 234, 236-239, 241, 242, 244-247, 250, 255, 259, 264, 265, 267-272, 274, 284, 287, 289, 295, 297-304, 308, 311, 320, 321, 328, 329, 351, 352, 354-357, 361-365, 371-374, 376, 378-382, 384-386, 388, 391, 396, 397, 400, 401, 404, 405, 412-415, 417, 418, 423, 424, 436, 439, 448, 449, 451-455, 457, 459, 460, 472, 475, 476, 479, 481, 482, 485-488, 490-493, 508, 511, 514, 516-519, 521, 522, 527, 530, 534, 535, 537, 538, 543, 544, 553, 555, 559, 561-564, 568-573, 582-586, 588, 589, 591, 592, 594, 595, 604, 606, 609-611, 614, 615, 619-622, 624, 625, 628, 633-636, 661, 664-666, 670, 689, 713-716, 718-721, 723-725, 728-734, 736, 737, 740, 741, 743-745, 747-749, 754, 757-759, 761, 763-765, 770, 771, 774, 776, 779, 780, 786-789, 791-794, 796, 797, 808, 811, 812, 815, 817, 819, 821, 823-826, 828-831, 855, 926-928, 930, 933-937, 941, 944, 946-948, 950-954, 959, 962, 964, 966-968, 971, 973-975, 978, 981, 982, 984, 1042-1045, 1047

South America, 193, 472, 518, 522, 527

South Carolina, 124, 128, 135, 167, 169, 173, 181, 191, 210, 217, 219, 222, 225-227, 231, 234, 237, 242, 246, 247, 250, 259, 274, 299, 374, 396, 397, 454, 487, 488, 490, 535, 537, 559, 561, 568, 609, 611, 730, 731, 734, 737, 749, 774, 776, 797, 819, 828, 934, 936, 950, 951, 954, 964, 967, 968, 981, 1045

Southeastern Baptist Theological Seminary, 1048

Southern abolition movement, 65

Southern blacks, 300, 320, 516, 517, 529, 535, 570-572, 577, 585, 587, 607, 724, 731, 773-776, 778, 792-794, 796, 797, 824

Southern Cause, 10, 570, 792

Southern Confederacy, 2, 11, 19, 108, 121, 130, 132, 135, 184, 188, 298, 619, 625, 627, 725, 796, 940, 941, 965, 969, 971, 979, 980, 1043, 1044

Southern families, 298

Southern Illustrated News, 655

Southern plantations, 424, 824

Southern ports, 171, 207, 664

Southern slave owners, 297, 300, 303, 352, 355, 415, 422, 493, 589
Southern states, 19, 35, 69, 73, 101, 104, 111, 115, 116, 118, 121, 132, 169, 175, 183, 192, 201, 207, 211, 217, 223, 224, 234, 246, 261, 264, 265, 267, 281, 303, 311, 352, 356, 416, 418, 423, 439, 448, 455, 485, 501, 508, 537, 586, 592, 595, 596, 619, 623, 624, 658, 664-666, 715, 721, 722, 731, 740, 749, 753, 754, 757, 765, 786, 826-828, 927, 935, 944, 947
Southern whites, 356, 369, 544, 588, 595, 724
Southerners, 11, 12, 15, 16, 19, 29, 35, 47, 64, 65, 104, 111, 134, 136, 139, 176, 187, 199, 211, 236, 265, 268, 271, 282, 297, 298, 300-304, 329, 351, 353-356, 404, 414, 415, 423, 493, 517, 519, 542, 544, 571, 608, 619, 620, 623, 626, 658, 662, 665, 677, 725, 728, 738, 761, 797, 821, 825, 829, 831, 928, 972, 982
sovereign powers, 267
sovereign states, 18, 187, 638, 662, 831
sovereignty, 31, 36, 38, 39, 42, 43, 45-49, 52, 54, 56-58, 60-63, 65, 84, 85, 93, 96, 97, 113, 126, 181, 183, 241, 255, 257, 267, 324, 327, 354, 357, 417, 426, 444, 509, 510, 634, 637, 649, 654, 691, 692
Spain, 376
Speed, James, 845
Speed, Joshua F., 155, 619, 802
Speer, William S., 350
Spencer County, Indiana, 27
spies, 148, 150, 584, 646, 654, 664, 683
Spooner, Lysander, 75, 207, 208, 294-296, 725
Spring Hill, Tennessee, 4
Springfield, Illinois, 16, 32, 118, 138, 185, 234, 284, 289, 296, 413, 464, 496, 505, 520, 751, 803, 806
St. Paul, Minnesota, 669
standing army, 211
Stanton, Edwin M., 146, 263, 282, 531, 651, 652, 666, 730, 739, 778, 843
Star of the West, 270
Stars and Bars, 73
Stars and Stripes, 73, 948
starvation, 35, 172, 221, 249, 487, 570, 607, 608, 658, 738, 776
state sovereignty, 31, 36, 324
states' rights, 36, 37, 62, 63, 65, 76, 101, 102, 106, 109, 116, 118, 127, 137, 139, 153, 183, 200, 224, 230, 265, 297, 303, 321, 352,

436, 437, 481, 482, 588, 625, 635, 715, 719, 757, 792, 817, 825, 828, 855, 958
states' rights movements, 825
status of income tax clarified, 183
Stephens, Alexander H., 59, 263, 365, 412, 413, 415, 515, 598-603, 625, 626, 666, 1045
Steubenville, Ohio, 122
stevedores, 729
Stevens, Thaddeus, 824, 825
Stewart, Alexander P., 1045
Stillman College, 1047
Stone, Dan, 288
Stonebraker, J. Clarence, 729
Story, Justice, 163
Stowe, Harriet Beecher, 67, 300, 417, 423
Stringham, Silas H., 221
Strode, J. M., 340
Stuart, Alexander H., 191
Stuart, Jeb, 1045
Stuart, Jeb (James Ewell Brown), 736
Stuart, John T., 802-804
Sturge, Joseph, 536
Suffolk County, Massachusetts, 65
suits against a state, 183
Sumner, Charles, 71, 215, 290, 294, 296, 329, 564, 824
Supreme Court, 37, 49, 54-56, 87-89, 129, 134, 152, 173, 313, 317, 320, 344, 345, 349, 414, 426, 427, 429, 433-436, 467-469, 479-481, 511, 617, 640, 665, 706, 712, 819, 822, 828, 947
sutlers, 797
Sweden, 118
Sweet, Martin A., 337
Tam O'Shanter (Burns), 804
Taney, Roger B., 152, 431, 453, 479, 499, 631, 666
Tappan, Lewis, 283
Taylor, Richard, 795, 1045
Taylor, Sarah K., 1045
Taylor, Susie King, 771
Taylor, Zachary, 131, 140, 795, 830, 855, 1045
Tea Party, 831
teamsters, 584, 794, 797
Ten Percent Plan, 591, 821

Tennessee, 2-4, 14, 81, 128, 160, 193, 204, 252, 259, 356, 374, 451, 488, 568, 580, 605, 636, 724, 746, 749, 770, 819, 927, 937, 940, 945, 956, 958, 967, 969, 980, 1044, 1046, 1047
Tennessee River, 605
Texas, 113, 114, 169, 173, 190, 233, 251, 256-258, 333, 334, 336, 339, 356, 376, 379, 380, 386, 461, 487, 488, 559, 561, 568, 580, 611, 749, 819, 942, 956, 962, 964
Thackeray, William M., 297
Thanksgiving Day, 758, 759, 764
Thayer, Eli, 354
The Crisis, 105, 550, 976
The Day-Book, 656
The Democrat, 656
The Farmer, 603, 656
The Federalist, 947
The Federalist Papers, 947
The Herald, 656
The Impending Crisis of the South (Helper), 518
The Liberator, 67, 70, 300, 302, 537, 774
The Lost Cause (Pollard), 229
The Missourian, 656
The New York World, 656
The Order of the Star Spangled Banner, 282
The Prayer of Twenty Millions, Greeley's, 579
The Rise and Fall of the Confederate Government (Davis), 115, 122, 127
The Second Treatise of Government (Locke), 64
The Sentinel, 302, 656
The South, 7, 8, 10, 11, 19, 24, 31, 37, 47, 59, 65, 68, 73-75, 100-103, 109, 111, 112, 116-119, 121, 124, 134, 135, 138, 141, 146, 153, 169, 173-176, 178, 183, 187, 190-192, 197, 198, 200, 202, 204, 206-208, 210, 211, 214, 216-219, 223-226, 228-231, 234, 236-238, 241, 242, 244-247, 255, 264, 265, 267-272, 274, 284, 287, 295, 297-304, 320, 329, 351, 352, 354-357, 361-365, 371-373, 379, 380, 382, 384-386, 391, 397, 400, 401, 405, 412-415, 417, 418, 423, 424, 436, 448, 449, 451, 453, 455, 459, 476, 481, 485, 487, 491, 492, 508, 514, 516, 517, 519, 521, 534, 535, 537, 543, 544, 553, 563, 568-571, 573, 582-584, 586, 588, 589, 591, 592, 594, 595, 604, 606, 609-611, 614, 619-622, 624, 625, 628, 633, 634, 636, 661, 664-666, 670, 689, 713-716, 719-721, 723-725, 728-730, 732, 736, 737, 740, 741,

743-745, 748, 754, 757-759, 763-765, 770, 771, 774, 776, 779, 780, 786-789, 791, 793, 794, 796, 797, 808, 812, 815, 817, 821, 823-826, 828-830, 926, 927, 933, 935, 937, 941, 947, 948, 951-953, 959, 962, 966-968, 973, 974, 981, 982, 1047

The South Since the War (Andrews), 736
The Southern Cross (poem), 631
The Southern Illustrated News, 655
The Star-Spangled Banner (Key), 520
thievery, 608
Thirteenth Kentucky Cavalry, CSA, 725
Thomas, E. M., 545
Thomas, George H., 66, 726
Thomas, Lorenzo, 575, 777, 778
Three-Fifths Clause, 416, 417
Tiffany, Charles, and slavery, 69
Tocqueville, Alexis de, 126, 534, 535
Todd, Dr., 107
Todd, Francis, 282
Toombs, Robert, 231, 324, 479
Torah, 420
torture, 177, 697, 729, 735, 745, 746, 779
Totten, Joseph G., 219, 221
Tourgee, Albion W., 829
treason, 112, 120, 133, 255, 265, 266, 268, 269, 296, 377, 540, 555, 558, 580-583, 631, 641, 654, 657, 659, 667, 679, 681, 682, 696, 697, 711, 713, 714, 728, 766, 817, 821, 974
Treasury Department, 144, 811
Treaty of Washington, 75
Treaty with Great Britain, 68, 400
trial by jury in civil cases, 183
Truman, Harry, 175
Trumbull, Lyman, 314, 330, 331, 334, 344, 345, 369-372, 426, 451, 457, 465, 466, 591
Truth, Sojourner, 72, 73
Turchin, John B., 747
Turkey, 421
Turner, Levi C., 291, 292
Turner, Nat, 300
Tuskegee, Alabama, 571
two-term limit on president, 183

Tyler, Erastus B., 631
Tyler, John, 128, 206, 360, 415, 855
Tyler, Lyon G., 415
Tynes, Ellen B., 1045
tyranny, 20, 32, 108, 111, 118, 123, 415, 953, 955
U.S. army, 73, 572, 573, 576, 587, 656, 851-854
U.S. Capitol, 70, 289, 780
U.S. Capitol, constructed by black slaves, 70, 780
U.S. Census, 69
U.S. Confederacy, 1044
U.S. Congress, 30, 70, 202, 210, 608, 744, 779, 812
U.S. Constitution, 23, 31, 51, 68, 74, 120, 121, 124, 126, 139, 141, 146, 153, 168, 173, 177-179, 181, 294, 350, 363, 416, 563, 589, 655, 663, 767, 811, 827, 926
U.S. flag, 73
U.S. government, 33, 74, 117, 138, 194, 218, 246, 265, 268, 415, 418, 419, 492, 496, 598, 621, 624, 662, 668, 758
U.S. military, 290, 665, 774
U.S. navy, 576, 587
U.S. Supreme Court, 414, 665
U.S.A., 36, 205, 217, 268, 287, 715, 753, 765, 821
Ullman, Daniel, 577
unalienable rights, 630, 637, 638, 655
Uncle Tom's Cabin (Stowe), 417, 423
Underground Railroad, 571
Underwood, J. R., 145, 202
Union, 4, 6, 7, 15, 19, 25, 27, 32, 34-38, 41, 43, 45, 50, 76, 77, 79, 92, 95, 96, 99-102, 110-120, 123, 125-129, 132-137, 142, 144, 145, 147, 155, 156, 165, 171, 173, 174, 176, 178-183, 187, 188, 192, 197-200, 202, 205, 208, 211, 213, 214, 217-219, 223, 225, 227, 231, 232, 236-238, 241-243, 245-254, 256, 257, 259-265, 267-270, 276, 280-282, 284, 285, 291-293, 295, 296, 310-313, 320, 322, 323, 327, 329, 332, 333, 337, 339, 343, 356, 359, 361-363, 366, 368, 371, 373-377, 379, 384-386, 398, 400, 401, 405, 406, 408, 409, 411, 412, 414, 415, 418, 424, 426, 430, 440, 441, 443-446, 448, 454, 455, 459-461, 473, 474, 478, 486-488, 501, 503, 506, 516, 519, 534, 535, 543, 544, 553, 567, 568, 571, 573, 574, 576-578, 580-585, 588, 591, 592, 594-598, 601, 602, 606, 611, 616, 618-620, 624, 634-636, 645, 655, 657, 658, 661-665, 669, 678, 680, 682, 683,

686, 690-695, 698, 701, 702, 708, 711, 713, 715-718, 720-722, 725, 727, 730, 731, 733, 734, 739, 745, 749, 752, 756, 758-769, 771, 772, 774, 776-778, 780, 781, 786-789, 796-798, 812, 816, 818, 819, 821-829, 831, 855, 927, 936, 938, 946, 952, 954, 958, 959, 963, 964, 975-977, 979, 981, 982, 984
Union army, 544, 585, 781, 927, 936
Union Central Committee of Baltimore, 580
Union officers, 280, 763, 772
Unionism, 142
United Daughters of the Confederacy, 720, 792, 796
United States Colored Troops, 790, 976
United States of America, 36, 74, 105, 116, 124, 125, 178, 274, 491, 492, 538-540, 556, 557, 560, 562, 593, 664, 749, 759, 768, 820, 826, 929, 958, 959, 966, 974, 975
United States Territories, 53, 311, 359, 442
University of Alabama, 609, 928, 959, 1047
University of Florida, 1048
Unmelted Pot, U.S. as an, 538
USCT, 790
Usher, John P., 850
Utah, 32, 378, 379, 385-387, 409, 410, 421, 460-462
Vache, Island of, 531
Vallandigham, Clement L., 624, 656, 658-661, 664, 678, 685, 687, 689-695, 698-701, 703, 704, 707, 709-712, 714, 715
Van Buren, Martin, 855
Vance, Robert B., 1045
Vance, Zebulon, 1045
Vanderbilt University, 937, 960, 976
Venable, Charles S., 1045
Vermont, 342, 824, 830
Vertrees, Peter, 792
Vietnam, 175, 272, 961
Vietnam War, 272
View of the Constitution of the US of America, A (Rawle), 125
Villard, Henry, 24
Vinton, Samuel F., 167
Virgin Mary, 23
Virginia, 8, 11, 26, 51, 65, 89, 90, 94, 107, 121, 122, 124, 126-128, 150, 151, 160, 165, 171, 181, 182, 191, 193, 194, 206, 210, 227, 229, 251, 252, 259, 264, 298-301, 351, 373, 374,

>   389, 393, 415, 451, 453, 486, 488, 501, 506, 536, 550,
>   551, 559, 561, 568, 598, 599, 615, 666, 725, 731, 740,
>   742, 749, 754, 757, 765-769, 793-796, 815, 824, 833, 843,
>   851, 928, 931, 934, 937, 939, 941, 942, 946, 948,
>   950-952, 957, 960, 961, 964, 976, 978, 984, 1044, 1045

Virginia Military Institute, 725
Voltaire (Francois-Marie Arouet), 422, 801
Voss, Arno, 340
voting age set to eighteen years, 183
Wade, Benjamin F., 781
Wade-Davis Bill, 29
Wake Fores, North Carolina, 1048
Wakefield, Judge, 810
Wakeman, Abram, 117, 831
Walden Pond, 67
Waldos, New England slaving family, 67
Wall Street Boys, 75, 207, 211, 415, 754
Wanton, Joseph, 66
war crimes, of Sherman, 728
war crimes, Southern, fabricated by the North, 745
war crimes, Yankee, 729-731, 734, 735
War Department, 62, 69, 117, 174, 194, 196, 248, 572, 577, 643, 647, 653,
>   654, 772

War for Southern Independence, 415, 661, 830, 1043
war measure, 559, 561, 599-602, 606
War Powers Act, 175
war powers, and Lincoln, 147, 264
war powers, presidential abuses of, 175
war, power to declare, 169, 721
Ward, Artemus, 30
Ward, James H., 221, 222
Warren, Joe, 792
Washburne, Elihu B., 243, 353, 478, 533, 813
Washington Act, 410
Washington College, 301, 730
Washington County, Rhode Island, 66
Washington, Booker T., 571
Washington, D.C., 4, 13, 23, 70-73, 121, 138, 200, 207, 228, 265, 276, 289,
>   352, 418, 520, 526, 532, 574, 726, 736, 751, 752, 780,
>   790, 803, 830, 927, 929, 932, 936, 938, 943, 950, 952,
>   959, 960, 966, 975, 977-979, 982, 983

Washington, George, 33-35, 65, 91, 103, 126, 139, 235, 260, 261, 299, 354, 456, 547, 612, 626, 669, 730, 813, 855
Washington, John A., 1045
Washington, Thornton A., 1045
Waters, Maxine, 16
Watkins, Sam, 724
Wayland, Francis, 302
Webster, Daniel, 67, 103, 201, 411, 520, 679
Webster, Massachusetts, 520
Weed, Thurlow, 755
Weitzel, Godfrey, 121
Weld, Theodore, 283
Welles, Gideon, 192, 219, 233, 244, 846
Welsh, 1043
West Africa, 69
West Indies, 65
West Indies, and Yankee slavery, 65
West Point, 125
West Point Military Academy, 217
West Point, Tennessee, 1047
West Virginia, 559, 561, 568, 666, 754, 765-769, 1044
Westchester, New York, 69
Western states, 352, 369, 516, 754
Western Territories, 352, 353, 355, 363, 365, 369, 370, 372, 418, 590, 620
Western Territory, 374
Whigs, 285, 332, 362, 380, 402, 412, 448, 451, 500
whip, 70, 92, 230, 236, 300, 423, 979
whipping, 71, 92, 236, 305, 508
white dream, Lincoln's, 513, 528
White House, 13, 24, 29, 70, 109, 121, 153, 184, 187, 191, 242, 277, 289, 290, 419, 543-545, 550, 551, 553, 625, 677, 732, 780, 801, 813, 931, 953, 962, 968, 975, 978
White House, Confederate, 543
White House, constructed by black slaves, 70, 780
white labor, 293, 358, 370, 519, 529, 530
white men, 84, 101, 321, 342, 366, 367, 370, 452, 453, 484, 495, 496, 504, 505, 520, 525, 543, 546, 547, 578, 616, 740, 773, 778, 785, 788, 791, 796
white racism in Illinois, 304, 305, 508
white servitude, 928, 944
white slave owners, 66, 421

white slavery, 287
white slaves, 928, 952
white supremacy, 185, 282, 364, 371, 414, 494, 508, 518, 519
white supremacy, built into Lincoln's platform, 371
White, C. A., 698, 710
White, J. W., 698, 710
whites, 37, 62, 65, 68, 70-73, 135, 186, 283, 289, 290, 293, 300, 304, 308, 320, 321, 341, 342, 355-357, 369, 370, 372, 389, 390, 394, 396, 408, 416, 419, 423, 495, 496, 505, 508, 514-516, 518, 519, 521, 529-532, 534, 535, 537, 542, 544, 548, 550, 551, 570, 571, 573, 578, 579, 588, 590, 594, 595, 605, 608, 671, 672, 720, 724, 751, 753, 770-773, 779, 790, 792, 795, 797, 950, 974, 1045
Wiggins, Thomas, 793
Wilcox, Elijah, 340
Wilkinson, James, 659
Willard's Hotel, 138
Williams, E. B., 340
Wilmington, Delaware, 210
Wilmot Proviso, 340, 357, 358, 378, 383, 384, 386, 387
Wilmot, David, 357, 358, 369, 378
Wilson, Henry, 294
Wilson, James, 417
Wilson, Woodrow, 206, 538, 1046
Winder, Charles S., 1045
Winder, John H., 1045
Wisconsin, 49, 50, 86, 94, 160, 193, 373, 374, 516, 572, 937, 951
Wise, Henry A., 90
Witherspoon, Reese, 1046
Womack, John B., 1045
Womack, Lee Ann, 1046
women, 2, 183, 187, 358, 496, 505, 516, 520, 521, 528, 536, 549, 603, 620, 666, 668, 671, 727-731, 736, 747, 754, 776, 777, 787, 797, 811, 812, 830, 930, 931, 936, 944, 971
women given the vote, 183
Wood, Fernando, 28, 69
Woods, William B., 828
Wool, John E., 243, 244
Work, Henry C., 737
World War II, 73, 175, 210
wounds, 573, 620, 761

Wright, A. R., 145
Wright, Silas, 167
Wyoming, 749
Yancey, William L., 171, 753
Yankee crimes, against Southern blacks, 730, 731
Yankee industrialists, 207
Yankee myth, 2, 64, 177, 215, 492, 515, 619, 926, 971
Yankee mythology, 23, 189, 570, 572, 821
Yankee propaganda, 65
Yankee racism, 536, 790
Yankee slave traders, 70
Yankee slave trading, 75
Yankee war crimes, 731
Yankee war criminals, 142, 725
Yankeedom, 514
Yankees, 67, 74, 103, 211, 282, 285, 296, 301, 302, 356, 369, 389, 399, 419, 514-516, 520, 521, 551, 658, 723, 725, 726, 731, 742, 786, 792, 795, 796, 952
Yates, Richard, 409, 465, 508
Zollicoffer, Felix K., 1045

Keep Your Body, Mind, & Spirit Vibrating at Their Highest Level

YOU CAN DO SO BY READING THE BOOKS OF

SEA RAVEN PRESS

There is nothing that will so perfectly keep your body, mind, and spirit in a healthy condition as to think wisely and positively. Hence you should not only read this book, but also the other books that we offer. They will quicken your physical, mental, and spiritual vibrations, enabling you to maintain a position in society as a healthy erudite person.

KEEP YOURSELF WELL-INFORMED!

The well-informed person is always at the head of the procession, while the ignorant, the lazy, and the unthoughtful hang onto the rear. If you are a Spiritual man or woman, do yourself a great favor: read Sea Raven Press books and stay well posted on the Truth. It is almost criminal for one to remain in ignorance while the opportunity to gain knowledge is open to all at a nominal price.

We invite you to visit our Webstore for a wide selection of wholesome, family-friendly, well-researched, educational books for all ages. You will be glad you did!

Five-Star Books & Gifts From the Heart of the American South

SeaRavenPress.com

MEET THE AUTHOR

"ASKING THE PATRIOTIC SOUTH TO STOP HONORING HER CONFEDERATE ANCESTORS IS LIKE ASKING THE SUN NOT TO SHINE." — COLONEL LOCHLAINN SEABROOK

LOCHLAINN SEABROOK, a neo-Victorian and world acclaimed man of letters, is a Kentucky Colonel and the winner of the prestigious Jefferson Davis Historical Gold Medal for his "masterpiece," *A Rebel Born: A Defense of Nathan Bedford Forrest*. A classic littérateur and an unreconstructed Southern historian, he is an award-winning author, Civil War scholar, Bible authority, the leading popularizer of American Civil War history, and a traditional Southern Agrarian of Scottish, English, Irish, Dutch, Welsh, German, and Italian extraction.

A child prodigy, Seabrook is today a true Renaissance Man whose occupational titles also include encyclopedist, lexicographer, musician, artist, graphic designer, genealogist, photographer, and award-winning poet. Also a songwriter and a screenwriter, he has a 40 year background in historical nonfiction writing and is a member of the Sons of Confederate Veterans, the Civil War Trust, and the National Grange.

Above, Colonel Lochlainn Seabrook, "the voice of the traditional South," award-winning Civil War scholar and unreconstructed Southern historian, America's most popular and prolific pro-South author, his many books have introduced hundreds of thousands to the truth about the War for Southern Independence. He coined the phrase "South-shaming" and holds the world's record for writing the most books on Nathan Bedford Forrest: nine.

Known to his many fans as the "voice of the traditional South," due to similarities in their writing styles, ideas, and literary works, Seabrook is also often referred to as the "new Shelby Foote," the "Southern Joseph Campbell," and the "American Robert Graves" (his English cousin). Seabrook coined the terms "South-shaming" and "Lincolnian liberalism," and holds the world's record for writing the most books on Nathan Bedford Forrest: nine. In addition, Seabrook is the first Civil War scholar to connect the early American nickname for the U.S., "The Confederate States of America," with the Southern Confederacy that arose eight decades later, and the first to note that in 1860 the party platforms of the two major political parties were the opposite of what they are today (Victorian Democrats were conservatives, Victorian Republicans were liberals).

The grandson of an Appalachian coal-mining family, Seabrook is a seventh-generation Kentuckian, co-chair of the Jent/Gent Family Committee (Kentucky), founder and director of the Blakeney Family Tree Project, and a board member of the Friends of Colonel Benjamin E. Caudill. Seabrook's literary works have been endorsed by leading authorities, museum curators, award-winning historians, bestselling authors, celebrities, noted scientists, well regarded educators, TV show hosts and producers, renowned military artists, esteemed Southern organizations, and distinguished academicians from around the world.

Seabrook has authored over 50 popular adult books on the American Civil War, American and international slavery, the U.S. Confederacy (1781), the Southern Confederacy (1861), religion, theology, thealogy, Jesus, the Bible, the Apocrypha, the Law of Attraction, alternative health, spirituality, ghost stories, the paranormal, ufology, social issues, and cross-cultural studies of the family and marriage. His Confederate biographies, pro-South studies, genealogical monographs, family histories, military encyclopedias, self-help guides, and etymological dictionaries have received wide acclaim.

(Photo © Lochlainn Seabrook)

Seabrook's eight children's books include a Southern guide to the Civil War, a biography of Nathan Bedford Forrest, a dictionary of religion and myth, a rewriting of the King Arthur legend (which reinstates the original pre-Christian motifs), two bedtime stories for preschoolers, a naturalist's guidebook to owls, a worldwide look at the family, and an examination of the Near-Death Experience.

Of blue-blooded Southern stock through his Kentucky, Tennessee, Virginia, West Virginia, and North Carolina ancestors, he is a direct descendant of European royalty via his 6th great-grandfather, the Earl of Oxford, after which London's famous Harley Street is named. Among his celebrated male Celtic ancestors is Robert the Bruce, King of Scotland, Seabrook's 22nd great-grandfather. The 21st great-grandson of Edward I

"Longshanks" Plantagenet), King of England, Seabrook is a thirteenth-generation Southerner through his descent from the colonists of Jamestown, Virginia (1607).

The 2nd, 3rd, and 4th great-grandson of dozens of Confederate soldiers, one of his closest connections to Lincoln's War is through his 3rd great-grandfather, Elias Jent, Sr., who fought for the Confederacy in the Thirteenth Cavalry Kentucky under Seabrook's 2nd cousin, Colonel Benjamin E. Caudill. The Thirteenth, also known as "Caudill's Army," fought in numerous conflicts, including the Battles of Saltville, Gladsville, Mill Cliff, Poor Fork, Whitesburg, and Leatherwood.

Seabrook is a direct descendant of the families of Alexander H. Stephens, John Singleton Mosby, William Giles Harding, and Edmund Winchester Rucker, and is related to the following Confederates and other 18th- and 19th-Century luminaries: Robert E. Lee, Stephen Dill Lee, Stonewall Jackson, Nathan Bedford Forrest, James Longstreet, John Hunt Morgan, Jeb Stuart, Pierre G. T. Beauregard (approved the Confederate Battle Flag design), George W. Gordon, John Bell Hood, Alexander Peter Stewart, Arthur M. Manigault, Joseph Manigault, Charles Scott Venable,

Thornton A. Washington, John A. Washington, Abraham Buford, Edmund W. Pettus, Theodrick "Tod" Carter, John B. Womack, John H. Winder, Gideon J. Pillow, States Rights Gist, Henry R. Jackson, John Lawton Seabrook, John C. Breckinridge, Leonidas Polk, Zachary Taylor, Sarah Knox Taylor (first wife of Jefferson Davis), Richard Taylor, Davy Crockett, Daniel Boone, Meriwether Lewis (of the Lewis and Clark Expedition) Andrew Jackson, James K. Polk, Abram Poindexter Maury (founder of Franklin, TN), Zebulon Vance, Thomas Jefferson, Edmund Jennings Randolph, George Wythe Randolph (grandson of Jefferson), Felix K. Zollicoffer, Fitzhugh Lee, Nathaniel F. Cheairs, Jesse James, Frank James, Robert Brank Vance, Charles Sidney Winder, John W. McGavock, Caroline E. (Winder) McGavock, David Harding McGavock, Lysander McGavock, James Randal McGavock, Randal William McGavock, Francis McGavock, Emily McGavock, William Henry F. Lee, Lucius E. Polk, Minor Meriwether (husband of noted pro-South author Elizabeth Avery Meriwether), Ellen Bourne Tynes (wife of Forrest's chief of artillery, Captain John W. Morton), South Carolina Senators Preston Smith Brooks and Andrew Pickens Butler, and famed South Carolina diarist Mary Chesnut.

Seabrook's modern day cousins include: Patrick J. Buchanan (conservative author), Cindy Crawford (model), Shelby Lee Adams (Letcher Co., Kentucky, photographer), Bertram Thomas Combs (Kentucky's 50th governor), Edith Bolling (wife of President Woodrow Wilson), and actors Andy Griffith, Riley Keough, George C. Scott, Robert Duvall, Reese Witherspoon, Lee Marvin, Rebecca Gayheart, and Tom Cruise.

Seabrook's screenplay, *A Rebel Born*, based on his book of the same name, has been signed with acclaimed filmmaker Christopher Forbes (of Forbes Film). It is now in pre-production, and is set for release in 2017 as a full-length feature film. This will be the first movie ever made of Nathan Bedford Forrest's life story, and as a historically accurate project written from the Southern perspective, is destined to be one of the most talked about Civil War films of all time.

Born with music in his blood, Seabrook is an award-winning, multi-genre, BMI-Nashville songwriter and lyricist who has composed some 3,000 songs (250 albums), and whose original music has been heard in film (*A Rebel Born, Cowgirls 'n Angels, Confederate Cavalry, Billy the Kid: Showdown in Lincoln County, Vengeance Without Mercy, Last Step, County Line, The Mark*) and on TV and radio worldwide. A musician, producer, multi-instrumentalist, and renown performer—whose keyboard work has been variously compared to pianists from Hargus Robbins and Vince Guaraldi to Elton John and Leonard Bernstein—Seabrook has opened for groups such as the Earl Scruggs Review, Ted Nugent, and Bob Seger, and has performed privately for such public figures as President Ronald Reagan, Burt Reynolds, Loni Anderson, and Senator Edward W. Brooke. Seabrook's cousins in the music business include: Johnny Cash, Elvis Presley, Lisa Marie Presley, Billy Ray and Miley Cyrus, Patty Loveless, Tim McGraw, Lee Ann Womack, Dolly Parton, Pat Boone, Naomi, Wynonna, and Ashley Judd, Ricky Skaggs, the Sunshine Sisters, Martha Carson, and Chet Atkins.

Seabrook lives with his wife and family in historic Middle Tennessee, the heart of Forrest country and the Confederacy, where his conservative Southern ancestors fought valiantly against Liberal Lincoln and the progressive North in defense of Jeffersonianism, constitutional government, and personal liberty.

LochlainnSeabrook.com

MEET THE INTRODUCTION WRITER

D R. J. MICHAEL HILL is the President of the League of the South, a former Professor of History at the University of Alabama, and a former Professor at Stillman College. He received his B.A., M.A., and Ph.D. at the University of Alabama.

A specialist in history, politics, economics, and social and cultural issues, Dr. Hill is the author of numerous scholarly articles, book reviews in academic journals, and books, including: *Celtic Warfare, 1595-1763* (Edinburgh, 1985), and *Sorley Boy McDonnell and the Rise of Clan Ian Mor, 1510-1590* (London, 1993).

A member of Christ Our Hope Reformed Episcopal Church in West Point, Tennessee, Dr. Hill is also a freelance author and lecturer who served as an Alabama delegate to The Southern National Congress. He is married with three children and lives in Killen, Alabama.

WWW.DIXIENET.ORG

MEET THE FOREWORD WRITER

ROBERT LOVELL has an Associate of Arts degree from the University of Florida, a B.S. in Education from Florida State University, and a Masters degree in theology from Southeastern Baptist Theological Seminary in Wake Fores, North Carolina.

He has served as Chairman of the Lake County Florida Republican Party and was voted the most valuable member in 1980. He then served ten years as Republican State Committeeman, elected county wide twice. He served twenty-two years on the Leesburg City Commission and was elected mayor five times.

In 2007 Mayor Lovell was presented the prestigious Community Service Award by the Lake County League of Cities. He has been a Civil War re-enactor for the past twenty years and presently serves as a Lieutenant Colonel and Aide-to-Camp to General R. M. Hardy commander of Hardee's Corps (a multi-state re-enactment organization).

Mayor Lovell is a 5th-generation Floridian and has two great grandfathers who served with distinction in the Confederate Army. He did an adult lecture series for ten years with the local community college on "Characters of American History" and published his autobiography, *Cracker Outlaw*, in 2008.

LOCHLAINN SEABROOK ~ 1049

If you enjoyed this book you will be interested in Colonel Seabrook's other popular related titles:

- ☞ EVERYTHING YOU WERE TAUGHT ABOUT THE CIVIL WAR IS WRONG, ASK A SOUTHERNER!
- ☞ ABRAHAM LINCOLN WAS A LIBERAL, JEFFERSON DAVIS WAS A CONSERVATIVE
- ☞ ALL WE ASK IS TO BE LET ALONE: THE SOUTHERN SECESSION FACT BOOK
- ☞ EVERYTHING YOU WERE TAUGHT ABOUT AMERICAN SLAVERY IS WRONG, ASK A SOUTHERNER!
- ☞ CONFEDERATE FLAG FACTS: WHAT EVERY AMERICAN SHOULD KNOW ABOUT DIXIE'S SOUTHERN CROSS
- ☞ LINCOLN'S WAR: THE REAL CAUSE, THE REAL WINNER, THE REAL LOSER

Available from Sea Raven Press and wherever fine books are sold

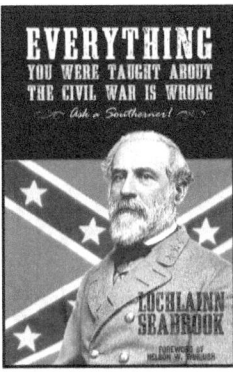

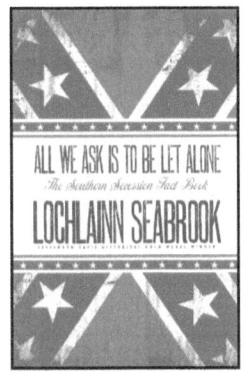
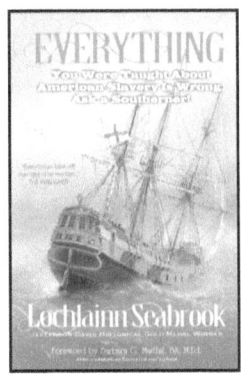

ALL OF OUR BOOK COVERS ARE AVAILABLE AS 11" X 17" POSTERS, SUITABLE FOR FRAMING

SeaRavenPress.com • NathanBedfordForrestBooks.com

www.ingramcontent.com/pod-product-compliance
Lightning Source LLC
Chambersburg PA
CBHW021216300426
44111CB00007B/331